JANÁČEK: YEARS OF A LIFE
VOLUME I

Janáček: Years of a Life

JOHN TYRRELL

VOLUME I (1854–1914)
The lonely blackbird

faber and faber

First published in 2006
by Faber and Faber Limited
3 Queen Square London WC1N 3AU

Typeset by RefineCatch Limited, Bungay, Suffolk
Printed in England by CPI, Bath

A CIP record for this book
is available from the British Library

ISBN 978–0–571–17538–3
ISBN 0–571–17538–4

2 4 6 8 10 9 7 5 3 1

TO JOHN WARRACK

Contents

Plates

Plates 28 and 31 from Institute of Ethnology (Academy of Sciences of the Czech Republic), with kind permission. Plate 6 from the Abbey of St Tomáš, Staré Brno, with kind permission. Plate 32 from John Tyrrell (private collection). All other photographs from the Janáček Archive of the Music Division of the Moravian Regional Museum, Brno, with kind permission.

Maps

Tables

Introduction

Janáček would have hated this book. In a letter to Max Brod about the biography he was writing, Janáček gave the following instruction: 'Definitely refuse all extra ballast which XY is asking you [to include]. What is at stake is your poetical work and not sober facts.' Nevertheless, Brod steamed ahead and a week later asked Janáček to respond to thirty questions about his life, which, to the composer's credit, he did. Janáček would no doubt have regarded the present project as an even worse example of 'ballast' and one that is furthermore quite unredeemed by any pretence at 'poetry'.

Like others of my generation I came to Janáček's life and works through Jaroslav Vogel's classic biography. I could have had no better guide. Vogel was a creative artist – a composer himself and a fine conductor of Janáček's music – with personal knowledge of Janáček. Through his broad culture and sympathies he was able to write for an international readership and produce a warm-hearted, generous book that has stood the test of time: it has been constantly in print in several languages. Written in an accessible style, it nevertheless takes account of the Czech scholarly discoveries of the 1950s (good years for Janáček publications although dark years for the country). Its chief limitation is its haphazardness in identifying sources, something I hope I have done better in this present work.

The first part of Vogel's biography stands in the shadow of an earlier book, Vladimír Helfert's detailed biography of Janáček's early life, published as the Nazis thrust their way into Czechoslovakia. Like many other Czech intellectuals, Helfert was imprisoned throughout the Second World War, and on his release from a concentration camp was broken in health and spirit. He died in 1945 without writing any of the

xvii

succeeding volumes of the biography that he had planned. There would have been another three or four and, had they been written, they would have made endeavours such as mine redundant. One of the finest Czech musicologists of his day, with a wide range of interests and, initially, a sceptical attitude towards Janáček, Helfert was the ideal biographer. He was a near contemporary of Janáček, able to draw on current memories, and trawl local archives and newspapers. My debt to Helfert will be evident from the many footnote references to his biography (*LJPT*) in the earlier part of this volume. If it is not an easy book to use, this is a reflection of an age in which density rather than accessibility was thought a scholarly virtue. A modern editor would have insisted on a more user-friendly approach with a clearer signalling of contents. Helfert's views on the Janáčeks' marriage, for instance, might not then have been buried unannounced in a seventy-page chapter on Janáček as a composer.

Since Brod, Helfert and Vogel wrote their biographies much more has come to light and in some cases been published. Janáček's extensive correspondence with his two major publishers Universal Edition and Hudební matice is now available, the lost letters to Rosa Newmarch have turned up (in Panama!), Zdenka Janáčková's memoirs (partly used by Helfert and Vogel, often unattributed) have now been published in English and Czech editions. Janáček's early letters to Zdenka (in German) have also been published (Helfert had access to them in only manuscript), while the later letters (in Czech), a much underused source, have become fully accessible, as have the letters to his daughter Olga. In particular, all of Janáček's letters to Kamila Stösslová are available in a fine Czech edition (and most of them also in English). Even Janáček's Kamila Album, kept under lock and key in some inner sanctum of the Janáček Archive for many years, has been published. Altogether in the eighty years since Brod wrote his biography, and the fifty years since Vogel wrote his, many 'sober facts' have turned up that need sifting and assessing to provide a more comprehensive picture of the composer.

To some it may seem that a biography is a foolish and oldfashioned enterprise, or one that should be undertaken only if accompanied by health warnings and disclaimers to disarm critics. This is not my view. I am, however, aware that even the attempt to draw out an account of Janáček's life based on documents is a subjective one: I have chosen this rather than that document; I have quoted more from this one than that; I have understood something in a particular way; or I have let a particular view prevail. In the end this is because I believe that one letter may be more important for understanding Janáček than another one, or one interpretation may be more plausible than any other I could have chosen. I can only hope that many years of working with the sources and thinking about them has led me to a view that others will also find persuasive. But I know that 'facts' change, that new documents turn up, that old ones can be differently interpreted, that different generations will find different emphases and that a biographer inevitably writes himself or herself into the story. I have at least tried to indicate my sources, my guesses and my hunches.

In the case of Janáček the would-be biographer has a head start over, say, Schubert, who left pitifully few letters, seldom dealing with serious matters. Thousands of letters that Janáček wrote have survived, and so have even more letters written to him. His last years are illuminated by almost daily correspondence with Kamila Stösslová. Janáček, furthermore, was a prominent member of his community, contributing as teacher, writer and journalist. He wrote on almost every subject that came up and it is not hard to discover his opinions on many topics. One of the aims of this biography has been to try and make sense of all this primary material, providing a sound, detailed, footnoted, chronological framework and putting it together in a way that illuminates Janáček's day-to-day life and his creative life. In this I have been more active in seeking out new sources than in taking into account the views offered by those biographies published during the gestation of my book.

I have been able to take advantage of Dr Theodora Straková's lifetime work on Janáček's writings by making use of the detailed list that she published in 1997 (in *JAWO*); her catalogue numbers make possible brief, instant references to particular writings. For the first time, her list allowed one to see the spread of interests that Janáček committed to paper. Dr Straková's magnificent two-volume collection of Janáček's 'literary' writings (*LD*), issued not long before her ninetieth birthday, offers Czech readers the opportunity to get to know this material, with the many insights it provides into Janáček's personality. In the light of this, my biography attempts to place Janáček's compositions in the wider context of his extensive literary writings, theoretical concerns and ethnographic researches.

Until now most Janáček biographies have been 'life and works'. When Vogel wrote his biography he was writing for people such as my younger self, who needed basic information about Janáček's compositions. I regard this phase as now almost complete. In the past thirty years the recording and publication of most of Janáček's works, and the generous provision of sleeve notes, CD booklets, detailed programme notes for concerts and opera performances has meant that the introductory nature of what Vogel was trying to do has been overtaken by events. Subtitling my biography 'years of a life' attempts to suggest something different, where the main thrust of concentration is indeed on the life of Janáček, year by year. This does not mean, however, that I have excluded discussion of Janáček's music. Instead I have seen the works as part of his biography: with Janáček, life and works are so interconnected that it is often difficult to discuss one without the other. But, in order not to exclude an important part of a potential readership, I have used music examples only when it seemed the most economical way of saying what I needed to; this is confined to a few more specialist chapters.

This book is divided into seven parts, four of which make up vol. i (up to the outbreak of the First World War and Janáček's sixtieth birthday in the summer of 1914) and three of which make up vol. ii (to Janáček's death in 1928). Parts are further divided into two types of chapters: chronological and contextual.

The chronological chapters provide a straightforward narrative that for much of the time is delivered at the rate of one year per chapter, though earlier years (where information is more sparse) are grouped together and crowded later years (in vol. ii) are split. Any reader wishing for a chronological account of Janáček's life and works could simply concentrate on these chapters and ignore everything else. Threaded between the chronological chapters is a varied series of chapters on particular topics, some of them constituting sequences throughout the book, e.g. 'Music as autobiography I' (and subsequently II, III and IV). Such chapters often range over several years. They comment on aspects of Janáček's life, personality, music, environment, mentors and enemies, providing context and detailed explanations.

I cannot imagine there will be many readers of a book of this size who will start at the beginning, end at the end and will stick to the printed order. Many will select according to need or interest and may very well start dipping into some of the topics since they are shorter and have more intriguing titles. Because of this, I have tried to make all chapters relatively self-sufficient (inevitably with a little duplication); cross-references are given where helpful.

By the clear division of material I have tried to address the chief concerns of biography: to provide facts and a shaping commentary. More skilful biographers than I have contrived to combine the two modes of operation in a seamless narrative but in any reflective biography there will be 'topics' (even if not signalled as such) that will interrupt a chronological flow. What I have written here has all the joins showing and boasts no concealing art at all and no 'poetry'. There are some readers who will prefer a more directed, opinionated narrative and wish to be swept up in a grand authorial vision of the subject. I believe there is also merit in a more transparent plan that might encourage the reader to find his or her own route through Janáček's life and enable a more proactive reading of the materials offered.

Author's note

BIOGRAPHICAL INFORMATION

Unless specifically stated, I have used standard Czech sources of biographical information: *ČSHS* for musicians, *OSN* and *MSN* for non-musicians.

CATALOGUE NUMBERS

Numbers in roman/arabic (e.g. III/6 for *Amarus*) are those of the Janáček catalogue (*JAWO*). A list and explanation of all such sigla are given in the indices at the end of this book.

CROSS-REFERENCES

Those in this volume are to chapter numbers; those for vol. ii (in progress) are by chapter title.

CURRENCY

For a full explanation of units of Czech currency and abbreviations, see chaps. 41 and 67.

DATES OF COMPOSITION

Unless new information or hypotheses are offered, dates of Janáček's composition are based without further acknowledgement on those given in *JAWO*.

DATES OF RUSSIAN LETTERS

For letters written in Russia up to 1918, new style dates (signalled 'N.S.'), i.e. the equivalent Western date, are given where possible. The Russian date of writing is twelve days behind the Western in the nineteenth century and thirteen in the twentieth.

EMPHASES IN QUOTATIONS

Unless specifically stated otherwise ('emphasis added'), italic-type in quoted material denotes emphases in the original source (usually underlining).

FOOTNOTES AND ENDNOTES

There are two forms of note: footnotes (signalled with symbols), which provide additional information and explanations; and endnotes (signalled with numbers), which in conjunction with the bibliography provide sources.

Locations of documents are supplied only for unpublished letters. Where a reliable English translation of published correspondence exists, reference is made to that rather than to a Czech source. Initials are used for the following individuals:

AR   Artuš Rektorys
KK   Karel Kovařovic
KS   Kamila Stösslová
LJ   Leoš Janáček
OJ   Olga Janáčková
ZJ   Zdenka Janáčková
ZS   Zdenka Schulzová (the maiden name of the above)

FORMS OF NAMES

The Czech Academy regularly revises the spelling of Czech in an attempt to make it match pronunciation (see *JAWO*, xviii). For English, which is much more *laissez-faire* and resistant to spelling reforms, this creates a problem with proper names (of works and of people). Although this solution is not liked by my Czech colleagues, I have stuck to what people called themselves, and to what Janáček called his works. For instance. Zdenka Janáčková always signed herself as 'Zdenka' and Janáček always referred to her as 'Zdenka'. In this book she is known as such and not as 'Zdeňka', which is how modern Czech sources refer to her. Similarly, I have retained the forenames of members of Janáček's family presented, for instance, in Helfert's biography (1938), rather than later versions such as Svatava Přibáňová's article (1984) on Janáček's family tree. Thus Amalie and Rosalie (as found in birth registers and other documents) are used for the first names of Janáček's mother and sister and not the respelt modern versions of Amálie and Rozálie.

PRONUNCIATION

For readers who like to have a stab at pronouncing the Czech names they will encounter in this book, I offer a few general principles.

The Czech language stresses the first syllable of every word. The only exception is in preposition-plus-noun combinations such as 'na Moravě' [in Moravia], which is stressed as if it were a single word.

Vowels are open, more or less as in Italian, and never diphthongized as in English. They come in two forms: short and longer, the long ones signalled by an acute accent (thus the second 'á' in 'Janáček' is longer than the first 'a'). For historical reasons a long 'u' is written 'ů' in some positions. The letter 'y' (both 'y' and 'ý') is considered a vowel, differentiated from 'i' by grammar rather than by sound. The letter 'j' is pronounced as an English 'y' (as in Janáček: 'YA-nah-check') and is often used to create diphthong-combinations ('aj' is pronounced 'ai-ee'; 'ej' is pronounced 'eh-ee' etc.).

Consonants are more or less as one might expect them in English, though without aspirates (the Czech 'b' and 'p' are 'cleaner' sounds than the English 'b' and 'p'). Here are a few more exceptions:

'c' is pronounced 'ts', e.g. Laca (LA-tsa).

The combination 'ch' is similar to the final sound of the word 'loch', e.g. Tichon (TI-chon).

The letter 'r' is always rolled.

The letters 'r' and 'l' can take the place of vowels, e.g. Brno (BiR-no).

Diacritic signs (i.e. the Czech *háček* [hook], which after 't' and 'd' is written as an apostrophe, but is otherwise written as an inverted circumflex) modify some consonants, and the vowel 'e', e.g.

č represents the sound 'ch' (as in 'cheek'), e.g. Janáček (YA-nah-check)

ď represents the initial sound in the word 'dew', e.g. ďábel (DYAH-bel)

ě represents the sound 'ye', e.g. Kateřina (KA-tye-ree-na)

ň represents the initial sound in the word 'new', e.g. pastorkyňa (PAS-tor-kee-nya)

ř is a Czech speciality, a rolled 'r' with friction, e.g. Kovařovic (KO-va-rzho-vits)

š represents the sound 'sh' (as in sheet), e.g. Šárka (SHAHR-ka)

ť represents the initial sound in the word 'tune', e.g. Káťa (KAH-tya) ž represents the sound 'j' (as in French *jeu*), e.g. Žárlivost (ZHAHR-li-vost)

In some northern Moravian dialect words the Polish ł (sounding 'w') is used, e.g. łáska (WAH-ska).

TRANSLATED TITLES
Czech (and Russian) works are generally given in English; the original titles can be found in the index.

TRANSLATIONS
Unless otherwise stated, all translations are my own, though I have had considerable help from those more skilled than I am in the particular languages involved: Czech, Russian and German. Where the translation comes from one of my earlier books and I think I can do better, I have not hesitated to make improvements or corrections.

Acknowledgements

I gratefully acknowledge the award of a British Academy Readership in the Humanities in 1992–4, which enabled me to clear the ground; much of the work I did then was used in the Janáček catalogue published in 1997 (*JAWO*). In 2000 I joined Cardiff University as a Professorial Research Fellow, which allowed me to work regularly on the book. A further grant from the British Academy enabled me to engage a Czech research student for one year; another from the Arts and Humanities Research Board to pay for commissioning specific chapters on Janáček's health and wealth. Publication has been considerably easier by generous grants from the Erna V. Fischer Trust Endowment for Czech Music at the Universiy of California, Santa Barbara, Department of Music and the Czech and Slovak Music of the USA. I am most grateful to Dr Derek Katz for his kind help in these matters.

I am grateful to the many scholars who have answered my questions: I am particularly in the debt of Milena Flodrová whose unrivalled knowledge of Brno archives and whose researches on my behalf have uncovered all sorts of fascinating, previously unknown facts. Others who have put their own research at my disposal or have helped me in various matters include Mark Audus (Nottingham), Dr Paul Banks (London), Dr David Beveridge (Prague), Prof. Geoffrey Chew (London), Harry Haskell (Guilford, CT), Dr David Wyn Jones (Cardiff), Dr Vojtěch Kyas (Brno), Dr Gunhild Oberzaucher-Schüller (Salzburg), Dr Jonathan Pearl (Santa Barbara), Prof. Robert Pynsent (London), Dr Rupert Ridgewell (London), Simona Sedláčková (Brno, Dr John Snelson (London), Prof. Miloš Štědroň, Heinz Stolba (Vienna), Mark Summers (London), Veronika Vevjodová (Brno) and Robin Thomson (Ashgabat). In addition to contributing expert chapters on

Janáček's health, Dr Stephen Lock (Aldeburgh) has also checked the manuscript from a medical standpoint. Without the timely assistance of Jim Page this book might never have been published.

The scale of the book has tested friends and colleagues to the limit of endurance. They have been generous in reading to various drafts and giving me many valuable suggestions reflected in the final form of the book. I am grateful to them all: Mark Audus, Geoff Chew, Jim Friedman, Yoko Kawaguchi, Margot Levy, Simon Rees, Nigel Simeone, Jan Špaček, Philip Weller and Šárka Zahrádková.

The book could not have come into the world without much help from my friends and colleagues in Brno: I am particularly grateful to Dr František Malý, head of the Music Section of the Moravian Regional Museum, who has allowed me generous access to the splendid holdings of the Janáček Archive and to his entire staff who have made me so welcome there over many decades. Janáček experts on the staff, Dr Svatava Přibáňová and Dr Jiří Zahrádka, have generously shared their treasures with me, have patiently answered my many questions over a long period, and have deciphered various illegible handwritings. The present Janáček curator, Dr Jiří Zahrádka, has given much practical help and moral encouragement; he has considerably enhanced the book with his series of ground-breaking chapters on Janáček's finances. I owe a particular debt to Jan Špaček. He has been my chief research assistant in Brno for over five years and his enthusiasm for 'Naše věc' [Our thing] has been an inspiration. This book has benefited immensely from his systematic transcription of many letters, his searching out of obscure items in journals and newspapers, and in the final stages, of checking my translations. Similarly, Simona Sedláčková and Ludmila Němcová have ably assisted in many aspects of my archival work: without their transcriptions my database would be much the poorer.

It is good to be able to thank old friends who have worked on earlier books of mine, and have continued to help me in the preparation of this one: in particular I am grateful to Ruth Thackeray for advice on the many tricky problems of presentation and her alert copy-editing of the manuscript, and to Marion Hubbard who for almost twenty years has drawn the maps for my books and has contributed five to this one.

The book has been built on a database created over fifteen years, beginning at a time when databases and diacritics seemed to be incompatible – except for Nota Bene. The specialist software that this firm provides, with an integrated suite of word processing, database, textbase and indexing facilities in so many languages has been invaluable; the helpfulness of its staff legendary.

Finally I am grateful to Faber and Faber for their taking on such a large and commercially unrewarding project.

Map 1   Bohemia and Moravia.

KEY

1 Lašsko
2 Valašsko
3 Haná
4 Silesia
5 Slovácko
6 Horňácko
7 Horácko

Javorník
Cukmantl
Gräfenberg
hoceň
Česká-
Třebová
Neplachovice
Opava
Moravia
Nové
Zámky
Olomouc
Hranice
oskovice
Prostějov
Teplice
nad Bečvou
Přerov
Vyškov
Švábenice
Koryčany
Hodonín
Kostice
Brno
ce
av

Gleiwitz
Ostrava
Frýdek-
Místek
Příbor
HUKVALDY
Bocanovice
Valašské
Meziříčí

POLAND

Cieszyn
Český-Těšín
Jablunkov
Mosty

HOSTÝN
Rovné
Terchová
Zakopane
Štrbské
Pleso
Demänovská

LUHAČOVICE
Uherské-
Hradiště
Velká

Čičmany
Trenčianske
Teplice
Slatina nad
Bebravou
Sliač
Detva

Slovakia

Bratislava

Scale
0   50mls
0   75kms

I

A LATE STARTER
(1854–80)

Images of Janáček

The most familiar image of Janáček is of an old man: a vigorous old man, but nevertheless white-haired and at least sixty-two. Here are two descriptions of him, one by Max Brod (who translated many of his operas into German), the second by Rudolf Těsnohlídek, the author of the novel on which Janáček based his opera *The Cunning Little Vixen*:

An unknown old man stood in my room. It was Sunday, still quite early. A moment before, I had been sleeping deeply. Was I still dreaming? – This head with its high, beautifully domed forehead, twinklingly serious big open eyes, and curved mouth: it was Goethe's head, as drawn by Stieler, but transposed here into softly Slavonic lines ... A name sounded in my dream. 'Leoš Janáček'. It was the composer of *Jenůfa*. [. . .] His glance bewitched me. Still more his words, whose holy naivety moves me still today.[1]

Leoš Janáček was waiting in the little garden of the Conservatory. He sat among the bushes, with thousands of tiny little blossoms above his head; that head of his was just as white, and seemed to be the largest of the flowers. He smiled; and I knew at once that this was the smile which life awards us like a gold medal for bravery in the face of the enemy. For bravery in sorrow, humiliation and anger.[2]

Against such lyrical, indeed beautiful, descriptions one needs to put others, such as a reminiscence of Jascha Horenstein. Looking back in old age at the International Society of Contemporary Music (ISCM) Festival held in Frankfurt 1927, where he was conducting a rehearsal, he took Janáček for the superintendent of the building: 'very bourgeois, very middle-class, one would say lower middle-class', with his watch and chain, and formal wear, 'as pleasant as the owner of a Gasthaus, or an Austrian or Czech coffee house'.[3] František Weyr, professor of law at Masaryk University, who had dealings with Janáček after the First World War, also didn't think he looked much like an artist. He was too carefully presented, Weyr thought, with his 'massive mane of already snow-white hair and cultivated moustache of the same colour'.[4]

Těsnohlídek depicts Janáček in repose, but most descriptions emphasize his energy and vigour, as for instance his appearance at a party in Prague after his return from England in 1926: 'an animated seventy-year-old of keen and cheerful appearance; a mane of thick silver hair above his high-domed forehead'. This was someone who talked and gesticulated so energetically 'that from time to time you think his old-fashioned shirt cuff might go flying'.[5]

Animation and energy are the overwhelming impressions that come across from one of the few pieces of cine footage of Janáček to survive. In the few seconds that it runs, it shows him greeting Mrs Maria Calma-Veselá on board a steamer during the ISCM Festival in Prague 1925. He pumps her arm with one hand while vigorously gesticulating with the other. The arms flail, the body is in constant motion, the eyes twinkle. He is shorter than the carefully posed photographs suggest. He is not well proportioned, the head is too big for the small body and by this stage – he was almost seventy-one – he is distinctly tubby.

It seems extraordinary that no-one bothered to record his voice. He was involved with early cylinder phonographs: one hopes for a barked introduction, or a word of encouragement to his folksingers, but the cylinders have no tales to tell other than the songs that they recorded. One has at least some idea how he spoke: it was *kratce* [short], as in many jokey representations of his speech omitting the acute accent (the long-vowel sign): not the standard Czech (*krátce*) with a long 'á' ('aah') but a short 'a' ('uh') instead. This trait is usually accounted for by a reference to his short-vowel Lachian dialect, which, it is said, he never lost. However not only were his vowels short, but also his sentences. And when he wrote letters – and sometimes formal prose – the paragraphs were just as short too: often a single sentence implying some sort of pause and possibly a shift before the next staccato rapid fire.

Most people who came across Janáček remembered the hair. In 1913 – he was then nearly sixty – he had begun to lose it and, consulting his doctor, was given 'some sort of water'. Thereafter, as his housekeeper Marie Stejskalová recalled, 'the master always moistened his hair with it. It helped; his hair seemed to thicken even more and took on that

4

lovely white colour admired by everyone and about which so much was written. It shone around the master's head like white fire.'[6]

Earlier images, before his hair turned white, still depict him as rather unusual and arresting in appearance. Here he is in 1906, just fifty-two, spotted on a rare visit to Prague by a couple of musical journalists: 'Janáček from Brno', as they identified him, with an 'interesting head', out of which shone 'two dark and fiery eyes', a 'Napoleonic figure' and crowned with a mop of 'overgrown hair' (xv/182).

When she first encountered him in 1877 (she was twelve at the time) his future wife Zdenka remembered Janáček as 'slim then, a figure smaller rather than larger, his pale face made a strong contrast with his hard, curly full beard, thick black curly locks and very striking brown eyes.' She was particularly taken 'with his small, full white hand'. In manner he was at first reserved, though she did not find him as strict as she expected him to be, 'let alone ill-natured, as was frequently said of him'.[7] Janáček's pupils at the Brno Teachers' Institute (where he taught for most of his life) found him 'strikingly taciturn, reserved and strict in every way' and treated him with some caution when he appeared, with his 'wonderfully shaky step', his 'tiny figure shuffling his way' round the benches, and, without a word, sitting down at the piano, 'his black locks waving luxuriantly in a gleam of sunlight'.[8]

What is abundantly clear is that his feelings were near the surface, reined in with difficulty. 'Deeply sensitive, with a soul of rich moods, agitated by the gentlest touch, sharply choleric at the strongest impulse',[9] was how a fiftieth-birthday tribute put it, a reference to his exceptionally short fuse, even in professional situations. Weyr's impression was of someone who had something 'aggressive and challenging' about him and he soon felt that 'it wasn't perhaps pleasant to come into conflict with a man of such an explosive temperament even when it was just some general difference of opinion that was at stake.'[10] 'Janáček can never bear any criticism from anyone and considers himself always infallible',[11] was how his exasperated father-in-law put it in 1883, not long after Janáček married Emilian Schulz's daughter. When criticized at a meeting of the staff of the Teachers' Institute, it was reported (in an official, minuted complaint) that he had 'waved his arms', spoken 'with an angry voice' and had stumped off 'demonstratively', having called the teaching staff a 'nasty lot of good-for-nothings'.[12]

In more conciliatory circumstances it was not the short fuse that caused problems so much as the fact that potential colleagues found it difficult to operate at the speed needed. Viktor Dyk, one of the innumerable librettists for *Brouček*, remembered the demands put upon him, a letter coming out of the blue from the suddenly famous composer of *Jenůfa*, 'four pages, written with a characterful, energetic hand', making a surprising request:

He was composing *The Excursion of Mr Brouček to the Moon*. And it was I, yes I, who could help him. He had tried elsewhere, but none of those to whom he turned was giving him satisfaction. What was needed was me, what was needed was concise speech, trenchant verse, or so Janáček wrote. Half request, half order. And before I got round to replying, a reminder came, and then a second reminder: I *must* do it, if his work was not to be killed off and destroyed. And for him, the composer who had had to wait so long, it was impossible to wait patiently. In the end – the reader must not imagine that this all lasted more than four or five days! – he appeared before me.[13]

And when Viktor Dyk was arrested (this was in the middle of the First World War), Janáček attempted to continue working with his librettist 'as though absolutely nothing had happened' and was bemused by the thought that the military censorship might slow things down. 'Leoš Janáček, continually bombarding me with letters and in cases of need always willing to surprise me with a visit in Prague, lost interest in his collaborator as soon as he ceased to be a collaborator.'[14]

When Jan Mikota took over the difficult job of handling Janáček for the publishing wing of Hudební matice he found that the 'social and commercial tone' that he sought to instigate soon disappeared. Above all Janáček wanted negotiations to be as brief as possible, without long consideration: just 'yes' or 'no'. Answers were curt, sharp and surprising: Mikota had never come across anything like it.[15]

Those who were nearest to him, such as his wife Zdenka, found him not only bossy, demanding and needing instant attention, but also sometimes mean, heartless and cruel. Even allowing for the friction of day-to-day married life and the fact that Zdenka's memoirs portray only too well the image of a wounded wife, there are many stories, such as his treatment of her in the later stages of pregnancy or inflicting his mistress Gabriela Horvátová on her in a most public way, that are difficult to explain other than through a cruel streak or at least insensitivity. Kamila Stösslová, the love of his later life, saw a more agreeable and relaxed person: she seems to have released in him a long-suppressed sense of fun. All other commentators found him without any spark of humour: 'I don't remember', Weyr wrote, 'that I ever heard from his lips some involuntary witticism or hearty laughter'.[16] According to František Kolář, who knew him from at least 1905* and twenty years later in Luhačovice, he hated jokes and people soon learnt not to tell them in front of him.[17] The worldly Gabriela Horvátová, invited to comment on him in her old age (by which time she had memorialized the hitherto despised Zdenka as an 'angel') recalled that there were 'six' Janáčeks: with his mercurial changes of mind one never knew which one she was going to get.[18] On the whole, however, women got closer to him than men: he had male colleagues and professional friends, but after the death of his brother František he had no really close male friends. Always susceptible to women (Kolář tells how he would perk up when he saw a pretty girl and adjust his moustache and tie in a shop window),[19] he would reveal more of himself to Gabriela Horvátová and especially Kamila Stösslová than to anyone else.

Much of what appears to be cruel in him can be explained by his upbringing: a young boy from a poor family sent away from home at the age of eleven – a crucial stage of his upbringing – and denied the company of his siblings and the love of his parents. His belligerence can be explained by his having to fight his way up from poverty and neglect, and the fact that, for much of his career, he considered his talents and achievements undervalued. Until late in life he certainly had a chip on his shoulder which can account for much of his behaviour. When recognition came, first national, then international, the bitterness largely faded. Weyr recalls the 'exceptionally conciliatory appearance' of the white-haired old gentleman who in a sprightly and contented way walked the streets of Brno.[20]

More difficult to explain, however, is how this country boy became an important and original composer. Destined and trained to be a teacher (and teaching remained important to him throughout his life), he became an opera composer. Although, like so much else, opera came late to him, he blossomed in old age to compose at white heat some of the most immediately captivating, varied and original operas of the twentieth century, some of the very few to find a permanent place in the repertory. And, in the gaps between writing the operas, he would turn

---

* He had memories of Janáček at the 'Volkstag' (see chap. 51) and was a member of the Russian Circle.

out, even more speedily, arresting works in other genres: the *Glagolitic Mass*, two splendidly vibrant string quartets, a celebratory Sinfonietta, and some extraordinary and visionary choral music. As in the case of Haydn, stuck out in the marshes of Eszterháza and 'forced to become original', Janáček in another province of the Habsburg Empire similarly became his own person, an anomaly difficult to pigeon-hole in the annals of twentieth-century music.[†] Although his belated musical education took place at leading institutions in Prague, Leipzig and Vienna, autodidactism and self-help were in his blood: something of the naive rustic remained with him throughout his life so that he came across to his contemporaries as ill-educated and homegrown. But in his own way, and in his own time, he found his own path and his own voice. When he emerged into prominence in old age he came to be seen as one of music's true originals, one of the most engaging composers of the twentieth century.

[†] Early histories tended to characterize him as a 'late nationalist', see for instance Donald Jay Grout's influential *A History of Western Music Revised* (Dent, London, 1960), 641–2. Even Adorno, never usually at a loss, found it hard to place him (see vol. ii: Janáček and Modernism).

8

2

Nations and languages

Czech, Bohemian, Moravian

'First of all, I presume I am a Czech composer and not just a *Moravian* one as they nowadays like to pretend in Prague.' Janáček was commenting, if such a neutral word can be applied to his usual tone of outraged indignation, on the description of himself as a 'Moravian composer' in the most recent edition of the *Riemann-Einstein Musiklexikon*.[1] When he made this statement in 1926, the differences between Czechs and Moravians were certainly smaller and fewer than they had been. Moravians lived in Moravia, Bohemians next door lived in Bohemia and both spoke the same language, Czech. Janáček's insistence that he was a Czech composer underlined that he was one of the Czech-speaking nation, not merely a composer from the province of Moravia. He was, as the great Czech historian František Palacký described himself, 'Moravian by birth, Czech by nationality'.[2]

There was, however, a linguistic problem when Janáček claimed that he was a 'český skladatel' [Czech composer]. In English the adjectives 'Czech' and 'Bohemian' have differentiated if overlapping meanings. Whereas 'Czech' refers to any aspects pertaining to the people (e.g. customs, culture, music, and especially language) from the combined area of Bohemia, Moravia and Czech Silesia, 'Bohemian', in modern parlance, refers only to the province of Bohemia (as well as, of course, to people of unconventional lifestyle, a meaning I shall now ignore). Thus not all Czechs are Bohemians; some, like Janáček, are Moravians. Similarly, Czech music can be written by Bohemians, Moravians and even a few Silesians, but Bohemian music can be written only by those from Bohemia, thus excluding Janáček.

The Czech language cannot make this distinction: 'český' has to do

9

service for both 'Bohemian' and 'Czech'. The famous string quartet in which Josef Suk played most of his life is known in Czech as the 'České kvarteto'. Its translation into English can cause problems. Both forms, 'Bohemian Quartet' and 'Czech Quartet', are used and both are correct since all members of the quartet came from Bohemia ('Bohemian') and all of them spoke Czech ('Czech'). Even if English is more precise adjectivally, both Czech and English are inadequate when it comes to nouns. Apart from uncomfortable neologisms such as 'Česko', 'Czechia' and 'Czecho' there is no single official word in either language to denote the Czech-speaking region. One has to make do with 'the Czech lands', 'the Czech provinces', 'Bohemia and Moravia' (as in the old Czechoslovak weather forecasts) and today, of course, the 'Czech Republic'.

A thousand years before Janáček made his claim about being a 'Czech composer', Moravia had been at the heart of the Great Moravia, in which the Bohemians, together with the Lusatian Sorbs, the Silesians, the Vistulans, the Slovaks and the Pannonion Slavs,[3] were just another subservient people. It was to the Great Moravia that Cyril and Methodius, the 'Slavonic missionaries' sent by Byzantium, came in 862 and gave the region an alphabet (at first Glagolitic, later Cyrillic), a language (Old Slavonic, based on Macedonian dialect and at the time perhaps intelligible to other Slavs) as well as a Christian religion. The awareness that the celebration of this event fostered in Moravia 1000 years later was essentially Pan-Slavonic, locating Moravia at the hub of a vast Slavonic empire (as the mythopoeic versions of the time saw it) that could stand up to its vigorous German-speaking neighbours. This was the vision of Moravianness that Janáček embraced as a young boy (see chap. 7), one that would inflect his views and his music up to the end of his life. It is this that distinguishes him from the composers born in Bohemia such as Smetana and Dvořák. The people in Prague who 'pretended' that Janáček was 'Moravian' had in fact put their finger on something. Even if Janáček was 'Czech' by nationality he, like so many Moravians of his generation, felt a strong regional identity that arose from different founding legends, different customs, different dialects, different folk costumes, and, most of all for Janáček, different folk musics.

Great Moravia soon crumbled. At the death of Methodius in 885, Rome brought it under its Bavarian espiscopate, and the followers of Cyril and Methodius took their mission – with more permanent results – to other Slavonic regions such as Kievan Rus and the Bulgarian Empire. Within a couple of centuries the centre of power in the Czech-speaking lands would shift to Prague, the capital of the Kingdom of Bohemia. The lands attached historically to the Czech crown consisted of three provinces, Bohemia, Moravia and Silesia. Silesia came and went according to political circumstances: today most of it is in Poland. Bohemia and its sister province Moravia have been linked in every political grouping but have always been somewhat separate (the 'Kingdom of Bohemia', the 'Margravate of Moravia', established in 1182).

As long as whoever wore the Czech crown resided in Prague, then the Moravians' closest relations would be with Bohemia and its capital, even when the Czech crown was also worn by the Holy Roman Emperor, as it was, for instance in the days of Charles IV, the 'Charles' of the Charles University, the Charles Bridge and the Karlštejn castle. The top layers of government were especially close. The Margrave of Moravia was generally a post held simultaneously by the King of Bohemia (or a close relative). Moravian and Bohemian gentry (the 'Estates') formed a unified group, owning lands in both provinces.[4] Two events, however, drove the Bohemians and the Moravians apart. One was the fifteenth-century religious wars of the Hussites, a proto-Protestant sect with a greater following in Bohemia than in Moravia, which remained more staunchly Catholic.[5] Even more crucial, however, was the Battle of the White Mountain where the Bohemian and Moravian Estates confronted their Habsburg ruler and lost. Its date, 1620, became as epochal and resonant for Czech history as 1066 is for English history – though it was essentially the 'Renewed Constitution' of 1627 that enshrined the new provisions. The guaranteed freedoms the Czechs had enjoyed even under the Habsburgs (from 1526 the elected Czech dynasty) were eroded in an increasingly centralized Austrian empire, which sought to impose its Catholic religion and its German language on its subjects. For the purposes of administration, Bohemia and Moravia became separate provinces reporting separately to Vienna, a typical Habsburg strategy to divide and rule. They had separate governors representing the Austrian crown, separate parliaments, until 1775 separate customs and excise, and until 1756 different systems of weights and measures.[6] In 1749 Moravia gained a separate administrative status equal to that of any other Austrian crown land[7] and from then until 1918 there were no formal administrative links between Bohemia and Moravia. Nearer to Vienna than to Prague, Brno was sometimes described as a suburb of Vienna,[8] especially after the opening of the railway link between Vienna and Brno in 1839.

As a visitor from Slovakia, Jozef Miloslav Hurban, reported in 1839, those Moravians who continued to speak Czech in the face of increasing Germanization claimed that they spoke 'moravsky' ['Moravian'], and were surprised when they were told it was little different from the language spoken over the border in Bohemia,[9] a statement that says volumes about the paucity of contacts between the two provinces. The statement also underlines how little the National Revival, well under way in Bohemia, had travelled over the border to Moravia. This seismic shift in national self-awareness had begun in Bohemia at the end of the eighteenth century. With the growing interest shown in Czech folk cultures and the advances in Czech literature, Czech theatre and Czech opera, Czech as a literary language began to fight back from near extinction.

When Janáček was born in 1854, Vienna was the capital of a multi-national empire that included present-day Austria, Hungary, the Czech Republic, Slovakia, Croatia, northern Italy and parts of Poland, Romania and the Ukraine. The regime had to weather the storm of the pan-European nationalist uprisings of 1848 but the empire's integrity would soon be destabilized by a series of military defeats that led to a policy of accommodation with its many constituent peoples. The loss of Austria's Italian provinces in 1859 hastened the fall of the absolutist government and brought about a more liberal era. Consequences of this were the relaxed laws of association and the easier formation of Czech societies, pressure groups and cultural organizations such as the Hukvaldy Singing and Reading Club, which Janáček's father founded in 1865.[10] The 1860s became a period of fervent Czech nation-building seen in the creation of iconic Czech nationalist organizations such as the Sokol gymnastic movement, the 'Hlahol' choral society and the Provisional Theatre (the later National Theatre), all based in Prague.

Similarly Austria's defeat in the Austro-Prussian War of 1866 led to the *Ausgleich* [Compromise] of 1867 in which the German Austrians divided the empire with the Hungarians, its most populous and vociferous minority. Separated by the river Leitha there was now an Austrian half (Cisleithania) and a Hungarian half (Transleithania). The much-used official formula 'kaiserlich und königlich' ['imperial and royal'] conceded local kingdoms as well as proclaiming an all-embracing empire. The Czechs, who came under the more benevolent Austrian rule, resented these new arrangements: although they had proved their loyalty in the Austro-Prussian War, the Dual Monarchy appeared to privilege the Hungarians and encourage the aspirations of German chauvinists living in the Czech lands. Such events contributed to Czech disaffection with the empire,[11] and reinforced the cravings for political independence – and also the need to bring the Moravians on board.

However, there was a huge difference in national consciousness between the two provinces. By the 1880 census Prague had become a predominantly Czech-speaking city with over 82% Czech speakers.[12] In contrast Moravian cities lagged behind with Brno remaining predominantly German-speaking up to 1918.[13] There were many reasons for this, including a more relaxed attitude in Moravia towards language (many institutions used Czech or German indiscriminately), and the fact that Bohemia had in Prague a clear cultural centre, whereas in Moravia culture was spread between Brno and Olomouc (the seat of a university until it was closed in 1860).[14] Most significant of all was the fact that intellectual life in Moravia was spearheaded not by the middle classes (as in Bohemia) but by the lower clergy.[15] Many of the clergy in Moravia looked askance on the dangerously 'Hussite' Bohemians and felt that if they wished to keep Catholicism alive they were better off looking towards Catholic Austria.[16] And they were proud of the ancient religious traditions. Jozef Miloslav Hurban, the Slovak visitor in 1839, noticed the cult of Cyril and Methodius in the altars and statues wherever he travelled in Moravia.[17] While in Bohemia national awareness was built on the founding legends of Libuše, the Přemyslid dynasty, and the heroic exploits of the Hussite armies, in Moravia the Catholic church laid more emphasis on the proselytizing saints, Cyril and Methodius, and in the 1860s the celebration of their mission was used to emphasize the region's Slavonic roots and the glories of the Great Moravian Empire.

Vladimír Helfert[18] noted another difference between Moravia and Bohemia: the 'modern' orientation of music in Bohemia. Its leading nineteenth-century composer, Bedřich Smetana, was an adherent of Liszt and thus a fully fledged neoromantic. Bohemian Czech music after Smetana continued to reflect avant-garde trends in German music – part of the 'progressive' programme fostered by leading Czech theorists and ideologues of the time. By contrast Moravia's leading nineteenth-century composer was the monk Pavel Křížkovský, whose music looked back to early Romanticism and was nearer to its Moravian folk roots. There were few adherents of neoromanticism in Moravia and significantly Janáček, when he went abroad to study, chose Leipzig, the city of Bach, Mendelssohn and Schumann, which in 1879 was still conservative in ambience and approach.

Moravia was 'abolished' in 1949. Although in 1918 there had been attempts to centralize the newly created Czechoslovakia by scrapping a layer of administration at provincial level and by heading off any separatist inclinations that might be felt in the newly-acquired Slovakia, Subcarpathian Ruthenia and indeed in Moravia itself, it needed the more vigorous efforts of the new Communist government in 1949 to destroy a political entity that had lasted for eight hundred years. Despite this, the concept of 'Moravianness' lingered on. When in 1991, a couple of years after the fall of Communism, a new census allowed 'Moravian' as a nationality, more than half of those in southern Moravia considered themselves Moravian (rather than Czech, Slovak or Silesian).[19]

Moravia and its regions

Within Moravia itself there are sharp ethnographic divisions, all of which are important in the context of this book. Apart from the rump of Silesia that administratively became part of northern Moravia, the most important ethnographic areas are Valašsko and Lašsko in the north and Slovácko in the south, and, to the west of all of them, Haná (see Map 1). Janáček was born in the north in what at the time was considered to be Valašsko; his third opera *Jenůfa* was set in Slovácko; his first choruses to become popular (IV/28) were in the Haná dialect. In this sense Janáček could claim full citizenship of Moravia, especially after his involvement with Moravian traditional music from 1888.

Between each of these ethnographic regions there are distinctions and folk memories that help explain their differences. Haná, its name merely commemorating a river, is the central Moravian region, fertile with good agriculture and rich peasants. Slovácko looks east to its neighbour Slovakia ['Slovensko']. Its dialect shares similarities with Slovak and its name is often translated as 'Moravian Slovakia'. There is frequent confusion in documents of the time, with 'Slovensko' used where 'Slovácko' is intended. Equally tellingly, there is no proper name for the inhabitants of Slovácko. Whereas a man from Slovakia is a 'Slovák' ['Slovak'], a man from Slovácko is a 'moravský Slovák' ['Moravian Slovak']. Like Haná, it is rich agriculturally and is particularly famous for its wine culture: wine and folksong are intertwined here as in no other Czech region.

Valašsko is a rich word, cognate not only with Wallachia in Romania but also with a host of other words denoting non-Germanic foreignness, usually Celtic or Italianate. Its etymological roots go back to the Celtic tribe in southern Gaul known to the Romans as the 'Volcae' and conjecturally to the ancient Germans as the 'Walhōs'. This name was applied by the Germans to the Celts in general (cf., in a British context, Wales, Cornwall and surnames such as Wallace and Walsh) and later taken over by the Slavs, though here the foreignness denoted was Italianate. Up to the early twentieth century Czechs used the word 'Vlach' to denote an Italian and 'Valach' (cf. Wallach) a Romanian.[20] The adjective 'vlašský' was routinely used in the nineteenth century in the phrase 'vlašská opera' ['Italian opera'].

Archaeology as well as etymology suggests that the Valachians of Moravia were not originally from the area and, although they lost the Italianate language they once spoke, they were often thought to be a race apart. Unlike the rich Haná or Slovácko regions, these were mountainous regions where agriculture was poor, and sheep and goats were the main form of farming. The word 'valach' (with a lower-case 'v') today still means a shepherd.

The eastward references of both Slovácko (pointing towards Slovakia) and Valašsko (pointing towards Wallachia in Romania) have a musical significance. Draw a line down the middle of Moravia roughly at the eastern border of Haná. On the western Haná side the musical folk traditions look towards those of Bohemia and western music in general; on the other side they look east. It is this division that aligns Janáček far more with his Hungarian contemporary Béla Bartók than with the Bohemian composers Smetana and Dvořák. Both Janáček and Bartók drew musically on the exotic folk traditions of an area that included half of Moravia, Slovakia, Hungary, Romania and even parts of Turkey.

Today Janáček is not regarded ethnographically as 'Valachian' but 'Lachian'. This is a comparatively new concept: the words 'Lašsko' or 'Lach' ['man from Lašsko'] are not found in nineteenth-century

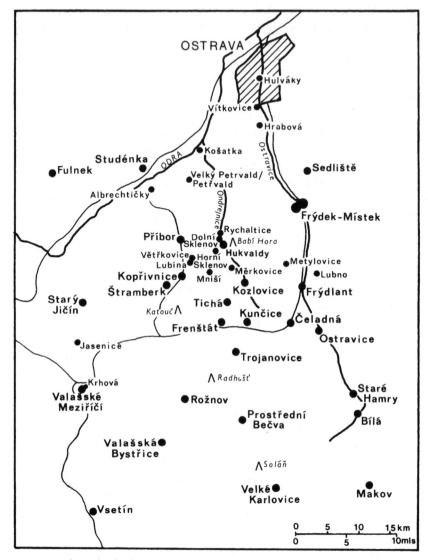

Map 2   Lašsko and Valašsko.

Czech reference books.[21] According to Janáček's colleague and later collaborator František Bartoš, nineteenth-century Lachs called themselves either 'Moravians' or 'Valachs'.[22] Janáček routinely employed the adjective 'Valašské' for 'Lašské' during the nineteenth century, for example in his orchestral arrangements of local dances (1889–91), enthusiastically promoted and published as *Valašské tance* [Valachian Dances] (vi/4), although these dances originate from villages around Janáček's native Hukvaldy, in what is today called 'Lašsko'. Similarly, the scenario (1889) for his ballet based on *Valachian Dances* (x/20) stipulates a setting in 'Valašsko', but with the Hukvaldy castle (now in 'Lašsko') in the background.

In the first volume (1886) of his important work on Moravian dialectology (*Dialektologie moravská*) Bartoš began to make a distinction between the dialects of Valašsko and Lašsko. His distinction slowly began to be accepted as standard in the twentieth century, and with it a differentiation of the two areas, though such a division remains informal. When planning in 1903 the Moravian contribution to the putative Pan-Slavonic Exhibition in St Petersburg (xv/316), Janáček distinguished ethnographically three types of Moravians: 'Slováci' ['Moravian Slovaks'], 'Laši' ['Lachs'] and 'Valaši' ['Valachs']. Twenty years later, when he brought together for publication six of his *Valachian Dances*, he retitled them *Lachian Dances* (vi/17). Generally the Lachian dialect is distinguished by its substitution of short vowels for long ones (denoted in spelling by the use of an acute accent: thus 'Janaček' rather than 'Janáček', with its long though unstressed second syllable). Neighbouring Polish has also had an influence in the Lachian habit of stressing the penultimate syllable, rather than the first syllable as in standard Czech.[23]

The Czech language effortlessly adds '-sko' (or '-ko') to the end of a word to denote a region, and words such as 'Lašsko' (i.e. the region of the Lachs) can often sound more official than they actually are. When in 1948 Jaroslav Procházka published a book on Janáček's Lachian roots, he conceded that the term 'Lašsko' was geographically and even ethnographically imprecise, and for the purposes of his book suggested both a 'narrower Lašsko' and a 'wider Lašsko' that encroached on to Silesia and parts of Haná (such as Přerov).[24] Realistically, however, Lašsko might be defined as an area contained between the rivers Odra and Ostravice (which goes through the twin town of Frýdek-Místek) and with the river Ondřejnice running down the middle. Larger towns are Místek, Příbor, Frýdlant, Štramberk and Frenštát (at its southern border; its northern border would stop short of Ostrava). Janáček's native village of Hukvaldy is almost at its heart. Lašsko is an area that is at the crossroads, intersected by the old imperial road linking Vienna to Těšín and beyond. To the north-east there is Poland, to the south-east

Slovakia. To the north-west there is Silesia, and to the south-west Valašsko.

Although he didn't see it this way, Janáček's birth as a subject of the Habsburg Empire was not a disaster. For all the many petty humiliations suffered by a minority-language speaker in a multi-ethnic nation there were undoubted advantages: a stable society, a sound educational infrastructure, a decently paid and decently pensioned job in education, a well-run bureaucracy, good communications and a postal service in which letters arrived the next day sometimes even the same day. Janáček's sixty-four years under the Habsburgs certainly advanced his career. His initial dealings with his publisher Universal Edition were undertaken when Vienna was still the capital city: by the end of the First World War it was a capital city anxious to give an impression of trying to be fair to its minority nations. Had Janáček not been an Austro-Hungarian subject, it is possible that the Vienna Hofoper might have been less eager to stage *Jenůfa* and send it on its international way into the German-speaking world.

Just as one can be a subject of the United Kingdom of Great Britain and Northern Ireland but yet feel oneself to be more of a Scot than anything else, so Janáček, despite working until retirement from the Teachers' Institute as an Austrian civil servant, would not have dreamt of defining himself in terms other than Czech and Moravian. Here language and culture were the chief determinants of nationality, overlaying even place of birth. One only needs to compare Janáček with another famous son of the area born two years later, just five miles away from Hukvaldy in Příbor – Sigmund Freud – to see how important language and culture were at the expense of place of birth. It would hardly have occurred to Freud to define himself as Moravian (let alone Lachian), but then he was a Jew and a German speaker, and at the time German was for him the language of social mobility that would take him to Vienna and its cosmopolitan, but German-speaking, culture. In the new Czechoslovakia of the postwar era, Jews would have the choice of aligning themselves with the new country (as did Janáček's friends the Stössels), as Germans, or somewhere in between Czech and German culture (as did Janáček's translator and great promoter Max Brod).

Czech and German

Like all Czechs of his period Janáček received a substantial part of his education in German. By the time of his birth, German had become overwhelmingly the language of education in the Habsburg Empire, and Czech, if it was used at all, was limited to rural primary schools. In the remote village school in Hukvaldy where Janáček's father taught, the school register was kept in German until the beginning of the school year 1863–4 (when it began to be kept in Czech),[25] but there is no evidence that German was used as a medium of instruction in Janáček's education there. From the moment Janáček was sent to Brno as a choral scholar in 1865, however, his education continued in German. Like all the primary schools in Brno at the time Janáček's school was a German-medium one and it seems (see chap. 7) that he repeated a year there expressly to improve his knowledge of German. Though no doubt contributing to his abiding dislike of German and German speakers, his German-medium education gave him a confident command of the language. He showed off his German to his uncle Jan Janáček with a little poem he wrote in his first surviving letter to him on 18 May 1866, when he was not yet twelve (see chap. 7). When he qualified as a teacher he was attested to teach at all national primary schools (which in effect meant being able to teach in German). In the introduction to his edition of Janáček's letters to Zdenka Schulzová from Leipzig and Vienna, some seven hundred pages all in German, Jakob Knaus commented on how extensive Janáček's German vocabulary was, and on how seldom he made mistakes or couldn't find the right expression.[26]

By the time Janáček began his German education in Brno, Prague had its Czech Provisional Theatre and many other cultural institutions. Changes in education came rather more slowly, and not soon enough to help Janáček. It was only during the third year that the Men Teachers' Institute in Brno was divided into Czech and German institutes and the rest of his education there could take place in Czech. By the time he was setting out as a young man to forge his career he was able to conduct choirs in Czech, teach in Czech, and establish an Organ School that, although officially German-Czech, nevertheless conducted most of its affairs in Czech.

Janáček claimed that even as a little boy he had been frightened of the German estate workers in Hukvaldy[27] but this is a reminiscence of many years later. The earliest contemporary evidence for Janáček's anti-German sentiments can be found in a letter to his uncle Jan in

1869: having wondered whether his uncle was a 'faithful Czech or a faithful German' he followed with a bloodthirsty poem about what might happen to the enemies of the Czechs (see chap. 7). This clear nationalist, pro-Czech, anti-German stance nevertheless did not prevent him from associating with a typically Germanized middle-class family of the time, the Schulzes, where despite the husband's Czech background (and the fact that he ran a Czech-speaking educational institute), German prevailed as the spoken language within the family and the young daughter of the family, Zdenka, was brought up in German. Janáček did not object to teaching her the piano in German, and subsequently even courted her in German. When in 1879 he went to study in Leipzig and Vienna, his love letters to his future wife were written entirely in German.

The linguistic fates of two of Janáček's brothers, Bedřich and František, provide an instructive parallel. Both worked abroad and both soon found themselves in circumstances where German was the lingua franca. The letters written to Leoš Janáček by Bedřich (by then 'Friedrich' or 'Fritz' and working in Klagenfurt as an engineer) are in German. His one surviving communication in Czech, a postcard from a holiday in Cordoba,[28] is in such poor Czech that it is virtually unintelligible, a reflection both of the fact that his Czech was spoken rather than written, and that even his spoken Czech was rapidly disappearing. Many more letters survive from Janáček's younger brother František and these provide a fascinating insight into the Janáček family's mixed linguistic background. František established himself in what is now Poland (though then part of Prussian Silesia) and married a Polish woman. Until 1895, when he moved to Russia, he wrote to Leoš in the brothers' best language of written communication, German.[29] In his second letter from St Petersburg, which appears to be reporting remarks by Leoš, he agreed that it was wrong not to try and write in his mother tongue, and thereafter he did, if with some difficulty at first.[30] Whereas Friedrich's Czech had all but disappeared, František's was in reasonable repair, topped up by trips to Prague and summer holidays spent with the family in Hukvaldy and his taking Czech newspapers.[31] It was only written Czech that caused a few problems such as slips in spelling and some contamination from Russian. František continued to write long letters to his brother Leoš in Czech, and it was only as Janáček's Russian improved that written communication between the two of them moved into Russian.

As soon as Janáček returned to Brno after his studies in Leipzig and Vienna he began to demand that Zdenka Schulzová spoke Czech with him, an uncomfortable transition for her as her Czech was rudimentary. His insistence on speaking Czech within the Schulz family was a major factor in poisoning the previously excellent relations between him and his future in-laws (see chap. 17). It could be argued that Janáček's linguistic intransigence not only upset relations with his in-laws but led to the early breakdown of his marriage with Zdenka.

Janáček, however, won this linguistic battle. Both his children were brought up in Czech and his daughter Olga spoke so little German that when in 1899 Bedřich/Friedrich Janáček and his family (who spoke no Czech) arrived in Hukvaldy for the summer, Olga was virtually unable to communicate with her cousins (see chap. 36). On one of the Hukvaldy holidays Olga attracted the attention of an under-huntsman on the archbishop's estate, and the young German found himself having to communicate in 'wretched Czech', though not for long since when Janáček turned up he soon put an end to the affair.[32]

Janáček's anti-German attitude was so well known that his pupil Jan Kunc devoted a whole paragraph to this topic in his biographical article on Janáček for *Hudební revue* in 1911. Kunc recounted how Janáček never went to Brno's German opera or German concerts, although he would have heard a much better orchestra than that used in Czech endeavours in Brno. It was not until 1906 that Janáček ventured into the German Theatre in Prague expressly to hear Strauss's *Salome* (not given in Czech until 1923). Another sore point was local transport. 'Until recently [Kunc recalled in 1911] he would never go into Brno trams, waiting until the [place] signs would be at least in both languages; only recently his heart condition forced him to give up this principle.'[33] Brno was sufficiently small for Janáček to get around on foot, but when in 1907 the Organ School moved there was now a brisk walk of well over half an hour. The trams that plied between Staré Brno and central Brno were owned by Germans and carried only German place names.

Similarly, if Janáček sent a postcard that carried only German wording, he usually crossed it out and wrote a Czech translation over it. In the summer of 1907, for instance, when he was travelling in Jablunkov, Silesia, he sent Zdenka a postcard from 'Jablunkau östr. Schlesien', as the monolingual card had it. He put a stroke through the 'au' (writing 'ov' above it), and crossed out the next two words. Similarly he replaced the caption for the picture of the town square

('Hauptplatz') with its Czech equivalent 'náměstí'. On the other side of the card he took the trouble to write out 'Korespondenční lístek' in exchange for an innocuous 'Postkarte'.[34] This practice – similar to Welsh-language enthusiasts' emending of monolingual road signs – continued for the rest of his life. Even when his country became Czechoslovakia, Janáček resisted going to what he regarded as German regions such as Marienbad (by then Mariánské Lázně) and, despite doctor's orders, set off for his Czech spa of Luhačovice instead. In 1925 the question arose of where the statue of his old teacher Pavel Křížkovský should go. Janáček objected to its being sited in a 'German' location (near the German Turnhalle) and instead proposed a more 'Czech' location such as near the Reduta theatre or the Lužánky hall (xv/280). For Janáček German was a symbol of his nation's lack of independence: fighting against the use of German (whatever its practical advantages and cultural riches) was casting a blow for Czech.

Ironically, of course, Janáček needed German when his career took off. It was a matter of some astonishment to his Czech publisher Hudební matice that Janáček cheerfully signed up with Universal Edition in Vienna when it came to providing a German-language piano-vocal score of *Jenůfa* rather than dealing through them and their approved foreign publisher. Janáček's early mastery of German now facilitated his professional contacts. He wrote all his letters to Universal Edition or to German-speaking interpreters of his music such as Otto Klemperer in German. With the German translator of his librettos Max Brod (who knew Czech well), correspondence was in German-Czech: Brod wrote in German (with the odd phrase in Czech where useful) and Janáček wrote back in Czech.

When *Jenůfa* was given its German première in Vienna in 1918, and Zdenka Janáčková accompanied her husband there, she noted drily: 'It was so strange that he spoke German here the whole time, he who couldn't bear to hear a single word of German at home.'[35] When he went to Berlin for the première of *Jenůfa* on 17 March 1924 'he even made speeches in German'. Janáček the pragmatist won out when it came to promoting his music, though there were occasional flickers of annoyance when, for instance in 1925, Hudební matice produced a leaflet on Janáček for use at the forthcoming Venice Festival and sent it to him to look at. Why, he asked, was it 'in German for Italy?' There were other means of understanding one another 'than the intrusive German'. And why was Hukvaldy called 'Hochwald'? 'Not a single German there.'[36]

3

The Janáčeks

In his authoritative biography of 1938 Vladimír Helfert traced the Janáčeks back to the second half of the seventeenth century to Těšín, the border area with Poland. In 1697 Kašpar Janáček moved from Těšín and settled in the Silesian town of Frýdek, then an important textile centre. Originally apprenticed as a weaver, he now became a draper and a member of the local drapers' guild. Helfert's account of the Janáček family as drapers in the eighteenth century emphasizes the Czech-speaking tradition of the area and its Silesian character – an orientation towards Opava in the north rather than Olomouc, Brno or Vienna in the south.[1] After the death of Kašpar's grandson, Jan Janáček (born 1742) there is an abrupt change: later male Janáčeks are schoolteachers and live not in Frýdek but on the Czech side of the Silesian/Czech border in nearby villages such as Albrechtičky and Hukvaldy. Although Helfert makes much of this break, it is perhaps more startling than he revealed. The last child of Jan Janáček (by his third wife, Dorota Zuzana Brojačová, 1748–1808) was given in the birth register as posthumous. Helfert did not provide a death date for Jan Janáček and failed to notice that the word 'posthumous' after Jiří Janáček in the birth register was either ironic or compassionate. Jiří Janáček was born on 17 April 1778, almost four years after the death of Jan Janáček on 6 June 1774.[2] All Jiří inherited from his 'father' was the family name.

No wonder that Dorota Janáčková, living in very reduced circumstances, would seek to leave Frýdek, where the circumstances of the birth of her little boy Jiří were well known. In 1784, at the invitation of Father Antonín Herman (1753–1801), she moved to the village of Velký Petřvald (now Petřvald) to serve as his housekeeper. Helfert allowed himself the speculation that the reason for this move was 'personal, perhaps of a quite intimate character'.[3] Jiří was then six and Herman became his mentor and guardian and in many ways a father to him. Whether Herman was his actual father one will never know, but in one way or another Herman was able to pass on to the young boy an education and world view completely different from that of the draper and small trader Janáčeks of the seventeenth and eighteenth centuries.

Herman came from a well-to-do aristocratic family. He was ordained as a priest and in 1778 (the year of Jiří Janáček's birth) joined the Augustinian monastery in Fulnek, where he led a comfortable existence in a 'cell' kitted out with fine furniture, fifty-six paintings, many books and a complete riding outfit. In 1784 this privileged life came to an end when Joseph II's reforms closed down the monastery and its twelve monks were dispersed and forced to work as priests in the community. Thus at the age of thirty-one Herman unexpectedly found himself as a chaplain in Velký Petřvald, a small village with a sixteenth-century wooden church and generally primitive conditions. There he quietly drank himself to death.[4] But he made sure that Dorota's son thrived. He provided his first schooling himself, awakening in him an interest in bookbinding, gardening and growing vegetables. Above all he sent him off to train as a teacher.[5] And so the Janáčeks became kantors.

Today the word 'kantor' is used colloquially in Czech to mean a schoolteacher. Earlier, however, it also embraced the notion of a musician (the word itself derives from the Latin *cantor*, 'a singer'). Outside the main towns, teachers were often chosen for their musical abilities in the knowledge that they would be able to augment their incomes by doubling up as organists or choirmasters. As a result many schoolteachers in even the most remote parts of the Czech lands were competent musicians, and music teaching would thus figure in the school syllabus, a phenomenon described approvingly by Burney in his *Present State of Music in Germany* (1775). From the seventeenth century to the nineteenth (significantly the period of maximum Habsburg national oppression) it was the Czech kantors who kept alive Czech language and culture. Kantors rightly took their place in the pantheon of Czech nationalist icons: the affectionate if sentimentalized portrait of a kantor in Dvořák's opera *The Jacobin* is typical. More concrete information can be found in Jan Trojan's remarkable study of the kantor tradition in Moravia, which lists over five thousand

Moravian kantors at work during this period.[6] Many were members of kantor families, with teaching posts often handed down from father to son. Jiří Janáček's case was typical. Of his four sons, the two oldest (Josef and Jan) became priests, the two youngest (Jiří junior and Vincenc) became schoolteachers. In turn some of the sons in the next generation became schoolteachers too.

Kantors, particularly good ones, did more than teach in school and look after the music in church. In many cases they represented sources of further education and self-improvement and led the community in a variety of ways. Jiří Janáček senior, his interest in horticulture awakened by Father Herman, became an expert gardener and cultivator of fruit trees, known as far as Brno for his grafting techniques and supplying many fruit trees to the surrounding areas.[7] His other interests included bookbinding, wood-carving, gilding[8] and organ building. With the local tailor Jan Huvar he built the organ (including pedals and seventeen stops) in his local church at Albrechtičky, an instrument that remained in use up to 1891.[9] Jiří junior specialized in beekeeping. Among the earliest memories of his son Leo were the forty-eight hives his father kept;[10] images of the hive continued to enliven Janáček's writings into his old age.[11] Jiří junior also founded the Hukvaldy Singing and Reading Club. Its aims were broadly educational: reading instructive magazines and articles and the cultivation of Czech folksong.[12] In 1865 it was one of the first such clubs in the region and represented an attempt to counter the pressure for Germanization that came from the archbishop's administrators (who used German routinely up to 1909).[13]

Above all, both Jiřís were fine musicians. Jiří senior's musical talents had been developed during his training as a schoolteacher in Ostrava (then just a small town rather than the industrial city of today). He was a passionate musician, a competent organist who knew how to improvise preludes, and a fine singer who could bring tears to the eyes of his listeners.[14] Jiří junior (1815–66) had an even more extensive musical training, acquired from two famously musical kantors: at school in Velký Petřvald (under Josef Richter) and as a teaching assistant to Alois Urbánek in Neplachovice. In nearby Opava there were more musical opportunities, as there were in his later posting to Příbor, a town with an important musical tradition.[15] Like his father, Jiří junior was an excellent organist, but in addition he was a pianist good enough to teach his son Leo to play Beethoven piano sonatas.

Another son, Josef, remembered his father having a large collection of sheet music by various composers.[16]

Poised between school teaching and music-making, kantor families would occasionally produce outstanding musicians able to earn a living through music rather than through teaching. This was the case with the Foerster and Suk teacher families, who nurtured two of the finest Czech composers of the twentieth century, Josef Bohuslav Foerster and Josef Suk. And it was also the case with the Janáčeks, whose musical training deepened with each generation. However the humble circumstances of the family meant there was no question of Leo Janáček doing anything other than following the family tradition and becoming a schoolteacher. Whereas little Josef Suk (1874–1935) went to the Prague Conservatory in 1885 at the age of eleven, Janáček did not get to the Prague Organ School until 1874, by which time he was twenty and had completed his training as a primary schoolteacher.

Jiří Janáček senior took up his teaching post in the village of Albrechtičky in 1799 and remained there until the end of his life. He was an outstanding and energetic teacher who increased the school roster (school attendance was not obligatory at the time) and constantly won excellent reports from the school inspectors on the quality of his work and the commitment of his pupils.[17] A great deal is known about his work since one of his teacher sons, Vincenc Janáček (1821–1901), wrote a full account of his father's life. Helfert made considerable use of this manuscript (it has subsequently been published)[18] and was able to verify many of its claims independently. Jiří senior taught until his retirement in 1842; he died in 1848, shortly after Jiří junior took up his teaching post in Hukvaldy on 26 September 1848.

By the time Jiří Janáček junior moved to Hukvaldy, he had held various temporary teaching posts, including one in the town of Příbor, where he met his future wife Amalie Grulichová (1819–84; see Plates 1 and 3), the daughter of well-off tradesfolk in Příbor. Her father, originally a tailor, ran a pub, and Amalie brought a dowry of 200 zl, roughly equivalent to her husband's annual salary. Like her husband, she was a good musician. She had a fine voice, and played the guitar and the organ: after her husband's death she served as village organist in Hukvaldy until the replacement teacher arrived. She was small and fair, her husband Jiří tall and dark,[19] and with an explosive temperament.[20] Both were said to be strict with their children.[21]

While Jiří senior thrived in Albrechtičky, Jiří junior had a much less happy time in Hukvaldy. He was thirty-three when he arrived and already the father of five. His post was not well paid in comparison with others in the area,[22] and the schoolhouse (in which the Janáčeks also lived; see Plate 2) was unsuitable for its purpose. Converted in 1816 from an earlier building,* the walls were damp, the roof leaked, door frames rotted, and the stove hardly worked. Complaint after complaint had been made to the authorities by Jiří junior's predecessor but to no effect.[23] When faced with a similarly inadequate schoolhouse in Albrechtičky, Jiří senior had enterprisingly resorted to malicious damage – he weakened and then dislodged the timber supporting the roof [24] – and got his new building within a year; his son simply sent in annual complaints or applied, in vain, for other postings.[25] The conditions took their toll on his family. Of Jiří senior's seven children six survived infancy. Of Jiří junior's nine children born in Hukvaldy one was stillborn and another four died in infancy. A comparison of the size of their families also sheds light on the characters of the two fathers. Both submitted their wives to a quarter-century of childbearing. But whereas poor Amalie Janáčková produced her total of fourteen children at a rate of one every one or two years, her mother-in-law Anna Janáčková produced her seven children at a more leisurely pace; the later ones (including Jiří junior and Vincenc) were born at five- or six-year intervals. The result was that Jiří senior's limited resources went further in a smaller and better spaced family, whereas Jiří junior was able to do rather less for his more numerous family, the youngest of whom was only seven when he died.

It was not until 1858 that Jiří junior's pleas were heard, and repairs made to the schoolhouse. It was too late to save his health. After August 1858 he was unable to teach regularly because of rheumatism and a heart condition. He died in 1866, at only fifty.[26] Jiří junior did not lack enterprise, as is evident in his extra-curricular activities, but he settled in Hukvaldy during exceptionally difficult times with failing harvests and high inflation[27] and seems to have lacked the toughness of his father. Jiří senior got what he wanted through hard work, pushiness, guile and force of character. These were characteristics that were inherited by his grandson, Leo.

---

* Přibáňová (1984, 15) has 'ledovna' ['ice house']; NH (1994, 22) has 'bednárna', a workshop for making barrels. LJPT (1939, 37) has an inexplicable 'bedovna'.

4

Hukvaldy

Rieger's encyclopedia[1] describes Hukvaldy as a fortified castle, the largest in Moravia, belonging to the bishops of Olomouc, the ecclesiastical capital. The castle withstood sieges by the Hussites (1420–30), by the Duke of Mansfeld (1622), by the Swedes (1645), and by the Hungarians, the Turks and the Prussians (1742–58) and had been the seat of administration in the area up to 1760. In that year, however, this function was taken over by the 'new castle' built in the valley beneath. The old castle burnt down in 1762, leaving the picturesque ruin that remains to this day.

Rieger's entry on Hukvaldy does not register the complicated changes in ownership of the castle. Although the Olomouc bishops (archbishops from 1777) were mostly the owners from 1250, it was in their possession continuously only from 1620. It was the Olomouc bishops, too, who in 1567 established the local brewery and the game reserve,[2] both of which survived into Janáček's day and are frequently mentioned in his accounts of the area. The article also fails to mention that a village had begun to grow up beneath the castle in the second half of the eighteenth century. In addition to the brewery there was a roadside inn, a mill, a distillery and from 1759 a chapel, later consecrated to St Maximilian.

Janáček's earliest years in Hukvaldy coincided with the tenure of Archbishop Fridrich Egon zur Fürstenberk (1853–92), who devoted great attention to the village, reconstructing the 'new castle', repairing the school (too late, however, to prevent its damp conditions contributing to the death of Janáček's father Jiří) and founding a horse farm in the game park: the 'Andalusian' horses[3] about which Janáček enthused to Kamila Stösslová in 1918.[4]

By the time Jiří Janáček settled there in 1848, Hukvaldy and the two neighbouring villages, Horní Sklenov and Dolní Sklenov (which together formed an administrative unit) comprised 137 buildings. Its inhabitants were mostly poor cottagers – 264 men and 309 women – who cultivated flax and eked out a living by weaving the yarn into linen, later sent off for sale to Opava and Olomouc. There were said to be looms in all the cottages. Sheep were also reared in this poor mountain village.[5]

The 1890 census records the village of Hukvaldy alone (i.e. without the two Sklenovs) as having 86 buildings with 551 inhabitants. The short entry on Hukvaldy in Otto's encyclopedia[6] describes it as a village and parish castle chaplaincy falling under the Místek district. In addition to the features described above, the entry mentions a post office with telegraph facilities, a police station, a savings bank, and a steam saw mill. It also mentions the two-class school, the birthplace of Leo Janáček.

5

Childhood
(1854-65)

When Leoš Janáček was born in Hukvaldy on 3 July 1854 (christened the next day as Leo Eugen Janáček) he had six surviving siblings. However, only one of these, his sister Rosalie,* was near enough in age to be part of his child's world. It was Rosalie who is mentioned in Janáček's feuilleton *Without Drums* (XV/199) as being taken with him by their father to perform in church, Leo singing treble and Rosalie playing the viola. Janáček does not specifically name her (she is described only as a 'sister') but by then the older sisters hardly qualified as 'us children'. By the time Leo was seven (a reasonable age for singing a solo in church) Rosalie Kateřina (born 1850) was eleven. Viktorie (born 1838) was twenty-three; she had married at not quite seventeen and continued for a while to live near the school.[1] The next two sisters, Eleonora Amalie (born 1840; see Plate 4) and Josefa Adolfina (born 1842; see Plate 5), were twenty-one and nineteen, and, like Viktorie, were old enough to act as surrogate mothers for the younger children (see table 5.1).

Both Eleonora and Josefa trained as teachers of needlework and domestic crafts and both figure in Janáček's later story. Eleonora, 'gentle, kind and attentive', was remembered fondly by Zdenka Janáčková as the best of the brood.[3] Josefa was altogether tougher. She was the only one of the family to live permanently in the area and later married the Hukvaldy schoolteacher Jindřich Dohnal. In her old age she stayed in Janáček's Hukvaldy cottage and served as his housekeeper when he was in residence and as caretaker when he was away.

* All names here are given according to the birth register, not according to how the children were ultimately known, or according to present Czech spelling rules (see Author's note).

Table 5.1: The children of Jiří Janáček and Amalie Janáčková[2]

born	died	name	comments
born in Příbor			
1838	1894	Viktorie	married Ondřej Červenka, emigrated to America but returned and died in Hukvaldy
1840	1919	Eleonora Amalie	trained as a handicraft teacher; moved to Švábenice, where she died
1842	1931	Josefa Adolfina	trained as a handicraft teacher; married Jindřich Dohnal (later divorced), died in Hukvaldy
1844	1919	Karel Jiří	trained as a teacher, worked in Krhová, near Valašské Meziříčí
1846	1918	Bedřich Vincenc	emigrated to Germany, in charge of factories in Ebenthal near Klagenfurt, then in Warsaw, moving to Vienna at the end of his life
born in Hukvaldy			
1849	1849	unnamed twin	stillborn
1849	1849	František, twin of above	lived two months
1850	1868	Rosalie Kateřina	died of typhus in Příbor
1852	1852	Jiří	lived fifteen minutes
1854	1928	**Leo Eugen**	
1856	1908	František Josef	worked in Prussian Silesia and St Petersburg as an engineer; returned to Hukvaldy when his health failed
1858	1941	Josef	trained as a teacher; worked partly in Russia, ending up in a smallholding near Rožnov
1861	1861	Adolf	lived six days
1863	1863	Marie	lived six months

By the time Leo was seven, some of the older children had left the nest. At some stage Viktorie and her husband the weaver Ondřej Červenka are said to have emigrated to America[4] (she returned much later to Hukvaldy where she died in 1894).[5] Eleonora settled in Švábenice (nearer Brno than Hukvaldy). Karel Jiří (born 1844; see Plate 8) trained as a schoolteacher and though he returned in 1865 to serve as his father's assistant,[6] he left Hukvaldy after his father's death and took up a teaching post in Krhová near Valašské Meziříčí. Bedřich Vincenc (born 1846; see Plate 9) left home early and found work in Germany.

The five children born in Příbor all had long lives apart from Viktorie, who died at fifty-five. In 1849, a year after the Janáčeks settled in Hukvaldy, Amalie was delivered of twin boys, one stillborn and unnamed, the other named František, who, however, lived only a couple of months.[7] In 1852 another son, Jiří, was born, though his life was even shorter: just fifteen minutes.[8] No wonder Leo, born two years later, was said to be his mother's favourite[9] – the first son born in Hukvaldy to survive. He was followed in 1856 by another František (or rather František Josef; see Plate 7). Although František spent most of his life abroad, a closeness in age translated into a closeness in affection with his brother Leo. Of all his siblings František was the one with whom Janáček stayed most in touch, exchanging letters with him, visiting him in St Petersburg in 1896, sending his daughter Olga to stay with him in 1902, and regularly spending time with him in Hukvaldy, where František returned in 1905.

The Janáčeks' next child Josef (born 1858; see Plate 10) also lived, but was the last to do so. From the nine children born in Hukvaldy only four survived childhood: a harsh testimony to the Janáčeks' poor living conditions there. Leo was seven when his brother Adolf was born in 1861 and would thus would remember his six-day life and the six-month life of his sister Marie born two years later. Janáček's own recollection (used by Brod in his biography, 1924) was that he was the seventh out of eleven children.[10] This suggests that he was unaware of the dead twins of 1849 and the short-lived Jiří of 1852 but that he remembered all those that followed. These sad childhood memories were compounded by the death of his own son Vladimír at two and a half. It was not by chance that Janáček would go on to set an opera text (in *Jenůfa*) about the death of a baby.

On 1 May 1859,[11] when Leo was getting on for five, he started attending his father's school. Many years later he wrote down his recollections:

The Hukvaldy school. A large room, old benches, pockmarked. One class on the left – for the very small; one on the right – for those more grown up. Two blackboards: Father and the under-teacher taught at the same time. How not to get in each other's way? In the corner a large stove; a bed beside it; on it the under-teacher slept.[12]

The 'under-teacher', however, arrived only at the end of 1859. Leo experienced a succession of four[13] of which his brother Karel was the fourth. (The fifth and last of Jiří Janáček's assistants arrived after Leo had already left for Brno.) As one of the 'very small' Leo naturally started in the lower class while Rosalie was by then in the upper class. In October 1861 Leo progressed to the upper class.

Leo was not his father's best pupil. The only indication of how he did at school comes from the *Kniha cti* [Book of honour], an elaborately bound record of the Hukvaldy school from 1818 to 1877 in which pupils who particularly distinguished themselves at the annual school inspection are singled out. Naturally the local schoolmaster would have done his best to get his own children into the top group, and Jiří Janáček managed to do so with most of his children. Karel, Josefa and Bedřich all received three annual mentions (Rosalie seems to have been the star pupil, with four); Josef received two and Viktorie one. Those who don't figure in this group are the gentle (but perhaps unacademic) Eleonora, Leo and František – another sign of early bonding between the two brothers. Leo appears only in the second league, where he is mentioned each year from 1860 to 1864.[14] The one occasion that young Leo distinguished himself was in 1861 (he was then seven) where within his 'Group II' he was given a mark of 'very good' in reading.[15]

Not much is known about Leo as a young boy. Musical he certainly was, otherwise he would not have been accepted as a choral scholar in Brno and in Kroměříž, nor would his future path as a musician have been so smooth. High-spirited and enterprising he probably was too, if one can believe his nice story (*Without Drums*, xv/199) recounting how he and a young friend (Jan Hláčík) stole drums for the ceremonial celebration of high mass. One may wonder why early biographers did not interview any of Janáček's siblings about their early life, but by his death only two were living, the then very elderly Josefa and Josef, the black sheep of the family. In his book published in 1930 Adolf E. Vašek acknowledges help from Josef and includes family details that can have come from no other source. However these are only scraps and perhaps serve only to illustrate that Josef had little to do with his famous older brother.

There remain Janáček's own much later reminiscences and, like all such memoirs, they need to be treated with caution. His earliest memory (he was then three) was of a fire that gutted the nearby brewery in 1857:

Fire. Fiery tongues of the blaze crept over the roof of the brewery – right next to the school – and at night in the summer! They carried us children in eiderdowns to the slopes of the park there above the [statue of the] Virgin Mary. I remember my cries.[16]

He also remembered the animals: the cow in the stable, the ducks in the school court, his father's forty-eight beehives; also the cottage of his sister 'Vikýna' (Viktorie) with its weaver's loom, and the single shop 'U Gobrů',[17] later to become the Hotel Mičaník. There were memories of church-going, trudging through the snow to midnight mass, wax candles in hand[†] (to be lit in church), their way illuminated by twinkling lanterns, or the pilgrimage to St Ondřej in the old castle, an annual event that took place on 30 November, by which time it was difficult getting up the steep slope after the first snow had fallen.[18] Other memories were of the surrounding countryside: collecting bilberries, and the ants that bit, getting lost on Babí hůra (the thickly wooded hill nearby), and the stream running down from it where (he was told) children came from. There were also darker memories of German officials working on the archbishop's estate: 'a noisy throng of strange, unpleasant people – always there at the entrance like dark bees there around the hive'. Germans were to be avoided.[19]

Not until a year before he died, when he was specifically asked to comment on his feelings about Beethoven, did Janáček relate how his father taught him the piano:

The old Wolfenbüttel edition of Beethoven's sonatas is well known: *Wolfenbüttel, chez Louis Holle, métronomisées par Ignaz Moscheles.*
That's the format I've got before my eyes to this day: I think it was published in fascicles with greenish wrappers.
As an eight-year-old boy I battled with many of the sonatas on the old piano.
Oh, the notes melted into my tears like the bloody spots on the back of my left hand.
I'm sure I never got the bass right! And when my father stood over me with a brush in his hand, its bristles would suddenly bore into my left hand.

[†] Vašek 1930, 19, explained in a footnote that the mystifying 'sloup' ['column', 'shaft'] that each carried was in fact a candle.

Since then I've known that notes should sweat blood when they are written and sweat blood when they are badly played.

And Father? No doubt he trembled at the thought that I wouldn't turn out to be what he wanted me to be. (xv/291)

Three years later, with Jiří Janáček's health failing, it was time to do something about Leo. According to Janáček's autobiography, Jiří took his eleven-year-old son to two choral scholarship interviews, one in Kroměříž, one in Opava. The plan for Kroměříž, a musically and culturally important residence of the Archbishop of Olomouc, with places for eleven choral scholars, presumably made use of whatever connections Jiří Janáček had with the archbishop's estate in Hukvaldy.[20] Jiří prepared his son in the Kroměříž park by grilling him about scales, but in fact Leo seems to have been accepted without examination: Janáček remembered that in the interview with a German priest in a black habit he took no part – 'as if I wasn't there'. If this is so it seems surprising that he was accepted (as Janáček went on to say in his autobiography),[21] a fact that Helfert's examination of Kroměříž archives was unable to prove or disprove.[22]

But Jiří Janáček went for the alternative plan, initiated through the interview in Opava, which seems to have been more rigorous. Here Jiří Janáček made use of his chance acquaintance with the composer Pavel Křížkovský (1820–85), whom he had first encountered when he was a teaching assistant at Neplachovice. Vincenc Janáček tells a charming story of how his brother became friendly with the 'little orphan'‡ Pavel Křížkovský, 'whose mother begged him to teach the lad music and singing, which he did and later prepared him for a choral scholarship at the church of the Holy Spirit in Opava'.[23] Helfert was able to confirm Jiří's one-year tenure in Neplachovice (1831–2) but also made the point that there was only a five-year gap between the two boys – Křížkovský was eleven, and Jiří sixteen[24] – so that Jiří fell more into the role of sympathetic older brother than teacher. Since 1848 Křížkovský had been in charge of the music provision at the Augustinian monastery in Brno. This connection forged what turned out to be a crucial link in the life of Jiří's son Leo.

In 1865, when Jiří was attempting to get Leo enrolled as a choral scholar, Křížkovský was ill with a throat infection[25] and that summer was convalescing in Opava, where his family still lived. Janáček

---

‡ A kindly way of referring to a child born out of wedlock.

remembered the coach journey to Opava (the rail link was built later):[26] 'I see only the interior of the high coach. Crumpled eiderdown. I see neither the horses, nor the coachman. Nor the countryside disappearing into the night, slept through in the bowels of the coach. Then the Opava square, an ant hill. I, frightened by everything.'[27]

In a reminiscence of Křížkovský Janáček also remembered something about his interview:

I was at his place with music, then a lad of about eleven. He played something. 'I should listen to it!' He sang and played at the same time on the piano. Some sort of sad song, something about a grave.[S] 'How did I like it?' I don't know what I answered. The composer probably wanted an outsider's verdict. (xv/166)

It seems enlightened of Křížkovský to have wanted the opinion of an eleven-year-old on his piece. Maybe it was Janáček's response to the 'sad song' that sealed his acceptance for a choral scholarship in Brno.

[S] What the 'sad song' was is a matter of dispute. Vašek (1930, 41) was the first to assert that it was *Autumn and Maytime*, and this has been reproduced in later Janáček literature (*LJPT*, 51, fn. 2; *LJOLP*, 174, fn.*). However this piece was composed in 1870 (see Straková 1955b, 22, and *NG2*), five years after the interview.

6

Brno I: 1860–1914

Before 1860, Brno had been transformed by two major events. One was the train link to Vienna in 1839, the first steam passenger train in the Czech lands. Above all, this increased Brno's value to the empire as an industrial town, now brought much closer to the imperial capital, and ensured that it would overtake Olomouc in size and importance. Another was the demolition of the city ramparts after 1852, which led to the creation of the ring road and parks, and released space for new buildings such as the Stadttheater, the 'theatre on the ramparts'. Existing parks such as the Lužánky park, a favourite haunt of Janáček, had been open to the public since 1786.

Some societies had been founded before 1860, for instance the first German Readers' society (1837), the male choral society Männergesangverein (1848), the German Musikverein (end of 1850s) and even some Czech societies such as the Jednota národní sv. Cyrilla a Methoda [The national society of SS Cyril and Methodius] (1848) and the Čtenářský spolek· Beseda [Readers' Club Beseda], which arranged musical evenings on Saturdays for members (1849). However the real transformation in Czech Brno is evident in the multitude of new societies which were permitted after the relaxing of laws allowed by the October diploma of 1860.

Although the population of Moravia as a whole was predominantly Czech-speaking in the nineteenth century (70.34% in the 1890 census), in the major towns such as Brno and Olomouc the situation was the opposite. Language was not considered in the 1869 census but there is no reason to believe that the balance of Czech and German speakers in Brno would have been much different from the census figures before the creation of Czechoslovakia in 1918, i.e. the Czech speakers hovered around a third. This was in contrast to Prague, where the proportions were reversed. Part of the Brno reason for this is that, with a German majority on the Brno town council, Germans were keen to keep it so, and the provision of Czech-medium schools was conceded reluctantly and usually only after appeals above their heads. Nevertheless, it is clear that from the 1880s there was much more opportunity for a pupil to be educated in Czech (a change that was too late for Janáček to benefit from apart from his final two years of teacher training). Surprisingly this seemed not much to have altered the balance of Czech and German speakers, if the census figures are correct (they were frequently contested by the Czech lobby). The call for a Czech university, however, was resolutely refused, and the conflict of Germans and Czechs over this in 1905 provided the context for Janáček's *1.X.1905* for piano (VIII/19). A Czech university came about only after the First World War.

Staré Brno [Old Brno], previously a separate market town, had been absorbed into Brno in 1850, but it retained much of its individual identity, and was able to sustain many separate institutions such as the Starobrněnská beseda (see below). In 1869, the year Janáček completed his basic schooling, it had 7823 inhabitants, a figure that grew to 8952 in the 1890 census (the last separate figure before the First World War).[1]

The tables that follow are intended to reflect the growth in Brno as a town and in particular that of its Czech element before the First World War and to provide reference dates for many of the Brno institutions, buildings, societies and journals mentioned in this book.

Table 6.1: Population of Brno 1869–1910
N/A = not available[2]

year	total	Czech-sp	%	German-speaking	%	others
1869	73,771	N/A	N/A	N/A	N/A	N/A
1880	82,660	32,142	39.6	48,591	59.2	1927
1890	94,753	28,202	30.3	63,622	68.3	2329
1900	109,346	38,365	33.3	68,702	65.2	2279
1910	125,808	41,943	33.2	81,617	65.3	2248

Table 6.2: Transport within and from Brno 1860–1914[3]

1863	Beginning of horse-drawn omnibuses: two routes going at hourly intervals, including one running between the railway station and Lužánky via the main square (to 1869)
1869	Rail link Brno–Olomouc–Šternberk (with a branch line to Přerov)
1869	Horse-drawn trams: five routes, including one from Staré Brno to Pisárky and one from Staré Brno to Moravské náměstí via the railway station (to 1875)
1877	Horse-drawn trams: two routes, including Staré Brno to Královo Pole via the railway station (to 1881)
1883	Rail link 'Vlárský průsmyk' [The Vlár (river) pass]: Brno–Slavkov–Bučovice-Kyjov–Veselí nad Moravou–Kunovice [to Trenčianská Teplá in Slovakia] (completed 1886)
1884	Steam trams ('Karolinka' and other women's names) (to 1900)
1885	Rail link 'Tišnovka': Brno–Tišnov
1900	Electric trams, the German-owned 'Elektrische Linie' (trams are still known in Brno slang in a Czech corruption of this, 'šalina', i.e. ElektriSCHE LINIE)

Table 6.3: Education in Brno 1860–1914[4]

When Janáček went to Brno all tuition at primary schools there was in German; he himself attended the German primary school at Lackerwiese ulice (now Jircháře, 1865–6). From 1867 high school tuition was permitted in Czech at the Gymnasium; Janáček, however, as a schoolteacher designate, attended the German Realschule in Staré Brno (1866–9).

1867	First Czech-language gymnasium [Gymnasium I]
1869	Lehrer-Bildungsanstalt [Men Teachers' Institute] at former Minorite monastery; Janáček trains there 1869–72
1869	Deutsche Lehrerinnen-Bildungsanstalt [Women Teachers' Institute]
1871	Lehrer-Bildungsanstalt divided into separate Czech and German institutions; the German K.k.Lehrer-Bildungsanstalt mit deutscher Unterrichtssprache at Alejní ulice (now třída Kpt. Jaroše) and from 1893 at Schmerlingova (now třída Kpt. Jaroše); the C.k. (Slovanský) Ústav ku vzdělání učitelů s vyučování jazykem českým [Imperial and Royal (Slavonic) Institute for the training of male teachers in the Czech language] at the Minorite monastery and from 1878 at Poříčí no.5; the Czech Institute includes a Czech-language practice school for primary schoolchildren; Janáček teaches at the practice school 1873–6 and at the Teachers' Institute 1873–1904
1872	Deutsche Lehrerinnen-Bildungsanstalt divided into separate Czech and German institutions: the K.k. Lehrerinen-Bildungsanstalt mit deutcher Unterrichtssprache at Deblínská (street no longer existent, now part of the Janáček Opera) and the C.k. Ústav ku vzdělání učitelek s vyučovácím jazykem českým [Imperial and royal institute for the training of women teachers in the Czech language] at Wawrova (now Hybešová) ulice; Janáček teaches Czech women teachers 1876–8; Czech Women Teachers' Institute includes a Czech-language practice school for primary schoolchildren
1877	First Czech-language private primary school (one class of 33 children, growing to 232 in second year)
1880	First Czech Realschule

Table 6.3:—*continued*

1881	First Czech-language public primary school for boys and girls; further ones opened in 1883 and 1886 (in Staré Brno)
1882	Brno Organ School; founded by Janáček; he is director and chief teacher of theory and composition 1882–1918
1885	First Czech industrial school; other types of Czech vocational schools (commercial, weaving, textile)
1885	Gymnasium II in Staré Brno; Janáček teaches there 1886–1902
1886	Further expansion of Czech schools by dividing existing ones
1886	'Vesna' school for girls (see under table 6.5); František Mareš becomes director in 1888; by 1900 'Vesna' evolved into a series of schools, providing instruction for girls both at an academic and at a practical level. Olga Janáčková learnt sewing there; Marie Stejskalová attended school there for a year and Janáček's niece Věra came from Prague to attend school there
1899	German technical schools divided into Czech and German technical schools
1900	By now eighteen German and six Czech junior schools (two girls', two boys' and two mixed) as well as some private Czech schools
1907	Brno Organ School moves to final location, Giskrova (now Kounicova) 30

Table 6.4: Buildings in Brno 1860–1914[5]

1863–7	'Červený kostel' ['Red church'], Protestant church in red-brick neogothic style
1867–8	Club building for German Turnhalle (gymnastic society) in red-brick neogothic style, reconstructed in 1878 after a fire
1868–70	Hotel Grand, reconstructed *c.* 1900
1868–71	Commercial Academy and Museum
1869–71	Girls' High School, demolished 1945 [site of Janáček Theatre]
1870	German Interimstheater, demolished 1883
1871–2	Besední dům (the chief Czech cultural home); opened 3 April 1873
1871–2	Kounic Palace
1872–4	Pražák Palace; Czech Provisional Theatre housed in its great hall 1881–4
1873	Lehrer-Bildungsanstalt
1875–8	Regional Assembly – Regional House I
1877	Main Post Office and Telegraph Building
1878	Czech Teachers' Institute; new building in Staré Brno
1881–2	Stadttheater (German Theatre; 'theatre on the ramparts', now the Mahen Theatre), the first in Europe with electric lights, opened 14 November 1882
1882–4	New building for Gymnasium I in Alejní ulice (now třída Kpt. Jaroše)
1881–3	Arts and Crafts Museum, now the Moravian Gallery
1883–4	Czech Provisional (National)* Theatre, adapted from the former public house and dance hall Orfeum, opened 6 December 1884
1888–9	Hotel Europa (Hôtel de l'Europe), an Art Nouveau building on the corner of Janská and Masaryková in which Gabriela Horvátová usually stayed (see vol. ii: 1916b)

* Over the years there was much variety in titling with 'Provisional' and 'National' alternating, sometimes used together. 'Provisional' implied that a better building would eventually materialize; 'National' emphasized the role of the theatre. 'Czech' was not part of the title but was implied by the language and is used in this book as a useful distinguishing word. Up to 1918 this is the building that the phrase 'Czech Theatre' means in this book within the context of Brno.

Table 6.4:—*continued*

1888–91	Deutsches Haus (German cultural centre), demolished 1945
1889–08	Regothicization of SS Peter and Paul (Brno Cathedral)
1894	Czech Provisional National Theatre expanded with a second gallery and renamed National Theatre, demolished 1945
1896–7	Czech lyceum and hostel 'Vesna'
1906–9	Palace of Justice
1907–17	Regional House II

Table 6.5: Czech-language clubs and societies (non-musical) in Brno 1860–1914[6]

1861	Český čtenářský spolek [Czech Readers' Club]: it organized the building of Besední dům (see table 6.4); Janáček was a member from 8 July 1874
1862	Moravský tělocvičný spolek [Moravian Gymnastic Society (the forerunner of the Brno Sokol); Janáček was a Sokol member from 26 February 1876
1867	Slovansko-zpěvácký spolek techniků brněnských 'Zora' [Slavonic choral society of Brno technicians 'Zora' ('Dawn')] from 1871 the Akademický čtenářský spolek Zora [Academic readers' club 'Zora']; not exclusively a choral society, it cultivated a Czech patriotic agenda with lectures, besedas, folk music activities
1868	Řemeslnická beseda Svatopluk [Craftsman Society 'Svatopluk']: the first exclusively Czech cultural group for workers and apprentices; includes choir
1870	Ženská vzdělávací jednota Vesna [Women's educational society 'Vesna' ('spring')]; founded originally as a women's educational society, with its own women's choir, it developed into one of the focal points of Czech Brno, founding schools (see table 6.3), organizing concerts, lectures and other cultural activities; Janáček had many connections at 'Vesna'; he lectured there occasionally, and 'Vesna' pupils sang his *Folk Nocturnes* (IV/32) at its second performance
1881	Literární odbor [Literary section] of the Readers' Club; renamed the Literary Club in 1882
1888	Beseda starobrněnská [Staré Brno Beseda]: acquired its own premises in Klášterní náměstí in 1900, running a library and organizing lectures and various entertainments; Janáček, Zdenka and Olga were all members; disbanded 1917
1898	Ruský kroužek v Brně [The Russian Circle in Brno]: Janáček was one of the founders and served in various functions, including chairman from 1910; disbanded 1915 and briefly revived 1919–21
1899	The Moravská ženská útulna [Moravian Women's Shelter]: founded as a shelter for needy young women from the country seeking work in Brno; soon began taking in orphans and abandoned children; Janáček, Zdenka and Olga all supported it in various practical ways (see chaps. 36 and 39)
1900	Klub přátel umění v Brně [Club of the Friends of Art in Brno]: included separate sections for literature, fine art and music (see table 6.6)

Table 6.6: Musical clubs and societies in Brno 1860–1914[7]

1860	Beseda Brněnská [Brno Beseda],[†] from 1879 Filharmonický spolek Beseda brněnská [Philharmonic Society the Brno Beseda]; Křížkovský was conductor 1860–3; Janáček was conductor 1876–9, 1880–1, 1883–8. Janáček founded the Beseda music school in 1882 (and was director until 1889); Janáček's journal *Hudební listy* published under its aegis
1861	Brünner Männergesangverein (renewed)
1862	Brünner Musikverein; including a music school
1864	Techniker-Gesangsverein
1867	Brünner Typographen-Sängerbund
1867	'Zora', men's choral society (see table 6.5); Janáček had good relations with the choir and took part on 29 April 1882 in a concert celebrating its fifteen years of existence
1868	'Svatopluk', men's choral society (see table 6.5); Janáček was conductor of the choir 1873–4, 1875–6
1870	'Vesna', women's choral society (see table 6.5; the 'Vesna' choir often joined forces with the Brno Beseda (originally just a male-voice choir) in concerts
1873	Brünner Musikclub
1881	Brünner Kammermusikverein
1881	Jednota na zvelebení církevní hudby na Moravě [The Association for the Promotion of Church Music in Moravia]; it oversaw the founding of the Brno Organ School in 1882 (see table 6.3)
1883	Pěvecko-zábavní spolek Hlahol v Brně [The singing and entertainment society 'Hlahol' in Brno]; its members occasionally came together with the Beseda for concerts conducted by Janáček during the 1880s
1885	Typografická beseda Veleslavín v Brně [The typographers' society 'Veleslavín' in Brno]; its members occasionally came together with the Beseda for concerts conducted by Janáček during the 1880s
1895	Česká národní kapela [Czech National Orchestra]; Janáček conducted it in 1898, 1899 and 1900
1902	Brünner Philharmoniker, the first Brno symphony orchestra, founded on the model of the Vienna Philharmonic
1903	Pěvecké sdružení moravských učitelů [Moravian Teachers' Choral Society, literally Choral society of Moravian male teachers], founded by Ferdinand Vach, originally based on graduates from Kroměříž, the society was renamed as above in 1904; although generally rehearsing in Prostějov during this period, it frequently appeared in Brno and gave the first performances of many of Janáček's choruses, including *Maryčka Magdónova* (IV/35)
1905	Klub přátel umění v Brně [Club of the Friends of Art in Brno], music section; Janáček was a committee member from the start and held various functions, including chair of the whole club in 1909; The club organized concerts and published the piano-vocal score of *Jenůfa* in 1908, the music of *In the Mists* (VIII/22) and a miniature score of *The Fiddler's Child* (VI/14) in 1914 as a sixtieth-birthday tribute to Janáček
1906	Orchestrální sdružení [Orchestral Association]
1912	Moravský smíšený sbor učitelský v Brně [Moravian Teachers' Mixed Choir in Brno], founded by Ferdinand Vach to perform large-scale choral-orchestral works, such as Janáček's *Amarus* (III/8)

† The primary meaning of the word 'Beseda' is a friendly conversation or neighbourly gathering for a chat. In the nineteenth century several subsidiary meanings developed, including a social organization or club (as here) or a type of social entertainment or informal concert.

Table 6.7: Brno-based Czech language newspapers and journals 1860–1914[8]

1863	*Moravská orlice* [The Moravian eagle]: daily paper; Janáček contributed twenty-three reviews and articles between 1875 and 1920
1869	*Časopis Matice moravské* [The journal of the Moravian Matice (= foundation)]
1884	*Hudební listy* [Musical pages]: musical journal founded and edited by Janáček; it ran until June 1888
1885	*Hlídka literární* [The literary sentinel] (renamed *Hlídka* in 1896): a Catholic monthly journal for literature and aesthetics, edited by Dr Pavel Vychodil at the Benedictine monastery at Rajhrad near Brno; Janáček contributed twenty-one articles and reviews (especially in the series 'Czech musical currents') between 1886 and 1917
1889	*Moravské listy* [Moravian leaves]: daily newspaper edited by Adolf Stránský; Janáček wrote forty-six reviews and articles between 1890 and 1892; renamed *Lidové noviny* in 1893
1893	*Lidové noviny* [The people's newspaper]: daily newspaper edited by Adolf Stránský; Janáček wrote sixty articles and reviews and five music supplements between 1893 and 1928; he was also the subject of several interviews, usually conducted by Adolf Veselý; the Janáček family subscribed to this newspaper, which was the source for several of Janáček's works, including *The Diary of One Who Disappeared* (v/12), *The Cunning Little Vixen* (1/9) and *Nursery Rhymes* (v/16 and 17)
1909	*Moravské hudební noviny* [Moravian musical news]: musical journal edited by Laďa Kožušníček and Miroslav Lazar; it ran until 1911

7

From schoolboy to schoolmaster:
Brno 1865–74

The Augustinians had been in Brno from 1350, their St Tomáš Monastery occupying a prime site in central Brno. Between 1782 and 1784, however, Joseph II dissolved most of the monasteries in his empire, sparing the Augustinians because of their important role as teachers (Joseph's targets were essentially the contemplative and mendicant orders). However, the Augustinians' accommodation was thought much too luxurious for them and it was taken over by the regional governor for his offices (today it provides one of the exhibition spaces of the Moravian Gallery). In exchange the Augustinians were offered an ex-Cistercian convent in Staré Brno. It was in a dilapidated state but it included a wonderful red-brick church (unusual in the area) dedicated to the Assumption of the Virgin Mary, one of the finest examples of Brno Gothic. By the time the Augustinians had finished making their new accommodation habitable, some of the rooms such as the chapter hall and the library were as elegantly furnished as in any aristocratic country house.[1] This is where the Augustinians resided when the eleven-year-old Leo Janáček arrived in Brno in the autumn of 1865.

The monastery's dedication to St Tomáš derived from the Augustinian church in central Brno and the association lingered on after the Augustinian monastery transferred to its new location in Staré Brno.* By the twentieth century it became known as the Staré Brno monastery, or as the Queen's Monastery, after Queen Eliška Přemyslovna, who had founded it in 1323. In the 1950s the monastery was closed down

---

* In his correspondence Gregor Mendel often signed himself as being at the 'Monastery of St Thomas' (see Stern and Sherwood, 1966, 71, 78 and 80).

by the Communist administration, the monks dispersed and the accommodation put to other use. After restitution in the 1990s, a few monks returned, as did the old name: the designation 'St Tomáš' has once again been promoted in official literature put out by the monastery.

The Augustinian community in Staré Brno consisted of about a dozen monks[†] (properly 'canons regular') together with a varying population of novices, lay brothers[2] and up to a dozen choristers. Ruled by St Augustine's belief of 'per scientiam ad sapientiam' ['through knowledge to wisdom'], Augustinians valued education and emphasized teaching and research. In the Staré Brno monastery an atmosphere was created that was conducive to study and a safe haven for single men of a scholarly disposition, however uncongenial it might have been for a lonely boy. About the time Janáček was there, there was a remarkable constellation of scholars including Franz Theodor Bratránek (a notable Goethe expert), the botanist Aurelius Thaler, the philosopher Matouš Klácel (ultimately deprived of his chair in philosophy for spreading Hegelian ideas), the finest composer in Moravia, Pavel Křížkovský, and the father of genetics, Gregor Mendel. The food was excellent (the kitchens were well known in Moravia and attracted many trainee chefs during the thirty years that Louise Ondráčková was in charge)[3] and the discipline, in comparison with the more spartan monastic orders, relaxed. As one of the chief centres of spiritual and intellectual life of the town, St Tomáš offered an atmosphere probably not much different to that of an Oxford college. In the early nineteenth century the monastery began providing tuition at the Philosophical Institute, a proto-university in a city that did not have a university until 1919.

Much of this civilized and enabling atmosphere was created by Cyrill František Napp (1792–1867), elected abbot in 1824 at the age of thirty-two (a tax was paid for every new abbot so they tended to choose young ones). He had been born into a wealthy family in Moravia and throughout his life confidently held various secular positions in Brno such as director of the Moravian and Silesian Gymnasia and member of the standing committee of the Moravian diet (the highest territorial authority), where he became deputy lord-lieutenant.[4] He was duly decorated by the state as a knight of the Order of Leopold and Franz

---

[†] Eleven of them are captured in a rare photograph taken probably between 1861 and 1864 and reproduced on Plate 6.

Josef. An attractive figure of the Austrian enlightenment ('excellently knowledgeable, both genial and serious'),[5] he had studied oriental languages, which he taught at the Brno Theological College, and had unusually wide intellectual and practical interests including education, fruit growing, wine-making and sheep breeding.[6] Although not a trained musician, he had, before his election as abbot, been in charge of music provision at the monastery for two years (1816–18); surviving records of what was performed during his tenure are testimony to his wide knowledge of the repertory and his enterprise in searching out worthwhile new works.[7] He maintained friendly relations with some of the leading figures in Czech patriotic circles such as Josef Dobrovský (1753–1829) and František Palacký (1798–1876);[8] these became welcome guests at the monastery and contributed to its reputation as a centre of the Czech Enlightenment in Brno.[9]

As a first-rate manager and administrator Napp was responsible for the improvements in the monastery's financial fortunes by introducing productive new methods in the farms from which it derived its income.[10] Although something of a grandee, he was immensely supportive of the monks in his charge. Křížkovský's letters home emphasize both Napp's human qualities (for example making sure that during Křížkovský's frequent bouts of ill-health he had first-class medical attention in Vienna, and adequate periods of recuperation)[11] and his generous support of musical activities at the monastery. Equally, however, he encouraged the interest in meteorology and botany of one of his more remarkable monks, Gregor Mendel (1822–84). Thirty years older than Mendel, Napp seems to have sensed his potential, and made sure that he had free access to the monastery greenhouse for his experiments. When these thrived he had a much larger glasshouse built for him, this time heated by a stove.[12] It was here that the famous experiments in peas were conducted and their results presented at two meetings of the Brno Naturforschender Verein at the Brno Realschule on 8 February and 8 March 1865, a few months before Janáček became a choral scholar.

When the Augustinians moved to Staré Brno they transferred not only the name St Tomáš but also a bequest made to the monastery in 1648 by Countess Sibilla Polixena z Montani (née Thurn-Wallesessin), usually known as the Thurn-Wallesessin Foundation. The bequest had originally been made with the object of establishing a hospital but there was not enough money for that and instead the monastery undertook to maintain six poor, deserving and musical boys during their studies in return for their singing at monastery services. A boy supported by such a choral foundation was known in Czech as a *fundatista*, for which the nearest English equivalent is a choral scholar. As Vladimír Helfert points out,[13] this practice is comparable with the first Italian musical conservatories, which developed from charitable institutions intended to look after and educate abandoned children. With one or two hiccups (e.g. after the 1848 Revolution, when the value of the Thurn-Wallesessin fund decreased so much that the accommodation of choral scholars was temporarily suspended), the Brno foundation was surprisingly long-lived, with moments of glory in the early part of the nineteenth century, as Janáček discovered when he did research for his autobiography.[14] He found references to a seventy-piece orchestra playing Beethoven's First Symphony to celebrate the name day of Abbot Napp, and performances of 'the largest mass in the world, Cherubini's Coronation Mass', Beethoven's 'Eroica' Symphony, Weber's overture to *Oberon,* and Auber's *La muette de Portici* (presumably the overture). Although these heydays had passed, the choir was still in reasonable shape under its very distinguished conductor when Janáček arrived in 1865. Janáček himself saw a continuity between the Thurn-Wallesessin Foundation, his own Organ School (which opened in 1882) and ultimately the Brno Conservatory which the Organ School became in 1919.[15]

The choral scholars lived in the monastery; food and medical attention were provided, as well as the smart light-blue, white-bordered uniforms, which gave the boys their local nickname of 'bluebirds'.[16] Everything else, such as money for school fees, laundry, shoes and other clothes, needed to come from home or elsewhere. The scholars observed a quasi-monastic regime, rising at five and getting in a sung mass before breakfast and school. There were daily singing rehearsals in the evening between six and seven, and extra rehearsals on Sundays.[17] There was not much in the way of holidays. In the week between the two half-year terms the scholars had extra singing rehearsals and occupied themselves with copying out music or revising.[18] In his first summer holidays (1866), all of Leo's co-scholars managed to get away, but he was too poor to travel and remained in the monastery. It is likely that he spent the next two summers in the same way.

By the 1860s the Thurn-Wallesessin Foundation provided for up to ten choristers, and although they had predominantly unbroken voices (trebles and altos), there were also a couple of older boys who sang tenor or bass. This small group provided the core of the music in the monastery and, with only two or three to a part, the boys learnt self-reliance and confidence at an early age. In commenting upon Křížkovský as a conductor Janáček said how dependable the choristers were after their daily training: 'as sure as flutes'; 'To conduct us was completely unnecessary' (xv/166).

Leo's arrival at the monastery came at a time of transition. Up to and including his first year, the choral foundation continued to operate as a conservatory, with instrumental tuition offered on a range of instruments and with the expectation of performing the orchestrally accompanied masses and other elaborate church music by Haydn, Beethoven and Cherubini. However by then the winds of change were blowing in the form of the Cecilian movement, which maintained that this musically rich repertory was essentially concert music and what was needed was a return to the unaccompanied choral music of the sixteenth century and earlier. Orchestral accompaniments were frowned on and the only form of accompaniment permitted was the organ. It took some time for the choirmaster at the Staré Brno monastery, Pavel Křížkovský, to come round to this view. The first sign of things to come was in the summer of 1866, and the process continued and accelerated so that by 1869, Janáček's last year as a chorister and a year that climaxed in the patriotic celebrations in Velehrad for the 1000th anniversary of the death of St Cyril, the music provided was strictly in accordance with the new movement.

Janáček could play the piano and the violin reasonably well when he arrived at the monastery. While pianos were available (Křížkovský records passing on his older one to the choristers when Abbot Napp bought him a new grand piano),[19] no instrumental tuition was provided after 1866 and any teaching was done either among the boys themselves or in the town. In a late reminiscence (xv/298), Janáček recalled trudging off for violin lessons to 'Vilemína Normanová-Nerudová, my teacher', from the famous Neruda clan[‡] (see chap. 12).

[‡]However, Janáček's memory may have served him ill. Although Wilma Neruda, later Lady Hallé, was born in Brno, by the time Janáček arrived in Brno she was in Sweden pursuing her highly successful career as a virtuoso violinist.

A benefit of these reforms was a particular concentration on voices, which may help to explain Janáček's preoccupation with voices throughout his life, and his skill in writing for them, both in choral music and in opera.

It was Amalie Janáčková who delivered her young son to the monastery, presumably in August 1865. Janáček does not explain how they made the journey. If they went by rail (and surely he might have commented on the excitement of his first train journey) then it would have involved a circuitous journey down the Ostrava-Břeclav line and then up from Břeclav to Brno (the more direct line via Přerov was constructed only from 1869). Otherwise the journey would have involved walking and some form of horse-drawn transport. Some of the most vivid and heart-breaking writing in Janáček's autobiography relates to his arrival:

Fearfully mother and I spent the night in some dark cell – it was on the Kapucinské náměstí. Me with eyes open. At first light, out, out, out!

My mother left me at the Klášterní náměstí with a heavy step. Me in tears, she too.

All alone. Foreign people, not warm-hearted; foreign school, hard bed, bread even harder. No cuddles.

My world, exclusively mine, is founded. Everything fell into it.[20]

When Leo arrived at the monastery in Brno one familiar face should have been that of Pavel Křížkovský, with whom he had had a friendly interview in Opava a few months earlier. However Křížkovský was still away convalescing. A throat ailment led to his prolonged absence from the monastery and Leo probably encountered him in Brno first in early February 1866, and then for only two months.[21]

While struggling to come to terms with this harsh new world, Leo had his misery compounded by bad news from Hukvaldy: on 8 March 1866 his father died at the age of fifty. 'The unimagined cruelty of it' was his single comment in the autobiography.[22] Would he have thought through the implications for his family? By then most of his Příbor-born siblings were off his mother's hands (the youngest, Bedřich, was twenty) and his sister Rosalie was sixteen, but there were still the two younger boys, František and Josef, to care for. Amalie Janáčková struggled on in Hukvaldy until the new teacher arrived in October. Then, it is assumed, she and the three children returned to her home town of

Příbor, where she had relatives.[23] Soon after, Křížkovský, having been present in Brno during most of February and March, was away again, this time recuperating in Vienna.[24] Whatever comfort and counsel the young Leo might have had would have come from even less familiar figures in the monastery. After his father's death Leo's financial needs were taken over by his uncle Jan Janáček (1810–89), who was then parish priest in the tiny village of Blazice. It seems unlikely, however, that the Revd Janáček would have made the then laborious journey to Brno to break the news to his nephew. Janáček's bleak comment 'the unimagined cruelty' rather suggests that the news came to him impersonally.

On 18 May 1866 Janáček sent his uncle a twelve-line poem in German, congratulating him on his name day. Conventionally sentimental, it nevertheless shows a good command of German for a twelve-year-old brought up in the depths of the Czech-speaking countryside. It is followed immediately by a prose translation in Czech and all his surviving letters to his uncle thereafter except one are in Czech. There are eleven of them altogether, written up to August 1869, when Leo's time as a choral scholar at the monastery came to an end. No letters from Jan Janáček from this period have survived, but Leo mentions several times in his that he has heard from him, for example in his second letter (21 June 1866), which gives some idea of what normally passed between them:

You asked me in your last letter for which months I have paid school fees and the laundress. I have paid them for the months of April and May. Furthermore I ask you respectfully if I may go to physical training and for that I pay 20 kr and I ask you further to send me 1 fl 60 kr;[§] I had my shoes mended. I thank you respectfully and kiss your hand and remain, your devoted grandson, Leo Janáček.[25]

More often than not, Leo signed off as a 'grandson'. He was aware of his exact relationship to Jan Janáček (his first letter had been addressed to 'Lieber Onkel' and correctly translated into Czech as 'Milý strýčku') but the frequent occurrence of 'grandfather' does seem to imply a remoteness in the relationship. Many of the letters are as businesslike as the one quoted above, and only occasionally do boyish enthusiasms break through.

§ fl = florenus (florin), an alternative expression for zl (see chap. 41).

The choral scholars went outside the monastery for their schooling. At the age of eleven Leo had already completed the compulsory six-year primary schooling in Hukvaldy, but presumably it was felt that in the light of a village-school education and Leo's plans as a teacher he should repeat the final year, which he did at a school in the Lackerwiese ulice (now Leitnerova-Jircháře ulice), some fifteen minutes away on foot with the 'smelly tanning factory' beyond (xv/298). This was not the nearest possibility (there was a primary school in Staré Brno), but the choice was perhaps suggested by Křížkovský, who taught religion and singing there. The school was reasonably new at the time, having been built as a four-class school in 1844, with a fifth class added in 1858.[26] As at all the primary schools in Brno at the time, tuition was in German: out of the eighty-one students in the fourth class, he was one of only four singled out as 'Czech' in the school records, i.e. with an inadequate knowledge of German. Despite what was clearly a miserable time for him away from home, his health was fine, with no records of illness or missed classes.[27] Furthermore he seems to have got on well with the music-making at the monastery:

Lots of music stands; instruments are carried in. A violin for the lame Mr Baroch. The positive organ [i.e. a small movable organ] in front, Hanáček, organist and headmaster, pulls out the very long stops.

Me a treble, Hönig double bass; there were even oboes and trumpets; Křížkovský with a viola of double height; playing without conductor. We knew how to: Horák's masses, Kempfer's [Kempter's] masses. But also Beethoven's [Missa] solemnis, Mozart's, Haydn's [masses]. How they praised me when I doubled once at the positive organ for Mr Hanáček!

And once at the Resurrection, when I grabbed the baton and conducted Schnabel's Regina caeli![28]

This lively picture would seem to come from Leo's first year (1865–6) in view of the instrumentalists around and the elaborate repertory (though Beethoven's Missa solemnis seems improbable). If the Schnabel piece was performed at Easter[II] (as implied by 'Resurrection') then Křížkovský was back in Vienna, and so the ensemble may have lacked firm direction and thus given Leo the opportunity to have his first stab at conducting.

Political and other events soon crowded in. The Austro-Prussian War, a culmination of the long-term rivalry of Prussia and Austria for

[II]In 1865 Easter fell on 16 April.

leadership of the German-speaking world, broke out on 12 June. Three weeks later, on 3 July, the Prussians had won their decisive battle at Sadová (Sadowa) and began occupying Austrian territory until peace negotiations were hammered out. Prussian soldiers entered Brno on 13 July, a hundred of them billeted at the monastery. Janáček comments in his autobiography how all his fellow bluebirds 'flew away' to safer climes. He alone of his companions was left to witness the events as they unfolded:

The Klášterní náměstí filled with Prussians. As if they'd descended like black swarms.
Only yesterday our 'own' soldiers were there. They ran away. [. . .]
From Pekařská ulice to Křížová ulice one walked along a little bridge.
A cross by the bridge.
Armoured units passed frantically, and then in the sudden curve one cart skidded and turned over. Sacks flew out, and coffee spilt out from the torn ones. The narrow pass blocked.
I witnessed all of this commotion! (xv/298)

War brought with it an outbreak of cholera in Brno[29] and Janáček remembered singing at many funerals. However, it was the music of the Prussians that made the biggest impression on him, one that continued to haunt him for over sixty years: 'the tin drums rolled and above them the high piccolos squealed. Predatory music. Even today it lingers in my ears and buzzes. I, a lad of twelve, with my eyes out on stalks, followed the wild tumult of the Prussian army on Pekařská ulice, and on the Vídeňka [Vídeňská ulice] here in Brno' (xv/253).

A peace treaty was signed in Prague on 23 August and by 13 September the Prussians had left Moravia, and Janáček's companion choristers returned. But things had changed for ever: 'The instrument stands deserted. Old works no longer resurrected. Mozart and Beethoven put aside.'[30] Wind instruments were no longer taught. 'Old Baroch, the last of the violin teachers, died soon afterwards in his little house in Hluboký vývoz.'[31]

And there was a substantial change in Leo's schooling. Now twelve, he began his senior schooling, much nearer the monastery, in the Staré Brno Realschule then situated in the Staré Brno Town Hall. 'Real' indicates the inclusion of 'real-life' or 'modern' subjects as opposed to the Greek and Latin taught at a Humanistisches Gymnasium. While the Gymnasium route would take students to arts-based university courses, the more practical orientation of Leo's senior school was appropriate for a boy aiming to become a primary schoolteacher. At what was technically an 'Unterrealschule' ['Lower Realschule'], he studied a mix of subjects which included Czech, German, mathematics, history, geography, nature studies, chemistry and religion, as well as drawing, calligraphy, 'measuring' and singing. When Janáček came to recall these years he remembered only two of his teachers, Horálek the mathematician and Rain [recte J. Weiner] the Czech teacher,[32] significantly both of them enthusiastic Czech nationalists.[33]

In a letter he wrote to his uncle in March 1867 Leo mentioned that he could not send the school report for the first half-year semester until his school fees had been paid. Meanwhile he was very short of cash. Jan Janáček had sent him 5 fl but much of this had already been swallowed up by the school fees, textbooks, stationery and by what appears to have been his one luxury: 'milk every day'. His shoes were in crisis (two pairs could no longer be repaired, according to the grumpy shoemaker – Janáček remembered his unpleasant encounters with him over sixty years later, xv/298) and the third and final pair was beginning to fall apart. He needed a suit for singing at funerals.[34]

Although the more ambitious musical ventures at the monastery had ceased, Janáček remembered other musical occasions in which he took part, none of them verifiable and most of them dubious. 'We sang, us boys on the Brno stage in Meyerbeer's opera Le prophète', he recalled in his autobiography.[35] Helfert and others after him discovered that there were no performances in Brno of Le prophète between 1857 and 1874, and so suggested that what Janáček actually sang in was Meyerbeer's L'Africaine, given, somewhat improbably in view of its staging requirements, at the tiny Reduta theatre in Brno, with a première on 2 April 1867. But, unlike Le prophète, whose Coronation Scene calls for a boys' chorus and a couple of boy soloists, L'Africaine made no such demands, so there is no reason why the theatre would take on boy singers with all the difficulties that this presents. The opera ran in repertory in Brno for a total of seventeen performances that year;[36] did they all involve the monastery choristers? Equally puzzling is Janáček's comment that he accompanied Miss z Ehrenbergrů at a concert at the Lužánky hall – 'and I was eleven years old'.[37] One of the stars of the Prague Provisional Theatre (she created the role of Mařenka in The Bartered Bride), the soprano Eleonora z Ehrenbergrů was at the height of her fame and powers, and any performance by her in Brno would have been a newsworthy event. But Helfert, whose research included diligent scouring of contemporary newspapers, failed to find any such concert mentioned. And why would they have an eleven-year-old boy, not especially remarkable as a pianist, accompany the great lady? On the other hand these are precise and distinctive reminiscences: it seems unlikely that Janáček would have completely made them up. The only one of Leo's youthful musical exploits reported by the older Janáček that sounds plausible is his singing a solo alongside Miss Marie Hřímalá in a Beethoven mass. It might not have been Beethoven's 'second' mass[38] (i.e. the *Missa solemnis*) but rather his Mass in C; there are reports from other sources that Hřímalá would occasionally help out in performances at the monastery.

By June 1867 Leo was even more in debt, recounting his woes in a letter to his uncle. He had had to borrow money from the 'Adjunct' (Father Method Vyskočil, who was in charge of the choristers) for stationery, school fees and laundry. Although Křížkovský meanwhile settled the school fee with the director of the Realschule (his colleague from the Benedictine monastery at Rajhrad, František Mathon), Leo still needed 6 fl 20 kr to repay the loan to Father Vyskočil, and an extra 2 fl for laundry and 1 fl 20 kr for new shoes. Meanwhile he also desperately needed a new coat. Even 'Mr Regens' (i.e. the Regenschori, choirmaster Pavel Křížkovský) had asked whether he didn't have another coat. He should have gone for 'holy confirmation' but was unable to since he had no suitable clothes:

However, a couple of days later I got a letter from you saying that you couldn't send me a coat or shoes until I sent you the measurement [for the coat] and the school report. Now my shoes were so worn out that they couldn't be mended, and everyone was laughing at me, so I spent the money on shoes.

Jan Janáček seems to have been holding out for the school report before sending any more money. So this time Leo enclosed both the report and his measurements for a coat. Exceptionally there is a note on the letter in another hand, presumably Jan Janáček's, 'geschickt' ['sent']. If Leo was reluctant to send his school report, there was much worse to come: for his first two years at the Realschule he was not a good student. Although in the first semester he came fifteenth out of fifty-seven, in the second semester he had dropped to twenty-fifth, with fifth-class grades (out of a scale of seven) in geography, arithmetic and nature studies, fourth-class grades in Czech and German, and a second grade only in singing (taught by Křížkovský).[39] This letter contains one of the few hints that Leo visited his uncle. He had also asked for a further 1 fl 40 kr for a cap: 'When I was at your place, I got a black one, and the shop was crowded and it was already damaged and now cannot be worn.'[40]

However this is the only reference in all eleven letters to 'your place', and from the dates of Leo's later letters to his uncle it is clear that during the summer months of 1867 he stayed at the monastery. It seems odd that he didn't try to see his mother and siblings, but the journey would have cost money, and all money had to be borrowed from his careful uncle. It is possible, however, that his mother managed to see him, if one can believe the story reported by Vašek in 1930. This is attributed to 'an account of relatives' (perhaps told to young Josef Janáček, when Amalie Janáčková returned):

It happened once that one of his parents came to Brno, asking among other things how [Leo] was getting on and what he was doing. Pavel Křížkovský opened the doors of the classroom and called out:

'Come and see what he's doing!'

Leošek in a group of friends was just at the moment doing acrobatics, standing with his head down and his legs in the air doing a handstand with the robust and raw joyfulness of a country lad.[41]

Another tale demonstrating Leo's high spirits as a chorister, this time from Janáček himself, surfaced at the end of his life in the feuilleton *For a few apples?* (xv/296). In it Janáček described how he and his young friends crept into the monastery garden at night to steal apples but were detected:

We leapt over fences and just wanted to escape through the cloisters.

At the corner with a lighted candle held high stood our – our [choir] director Pavel Křížkovský!

As, one after the other, we needed to pass him, a minor scale was played on us.

For a few apples in our pockets – a minor scale in every octave. I got a slap across the face in the highest octave.

On 22 July 1867 the Abbot Cyrill Napp died at the age of seventy-five. On the order of the bishop, his funeral was as grand as church regulations allowed and even Křížkovský, describing it to his old mother in Opava, was pleased with the event: 'there was never such a grand funeral as the funeral of Mr Prelate', naturally with equally grand music provided by the monastery choristers under his direction.[42] For all Křížkovský's desire to steer the music provision along the more austere paths of Cecilian reform, the old ways lingered on. In the same letter he reported on another splendid occasion a few months later, when at the visit of the papal nuncio Falcinelli from Vienna, the bishop asked Křížkovský to direct the music at a celebratory mass at Petrov, the Brno Cathedral. Thus on 20 October Leo and his fellow choristers from the monastery joined the cathedral choir in Cherubini's Solemn Mass in C under Křížkovský's direction. This was another great success, with Křížkovský's winning plaudits from the distinguished guest who, according to Křížkovský's letter to his mother, declared that he could scarcely hear music better performed in Vienna.[43] And there were other non-Cecilian events (even if less grand) such as the 'serenade' a week later that Křížkovský prepared for the fiftieth anniversary of the prior's consecration as priest.[44]

Napp's successor was none other than Gregor Mendel, a very different figure. Whereas Napp was urbane and confident in his dealings with the town, Mendel gave the impression of a country bumpkin not entirely at ease with the position in which he found himself (the most important cleric in Brno after the bishop). Though said to have a 'waggish' sense of humour, he was fairly introverted. He came from German-speaking peasant stock in Silesia; his Czech was acquired later and was not fluent, and his scientific work and correspondence was conducted entirely in German. Unlike his predecessor, he showed no interest in music or the music provision in the monastery – another reason perhaps why Křížkovský was able to further his Cecilian reforms without much opposition.

Mendel's accomplishments in the field of genetics were almost unknown during his lifetime (his celebrated paper 'Versuche über Pflanzen-Hybriden' ['Experiments on plant hybrids'], 1866,[45] lay unread until rediscovered by the scientific community in 1900), and his colleagues at the monastery had no idea that among them they had a figure of world class. Mendel's early obscurity is reflected by the fact that, fifteen years after his death, the hugely comprehensive *Ottův slovník naučný* [Otto's encyclopedia] had no article on him,[¶] an

---

[¶] It would have been in vol.17, which came out in 1900.

omission rectified only in the supplementary volume of 1909. The statue erected to him in Klášterní náměstí in 1910 was a matter of international funds and local mystification.[46] Even Helfert in his 1939 biography mentions Mendel only in passing (as the then 'prelate'). Vogel does not even do that.

It is one of the strange facts of Janáček's life that for two years he was under the charge of Mendel: two of the most famous people associated with Brno connected in this way. Mendel had contact with Leo at least twice a year since he needed to see his semester report (see below). And from 1872 when Janáček took over Křížkovský's post as choirmaster at the monastery during the latter's permanent absence in Olomouc, he would have had some dealings with Mendel from time to time.

Now in his second year at the Realschule, Leo once again had problems with his school report at the end of the first semester. He had, he wrote to Uncle Jan on 21 March 1868, been looking forward to a good report but it turned out that he had failed in arithmetic because he had been ill and had missed the exam. He was allowed to take a supplementary exam at the beginning of the new semester. Whereupon he got a 'first-class report', though he was unable to send it until he had shown it to Mendel. As usual there were more requests for money: he needed '10 zl by Thursday' to replace the trousers ('too small') and coat ('already completely worn out'). Interestingly, the letter is written in German (and then translated into Czech), the last time he would do this. Written a few months before Leo's fourteenth birthday, it is assured and relaxed and even indulges in a bit of story-telling: how he was expecting a good result and how 'Mr Assistant Michálek', a former choral scholar now a teacher at the Realschule, had teased him (he was just ten years older than Leo) by asking him what he was expecting and then giving him the bad news that he had failed arithmetic.[47]

But this more confident dealing with his uncle was disrupted by a quarrel. It is documented only by the nephew's abject apology, sent some time after 5 July 1868, but may be explained by his poor grades: he was on the cusp of failing geometry and arithmetic, hardly better in Czech, German and nature studies, though continuing to be excellent in singing. Only half of the missed classes had been excused.[48]

Dearest Uncle

First forgive me for the ill I've you done in this half-year. Only now do I see what wrongs I've done you. Only now do I see my stupid anger at you, now I see that your arrival will always be useful for me; now I see your great goodness.

God forgive me for it!

Uncle forgive me for it!

I've shed many tears when I've remembered it. I want to be true to you for ever and remain your loving grandson.

In addition to the fluctuations in family relationship ('uncle', 'grandson'), and the earliest instance of Janáček's dramatic single-sentence paragraphs (here with distinct liturgical echoes), the letter is revealing in its reference to uncle Jan's 'arrival', presumably to sort out the matter face to face and maybe also to tell his nephew about the death (18 April 1868) of his sister Rosalie from typhus at the age of eighteen.[49]

Once this heart-felt appeal is out of the way, the letter reverts to begging mode (more shoes, laundry, stationery), including a very singular request for a coat and trousers made from 'Russian linen'. Taken together with the signature 'Lev Janáček'[50] this suggests a shift in the youngster's outlook on the world. He had just passed his fourteenth birthday and now suddenly adopted the Russian form (Lev) of his first name Leo (see chap. 14). This is the first instance of the Russophilia that would characterize Janáček for the rest of his life (see chap. 9).

When he next wrote, on 19 August 1868, the second semester was over, and holidays were beginning, though clearly he had little free time: he had wanted to write earlier but had to copy out music. He enclosed his report. In his reformed mode, he had got a first-class pass in conduct (which he declared he didn't deserve). It is evident from the late date and no mention of any plans for visiting that he would not be spending any of his summer with his uncle.[51]

After the quarrel with his uncle (one of the few signs of teenage rebellion) Lev seems to have made a real effort in his last year, especially in the second semester. In the first semester his best subjects (all third-grade) were conduct, German, Czech, nature studies, drawing and French, with a fifth for mathematics. From the 'inconstant' grade for 'industry' it is also clear that he had not worked consistently hard: he came thirtieth out of the forty in his class. Interesting is the early exposure to French,** if only for one term (the subject is not included in his final report).[52]

Much of Janáček's final year at the Realschule was dominated by the excitement over the celebrations of the 1000th anniversary in 1869 of the death of St Cyril. If Lev had become pro-Russian in 1868, this was now transformed into the pro-Slavonic stance that many clerical circles had adopted in Moravia, both a subtle expression of anti-Austrian feeling and to some extent also a proclamation of Moravia's separate path from that of the hot-headed nationalists of Bohemia. The first manifestation of this was the celebration on 14 February at the Dominican church with a choir assembled by Křížkovský from the cathedral and from his monastery choristers, plus two male soloists. It is clear from the works that Eichler mentions (Křížkovský's biographer Karel Eichler was organist on that occasion) that Křížkovský had taken account of the Cecilian reform, choosing the Mass in A major by Karl Greith (one of the chief theoreticians of the movement),[53] and an unaccompanied motet *Ecco, quomodo moritur justus*, by Jacobus Handl.[54]

This occasion, however, was dwarfed by the celebrations at Velehrad later in the year. By 26 May Lev was bubbling over with enthusiasm:

Dear Uncle, it will be already known to you that this year there is a large celebration at Velehrad for which the reverend gentleman, Father Křížkovský has been appointed director, which he has accepted. Whereupon twenty singers will leave for Velehrad on 5 July from Brno, among whom will be me, as will all the choral scholars. The journey, food, accommodation will be paid by the reverend gentleman, the Archbishop†† of Olomouc [Fridrich Egon zur Fürstenberg]. You don't know how much I'm looking forward to the sacred ground where once great Svatopluk [a ruler of Great Moravia] and the Slavonic apostles Ciryl [Cyril] and Metod [Methodius] had their post, that I will see it; I am not worthy to tread in their footsteps. I have one request for you, dearest Uncle: Please buy me a Slavonic suit. [You need do] nothing more than buy somewhere in the vicinity, perhaps in Bystřice, so-called 'Russian linen' of slightly better material, it won't be so expensive there, then send it to me in Brno and in the monastery there is now a tailor who would sew it for me cheaply.[55]

** Helfert (*LJPT*, 90) has him starting French only in November 1872.
†† Janáček has 'arcikníže', literally 'arch priest'.

All this – apart from the 'Russian linen' (a subject of further requests) – came about as Lev described. In his account Eichler described a week of celebrations in Velehrad topped and tailed with the feast of SS Cyril and Methodius on 5 July and its octave on 12 July, with assorted feast days in between. Among the older composers represented (for instance in graduals and offertories) were Vittoria, Palestrina, Anerio and Handl; nineteenth-century composers included Franz Xaver Witt, Johann Gustav Eduard Stehle, Bernhard Mettenleiter and others of the Cecilian persuasion. There were no festive masses by Mozart, Haydn, Beethoven or Cherubini: the whole celebration was conceived entirely according to what was appropriate to the newly reformed church music. The papal nuncio Falcinelli got a whiff of what was to come when he officiated at a pontifical mass on the feast of SS Peter and Paul (29 June) in Brno Cathedral with music provided by Křížkovský and a large group of singers including the Staré Brno choristers singing a mass by the reformist Franz Witt. 'The result was splendid', Eichler reported but with exquisite tact noted that 'the nuncio did not show his satisfaction in the same demonstrative way as two years ago' (when he was offered Cherubini). So it is unsurprising that the nuncio didn't get to Velehrad. More surprisingly, neither did the Archbishop of Olomouc ('indisposed') although he seems to have paid for most of the celebration.

The papal nuncio did however give his blessing to the event by turning up at the Staré Brno monastery on 1 July, where he was welcomed by a serenade. Two days later, on Saturday 3 July, Křížkovský and his singers set off for Velehrad, where a busy schedule of services and performances awaited them. The group was made up of the Staré Brno choristers augmented by a few enthusiasts, altogether twenty singers (five per part),[56] a small group for such an ambitious undertaking. Křížkovský was particularly anxious that the voice of his leading alto, Lev Janáček, would not break during all this heavy usage (Lev celebrated his fifteenth birthday on the day he left for Velehrad). Apart from a big event which Janáček may have attended in Velehrad on 18 August, conceived as a sort of culmination of the Cyril and Methodius celebrations and which attracted an audience of 40,000 including 250 priests, this was now the end of Lev's singing career. By September 1869 he was no longer a choral scholar at the Staré Brno monastery.

The Cyril-Methodius celebrations of 1869, and their detailed preparation, marked an important stage of Janáček's understanding of his nationality. Already 'Lev', he was turning into the fervent Czech patriot of later years, and was now uncertain about where his uncle Jan stood. His letter of 26 May, with its eager anticipation of the Velehrad celebration, is prefaced with these extraordinary words:

Please forgive me that I've not written to you for so long. I've already written a couple of times to you – and then I burnt the letters – for I don't know whether you are a faithful Czech or a faithful German – or a little bit of both. Ah, dear Uncle, you don't know how I love these Czechs, you won't believe how I hate these Germans, these Germans who don't have their own homeland, who came into our beautiful Czech lands, to take our beautiful homeland away from us, attach it to themselves and then Germanize us.

And in case poor Jan Janáček (probably, like so many other Czechs of the time, 'a little bit of both') hadn't got the point it was hammered home at the end of the letter with a poem entitled 'To the Murderers!' beginning 'Silence, wretched prophets' (those who had prophesied doom for the Slavs). 'Thus we will punish our enemies', Lev commented, as he sent it. Janáček's first recorded creative endeavour in Czech[‡‡] consists of forty-eight lines of jingoistic doggerel arranged in six eight-line stanzas. The final two lines provide the stirring refrain commanding both the prophets of doom or the murderers to be silent. It has a jaunty rhythm, and its lines of six or seven syllables are mostly stopped with emphatic rhymes. Much of the imagery is conventional, not to say bloodthirsty. What is interesting is the geographical vocabulary. There is a single reference to 'king and fatherland' that could perhaps suggest the old Bohemian kingdom (the word 'Czech' does not appear at all), but most of the time the poem is peppered with 'Slav' words: 'Slavstvo' ['Slavdom'], 'Slovan' ['a Slav'], 'Slovanský', 'Slávský' ['Slavonic']. The celebration of SS Cyril and Methodius had ensured that Lev Janáček would become a Pan-Slavist (see chap. 9).[57]

Whatever Jan Janáček may have made of the poem, he would have been pacified by the prompt sending of a satisfactory school report, which Lev copied out in a letter dated 6 August (the school year having ended on 30 July).[58] The report put him into the top category, and he was sixteenth among the forty pupils in his class, a considerable

‡‡ The name day poem for his uncle was in German (see above).

improvement from the first half year, and a remarkable one in view of the fact that he had got by without textbooks, as he rather pointedly told his uncle. Included in Lev's copy is an explanation of the grading system with five grades for conduct (he got a top grade here), five for industry (he got a second grade), and seven for progress. In the last he got to the second grade ('excellent') for nature studies, and the third category ('praiseworthy') for German, Czech, geography and history, drawing, calligraphy and singing. This is much the best of all his school reports. Only in arithmetic, chemistry and architecture ['Baukunst'] did he sink into the fourth grade ('satisfactory'). He had missed sixty-eight teaching hours, all excused.

There were more requests for clothes, which once again took on a nationalist aspect. The previous requests for a suit of Russian linen seem to have been ignored, for now what was wanted was a 'beautiful light Sokol[§§] suit' for 6 zl rather than a much more expensive German one. His most fervent wish, however, was 'for you to let me home again' – the first time in four years. He didn't need money for this: he had been paid his first professional fee of 7 zl 50 kr for his participation in the Velehrad celebrations.[59] When (if?) he did get home is not clear. He wrote again eight days later (his final surviving letter to his uncle) in which it is clear that he still hadn't moved from Brno. The demands for clothes continue and are given in detail: Janáček seems to have been turning into a natty dresser, with very specific requests, including high boots and long baggy trousers that could be laced up at the bottom and tucked into the boots.[60] It sounds as if he were aspiring to a Russian appearance, the sort of thing that Tolstoy wore when dressing up as a peasant. Lev presumably attended the big Velehrad celebrations on 18 August and perhaps from there made his way to see his mother, not to Hukvaldy, but to Příbor, where he was able to visit the grave of his sister Rosalie.[61]

In September 1869 Lev Janáček began his post-school studies at the Men Teachers' Institute in Brno, the k.k. Lehrer-Bildungsanstalt (see table 6.3). It is thought that Křížkovský found him rented accommodation near the monastery (according to the 1870 census he was registered as the thirtieth boarder at the Augustinian boarding house at

---

[§§] Although primarily a gymnastics organization, the Sokol movement had strong nationalist elements and devised fanciful patriotic outfits for special occasions.

Klášterní náměstí no. 1)[62] and, in return for helping out with the choir, Lev continued to take meals at the monastery.[63] A few months before, the teacher-training course at all such teaching institutes in Austria had been extended to four years. Janáček's training at this 'middle school' continued in German, but in his third year (1871–2) the institution became Czech, the 'Imperial and Royal Slavonic Men Teachers' Training Institute'.[64] This also led to a change at the top: on 15 November 1871 Dr Josef Parthe had to step down as director in favour of the Czech-speaking Gustav Zeynek, who in turn left to be a school inspector in Opava and was replaced on 30 September 1872 by Emilian Schulz,[65] a change that would have long-lasting consequences for Janáček. Janáček's life came to be intimately bound up with the Schulz family (see chap. 13).

Lev in fact got through the four-year course in three years. When he graduated at the age of eighteen he was expected to spend two years as an unpaid assistant teacher; Křížkovský's account book shows that Jan Janáček continued to support his nephew for the first two years of his training.[66] In his second year Lev received a state scholarship of 50 zl, increased the next year to 100 zl. It was not a princely sum but was comparable with a low annual wage (for instance a member of the chorus at the Prague Provisional Theatre earned 120–180 zl a year in 1862)[67] and allowed him to be independent of his uncle. Although the letters had already ceased (or at least have not survived), later correspondence and reminiscences suggest that the two kept in touch and that Janáček visited his uncle occasionally, especially after 1870, when the latter moved to Znorovy (as it was called in the nineteenth century; in 1924 it reverted to the earlier name of 'Vnorovy').

The three years of teacher training (1869–72) are almost blank in terms of surviving records, though there is one intriguing personal reminiscence. For all its opening claims to date from Lev's time at the Staré Brno monastery, the reference to 'trudging' to the 'institute' (i.e. in central Brno) places it within this period. Furthermore the distinctive personal appearance would not have been allowed by the monks (it sounds as though Lev had succeeded in badgering his uncle to let him have high boots):

As a choral student at the Staré Brno monastery foundation, Janáček wore his hair in long flowing locks that reached his shoulders. On his head he wore a

Sokol cap¶¶ and on his feet, high boots, *faldovačky*.*** In this way he trudged day in day out to the institute, a stack of books tucked under his left arm. He was already then an excellent pianist and in the monastery he had an equal partner with whom, under the guidance of the great Křížkovský, he played Beethoven symphonies. There were precious moments of artistic enjoyment whenever these two enthusiasts sat down to the piano.[68]

This reminiscence was published in 1940 by Father Augustin Neumann,[69] whose uncle František Neumann††† (a choral scholar at the monastery for five years and later headmaster of a school in Bosko-vice) seems to have been Janáček's piano duet partner. Furthermore František Neumann remembered a song written by the young Lev, *If you don't want me, so what?*, quoting the tune from memory. Astonishingly the song survived (v/1): the Janáček archive has a version in Janáček's hand for piano and voice,[70] the tune identical with Neumann's except for the key. Janáček seems to have remembered this for a 'Svatopluk' concert a few years later (23 January 1876), where this title is given as the second of a group of 'Three Songs'. The outer two are familiar as choruses (*Ploughing* iv/1 and *True Love* iv/8). Was this song perhaps given as a contrasting solo between the two choruses, or was it recycled as a chorus, as a surviving part suggests? Either way, the solo version would appear to be Janáček's first surviving composition.‡‡‡

In his autobiography Janáček passed by the teacher-training years with two short sentences: 'The Teachers' Institute in the Minorite monastery. I think with gratitude of Dr Parthe from psychology.'[71] Lev concentrated on the subjects that he was to teach – Czech language, history, geography, music (singing and organ) – plus of course educational methods and theory. Dr Parthe's lectures on psychology, Helfert suggests,[72] gave Janáček an early taste for an interest which importantly informed much of his own theoretical work in music.

These three blank years in Janáček's life encourage one to speculate. At this stage of his life Lev Janáček was following in the family

---

¶¶ A flat pill-box hat, usually with a feather.
*** High lace-up boots, from the German *Falte* [a fold].
††† This a different František Neumann from the conductor, whose first contacts with Janáček date from 1906 and who went on to be the conductor of many Janáček premières.
‡‡‡ Janáček's *Graduale in festo purificationis BVM 'Suspecimus'* (ii/9) might be seen as a rival in view of the 'about 1870' that its discoverer, Bohumír Štědroň, suggested for it in his Janáček catalogue. But this early date seems unlikely on stylistic grounds (see chap. 12).

footsteps, on his way to becoming a schoolteacher, though one in whom a musical talent had already been detected, encouraged and to some extent trained. At the end of his five-year teacher training, with almost no money at his disposal, Janáček spent a year in Prague furthering his studies exclusively in music so that he could qualify specifically as a music teacher. Whatever else happened while he was at the institute in Brno, it presumably dawned on him that if he did not wish to spend the rest of his life as a general schoolteacher he would need to do something about it. A youthful ambition as a 'forester' (recorded in his first year at the Realschule)[73] seems to have been discarded early on, and music took its place. Meanwhile he had little option but to put his head down and get his standard teaching qualifications out of the way.

Given his continuing connections with Křížkovský, Lev probably attended the concert at the Brno Beseda on 9 January 1871 celebrating Křížkovský's fiftieth birthday.[74] He is equally likely to have taken part in the music Křížkovský composed for the service on 26 July at St Tomáš's church, where a statue commemorating the great Moravian folk-music collector (and Křížkovský's mentor) František Sušil was unveiled. That evening there was a special concert at the Lužánky hall at which Křížkovský's settings of Sušil's words were performed, as well as solo folksongs sung by Jan Ludvík Lukes,[75] a former Brno Augustinian choral scholar and now the leading tenor soloist at the Provisional Theatre in Prague. There is an indication, too, that Lev took part in a concert in Brno on 6 May 1872 involving the 'Zora' choir, the Brno Beseda and 'Svatopluk' – a symbolic event in view of his later associations with the last two organizations.[76]

On 20 July 1872 Lev completed his studies at the Teachers' Institute, passing the qualifying exam with a general result of 'good', and 'very good' in geography, singing and organ.[77] Four days later he was given a temporary certificate, ungraded, which allowed him to work as an under-teacher or provisional teacher at primary schools with German or Czech as the language of instruction.[78] When he began his two years unpaid teaching practice – and there is no information about how it might have come about – Lev was lucky. Instead of being sent off to some village school, he was allocated to the 'practice school' attached to the Teachers' Institute. Furthermore it was the only primary school in Brno at the time to provide instruction in Czech, all the others being run by the 'town', which was then in German hands. The person who signed the certificate allowing him to do so (with the approval of the Regional School Board), dated 25 November 1872, was none other than the new Czech-speaking director of the institute, Emilian Schulz.[79]

The fact that he was now a young professional rather than a student seems to have allowed Lev time for other forms of self-improvement. He resumed his studies of French (briefly begun for a single semester at the Realschule in 1868–9, see above): Helfert records his copying out French sentences and other materials between 8 November 1872 and 24 July 1873.[80] In the next academic year (1873–4) he completed a course of academic lectures given by Professor Antonín Matzenauer on Czech language and literature at the Moravian Regional Academy.[81] There was also more time for music-making outside the monastery and the schoolroom. On 19 January 1873 Janáček accompanied the violinist Otakar Kopecký at the piano when he played at a concert given by the 'Svatopluk' society.[82]

During the second of his two unpaid teaching years, Janáček began to look ahead. Early in 1874 Schulz had requested a testimonial from Křížkovský with a view to Janáček's pursuing further musical training:

With reference to the application of Mr Lev Janáček I am very pleased to state my opinion, namely that in the light of his unusual musical gifts, especially for playing the organ, should Mr Janáček be given the opportunity of getting an all-round knowledge of the musical system and devoting himself exclusively to this art for a longer period under excellent teachers, a splendid result could be expected since his truly exceptional talent justifies such a hope.
Pavel Křížkovský, choirmaster[83]

Křížkovský's opinion, given on 12 January 1874, was based on observing Janáček as a performing musician: as a conductor (who had taken Křížkovský's place in the monastery) and as an organist. He would have had little notion of Janáček's talents as a composer since at the time Janáček had written only a handful of male-voice choruses for 'Svatopluk' (see chap. 10), performed in Brno when Křížkovský was in Olomouc. It is possible, however, that Křížkovský might have seen these few pieces, since he returned to Brno for a while during the summer of 1873[84] and Janáček could have shown his old teacher the music, most of it in the Křížkovský mould.

Before he could further his musical studies, however, Janáček needed to complete his teacher training with final qualifying exams. Janáček's request to the ministry to take these early, in April 1874,[85] did not succeed and instead he took them in October, two years after he began his teaching practice. By 6 October he was already in Prague attending lectures at the Prague Organ School, as the dates of his lecture notes testify;[86] if the exams were later than that, presumably he travelled back to Brno to take them. According to the detailed certificate awarded him on 18 November 1874[87] he was now fully qualified as a teacher for all primary schools (Czech and German), and in middle schools where Czech was the medium of instruction as a 'literní' teacher, in which the focus was on reading, writing, languages, history, geography and singing rather than drawing and handicrafts or more technical and vocational subjects.

The examination certificate is wonderfully detailed in describing the written and oral questions that he was asked, and provides comments on his responses. In Czech as a teaching language, when he was asked in his oral exam to talk about the 'relation of poetics to aesthetics' and the 'vowel shift', he was assessed as 'showing great knowledge in grammar, literature and poetics'. His writing style was found to be refined and correct with the overall comment 'very good'. In geography the examination included a description of Sweden and Norway; a cultural review of France; a comparison of the British Isles with the Italian peninsula; an account of European lakes; and a cultural review of the Kingdom of Bohemia in comparison with Moravia. Here Janáček was assessed as 'very good' in both written and oral examination.

In history the examination included the internal conditions of Rome after the Punic wars; the Czech king Václav IV and his time; the culture and religion of the old Egyptians; the French encyclopedists. Here the examiners commented on Janáček's 'exceptional knowledge of ancient history with great certainty in chronology' and he was again assessed as 'very good'. What is remarkable is that someone whose chief ambitions were now in music showed so much interest in and knowledge of these subjects.

The only parts of his examination that were assessed merely as 'good' (thus bringing the overall result down to a second-class certificate) were some aspects of teaching theory (such as the school system and education laws) and the practice class, where his explanation of the earth's rotation, although 'clear', did not command the attention of all the pupils. Part of what Janáček was up to in Prague was perhaps to ensure that explaining the rotation of the earth did not need to form part of any future life and that if he was to be a teacher, it would be a teacher only of music.

8

Pavel Křížkovský

Torn between his monastic vows and his talents as a performing musician and composer, Pavel Křížkovský (see Plate 27) is an intriguing figure in Moravian music of the nineteenth century. He was born in 1820 and, like many a poor country boy (in his case illegitimate), he trained for the priesthood. But this was only after considerable exposure to music from an early age, for instance as a choral scholar in Opava, where he was aided by Janáček's father, the young Jiří Janáček. He went on to university studies in Olomouc – poverty prevented his completing them – before arriving in 1843 in Brno, where he kept himself alive by teaching the piano and, it is thought, at the same time taking lessons with a leading musical theorist, Gottfried Rieger. He became a novice at the Augustinian monastery in Brno under Abbot Napp in 1845, a monk a year later and a priest in 1848, but he still continued with his musical activities – chiefly composing and performing – taking a full part in the concert life in Brno. He was one of the founders of the Brünner Männergesangverein (1848), he played the viola in string quartets at public concerts and in 1860, when the new, exclusively Czech, Brno Beseda was established, he became its first conductor. He held this post until 1863, when the Bishop of Brno, Anton Ernst Schaffgotsch, finally put his foot down and restricted his secular activities. Thereafter Křížkovský's concert-giving was confined to church venues, notably at the Augustinian monastery, where he had become choirmaster in 1848, and at Olomouc Cathedral, where he was choirmaster from 1872.

Judging from the occasional references in his letters to his uncle, Leo's attitude towards Křížkovský was respectful rather than affectionate. A portrayal of him as a benevolent but distant figure occurs in his autobiography (1924):

Father Pavel Křížkovský. I remember him as a sick man in Škrochovice near Opava. Me a little singer – a treble soloist. I sing a solo in Beethoven's Mass. Uncompromising, always strict during rehearsing. Unmethodical: he would be taken up with the overall effect. Before we got the hang of it! He called me to him, played me his song, asking me how I liked it. 'Play me on the piano what occurs to you!' Who knows what occurred to me then!¹

Janáček's reminiscences are as 'unmethodical' as Křížkovský's rehearsal techniques had been. In a tribute to his mentor published in 1902 (xv/166) Janáček implies that Křížkovský's playing him one of his songs and soliciting his opinion was part of the Opava interview. Presumably, too, Křížkovský heard him sing then, but when did the rest occur? According to the 1902 memoir, Křížkovský's request for Janáček to improvise happened later, when he was delivering music to Křížkovský's cell in the Brno monastery. It is striking that neither in 1902 nor in 1924 is there any comment about fatherly care: the memories recorded in both places are only those connected with music. More eloquent is the brief comment in Janáček's 1902 memoir: 'Křížkovský would never speak at all about himself, let alone to me, just a boy' (xv/166). Although there was much that could have brought the two together – their family connections, their similar fates in being sent away as youngsters to be choral scholars, Leo's undoubted musical talent – no such father-son bonding took place. And no adult relationship developed either. By the time Janáček had grown up, Křížkovský was in Olomouc. Janáček took his young bride to meet him on his honeymoon in 1881, but all she recalled was Křížkovský's lending her husband money.²

Even if there was no emotional bond, Křížkovský's impact on the young Leo was deep and long-lasting. In the Chorale Fantasy (viii/4), his graduation composition at the Prague Organ School, Janáček symbolically included a contrapuntal working-out of the closing chorale from Křížkovský's cantata *SS Cyril and Methodius*.³ Janáček's writings about Křížkovský extend across his entire adult life from 1875 – from his first published article (about Křížkovský's reform of church music, xv/1) – to fifty years later when he wrote a short piece for *Lidové noviny* about the location of Křížkovský's statue in Brno (xv/280). In between there is a detailed article about Křížkovský's importance to Moravian folk music and to Czech music in general (xv/166) and a commentary on his chorus *The Drowned Maiden* (xv/167), both published in 1902. Janáček wrote more about Křížkovský than about any other composer apart from Dvořák and Smetana.

Janáček's most substantial article on Křížkovský (xv/166) was originally delivered as a lecture on 26 February 1902. This medium might have allowed a more personal approach but, apart from the couple of reminiscences quoted above, the piece is concerned only with Křížkovský as a composer and his relationship to his folk texts, and as a conductor. All had an influence on Janáček – Křížkovský was the most important musician he had yet encountered.

Křížkovský's Czech sympathies, shared by many of the monks at the Augustinian monastery, were also important in shaping Janáček's outlook. František Bílý (1854–1920), Janáček's near-contemporary at the primary school in Lackerwiese ulice, recalled how Křížkovský, who taught religion there, came across to his pupils as sympathetic because he taught his subject in Czech, despite its being officially a German-language school.[4] Křížkovský's Czech sympathies were evident in many other ways. Born 'Kriskowsky' (according to the birth register) and signing himself at first as 'Krischkowský', he had adopted the purely Czech form of his difficult surname by the 1860s.[5] Although he had been one of the founders of the Brno Männergesangverein, which despite its name was essentially a mixed German and Czech organization, he soon devoted his services exclusively to the Czech-only Brno Beseda. Apart from liturgical settings in Latin, his vocal music is overwhelmingly in Czech; he set only a couple of German texts.

Křížkovský's compositional output is small and well over half of it, again understandably, was sacred or liturgical. Janáček wrote enthusiastically about the liturgical music (xv/1, 1875), but in his 1902 lecture he passed it by with hardly a word. Nor has it been of any interest to many others after the first substantial biography (1904) by Dr Karel Eichler, who as a priest himself took a more professional interest in this area. The collected edition of Křížkovský's works begun in 1949 published most of his secular choruses and songs in its 'Volume 1' and left it at that. The sympathetic discussion of Křížkovský by Jiří Vysloužil in 2001[6] concentrates almost exclusively on his secular choruses.

Křížkovský's eighteen secular choruses,* mostly for unaccompanied male voices and, with a couple of important exceptions, all based on

---

* As listed in NG2; twenty-five if alternative versions are included.

folk texts, are at the heart of his compositional endeavour and are the reason why he was important to Moravian music and in particular to Janáček. His choruses turned up regularly at Brno Beseda concerts and formed part of the standard choral repertory of the period in Moravia. Janáček himself conducted many of them. Their success, he stated in his 1902 article, was 'huge', and he went on to mention half of them by name with comments on their structure and character that derive from an intimate knowledge of these works. Many of them he referred to not by their titles but by their folksong texts, which he knew equally well.

The texts all came from the huge collection made by another Moravian musician priest, František Sušil (1804–68). His *Moravian Folksongs* was published from 1835, first only as booklets with words. The revised edition of 1860 (now with tunes added) contained 2091 tunes and 2361 texts.[7] This collection was Křížkovský's quarry. His simplest choruses are not much more than arrangements harmonized for four-part male chorus, as for example his early choruses *Enchantment* and *The Faithless Heart*. In other cases Křížkovský would take the words only and, in his setting, attempt to recreate an authentic folk tune.

Křížkovský's early choruses are often described as *ohlasový* works, works that are an 'echo' (*ohlas*) of folk art. An early manifestation of the Czech folk revival, the *ohlas* tendency was first seen in literary works attempting to imitate folk texts, for example *An Echo of Russian Songs* (1829) and *An Echo of Czech Songs* (1839) by the Czech poet František Ladislav Čelakovský (1799–1852) – Czech reflections of Romantic trends elsewhere, such as James Macpherson's 'Ossianic' poems. Musical 'echoes' are of course more problematic than literary ones since anything more complicated than an unaccompanied tune will remove it from the sphere of traditional music to the sphere of art music. Nevertheless, a nod in the direction of traditional music can be seen in features such as the use of traditional texts, the syllabic setting and a general simplicity of means. Janáček commented approvingly in his article on Křížkovský's uncomplicated rhythms, the intelligibility of the words and the way that his settings arise from the spirit of the original folk materials.

Janáček emphasized that the *ohlasový* genre was important in the development of Czech-sounding music, in contrast to the German-influenced Liedertafel style (XV/166). According to Janáček, Křížkovský was the first Czech composer to give Czech its 'singing robe', a 'robe' that Křížkovský had noticed in folksong and which he went on to incorporate in his own works. Admittedly Smetana, regarded elsewhere as the father of Czech music, came before Křížkovský with his polka-based concept of Czech music. But the Smetana polka style, Janáček suggested, could only go so far. He could also have said that the *ohlasový* style could only go so far too, as Křížkovský himself discovered.

Křížkovský's *Love-Gift* (the first chorus mentioned in xv/166), begins as a straight homophonic arrangement of tune no. 998 from Sušil. Far more than just an arrangement, however, it turns into a substantial, six-minute piece with a three-part structure (Allegro, Moderato, Presto) and has the exhilarating character of a vocal scherzo. Janáček's article goes on to discuss *The Drowned Maiden I* (1848), a simple exchange between a girl and her young man who is going off to war. She waits seven years for him and when he doesn't return she drowns herself. The piece features many changes of key and tempo to characterize the two protagonists, an aspect that Křížkovský built on in his more extended setting of 1860. In this later version (*The Drowned Maiden II*) there is a larger cast of characters, their direct speech suggested by breaks and by changes of tempo. A ritornello – in effect variations of the main tune – holds this extended chorus together. Notable too is the use of a solo voice. Here it is used only for textural contrast (the solo voice does not represent a particular person), but all the ingredients are in place to turn this male-voice chorus into an unaccompanied cantata. Many of these features are suggested by the essentially balladic nature of the text and juxtapositions of dialogue.

Most of Janáček's early choruses for 'Svatopluk' (1873–6) are *ohlasový* works (some actually designated as such)[†] and Křížkovský's stamp on them is evident (see chap. 10). One of the least known is the male-voice chorus *You cannot escape your fate* (iv/9). Its title may seem to look forward to *The Diary of One Who Disappeared* (v/12); however this is not a fate-ridden tragedy but a much more light-hearted affair. In this Serbian folksong a girl foolishly throws an apple into the air and declares that she will marry whoever it falls on. It falls on an old man, whom she doesn't want to marry, so she packs him off on various errands culminating in sending him to war – but he comes back even

---

[†]e.g. *True Love* (iv/8), which Janáček described to the 'Svatopluk' committee on 6 January 1876 as one of a cycle called *Ohlas národních písní* [An echo of folksongs] (*LJPT*, 333, fn. 2).

from war and so she capitulates saying 'no-one can avoid his fate'. Setting these words, Janáček wrote a type of scherzando chorus in the manner of Křížkovský's *Love-Gift*. As in Křížkovský's choruses, the harmonic style is simple, without the fancy modulations of Janáček's *Vocal Duma* (iv/10) (suggesting that iv/9 was written with 'Svatopluk' rather than the Beseda in mind, though publicly performed by neither choir).

Later Janáček choruses, such as the Bezruč ones (iv/33–6), which he began composing in 1906, are similarly little dramas along the lines of *The Drowned Maiden*, with individual roles characterized and brought alive, sometimes by the use of solo voices. Petr Bezruč's texts are balladic and have a directness and simplicity of diction that allow them to come across as developed versions of traditional texts. Although Janáček's musical style is much more experimental than Křížkovský's, the techniques of dramatizing his settings as mini-cantatas held together by a varied ritornello directly mirror Křížkovský's method in *The Drowned Maiden* (see chap. 54). One might have thought that Janáček's analysis of Křížkovský's *The Drowned Maiden* (1902, only a few years before the first of the Bezruč choruses) would have referred to some of these features. However, creativity works in different ways. Janáček's approach to the piece was to sketch in (with a series of music examples) a 'mesologický doprovod', i.e. an accompaniment that suggests the natural environment against which the scene takes place. In this way he showed his own response to the inherent drama of the piece. It was clearly a piece that haunted him and continued to throw up parallels, such as his settings (1906–7) of Bezruč's *Maryčka Magdónova* (iv/34 and iv/35) with its young heroine drowning herself, or his attempt to drag Pavla Křičková's poem with the same title as Křížkovský's chorus – *Utonulá* – into the inspirational vortex of his *Danube Symphony* (ix/7; see 1923).

If Křížkovský can be regarded as the first of Janáček's 'mentors', it is less because of any personal relationship than because Křížkovský was a crucial precursor. He was his composition teacher, however, only by example. Janáček began composing only after Křížkovský left Brno for Olomouc in 1872.

Janáček was a more direct pupil of Křížkovský as a conductor and had a high regard for him in this capacity: 'No-one who sang or played under him will ever forget any of the pieces they rehearsed. No-one could reach so boldly, so surely, as he could into the depths of a soul, into the expression of another soul, of another composer.' Janáček always remembered how the Credo of Michael Haydn's D minor Mass sounded under Křížkovský's direction and had many vivid memories of such music-making, where the monastery musicians were joined by others from the town such as the oboist Josef Štross and the soprano Marie Hřímalá. Janáček regretted how such festive music gave way to the austerities of the Cecilian church music reforms and he found Křížkovský's conversion hard to explain (xv/166).

Janáček took over Křížkovský's two main musical posts in Brno: at the Augustinian monastery in Staré Brno in 1872 and at the Brno Beseda in 1876. Janáček's unsystematic rehearsal techniques, his authoritarian stance, uncompromising standards and his commitment to the music he was conducting all sound very much like a younger model of Křížkovský. And Křížkovský himself seems to have sensed this, if Jan Kunc (presumably relying on Janáček's own recollection) reported his comment correctly: 'You'll see how that fellow will soon outstrip me.'[8]

Significantly, when Janáček published his first article in January 1875 (xv/1) it was devoted to his old teacher. Křížkovský was of course still very much alive and would be bound to read the article, printed in *Cecilie*, the leading Czech church-music journal. So it is hardly surprising, despite Janáček's proverbial tactlessness, that it is full of praise for Křížkovský's achievements as a conductor, as a church-music reformer, and as a composer of secular and sacred works. Perhaps this public declaration was the only way that he could express some sort of thanks to his old teacher. Five years later, at a time when Janáček had triumphed as conductor at the Beseda and was forging ahead with his studies in Leipzig, one gets a glimpse of what Křížkovský thought of it all. Berthold Žalud, keeping Janáček in touch with Brno gossip, mentioned Křížkovský in one of his letters:

Křížkovský was here for about a week. He is now more cheerful. He regrets that you are lost to church music. I countered [this by saying to] him that someone who knows all types of music will certainly benefit church music more than a musician who has grown up one-sidedly. [. . .] He said that it's a great happiness for you that you've got to Leipzig.[9]

In 1883 Křížkovský suffered a stroke and was paralysed down his left side; later that year he retired to the Augustinian monastery in Staré Brno.[10] Presumably Janáček saw him from time to time during his regular rehearsals and services at the monastery, and even at the Beseda concert on 29 March 1885, where Křížkovský heard him conduct Liszt's *Mazeppa* among other works.[11] That was, however, the last concert Křížkovský attended. On 8 May 1885 he was found dead in his cell. His funeral at the monastery church on 11 May was a large-scale affair, bringing together musical and spiritual Brno to celebrate both sides of his life. Janáček tended to avoid funerals and did not even attend his mother's in Hukvaldy the previous year, but on this occasion he conducted the Beseda chorus, the monastery choral scholars and a brass band in the chorus that Křížkovský himself had composed for Sušil's funeral in 1869: *Take your rest.*[12] And in another act of homage, some ten years later, Janáček made his own setting for male-voice chorus of these words (IV/24). He derived great pleasure when the work, lost for thirty years, turned up at the end of his life.

9

Pan-Slavism I

Pan-Slavism, the movement for the union of all the Slav peoples, was a response to the writings of the German philosopher Johann Gottfried von Herder (1744–1803). Twenty years before Napoleon's European wars began to stir up thoughts of nationalism among hitherto submerged or unimagined nations it was Herder who had stressed the importance of the mother tongue (rather than dynastic loyalty) in determining national loyalties. Furthermore, it was Herder in his *Ideen zur Philosophie der Geschichte der Menschheit* (1784–91) who had contrasted the Slavs with the more 'advanced' Germanic and Latinate nations and, as a disciple of Rousseau, had seen in their backwardness and artlessness their passport to a glorious future. The Slavs, he proclaimed, were the future leaders of Europe.[1]

In Hans Kohn's definition, Pan-Slavism proposes an alliance, whether culturally or politically, of all the Slavs. Some writers such as John Erickson have sought to reserve the term 'Pan-Slavism' for the political movement and 'Slavism' or 'Slavophilism' for a cultural movement where boundary change is not envisaged.[2] While this distinction is useful in a general discussion, it is not always practical since it is difficult in some cases to separate the two: many political ends were pursued subversively under the banner of culture, and some Pan-Slavists were unclear what they wanted. In this book the term 'Pan-Slavism' covers all manifestations.

The conflicting and complicated nature of Pan-Slavism is well demonstrated by comparing it with Pan-Germanism. At the start of the nineteenth century German speakers were dispersed among numerous kingdoms, grand duchies, prince-bishoprics, one empire and other assorted states. For those who believed the Germans should aspire to being a single people living within a single political entity there were two hopeful signs. One was the fact that, despite their various dialects, all Germans spoke roughly the same language. Second was the fact that most of the states where Germans lived were self-governing and could therefore come together in some sort of voluntary association – as most of them did in 1871. The more numerous Slavs, on the other hand, spoke up to a dozen languages, mostly mutually unintelligible, and apart from the Russians almost all were subject peoples, distributed among three multi-ethnic empires: Habsburg, Ottoman and Russian.

While Pan-Slavism by definition involved all Slavonic nations, in practice the term was frequently merged with Russophilism. Russia was by far the largest Slavonic nation and the only one with a long history of political independence. It had a distinctive culture, literature and musical tradition that could be admired and imitated. An awareness of Russian Slavs running their own affairs was a hopeful inspiration to subject Slav nations.

To most non-Russians Pan-Slavism and Russophilism were usually veiled expressions of nationalism and of aspirations towards independence. Such manifestations of nationalism varied according to which empire they were subject to and according to what religion they professed. In his classic exposition of Pan-Slavism, Hans Kohn contrasted the east and south Slavs with their 'Illyrian' aspirations to the 'realistic' Czechs and the 'messianic' Poles.[3] The Poles had long experience of Russia: the two countries were divided not only by a common border but by centuries of bitter conflict. During the eighteenth century Russia had joined enthusiastically with Prussia and Austria in partitioning Poland out of existence. No Slavonic solidarity there, though it should perhaps be remembered that Russians saw Pan-Slavism rather differently as the unity of Slavdom under the hegemony of Russia, with all other Slav peoples abandoning their quaint 'dialects' for Russian and their Catholicism for Orthodoxy.

The east and south Slav nations that had been part of the Ottoman Empire took a different view of Russia and hence of Pan-Slavism. To them the Russians were potential liberators and they could view much of the nineteenth century as a triumphalist history in which one by one the Slav nations threw off the Ottoman yoke, often with Russian assistance. And any firmer embrace with Russia was not to be feared since many of these east and south Slav nations had belonged to the same Orthodox world that had been shattered by the fall of Constantinople in 1453. One could argue that what was on offer was a return to an idyllic Slavonic and Orthodox past.

The Slavs of the Habsburg Empire occupied an area somewhere in between. The Czechs had had their own brand of Protestant Christianity (based on the teachings of Jan Hus, ?1372–1414) but by the nineteenth century most were Catholics like their Habsburg masters, so that religion was no longer a sign of difference, as in the two other empires. Although they were divided on the issue, the Czechs, like the other Catholic Slavs in the Habsburg Empire (the Slovaks, the Croats and the Slovenes), produced some of the most enthusiastic non-Russian Pan-Slavists. For Czechs an interest in Russia, even one covertly disguised as 'Pan-Slavism', was something of a political statement, the unspoken political affiliation of the conservative *staročech* [Old Czech] party.[4] Enthusiasm for Russia denoted a lack of enthusiasm for Austria-Hungary, and was regarded with suspicion by the Habsburg authorities: the last thing they wanted was too much cosying up by the Czechs to the Russians, let alone any thought of the Russians 'liberating' their Czech brothers. If the Czechs had taken a more detached view of Russia they might have noticed that another Slavonic nation – the Poles – had not been protected by their Russian brothers. It was an uncomfortable thought for Pan-Slavists (should any of them have got round to thinking it) that the Poles and Ukrainians of Galicia had more autonomy within the Austrian Empire than Poles and Ukrainians within the Russian.

Pan-Slavism was given particular impetus by the events of the revolutionary year of 1848. Not long after the fall of the autocratic Austrian chancellor Metternich and the regime's panicky promises of a liberal constitution, the Czech historian František Palacký presided over the first Pan-Slavonic Congress in Prague, where the solidarity of all Slavonic peoples was proclaimed. Among the delegates there were huge differences in attitude. At one end of the political spectrum there was Bakunin's revolutionary dream of the destruction of existing empires to be replaced by a federation of independent Slavonic nations; at the other was Palacký's more cautious preference for working within existing political frameworks. Palacký saw danger in a collection of dwarf nation-states that might be the successors to a dismantled Austria, all too small individually to resist the embrace of the Russian bear. His predictions came true a century later. Famously Palacký had proclaimed that 'If the Austrian state had not existed for ages, we would be obliged in the interests of Europe and even of mankind to endeavour to create it as fast as possible.'[5] Palacký would no doubt have welcomed the enlarged European Union of the twenty-first century as simply a bigger and better 'Austria'.

As it was, Russia, which could have led a Slavonic revolt in 1848, preferred to come to the aid of Austria in quelling the rebellion and restoring the status quo. Despite the freedom of cultural expression permitted by the October diploma of 1860, political expression in the Czech lands remained risky or impossible until the collapse of the Habsburg Empire in 1918.

Among composers, the most important Czech Pan-Slavist was Dvořák (1843–1904). For all the later perception of him by Smetana's supporters as having sold out to foreigners with his many commissions, publications, trips abroad and considerable following outside the country, it is clear that the inspiration of much of his work is essentially Czech, but within the context of the wider Slavonic world. So, in addition to the *Czech Suite* and the *Hussite Overture*, there are the *Slavonic Dances* and *Slavonic Rhapsodies*. Most of his operas had Czech subjects but two, *Vanda* and *Dimitrij*, had Polish or Russian subjects. And he had a particular penchant for that most Slav of all genres, the *dumka* (see below). All these characteristics set Dvořák apart from Smetana, whose nationalism was expressed musically in purely Bohemian Czech terms.

It was perhaps for this very reason that Janáček would favour Dvořák rather than Smetana. The earliest expression of Janáček's Czech nationalism was his enthusiasm for the Cyril and Methodius celebration at Velehrad in 1869, an echo of a Pan-Slavonic world that linked Russia and Moravia. It is striking that the poem that Janáček sent to his uncle did not include references to Prague, Bohemian history or myths, but instead invoked the wider Slavonic world (see chap. 7).

It was not long before Janáček, in his Pan-Slavonic orientation, would gravitate towards Russia, its language and its culture. He had already demanded from his uncle Jan 'Russian linen' for a suit. Defiantly, he adopted the Russian name of 'Lev' from the age of fourteen to replace the more German form 'Leo', and 'Lev Janáček' remained his professional name for over a decade until softened into 'Leoš' in 1880 (see chap. 14). Quite when young Lev began learning Russian is unclear, but certainly not earlier than 1873 (i.e. when he was studying at the Brno Teachers' Institute): the two Russian grammars surviving in his library were books published in that year. Helfert records Janáček writing notes of an 'intimate nature' in his exercise books in cyrillic script in 1874 (see chap. 11). The fact that these are merely a transliteration of Czech words suggests that all he had done so far was to master the script. Had he got further he might have concealed his thoughts more thoroughly by writing them in Russian.

Janáček's first work inspired by a Russian author, the lost melodrama based on Lermontov's poem *Death* (x/3) and performed by the Brno Beseda in 1876, was for the time an isolated instance. Even though it was another thirty years before he returned to Russian authors for compositional inspiration, a sympathy was clearly there. His two children, Olga (born 1882) and Vladimír (born 1888) were both given names that were popular in the Czech lands, but were nevertheless Russian borrowings and, incidentally, the names of Pushkin's pair of lovers in his *Eugene Onegin*.

Although it is not something much associated with Janáček it is possible that the import of the instrumental *dumka* into Czech music came to Dvořák via Janáček. Vocal *dumi, dumki* or *dumky* are a characteristic of Polish and Ukrainian music, terms used for laments or pieces of a ruminative nature throughout the nineteenth century. One of Janáček's earliest choruses has the ambiguous title *Zpěvná duma* [Vocal duma] (iv/10). While the first word can be translated variously as 'singable' or 'tuneful' the second word invokes the Slavonic world. In Czech the word *duma* is a Slavonic borrowing (from Russian or Ukrainian), a fancy word for 'thinking' or 'meditating' and hardly part of normal Czech vocabulary. The much more common secondary meaning (and more usually given in the diminutive, *dumka*) was 'a mournful song, lament, heroic elegy'. This much Janáček would have gleaned from the second volume (1862) of Rieger's encyclopedia,[6] which was the chief Czech work of reference until Otto's much larger encyclopedia began coming out in the late 1880s. Rieger goes on to explain that among the Ukrainians, *dumy* are 'a special type of national epic poetry'. The Rieger entry is detailed and substantial, including a ten-line example of a typical *duma* and a discussion of its rhyme and assonance features and the numbers of syllables per line. It speculates about the possible origins in the Russian epic *Slovo o polku Igorev*, and provides an interesting cultural commentary on the word, more as a genre than as a specific form. Although Polish and Ukrainian musical *dumky* were in existence well before Rieger was published, there is no consideration here of any musical settings. The author of this part of the Rieger article discusses the word purely in cultural and literary terms.

Whether he read about the *dumka* in Rieger, or whether he came across it in some other way, Janáček clearly had some notion of what the word meant. The text that he set in his chorus came from František Ladislav Čelakovský's collection *An Echo of Czech Songs* (1839), a pastiche folksong (about a grief-stricken girl) called *The Breaking of a Promise*. *Vocal Duma* is thus Janáček's own title, but what he intended by it, by far his most ambitious chorus to date (see chap. 12), is more difficult to fathom, though its abundant melismas are perhaps an expression of lamenting, of keening, and in this way reflect the sub- ject matter. Helfert, signalling this as Janáček's most important com- position to date, saw in it aspects of the Cecilian reforms in church music and its return to the modal and *a cappella* music of the sixteenth century.[7] Jarmil Burghauser, on the other hand, suggested Russian Orthodox church music as being 'much more striking than the influ- ence of Catholic church music',[8] though apart from a few very low bass notes and the odd fervently incantatory section there is not much that would support this view (and it does rely on assuming that Janáček had actually heard Russian church music at this stage – by no means proven). Despite the *duma* of the title, it is difficult to argue that any- thing specifically Slavonic was intended in its music, merely the general suggestion of a lament.

But clearly the title lingered in Janáček's memory and a few years later he used the term *dumka* for two instrumental pieces. One is lost, a *Dumka* for piano performed in Rožnov on 8 September 1879, its existence known only through a concert programme and a press report confirming Janáček's participation (x/4).[9] The other is a *Dumka* for violin and piano said, on the basis of Janáček's recollection, to be composed in '1880',[10] i.e. during his time in Leipzig and Vienna (VII/4). There are good reasons, however, for placing it a few years later, though no later than March 1885, when it was performed (see chap. 23). For all its moody, ruminative character it doesn't dispel the feeling that at this stage of his life Janáček's Pan-Slavonic compositions are more a matter of Slavonic aspiration than of specific Slavonic colouring.

10

Early professional life: before Prague (1872–4)

Janáček's professional life started in September 1872 when, at eighteen and having finished his teacher training, he began work as a school-teacher at the Czech-language practice school attached to the Teachers' Institute in Brno. At much the same time he began his freelance career by taking over Křížkovský's duties as choirmaster at the Staré Brno monastery when Křížkovský left for Olomouc Cathedral. He was paid no stipend at either institution. The Teachers' Institute didn't pay because they demanded two years' unpaid work from novice teachers before putting them on the payroll. The monastery didn't pay because there was no provision for it – the job was meant to be done by one of the monks. Quite what Janáček lived on for the next two years is not clear but the monastery gave him free meals in return for his work and the occasional one-off fee, for instance a payment of 10 zl on 16 April 1875 for extra work involved in the Easter services.[1] Some fees came too from giving private music lessons: when Janáček went to Prague in 1874 these were handed over to his friend František Neumann (see chap. 11).

Officially Janáček's post at the monastery can be dated to 2 October 1872 when he began filling in the choristers' attendance register,[2] but what with Křížkovský's poor health he probably stood in for him at earlier times after he ceased to be a chorister in the autumn of 1869. In August 1872, when the society 'Svatopluk' was considering appointing Janáček its choirmaster, he was reported even then to be 'director of singing at the Staré Brno monastery'.[3]

How long Janáček remained at the Staré Brno monastery as choir-master is unclear. Helfert found four different dates suggested for when Janáček stopped (1884, 1885, 1888, 1891), the first two probably connected with the death of Křížkovský. '1888' was what Zdenka Janáčková remembered,[4] though not in her memoirs, where the subject is hardly mentioned. A reference in Janáček's notebook for 1889–90 to an annual payment from the monastery for that year[5] would seem to confirm his involvement at least until then.

The very fact of this uncertainty is eloquent. Janáček was not doing much more than letting things tick over. The reformist programme that Křížkovský initiated and Janáček maintained was restrictive in its approach to repertory. Schaffgotsch, Bishop of Brno, was emphatic that the Augustinian church should not become a concert venue, so that even the public concert planned on 30 August 1876 for the inauguration of the new organ had, after the bishop's intervention, to be a private-invitation event.[6] From March 1873, when Janáček became choirmaster of 'Svatopluk', and later, when he became choirmaster at the Brno Beseda, he had more scope elsewhere. It would seem that for the free meals he received, and perhaps out of loyalty to Křížkovský, Janáček simply stayed on at the monastery without particularly exerting himself. And, it must be said, there wasn't much incentive. He was not paid a regular stipend until after his marriage in 1881 (when according to Zdenka he got 15 zl a month).[7]

Apart from conducting the monastery choir, Janáček's first permanent freelance employment was as choirmaster of 'Svatopluk'. With characteristic thoroughness, Helfert devoted many pages to 'Svatopluk', its antecedents and its profile as a cultural society in Czech Brno.[8] The Řemeslnická beseda 'Svatopluk' [Craft society 'Svatopluk'] was founded in 1868 as a self-help working man's club, rather conservative in nature, and attracting not so much industrial workers as craftsmen and small traders. As with most such clubs of the time there was a patriotic subtext to its activities, its name commemorating the famous ruler of the ninth-century Great Moravia. It might seem odd that the society should latch on to an eighteen-year-old as a prospective conductor for its male-voice choir but, as Helfert explained, Janáček had an ally in the chairman Dr Josef Illner (1839–94), who had heard about his success at the monastery;[9] furthermore there were few other suitable candidates among the tiny Czech-speaking population of Brno. For reasons that Helfert considered to be a matter of honourable principle Janáček declined the annual stipend[10] despite the modest state of his finances. Perhaps the young Janáček was unsure of his ability to adjust to such different circumstances. Instead of a choir of a dozen young boys and a few novices, all of whom could read music and were obliged to go to rehearsals and who week after week turned in performances of a range of music including the polyphonic repertory of the sixteenth century, he was now faced with a choir of about forty men of various ages,* often with little cultural and musical background and with no particular obligation to attend rehearsals. But Janáček need not have worried. He was a success from the start: attendance at rehearsals noticeably improved[11] and after a couple of concerts the press began characterizing the choir as the best in Brno.[12]

Janáček's tenure of 'Svatopluk' is generally regarded as one of the turning-points in his life. This is no doubt true – his first compositions date from this period† – but it is worth remembering what a short period it was and how few events were involved. Janáček took up his post on 1 March 1873‡ and continued until the summer of 1874, when he went to Prague for his year of study at the Organ School. Although he was reappointed after his return in the autumn of 1875 and held the post for a further year, this was overtaken by other events (see chap. 12). It is the pre-Prague 'Svatopluk' period that is the crucial one.

During eighteen months in 1873–4 Janáček presided over eight 'Svatopluk' events: four concerts and, in the summer months, four excursions to nearby villages (two of them now suburbs of Brno):[13]

Table 10.1: Janáček's concerts and entertainments with 'Svatopluk' 1873–4

---

27 April 1873: Beseda§ at the pub 'U bílého kříže' ['At the white cross'], Pekařská ulice; premières of *Ploughing* (iv/1) and *The Enforced Bridegroom* (x/2)

5 July 1873: Beseda for blessing the society flag at the Besední dům; première of *War Song (2)* (iv/3)

10 August 1873: Excursion to Žabovřesky

9 November 1873: 'Concert beseda' at the Besední dům; première of *The Fickleness of Love* (iv/4)

14 March 1874: 'Concert beseda' at the Besední dům; première of *Alone without Comfort (1)* (iv/7) and second performance of *Ploughing* (iv/1)

31 May 1874: Excursion to Židenice

19 July 1874: Excursion to Žabovřesky

6 September 1874: Excursion to Šlapanice; performances of iv/1, iv/3 [or iv/2?], iv/4, iv/7

---

* According to the *Kalender für die musikalische Welt* for 1880 (p.177), 'Svatopluk' had then, i.e. some years later, forty-two members.
† With one possible exception (v/1), see chap. 7.
‡ He was elected on 13 February and took over formally on 1 March, see *LJPT*, 195–7.
§ The term 'beseda' is used here in its sense of informal concert (see chap. 6).

The excursions were partly recreational, partly to recruit members from further afield. Current members would process through the village, the choirmaster at the head, then the choir, then flagbearers with flags, committee members and others.[14] All this would climax in a musical event, though one generally shorter and less demanding than the Brno concerts. At the first excursion in which Janáček participated, to Žabovřesky on 10 August 1873, a few relatively easy choruses were performed – according to press reports (such events were regularly written up in *Moravská orlice*) as precisely as in Brno.[15]

Four concerts and four excursions in eighteen months do not sound much, but it is a good indication of how high Janáček set his sights. Opportunities for participation at other society events were turned down on the basis of not enough rehearsal.[16] Given weekly chorus rehearsals, the music must have been drummed into his singers with unrelenting vigour.

The programme for Janáček's first appearance with the choir (27 April 1873) gives a good idea of the general approach that Janáček inherited. The event, designated as a 'beseda', i.e. not a concert, was held at a pub. The programme began with an unspecified 'overture' and ended with a dance: such instrumental topping and tailing was characteristic of the time and signalled the presence of one of the several military bands that readily took part in such events. There was also an unnamed cello solo performed by František Mráček (from the German Theatre orchestra in Brno, and a favoured participant in Czech cultural events), and a Miss Mudrová delivered a recitation (a popular genre of the time). The 'Svatopluk' male-voice choir itself was heard in four short pieces (all designated 'premières'): one by a minor composer of patriotic choruses, Josef Drahorád; another for mixed voices (joined perhaps by the ladies from the 'Vesna' society) by a leading Prague choral and operatic composer, Karel Bendl (1838–97), and two choruses by Janáček, his *Ploughing* (IV/I) and *The Enforced Bridegroom* (X/2). Janáček's choruses, specially written for the occasion (he produced a new chorus for each of the 'Svatopluk' besedas until his departure for Prague), marked the beginning of what became an important genre for him, and one that he would cultivate throughout his life.

Janáček's increasing confidence and artistic ambitions as conductor and music organizer can be tracked by considering the next three besedas. The most significant aspect of the second (5 July 1873), still billed simply as a 'beseda', was that it took place not in a pub but in the recently opened Besední dům (see chap. 6), which from then on became the choir's Brno home. The other two were billed as 'concert besedas'. That of 9 November 1873 had a subscription list for the first time and 400 copies of the programme were printed. Furthermore, it was specifically advertised as being 'without dancing', thus losing the overture at the beginning. Omitting the dancing signalled that what was intended was no longer light entertainment but something more serious. Janáček's organizational energy is evident in his attending to such details as the programmes and the subscription list and even arranging for a bouquet for Miss Mudrová, who appeared as reciter again.[17]

The different presentation was matched by the increasingly aspirational contents. Although the function of the second beseda was essentially to dedicate the society's banner on its fifth anniversary (a circumstance fraught with ticklish political implications and needing skilful negotiation for it to happen at all),[18] it nevertheless included music by Schumann and Mendelssohn. The young violinist Václav Kopta, recently returned from America, played a movement from the latter's Violin Concerto and two other pieces. The choruses comprised mixed-voice works by Mendelssohn (joined by the 'Vesna' ladies) and Norbert Javůrek's male-voice chorus To Moravia as well as Janáček's specially written contribution for the banner ceremony, his War Song with brass and piano accompaniment (IV/3). Similarly, the third beseda was both an artistic success and a financial one, making a profit of 87 zl 85 kr, and included the first performance of Janáček's The Fickleness of Love (IV/4).

It was the final beseda (14 March 1874), however, that showed how much had been achieved during Janáček's short tenure. It was attended by Count Serényi and other local aristocrats, perhaps because of the drawing powers of the baritone Josef Lev (1832–98) from the Provisional Theatre in Prague, who sang among other things an aria from Rossini's La Cenerentola. The instrumental portion included a piano trio, and among the choruses was Křížkovský's SS Cyril and Methodius, one of his longest and most ambitious. Once again Janáček wrote a new chorus, his Alone without Comfort [1] (IV/7), and Ploughing, now a popular favourite, was heard again.

Janáček's final public event with 'Svatopluk' before going to Prague was the last of the summer excursions. More ambitious than its predecessors, it took place in Šlapanice on 6 September 1874. After the choir's rendition of a mass by Josef Drahlovský in the morning (expeditions were usually on Sunday), the 'afternoon entertainment' consisted of six choruses, two recitations and two cello solos. Of the six choruses, one was by Křížkovský, his *Recruit's Prayer*, and four were by Janáček. What in fact Janáček presented was, with one exception, his entire male-chorus output performed so far, three of them grouped together as *Three Songs*. It is as if Janáček, in his final 'Svatopluk' event for the time being, was providing a mini-retrospective of his compositions.

The chorus omitted was *The Enforced Bridegroom* (x/2); while the music is lost the words survive in the programme of the first performance.[19] The fact that it was not performed at Šlapanice suggests either that it had been lost by then, or that Janáček was unhappy with it.[II] The four choruses sung on this occasion follow two traditions. *War Song*, with its affirmative unison opening and generally masculine vigour, is characteristic of the typical patriotic choruses of the time (such as those by Tovačovský[¶] etc.). Its different character from Janáček's other early choruses, and the fact that it was accompanied, arise from the festive occasion for which it was written. Janáček completely disowned the piece when it turned up many years later (he couldn't believe he had written it).[20] It exists in two forms, unaccompanied (IV/2) and accompanied (IV/3). The two versions share the same text and the same music at beginning and end, though the accompanied one has a more developed middle section. In the absence of dates on manuscripts one can speculate that Janáček first wrote the unaccompanied version and then expanded it to fit the ceremonial occasion at which it was performed. Alternatively, the unaccompanied version could have been made for the Šlapanice excursion. The fact that contemporary parts have survived for both suggests that both were performed.

The three other choruses performed at the 'Svatopluk' besedas are all settings of folksong texts and, as Helfert emphasizes, are not at all in the patriotic male-voice chorus tradition but instead follow on from Křížkovský and his fascination with Moravian folksong. Křížkovský

[II]The *Moravská orlice* review (29 April 1873, quoted in *LJPT*, 333) declared that it was difficult to perform and it had 'something of *Lohengrin*' about it. This lost chorus is the source of many subsequent confusions; see *JAWO*, 297–8.

[¶]Arnošt Förchgott-Tovačovský (1825–74), choirmaster from Tovačov in Moravia and one of the most popular composers of Czech patriotic choruses of the time.

took his texts and tunes from Sušil's collection of Moravian folksongs but Janáček seems to have gone further afield: only *Ploughing* is based on a Sušil text. Since the provenances are unknown it is not possible to say whether these are in fact, like Křížkovský's earlier choruses, merely arrangements of folk tunes or the more developed stage of 'echoes' of folksong in which the composer attempts to re-create a folk style without direct quotation (see chap. 8). Like the early choruses of his mentor (and one has to remember how little secular music Janáček knew at this stage of his life), Janáček's arrangements are all simple, homophonic and – in the case of *Ploughing* – strophic, i.e. each verse has the same music. The two later choruses, IV/4 and IV/5, are formally more adventurous though still with many repeated elements. Striking about IV/4 (especially in view of Janáček's later interest in speech melody) is the free metre dictated entirely by the words. No time signature is assigned and it would be confusing to give one in a piece where the first five bars consist, respectively, of 9, 8, 8, 6 and 7 eighth notes. This piece opens evocatively as a solo for Tenor I, with other parts coming in later, a typical leader-and-chorus formula in folk music.

Helfert made much of the complexity of the final chorus, *Alone without Comfort [1]* (IV/7), as evidence of Janáček's 'development', but emphasized that he had not seen the original version.[21] In fact he was commenting on the version that Janáček wrote a quarter of a century later (IV/26), which in its harmonic style alone clearly shows how far Janáček had travelled by then. However he had certainly not travelled that distance in just a few months, although there are a few surprising harmonic juxtapositions in IV/7 and a modestly imitative opening, which the earlier choruses lack. Perhaps the most striking development in these three choruses is not in IV/7, but in IV/4 with its triplet decorations, seemingly to illustrate the flowing of water mentioned in the final verse. The men from 'Svatopluk' must have had quite a time with it.

When Janáček returned from Prague he continued writing choruses for 'Svatopluk', for example his *True Love* (IV/8) performed at a 'Svatopluk' beseda on 23 January 1876. But two early choruses may well have been written together with the pre-Prague set, namely *I wonder at my beloved* (IV/5) and *The Drowned Wreath* (IV/6). That they appear to be from the 'Svatopluk' period is suggested by the fact that the performance materials were found in the 'Svatopluk' archives, though there is no record of their being performed (and the press was assiduous in documenting 'Svatopluk' events). In their simple harmonic style and texture both are nearer to ɪᴠ/ɪ than to ɪᴠ/7. Like ɪᴠ/ɪ, ɪᴠ/6 has a folksong text from Sušil. And, of all Janáček's choruses, it is the only one that is demonstrably an arrangement** rather than an 'echo' since the first eight bars are based on the tune that Sušil collected.[22] One suspects that the same may be true of the even simpler ɪᴠ/5 but no-one so far has found the source of the words, let alone the tune. If one wishes to place these two choruses into the context of Janáček's work they seem to fit well with ɪᴠ/ɪ, i.e. taking them back to 27 April 1873, rather than the later dates that Helfert suggested.[††] It is possible that for his first venture at 'Svatopluk' Janáček in fact wrote four choruses, ɪᴠ/ɪ, ɪᴠ/2, ɪᴠ/5 and ɪᴠ/6, and chose to perform the two that worked best. Janáček had chosen well: ɪᴠ/5 and ɪᴠ/6 were never publicly performed by 'Svatopluk'; ɪᴠ/2 was soon lost; *Ploughing* (ɪᴠ/ɪ), however, was encored at its first performance[23] and received more subsequent performances than any other of his early choruses.

** Helfert stated that *Ploughing* (ɪᴠ/ɪ) was also an arrangement. It certainly sounds like one, but Helfert had to assume that 'Janáček heard it somewhere and wrote it down' (*LJPT*, 331).
[††] His '1875–76' (*LJPT*, 333) may simply be repeating Veselý's dates for all of Janáček's 'Svatopluk' choruses (Veselý 1924, 155–6), dates which Helfert elsewhere corrected to 1873–4.

11

Musical studies: Prague 1874–5

Janáček's musical training before he went to Prague was mostly practical. His long years as a chorister meant that his sight-singing was excellent and he was a good keyboard sight-reader too, if the story of his playing through duet arrangements of Beethoven symphonies is true. He was a fine organist; this is something Křížkovský specifically commented on in his testimonial (see chap. 7) and he was a good enough conductor for Křížkovský to entrust him with the monastery choir. This experience with a small group of well-trained choristers had broadened when in 1873 he took on the amateur male-voice 'Svatopluk' (see chap. 10).

Of his theoretical knowledge one can only guess that it kept abreast of his practical needs. Helfert found evidence of Janáček's looking at Gottfried Rieger's manual on harmony and figured bass, first published in Vienna 1833. Janáček borrowed it (in its Brno 1839 edition) from the primary school in Lackerwiese ulice and hung on to it for the rest of his life. Another book found in his library was Jan Kypta's harmony manual (published in Brno 1861 on the recommendation of Křížkovský), this time purloined from the Teachers' Institute.[1] Presumably too the 'singing' that features in his years at the Realschule and the Teachers' Institute included some theory. Furthermore he was sufficiently equipped to compose simple and successfully performed pieces for four-part male chorus at 'Svatopluk'. Their musical idiom was restricted by their forces: anything too complicated and the amateur choir would have floundered. In his intensive year of music studies at the Prague Organ School Janáček would in particular deepen his knowledge of music theory.

To English ears 'organ school' might be an unfamiliar concept but it is one that is easily explained. A music conservatory trains all sorts of different musicians specializing as instrumentalists, as composers or as teachers. The Prague Organ School, and later the Brno Organ School, specialized in producing church musicians, providing organ and choir-training skills, a knowledge of church music repertory, and rudimentary compositional skills. The two famous Czech organ schools, however, both saw themselves as doing something more. Janáček's funding for setting up the Brno Organ School came from a church-based organization, which to some extent tied his hands, but in his imagination there was always a conservatory in the making (this dream came true in 1919) and from early on expert tuition was offered in piano and violin as well as the organ. The theoretical knowledge that Janáček demanded went way beyond church-music requirements. Similarly the ten-month course for village organists (the modest beginnings of the Prague Organ School in 1830) had by the time Janáček went there become a three-year course which in the final years offered instruction in musical forms and in instrumentation. Above all it taught composition – something the Prague Conservatory did not do at the time – and welcomed mature students (there was an age limit at the conservatory).[2] In 1874 the Organ School was by far the best place in Prague for a thorough theoretical and compositional training.

Prague itself was a big adventure for Janáček. For a start it was much bigger than Brno (at the 1869 census the population was 270,264, Brno a mere 73,771.)[3] It was also a more Czech city. It had become increasingly so during the nineteenth century: by the 1880 census (the first time that a citizen's spoken language was registered) only 17.54% of the people of Prague gave German as their first language;[4] in Brno at that time German speakers made up 59.20% of the population.[5] Prague was a strikingly beautiful city with a glamorous and iconic river running through it. Once the seat of kings and emperors, Prague commemorated past glories with wonderful buildings from the Middle Ages onwards. And it was a cultured city, alive with theatres, opera houses and concert halls, many in Czech hands. All this was in sharp contrast to Brno, where the only Czech-run cultural building at the time was the Besední dům.

Janáček undertook his Prague studies on almost no money at all. Luckily tuition at the Prague Organ School, unlike the Prague Conservatory, was free.[6] According to a brief report in the journal *Dalibor* Janáček was awarded a scholarship by the Moravian Regional

School Board: 'Mr Janáček is leaving for Prague, having obtained considerable support from the Regional Council, to devote himself to a thorough study of music and especially to be educated in composition.'[7] The only income that Janáček recalled in later life came from František Neumann (Janáček's piano-duet partner in the Beethoven symphonies), who inherited Janáček's piano pupils from Brno and very honourably sent him his fees to Prague: from time to time 5 zl would turn up.[8] On this Janáček lived in an unheated room in Štěpánská ulice[9] (he would 'steal' heat by quietly keeping the door ajar). His landlady provided breakfast; lunch was whatever he could afford – plums and a roll were specifically mentioned in one of his memoirs.[10] The guardian angel of his Prague stay was Ferdinand Lehner (1837–1914), the chaplain in the district of Karlín, where he trained the choir in the spirit of Cecilian reform. The year that Janáček went to Prague, 1874, Lehner founded the periodical *Cecilie* (later *Cyrill*), which espoused reformist ideals for church music. Křížkovský and Lehner were thus comrades-in-arms in the same cause, and Křížkovský presumably recommended Lehner to Janáček as a contact in Prague. He turned out to be very useful. Not only was he good for the odd meal, but he provided (as editor) Janáček's first journalistic assignment. He also seems to have been responsible for the piano:

Piano keys scribbled in chalk on the table. On it my fingers learnt to run up and down according to the notes of Bach's preludes and fugues. It was embarrassing, didn't I just long for the living note!

Hire a piano? Where to find the money?

But one fine day, all of a sudden, there was a piano standing in my little room in Štěpánská ulice. I related the inexplicable incident to Father Ferdinand Lehner, first chaplain in Karlín, the editor of *Cyrill*.

A knowing smile stole over his good-natured face.

At the end of the school year the piano vanished from my flat again just as quietly.

And for so many suppers he invited me, a hungry student![11]

Janáček's poverty in Prague meant that he could take little advantage of the rich cultural life offered by the Czech capital. There is no evidence that he went inside a theatre or an opera house. He attended free concerts in churches, one memorably conducted by Skuherský (see below) and it was probably at St Vojtěch's that he encountered Dvořák (see chap. 22) but otherwise Prague brought him few cultural benefits apart from his course. There is one exception, which he remembered

for the rest of his life: the one time he saw Smetana. 'How I managed –
on just 5 zl a month – to get into a concert in honour of Bedřich
Smetana I just don't know. I crept in near the orchestra. It was almost
dark with the musicians playing and the audience listening. So my
memory of Smetana is like that of a child's imagining God: *in the
clouds*' (XV/275). The concert took place at the concert hall on Žofín
island on Sunday 4 April 1875.* It was a moving event, a benefit
concert for the now deaf master at which were played two of the symphonic poems from his orchestral cycle-in-progress, *My Fatherland*.
The first was *Vyšehrad* on its second public outing, and the other was
the première of the second poem, the one which would become by far
the most popular: *Vltava*.

The orchestra was just ending and the deafening tumult united in the name
Smetana! Suddenly so many people flashed past and pushed that it became
almost dark. They led the ailing composer up the stairs. Only *his face*
imprinted itself on my soul. I still have it clearly in my mind: always in the
hubbub and as if in the mist. Certainly at the time my eyes devoured only him
and to all else I was deaf and blind. (XV/193)

The Prague Organ School was prepared to allow those with
'appropriate theoretical knowledge and education in organ playing' to
proceed directly to the second year.[12] With only one year free, and
considerable musical experience, this is what Janáček did; he also tried
to look in on some of the first-year classes but this proved difficult as
the teaching hours mostly overlapped.[13] He signed up for second-year
subjects: harmony, chorale, single and double counterpoint, imitation
and fugue, organ, figured bass and unprepared modulation,
unprepared 'preluding' (improvisation).[14] Backed up by his practical
experience, he passed through the second year with flying colours. He
was taking the course at considerable personal sacrifice and was
determined to make the most of it. The manuscript books he covered –
thirteen survive – are testament to his commitment and industry; his
progress can easily be charted by the carefully dated succession of
exercises.[15]

Janáček was lucky that while he was there the head of the Prague
Organ School and one of its chief teachers (there were only four)[16] was
František Zdeněk Skuherský (1830–92). Having graduated there

---

* Not '1874', as the title of Janáček's article *In the year 1874* (XV/275) suggests.

himself, Skuherský then worked abroad as a conductor (1854–66 in Innsbruck) and developed a modest reputation as an opera composer: three of his German-text operas had been performed in Czech translation at the Prague Provisional Theatre though none had stayed in the repertory. It is, however, as a theorist and teacher that he is remembered.[17] He wrote the first Czech textbooks on composition and on musical forms as well as two textbooks on harmony and an organ method; his harmonic theories were daring for the time and left their mark on composers as varied as Janáček and Alois Hába; and he was a systematic and rigorous teacher, remembered fondly by his many pupils for his tolerance and human qualities. By the time of Janáček's arrival at the Prague Organ School Skuherský was in his prime: a vigorous teacher and administrator. In the previous eight years he had overhauled the syllabus and created the three-year course. His treatise on musical forms, published in 1873, served as a textbook of examples for his classes (his other books, on composition, the organ and harmony, were published in the 1880s). In the Czech world Janáček could have gone to no-one better.

A clear picture of Skuherský's methods emerges from Janáček's exercise books. In his detailed study of these exercises, Helfert showed how Skuherský offered brief explanations of any new subject to be covered, then a few examples that were copied out in class. After that students were expected to write their own versions and in this way to master the material before moving on to the next phase that Skuherský presented. The aim was for students to learn routine compositional procedures, gain a technique for solving basic problems and at the same time develop their musicality (Skuherský's examples were rhythmically rich and strikingly melodic).[18] In this methodical way, Janáček and his second-year peers started with cadences of various types and keys, moving on to modulation. This was one of Skuherský's specialities and one of the most progressive aspects of his teaching. In exercises of a few bars students were expected to modulate from one key to another, usually very remote. Janáček clearly enjoyed this, turning out ten a day,[19] and it was the one thing that he remembered, though in a garbled form, in his autobiography. Here he described his entrance exam at the Organ School where he was asked the standard question of how a dominant seventh resolves. It seems inconceivable that he didn't know the required answer; the irregular resolution that he jotted down in his autobiography (his 'thoughts' while he remained silent at the exam)[20] is in fact the product of his adventurous modulation course.[21] In one sense the modulation course was too adventurous. As Vítězslav Novák vividly put it, having to teach from the published book: 'I soon had a deer park at home in which everyone was a stag.'[22] Nevertheless Janáček clearly found it stimulating and covered his exercise books with strange modulatory efforts that may well have contributed to his later oddness. Helfert wrote approvingly of what he found – its directness, lyricism and melodic richness.[23]

After modulation, students moved on to chorale harmonizations and eventually on to counterpoint, which was again taught systematically: from note-against-note to invertible counterpoint, and finally fugal expositions. Here again Skuherský was in the forefront: his was the first published treatise on counterpoint in Czech. His concern in this field was encouraged by his interest in Cecilian reforms, but his account of early music (for instance in his book on forms) is one that today would be considered ahistorical and unsympathetic. Ludvová cites his account of Palestrina as bemoaning perceived shortcomings such as a restricted harmonic palette.[24] This limited view may have coloured Janáček's later negative view of early music.

While clearly an industrious student Janáček occasionally allowed his thoughts to stray elsewhere. Helfert was struck by various passages in the Prague notebooks written in cyrillic. Deciphering them, he discovered that the words were not Russian but Czech and of an 'intimate nature', written in cyrillic script to disguise from prying eyes his musings on a distant beloved.[25] The young lady, Helfert discovered, was Ludmila Rudišová, the sixteen-year-old daughter of a factory owner J.B. Rudiš, to whom Janáček had taught the piano in Brno.[26] It was not a relationship that her father encouraged, and the beloved remained distant; endearingly, Helfert decided that this was the source of the lyrical effusions that he detected in the modulation exercises.[27]

During his time at the Prague Organ School Janáček also embarked on what would become a lifetime of self-education, in this case picking up subjects not taught there such as aesthetics and music history. On 3 December he began reading Josef Durdík's treatise on aesthetics, a process graphically revealed by paging through his copy.[28] For Janáček self-education meant annotation: many pages of the books that he acquired for study are covered with the dates of when he got to a certain point, much underlining, emphasizing important passages with lines in the margin, occasional glosses and, when he got more experienced, critical comments. The surprise is that he took to Durdík. Durdík's aesthetic was a formalist one that stressed form over content, preferred Classical to Romantic, and was wary of combining different artistic media such as words and music. From what one knows of Janáček the mature composer, of his preoccupation with opera, of the programmatic elements in his music and of his belief in the expressive qualities of music, a sympathy for formalist aesthetics is the last thing one might expect.

Josef Durdík (1837–1902) is not a familiar name these days and neither is the brand of philosophy he espoused (Herbartianism), but his stance is familiar from formalists such as Eduard Hanslick. Herbartianism, as Michael Beckerman explained in a sparkling essay ('Janáček and the Herbartians'),[29] was the 'official' philosophy of the Austro-Hungarian Empire. Other exponents from the region such as Robert Zimmermann (1824–98) and Otakar Hostinský (1847–1910) published in German and were thus better known than Durdík. As the founder of Czech musical aesthetics, Hostinský went on to become a most influential figure in Czech music in the late nineteenth and early twentieth centuries. Although Beckerman argued ingeniously for a 'concrete formalism' in Janáček,[30] one might also say that the young and impressionable Janáček was simply taking up a recently published book (1874), perhaps recommended by his superior at the Brno Teachers' Institute Emilian Schulz, himself an avid Herbartian. He had never come across anything like it, found it stimulating and read it right to the end, some of it twice. He then moved on to Zimmermann's *Allgemeine Aesthetik als Formwissenschaft*, in German, finding it more challenging; he even attempted to make Czech translations of certain parts. This led in turn to a much more durable interest, pursued over a longer period, in the theories of the German physicist Hermann Ludwig Ferdinand von Helmholtz (1821–94). By his later years Janáček had rejected Durdík and Zimmermann, dismissing them in his autobiography of 1924 with the brief sentence: 'fabrications and aesthetic ponderings (Dr R. Zimmermann, Dr J. Durdík, Dr Hugo Riemann, etc.) do not satisfy me.'[31]

As for Janáček's self-education in music history, at some unknown point he copied out biographical notes on Bach;[32] his readings from August Wilhelm Ambros's culturally conceived *Geschichte der Musik* (1862–8) are dated between 7 January and 22 April 1875, during which time he read the first volume, dealing with Chinese, Indian and Arabian music and the ancient traditions of the Egyptians, the Semitic nations and the Greeks. His copy of the next volume (Western music from early Christianity to Burgundian polyphony) bears no date; he seems to have given up some time during May 1875.[33]

And while all this was going on Janáček got back to composition. Presumably the successful performances of his choruses for 'Svatopluk' had whetted his interest and, significantly, composition had been singled out as the purpose of his studies when *Dalibor* announced his departure for Prague. When Helfert came to write about Janáček's compositional activities there he had to be content with the following statement: 'During his Prague studies Janáček wrote an independent composition: *Chorale Fantasy*. It was performed by the composer on 23 July 1875 at the concluding examination at the Organ School. [. . .] So far not found.'[34]

What Helfert did not know was that between December 1874 and the end of his Prague studies Janáček was busily composing, not just little modulation exercises or even the *Chorale Fantasy* for organ (VIII/4), but a series of at least ten pieces of which the *Chorale Fantasy* is the culmination. After his return to Brno in October 1875 Janáček began writing them out in an album, adding two more instrumental pieces, both called *Sonnet* (VII/1–2)† and composed in November 1875. Although dates of composition are offered for most of them in Janáček's super-neat manuscript, they appear in an order in which the November pieces come before two earlier ones.‡ Helfert in fact knew one of them, *Exaudi Deus [2]* (II/4), which Lehner published in *Cecilie*, and assumed it was written nearer the date of its publication in 1877. Although the album survived Janáček seems to have forgotten about it. His wife Zdenka eventually inherited it and passed it on to the Brno notary Dr František Weiner (1871–1934) along with other manuscripts. It was not until 1958, when the 'Prague Album' was acquired

---

† The Czech title *Znělka* derives from the verb 'zníti' ('to sound'), and covers a variety of meanings associated with the concept of something 'sounding', ranging from a signature tune or theme tune to the verse form.

‡ Straková 1959, 164, fn. 6. The album has subsequently been issued in a handsome facsimile edition, Leoš Janáček: *Sborník skladeb z pražských studií* [Collection of compositions from his studies in Prague], ed. Theodora Straková and Jiří Zahrádka (Editio Janáček, Brno 2001). Straková (1959, 163) believes that the two short November pieces were written in later, on spare pages of the album.

by the Janáček archive from Weiner's son (Dr Václav Weiner), that its contents became known.

Exaudi Deus [2] is typical of half of the contents of the album, i.e. one of the six motets to Latin words, some unaccompanied, some with organ accompaniment. While the general idiom and aims fitted in well enough with Cecilian ideals for Lehner to publish one of the pieces, it is also clear that the differences between the six pieces reflect what Janáček was learning at the time in Skuherský's classes. For instance on 9 December 1874 Skuherský began lecturing on church modes;[35] within three weeks, by 29 December, Janáček had composed his first Latin motet, *Graduale 'Speciosus forma'* (II/1), in the Lydian mode. The piece was timely in the sense that the text set was that for the Gradual for the 'Mass on the Sunday within the Octave of Christmas': in 1874 this fell on 27 December. Janáček's setting begins with a plainsong melody sung by unaccompanied basses. This is taken up in unison by tenors and basses, now with organ accompaniment, and followed by male voices in four-part harmony before much the same happens all over again, but instead for sopranos and altos. The extensive use of plainsong resulted in a free-flowing, ametrical setting with irregular numbers of notes per 'bar': a direct parallel to Janáček's setting of *The Fickleness of Love* (IV/4). The next piece, *Introitus in festo SS Nominis Jesu* (II/2), has another text dictated by the liturgical year, this time the introit text for Sunday 3 January 1875. It works in much the same way, here in the Dorian mode, but in contrast it concludes with a metrical chorale-like section in a regular 4/4: in December Skuherský had introduced his students not only to church modes but also to chorale harmonization.[36] ·

Apart from putting into practice lessons learnt from Skuherský, Janáček was also following Křížkovský's approach to the problem of how to present plainsong to congregations unaccustomed to this ametrical form of music sung in unison and unaccompanied. Křížkovský's trick, Janáček wrote (XV/1; see below), was to alternate unison passages with 'well-harmonized' sections for four-part male chorus or boys' (women's) chorus with appropriate organ accompaniment.

After the Christmas break (by 7 January 1875) Skuherský started lecturing in counterpoint.[37] This is reflected in Janáček's next piece chronologically (dated 3 February), the first of the two settings of *Exaudi Deus* for mixed voices and organ (II/3), which begins ambitiously in invertible counterpoint. Although it opens in a modal G minor, it acquires more accidentals as it continues and is the most tonally conceived of the pieces so far. The next two pieces – the second, unaccompanied setting of the *Exaudi Deus* (II/4) and a very short *Benedictus* with organ accompaniment (II/5), written over the next two weeks (10 and 17 February) – lose touch with Skuherský's counterpoint classes altogether and instead present simple, effective homophonic settings that a village choir might manage perfectly well.

After that there is a pause in these dated pieces and it was not until classes stopped on 6 June that Janáček began composing again. By then Skuherský had got to the end of his counterpoint classes, including fugal expositions;[38] the last of the Latin motets, the unaccompanied *Communio 'Fidelis servus'* (II/6), dated 20 June 1875, is the most ambitious with a proper fugal exposition and other contrapuntal sections throughout. The day before writing this Janáček had composed the first of the three organ pieces in the album, *Prelude* (VIII/2). He then continued with organ pieces, *Varyto* (VIII/3) on 24 June and, after the revision period at the Organ School began, *Chorale Fantasy* (VIII/4), completed on 7 July. Presumably Janáček knew that he had to present an organ piece for his final exams, so the first two may simply have been dry runs of increasing complexity and length (the three pieces last respectively three, four and seven minutes). *Varyto*, named after a mythical Czech harp (harplike gestures marked 'recit.' open the piece and interrupt it halfway through), is the first of the organ pieces to be written in three staves and is full of metrically contrasting textures. The *Chorale Fantasy* is an ambitious multi-sectional piece with many changes of tempo and texture. Some time after Janáček got back to Brno and copied these pieces out in the album, he seems to have had another look at them; perhaps he performed them at the monastery. Unlike the motets they contain pencil corrections and in the case of the *Chorale Fantasy* substantial suggestions for cuts.

Six or eight male-voice choruses written for 'Svatopluk' in 1873–4, six Latin motets written possibly for liturgical use in 1874–5, three organ studies, the last of which was for Janáček's final examination: these early works suggest a composer writing essentially for practical use. This doesn't sound like the thoroughly unreasonable and visionary composer of his later years. However, if one pages further in the Prague Album there is a pleasant surprise: an instrumental piece between *Exaudi Deus [1]* (II/3) and *Communio* (II/6). It is written for string quintet (including a double bass) and a 'chromatic trumpet' and bears the curious title *Sounds in Memory of Arnošt Förchgott-Tovačovský (2nd part)* (VI/1). Tovačovský was the most performed choral composer at the Brno Beseda, a prominent Moravian with pan-Slavonic ideals. His death on 18 December 1874 may have stimulated Janáček into composing a tribute to him. Although designated 'second part', there is no extant 'first part' and it stands as an independent slow movement. String writing did not form part of Janáček's course at the Organ School (this was third-year material) so the impulse for the piece must have been entirely personal. Quite what Janáček imagined with the curious 'chromatic trumpet' (i.e. a valve trumpet capable of playing a continuous chromatic scale) in the middle of the texture is hard to imagine. When he looked at the album some time later he attempted to correct some of the more obvious compositional slips (such as consecutive fifths) and in a very scrawly pencil wrote 'Violin III' over the trumpet part – a much more practical solution.

In comparison with the motets, which are all short (the longest lasts two minutes), this is a substantial piece that takes up twenty-two pages of the Prague Album and lasts for over five minutes. It begins with the tempo indication Grave, with a rhythmically distinctive motif that is developed fugally. This suggests that it was written after Skuherský had dealt with fugal expositions (8 May–4 June), and most likely after 7 June 1875, when formal teaching had ended.

Sounds stands out in the Prague Album for all sorts of reasons: the length, the unusual forces, the fact that this was surplus to Organ School requirements, but also, it must be said, because the rest of the stuff is rather dull and gives no hint of a strikingly original musical mind at work. *Sounds* is at least odd (full of strange flourishes) and, in its way, effective. The fact that Janáček did not go on to write many more liturgical pieces of a Cecilian persuasion or pieces for organ need not be a matter of regret. Organ and liturgy came together splendidly at the very end of his life, in his *Glagolitic Mass*. But by then he was fifty years older and a very different composer.

It was during his year in Prague that Janáček's career as a writer began and his friendship with Lehner bore further fruit: Janáček's first three published writings (XV/1–3) were all for Lehner's *Cecilie*. The first was an article of some 2000 words on Křížkovský and his role in the reform of church music (see chap. 8). It was written as he was working on his first surviving liturgical piece (II/1; see above) and he was clearly mindful, while describing Křížkovský's achievements, of what he himself was trying to do at the same time. Lehner presumably suggested the topic as a Christmas vacation assignment and published it promptly on 5 January 1875. This is a confident piece, written in a 'learned' style (full of fancy endings and grammatical constructions that were by then fading from the language), and its three references to aesthetics bear witness to his readings of Durdík. The next two articles, published in March and May 1875, were reviews of church music performances in Prague and Brno: a Gregorian mass conducted by Skuherský at the Piarist church in Prague on 24 January 1875 (xv/2) and a review of church music at Easter in Brno (xv/3). While the Easter piece is useful in providing a list of repertory at the Staré Brno monastery (Janáček was reviewing his own performance), the Prague review was much more problematic. A more sensible person than he would have bowed out of this undertaking or found some way of muting his criticisms. It was not Janáček's way, however, to see the incongruity and riskiness of criticising his present teacher, the very person who would be examining him a few months later. This is the first recorded occasion when his firmly and publicly stated view did him damage. There would be many similar occasions to come. His criticisms were detailed and concerned matters such as the correct accentuation of Gregorian chant in Skuherský's performance: long notes rather than stressed syllables were habitually accented (one of the remarkable aspects of Janáček's Latin settings is that the tonic stress in each word is carefully marked in the manuscript). Further lapses to which he drew attention included breathing in the middle of words, inappropriate speeds and the fact that, in a plainsong mass, the various graduals and other elements of the proper were drawn from polyphonic and other repertory (Palestrina, Durante). A few compliments here and there (for instance mentioning that the insertions went well, 'although inappropriate') come across simply as damning with faint praise.

The upshot was swift. Four days after publication (one wonders what private scores Lehner may have been settling by printing a piece that would clearly damage both Janáček and Skuherský), Janáček was suspended from the Prague Organ School. He wrote no exercise in his book that day, but instead, and very clearly in ink: 'This day [9 March 1875] will be memorable for me since force was used against me because of the truth. Lev Janáček.'[39] He hung around in Prague a little longer (there is a Prague date of 11 March in his copy of Durdík) but returned to Brno before the official Easter break and got on with his reading of Durdík and of Ambros on the Egyptians.[40]

But whereas Janáček's criticism of Kovařovic twelve years later (xv/70) was to poison his relationship with the conductor and seriously damage his career as a composer (see chap. 49), Skuherský's much greater human qualities were soon on display. An intervention on Janáček's behalf was made by Jan Lukes, a tenor at the Provisional Theatre and former Augustinian choral scholar, and Skuherský accepted his recalcitrant student back.[41] He seems not to have taken any lasting offence, judging from Janáček's excellent end-of-year results. This is entirely in keeping with others' experience of him: a decade later Skuherský appointed as lecturer at the Organ School one of his most talented students, Karel Stecker (see chap. 32), despite Stecker's critical review of his composition treatise.[42]

Once back in Prague Janáček returned to be a model student. In May 1875 he worked on his fugal expositions with Skuherský and read Durdík until teaching ended.[43] He made use of the revision period in June by writing a sixth Latin motet (*Communio* ii/6) and the couple of dry runs for his final organ composition. On 22 July there were theory exams and the next day practical exams: unprepared modulation, improvisation on the organ and the performance of four student compositions: two preludes, one fugue and Janáček's own ambitious *Chorale Fantasy*.

The Prague Organ School final examinations, which were open to the public, were considered important enough to be announced in the chief musical journal of the time, *Dalibor*; the results were also published a couple of weeks later. Though the standard, the reviewer claimed, was not as good as the previous year, the modulation and improvisation were nevertheless considered 'skilful'. Two of the compositions announced were not performed but H. Krause's *Prelude* and Lev Janáček's *Chorale Fantasy* both apparently showed mastery of the 'severe style': 'we recognize these two last mentioned as outstanding both in talent and in diligent and sincere effort.' Janáček also played Bach's Toccata and Fugue in C (presumably the Toccata, Adagio and Fugue BWV 564). Of the performers only Janáček and Antonín Kratochvíl were regarded as outstanding.[44]

On 24 July Janáček was awarded a final certificate. It proclaimed that he had attended the two-year teaching course for organists in 1874–5 'very industriously' and was now excellently equipped to fulfil the role of organist. Apart from figured bass, where he was merely 'good', he got the highest grade ('very good') in all other subjects: harmony, chorale, counterpoint, imitation and fugue, organ, unprepared modulation and improvisation.[45] Helfert put this certificate into perspective by pointing out the rigour of the course. Of twenty-two students in the second year, three withdrew, ten failed. Of the nine that passed, six were graded as 'competent' and only three were 'excellently qualified'. These included Janáček, who had the best results of the year.[46]

Janáček was now able to take the state examinations that would allow him to teach music in schools and at the Teachers' Institute. The exams took place in Prague on 13, 15 and 17 October 1875 in the presence of a distinguished commission which included Skuherský, the composer J.N. Škroup and the theorist Josef Förster. Janáček was examined in the literature and history of music, where he was pronounced only 'adequate', but in voice, organ and piano, and in the trial lecture, he was graded as 'very good'.[47] On the basis of this he was later named a provisional teacher of music at the Brno Teachers' Institute on condition that within a year he took an extra qualification in violin. He was appointed to teach singing in the highest class at both the Men and Women Teachers' Institutes and to be in charge of all teaching of 'music and singing'.[48] Janáček, who had not so far learnt the violin systematically, accordingly took a further violin examination on 7 November 1878 (i.e. he appears to have been granted an extension). It was only in an official decree of 14 May 1880 that he was appointed music teacher, now no longer 'provisional'.[49]

Janáček's association with the Prague Organ School did not end in 1875. He had completed the second year of the three-year course and decided to return for tuition in instrumentation and form. This time, however, he was not officially registered, but spent just a month there in the summer of 1877. In this time he filled out four exercise books of which the first (dated 20 June 1877) and the last (final date 13 July 1877) survive.[50] It is not clear with whom he worked, though Helfert concluded that he studied form privately with Skuherský. There is not much evidence for his studying instrumentation (another third-year subject) during this period although among the form exercises there are comments on unusual instruments such as the cor anglais, harp, bass clarinet and viola d'amore[51] – the first instance of Janáček's contact with an instrument that would haunt his later compositions. Although more substantial forms such as overtures, sonatas and symphonies are mentioned in the notebooks, it is clear that the practical examples that Janáček worked on were confined to song form (i.e. simple ABA forms) and rondo form (i.e. ABACA etc.).[52] His one example of rondo is unfinished, as if to symbolize Janáček's study of form in Prague: it had been unrealistic to try and squeeze into a month something that would normally stretch out over a school year. Janáček's studies of form would, however, continue abroad, at Leipzig and Vienna.

12

Early professional life: after Prague
(1875–9)

Janáček left Prague bursting with confidence. He had, for the first time, been able to devote himself exclusively to his musical education. He had enjoyed the benefits of a well-run, systematic music-theory course and a teacher who took his duties seriously and who commanded his respect. He had worked extremely hard, he had come out top in the examinations and returned armed with new qualifications in music. At the same time his day job changed. He had completed his two-year probation so now went on to the pay roll. And he moved from the practice school (where he taught general subjects to primary school boys) to the Teachers' Institute, where he taught 'music and singing' to male trainee teachers of fifteen years and upwards. This was his 'professional life' for the next twenty-eight years, his main source of income. Within a year of returning his annual salary at the Teachers' Institute was 1040 zl and since this was state funded he could expect regular increases every five years.

His material needs now attended to on a modest but stable basis, Janáček could turn his attention to other things. During his time in Prague he had made useful connections: Lehner, Skuherský and, possibly, Dvořák.* While contacts with the first two continued for a while, those with Dvořák endured until his death in 1904. From Skuherský Janáček developed a lasting interest in music theory; Lehner, on the other hand, encouraged Janáček as a writer, giving him opportunities to publish his first articles and reviews in *Cecilie*.

A few months after getting back to Brno Janáček published a series of five articles (xv/6–10) in the leading Moravian Czech newspaper of

---

* For a discussion of how they may have met, see chap. 22.

the time, *Moravská orlice*. Entitled *Something about Music in Brno*, the articles form a survey of the five leading secular choirs in Brno with details gleaned from Janáček's attendance at rehearsals and concerts. The first article (xv/6), on the Brno Beseda, is written fancifully as fly-on-the-wall reportage (he describes himself hidden from view in an invisible cloak); when the clock struck seven, he was expecting the hall to be jammed with singers, who together with the choirmaster would be panting with enthusiasm and love for art; the tremendous sound they made in 'some classical piece' would shake the walls. The reality, of course, was that by eight o'clock a total of six singers had wandered in; when parts were eventually handed out, the demanding classical piece that Janáček was expecting to hear turned out to be a quadrille made up of folksongs.

This first article has a journalistic flair which makes it clear why *Moravská orlice* was happy to print five 750-word articles by the twenty-one-year-old writer in which he systematically lambasted the low standards and poor repertory of 'Vesna', 'Zora' and the German Musikverein at their public concerts in November 1875. While the sarcasm of the first piece gives it a bit of life, the remaining articles are high-mindedly preachy and so much imbued with Durdík's formalist philosophy that Helfert used this as a reliable way of identifying the author (writing under the nom-de-plume 'á').[1] The only choir that avoided his strictures was 'Svatopluk', characterized in Janáček's final article with a sentimental picture of how its members, weary with toil and faint with hunger after a hard day's work, and longing to get back to family and food, nevertheless turned up in force for their singing rehearsal. The fact that Janáček had recently taken over again at 'Svatopluk' as choirmaster did not inhibit him from praising the standards of his own choir at the expense of the competition. One can understand why Janáček was never short of enemies in musical circles.

Controversies sell newspapers so it is equally understandable that *Moravská orlice* was happy to let this belligerent young man carry on tearing apart the performers and, if necessary, the composers in his occasional reviews of concerts over the next two years. It is rather less clear why they were prepared to print such specialist items as his analysis of Brahms's Piano Quintet, one of the pieces performed in Janáček's Chamber Music series (see below). The quintet had not found favour with the public, and Janáček, in a series of three articles (xv/17), had belatedly attempted to justify it. Even Helfert, who was happy to defend Janáček's attacks on standards in Brno, felt that this article was unsuitable for the daily press as was his review (xv/18) of Johann Christian Lobe's composition manual, printed in Czech translation in instalments in a new Czech music periodical.[2] Although Janáček continued to publish further specialist articles in Lehner's *Cecilie*, for instance his first music-theory article (xv/16) or his exposition of how singing was being taught at the Teachers' Institute in Brno (xv/20), what he really needed was a platform for exclusively theoretical writings.

After his devastating review of Schumann's *Manfred*, performed by the Brno Musikverein on 16 December 1877 (xv/21), Janáček suddenly fell silent as a writer for almost three years. Maybe even *Moravská orlice* found his comments potentially libellous, or maybe someone managed to persuade him that conducting the Brno Beseda and publishing reviews of his rivals' concerts were incompatible activities. Helfert made a good case for seeing this burst of journalistic activity in 1875–7 as a trial run for Janáček's own journal *Hudební listy*,[3] which was set up in 1884, and which allowed him opportunities for both regular reviewing and the longer theoretical articles that he clearly longed to write (see chap. 24). What the writings from the period 1875–7 demonstrate is Janáček's passionate self-expression at a range of levels, one of the most distinctive aspects of his persona.

The four years between the autumn of 1875 and Janáček's departure for Leipzig to continue studies were dominated by his activities as a conductor and musical organizer in Brno. On his return from Prague he resumed his work at the Staré Brno monastery. Soon, too, on 21 October 1875, he was also invited to resume the conductorship of 'Svatopluk'; he agreed to do so, again renouncing a fee.[4] Four months later, however, he was approached by the Brno Beseda to become its music director: he began attending Brno Beseda committee meetings in mid-February 1876.[5] In the light of the much greater possibilities that he found in the Brno Beseda, his efforts with 'Svatopluk' began to falter and on 26 October 1876 he resigned. There were no hard feelings. He had done wonders for the society; members were grateful but perhaps realized that his mission for music in Czech Brno lay elsewhere. For his part Janáček continued to feel warmly about 'Svatopluk': in 1893, twenty years after he had become choirmaster there, he wrote a male-voice chorus *Our Birch Tree* (IV/22) for the commemorative album published to celebrate twenty-five years of the society's existence.

Janáček's second tenure of 'Svatopluk' was, however, a pale reflection of the first. Apart from conducting a couple of choruses at a charity event on 28 August 1875 (i.e. before his official reappointment), Janáček officiated at only five more events:[6]

Table 12.1: Janáček's concerts and entertainments with 'Svatopluk' 1875–6

after 31 October 1875: Entertainment with the Brno Beseda and 'Zora'; programme unknown
23 January 1876: Beseda;[†] Janáček conducts choruses by Vašák, Bendl, V.E. Horák and his own *Three Songs* (including the première of *True Love* IV/8)
27 February 1876: Beseda; Janáček conducts three choruses
18 March 1876: Entertainment in honour of chairman Dr Josef Illner, who was leaving Brno; programme unknown
15 October 1876: Beseda in honour of Josef Illner (mostly choruses by Tovačovský)

Two weeks after the entertainment of 18 March 1876, Janáček conducted his first event at the Brno Beseda, after which his energies were firmly directed there. If 'Svatopluk' held any summer excursions, Janáček did not take part in them. The only reason for his participation on 15 October was that the beseda was conceived as a tribute to the society's former chairman (and Janáček's sponsor) Dr Josef Illner. Having been planned for the spring (23 April), it had been postponed, perhaps in the light of Janáček's new commitments to the Brno Beseda.

There was a clear deterioration in the aspirations of the 1875–6 'Svatopluk' concerts compared with those of 1873–4. The only autumn concert was a joint entertainment with other societies. The fact that no programme was printed or written up in *Moravská orlice* suggests that it was fairly light. The same goes for the 'entertainment' on 18 March 1876, the society's first farewell to its chairman. Furthermore the two spring concerts for which the programmes are known both ended with 'dancing', suggesting that Janáček had shrugged and given up his battle to raise the tone of the events (see chap. 10). Most eloquent of all is the fact that, with one exception, Janáček no longer used the society as a vehicle for his own pieces. Whereas in 1873–4 he had

---

[†] The term 'beseda' is used here in its sense of informal concert (see chap. 6).

written at least one new chorus for each proper concert, in the second series his own music was heard only at the beseda on 23 January 1876, which, with 500 programmes printed, two lightish violin pieces (Vieuxtemps and Wieniawski) played by Gustav Zinke, a recitation and a chorus by Bendl, was comparable with earlier concerts. The Janáček items formed a group (*Three Songs*) consisting of *Ploughing* (IV/1, a favourite piece now on its fourth outing) followed by *If you don't want me, so what?* (V/1) and *True Love* (IV/8). Since the status of V/1 is disputed (see the discussion in chap. 7), *True Love* was the only incontrovertibly new chorus that Janáček wrote for 'Svatopluk' in his second tenure. Although one of his most beautiful and affecting early choruses, it is also one of his simplest and shortest: two verses, very slow, of six unmeasured bars. When this is compared with the demanding first chorus that Janáček wrote a month later for the Brno Beseda (*Vocal Duma* IV/10), it is clear that his expectations for what he could achieve with his working men at 'Svatopluk' had become very modest.

In view of the fact that his regular officiation at the Sunday services at the Augustinian monastery had long since settled into auto-pilot routine, it is surprising that Janáček seems to have composed a few more motets for use there. Bohumír Štědroň's most exciting find, when he examined the Staré Brno monastery archives in 1947,[7] were three, hitherto unknown, liturgical pieces by Janáček, *Regnum mundi* (II/7), *Exsurge Domine* (II/8) and the *Graduale in festo purificationis BVM 'Suscepimus'* (II/9). Dating these pieces is difficult. Although II/8 and II/9 survive in Janáček's autograph, neither is dated, but there are copied parts for II/7 and II/9 dated respectively 1878 and 1879. This proves no more than that parts were written out by then, possibly with a performance in mind. A revision date of 28 January 1887 in Janáček's hand on the autograph of II/9 suggests that this piece at least was still being considered eight years later (and strengthens the case for Janáček's conductorship of the monastery choir continuing at least until then). Stylistically, however, the three motets would seem to belong with the liturgical pieces in the Prague Album, i.e. late 1874 to 1875 (see chap. 11). All three use the same initial formula as in II/1 and II/2, i.e. a unison plainsong opening with a continuation in four-part harmony (and similar alternations throughout); none employ the more contrapuntal devices found in II/3 and II/6. They differ from II/1 and

11/2 by dispensing with organ accompaniment. Although 11/8 is bland in its harmonic vocabulary, both 11/7 and especially 11/9 have a few unusual chords that are not found in the Prague Album pieces. This suggests something a bit later: i.e. the 1878 and 1879 dates on the parts are reasonable dates also for their composition. Together with the Prague Album pieces these three motets bring the total of Janáček's early Latin motets to nine. This was not quite the end of the line. In 1903 he wrote a *Constitues* (11/12) for performance at mass in Brno Cathedral on its feast day of 29 June (the feast of SS Peter and Paul). But by then he had relinquished his duties at the monastery and the new piece, written during his resumption of work on *Jenůfa*, was in a much more adventurous idiom.

It was through his connections at the Augustinian monastery that Janáček made his first trip abroad. In the summer of 1878 he had been invited by the firm of organ builders G.F. Steinmeyer to visit their factories in Oettingen in Bavaria – Janáček had presumably had contacts with them after he had inaugurated the new organ they had installed for the Augustinians in 1876. The firm was a comparatively new one (founded in 1847) and not as famous as it was to become (2400 organs by the mid-1990s),[8] so perhaps an invitation to a young but promising Czech organist was considered a good investment for the future. Janáček made a larger trip of it, visiting the Bavarian capital Munich on the way back, meeting up with his brother Bedřich somewhere in the Harz mountains (where he ran a ceramics factory), and then finally reaching Berlin. He would have liked to have seen Hamburg too, but the money ran out.[9] All this happened at the end of July 1878 when, according to Janáček's annotations in his copy of Helmholtz, he was in Prague (24–6 July), visiting Dvořák on 26 July.[10] He arrived in Oettingen by 31 July. This date is known from Janáček's manuscript of his *Idyll* for strings (VI/3), on which he noted that he began it in Oettingen that day. Inspired by the Steinmeyer organs Janáček also began a composition for organ, known as *In Oettingen 4 August 1878* (IX/2). He managed only twenty-four bars before abandoning it, the sheet later turned over and stuck down to form the title page of his *Idyll*.

Janáček described his German trip only briefly in his autobiography, and mostly as a tourist experience, such as the mention of the Glyptothek and Pinakothek in Munich. He was struck by the cheap white beer made from oats in Berlin, and in Oettingen by how few citizens went to the pubs there (he seems to have kept company with one of the sons of Georg Friedrich Steinmeyer, young Theodore Steinmeyer, whose death in February 1880 was with sadness recorded in a letter to Zdenka).[11] A habit that would be repeated in later travels was looking out for names of Slavonic origin in what was now German territory (as in the Harz mountains). But most of all he remembered losing his shabby suitcase, sent ahead by rail and which ended up somewhere else. Although 'a mere boy', he kicked up a fuss to get it back.[12] As he travelled around he continued with the *Idyll*, beginning to write it out in full score on 15 August and finishing it on 24 August. When, down to his last penny, he got back to Prague on 29 August he added an extra seventh movement.

The Brno Beseda had been founded in 1860 expressly as a male-voice choral society[13] and was thus a completely different sort of organization from 'Svatopluk', with a different agenda and a different constituency of members. The choir was its *raison d'être* and it was easy enough for Janáček to build further musical activities around it. This was helped by the fact that the members of the society, drawn from middle-class professionals or people of leisure, were generally wealthier than the members of 'Svatopluk' and more musically literate. Janáček soon turned the male-voice choir into a mixed choir, which with a partly bought-in orchestra was able to perform very demanding works for chorus and orchestra. In support of these activities Janáček later founded a music school to train young singers and instrumentalists (1882), and a journal, *Hudební listy* (1884). The Brno Beseda became the chief Czech concert-giving organization in Brno, still going in the 1950s, when its name changed to the 'Philharmonic Choir Brno Beseda'. 'Svatopluk', on the other hand, faded out in the 1920s, the need for it and what it stood for having passed.

Although there had been thin years in 1872–5, the Brno Beseda aimed to present four concerts a year, and this scheme was immediately resumed in Janáček's concerts in 1876–9 (see table 12.1). Like his first 'Svatopluk' concerts, Janáček's Brno Beseda concerts trod an increasingly ambitious path. Three of the four musical events after Janáček took over are billed, like most of their predecessors in 1860–74, as 'besedas' (see above) but, with the exception of a few deliberately light events ('entertainments'), usually in the summer, Janáček thereafter conducted 'concerts', not 'besedas'. As in the early 'Svatopluk' besedas, Brno Beseda musical events were topped and tailed by a military band (that of the 71st Infantry Regiment under its bandmaster Eduard Horný, 1838–1907), which supplied an overture and 'conversational music'. It took Janáček over a year to get rid of this, but by the concert of 22 April 1877, he had provided his own 'overture' (in the form of Dvořák's Serenade for strings) and thereafter, apart from 'entertainments', the overture and dancing were omitted.

From the outset Janáček had two aims: one was to turn the Beseda's male-voice choir into a mixed choir and the second was to form an orchestra. The mixed choir (36 men and 16 women) made its first appearance in Janáček's second concert and, although male-voice choruses were still performed, mixed voices were now available to widen the scope of the programmes. Creating an orchestra was more difficult. Janáček's plans, set out at the committee meeting on 14 February 1876, for performances in the first year of three of Smetana's symphonic poems from *My Fatherland*[14] were too ambitious (it was not until 1880 that Janáček conducted one of these pieces), but an ad hoc body could be assembled immediately by using Horný's military band for wind and brass and by bringing in string players, either from the German Theatre orchestra or Czech amateurs. Orchestral items (such as the first movement of Rubinstein's Third Piano Concerto) were attempted in the first year and became increasingly prominent in the second; chamber music was occasionally included, for example a Beethoven string quartet in the second concert. The real triumphs however were the major choral-orchestral works that were the sole items in the April concerts in 1878 and 1879, namely Mozart's Requiem and Beethoven's *Missa solemnis*. These were risky, high-profile events with top soloists from Prague, and which Janáček had to push through the Beseda committee with a financial guarantee provided by him and Mrs Amalie Wickenhauser (see below).

A feature of Janáček's concert planning was the presence of Dvořák's music, initiated with the Serenade for strings in 1877. Thereafter Dvořák's choruses began to be included as a matter of course, and a particular triumph was the concert on 15 December 1878, which not only included three newly orchestrated *Slavonic Dances* (their second performance) and one completely new one (a world première) but also had the composer himself playing the piano accompaniment for his choruses. The Beseda made much of the occasion by providing a ceremonial welcome before the concert, a laurel wreath during the concert and, after it, a party with toasts drunk to Dvořák, Janáček and Mrs Wickenhauser.

Table 12.2: Janáček's concerts with the Brno Beseda 1876–9[15]

(titles given of larger works, and all works by Janáček, Křížkovský, Dvořák and Smetana; others summarized)

1876

3 April: Beseda. Janáček conducts the première of his *Vocal Duma* (IV/10) and choruses by Bendl and François-Emmanuel-Victor Bazin (mixed voices with 'Vesna'); programme includes solo violin pieces (Spohr, Beethoven); military band conducted by Eduard Horný provides overture and 'conversational music'

13 May: Concert (the first with the Brno Beseda's new mixed-voice choir). Janáček conducts Rubinstein's Third Piano Concerto, first movement (soloist: Amalie Wickenhauser), male-voice choruses by Křížkovský (*The Recruit's Prayer*), and mixed-voice choruses (with string accompaniment) by Beethoven and J.S.Bach; programme includes Hiller's Duet for two pianos (Olga Neruda and Amalie Wickenhauser) and a Beethoven string quartet; military band conducted by Eduard Horný provides overture and 'conversational music'

13 November: Beseda. Janáček conducts male-voice choruses by Vojáček and Křížkovský (*The Love-Gift*), a women's chorus by Liszt (with harp and piano accompaniment) and the première of 'Part I' of his melodrama, *Death* for reciter and orchestra (X/3); military band conducted by Eduard Horný provides overture and 'conversational music'

14 December: Beseda. Janáček conducts old Czech songs and Mendelssohn's Psalm xlv for mixed chorus and orchestra; programme includes music for string quintet; military band conducted by Eduard Horný provides overture and 'conversational music'

1877

22 April: Concert. Janáček conducts Dvořák's Serenade for strings and Skuherský's symphonic poem *May*, Bruch's Violin Concerto (soloist: Gustav Zinke) and choruses by Bendl and Křížkovský (*The Drowned Maiden)*; 'conversational music' but no overture

10 June: Janáček leads Beseda trip to Adamov where the Beseda choir sings during High Mass

28 October: Concert. Janáček is soloist in Mendelssohn's Piano Concerto no. 1 in G minor (orchestra conducted by Ernst Wickenhauser), plays Rubinstein's Fantasia in F minor for two pianos op. 73 (with Amalie Wickenhauser) and conducts choruses by Bazin and his *Festive Chorus* (IV/12); Beseda choir is augmented by Staré Brno choristers and students from the Teachers' Institute

2 December: Concert. Janáček conducts the première of his Suite for strings (VI/2), Smetana's *Farmers' Chorus*; four of Dvořák's *Moravian Duets* were also sung

1878

14 April: Concert. Janáček conducts Mozart's Requiem (soloists from the Prague Provisional Theatre and the Brno German Theatre)

19 May: Concert. Janáček conducts male-voice choruses by Dvořák (*The Ferryman*), Křížkovský (*A Thrashing*) and Ludevít Procházka, and Haydn's Symphony no. 7 [i.e. no. 97] in C major

26 October: Musical entertainment. Janáček conducts male-voice choruses by Javůrek, Dvořák (*The Betrayed Shepherd*) and Křížkovský (*The Recruit's Prayer*); programme includes solo songs and pieces for piano, for cornet and for guitar

Table 12.2:—*continued*

---

15 December: Concert. Janáček is soloist in Saint-Saëns's Piano Concerto no. 2 in G minor (orchestra conducted by Ernst Wickenhauser) and conducts the première of his *Idyll* for strings (VI/3) as well as four *Slavonic Dances* by Dvořák; he also conducts the première of Dvořák's three male-voice choruses, *Sorrow*, *Miraculous Water* and *The Girl in the Woods*, published the next year as *From a Bouquet of Slavonic Folksongs*, with Dvořák playing the piano accompaniment

1879
  2 April: Concert. Janáček conducts Beethoven's *Missa solemnis* with 100-member chorus and soloists from the Prague Provisional Theatre; he is presented with a baton, tooled in silver, and an embroidered music case
14 July: Outdoor entertainment. Janáček conducts male-voice choruses by Dvořák (*The Ferryman, Sorrow, Miraculous Water* and *The Girl in the Woods*), Křížkovský (*The Complaint*) and Malát, and accompanies songs at the piano; programme includes cello solo by a member of the military band and 'conversational music'

As with the 'Svatopluk' concerts in 1873–4, Janáček used the Beseda as a showcase for new compositions, although the rate was rather slacker with roughly one new piece a year rather than one piece per concert. It is interesting that in all his years as conductor at the Beseda he wrote only one male-voice chorus specifically for what was essentially a male-voice choir, his *Vocal Duma* (IV/10), presented at his first concert on 3 April 1876. Thereafter he wrote occasional male-voice choruses for other venues, and at the Beseda experimented instead with other genres such as his melodrama *Death* (X/3) for reciter and orchestra; this was his first composition with an orchestral score and was performed on 13 November 1876. He went on to produce pieces for string orchestra which were premièred at the December concerts of 1877 (Suite, VI/2) and 1878 (*Idyll*, VI/3). All these pieces were much more ambitious than the little choruses for 'Svatopluk', the longest of which lasts only three minutes. His *Vocal Duma* lasts seven minutes, while the two string pieces are multi-movement works lasting respectively twenty and twenty-four minutes.

In *Vocal Duma* Janáček set not a folksong text (as he had done for all his 'Svatopluk' choruses apart from *War Song*) but a convincing fake by František Ladislav Čelakovský, *The Breaking of a Promise* (see chap. 9). The technical demands of Janáček's setting leap off the page. Where the 'Svatopluk' choruses moved along in hymnlike homophony, Janáček expected his Brno Beseda tenors and basses to be able to sing rhythmically independent parts with a huge amount of melisma. It was by far Janáček's most ambitious chorus to date. The changes are evident not only in the novel textures but also in the very different musical language, whose archaic-sounding modal melodies and strange modulatory excursions reflect some of Janáček's discoveries the previous year at the Prague Organ School. All this took Janáček's male-voice chorus style significantly further away from Křížkovský and the folksong-based choral writing of the 'Svatopluk' choruses. Contemporary reviewers were bemused by it. Even today the chorus sounds experimental and has moments of wild intensity in the gathering climax towards the end that look forward to Janáček's Bezruč choruses thirty years later (see chap. 54).

As a melodrama (i.e. a piece for spoken voice and accompaniment) Janáček's *Death* appeared to be cashing in on the enthusiasm for spoken recitations at Brno concerts. Despite the popularity of this genre among Czech composers it was not something that Janáček tried again, apart from a short satirical passage in the Moon Excursion of *The Excursions of Mr Brouček*. The fact that the piece was presented merely as 'Part I' of a work in progress, that a continuation was never performed and that the music has been lost suggest that Janáček was unhappy with it. Or perhaps Janáček was unhappy with the military band that performed it: his next orchestral pieces were for strings alone, which meant that Horný's military band was not involved. The chief interest of Janáček's *Death* is that its Lermontov poem was the first Russian text to inspire him – the first of many.

If the two string orchestra pieces were a direct response to Dvořák's Serenade for strings, which Janáček conducted at a Brno Beseda concert seven months before the first of his own works for strings, it took a while for any stylistic influence to register: clear in the *Idyll* (1878), hardly apparent in the Suite (1877) apart from the final movement. A key perhaps to Janáček's ambitions for the Suite are the titles printed on the original programme (but suppressed in the publication forty-nine years later): 1. Prélude; 2. Allemande; 3. Sarabanda; 4. Scherzo; 5. Air; 6. Finale. The first three of these (and arguably no. 5 too) suggest not the world of Dvořák's Serenade, but something much earlier, the Baroque suite. The third movement, for instance, has a two-part structure marked off with repeat signs and a deliberately backward-looking musical language that suggests a pastiche. As a Baroque sarabande, however, it is a failure. Sarabandes are triple-time dances; Janáček's quadruple-time piece has more the character of a bourée.

Furthermore there is a basic misunderstanding about the structure. Baroque binary structures are dynamic tonal journeys: they move to the dominant in the first half and return home in the second. Janáček's 'Sarabande' stays resolutely in G major apart from a surprise landing, quickly rectified, in E flat major (a typical Romantic gambit). What is abundantly clear from, say, the first movement (with its flourish of improbable modulations) is that while Skuherský's modulatory techniques had a huge impact on Janáček he had clearly not passed on the dynamic and structural basis of modulation that underpins music from the Baroque period onwards. Janáček uses modulation more to inject colour and emotion than as a structural device. This basic trait explains not only the rather unconvincing structures and occasional aimlessness of his early instrumental music but also the harmonically static nature of much of his later music. There is also a revealing nonchalance about the overall key structure of the Suite. Although the first three movements start off conventionally with a single key centre (G minor/G major) the final movement is left high and dry in B major, thus disregarding the unity of key structure that even Romantic composers generally observed in multi-movement pieces.

By the fourth movement Janáček seems to have abandoned any pretence of writing a Baroque suite and instead wrote an attractive Beethovenian scherzo (based on his own *Sonnet (2)* (VII/2). And by the finale, some of the impact of Dvořák seems to have kicked in. This alone in the Suite has a conventional key structure (minor to relative major and then back again) and the typical gestures of a sonata-form 'development' in the second half. Altogether the Suite is something of a ragbag of influences, perhaps even of Wagner (Helfert found traces of *Lohengrin* in the high upper-string writing in the second movement).[16]

In comparison, the *Idyll* is a much more unified piece. Apart from the late-addition Scherzo that goes back to the 'olden-style' simplicities of the Suite's 'Baroque' movements, this sounds much more like nineteenth-century string music, making use of both divided string effects and the full sound of the string orchestra. The structures are clearer; there is much less random modulation and enharmonic wandering. And above all there are distinctive moments such as the opening of the third movement, with its awkwardly lunging quintuplet movement, its dark Slavonic character and chromatic clashes, or the languid arabesques of the opening of the fifth movement.

Janáček was presumably pleased enough with the *Idyll* to make sure that Dvořák attended the première in December 1878, but only four-teen months later he wrote to Zdenka Schulzová from Leipzig that he now set little store by these two works,[17] a verdict he repeated about the Suite to Brod in 1924.[18] Nevertheless he conducted the *Idyll* at the Beseda's twenty-year jubilee concert in December 1880 and let the Suite be published in 1926. By then, however, the *Idyll* had dis-appeared. It turned up inexplicably in the possession of a provincial schoolteacher only in 1937.[19]

Besides his involvement with the Brno Beseda concerts, the Teachers' Institute also made its demands on Janáček's time and energy in these years. He composed a *Festive Chorus* for the laying of the foundation stone of the new building (IV/12), performed on 15 July 1877, and another for the consecration of the completed building (IV/13), per-formed a year later on 8 July 1878. The first chorus (IV/12) was an elaborate affair (sometimes known as a 'Triple Festive Chorus'), writ-ten for outdoor performance and involving a male chorus, a female chorus and four male soloists. Whether it involved a piano accom-paniment as well is a point of contention. Svatava Přibáňová[20] has argued against the description 'with piano accompaniment' (found for instance in the list of works in Janáček's autobiography)[21] on the basis that no such piano accompaniment has turned up, that the outdoor first performance may well have precluded a piano and that the con-temporary newspaper accounts of its performance omit any reference to a piano. Janáček may have confused it with the second chorus, which definitely has such an accompaniment (and was presumably performed inside, rather than outside, in the newly erected Teachers' Institute). The two choruses have indeed become hopelessly confused; even the notes to the 1994 Supraphon recording of IV/13 refer to 'three' versions of the same chorus.[22]

However IV/12 and IV/13 are entirely different works, setting dif-ferent words to different music. The only thing they have in common is belonging to the same genre of ceremonial-occasion chorus (such as *War Songs* IV/2 and IV/3). Written in the Tovačovský patriotic style (rather than folk-based à la Křížkovský) both choruses are thus charac-terized by affirmative unisons and massive chordal sound; there are also effective contrasts between choirs (IV/12) or between choir and baritone soloist (IV/13). What is also clear is that without some sort of accompaniment IV/12 does not make musical sense. Not only are there suspicious gaps of a few bars between some of the entries that suggest that something might be missing but also the entries themselves do not join up. Jan Trojan came to this conclusion, supplying his own piano accompaniment for the piece when it was first published in 1972. In comparison with the extraordinary *Vocal Duma* (IV/10), these are staid and unremarkable pieces, but they serve their purpose and suggest that Janáček had by now acquired the technical skill to handle this particular genre of choral music convincingly. He seemed pleased enough with the first chorus (IV/12) to give it a second airing a few months later in one of his Brno Beseda concerts. The second chorus (IV/13) is just as effective but was not performed again in Janáček's lifetime; the music was believed to be lost until the manuscript turned up in 1985 in the estate of Josef Růžička, formerly librarian at the Teachers' Institute.

Among his work with amateur choral groups was an All Souls' Eve event on 1 November 1875, when Janáček assembled some fifty members to sing a funeral chorus by Křížkovský at the Dobrovský's grave as part of the traditional All Souls' Eve ceremony of remembrance.[23] In the spring of 1876 he reportedly got up an amateur choir to sing church music at St Michal's (a church said to have a 'Slavonic' orientation), a venture, Helfert argued, that was to provide high-quality church music for a specifically Czech congregation.[24]

There was also the series of chamber concerts that Janáček organized between 1877 and 1879 with his piano teacher Amalie Wickenhauser[‡] (née Neruda). The Neruda family was one of Brno's musical treasures, the talented sons and daughters of the organist at Brno Cathedral, Josef Neruda. In 1845 Josef took his family to Vienna to further their musical education and from 1848 Amalie (pianist, 1834–90), Viktor (cellist, 1836–52), Wilma (violinist, 1838–1911) and Maria (violinist, 1840–1922) began to tour Europe as a family of Wunderkinder. The family's repertory consisted of high quality chamber music; with father Josef they were able to make up a string quartet, and with Amalie a

---

[‡] Czech musicological literature usually gives her name in a Czech form, 'Amálie Wickenhauserová'. Although for a while she favoured Czech music-making in Brno, she was a German (Zdenka Janáčková regarded her as such, see below) and this book refers to her by the main German form of her name, Amalie Wickenhauser. In his letters to Zdenka, when not contracting the name to 'Wick' or 'W', Janáček also called her Wickenhauser (see *IB*, 37–8). There are other variants such as 'Wickenhausser-Neruda' (sic; see facsimile in Kyas 1993b, 236).

piano quintet. When Viktor died on tour in St Petersburg, his role was taken over by another cellist son, Franz (1843–1915). As adults Franz and Wilma went on to make international careers, settling respectively in Copenhagen and England (Wilma became Lady Hallé after marrying Sir Charles Hallé in 1885). Amalie, on the other hand, stayed in Brno, having married the conductor of the German Theatre, Ernst Wickenhauser, and set up as a piano teacher. Janáček became her pupil in 1876 and at his Beseda concert on 13 May that year she played the opening movement of Rubinstein's Third Piano Concerto with Janáček conducting.

Two chamber concerts were planned to take place at the Readers' Club each January in 1877, 1878 and 1879. A small band of musicians participated; the string players in the first two years were Beseda stalwarts such as Gustav Zinke, Vít Pergler, Malý[§] and František Mráček; either Janáček or Wickenhauser appeared as pianists.[25]

There was also an isolated chamber concert at the Reduta theatre on 7 October 1877 that Janáček and Wickenhauser organized, in which

Table 12.3: Janáček's and Wickenhauser's chamber concerts in Brno 1877–9

1877

6 January: Mendelssohn's Piano Trio in C minor op. 66 (with Janáček); Haydn's String Quartet in G op. 76 no. 1; Schumann's Piano Quartet in E flat op. 47 (with Wickenhauser)

14 January: Beethoven's 'Spring' [Violin] Sonata in F op. 24 (with Janáček); Mendelssohn's String Quartet in E minor op. 44 no. 2; Brahms's Piano Quintet in F minor op. 34 (with Wickenhauser)

1878

6 January: Rubinstein's Piano Trio in F op. 15 no. 1 (with Janáček?); Beethoven's String Quartet in B flat op. 18 no. 6; Schumann's Piano Quartet in E flat op. 47 (with Wickenhauser?)

13 January: Saint-Saëns's Piano Trio no. 1 in F (with Janáček); Grieg's Violin Sonata [op. 8? or op. 13?] (with Wickenhauser); Brahms's Piano Quintet (as in previous year); Reinecke's Piano Duo in A (= arrangement of Schumann's *Manfred*; Wickenhauser and Janáček)

1879

5 January: Dvořák's Piano Trio in B flat op. 21 (with Wickenhauser); W. F. Bach's Sonata [Concerto?] in F for two pianos (Wickenhauser and Janáček); Rubinstein's Piano Quintet in G minor op. 99 (with Janáček)

12 January: Woldemar Bargiel's Piano Trio in B flat op. 37 (with Janáček); Reinecke's Piano Duo (as in previous year); Friedrich Gernsheim's Piano Quintet in D minor op. 35 (with Wickenhauser)

[§] First name unknown.

they played Schumann's Andante and Variations in B flat for two pianos, and Wickenhauser and her violinist sister Wilma, then 'Frau W. Norman-Neruda' on the programme,[26] contributed other items.

Janáček's Beseda concerts represent four years of solid achievement, properly hailed as such by Helfert in his biography. Czech Brno – even German Brno – hadn't seen anything quite so impressive as this expansion of concert life with large-scale choral works and symphonic works, and that brought the celebrated Czech composer Antonín Dvořák to Brno. Side by side with this was a succession of chamber concerts purveying the very best of the repertoire.

Helfert paints a hero's story depicting the twenty-one-year-old musician, the young, ambitious and hardworking Janáček and his relentless struggle against the philistinism of Czech Brno and its comfortable refuge in sentimental nationalism. In Helfert's view it is Janáček who single-handedly forged from the male-voice Beseda an organization that within a few years could mount with evident success Beethoven's *Missa solemnis* and who, equally, was responsible for the series of chamber concerts with their sober and tasteful selection of repertory. And unlike the comparable figure in Prague, Smetana, who for all his heroic actions in developing a forward-looking opera company at the Provisional Theatre, had a band of loyal supporters and advisers, Janáček was quite alone. As Helfert stated, 'he had no-one to lean on'.[27]

This hero story was questioned in 1993 in a remarkable article by Vojtěch Kyas, 'Did Janáček have no one to lean on?'[28] While there is no gainsaying Janáček's achievement at such an early age in making the differences he did, Helfert's final sentence about having no-one to lean on is not true: it paints Amalie Wickenhauser out of the picture.

What Helfert didn't notice was that virtually all the pieces played at the Readers' Club chamber series had been played by Wickenhauser or members of her family in Brno during the twenty years before. It is clear from Kyas's analysis that it was Wickenhauser, not Janáček, who determined the repertory of the chamber concerts. Although they shared equal billing in the pieces and equal credit for the organization, it would indeed be astonishing if Amalie Wickenhauser, with almost thirty years of public performances behind her, did not play the leading part in determining what was played rather than the young Janáček, whose experience of secular music was still extremely limited. Under her tutelage, Janáček, who had had no systematic piano tuition until then, was able to hold his own with established musicians in chamber music concerts and appear as soloist in two piano concertos.

Wickenhauser's guest appearances in the Beseda concerts were merely the outward manifestations of her dominating influence. Records of the Beseda committee meetings show that she was pulling the strings there too, ensuring where exactly she appeared in the programmes and providing the sheet music in some cases, and her husband Ernst Wickenhauser (a German and thus not a natural part of Czech Brno concerts) as conductor in others.[29]

In October 1879 Janáček went to Leipzig and on the few occasions Amalie Wickenhauser is mentioned in his letters to Zdenka it was only to disparage her: for her showy stage manner (in comparison with the no-nonsense Clara Schumann)[30] or her defective teaching (which meant, Janáček believed, that he had to begin all over again).[31] Wickenhauser was due to appear once more at a Beseda concert just as Janáček was returning from Leipzig, but excused herself at the last moment on grounds of ill-health.[32] Although she continued to perform until 1887 (she died in 1890 at the age of fifty-five),[33] she did so only in German-Brno concerts, at the Musikverein, as did any of her siblings returning to Brno.

It is clear from Janáček's remarks and from Wickenhauser's sudden 'indisposition' that there had been some sort of rift. Its cause was the advent of Zdenka.

13

The Schulzes

In 1877 Lev Janáček began giving piano lessons to Zdenka Schulzová, the twelve-year-old daughter of his superior at the Brno Teachers' Institute, Emilian Schulz, thereby beginning an association that led to his marriage with her in 1881; despite all the difficulties in their later relationship they lived together until his death over fifty years later. Zdenka's recollections of their life together were set down in *My Life*, a manuscript completed in 1936 that was made accessible to Vladimír Helfert and Jaroslav Vogel for the writing of their biographies but was unpublished until the 1990s.[1] It is one of the most important sources for Janáček's family life, though in some ways a problematic one.* Together with a few recollections that Zdenka gave to the scholars Helfert and Robert Smetana before her death in 1938,[2] it is the only source for Zdenka's early life.

Zdenka Schulzová was born on 30 July 1865 in Olomouc. Her father Emilian Schulz (1836–1923) was Czech, the son of a doctor in Obříství, a village between Mělník and Prague. After his education in Prague, he taught at the Realschule in Olomouc before becoming director of the Realschule in Kroměříž in 1872. He was there only a short time before taking up the post of director at the Teachers' Institute in Brno (on 30 September 1872),[3] just when Janáček was completing his training there. Zdenka remembers her father as 'uncommonly good-natured and cheerful', whistling Czech folksongs

---

* See Paul Wingfield: 'Zdenka Janáčková's memoirs and the fallacy of music as auto-biography', Beckerman 2003, 165–97. In evaluating Zdenka's memoirs, readers may wish also to consider the arguments set out in my Introduction to *MLWJ*, ix–xvii, overlooked by Wingfield in favour of a promotional newspaper article that appeared at the same time.

to himself, content with simple pleasures such as his pipe or a cigar and drinking in a café, and looking after a small menagerie that included an owl and a squirrel.[4]

This idyllic picture is one that comes from a devoted daughter who had no experience of her father in the workplace. It is a view that Helfert accepted (his biography of Janáček is dedicated to Zdenka) and from that source has been carried over elsewhere. However, buried in the Teachers' Institute archives, which Bohumír Štědroň examined in 1947, is evidence of a rather more abrasive personality, short-tempered with both staff and students, a man who had difficulties in keeping personal and professional life apart.[5] The picture that emerges from these and other documents is of a typical Austrian functionary who, despite his Czech background, was happy to instigate disciplinary proceedings against students for taking part in Dobrovský celebrations,[6] a pro-Czech manifestation (and thus seen as potentially anti-Austrian).

According to Zdenka, her mother Anna (1840–1918) was made of sterner stuff. She was brought up in Johannisberk (now Janský Vrch) in Silesia, the daughter of Gustav Kaluschka,[†] who had been private secretary to the Archbishop of Breslau (now Wrocław). Although allegedly Polish in origin, the Kaluschkas spoke German and had aristocratic pretensions. Anna developed into a 'type of strict, energetic and frugal townswoman who always cared about the social position of her husband'. In Zdenka's recollection she was 'beautiful, slim and elegant, with strict moral principles', running her household simply and thriftily and bringing up Zdenka in this way too.[7] It was Anna Schulzová who was the dominant partner. Schulz got on splendidly with his strict and frugal wife' taking life easily and giving way to her without being under her thumb. For example the Schulz family spoke German, Anna's language, despite the fact that Schulz was Czech and in charge of an institute for the training of Czech schoolteachers. So their only child Zdenka was brought up in German (speaking Czech only with the servants) and received her private education at home in German. Her father taught her history, geography, physics and German grammar though he lost patience with her over the last subject

---

[†]This is how Zdenka spells the family name; the 1880 census (Archiv města Brna) however registered her mother as Anna Kalušková (Kaluschke), born 1823 in Olomouc, and then staying with the Schulz family 'as a guest'. I am indebted to Milena Flodrová for this information .

and passed the task over to another member of his staff, who also gave her lessons in arithmetic and writing. Her favourite subject was needlework, taught by Miss Waltrová from the Women Teachers' Institute. She learnt the piano from about the age of eight, taught by Professor Antonín Vorel, from the Teachers' Institute.[8]

Zdenka led an isolated childhood. Not going to school, she had almost no friends of her own age, and the family made few visits and received few visitors apart from her grandmother and a couple of great-aunts on her mother's side. A visit to Feldkirch in Vorarlberg (Austria) for the marriage of a relative in 1877 was a big adventure. The trip back, via Munich and Vienna with visits to art galleries and the opera, was her first major cultural impression.[9]

In 1877, perhaps in the autumn at the beginning of the academic year, Professor Vorel felt that his hardworking piano pupil had made such progress that she would benefit from a new teacher. He advised Schulz to entrust her further musical education to Janáček.[10] Schulz was well aware of Janáček's outstanding musical talents: he had already ensured that his young employee was appointed provisional teacher at the Teachers' Institute. At that stage the institute was accommodated partly in the Minorite monastery in Brno while the Schulzes lived in a four-room, second-floor flat on Pekařská ulice.

I was very frightened of my teacher [Zdenka remembered]. I knew him a little from the institute and heard from his pupils that he was very strict. Even his appearance had something dark for me. He was slim then,[‡] a figure smaller rather than larger, his pale face made a strong contrast with his hard, curly full beard, thick black curly locks and very striking brown eyes. Already at that time I was particularly taken with his small, full white hand, which when he touched the keyboard became an independent being with a soul of its own. My fears were groundless; Janáček didn't indulge me, he didn't speak unnecessarily, he demanded that I learn my lesson perfectly as a matter of course, yet I couldn't say that he used to be particularly strict let alone ill-natured, as was frequently said of him. I did my best so he should be pleased with me: for one thing, I really liked playing the piano very much, for another I was proud of the fact that everybody told me what an excellent piano teacher I had. For about a year Janáček came to give lessons at our old apartment

---

[‡] In fact Zdenka describes him in her account to Smetana as 'very thin' and that, although his frame was firm and healthy with no signs of consumption, he appeared undernourished (Smetana 1948, 24).

in Pekařská ulice: then [in 1878] we moved into the director's apartment in the new institute building in Staré Brno.[11]

At thirteen Zdenka was mature for her age, 'with the appearance of a young woman', as she put it; in the new apartment, where there was a mirror opposite the piano, she began to be aware from glancing in the mirror that Janáček was taking a more than teacherly interest in her appearance, looking approvingly at the 'long golden plaits' that fell on her back.

And I noticed other attentions too. Before, he spoke to me only of things that directly concerned my piano playing, now he initiated conversation on other topics; he recommended my visiting this or that concert, he invited me to organ recitals in the Staré Brno monastery, trifles from which I got twofold pleasure: both as a pupil who had been singled out, and as a girl within whom a woman was awakening. I had three piano lessons a week. Janáček told me that we were being held back too much in them by [practising] playing four hands; that in future we'd have a separate lesson on this. He said that he'd come to us on Sunday mornings and that he didn't want any fee for it. And the height of his attentiveness towards me was that at the end of the winter, during one of the musical evenings that he got up with his pupils at the institute, he did me the honour of playing with me Dvořák's *Slavonic Dances* for four hands.[12]

Lev and Zdenka played one or more of Dvořák's *Slavonic Dances* at an informal concert at the Teachers' Institute on 2 March 1879. A month later, on 2 April, came the crowning event of Janáček's conducting activities at the Brno Beseda before his departure for Leipzig, a performance of Beethoven's *Missa solemnis* (see chap. 12). Zdenka was at the concert, observing her teacher's success 'joyfully' from afar, and at her next lessons enjoyed hearing all about it and seeing the presents he had been given, which he brought round to show her.

On Easter Monday [14 April 1879] my parents invited several teachers from the institute to supper. From the time we moved to the institute we received many more visitors altogether, especially Father's friends and colleagues. My teacher was also invited on that occasion, and made it clear that he came to our home frequently and liked doing so. We played the piano together, then he played solo; the atmosphere was exhilarating. I was helping to serve the guests and when I went into the room next door for wine, Janáček slipped in there behind me and kissed my hand. Now I was no longer in any doubt that he was courting me. From that time he came to us more and more frequently, he accompanied us on family walks, he danced attendance on Mama and

Grandmother so engagingly that both of them soon fell in love with him as their own son.[13]

Ten days later, on 24 April, Zdenka and Lev seem to have come to some sort of understanding: at any rate this was a date that Janáček remembered as being especially significant in their relationship: 'See, Zdenčinko, I always remember very gladly, very gladly indeed 24 April of last year! How quickly the evening went by then surprises me even today; and I have it still so clearly before me that I could remember every little detail, all the words of that evening.'[14] That day Janáček conducted the Teachers' Institute choir to celebrate the twenty-fifth wedding anniversary of Emperor Franz Josef.[15] Was Zdenka there with her family? Was there some gathering at the Schulzes' house afterwards?

There was another duet performance at the Teachers' Institute on 18 May, with Lev and Zdenka playing Dvořák's *Slavonic Dance* no. 8.[16] Matters then came quickly to a head:

On one occasion we were alone together in the room. We were talking calmly about something when suddenly he threw himself on his knees before me, he clasped me by the waist and, trembling all over with excitement, told me that he loved me and wanted to marry me. I was so taken aback by this unexpected outburst that I couldn't say a word. I simply nodded my head. Passionately he seized me and kissed me. The feeling that I felt at the time wasn't at all pleasant: I was scared out of my wits.[17]

In her later analysis of her reactions Zdenka explained how she was still a child in many ways; although drawn to her teacher she was 'not yet ripe for love'. By this time Janáček was beginning to make preparations for his year in Leipzig, a plan that had been initiated some time before 9 April (when Schulz wrote to Skuherský asking for a reference for Janáček), i.e. a few days before the Easter Monday incident. Zdenka reports that her father had been less keen than his womenfolk when he first noticed that something was going on between his daughter and Janáček but 'was far too good-natured to intervene in any way'.[18] If the Leipzig plan hadn't already been in train, one wonders whether Schulz might not have initiated something of the sort expressly to put some space between his young daughter and her impetuous young suitor. He certainly continued to encourage and facilitate the scheme. This much is evident in Janáček's fulsome gratitude in a letter written on 23 June 1879 from Vienna, where he had gone to enquire into the status of his application for unpaid study leave. In what was Janáček's first surviving dated letter to Zdenka, though also directed to the whole family, he commented: 'And so I think that one of my most longed-for dreams will be fulfilled; and that through the quite extraordinary goodness of Mr Director and his powerful intercession.'[19]

Leipzig came too late to forestall the further progress of marriage plans. There was an occasion in August when Janáček had had to excuse himself from a piano lesson because of an appointment elsewhere and Zdenka retired to sob quietly in disappointment. However he turned up after all, saw that Zdenka had been crying, and burst out: 'I'll ask for your hand at once.'

But before we could agree on anything Mama came after us. It was getting dark. We sat down on the settee, he in the middle, we on either side of him. While he chatted with Mama about this and that, I fell asleep. I don't know how it could have happened: perhaps weariness from crying in the afternoon. It had already got very dark when I woke up and began to take in the voice of Mama: 'But she's just a child, she's not ready for marriage. She must go on learning. And she also doesn't know yet how to run a house.'[20]

From what Zdenka overheard, her mother seemed more than ready to accept Janáček as a future son-in-law. Although Zdenka had 'no wealth to speak of' Mrs Schulzová declared that her daughter would have a dowry and that the Schulzes would be able to help out financially even after the wedding. Janáček would have none of this: he would not allow his young wife even to look after the household. Mrs Schulzová, however, had a better grasp of his financial position: he was poor, he had to support his widowed mother and any wife of his could not expect a lavish lifestyle. 'Then they fell silent. I forced myself to keep my eyes closed because I was ashamed of what I'd overheard. But I had to move at some stage. They both turned to me. Mama said to me: "So you want to leave me already, Zdenči?"'[21]

Zdenka's silence was taken as acquiescence. Mrs Schulzová undertook to secure her husband's agreement. As Zdenka described it, 'she had quite a hard time before she managed to stop him making objections. Publicly, however, we were engaged only after a year, although it was known in Brno circles that Janáček was courting me.'[22] There was one other opponent to this development, Janáček's piano teacher, Amalie Wickenhauser:

This tall, thin brunette came to like Leoš more than was permissible for a married woman. As far as I know from what he told me, he didn't give any cause for this. So long as she didn't suspect that he loved me, she was said to praise me and to praise even my piano playing, which she heard at performances at the institute. But when she discovered that he was engaged to me, she began to get jealous and to dissuade Leoš from marrying me, so that he stopped going to her for lessons.[23]

In her recollections to Robert Smetana, Zdenka dated the conversation between her mother and Janáček above to 'September'[24] rather than to August, as in *My Life*. If it was September, then it must have been very early, certainly before 8 September, the date of Janáček's next surviving letter,[25] which opens 'Oh my beloved Zdenka' rather than to 'Esteemed Miss', as in the Vienna letter. On 8 September Janáček was in Rožnov, on what is sometimes described[26] as the one and only concert tour of his life. This is overstating the case: he simply travelled from Brno to take part in a concert with a few other Brno musicians.

Within sight of the mountain Radhošt' (see chap. 36), Rožnov is at the heart of Valašsko; the occasion was a two-day celebration associated with the erection of a statue to the Czech historian František Palacký and culminating in a concert on the afternoon of 8 September in the hall of the local sanatorium. Janáček played Smetana's *Czech Dances* and his own *Dumka* for piano (x/4), whose mention in the programme is all that is known of this lost composition. Janáček himself did not refer to the piece in his letter to Zdenka, which is instead a diverting account of his arrival in Rožnov and the appalling food and beer that was sent up to his hotel room. He was hoping that the nighttime outline of Radhošt' would inspire him to compose 'something elevated', but he had to be content instead with munching sour bread. He hadn't even been able to meet his 'brother' (presumably his older brother Karel who was then a teacher in Krhová, Valašské Meziříčí, which Janáček would have passed through to get to Rožnov).[27]

And soon Janáček was off to Leipzig:

As a parting present I gave him a purse with 20 ducats that I'd received as a child from a lady we knew. He wept, he told me the whole time that he was afraid that I'd forget him. I had to promise him that I'd write to him as often as possible; he said that I'd be getting a letter from him every day. I was very lonely after his departure, but even at that time I was able to find relief from pain in work: I threw myself into my lessons, and in addition Mama began to get me doing housework even more. Besides, every day had some joy for me too: the letter from Leipzig.[28]

Janáček handsomely fulfilled his promise of a daily letter (see chaps. 15 and 16). His daily letters from Leipzig and Vienna, written usually in several bulletins a day, provide not only an account of his life abroad and his hopes, fears, disappointments, joys and depressions, but also reveal a great deal about the relationship between him and Zdenka, who had turned fourteen at the end of July. Her letters have disappeared so that what she wrote back can only be inferred from occasional comments in Janáček's. She probably spent most of the time encouraging him, calming him down, trying to get him to relax and not to work so hard. She also ran Janáček's errands around Brno, getting her father to send instalments of his Brno salary and visiting Janáček's mother. Occasionally Zdenka was pressed into giving advice, though much of the time the hectoring way in which her views were solicited (e.g. over the plan to transfer to Vienna)[29] makes it clear that she was simply expected to rubber stamp decisions that Janáček had already taken.

On just one occasion did she put her foot down, having misread his letters to understand that he intended to become a travelling virtuoso. The letters concerned give no such impression (Janáček had merely thought of going to study with Saint-Saëns in Paris)[30] but Zdenka seems to have got the wrong end of the stick, and it needed many pacifying letters from Janáček to explain that this wasn't his intention.[31] Most of the time, however, it seems to have been a passive relationship – as one might expect with the ten-year age gap between the two, and the fact that Janáček was having all the interesting experiences abroad, while fourteen-year-old Zdenka was learning wifely skills by helping her mother round the home.[32]

What is extraordinary about this correspondence is that it was conducted entirely in German, and that in all the letters up to Christmas 1879 Janáček continued to address his unofficial fiancée in the formal *Sie* form rather than the informal *Du*. The delicious irony of the passionate Czech nationalist Janáček writing his love letters in German is a topic that is addressed in more detail elsewhere (chap. 2). The *Sie* of these letters is a reflection of the more formal relations of the period and one, anyway, that stopped during the Christmas break. Originally, Janáček thought that he would be unable to get back to Brno for Christmas; the fact that the Schulzes then invited him to stay with them[33] and sent money for the fare[34] makes it clear that by then Schulz was reconciled to having Janáček as a son-in-law.

On the Sunday before Christmas [Zdenka recollected], just when I was writing to him again, a carriage rolled up in front of our apartment and out of it jumped my fiancé. For me that was the most beautiful Christmas present. And he just beamed. He stayed with us, upstairs in Father's office. For meals he was our guest. In those joyful days we got even closer, we began to say *Du* to one another and I got used to calling him 'Leoš', as his mother called him.[35]

Grandmother Kaluschka, seemingly so supportive, did not entirely approve of this when she visited her relatives in Vienna at the end of April 1880: 'Yesterday [Janáček wrote to Zdenka] I walked with Grandmother and with Aunt Marie and Fanny for the whole afternoon around the town. I prepared Grandmother properly, I must still tell her about the *Du*.' Despite the 'preparation', the news didn't go down well: 'Dearest Zdenčinko we'll have bad times with Grandmother but no matter. [. . .] She keeps on wanting to see you as a child and she remained standing in the Graben for quite a time when I told her that you're already wearing long clothes.'[36]

The Christmas holidays of 1879–80 were memorable for Zdenka for a further reason. It was then that Anna Schulzová got round to telling her daughter that she was pregnant. She was thirty-nine and with a single child of fourteen: the new addition was something of a surprise, and seemingly an unwelcome one, judging from the 'heated altercations' that Zdenka overheard between her parents. Nor did the news go down well with Leoš:

I suspected that he wouldn't like it. In fact, when we met again and he saw me tearful, he asked me what had happened to me. I told him what we could look forward to. Unpleasantly surprised, he pulled a face and he said only: 'Well, I'm amazed they weren't more sensible.'
From that moment onwards it was as if he had grown cold towards me.[37]

The meeting would have been in the first few days of the 1880s; Janáček was still in Brno for the rehearsal (5 January)[38] and concert (6 January)[39] of the Brno Beseda at which Dvořák conducted his F major symphony and *Slavonic Rhapsody* no. 2, and Berthold Žalud, Janáček's replacement as conductor of the Beseda, conducted choruses by Dvořák and Křížkovský.[40] Early on 8 January Janáček started the journey back to Leipzig, having to change trains with his heavy cases in Prague and Dresden.[41]

Zdenka presented the news of her mother's pregnancy as a turning-point in her relationship with Leoš; her claims that 'there was none of his earlier ardour' in his subsequent letters from Leipzig,[42] however, would not strike the reader. If anything, their more intimate form of address make them seem more ardent. Furthermore, Janáček made a point of acknowledging her as the source of inspiration for his post-Christmas holiday pieces. At least temporarily, she became his muse:

How, all-dearest Zdenči, do you come into the Zdenči-Leoš fugue [x/6 no.14]? Quite simply: I thought of you during the whole of the work and thereby we created it both together. With your name I will embellish all my works, my Zdenči, since I don't write anything without thinking of you at the same time.[43]

This was even more the case with Janáček's next piece, his Theme and Variations (VIII/6): 'They are really nice and I regard them as my first completely correct work, as my op. 1. You will like them, dearest Zdenči, and should they ever be published, they will carry your dear name.'[44]

When Zdenka's memoirs became generally available there was speculation that the new arrival in the Schulz household had more to do with Leoš than with the child's father Emilian Schulz. After all, as Zdenka, innocently relates, in the spring of 1879, when Leoš had accompanied them on family walks, he had 'danced attendance on Mama and Grandmother so engagingly that both of them soon fell in love with him as their own son.'[45] However the suggestion that Janáček may have been the father of Zdenka's little brother can easily be dismissed. Although Anna Schulzová may have found her daughter's suitor attractive she comes across as a woman of considerable self-restraint who would have firmly resisted any such impulses. She fell pregnant in about August 1879, at the very time she was discussing the possibility of her daughter's marrying Janáček, and such thoughts may simply have rekindled her own marriage, as might her efforts to bring her husband round to accepting Janáček as a son-in-law.

According to Zdenka's memoirs it was during Janáček's Whitsun break in 1880 in Brno that the Schulzes' baby son arrived[46] however, according to the register of births he was born the next weekend, on Sunday 23 May 1880§ (by which time Janáček had returned to Vienna). Janáček's couple of references to him in his letters from

§ I am indebted to Milena Flodrová for this information. He is registered as 'Leo Schulz', though was known throughout his early life at 'Leoš' and reverted to 'Leo' only when he moved to Vienna in 1907.

Vienna afterwards are not unfriendly. On 28 May he enquired about how 'Leošek' was getting on[47] – the name had already been decided on –[ll] and on 31 May he declared that he was looking forward to 'holding him',[48] a reference to the forthcoming christening where he would be standing in for his godfather.[49] This took place early in June, when Janáček had returned permanently from Vienna. However, his relationship to the Schulz family would now be very different. Until then Janáček had cast himself as the son of the family. Now he had a rival.

[ll] Smetana 1948, 25–6, alleges that it was in honour of the priest who would officiate at the christening and of Janáček himself.

14

What's in a name? Leo, Lev and Leoš

Janáček was christened Leo Eugen Janáček, but his middle name dropped away as swiftly as those of his siblings. It is rare for Czechs to style themselves with more than one forename, or even a middle initial. Where the Leo or the Eugen came from is a mystery: neither name celebrates a previous family member or a nearby saint's day. Interestingly Leo the Great (Pope Leo I) shares a name day of 10 November with St Eugene of Toledo:[1] having decided on Leo perhaps Janáček's parents took the easy option of adding in 'Eugen' as well. That said, Janáček celebrated his name day on 11 April, given for 'Leo' in older Czech calendars.[2] He did so in Vienna in 1880,[3] and the date was remembered among his family: for instance by his mother in the last three years of her life,[4] by his brother-in-law Leo Schulz thirty years later,[5] and by the trio of ladies (Zdenka, his niece Věra and her mother Joza Janáčková) wishing him well from Prague in 1915.[6]

Although the names Leo and Eugen are both used by Czechs, more Slavonic-sounding versions exist in the form of Lev and Evžen. In origin Leo is a Late Latin personal name (meaning 'lion') and had papal associations, with thirteen popes of this name. Its greatest disadvantage for the young Janáček was that it could be thought of as German, the short form for names such as Leopold and Leonard. In a letter to his uncle Jan Janáček just after his fourteenth birthday in July 1868 Janáček signed off not with his usual 'Leo' but with the Russian-sounding 'Lev' (see chap. 7), his earliest recorded venture into impression management. Although 'Lev' is an early vernacular calque in Russian (the Russian word for 'lion') it also means 'lion' in Czech and was common in older Czech generations.[7]

'Lev Janáček' was how Janáček was known professionally throughout the 1870s, for instance at 'Svatopluk' and the Brno Beseda. In the 1880s, however, 'Leoš' began to occur and would soon become Janáček's final choice for his asserted first name. From Zdenka's aside 'as his mother called him' one could infer that 'Leoš' had been Amalie Janáčková's pet name for him, perhaps since birth (her existing letters to him, the earliest of which is from October 1879, are all, however, addressed to 'Leo').[8] When Zdenka got to know the old lady during Janáček's time away in Leipzig, she too acquired 'Leoš': 'I got used to calling him "Leoš", as his mother called him.'[9] Janáček's first letter in the new year was signed 'Dein Dich ewig liebender Leo' [your ever-loving Leo][10] but two hours later this became 'Dein ewig Dich liebender Leoš'.[11] A combination of their two names was commemorated in Janáček's composition of the time, his 'Zdenči-Leoš Fugue (x/6 no.14), infused, he claimed, with a wild 'Leoš-Zdenči' spirit.[12]

However, there is evidence that Janáček was contemplating the change earlier than that Christmas of 1879. On 30 October 1879 he wrote to Zdenka: 'I'm beginning to acquire respect among the students, which is naturally enhanced to a certain extent by my name as it's written and heard (Leoš etc.).'[13] Was he giving out 'Leoš' (rather than Leo or Lev) as his first name in Leipzig as a way of sounding mysteriously (and impressively) foreign? Were the foreign surroundings contributing to his feeling Czech and making him want to show it in a way that Leo and Lev did not? Soon after that the Prague music periodical *Dalibor* published a short news item about 'Mr Leoš Janáček, the admirable director of the Brno Beseda'.[14] From the accuracy of the news that followed it is clear that *Dalibor* was printing information that Janáček had himself provided, presumably including this new approved form of his Christian name, the first time it had appeared in print. In professional contexts Janáček was soon signing himself regularly 'Leoš Janáček', as for instance in his letter written to Alois Vlk at the Brno Beseda on 22 February 1880.[15]

'Leo' up to July 1868, 'Lev' in the 1870s, and 'Leoš' thereafter is in fact too tidy. Official documents prefer to stick to what is on birth certificates, so that whatever Janáček contrived to call himself in print, on concert programmes or in letters, 'Leo' stubbornly remained for a good while, for instance in the ministerial decree of 14 May 1880 appointing him a full teacher of music.[16] And people, having got used to 'Lev', would use that too: in the Beseda minutes (13 February 1882) and a report in *Moravská orlice* (4 April 1882), for example, both refer to the resumption of the society's conductorship by 'Lev Janáček';[17] that form was also used by by Berthold Žalud (who should have known better) in a report of the Organ School exams in *Dalibor* in 1883.[18] Janáček's marriage certificate (1881) gives him as 'Lev' too – in combination with a rare 'Evžen'.[19] Jindřiška Bártová, in her investigation of Janáček's time at the Teachers' Institute, reports that Janáček began signing himself 'Lev', but when he had abandoned 'Lev', he signed himself as 'Leo' rather than 'Leoš'. It was only in 1887 that he systematically began signing himself there as 'Leoš'.[20]

Janáček published almost no music during his 'Lev' phrase, the one exception being his *Exaudi Deus [2]* (11/4; *Cecilie*, iv, 1877), where his name is given merely as 'L. Janáček'. On the title page of his *Ten Czech Hymns from the Lehner Hymnbook for the Mass* (11/10), he is given as 'Leoš Janáček'. This formulation is both early (1881) and significant since he was was in effect his own publisher and thus had full control of how he wanted himself styled.

Janáček began publishing articles in the 1870s and all those that bear his full name rather than 'L. Janáček' or a pseudonymic symbol are signed 'Lev Janáček', from xv/1 in 1875 to xv/20* in 1877. The first published writing that he signed 'Leoš Janáček' was in 1885, in a review of an Organ School concert (xv/42). In *Hudební listy*, his chief publication outlet in the 1884–8 period, Janáček signed his reviews with a symbol and gave his full name ('Leoš Janáček') only on the larger theoretical articles (e.g. xv/44, xv/45 and xv/61). One would have thought that he would be 'Leoš' thereafter, but there is an intriguing exception. The chapter on music (xv/94, section VII) that Janáček contributed to František Bartoš's long introduction to his *Moravian Folksongs Newly Collected* (1889) reverts to the signature 'Lev Janáček'. It is only a few pages long, and Bartoš in his efficient, not to say bossy, way might well have done the proofreading himself and chosen this familiar form of Janáček's name, though no longer the one that Janáček was using. It is clear that Bartoš never called Janáček by his first name: all his letters to him begin with the salutation 'Dear friend'. Or maybe for the purpose of folksong work Janáček continued to used 'Lev Janáček': in the first edition of the school collection *A Bouquet of Moravian Folksongs* (xiii/1), which appeared in 1890 the compilers were given as 'Fr. Bartoš and Lev Janáček', a formulation

* Not Leoš Janáček, as in *JAWO*, 361.

that continued as late as the enlarged third edition of 1901 (XIII/2). However the first fascicle of some of these songs issued with Janáček's accompaniment (V/2; 1892) used the form 'Leoš Janáček'. And by the time of Bartoš's and Janáček's vast collection of 1899–1901, *Moravian Folksongs Newly Collected* (XIII/3), Janáček's name is given firmly as 'Leoš Janáček'. Leo and Lev had disappeared for ever – at least as far as Janáček was concerned.

But not among his family. In letters to Zdenka his sister Josefa referred to him as 'Leo',[21] as did Zdenka when writing in German to Joza Janáčková.[22] And occasionally Zdenka called him 'Leo' to his face and was told off about it. In a letter to her dated 24 July 1921 Janáček asked her how long she had been writing 'Leo': 'I am only Leoš', he retorted.[23]

15

Musical studies: Leipzig 1879–80

Janáček's first thoughts for studying music abroad were to go to Anton Rubinstein in St Petersburg. On 7 August 1878 the Regional School Board in Brno refused Janáček's request for 150 zl to finance a vacation trip to study with the Russian piano virtuoso. The school board returned Janáček's request without debating it on the basis that they failed to understand the reasons he gave.[1] By the following spring this modest excursion had begun to turn into something more substantial that would take Janáček away from his teaching post during the entire school year. His piano teacher Amalie Wickenhauser suggested that instead he go to Leipzig: through her friends the Drbskýs she thought she might be able to pull strings with the regional governor to get him leave of absence. Wickenhauser's influence, however, was waning. As Janáček recalled in a letter to Zdenka, he took this suggestion to his employer at the Teachers' Institute, Emilian Schulz: 'But I trustingly placed the whole matter in your father's hands and didn't take any other steps – and I wasn't disappointed.'[2] Schulz wrote to Skuherský in Prague and received the following response:

With reference to the letter of the esteemed directorate of 9 April 1879 no. 123, I have the honour to say that I am delighted to be in the pleasant position of being able to report only in the most favourable terms 'on the musical talent and the capacity for further education' of Professor Leo Janáček.

I am firmly convinced that Janáček is of an eminently artistic disposition; in him can be found all the prerequisites for achieving competence, importance and beauty, namely: in him talent, intelligence, perseverance and enthusiasm are harmoniously united. As a consequence Janáček has already taken admirable steps both as a creative and as a performing artist. A comprehensive knowledge of musical literature, a subtle ear as well as rich understanding in the field of musical theory and aesthetics equip him as a conductor and a critic. He has given eloquent proof of all this on many occasions before the public.

Relying on these noteworthy factors allows me to express the wish that Janáček's special circumstances would recommend themselves to those in charge for further beneficial development.[3]

It is impressive how many of Janáček's qualities Skuherský had noticed at this early stage, qualities that would become more pronounced as time went on. Janáček would need every ounce of 'perseverance' to get him through what would be a long haul. This concrete and enthusiastic reference from the leading Czech musical theorist of the time was vital to the next stage of the process, namely a formal application by Janáček on 5 May 1879 to the Ministry of Culture and Education in Vienna to take unpaid study leave from his post at the Teachers' Institute. In it Janáček described his existing musical qualifications but also his aspirations: as a former pupil and present teacher at the Teachers' Institute he could not rest content with an ordinary education and therefore set himself a higher goal, one that he could achieve only by studying abroad at Leipzig and Vienna. His colleagues had undertaken to divide his hours among them so that the state would not incur any expenses. The request was supported by Schulz and posted on 13 May.[4] On 17 July Schulz was informed that Janáček would be granted a semester's leave providing this did not entail any extra expense.[5] With Janáček's sabbatical arrangements approved the way was clear for him to apply to Leipzig Conservatory. Although his application to the ministry mentioned Vienna as well as Leipzig, Vienna may have been included purely for diplomatic reasons. There is no suggestion in the early months of Janáček's voluminous correspondence with Zdenka that he would be moving on to Vienna and when on 12 December 1879 Janáček applied to the Regional School Board in Brno for an extension of leave into the second semester, he gave as his aim finishing his musical studies in Leipzig.[6] It was only when things went sour in Leipzig that Janáček began to consider the advantages of transferring to Vienna for the second semester.

Leipzig was presumably suggested by Wickenhauser as a musical city much associated with the music she played, the city of Mendelssohn and the Schumanns. In 1879 it had over 200,000 inhabitants, comparable with Prague and over twice the size of Brno.[7] Unlike both Prague and Brno, however, it was essentially a Lutheran city, dominated by churches such as St Thomas's (the Thomaskirche), where J.S. Bach had been Kantor. Other important musical associations included the Gewandhaus Orchestra, music publishers such as Breitkopf & Härtel and C.F. Peters, and the piano manufacturer Blüthner. The Leipzig Royal Conservatory where Janáček would study had been founded by Mendelssohn in 1843. By the late 1870s it was considered somewhat conservative in outlook but it was nevertheless one of the foremost German music-teaching institutions of its day, attracting many foreign students: distinguished former alumni from abroad included Grieg, Svendsen and Sullivan.

The conservatory replied to Janáček's request on 17 September, acknowledging his application and the compositions he had enclosed.[8] The letter does not name them but presumably he wouldn't have sent any of his Czech settings, which would rule out the surviving thirteen male-voice choruses. He probably wouldn't have risked the Latin motets either, bound up as they were with the Cecilian movement. The most likely candidates would be the two pieces for strings, the Suite (VI/2) and the *Idyll* (VI/3), his most recent and most substantial compositions to date. These were also the two pieces that Janáček mentioned when asked by his piano teacher in Leipzig about his compositions.[9] The conservatory invited him to take the entrance examination on 2 October.[10]

On Tuesday 30 September Janáček left for Prague, where he had lunch with Zdenka's grandmother and they drank to Zdenka's health and to Janáček's future marriage with her. Janáček already had a date in mind – 5 November 1881 – an advance booking of more than two years that caused Mrs Kaluschka some mirth. At eight that evening, as she wrote to the Schulzes in Brno, Janáček would be setting off by train 'to his new future'.[11] He arrived in Leipzig the next day at 6.30 a.m.[12]

Janáček's studies in Prague are documented by his surviving course-work notebooks and by an album in which he wrote out neatly the pieces that he composed there; about his day-to-day life one knows next to nothing. The situation in Leipzig is the reverse: no album of pieces, few study notes, but instead a detailed list of the concerts he attended and in his letters to Zdenka Schulzová a virtually hour-by-hour account of his life and thoughts. Not until the final sixteen months of his life in his letters to Kamila Stösslová would there be such a continuously detailed account of his emotional ups and downs and of the trivia, triumphs and frustrations of his everyday life.

Janáček wrote to Zdenka no fewer than 124 letters from Leipzig in the 144 days between 1 October 1879 (the day of his arrival) and 23 February 1880.[13] This period was reduced to 116 days by a comparatively long Christmas break (11 December 1879 to 8 January 1880), which means that when in Leipzig Janáček wrote at least one letter a day to Zdenka. And even this is a misleading representation since many of the letters are in fact multiple letters (usually four a day), dated and timed, and sent together for reasons of convenience and economy. Janáček's letters to Zdenka amount to 170 printed pages* in Jakob Knaus's tightly packed, small-type German edition (IB, 1985) or 270 pages in the more spacious (but slightly abridged) Czech translation (DZ, 1968).

Soon after his arrival Janáček located the Gewandhaus and reported to the conservatory. Armed with a list of available accommodation, he took the first room he saw, at Plauenstrasse no. 1,[14] about ten minutes' walk from the conservatory. Jan Racek published a couple of photographs of this, the 'Haus zum goldenen Apfel' – a large corner house on several floors including the attic – with a forbiddingly gloomy ground-floor entrance. Incongruously, it shows a rather battered cherub perched above the door with one foot on a large globe, no doubt 'golden' at some stage but very grubby at the time of the photograph.[15] It was here that Janáček made his way up to his second-floor room, owned by a Mrs Meyer, to whom he paid 24 marks a month with service but without laundry[16] (for which he paid separately). Relations with Mrs Meyer seem to have been cordial though their meetings were infrequent: she is not much mentioned in Janáček's letters. During the very cold December she undertook to borrow a thicker eiderdown for him[17] and she helped him occasionally with getting his fire going.[18] She also insisted, when he found the local bread inedible, on buying Stollen for him, the German sweet loaf[19] filled with dried fruit and marzipan. It was only at the end of his stay when he was trying to get his trunk sent off in advance that the helpful and knowledgeable servant is mentioned.[20]

A week after he arrived he described his little nest to Zdenka:

I'm now sitting and writing with a rug on my lap. My apartment consists of one room, in which there stands my piano, a stove, a table and next to it

---

* 167 pages plus 3 pages in the appendix.

something like a divan; next to that there is a quiet corner for my bed, my trunk, now also a chest and two chairs. I've got enough light since the windows look out on to the street. But, as I feel, I will have to heat at least a bit in the early morning.[21]

By December it was very cold indeed:

In the early morning it's always so cold in my room that I can't even touch the water. These days I have been so cold in the night that I had to make use of my rug during the night and huddle under it in bed. It's the fault of these single windows; I feel a draught from the windows in the middle of the room.[22]

Janáček attributed the coldness to the local habit of single glazing.[23] (He was used to a system of double glazing in Moravia that preserved not only heat but also perishable foodstuffs stored between the two windows – Janáček needed to find a different solution for keeping his salami.)[24] He was already over-budget, having allowed only 20 marks a month for his accommodation. The piano he had hired for 15 marks 50 pf a month, but this also came to more than he reckoned since he had to pay for three months in advance as well as transport to and from the flat.[25]

Lighting was with paraffin lamps, another drain on his finances, since it was almost dark by four during the winter; occasionally he would run out of fuel and have to go to bed early.[26] As for food, Janáček took a lunch at the Norwegischer Hof[27] (and was delighted when he returned after Christmas to find a Czech restaurant that was cheaper, with soup, roast meat and cheese for 90 pf, having had to pay 1 mark 30 pf before).[28] For the other meals he coped as best he could, brewing black coffee in the morning on his stove.[29] After a while Mrs Schulzová took pity on him and sent him regular food parcels every ten days or so.[30]

Janáček's existence in Leipzig was lonely, largely through choice. When, for instance, the three Vorlíček sisters (two violinists and a cellist) from Prague descended on him, he did his best to ignore them. He went to their matinée concert at the Blüthner hall on 15 February under protest,[31] and left the celebratory drinks party that evening in almost indecent haste.[32] He made no friends in Leipzig and it is only rarely that any fellow students are mentioned. In October, for instance, he sat between two students at Gewandhaus rehearsals: a 'Jew from Sweden', who wanted to play piano duets with him; and a certain

Bärman, who had previously studied in conservatories in Strasbourg and Berlin.[33] But by mid-November both had disappeared or had seats elsewhere.[34] It was almost unheard of that Janáček would go for a drink with anyone. One rare occasion was on 18 January when he had mistaken the time of a concert and found the Gewandhaus closed and dark. Cross at his mistake he allowed himself to be hauled off by a fellow student for a beer at the pub Feuerkugel, allegedly the haunt of Lessing and Goethe. There he and his companion chanced upon 'one of the best violinists, Bach by name, American by birth' and Janáček was delighted to learn that the American knew several sentences in Czech from his violin teacher, one of the many expatriate Czechs in American orchestras. 'I remained sitting there for an hour',[35] Janáček recalled, which he no doubt thought was a long time.

It's not surprising that Janáček didn't make friends. He was older than many of the students around him, a foreigner isolated in his strange world, and not clubbable by nature. He was also tremendously competitive and must have irritated many of his peers with his earnest, hard work, and his frustration at their slow rate of progress. Towards the end of his time he bumped into a second-year student at the Riedel Society Concert.[36] Asking what his group was studying with Grill (see below), Janáček was astounded to learn that they were only a little ahead of his first-year group, forced by his impatience to go much faster than normal. As he wrote to Zdenka in October 1879: 'I see how my colleagues find time for useless walking around with the obligatory cigar [. . .] I'm beginning to acquire respect among the students, which is naturally enhanced to a certain extent by my name as it's written and heard (Leoš etc.)'[37] (see chap. 14).

Janáček filled what little spare time he allowed himself with reading and going for walks. He had brought his copy of Zimmermann's *Zur Geschichte der Aesthetik* with him but seems not to have made much headway: he was probably too tired in the evening for such concentrated material and referred to it only once, near the beginning of his time in Leipzig.[38] He had also taken some lighter reading with him and by 23 November 1879 he was already on his last book; after Christmas he would return with a 'new supply'.[39] One knows about one item from this batch since between 17 and 22 January he made several references to it. The book was Bulwer Lytton's *A Strange Story*, the English novelist's tall tale of murder, magic and the occult. Janáček presumably read it in German (a cast-off from

Mrs Schulzová?)[†] since no Czech edition existed. He began it on 17 January.[40] The next day he read it for an hour after lunch but couldn't carry on because he found it 'excited' him too much.[41] By 19 January he had put it down altogether: 'It's impossible for me to get to the end on my own, it's so terribly disturbing – I won't go further than the first murder'[42] (of which the narrator-hero is wrongly accused). However, as he reported a few days later, he had looked ahead and realized that it was going to come right after all (the hero is released with apologies). Relieved, he went on reading it 'more peacefully but only in quite small doses so as to be able to control myself'. The problem, he wrote, was: 'I live through this sort of novel and share all "his" [i.e. the hero's] suffering, pain and therefore I can't read anything else.'[43] A few weeks later he reported that he had not been able to read anything at all: he had been too caught up in the fates of the main characters and as a result had become overwrought himself.[44] This is the first indication of Janáček's passionate identification with fictional characters, a trait that would be invaluable when he turned to writing operas seven years later.

One of Janáček's favourite walks was to the train station – this because he could imagine he was on his way home.[45] Occasionally he undertook something longer, such as the 'grand promenade' lasting an hour and a half, which took him twice round the inner city.[46] Judging from the map that Janáček drew for Zdenka, this route (beginning from his room) took in clockwise the theatre, the market place, the museum, the university, Pleissenburg (with its larger detached houses), St Thomas's church and the Bach memorial, a circle enclosing the old town with the conservatory almost at its heart.[47] By January 1880 his walks were taken in company – with Zdenka.[48] This little conceit caused some puzzlement at the other end and an explanation was demanded: 'What am I doing when I go for a walk with "you"? Well nothing around me exists: I hear nothing, I see nothing, but simply speak in spirit only with you.'[49] The 'silent presence' trope was something that Janáček would rediscover and greatly exploit in his relationship with Kamila Stösslová.

In Leipzig Janáček's walks never seem to have taken him out of the city. Engrossed in his own thoughts, he seldom seemed to notice his

---

[†] Mrs Schulzová appears to have read things first: 'If Mama [Mrs Schulzová] says that the new novel isn't so exciting then I'll read it' (LJ to ZS, 25 Jan 1880, *IB*, 148–9).

surroundings. Late one Sunday afternoon, however, after a snowfall, he wrote:

I've just come from a walk – how everything is alive and bustling! Everywhere on sledges, large and small. And the children of the whole town are all out, as if by agreement. The coachmen have such enormously long whips like shepherds have in our country and whip them so that it resonates. [. . .] My fingers are completely frozen, thus these scrawls. People look at me in my white winter trousers as if I'd fallen from the heavens – I'm the only 'white one'.[50]

Janáček's winter gear was certainly striking. There was, for instance, the 'long kaftan'[51] that he mentions wearing in mid-November, when the snow was falling. Was this worn in combination with the 'white winter trousers'? Janáček himself was entertained enough by his own appearance to write to Zdenka: 'Your father's large scarf around my neck serves me as a pretty collar, and if I hadn't got hair on my head I'd peep out from my nest like a condor.'[52]

Studying in Leipzig turned out to be a very different experience from Prague. Janáček was now five years older and in the intervening years had gathered considerable professional expertise. He had occupied a regular teaching post at the Teachers' Institute for two years and was much better off than he had been in Prague. His annual salary of 1280 zl yielded 106.66 zl a month, some of which went to support his mother and other obligations; when doing his sums in February 1880 (contemplating the move to Vienna), he reckoned that if he paid 35 zl a month for fees he would have only 35 for everything else.[53] This means his clear total each month was 70 zl, or 140 German marks. Two weeks after his arrival in Leipzig he had a fair idea of his outgoings to be able to draw up a budget:

Table 15.1: Janáček's Leipzig budget

	Janáček's estimates (marks)	monthly total in marks
lunch	1.50 to 1.55 per day	46.50
supper	0.75 to 0.80 per day	24.00
breakfast	2.0 for 2 weeks	5.00
laundry	1.14 per week	5.13
coal and wood	3.0 for 2 weeks	7.50
room	per month	24.00
piano	per month	16.50
total for month		128.63 marks

With only 140 marks at his disposal, this was very tight if he wanted to come out on his salary and this sum did not include incidental expenses such as paraffin (for lighting), paper, stamps, sheet music, concert tickets and above all his conservatory fees. The first quarterly instalment of the fees (100 marks up to Christmas)[54] was perhaps paid out of money he had saved up or the '20 ducats' that Zdenka gave him on his departure.[55] However when Mrs Schulzová's food parcels began arriving he could save on suppers. And while he reckoned that his room was expensive compared with those advertised in newspapers, he appreciated that it was very quiet, that he was left alone and that his room was cleaned when he was out. But the next semester he thought he would hire a cheaper piano.[56]

By 5 November he seemed to be coping: after paying the monthly charges he had 70 marks left, from which lunches would take up 45 marks and suppers 15 (Mrs Schulzová's food parcels had indeed helped); that left 10 marks for laundry, music 'and other trifles'. From the occasional comment to Zdenka one can infer that Schulz was drawing Janáček's monthly salary for him and sending it on to him.[57] Although money continued to be a worry, the fact that he could draw up such budgets and pay for a room, its heating and regular meals was a vast improvement on how he had had to live in Prague.

One of the most striking differences between Prague and Leipzig for Janáček was that he was now able to take full advantage of the concert life around him. Many concerts came free by virtue of his being a student at the Leipzig Conservatory. In his time the conservatory was still housed in a courtyard of the Gewandhaus building[58] and conservatory students had free admission to the rehearsals and orchestral concerts (mostly on Wednesdays) at the Gewandhaus, one of the most celebrated concert venues in Europe. At 1.30 on Saturday afternoons there were 'motet' concerts (sacred choral music and organ solos) at St Thomas's. Then there were regular 'solo' concerts given by the students at the conservatory on Fridays from six to eight. Janáček described them as 'musical soirées, held every Friday and where outside people can also attend',[59] a useful way of providing students with performing experience in public. Janáček went to virtually all of these concerts, skipping only 31 October, when he was desperately trying to finish his Romance (x/8 no. 2), and the last two in February 1880, when he had clearly had enough and was running out of time to finish more important work. He was also well enough off now to buy tickets for a few other concerts promoted by commercial agencies, the Riedel Society, the Euterpe Society and the matinée concerts arranged by Blüthner. These cost him between 2½ and 4 marks a time and the expense was usually noted down.

Janáček took his concert-going very seriously in Leipzig. There is hardly a week when he did not attend three concerts, sometimes more. He kept all his programmes, many of them annotated, and wrote up a list in his 'Diary of Musical Leipzig', the first of his seventy-one notebooks (of which more in later chapters). The most detailed record of his concert-going in any period of his life, the Leipzig Diary is a small pocket notebook, bound in light-brown leather, with rough pencil workings at the back and neat ink-written entries at the front. The first thirty-six pages provide a list of the concerts he had attended, to 17 February 1880, a week before his departure. Janáček listed each concert with its date and programme and added occasional comments. Each event is numbered, sixty-two in total, which is about right allowing for Janáček's occasional lapses in leaving out the odd number or duplicating others. The notebook is amplified by his comments on some of the concerts in his letters to Zdenka, and by the annotated programmes, which Janáček carefully retained.[‡]

At the motet concerts at St Thomas's Janáček heard organ music and choral music ranging from Palestrina, Lotti and Alessandro Scarlatti to nineteenth-century works, often by composers associated with the Leipzig Conservatory such as Mendelssohn, Moritz Hauptmann, Salomon Jadassohn and Janáček's organ teacher Wilhelm Rust. As an experienced choral conductor, Janáček had strong opinions on some of the performances. On his second visit to St Thomas's (11 October 1879) he felt that the eight-voice *Hilf mir Gott* by the little-known H. Kotzholt was too difficult for the choir, and together with Rheinberger's six-voice *Bleib' bei mir* was not sung with the same precision as the pieces the previous week. The next week the motet (Christian Theodor Weinlig's *Der Chaos in Dunkel der Nacht*) went better, but Rust made a real botch of Bach's organ prelude *Gottes Sohn ist*

[‡] See, for instance, the list Helfert prints in *LJPT*, 134–9. The information that follows is drawn from this (which incorporates programme annotations) and Janáček's list in his notebook BmJA, Z1. Comments in his letters to Zdenka are footnoted separately.

kommen BWV 703. The fact that Janáček was able to offer an opinion on the performance of an eight-part Palestrina Sanctus and Agnus Dei ('not well understood or performed') at the concert on 25 October 1879 is a credit to what he picked up of this repertory from Skuherský; it is nevertheless curious to come across his admiration (24 January 1880) for a fifteenth-century *Alta Trinità beata* ('very effective'). Sometimes he offered robust opinions on the works themselves: an eight-voice setting of Psalm cxiv by Ernst Friedrich Richter (a teacher at the Leipzig Conservatory better known as a theorist than as a composer) had, Janáček declared, a 'rather scholastic' canon in the middle (25 October 1879); the motet *Wie lieblich sind Deine Wohnungen* by Moritz Hauptmann (8 November 1879) was 'nothing but third progressions'.

In addition to the motet concerts Janáček attended a couple of more ambitious concerts given in St Thomas's by the Riedel Society. He was drawn by the unusual repertory of the concert on 1 February 1880, which included pieces by Josquin, David Perez (*Tenebrae factae sunt* for four voices – 'very nice') and his sole and disappointing encounter with Schütz (a couple of the *Psalmen Davids* – 'oldfashioned'). An earlier concert, 21 November, which included Bach's *Actus tragicus*, sparked off Janáček's anger at a Mass setting by Albert Becker that was, he proclaimed, a bad copy of Beethoven's *Missa solemnis*:

I know Beethoven's Mass by heart and followed the performance of Becker's Mass movement by movement: I always knew in advance what would be coming – and I was never wrong. Only the Credo was more independent – to its detriment [–] because had it also resembled it it would have been better! It's a mystery to me how the local critics can rank this absurdity so highly, for it was at their request that this pasquinade was repeated today.[60]

Most of the pieces played at the conservatory soirées were solo instrumental and chamber music, but concertos were also included, presumably with piano accompaniment. The repertory was unadventurous: mostly Haydn, Mozart and Beethoven through to Mendelssohn, Spohr and Schumann. On the whole Janáček had little to say about the music, apart from finding 'Mozart's Concerto for Violin and Viola in E flat' (presumably the *Sinfonia concertante* K364/320d) 'effective and difficult', Moscheles's Piano Concerto no. 3 in G minor op. 60 'oldfashioned' and Spohr's Violin Concerto no. 8 'in modo di scena cantante' 'very skilful'. At the first soirée he attended (10 October

1879) he felt discouraged that the instrumentalists, performing pieces in which he himself had taken part, did so more 'imposingly' and he wanted to rush away. However, as he consoled himself, these were final-year students who had been at the conservatory for three years, and he had only just begun.[61]

With few exceptions, performers interested him less than the music performed. Conductors were seldom mentioned – unless Carl Reinecke (1824–1910), the long-term Gewandhaus conductor, was not at the podium. When he was ill once and replaced by Arthur Nikisch, then second conductor at the Leipzig opera, Janáček wrote disparagingly:

I've just come from the Gewandhaus rehearsal. Reinecke is sick and it was taken by the first [*recte* second] conductor from the theatre. I studied the contrast between the two and I was very struck by Reinecke's thoroughness. The orchestra also immediately sensed the weaknesses of the conductor and just played through everything. The chorus was as wretched as ever.[62]

After the performance that evening Janáček softened his view and grudgingly characterized Nikisch (a year younger than him and soon to become one of the great conductors of his day) as 'quite good'. Although Janáček had intended to get to the orchestral concerts given by the Euterpe Society (the chief rival of the Gewandhaus)[63] he did so only once, at the very end of his stay. On that occasion he was able to compare Wilhelm Treiber's interpretation of Beethoven's 'Eroica' with Reinecke's: 'Treiber conducts well enough but judging according to the performance he hadn't rehearsed nearly so well. [. . .] [At the Gewandhaus] it was splendid.'[64]

Grieg's performance of his Piano Concerto on 29 October 1879 passed by without comment apart from his jotting down a theme; the celebrated pianist Vladimir de Pachmann got an honourable mention in the Reinecke Piano Concerto in G minor on 3 December 1879 ('played well'). Partly because he was able to compare her favourably with the now demonized Wickenhauser, Clara Schumann, performing Beethoven's Piano Concerto no. 4 on 12 November 1879, drew a more detailed comment. 'Her outward appearance', Janáček wrote to Zdenka, 'is respectable both in her hairstyle and in her clothes, nothing of the crazy or the diabolical aspects of a W[ickenhauser]. She played Beethoven's Concerto in G major with a lightness and correctness that's possible only when one has been giving concerts for fifty-one years already.'[65] (Clara was then sixty and had indeed made her début at the Gewandhaus at the age of nine.)

Janáček's unbridled admiration was reserved for Anton Rubinstein. He was already well acquainted with some of his music from his and Wickenhauser's chamber concert series; together with a Bach prelude he had played an étude by Rubinstein at his audition at the conservatory.[66] When Rubinstein turned up at a Gewandhaus rehearsal on 15 October 1879 (on his way to Hamburg for a production of his opera *Feramors*) Janáček could hardly contain his excitement:

But the most interesting thing for me was the presence of Rubinstein. From the beginning he sat in one of the last rows and listened very attentively; I observed him the whole time – during the piano concerto he was restless; I didn't like the concerto either, too little strength and energy [Dr Otto Neitzel from Strasbourg playing Beethoven's Piano Concerto no. 5 with a 'weak touch'].[67] After that he walked through the hall to the orchestra and then the applause rose up like a storm. He's a big man, with long dark hair, no beard, powerful features – if I knew more already – how I would have run up to him![68]

Had Janáček done so he could have told Rubinstein about the registered letter sent in 1878 asking to study with him: this had chased the Russian from Paris to Petersburg and came back unopened.[69] On 19 November, a month after this first glimpse, Janáček heard Rubinstein play a solo recital on which he splashed out a whole 4 marks (he had left buying his ticket to the last moment and the gallery at 3 marks was already full). That evening, at the late hour of 11.15, Janáček gave vent to his feelings in his letter to Zdenka:

Should I tell you about Rub[instein]? I've not heard a greater artist! Not enormous technique, anyone can learn that, but his conception and rendition of compositions – that's the real artist in him. He played at least twenty-five pieces,§ among them great works, naturally by heart. But in my opinion he played his own works [a fugue to open the concert, a galop to end it] the least beautifully – his soul rushes ahead of his body. His *pp* is wonderfully beautiful, his *fpp* long-lasting. He played solo from seven to 9.45 – and the fact that it didn't tire one is the mark of good playing. I'll hear him once again on Sunday at the chamber concert.[70]

The chamber concert was in fact on Friday 22 November and was devoted entirely to Rubinstein's own works: two quintets (for piano

§ *recte* fourteen, a programme ranging from Mozart's C minor Fantasia K475 to Schumann's Fantasy, with a large group of Chopin in between.

and wind in F major op. 55 and for piano and strings in G minor
op. 99), in which Rubinstein himself played the piano, and a string
quartet (C minor op. 17 no. 2). Janáček again had to pay for a ticket (as
he grumbled to Zdenka the day before)[71] but the concert seems to have
paid for itself many times over:

Yes, to be a great artist is beautiful! How I felt today at the concert! When I
hear Rubinstein's compositions I feel extraordinary: my spirit truly melts, it
takes wing, becomes free and, at the moment when I listen to it, paints free
pictures for itself. I like his compositions so much that it seems to me that some
day I should become his heir. This verve, this speaking 'to the soul' I find
nowhere else but in his compositions. It is so natural, uncontrived, he reveals
himself just as he is, how he feels, he doesn't go after any musical doctrines, he
seizes my innermost depths. And how far I am from his standpoint: I feel the
sorry state of my present work – I know that I'm cladding myself with an iron
cloak [of technique] – how long will I have to fight to rid myself again of these
constraints! But I'm told: it's necessary – and with the thought that it won't
last long I obey. But I long for the time when I could write freely, free of all
these conventions. [. . .] At the end of the concert I felt how I would have to
weep – but why did this, the very happiest moment, pass so quickly?[72]

This hero worship of another composer is without parallel in
Janáček. No doubt he was expressing himself without constraint in this
letter to Zdenka, written at 9.30 straight after the concert. In later life
his approving comments, for example about Dvořák or Tchaikovsky,
were written for public consumption when he was a bit older and more
circumspect. It is wonderful to catch him off guard like this, and one
can only marvel that such conventional if well-wrought music spoke to
him in this way. Most of it was in fact a quarter of a century old by then
– only the Piano Quintet op. 99, which Janáček knew from performing
it in Brno, was more recent. This fascinating letter also shows how
aware Janáček was of the restrictions of the training that he was undergoing and how he would need to break free when he had learnt his
craft. It remains very odd, however, that at the age of twenty-five the
epitome of compositional freedom for him was Anton Rubinstein.
When the butterfly finally emerged from its chrysalis it was to be a
very different composer from the one who had captured his soul on
22 November 1879.

Although Skuherský had declared that Janáček had a 'comprehensive
knowledge of musical literature', this statement was hardly true. From

the Augustinian monastery in Brno and from the Prague Organ School Janáček knew a fair amount of the sacred choral music repertory. From his own chamber concerts and to some extent from the Brno Beseda concerts, he knew some chamber music though what knowledge he had was patchy: it is clear, for instance, from his comments to Zdenka about the cycle of Beethoven violin sonatas given in Leipzig in January 1880 that he knew only two of the ten. As far as orchestral music was concerned, he was hearing much of the standard repertory for the first time.

Janáček's annotations for Beethoven's 'Eroica' Symphony (a rehearsal conducted by Reinecke at the Gewandhaus) suggest some acquaintance with the work ('Adagio not very nice, third horn weak, otherwise excellent'), as does his description of the 'Pastoral' Symphony, where he explains its programmatic aspects perhaps for Zdenka's edification.[73] However what he wrote about Beethoven's Eighth Symphony might well signal his first encounter with this Cinderella work: he noted the orchestral forces and that the first violin part was difficult, an observation supported by several incipits of tricky moments. The Beethoven piece that made the greatest impression on him, shortly before his departure, was the late String Quartet in C sharp minor op. 131:

Today there was again a concert which gripped me right to my soul. They played a string quartet by Beethoven, one of his last works where he didn't care at all any more whether people would like it, and instead expressed his innermost life in music. [. . .] Would that there were a little bit of that great soul in me too, I thought as I listened to it![74]

Expressing his 'innermost life in music' in a string quartet is what Janáček found himself doing in the last year of his life, an unexpected development for someone who after his studies virtually renounced chamber music.

All of the Brahms pieces that Janáček heard in Leipzig were apparently new to him. These included the First Symphony, where he observed that the Adagio was 'a little long', that there was a 'Slavonic motif' in the Andante, that the final movement was 'brilliant' but the general impression 'uncaptivating'. For the Haydn Variations Janáček noted the forces, and for other works he offered opinions: the opening movement and the scherzo of the String Sextet in G op. 36 (given at the fifth of a series of professional chamber concerts) were 'very splendid' but the *Schicksalslied* 'not good'. Although the Piano Quintet in F minor op. 34 had been played twice at the Janáček–Wickenhauser chamber series in Brno and Janáček had written an analytical article about the work (xv/17), Brahms seems to have been mostly terra incognita until now. When Wenzel commented that Janáček's Theme and Variations for piano (viii/6) reminded him of Brahms's *Handel Variations*, Janáček was flattered but had to confess to Zdenka that he had never 'seen' the music for the latter.[75]

With Schumann Janáček was much taken by his overture to *Genoveva* ('splendid'), quite liked his *Overture, Scherzo and Finale* ('very nice, finale less effective, Scherzo difficult to conduct, it didn't go well') and heard two symphonies, again probably for the first time. The Symphony in B flat (no. 1) passed by without comment but for that in D minor (no. 4) he noted the forces and his remarks indicate that the music was new to him: 'second movement original. The movements flow into the whole. Difficult.' Apart from a few songs Janáček heard little Schubert in Leipzig, but the 'Great' C major Symphony he characterized as 'very nice'.

Leipzig was a Mendelssohn city and Janáček encountered his music at all venues, including an all-Mendelssohn commemorative concert at the conservatory on 4 November, the thirty-second anniversary of his death. Janáček already knew Mendelssohn's music reasonably well from Wickenhauser and in Leipzig he came across several pieces (e.g. the Piano Trio in C minor) that he had performed himself. But other works were new to him, perhaps the *Hebrides* Overture and certainly the 'Scottish' Symphony in A minor. He commented on the keys of the first two movements, both 'excellent', and on the form of the final one. Although he remarked in a letter to Zdenka that it was one of the pieces that he was planning to perform in Brno and that he was hearing it 'again',[76] his acquaintance with Mendelssohn's overture to *Midsummer Night's Dream* seems to have been limited: he noted that only two horns and a tuba were needed. Was this all the brass that was used, or was Janáček unaware that the famous low notes were originally written for the ophicleide and that there were also two trumpets? Some of Mendelssohn's choral pieces that Janáček heard in Leipzig recommended themselves for future performance at the Beseda concerts, for example his setting of Psalm cxiv – 'effective and not hard; without soloists (chorus sang scandalously)'.

As a whole the Gewandhaus repertory was limited to Austrian and German Romantic music (stopping short of Liszt and Wagner). There was little that was earlier: just one Haydn symphony was performed (no. 99 in E flat)[||] and only two Mozart symphonies, the 'Jupiter' and no. 40 in G minor, both perhaps firsts for Janáček. In the 'Jupiter' he jotted down the numbers of wind and brass needed and commented on the difficulties of the fugal finale for the string instruments; in no. 40 he was much taken by the 'splendid [. . .] scherzo' (as he described the spirited cross-rhythm minuet). Little non-German music was played while Janáček was in Leipzig: apart from that by Rubinstein, there was no Russian music (let alone any Czech) and no French music, though England was represented by a piano concerto by Sterndale Bennett (Janáček solemnly noted from the programme that Schumann thought highly of Bennett). There were the occasional novelties. Janáček dismissed a symphony by August Reissmann given on 14 January (in the same concert as the Bennett) as 'formally correct, but without élan or originality'. Two new works attracted more extensive comments. 'I didn't approve of the first and last movements', he wrote to Zdenka about the *Ländliche Hochzeit* Symphony on 26 November, reckoning that Goldmark was overrated: 'They make too much noise about this composer.'[77] Quite what Janáček took exception to in the theme-and-variations first movement and conventional finale of this agreeable if slight work is hard to fathom; so are Janáček's thoughts about it in his Leipzig Diary, where he regarded it as being in four movements (rather than in five). The second new work, published only that year, was Max Bruch's *Das Lied von der Glocke*. Janáček heard this large-scale choral work both at rehearsal and at the concert that evening (5 November 1879) and covered his copy of the libretto with annotations about keys, rhythms, orchestral interludes and adding brief comments such as 'good', 'not good', 'shameful work', 'thematic'.[78] Once he got back from the rehearsal at noon he fulminated to Zdenka about it:

They are giving the 'highly regarded' work *Das Lied von der Glocke* (Schiller) set to music by Max Bruch. The work fills the whole evening but I didn't particularly like it: the composer belongs to the northern, grumpy style; he doesn't go in for free, fresh fantasy; the fugal places are good, but where his genius ought to show itself and count, for instance in the paragraph [Janáček

[||]Janáček gave it as 'no. 3 in E flat', presumably using the common Breitkopf & Härtel numbering.

quotes a section about the storm], the material overwhelms the composer, who whimpers and swims around without aim, without strength – noise without rules. I've already heard the odd thing from Bruch[¶] but it's all the same. But I'm glad that I've heard this, his greatest work.[79]

In later years Janáček would keep the programmes of concerts and operas that he attended and often annotated them but he gave up listing them systematically as he did in his Leipzig Diary. At his initial interview at the conservatory Janáček had been asked 'What do you really want from us?'; besides his ambitions as a pianist and organist, he said that he wanted to hear 'lots'.[80] The notebook thus provided an *aide-mémoire* of what he heard. There was also another motive: many of his annotations on the orchestral music performed refer to the forces (i.e. the number of wind and brass instruments needed) and the level of difficulty. Janáček was looking out for music that could be performed with his forces at the Brno Beseda.

What is striking in this flurry of concert attendance is that the future opera composer did not once visit the opera. The Neues Stadttheater, with Angelo Neumann as director, was undergoing a Wagnerian phase at the time and one might have expected Janáček to show some curiosity. Although his budget wouldn't have stretched to many visits, standing room in opera houses could often be very cheap and Janáček did manage to afford the ticket price for a few special concerts. One concludes that opera was simply not part of his musical world at the time.

Another major difference from Prague was the much larger and more varied institution in which Janáček was studying. Whereas in Prague Skuherský was almost his only teacher, in Leipzig there were many more. His timetable, according to what he wrote on the hard yellow wrappers in his notebook, is given in table 15.1.

Of these classes some mattered to Janáček more than others. The four-to-six slot on Mondays to Thursdays seems to have been voluntary: certainly Janáček makes no reference to attending. He gave up 'singing' almost at once, concluding within two weeks that he knew more than Messrs Reinecke and Klesse about choir practice and would

---

[¶]For instance the Violin Concerto in G minor, which he conducted at a Brno Beseda concert on 24 April 1879.

Table 15.2: Janáček's timetable in Leipzig 1879-80

Monday	9-10 (composition Mr Grill)
	3-4 (harmony Dr Paul)
	4-6 (score-reading, quartet, orchestra, conducting Mr Schradiek)
	6-7 (singing Mr Klesse)
Tuesday	3-4 (organ Dr Rust)
	4-5 (piano Dr Paul)
	4-6 (solo playing Mr Hermann)**
	6-7 (singing Mr Klesse)
Wednesday	12-1 (aesthetics Dr Paul)
	3-4 (piano Mr Wenzel)
	4-6 (solo playing Mr Reinecke)
	6-7 (singing Mr Reinecke)
Thursday	9-10 (composition Mr Grill)
	3-4 (harmony Dr Paul)
	4-6 (solo playing Mr Schradiek)
Friday	3-4 (organ Dr Rust)
	4-5 (piano Dr Paul)
	6-8 (general solo playing) [i.e. soirée]
Saturday	12-1 (aesthetics Dr Paul)
	3-4 (piano Mr Wenzel)
	4-6 (solo playing Mr Schröder)

gain nothing by going to their classes.[81] He relented only twice more, the last time on 14 January to curry favour with Reinecke to get into his orchestration classes[82] (the ploy seems not to have worked). Although aesthetics with Dr Paul would have sounded promising for Janáček with his burgeoning interest in the field, the only mention of the subject is his announcement on 16 October that he had to go to the university and enrol for it along with the history of music.[83] Presumably these are the 'lectures' mentioned on his report signed off on 12 December,[84] but Dr Paul's bland comment 'attends and shows a lively interest in the matter' need not be taken too seriously (see below). The core subjects, which, at least in the beginning, he attended assiduously were composition (with Grill), harmony (with Paul), organ (with Rust), piano (with Paul) and more piano (with Wenzel).

Organ was the first casualty. When Zdenka asked why he mentioned it so seldom in his letters he told her that there were no organs

---

** There was an overlap with his piano lesson with Dr Paul; Janáček mentions Hermann only once more in his letters and so disparagingly (LJ to ZS, 27-8 Nov 1880, *IB*, 106-7) that he clearly chose to go to Paul.

to practise on. He had been better off, he wrote, at the Organ School in Prague.[85] All that was offered for practising was a grand piano kitted out with pedals and stuck in an unheated wooden hut (Janáček had to practise with his greatcoat on),[86] and even this primitive venue was often occupied by another student.[87] A promising organist in Brno and Prague, Janáček had virtually abandoned the instrument by the time he left Leipzig although he got on well enough with the teacher: Wilhelm Rust (1822–92) was the chief editor of the critical edition of Bach's works between 1858 and 1881, the organist at St Thomas's from 1878 and Kantor of the Thomasschule from 1880. The last time that Janáček mentioned an organ lesson was on 23 January 1880 (a month before he left), when he commented to Zdenka that Rust had been half an hour late.[88] Perhaps that was the last straw.

He had better luck with the piano. He could practise in his room (he hired a piano on his first day), and he had two teachers to satisfy. At least in the beginning he worked hard at it; practising the piano is frequently mentioned in his letters. One of his teachers was the elderly Ernst Ferdinand Wenzel (1808–80), at seventy-one the oldest member of staff and himself a pupil of Friedrich Wieck, the father of Clara Schumann. Specializing in technique, Wenzel had taught the piano at the conservatory since its opening in 1843,[89] and Janáček particularly enjoyed Wenzel's reminiscences of famous Leipzig musicians he had known including Mendelssohn, Moscheles and Schumann.[90] Janáček's first lesson was disappointing. He had been playing all the wrong pieces, he was told, much too difficult for him, and was promptly put on remedial studies: Clementi's *Gradus ad Parnassum*, Cramer's *Etudes*, Moscheles's studies and Bach's *Inventions*.[91] Janáček set to, if somewhat grudgingly, and seemed genuinely concerned when Wenzel fell ill a few days before the Christmas break.[92] Wenzel kept Janáček working at the studies: on 14 January Janáček reported to Zdenka that he had at last finished with Clementi and had moved on to Cramer.[93] It was only when Janáček played three of his own fugues publicly on 14 February 1880 that Wenzel took real notice of him, seemingly offended that Janáček had never mentioned that he was also a composer.[94] Wenzel insisted on hearing the Theme and Variations (VIII/6), which Janáček was still working on at the time, and was most complimentary about the piece. By then, however, Janáček was on the point of leaving Leipzig. The fact that Wenzel then enquired whether some sort of financial support would keep him there longer[95] suggests a real regret at his precipitate departure.

Janáček also had twice-weekly piano lessons from the versatile Dr Oscar Paul (1836–98), one of the stars both of the conservatory staff (where he had taught from 1869) and at Leipzig University (where in 1872 he was appointed associate professor). Paul had studied at Leipzig University, taking his doctorate in 1860 under Moritz Hauptmann. He was now forty-three, a rising scholar whose books included the first German translation of Boethius's *De institute musica*, a study of the harmony of the Greeks, and a history of the piano. His harmony manual was published in 1880 and an English translation appeared in 1885. He had also studied the piano at the Leipzig Conservatory under Louis Plaidy and had considered a career as a pianist.[96] Paul had made flattering remarks about Janáček at his audition.[97] A few days later Janáček summed up for Zdenka what he thought of his piano teachers:

Dr Paul continually appears to be the brightest among them all: he is the opposite of Mr Wenzel, as he told me himself. With Dr Paul I'm playing these pieces:

1. *Die Schule des Virtuosen* by Czerny
2. [Louis] Plaidy: *Technische Übungen*
3. *Das wohltemperirte Clavier* by Bach
4. [Beethoven:] C minor Sonata for piano and violin [op. 30/2]
5. Nocturne in B major by Chopin [op. 32][98]

According to Paul, Janáček should practise for five hours a day, spending half an hour each on Plaidy, Czerny and Bach, a further half hour on Beethoven and Chopin together, a whole hour on Clementi (for Wenzel), and the remaining two hours on the organ.[99]

Later Paul added a Chopin Waltz in A flat[100] and Hummel's Piano Concerto in A minor op. 85[101] to the stock of pieces to be practised, but by January he had decided that the Hummel was 'too easy' and that Janáček should instead embark on Beethoven's 'Emperor' Concerto. Janáček was not averse ('Beethoven's most beautiful') but funds were low for buying more music and he would wait a bit.[102] However Janáček's attitude towards Paul was beginning to change. Two weeks later, on 3 February, he reported the following incident to Zdenka:

I practise as long and with as much dedication as a teacher can only dream of; now I come to the class (to Paul, piano) – he is completely out of sorts and at the same time rude to a female student who made many mistakes ('You with your stupid head!', he addressed her in front of everyone). Then it was my turn; I played one piece, he said nothing; I didn't even play the other piece I'd practised because I saw that he was exhausted and wasn't taking anything in. As I went off I asked him jokingly what I should be practising further; he mentioned Chopin's Ballade in A flat major. Today I had to smile to myself, otherwise it would have infuriated me.

Janáček went on to explain to Zdenka how he had been set the Hummel Piano Concerto (but felt he ought to be mastering technique first), then Beethoven's 'Emperor' (for which he felt he was not ready). And now Paul had clearly forgotten about both of these suggestions.[103] Later grumbles concerned the Chopin waltz, which Janáček had been practising in 'slow tempo' at Christmas:

Paul keeps saying: 'Just quicker!' And yet many melodic passages don't tell at the speed he wants. If the waltz were played like that it would be terrible to listen to. He doesn't demonstrate it because he can't do anything and I won't come forward now with my conception.[104]

With composition, his chief preoccupation in Leipzig, Janáček got off to a bad start. While waiting for classes to begin he wrote a piano sonata (x/5) and wanted to present it to his composition teacher Leo Grill. But this was not the way things were done. Grill said that he had no time to look at it either in class or out of class,[105] and the sonata was quietly abandoned.

At thirty-three Leo Grill (1846–1919) was ten years younger than Dr Paul though much more of a pedant. He led an unobtrusive life at the conservatory, teaching from 1871 until his retirement in 1907 at the age of seventy-one.[106] Although Janáček took what was called 'composition' with Grill, what he got instead was essentially musical form taught in the method familiar from Skuherský.†† In class Grill would describe a particular form and analyse a few examples of it; in the next class he would correct the students' attempts to imitate that form and go on to the next only once he felt that the class had understood everything. With Grill 'composition' started with the construction of short musical periods, described as 'songs'.[107] These were

---

†† The method described is not far removed from H.C. Koch's *Anleitung zur Composition*. It is surprising that purely Classical training of this kind, based on Haydn and Mozart, was still on offer almost a century later, and that it appealed so much to Janáček (I am grateful to Geoff Chew for this observation).

then built up into two-, three- and four-section pieces with the addition of contrasting middle sections and other links.[108] Once these basic principles were absorbed the class went on to simple ABA forms (such as minuets and marches), and then rondos of increasing complexity (four types were specified), culminating in sonata form. Janáček found this very frustrating. Within his first month he was told off for being too ambitious with 'long forms' rather than the 'short motifs' that Grill wanted,[109] and was mortified to hear that he had 'no feeling for rhythm'.[110] When that same month Paul enquired about his composition, Janáček complained that things were going too slowly since Grill wouldn't move on until everyone in the group understood the material. Paul suggested that he transfer: 'So I will at last be able to work according to my capabilities.' If he worked as Grill thought best, Janáček confided to Zdenka, he would 'remain a real musical dumpling', knowing only the rules.[111]

However things had already begun to change. Three days earlier, on 20 October, Janáček had succeeded in pleasing Grill[112] and by the end of the month he had come to the conclusion that having a 'pedant' (Grill) as well as a 'libertarian' (Paul) was a good combination.[113] Soon he got to the stage where Grill had no corrections and allowed Janáček to proceed on his own, while the others in the group had to keep repeating their assignments.[114] When Janáček thought again about dropping Grill's classes he decided to stay.[115] No doubt he was flattered by Grill's change of attitude towards him:

Today I had to laugh to myself at how Grill had to content himself with giving a special lecture only for me because the others are worlds apart from me. And he did so with such enthusiasm as I've never detected in him before. It was about minuets, polonaises etc. He also invited me to sit next to him during his examples so that I could see the music and he was highly delighted when I analysed some really interesting pieces by Beethoven for him.

How times have changed![116]

By early December he was even skipping Paul's classes so that he could do more for Grill: 'Today I excused myself from Paul in order to have the afternoon free since I did lots of work for Grill in the morning. Those long faces of my fellow students when Grill now lectures for me alone are a picture! But these wretched fellows will have to run in order to catch me up.'[117] A week later he was saying his goodbyes before returning to Brno for Christmas. Grill was now 'very friendly' and asked him to compose a minuet or a march over the Christmas vacation.[118] Janáček settled for the minuet, the 'Zdenči Minuet' (x/11) – so-called since it was written under her 'supervision'. When Janáček took it to Grill in January: 'He went on lecturing and didn't notice those lazybones. Just imagine, dearest Zdenči, for the whole lesson he busied himself with me; first he looked through my minuet and then he lectured until the end.'[119]

While Grill's 'composition' lessons were essentially lessons in musical form, Dr Paul's 'harmony' lessons seemed more like composition. Janáček's first assignments for Paul were a series of fugal exercises, starting with two-part fugues, progressing to pieces in three and four parts and culminating with a double fugue (which Janáček described to Zdenka as four lads brawling, then joined by another four until the police were called in to create order).[120] How many fugues he wrote is a matter of conjecture. Janáček reckoned to have written twenty during October alone;[121] Helfert counted seventeen altogether[122] but occasionally took intention for deed: a more sceptical analysis of Janáček's references to fugues in his letters to Zdenka (the only source) suggests no more than fourteen.[‡‡] Fugues were a direct continuation of what Janáček had done with Skuherský in Prague and, once he had settled down and got used to writing two-part fugues again, he was able to throw them off quickly and to impress his teacher with the 'giant strides' he had made in a short period.[123] He appears to have covered Paul's entire three-year fugue course in three months.[124] The final fugue he wrote was the 'Zdenči-Leoš Fugue' (x/6 no. 14), which Janáček took to Paul on 12 January.[125]

Janáček's easy mastery of fugues and Paul's enthusiasm for what he wrote gave Janáček considerable satisfaction in his first month, as well as a boost to his confidence, which had been badly shaken by Grill's caution. Paul could now move him on to writing 'romances' for piano and violin. There was a hitch at the beginning since Janáček was unsure what was needed. Having composed three, he took one to his lesson, only to find that Paul thought it was more of a 'scherzo'.[126] Altogether Janáček wrote seven romances in his attempts to produce a group of three that satisfied both himself and Paul.[127] Although Paul professed to find a 'Slavonic' spirit in Janáček's work – and even suggested the

---

[‡‡] See *JAWO* x/6 for an estimate and a critique of Helfert's counting. Even the fourteen recorded there may be one too many (fugues 2 and 3 may in fact be the same piece).

romances be called 'Czech Romances'[128] – it is hard to see the one surviving Romance (VII/3) as anything more than a run-of-the-mill Romantic genre piece, though the control of harmonic direction is an improvement on Janáček's earlier instrumental pieces such as the Suite for strings (VI/2).

While his regard for Grill gradually rose during November, Janáček began to lose faith in Paul, hardpressed, one learns, by a workload of forty-nine teaching hours a week.[129] Paul enthused rather than scrutinized rigorously and set lofty, unrealizable targets. On 6 November, for instance, he asked for a symphony 'by Easter'.[130] Janáček sketched a scherzo for it on 25 January 1880[131] but soon abandoned the project. On 19 January someone brought to Paul's class an old score which in addition to four standard voice parts had a 'quinta pars'. Early music was not one of Paul's strengths and he unwisely defined the 'quinta pars' as a voice part a fifth away from the tenor (instead of merely a fifth voice part), a mistake soon evident to all when a sixth voice joined in.[132] Janáček's opinion plummeted. A week earlier Janáček had taken his 'Zdenči-Leoš Fugue' to Paul: 'Paul liked my work very much; he found it faultless, although I myself know that I made two gross thematic errors; his cursory glance didn't satisfy me at all. So his praise left me quite cold.'[133] By the time of the 'quinta pars' incident Janáček was describing the 'gross thematic errors' in his final fugue as deliberate 'mistakes' set as a trap for the unsuspecting Paul.[134] After that Janáček didn't bother to write any more compositions for Paul.[135] 'I can look on Paul only with pity' was his withering comment as he made plans to leave Leipzig.[136]

Meanwhile Grill's stocks rose as he insisted on his students not running before they could walk, and in the end Janáček respected someone who clearly took pains and had a well-tried method. And nothing is sweeter than the praise of someone if one has had to work really hard to win it. Grill's enthusiasm for the 'Zdenči Minuet' in January is carefully recorded in his letters to Zdenka ('of all my works he liked it the most'),[137] whereas Paul's praise for the 'Zdenči-Leoš Fugue' a matter of days earlier was brushed aside.[138] By the end of January Janáček embarked on his most ambitious piece for Grill, the Theme and Variations for piano (VIII/6). It took him almost four weeks until the end of his stay.

As Janáček's time in Leipzig drew to an end he became so impatient to acquire from Grill as much as possible of his teachings on forms that he was prepared to pay for extra lessons, though found that they didn't come cheap: 6 marks a time rather than the 2 marks that he had budgeted. In the extra hours at Grill's home (a long walk away)[139] Grill would explain the new material to him and then correct Janáček's version at the conservatory.[140] Janáček began going on 31 January[141] and from 9 February went twice a week[142] (Saturday and Thursday), a plan that would cost a total of 48 marks for four weeks, but would allow him, as he explained to Zdenka, to analyse another four forms and work through four examples: 'I hope to be finished with them this month or two to three days later.'[143]

In the end he didn't quite get there. By Monday 23 February he was aiming to finish his 'last work, Rondo III' before his final lessons with Grill that week:[144] despite all the extra hours they had not got round to 'Rondo IV', the final type of rondo that Grill taught. But he had at least finished a 'fairly large piece', the Theme and Variations for piano. The last note was written on 22 February, and the next day Janáček took the final section for Grill's scrutiny.[145]

The number of works that Janáček wrote in Leipzig shows the same industry that was evident during his studies in Prague. Their composition is detailed on a virtually daily basis in his letters to Zdenka: one knows when he began them, when he ended them, when he took them to his teachers and often what they and he thought about them. From Janáček's letters to Zdenka it is possible to draw up a list of compositions and compositional exercises that he completed in Leipzig (see table 15.2).

Although most of the pieces arose out of specific assignments, a few were written spontaneously without prompting, such as the Piano Sonata (X/5) that Janáček began while waiting for classes to get going at the conservatory, the song cycle *Die Abendschatten* (X/7) – mentioned once in a letter to Zdenka and never again – and the Violin Sonata (X/12). But almost none of these pieces has survived: just one Romance and the Theme and Variations for piano (VIII/6). Zdenka was no doubt presented with 'her' variations on Janáček's return and hung on to them. And this survival of Janáček's near-final piece written during his Leipzig months does provide a useful snapshot of what he had achieved during this time. Although the variations reminded Wenzel of Brahms's *Handel Variations* for piano, the model was undoubtedly Mendelssohn's *Variations sérieuses* op. 54. What is immediately clear just from the sixteen-bar theme is the control of the part-writing

Table 15.3: Janáček's compositions in Leipzig 1879–80

JW	title	date	comments
x/5	Piano Sonata in E flat	4–6 Oct 1879	at least two movements
x/6	14 (?) fugues	9 Oct–14 Jan 1880	probably six two-part fugues; at least three three-part fugues; one double fugue; for Paul
x/7	Die Abendschatten	begun 26 Oct 1879	song cycle on words by Karl Friedrich Hermann Mayer; abandoned
x/8	7 Romances for violin and piano	27 Oct–17 Nov 1879	one (vii/3) survives
x/9	'Song' for Grill	9 Nov 1879	possibly just another exercise in musical periods
x/10	Sanctus	21–4 Nov 1879	including a fugue; for Paul
x/11	'Zdenči Minuet' for piano	by 8 Jan 1880	for Grill
x/12	Violin Sonata [no. 1]	14–18 Jan 1880	two movements
x/13	Scherzo from a symphony	25 Jan 1880	presumably in piano score; for Paul
viii/6	Theme and Variations for piano	29 Jan–22 Feb 1880	for Grill
x/14	3 Rondos for piano	16–23 Feb 1880	for Grill

(much more contrapuntal Janáček than usual) and the confident handling of key structure (as compared to the hit-and-miss oddities of the Suite vi/2). After the theme, with its unusual modulation to the relative minor at the midway point, there follow six variations of contrasting moods and tempos with an extended seventh variation providing a well-developed climax. Imagination and technique go hand in hand. Grill saw it in stages and his beady-eyed supervision shows: Janáček's Theme and Variations has the distinction of being one of his most carefully crafted pieces, with unusual delicacy in the figuration. This was the only formal set of variations that Janáček composed throughout his life: although not sounding remotely like the mature composer, this piece is evidence of his early mastery of imaginative variations of small motifs.

Janáček's studies in Prague had been a triumph, and the fact that he later copied out the compositions written in Prague is a good indication that he himself was pleased with what he had done there. Leipzig was a different matter. After his year in Prague his conducting activities had blossomed so that he now held the chief conducting post in Czech Brno. He was in lively contact with one of the finest Czech composers of his day, Antonín Dvořák, who at Janáček's behest began his regular visits to Brno. He was twenty-five, in love with his boss's daughter (and with her family's consent): there would seem to be a wonderful life stretching out before him. Leipzig, it was hoped, would give him further qualifications and provide the foreign seal of approval.

It speaks volumes that Janáček kept very little of what he composed there. As a seasoned pedagogue himself he soon became aware of the shortcomings of most of his teachers. While to Skuherský in Prague (and for that matter Křížkovský in Brno) Janáček represented a promising future for Czech music, to his teachers in Leipzig, Janáček was just another foreign student – they had hundreds. With his high standards and conscientious approach Grill was the exception, and Janáček worked hard for him; the others took a far more lofty view and although encouraging (as Paul was) this was not what Janáček needed. By February 1880 he had given up everything but Grill's lessons in form.

He had also begun to explore the possibilities elsewhere. One Sunday afternoon, 25 January, Janáček began sharing his thoughts with Zdenka and her father:

Dearest Father, is it precisely a one-year certificate from the conservatory that is necessary for attaining the title?[§§] Couldn't I study further in the next half year in Vienna, nearer to you, dearest Zdenči? Up to Easter I'd like to take one or two private lessons a week with Grill, with whom I'm really learning something new, and I'd certainly be ready with the whole teaching about forms since I'm anyway very far ahead and I can't always go on waiting for the others. With the piano by that time I'd also be very far so that I could make a claim on Professor Door[||||] as a teacher at the Vienna Conservatory. With the organ, it seems to me that I'm better off in Vienna; at the very least one of the largest instruments is built in the hall there. And then I'd be able to go round to your relatives, dearest Zdenči, to speak with them about you. [. . .] From a musical point of view there is so little for me here from Easter: concerts in the Gewandhaus come to an end. These and Grill have now become the only things where I could learn much.

What did Emilian Schulz and Zdenka think of such a plan? If positively, then he would write to the Vienna Conservatory to explore

[§§] Helfert (*LJPT*, 116) assumes from this reference that the 'title' was 'professor of music'.
[||||] Anton Door, professor of piano at the Vienna Conservatory 1869–1901. Janáček in fact ended up with Josef Dachs (see chap. 16).

the possibility of a transfer.[146] Within a few days Janáček had his answer, and on 28 January wrote off to Vienna[147] and began worrying about whether semesters worked the same way and when he could transfer.[148] And, impatient as ever, he then fretted when no answer arrived, writing again two weeks later, this time also to Franz Krenn, his potential composition teacher.[149]

A couple of days after that a positive answer arrived from the general secretary at the Vienna Conservatory;[150] at a cost of 136 zl Vienna could take him for the months of April, May and June and up to the end of term on 15 July. Janáček reckoned that this would leave him with 35 zl a month: not enough to come out on – but if for these four months he stopped supporting his mother and paying off his debt to the music dealer Winkler[¶] and if he could pay the conservatory in monthly instalments, then it would be possible.[151]

Although Janáček had first envisaged leaving Leipzig in mid-March,[152] this date was continually brought forward. When on 23 February he heard from the Vienna Conservatory that payment by instalments would be allowed and on the same day he received money from Schulz to pay for Grill's extra lessons and his train fare home,[153] there was almost nothing to keep him in Leipzig. He left the next day.[154]

The one thing that might have kept him longer in Leipzig would have been a performance of his Theme and Variations for piano. During the few weeks before his departure Zdenka was informed in minute detail about his preparation for and continual postponement of the performance of three of his fugues at one of the conservatory soirées. The fugues (unspecified apart from the final 'Zdenči-Leoš' one) were from the series that Janáček had written for Paul, and it was at Paul's initiative that a selection should be played publicly. On 22 January Janáček began copying them out for the purpose,[155] and practising them for a performance on Friday 30 January.[156] The programmes for the Friday soirées, however, seem to have been drawn up fairly randomly at the last moment so that Janáček played his fugues on none of the days he was told (30 January, 6 February or 13 February)',[157] and then, unexpectedly, he found himself playing them on 14 February,

---

[¶] Zdenka (*MLWJ*, 32–3) mentions his supporting his mother and the 'smaller debts' he had incurred before his wedding in the purchase of many books and pieces of music.

a Saturday (not usually a soirée evening), and had an unexpected triumph:

So it's behind me at last. During the first two fugues I was very agitated and had to force my fingers through sheer will power; but I got through them quite well. The Zdenči-Leoš fugue went very well; and I calmed down so much that I composed ornaments while playing. Paul said 'charming!' and one pupil (an Italian), who had a real fear of fugues, told me as I left that those were the first fugues whose melodies had a pleasant effect on him. That pleased me. Otherwise I didn't speak with anyone because as soon as I came off the platform I got dressed and walked home. Now I would like to play the variations and then nothing need detain me here any longer.[158]

But the compliments kept flowing, as Janáček reported to Zdenka a few days later. There was his piano teacher Wenzel, who now insisted on hearing Janáček's Theme and Variations for piano, the congratulations from 'many fellow students' and, according to Paul, also from other teachers at the conservatory. Although Janáček had been tempted to stay to give a performance of the Theme and Variations, which he finished a few days later, he felt he shouldn't stay simply because of them. He could, after all, play them anywhere else,[159] but there is no record of his doing so.

A few weeks before he left Janáček summed up in a letter to Zdenka what he thought he had achieved in Leipzig: 'That I've got to know the state of one of the most musical cities in the world, that I've heard many concerts and that I have, as I hope, thoroughly studied musical forms – these are the fruits of my time here.' He realized that this was a more modest aim than what he originally had in mind. It was, for instance, 'impossible to write symphonies, as Paul demanded'. He could perhaps have done so, but had he 'trusted this man' he would have ended up 'paying dearly' for it. In the end it was a remarkably philosophical and uncharacteristically patient Janáček that emerged:

The aim [of writing a symphony] I will achieve, calmly, with hard work and if I have a real talent, only on the path that Grill showed me. I must master all forms so that they become second nature to me: I must be able to write in any form without having to think further about it myself. Which needs practice and time. That has become my main aim and in this respect I am quite calm and pleased with myself.[160]

Years later, when he was writing his autobiography, his time in Leipzig was relegated to a single page. He remembered the wooden hut and the piano with pedals for organ practice that had eroded any wish to continue with the organ. Then there was the much too relaxed choir rehearsal; although not revealed in his letters at the time, here he alludes to rehearsing Beethoven's *Missa solemnis*, in which Janáček was designated a first bass. The Saturday concerts at St Thomas's are mentioned though without further comment. The Gewandhaus concerts, which took up a huge amount of Janáček's time and interest, were collapsed into a single event conducted by Nikisch (Janáček's view of Nikisch had clearly changed with the conductor's later fame; Reinecke, who had conducted all the other concerts at the Gewandhaus, was not mentioned at all). Even Rubinstein is remembered only because when playing the piano part of his 'sextet' (*recte* quintet) from memory he lost his place – another detail not mentioned at the time. Another recollection was how he detected a 'Slavonic colouring' in the local Leipzig dialect and how Leipzig University had a 'famous lion' taken from Prague at the time of Hus. As for teachers, he remembered Wenzel's dozing off during piano lessons, Dr Paul as being superficial' and Grill as being 'good'.[161]

While Leipzig had not lived up to Janáček's expectations, his five months there were nevertheless valuable in several ways. Seeing at first hand the shortcomings of a well-regarded international musical institution and the happy-go-lucky attitude of most of the students boosted his own confidence. The poor provision for organ practice shut off one of his areas of interest (leading to an increased concentration on others) and although he continued to play the piano, any ideas about a concert career that Wickenhauser may have inspired in him were quickly set aside when he observed the talented students around him. Perhaps the most positive outcome was the secure technical grounding that he built up with Grill, which enabled him to work quickly and extract the maximum out of any musical material. Janáček himself was to realize this soon after his arrival in Vienna:

Altogether I'm working very easily now, since I know now how to grasp every thought and round it off; that's Grill's legacy. My fellow students today *wait* for a perfect thought, but for that not only talent is necessary but a certain technical competence, which they totally lack.[162]

16

Musical studies: Vienna 1880

It is all too easy to see Janáček's studies in Vienna as comparable with those in Leipzig: a second semester spent abroad in another German-speaking city. But Vienna for him was as different from Leipzig as Leipzig had been from Prague. For a start Janáček was based there for far less time: just two months, whereas he spent five months in Leipzig. In Vienna he didn't feel nearly so isolated since he could take the occasional long-weekend break, usually going on the cheap overnight goods train to Brno. At least seventeen hours by train from Brno via Prague, Leipzig had been just too far and too expensive for such jaunts. So Janáček's time in Vienna (from 31 March) was eroded by two long-weekend breaks (Friday evening to Tuesday morning, 16–20 April and 30 April–4 May) and a ten-day break at Whitsun (14–24 May). Altogether he was in Vienna for only 48* days (compared with the 116 in Leipzig) and during this time he wrote 33 letters to Zdenka (compared with the 126 written in Leipzig).

Although a German-speaking city and a large one at that (871,000 at the 1890 census – i.e. four to five times bigger than Prague), Vienna felt much more like home, with the same currency, a substantial Czech population (just under 10%),[1] and many shared features of culture, cuisine, architecture and outlook. It was, after all, Janáček's capital city at the time and involved no crossings of international borders. And he had friends in Vienna. Almost the moment he got there he made contact with Alexander Lorenz and his family. Lorenz was related to Anna Schulzová's side of the family, perhaps a first cousin. Mrs Schulzová's aunts Fanny and Marie (mentioned in Zdenka's memoirs)[2] were

---

* Or possibly a few more; see chap. 17 for a discussion of when Janáček left Vienna.

frequent visitors and Mrs Schulzová's mother, Grandmother Kaluschka, came for a short stay during Janáček's time there. Alexander was probably a bit older than Janáček, with a wife and some curly-haired and undisciplined children,[3] and worked in a bank,[4] but he was not old enough to be referred to as anything other than 'Alexander'. Janáček made almost daily visits there during his early days in Vienna (the Lorenzes lived a forty-five-minute walk from Janáček's dwelling)[5] and the friendly atmosphere, and the possibility of his being able to talk endlessly about Zdenka, seem to have made him more at home.[6] Only towards the end of his stay, when he was running out of time, did he begin to restrict his visits.[7]

Other aspects of life weren't so easy. Janáček had been happy in his quiet accommodation in Leipzig and offered a full description and many references to it in his letters to Zdenka, but the room he found in Vienna (Vienna I, Riemerstrasse no. 9, 3rd floor, with a Mrs Leithner) was merely described as a 'ghastly hole'. It cost him 12 zl a month, near the bottom of the market (the conservatory recommended accommodation at 20 zl a month),[8] but he needed to count his pennies since the course was eating up half his monthly income. Apart from a 'miserable pianino'[9] (i.e. a small upright piano) that he hired, next to nothing is known about his room. There was no heating[10] and, although the weather was warmer by then, he complained of the cold even in May.[11] Lighting seems to have been with candles[12] rather than paraffin lamps. Above all it was noisy. More than once Janáček complained of music coming from other parts of the building[13] or of buskers outside[14] stopping him from getting on with his composition.

Money was even more of a consideration than it had been in Leipzig. His finances, he reported on the day after his arrival, were 'awful'. Having paid the monthly registration fee of 42 zl 50 to the conservatory, 7 zl for a month's piano hire and 3 zl for its transport, he had just 24 zl left.[15] A few days later, having shelled out 4 zl 50 for music, he had, as he told Zdenka, not a single krejcar left.[16] That was presumably having set aside money for meals, which cost him about 1 zl a day ('soup and beef' for lunch; 'goulash or something smaller' in the evenings).[17] There was no question of his going to the conservatory concerts, for which students were charged 50 kr.[18] Schulz seems to have helped out with the odd loan.[19]

After Leipzig Conservatory, where he tried everything on offer, Janáček went to the Vienna Conservatory with a very specific agenda: to continue his studies in piano and composition. So whereas Leipzig had a cast of many teachers that figure in his correspondence, with starring roles for Paul, Grill, Wenzel, Rust and Reinecke, there were in Vienna just two: Franz Krenn (1816–97) for theory and composition, and Josef Dachs (1825–96) for piano. Janáček had considered resuming organ lessons too, but the conservatory advised him that doing so would double his costs and so he decided against it:[20] a final nail in the coffin of his career as an organist. In his letter to Zdenka of 2 April he declared that he was accepted into the second year (out of three).[21] As Hartmut Krones has shown, this refers to composition; for piano he was placed in the first year.[22] His timetable at first was as set out in table 16.1:

Table 16.1: Janáček's timetable in Vienna 1880[23]

Monday	3–5	composition	Krenn
	5.30–7.30	piano	Dachs
Wednesday	3–5	composition	Krenn
Friday	3–5	composition	Krenn
	5.30–7.30	piano	Dachs

After a couple of weeks, however, Janáček stopped taking piano lessons. He may have been prompted to do so by his disappointing performance in Dachs's classes:

I've just come from the conservatory: today's lesson much distressed me. I can't get by with my Leipzig touch: with it I don't produce the right tone on a Bösendorfer. The action is so heavy one has to hit it. When I'd played one scale I was so tired that I couldn't repeat it.[24]

On 21 April, straight after returning from his first long weekend in Brno, he stopped piano lessons altogether,[25] presumably as a result of discussions with Zdenka and her father. Since according to his registration certificate Janáček's main subject was piano, and composition was merely a voluntary extra, Janáček needed official permission for it to become his main subject. But this was granted on 22 April, as stated in the handwritten amendments on his registration certificate.[26] This meant that he could devote himself fully to composition without spending several hours a day practising. However, he continued to keep up the piano on his own, often referring in his letters to playing the piano. Not long before he left Vienna he bought, umprompted, the third volume of Czerny's virtuoso school having got to the end of the second volume.[27] Giving up piano lessons had of course far-reaching consequences. Janáček's ambitions as a concert pianist that had taken him to Leipzig were now finally laid to rest: from now on he would concentrate his efforts as a composer, teacher, writer and, for a while, as a conductor.

Chiefly because of his restricted finances Janáček got to only three musical events in Vienna: a concert by the Vienna Philharmonic at the beginning of his stay, and two operas. The concert ticket came from his composition teacher Franz Krenn; the programme included Beethoven's *Egmont* music and an unspecified piece by Wagner. 'The performance', Janáček wrote to Zdenka, 'was outstanding but the impression was not exceptional in any way – at least for me. The hall, splendid in all respects, seemed too large to me – the tone of all the instruments is bound to be so thin and mean.'[28] Apart from his restricted finances, this may explain why Janáček made no further attempt to attend concerts in Vienna.

Nevertheless it was in Vienna that Janáček got twice to the opera, his first recorded encounters apart from his possible appearances as a chorister in a Meyerbeer opera (see chap. 6). Janáček's first visit was on 14 April 1880. He was feeling flush with funds since Schulz had sent him money for his train fare, and he proposed to go to the opera twice in the remaining days before his first long weekend in Brno.[29] In the event he went only once, to Weber's *Der Freischütz*. Writing to Zdenka afterwards, he had almost nothing to say: the music didn't much interest him; no doubt, he wrote, the piece had been played too often.[30] The second trip was on 31 May, shortly before he left Vienna for good, and was feeling at a loss. At the Hofoper he saw *Les deux journées*, Cherubini's 'rescue opera' set during the French Revolution and more of a repertory piece then than the rarity it has become today. Again he barely reacted. Apart from a 'single place', he wasn't taken by the music, though, as he said, he was tired and hardly in the right mood. Tiredness, however, did not get in the way of his enjoying the ballet given with it to fill up a short evening:

Until now I always had, from hearing about it, a great prejudice against ballet and was much biassed against it. Yesterday I saw a ballet for the first time and I must say that I liked it very much. At some individual moments it was truly brilliant. It was called *Dayla*. As you related, dear Zdenčinka, one thinks one is seeing bushes and other decorations – and suddenly everything moves and it is revealed as a whole swarm of fairies.[31]

Dayla, or rather *Dyellah oder die Touristen in Indien*, was a 'fantastic-comic ballet in two acts', first given at the Hofoper in 1879 with choreography by Pasquale Borri and music by Antonio Baur. With its transformations, its 'fairies' and its brilliant moments, it was a formative event in Janáček's life: this enthusiastic response to the combination of stage and music perhaps planted a seed for the extensive use of ballet in his operas such as *The Cunning Little Vixen* and the Moon Excursion of *The Excursions of Mr Brouček*.

Janáček had few other entertainments while in Vienna. Towards the end of his stay, he went to the Prater pleasure ground.[32] And while he was waiting for the crucial qualifying exam, he took advantage of the public holiday by going to the Graben (a street near St Stephen's Cathedral) to see the Emperor Franz Josef at the Corpus Christi celebrations:

So I saw all that splendour at last – but for 50 kr. I had already wanted to go home because it wasn't possible for me to find a place in that throng. But in the end I bought a seat for myself on the stands near the Stephanskirche [i.e. St Stephen's Cathedral]. I liked most of all the part of the procession from the Blessed Sacrament to the back; that must have been where the emperor was too because his bodyguard with its trumpeters followed straight afterwards. I saw the emperor's carriage in another place. But I nevertheless couldn't see the emperor himself because I was a little too far away.[33]

The nature of Janáček's life in Vienna, largely devoid of such diversions, throws even more into relief the one thing that he pursued consistently while he was there: composition. Information about this, however, is entirely restricted to what Janáček told Zdenka in his letters. Whereas a couple of the Leipzig pieces survive and give one some indication of his progress there, nothing remains of his Viennese works, though their more ambitious nature does suggest that he had moved on. Instead of basic compositional exercises, fugues, piano variations and romances for violin and piano, Janáček wrote the works shown in table 16.2, all of which are lost.

Janáček's composition teachers at Leipzig, Paul and Grill, had been respectively forty-three and thirty-three years old. Janáček's composition teacher in Vienna, Franz Krenn, was much older, sixty-four,

Table 16.2: Janáček's compositions in Vienna 1880

JW	title	date	comments
x/15	[Piece in sonata form], piano	10–13 April 1880	
x/16	Violin Sonata [no. 2]	20 April–13 May 1880	four movements: Allegro, Moderato (Adagio), Scherzo, Finale; second movement played at the qualifying round of the composition competition (Vereinsmedaille) on 28 May 1880
x/17	Frühlingslieder [Spring Songs]	22 April to 7 May 1880	song cycle for high voice and piano after Vincenz Zusner's poems, nine songs
x/18	String Quartet	27 May–2 June 1880	three movements completed, the third of which was a scherzo

and thus nearer in age to his Leipzig piano teacher Wenzel, the one Janáček remembered dozing off during the classes. A composer and organist, Krenn had taught harmony at the Vienna Conservatory since 1869 and was well enough known for Janáček to have heard about him and to have written to him from Leipzig (see chap. 15). Krenn was affable but undemanding with a *laissez-faire* attitude. Janáček's initial impression was that he was 'a fellow with good views but with too little well-grounded knowledge'.[34] At his first lesson Janáček discovered that many of the 'rules' that Grill had inculcated were not followed in Vienna:

I don't like the fact that Krenn is so old but at the same time looks down with such ridicule on all rules of the old style that must, after all, always and forever form the basis of all solid work. So he said yesterday, 'Where others may not let two voices converge on the same note (counterpoint), "here in Vienna" it's allowed.'

Janáček 'might have had lots to say to him about this utterance', but instead he kept his counsel and simply observed:

The theory class was almost disgusting for me: here boys are writing symphonies, quartets and God knows what else and can't put together a solid [musical] phrase. I must submit to it and calmly work for myself. [. . .] If, dear Zdenči, you'd seen the puffed-up faces of my fellow students you would have had to laugh with me. What an opinion he[†] has of himself! But he is already writing symphonies for large orchestra and consequently sits 'on Beethoven's right hand' – and the teacher confirms him in this delusion! If only I didn't have to listen to it. I don't know where to look when they play through their work![35]

A couple of days later Janáček was still maintaining his silence:

So far in Krenn's class I sit as quiet as a mouse because I'm giving in my first work only on Friday. Krenn must now believe that I am taken, God knows why, with his teaching results since he said to me in parting: 'If only you'd come straight to Vienna!' [i.e. not first to Leipzig]. I couldn't respond to him since he would have been a little taken aback by my reply.[36]

In the end Janáček found himself appreciating all his hard work in Leipzig and the compositional skills he had acquired there: 'I also want to work further only on Grill's foundations and not let myself be influenced by this Wagnerian bombast.'[37] As it was, Krenn was happy enough to let him get on with whatever he wanted, as Janáček discovered when on Friday 9 April he took his first exercise to him, the 'last rondo', begun on 3 April.[38] Janáček was in fact continuing with his systematic exploration of forms initiated in Leipzig (Grill had seen the 'third rondo' on 23 February). 'So Krenn liked my work after all; it's so nice that he's now content with my style.' It would seem that Krenn then assigned a more ambitious task, a sonata form movement for piano (x/15), which Janáček began the next day.

At the lesson Krenn seemed chatty and even conspiratorial: 'He spoke with me a long time also about the mad way with which the other fellow students throw themselves into the Wagnerian manner of writing; he criticizes it but he's not energetic enough about it: Grill would have shown them by now!' When Krenn asked him why he hadn't come straight to Vienna, Janáček answered him, 'completely honestly', that he'd learnt a lot in Leipzig and that he didn't regret his going there for a moment. Krenn, as he told Janáček, thought highly of the Prague Organ School: 'those who come from it are always the best contrapuntalists.'[39]

What Janáček did not yet know, and discovered much too late, was that although Krenn might indulgently accept all that was presented to him, such an inclusive attitude was not shared by other teachers at the conservatory. In other words, if Janáček persisted in composing in the

[†] Janáček appears here to have one particular fellow student in mind.

way approved by the Leipzig Conservatory he would be producing music that many at the Vienna Conservatory, especially those on the examination board, would regard as outmoded and oldfashioned, whatever its technical excellence. So from the moment he started in Vienna misfortune loomed. His teacher Krenn failed to warn him and Janáček's contacts with his fellow students were so limited that he didn't pick up useful information from them.

Once satisfied with his sonata-form piece, Krenn encouraged Janáček to begin composing a violin sonata (X/16). He composed its four movements over a period of three weeks (20 April–13 May), between his first and third breaks in Brno. This is the first recorded instance of Janáček's planning the composition of a work according to his own deadlines marked by holidays and other treats. As he wrote to Zdenka, 'one way or another I must have the whole sonata finished before I come to you for the Whitsun holidays.'[40] Janáček would use this approach on a far larger scale when composing operas in his final years (see vol. ii: How Janáček wrote operas).

Krenn also drew Janáček's attention to the Vincenz Zusner Prize at the conservatory: 20 ducats for the best settings of any two poems by the Viennese poet (1803–74), to be submitted by 15 May. Janáček launched into this as soon as he'd found some Zusner in the conservatory library on 22 April, his *Frühlingslieder*,[41] and went on to set not just two songs but a whole cycle (X/17). While Janáček took movements or sections of movements of the Violin Sonata to Krenn on a regular basis, the Zusner songs had to be written independently. Their progress was charted in almost daily bulletins to Zdenka, along with reports on the sonata.

There are fourteen poems in Zusner's *Frühlingslieder*, which Janáček copied out in his notebook.[42] He got on fast: within six days (23–8 April) he had written six songs, and after his second weekend break in Brno he had another burst of creative energy and produced three more (5–7 May).[43] Any plans for further songs were sacrificed to getting on with his violin sonata.[44] The nine that can be tracked in his correspondence were already seven more than were needed for the competition. Nevertheless it looks as though all of these were submitted on 11 May. Since entries had to be written in another hand, Janáček employed his friend Metoděj Janíček (then covering for him at the Augustinian monastery) as an unpaid copyist, which he did 'beautifully and almost without mistake'.[45]

From the day he embarked on the song cycle Janáček fantasized about winning: 'You can't imagine how pleased I'd be if I were to get at least second prize! Not because of the money but because of the recognition; after all it's my first free work after my studies.'[46] Writing songs affected Janáček in new ways: 'And because last night I finished one song I had nothing but dreams about music. Then I was so scared in the dream that I – wept and that woke me up.'[47] By the evening of 25 April Janáček was too tired to do anything more than write out the tune without accompaniment. But

this morning I got down to work and saw that I could put the melody of the voice part quite nicely into the accompaniment *one bar later* and that it would sound very good together. It pleases me that without thinking I wrote a song on a 'canon' like this and that it came really 'from God's grace'.

In this way the song acquired greater musical value.[48]

The final song, Janáček told Zdenka, included a reminiscence of the first song and would, he hoped, round off the cycle nicely.[49] Looking through them, he declared that most of all he liked the second, the penultimate and the last. As for the rest, they were 'characteristic' but not sufficiently melodic.[50] Happy anticipation followed: 'all that is missing now is the prize.'[51] After the Whitsun recess Krenn informed the compositions class that there were nineteen entries, and none of them bad, 'so giving the prizes will be very difficult'; 'Whoever gets first prize can indeed take honour from it.' Janáček was already getting the jitters, he told Zdenka, when thinking about this happy prospect.[52]

Krenn had little to say about the Violin Sonata, though he began by offering 'lots of praise'.[53] It was Janáček himself who was more critical, for instance declaring to Zdenka that his original draft of the final movement was 'bombastic, empty rubbish'.[54] By the time he had heard the third movement, Krenn felt that the work was good enough to be submitted for the qualifying round of the conservatory's annual competition, the Vereinsmedaille.[55] All that was needed at this stage was a single movement. Successful candidates then went on to complete the work for the final round.

The second movement was duly rehearsed on 26 May with Janáček's fellow student Victor von Herzfeld (1856–1920, from Bratislava and a future teacher at the Budapest Conservatory)[56] playing the violin part. Janáček was anxious about Herzfeld's participation from the outset since Herzfeld had also entered with his own piece for the competition and might not, Janáček feared, play the sonata 'with the necessary fire'.[57] In the event Janáček took even more against him at the rehearsal when, having got up the first movement as well as the requested Adagio, Herzfeld kept hovering over him fishing for compliments. But none were forthcoming since Janáček regarded his rendition as unrecognizable. And Herzfeld irritated Janáček by calling out 'bravo' during the rehearsals of the other competition pieces so that Janáček began doubting his own judgement.[58] The qualifying round of the competition, at which single movements of the submitted works were played, took place between 3 and 6 p.m. on 28 May 1880. The moment it was over Janáček wrote to Zdenka about the outcome:

[6 p.m.] My dearest Zdenči, I'm writing to you but with what feelings I cannot tell you. I have come into conflict with my innermost self – but on the other hand I have to laugh at how easy it is to judge someone. You know that Krenn told me even after the first movement of the violin sonata that I ought to enter the competition:[‡] today the distinguished commission composed of the director [Julius] Epstein (piano teacher) and two members of the directorate after listening to the Adagio didn't admit it to the competition. They weren't, as Krenn told me, taken by it. I don't hold it against those gentlemen since I wouldn't have been taken by even a Beethoven Adagio if beforehand I had listened without interruption for a full three hours to student works.

Krenn was most animated when he regretted that he hadn't succeeded with his proposal. You will certainly be asking yourself now what I say to all this. My own personal conviction remains that my sonata was the best work of all those submitted. The jury didn't look at the work at all: each piece was played through one after the other from 3 to 6 p.m. and a judgement was made. My chief concern when I composed the sonata was that it was formally correct and, as far the *work* was concerned, perfect. As for the other sonatas, only one movement from each was ready and nothing more; not one of these movements was in sonata form and as far as any technique is concerned there's nothing to say. But the jury didn't look at that because not a single member was an expert in that field.[59]

The next day Janáček wrote a letter of complaint to the directorate of the conservatory, duly copied into his next letter to Zdenka on Saturday 29 May:

[‡] According to Janáček's letters to Zdenka this occurred only after Krenn heard the third movement; see above.

The undersigned takes the liberty of submitting the following request to the esteemed directorate:

According to the words of Prof. Krenn I wasn't admitted to the competition because my Adagio was without élan, although it gave evidence of good schooling. Based on this verdict may I make the following points:

1. I concede that an Adagio will never make an impression if it is considered in such a programme as an examination.
2. One cannot make a complete judgement on this Adagio since it is an extract from a whole work.
3. If I were to have chosen myself I wouldn't have played this number but the Scherzo and the Finale.
4. For a long time I've listened to and studied the works of my fellow students and I am convinced that the sonata forms in which they wrote them are not at all correct and that they contain harmonic and contrapuntal mistakes that I undertake to demonstrate.

Janáček followed this with the request that he play the piece once more before the jury. However, as he then went on to comment to Zdenka, he wasn't expecting too much. If they didn't concede to his request he would publish the whole affair in a musical periodical. The incident, however, had not turned him away from his present direction, 'for which I thank Grill in Leipzig'.

I won't submit to musical unstylishness, the chasing after effects and the pompous throwing around of bombastic sequences of chords; the time for this has passed. I must only deplore those teachers who educate their pupils in that sphere. The director [Josef Hellmesberger] is a violinist and was schooled at the conservatory here; as a violinist he has after all no solid theoretical training; Epstein is a pianist and a virtuoso to boot. Krenn is the only theoretician – and he is for me.[60]

The letter and these reflections seem to have calmed Janáček down. By the next day his plan was to tell Krenn on Monday that he had written his complaint and that he wouldn't attend further classes until he knew the outcome. If his request for the jury to be reconvened to hear his piece again was disallowed, he would send his sonata to the critic Eduard Hanslick (and Dvořák's advocate) 'with an appropriate explanation and ask him in full trust for an opinion'. He wouldn't leave Vienna until 12 June in order to find out how he did in the Zusner song competition. Meanwhile, he wrote, he would work 'further on the quartet'.[61]

The String Quartet (x/10) thus became useful occupational therapy while Janáček awaited the outcome both of his letter to the directorate and of the Zusner competition. As early as 25 April he had thought of writing a quartet to submit for the Vereinsmedaille competition.[62] However the Violin Sonata and the songs had intervened, and only when he had completed them and returned from his Whitsun trip to Brno did he turn his attention to writing a quartet, beginning on 27 May. He had already spent a couple of days studying Beethoven string quartets that he had borrowed from the conservatory library.[63] He made good progress, with a first movement almost complete the next day ('Krenn will be astonished that I've already got so far').[64] There was a hiatus while Janáček absorbed his shock and outrage at the result of the first round of the Vereinsmedaille competition, but his discipline was such that he completed and copied out the first movement on Sunday 30 May, adding a second (presumably slow) movement the next day (by 9.15 p.m. he was copying it out), and a scherzo the day after, drafted in a single one-hour session, and comforted himself with the reflection that if he were untalented he could not have achieved this.[65] However, this was his last letter to Zdenka from Vienna, and no more was heard of this work. It is not known, for instance, whether he added a final movement: like all the other works from Vienna, the music has disappeared. Although Janáček muttered on about sending the Violin Sonata to Hanslick,[66] and even to Skuhersky,[67] once he had made a copy of the manuscript there is no record of his having done so. He did not, however, destroy the music of the Violin Sonata immediately, since he played it with Gustav Zinke on 6 January 1881 at a Brno Beseda chamber concert.

In the event he didn't stay to hear the outcome of his complaint. It would, however, have been negative, both because the rules did not allow for any appeals, but more especially because, as Krones has shown, Janáček had not been qualified to enter the competition in the first place since he was not taking the necessary subsidiary subjects (a state of affairs of which Krenn was presumably ignorant).[68] It was just as well Janáček didn't linger on in Vienna to hear the news. His rival Herzfeld came first in the Vereinsmedaille competition and second in the Zusner song competition – results that Janáček would have found impossible to accept.[69]

Janáček's studies away from Brno had increasingly diminishing returns. Prague was a huge success: a fine teacher, a great leap forward in his technical resources (particularly harmonic), a series of pieces he was proud of, and a triumphant graduation from the Prague Organ School. Significantly he attempted to go back there for a top-up a couple of summers later. Leipzig, too, had its benefits. While there he developed further technical prowess, this time in note-by-note progression and in increasing artfulness in the manipulation and variation of musical motifs. He heard all the non-operatic music performed during the winter season of a celebrated German musical city; he developed his piano skills but also began to realize that his strengths lay elsewhere. This time he left, abruptly, without graduating, but what he did was sufficient to enhance his status as a teacher, and he looked back with gratitude on what Grill had taught him.

But Vienna was a disaster.[5] He heard almost no new music, and this time learnt nothing new from his teacher. He wrote a couple of more ambitious pieces but could have done that anywhere, and his mortifying experience with the qualifying round for the composition competition was a terrible blow to his self-confidence. Such gains as there were from Vienna were primarily negative: his time there brought to an end any ambitions as an organist and pianist (and thus channelled Janáček's future path into composition). Since Janáček had nothing but contempt for Krenn's *laissez-faire* methods he achieved self-reliance and thereafter felt no need to go elsewhere to develop his compositional skills. After Vienna Janáček would become increasingly self-educated. Although the paths he chose were odd ones, it was nevertheless these paths that made him the distinctive composer that he became. In Vienna Janáček wrote standard forms of chamber music and a song cycle. His brush with the conservatory soured his view of these genres for a long time to come. He would return triumphantly to a song cycle, a violin sonata and to string quartets at the end of his life, but in a completely different idiom. While his two experiences of opera in Vienna were disappointing, this is nevertheless the direction in which he turned during the next decade, a direction that he pursued for the rest of his life.

[5] In his account of Janáček's contacts with Vienna Jiří Vysloužil takes a more favourable view of Janáček's time in the city, a view based chiefly on the friendly review in *Dalibor* of Janáček's Violin Sonata (x/16) when it was played in Brno in 1881, and elements of Brucknerian influence that Vysloužil detects in some of Janáček's later works (Vysloužil 1992, 259–63).

II

THE YOUNG PROFESSIONAL
(1880–8)

17

June 1880–December 1881

Janáček returned to Brno in June 1880 with his tail between his legs after the Vienna débâcle. Exactly when, however, is difficult to determine. According to his last letter from Vienna, on Tuesday–Wednesday 1–2 June, he would be sending his trunk directly to Brno on Friday 5 June[1] and arrive in Brno on 12 June, having spent a couple of days going to see his uncle, Father Jan Janáček, in Znorovy. He had paid for accommodation until the middle of the month,[2] and for piano hire until 10 June.[3] In his Wednesday letter he also announced that he was going that afternoon to the Viennese amusement park, the Prater, the second time in two days. This time it would be with Zdenka's relative Alexander Lorenz, whom he felt a bit guilty about, having seen him only a couple of times since his most recent return from Brno.[4] The puzzle, however, is why this is Janáček's last letter from Vienna. If he had left, as planned, at the end of the next weekend why did he not go on writing to Zdenka for a few more days? He had been in daily contact with her all this time and there is no indication in this last letter that he wouldn't be writing to her as normal, indeed several times a day. Either a few letters from Vienna have disappeared (unlikely, since Zdenka meticulously hung on to everything she received from her future husband) or, as in Leipzig, Janáček left abruptly without warning and simply turned up in Brno. This is more likely. There was nothing to keep him in Vienna apart from the fact that he had paid in advance for accommodation and the piano. He was not going to classes; the string quartet he was writing could be written anywhere. He might, against all hope, have wondered whether the conservatory would relent and let him proceed to the next round of the composition competition. The efforts of his composition teacher,

Franz Krenn, had already failed, however, and by now Janáček knew enough of what was expected in Vienna and how his own music differed. His official reason was waiting for the outcome of the Zusner song competition, due to be announced on 12 June.[5] But why wait for what was – in view of the qualifying round of the other competition – likely to be yet another humiliation? Perhaps it took time for all this to sink in; perhaps Zdenka wrote to him telling him to come home. Perhaps he was on the same train as the trunk he planned to send on Friday 5 June. He was certainly back in Brno by 11 June, since he conducted the Beseda choir in a 'serenade' on the visit of Emperor Franz Josef that day.[6]

So Janáček returned to Brno perhaps in early June, no doubt wishing that he hadn't gone to Vienna in the first place. He was considerably in debt and had nothing to show for it apart from three compositions and a short, bland reference from Krenn.[7] Then there would be the uncomfortable business of explaining to his friends and foes in Brno why he had returned so soon. He couldn't move back to his mother's flat in Staré Brno since, while he was away studying, she had tried to make ends meet by taking in students. Instead he found lodgings in Měšťanská no. 50, a large tenement block owned by Josef Freyschlag; according to the 1880 census he rented flat no. 44.[8]

There was not much to be done in Brno at this stage. His teaching was still covered, he was not going back to the Augustinian monastery until July,* and little went on at the Brno Beseda during the summer. So all he could do was mooch around at the Schulzes feeling sorry for himself. Zdenka, no doubt, was kind and sympathetic, but one wonders what her family made of it all, especially since there was a newborn baby in the house. Mrs Schulzová was weak from a difficult labour[9] and this, rather than the woes of a demanding, debt-ridden and troubled prospective son-in-law, was dominating their thoughts.

Janáček was at least evidently welcome at the christening, which took place at the Schulzes' flat some time in June. At the ceremony he stood in for the official godfather, Julius Kaluschka from Kolín, and

---

* He informed Zdenka that he would be writing to Křížkovský offering to take over the choir again from 1 July 1880 (LJ to ZS, 31 May 1880, *IB*, 239–40).

was one of the three Leošes in the room: himself, the officiating priest and little Leoš Schulz.[10]

By the autumn, Janáček had resumed most of his former activities in Brno, which of course included the Brno Beseda. There had been forthright correspondence between Janáček and the Beseda during his time away, chiefly regarding his distaste for conducting entertainment concerts, and the Beseda's view that this was part of his job.[11] Since Janáček was not being paid, however, there was not a lot that the Beseda could do apart from urging him to comply with its regulations. When Janáček stood his ground, a compromise was agreed by which the choirmaster's functions were divided between a director, who conducted the concerts, and his deputy, who conducted the entertainments – this fell to Janáček's friend and colleague, the accommodating Berthold Žalud. Janáček's concerts with the Beseda from 1880 are summarized in table 17.1.

Janáček's first task was to take charge of the jubilee concert on 12 December 1880 celebrating twenty years of the society's existence. He chose an all-Czech programme which acknowledged the strides made in Czech music during those twenty years: orchestral pieces by Dvořák and Smetana topped and tailed the concert, with choral pieces and Janáček's *Idyll* for strings (vi/3) in the middle. Dvořák's *Rhapsody* for large orchestra acknowledged the composer's connection with the Beseda that Janáček himself had fostered, but Smetana's *Vltava* from *My Fatherland* was the realization of a plan that Janáček had announced on taking over the Beseda in 1876.[15] Janáček had written dismissively to Zdenka about his *Idyll* from Leipzig, so its inclusion here (or rather, just five movements from it) suggests that he now thought better of it. The choral pieces consisted of one of Janáček's favourite Křížkovský male-voice choruses, *The Love-Gift*, a sparkling vocal scherzo, and two pieces written especially for the concert, his own *Autumn Song* (iv/14) and František Pivoda's *Spring Moods*, both for mixed voices. Janáček had suggested just a few weeks after his return from Vienna that 'Slavonic' composers be invited to send in works for the jubilee concert,[16] but in the end there were just two, with Janáček's perhaps written to make up the numbers.

Janáček's *Autumn Song* occupies an odd place in his oeuvre. It is the first of only three choruses he wrote for unaccompanied mixed voices; it came in the middle of a long break between the first flush of

Table 17.1: Janáček concerts with the Brno Beseda 1880–8[12]

(titles given of larger works, and of all works by Janáček, Křížkovský, Dvořák and Smetana; others summarized)

1880

12 December: Jubilee concert celebrating twenty years since the founding of the Brno Beseda; Janáček conducts Dvořák's *Rhapsody*, Smetana's *Vltava*, and five movements of his own *Idyll* for string orchestra (vi/3); choruses include his *Autumn Song* (iv/14) (première), Křížkovský's *The Love-Gift* and Pivoda's *Spring Moods*

1882

2 April: Concert; Janáček conducts Dvořák's *Stabat mater* (soloists from Prague)

20 May: Concert; Janáček conducts Tchaikovsky's Serenade for strings, and, with Ferdinand Lachner as soloist, Max Bruch's Violin Concerto in G minor, Dvořák's *Mazurek* and Saint-Saëns's *Introduction et rondo capriccioso*; choruses include Křížkovský's *Spring*, Dvořák's *Village Gossip* and Bendl's *Golden Hour*

1883

18 March: Concert; Janáček conducts Dvořák's Symphony no. 6 in D, Smetana's *Vltava*, Brahms's *Schicksalslied* for choir and orchestra; programme includes arias sung by the tenor František Broulík from the Vienna Hofoper; the Beseda choir is augmented by graduates of the Teachers' Institute; pupils from the Organ School also sing in Křížkovský's *The Shepherd and the Pilgrims*[13]

16 December: Concert; Janáček conducts Dvořák's overture *My Homeland*, Brahms's *Hungarian Dances*, Schumann's *Nachtlied* for chorus and orchestra, and male-voice choruses by Václav Veit, Pivoda and Karel Slavík

1884

30 March: 'Historical concert'; Janáček conducts Dvořák's *Legends* for orchestra, Saint-Saëns's *Danse macabre*, Palestrina's *Missa brevis*, Vecchi's *Missa pro defunctis* for eight-part choir, and Křížkovský's *The Shepherd and the Pilgrims*

1 June: Joint concert of the Brno Beseda and Prague 'Hlahol'; Janáček conducts two choruses, Bendl's *Trust in God* and Dvořák's *The Betrayed Shepherd*; programme includes choruses sung by 'Hlahol' or by the combined choirs, songs and arias with Marie Petzoldová-Sittová from the Prague National Theatre as soloist

1885 (only one full concert as the Beseda was low on funds)

29 March: Concert; Janáček conducts Liszt's symphonic poem *Mazeppa*, Dvořák's Nocturne for strings, choruses by Slavík, Karel Knittl and Dvořák (*The Beloved as Poisoner*); programme includes Dvořák's ballad *The Orphan*

1886

10 January: Jubilee concert celebrating twenty-five years since the founding of the Brno Beseda; Janáček conducts Dvořák's Symphony no. 7 in D minor and *Hymn: the Heirs of the White Mountain* for chorus and orchestra, and Křížkovský's chorus *The Drowned Maiden*

17 January: Programme of 10 January repeated as 'First Czech popular concert'

18 April: Smetana memorial concert; Janáček conducts Smetana's *Farmers' Chorus* for male voices; programme includes Smetana's String Quartet 'From my Life' and a lecture on Smetana by Otakar Hostinský

14 November: Brno Beseda concert enlarged with members of 'Svatopluk', 'Hlahol' and 'Veleslavín'; Janáček conducts march from Fibich's opera *The Bride of Messina*, Smetana's *Vyšehrad* and, with Josef Hofmann (billed as 'Josua Hofmann') as soloist, Beethoven's Piano Concerto no. 1 and Weber's Polonaise, arranged by Liszt for piano and orchestra; Janáček also conducts Dvořák's *Hymn of the Czech Peasants* for chorus and orchestra, his male-voice chorus *The Forsaken One*, and the première of two of his own *Four Male-voice Choruses* (IV/17): *O Love* and *Ah, the War*; the nine-year-old Hofmann also plays several solo piano items

21 November: Programme of 14 November repeated as 'Second Czech popular concert'; Hofmann includes his own newly composed *Reminiscence of Brno*

1887
24 April: Academy at the Czech Theatre, consisting mostly of solo items (piano, voice); Janáček conducts male-voice choruses by Josef Leopold Zvonař, Ferrario, Bendl and Dvořák (*The Fiddler*)

27 November: Concert; Janáček conducts Dvořák's *Legends* for orchestra and Georg Goltermann's Cello Concerto in A minor (with A. Hekking as soloist), and a chorus by Bendl for baritone, mixed chorus and piano

1888
29 April: Concert; Janáček conducts Dvořák's *The Spectre's Bride* (soloists include Marie Petzoldová-Sittová, Eduard Krtička and Hugo Krtička from Prague) in Dvořák's presence; this was one of the few Beseda concerts to make a profit[14]

---

choruses for 'Svatopluk' and the Beseda up to 1876 and the choruses of 1885 (IV/17); and it is the first piece that Janáček composed after his dispiriting experience in Vienna. It would be nice to report that by 18 September (the date of composition entered on the autograph) he had regained his spirits and confidence and was transcending that experience by writing a fine piece. But in fact it is one of his worst: aimless, characterless and incompetent. Its problems begin with the words, by one of the most distinguished Czech poets of the century, Jaroslav Vrchlický (1853–1912). They are written in high-style iambs, an uncomfortable metre for Czech with its first-syllable stress. Czech poets get round this by beginning each line with a monosyllable, which inevitably increases the number of words such as the Czech equivalents of 'oh' and 'how'. This not only gives the text a more precious and 'poetic' flavour but, with its end-stressed lines, encourages Czech composers to place an erroneous wallop on the final syllable of multi-syllable words. Compared with his earlier, beautifully stressed, mainly trochaic, folk-poetry settings, Janáček's setting of Vrchlický's words is appalling, with many mis-stressed third syllables. Furthermore the lyrical verse is far too fragile to take the somewhat pompous 'festive' mood that Janáček imposed upon it.

This uncharacteristic indifference to the words is compounded by a tonal rambling that looks back to Janáček's post-Skuherský phase, but also by mawkish chromatic part-writing that seems to be derived from his studies abroad. The most interesting aspect of the piece is its texture. The four voices are subdivided (into nine parts in the penultimate chord) and there are exposed lines presented in octaves as well as some thick low chords in the basses that are the only glimmer of the future composer. After this it seems surprising that Janáček went back to Vrchlický, but he went on to become the poet that Janáček set most frequently. Janáček's *Autumn Song* didn't go down well with members of the choir, chiefly because its demands meant that he spent much more time rehearsing it than Pivoda's unassuming *Spring Moods* and Křížkovský's familiar *Love-Gift*, an accusation that fuelled Janáček's first altercation with the Beseda.

This occurred a few weeks later. The chamber concert on 6 January 1881, now under the aegis of the Brno Beseda, was an echo of the winter chamber concerts that Janáček had organized with Wickenhauser before his time in Leipzig. It opened with Mozart's Clarinet Quintet – Janáček's attendance at the Vorlíček sisters' concert in Leipzig on 15 February 1880 had been some use at least in alerting him to this piece – and included vocal numbers sung by Josef Lev, the baritone star from the Czech Provisional Theatre whom Janáček had tempted to Brno to sing at a 'Svatopluk' concert in 1874. The bone of contention however was the inclusion of two pieces by Janáček, his Minuet and Scherzo for clarinet and piano (X/19), newly written to complement the Mozart quintet, and his Violin Sonata (X/16), whose slow movement had been Janáček's ill-fated entry for the first round of the Vienna Conservatory Vereinsmedaille competition. Two days later the review in *Moravská orlice* stated:

It would certainly have been only to the advantage of the concert had one of the two Janáček numbers been exchanged for a piece by Dvořák or Fibich. Mr Janáček's works, no doubt very worthy, reveal an unusual talent but so far on the whole remain highly promising experiments, whereas surely one of the main requirements of a chamber concert is that the programme should consist of flawless or perfect works.[17]

The first Beseda committee meeting after these events, on 15 January 1881, was a heated affair, whose tensions are evident from the minutes. The chief executive, Professor František Višňák, stated that the discontent both of those members taking part and of those in the audience should be noted. When Janáček demanded an explanation, he was told that members of the choir had complained that the performance of Křížkovský's *Love-Gift* was not up to speed because Janáček had spent more rehearsal time on his own piece. Janáček responded that this was a 'lie'; when asked by the chair to consider his words, he proclaimed 'in great agitation' that he was giving up the post of music director and stumped off.[18] The Beseda 'noted' his resignation and promptly reappointed his deputy Berthold Žalud, who had held the fort during Janáček's absence abroad.[19]

Janáček jotted down some of his reactions in his notebook: 'They say I've got many enemies? Should that matter to me? God forbid! I'll fight as long as I feel!'[20] However the 'fighting' seems to have given way to angry resignation. The two pieces played at the chamber concert were seemingly destroyed (they have never been found) and Janáček's connections with the Beseda ceased for a year. Although he resumed his conductorship in February 1882, it was not until November 1886 that he performed another of his own works there.

Janáček's public persona is well documented in his various activities in the early 1880s: the founding of the Brno Organ School in 1881, the periodical he edited, *Hudební listy* (1884–8; see chap. 24), and in his stormy relationship with the Brno Beseda. But what is hardly documented at all is his emotional life. This is in stark contrast to the previous seven months in Leipzig and Vienna, where he related his day-to-day life and his emotional ups and downs almost hourly in his letters to Zdenka. The above brief entry in his notebook is a rare exception. One inevitably has to rely on the much later memoirs of his future wife Zdenka Janáčková, and she is hardly an impartial witness. The early years of the marriage were undoubtedly the worst years of Zdenka's youth, sheltered as she had been by a protective family and ill equipped as she was to cope with the turbulence around her. But one has only her side of what went wrong.

As she recalled in her memoirs, Zdenka had expected that on Janáček's return to Brno they would continue with the 'happy idyll of a betrothed couple'. Announcements of their engagement, now made formally by Amalie Janáčková and the Schulzes, were sent out on 1 July 1880.[21] However, as Zdenka also admits in the memoirs, there were problems almost at once. For a start there was Zdenka's little brother, who was poorly and caused much worry and made much work: Zdenka shared all this with her mother, still weak from her confinement. It was good experience for a bride-to-be but it kept her away from her fiancé. Self-centred as ever, he took it badly.[22]

This was compounded by Janáček's sudden and fiery self-assertion of his Czech nationality. Though long-standing, Janáček's national awareness seems also to have been fitful. Either it didn't much matter to him for a while that his dealings with Zdenka and most of her family were in German, or this was a cynical calculation on his part. His argument might go as follows: marrying into a comparatively wealthy middle-class family was a big step up for a poor village boy; seeming compliance with this semi-Germanized world was a price worth paying until things were secure enough for him to assert his nationality. In other words, he waited patiently until the formal announcement of his engagement to Zdenka Schulzová on 1 July 1880 and then declared that he was Czech and Zdenka would have to be Czech too. But 'waiting patiently' was never Janáček's strong suit. It seems more likely that his time in Leipzig, in a completely German environment, polarized his feelings and brought his dormant Czechness to the surface. From his early months in Leipzig he began asserting a newly adopted Czech form of his first name (see chap. 14). Since Zdenka's Czech was rudimentary and non-literary there was no point in writing to her in Czech, let alone trying to get her to reply in Czech: this was something that would have to wait until his return to Brno in June 1880. But now the fun began:

After his return from Vienna he began to urge me to speak Czech with him. Why shouldn't I do that for him when I loved him more and more? I knew a fair amount of Czech, but only from our servants, with whom I had to make myself understood in their native language because none of them knew German. Mama always picked only Czech servants; she said that they were more hardworking and loyal than German girls. I was afraid that I might have learnt to speak somewhat incorrectly from them and that Leoš would laugh at me. But he replied to me in a serious tone: 'This is something we Czechs don't do, we're glad when someone wants to learn our language.'[23]

Janáček had always spoken Czech with Emilian Schulz; now he spoke Czech with Zdenka too. This caused problems since Mrs Schulzová knew little Czech and her mother Mrs Kaluschka, permanently resident with the family after the birth of Leoš Schulz, was actively hostile:

When one said 'Czechs' to her she imagined servants and a few of the most wretched paupers. According to her, anyone who didn't speak German wasn't an educated person. And now I, her little darling, her pride and joy, was beginning to speak the language of these despised creatures! And what's more, in company! And at the instigation of her [i.e. my] fiancé![24]

Janáček made matters even worse by refusing to speak German at all, so that any dealings with Mrs Schulzová or her mother had to be done via Zdenka, a provocation that now began to upset Mrs Schulzová as well: 'It was embarrassing and made no sense when after all he knew perfectly well that Mama and Grandmother really couldn't speak Czech; and they in turn had vivid memories of how, not so long ago, he'd conversed pleasantly with them in German.'[25] Zdenka recalled that this 'cross-fire' went on into the winter, by which time planning for the wedding was in full flood. Together with eleven other girls she was having cooking lessons in the famous kitchens of the Augustinian monastery, and her trousseau was being assembled. Schulz found a flat for the young couple to occupy when they were married, and their furniture was bought by the Schulzes, including a new Ehrbar baby grand piano (made in Vienna in 1876) that Leoš chose himself at Gregor's piano shop, and which remained his piano for the rest of his life.[†]

It is from this period that Janáček's hostility to his future in-laws can be dated. This was seemingly a complete volte-face and is not easy to explain. His letters from Leipzig and Vienna show every sign of respect and affection for the Schulzes. Emilian Schulz emerges as a stout supporter of Janáček's career, making sure that the young man found work in Brno, and that he got leave of absence for his studies abroad, while Mrs Schulzová attended to his material needs by frequent invitations to meals when in Brno and with food parcels when away. During Janáček's trips back to Brno from Leipzig and Vienna he became a permanent guest at their place, sleeping in Director Schulz's study. All the family's behaviour comes across as supportive and even loving. Before and after the wedding Emilian Schulz was an avid supporter for Janáček's proposal for the Brno Organ School (see chap. 21), perhaps because he truly believed in it, perhaps as a way of ensuring a better future for his daughter.[‡]

[†] It can be seen today in the Janáček house in Brno, and was in good enough shape in 2004 to allow Jan Jiraský to make a recording of *In the Mists* on it (ArcoDiva, UP 0071–2 131); see also chap. 24.

[‡] According to Zdenka's reminiscences given to Robert Smetana, the Organ School would provide a 'further economic basis' for the young couple (Smetana 1948, 25).

The arrival of Leoš Schulz changed the dynamics of the household (as indeed did the more permanent residence of old Mrs Kaluschka); Janáček's new-found Czechness and his demands for Zdenka to follow suit did not help. And Schulz's being both Janáček's boss and his prospective father-in-law may have produced tensions. All of these factors may have contributed to Janáček's change of attitude. Nevertheless it remains odd that what became a permanent and deep-seated antipathy by Janáček towards the Schulzes should have developed so quickly. His hostility affected Zdenka, who eventually decided to confront him; he stormed out of the house without a word. It was Mrs Schulzová, perhaps feeling that Zdenka would later reproach her parents for having been made to choose them rather than Janáček (as Zdenka speculated), who repaired the damage with a conciliatory letter.

But the Schulzes, too, had their doubts about the way things were going, and began to pursue the question of what language the banns would be proclaimed in. Zdenka thought that her mother's wish for German 'out of regard for our relatives' might have been a deliberate ploy to provoke a split between her and Leoš (who once again stormed out of the house). 'Child, you won't be happy with him,' was now Anna Schulzová's verdict. Zdenka's reply: 'I'd rather be unhappy with him than happy with someone else' may well have been 'half from the depths of [her] love, half out of childish wilfulness'[26] but it is also evidence that Zdenka, like her fiancé (see chap. 15), had read Bulwer Lytton's *A Strange Story*: 'Better be unhappy with one we love, than be happy with one we love not.'[27]

And so the preparations for the wedding stumbled on. This time it was Zdenka who had to make peace with her grumpy suitor: 'Scowling, angry, at once he began to dictate the conditions for a reconciliation. That if the wedding was to happen at all, it would have to be in Czech, and if we had children they'd have to be brought up in Czech.'[28] These were not conditions that Zdenka herself questioned, but the stormy way the reconciliation came about increased Janáček's alienation from the Schulzes.

Originally scheduled for after the summer holidays (in 1879 Janáček had predicted to Mrs Kaluschka that it would be on 5 November 1881),[29] and at least after Zdenka's sixteenth birthday on 31 July 1881, the wedding was in the end brought forward to Wednesday 13 July. In her recollections given to Robert Smetana, Zdenka remembered that a month before the wedding she had been prepared for confirmation by

Father František Ruprecht (1841–1903), the professor of religion at the Teachers' Institute. Later, the engaged couple both took catechism classes and Janáček 'also attended confession'.[30] Apart from concerts in St Thomas's, Janáček had entered a church in Leipzig only once when he went to Mass on 25 January 1880;[31] this, together with the fact that he had to prepare himself from Zdenka's catechism book since he had 'forgotten the regulations', shows the extent to which his religion had lapsed. Any religious activity now seems to have been undertaken purely to satisfy demands made by the church in order to have a church wedding. The couple took holy communion before the wedding,[32] perhaps the very last time that Janáček did so.

The famous wedding portrait of Leoš and Zdenka (see Plate 12) was also taken before the wedding. In her memoirs Zdenka explained how with the photography of the time brides in white came out as 'large unshaded blobs'. Although Zdenka was to be married in a fashionable rose-coloured gown,[33] she played safe by being photographed beforehand in an elaborate black dress, sitting in a carved wooden chair with Janáček standing protectively by her, one arm resting on the chair, the other held elegantly behind him. Naturally he was wearing his *čamara*, the braided jacket promoted by the Sokols and Czech nationalists for ceremonial occasions, rather as a Scot might favour a kilt for formal wear.

The wedding took place at five o'clock in the Augustinian monastery church, conducted by Father Ruprecht with Father Anselm Rambousek as assistant. Zdenka records many details of her accessories and of the ceremony, but the most fascinating aspect was the problem over Amalie Janáčková. Three hours before the service was to begin Janáček insisted on Zdenka's accompanying him to see his mother. He explained that she would not be coming to the Schulzes' house before the service or even to the church 'because she hadn't got the right clothes'. Zdenka, her hair in curlers, demurred and it was her uncle Julius Kaluschka who in the end took her off to see Amalie Janáčková. There she learnt that it was not a question of whether Janáček's mother had an appropriate outfit but that Janáček himself had forbidden her to attend either event. It is understandable that Janáček thought that his mother might be ill at ease among the Schulzes and their German relatives but it seems extraordinary that he didn't want her at the wedding ceremony either. Zdenka may have misremembered the details: in her account to Smetana, for example, she relates that

Mrs Janáčková (and one daughter) attended the church service though not the Schulz reception beforehand and that this was purely a matter of linguistic convenience. 'Janáček's sister' was not identified except as being a domestic science teacher. This means either Eleonora or Josefa, and is more likely to be Eleonora, who was then closer to her mother and lived nearer than Josefa (i.e. in Švábenice, not in Hukvaldy).

The bridesmaid was a childhood friend of Zdenka's, Gusta Horničková, the best man was František Dlouhý (1852–1912), one of Janáček's colleagues from the Brno Teachers' Institute, and the witnesses were Vincenc Neubauer (an estate manager, perhaps a friend of the Schulzes), Alexander Lorenz (Zdenka's relative with whom Janáček had spent so much time in Vienna) and Janáček's friend the painter Josef Ladislav Šichan[34] (1847–1918), who presented the couple with oil portraits of themselves.[5] The wedding party included some twenty guests who departed in carriages from the Teachers' Institute. After the wedding they proceeded to the Besední dům for a reception in the Small Hall. Music had been provided at the church by some of Janáček's pupils at the Teachers' Institute, who had returned from their holidays for the occasion. But there was also unexpected music at the reception: members of the German Theatre orchestra who had played at Brno Beseda concerts struck up dance music in the room next door as a special surprise for their conductor. Zdenka declared that they 'of course danced to their music', but 'they' may not have included Janáček – a poor dancer as Zdenka reveals later in her memoirs.[35] Zdenka remembered (in her account to Smetana) that Janáček 'drank very abstemiously'. Nevertheless he 'glowed with happiness'. Father Rambousek (1824–1901), soon to become Mendel's successor as abbot at the monastery, made a 'witty speech' and the festivities continued until three in the morning.[36]

'We all grew merry, especially with the champagne, Leoš drank a toast to calling my parents *Ty*.' This is generally how friends acknowledge the time has come to use the intimate form of 'you' (*Ty*). But in Janáček's case he seemed to have thought better of it: 'the next day, when we then went from the new flat to my parents for lunch, he was again cool as ice and surprised my parents by calling them *Vy*.'[37]

[5] For many years only the one of Janáček was known, but Eva Drlíková tracked down its partner in Vienna, and reproduced it in *OM*, xxxiv/4 (2002), cover.

Zdenka's memoirs also record the honeymoon trip in some detail. The couple left the next day by train, serenaded at the station by Janáček's pupils from the Teachers' Institute.[38] They went first to Zdenka's paternal grandfather, a doughty Czech patriot, who lived with an unmarried daughter in Obřístí, Bohemia, one of the few references Zdenka makes to the Czech side of her family. Thereafter they spent a week in Prague, where they met some of the friends Janáček made during his year of study there. There was Ferdinand Lehner, the priest and choir director who had taken a kindly interest in Janáček as a student in Prague, the baritone Josef Lev, who had sung for Janáček a few months earlier at the chamber concert and who now showed them round the newly completed National Theatre (a brief glimpse before it burnt down a few months later), and most memorably Antonín Dvořák:

Leoš and I were travelling somewhere by carriage when Dvořák came walking along the pavement in the opposite direction. Leoš let out a cry of joy, gave orders to stop and called out to the Maestro, saying he wanted to introduce me. Dvořák came up to the carriage, stuck his head inside, opened his eyes wide at me and exclaimed: 'What have you been doing marrying a child!'[39]

Although this passage suggests that Dvořák had not met Zdenka before, they had probably been introduced during Dvořák's visit to Brno for the Beseda concert on 6 January 1880, at which Janáček and Zdenka had heard Dvořák conduct his Symphony no. 5 in F.[40] 'After that', Zdenka recalled, 'he was very often with us', taking part for instance in a joint trip to Karlštejn, the splendid Gothic castle outside Prague built by Charles IV. Zdenka remembered Dvořák as 'a simple, dear person with ridiculous ideas', one of which was his interest in the 'call of the castle guard', which they'd heard about from the guide, and which Dvořák, seemingly seriously, kept on repeating to himself all the way back to Prague.[41]

Evidence of Janáček's antipathy towards the Schulz family, however, was again on display when the honeymoon couple bumped into Grandmother Kaluschka at Petzold's restaurant in Prague: 'I wanted to rush over to her, but my husband looked so disapproving that I didn't dare. We greeted each other only perfunctorily and I made an excuse that we had to leave because we were invited elsewhere.'[42] Matters did not improve on their way home or on their return:

Leoš behaved with similar stiffness towards Uncle Gustav [Kaluschka], at whose house we broke our journey on the way home. It didn't help that my uncle was hospitable and did all we could have wished: he was a German and Mama's brother and that was unforgivable. Only my little cousin, who didn't know any German at all, found favour; Leoš chatted the whole day with him. [. . .] Home wasn't much better. Papa came to the station for us, he took us home for a meal, then he accompanied us to our own flat. There were plenty of signs there that during our absence he and Mama had lovingly taken the trouble to make everything as cosy as possible for our return. The salon, the bedroom, the dining-room, Leoš's study, everything had been carefully cleaned and tidied, but my husband didn't even thank Father, didn't even show that he took pleasure in all this.[43]

After a week the couple went off on the second stage of their honeymoon, starting with a visit to Janáček's priest-uncle, Jan Janáček, in Znorovy. Although Zdenka by now was pining for her mother and would have preferred to stay at home, she found Father Janáček 'a very nice, affable gentleman, we got on famously together'. From there they made several trips in the vicinity, including one to the Moravian folk centre of Strážnice, and then went on to Velehrad, the scene of the Cyril and Methodius celebrations in 1869, and to Janáček's birthplace Hukvaldy. Zdenka was struck by the 'pleasant company of teachers and estate officials with whom we mixed at the Stará hospoda [Old inn]'.[44] No doubt hearing a bit of German from the archbishop's estate officials helped. It was in Hukvaldy that Zdenka met Janáček's sister Josefa, who taught domestic science in the local school. She was now thirty-nine, unmarried, but 'great fun', not a view that Zdenka later held, or indeed one that emerges from her letters. However, she smoked, and taught Zdenka to smoke, so perhaps she came across then as engagingly 'naughty' and clearly very different from the other more serious ladies in Zdenka's life. However, neither Zdenka nor Leoš became regular smokers (Janáček is reported as smoking the occasional cigar).[45] Zdenka claimed that she and her husband would occasionally smoke 'for fun' in company.[46]

In these honeymoon trips Janáček had clearly tried to give his bride a taste of his earlier life: Hukvaldy, his uncle Jan, his Prague mentors. But one more important gap remained: Father Pavel Křížkovský, whom they visited on the way back, in Olomouc, where he was choirmaster at the cathedral. Zdenka remembered the visit mostly because of Janáček's miscalculation over the budget. They had to skip lunch because they had run out of money and seemed not to have enough to get them back to Brno. Křížkovský, a 'good soul', lent them 5 zl.[47]

Shortage of money is a topic frequently mentioned in Zdenka's memoirs. She was used to a home carefully if not frugally run, and to the higher level of income appropriate to a director of a teaching institution rather than that of one of his junior members of staff. Janáček's annual salary, then 1243 zl, from the Teachers' Institute was now augmented both by 15 zl a month from the Augustinian monastery (which continued to give him lunch and supper) and by an allowance of 25 zl a month from Schulz, who also provided his daughter with money for fuel. Although Zdenka characterized all this as 'quite decent', she had also quickly come to the conclusion that her husband was not good with money and tended to 'fritter it away'. A joint kitty proved a disaster: Janáček had spent it all well before the end of the first month. After that she insisted on his giving her house-keeping money separately: 'I came out well on my share, but he could never properly work out his.' Of course, as Zdenka acknowledged, he continued to support his mother and his youngest brother Josef (now twenty-three), and to pay off his debt to the Brno music dealer Winkler. 'But all that could have been put right nicely if he'd entrusted it to me, or had at least consulted me, for I always had much more financial sense than he did. But he never let me in on anything important, he preferred to do stupid things.'[48]

Zdenka had other complaints. The affectionate diminutives 'Zdenči' and 'Zdenčinka', with which Janáček's letters to her from Leipzig and Vienna are liberally sprinkled, were soon abandoned for a straightforward 'Zdenko' (i.e. the vocative of 'Zdenka'); this, spoken in his 'clipped manner', struck her as harsh and 'sometimes almost tyrannical'.[49] Then there was his insistence on her not reading German books any more; instead he borrowed light fiction for her from the local library, usually translations into Czech, which she had to plough through on her own; it took a year or so before she was comfortable with reading in Czech. Furthermore Janáček soon stopped giving her piano lessons; as he needed the piano for his own work, she sometimes didn't get to the instrument for days, and in the end gave up playing altogether.

Although she doesn't spell it out in her memoirs, it sounds as if Zdenka's life had suddenly become rather empty, without her former hobbies (reading in German, the piano), without much contact with her family and without being able to care for her little brother. Even if, as she said, there was 'plenty of work' in a flat without electricity or running water (which needed to be carried in from the pump in the courtyard), she did have a daily help for the 'worst work', and since Janáček took his meals at the monastery there was not a lot she had to do in the kitchen. Much of the time Janáček was simply out working: 'In the morning, teaching at the institute, every day at noon a rehearsal with the choristers at the monastery, in the afternoon teaching again, often rehearsals with the Beseda Philharmonic and lots of other occasional work.'[50] What upset her the most were the much restricted contacts with her family. They were not allowed to visit, and she was 'virtually forbidden' to go to them. She seems to have been stuck at home for much of the time feeling sorry for herself.

Why was it so important to Janáček that Zdenka didn't see her parents? Zdenka came up with three explanations. One was his newly discovered linguistic intransigence, and the fact that if Zdenka went home she would talk German with her mother. A second was his jealousy towards parents to whom she was evidently devoted. And a third was the position of his own mother. Amalie Janáčková, then sixty-two, is a shadowy figure who after her husband's death in 1866 almost drops out of the story until the years leading up to her death in 1884. It is understandable, once Janáček went to Brno as a choral scholar and was supported by his uncle, that she devoted her limited resources to her younger sons, but it almost seems as if she ignored the schoolboy Leo altogether. One visit is recorded (see chap. 7) but not a single letter. Janáček visited her at the end of his Brno school studies in the summer of 1879; she was then living in Příbor, where she moved in 1866 after her husband's death.

The next one hears of Janáček's mother is not until many years later, when she moved to live with Janáček in Staré Brno in Měšťanská ulice no. 15 – she was officially reported as living there in 1881.[51] Svatava Přibáňová suggests that the move was after 1877, when her youngest son, Josef, left the nest for Russia.[52] In the 1880 census she had had four students living with her (one reason why Janáček couldn't stay with her on his trips back from Leipzig and Vienna). Although officially 'domiciled' in Hukvaldy, she could, within Austro-Hungarian law, live where she chose to and the pension she received after the death of her husband Jiří Janáček could be sent to the nearest parish office (in her case that of St Marie, Staré Brno). All her sons, however, continued to support her financially.[53] Janáček appears to have had minimal contact with her when abroad, generally not writing to her but instead sending messages via Zdenka, who went to visit her from time to time, accompanied by her mother. As Janáček put it some three weeks into the beginning of his time in Leipzig: 'You can always tell my mother, dearest Zdenka, how I'm doing and that should anything special happen I would write to her.'[54] Amalie's earliest surviving letter to her son dates from October 1879 and was prompted by a letter from 'Mr Dvořák' wanting back the performing materials for his Piano Concerto, which Janáček had been considering performing at the Beseda. Her letter is practical and businesslike rather than especially affectionate or lonely, though she mentions that she had complied with Janáček's wishes conveyed by Zdenka and 'Mrs Director' (i.e. Mrs Schulzová) 'with pain'. What request might have caused her pain? She seemed unconcerned, however, that her son was not communicating directly with her. Although she instructed him to 'write soon',[55] it was not for many months that he did so, or at least told Zdenka that he would.[56]

Zdenka had little to say about her mother-in-law in her memoirs: 'As far as I could tell from our rare meetings with her, she wasn't a bad person. She got on very nicely with me and with my parents. Soon after our wedding she moved in with her daughter Eleonora in Švábenice near Vyškov.'[57] There was, however, a story behind this which Zdenka unearthed only after Janáček's death:

Among Leoš's papers I found her letters from the first year of our marriage; nowhere there did she come across as unfriendly towards me, reproaching Leoš only with the fact that he'd promised that she'd live with us after the wedding and that he then didn't keep his promise. To me it seemed odd: even before the wedding Leoš had come to an agreement with my parents that we young people would remain on our own. Leoš never showed me these letters from his mother, but I think that they preyed on his mind. Perhaps, since he didn't have his mother around, he thought that I shouldn't have contact with my parents: he always had such childish ideas.[58]

There is indeed a short undated letter to Janáček from Amalie Janáčková, whose references to the imminent end-of-year holidays suggest it was written in mid-December 1881. Having thanked her son for money, she added: 'you mustn't fear that you will ever see me in Brno for with a bleeding heart I left Brno for ever.'[59]

This incident may well be the key to it all, the source of immediate friction in the new marriage and the source of much resentment to come. Forty years later Janáček exploded with anger at Zdenka's idea of bringing her widowed father to live with them, and remembered his bitterness about not being able to help his mother: 'I too had a mother, a poor wretched mother – and she couldn't live with me: but not on my account!'[60]

A final reason that Zdenka offers for her husband's behaviour is that he simply wasn't used to family life, thrown out of home when he was young and having to fend for himself thereafter: 'Life among strangers certainly didn't teach him tenderness.' And Zdenka, as she readily admitted, was too young (she was still only sixteen) and inexperienced: 'I just knew one thing: that at home with my parents there was warmth and I felt good there. Like a thief I used to steal off more and more often to my parents and I used to cry a lot at mother's. She was also unhappy at this but she couldn't help me.'[61]

The one thing that seems to have given Zdenka pleasure in her first year of marriage was that she had a social life: she threw herself into the activities mounted in Czech Brno, and this certainly would have pleased her husband. She joined the Czech Ladies' Committee for Charitable Works, which looked after children in Czech children's homes, collecting money for them and making clothes. She joined 'Vesna' (which began life as a choral society in 1870 but later branched out to become an educational establishment for girls). She attended lectures and got to know the worthy women who ran the organization. Other means of Zdenka's integration with Czech society came through the Czech Readers' Club:

Very often we also used to go to the Readers' Club in the Besední dům, where Czech intelligentsia gathered. We felt at home here, as if on a firm island in the middle of the German sea around us. Over a glass of beer we'd sit in pleasant conversation there with Father Ruprecht or the painter Šichan.

Zdenka mentioned many of the people she met there. Among them she noticed that one, the wife of the politician and lawyer Dr Šrom, was German and that people spoke to her 'cheerfully in her native tongue and nobody reproached her for it. Sometimes I thought regretfully how sharp Leoš was with Mama and Grandmother: I began to realize that this intolerance wasn't a characteristic of all Czechs but only of my husband.'[62]

Zdenka's greatest pleasure was dancing. This had begun before she married Janáček, and one of her most vividly recounted memories was her first dance, the fancy-dress ball at the Readers' Club in which she went as Marguerite – Gounod's *Faust* had been recently performed in Czech by the touring Pištěk company. Janáček accompanied her himself dressed up as Faust:

He wore a black velvet coat which suited his pale face, his black beard and curly hair, and his dark eyes very well. At his side he had a sword. I had a blue dress just like all Marguerites have in the theatre, and on my breast and at the end of my loose plaits, I'd fastened posies of yellow daisies – marguerites. And today, after all those years, I must say that we really made a handsome couple.[63]

18

Janáček as teacher

Like his father and grandfather before him Janáček spent his working life teaching. His early years were all directed to training for this purpose, his means of earning a living. The chief difference between him and his forebears was that he ended up as a specialist music teacher in a town rather than a general teacher in a small village. Furthermore Janáček had several teaching jobs, some held simultaneously, at the following institutions:

1872–6   Practice school at the Men Teachers' Institute
1873–1904 Men Teachers' Institute
1876–8   Women Teachers' Institute
1882–1920 Brno Organ School (Conservatory in final year)
(1882–9   Beseda music school)
1886–1902 Staré Brno Gymnasium II
1920–5   Master School in composition (Brno branch of Prague Conservatory)[1]

The practice-school job essentially kept Janáček in Brno at the beginning of his career and was his only general (rather than specifically musical) teaching post. It was unpaid until 1876.* In 1873 Janáček was listed as a stand-in teacher at the Teachers' Institute.[2] Only after two years of teaching practice, his Prague music studies in 1874–5 and his passing of state examinations in October 1875 could he be designated an 'imperial and royal music teacher'; this title was conferred on him on 30 August 1876, at first provisional, and on 14 May 1880 regular.[3]

---

* *LJPT*, 271 reports that from 17 February 1874 Janáček could 'claim remuneration', but there is no record of any such remuneration being given him until 1876 (see chap. 42).

In the ministerial decree of 30 August 1876 Janáček was also charged to oversee the teaching of singing and music at the Women Teachers' Institute and teach there, if needs be.[4] The archive of the Women Teachers' Institute supports this, but provides no further details of his activities.[5] He was not paid for what he did and presumably he was not there for very long.[†] Although this mainly supervisory post may have included teaching, this is not true of Janáček's post at the Beseda music school; as director there he was concerned merely with overseeing and organizing the provision of instrumental teachers (see chap. 20).

Janáček's chief teaching posts were the three long-held ones: at the Men Teachers' Institute (from 1873), the Brno Organ School (from 1882) and at the Staré Brno Gymnasium II (from 1886). As the list above shows, Janáček shed two of these three as he approached fifty, keeping on only the Organ School. A year after it became a conservatory in 1919, Janáček stepped down and in compensation was appointed to the academy-level post attached to the Prague Conservatory, in which capacity he looked after a few young Brno composers. Because of his particular involvement with the Brno Organ School, Janáček's years there will be addressed separately (chap. 21). The present chapter is primarily concerned with Janáček as a teacher at two institutions: the Men Teachers' Institute and the Staré Brno Gymnasium.

The Teachers' Institute made up over half of Janáček's income (see chap. 41). By the mid-1880s he was earning a total of 1340 zl with regular increments thereafter. In contrast the Gymnasium job yielded only 240 zl a year with no increments; the Organ School's 370 zl (or 740 K) was not increased until 1903. To some extent these levels of pay reflected the number of hours Janáček worked at each institution (just four, for instance, at the Gymnasium), though the Organ School included a huge amount of administration undertaken without secretarial help.

At the Teachers' Institute Janáček's teaching load was officially twenty-four to twenty-five hours a week during which he taught singing, piano, violin and organ, and attended church services and staff meetings. Classes at the institution took place five days a week from eight to six (with a one-hour lunch break) and from eight to twelve on Saturdays.[6] 'Music and singing' was an obligatory subject for all trainee

---

[†] According to records in the Brno Town archive, he was there until 1878 (information from Jiří Zahrádka).

teachers throughout the four-year course. The syllabus included music theory, harmony, singing practice (both solo and choir), the history of music, folksong and methods of teaching music. Students were expected to play the piano and the violin; the more accomplished ones took the organ as well.[7] Janáček was the only official music teacher at the Teachers' Institute and, since he was not able to cover all the teaching himself, he shared the load with other musical members of staff.[8] While the syllabus was laid down centrally (and aimed to support the Austro-Hungarian state ideology and its religion), Janáček, as the first official music teacher, had some input into what was taught and how.[9]

Today it seems a sympathetic aspect of the teaching syllabus that music was regarded as important; however, its inclusion laid a huge burden on the teachers as the trainees would not necessarily have much in the way of musical aptitude or experience. The group teaching of a large number of students posed many problems, as one of Janáček's students recalled:

I see [Janáček] – as though it were today – how reluctantly he walked to the conductor's stand in the music room to conduct such works as Pleyel's duets during which he heard those forty (!) violinists of all sorts playing on all sorts of violins with all sorts of skill and, mostly, lack of skill.[10]

The difficulties Janáček faced were graphically described by a student who, with seventeen others, attended a one-year course at the Teachers' Institute in 1893 in order to complete various final-year subjects, including 'music and singing'. Out of this group only three had previous musical training; some of the rest attempted to acquire rudimentary skills on the violin during the holidays before enrolling at the Teachers' Institute. Apart from the violin, which one of his colleagues taught, Janáček was wholly responsible for the group. He had to listen to fumbling attempts on the piano (exercises from the standard Czech piano method by Jan Malát, and the least demanding Clementi sonatas); in the second semester, on the organ, students were expected to play short preludes in all major and minor keys. Singing was taught in group classes, using exercises from the Czech singing method by Pivoda[‡] in the first semester, and in the second learning

---

[‡] Janáček's contacts with František Pivoda (1829–98) go back at least to Janáček's time in Leipzig: in a letter of 7 August 1880 (BmJA, A 4313) Pivoda reminds Janáček of his promise, made from Leipzig, to let him know which parts of his singing method he already had and which ones Pivoda could still send him.

Czech folksongs from the recently published Janáček-Bartoš *Bouquet of Moravian Folksongs* (XIII/1). Students also attended Masses at the Staré Brno monastery church, with Janáček playing the organ.[11]

Janáček's notebooks include his school registers, with names written out neatly (by Zdenka?), and these give some idea of his workload. In 1881–2, the first year with surviving lists, Janáček taught students in all four years of the course: I – 34; II – 43; III – 68; IV – 74 (a total of 219 students). All of them learnt singing, and he needed to hear them individually several times a year in order to grade them. Additionally those in the first and second year took the organ with Janáček, and in the third year all sixty-eight learnt the violin with him.[12] The numbers and subjects varied from year to year (with other colleagues taking on some of the instrumental tuition), but in all years Janáček was responsible for singing.

A few years later, in 1887–8 for instance, the size of the groups in the first two years had increased, while the third and fourth had diminished: I – 60; II – 53; III – 54; IV – 40 (a total of 207 students). In this and other years he gave indications in the register of his students' voices: tenor, baritone, bass or alto. There were sixteen altos among the sixty students of his first year, i.e. a quarter still had unbroken voices when they arrived at the Teachers' Institute. In the first years his notes (giving grades and the dates on which he graded them) indicate that he graded the first-year students up to three times over the year; those in their third and fourth years were graded up to six times each in singing, violin and organ. In other words, in these two year-groups alone he needed to see over one hundred students individually up to eighteen times. Even if he contrived to get through this in just ten minutes each, this represents a commitment of at least three hundred hours over the year. In this year he provided a careful summary in the register of his final grades, using the usual five-point scale in which a five was a fail, a scale that persists to this day in the Czech Republic. In the first year he awarded two firsts, eighteen seconds, nineteen thirds, seventeen fourths and one fail; by this stage, three out of the sixty had dropped out. In the second year there were three firsts, seven seconds, eighteen thirds, twenty-four fourths and no failures. In that second-year group two students died,[13] not an unusual occurrence. Scarlet fever, flu (in 1890) and cholera (in 1892) all took their toll among the students; many suffered from tuberculosis, with up to three cases of death a year in the institute.[14]

Janáček was one of the strictest teachers at the Teachers' Institute. Although grading was inevitably subjective, based purely on teacher observation, results nevertheless could be compared across the board. For instance in 1895 Janáček gave fourth-class marks to twenty-five out of forty-four students in their final year, results that were out of line with other teachers' gradings and would influence the students' final grade. Schulz invited Janáček to revise his grades, but was countered with an outraged refusal, as the staff minutes record.[15]

With such numbers, and at a time when teachers commanded much greater authority than they do now, conditions were harsh. Students were often expelled for out-of-class misdemeanours that today would be shrugged off, such as rowdy behaviour on the streets at night and visiting bars, or in acts of unspecified 'indecency'. Jindřiška Bártová's archival research unearthed some curiosities such as a student being sent down for showing his neighbour on the bench a 'very indecent picture', which turned out to be a scene from a 'Turkish harem'. Even the dress code was restrictive, for instance the wearing of fashionable hats with wide brims was forbidden; students were not allowed to draw attention to themselves with flamboyant clothes. Politics, too, could be problematic. Investigations were conducted in 1878 about the distribution of a Russian primer (interest in Russia and its language was regarded as a political statement), or the purchase of a wreath for the grave of the Czech (and pro-Slavonic) patriot Josef Dobrovský.[16]

Jan Kunc (1883–1976), who went on to become director of the Brno Conservatory, experienced Janáček as a teacher both at the Teachers' Institute and at the Organ School. In his remarkably frank account of Janáček in *Hudební revue* (1911) he contrasted Janáček's liveliness as a teacher at the Organ School with the somewhat withdrawn, taciturn impression he made at the Teachers' Institute. Kunc attributed this to Janáček's huge teaching load, the rigid syllabus and the fact that he had to deal with large numbers of unmusical and unmotivated students. Instrumental teaching seems to have been the major bugbear. Kunc recalled the 'calculatedly cold' way with which Janáček tapped his pencil to indicate to students playing through their prepared organ pieces that they should begin again. Group singing was drilled with great precision. Janáček didn't teach many pieces, but what he did was done extremely thoroughly.[17] Single-voice folksongs and Pivoda's exercises formed the basis for the singing in the first three years; by the fourth year Janáček's students, for instance in 1883, were singing 'patriotic choruses' (Norbert Javůrek's *To Moravia*, Alois Jelen's *Love for one's Homeland*) and 'social choruses' (Josef Leopold Zvonář's *Excursion Chorus* and Dvořák's *The Betrayed Shepherd*). Janáček maintained that these were practised 'precisely, up to concert standard' – this despite the 'undeveloped voices' and disproportionate distribution (mostly 'childish' basses with only a sprinkling of tenors).[18]

Bártová's study of the monthly records provides further details of the repertory that Janáček introduced: Czech songs by Bendl, Malát and Fibich were those that he used the most. Music history formed a part of 'music and singing' and here Janáček would talk about Palestrina, Handel, Haydn, Mozart, Beethoven, Křížkovský and Smetana (interestingly, Dvořák is missing from this group). According to his teaching, the 'most significant living composers' included Gounod, Rubinstein and Brahms.[19] In addition to class teaching Janáček was responsible for the music sung at church services. When the dispute with Schulz blew up in March 1883 (see chap. 20) Janáček's defence gives some idea of what was involved: hymns for ordinary Sundays and special ones for particular church seasons, with the second years being able to sing Latin plainsong. And Janáček was also responsible for organizing various informal concerts (the so-called *akademie*) and other festive events at the Teachers' Institute with his students taking part. On a couple of special occasions (laying the foundation stone for the new building and its opening a year later), Janáček wrote new choruses for students to perform (IV/12 and IV/13).

In trying to map aspects of Janáček's personality, Helfert devoted less space to his school teaching than to other activities.[20] The day job, one can argue, was chosen for Janáček; more interesting are the things that he chose himself: his conducting, his composition, his writing, his folksong work and his directorship of the Organ School. However, it is clear from Janáček's published writings that music teaching in schools was a major concern for him during the decade 1877–87. He published four articles about aspects of teaching (XV/20, XV/39, XV/78, XV/82)[§] as well as a singing-teaching manual a decade later (1899; XV/162). Many of Janáček's other activities could be regarded as complementary to his endeavours as a school-music teacher. His theoretical writings

---

[§] Vysloužilová 1976, 215 lists a fifth article in *Hudební listy*, ii (1884–5), on music teaching at junior schools; however this is signed with a plus (+) rather than Janáček's usual triangle. Dr Straková did not include it in her list of Janáček's writings in *JAWO* or reprint it in *LD*.

may have been conceived at a more advanced level, e.g. for students at the Brno Organ School, but much of his folk-collecting activities fed directly into this school teaching. His collection *A Bouquet of Moravian Folksongs* (XIII/1), edited with his superior František Bartoš at the Staré Brno Gymnasium and first published in 1890, was used for class singing both at the Teachers' Institute and at the Gymnasium, and it is reasonable to assume that the accompaniments that he wrote for fifty-three of these (V/2) were intended for these purposes too.[21] Janáček's singing manual (XV/162) was designed for use at the Teachers' Institute, and although, on the basis of two negative reports, the Ministry of Culture and Education did not approve its use at teaching institutions,[22] its pages demonstrate how seriously Janáček took his work and provide a useful insight into his approach. Its 104 exercises begin with the naming and notation of notes and proceed, through a variety of note values, rhythms, metres, tempos, intervals, keys and dynamics, mostly in single-voice tunes with piano accompaniment, to a few two-part exercises at the end. Nevertheless, it would be difficult to make out a case for Janáček as a teacher to be as influential in this respect as, say, Kodály. He had no impact on the teaching of music beyond the institutions in which he taught, or the students he taught. There is no 'Janáček method' to survive him. The contributions he made, and these are controversial, were more in the field of music theory than in the teaching of music to schoolchildren.

Later reminiscences by Janáček's former students from the Teachers' Institute, recalled only when he had become famous, need to be taken with a pinch of salt as they inevitably give a more glowing account than may have been the case. Nevertheless they provide a picture of Janáček in a less familiar context:

At that time he had not yet been 'drunk with glory'[II] but he was obviously an exceptional figure on the teaching staff. All his pupils felt this. Even if our teacher was strikingly taciturn, reserved and strict in every respect, we nevertheless always welcomed him with special respect whenever he entered the music room, the great hall of the period. With his wonderfully shaky step, his tiny figure shuffling his way round our benches, our teacher would sit down at the piano without a word, his black locks waving luxuriantly in a gleam of sunlight. [. . .] And when we sang folksongs from the Bartoš-Janáček *Bouquet*

[II] Janáček's pithy description of his trip to London in 1926.

and the maestro accompanied our song on the piano, it was evident to everyone that a rare artist stood before us whom, of course, not everyone
understood.[23]

Another reminiscence, although celebrating Janáček's 'great kindness', 'charming smile' or the 'kind expression in his eyes', nevertheless
went on to describe his 'fiery temper', irritability and 'fits of uncontrol-
lable anger':

If at some stage someone in the choir got something wrong he knew immediately which unfortunate throat had perpetrated the wrong note, and went for
the culprit with baton or pencil, both of which were equally dangerous
weapons in his hands. But we soon got used to it and even used to be proud of
it. 'I had it coming for me today! Did you see how his baton bounced off my
skull!' [. . .]
Leoš Janáček was never one of those teachers who entered things in
class-books or who sent in complaints to the director. He dealt with us on
the spot: with a baton or a pencil or with scores, and with thorough, robust
scoldings that invariably began 'Bah, you lazybones!'[24]

In 1886 Janáček added to his duties the teaching of music and singing
at the Staré Brno Gymnasium. Quite why he took on this post seems
at first hard to explain. It is evident from the account above that
he regarded the Teachers' Institute job as a chore. Why would he
have wanted more of the same, especially when he had so little time
to himself? The monastery choir, the directorship of the Beseda choir
and school, and his editorship of *Hudební listy* were all going strong.
The answer probably lies in a combination of personal contacts with
František Bartoš (1837–1906; see Plate 29) and the sudden death of his
old friend and colleague Berthold Žalud. The Staré Brno Gymnasium
('Gymnasium II') was originally (1883) a branch of what was then the
only Czech-language Gymnasium for boys in Brno (Gymnasium I). In
1885 the branch became an independent 'lower' Gymnasium. Bartoš
had taught at Gymnasium I since 1869 and transferred to the new
establishment, which, as it happened, started life in the building of the
Teachers' Institute. Janáček and Bartoš already knew one another from
Czech cultural circles;[25] now they would have bumped into one another
on a daily basis. Žalud had been appointed teacher of 'music and singing' at the Staré Brno Gymnasium from its inception; following his
death from tuberculosis on 19 July 1886 a replacement was needed for
the autumn at short notice. Bartoš, a senior figure at the Gymnasium

who himself became director in 1888, could well have persuaded Janáček that his duty as a Czech patriot and a friend was to take over Žalud's post.

No doubt Bartoš could have stressed that this was not an onerous task, and involved a commitment of a mere four hours a week during term. Pupils had what were essentially singing lessons (though elements of theory and music notation were included) partly to provide a choir for the church services that they were obliged to attend – religious education was a crucial part of the curriculum.[26] Until the academic year 1899–1900 the students who chose to take 'voluntary singing' were divided into two groups, division I and division II, each division attending two one-hour classes a week. Numbers varied, but for instance in the teaching year 1890–1 Janáček had twenty-nine pupils in the first division and twenty-six in the second;[27] in the next year the figures were twenty-three and twenty-four.[28] According to his blueprint published in *Hudební listy* in December 1887 (*Proposal for a Singing-Teaching Course at Gymnasia and Realschulen* xv/78) Janáček counted on rather larger numbers, up to thirty boys between ten and thirteen in division I and up to forty boys between eleven and sixteen in division II. In division I they mostly sang folksongs, in division II a more demanding repertory. For instance in the autumn semester of 1900 Janáček rehearsed with his higher division a choral arrangement of Weber's 'Prayer' from *Der Freischütz*, Caspar Ett's *Veni Sancte Spiritus*, Haydn's *Schöpfungsmesse*, Liszt's *Ave Maria*, Fibich's *Missa brevis* and his own chorus for mixed voices, *The Wild Duck* (iv/18); this last was performed at the Besední dům at the seventh concert of Brno Czech middle schools on 17 March 1901, the first known performance of this 1885 chorus.[29]

Something of Janáček's approach to his task can be gleaned from his proposal (xv/78), but evidence of what actually went on is provided by some of the surviving class 'catalogue' books (from 1894–5 onwards), in which Janáček noted down what he did in each class. In Bohumír Štědroň's study of these he printed a facsimile of Janáček's work in the week of 11–15 March 1895. It is clear from this that Janáček gave four classes, all from four to five in the afternoon: on Monday and Thursday (11 and 14 March) in division I, and Tuesday and Friday (12 and 15 March) in division II. In the class book Janáček noted down the differing exercises (from Pivoda's singing method) that he conducted with both classes, and Tovačovský's song *Spring is coming*, which he practised with both groups. The names of missing students are recorded (a total of seven students over the four classes, six of them 'excused'). There is also a note in the 'remarks' column showing that the director Bartoš attended the Friday afternoon class.[30] This detail is most significant: one of Janáček's complaints in his dispute with Schulz (see chap. 20) was that at the Teachers' Institute the director took no interest in what he did in his classes, but, as Štědroň noted, there is plenty of evidence that Bartoš found the time to sit in on some of Janáček's classes and offer moral support and encouragement.[31] The result was that Janáček stayed in his post at a most pressured time, even beyond Bartoš's retirement in 1898, and that he took the job seriously enough to write and arrange music for his young charges.

From 1898 this 'lower' Gymnasium was gradually expanded with more advanced classes, with the result for Janáček that in the autumn of 1899 he had to add a third, more advanced class,[32] and this seems to have led to his seeking out more demanding repertory and in a couple of cases making his own arrangements of music for use there. This is the origin of two arrangements he made in 1901, that of Grieg's *Lankjending* op. 31 and Liszt's *Missa pro organo* LW E33. The Grieg arrangement (XII/3) is of an accompanied chorus, whose orchestral accompaniment Janáček transcribed for piano and harmonium. For the next academic year Janáček, even more curiously in view of his previous hostility to Liszt's music (see chap. 23), arranged his Organ Mass (XII/4). In this case he derived voice parts from the organ part that remained, mostly without change, as an accompaniment. Janáček's autograph survives, and a single date at the end of the Gloria – '24 September 1901' – gives an indication of when he was working at it. Rehearsals began on 16 October (by which time Janáček had completed the whole arrangement and had copies made) and went through the piece systematically at the rate of two classes a week throughout October and November, leading to a performance of the Credo on 24 November. By 16 December, the last class before the Christmas break, Janáček was rehearsing the whole work. There were more rehearsals the next year and possibly, Bohumír Štědroň speculated, a performance.[33] This is a much more ambitious programme than anything he achieved at the Teachers' Institute. One could argue that with younger students, who took Janáček's music and singing classes as an extra rather than as an obligation, Janáček had more committed singers, but the difference in leadership at the top – Schulz on the one hand, Bartoš on the other – was probably the crucial factor in determining how he felt about the two institutions.

Janáček soldiered on at both the Teachers' Institute and the Gymnasium until he approached fifty. When he took early retirement on the grounds of ill-health he suddenly acquired much more free time and this had a marked impact on his productivity as a composer. This is the period when he began two new operas, *Fate* and *Brouček*. When in 1920, in the middle of the composition of *Kát'a Kabanová*, Janáček gave up his final major teaching commitment, the Organ School/ Conservatory, his compositional career, despite his advanced age, blossomed as never before.

19

Janáček as music theorist

Janáček began writing about music theory in 1877 when he was twenty-three, and continued doing so for most of his life. His writings on the subject were collected in two volumes, published in 1968 and 1974, carefully edited by Zdeněk Blažek,[1] and have thus been readily available for over thirty years. Nevertheless they have attracted less detailed attention than almost any other aspect of his output. The leading American Janáček scholar, Michael Beckerman, devoted his doctoral studies to the subject, and having delivered himself of a slim published volume (1994), full of common sense and pithy observations, moved swiftly on to other matters.

Beckerman's introduction explains why scholars have tended to shy away from what is after all a substantial and arguably central part of Janáček's activity and one that would surely have been expected to shed light on his own work as a composer. The chief problem is that it is sometimes difficult to understand what Janáček was trying to say as a writer. He often seems to be wrestling with more than one idea at a time: to make sense of what he is saying one sometimes needs to take his writings apart and reassemble them in a different order. Then there is what Beckerman calls the 'feuilleton' style that Janáček sometimes adopts in his theoretical works, a type of fine writing which, with its flowery expressions, occasionally illuminates but more often than not obscures difficult concepts. Finally there is the home-made vocabulary: standard theoretical concepts such as rhythm, counterpoint, etc. are discarded in favour of Janáček's own terms. Both Blažek and Beckerman felt the need to provide glossaries of several pages explaining what they thought these terms meant.[2]

It is not entirely straightforward to determine what is a 'theoretical

215

writing' by Janáček, and what is perhaps something else. Beckerman printed a list of eighteen items (see table 19.1) but there are others which could have been included. Excluded here, for instance, are Janáček's analyses of individual compositions. Musical analysis and musical theory are usually differentiated, but there is common ground

Table 19.1: Janáček's writings on music theory
The following is a list of Janáček's writings accepted by Blažek (in *HTD*) as essentially about music theory, minus the late but slight xv/300 which Beckerman excluded, plus one more that Beckerman has added.

JW	title	publication	no. of pages in HTD
xv/16	General Clarifications of Melodic and Harmonic Matters	Cecilie, 1877	5
xv/26	Essays in Music Theory	HL, 1884–5	15
xv/44	On the Perfect Concept of Two-Note Chords	HL, 1885–6	25
xv/56	Bedřich Smetana on Musical Forms	HL, 1886	5
xv/61	On the Concept of Key	HL, 1886–7	21
xv/68	On the Scientific Nature of Harmony Treatises	HL, 1887	2
xv/76	On the Triad	HL, 1887–8	51
xv/80	A Brief Word about Counterpoint	HL, 1888	2
xv/147	A New Current in Music Theory	LN, 1894	–
xv/151	On the Composition of Chords and their Connections		
	first edition: privately published, Brno	1896	–
	second edition: František Urbánek, Prague	1897	113
xv/190	Modern Harmonic Music	Hlídka, 1907	7
xv/191	My Opinion about Rhythmic Organization	Hlídka, 1907	44
xv/192	On the Practical Aspects of Rhythm	Dalibor, 1908	4
	part of a larger unpublished study:		
xv/317	Resultant, Relative and Simple Harmony	–	14
xv/197	The Weight of Real-Life Motifs	Dalibor, 1910	4
xv/202	Complete Harmony Manual		
	first edition: Píša, Brno	1912–13	–
xv/210	On the Course of the Composer's Mental Activity	Hlídka, 1916	17
xv/331	The Intellectual and Psychological Basis of Musical Imagination	(unpublished, 1917)	5
xv/202	Complete Harmony Manual		
	second edition: Píša, Brno	1920	59

since any analysis will rest on certain theoretical postulates and, especially with Janáček, these may well be innovative and have a theoretical value of their own. One huge area of Janáček's speculative theoretical activity, his 'speech-melody theory', has largely been excluded. What Janáček was attempting to do in this area seems to be a different enterprise, addressing a different audience but, as Beckerman points out,[3] there are many common elements (for the purpose of this book speech melody is discussed elsewhere, see chap. 35). Similarly, Janáček's work with folksong has many theoretical concerns but again the constituency addressed is different, and this aspect of Janáček's work is also dealt with elsewhere (chap. 28). Finally it could also be argued that there is a substantive difference between speculative music theory and practical works (such as harmony manuals) intended for students. Blažek and Beckerman have regarded Janáček's harmony manuals as practical application of his ideas and have included them.

As will be clear from a glance at this list, Janáček's theoretical writings bunch round a few specific periods, unlike his more general literary writings, which have a more even spread throughout his life. To some extent these groups reflect Janáček's absorption of and coming to terms with theoretical concepts and discourses from particular writers and scientists. He was originally attracted to the formalist philosophy of Durdík and Zimmermann (see chap. 11), in particular the strong elements of positivism evident in Durdík's attempt to incorporate findings from mathematics and the natural sciences.[4] This led to an interest in Helmholtz's studies in musical psychology. Such concerns were reflected in his writings of the 1880s. Increasing interest in elements of experimental psychology introduced Janáček to the writings of Wilhelm Wundt; his second edition of his own harmony book in 1920 incorporates some of Wundt's ideas and concepts. In his discussion of this periodization, Beckerman goes further, declaring that after each burst of theoretical activity came a burst of creative activity, as if, having got something sorted in his mind, Janáček was then free to compose.[5] There is certainly something in this; the choruses of 1885 (IV/17) and 1888 (IV/19) and his first opera Šárka come towards the end of Janáček's first theoretical endeavours, and the great works of his last years come after the final theoretical writings, whereupon Janáček left theory alone: he had solved everything to his satisfaction.

However this is not the whole story. One should also feed in

Janáček's preoccupation with folk music (and its theory) which led to the folksong-based works of the early 1890s. Even more arresting is the 'discovery' of speech melody in 1897 that, among other things, led to Janáček's stopping work on *Jenůfa* and a prolonged period of exploring this new theoretical concept in smaller works before returning to the opera several years later. It could also be argued that Janáček's patchy pattern of creative activity in the early years of the century up to 1916 has less to do with theoretical considerations and more with his physical and psychological health. Equally the compositionally barren years of the early 1880s reveal not only Janáček's struggling with theoretical concepts but also his lack of time (when as a young professional he had to keep many pots boiling to provide for himself and his family) and the lack of repose in his home life. In other words, for Janáček to be composing at full pitch he not only needed to have a clear head theoretically; he also needed a stable home life, reasonable health, time for composition, and some evident demand for his works. It was only by 1920 that all these conditions were met and that Janáček composed quickly and easily, despite his advanced age.

Apart from speech melody and folksong, Janáček's theoretical preoccupations could be said to dwell in particular on two phenomena: how chords connect with one another, and the nature of rhythm. Despite the avid engagement with form that characterizes his later studies in Prague (1877) and his studies in Leipzig and Vienna (1879–80), musical form was not something that occupied him in his theoretical writings apart from a short essay on Smetana (XV/56). In his 1924 article on Janáček's theoretical teachings, Osvald Chlubna devotes about half of it to form (presumably derived from Janáček's lecture notes) but makes it clear that Janáček's teaching in this field was based on existing literature and had little personal about it,[6] a view that is borne out by the exposition that follows and indeed by the stenographic notes of Janáček's lectures taken by one of his students, Mirko Hanák, in 1909.[7] Counterpoint, too, is a subject about which Janáček had little to say. He gave it a new term (*opora*, literally 'support'), but essentially wished to replace the teaching of counterpoint with the theory of rhythmic organization.[8] Jan Kunc, a pupil of Janáček at the Brno Organ School and later director of the Brno Conservatory, characterized the teaching of counterpoint at the Organ School as 'quite weak'.[9]

On the other hand, the way chords follow one another and connect with one another, with implications for melody, dissonance and harmony, is central to Janáček's theoretical endeavours. His views were formed from his training in Prague with Skuherský who, well in advance of his day, believed that any chord could follow any other and it was the skill of the composer that was able to make this sound right and natural. What Janáček sought was an acoustical-theoretical basis for this that connected the root note of the first chord of two with the individual notes of the second chord, observing whether they were more consonant or less consonant with this root note. This is an unusual view, not one generally accepted by music theorists. These so-called 'connecting forms' nevertheless became a cornerstone of Janáček's harmonic theory and he explained all harmonic phenomena through them.[10] He suggested that there were four types of connecting forms, which he labelled conciliation, excitement, intensification and substitution. The difference between these connecting forms explained the difference in emotional effect that the chords generated.*

This is how Janáček introduced the topic in his first harmony textbook (1897):

In a quiet room play the (incomplete) dominant seventh chord (g–b–f′) strongly with the right hand; with the left play the triad (a flat–c′–e flat′) without however taking the fingers of the right hand off the keyboard. Listen to the now resulting chaos – it reflects, although in the most glaring way, the effect of combining the sensation tones [*pocitové tóny*] aroused by notes of the second chord with the false sensation tones [*pacitové tóny*] remaining from the first chord. [. . .]

Let us now repeat the process artificially. We will hear more clearly a very alluring and interesting reconciliation of this sounding chaos. Raise the fingers of the right hand from the keyboard slowly one by one beginning with the highest note (F), and ending with the lowest (G). What a pleasant emotion now grips us and accompanies the whole process of clarification! This is not surprising: after all, as the harmonic combination of the sixth arising from the sensation tone A flat and the false sensation tone F [. . .] dies away, finally the clearer, more pleasant fifth is heard. Similarly all these other harmonic combinations of the sensation tones of the second chord with those still sounding

---

* Despite the wayward appearance of such a description it is closer than it might seem to Germanic traditions of harmonic theory, for instance Schoenberg's theory of strong and 'superstrong' chords, whose strength derives from the notes in common or not in common between successive chords (I am grateful to Geoff Chew for this observation).

from the first chord turn into pleasanter intervals. After the storm, peace; after the grey cloud, the brightness of the sun – that's the way it works. [. . .]

In this way, we could name those combinations with a disturbing effect, those with a calming effect, etc. Here is the source of our absolute musical feeling capable of the highest intensification in the most subtle nuances. This is the source of truth that everybody, layman or expert, will be subject to, providing only that they have healthy hearing. (xv/151)

What is perhaps most characteristic about this extract is the way in which harmonic phenomena are interpreted by means of an emotional, psychological and metaphorical vocabulary – 'pleasant emotion', peace after the storm, the sun breaking through grey cloud – in an attempt to pinpoint a 'disturbing effect' or a 'calming effect' (i.e. two of the connecting forms, 'excitement' and 'conciliation') and the notion that these spring from 'our absolute musical feeling'. Behind all this was the thought that any theory of harmony should not be merely a mixture of practical descriptions but that students need something more 'psychological' that would allow them to develop their thoughts on harmony individually.[11] One intriguing possibility in explaining the background to Janáček's harmonic theories is his Ehrbar piano, acquired as part of Zdenka's dowry in 1881. It could be argued that the distinctive sound created by its leather hammers, its richness of harmonics and in particular its fine sustaining powers had a decisive effect not only on Janáček's music, but on some of his theoretical notions. Is it possible that, as Janáček hammered away at it and heard the traces of previously struck chords and the way they clashed with new ones, his theory took shape, a theory that, after all, seems to relate more to the piano than to voices or to any other instrument?

Janáček's idea of connecting forms goes back as early as 1884–5 (*Essays in Music Theory* xv/26). A year later (in *On the Perfect Concept of Two-Note Chords* xv/44) he combined this with some sort of physiological explanation: the first time a Czech theorist had applied physiological and psychological aspects in explaining harmony.[12] It is essentially this preoccupation with trying to discover the reasons behind harmonic phenomena that makes Janáček so distinctive a music theorist, that makes his discourse so utterly different from any other and, whatever the shortcomings in clarity or consistency, make him original and provocative.

In xv/44 Janáček criticizes all previous theories of harmony for 'ignoring the relation of all the notes of a sounding chord to all the notes of a chord that has ceased to sound.' Thirty-five years later he was saying much the same thing: 'I do not take much pride in this treatise itself, but certainly in the idea of explaining the effect of chord connection as a clash between the traces of one chord and the initial sounds of the next chord, and the subsequent resolution of this tangle [*spletna*] in our consciousness as the basis of aesthetic form.'[13]

This *spletna* was another theoretical concept unique to Janáček. He believed that as one chord gave way to another there was a so-called 'chaotic moment' when both chords were heard together. He was delighted to find in Wundt's studies of hearing what he believed to be physical proof of this. Since then, however, Wundt's findings have been discounted, which means that the concrete 'proof' that Janáček believed to underpin his theory now undermines it. It would, as Beckerman points out, have been better if Janáček had left this as a way of thinking about chords derived from his own observation rather than something that was universally applicable.[14]

In his survey of harmonic systems the Czech theoretician Jaroslav Volek attempted to put Janáček's theory into the wider context of harmonic theories of the time and concluded that Janáček had one essential difference from all others. This was that he seemed, at least theoretically, not to take account of harmonic function, i.e. the idea that chords are not inert but have particular functions described as tonic, dominant or subdominant. All chords in the harmonic era can be subsumed within these three functions and they provide a useful tool for explaining how harmony 'works'. Janáček, however, explained his chords in terms of the part-writing or voice-leading of individual notes, a concept that goes back centuries. Consequently Volek charac-terized Janáček's endeavour as essentially a conservative one, reflecting theoretical thinking up to 1850 at the latest.[15]

Other criticisms have been made on a more down-to-earth basis. In his Janáček biography, Jaroslav Vogel, for instance, proposed that Janáček saw independent chords where other theorists might see sus-pensions (thus greatly adding to the complexity of the description and giving the feeling that one wasn't seeing the wood for the trees), and that his description of chromatically altered chords is much too poetic and esoteric (or just plain waffly) to convey the simple technical mean-ing that would help an average student.[16] Although Janáček's pupil Josef Blatný (later a teacher at the Organ School) attempted to rebuff these criticisms,[17] there is no denying that Janáček's harmony books are poorly organized and that most Czechs who have espoused them have found them difficult to use in teaching. Even as fine a musician as Jan Kunc clearly found XV/151 (used as a textbook during his time at the Organ School in 1902–3) hard to understand.[18] It is not altogether surprising that a year after Janáček left the Brno Conservatory it was decided to abandon his harmony book as a textbook.

What should be the most interesting question of all, how Janáček's harmonic theory illuminates his own practice, tends to yield rather disappointing results. It is hard to see how a talented student who persevered with Janáček's harmony manual could write music that would sound in any way like Janáček's and, furthermore, it is hard to see how any of these observations illuminate Janáček's own practice, however truly he felt them.

More pertinent to his own music, however, was Janáček's concept of rhythm. As Jiří Kulka has noted, this is idiosyncratic in that it does not distinguish between rhythm (i.e. alternations of notes of various lengths) and metre (i.e. alternations of accented and unaccented beats).[19] Instead he saw the rhythmic sphere as a series of layers relating to levels of rhythmic activity going from slow to fast. An individual unit of time was defined as a *sčasovka* (a word derived from *čas* = time) and the whole rhythmic-metric organization as *sčasování* (a word Janáček invented to describe musical events in time, especially as related to psychological phenomena).[20]

Such rhythmic units can often be applied to one aspect of Janáček's musical language, namely his expressive use of ostinatos. A character-istic group in Janáček's music of, say, four notes continually repeated as an ostinato is a typical *sčasovka*, and this itself will represent one of the rhythmic layers in Janáček's music. Furthermore the very concept of (semi-)independent layers is one that is central to Janáček's music both in its compositional approach of adding complicating montage layers and in the emotional effect. David Pountney once made a telling analogy between these ostinato layers and their emotional effect and the 'lines of forces' that surround images in certain Munch paintings.[21]

Unlike Janáček's ideas on harmony, which go back to the 1880s, his ideas on rhythm come comparatively late in his theoretical thinking, in the 1900s, some twenty years after he began working as a music eth-nographer. There is a difference, he wrote, between a trained composer, able to notate music, and a folk composer. A trained composer 'has in mind empty, evenly measured time and fills it with a tune; the folk composer has in mind the words, i.e. a certain number of melodically fixed notes'. Elaborating these in his own way, he understands time not as an abstract scheme ('empty, evenly measured time') but as a succession of events 'full of spiritual content' (xv/163). Janáček's concept of rhythmic organization takes its cue from this, not a formal, empty scheme for structuring the musical flow in time, but something that conveys artistic and emotional content.[22] Janáček's concept of *sčasování* attempts to take account of psychological, social and cultural aspects.[23]

If one wanted to see some common thread in Janáček's theoretical thinking it is this: that music cannot be detached from life. There is a direct link between music and emotion, music and psychology, music and the environment. Much of what Janáček was after in his notion of speech melody was trying to tease out this link from the smallest scraps of human utterance with a view to finding a 'window into the soul'. His theories of harmony and rhythm were similarly aware of this psychological dimension. Such theories will not necessarily be helpful for any other composer's musical practice but they have much to say about how Janáček himself experienced music and thus sheds light on the roots of his own creative imagination. Sound in music, the theoretician Josef Hutter had said to Janáček, meant something only if it was pure. Janáček's retort lies at the heart of all his compositional and theoretical endeavours: 'And I say that it means nothing unless it is thrust into life, into blood, into an environment. Otherwise it's a worthless toy.'[24]

20

1882–summer 1884

In the later pages of her memoirs Zdenka was surprisingly forthcoming about her sex life with Janáček. She has nothing to say about it in the beginning but this would appear to have been one of the more satisfactory parts of her early married life since within a couple of months she fell pregnant. The watchful Mrs Schulzová confirmed Zdenka's own findings and advised her to tell Janáček, in the hope that he might now be more considerate to his young wife. But Janáček appeared to show no interest and no signs of changing his ways. When Mrs Schulzová took what was an unusual initiative for her by coming to see him and asking him to be 'kinder' to her daughter, she was shown the door.

Zdenka took 'approaching motherhood' in her stride, continuing to dance even in the Carnival balls (i.e. in January and February 1882); she was, however, beset by other anxieties such as Janáček's contemplated departure from his post at the Teachers' Institute to make a living instead as a private teacher.[1] Janáček's application to the Regional School Board was in fact merely for a transfer to another institution, giving as his reason disagreements with his father-in-law, who was at the same time his boss. Nevertheless the application, made on 22 December 1881,[2] cast a pall over Zdenka's first Christmas as a married woman and her first attempt to present the traditional Christmas Eve meal. While she skivvied anxiously in the kitchen, her husband ignored her and instead devoted his energies to entertaining their only guest, the painter Josef Ladislav Šichan.[3]

After Christmas Schulz managed to block Janáček's application: his comments to the Regional School Board on 1 January 1882 suggest that the disagreement with Janáček was trivial, merely reflecting the latter's irritation that Schulz had refused to pay for an outside artist to perform at one of the institute's informal concerts. On 16 January the board told Janáček to wait for a job to turn up and apply for it in the normal way.[4] Schulz's attempts to play down such disagreements can be construed as his wisely taking the long view: only a couple of weeks before his application to move Janáček had been elected director of the proposed new Brno Organ School by a committee that Schulz headed as chief executive. With this exciting prospect in view Janáček was clearly not going to leave Brno.[5] Nevertheless Schulz was sufficiently worried about Janáček's itchy feet and his daughter's future to increase his financial support for the couple by taking out an insurance policy with the company Slavia that would pay out a lump sum to her on his death.[6]

Janáček had parted company with the Brno Beseda in January 1881 and seems to have been genuinely surprised when he received the society's good wishes for his wedding. From his honeymoon in Prague he sent back his thanks on the famous 'wedding' photograph, now made into a postcard for this purpose.[7] But in fact Janáček had not remained completely aloof from the society during 1881. Among his collection of programmes, he kept those for the Beseda concerts on 3 July (a co-production with 'Rastislav') and 15 November.[8] If he had gone to the next one, on 14 December 1881, he would have found the society in crisis. Žalud, who died of tuberculosis a few years later, had been forced to give up the conductorship on grounds of ill-health, and the only replacement that could be found was Jan Nesvadba, a willing but uncharismatic conductor of the second rank whom Janáček had replaced at the Beseda in 1876. When a new committee was elected on 5 February 1882, it was decided that fences had better be mended with Janáček and a delegation was sent to plead with him to return. He accepted at once and on 17 February 1882 returned to the society in triumph.[9]

The change was immediately apparent. Whereas Nesvadba's December concert consisted mostly of choral pieces interspersed with a few instrumental pieces with piano accompaniment (including a 'song' for cornet à piston with violin and piano accompaniment), Janáček's first concert after his return was another large-scale choral work, Dvořák's *Stabat mater* (on 2 April 1882), and his second concert (20 May 1882) had several orchestral pieces among the choral items (see

Table 17.1). In addition to Tchaikovsky's Serenade for strings there were three pieces featuring a promising young violinist from Prague, Ferdinand Lachner, who was the soloist in Bruch's Violin Concerto and other pieces for violin and orchestra.

For the time being, Janáček's superior skill as an organizer and a conductor were acknowledged and his vision for the Beseda as something more than a patriotic choral society was accepted. This was evident in his proposal, at a committee meeting on 5 April 1882, that the Beseda solve the problem of getting string players for the orchestra by training young violinists at a special Beseda school. This was an old idea of his, but now in his strong position he was able to push it through. Accordingly the school opened at the end of September 1882 with Vít Pergler (1844–1938) as teacher and Janáček as supervisor. The success of the school was immediate. The number of prospective pupils was such that two more teachers had to be engaged, and by the beginning of the second year there were eighty-five students on the books. Soon the school's profit allowed it to subsidize the loss-making concert activities,[10] and in 1887 the school was expanded to take in pianists and cellists.[11] This was one of Janáček's most durable initiatives at the Beseda: the school survived until it was absorbed by the newly formed conservatory after the First World War.

Just before the Beseda violin school opened its doors, Janáček's even more ambitious venture, the Brno Organ School, also took in its first group of nine students. Classes began on 15 August 1882, with Janáček himself teaching theory. This was the modest beginning of an institution that would increasingly dominate Janáček's life in the next thirty-eight years (see chap. 21).

Together with the Organ School (teaching was mainly in the evenings in the early years), Janáček's continued work at the Augustinian monastery (a lunch-time rehearsal and mostly weekend services), his day job at the Teachers' Institute and his resumed conducting activities, Janáček had much on his plate and was not able to devote as much time to his young wife as he might. And composition had not been completely neglected. When they were on honeymoon in Prague the Janáčeks had visited Ferdinand Lehner, and it was on this trip perhaps that Janáček heard about Lehner's then unpublished hymnbook and undertook to provide organ accompaniments to some of the hymns for publication in the music supplements to *Cyrill* (the successor to *Cecilie*).

Janáček completed ten of these and sent them to Lehner, who acknowledged receipt on 22 November 1881 and asked for additions and an introduction.[12] Janáček sent these too, only to discover that Lehner had shown them to the organist and composer Adolf Průcha and the theorist Josef Förster, who expressed reservations about some of Janáček's harmonizations. Although Lehner suggested a meeting between Janáček and Förster,[13] Janáček took umbrage and demanded his settings back. He went on to publish them himself with Karel Winkler, a thirteen-page booklet entitled *Ten Czech Hymns from the Lehner Hymnbook for the Mass* (II/11). It was Winkler's first musical publication: 'W1', as the plate number has it.

Today it is difficult to see what all the fuss was about. The severe, mildly modal style of Janáček's organ accompaniment was in keeping with Cecilian practice and was comparable with that of Janáček's Latin motets. Lehner had, after all, published one of Janáček's motets (II/4) in *Cecilie* in 1877. Were Förster and Průcha perhaps bothered by some of the more 'modern' harmony that had now crept into Janáček's 'severe' style after his time in Leipzig and Vienna? Whatever the people in Prague felt, there seems to have been enough local demand for the print-run to sell out and Winkler to publish a second edition in 1889. And Janáček himself presumably felt good enough about them to allow this and even to add three more harmonizations and tidy up the earlier pieces. But he had now parted company from Lehner: the three new hymns came from a quite different source.

It is important when considering the picture of misery that Zdenka presents to remember that one is getting only her side of the story. Nevertheless some of the incidents she reports do suggest an almost maliciously cruel young husband, a cruelty that may even explain Janáček's success many years later in portraying the callous and heartless Kabanicha's treatment of her daughter-in-law in *Káťa Kabanová*. An example of his insensitive treatment is that, in Zdenka's final couple of weeks of pregnancy, he decided to rent a different flat, in Klášterní ulice no. 2 (he had never liked the one that Schulz chose for them since it was 'very near' Zdenka's parents).[14] Virtually all the organization and physical work involved fell to a heavily pregnant Zdenka: they moved on 14 August 1882 and she went into labour the next day. Another incident she reported was the marriage of Berthold Žalud, on 8 August, just a week earlier. Zdenka was considered to be too close to childbirth to go to the wedding and reception but Schulz and Janáček attended the wedding at St Jiljí, Komárov,* where both served as witnesses. Zdenka asked her husband to be back by ten in case she went into labour. He hadn't returned by 10.30 p.m. so she went to sleep at her parents' house (her mother had stayed at home with her young son). When, fearing that Janáček would take it badly, Zdenka rushed back 'before five' to her flat, she found that the door was bolted from the inside:

I rang, I knocked, I cried, I banged on the door, but he didn't open up for me. And he wasn't sleeping. He was walking to and fro behind the door whistling a song. There was nothing for it but to go home to my parents again. And then on the way I decided that I'd rather not return to my husband again. But when I came out with this at home my parents gently and earnestly talked me out of it and so towards about eight I set out on the journey again. The door was no longer bolted, I went in and reproached my husband with what he was doing to me. He said roughly: 'You should have stayed at home, after all nothing would have happened to you.'[15]

It had been long agreed between the young couple that Zdenka would return to her parents' house for the birth. But when on 15 August, the day after the move, Zdenka had labour pains, Janáček simply got angry when he heard the news and let her leave without saying goodbye or helping her in any way:

I dragged myself home on my own and there began immediately a difficult and prolonged labour. In my agony I called continually for Leoš. When it had already got towards noon, my parents sent for him. They knew that he was in the monastery: that day, the Feast of the Assumption of the Virgin Mary, there was a banquet there to which my husband was usually invited. He heard the message, but he didn't come. At two o'clock I gave birth to a little girl. My parents sent to the monastery again. Later I learnt that my husband was just lighting up a cigar when the messenger sought him out. He calmly began smoking and didn't show the slightest excitement or even inclination to have a look at the child. Only at the urging of one of the priests, Father Augustin [Augustin Krátký], did he finally consent and got up from the table. He came to my parents' place; he didn't greet them, it was as if he didn't see them. He scarcely glanced at the child, he kissed me coldly and then at once went away again.[16]

---

* At the time a village near Brno; from 1919 part of Brno.

Perhaps, Zdenka speculated, it upset him that they hadn't had a son. During her pregnancy Janáček had often said 'It must be a boy.' After two weeks at her parents' house Zdenka returned with little Olga, as the new arrival was called. The presence of a sickly baby in the flat exacerbated what was already a fractious and unhappy situation. Olga cried in the night; Janáček flew into a rage because of it, saying that he needed his sleep. Olga needed a doctor; Janáček said there was no money for this. He seemed not to bond with his daughter at all: 'I doubt if he ever nursed the child, or ever played with her.' Arguments kept on breaking out, and in one such scene, Janáček struck his wife (who had Olga in her arms). This outbreak of physical violence was not quite the last straw. That was Janáček's threat to bring back his mother (who had kept house for him while Zdenka was away) to 'sort out' Zdenka. Zdenka had always been somewhat afraid of Amalie Janáčková and countered this threat by saying that if Janáček's mother came she would 'go home'. These words speak volumes: one of Janáček's reasons for restricting her visits to her parents was his resentment that she regarded her parents' flat, rather than their own, as 'home'.

And this – in the end – is what happened. Janáček, still insisting that his mother would join them, went off to work. Zdenka got dressed, and took herself and Olga back to her parents. Mrs and Mrs Schulz were not surprised. It was, as Zdenka mused later, a 'strange separation'. Her husband didn't come for her, didn't ask for her, didn't write to her. She couldn't understand why she'd been let go so lightly. After all, only a couple of years earlier, Janáček had been writing daily loving letters to the one person who understood him ('after all I don't know how to speak as freely with anyone else as I do with you').[17] Perhaps in this period Janáček had come to realize all the limitations of marrying such an inexperienced young girl from such a different background and one who remained strongly bonded to her parents. Maybe he was even relieved, at least in the beginning, that he was rid of her and the little daughter he hardly noticed apart from her crying in the night.

Oddly, since the row had been ostensibly provoked by Janáček's threat to bring his mother to stay, Amalie Janáčková remained in Švábenice, oblivious to what had happened, and Janáček made no attempt to tell her about it. She wrote to her son on 7 December 1882 thanking him for his 'support' (i.e. money), telling him how she had fallen out with her daughter Eleonora in Švábenice, and sending greetings to them all and a present for the new baby.[18] The disagreement with Eleonora might have been yet another reason for Janáček to bring his mother to keep house for him again, but significantly he kept quiet about it all and did not respond to her letter, which meant that she followed it up a week or so later with another one, asking whether he had received her package and whether the baby jackets she had knitted for Olga were big enough.[19] This time Janáček did reply, seemingly without spelling out what had happened and simply mentioning that the jackets were too small, a response that Amalie didn't believe at all, attributing it to malice and ingratitude on Zdenka's part. But she picked up that all was not well and demanded to know the reason.[20]

Janáček's next letter – none of these have survived – proposed that his mother come and stay after Christmas. Amalie responded by saying that getting to Brno involved some walking, which she found 'impossible for an old person such as myself'. She had not yet turned sixty-three and had made the journey back from Brno in September so unless her health was deteriorating then (it did so in 1883), Janáčková was merely piqued by her son's offhand treatment and his changes of mind. She had heard from Janáček's former maidservant that he would give her a home – the 'small room' would be her dwelling, and this had been further confirmed to her by Janáček's colleague Žalud. Perhaps it was for the best, she wrote, but Janáček should at least be honest about his reasons. The 'small room' would be quite enough for herself and Lori (i.e. it wasn't just Amalie Janáčková but her unmarried daughter Eleonora as well who had expected to be housed), and they would have been delighted had this happened. Janáček however, she said, had declared that he didn't want to live in a 'double house-hold'. She hadn't got in his way ('after all I sat whole days in that small sitting-room') and Janáček could have saved a bit of money for himself. Instead he was now harming his health and shortening his life.[21]

Seeking comfort from his mother was clearly not an option. So Janáček appears to have spent at least part of his Christmas break in Prague, seemingly with Dvořák. The only indication that survives for this is a brief entry in his notebook for 1881–2:

December 1882: I played with Dvořák:
1. Music to Tyl [i.e. Dvořák's overture and incidental music to Šamberk's play *Josef Kajetán Tyl* B125]
2. String Quartet no. 3 in C major [i.e. no. 11, B121]
   movements II, III and IV great; I weaker.[22]

Dvořák was showing off his recent works. The play by František Ferdinand Šamberk was first given at the Provisional Theatre in February 1882 and the string quartet had been performed in Berlin only the month before Janáček's meeting with Dvořák. Janáček also attended a performance in Prague of Beethoven's *Missa solemnis* given by the Prague choral society 'Hlahol' at Žofín, on 13[†] December 1882.[23]

While Amalie Janáčková was writing her disgruntled letters from Švábenice, the Schulzes, similarly, weren't too pleased with the situation. They had accepted Zdenka back 'without reproach' but nevertheless Schulz himself didn't want his daughter to 'have the stigma of being a woman who had run away from her husband' and wished the matter to be settled legally. The advice from the lawyer Dr Bedřich Hoppe, an old family friend, was to ask for a 'voluntary divorce' (i.e. without a trial) so that the couple could easily come back together if they wished to. Conciliation was also tried. Hoppe saw Janáček, and as a result of this Father Anselm Rambousek (who would have been in regular contact with Janáček at the Augustinian monastery) came to see Zdenka to enquire whether she would like to return to her husband. Zdenka claims that when she told him her side of the story and sought his advice, Rambousek told her to stay put. The 'divorce' hearing followed in due course, with Schulz acting for the under-age Zdenka and refusing alimony from Janáček. It was agreed, however, that Janáček should contribute 25 zl a month for the child. In turn Janáček insisted on the right to see Olga once a week, and Zdenka made it a condition that she should be present at this meeting (in case, she confessed in her memoirs, Janáček tried to abduct his little daughter, though from his total lack of interest this worry would appear to be groundless).[24]

What took place with rather more unpleasantness was the removal of Zdenka's goods and 'dowry' from the flat, which the court had allowed. Zdenka, the caretaker of the Teachers' Institute and Schulz arrived at the flat to be greeted by a very surly Janáček who told Schulz that he had no right to be there:

[†]Racek gives no date but 'Hlahol' performed the *Missa solemnis* twice, on 8 December and 13 December 1882 (*Památník Hlaholu 1861–1911*, 41). Janáček was still in Brno on 9 December – he attended a Beseda committee meeting on 8 December (*LJPT*, 227, fn. 2), so would have gone to the second performance.

And then something boiled over in my usually kindly father. 'You ungrateful boy!', he shouted and ran up to Leoš, who didn't expect anything like that. Leoš fled and started calling to the police for help. The caretaker and I rushed up to Father, held him back, and I pacified him and pleaded with him until he agreed to go home. The next day he didn't come with me. I saw to it myself that my things were taken away in good order.[25]

This is a rare glimpse of how things now were between Schulz and Janáček, men who would naturally bump into one another on virtually a daily basis at their place of work. The relationship had been deteriorating fast after Zdenka's flight home, as is clear from a complaint that Schulz made against Janáček to the Regional School Board on 16 March 1883. Whereas in January 1882 Schulz had asked the board to ignore Janáček's request for a transfer, a year later he was demanding 'disciplinary measures against the music teacher Leoš Janáček' and changes in his condition of service, 'for it has become impossible for the director and the named teacher to remain at the same institute'.

Schulz's criticisms were mostly the trivial irritations of day-to-day institutional life. For instance, after Schulz had refused to pay for his 'outside artist' in November 1881, Janáček had allegedly abandoned institute concerts and neglected the students' singing in church or at the 'Habsburg Jubilee'. He had made difficulties filling in for a sick colleague. He had grumbled about timetable changes whereby he had acquired a couple more hours of teaching. He had protested that Schulz had not given a sufficiently serious punishment to a student for insulting him.

There were also suggestions of a conflict of interests between Janáček's work at the institute and his role as music director of the Brno Beseda (see Table 17.1). Janáček had set himself an ambitious programme for the Beseda's spring concert on Palm Sunday, 18 March 1883. The star attraction was undoubtedly the soloist František Broulík, an outstanding Czech tenor of the period, then engaged at the Vienna Hofoper; and Janáček certainly had his time cut out rehearsing a demanding programme of Dvořák's Symphony no. 6 in D, Smetana's *Vltava* and Brahms's *Schicksalslied*. Schulz complained that Janáček had left classes early on Wednesday 14 March 1883 in order to rehearse for the concert and had got some of his friends at the Beseda to insist that he had time off to take rehearsals on 16 and 17 March.

But there were also accusations that had broader implications in any examination of Janáček's marital problems. Janáček, Schulz reported, had said that he ought to be removed from his office as director 'because he speaks German at home with his wife' (Janáček's 'national fanaticism', Schulz concluded in a parting shot, gave the impression of madness). And there was plenty of evidence of Janáček's hot temper: that when criticized on any of these points he had 'waved his arms' and had spoken 'with an angry voice' (all those at the staff meeting, Schulz declared, had been struck dumb 'by such a coarse action'), or had stumped off 'demonstratively', and had called the teaching staff a nasty lot of good-for-nothings.[26]

Janáček did not take Schulz's ten-point letter lying down. The strength of his feeling is shown by the very long letter that he wrote to the Regional School Board on 18 April 1883, the day after Schulz made further accusations of Janáček's conduct at a staff meeting. There was one area of agreement between him and his father-in-law: both felt now that they couldn't work together and Janáček repeated his request for a transfer. Director Schulz, he claimed, 'hated' him and called him terrible names, so bad that he couldn't write most of them down in a letter. But above all there had been the incident in Janáček's flat where Schulz had come to help Zdenka remove the furniture. Janáček gave his own version of the event:

On 2 March of this year, without having any right to be in my flat, he tried to seize me, throttling me with such terrible passion that I was in danger and it was only with difficulty that I could get away from my flat in order to call policemen to my defence. These remained the whole time of the unseemly visit of Mr Director at my flat to protect me.

I can prove with witnesses who were present that I didn't give cause for this scene and that what I say is true.

In their accounts Janáček and Zdenka agreed on the basics: that 'something boiled over' in Schulz and led to his physical attack on Janáček, though no doubt Janáček enjoyed calling for the police and making the most of this incident. The rest of Janáček's letter was a defence against Schulz's criticisms: that there had been plenty of student participation at church services, with specially taught seasonal music; that Schulz continually cast aspersions on his work 'although up till now for all these years he never came to inspect me even once'; that he hadn't sloped off early for the Beseda rehearsal (just twenty minutes early); that this was the first time it had happened (and Schulz was partial to doing it himself). But above all, Janáček protested, 'In all sorts of ways Mr Director Schulz seeks to belittle and cast doubt on my activity in school both among the higher officials and at staff meetings.' For all the personal and domestic conflicts that lie behind this, there seems to be a genuine regret that Janáček's 'love for teaching, perseverance and enthusiasm for things of the mind and for further education' was not appreciated by his superior:

I also ask the Supreme Imperial and Royal Regional School Board kindly not to consider my request as an expression of anger and hate; I know that I am only a subordinate teacher of music, I know my duties and I want to carry them out conscientiously; I take exception only at being considered a person unworthy of honour, which by right I don't deserve at all.[27]

The Regional School Board, in the person of its inspector Vincenc Prousek, took the affair seriously and did not prejudge it. Janáček was asked to comment specifically on Schulz's ten points, with his answer minuted (he conceded that he may have 'waved his arms' but otherwise refuted all criticisms). Since in his letter Janáček had suggested that he was not alone on the teaching staff in finding Director Schulz difficult, three of his colleagues were also cross-examined and they confirmed that Schulz had made comments about Janáček 'of an insulting nature' and that Schulz also treated the teaching staff 'in an insulting manner'. There were, it seemed, faults on both sides: 'The director brought his domestic disagreements into his official business', and while 'Janáček sometimes affected the students unpleasantly with his excitable nature, the director often chided the students with rough words.'[28]

All this was then put again to Schulz, who on 13 June declared that Janáček was now behaving decently towards him, as indeed he was towards Janáček. The problem was, Schulz explained, that Janáček always considered himself infallible. But Schulz felt they could now carry on working together at the institute. The next day he wrote a personal letter to the inspector, regretting that his staff had shown so little sympathy for him although they knew the pain he had been caused 'by the action of a man, a wretched thief of family happiness'. Prousek made his adjudication two weeks later, on 28 June 1883. The dispute, he concluded, essentially arose through domestic family matters, and disciplinary measures were unnecessary. Both director and teacher had displayed 'some unseemliness on school duty' and the best solution would be if they could be kept apart. But this was impossible, and since both had given assurances to avoid any future conflict, Prousek recommended that Janáček remain as a teacher at the Teachers' Institute in Brno.[29]

With this violent upset out of the way, the two men continued to work together at the institute until Schulz's retirement in 1899 without the need for further intervention. When Janáček made various applications for financial support to the Ministry of Culture and Education or the Regional School Board, Schulz backed him with covering notes. Schulz furthermore remained as chief executive to the committee that oversaw the Organ School until 1895. The two men never got on well again – something that would affect Janáček's relation with his wife – but at least they were not at each others' throats.

One of Schulz's complaints, that Janáček's commitments at the Beseda interfered with his duties at the institute, also would have been less justified in the next few years. Under the new arrangements Janáček did not have to officiate at 'entertainments', so he was not involved in the informal concerts that were arranged in June, October and November 1883. The only other concert he conducted that year was on 16 December, and this too was on a more modest scale, mostly male choruses. The orchestra performed only in an overture by Dvořák from his incidental music to *Josef Kajetán Tyl* (which Janáček had played through with the composer during the previous Christmas holidays; see above), and in the accompaniment to Schumann's *Nachtlied*. The next year, Janáček's spring concert on 30 March 1884 was also less ambitious, at least in terms of forces (see Table 17.1). The orchestra played in two rather easier pieces, Saint-Saëns's *Danse macabre* and Dvořák's *Legends*. What, however, is notable about this concert is that it was billed as a 'historical concert' and that it contained two items quite out of the ordinary Beseda repertory: a Sanctus from Palestrina's four-part *Missa brevis*, and Orazio Vecchi's eight-part *Missa pro defunctis*. Three months later (1 June 1884) the last Beseda concert of the season was a joint venture with the leading Prague choral society 'Hlahol', in which the conducting was shared between Karel Knittl and Janáček. Among the eleven items were vocal and piano solos, and 'Hlahol' and the Beseda divided the choral items so that Janáček conducted only two (Bendl and Dvořák); again, an assignment that would have made few demands on his teaching time.

After the furniture incident Janáček had returned his ring to Zdenka, but she, as she told him, would continue to wear hers 'because I thought that we should continue to be faithful. With that we parted.'

With this unpleasantness out of the way, life changed much for the better for Zdenka. Her parents called in a children's doctor for the ailing baby. When it was discovered that Olga was digesting her food badly, raw meat was prescribed and she immediately recovered.

And an absolute miracle happened to me. Within a short while I positively blossomed. Life was so carefree under Father's protection and such fun with the two young children, my brother and daughter, who appeared like siblings and who so liked one another too. Not to mention Mama, who was clearly glad to have me home. At that time Grandmother was no longer with us, she'd gone off to Uncle Gustav [Kaluschka] in Kolín, and Mama and I most happily shared the housework and caring for the children. I felt that I'd found my niche and this cheered me up. I worked willingly and at everything: in this way I tried at least a little to repay my parents for the unpleasantness which I'd caused them.[30]

In her new blossoming state Zdenka even had admirers, for instance a nice young lawyer 'from a prominent Brno Czech family'; she had met him in Vienna while on a visit there with her father. He continued to pay court to her when he began to work in Brno and sometimes encountered her at balls: 'He was always very attentive to me, kind, absolutely correct. Never did he overstep the bounds of propriety by so much as a single word. In this way we were acquainted with one other for very many years.'[31] However, as Zdenka primly added, 'Leoš was the first and only man in my life, and after we parted I'd remained absolutely faithful to him, although people told me tales that he wasn't paying me back in kind.' For Zdenka, who was still only eighteen, life seemed

exquisite now that I'd passed through that gloomy intermezzo of a marriage torn apart by conflicts. At home everything was now so peaceful, so harmonious, there were no misunderstandings, there were no arguments, there were no financial difficulties, the children were healthy. In this happiness I bloomed in such a way that people began to call me a 'Staré Brno rose'.[32]

Life, however, was considerably less rosy for Janáček in his separated state. The flat was almost empty now that the furniture had gone, including the Ehrbar baby grand, so he had to borrow a piano. The real surprise is that Amalie Janáčková didn't move in. In her edition of

Amalie's letters Svatava Přibáňová suggests that Janáček kept his mother away in the hope that Zdenka would return.[33] And yet, at least as Zdenka reported it, there seems so little evidence in the early stages that this was his wish. Zdenka recollected seeing her estranged husband almost every day when she went out shopping: 'We walked past one another as if we didn't know one other.' Mrs Žaludová (the new wife of Berthold Žalud), who lived in the same building, cleaned for him. Meals were not a problem since he continued to get them from the monastery.[34]

At the end of the school term, in the summer of 1883, Janáček went to Prague for an extended visit. It is understandable that he wanted to get away after such a bruising time: his young wife leaving him, a very serious quarrel with his employer and thoughts of trying to quit his settled post at the Teachers' Institute. Janáček, it would seem, was at the crossroads: in his personal life, in his professional life and with great uncertainty about his creative ambitions. Although in Leipzig and Vienna he had found himself focussing on composition (at the expense of any thoughts of becoming a virtuoso pianist or organist), during the early 1880s Janáček was at his least productive as a composer. After the battering to his self-esteem that he received in Vienna and then at the Beseda in early 1881, he seems to have had no stomach to compose anything at all.

Janáček's stay in Prague is confirmed by a letter to the music historian Josef Srb-Debrnov where he states he has been 'industriously studying for the whole holidays'.[35] 'Studying' included more Durdík – Janáček acquired his short book *On the Fashionable Philosophy of our Day* (Prague, 1883), which he inscribed 'Prague, 7 August 1883'[36] – and what seems to have been a crash course in opera. According to the annotations in the opera librettos he bought during this period, he was in Prague between at least 22 July and 3 September 1883, attending at least eight opera performances. After it had burnt down in 1881 the National Theatre was in the process of being rebuilt (the restored building reopened in November 1883); in the summer of 1883, however, there was a season in the New Czech Theatre, an enormous outdoor theatre seating three thousand, and it was there that Janáček had his most sustained exposure to opera so far. Whatever the shortcomings of the staging in a summer theatre, there was a magnificent bunch of soloists that could turn in, for instance, a *Trovatore* that had not been rehearsed (as Janáček surmised in his comments) but which nevertheless captivated him sufficiently to encourage him to see it three times. He also saw Meyerbeer's *Le prophète* twice and single performances of Halévy's *La Juive*, Verdi's *Un ballo in maschera* and Smetana's *The Secret* (see chap. 25). Opera seems at last to have made its mark on Janáček at an empty and confusing time for him when other certainties had crumbled. After opera came to Brno with the opening of the Czech Provisional Theatre that opened in December 1884, there was no looking back.

On arrival at the Hotel Garni in Václavské náměstí (the very last hotel suggestion for Prague in Baedeker, one without the commending asterisk),[37] Janáček seems to have written to Dvořák. It was at the Hotel Garni that Dvořák's letter of 22 July reached him: 'Dear friend, It would give me much pleasure if you were to visit me here at Vysoká. Come soon, however: on Saturday [28 July] I'm going to look at the venerable Orlík, perhaps you could come with me.' Dvořák's precise indications about train timetables followed, involving a three-hour journey to Příbram and then an hour's journey by 'post' to Bohutín, where Dvořák would wait for him and take him the half-hour walk to Vysoká, the summer residence of his brother-in-law Count Kounic.[38] This plan appears to have been realized: Janáček's later reminiscence (xv/201) mentions a trip with Dvořák to Orlík (a castle spectacularly perched on the bank of the Vltava) and he stayed, it seems, about ten days at Vysoká with Dvořák and his family, thereby missing the opportunity of seeing another Verdi opera in Prague, *Rigoletto*, which was staged at the New Czech Theatre on 31 August.

When Janáček returned to Prague (for *La Juive* on 7 August), he transferred from the Hotel Garni to Dvořák's Prague flat in Žitná ulice (it was there that Dvořák's later letters were addressed). Dvořák issued further invitations for trips, on 23 August to Prachatice: Dvořák would meet the train at Tochavice (a couple of stops further south from Příbram) and together they would go on by train to Písek and Prachatice.[39] The real goal, however, was Husinec, the birthplace of the religious reformer Jan Hus, a 5-km walk from Prachatice. As far as Dvořák was concerned, this was creative research: he was in the middle of his *Hussite Overture*, which he had begun on 9 August. Dvořák and Janáček arrived that afternoon at the Hus memorial in Husinec, a trip documented by Dvořák's writing a couple of musical incipits in the visitors' book with Janáček, more modestly, simply adding his name.[40]

This time Janáček had no more than an overnight stay at Vysoká: he was back for *Trovatore* (now for the third time) on 26 August.‡

Perhaps on the advice of Dvořák, Janáček did try a little composition. The Durdík book contained his Czech translation of *Ave Maria*, from Byron's *Don Juan* (Canto 3, verse 102), and Janáček set this for male-voice chorus (IV/16). It is not known when, but it would make sense that he did so during this summer break in Prague and Vysoká (in 1890 Janáček let the piece be published in the musical supplement of an obscure music periodical *Varyto* the composer given as 'LJ'). After the *Autumn Song* disaster in late 1880 Janáček was no longer composing for the Beseda choir, so if he intended it to be performed, *Ave Maria* may have been intended for the Teachers' Institute. It is a good piece for inexperienced but well-drilled singers: short, not very demanding in its notes but with constantly changing dynamics, and many speed changes. Its contrasting middle section makes use of a few soloists whose need for greater skill is demonstrated in the more exposed imitative writing.

Was it in Prague or Vysoká that Janáček wrote his two *Pieces for Organ* (VIII/7)? Again there is no evidence of when they were written apart from a *terminus ante quem* of 1884, when Janáček had them privately printed at the Benedictine press at Rajhrad near Brno (a connection that he would use for printing music for many years to come). Helfert thought well of these pieces, comparing their harmonic language with that of *Parsifal*,[41] but it must be confessed that they probably give more indication of the type of improvisation that Janáček perhaps did at the monastery, with bold modulatory tactics and a style that one can either designate as 'rhapsodic' (as Helfert does) or, less charitably, as meandering. Janáček would not write another solo for the instrument until the magnificent movement in his *Glagolitic Mass*. The compositions of the period may have been good occupational therapy, but in a sense they are hardly more than flickering reflections of what he had done much earlier, the two organ pieces continuing the line of those written during the time of his Prague studies, and *Ave Maria* looking back in its forthright simplicity to the type of choruses he wrote for 'Svatopluk'. But maybe something had shifted: after another thoughtful silence of about two years Janáček would write a group of choruses (IV/17) that were by far his most successful to date, a

‡ Janáček gives the date of 25 August in the libretto; Smaczny 1994, 114, has 26 August.

precursor of his great choruses of the twentieth century, and a few years later he would begin his first opera.

It is possible that Janáček saw more operas in Prague. Gluck's *Orfeo ed Euridice*, Mozart's *Le nozze di Figaro* and Rossini's *Guillaume Tell* were all performed at the New Czech Theatre during Janáček's summer retreat in Bohemia and these would all have been new and probably of interest to him, but documentary evidence that he saw them is lacking. He did, however, see Smetana's late opera *The Secret*, presented at the New Czech Theatre on 3 September. That day he heard once more from Dvořák:

> Dear friend, it seems I'm unlikely to catch you in Prague since I'll be finished with the [*Hussite*] overture only towards the end of the week. I am really sorry that I won't be granted spending another pleasant moment with you; if however you stayed on longer after all, before I arrived, we could have a look at Sychrov. If you won't be staying then I'll say goodbye; I'm glad to hear that the stay at my place was pleasant for you.[42]

In the autumn of 1883 Zdenka was walking down the street and noticed her husband in the café 'U Simonů', on Měšťanská ulice. On seeing her, he made a 'deep bow'. Soon afterwards, the same thing happened when meeting him in the street. This time Zdenka courteously thanked him. And soon after that she received a request, apparently the first, for him to see his one-year-old child under the conditions of the 'divorce'. Since Zdenka had insisted in the court agreement that she be present at such meetings, it meant of course Janáček's seeing Zdenka too:

> So I got Olinka[§] dressed up – she was already walking and had exquisite curly hair – and went with her to the Žaluds in accordance with the divorce settlement. They sent for Leoš. He came after a while, we greeted one another and I went on chatting with my hostess. My husband went up to Olinka and stood helplessly over her. She didn't know him and he didn't know what to say to her. Then our hostess got up, took Olinka in her arms, and went outside. We remained on our own. Immediately he got up his confidence: 'Did you go away for the holidays, Madam?'
> I answered very briefly, but this didn't deter him. He went on asking me things, and according to the questions I saw that he was well informed about my every step. He showed pleasure in the fact that after our divorce I went on

---

[§] Olga, especially as a child, was known by the diminutives 'Oluška', 'Olinka', 'Olguška'.

mixing only with Czech society. And suddenly he blurted out jealously: 'And have you been having a good time?'

Even Zdenka's defiant answer, 'Yes, I've enjoyed myself', did not deter him and Janáček asked to see Olga a week later, the first of many regular meetings, which Zdenka soon realized were simply a pretext for seeing her:

He always just caressed the little girl and thereafter didn't take any notice of her. But he hovered around me, he entertained me, he was delightful – and he knew how to be when he wanted: once again it was the same charming Leoš from the time before our wedding. I was reserved at first, but I soon melted; repressed love flared up within me once more. Again I longed to see him, to hear his voice, his expressive clipped speech.[43]

Another ploy was to accompany Zdenka to the German Stadttheater in Brno, which had opened in November 1882. The Schulzes had a permanent subscription for one seat, which Zdenka and her mother took turns in using. One evening Zdenka found Janáček waiting to accompany her at the end of Pekařská ulice, the long street that connects Brno to Staré Brno. He was there waiting for her after the show:

Strange: we, who during our marriage had had nothing to say to one another apart from our arguments, suddenly had in common so many topics for conversation that Leoš asked me if he could wait for me again next time. It became a matter of course that we'd walk together to and from the theatre. In a short while he asked me to return to him, to forgive him, saying that he knew that he'd behaved badly towards me.

What had brought about Janáček's change of heart? He had enjoyed his creature comforts associated with the Schulzes, and had in Zdenka a wife who cooked well and was well-trained to be a home-maker. A year of fending for himself (and he was never very practical in the kitchen) may have brought home to him that the losses of living apart outweighed the benefits. Maybe the friends who had informed him of Zdenka's doings had tried to persuade him that he ought to get back together with her. Maybe Dvořák had had a word with him during the summer; certainly Janáček would have had an opportunity at Vysoká of seeing for himself how happy his friend was, surrounded by his large family. And there was his old mother, who in April 1883 wrote to him for his name day in his 'sadness and loneliness' and pleaded that Janáček return to his wife: 'it would be a great unhappiness both for you and for her if at such a young age a husband and wife were to be divided from one another; I think, and am sure I'm not wrong, that this would be your most fervent wish.'[44]

Naturally Zdenka was wary: 'Some things were too deeply imprinted on my soul', she commented. But Janáček persisted, acknowledging that he had been unkind also to the Schulzes. He sent a letter of apology to Mrs Schulzová. Easily charmed, Anna Schulzová 'forgave him everything' and they agreed that he'd speak Czech and she German. This was easier than it might have been earlier because of a surprising decision on her part to send Leoš Schulz to Czech schools and to bring him up in Czech, which inevitably led to communicating with her boy in Czech.[45]

Anna Schulzová was keen that her daughter should return to Janáček. They were both fearful of the social stigma that divorce aroused at the time in the tiny Brno Czech community and Mrs Schulzová felt that a child ought to be brought up in a 'normal family circle'. Furthermore, Janáček's 'continual pleas and attentions' weakened Zdenka's resistance so that in early spring 1884 Zdenka decided that she would go back to her husband. Unenthusiastic about the marriage in the first place, Emilian Schulz 'wouldn't hear of it': 'he didn't understand why I wanted to return to what I'd been so glad to run away from.' It took a concerted effort on the part of Zdenka and her mother before Schulz agreed at least not to stand in their way.

On Holy Saturday, 12 April 1884, some eighteen months after Zdenka left her husband, Janáček was invited to supper again, a somewhat stiff occasion: 'Papa did indeed control himself: he welcomed him; he was cool but he was courteous, even if he spoke as little as possible.' The 'divorce' was quickly annulled and within a week all was ready for Zdenka to return to her husband. Except that when it came to it, she couldn't quite bring herself to do so: 'I put it off almost until the beginning of the summer holidays.'[46]

On 13 June Janáček made an application to the Regional School Board for financial support, saying that he had been ill for three months with catarrh on his lung. He needed to go to the spa at České Teplice for 'chronic rheumatism' (the first sign of an ailment that would increasingly afflict him; see chap. 64). He was also supporting a 'seriously ill mother'. He enclosed a letter of recommendation from the directorate (Schulz now supporting him) and a doctor's certificate from Dr Fred. Kroczak of 8 June 1884.[47]

It was Janáček's health that finally brought Janáček and his wife back together. Although no more was heard of the rheumatism at the time, according to Zdenka's memoirs they both got coughs and the doctor diagnosed inflammation of the bronchial tubes and recommended Gleichenberg for it, a spa in Styria, Austria, where the waters were considered particularly beneficial in treating catarrh in the mucous membranes. The Regional School Board took their time (over the summer holidays) to decide to allocate Janáček 60 zl.[48] But well before then the prospect of a spa holiday (courtesy of the Schulzes' largesse) speeded up Zdenka's decision. Furniture was moved back again into the flat in Klášterní náměstí, little Olga was left there with a newly engaged servant, and Zdenka and Leoš went off to Gleichenberg as man and wife for a three-week trip.[49] Such was Janáček's standing in Czech Brno that this holiday was mentioned in a short announcement on 17 August 1884 in *Moravská orlice*.

21

The Organ School

Of Janáček's various posts, that of director of the Brno Organ School*
was the most durable: he presided over the school and its successor, the
Brno Conservatory, for a total of thirty-eight years, more than half his
life; even his main job at the Teachers' Institute was shorter, a bare
thirty years. Although many other of his activities, his conducting,
his folk-music collecting and later his composition, stamped Janáček as
a distinctive figure in Brno musical society, the Organ School was
unique. It was his invention; no-one else was director of the Organ
School, and by the time it had become the Conservatory and was later
taken over by others, its nature had changed from a privately funded
institution, whose official mission was to produce organists and choirmasters, to a publicly funded institution aiming to produce musicians
of all sorts. The Organ School's success was entirely due to Janáček's
drive in keeping it going through difficult times, in getting good
teachers for it, and in his constant wish to improve what it offered. For
all his international reputation as one of the outstandingly distinctive
composers of the twentieth century, one needs to remember that as
founder-director of the Organ School he was also vitally important to
the development of music in Brno and Moravia. Many of the region's
leading twentieth-century musicians were trained at his Organ School
and themselves shaped the next phase.

With its first-floor portico adorned with Corinthian pillars and
pediment, the pseudo-Renaissance Organ School overlooked one of the
main thoroughfares out of central Brno. Since 1990 the road has been
called Kounicova, as it was in 1918, but before then it was Giskragasse

---

* For comments on the concept of an organ school, see chap. 11.

or Giskrova ulice. The building was known originally as the 'Greek Villa', a small but imposing two-storey building, almost square, with simulated rustication on the ground floor. On the first floor, pediments above the windows add gravitas and continue the Greek theme. Access to the building was not from Giskrova but, in this corner-site building, from Smetanova ulice, as it has been known since 1921. Originally a blind alley,[1] it is now a street which descends through leafy avenues and across another main road to the Lužánky park, one of Janáček's favourite haunts. There is a small entrance on the side of the building off Smetanova but the main gate is further on, through tall railings and a courtyard that leads up to the covered entrance. When it was acquired for the Organ School in 1907 the building was thought to be the height of opulence, having been built originally by the Russophile lawyer Ctibor Chleborád as a possible Russian consulate – hence its architectural pretensions – and then used by the factory owners Haas & Kordina as a private residence.[2]

Coming to it today the visitor can be misled into thinking that the Organ School has always been housed in this small but impressive building. It needs some effort of will to remember that this was its home for only eleven years before it became a conservatory, and that for its first twenty-five years the school had survived in humbler and far less suitable buildings. The 'Greek Villa' was the Organ School's fourth home. Its various locations can be summarized as follows:

1882–6:	Teachers' Institute, Staré Brno
1886–96:	'U modré koule' ['At the blue globe'], Starobrněnská no. 7, Brno
1896–1907:[†]	'Tachovský House', Jakubská ulice no. 1/Česká ulice no. 8, Brno
1907–19:	'Greek Villa', Giskrova [later Kounicova] no. 30, Brno

In 1919 the Organ School became the Brno Conservatory and remained there until after the Second World War, when a move to a bigger building became possible. In the 1950s, largely owing to the imaginative efforts of Dr Theodora Straková, the building was

---

[†] JVŠ, 24, gives the date of the move to the 'Greek Villa' as 15 August 1908, but it is clear from correspondence and from the relevant annual reports of the Organ School that the move took place over the summer of 1907, and that the new building was in use in the autumn of 1907. '1908' (but not '15 August') reflects the completion of necessary adaptations to the new building (see below).

acquired by the Moravian Regional Museum to house its musical archives. So the growing Janáček collection, together with rich church-music archives amassed after the Communist dissolution of the monasteries, returned to Kounicova (or rather Leninova, as it was between 1946 and 1990). The Janáček archives have remained there as part of the Music Division of the Moravian Regional Museum.

The changes of venue accompanied a gradual increase in the size of the Organ School and the improvement in its fortunes. Originally it consisted of a single narrow room in the Teachers' Institute, its one window looking on to the courtyard and so dark that it had to be lit by a paraffin lamp during the day. At its opening in 1882 the Organ School possessed an organ with one set of stops, basically a harmonium with pedals. In Ludvík Kundera's account this instrument, a blackboard and benches for 'five to six students', constituted the Organ School's entire equipment at the time.[3] Since the first-year intake in this building was generally nine or ten,[4] there must have been a few extra chairs. The room could be used only out of hours as it was used by the Teachers' Institute during the day.

Four years later the Organ School moved out of Staré Brno to premises on the first floor at the back of an apartment block 'U modré koule' ['At the blue globe']. To get to the school one went through a courtyard up wooden steps to a gallery and through a small anteroom into the single teaching room. This too was shaded by the shrubs from the garden but there were now two windows. And there were now also two organs, a newly acquired one in the teaching room and the old one in the anteroom. There were four tables and fourteen chairs[5] (though again one wonders how they coped with the exceptionally large first-year class in 1891 with twenty-six students).[6] The big improvement was that, unlike the room in the Teachers' Institute, the rooms with their two organs were available for practice throughout the day except when classes were going on. During its ten-year stay at 'U modré koule' the Organ School hired a piano, and, after making collections for this purpose, bought a new piano (for 300 zl) and a third organ (for 1345 zl), a two-manual instrument with seven stops and fifteen couplers.[7]

In 1896 the Organ School moved again, further into the centre of Brno, to the first floor of another corner house, on Jakubská ulice no. 1 and what was then Rudolfská (now Česká) ulice no. 8. This time a suite of four rooms was at its disposal, two larger teaching rooms, one with a piano, the best Mölzer organ and room for sixteen students, the smaller one with the older Rieger organ and with room for six students. In winter, however, teaching tended to be confined to the smaller of the two rooms to save fuel. Improvements came too during these ten years. A new Mölzer organ was bought (for 3190 K) and electric motors were fitted on all three organs so that the wind supply was automatic; previously some hapless student had to pump away for one of his colleagues.[8]

The 'Greek Villa', where the school began moving in the summer of 1907,‡ outstripped all its predecessors. There were now eighteen teaching rooms, including a small concert hall on the first floor and an office for the director. The number of organs went up to four (a new one was bought in 1909 for 3500 zl) and there were five pianos.[9] A contemporary photograph of the main teaching room (now the reading room of the museum) shows a room equipped with two blackboards, a piano and seating for at least eighteen students,[10] though they must have squeezed in more, since first-year intakes in the new building were usually in the thirties.[11] Janáček's life was made considerably easier when he and Zdenka moved into a house built for them in the grounds (see chap. 60).

In his autobiography Janáček claimed that he dreamt up the idea of the Brno Organ School on 12 June 1878 as somewhere to teach his 'logic of harmonic connections'.[12] The precise date would appear to come from his reading of Helmholtz's *Die Lehre von den Tonempfindungen* (he got to p. 366 that day),[13] where he found confirmation of one aspect of his theory (see chap. 19). The four paragraphs he devotes to this in his autobiography all reinforce the idea that the Organ School was founded expressly to teach a theory of harmony that had been confirmed by his reading of Helmholtz. This, of course, is a reminiscence almost fifty years after the event and although Janáček certainly used the school to promote his theory, this was a later development. His studies at the Prague Organ School in 1874–5 were crucial in suggesting to him that a similar institution could be established in Brno ('I travelled to my Prague studies with this idea and in its realization I see one of my greatest tasks').[14] Janáček hinted at this in one of his

---

‡According to the Organ School's annual report for 1907 (published a year later) the move was completed by 1 August 1907; the next report (for 1908) records that all adaptations of the new building were completed by 15 December 1908.

earliest published articles, a report on Easter music given in Brno 1875, where he stressed the need for educated musicians in directing church choirs (xv/3). The earliest concrete dated information about his plans comes from one of his letters to Zdenka from Leipzig: 'Today [26 October 1879, i.e. less than a month after he had arrived] my head was continually teeming with thoughts about the practical value of founding an organ school; and so I have already found many materials on all sides.'[15]

However, what needs to be remembered about the Organ School is that it was a private institution, created within church circles for the express purpose of training church musicians, and its coming into existence did not depend on Janáček's whim. Although his time at the Prague Organ School was formative and led to his thinking about setting up something similar in Brno, and although his experiences at the conservatories of Leipzig and Vienna, both positive and negative, gave him more ideas as to how a teaching institution should be run, Janáček could not act on his own: he needed an influential, well-connected committee whose job it was to seek permission from local authorities to establish such a school, to raise funds and to act as the respected overseers for the work of the school.

According to the Organ School's first annual report (1881–2) it was in May 1881, i.e. a year after Janáček had returned from his studies in Vienna, that 'some Brno gentlemen got together and discussed what to do about the decline of church music'.[16] By 4 June they had decided to form a society (along the lines of the corresponding Prague society) called the Association for the Promotion of Church Music in Moravia[17] and four days later *Moravská orlice* printed the names of these concerned Brno gentlemen. They included well-placed representatives of the administration and education, Janáček himself, supporters of his aims such as Father Anselm Rambousek (see chap. 17) and Dr Josef Chmelíček (1823–91), a teacher at the theological college in Brno, and crucially the director of the Teachers' Institute, Emilian Schulz,[18] whose daughter was due to marry Janáček a month later.

As chairman[19] of the society there was a leading local aristocrat. This, for the first twenty-seven years, was Jindřich Count Belrupt-Tissac (1825–1913), who had been present at the initial discussions; in 1908 he was succeeded by Jindřich Count Harrach. A church dignitary served as vice-chairman (Canon Dr Zeibert to 1900, thereafter Abbot Bařina of the Augustinian monastery). The most important function, however, was that of the chief executive [*jednatel*], at first Emilian Schulz, from 1895 Dr Alois Kolísek (1868–1931, a priest returned from Rome with a newly acquired doctorate in theology), and from 1905 Janáček's lawyer Dr Felix Rudiš (1856–1947). In addition to an inspector and a treasurer, there was a small committee that over the years included a variety of men (no women at all) from the church, educational establishments and local administration.

The Organ School was in effect a Czech-speaking institution. In his account of the first-year exams Janáček's friend Berthold Žalud made the point that they were conducted in Czech, and certificates were awarded in Czech because the students were all Czech[20] – which implies that had any German speakers enrolled different arrangements would have to have been made. Not all the members of the committee, however, were fluent Czech speakers: Dr Josef Chmelíček (1823–91), for instance, declined Janáček's invitation to lecture in music history on the grounds that he was too old and that his Czech wasn't good enough.[21] Subscribing members of the society were drawn from both communities. This is reflected in the annual reports issued to members bilingually, at first German, then Czech and from 1905 the other way round. The first exclusively Czech report (that of 1918–19) came only after the proclamation of the Czechoslovak state.[22]

An important function of the committee was to raise funds. Although funds were occasionally solicited for specific aims, such as the purchase of a new organ, the chief funding mechanism was to persuade members of the public to become members of the society and to pay regular dues. Kundera's figures show how membership rose to 297 in 1884–5, slumped to 142 in 1892, but from 1906 (when the last move was mooted) began to rise steadily, achieving almost 500 members in 1918.[23] The fact that a substantial part of the school's income came from this source, from people concerned chiefly with the training of church musicians, meant that, whatever greater plans Janáček had for producing composers and for musicians other than organists, or indeed for promoting his theories of harmony, his hands were always going to be tied: as far as the members were concerned, the over-riding function of the school was to provide well-trained organists and church choirmasters.

Students paid fees: annually 5 zl at first, from 1899 10 K monthly (and later up to 16 K), though provision was made in the cases of the poorest students to waive some of the teaching fee.[24] But financial support increasingly came from local government and the state, and here the broadly drawn and highly placed committee members were especially useful. Local government, i.e. the office of the Moravian Governor, contributed 100 zl in the first year, an annual sum which rose with regular increases up to 2000 K in 1908.[25] After being lobbied in 1888, the Austrian Ministry of Education and Culture conceded a subvention of 200 zl in 1890, but soon increased it continually and substantially: in 1902 to 800 K; in 1905 to 1500 K; and in 1906 to 4500 K. Not that these sums impressed Janáček: in 1908, for instance, he demanded (in vain, of course) that the 4500 K subvention should be immediately raised to 19,500 K, which would allow an annual salary of 6000 K to the director, and 3000 K each to the teachers of counterpoint, organ and singing. Nevertheless by 1913, just before the war, the school was receiving a total of 15,350 K from this source. In 1906, when the purchase of the new building was being negotiated, its cost of 88,000 K[26] was defrayed partly by loans of 30,000 K from the state and 20,000 K from the Moravian Government.[27]

Financially and artistically the Organ School made steady progress up to the beginning of the First World War. Its fortunes during the war will be described in vol. ii, but essentially the war eroded its financial stability with the cutting back of the subsidies[28] and by the call-up affecting both staff and students (predominantly male, though female students had been admitted from the late 1880s). Some courses had to be abandoned, as was the teaching of wind instruments.[29] That the school kept going was a tribute to Janáček's will and determination. It was thus well placed for its nationalization after the war and its rebranding as a conservatory in 1919.

The regulations for the new society, the Association for the Promotion of Church Music in Moravia, were approved by the Moravian governor on 4 June 1881[30] and, with this hurdle achieved, fundraising could begin with invitations in newspapers and specialist journals for the public to support the society's aims by becoming members. On 1 July 1881, for instance, *Dalibor* published an announcement (xv/23) about the proposed new institution, its organization and mission that, although signed by the 'organizing committee', was clearly written mostly by Janáček.

Further developments took place after the summer (during which Janáček married Zdenka Schulzová), such as the members' general assembly on 23 November 1881, where the society's aims were set out,[31] and the executive committee and its officers were formally elected. On 7 December 1881 this body convened to elect its director, Leoš Janáček, a foregone conclusion by then. Janáček would remain in this role for the next thirty-eight years, and despite his prickly nature and hot temper, relations with his committee remained generally harmonious throughout this long period.[32] More difficult were Janáček's relations with part of the clergy (who generally supported the school), for instance when they discovered that his opera *Jenůfa* was based on an 'immoral' libretto.[33] Janáček was able at least to satisfy the enquiries of Bishop Huyn about the church-going activities of the students by assuring him that his students sang at Mass every Sunday at the Minorite church, and that this needed one hour of special rehearsal.[34]

Teaching began at the end of summer 1882. Eighteen students applied and were interviewed on Sunday 13 August 1882. Of these, nine were admitted[§] and classes began on 15 August.[35] Public exams took place eleven months later, on 19 July 1883, and were reported at some length by Berthold Žalud in *Dalibor*, in which he emphasized the clarity and correctness of the answers and the ability, even of the youngest student, the sixteen-year-old František Kolářík, to harmonize a given soprano line using passing notes and suspensions. Žalud expressed surprise that public exams took place at all for what were only first-year students. But originally Janáček had devised only a one-year course, during which it became clear that a second year was needed, and Žalud was able to report that in 1883–4 a second year and a new first year would run concurrently.[36]

But even two years turned out to be not enough and in 1887–8 a third year was added.[‖] However, the accommodation was at first so limited and finances so tight that it was difficult to run more than one year at a time. In the first twenty years, there were only eight first-year intakes so that students wanting to enter the school sometimes had to wait a year or even two for a new first year to open. This meant that

---

[§] This is the story that Kundera tells on *JVŠ*, 20. His chart on p. 141 erroneously opens the school a year earlier but is correct from 1883–4. Helfert's summary of the first eight years (*LJPT*, 280) supports this except for stating that there was a second- and third-year intake in 1885–6. This is impossible since the third year opened only in 1887–8. In 1885–6 the intakes were for the first and second years only.

[‖] *JVŠ*, 20, supported by chart of intake on p. 141. Helfert (*LJPT*, 279–80), however, implies that a three-year course was envisaged from the beginning.

numbers remained small.[37] On the whole first-year intakes tended to be in the teens and with a high drop-out rate; third-year groups could go down to as few as three to five students. By 1905–6 finances had stabilized, with an increased state grant, and all three years ran simultaneously for the first time. With thirteen students recruited and a new refresher 'ten-month course for country organists' (a successful new venture that ran annually until numbers dwindled during the war), the total enrolment was forty. With the move to the new building in 1907 numbers thereafter increased into the high fifties and even more in some years.

Once the course had settled down into its three-year shape, each year was accorded a specific aim: the first year was to supply all that was needed in practical and theoretical knowledge to train a village organist, the second enough to train a town organist and the third year a choirmaster.[38] Thus students did not need to go through all three years of the course and, if they were of sufficient quality and experience, they were allowed to enter the second or even the third year.

When the school opened there were just three teachers: Jan Nesvadba (1829–99) for singing, Jan Kment (1860–1907) for organ and Janáček for theory. Twenty-five years older than Janáček, Nesvadba was a reliable choirmaster who, like Janáček, had conducted both the Beseda and 'Svatopluk' at various times. Kment, freshly graduated from the Prague Organ School, was in his first post. Both served Janáček loyally in the early years of the institution. As student numbers grew, the number of staff increased[39] together with the subjects that could be offered. Music history was added in 1885 as a new subject. Knowledge of the liturgy was necessary for church organists, and this was taught from 1887. A particularly distinctive aspect of the course was the teaching of psychology and aesthetics.[40] Although an Organ School implies that the only instrument students needed to study would be the organ, Janáček always saw his school as broader, and in 1891, a few years after he ceased to be head of the Beseda instrumental school, he introduced compulsory piano lessons[41] and twelve years later compulsory violin lessons.[42] In time this allowed students to specialize, so that by 1917–18 a student could choose one of three routes – as an organist-composer, a pianist or a violinist; this of course meant that the appeal of the school was greatly enhanced.[43] And with the specialization that this also implied, Janáček made valiant efforts to offer organ tuition at an advanced level and thus further increase standards and status.

However, his attempts to secure state funding for a 'master school' in organ[44] failed despite public concerts of the two candidates for this post (see chap. 60). Once the school moved to the new building, the many new teaching rooms allowed new instruments to be taught: clarinet, flute, horn, trumpet and oboe.[45] With the view that organists might need to take part in the musical life of the towns where they worked, students were required to learn one of these. As with the organ, piano and violin, all instruments were taught in groups of up to eight students.[46]

What is clear from the list of teachers given in Kundera's study[47] is how stable the teaching staff was over the years, with stalwarts such as Jan Kment, Emerich Beran (1868–1940) and in particular Max Koblížek (1866–1947) – the last two themselves graduates of the Organ School. Janáček was particularly lucky to have fine and devoted piano teachers such as Marie Kuhlová (1862–1951) and Marie Dvořáková (1887–1953). Many of the teachers were also active performers and took part in the concert-giving activities of the school, which meant that they were the earliest performers of Janáček's chamber and solo instrumental compositions: Dvořáková gave the première of *In the Mists* (VIII/22); the cellist Rudolf Pavlata (1873–1939, who taught score-reading and instrumentation and conducted the orchestra) with the pianist Ludmila Prokopová (1888–1959), the première of *Fairy Tale* (VII/5); the violinist Pavel Dědeček (1885–1954), the pianist Růžena Fialová and Rudolf Pavlata the première of Janáček's Piano Trio (X/22). By the time of the school's greatest heyday, at the outbreak of the First World War, the regular staff reached eight including Matouš Balcárek, who taught psychology and teaching practice, and Dr Albín Zelníček, the long-term liturgiologist (from 1907 until 1919).

Janáček himself taught 'theory' for the entire duration of the Organ School. This covered a wide range of subjects: harmony, counterpoint, composition, improvisation, figured bass, score-reading, and in the third year orchestration, form and opera. Janáček was happy to pass on figured bass to others (Emerich Beran began teaching it in 1891), and when František Musil (1852–1908) joined the staff in 1905 he was able to relieve Janáček of counterpoint, orchestration and score-reading. But Janáček never relinquished composition and harmony: his idiosyncratic approach is summarized in chap. 19 and it was the teaching of Janáček's theories that became one of the most distinctive aspects of the Organ School, after a while supported by his published harmony treatises of 1896–7 (xv/151) and 1911–12 (xv/202). Although a second edition of xv/202 was published in 1920, Janáček had by then stepped down from the directorship. In the newly created Brno Conservatory, his harmonic theory was abandoned with unseemly haste.

Ferdinand Vach (1860–1939, see chap. 39), the conductor of the Moravian Teachers' Choral Society (see chap. 51) and one of the leading choir-trainers in Moravia, joined the staff in 1905 and immediately began organizing the performance of larger choral works. These were often elaborate affairs, usually two a year, held mostly in the Jesuit church (the church of the Assumption of the Virgin Mary, Jesuitská ulice), though the larger ones took place in the Besední dům. They frequently involved outside soloists (the tenor Stanislav Tauber sang regularly), and even orchestras (the military band of the 8th Infantry Regiment). Works performed included Palestrina's *Missa Papae Marcelli*, Dvořák's *Stabat mater* and Mass in D, Haydn's *Creation* and, for the twenty-fifth anniversary of the school, Cherubini's Requiem. Janáček was not directly involved in these performances except in 1909, when he stepped in for a sick Vach and conducted one of the most ambitious, Gounod's oratorio *Mors et vita*.[48]

The move to Giskrova provided the Organ School with a small performing space on the first floor and from 1908 Janáček began to organize regular chamber concerts given by members of his staff, notably Prokopová, Dědeček and Pavlata. By the next academic year (1909–10) these 'sonata hours', as they were called, became a planned series of mostly piano trios, with Janáček providing spoken introductions. This was the venue for Janáček's *Fairy Tale* for cello and piano (vii/5). In 1910–11 the programmes became more diverse, including both vocal and orchestral items (early Haydn symphonies). With the increasing range of instruments taught, the next year the concert series became 'symphonic concerts', which took place in the nearby Lužánky hall. In addition to chamber music involving the resident trio, these included four of Beethoven's symphonies (nos. 5–8) conducted by Pavlata, a series which continued in 1912–13 with Beethoven's symphonies nos. 1–4. The symphony concerts in 1913–14, again under Pavlata, concentrated on concertos and symphonic poems, though smaller solo and chamber works were included, such as the first Brno performance of Janáček's piano suite *In the Mists* (viii/22). This, however, was the last year of symphonic concerts: the war restricted the Organ School's budget and available players. The concert series reverted to 'sonata hours' in the Organ School, a series of four concerts in 1914–15. There were three more concerts in 1916 and 1917 including, uncharacteristically for Janáček, a memorial concert for Emperor Franz Josef in December 1916.[49]

Most accounts of Janáček's directorship of the Brno Organ School stress how much he had to do to keep it going, and how many of the initiatives, some of them very imaginative, came directly from him. Even when the school expanded there was no secretarial help. It was Janáček who built up the library, not just of organ works and theoretical works, and, despite the very limited finances, carefully chose works for it: his first purchase was a score of Berlioz's Requiem.[¶] Helfert's list of works acquired during the early years of the institution gives some idea of Janáček's breadth of interest: church music by Lassus, F.X. Haberl and F.X. Witt (leading Cecilians), but also Dvořák's *Legends* for orchestra, Brahms's Symphony no. 2 (quite new at the time) and Mendelssohn string quartets.[50] In the Giskrova building there was a dedicated reading room for students, equipped with musical periodicals, which was open even on Sundays.[51]

It was Janáček's initiative that led to final-year students having to graduate with the composition of a Latin mass for chorus and organ, which would then be performed publicly.[52] This is the background to Janáček's own unfinished Mass in E flat from 1908 (IX/5), composed in class as a demonstration of how to go about such things. Another initiative was the publication of annual volumes of student compositions (mostly offertories), issued free to members of the Association for the Promotion of Church Music in Moravia. Volumes with these compositions came out in 1914 and 1915, but further volumes were thwarted by the war.[53] Janáček was keen to involve his students in experimental work: in music psychology and perception (the basis for his article *On the Course of the Composer's Mental Activity* XV/210, which he published in *Hlídka* in 1916), in the plan to draw up

---

[¶]*LJPT*, 281; however, negotiations had been going on for its purchase well before the school opened. On 21 December 1881 the publisher and bookseller Urbánek reported his searching for it to Janáček (BmJA, A 5) and by 2 January 1882 had found a copy for 19 zl (BmJA, A 100).

a 'Dvořák theme dictionary' (see chap. 60), and in helping him with collecting Moravian folksongs.[54]

Janáček wanted his students to have every opportunity of hearing a good range of music, and negotiated free entry for Organ School pupils to the concerts given by the Brno Beseda and Musikverein and to the operas at the Czech theatre.[55] It is more difficult to assess whether he was genuinely concerned with his students' development of independent thought. On the one hand originality was emphasized (and it was generally thought that students who went to the Prague Conservatory acquired more technical proficiency but less originality than in Brno),[56] but on the other hand Janáček's teaching involved students repeating virtually verbatim the phrases with which he had lectured, or coming up with answers that exactly corresponded to his own understanding:

When he spoke on a subject it was clear that he had the material exactly divided up and logically arranged, expressed as far as possible with the most appropriate words and as concisely as possible. When we went over it he wanted us to express ourselves with the same words: 'Precision of thought is reflected in precision of speech', was his slogan.

There would be heated scenes, Jan Kunc went on to explain, when Janáček wasn't happy with any of the answers he got. One after the other, Kunc and his fellow students would stand up and sit down again having failed to give Janáček the answer he wanted, sometimes prompting his pacing up and down the room, or even explosions of anger at the students' 'superficiality and imprecision'. The scene would be repeated the next day until eventually someone came up with the 'right' answer.[57]

Those students who left memoirs of the Organ School looked back with affection at the institution, and at their contacts with Janáček. All stress how central was his role. Rudolf Kvasnica, a pupil in 1910–14** and a member of staff from 1916, recalled how much Janáček enjoyed lecturing and teaching. He was also very strict, demanding discipline from staff and students, and sat in on many lectures and classes. His theory classes were considered to be particularly difficult, inducing panic among the students as they waited to see how their homework would be judged.[58]

** He was taken for a year's trial in 1910 (Kvasnica 1974, 172), entered the normal course in 1911–13, and took the advanced course in 1914 (JVŠ, 145).

His eyes were everywhere [recalled Chlubna]. In the corridors and classrooms there had to be calm and order. He didn't tolerate loitering or slovenliness. Even outside school he took an interest in his charges' life and work, their music-making – and he punished their shortcomings. However he had a soft and good heart. He helped where he could. And therefore he enjoyed unparalleled honour and respect, both human and artistic, and was indeed our real 'old gentleman' and ruler of the school.[59]

22

Antonín Dvořák

While Janáček's attitude towards the major figures in Czech music before him such as Bedřich Smetana (1824–84) and Zdeněk Fibich (1850–1900) was ambiguous, if not actively hostile (see chap. 49), his attitude towards Antonín Dvořák, the other major composer in the Czech pantheon, was completely different. Dvořák was born in 1841 and thus half a generation older than him: old enough to be model and mentor, young enough to be a friend. And friend he was almost from the beginning. They probably met in Prague during Janáček's studies there in 1874–5, but how they became acquainted can only be conjectured. It is most likely that Janáček encountered Dvořák at St Vojtěch's, where the latter was organist: many years later Janáček recalled Dvořák's improvisations there on the organ (XV/181). And there were other possibilities, as Jarmil Burghauser suggested, such as the fact that Janáček's Prague lodgings were near Dvořák's flat in Prague,* and that Janáček, like other Moravian students in Prague, may have gathered at the Neff household where Dvořák was a favoured visitor.[1] If their first meeting had been unusual or in some way distinctive, then Janáček might have remembered it. But this was never the subject of any of his subsequent reminiscences. Instead he remembered their later tour:

An expedition with Dr *Antonín Dvořák*.
We stood awhile near the little church at Říp. From there to *Strakonice*, to

---

* Burghauser's point was based on his assumption that Dvořák was living then at Štěpánská ulice. In fact Dvořák moved there only in November 1877. From May 1874 he lived at Na rybníčku 14, which was as close or even closer to Janáček's lodgings (I am indebted to David Beveridge for this information).

Orlík. We walk down from the castle, right to the Vltava. We sit at a table. Dvořák says:
'I think it's goat and not venison.'
We enjoyed it during lunch. So we spent the night there.
We had a look round *Husinec.* We caught sight of *Prachatice.*
A little bit of the journey from Prague by train, a bit back too. The rest on foot.
In any event what was said during three days was minimal.[2]

In his autobiography, Janáček (or his editor Adolf Veselý) put a date to this: 1877. This places it during the month Janáček spent in Prague in the summer of 1877 in his 'top-up' course at the Prague Organ School. It is of course possible that Janáček made contact with Dvořák then, but there wouldn't have been much time for leisurely three-day expeditions, given Janáček's ambitious goals for his Prague studies. As it is, three[†] of the places mentioned were part of Janáček's peregrinations with Dvořák in his much more leisurely summer spent in Prague in 1883. Janáček had already mentioned these 'wanderings' in a reminiscence of Dvořák published in 1911 (XV/201), though without offering a specific date. Thirteen years later the memory was still there – especially of Dvořák's silences – but a date was unwisely added.

The summer of 1883 was when Janáček enjoyed his most extensive contacts with Dvořák, a time that included a ten-day stay with him and his family at Vysoká (the summer residence of Dvořák's brother-in-law, Count Kounic) and several expeditions with him to local beauty spots. When not at Vysoká Janáček stayed in the Dvořáks' flat in Prague. Since this was during the period when Janáček had split up from his wife and was at his most vulnerable, it is reasonable to speculate that Dvořák, an enthusiastic family man, exerted some influence on his hot-headed young friend both in repairing some of the psychological damage by getting him to compose again, and in persuading him to make it up with Zdenka. When Janáček returned to Brno in September 1883 he resumed contacts with her which led, a year later, to their reconciliation (see chap. 20).

Janáček's friendship with Dvořák was both personal and professional. What soon consolidated it was the fact that Janáček, in his

---

[†]The two that weren't visited in 1883 are Říp and Strakonice. Whereas Strakonice is in the area (34 km from Orlík), Říp is north of Prague, some 130 km from Strakonice. It is possible that forty years later Janáček confused several trips, but there is no corroborative evidence that he and Dvořák were ever together at Říp or Strakonice.

position as conductor of the Brno Beseda, could ensure that Dvořák's music was frequently performed in Brno – to the extent that disapproving commentators regarded it as a 'cult' (specifically, an anti-Smetana cult) in which Brno became 'the most Dvořákian city' in the Czech lands.[3] The earliest Dvořák composition that Janáček conducted at the Beseda was the Serenade for strings in 1877; thereafter Dvořák became a regular favourite (see tables 12.2 and 17.1). The music that Dvořák wrote was much the sort of thing which could be cultivated by a middle-of-the-road music society such as the Brno Beseda. His choruses became staple fare there – even during the times when Janáček wasn't music director. Dvořák wrote attractive orchestral works such as the *Slavonic Dances, Legends* and symphonies that could be managed by the orchestra, while his large-scale choral-orchestral works such as the *Stabat mater, The Spectre's Bride* and *St Ludmila* could feature as the climax of the Beseda's musical year. Smetana, in contrast, concentrated on operas. Apart from his early *Triumf-Sinfonie* (with its unacceptable – from a patriotic Czech vantage point – use of the Austrian national anthem) Smetana wrote no symphonies, not many choruses and only one short choral-orchestral work. His symphonic poems, though gamely attempted by Janáček and his band in Brno, were very demanding for a fledgling orchestra.

The Brno performances of his works brought Dvořák on several visits to Brno (see table 22.1 below) so that together with meetings in Prague personal contacts were regularly maintained. Though they may have had little to say to one another, Dvořák and Janáček had many shared interests, for instance in the Pan-Slavonic view of music exemplified by the *dumky* they both composed (see chap. 9). Above all, Dvořák provided models. Soon after Janáček conducted Dvořák's Serenade for strings at the Beseda, he composed two pieces for string orchestra, his Suite (vɪ/2) and his *Idyll* (vɪ/3). Janáček's *Valachian Dances* (vɪ/4) a decade later were a response to Dvořák's popular *Slavonic Dances*. Janáček made arrangements of six of Dvořák's *Moravian Duets*, expanding them from two female voices and piano to vocal quartet and piano (xɪɪ/2). Despite aspirations to write a symphony during his studies in Leipzig in 1879–80,[4] Janáček never followed the impressive example of Dvořák in this field. When there was a possibility of Dvořák's turning up in Leipzig to attend a performance of his *Slavonic Dances*, Janáček thought that they might go back on the train together to Prague so that he could pick Dvořák's

Table 22.1: Meetings (planned as well as realized) between Janáček and Dvořák

(sources given if not discussed in this chapter)	
1874–5	Janáček probably meets Dvořák during his year in Prague, perhaps at St Vojtěch's.
1877	July: Janáček possibly meets Dvořák during his further studies in Prague.
1878	26 July: Janáček drops in to see Dvořák in Prague on his way to Oettingen.[8]
1878	15 December: Dvořák visits Brno to hear Janáček conduct a Beseda concert that includes four *Slavonic Dances* and Janáček's *Idyll* (VI/3). He plays the piano for the première of three of his male-voice choruses, *Sorrow*, *Miraculous Water* and *The Girl in the Woods*.
1880	6 January: during Janáček's Christmas–New Year break in Brno, Janáček and Zdenka Schulzová attend a mostly Dvořák concert, given at the Brno Beseda with Dvořák conducting his Symphony no. 5 in F and his *Slavonic Rhapsody* no. 2 (see chap. 17).
1880	21 February: Janáček hopes to meet Dvořák in Leipzig for a performance of the *Slavonic Dances*; he goes to meet the train, but Dvořák doesn't turn up.[9]
1881	Second half of July: Janáček and Zdenka meet Dvořák in Prague on their honeymoon. They make a trip with him to Karlštejn by train and also see Dvořák several times during their time in Prague (see chap. 17).
1882	2 April: Janáček invites Dvořák for a performance of his *Stabat mater* at the Brno Beseda that he is conducting; at the last moment Dvořák is unable to come since his father falls seriously ill.[10]
1882	About 13 December: after his separation from Zdenka, Janáček visits Dvořák in Prague during his Christmas holidays and plays some of Dvořák's recent music with him (see chap. 20).
1883	28 July: Janáček accompanies Dvořák on a trip to Orlík, and then stays on for about ten days with the Dvořák family at Vysoká (see chap. 20).
1883	About 7 August until at least 4 September: Janáček spends the rest of his summer trip to Prague at the Dvořáks' flat (see chap. 20) apart from one more trip with Dvořák (see next entry).
1883	23 August: Janáček accompanies Dvořák to Prachatice and Husinec; he probably stays overnight at Vysoká before returning to Prague (see chap. 20).
1885	8 October: Janáček has lunch with Dvořák in Prague and consults him over a planned performance by the Brno Beseda of *The Spectre's Bride* (see chap. 23).
1886	10 January: Janáček conducts the Brno Beseda in a concert that includes Dvořák's Symphony no. 7 in D minor and *Hymn: the Heirs of the White Mountain*; Dvořák is invited to attend but declines as he is orchestrating *St Ludmila* (see chap. 23).
1887	Early November: Janáček goes to Prague to consult Dvořák about *Šárka*, which he had sent him in August (see chap. 26).
1888	29 April: Janáček conducts Dvořák's cantata *The Spectre's Bride* at the Brno Beseda. Dvořák comes to Brno for the occasion; Janáček remembered saying goodbye to him and the soloists at the station (see XV/201 and chap. 23).
1889	5 October: Janáček plans to be in Prague to pick up the score of *Valachian Dances* (VI/4) from Dvořák, where he had asked for it to be sent.[11]
1890	Dvořák in Brno?[12]
1892	18 April: Dvořák takes part in a chamber concert in Brno before leaving for America. Janáček reviews the concert for *Moravské listy* (XV/141).

Table 22.1: Meetings (planned as well as realized) between Janáček and Dvořák

1897	8 May: in Brno Dvořák conducts the newly created Czech Philharmonic in his Symphony no. 9 'From the New World', *The Noon Witch*, *The Golden Spinning Wheel* and the overture *Carnival*. Janáček is there and is much taken with the symphony. He makes arrangements to see Dvořák after his visit to Kroměříž in order to pass on the score of his cantata *Amarus* for Dvořák's perusal. However, Janáček misses Dvořák at the station. and has to send the score to Prague (see chap. 36).
1904	1 March: Janáček times a trip to Prague to coincide with the dress rehearsal of Dvořák's last opera, *Armida*. The rehearsal is a disaster and Dvořák is very irritated. It is the last time that Janáček saw Dvořák, who died two months later (see chap. 47).

brains about 'which movements from Beethoven and other classics he most recommended for study'.[5] And when Janáček's studies began to fall apart in Vienna he considered going to Prague to study with Dvořák.[6] The first piece by Janáček that Dvořák heard was the *Idyll* for strings, performed by the Brno Beseda on 15 December 1878. Did he offer an opinion of Janáček's composition? Although Janáček dismissed the *Idyll* in one of his letters to Zdenka from Leipzig, he performed it a second time in Brno at the high-profile Beseda Jubilee Concert on 12 December 1880, so if Dvořák had expressed a view, it couldn't have been all bad. From the mid-1880s, when Janáček began returning to composition after his post-Vienna, post-divorce trauma, he began sending Dvořák pieces to look at. He had not done so before and the that he did so now suggests that the idea may have come from Dvořák in an attempt to buck him up at a bleak time. The first pieces he sent to Dvořák were the four choruses of 1885 (VI/17) – significantly dedicated to Dvořák. Then followed the opera *Šárka* and another three choruses in 1888 (IV/19) and, nine years later, the cantata *Amarus* (III/6). Dvořák was not a particularly zealous mentor. He wrote Janáček a nice letter about the 1885 choruses (though he worried about the modulations; see chap. 23), but it took a lot of work on Janáček's part to extract some sort of comment on *Šárka* and *Amarus* (see chaps. 23 and 36). Dvořák apologized for not looking at the 1888 choruses; in fact he never sent them back and they were discovered in his estate years later. One wonders whether he lost them on purpose. If he had been nonplussed by the 1885 choruses what would he have made of these even more experimental ones? Dvořák's verdict on

Amarus was not that different from what he had written a decade earlier about the 1885 choruses, i.e. he found the modulations problematic and felt that Janáček could do better melodically. But what would be particularly influential on Janáček's exploration of 'speech melody' was his advice, over *Amarus*, that he should try and improve his declamation (see chap. 36). This was what Dvořák was prepared to tell Janáček to his face. To his pupil and son-in-law Josef Suk he expressed a less guarded opinion of Janáček's music: 'Yes it's strange but it was written by someone who thinks with his own head!'[7]

When Janáček returned to composition in the summer of 1883 he had discovered opera. However, Dvořák's operas up to this period offered less attractive models for him. Apart from the heroic *Dimitrij* and *Vanda*, most were small-scale comedies that hardly held the stage (Janáček knew only *The Cunning Peasant* and had reservations about its libretto; see chap. 25). Dvořák took time to learn his craft in this genre and it was only in his final decade that he composed his masterpiece *Rusalka* – by which time Janáček was well under way with his own, very different masterpiece, *Jenůfa*.

In the 1890s one of the most striking changes in Dvořák's own aesthetic was evident in his renewed interest in opera and his sudden espousal of the symphonic poem, e.g. in those based on the ballads of K.J. Erben: *The Water Goblin, The Noon Witch, The Golden Spinning Wheel* and *The Wild Dove* (all 1896). This new passion for programme music by his older friend chimed in with Janáček's own shifting aesthetic, and he devoted detailed analyses to all four symphonic poems (XV/152, XV/153, XV/154, XV/156; see chap. 33). Furthermore, the method of composition by taking lines of text and setting them, and then suppressing the words, is a technique that Janáček himself tried out in his overture to *Jenůfa, Jealousy* (VI/10) (see vol. ii: Janáček and programme music). The timing is fascinating; *Jealousy* was composed by February 1895, a year before the first of Dvořák's symphonic poems on Erben. When Janáček produced his analysis of *The Water Goblin* he made reference to Dvořák's method of composition. There is no proof (e.g. in surviving letters), but it does sound as though they may have discussed this method earlier, with Janáček trying it out first and spotting immediately what Dvořák had done when he saw Dvořák's score. In one of the last concerts that Janáček conducted (20 March 1898), he gave the première of the last of Dvořák's Erben symphonic poems, *The Wild Dove*.

As table 22.1 shows, Janáček saw Dvořák regularly throughout the 1880s. Their infrequent meetings thereafter do not reflect any cooling in the friendship but instead can be explained by a number of other factors: Janáček's resignation from the Brno Beseda in 1888 (and thus now lacking a pretext for inviting Dvořák to Brno), Janáček's active involvement with Moravian folk music (which took over much of his free time), and Dvořák's own period in America (1892–5). Although Dvořák was back home again in 1897, Janáček had by then begun to find his feet as a composer and perhaps felt less need for endorsement by his distinguished friend.

Apart from the four Erben analyses, Janáček published analyses of Dvořák's String Quartet op. 105 (xv/153) and *The Spectre's Bride* (xv/86) and frequently invoked him in his theoretical articles. Here for instance is an early comment in *Hudební listy* on what seems an unlikely topic, both for Dvořák and for Janáček:

I am convinced that Dvořák's scores are in this respect [i.e. both melodic and harmonic] masterly works of counterpoint.

As a rule he is never satisfied with a clear, interesting harmonic basis to a *single* melody; he proceeds here simultaneously with two, three and up to as many as five expressive motifs.

'Every instrument has its own [tune]', I heard a member of the audience saying during the last concert of the Philharmonic Society in Brno [i.e. the Brno Beseda].

I would compare his scores to an outstanding picture: a single idea speaks from many groups of various people; each face, however, has its own particular expression.

On every page of Dvořák's scores you see many interesting figures all sounding together in one beautiful harmonic thought, without, however, a single one resembling another.

[. . .] What is most important, *Dvořák never leaves a motif in one voice* until one tires of it; hardly has one got to know it than a second one beckons invitingly. You are kept in continual, pleasant excitement. (xv/80)

Later, when his Prague contact Artuš Rektorys was planning a memorial volume on Dvořák and asked for a contribution, Janáček conceived the idea for a 'Dvořák theme dictionary', arranged according to the initial intervals, that would provide an insight into this 'real treasure trove of musical thought'. It would be a 'sizable book', Janáček wrote (and he would get his students to help him), though one that never came to fruition since Rektorys jumped ship from the periodical *Dalibor* (sponsoring this project) just as Janáček was getting excited about it (see chap. 60).

A year later Janáček wrote his most substantial reminiscence of Dvořák (xv/201): it included a glimpse of Dvořák improvising 'discreetly' on the organ at St Vojtěch's, his trips to Brno, their walking tour, his stay at Vysoká, and 'frequent trips to Prague'. A good third of the article is devoted to examples of Dvořák's letting off steam: at Škroup's song *Kde domov můj* (Where is my homeland?, now the Czech national anthem), which served Dvořák as the basis for his incidental music to *Kajetán Tyl*, at Berlioz's Requiem (sadly, Janáček doesn't elaborate), and especially at the unsatisfactory dress rehearsal of his last opera *Armida*. And he remembered his shock when, soon afterwards in Warsaw, he learnt of Dvořák's sudden death at sixty-two (see chap. 47). Buried in the article is one of the most personal comments that Janáček ever wrote about anyone:

Do you know the feeling when someone takes the words out of your mouth before you've said them? I always felt like that in Dvořák's company. His person and his works are interchangeable for me. In this way he took his melodies from my heart. Nothing on earth will break that sort of bond.

23

Autumn 1884 – summer 1888

While Janáček and his wife recovered their health and some of the
sparkle of their marriage in Gleichenberg, Amalie Janáčková's health
began to fail. She had been poorly since Easter 1883 and had written to
Janáček then saying how she had been dividing her time between her
children Karel (five days), František (eight days) and Josefa (sixteen
days) but had to retire to bed when she was with Karel, and at Josefa's
had spent the entire Easter holidays in bed.[1] Later that year she sent a
brief note to Leoš with some cherries that she'd received as a present for
her name day. She couldn't write any more: 'I am very sick', she concluded.[2] Some time that winter, she elaborated on what had kept her in
bed and prevented her from writing: 'gout, and stomach catarrh, and
hardening of the liver'.[3] This combination of symptoms turned out to
be stomach cancer. She managed a couple of short letters to her son in
April 1884, one for Leoš's name day (11 April) and one ten days later,
and even suggested that she would be travelling to Brno to bring a
present when she was 'better'[4] – no doubt she would have been glad to
see her son settled back with his wife and daughter. But such hopes
were vain. The news from Švábenice early the next month was such
that Janáček, not the oldest son but seemingly taking charge, began
summoning his siblings there. František arrived there on 6 May;[5]
Bedřich began making arrangements to travel from Germany[6] but did
not get there in time to see his brother Leoš. In his letter to him on 29
May Bedřich suggested getting in touch with a doctor in Leipzig, Dr G.
Langbein, and asking him for advice.[7] After the May crisis passed,
Amalie Janáčková was taken from Švábenice to Hukvaldy to stay with
her daughter Josefa[8] and it was from Hukvaldy at the beginning of
October 1884 that Amalie, now sixty-five, wrote to Leoš a final letter:

Certainly for the last time in my life I'm writing a letter to you and ask you also for the last time to pick up my widow's pension and send it to me. And I also say farewell to you and wish you happiness and health and contentment in this world and not to forget your loving mother.

I kiss Zdenka and Olguška heartily and I am inexpressibly sorry that I won't see any of you again.

Farewell, your mother Amalia Janáček [sic]

Greetings to all those I know.[9]

On 25 October Josefa wrote to Leoš from Hukvaldy:

I'm letting you know briefly how mummy is getting on; a fortnight ago she had great pains in her legs and they started swelling up more and more, so much so that now she lies in bed all swollen and without movement. [. . .] Dear brother, for God's sake please, when I let you know about her death come to the funeral, it's mother's only wish, you're still her special favourite, please don't leave me on my own for I don't know how I would organize everything, there's no ready money at all.[10]

This heart-felt plea went unanswered. Although Janáček had convened the family gathering in Švábenice in May, something prevented his going to Hukvaldy in November. Zdenka claims that her husband was unwell ('he was coughing badly again'),[11] and certainly illness had kept him away from Brno Beseda committee meetings.[12] However it seems hardly likely that it was just a cold that prevented his attending his mother's deathbed or funeral. He had no immediate responsibilities at the Beseda. Although his arrangements (XII/2) of some of Dvořák's *Moravian Duets* were given by the Beseda on 8 November, he himself was not conducting, and thus not taking rehearsals. His teaching responsibilities at the Teachers' Institute and at the Organ School could surely have been set aside for a day or two to allow him to say goodbye to his mother. So perhaps it was something else that kept him away: awkwardness between his mother and Zdenka, or some feeling of guilt at not having been able to give her a home in her final years that made it all too painful.

So Josefa struggled on alone. Amalie Janáčková died on 16 November and a week later Josefa wrote to her brother describing their mother's last days and hours: how her legs and arms swelled up like kettles until she couldn't move, how a week before she died she got a dry cough, and the next day she began spitting blood but in the end became too weak even to get rid of the blood. Until the last moment she had hearing, memory and feeling; half an hour before she died she said her goodbyes. Only one of Josefa's siblings, František, turned up for the funeral, and Eleonora, although ill, got to Hukvaldy at the end of the day. Josefa describes the country obsequies:

I ordered a funeral with sung mass and [holy] water, I didn't invite the priest to the house, that would have cost 10 zl more. The Hukvaldy reverend accompanied us up to Sklenov [the neighbouring village, on the way to Rychaltice, where Amalie was buried], the musicians offered [their services] themselves, the under-teacher Prpik [Prpík] with the beseda singers sang to me at home and at the grave, the schoolchildren went in the procession to Sklenov. I was desperately sad when I got your letter and one from Karel saying that you weren't coming, I was expecting for certain that you two would come, Karl [Karel] sent a nice wreath and 10 zl.[13]

As Josefa made a point of mentioning Karel's contribution and is silent about anything from Janáček one can only conclude that he sent nothing. From now on all funerals became unbearable for him, and he would avoid them if possible.

'After the death of his mother Leoš was very sad for a long time', Zdenka commented, and she dated the new coolness between him and her parents from this moment. Things had been nicely patched up between Janáček, his wife and her parents by the time of their trip to Gleichenberg, with Zdenka reporting frequent visits between the two families when they returned. These had been interrupted by Zdenka's little brother Leoš contracting scarlet fever and Zdenka's caution about Olga getting it too.[14] However, after Janáček's mother's funeral things suddenly got worse:

From that time he clearly avoided visiting my parents. I saw from his face that it even upset him if I took Olga with me. In the end it settled into the pattern that she'd go with me only on Sunday morning. However, he didn't stop me from visiting my parents by myself when I wanted to. Vainly I and my parents racked our brains as to what had happened. There was no obvious reason why Leoš had become estranged again. I didn't dare ask him outright, I was frightened of maybe disturbing the peace in which we were now living.[15]

Eight days after his mother died Janáček attended his first Brno Beseda committee meeting for a while and made a new proposal: that the Beseda should found a musical periodical that would in particular review the productions of the new Czech Provisional Theatre in Brno, both opera and drama, as well as publishing articles on a range of musical topics, particularly music theory, church music and music education. The committee gave its blessing and within a very short time *Hudební listy*, as the new journal was called, began coming out (see chap. 24). The new Czech theatre opened on 6 December 1884 with a thirty-year-old Czech play, Josef Jiří Kolár's tragedy *Magelóna*; the next evening Smetana's *The Bartered Bride* was given as the first opera. An operetta, Suppé's *Der Gascogner*, followed on 9 December and Verdi's *Il trovatore* on 11 December. Janáček was present for all three musical evenings, and his comments on them constitute his first opera review for *Hudební listy* (xv/27), published in the first number on 13 December. Operetta constituted a large part of musical repertory at the theatre and in addition to *Der Gascogner*, Janáček found himself having to review Planquette's *Les cloches de Corneville*, Lecocq's *Giroflé-Girofla* and two more pieces by Suppé, his *Donna Juanita* and *Boccaccio*, in the first three weeks alone (xv/28, xv/29).

For the next three months Janáček was on a treadmill, producing a weekly issue of the new journal single-handed, and reviewing operas on a regular basis until the end of the opera season on 31 March 1885. This may well have been good occupational therapy for him after his mother's death. Zdenka mentions the 'theatre outings' as a feature of the 'busy social life' that resumed once she had returned to Janáček, but *Hudební listy* and its constant pressures were not mentioned in her memoirs. Instead she alludes to their frequent appearances in 'Czech society' and particularly at balls. Jan Havlíček, a leading light in the Brno Beseda and a fervent Czech patriot, proclaimed that when she wasn't there 'it was no ball at all' and that none of the other ladies could keep dancing as long as her. Zdenka agreed: 'I could go on dancing till dawn. Leoš liked it. He learnt the beseda [a quadrille based on Czech folksongs] and used to partner me in it.'[16] This however was Leoš's only accomplishment in this field since, according to Zdenka, 'he couldn't dance in time. He was impossible at round dances.'[17] Maybe there was something, after all, in Grill's comment in Leipzig that Janáček had no sense of rhythm.[18] Nevertheless, Janáček enjoyed going with Zdenka to the balls and 'glowed with pleasure' when he saw her success.[19]

Despite the pressures of *Hudební listy* throughout the winter Janáček needed to keep up regular rehearsals with the Beseda choir and orchestra for the chief concert of the year (in fact the only proper one – the Beseda was low on funds).[20] This took place on 29 March and furthered the Brno cult of Dvořák with three pieces by him: his ballad *The Orphan*, a male-voice chorus *The Beloved as Poisoner* and his Nocturne for strings (Janáček's concerts with the Brno Beseda 1880–8 are summarized in table 17.1). The really ambitious part of the concert, however, was the final item: Liszt's symphonic poem *Mazeppa*. Its inclusion was noteworthy given Janáček's previous antipathy toward programme music and the neoromantic school. In Leipzig he had proclaimed that Liszt's day was over: 'How depressing it must be for a creative spirit in his later years to come to the realization that in his best years he was on the wrong path, that he put so much effort into his greatest work – for nothing!'[21] Now, however, he embraced the programmatic aspect by having Victor Hugo's poem, which served Liszt as his programme for the piece, recited before the music was played.[22] The event signals a shift in Janáček's aesthetic views, one that would eventually lead to writing symphonic poems of his own.

The event was significant too in that it was the last concert that Křížkovský attended. A stroke had compelled him to give up his post in Olomouc, and he had retired to the Staré Brno monastery in 1883. No doubt he encountered Janáček from time to time during regular services there and would have seen for himself how his protégé was flourishing: his creaky marriage patched up, his continuing successes at Beseda concerts and his important new initiatives such as *Hudební listy* and the Organ School. Křížkovský died on 8 May 1885 and three days later Janáček presided over the music at his funeral (see chap. 8).

Another demand on Janáček's time was the Organ School and in particular his attempts to raise its profile and seek funds to develop it. Two public concerts took place: the first was a concert aimed at the German community on 22 February 1885 at the Lužánky hall, which Janáček, presumably because of his anti-German attitude (see chap. 2), didn't even bother to attend; he himself organized the second, held on 8 March at the Teachers' Institute. Professionals gave their services free and joined pupils from the institution, who sang Jakobus Handl's celebrated funeral motet *Ecce quomodo moritur*, an odd choice for such an occasion, but Handl's fifteen-year sojourn in the Czech lands counted in the work's favour with Janáček. A promising student, František Kolářík, played Bach's Toccata in C. Janáček took a large part himself. He performed Bach's 'concerto for two organs' (one of the concertos for two harpsichords BWV 1060–2?) with the organist at

Brno Cathedral František Musil and a string quintet accompaniment.[23] He accompanied the violinist J. Sobotka from the local theatre orchestra* in the première of his *Dumka* for violin and piano (VII/4; see below). Janáček and Musil also improvised on the organ: 'more like well-thought-out compositions than a simple creation of a momentary mood' was the verdict of the *Dalibor* critic.[24] Janáček himself was unhappy with the event and went to the trouble of writing a damning review of certain aspects in *Hudební listy* (XV/42). It seems extraordinary that having persuaded various professionals to give their services he then went on to publish critical comments on their performances. Thus the pianist from Vienna, Miss Wallová, had a 'coarsegrained Viennese touch' and messed up the octaves in Julius Schulhoff's *Caprice*. Mr Sobotka played too fast and took time to warm up and only came alive in the cadenza of the Mendelssohn Violin Concerto. And although Musil's improvisation went down well with the public, the Bach concerto (with Janáček) 'completely disappointed us'. The overall impression 'was not integrated, unified and powerful. The ensemble frequently went wrong.' It's not surprising that this concert given to raise funds for the Organ School was the last of its type.

Janáček did not spare his own students (who were out of tune in the Handl, and didn't come in together after pauses) or himself: in his improvisation, *pace* the *Dalibor* review, he seemed (according to reports) to have been playing whatever came into his fingers. In his reviews in *Hudební listy* Janáček always signed himself with a triangle, but here he gave his full name, making it quite clear to all that he was unhappy with his own contribution and wasn't afraid to say so.

It seems almost inconceivable with all this going on that Janáček – at last – got back to composition. He had hardly written a note since he had got married. There had been the harmonizations for Lehner's hymnbook (II/10), more a matter of routine accompaniment than real composition, and the little chorus he had written during his therapeutic summer in Prague, *Ave Marie* (IV/16). With the opening of the Czech Provisional Theatre in Brno he had begun to toy with an opera of his

---

* Janáček perhaps spotted him at a Beseda concert on 8 November 1884: he played Jindřich Hartl's Mazurka on both occasions. His full first name is unknown, but the initial 'J' is given in the programme of the Beseda concert. *LD*, i, 78, states that he was 'from Prague', but the *Dalibor* review makes clear that he was a member of the orchestra of the 'local [i.e. Brno] town theatre'.

own, *The Last Abencérage* (XI/1), but this had got no further than a scenario (see chap. 26). Somehow in the spring of 1885 he had found the time and the will to write a set of choruses, and furthermore had had the confidence to offer them to the Prague publisher F.A. Urbánek.[†] Presumably he composed them in April–May, once he had put *Hudební listy* to bed for the season (it 'rested' until the opera season started again in the autumn) and had got the big Beseda concert out of the way. Janáček's letter to Urbánek does not specify which works he was offering,[25] but his *Four Male-Voice Choruses* (IV/17) seem to be the best candidates. On 24 August Urbánek declined to publish the choruses,[26] and Janáček simply passed them on for publication to the Brno firm Karl Winkler that had published his Lehner hymn settings a couple of years earlier. It's not surprising that Janáček wanted them published: the set includes two of his most evocative choruses, the haunting *O Love*, a strophic chorus, distinctive through its gently rocking 7/4 metre, and *Ah, the War*. Although the regular opening of the latter suggests another strophic chorus, the strange modulatatory course that the piece embarks on takes it into new realms: a successful combination of the oldfashioned *ohlasový*-type chorus (see chap. 8) with the experimental thrust of his *Vocal Duma* (IV/10).

The first three choruses were all based on traditional Moravian folk texts, but the final one is a setting, rare for Janáček at the time, of a contemporary poem by Jaroslav Tichý, a teacher at the Brno Czech Gymnasium I. Janáček in fact printed this poem in *Hudební listy* (in 1 November 1886) as one 'suitable for setting'. Had he already produced his own setting and was curious how others might approach it? Or did he take his own advice having printed it? If this is the case then this chorus could not have been included with the others that he offered to Urbánek in June 1885.

Unlike almost all of Janáček's choruses up to now the *Four Male-Voice Choruses* (IV/17) were written with no specific performance in mind. After the *Autumn Song* (IV/14) incident in 1880 (chap. 17), Janáček had resolutely not performed any of his own pieces at the Beseda. So this collection seems to have been composed for its own

---

[†] Janáček's associations with the publishing family Urbánek would stretch over many years. His earliest dealings were with the founder of the firm, František Augustin Urbánek (1842–1919). In 1891 he was briefly in correspondence with his brother Velebín (1853–92; see chap. 29) and from 1908 dealt mostly with František's son Mojmír (1873–1919, see chap. 56).

sake, and Janáček decided, by offering it to a publisher, to send it out into the world to find its own fate. When he did conduct two numbers from it a few months after publication, it was not a purely Beseda chorus that sang it, but one enlarged with members of three other choral societies (see below). Ironically, it needed Janáček's departure from the Beseda for another of the *Four Male-Voice Choruses* (no. 1: *The Warning*) to be performed at a Beseda concert, conducted by Josef Kompit on 23 May 1889.

Middle-class Czechs, if they could, would take summer holidays seriously, often spending most of the time away. Those with country backgrounds would often return to their native villages, and this is what Janáček eventually did, with the not wholly enthusiastic co-operation of Zdenka. The regular trips to Hukvaldy began only in 1888, however it seems likely that Janáček got there in August 1885, perhaps on his own. For one thing he needed to pay his respects to his mother's grave: on 15 June Josefa asked him to contribute to Amalie Janáčková's grave in Rychaltice – she had paid for a 'gate' and had planted a large ornamental rose.[27] Janáček was in Brno throughout July 1885 for teaching duties (including the public examinations of the Organ School on 14 and 15 July),[28] but may well still have been there on 9 August for a charity concert in aid of 'Radhošt', a society support-ing Moravian, Silesian and Slovak academics. The fact that Dvořák himself should have participated (according to the printed programme) and that Janáček kept the programme[29] suggests that he stayed in Brno to attend it.[‡] But it seems possible that soon after then, he slipped off to Hukvaldy. The idea may have come from Josefa, who in her letter about their mother's grave had enquired where he would be spending his holidays and mentioned that František's wife Máša (Marie) from Gleiwitz had been with her for a couple of weeks.[30] Later recollections in Janáček's article *At Harabiš's* (xv/257) suggest he visited then (though the date he gives there of 1881 may be a confusion with his honeymoon trip to Hukvaldy). It is possible, too, that some of his earliest notations of folk music (from an area around Hukvaldy, from Kunčice to Petřvald) support this (see chap. 28).

A combination of Beseda and *Hudební listy* business took Janáček

---

[‡]Dvořák, however, didn't. He discovered that he was not permitted to conduct a military band (that partly provided the orchestra) and so stayed at home (Šourek 1954, ii, 239).

on a rare trip to Prague, probably on 8 October 1885. This was prompted by concerns over his next planned oratorio concert with the Beseda, a performance of Dvořák's 'dramatic cantata' *The Spectre's Bride*, to celebrate the society's twenty-five years of existence. As usual it was the soloists who were the problem: František Adolf Šubert, the energetic administrative director at the National Theatre in Prague, was generally reluctant to let his contracted soloists sing elsewhere, but Janáček felt that a plea in person might do the trick. The proposed visit took place in the morning before 11.30. There was a lunch with Dvořák, and in between a brief trip to see the two Josef Försters/ Foersters. Josef Förster (1833–1907, the father) was a respected music theorist and Janáček was hoping to get him to contribute an article to *Hudební listy*. His son Josef Bohuslav Foerster (1859–1951, who rendered his surname differently) was a composer and music critic, then on the Prague newspaper *Národní listy*; Janáček wanted him to write the Prague opera reviews in *Hudební listy*.[31] Both promised their services, though in the end it was only the son who obliged by sending Janáček regular reviews during the second year of the journal. This is the first recorded meeting between the two composers, who maintained a distant and somewhat competitive friendship until the end of Janáček's life. The relationship would be complicated by the fact that each turned a Moravian play by Gabriela Preissová into an opera, and that Foerster's *Eva*, so successful at first, was later overtaken in national and international popularity by Janáček's *Jenůfa*.

In the afternoon Janáček saw František Pivoda, the well-known Prague singing teacher who had already been helpful in rustling up Prague soloists for Janáček's larger-scale ventures with the Beseda. Whatever soloists emerged from Janáček's discussions with Šubert, Dvořák and Pivoda, the outcome was thwarted by Dvořák's English publisher Novello, who wanted 530.40 marks for performance materials and rights[32] – too much for the Beseda at the time. Janáček gave the work three years later in Brno, and for the anniversary concert found something cheaper. The visit to Pivoda, however, at least produced the promise of a substantial article for *Hudební listy*: the serialization of his article *Singing and the Public* provided Janáček with useful material that helped fill up a regular slot in the second volume. About this time there is evidence of more such purposeful activity on Janáček's part to find *Hudební listy* contributions, such as his contacts with Jan Herben[33] (who contributed articles on Prague theatre) and with the Moravian novelist Václav Kosmák in November 1885[34] that led to Janáček's serializing his *About the Fair: a Picture of Musical Life from Earlier Times* across many issues in the second and third volumes. It turned out to be a useful contact that Janáček revived four years later, when contemplating a folk-based ballet (see chap. 27).

The Beseda's twenty-fifth anniversary concert took place, slightly late, on 10 January 1886 with a mostly Dvořák programme. Usually willing to come to Brno for these events, Dvořák declined Janáček's invitation: he was hard at work orchestrating his oratorio *St Ludmila* and in his purposeful way wished to get on with that.[35] The concert was notable in being repeated a week later as a 'popular concert' with reduced ticket prices – a way of extending the Beseda's potential audience. This was Janáček's initiative, pushed through against opposition from his colleagues on the committee, and was sufficiently successful for the experiment to be repeated later that year.

Another venture with the Beseda later in the season was less satisfactory: Bedřich Smetana had died in May 1884 and it was felt that the Beseda should commemorate the event in some way, if two years late. Some of the Prague-Brno antipathy that existed in Brno is evident by comparing the enthusiastic espousal of Dvořák, seen in the plans and realization of the twenty-fifth anniversary concert, and what was eventually produced for the concert in honour of Smetana. Janáček had proposed the event,[36] but an unspecified illness kept him from properly rehearsing the single chorus that was included. The rest of the concert consisted of a lecture by Smetana's friend and passionate advocate, the leading Prague music aesthetician Otakar Hostinský, and a reluctant performance of Smetana's String Quartet 'From my Life' by Pergler's Quartet. The wrangling that this lacklustre concert provoked afterwards was a factor in Janáček's offering his resignation on health grounds.[37] The resignation was not accepted, and Janáček soldiered on for two more years as music director, though the incident is symptomatic of the simmering dissatisfaction that ran throughout his association with the Beseda during the 1880s.

It was presumably on health grounds that Janáček made his first visit to Luhačovice in the summer of 1886. The heyday of Janáček's regular trips to Luhačovice came only later, in 1903 at a time when the spa was being developed commercially (see chap. 45). In 1886, however, the spa was small and in private hands, and, before the rail link was opened, difficult to get to. The reference in Zdenka's memoirs to this happening in '1886' was for a long time unconfirmed, but the chance purchase by the Moravian Museum of one album and a single leaf from another provides corroboration of a most interesting nature. The leaf, with the folksong *Voděnka plyne* [*The water flows*], in Janáček's hand, has his signature and inscription 'Luhačovice, VIII/1886'.[38] This suggests little other than that Janáček was in Luhačovice that month, and was now showing a growing interest in folksong. The surviving album,[39] on the other hand, reveals rather more. Albums were a feature of the period: friends and acquaintances would be encouraged to contribute entries – poems, drawings, paintings and even music. This one, roughly A5 format, is expensively bound with an image of a woman with a large hat engraved on the leather. The entries, some of which are immensely accomplished (for instance that of a pretty young man with a lute in one hand and cherub in the other, inscribed Brno 1884), date over a long period and start – somewhat surprisingly – in Hukvaldy ('Hochwald, am 24. Feb. 1884', i.e. in German), which suggests that a connection was made between Janáček's contacts there and the (unknown) owner of the album. Other entries, all from Moravia, are inscribed in Místek and then Prostějov (30 June 1884) and Brno 1884 – the owner clearly travelled a fair amount with the album always at the ready. The Luhačovice entries all date from August 1886. After a four-line inscription by one Rainer Tlusťák comes Janáček: 'In kind remembrance of the wonderfully beautiful Luhačovice times, yours for ever devoted, Leoš Janáček VIII/1886.' This is followed by a four-line quotation from the first tenor part of his chorus *Ah, the War* from the *Four Male-Voice Choruses* (IV/17), whose publication in Brno was now imminent. If the placing in the album is significant, this inscription presumably predates the next Luhačovice entry (A. Šrámek), 16 August.

Zdenka recalled the Luhačovice trip in her memoirs. Rather pointedly she wrote that their income was 'hardly enough for Leoš's trip', so she stayed at home 'scrimping and saving as much possible' (this is an early example of Zdenka the Martyr, as frequently portrayed in the pages of her memoirs), and that 'on the other hand I felt that my husband wanted to be alone'. When he was first in Luhačovice in 1886, Zdenka recalled, her parents were also there, and she went briefly with Olga to visit them all. She had a terrible time since her six-year-old brother had a cough and, anxious that Olga might catch it from him, she avoided her parents. And she saw little of her husband either: 'He was in the midst of an amusing company, which meant he couldn't devote himself to us. And when Olinka kept on going up to him and got in his way he was very, very unkind to her.' So Zdenka went home earlier than she'd intended. 'We remained out of sorts with one another so that he didn't even write and tell me when he was returning. I was on a visit to my friend Mrs Žaludová in Královka beyond Komárov at the very time he arrived home.' On 19 July 1886 Janáček's colleague Berthold Žalud died a 'poetic' death (conducting an orchestra; he suffered from tuberculosis and had been sickly for some years). Zdenka, perhaps, went to comfort the new widow and was thus away when Janáček returned:

I was most surprised when on my return I saw that he'd already been back from Luhačovice a long time. I reproached him for not even sending me a message via the servant. 'You know', he said to me, 'I was in such high spirits from that company that I had first to go and calm down on my own.'

On his own. I regretted it. I felt that something stood between us. But when everything continued in its old tracks I forgot about it. Early one morning – it was already well into the autumn (the heating in the stoves was on) – my husband was getting ready for school. I was brushing his suit. I was taking everything out of his pockets so that it wouldn't get in my way during the work, when suddenly I caught sight of a letter without an envelope with the greeting 'Geliebter Leo'. Who could have been writing to my husband in this way? I looked at the signature 'Ihre Sie liebende Marie' [Your loving Marie]. I didn't see any more. Leoš rushed up, tore the letter from my hand and threw it into the stove. In a trice I realized the connection between this billet-doux and my husband's desire to be alone; it dawned on me whose was the crumpled lady's handkerchief which he'd brought in his luggage from Luhačovice and of which he swore that he didn't know how he came by it. And I'd actually believed him then! I had the handkerchief washed and kept it carefully. I got terribly angry that I'd been deceived in this way. I rushed to get the handkerchief, I tore it to pieces and threw them at my husband's feet. And I told him my opinion about it all in no uncertain terms. He was contrite, he begged me not to get angry, saying that there had been nothing bad in it. I never learnt anything more from him. But when I complained about it to Mama, she let slip that they already knew about that affair of Leoš's in Luhačovice. They'd kept quiet about it so as not to provoke him any further. I soon calmed down when I didn't notice anything else suspicious.[40]

This account throws up a number of revealing points. The first is that this affair in Luhačovice, for all Janáček's antipathy to the language, was seemingly conducted in German. Furthermore one of the entries in the album is a beautifully illuminated 'M' surrounded by flowers: it would seem that the mysterious 'Marie' was the owner of the album. But, for all Zdenka's anger, this could hardly have been much of an affair, since the few words she quotes, 'Ihre Sie liebende Marie', are in the formal style of address. There is, however, also the beginning of a pattern here. Janáček picked up other ladies in Luhačovice who figure much more prominently in his later personal and creative life – Camilla Urválková and Kamila Stösslová for example – and perhaps the connection was made in Janáček's mind as early as 1886 between holidays there and amorous adventures.

Janáček was back in Brno by 30 August 1886: on that date he began sending copies of the recently printed *Four Male-Voice Choruses* (IV/17) to well-placed people in Prague. There was Karel Knittl at 'Hlahol'[41] (the leading Prague choral society) and Janáček's Prague adviser, the singing teaching František Pivoda, who commented perceptively on their 'remarkable daring' and the problems of intonation that the choruses would cause so that only the best singing groups would be able to manage them.[42] Dvořák, to whom Janáček had dedicated the choruses, wrote much the same:

Dear friend
    I got your choruses and thank you for them as indeed for the dedication, which greatly honours me and which gives me real pleasure because it is a gift with great promise and in these times a truly special one. As soon as I had got them, I read them through several times assiduously and I must honestly admit that I was taken aback in many places, especially as far as your *modulations* were concerned, and wasn't sure what to make of it all.
    I didn't go straight to the piano, I didn't play them; I think after all that I understand something just by looking at it with a theoretical eye. But when I had played them through once, twice, three times, my ear did get used to it and I said to myself: alright, it could be like that but we might still argue about it.
    But what of that? Your choruses are a real enrichment of our poor literature (in that genre). Briefly: they are original, the main thing is that emanating from them is a *true Slavonic spirit*, it's none of your *Liedertafel*. There are places in them which will have an enchanting effect and I'd be really pleased to hear them as soon as possible. I congratulate you on this small but significant composition and wish you many more like it![43]

The dedication to Dvořák and the sending out of copies is another mark of Janáček's increasing self-confidence. Dvořák had been present in Brno when Janáček conducted his *Idyll* (VI/3) in December 1878, and perhaps looked through the score then, but the comments in this letter represent the first time that Dvořák committed any thoughts on Janáček's music to paper and as such are particularly valuable. They encouraged Janáček to show the older composer several more of his compositions and, more importantly, to embark on his first opera, *Šárka* (I/1; see below).

Although none of these copies resulted in any Prague performances ('Hlahol' got round to it only in 1906), the publication had in the end enormous consequences for Janáček's future career. Quite without prompting, a prominent choral society, 'Smetana' in Plzeň, lighted upon it before 'Hlahol' did and gave *Ah, the War* on 25 March 1905 with such success that it took it abroad that summer to Spa, in Belgium – the first performance of any Janáček piece outside the Czech lands. But even better, the enthusiastic account they sent to Janáček of this event spurred him into composing his group of Bezruč choruses the next year (see chap. 51).

Žalud's death in the summer of 1886 had unexpected consequences for Janáček: he found himself having to fill in for him at the Staré Brno Gymnasium, perhaps at the suggestion of one of the senior members of staff, František Bartoš (see chap. 18). It was not a big commitment, just two hours twice a week teaching 'music and singing' to Gymnasium schoolboys, but it came on top of everything else he was doing, including a move to more spacious accommodation for the Organ School, now further out of Staré Brno (see chap. 21). Other obligations crowded in at much the same time: on 25 September Janáček was named a member of the examining commission for teaching at Czech primary and middle schools:[44] he remained on the commission until his retirement in November 1903. On 30 September, as choirmaster of the Beseda, he got together with the choirmasters and members of other Brno choral societies ('Svatopluk', 'Veleslavín', the local 'Hlahol' and the Cyril Association) with a view to holding joint rehearsals. Sixty singers turned up (including a disappointing twenty-nine from the Beseda).[45] One result of this short-lived initiative was the joint concert in November at which Janáček conducted two choruses from the newly published collection (IV/17). However worthy these may have been they were completely overshadowed by the part in the concert played by the nine-year-old Josef Hofmann from Warsaw. Janáček, who had facilitated this opportunity (and was warmly thanked by Hofmann's father after successful tours in Berlin and Copenhagen),[46] was most taken by it all, and wrote up a special account of it in *Hudební listy* (xv/60). His instinct in this matter turned out to be sound: Hofmann went on to become one of the most important pianists in the first third of the twentieth century, and the first professional musician to record, cutting several cylinders in 1887.[47] As in the earlier Beseda concert the previous year, this one was also repeated as the 'Second Popular Concert' a week later.

After the unsuccessful Smetana memorial concert and the murmurings in Prague about Brno's lack of interest in Bohemia's most adulated composer, Janáček presumably felt piqued into suggesting that some larger-scale Smetana piece be performed. In the end it was *Vyšehrad*, the first symphonic poem of *My Fatherland*, that was given, but at the committee meeting on 14 September Janáček had suggested that he conduct the third symphonic poem in the cycle *Šárka*.[48] It is probably just a coincidence that a few months later Janáček would begin writing his first opera with the same title, but one can argue from other circumstances at the time that Janáček's mind was beginning to turn towards writing an opera himself. His opera reviews in *Hudební listy* over the last two seasons had been very snappy affairs, concerned almost exclusively with performance, but he now began to write longer opera reviews that suggest a greater engagement with and curiosity about the genre: these include an analysis (xv/63) of the prelude to Gounod's *Faust* in December 1886 and, in mid-February 1887, at about the time that he might well have been considering his own opera, a detailed review and analysis (xv/73) of certain aspects of *The St John's Rapids* by Josef Richard Rozkošný.

The subject for Janáček's first opera turned up on 1 January 1887: Julius Zeyer's libretto *Šárka*, intended for Dvořák and eventually published in three instalments in the theatre magazine *Česká Thalie* (see chap. 26). Quite when Janáček was alerted to it by Karel Sázavský is not known, but an excellent opportunity would have been on 16 January 1887 (by which time the second instalment had been published), the date of Janáček's first appearance at a committee meeting of the Brno Theatre Družstvo. This was the organization responsible for managing the theatre (hiring the touring companies that performed there), to which Sázavský also belonged. As a leading opera critic and as someone with an increasing interest in the theatre,[§] Janáček was presumably voted in as a way of neutralizing his attacks in *Hudební listy*. His inclusion in the committee was perhaps yet another source of confidence that seems to exude from the thirty-three-year-old Janáček at the time. This is clear from some of his journalism in *Hudební listy* that month. On 15 January, for instance, he took issue in a review (xv/ 68) with an article coming out in instalments in *Dalibor* written by Otakar Hostinský. Janáček knew Hostinský from the Smetana memorial concert, over which they had exchanged several letters.[49] It may even be that his critical pen was sharpened by the fact that Hostinský had not responded positively to Janáček's invitation to publish his Brno lecture in the pages of *Hudební listy*.[50] In the same issue of *Hudební listy* Janáček also published his devastating and, as it happened, disastrous review of Kovařovic's opera *The Bridegrooms*, presented at the Brno Czech Theatre (xv/70; see chap. 49). Janáček had already begun enlivening his opera reviews by writing them in dialogue form. Kovařovic's opera was given the same treatment, which, seen in isolation, comes across as particularly demeaning. Janáček was not to know that within thirteen years Kovařovic would be chosen for one of the supreme jobs in musical Prague: director of the National Theatre opera, with the power to make or break aspiring opera composers – not least Janáček.

On 15 February 1887 Janáček published his review of Rozkošný's opera (xv/73) and a week later the Czech Theatre season ended, which meant that the fortnightly pressure to get *Hudební listy* to press was now over for the next half year and Janáček, now bristling with confidence, could turn to composition again – to his first opera, *Šárka*. There are no dates on the copy of the score; all that is known is that on 6 August 1887 Dvořák thanked Janáček for sending it. Dvořák's thanks were addressed to 'Leo Janáček aus Brünn', then staying at 'Dr Angelis Wasser Anstalt' in Cukmantl, a spa resort in Silesia. This suggests the following course of events: that some time from about March onwards Janáček got on with his three-act opera, writing it in piano-vocal score and completing it in time for him to have it copied in Brno, and for him to take the copy with him to Cukmantl. During his

---

[§] On 10 June 1886 Janáček's presence and interventions were reported at a meeting of the Družstvo where the future of the Brno Theatre was debated (*LJPT*, 268–9).

stay Janáček checked through the copy and then posted it to Dvořák, giving his temporary address at the 'water institute' (in his autobiography Janáček remembered the spa being owned by a 'Dr. Anděl', who maintained 'Czech company').[51]

The copied score is of additional interest in that it is the first known to be written for Janáček by the oboist Josef Štross (1826–1912, whom Janáček had remembered from his performances at the Staré Brno Monastery in the 1860s). Štross went on to copy many more of Janáček's works up to the first version of *Fate*, when he was almost eighty.

Janáček had to wait a long time for Dvořák to give a verdict on the opera. On 3 October Dvořák wrote again, seemingly responding to a letter from Janáček saying that he was coming to Prague (Janáček's impatience would no doubt have been tempered with respect for his eminent friend). However Dvořák wasn't sure where he would be and rather impracticably (considering it was term-time) suggested that Janáček might like to come to his country place in Vysoká, where they could go through the opera in a day or two.[52] Another exchange of letters followed at the end of the month with Dvořák again writing, apologizing for his silence and now suggesting that Janáček come to Prague 'but not before 29 October' (since Dvořák had to be in Berlin). 'But I imagine that you are in no great hurry over the matter', a comment that casts doubt on Dvořák's knowledge of Janáček's character.[53] Presumably Janáček did get to Prague after 29 October, and presumably one upshot of this was that whatever Dvořák told him about his first opera, he also made it clear that he'd better write to the author of the text, Julius Zeyer, for permission to use it. Janáček did so: on 10 November Zeyer wrote back in strong terms, refusing his permission, though not forcefully enough to dissuade Janáček from writing again, prompting Zeyer's even more vigorously worded second letter (17 November; see chap. 26).

Surprisingly this rebuff seems not to have dampened Janáček's spirits. In early 1888 he had much on his plate. He made a special expedition to Prague for a big Tchaikovsky concert, given by the Umělecká beseda in the composer's presence on 19 February, including major works such as the First Piano Concerto, the Violin Concerto and two overtures, *Romeo and Juliet* and *1812*. It was Janáček's first extensive experience with a composer who would go on to exert considerable influence on him. In view of Janáček's later enthusiasm his extensive review in *Hudební listy* (xv/87) is surprisingly cool. The few positive comments with which he kicks off are distinctly odd: 'an outstanding contrapuntalist – of Berlioz's school, and excellently versed in existing forms'. While the *Romeo and Juliet* overture and the Piano Concerto were 'imposing', the *1812* was barely unified, 'almost rhapsodic'. What seems to have upset Janáček was that Tchaikovsky failed to find much use of Slavonic materials: this was confined to particular movements such as the third movement of the Piano Concerto or individual motifs in the *1812*. Instead he then filled his review with a long list of Tchaikovsky's works copied from the programme. It would be several years before Tchaikovsky would make any real impact on him.

On 29 April Janáček performed Dvořák's *Spectre's Bride* at the Beseda in the teeth of opposition, with splendid soloists from Prague (including the leading diva Marie Petzoldová-Sittová) and the event even made a small profit. This was the climax of his activities at the society: Dvořák came specially, the concert had enthusiastic press coverage; composer and conductor were the subject of many ovations; and Janáček himself received a special gift of 100 zl from the Beseda.[54] On the back of this success Janáček embarked on three new choruses, the *Three Male-Voice Choruses* (iv/19). They were copied out neatly and Janáček dated one (14 May) and sent them off to Dvořák again, perhaps on 15 May, one day before Zdenka gave birth to a child, a boy, christened Vladimír (see chap. 27). It is perhaps against this wholly optimistic background that one can understand why Janáček felt it was worthwhile having another go at *Šárka*. Despite his later reminiscence that his consultation with Dvořák had gone 'quite well',[55] it was nevertheless necessary for him to revise the work and produce what was essentially an entirely new version (see chap. 26), completed in the month after Vladimír was born: Štross's copy was dated 16 June 1888.

On 5 May, a few days after the *Spectre's Bride* concert, the Beseda committee voted that Janáček should henceforth conduct all concerts and rehearsals. This request was less innocent than it sounded. The running dispute between Janáček and the committee right from the beginning of his time at the Beseda had been over the 'entertainments', which he had refused point blank to conduct, a battle that he had won in the past because he did his job unpaid (making it difficult to exert pressure on him) and because no-one else seemed capable of taking over from him. Now however it became a matter of personal pride between him and the chairman Dr František Hodáč, who resigned to force a showdown: the committee should choose between him and Janáček.[56] The committee met again on 23 May, this time without Janáček, and asked Hodáč to withdraw his resignation, a resolution that indicated a majority against Janáček, though Hodáč stuck by his decision. A week later the committee met again, now with Janáček. Flushed with delight at the recent birth of his son, Janáček behaved in a surprisingly conciliatory way, offering to meet separately with Hodáč (who wasn't there) and to try to hammer out some compromise. Despite the financial success of the *Spectre's Bride* concert, committee members expressed the thought that Janáček's activities had cost the society money, a criticism that was easily rebuffed by observing that the Beseda music school, which he had set up despite opposition from the committee, had become very profitable, a 'milch-cow' for the society financing many other activities, as Janáček pointed out. Even *Hudební listy*, in deficit for the first two years, was now in profit (as the treasurer confirmed), despite the statement to the contrary of the vice-chairman.[57]

Although the meeting broke up without Janáček's resignation, a day or two of reflection settled Janáček's mind and on 1 June he wrote to the vice-chairman Antonín Váňa:

I announce respectfully to you that I am giving up the post of director of music at the Philharmonic Society Brno Beseda.

Already for the second time under my direction during the past ten years I was the target of an inconsiderate and demeaning attack.[...] The first time I couldn't take it, still less the second time and certainly I will never again take part in creating such conditions from which such an unexpectedly good concert could take seed. I inform you furthermore that in terms of contents *Hudební listy* is closed and according to the wishes of the esteemed committee it is not necessary to publish it any more.[58]

That day the final issue of *Hudební listy* appeared, a bumper issue with four items by Janáček. Two years earlier Janáček had resigned, but had been persuaded to stay on. This time, however, the Beseda simply accepted his resignation as music director and entrusted the chief executive to write him a letter thanking him for his services, which he did on 8 June.[59] Curiously Janáček did not resign at the same time from his directorship of the Beseda music school, an anomaly that was resolved only after another year.

Perhaps Vladimír's birth put a new perspective on things. Perhaps, too, Janáček's rejuvenated interest in composition was beginning to seem more important than struggling on against the opposition at the Beseda. Dvořák got back to him about the choruses (IV/19): he'd been in Vysoká for four weeks and only now had someone collected the post; he would comment on the choruses in due course. He never did. In fact he never returned them to Janáček – they were found in his estate years after Janáček died. Had Dvořák looked at them he would have found them even more experimental than the 1885 choruses. While three of the group were, like the majority of Janáček's earlier choruses, based on Moravian folk texts, only one of the three 1888 choruses is. This is *The Jealous Man*, a folk ballad about a young man, presumably a brigand, who lies dying attended by his girl. He asks for his sword so, he says, he can see how pale his cheeks are. The girl knows better. She gives him his blade but jumps nimbly out the way. As the lad acknowledges, he would have killed her to prevent someone else having her after his death. This text haunted Janáček for years and he next came back to it when he wrote the prelude *Jealousy* to his opera *Jenůfa*. This first attempt at setting it is innovative in its texture: a solo baritone voice is added to the four-part male chorus to declaim the direct speech of the brigand, and choral voices are used almost like an instrumental accompaniment at times. In its sectionalized form reflecting the stages of the story it anticipates the Bezruč choruses of fifteen years later.

The Jealous Man is the longest and most elaborate of the three choruses. The two others, both setting recently published texts by Smetana's librettist Eliška Krásnohorská, are experimental chiefly in their harmony: bold juxtapositions and modulations rather at the expense of rhythmic interest, which, in the first chorus (*Parting*) especially, is repetitive and inert. This is about the furthest Janáček travelled in this *Art nouveau*–Decadent direction, something that his sudden espousal of Moravian folk music would reverse within just a few months.

The second chorus, *The Dove*, contains an intriguing puzzle. Its words about a faithful dove looking for its wounded mate (with a very effective repeated 'calling motif' in the first basses against static other voices), recalls Janáček's affecting chorus *The Wild Duck* (IV/18) but its chief motif looks back to the tune of the middle section of Janáček's

Dumka for violin and piano (VII/4). The date of composition of the *Dumka* is not known: many years later, Janáček guessed '1880' and Helfert speculated that it might have been one of the lost Romances from Leipzig, retitled. However this characterful, moody piece is a world apart from the sedate surviving Romance (VII/3) and sounds nearer in time to *The Dove*. It is tempting to think that the middle section of the *Dumka* is a later elaboration of *The Dove* but the dates don't work: the latest that the *Dumka* can be dated is shortly before it was performed on 8 March 1885 (at the benefit concert for the Organ School), which is a couple of years before Krásnohorská published her poem. Perhaps Janáček wrote the *Dumka* especially for the concert? In later years, despite all his speech-melody posturing, Janáček would occasionally fit words to existing tunes. This is precisely what seems to have happened here. It's a haunting little tune, and one can understand why Janáček used it again. Perhaps he discovered that its six notes fitted the six-syllable lines of Krásnohorská and he went along with it.

Some time after Štross had completed his fair copy of *Šárka* (second version) Janáček got down to the task of orchestrating it. Once all his teaching obligations were out of the way (the Organ School public examinations were on 11 July that year),[60] Janáček set off for his summer holiday, this year in his native Hukvaldy. Although completing the scoring of *Šárka* was on the agenda, other, much more interesting things took over, preventing him from orchestrating the final act.

24

Hudební listy

For four years Janáček ran, virtually single-handed, the musical periodical *Hudební listy* [Musical leaves/letters]. On the banner heading he is designated 'executive editor'; the 'owner and publisher' was the Brno Beseda. The Beseda bore the financial burden and saw to distribution. When Janáček abruptly parted company with the Beseda in 1888 the journal folded.

Most astonishing about *Hudební listy* was the speed at which it happened. On 24 November 1884, at a meeting of the Beseda executive committee, Janáček proposed starting a new musical journal, a motion immediately approved by the committee.[1] At the next executive meeting, on 8 December, Janáček suggested the title *Hudební listy* and sketched in his ideas for the new journal.[2] Five days later, on Sunday 13 December 1884, the first issue was published. There was no editorial board or advisory committee; the conception and the execution of the journal was Janáček's alone.

It should be said, however, that this is not quite the feat that it may sound. The first issue was a mere four pages long, a folded A3 sheet: this was its usual format throughout the first year of publication. Although a four-page fascicle is not much, the pressure was relentless: the journal came out every week for thirteen weeks, at first every Sunday, then every Monday. This frequency was reduced in the next volume (1885–6), when the journal appeared twice a month but at double the length, a pattern that continued through the third volume (1886–7). In the fourth volume (1887–8) the frequency was further reduced to monthly, but with the length doubled again (see table 14).

The journal thus grew from a single folded sheet in its first year to four folded sheets in its last; irregularly sized fascicles (such as the final

Table 24.1: *Hudební listy*: dates, fascicles, pages

vol.	date of first fascicle	date of last fascicle	pages per fascicle	no. of fascicles	total no. of pages
i	13 Dec 1884	9 March 1885	4	13	54
ii	19 Oct 1885	23 Feb 1886	8	9	80
iii	15 Oct 1886	1 March 1887	8	10	82
iv	1 Nov 1887	1 June 1888	16	8	128

one in vol. ii) came usually at the beginnings or ends of the volumes, when material had accumulated over the summer or needed to be printed before the journal closed for the holidays.

The launch of the journal coincided with the opening of the Provisional Theatre in Brno on 6 December. Publication of the journal, Janáček announced both to the Beseda committee and to subscribers, would coincide with the theatre season: basically over the winter to March. In its last year, however, the journal continued well beyond the theatre season until June, and the next (unrealized) volume was announced for 1 September, i.e. well ahead of the theatre season. *Hudební listy* thus crept up from a publishing period of three months in its first volume to eight months in its final one, and plans were in train to extend it further, perhaps to ten months, had the next volume not been scuppered by Janáček's quarrel with the Beseda.

The pattern of publication, reflecting the theatre year and the academic year rather than the calendar year, was a common one at the time and had much to recommend it. It allowed a small editorial staff to take a long summer holiday when little else was going on and encouraged the leisurely accumulation of fresh ideas, plans and articles for the next year. For a one-man band, such as Janáček's *Hudební listy*, it was ideal.

Janáček's announcement at the beginning of the first issue (xv/25) set out what he intended with the journal. A new era, he declared, had begun in Brno with the opening of the Czech Provisional Theatre. It had been resolved to publish a weekly journal, *Hudební listy*, which, during the time of the theatre season, would review both opera and theatre in Brno briefly, concretely and impartially. These reviews were a main feature of the journal throughout its existence and gave it its subtitle: 'a periodical devoted to music and to theatrical art'. There would also be essays on the theory of music, and on the history and aesthetics of music. There would be topical issues and news of outstanding musicians. Any new music sent to the journal would be reviewed. Aspects of church music would be covered as well as the musical education of the younger generation. An important mission would be to defend and support 'our Czech musical school'.

This agenda was more or less realized. Opera and drama reviews remained central and, from the second volume, covered the National Theatre in Prague as well as the Czech Theatre in Brno. The reviews were preceded by more substantial general articles, sometimes serialized over many issues. There were smaller news items at the end. Here, as a typical example, is a breakdown of the contents of the first fascicle of vol. ii:

Table 24.2: *Hudební listy*: contents of vol. ii, fascicle 1

Leoš Janáček: *On the Perfect Concept of Two-Note Chords* (xv/44). This is one of Janáček's longer theoretical articles that formed the backbone of all four volumes, in this case one that ran at the rate of a couple of pages a fascicle throughout eight of the nine fascicles in vol. ii, and into the first three fascicles of vol. iii. In the two pages here there are six music examples, including two reduced-score illustrations of music by Liszt and Dvořák.

Unsigned: *From Music History*, part of a serialized article (here just over a page) dealing briefly with music of the Chinese, the Hindi, the Egyptians, the Jews and the Greeks. The article ran over seven fascicles in six brief instalments, by which time it had got to the ninth century and Gregorian chant. At the end the source was declared to be Skuherský's book *On Musical Forms* (1873, 2/1884).

Leoš Janáček: *Missa Quinti toni: Auctore Orlando di Lasso* (xv/45). This short article (two and a half pages with a brief conclusion in the next fascicle) on a mass by Lassus comes under the heading 'Church music' (thus satisfying one of Janáček's stated objectives) and is notable for its numerous music examples and its dwelling on stylistic rather than biographical matters.

History of Organ-Building in Moravia: a summary (half a column) of five organs, giving locations, makers (and usually dates and costs) and brief specifications of manuals, stops, etc. Particulars were sent in by local choirmasters, priests or teachers. Another four organs were described in ii/3, but what seemed like a good idea never got any further.

Theatre News: Under 'National Theatre in Brno' there are over three and a half pages of theatre and opera reviews contributed by three reviewers: 'P.H.' (Fr. Prav. Hnilička), mostly for theatre reviews; 'J.K.', for opera; and Janáček, whose contributions are signed with a triangle. It continues with a brief survey of opera in Prague (by 'J.F.', i.e. the composer and critic Josef Bohuslav Foerster), a news item about the operas to be performed in Plzeň, and (illogically under this heading) a review of the Brno Beseda's third concert of the season. Later fascicles included detailed accounts of plays staged in Prague. Janáček's part in this section is comparatively small, but he contributed a review (sometimes covering several operas) to almost every fascicle apart from the latter part of vol. iv, where the journal continued after the end of the operatic season on Brno. Generally there were few concert reviews.

Table 24.2:—*continued*

Vlad. Šťastný: *From the Forest*, a short poem 'recommended to composers'. Janáček
occasionally included literary items, such as *About the Fair: a picture of musical life from
earlier times* (serialized in this volume and fitfully throughout the next) by the popular
Moravian writer Václav Kosmák. Another poem recommended to composers in II/2,
Jaroslav Tichý's *Your Eyes*, Janáček himself set as the final chorus in his *Four Male-Voice
Choruses* (IV/17). A further compositional impetus came in IV/4, when Janáček reprinted
an extract from Svatopluk Čech's novel *The True Excursion of Mr Brouček to the Moon*
soon after its publication in 1888. It was twenty years, however, before this seed grew into
Janáček's fifth opera.

A final page devoted to short news reports (of events in Vienna, news about Délibes, Hans
von Bülow and Dvořák), news of musical societies, a list of periodicals received and a
repertory list for Prague and Brno theatres for the past week, a retrospective feature later
extended to the past fortnight. This had begun in vol. i as a future listing, but was clearly
hard to organize. By the later volumes any listing was abandoned and the news reports in
general became increasingly thin.

This pattern and balance was maintained throughout the volume.
Janáček's chief concerns were to have enough long articles that could
be serialized in larger or smaller chunks, and to keep the opera and
theatre reviewing going. During vol. ii Hnilička's theatre reviews
passed over to Janáček's colleague (and best man) František Dlouhý. In
Prague, opera reviews passed in vol. iii from Foerster to the well-known
singing teacher František Pivoda.[3] Prague theatre reviews were in the
hands of the writer Jan Herben (1857–1936).[*]

Of the areas that Janáček sketched out in his preliminary announcement, the theory of music was by far the best represented. Although
he had solicited (and been promised) something from Josef Förster (see
chap. 23),[4] this aspect was entirely covered by Janáček's own long
articles, and anyone looking at the four-year run of the periodical
might suspect that this was its chief *raison d'être*. *Essays in Music
Theory* (xv/26) kept vol. i going; *On the Perfect Concept of Two-Note
Chords* (xv/44) took up all of vol. ii and some of vol. iii; *On the
Concept of Key* (xv/61) filled up the rest of the volume. And *On the
Triad* (xv/76) ran throughout vol. iv. This is a very substantial article,
a short monograph that takes up over fifty pages in a modern reprint,
and was twice the length of any of its predecessors. The longer fascicles
and longer publication span of vol. iv allowed its complete publication.

---

[*] On 10 November 1885 Janáček announced to František Šubert at the Prague National
Theatre that Herben would be reviewing plays and asked for a free pass for him (Prague,
Státní ústřední archiv v Praze, fond Reg. Národního divadla v Praze, D-148, i, 212).

Janáček also published shorter articles, often with a theoretical or analytical thrust. These are listed here with their respective fascicle numbers in *Hudební listy*. Most are a couple of pages long and only a few needed to be spread over more than one fascicle. Theatre and concert reviews by Janáček and polemics arising from them are not included in this list:

Table 24.3: Janáček's articles in *Hudební listy*

JW	title	vol./fasc.
xv/26	Essays in Music Theory	I/1, 2, 3, 4, 5, 6, 7, 9, 10, 11, 12, 13
xv/30	'Tristan and Isolde' by Richard Wagner	I/4, 5, 6, 8
xv/39	Singing at Primary Schools	I/12
xv/44	On the Perfect Concept of Two-Note Chords	II/1, 2, 3, 4, 5, 6, 7, 8; III/1, 2, 3
xv/45	Missa Quinti toni: Auctore Orlando di Lasso	II/1, 2
xv/53	Church Music [review of Fibich's Missa brevis]	II/8
xv/56	Bedřich Smetana on Musical Forms	III/1
xv/58	Hymnbooks	III/2, 4, 7
xv/61	On the Concept of Key	III/4, 5, 6, 7, 8, 9, 10
xv/63	The Prelude to Gounod's 'Faust'	III/5
xv/66	A Musical Academy in Prague [the need for musical theorists]	III/6
xv/68	On the Scientific Nature of Harmony Treatises [review of Hostinský's article on harmony manuals serialized in Dalibor]	III/7
xv/71	Something Topical After All! [the need for an Academy of Music]	III/8
xv/65	Review of Ludvík Kuba's Slavdom in its Songs	III/10
xv/74	The Theatre Season is Over [suggestions for improvements]	III/10
xv/75	An Old Music Manuscript [from the Staré Brno monastery]	IV/i
xv/76	On the Triad	IV/1, 2, 3, 4, 5, 6, 7, 8
xv/78	A Proposal for a Singing-Teaching Course at Gymnasia and Realschulen	IV/2
xv/80	A Brief Word about Counterpoint	IV/3
xv/81	On the Transposition of Choral Songs	IV/3
xv/82	On Teaching Singing to the First Class of a Primary School	IV/3
xv/84	Intelligent Work [the psychology of musical motifs]	IV/4
xv/86	A Special Phenomenon [the chord of the seventh in Dvořák's Spectre's Bride]	IV/5
xv/88	Ease in Invention [on motif repetition]	IV/6
xv/90	Difficult Intonation [how to sing difficult voice parts in tune]	IV/7
xv/91	Ricercar [on improving musical standards in Brno]	IV/8

Janáček published few of these shorter articles in the first two volumes but made up for it in the next, when there is hardly a fascicle without one (IV/3 exceptionally has three). Janáček himself contributed five articles on church music (XV/45, XV/53, XV/58, XV/75, XV/81); five – arguably six – on music education (XV/39, XV/66, XV/71, XV/78, XV/82, XV/90); one review of new music (XV/53) and two of important books and articles (XV/65 and XV/68). In the final issues of the last two volumes Janáček published an end-of-term report on the theatre (XV/74, XV/91) with suggestions for how to improve musical standards in Brno. However, the interest that Janáček showed in theoretical and analytical aspects of music is overwhelming.

An obvious drawback of *Hudební listy* is how much it remained a platform for Janáček alone, and how few other voices, apart from those of the reviewers, were heard in it. Here is a list of the articles not written by Janáček:

Table 24.4: Articles by other authors in *Hudební listy*

author	title	vol./fasc.
[Berthold Žalud][5]	*Church Music: something from the history of organs*	I/3
	On the Present State of Church Music in Brno	I/6, 8, 9,13
K. Kobinger	*How German Writers Criticize Richard Wagner*	I/7
[Berthold Žalud]	*Singing at Middle Schools*	I/8
'O'	*Singing at Primary and Town* [i.e. secondary] *Schools*	I/10, 11
[Berthold Žalud]	*The Contents and Form of Musical Work*	I/10, 13
Kašpar Pivoda	*Singing at Primary Schools* [response to X/39]	I/13
František Skuherský	*From Music History*	II/1–5, 7
František Pivoda	*Singing and the Public*	II/3–9
[unsigned][†]	*Bohumil Rieger: conductor and music teacher in Brno*	II/3
+	*Something about Teaching Singing at Primary Schools*	II/5–7
Fr. Prav. Hnilička	*A Brief Outline of Twenty-Five Years of Activity of the Brno Beseda*	II/7–9
–aa–	*On Musical Events in Warsaw*	III/2, 8, 10 IV/2, 4, 8
K. Sázavský	*Singing in Primary School and in Life*	III/8
H-č	*St Ludmila* [review of first performance]	III/10
A. Konrád	*Sacred Polish Song* [extract from longer monograph]	IV/1, 2, 3
J.J.Fux	*Gradus ad Parnassum* [reprint of a Czech translation]	IV/4–8
Jan Blahoslav	[on music, from his *Czech Grammar*, 1569]	IV/7
Fr. Bartoš	[extract from *Our Children*]	IV/8
Fr. Bartoš	[extract from *Moravian Folksongs*, on ballads]	IV/8

[†]A possible author was Janáček's supporter and inspector of the Organ School, Prof. Chmelíček, a former pupil of Gottfried/'Bohumil' Rieger.

This list demonstrates that Janáček was relatively successful in attracting other writers in the first and second years, in particular stimulating a lively debate on music education. But in the final two years (especially after the death of Berthold Žalud, who had contributed a number of articles in the first year) Janáček published no new articles by other writers, apart from reviews (including regular reports from a correspondent in Warsaw). Although the extracts from recently published books by Konrád and Bartoš were sensible ways of drawing attention to these publications, the serialization of Fux's *Gradus ad Parnassum* looks like desperation. No doubt the dearth of contributors arose from the fact that they were unpaid, and in the end Janáček probably found it easier to write his own articles than to persuade others to write for him. It did mean, however, that 'music history', mentioned in the preliminary announcement as a featured area, was ill-served in the final two years.

The fact that *Hudební listy* increasingly reflected Janáček's own interests meant that the ideal reader of the journal was someone just like him with a passionate interest in music theory, an increasing interest in opera and theatre, and a professional interest in church music and music education. As Helfert put it, the journal had a completely individual character as an 'encyclopedia of Janáček's critical and theoretical views of the time'.[6] A comparison with its only real Czech competitor of the period, *Dalibor*, points to other essential differences. *Dalibor* was published in Prague by F.A. Urbánek and was promoted as a 'periodical for all branches of musical art'. To take, for example, its vol. viii (1886), published in the middle of the *Hudební listy* run, this is a sturdy volume of 476 pages of a smaller format than *Hudební listy*, issued weekly in eight-page fascicles throughout the calendar year and, as a trade journal for Urbánek, it contains advertisements and news of its publications and those of his brother, the publisher Velebín Urbánek (*Hudební listy* carried no advertisements). The cost for a journal that was five times larger than *Hudební listy* was comparable: 1 zl for three months. A typical issue had much the same plan: one or two long articles, a substantial review section and brief news items at the end. Where *Dalibor* scored was the much wider selection of articles and writers (some forty general articles that year by at least twenty different writers), the coverage of concerts (rather than merely operas and plays) and the much more extensive provision of news and reviews. *Dalibor* had a wider constituency, for which it provided such regular items as 'letters from Brno', reports from twenty-two smaller Czech centres and reports from abroad (Zürich, Hamburg, Lwów, Paris, St Petersburg, Vienna and even two from Milwaukee). The fact that it was broader-based and more general in its readership gave it a much longer life then *Hudební listy*. It survived from its beginning in 1879 until 1913 and was revived in 1919–27, though by then it was a pale shadow of its former self and had been nudged aside by other journals such as *Listy Hudební matice/Tempo* and *Smetana*.

As with most journals, readers of *Hudební listy* no doubt took what they wanted, and one wonders how many people actually read Janáček's long articles on music theory. Among the subscribers listed in the first year there are not many obvious candidates. After six issues there were only nineteen named subscribers: the small number is a reflection of the haste with which the journal came into being, and the lack of any sort of attempt at promoting it. Nevertheless by the end of the year things had improved, and *Hudební listy* listed more new subscribers in the last three issues, making a total of eighty-seven. This number rises to ninety-six, if one includes the extra nine copies that Pivoda had taken for his singing institution. In a letter of 2 February 1885 Pivoda explained to Janáček how, having failed to attract subscribers from his pupils, he decided to give nine of the richer ones a free subscription in the hope that they would then take them over themselves.[7] Pivoda's generosity could cynically be regarded as a way of keeping in with a useful contact in Brno who promoted his singing method but also as an acknowledgement that Janáček was carrying on where Pivoda left off: he was the last editor of a journal for choral societies, also entitled *Hudební listy*, which had folded in 1875.

Of the eighty-seven subscribers only ten were clearly trained musicians. The rest included a large proportion of teachers, school directors and inspectors (twenty-three, excluding music teachers) and clergy (sixteen, including Janáček's old uncle Jan Janáček, a very solid representation from Brno Cathedral, but none from the Staré Brno monastery). It was predominantly bought by people in Brno (almost half) and in nearby towns and villages. Apart from Pivoda's ten subscriptions, there were only seven subscribers in Prague (four of them from the 'Hlahol' executive). The subscription list was overwhelmingly male: only four women were listed.

Judging from the heart-felt plea in the final fascicle of vol. i for subscribers who had not yet paid to do so now, to 'reduce the deficit', one can assume that many more copies were sent out and the total number may have been nearer 120. Subscribers were not listed in later years, but from the deficits given by the Beseda treasurer for the first two years[8] it is possible to get some idea of the size of readership (see table 24.5):

Table 24.5: *Hudebni listy*: subscriptions (*extrapolated figures in square brackets*)

vol.	cost of subscription	no. of subscribers	total take	deficit	overall cost	total no. of pages
i	1 zl	97	97 zl	17 zl	114 zl	54
ii	1.30 zl	[141.5]	[184 zl]	3 zl	[187 zl]	80
iii	1.30 zl	?	?	'profit'	?	82

There was a substantial price rise (to 2 zl) in the fourth and final year but also a corresponding increase in length. No profit/deficit figures are available for that year, but it is hardly likely that the Beseda would have gone on publishing the journal into June if it was running at a deficit. It is, however, equally unlikely that the number of subscriptions would have got much beyond 150.

What is clear, however, is that in this form it was self-sustaining, providing Janáček was willing to go on with it. With one other person in the Beseda seeing to subscriptions and distribution, its costs were merely those of printing, and these, even without advertisements, were balanced by the subscriptions. In terms of size and months covered, the journal had increased substantially over the four years and seemed set to continue.

The end happened quite abruptly. Janáček had put the last issue to bed, completing the two serializations, and giving a date of '1 September 1888' for the next issue, when a row blew up over a different issue at the Beseda, and Janáček walked out (see chap. 23). The fact that it was basically a one-man show meant that there was no interest at the Beseda in continuing it (the committee thought that it was still costing them money, and the treasurer needed to point out that they were in fact in balance). On the other hand Janáček had no means of continuing it outside the aegis of the Beseda, though interestingly in this last issue he had speculated about the journal moving to a specially formed company made of leading choral societies, booksellers and other interested people (xv/86).

In retrospect it seems odd that the Beseda bothered with *Hudební listy* at all. It was never a Beseda journal in the sense of providing news from the society and it covered almost none of the Beseda concerts – perhaps as a matter of principle Janáček was scrupulous in keeping his name out of the journal, both as a composer and as a conductor. Maybe Janáček was relieved at the demise; certainly he never made any further attempt to begin another musical periodical, although his journalistic instincts continued to be exercised, for instance in his regular reviews for *Moravské listy* in 1890–2. He found other outlets to publish his theoretical articles and his opera reviews. And, as it was, his abundant energies were about to be transferred to his passionate interest in traditional Moravian folk music.

25

Janáček's knowledge of opera I: up to *Šárka*

In view of his musical education and experience until his mid-twenties, an opera composer is about the last thing one might have expected Janáček to be. His earliest aesthetic formation, deriving from Herbart's and Durdík's formalism had no place for a genre that attempted to combine several arts. Even if he had had the curiosity, he was too poor to get to the opera in Prague during his studies in 1874–5. His energetically pursued savouring of musical life in Leipzig omitted opera altogether, and when in Vienna he did get to see a couple of operas (Cherubini's *Les deux journées* and Weber's *Der Freischütz*), he didn't care for them. All this, however, changed in the early 1880s.

Although an excellent German opera house opened in Brno in 1882 on the former ramparts (the new Stadttheater), Janáček on principle did not step inside this building until 1919. Ironically this would be the opera house in which all his later operas received their premières. The building still stands, if frequently renamed; since 1965 it has been known as the Mahen Theatre.

Apart from a half-remembered performance of a Meyerbeer opera in which he may have taken part as a child singer (see chap. 7), Janáček's only known early exposure to opera in Brno was during a couple of seasons in 1881 and 1882 by the visiting Pištěk company (Janáček was abroad during their first visit in 1879–80). The one opera that Janáček is known to have seen there was Gounod's *Faust*, but this was a sufficiently formative experience for him to publish a review in *Moravská orlice* (xv/22) and to appear soon afterwards as Faust at a fancy-dress party (with Zdenka as Marguerite and his friend Berthold Žalud as Mephistopheles; see chap. 17).

Janáček's first prolonged exposure to opera came in the summer of 1883, which he spent in Prague, having split up with Zdenka. Here he saw Meyerbeer's *Le prophète*, Halévy's *La Juive*, Verdi's *Il trovatore* and *Un ballo in maschera*, and Smetana's *The Secret*. That this was a watershed is clear from the fact that he went to extra performances of the same operas (*Le prophète* twice, *Il trovatore* three times) and that he bought librettos and covered them with comments.[1]

In the winter of 1884 the situation in Brno was transformed by the opening of the Czech Provisional Theatre. Although this adapted dance hall on Veveří ulice with its tiny stage and its equally tiny auditorium was modest (sanctioned to take an audience of 771 of which half had to stand), it was the only theatre for the Czech theatre-going and opera-going public from 1884 until 1919, when Czechs were able to share the opulent German Theatre; it was demolished only in 1952. That the theatre was thought to be only a makeshift beginning is reflected by its name ('Provisional'). When it was clear that a new building was impossible, a second gallery was added in 1894, bringing the capacity to a thousand and leading to a resigned name change to the 'National Theatre'.[2] This was the theatre in which Janáček's second and third operas, *The Beginning of a Romance* and *Jenůfa*, were first given. The companies (contracted for a year or two) that squeezed into this venue were equally modest. Jan Pištěk's company in 1884 had a total of eight soloists, František Pokorný's company the next year had two conductors (including Karel Kovařovic), but a chorus of only twelve and an orchestra of eighteen.[3] In the early days, missing orchestral parts needed to be filled in on a harmonium.[4]

It was here too that Janáček cut his teeth reviewing a total of thirty-three operas and operettas (several times, in many cases) for his journal *Hudební listy*, which he started partly for this purpose. His reviews provide most of the information about what he saw and what he thought about it, and this can be amplified by his collection of piano-vocal scores and librettos of operas, though one cannot be sure when all these annotations were made. Janáček's regular reviewing, until the journal folded in the summer of 1888, provides the background for the composition and revision of his first opera *Šárka* (1887–8) and for the opera that he contemplated before that, *The Last of the Abencérages* (1884–5).

What Janáček knew at this stage represents a narrow segment of operatic repertory. Apart from Gluck's *Orfeo*, he knew nothing from the eighteenth century and apart from Wagner's *Tristan* nothing recent from the international repertory. Since on the whole the Czechs left the Germans to perform German operas (which Janáček thus missed out on since he refused to set foot in the German Theatre) and since Russian operas had not yet got to Brno, 'international repertory' meant largely Italian and French operas. Czech opera patriotically formed a substantial part of what was performed (thirteen of the thirty-three operas and operettas that Janáček reviewed). Janáček was in favour of this high proportion (xv/41), though was critical of many of these works and expressed his reservations quite openly – this itself is striking given the fact that for much of the time he commented on performances rather than the music, and his remarks on the operas themselves are comparatively rare. Apart from a few operas by Smetana, Dvořák and Blodek (his unassuming one-acter *In the Well*), the Czech operas performed in Brno in these years were by composers who made some impact in Prague at the time but whose works would not survive into the twentieth century: Bendl, Šebor, Rozkošný and Hřímalý.

Janáček characterized Karel Bendl's *The Elderly Suitor* as 'tuneful' but hardly original. Its problems, he thought, resided in the fact that it attempted to make use of folksongs but that Bendl's general style had nothing to do with either Czech or Moravian folksong, and the collision of these two styles was 'a basic shortcoming' (xv/33). Josef Paukner's *The Treasure*, the only Czech opera given in Brno during this period that had not already been presented in Prague, was dismissed even more briskly. Fresh, flowing melody was conceded but again it was not very original, he thought, and the orchestration had not been thought through; many of the introductions ought to be omitted (xv/41). Janáček promised a discussion of the libretto 'elsewhere' but never got round to it.

Janáček professed that he had been looking forward to Karel Šebor's *The Frustrated Wedding*. Twenty years earlier Šebor had been seen as a rival to Smetana; however by the late 1870s, when he wrote his last completed opera, he had fallen on hard times and the trivial, folksong-bound libretto offered no opportunities for his strong dramatic talent. So, Janáček commented, the opera had its moments with a good overture and well-set words showing his flair for effective characterization but it lacked the charm of Smetana's *Bartered Bride* or *The Kiss* (xv/46). Vojtěch Hřímalý's *The Spell-Bound Prince* was dismissed in a single sentence as a comic opera with forms based on 'merry polkas and fast waltzes' into which 'playful whirl' the Angelus and Ave Maria in Act 1 come as something of a surprise (xv/52).

Josef Richard Rozkošný's *St John's Rapids* was one of the few Czech operas of the time to be published in piano-vocal score. Although no copy survived in Janáček's library, it seems likely that his rather more considered comments were based not merely on hearing the opera in performance but on playing it through himself from the score. Janáček liked its clarity and transparency, despite – his usual comment – its lack of originality in melody and especially harmony. Whole scenes, he thought (e.g. in Act 4), resembled Gounod's *Faust*, though this was the fault of the libretto. He found it all rather pale and cold. How to explain this? Janáček did so, interestingly, by considering the metre of the libretto, finding that it was mostly in iambs, which is hardly surprising, given the fact that Eduard Rüffer's libretto was written first in German (in which iambic pentameters were seen as both normal and 'elevated') and then translated.[5] This gave it a sameness which had a dulling effect. Similarly the use of oldfashioned forms (simple ABAs, for instance) detracted from any dramatic effect it might have had, as did the Gounod-like shifts in tonality (xv/73).

Seen in this context, Janáček's comments on Karel Kovařovic's *The Bridegrooms* (xv/70), the *cause célèbre* that later scuppered his chances of *Jenůfa*'s acceptance by Kovařovic at the National Theatre (see chap. 49), come across as less devastating than the impression that this much-reproduced review gives when seen in isolation. However it is tone here rather than content that did the damage. At least Rozkošný could perhaps have taken comfort from a serious, 500-word piece which included examples from named scenes; *The Bridegrooms* was dismissed in less than a hundred words in an imaginary sarcastic dialogue, an approach Janáček had already begun employing to liven things up in his journal.

Had he been a regular reader of *Hudební listy*, Kovařovic might have noticed that Janáček was equally critical of some of Smetana's operas. *Dalibor* came through mostly unscathed ('the effect was powerful', 'islands of delightful tunes, well-thought-out forms of a Czech nature', xv/85), though his comments were not sufficiently enthusiastic to escape censure from the Prague journal *Dalibor*.* However the Smetana opera

---

* Correspondence followed in which Janáček responded to the scornful reprint of a couple of sentences from his review with a version that gives the sentences in their full context (xv/89).

that seems to have truly vexed Janáček was *The Two Widows*. Here, without the benefit of a score, and at first hearing (as he writes), Janáček came up with eight numbered points, six of them critical, including the fact that the style of opera was not unified, that Act 1 was much more successful than Act 2, that the melodrama in Act 2 'aroused resistance' (a comment that explains perhaps why Janáček destroyed his own melodrama *Death* XI/3 and thereafter employed the technique only for satirical purposes), that neither libretto nor music brought the piece to a climax and that it was a mistake to mix the subsidiary country couple into the main action. An example of non-unified style that Janáček gave, i.e. the rather more wistful music connected in Act 2 with Anežka that he felt was out of keeping with the more genial general style of the piece, strikes one today as a misunderstanding. One of Smetana's strengths in *The Two Widows* and *The Bartered Bride* is the darker colours he summoned up for the more painful situations in which his heroines found themselves. But otherwise Janáček's comments seem fair. And, on the other hand, he was impressed by the interesting modulations and striking melodic phrases that he noticed. As a whole he found it more interesting than *The Bartered Bride* (xv/77).

Almost the only Czech operas on which he offered no critical comments were Smetana's two most popular, *The Kiss* and *The Bartered Bride*, the latter by then an indestructible part of Czech repertory and which, at thirty performances during Janáček's *Hudební listy* years, was double that of any other opera. Dvořák's one-act comedy *The Cunning Peasant* (seemingly the only opera by his friend and mentor that Janáček knew at this stage) he criticized chiefly because of its libretto (the 'cunningness' seemed to be attached to the wrong person) and its lack of convincing motivation (xv/52). Surprisingly the Czech opera for which he had unstinting praise was Vilém Blodek's modest one-act comedy, *In the Well*, particularly for its effective and lively choruses (xv/36). Later, when attempting to justify his second opera *The Beginning of a Romance* to František Šubert, he declared that he was aspiring to 'at least the level of musical expression' of Blodek's opera (see chap. 29).

Following Smetana's example as opera critic twenty years earlier, Janáček lashed out against the operettas with which the company attempted to attract a wider audience. He had many objections: the company had neither the sets for it nor the necessary forces; there were no good aesthetic, artistic or 'even moral' reasons for performing such works: the spirit of such operettas isn't 'ours' (i.e. Czech) and it spoilt good health (!) and taste. This attitude has its roots in the elevated mission that music represented for cultured Czechs in the nineteenth century (with the unspoken view that music was not mere entertainment) and was perhaps also a dig at the frivolous Viennese, who cultivated the genre so enthusiastically. The wonder is that Janáček bothered to attend operettas, let alone to write about the performances, though perhaps this was merely an excuse for expressing his strong views, e.g. that Lecocque's *Giroflé-Girofla* totally lacked any artistic merit (xv/28) and that the effort and time spent on staging Genée's *Der Seekadett* was a waste and detrimental to healthy human minds (xv/32). Janáček even saw Lortzing's opera *Zar und Zimmermann* in this light: musically empty. A more dignified performance of the part of the tsar might have saved it, he wrote, but, fatally for Janáček, it had crossed the line from comic opera into operetta (xv/83).

Perhaps because there were no novelties in the international repertory performed, Janáček did not see the need to comment on musical aspects rather than their performance, so his views can only be inferred. From an elderly Zdenka Janáčková, Jan Racek gleaned that Janáček liked Verdi.[6] Although there is not much support for this in terms of printed statements from Janáček, it is not an unreasonable conclusion: the fact that he saw *Trovatore* three times in Prague in 1883 represents some sort of evidence, as does the occasional comment on some of the other operas, that Germont's 'Di Provenza il mar, il suol' was one of the most beautiful passages in *Traviata* (xv/32) and that he liked *Ernani* (xv/110), though not sufficiently, it seems, for him to bother to review its single Czech performance on 27 October 1886. Gounod's *Faust* was another favourite, judging from his enthusiastic comments going back to 1880, when he saw it performed by the Pištěk company. Although his essay on the orchestral introduction to the opera was critical of the way the key shifted (without 'proper transposition'), the fact that he bothered to publish 400 words on the subject with two musical examples and two charts (xv/63) does at least indicate an engagement with the piece.

The only other opera that he subjected to some sort of musical analysis was the prelude to Wagner's *Tristan und Isolde*. He had not seen the opera – he would not do so until he was almost seventy – but he did possess a score and in an article (serialized over four issues of

Hudební listy in 1885) he proceeded to launch into a bold criticism of its harmony, illustrated with seven musical examples. His summary offered it as a 'small contribution' to clarifying the basis of Wagner's composition. He had, he wrote, noted some 'incorrectnesses and roughness in its harmonic links'; he found that Wagner hadn't after all done away with all traditional forms, though since Dvořák made use of *all* (Janáček's emphasis) Wagner was by implication rather one-sided. However, what Wagner had created in the field of dramatic music belonged undeniably to the best there was (xv/30).

In general it could be noted that apart from *Tristan* all the operas Janáček knew and commented on were number operas, and his comments seldom affect the construction of the opera. Criticisms tend to be limited to aspects such as 'defective harmony'. Perhaps the one clue to the future opera composer is his awareness of some composers' ability to express character (as in Šebor) or psychological depth (Smetana's *The Kiss*).

Table 25.1: List of operas that Janáček had seen, studied or commented on up to 1888

Unless otherwise stated, all operas that Janáček attended were performed at the Brno Czech Theatre (Provisional Theatre, National Theatre etc) and reviewed in *Hudební listy*.

PNCT = Prague, New Czech Theatre;
lib = copy of libretto in Czech in Janáček's library; Ger. lib = copy of libretto in German in Janáček's library;
VS = copy of piano-vocal score in Janáček's library; Ger. VS = German piano-vocal score in Janáček's library

composer: title	date, place of first performance	dates of LJ's attendance	publication details of review by LJ (other writings as specified); other information
Auber: *La neige*	1823, Paris		VS
Auber: *La muette de Portici*	1828, Paris		lib
Balfe: *The Bohemian Girl*	1843, London		1 Jan 1888 (xv/83)
Bellini: *Norma*	1834, Rome		1 Nov 1885 (xv/47); lib
Bendl: *The Elderly Suitor*	1882, Chrudim	31 Jan 1885	19 Jan (xv/33) 2 Feb 1885 (xv/35)
Bendl: *Lejla*	1868, Prague		Janáček acquainted with VS (Prague, 1874–80); see chap. 26
Bizet: *Carmen*	1875, Paris		15 Nov 1886 (xv/60) 1 Dec 1886 (xv/62) 15 Jan 1887 (xv/69); lib

Table 25.1:—*continued*

composer: title	date, place of first performance	dates of LJ's attendance	publication details of review by LJ (other writings as specified); other information
Blodek: *In the Well*	1867, Prague	5 Feb 1885	9 Feb 1885 (xv/36)
			15 Oct 1886 (xv/57); lib
Cherubini: *Les deux journées*	1800, Paris	Vienna, 31 May 1880	
Dvořák: *The Cunning Peasant*	1878, Prague	29 Dec 1885	1 Jan 1886 (xv/51)
			1 Feb 1886 (xv/52)
			1 Feb 1887 (xv/72)
		20 Nov 1887	1 Dec 1887 (xv/79); lib
Fibich: *The Bride of Messina*	1884, Prague		lib (2 copies); VS
Flotow: *Martha*	1847, Vienna	6 Feb 1885	9 Feb 1885 (xv/36); lib
Genée: *Der Seekadett*	1876, Vienna	4 Jan 1885	12 Jan 1885 (xv/32)
Gluck: *Orfeo ed Euridice*	1762, Vienna		In Sept 1887 Janáček proposed that the Brno Beseda stage a performance.
Gounod: *Faust*	1859, Paris	Brno, Pištěk's opera company 1880	12 Oct 1880 (xv/22)
			16 Feb 1885 (xv/37)
			23 Feb 1885 (xv/38)
			1 Dec 1885 (xv/49)
			1 Feb 1887 (xv/72); analysis of introduction 15 Dec 1886 (xv/63); Ger. VS, Ger. lib
Halévy: *La Juive*	1835, Paris	PNCT, 7 Aug 1883	1 Jan 1887 (xv/67); lib; Ger. lib
Hřímalý: *The Spell-Bound Prince*	1872, Prague		1 Feb 1886 (xv/52); lib
Kovařovic: *The Bridegrooms*	1884, Prague		15 Jan 1887 (xv/70)
Lecocque: *Giroflé-Girofla*	1874, Paris	18 Dec 1884	20 Dec 1884 (xv/28)
Lortzing: *Der Waffenschmied*	1846, Vienna		15 Nov 1886 (xv/60)
Lortzing: *Zar und Zimmermann*	1837, Leipzig	20 Dec 1887	1 Jan 1888 (xv/83)
Marschner: *Der Templar und die Jüdin*	Leipzig, 1829		Ger. lib
Meyerbeer: *L'Africaine*	1865, Paris		Ger. lib

Table 25.1:—*continued*

composer: title	date, place of first performance	dates of LJ's attendance	publication details of review by LJ (other writings as specified); other information
Meyerbeer: *Le prophète*	1849, Paris	PNCT, 22 July 1883	Janáček recalled singing in it as a chorister in Brno in the 1860s, but this fact is disputed (see chap. 7); lib
		PNCT 9 Aug 1883	
Paukner: *The Treasure*	1885, Brno	2 March 1885	9 March 1885 (xv/41)
Planquette: *Les cloches de Corneville*	1877, Paris	14 Dec 1884 28 Jan 1885	20 Dec 1884 (xv/28) 2 Feb 1885 (xv/35); lib
Rozkošný: *The St John Rapids*	1871, Prague	13 Feb 1887	15 Feb 1887 (xv/73)
Šebor: *The Frustrated Wedding*	1879, Prague	8 Oct 1885 10 Oct 1885	19 Oct 1885 (xv/46) 1 Feb 1886 (xv/52)
Škroup: *The Tinker*	1826, Prague	27 Oct 1885	1 Nov 1885 (xv/47)
Smetana: *The Bartered Bride*	1866, Prague	7 Dec 1884 17 Dec 1884 26 Dec 1884 2 Feb 1885	13 Dec 1884 (xv/27) 20 Dec 1884 (xv/28) 27 Dec 1884 (xv/29) 2 Feb 1885 (xv/35) 1 Nov 1885 (xv/47) 15 Dec 1885 (xv/50)
		21 Feb 1886	24 Feb 1886 (xv/55) 15 Nov 1886 (xv/60) 12 Dec 1886 (xv/62) 15 Dec 1886 (xv/64)
Smetana: *Dalibor*	1868, Prague	16 Jan 1888	1 Feb 1888 (xv/85); defence of review, 1 April 1888 (xv/89)
Smetana: *The Kiss*	1876, Prague	13 Dec 1884	20 Dec 1884 (xv/28) 3 Jan 1885 (xv/31)
		1 Feb 1885	2 Feb 1885 (xv/35) 15 Oct 1886 (xv/57)
Smetana: *The Secret*	1878, Prague	PNCT, 3 Sept 1883	
Smetana: *The Two Widows*	1874, Prague	10 Dec 1887	1 Nov 1887 (xv/77)
Strauss: *Die Fledermaus*	1874, Vienna	28 Dec 1884	3 Jan 1885 (xv/31); lib

Table 25.1:—*continued*

composer: title	date, place of first performance	dates of LJ's attendance	publication details of review by LJ (other writings as specified); other information
Strauss: *Das Spitzentuch der Königin*	1884, Vienna	25 Jan 1885	26 Jan 1885 (xv/34)
Strauss: *Der lustige Krieg*	1881, Vienna		lib
Suppé: *Boccaccio*	1879, Vienna	26 Dec 1884	27 Dec 1884 (xv/29) 1 Nov 1885 (xv/47)
Suppé: *Der Gascogner*	1881, Vienna	9 Dec 1884	13 Dec 1884 (xv/27)
Suppé: *Donna Juanita*	1880, Vienna	21 Dec 1884	27 Dec 1884 (xv/29); lib
Verdi: *Un ballo in maschera*	1859, Rome	PNCT, 25 July 1883	
Verdi: *Ernani*	1844, Venice	27 Oct 1886 (?)	LJ mentions it on 1 Nov 1886 (xv/59) but did not write a formal review
Verdi: *La traviata*	1853, Venice	7 Jan 1885 3 Oct 1885 27 Feb 1885	12 Jan 1885 (xv/32) 2 March 1885 (xv/40) 19 Oct 1885 (xv/46); Ger. lib
Verdi: *Il trovatore*	1853, Rome	PNCT 27 July, 22 and 26 Aug 1883 11 Dec 1884 6 March 1885 13 Oct 1885	– 13 Dec 1884 (xv/27) 9 March 1885 (xv/41) 19 Oct 1885 (xv/46)
Wagner: *Tristan und Isolde*	1865, Munich		analytical article, 3 Jan–2 Feb 1885 (xv/30); Janáček also proposed conducting prelude on 27 Nov 1887, though this plan was not realized
Weber: *Der Freischütz*	1821, Berlin	Vienna, 14 April 1880; 24 Feb 1885 20 Feb 1886	– 2 March 1885 (xv/40) 24 Feb 1886 (xv/55)
Zajc: *Die Hexe von Boissy*	1866, Vienna	25 Dec 1885 (?)	1 Jan 1887 (xv/67)

26

Janáček's first opera: Šárka in 1887–8

Hardly had he started reviewing operas staged at the Provisional Theatre in Brno than Janáček began thinking about writing his own. This was *The Last Abencérage* (XI/I), based on François René Chateaubriand's *Les aventures du dernier des Abencérages* (1826). Janáček was improving his schoolboy French at the time and acquired editions in French of Racine's *Athalie* and Molière's *L'avare*.[1] Chateaubriand's tale – some forty pages in a modern paperback – is about Aben Hamet, the last ibn Serazh (Zerag), a rich Moorish family established in Cordoba and Granada from the eighth century. Spanish romances of the fifteenth and sixteenth century describe the family's rivalry with the Zegers, resulting in death and exile.[2] Cherubini's opera *Les abencérages ou L'étendard de Grenade* (1813), although derived from the same subject matter, predated Chateaubriand's tale by thirteen years and was quite unknown to Janáček. Chateaubriand's tale can be summarized as follows:

Aben Hamet returns to Spain from exile and falls in love with Donna Blanca, who, although betrothed to Count Lautrec, returns his love. This leads to a duel with her brother, Don Carlos. However, as soon as Aben Hamet discovers that Donna Blanca comes from the family that persecuted his ancestors he leaves her and returns to exile and death. Donna Blanca expires.

According to his annotations in a Czech school edition in French (Šimáček, Prague, n.d.), Janáček read Chateaubriand's tale between 16 August 1884 and 23 January 1885. At about the same time he jotted down a scenario in his diary for 1885, the names modified for a Czech audience:

Act 1
Madrid, Don Rigo's palace, a small square
Action:
Aben Hamet has lost his way
Donna Blanka's scene
Don Carlos's scene in procession with Lautrek
Change of scene: A garden with a view of the Alhambra
Donna Blanka with her women
Don Rigo
Aben Hamet
Declaration of love

Act 2
A hall in Generalif; a banquet
Carlos's reproach to Blanka
Lautrek and the aristocracy
Aben Hamet
Lautrek's song
Blanka's song
Aben Hamet's song
Challenge, duel. Aben Hamet reveals himself

Act 3
Africa. Countryside around the ruins of Carthage, the building site of the Zegers.
Aben Hamet's Moorish grave. Doves lap from the water contained above the grave.
Donna Blanka dies.[3]

Remote as this subject matter seems for Janáček, there was a Czech precedent in Karel Bendl's 'grand opera', *Lejla* (based on Bulwer Lytton's novel *Leila, or The Siege of Granada*), set in the same exotic locale. This was one of the most successful Czech operas of the period (first given at the Prague Provisional Theatre in 1868) and one of the few to appear in print at the time (two vols: 1874 and 1880). Janáček's scenario, with its grand settings, its formal scenes and its succession of songs in Act 2 and other suggestions of set numbers, runs along the same lines. His proposed voice types, with soprano and tenor lovers, aristocratic bass (Don Carlos) and baritone rival (Lautrek), follow both *Lejla* and also *Il trovatore*, which Janáček saw three times in Prague the previous summer. However, even if Bendl was an encouraging model for this sort of subject matter, *The Last Abencérage* failed to get further, probably because of the question of the libretto. It was decades before Janáček had the confidence to concoct a libretto himself from a novel (rather than a play), and if he was going to get further he would have needed someone to carve out a verse libretto for him in accordance with the scenario's implied aesthetic of solo numbers, double arias, concertato finales, etc. There were no obvious potential Czech librettists in Brno at the time; Janáček's best bet was to find a ready-made libretto.

One turned up two years later, by which time Janáček had reviewed many operas for *Hudební listy* and had greatly expanded his experience of the genre. While one can argue that *The Last Abencérage* was Janáček's 'own choice' (however unlikely and unsuitable), it is less easy to contend that *Šárka* was exactly what he would have chosen.

The libretto for *Šárka* was built on one of the most popular Bohemian-Czech founding myths. In musical works alone this myth is the basis for the symphonic poem *Šárka* (1880) from Smetana's orchestral cycle *My Fatherland*, Fibich's best-known opera (*Šárka*, 1897) and Ostrčil's opera *The Death of Vlasta* (1904). Zeyer's *Šárka* continues the story told in Smetana's opera *Libuše*, premièred at the opening of the National Theatre in Prague in 1881:

The action of *Šárka* takes place in the 'maidens' war', the armed revolt of Czech women against the patriarchy. Women's power declined after the marriage of Libuše and even more so at her death, when her consort Přemysl was left in sole command. In protest the women form an army of women warriors. Their success, especially the exploits of Šárka, the boldest of the women, caused consternation among the men. Ctirad offers to hunt Šárka down and equips himself for his task with magic weapons. In order to deal with this new challenge, Šárka has her women bind her to a tree at a place in the forest where Ctirad will pass. He discovers her and is deceived by her explanation that she has been left to die by one of her rivals. His pity is aroused, and then his love. Too late he realizes that this is an ambush; Šárka relieves him of his magic weapons and then, with her horn, summons her women, who make quick work of him. But Šárka has fallen in love with him. In remorse she throws herself on to his funeral pyre.

Julius Zeyer (1841–1901) was a leading poet of the time, internationalist in outlook from his family background (a father of French Alsatian descent, and a German-Jewish mother), extensive travels and his association with the outwood-looking 'Lumír' group of Czech poets. At the request of Dvořák, Zeyer produced a libretto by adapting the fourth part (*Ctirad*, 1879) of his five-part verse epic *Vyšehrad*; perhaps on the lookout for something more internationally attractive, however, Dvořák was reluctant to set *Šárka* – a couple of years later he launched into his opera *Dimitrij*, set on Russian soil. Zeyer waited several years, during which *Šárka* found its way – equally fruitlessly – to the ailing Smetana, before he went ahead and published his libretto in a new theatrical magazine, *Česká Thalie*.[4] It came out in three fortnightly instalments (1 January, 15 January, 1 February 1887) and it was there that Janáček read it, his attention drawn to it by Karel Sázavský (see chap. 23).

Inspired by SS Cyril, Methodius and Great Moravia (see chap. 7), Janáček's national awareness was principally Moravian. Given a free hand, would he have been attracted to subject matter that was unmistakably Bohemian-Czech? Even if he had opportunistically embraced this subject matter (since it was the sort of thing that clearly went down well in Prague), how happy would he have been with the operatic conventions that lay behind Zeyer's libretto? Unmediated, an opera libretto can constrain a composer into a particular set of operatic conventions and thus determine the type of opera that emerges. Smetana himself, for instance, simply took what came, and the type of operas he wrote depended largely on whoever happened to be writing his librettos: many ensembles in the operas to Krásnohorská librettos, almost none in the ones to Wenzig librettos.[5] Janáček, writing his first opera based on a text by one of the grandees of Czech letters, could hardly be expected to change the type of opera that Zeyer's libretto predicated, let alone suggest – Verdi-like – that Zeyer give him an extra ensemble here, a duet there. But Janáček's preferences at the time for number opera – opera clearly divided into 'numbers' (arias, duets, ensembles etc.) – can be read into his scenario for *The Last Abencérage* as well as the commissioned libretto for the next opera, *The Beginning of a Romance*, and even his home-made libretto for his third opera, *Jenůfa*, in its earliest version (see chap. 48).

Zeyer called his libretto a 'music drama', a term that points clearly to Wagner. Wagner haunts the subject matter (a Walküre-like women's chorus, magic weapons, and a love-in-death union in the immolation of hero and heroine) and even the lengthy stage directions, such as those for the change of scene in Act 1: 'The music begins quietly and tremblingly and grows gradually into a veritable flood. Gradually with the music the underground tomb in the courtyard of the castle becomes clearer. Through the darkness Ctirad can be seen slowly making his way down the broad stairs cut into the rock [. . .].' In accordance with this aesthetic, Zeyer's text avoids simultaneous solo singing (duets, trios etc.) and was conceived as a succession of monologues or dialogues rather than providing obvious cues for Italianate duets and ensembles. However, it freely allows choruses. A chorus of male heroes debates with Přemysl at the opening and punctuates the first scene with reactions to events such as the arrival and welcoming of Ctirad. Similarly a chorus of warrior women supports Šárka and comments on her plans throughout the second part of Act 1 and the first part of Act 2. The third act is dominated by choruses – male heroes, women from the people, choruses of girls and choruses of youths – to such an extent that the act takes on a static, oratorio-like character. There are several occasions in this act where Zeyer directed soloists and chorus to sing together but the only indication of soloists singing together is at the end of the long Ctirad-Šárka scene in Act 2, when four lines for each of them are noted as being sung 'simultaneously'.

Zeyer's alternation of choruses and solo parts breaks up what would otherwise be a steady flow and suggests set numbers, for instance at the beginning of Act 2, when choruses of warrior women frame Šárka's invocation to the moon. Further set-number suggestions can be read into Ctirad's monologue in Act 1, when he is alone for a long scena-type aria, or in Act 2, when the exchange between Ctirad and Šárka is conducted mostly in strophe-like stanzas rather than single-line exchanges that would be found in a more naturalistic conversation. The fact that the entire libretto is written in iambs (mostly unrhymed pentameters, though there are also some shorter lines)[6] gives it a high-flown 'poetic' feel. For all its Wagnerian allusions and its genre title 'music drama' this is an operatic libretto with plenty of scope for musically extended arias and other set numbers, though it stops short of providing opportunities for Italianate ensembles.

By August 1887 Janáček had set Zeyer's text in a piano-vocal score, had it copied out and sent it to Dvořák, who acknowledged its arrival at his holiday home in Vysoká on 6 August 1887.[7] If he was surprised to see the text he was meant to be setting himself surfacing in this way, his short letter to Janáček did not betray it; perhaps he had not properly looked at it at the time. It took some time, however, for Dvořák to talk to Janáček about it, a meeting that did not take place before November 1887 (see chap. 23). Janáček later remembered that

Dvořák's assessment went 'quite well',[8] but it could not have been wholly enthusiastic since he then completely rewrote the piece. There are thus two separate and distinct early versions of *Šárka*, one completed by mid-1887, and a second that was copied out by 18 June 1888, a version that Janáček then went on to orchestrate, though completing only Acts 1 and 2. Janáček's much later revisions in 1918 of the 1888 version were radical and transformed the piece into something quite different; these will be discussed in vol. ii. The present chapter is concerned only with the 1887 and 1888 versions and the light they shed on Janáček's opera aesthetic of the time.

In his reaction to Janáček's *Four Male-Voice Choruses* of 1885 (IV/17) Dvořák had asked for 'more melody'. Either he asked for it again in *Šárka*, or Janáček remembered this earlier criticism and set to work accordingly. This is clear from the expansion of lyrical passages, for instance in the two aria-type set pieces in Act 1: Přemysl's welcome to Ctirad after learning his name and his mission ('Bud' chrabrým') and, a little later, Ctirad's reflections on approaching Libuše's tomb to collect the magic weapons ('O svatý stíne').* In both cases Janáček added what could be regarded as a second verse. The new verses were without words: these had to be filled in later, in the former case only shortly before the opera's première in 1925. A similar instance is the extension of the Act 2 love duet for Šárka and Ctirad. Here again Janáček expanded his material musically – well beyond the dimensions of the original text.

An allied feature of the 1888 version is that the choruses became more substantial, both in texture and in length, especially in the first two acts. In Act 1, for instance, Ctirad's monologue is interrupted by the offstage strains of the women's war-chorus ('O běda kam zapadne náš sbor'). In the first version this was a mere 2-bar phase; in the second version it grew to a 20-bar chorus and, a little later, a new 32-bar chorus was added, derived from the same material. Similarly the chorus in which the women attempt to dissuade Šárka from her plan to seize the golden crown from the entombed Libuše ('O Šárko, nejdi blíž!') was expanded from 8 to 44 bars, their chorus of fear as Šárka carries

---

* As only the 1918 version of *Šárka* is published, I have given a few specific details of changes, with text incipits to help identify the passages in question. When comparing these comments to the published piano-vocal score (UE, 2002) readers should bear in mind that in his 1918 revisions Janáček made many changes to the solo voice parts.

on unconcerned ('Nás jímá strach') grew from 8 to 49 bars and the final chorus of the act, as the women run off in disarray ('Nás hltí tma'), has a 14-bar addition. The pattern is the same in Act 2: the opening chorus ('Juž zbledly hvězdy') was expanded from 9 to 38 bars and the womens' comments on Šárka's strange behaviour and methods ('O jak jsou tajemny') from 10 to 21 bars. In other words, in comparison with the 1887 version, Janáček's set numbers in 1888 became much more obvious, with second verses added.

Given all his other commitments, Janáček would have had little time for rewriting Šárka before his Christmas to New Year break. Soon after that there was a new première in Brno that would have an effect on Šárka – Smetana's Dalibor, given on 16 January 1888. Janáček was there and published his review two weeks later (xv/85). It is much more substantial than his usual opera reviews of the time and suggests that the work had a considerable impact on him. Dalibor had first been given in Prague twenty years earlier, but performances at the time were rare. Janáček had not come across it on stage before; he may, however, have prepared himself for the Brno première by studying the piano-vocal score that had been published in 1884:

We have had a decent time [Janáček wrote in Hudební listy] preparing for an uncommon treat on 16 January, Smetana's Dalibor was performed in Brno for the first time. Its effect was powerful, complete – like some sort of trance. We are, however, slowly coming out of this intoxication and already the second performance in no way prevented our following it calmly and comparing individual parts. (xv/85)

Janáček's review then goes on to enumerate these parts, drawing attention to 'tunes of well-thought-out forms, and of Czech character'. In his comments on particular numbers he also mentions more general technical devices such as transitions. And there is a statement that could almost refer to Janáček's later operatic style: the fact that apart from her duet with Dalibor 'Ó blaho neskonalé lásky', 'Milada sings in "an uncommon language for Czechs": i.e. with tunes formed chiefly according to the cadence of the rhythm of speech. Melodies that are more beautiful musically go into the orchestra'.

Although there are some obvious set numbers in Dalibor of a comparatively oldfashioned nature (strophic choruses, a cabaletta duet to conclude Act 1), the general impression that the opera gives is much more one of continuous thematic development. Dalibor has sometimes

313

been described as 'monothematic', suggesting that Smetana used Lisztian-type thematic metamorphosis to generate his melodic material and thereby create a musically unified, developmental flow that links larger scene sections. It is this aspect that Janáček latched on to in his 1888 revision of *Šárka*, and there are substantial sections that became thematically connected in this way.

For instance, when revising the beginning of Act 3, Janáček did so by scrapping a number of sections based on different themes in favour of a more unified section based on the continuous development of a single theme, that of the opening prelude. Similarly in Act 1 Helfert demonstrated[9] how the second half was based on developments of a descending theme, sometimes in combination with another (his ex. 76). This, however, was achieved only in the 1888 version; its counterpart in 1887 was built on a greater number of themes and sections. This tendency towards reducing the number of themes and instead developing and varying what is there anticipates Janáček's method in his mature operas of using a first version as something to generate ideas and to grasp the shape of the work before rigorously pulling it together in a completely rewritten second version (see vol. ii: How Janáček composed operas).

Helfert saw Janáček as directly following Smetana's practice in *Libuše* – logically enough, since the libretto followed on from that of *Libuše*. Although Janáček did possess a piano vocal-score of *Libuše*, his markings, with their reference to Hipp's chronoscope (see vol. ii: 1922), would appear to be of a much later date and there is no direct evidence that he saw the opera on stage before 1909 (XV/195). *Dalibor*, performed in Brno at the time of Janáček's revisions of *Šárka*, seems a more plausible model. Quite apart from whatever improvements Dvořák may have suggested, Janáček's new version of *Šárka*, prepared over the first few months of 1888, was written in the shadow of Smetana's *Dalibor*.

When one considers Janáček's *Šárka* one must remember how ambitious a piece it was for Janáček at the time. Although it is a short opera, lasting little over an hour, it was nevertheless by far the longest piece he had written to date. Apart from student exercises and an early song (V/1) he had written no music for solo voice; apart from the destroyed melodrama *Death* (X/3), allegedly with an orchestral accompaniment, he had written no music for full orchestra, although he had considerable experience in conducting orchestras. The one genre in which he had some expertise to draw on was writing for chorus – the many choruses that Zeyer included may have been one of the attractions of the piece – even if most of his earlier choruses were unaccompanied. Helfert rated it highly: 'At the time it was written, Janáček's *Šárka* was the most perfect and stylistically the purest Czech tragic opera of its time besides [Fibich's] *The Bride of Messina*',[10] a verdict delivered in 1924 during Janáček's lifetime, and which gave the composer much pleasure.

However, Janáček's 1888 *Šárka* was destined never to be heard. When he saw Dvořák in Prague, Dvořák presumably drew Janáček's attention to the fact that the libretto had been written for him (i.e. Dvořák) and that Janáček had better clear it with Zeyer and get formal permission. Janáček's letters to Zeyer have disappeared, but those Zeyer wrote to Janáček exist, and must have given him quite a shock:

Esteemed Sir [Zeyer wrote on 10 November 1887]
  I much regret if this will be unpleasant for you but I cannot consent to your composing music to my *Šárka*. Believe me, I have very strong reasons.
  Besides, you yourself can take some of the blame in this matter. Allow me to say to you that you should surely have asked me first before sending into the world your outline for an opera to my text. Your music will certainly not be lost because of this; you can use it in some other way. In any event, my name would only harm you with the management of the National Theatre since I have only opponents there.
  Forgive me if I have possibly caused you a nasty moment, remember that you have also caused me one.[11]

When, many years later, Janáček commented on this, he declared that he had not known how the opera would turn out and so he had written it first, and only when Dvořák had seen it and his verdict 'turned out quite well' did he ask Zeyer for his permission. Not taking Zeyer's 'no' for an answer, he wrote again, and this time received a longer and much more emphatic letter:

It seems [Zeyer wrote again on 17 November 1887] that you did not receive my first letter and so it becomes my very unpleasant duty to tell you once again that I *do not give my consent* for you to use my *Šárka* as a text for your opera. I have very serious reasons for this, which have absolutely nothing to do with you personally and therefore there is nothing in my conduct to cause you offence.

Zeyer, on the other hand, was himself offended, presumably by Janáček's mentioning that he had made a few changes for which he wanted his approval. Janáček must also have invoked Dvořák, and this didn't go down well either:

I must add that either Mr Dvořák or you are mistaken [the same letter continues]. I did not offer either him or anyone else my *Šárka*. He invited me, through the good offices of Prof. Sládek, to write a text for an opera for him. I was glad to comply with his wishes. He did not agree with my views on opera, he did not like my text and so he did not compose *Šárka*. I could not really hold this against him, and we remained good friends.[12]

It is characteristic of Janáček that he simply ignored the implications of what Zeyer wrote and, in denial, went on to produce a complete second version of his opera. It was only when he got to orchestrating the final act that he lost heart. Had Zeyer not only given his permission for Janáček to use his libretto but lent his influence to securing a performance of the work in Prague, one wonders whether the whole course of Janáček's life might not have been changed. Would a *Šárka* by Janáček performed in Prague, in say 1889, have won the golden opinions that Helfert gave it in 1924? Had it been performed and been successful then, might Janáček have gone on writing works in this vein – works which today might be as seldom performed as *Šárka*? But because of Zeyer's interdict *Šárka* never got even to Brno. It was a bitter blow at the time, but it did Janáček a favour. Instead of pursuing a path well trodden by others in Prague and beyond, Janáček turned abruptly away from this style and subject matter. Moravian folk music, an interest lurking in the background for a couple of years, became a passion, cultivated with all Janáček's impulsive energy. Out of it came a distinctive stylistic amalgam that would characterize Janáček's later music.

III

THE BLACK RIBBON
(1888–1903)

27

Summer 1888–90

In the eight months up to June 1888 Janáček had suffered three substantial blows to his self-esteem. In November 1887 Julius Zeyer refused permission for his opera text *Šárka* to be set to music, with the result that Janáček's first opera was dead in the water as far as a production was concerned. In June 1888 Janáček's edgy relationship with the Brno Beseda collapsed again and he resigned, and this time no-one tried to get him to reconsider. And with the end of the Beseda relationship came the end of his journal *Hudební listy*.

It says much about Janáček's obstinate nature that none of these upsets seemed to have made much difference and, if anything, simply strengthened his will. With *Šárka* he went on to write a new, second version of the opera and began orchestrating it. Although he no longer ran his own journal, he transferred his journalistic activities elsewhere: within two years he was writing regular reviews for the new Moravian newspaper *Moravské listy*. Conducting stopped, but that perhaps was a blessing: he no longer had to deal with truculent members of the Brno Beseda executive committee who had a less cultivated agenda for Brno, nor did he have to cajole reluctant choir members into turning up for rehearsals. Instead, all his excess energy (and it needs to be remembered that his three day-jobs continued: the Teachers' Institute, the Czech Gymnasium II, the Organ School – and maybe still the Staré Brno monastery choir) was directed elsewhere; Janáček reinvented himself as a musical ethnographer.

This transformation had already been quietly in progress for a couple of years even before 1886, when Janáček reviewed Kuba's collection of Slav folksongs (xv/65; see chap. 28). Now that he suddenly had more free time, he poured it into this new outlet. The fact that he was a new father seems only to have increased his *joie de vivre*. His son Vladimír (see Plate 13) was a source of intense pride and pleasure from the start. As Zdenka recalled:

He was happy, he was proud of the little fellow, he held him in his arms, he played with him – how different he'd been with Olga, and only because she wasn't a boy. He even put up with the fact, although with evident distaste, that for the puerperium, Mama was with us in order to look after me. The christening was the most lavish imaginable. Papa was the godfather,* the god-mother Lorka [Janáček's sister Eleonora]. We called the boy Vladimír to have a counterpart to Olga.[1]

It was no doubt also a source of happiness for Zdenka to discover that she had at last got something right. The beginnings, however, were difficult. When Vladimír was born on 16 May 1888 she was already exhausted, having had to nurse Olga, who in February became ill with an infection of the joints and around the heart. The new arrival was very weak, Zdenka had little milk and the doctor declared that only a wet-nurse could save the child. Janáček, however, refused to pay for one, and it was only after an appeal to Zdenka's father that a compromise was reached: Schulz paid the 12 zl a month for the wet-nurse, the Janáčeks paid for her food. Except of course Janáček didn't give Zdenka any extra for this, so that, as she eagerly relates, she cooked well for Cilka, the wet-nurse (who needed to be well nourished), while she herself made do on scraps – Zdenka the Martyr again. However, her sacrifice paid off: the little boy began to thrive, domestic peace returned, and after six months, when Vladimír was weaned, Cilka had become so much part of the family and was so devoted to her little charge that she stayed on as a domestic servant.[2]

By the time Vladimír was born, Olga was getting on for six and was an intelligent, pretty, cheerful if occasionally difficult child, having inherited her father's stubbornness. Zdenka reports that Janáček had come to love her 'in his own way' but remained rather detached: he didn't miss her when he was away, and was generally a severe father who 'knew the rod rather than the caress'. With his little son it was a different matter:

* Schulz was not Janáček's first choice. Karel Janáček, who was godfather to Olga, wrote on 29 May 1888 (BmJA, A 4657) excusing himself – he had unavoidable duties that day – and suggested that Janáček ask his father-in-law, which, he wrote, was a more 'frequent' practice.

As we watched him grow up, we took greater and greater pleasure in him. Dark eyes after Leoš, golden-haired, dark eyebrows, lovely white skin – an exquisite child. He was always high-spirited, he laughed and sang the whole day long. For his age he was uncommonly clever: already at two and a half he spoke entirely correctly. He wore a broad hat and carried a little stick when he went for walks. He greeted the ladies and gentlemen whom he knew; he'd say 'rukulíbám'[†] and with charming politeness raised his broad hat at the same time. And he was a good child. When he was given some little treat, he didn't put the morsel into his mouth without first sharing it out with all of us. He liked his former wet-nurse Cilka best of all. When 'Nána', as he called her, was with him, I could go about my social duties without anxiety: the little boy didn't miss me. Cilka also doted on him and found it difficult to part with him when she left after two years in service with us.

Leoš avidly registered the first signs of musical ability in his young son: his little songs, well in tune, and his interest in the piano. When Leoš worked, Vladíček sat down next to him, observing him fixedly, and listened. And when Leoš went off, the little boy climbed on to the piano stool and began to 'play', and with a pencil scrawled in the music as if he were writing. His Daddy would take him up in his arms and say happily: 'My lad, you'll be a musician.'[3]

Towards the end of the school term, in the summer of 1888, Janáček's domestic worries over his ailing family and his professional batterings finally seem to have got the better of him and, with the support of Schulz, he applied to the Regional School Board for funds to go to the spa in Gräfenberg[‡] to treat his 'rheumatic pains and nerves'. He had suffered long and dangerous illness in the family, he wrote to the board on 19 July, and had almost exhausted his financial means.[4] Presumably the application to go there was unsuccessful: there is no record of payment by the school board and, judging from the fuss over the wet-nurse, it seems unlikely that Janáček could have financed the trip himself; Gräfenberg (today's Lázně Jeseník) doesn't feature in the list of spas in his autobiography. Instead he seems to have gone to Hukvaldy and continued his folk-music collecting in the area, as a press report of 17 January 1889 claims: 'As we have heard, the outstanding artist and musical composer Mr Leoš Janáček studied Valachian dance music during this last summer and has collected much valuable material.'[5]

Apart from a few reviews of folksong collections that Janáček published (see chap. 28), this is the first public acknowledgement of

[†] 'I kiss your hand', a greeting to ladies in polite society, even then somewhat antiquated.
[‡] The famous Silesian spa where Vincenc Priessnitz had devised his water cure (see chap. 45).

Janáček's activity in this field. It is tantalizing that this crucial summer, this turning-point in Janáček's career, is so little documented, but this much at least is clear: that some time after 16 June 1888, when Josef Štross dated his copy of the piano-vocal score of *Šárka* (second version), Janáček went on to orchestrate two acts – and then stopped. And some time before January 1889 Janáček had arranged for full orchestra some of the folk dances that he had collected in the Hukvaldy area. He got Štross to copy out the full-score version of two acts of *Šárka* and then put all the scores away; they would not re-emerge until thirty years later. Instead, *Moravské noviny* could hardly keep up with the news items about Janáček's ethnographic activities into which he now poured his energies. The anonymous announcement on 17 January 1889 about Janáček's summer was followed four days later by a report that 'Vesna' would be practising the ritual folk dances and songs *The Little Queens*, based on material made available by Janáček, as well as 'Valachian folk dances'.[6] A month later *Moravské noviny* announced that these rehearsals would now lead to a public performance:

The music accompanying the Valachian dances was composed by the collector, the musical director Leoš Janáček, and it can be said in advance that these graceful dances, which have never before been danced outside our Valašsko, will be the most splendid number of the entertainment and will certainly become the adornment of Czech dancing entertainments.[7]

Yet another announcement specified that the 'entertainment' would take place on 21 February 1889 at the Besední dům under the auspices of 'Vesna', and would begin with *The Little Queens*, after which Valachian dances such as the handsaw dance, the smoke dance, mazurka and others would be performed.[8]

The press reports of the entertainment are unclear about which version of *The Little Queens* was used. Performed by women or girls from 'Vesna' under the supervision of Mrs Lucie Bakešová, it might have been the piano-accompanied arrangements that Janáček made (IV/20), or merely the version that had been collected by Bakešová and her husband František Bakeš, which had already been given several times, for instance at Ořechov near Brno on 15 July 1888. But it is clear that the performance of the *Valachian Dances* for orchestra on 21 February 1889 constituted the first outing of two dances (*Oldfashioned Dance I, Handsaw Dance*) from the complex of Janáček's *Valachian*

Dances (vi/4) (see chap. 30). The announcement quoted above makes it sound like more than two dances, but Janáček's arrangements combine several: his *Oldfashioned Dance I* included the *Mazurka*, and the *Handsaw Dance* included the *Smoke Dance*. The orchestra was the band of the 8th Infantry Regiment conducted by its bandmaster Josef Opelt, the 'forty dancers' rehearsed by one Jan Šimůnek. The evening was considered to be a great success and the *Valachian Dances* such a hit that another performance was announced for 3 March in the Besední dům, this time under the aegis of the Czech Readers' Club.

The concert of 21 February marked several beginnings. In addition to Janáček's new image as someone working with Moravian folk music, it is also the start of his collaboration with the folksong collector Lucie Bakešová (1853–1935). From the Bakeš estate in Ořechovičky near Brno, she had already initiated an energetic programme for stimulating performances of folk dances and folk rituals. Soon Janáček and Bakešová (together with another collector, Xavera Běhálková) would begin the publication of a series of folk dances arranged for piano by Janáček with choreographic descriptions by Bakešová (viii/10) and together they would take a major share in organizing the Moravian folk-music contribution to the 1895 Ethnographic Exhibition in Prague. Bakešová was a year older than Janáček and, although she was respectful of his status as a professional musician, her impatience and forthright plain-speaking sometimes outstripped her tact. After 1895 the friendship cooled.

The performance of the *Valachian Dances* was also the first time that a piece by Janáček for full orchestra had been given, with the exception of the orchestral accompaniment to his melodrama *Death* (x/3), heard once in 1876 and seemingly destroyed. Janáček had been thinking orchestrally while orchestrating *Šárka*, and it seems to have been a logical transition for him to have taken his folk music activities into this sphere. In this way he graduated from the collecting of folk dances in his native area to promoting them publicly in Brno, re-creating for a large symphony orchestra dances that in their native habitat would often be accompanied by no more than a single instrument such as a cimbalom.

While Janáček would add to his collection of folk dances over the next two or three years and get them performed locally, he soon had more ambitious plans for them. Fired up by their success on 21 February he wrote immediately to František Adolf Šubert, the director of the

National Theatre in Prague, about the dances that had been performed that evening:

I collected them in my native region and composed the music to them.

The success, owing to their earthy character and charm, was complete. Even the critics write in this vein.[5]

So I am asking you respectfully whether these *Valachian Dances* might be accepted for performance at the National Theatre?

If such a performance would coincide with the intentions of the National Theatre, I'd be willing to send to the esteemed directorate both the score and the written-out parts as well as photographs of important moments with the relevant descriptions.

According to what I've heard, these dances are to be repeated on 2 March. I would send you a respectful invitation when the matter is decided for certain, so that you could see for yourself the effectiveness of both music and dances.[9]

The comment about the 'photographs of important moments' is an indication that Janáček's aim was not merely the stylized re-creations of folk dances for symphony orchestra, but arrangements that to some extent allowed for the original dance steps. In collecting, Janáček often noted the steps and wrote down choreographic descriptions, and it is evident that despite his own lack of skill in dancing (see chap. 23) he was well informed in these matters. Thus when there was a performance of these two dances planned in Olomouc, and enquiries were made as to what exactly the dancers were meant to be doing, he was able to send precise instructions:

According to the wishes of Mrs Lucie Bakešová I venture to give you a few indications concerning the performance of the *Valachian Dances*. It's complicated at the beginning of *Oldfashioned Dance/Ribbon Dance* since I have combined two dances.

It contains:
1) a similar march-step to that of a polonaise.
2) turning on the spot.
3) a march movement, hands aloft holding ribbons.
4) slow turning with raised hands.
5) quick turning.[10]

Then follow detailed instructions concerning where in the music these figures should be undertaken.

---

[5]There was of course no time for reviews since Janáček was writing just after the concert. Perhaps he was referring to the pre-concert publicity.

František Adolf Šubert was a dominant figure at the National Theatre for some twenty years. He and Janáček had already clashed over the use of National Theatre soloists in Beseda concerts (see chap. 23) and he would go on to play a part in Janáček's life both in negotiations at the National Theatre during this period, and also several years later when he became director of the new Vinohrady Theatre in Prague. The National Theatre, which performed drama, opera and ballet, was always on the lookout for popular novelties, and Šubert responded quickly and positively to Janáček's proposal: he would send his ballet master, Augustin Berger, to Brno for the repeat performance to see whether the National Theatre could make use of Janáček's dances.[11] Berger was indeed there on 2 March 1889, and three days later Šubert wrote to Janáček again:

According to the report from our ballet master Berger, we could make use of the two dance numbers he saw in Brno only as insertions and not as an independent dance. For this reason I'd be ready to insert these two dances into the whole-evening ballet that we are preparing now, namely *A Tale of Happiness Found* by Berger and Kovařovic. Please let me know for how much you would, dear sir, let us have the two dances, i.e. the score of these compositions.[12]

Janáček was delighted: 'Kindly make me an offer', he telegrammed back to Šubert,[13] but once he'd thought about it more he changed his mind. Maybe he didn't care for having a work of his inserted into one by Karel Kovařovic, whose last opera he had so contemptuously dismissed in his review (XV/70), or perhaps he saw greater opportunities beckoning. A few days later he wrote back:

Thank you for the trust and favour expressed [in your letter].

I have, however, many concrete objections to the performance of my *Valachian Dances* as insertions in the ballet *A Tale of Happiness Found*.

My spirit speaks to me more to compose an independent ballet in a unified style from the rich and effective Valachian motifs. I have also said as much to Mr Berger.

So I am offering such a work [i.e. an independent ballet] to the esteemed directorate.

In order for you to build up confidence I am willing to send you the score and parts of a single dance. After hearing it, kindly tell me whether there are enough vigorous motifs in the piece so that I would be able to compose a whole work.

At the same time I should say that I already have most of the work done and

that the whole piece could be ready before the summer season. For this purpose I have offered to collaborate with Mr Berger.
Kindly let me know whether you agree with my proposal.[14]

Naturally the National Theatre was not going to be sold an entire
ballet on the basis of a single dance by a then unknown composer
and demanded to see the whole score and the whole scenario before
making up their minds.[15] So Janáček set to work. Even if he was not
exaggerating when he wrote that he had much of the music ready, there
was still the question of the scenario. Here he made use of the contacts
built up during his editorship of *Hudební listy* and turned to the Moravian novelist Václav Kosmák, whose *About the Fair* he had serialized in
the journal. Within a couple of weeks he had coaxed something out of
Kosmák, Janáček's first active collaboration with a librettist. As soon
as Kosmák got down to work he realized that this couldn't be a ballet
with a story enacted purely through music but that there would need to
be spoken dialogue as well, and so he set up a meeting with Janáček
to talk it through.[16] A second surviving note from Kosmák accompanied a draft of the putative ballet: 'Here is a sketch of the idyllic
scene, *Valachian Dances*. According to your wishes, I've compressed
everything into *one* scene. It can be changed a lot if anything occurs to
you, and wherever you want.' All this was produced very quickly,
probably by the end of March 1889, and it sounds from Kosmák's
postscript as if speed rather than quality had been the priority: 'Don't
announce in Prague or in the newspapers that it's I who wrote the
libretto.'[17] Maybe Janáček had doubts too, and sent to Šubert an
account of the scenario for a preliminary appraisal:

I want to submit *Valachian Dances*, an idyllic picture in one act, to the directorate. Before I write the libretto into the score, I'd be glad, however, to know
whether it isn't too superficial, insufficiently detailed perhaps, and whether it
can be recommended at all in this form. I also ask you, if it doesn't take up too
much time, to give me your very brief verdict.

  Contents: The Hukvaldy Burgrave is arranging a celebration in honour of
the officer who has arrived at the manor with a press-gang. The festivities are
interrupted when Vojtěch and Václav rush on to the stage seeking protection
with the Burgrave's wife from the press-gang pursuing them. One young man
from the village has to be conscripted, the choice, however, is difficult. The two
that have been caught are twins and both are engaged. On a whim the officer
pronounces they should compete by dancing. This doesn't help since each
dances as beautifully as the other. They draw lots and the choice falls on

Vojtěch. General emotion and regret. Janek, however, a clumsy fellow whom all the girls despise, wants to be a soldier and continually brags and pushes himself forward. Moved by the ardent love of Anežka and Vojtěch, the Burgrave's wife begs the officer to take Janek in exchange for Vojtěch. Gallantly, he agrees.[18]

Janáček followed this summary of the plot with a cast list of sixteen characters, filling out those named above with typical village types such a clerk, a bailiff, the mayor and a forester, as well as a chorus that includes soldiers, the 'Valachian people' and 'musicians with a cimbalom player'. The action is to take place in the manor gardens, with the Hukvaldy ruins in the background; the period is 'rococo from the time of Maria Theresa'.

Then follows an account, number by number, with some dialogue included (though from Janáček's comment at the end that 'it goes without saying that nothing is spoken and only acted' this may have been merely an indication of what needed to be mimed by the dancers). The fact that the first four numbers are given in considerable detail and the remaining seven with just a line or two suggests that the scenario was still being fleshed out. In his letter Janáček stated that he had finished his music, which needed just a couple of weeks for the copyists to be finished.[19]

On 10 April 1889, four days after the première at the Prague National Theatre of the 'fantastic ballet' *A Tale of Happiness Found* by Kovařovic and Berger (without of course any contribution from Janáček), Berger sent a note to Janáček saying that he very much liked the scenario and it would be placed before Šubert on his return from holiday the next day: Berger couldn't take a decision on his own to accept it. As a postscript he mentioned that he was sending back a folk costume to Zdenka 'only now'. This suggests that there had been some friendly interchange between him and the Janáčeks when he came to Brno for the concert on 2 March and that he had returned to Prague with a Valašsko folk costume as a model.[20]

It was a month before Šubert got back to Janáček. On 13 May he wrote: 'The action of your ballet announced to me is fine but very simple in its nature. Its effectiveness will thus depend on the music and on the character of the dances.' He would be able to make a decision only once Janáček had sent on the score and the libretto. As with Berger's note, the tone was encouraging: 'It would be very nice for me', he concluded, 'if it turned out that we can give your work with good results – especially since it will be a Czech-Moravian national ballet.[21]

While Janáček, his copyists and Kosmák worked away, there was yet another performance of Janáček's *Valachian Dances* in Brno, this time at a concert on 23 May 1889 of the Brno Beseda under its new conductor Josef Kompit. It was a typical mixed programme of orchestral and vocal pieces, including Janáček's *The Warning* from his *Four Male-Voice Choruses* (IV/17), seemingly the première of this individual chorus. Among the orchestral works, together with Dvořák's *Czech Suite* and the prelude to Smetana's *Libuše*, were 'L. Janáček: *Valachian Dances* (new)', as the printed programme put it. It is only from reviews, for example the one published in *Dalibor*,[22] that one learns that, while Kompit was in charge of the vocal works, the orchestral items were in the hands of bandmaster Opelt, again conducting the band of the 8th Infantry Regiment. It is tempting to speculate that Opelt simply repeated the two dances he had already conducted in February, but the word 'new' in the programme is arresting and suggests that different ones were given:[II] after all there were many more to choose from as Janáček had now written a whole ballet made up of Valachian dances. A review, originally printed in the Brno newspaper *Hlas*, suggests that a new type of Janáček was beginning to emerge as a composer:

Without doubt a new period in Janáček's creative activity began with the publication of a collection of male choruses two years ago [IV/17], in which the composer continued down a path already evident to the alert observer in his earlier pieces. [. . .] And we consider the greatest merit of Janáček's compositions is that he holds to the path taken, that he writes as his inner self dictates, free of any attempt to conduct himself according to recognized models, free even of the fear of suggesting some composer or other by some turn of phrase. [. . .] As far as the harmonic voice-leading and orchestration is concerned, Janáček doesn't go down the old, well-trodden paths but conducts himself according to the demands and possibilities of a modern direction for music.[23]

Once the concert was out of the way and the music no longer needed in Brno, Janáček sent the score and parts of his *Valachian Dances* ballet to Prague, accompanied by a letter hoping 'that the music will be so substantial that the piece would be worthy of performance'. He

---

[II] In her detailed study of Janáček's dances, Jarmila Procházková has suggested that these were a *Smoke Dance* and a *Lachian Triple Dance* (Procházková 1992–3, 316).

suggested a few last-minute metronome marks and then left the work 'in the hands of the Lord God'[24] and, of course, those of Šubert. Some time after that there were the Organ School exams – this was the first year that women had been admitted[25] – and then, accompanied by his daughter Olga, he went off to Hukvaldy for the summer.

Zdenka didn't join them. In her memoirs she mentioned how Janáček's sister Josefa had come to stay the previous Christmas and had offered her views on weaning Vladimír. Zdenka had taken umbrage ('I told her that as an unmarried woman without experience this was something she simply didn't understand') and Josefa lost her temper, while Janáček took her side against Zdenka. 'It was clear that Josefka and I wouldn't get on. And indeed despite all attempts at friendship, our mutual dislike extended throughout our lives until her death. It upset Leoš, he wanted to bring us together. But he was always a bad psychologist and a bad diplomat: his attempts at reconciliation drove us even further apart.' Going to Hukvaldy to stay with Josefa that summer was one such attempt:

It suddenly became important for him that we should spend the holidays all together, although for so many years before he'd wanted to be on his own. How gladly I'd have gone with him to any other place. But the memory of the ruined Christmas took away my appetite for a stay with my sister-in-law. My husband, however, insisted on Hukvaldy, and only Hukvaldy. And here I rebelled: I sent Oluška off with him and for my part remained at home with the little boy.[26]

As Zdenka ruefully recalled, this turned out to be a bad idea: 'Leoš was so angry with me that he didn't send me a single line throughout the summer.' Indeed for Zdenka's twenty-fourth birthday on 30 July, it was the seven-year-old Olga who sent good wishes from Hukvaldy, her first surviving communication.[27] 'And later I [Zdenka] found out that he'd taken his revenge on me through something far worse.'[28]

'I'm certainly an impatient fellow in your eyes', Janáček wrote to Šubert some time during the summer. 'I can't help it, however, as I've not received any answer either to my parcel or to my letter sent two months ago.' He was thinking of going to Prague early the next month and hoped that by then the matter of his ballet would be decided. On Janáček's letter Šubert scribbled the instruction that the conductors should deliver a report,[29] which they duly did. It was entirely negative:

'*All three*' felt that Janáček's ballet would not be a success for Janáček or for 'our national institute' and Šubert was returning the score.[30] However, it took considerable effort on Janáček's part over the next two months to get back his score and orchestral parts:

Now for the third time [Janáček wrote to Šubert in December 1889] and always in vain I'm asking for you to send back the *orchestral parts* of my *Valachian Dances*.

Since they are on the programme for the gala theatre performance in aid of the lottery for the 'Provisional National Theatre in Brno' on *Saturday* the 21st of this month, it is high time for you to send them to me *immediately* by return of post.[31]

As Janáček resignedly cut his losses with Prague he began to explore how else he might capitalize on the local success of his dances: 'I've written *Valachian Dances* for orchestra', he wrote to the leading Prague music publisher F.A. Urbánek on 5 December. 'Some of them, finished last year, were given three times in Brno and much liked according to the reviews in *Dalibor, Moravská orlice*, etc. I've now finished the whole cycle, eight dances.'[32] By 'three times in Brno' Janáček was presumably referring to the performances on 21 February, 2 March and 23 May described above, though this is the first allusion to the number of dances that Janáček had written by now. Urbánek responded immediately with a request to look at the dances and for Janáček's conditions.[33] Also on 5 December Janáček wrote to another, smaller, Prague publisher, Bursík & Kohout. Janáček's letter has disappeared, but their answer (written the same day as Urbánek's one) survives and presumably seemed to Janáček more positive and promising than Urbánek's: they were willing to publish Janáček's *Valachian Dances* first for piano (two or four hands) and then for orchestra, though of course they wanted to have a look at them first.[34]

Meanwhile Janáček's attempts to get the orchestral parts back from Šubert had got no further and it was only his desperate note, written on 14 December, a week before the charity concert, that finally got results.[35] The concert, a bizarre mixture that included Act 1 of Smetana's *Dalibor*, a one-act play *Telegram* by Gustav Pfleger-Moravský, and a 'scene prologue' by the Moravian novelist Josef Merhaut, *Moravia before the Cathedral of Art*, did indeed include two of Janáček's *Valachian Dances* (it's not known which). This time the reviews (e.g. in *Moravské listy*) were less favourable:

The *Valachian Dances*, composed by L. Janáček, with which the performance opened, seem to be somewhat overfull and oversaturated, the melody runs in a lively fashion from one voice to another while the other voices take care of a contrapuntal accompaniment out of some sort of noisy necessity. Too much striving for idiosyncrasies, both instrumental and harmonic, is evident overall, though one cannot deny the conscientious quality of the dances – perhaps overdone – and their national colour. So far everything seethes and makes a noise, pushing its way by force into the score. We don't doubt that in Janáček we have a gifted force as a composer who in time will develop and find understanding and appreciation.[36]

Part of the problem may have been that Janáček's dances were at a disadvantage in the company of Dvořák's effortlessly crafted and orchestrated *Slavonic Dances*. Two of the three earlier performances of the *Valachian Dances* had been with dancers, thus emphasizing the folkloristic element even more; detached from this element and performed merely as art music, they came across as clumsy and overdone. Janáček's orchestration has always been controversial, but in these very early pieces he was still learning his craft.

Despite this setback another performance of the dances went ahead the next month, on 12 January 1890, this time at a costume ball at the National House, Olomouc. The dances (once again the *Old-fashioned Dance I* and the *Handsaw Dance*) were clearly context-sensitive: danced by women in local costumes, together with other dances from Haná arranged by the Olomouc composer Antonín Petzold, they were rated a great success in the reviews, 'a divine fruit' worthy of the company of Smetana, Dvořák and Křížkovský.[37] The orchestra was another military band (that of the 93rd Infantry Regiment), the conductor Cyril Metoděj Hrazdira (a graduate of Janáček's Organ School), who would go on to conduct the première of *Jenůfa*.

Janáček himself wasn't at the costume ball. A warm-hearted letter from Ignác Wurm (a distinguished Moravian patriot, unusually both a priest and a member of the Austrian assembly) offered accommodation and looked forward eagerly to his arrival.[38] But a second letter from Wurm regretted that Janáček hadn't been able to enjoy his triumph, having gone down with flu.[39] Brno had been overwhelmed by a flu epidemic that affected most of the teaching staff of the Teachers' Institute in Brno,[40] As Zdenka recalled, the entire Janáček family was afflicted:

Christmas Day we still celebrated cheerfully. My parents were invited to our place, everything went beautifully, only Olinka was coughing a little. The next day she got measles. My brother and Vladíček caught the infection from her. Then Cilka had to go to bed: she had flu. Immediately afterwards Leoš fell ill. It was like a field hospital at our place. Neither of my parents came to us because they didn't want to spread the infection from my brother, we couldn't send anyone to them because people were frightened of the new illness and didn't want to go anywhere where somebody was ill. I rushed from bed to bed in an unhappy daze until one day I caught it as well. [...] No one came to us, elsewhere whole families also fell ill, day and night the streets rumbled with the sounds of doctors' carriages. But as far as I know nobody died of flu then and at Carnival people were already dancing again merrily.[41]

In March 1890 Bursík & Kohout wrote again to Janáček: they would be prepared to publish two of his dances in full score providing he could guarantee a sale of twenty copies at full retail price (in his letter to them of 3 March Janáček had apparently mentioned an admirer who might buy a few copies).[42] Another letter a week later added that if the orchestral arrangement was liked the firm would then go ahead and publish the piano arrangements for two or four hands.[43] Armed with this information, Janáček wrote to Mrs Bakešová, who would be responsible for the choreographic descriptions:

Dear Madam

I venture to give you news about how far negotiations for printing the dances have proceeded.

I have come to an agreement with the firm Bursík & Kohout. In the beginning they didn't want to publish the score at large expense for a small sale. After my pleading they eventually agreed to publish two dances in full score – as a trial and on condition that I find a patron who will buy twenty copies of the score. I remembered the promise of the owner of the estate in Rychaltice in Valašsko, that he wanted to support the printing and promotion of the dances in an appropriate way. So I've written to him now. Of course I don't yet have an answer.

After the scores are published, piano arrangements for two and four hands will come out.

A special selection of the songs A Bouquet of Moravian Folksongs [XIII/1] (174) will be published in pocket format in a fortnight. You will be sure to like it. The print-run will be 3000 copies; so we hope that it will be sold out within a month![44]

This letter provides an excellent picture of Janáček's publishing activities in 1890–1, his most productive year so far in this sphere.

Janáček's 'patron' responded positively and on 18 April Bursík & Kohout wrote to say that they had already published two of Janáček's *Valachian Dances*, though without the titles in Russian, as requested.[45] The score, with its beautifully engraved title page, was dedicated to 'Marie Jungová', a native of the region who had guided Janáček in his folkloristic investigations and taken him, for instance, to hear the cimbalom player Jan Myška.[46] It has been assumed[47] that her husband Arnold Janda was the 'patron', but it seems more likely to have been her father, Josef Jung senior, a well-known local landowner and a friend of Janáček's. Janáček's letter to Bakešová states that the patron was 'the owner of the estate in Rychaltice in Valašsko' (whereas Janda had been, since 1884, a state engineer in Kroměříž). Furthermore, if Janda was paying for the publication, would he not have been offended that it carried the name of his wife with her maiden name rather than her married name? There is one more curiosity about this publication: it is given an opus number, op. 2.[¶] This would appear to signal the importance that Janáček attached to the publication, though he soon went off the idea of opus numbers (his Suite with folk dances is 'op. 3', with which the numbering ends).

Despite Janáček's confidence, and despite the subvention (estimated by Bursík & Kohout to be a maximum of 5 zl a copy, i.e. 100 zl),[48] the publication seems not to have been a commercial success as the firm did not follow it up with a piano version. The next year Janáček and Bakešová undertook this themselves, publishing *Folk Dances in Moravia* (VIII/10) privately. But the *Bouquet of Moravian Folksongs* (XIII/1), if it didn't sell out its 3000-copy print-run in a month, did so within a couple of years, with a second edition issued in 1892.[**] This tiny booklet, a collection of 174 songs, was put together by Janáček and his superior at the Czech Gymnasium II, František Bartoš, and was designed for use in schools and educational establishments: folksong words and tunes for class-singing that could help to reinforce the Moravian folk heritage among young people in town schools. It would become a vital adjunct to Janáček's own work as a teacher, and he went on to provide harmonizations for almost a third of the songs (V/2).

Soon it was time for another summer holiday, and this time Zdenka

---

[¶] Janáček's op. 1, mentioned as such in a letter to Zdenka, though not on the actual manuscript, was his Theme and Variations (VIII/6) of a decade earlier; see chap. 15.

[**] Not 1893 as in *JAWO*, 341.

felt she would have to go to Hukvaldy with her husband and the children, Josefa notwithstanding. But in fact the problems came from quite a different quarter:

At first I didn't regret it. This time, misgivings about my sister-in-law seemed misplaced; she was kind to me, we kept house together and got on well. And Hukvaldy was really beautiful – the castle, the deep forests, the mountains; in a short while I fell in love with everything. The people were welcoming, kind, one fitted in among them as if in a family. At first Leoš spent a lot of time with the children and me. He took us for walks, he showed us the herds of fallow deer in the park, he taught us how we could get almost right up to them. I was interested most of all in the herd of black Spanish horses. [. . .] For me it was a delight to see so many beautiful animals here together, to be able to stroke them, speak to them, give them sugar, look into their beautiful fiery eyes, and observe how their arched nostrils flared proudly. At six in the evening the horn was sounded on the Hukvaldy stud-farm and then the whole herd galloped home. It was dangerous to get in their path at that moment, but the magnificent wild ride was splendid to watch from the sidelines. [. . .]

And here again of course the inevitable shadow had to fall. Once my husband and I were walking from the park. As we were approaching the brewery, a carriage in which a lady was sitting was just going into the gates. Leoš entirely brightened up, he took off his hat and waved it in greeting. The lady returned the greeting in a friendly fashion. 'You know, that's Mrs Rakowitschová', he said to me.[49]

Františka Rakowitschová (1864–1950) was the second daughter of Josef Jung and a sister of Marie Jungová (the dedicatee of the *Valachian Dances*), married to a forestry official who worked in Hukvaldy on the estate of the Archbishop of Olomouc. According to Zdenka, she was 'a chestnut brunette with wide lips, slow-witted, she got bored in women's company, she enjoyed being with men, she smoked a cigar and had no interest in art.' Now that Mrs Rakowitschová had arrived in Hukvaldy with her children Janáček's behaviour changed completely: 'We no longer meant anything to him, he was now in the service of this lady. On excursions, in the inn, at chance meetings, everywhere he saw only her.' Observing Janáček and Mrs Rakowitschová together in company, for instance at an expedition by the whole village to the Matulov wood, Zdenka noticed how Janáček 'hovered around her' and how this affair seemed to be public knowledge: 'What I didn't see, people filled in with hints and knowing smiles. I learnt that my husband had already had a good time with Mrs Rakowitschová the previous

334

[summer] holidays.' At night when Zdenka and the children were already in bed, she would hear her husband sneaking out quietly and returning late. She was of course mortified, especially since her rival was older than her, less 'refined' and less intelligent and, it seems, fairly heartless (some time later Zdenka stumbled upon a postcard from her to Janáček that declared, in German and in the intimate 'Du' form, how 'unpleasant' it was that Janáček's wife was around). When Zdenka finally confronted her husband – unsuccessfully – she then found that Josefa was no comfort either: 'Men must have their fun and games, mustn't they, it's their prerogative', was all she said.

When Vladíček got a cold sore from the damp, I made it my excuse for going home with him. My husband was clearly glad. When after the holidays he returned with Olinka we didn't discuss Hukvaldy, but the tension between us remained. Here in Brno I bore it calmly. I got even more closely attached to the children. They were my surest support, they were now my everything.[50]

When Janáček himself returned to Brno, he resigned from the directorship of the Brno Beseda school.[51] It was odd that he hadn't done so a year earlier, when he relinquished the conductorship and *Hudební listy*. Perhaps the last straw had been when he got back to Brno and heard that the new conductor, Josef Kompit, had begun rehearsing another large-scale piece, Dvořák's *St Ludmila*. It was a piece close to Janáček's heart and one that four months after his own departure in June 1888, when the Beseda had failed to find a replacement for him, he had offered to conduct.[52] Now that Kompit was doing it himself without offering Janáček even a guest appearance, he severed his last connection with the society, a relationship that stretched back to the 1870s. Naturally it embittered future contacts. The organization that might have been a launch-pad for some of Janáček's larger-scale choral-orchestral works (such as the cantata *Amarus* of 1897) was now seen as the enemy.

The reason Janáček gave for resigning from the Beseda school was 'too much work'. This, however did not prevent his taking on something much more onerous: serving as music critic for a new daily paper established the previous year, *Moravské listy*. By October he was hard at work reviewing Smetana's *Bartered Bride, The Secret, Dalibor*, Balfe's *Bohemian Girl*, a concert by the violinist Ondříček, and *Rigoletto* (xv/96–101), all in much the same terse way that he had done for *Hudební listy* a few years earlier.

That month Olga got scarlet fever and after five weeks, 'when she was already peeling', Vladimír, now two and a half, caught it from her:

The illness took its course with him very violently. It was accompanied by an infection of the brain membranes[††] and our hope and pride was gone in two days. He became ill on Friday evening, he got convulsions in the night between Saturday and Sunday, he sank into unconsciousness and never came round, although the doctor arrived immediately. He died in convulsions on Sunday 9 November 1890 at 11 a.m.[53]

It seems inconceivable that Janáček would have staggered out to a concert given by the hated Beseda that same evening and written a review of its not very ambitious mixed programme.[54] A review (xv/102) did appear three days later in *Moravské listy*, though unsigned, so perhaps a colleague filled in for the grieving father. By a strange coincidence, on that very evening in Prague there was the first performance of a new play by the young Gabriela Preissová: *Her Stepdaughter*. A few years later Janáček would seize on it for his third opera, *Jenůfa*.

Vladimír's sudden death could not have come at a worse time for Janáček and his wife. The Rakowitschová affair had opened up a gulf between them:

Each of us was alone in our pain [Zdenka recalled]. For some time now, Leoš and I had not lived as man and wife. There were no intimacies between us, not even affectionate words. As long as Vladíček was around, it was bearable. It was my consolation that at least my husband loved the boy, but now it was terrible. Next to one another, mutual unhappiness, mutual pain, and yet each one so alone.[55]

Czech Brno sent condolences. People wrote letters or came round to the flat to leave their visiting cards, filled with a few words of comfort. The Janáčeks kept them all, however short: fifty-two cards or letters survive in the Janáček Archive. But the death of Vladimír endured as an open wound in Janáček's relationship with Zdenka. It was not talked about, though references to it occasionally burst out at times of special tension (see vol. ii: 1916c). Both had different recollections of what happened next. This is Zdenka's version:

After a while this terrible blow produced a strange reaction within me: an enormous desire to be a mother again. Everywhere I went I thought only about

[††] Streptococcal meningitis. This is rare today because of antibiotics.

having Vladíček again, albeit in a different form. It was so strong that it over-came my self-control and forced me to something that in normal circumstances I'd never have done: I went to Leoš and begged him to give me a child.

I'll never be able to forget what happened next. With a grimace, he looked at me and said harshly: 'Hm, that's what you would want, but I don't.'[56]

Almost forty years after Vladimír's death it was Janáček who believed that it was Zdenka who refused to have more children.[57] Maybe the refusal that he had in mind had come earlier, one that might explain the six-year gap between the births of Olga and Vladimír. In the 1880s Janáček used his notebooks mostly as class registers, but there is an intriguing scrap he jotted down in that for 1885, '16 January 1885: Zdenka said that for her a ball is nicer than a young child.'[58] By her own account, Zdenka was a keen dancer. Wherever the refusal lay, Zdenka was probably right when she reported that Janáček 'remained cold and remote for years'.

The impact of Vladimír's death on Janáček can only be surmised. The teaching term was in full flow at the Teachers' Institute, the Czech Gymnasium II and the Organ School; one cannot imagine his taking off more than a day or two to mourn. Certainly by 19 November he was back to his reviewing duties, attending a performance of Meyerbeer's *Les Huguenots*, of which his review appeared a few days later in *Moravské listy* (XV/103).

Janáček seems to have left no record at the time of his feelings, except perhaps musically. When searching out *Šárka* material from the decorated peasant chest in which Janáček stored his compositions, Břetislav Bakala came across a short piece for orchestra that he took to be an extra overture for the opera. Like the other *Šárka* materials it had been copied out by Josef Štross and was in much the same musical idiom. The piece was acknowledged by Janáček in that, under the title of *Skladba* [*Composition*] and dated 1890, it was listed among his orchestral pieces in his autobiography (1924); the date was not entered on the manuscript and could have come only from the composer him-self. In his biography Vogel suggested that the piece may have been written 'under the stress of a tragic circumstance, which could have been the death of Janáček's second child Vladimír'.[59] There is much to support this view. There was no reason for Janáček to write an extra overture for *Šárka* – the existing one works perfectly well and is nicely integrated into the first vocal number. The only other evidence for the *Šárka* explanation (the brief thematic link with the opera) can be dismissed as a coincidence. Instead the work, now known as Adagio (vi/5) after the initial tempo indication, has all the trappings of a late romantic tragic piece: the slow pace, a clear D minor (not a key usually associated with Janáček), a mournful opening theme, announced on the bassoon amid other subfusc orchestral colours – violas, tremolo cellos, funeral-march drum beats from a pizzicato double bass. Although the gloom lifts in a more hopeful middle section (this is where the *Šárka* quotation comes), tragedy resumes in the final section with a return of the main tune, which after a full orchestra version is reduced to a plangent cor anglais against the funeral-march beat (now on the timpani itself) and a final, solo horn version. Placed against Janáček's folk-based compositions of the time, the piece is a complete oddity. By January 1891 the folk-based activities and compositions were resumed with increasing energy.

28

Janáček as music ethnographer

For Janáček the 1880s were filled with new initiatives that would shape the rest of his life, but none as important and far-reaching as his contacts with Moravian folk music. Whereas his exploration of music theory was intense but came in bursts and faded away in his later years, when composition became his chief concern, folk music, once he came to terms with it from the mid-1880s, remained a permanent interest.

Furthermore, while music theory informed Janáček's teaching but its connections with music are less easy to spot, there is no doubt of the connection between his explorations in Moravian folk music and his own creative work. For the five-year period between 1888 and 1893, almost everything he composed was directly connected with it, and afterwards many of the characteristics of Moravian folk music became part of his own style. By the time he emerged from the crucible of folk music he was a substantially different composer, and within a few years began to write music that sounded recognizably like that of his later works. Moravian folk music was the element needed to complete Janáček's musical formation.

It is tempting to assume that Janáček's interest in Moravian folksong began only in the summer of 1888 in the wake of two enormous upsets in his professional life: Zeyer's refusal to grant him permission to use the text of *Šárka* (which meant the end, for the time being, of his hopes to be an opera composer), and the final row with the Brno Beseda and the demise of *Hudební listy*. Janáček, one can imagine, angry at the ingratitude after all he had done for classical music, stomped off to seek new and more rewarding pastures. But the *Šárka* débâcle had already taken place in November 1887, and Janáček remained in denial for almost a year as he continued to work on his opera. Moreover, there are several indications of his interest in Moravian folk music long before the summer of 1888. This interest had been quietly growing in the background for three or four years and simply came to the fore when other ambitions were thwarted.

Janáček had been detached from his rural roots at the age of eleven and whatever he may have imbibed from this folksong-rich area during childhood can be only a matter of speculation. While his coming to Brno severed his early ties, it shouldn't be forgotten that by the 1860s the great Sušil collection of Moravian folksong had been published in its definitive version and that, through the close links between Křížkovský and Sušil, copies of it would have been readily available at the Staré Brno monastery: Janáček's hearing and identifying a Czech folksong sung in Leipzig is one scrap of evidence of his knowledge at the time.[1] Bohemian and Moravian folksong, albeit in a salonized form, was often included in concerts and once Janáček began conducting at 'Svatopluk' and the Brno Beseda, his knowledge of the *ohlasový* repertory also increased: from his article on Křížkovský and folksong (XV/166) it is clear that he was well aware of the Sušil models that lay behind Křížkovský's settings (see chap. 8). He himself went on to write in this manner in his early choruses. His encounter with the original raw material, however, was limited until he started seeking it out himself.

The single most important factor in stimulating Janáček's interest in the area was his contacts with the scholar and folksong collector František Bartoš, seventeen years his senior. When it opened in Brno in the autumn of 1885, the new Czech Gymnasium II was housed in the Teachers' Institute where Janáček worked; it is reasonable to suppose that he and Bartoš came into almost daily contact there, though as Straková argued in the preface to her edition of their collected correspondence,[2] the two men would also have known each other from Czech cultural circles in Brno long before, in the Czech Readers' Club and in 'Vesna'. At least in its first year (1884–5) Bartoš subscribed to Janáček's *Hudební listy*. When Janáček joined the staff of the Gymnasium II in 1886 their contacts became ever closer. Both originally from the country and lovers of nature, they were often seen walking together on the wooded paths leading up to the Brno Špilberk castle.[3] Bartoš took a keen interest in Janáček's singing classes at the

Gymnasium and often sat in on them (see chap. 18). They were both involved with the Moravian contribution to the 1895 Ethnographic Exhibition and their most sustained collaboration – *Moravian Folksongs Newly Collected* (XIII/3) – came about as a result of it. They remained colleagues until Bartoš's retirement in 1902, and were in frequent contact until his death in 1906.

Towards the end of 1886, at the invitation of the editor of *Hlídka literární*,[4] Janáček reviewed Ludvík Kuba's collection *Slavdom in its Songs*. Janáček's long review (XV/65), over ten pages in a modern reprint, is a milestone in his association with folk music, important for determining his knowledge of the field at this stage. Much of the review is taken up with his detailed comments on the accompaniments that Kuba provided. However, it also provides this piece of personal information:

In *Vnorovy* in Moravian Slovakia the people like singing; I enjoyed listening from a distance to the songs of the sturdy young people as they bathed, especially on a Saturday until late into the warm summer nights. I stood so far away that I could sense the consonants, especially on the long notes, only from *the clearly evident breaking of the notes*. It was an interesting phenomenon. I remember to this day the incredibly beautiful tune of one such song. With such buoyant force it sounded for a long, long time, especially the last note of individual sections of the song, and then suddenly got lost in the pastures and leafy banks of the quiet Morava river [ex. 1].

Ex. 1

Hardly having waited until morning, I called together well-known women singers from the district and asked them to sing me that same tune which I took down from them. And amazingly – I hardly recognized it. The long dying notes disappeared, the sharp rhythm disappeared and a colourless, metrical version took over. It was evident that they sang and made musical poetry with quite another joy in the wonderfully beautiful, open countryside rather than in the closed, stuffy room where, furthermore, they were being observed. – Since then I write down songs for myself from a distance and – by stealth; and I'm convinced that I am always taking down the best variant. (XV/65)

This charming reminiscence offers a number of useful points. The tune Janáček quotes is in fact the beginning of *O Love* from *Four Male-Voice Choruses* (IV/17), the words taken down by him and surviving in his notation.[5] Since these choruses were sent to the publisher Urbánek on 20 June 1885 (see chap. 23), and were composed that spring (at the latest), the Vnorovy notations must go back at least to the previous summer, i.e. 1884. Vnorovy (then 'Znorovy') was where Janáček's uncle Jan Janáček lived and worked from 1870, and it is assumed that this encounter with folk music took place during one of Janáček's visits there.

Some writers[6] have placed the Vnorovy incident to 1874–5 on the basis of Janáček's much later reminiscence of a girl he was in love with, Běta Gazarková (XV/292), according to which his meeting took place in Vnorovy when he was a 'student'. However the way Janáček describes his notations in the quoted extract (XV/65) above would seem to come not from a youngster tormented by calf love but from an older person (not taking part in the bathing himself; imperiously summoning the women to sing for him) with a much more critical cast of mind. Janáček could have chosen to visit Vnorovy during several summers in the early 1880s when he was becoming an increasingly important professional. Although he went with Zdenka to Vnorovy in 1881 during their honeymoon trip, it rather sounds from his account above as though he was on his own. This would have been possible in 1882 after the birth of Olga (when Zdenka went to her parents for two weeks); not in 1883 (Janáček spent all the summer in Prague); and most likely in 1884, before he repaired his marriage with Zdenka.

Another reason why 1884 may be more convincing than 1874–5 for the Vnorovy notations is that Janáček began regularly taking down folksong notations in his home region around Hukvaldy soon afterwards. His first trip to Kozlovice (where he observed the folk dancer Žovka Havlová) dates from the summer of 1885.* The notations he made in Kunčice pod Ondřejníkem and Čeladná are dated 1886,[7] and an authorized copy of his arrangement of the dance *Furcoat/Cross*, taken down in Petřvald, is dated 1886. Janáček made repeated visits to most of these places (and to nearby Mniší and Větřkovice) in the years up to 1888.

---

* If one can trust his statement in 1898 that he had met her thirteen years earlier (XV/158).

Collecting Folk Materials

As Jiří Vysloužil makes clear in his survey of Janáček's folkloristic activity, it was Janáček the composer who collected, rather than Janáček the scholar.[8] So it was the more colourful regions and the more interesting instruments or combinations of instruments that most attracted his attention. He hardly bothered with anything on his doorstep, near Brno, but instead he made repeated expeditions to two ethnographically distinctive regions: Valašsko/Lašsko and Slovácko (see chap. 2) with occasional forays to out-of-the-way places such as Silesia or Slovakia. And although he collected a fair number of solo songs, he was particularly taken by a few exceptional phenomena such as the folk ensembles of southern Moravia, the multi-part singing in Slovakia, and quirky instruments such as the cimbalom (a dulcimer played with a hammer in each hand) and the bagpipes (a sweeter, gentler instrument than the warlike bagpipes of Scotland and, unlike the Scottish instrument, with a tuning system that allowed it to be played in combination with other folk instruments). Janáček's notations are some of the earliest made of Moravian ensemble folk music, with its distinctive texture involving a band of at least three instruments: the *hudec* (a word meaning a folk musician, but here specifically the first violinist), a *kontráš* (a second violinist often playing an accompanying, contrasting, even contrapuntal part), and a cello or double-bass part, with occasional extras such as another violin, a clarinet or a cimbalom. Equally remarkable are the multi-part (usually two-part) folksongs: Janáček described these vividly when he was interviewed in 1906 by a reporter from *Dalibor* (see chap. 53) and re-created them in his *Folk Nocturnes* (IV/32).

The number of items Janáček notated is not huge – Vysloužil estimates it at around three hundred[9] – but, as can be seen from table 28.1, over a period of almost thirty years he regularly went into the terrain to make folk notations. Only with the First World War did this activity cease – Janáček was sixty by then – and after the war his life changed.

In tandem with his own collecting was the large-scale organization of activity promoting Moravian folk music. This began with the Ethnographic Exhibition held in Prague in 1895. Among other musical tasks, Janáček was responsible for getting together the 'Moravian Days' that brought whole ensembles of folk musicians to Prague from several regions of Moravia (see chap. 32). The systematic collection of Moravian folk music was given further life by *Das Volkslied in*

Table 28.1: Janáček's collecting of folk materials

Based on the detailed list by Vysloužil (*LJOLP*, 94–117), which is organized by location and includes song and dance titles and names of performers, this table omits details of individual songs and dances, and names only the more significant performers. Additions reflecting more recent research are taken from the summary list by Procházková (1998d) and from Janáček's correspondence. I have not included (as do Vysloužil and Procházková) Janáček's trips to various regions made merely to rehearse singers and players for the 1895 Ethnographic Exhibition. Janáček notated some folk performers not in their native region but elsewhere. Here the second column reflects where Janáček heard them, with their origin given in the fifth column. Dates are particularly uncertain in the 1880s.

Regions (under *area*) are as follows:
B = Brno region; L = Lašsko; S = Slovácko; Sil = Silesia; Ska = Slovakia; V = Valašsko.
In border areas both ethnographic regions are shown.
Other abbreviations (in *types of notation*):
cd = choreographic descriptions   cimb = notations for cimbalom
ens = ensemble music (usually for strings)   ph rec = phonograph recording
spm = speech melodies

Notes include important performers, Janáček's published descriptions of his folk trips and uses of the material in compositions (but not editions).

date	place	area	types of notation	notes
?1884, summer	Vnorovy	S	songs	xv/165; includes tune and words used in *Ó lásko* (iv/17)
1885	Kozlovice	L	songs, dances, cd	Žovka Havlová; xv/145; xv/158; used in vi/4 etc.; viii/10
1885–6	Kunčice pod Ondřejníkem	L	songs, dances, cimb	xv/145, xv/257; used in vi/4 etc.; viii/10
1885–6	Čeladná	L	songs, dances	xv/145, xv/257; used in vi/4 etc.
1885–8	Mniší	L	songs, dances	Josef Křístek
1885–8	Petřvald	L	songs, dances, cimb, cd	Jan Myška; xv/143; used in vi/4 etc.; viii/10
1885–8	Větřkovice	L	songs	Matula; xv/158; used in iv/27 and v/9
1888	Tichá u Frenštátu	L	Kolo dance (for piano), cd	
1891	Mniší	L	songs	Josef Křístek; xv/158; xv/168; used in iv/27 and v/9
1891	Košatka	L	songs, dances, cimb	Mikeska (cimb)
1891, Aug	Tichá u Frenštátu	L	songs, dances, cd	
1891, 8 Sept– ?	Velká nad Veličkou	S	ens	Pavel Trn (vn)

Table 28.1:—*continued*

date	place	area	types of notation	notes
1892, July	Luhačovice	–	cimb	players from Březůvky (S/V); xv/145
1892, Sept?	Strážnice	S	ens, songs, dances, cd	Pavel Trn (vn)
1892, Sept?	Lipov	S	ens	Jiří Valášek; xiii/3
1892, Sept?	Blatnice	S	cd	
1892, 1–19 Sept	Velká nad Veličkou	S	ens, songs, dances	
1893, July?	Jasenice	L/V	songs, ens, cd	Janáček added tunes to cd by Pernický and Zapletal; xv/145; xiii/3
1893, Aug	Valašská Bystřice	V	cimb	Jan Mikuš (cimb)
1893, 27–9 Aug	Velká nad Veličkou	S	songs, dances, ens	Pavel Trn (vn)
1893, 1 Sept – ?	Polanka	V	cimb, ens.	Jan Míček (cimb); xv/143
1895–7	Starý Jičín	L/V	dances	xv/163
1897, 16 Oct	Kostice	S	songs, spm	
1898, 11 Sept	Horní Sklenov	L	songs, spm	xv/163; xv/245
1899, May–June	Březová	S	songs, bagpipe, spm	
1900, 6 Sept	Kunčice pod Ondřejníkem	L	cimb	F. Klepáč (cimb); xv/163
1901, Sept	Makov	Ska	multi-part songs	iv/32
1901, Sept	Velké Rovné	Ska	multi-part songs	iv/32
1906	Ostravice	L	songs, ens	
1906	Sehradice	V	songs?	
1906, Jan	Bílá	V?	weavers' songs	
1906, 12 April to 3 July	Horní Sklenov	L	songs	
1906, 13 May	Ořechovičky	B	photographing folk rituals, folk plays	with Lucie Bakešová
1906, 27 July	Lubno	L	cimb; drawing of cimb	Ignác Kotek (cimb); xv/186; xiii/5
1906, 26 Aug	Lubina	L	bagpipes, ens	Úhelný (bagpipes)
1907	Trojanovice	L/V	songs to the folk play *The Three Kings*	
1907	Valašské Klobouky	V	survey, spm	
1907, 1 Jan	Frenštát	L	songs, cimb	
1907, 21–2 July	Jablunkov, Bocanovice, Mosty u Jablunkova	Sil	songs, spm	xv/188
1907, 23–4 July	Valašská Bystřice	V	tunes	texts already taken by František Bobek
1908	Ludkovice	S/V	songs	
1908, summer	Luhačovice	S/V	songs	xiii/5
1909, 29 April	Beloveža	Ska	song tunes	

345

Table 28.1:—*continued*

date	place	area	types of notation	notes
1909, 19–20 Aug	Prostřední Bečva	V	songs, spm	Jan Juříček (singer)
1909, 28 Aug	Metylovice etc.	L	songs, survey	
1909, Nov	Modřice	–	ph rec of songs	singers (including Eva Gabel) from Slatina nad Bebravou (Ska); v/9
1910, 3–7 Sept	Moravec	–	ph rec of songs	with Hynek Bím and F. Kyselková; singers from Terchová (Ska)
1911, 2 July	Vnorovy	S	ph rec of songs	with Bím
1911, 20 Aug	Velký Ořechov	–	two-part Moravian Slovak songs	with Bím; singers from Čičmany (Ska)
1912, 12–25 May	Brno	–	ph rec, notation of multi-part songs	singers from Terchová (Ska)
1912, 5 June	Kozlovice	L	Christmas plays *Valachians* and *The Three Kings*	
1914, 24–7 July	Valašská Bystřice	V	photographing 'song environment'	with Dušan Jurkovič
undated	Sedliště	L	dances	

Österreich, an Austrian-government-funded project initiated by Universal Edition with the aim of publishing a multi-volume compilation of the traditional music of all the peoples in the Austrian half of the empire. Janáček eventually took charge of a committee overseeing folksong collecting work in Moravia with a small budget to finance its activities. It took up much of his time, as will be clear from the many references to it after 1905.

Janáček was reasonably systematic about his transcriptions: field notations were jotted down in whatever he had to hand, but afterwards he usually wrote them out again with details of performers, venues and subsequent reflections (such as analysis of structure, comparable versions).[†] From the point of view of the modern ethnographer, much of what Janáček did may seem outdated, and yet much was forward-looking and modern for his time. As early as October 1892 he was keen to acquire a phonograph to record performers (rather than merely relying on his ear),[10] though it was only

[†] This is nicely demonstrated in the three facsimiles supplied in Procházková 2004.

much later that he was able to acquire one for his folksong committee. This was used from 1909 (he put the collector Hynek Bím in charge) and Janáček went along on several of Bím's expeditions and occasionally attempted to notate directly from the cylinders.[11] The wax cylinders still exist and the recordings made have been released commercially.[12]

Janáček was equally keen to cover all aspects of folk activity, rather than merely music, and to place it into its environmental context. From the start he took an interest in the steps in the dances he notated.[‡] According to Zdenka's reminiscences given to Robert Smetana, Janáček often consulted his wife, a keen dancer, on what he had taken down.[13] He made several attempts to take photographs of dancers, and of the environment. One could also regard the notation of speech melodies, which he made on location from 1897 onwards, as part of this broader attempt at contextualizing the folk activity, rather than merely a personal quirk An important aspect of the Moravian contribution to the 1895 Ethnographic Exhibition that stemmed from Janáček was the insistence on always performing the folk rituals of which the music was an intrinsic part.

In her examination of Janáček's procedures as a collector,[14] Jarmila Procházková concluded that he was generally inconsistent about the use of key signatures, though he flexibly recognized the use of non-classical modes, and the simultaneous use of different notes (e.g. in voice and instrumental accompaniment). Particularly forward-looking was his approach to microtonal variation; he noted sharpness or flatness as a tonal phenomenon rather than as a shortcoming by the performer. Nor, like older collectors, did he attempt to force folksongs into regular metres.[15] Janáček may not have been as systematic as his contemporary Bartók in his approach to fieldwork, but he did bring to it his exceptional sensitivities as a musician and picked up intuitively many important aspects of what he heard.

Editions
Janáček's editions begin with the popular pocket-format *Bouquet*, published with Bartoš in 1890 (XIII/1), a compilation of suitable materials for singing in school. The edition of 3000 copies sold out in a couple

---

[‡] See 'cd' entries in table 28.1.

of years and was reprinted in 1892. In 1901 another edition came out (XIII/2), enlarged from the original 174 songs to 195. One could regard this collaboration with František Bartoš as a confidence-building exercise for the enormous scholarly edition *Moravian Folksongs Newly Collected* (XIII/3; containing 2057 items), on which the two men worked for many years. It is clear from Janáček's correspondence, for example with Hynek Bím,[16] that the original intention was to issue the edition in time for the Ethnographic Exhibition in 1895. But it turned into a much larger project, taking almost a decade to realize and eventually completing publication in 1901.

Janáček collected only a small number of the items in XIII/3 himself. His and Bartoš's task was one of co-ordinating the work of other collectors, assembling and finally editing. Merely seeing the material through the press, fascicle by fascicle, took up a huge amount of Janáček's time up to 1901, one of several factors that held up his own work on *Jenůfa*. After František Sušil's groundbreaking edition of 2091 songs, this remains the most substantial edition of Moravian folksongs; like the Organ School, it is another monument to Janáček's non-compositional activity.

Apart from a small selection of songs that Janáček and Pavel Váša published in literary supplements to *Lidové noviny* in 1911 and 1912 (XIII/4), this was the last folksong edition that appeared in Janáček's lifetime. There should have been another large-scale edition generated by the *Volkslied in Österreich* project. Work began in 1908 and was seemingly complete by 1913, but publication was halted by the First World War. The Czech part continued under new Czechoslovak ownership in 1919, with folksong committee meetings in Prague remaining a regular fixture in Janáček's diary. However the new republic seemed reluctant to involve itself at any serious financial level with the folkmusic activities that the Austrian government had subsidized. The result was that the much-longed-for edition of Janáček's *Moravian Love Songs* (XIII/5) came out posthumously, seen through the press by the co-editor Pavel Váša, and even then in a very leisurely fashion between 1930 and 1936.

Writing about Folk Music

Janáček's involvement with folk music as a writer and scholar proceeded virtually simultaneously with his own collecting activity. The Vnorovy notations may have been a way of idling away a summer, but having to write a long journal review made him think about the matter from a more theoretical and critical angle, and his *Hlídka* review (xv/65) was soon followed by other writings. In his edition of Janáček's folksong writings, Vysloužil lists fifty-one items plus another ten fragments and other documents about folk music which, reprinted, come to over five hundred pages. However, only about half of these were published in Janáček's lifetime (listed in table 28.2 below); the unpublished materials are mostly trial versions for prefaces to collections (particularly the posthumous *Moravian Love Songs* XIII/5) and

Table 28.2: Janáček's published writings on folksong

JW	date	title	description or comment
xv/65	1886	Slavdom in its Songs	Review of Kuba's collection
xv/93	1888	Moravian Folksongs	Review of Bartoš's collection
xv/94	1889	Some Words on Moravian Folksongs: the musical side	Janáček's contribution to the preface to Bartoš's collection *Moravian Folksongs Newly Collected*
xv/95	1890	Dimitrij Slavjanskij	The Russian Slavyansky as a successor to Sušil in collecting and popularizing folksong
xv108	1890	A Bouquet of Moravian Folksongs	With František Bartoš: preface to folksong collection XIII/1
xv/109	1891	Valachian and Lachian Dances	Analysis of four Valachian dances played at the concert in Brno on 4 Jan 1891
xv/117	1891	Folksongs for Primary Schools	Review of Vorel's collection
xv/129	1891	On Folksong: a feuilleton	On styles of folk music and problems of origin
xv/140	1892	On Folksong Collections	Problems of collection and notation of folksongs, and criticism of Hostinský's views
xv/143	1893	The Music of Truth	A trip to Slovácko and Valašsko in Sept 1893; description of local dances
xv/144	1893	Melodic Turns of Phrase in Folksongs	Classification; application of Janáček's theory; tonality
xv/145	1893	Outlines of Musical Folk Dances in Moravia	Expansion of xv/109
xv/146	1894	Music at the Ethnographic Exhibition	Plans for Moravian representation
xv/148	1895	Programme of the Moravian Folk Festivities at the Czechoslavonic Ethnographic Exhibition	Printed programme

Table 28.2:—*continued*

JW	date	title	description or comment
xv/158	1898	The Settlement 'Pod Hukvaldy'	Hukvaldy and its surroundings described in words and with quotations of local songs and dances
xv/163	1901	On the Musical Side of Moravian Folksongs	Janáček's introduction to xiii/3
xv/164	1901	Some Lachian Dances	Songs and dances collected by František Pinoczy with Janáček's comments; analysis of Silesian dances
xv/166	1902	The Importance of Pavel Křížkovský in Moravian Folk Music and in Czech Music as a Whole	Includes comments on Křížkovský and folksong
xv/177	1905	Why do we have so many polkas and waltzes?	The relationship between tune and choreography: the simpler the steps the more versions of a dance
xv/182	1906	An interview with Leoš Janáček	Includes Janáček's comments on the two-part songs in Makov and Velké Rovné, Slovakia
xv/183	1906	Collecting Czech Folksong in Moravia and Silesia	Brochure for the working party for Czech folksong in Moravia and Silesia and a two-part flier for collectors
xv/186	1907	Thoughts along the Way	A trip among musicians in Lubno, Silesia
xv/196	1909	Rhythm in Folksong	On the notation of rhythm and barring of folksong
xv/200	1911	Under the Sword	A trip to Strání; Janáček's views on the origin of the sword dance and its traditions
xv/212	1917	The Cradle of the Earliest Czech Folksong	Speech and folksong
xv/218	1919	He Didn't Live to See	Obituary reminiscence of Martin Zeman
xv/235	1922	Questions and Answers to Dr Alois Kolísek	On the psychology of creation in folksong; folksong as a reflection of the spiritual wealth of the nation
xv/257	1924	At Harabiš's	Janáček's encounter with the Kunčice musicians and getting to know Lachian dances [in 1885–6]
xv/286	1926	A Note (in Memory of František Bartoš)	The psychology of creation in folksong
xv/288	1926	On Tonality in Folksong	Tonality as the co-creator of the psychological effect of folksong
xv/301	1927	On the Most Durable Thing in Folksong	Rhythm in folksong
xv/310	1928	My Lašsko	Reminiscences of Lašsko and its dances

other theoretical speculations; their existence and extent indicate the seriousness with which Janáček approached the subject. This is also evident, for instance, in the preface that he contributed to xiii/3. The collection itself is huge – 1196 pages. Janáček's introduction (xv/163) is on an equally large scale and, in Vysloužil's edition, takes up 136 pages, which represents over a quarter of all Janáček's writings on folk music, published and unpublished.

Most of the rest is more modest. A good number of pieces are pleasantly written feuilletons, often directed at a general readership (e.g. for *Lidové noviny*), in which Janáček would recall a trip to a particular ethnographic region, and the pleasures and difficulties of collecting materials there, often put into a wide social context: travelogue as much as musical comment. A few writings arose from the organization of folksong collecting (reports and directives for collectors), but in his last decade, after active collecting ceased, Janáček became more thoughtful and speculative in his writings, dwelling in particular on the psychology of the creation of folk music.

Theoretical Concerns

On 18 December 1898 Janáček gave the first performance at 'Vesna' of his *Hukvaldy Folk Poetry in Songs* (v/4), preceding these folksong arrangements for voice and piano with an illustrated lecture. The lecture was reported at some length in *Moravská revue*, and Janáček's views about folksong emerge with a clarity that is not always apparent in his own writings.

Janáček divided Moravian folksongs into three types: *bohatýrský, popěvný* and *kolový*. For the sake of simplicity they will be referred to here respectively as 'heroic', 'lyrical' and 'circular', but like all of Janáček's terms they lack direct equivalents in English. A *bohatýr* is a hero from legendary times, and with this term Janáček wished to signal that *bohatýrský* was the oldest stratum of folksong. *Popěvný* is cognate with *nápěv* [tune], and by this term Janáček indicated not only that this type of folksong was more lyrical than the heroic type, but that it was made up of a store of short motifs that were constantly repeated throughout the song (another word he used to describe this type was *zálohový*, an adjective from *záloha* [reserve]). He regarded them as less valuable than the older, heroic stratum, much more common and easier on the ear. The third type was essentially an ABA form, the original motif returning at the end. This, Janáček reckoned, had a Serbian origin (he took his term from the Serbian *kolo* or round dance) and the type travelled west before coming to the Czech lands.[17] Later, in his introduction to *Moravian Songs Newly Collected*, these terms were modified further: 1. *bohatýrský*; 2. *tematický* [thematic] (*zálohový*); 3. *kolečkový* (*úpadkový*), where the circularity (*kolečkový*) is directly characterized as being in decline (*úpadkový*) (xv/163).

As is illustrated here, Janáček was specifically concerned with classification (there were further types of classifications for dances),[18] and this inevitably involved description and analysis: of melodies, keys, rhythms, etc. His overall concerns are well demonstrated by the topics that he chose when in 1922–3 he lectured on folksong: individual types, notation, key, and the folk composer's psychology of creation.[19] Notation became a particularly urgent concern when Janáček later took charge of a whole team of collectors: how to give instructions that would unify the result while allowing room for individual peculiarities.

Early on in his consideration of folksong Janáček locked horns with the chief Czech theorist Otakar Hostinský, whose clear-sighted views of how to handle word-setting in Czech (taking account of correct stress and vowel length) spilt over into views on how to notate Czech folksong, which did not always adhere to such prescriptions. Janáček took a liberal and more modern stance, notating incorrect stresses (if that is indeed what the singers did), believing that the rhythm of the words and the rhythm of the tune were independent elements, though naturally bearing one upon the other. Janáček used rhythm as the chief element in classifying folksongs.[20] Rhythmic aspects overlapped with his theoretical concerns in art music, as did psychological reflections. A glance at the subject index of his collected writings on folksong edited by Vysloužil (*LJOLP*) shows how psychology and rhythm are two of the topics most discussed.

Janáček was well aware of the work of his Moravian predecessors, Sušil and Bartoš – his much annotated copies of their publications[21] bear witness to the critical distance that he himself travelled. In general Bartoš took an idealist attitude towards folksongs, typical of the period, and was not beyond bowdlerizing sexual references in texts.[22] Janáček was more of a realist,[23] not only restoring suggestive texts, but also making sure that tunes were taken down as objectively as possible, the notation not constrained by the metrical and tonal expectations of nineteenth-century classical music.

In this he was influenced by Russian collectors, particularly Ivan Pratsch, the earliest important Russian collector, whose collection (together with L'vov), was first issued in 1790.[24] This volume in Janáček's library[25] became a useful source for Russian folk tunes that he dipped into for his later 'Russian' operas, *Kát'a Kabanová* and *From the House of the Dead*. Despite the resonant words about the universality of folksong that he delivered in a speech in London in 1926 (xv/283), Janáček seems to have taken little interest in the non-Russian folk collections in his library, for instance Cecil Sharp's collection of Somerset folksongs, the volume of Negro spirituals given to him by the American student Edmund Cykler (see vol.ii: 1928a), or English ballads, songs and bagpiper melodies presented to him by H.C. Colles of *The Times*. There is not a single mark by Janáček in any of these books.[26]

In the years from 1885 until his death Janáček's attitude towards Moravian folk music naturally changed and, after his initial enthusiasm for making Valachian folk dances the basis for orchestral dances and other works, he soon began to avoid direct use of folk material in his own works, apart from his piano accompaniments to folksongs. Behind this lies Janáček's perception that, although anonymous, 'folksong' usually had a composer, and so the use of folk music in art music could be seen as an exploitation, an infringement of intellectual property (xv/166).

Although Janáček's role in collecting Moravian folk music and organizing its collection by others dwindled after 1914, folk music remained a concern up to his last years. One way to understand this persistence is to see Moravian folk music as a resource for Janáček very similar to speech melody (the two became entangled in some of his theoretical discourse and at one stage he theorized that speech melody could have been the basis for folksong; see chap. 37). It is clear that neither speech melody nor Moravian folksong provided raw musical material for the mature composer, but both sharpened his awareness and musical sensibilities so that his continued work with them provided training and sustenance. Each needed a different approach: with speech melody it was simply a matter of taking them down as Janáček overheard people speaking, and developing an insight into their nature by trying to build up an awareness of location, circumstance, emotional aspects and so on. Folksong was a broader occupation, ranging from fieldwork and organizing, to editing and publication. Significantly, however, almost into his final years, Janáček would occasionally touch base by making more folksong arrangements (see chap. 31). There was no doubting his engagement. In the following extract Janáček vividly conveys his excitement at hearing for the first time (1899) the slow songs from Březová:

The way that I heard people singing there was something I had never before imagined as a slow [*táhlý*, i.e. drawn-out] song. What I could read from the notation was far from reality. It was a flood which I struggled in vain to make sense of. I burned with shame until my ears throbbed. From the mouths of my women singers flowed a stream of sound that broke up, as if by itself, here into shorter held notes, there into longer. The expression on their faces was simply a passion for singing. If only by a shake of the head a woman might betray that she was counting! Nothing. So I establish it faithfully note by note [ex. 2]. I consoled myself that I'd sort out the confusion as soon as I found the time. (xv/315)

Ex. 2

V tom bre-zov - ském   po - ľi   roz-ma-rýn   ze - ľe-ný,

ked' ve-ter za-ve - je,   ce-łé po - ľe   vo-ní.

29

1891–3

'On Sunday the 7th [of January 1891]', Janáček wrote to Mrs Bakešová, 'we will practise four new Valachian dances: a trainer from Hukvaldy will be arriving. Since, as you must certainly already know, you have to talk about "The beauty in the movements" of these dances, I respectfully invite you to it.'[1]

Within six weeks of Vladimír's death Janáček was back to folk-music activities, seeking perhaps to take his mind off his loss with hard work. During the first half of 1891 he would write a new ballet and a new opera, and keep up his reviewing activities for *Moravské listy* in addition to his three teaching jobs. The concert on 7 January* at the Great Hall of the Besední dům included a performance of four of his *Valachian Dances* for orchestra with Janáček conducting the orchestra of the Brno Theatre, the first time he had appeared publicly as a conductor after his parting with the Brno Beseda. In the same concert, ten of the piano arrangements that he had made of *Folk Dances in Moravia* (VIII/10) were played by two women students from the Organ School, Antonína Nikodemová and Anna Kumpoštová. This served as a launch for the pieces: the first fascicle with six dances was in the shops by 22 February.† The audiences were well prepared, both by an article that Janáček published in *Moravské listy* (3 January 1891; XV/109), in which he analysed and described the dances, and by a series of talks the next day at the Besední dům under the auspices of 'Vesna' given by Janáček and his associates in the publication of VIII/10:

---

* Not 4 January, as in *JAWO*, 185 and 187.
† As is clear from a letter to Janáček from Bursík & Kohout (22 Feb 1891, BmJA, A 25), discussing commission terms.

The very numerous select audience filled the ground floor hall of the Besední dům to the last place and with stormy agreement attended Mrs Lucie Bakešová's ingenious demonstrations from the point of view of cultural history, the excellent description of the Haná dances by Miss Xavera Běhálková and the surprising analysis by Mr Leoš Janáček, together with the artless performance of the Valachian dances and songs.[2]

The concert itself was an even greater success, the *Valachian Dances* in particular:

Much more characterful and effective, however, were the *Valachian Dances*, performed by the large orchestra, conducted by their composer and collector. All four dances, *And I forlorn* [*Oldfashioned Dance II*], the *Blessed Dance*, Furcoat and the *Čeladná Dance*, were received with stormy applause. The ballet master of the Prague National Theatre, Mr Aug. Berger, who was there, expressed the highest praise about the character of the dances and their excellent performance. Mr Janáček was given a wreath by the ladies from 'Vesna'. The entertainment during the general dance that took place after the folk dances was very animated.[3]

The presence of Augustin Berger, with whom Janáček had had friendly contacts two years earlier, is notable. Presumably he had been specially invited and felt sufficient interest or obligation to make the journey to Brno. And it seems to have been Berger who urged Janáček to contact Šubert again, despite the débâcle of the *Valachian Dances* ballet two years earlier:

Perhaps my letter is excused after Mr Berger's report, perhaps I come at the right time in offering *newly* composed Valachian dances to the National Theatre.

They are four in number and have been generally liked here for their earthy character, charm and variety.

Since the musical material is in good order they could be staged immediately.

I got the impression that Mr Berger mentioned *The Farm Mistress* as a suitable home for them. So kindly tell me your decision.[4]

This time Janáček's aims were more modest, with no question of his offering to compose an independent ballet. Instead the four dances could perhaps be used in the Moravian play by Gabriela Preissová that had caused a stir when it opened in Prague in 1889 and remained in the National Theatre repertory until 1897. Preissová was in the news at the time. Her second play set in Moravia, *Her Stepdaughter*, had been given in Prague in November 1890; on 10 January 1891 it opened in

Brno and she introduced it with a talk at 'Vesna' about her Slovácko plays.[5] Did Janáček get to her lecture? It was part of the same series of talks on Moravian folk culture in which he himself had lectured on 3 January 1891. It would seem surprising in view of their many mutual acquaintances, including František Bartoš and indeed his own connections with Preissová,[‡] if he had not at least got to a performance of the play. Later that year Janáček would investigate the musical aspects of Slovácko for himself and it would be a revelation.

Šubert would probably have been aware of Janáček's increasing prominence. The Bursík & Kohout full score of two of the *Valachian Dances* was reviewed by the composer Josef Nešvera in *Moravské listy* on 10 January. Furthermore the concert at the Besední dům had been such a success that it was repeated on 11 January to an even bigger audience, and written up in a full three-part article in *Moravská orlice* that gave detailed descriptions of the costumes, the names of the dancers and so on.[6] The publication of the orchestral score of the two dances allowed their performance elsewhere, for example in Písek, Bohemia (16 January), where the dances were given at a carnival season ball together with other Moravian dances such as Kovařovic's arrangements of *The Little Queens*.[7] Meanwhile in Brno an entertainment given by 'Vesna' and the Brno Beseda on 20 January included Janáček himself playing some of the dances at the piano: 'it climaxed with the delightful Valachian and Haná dances, which at general insistence were played by the composer Mr Leoš Janáček himself with the rarest willingness.' It sounds too as though, two months after Vladimír's death, Zdenka was also pulling herself together since the report mentions that she 'served at the tea urn'.[8]

The outcome of Janáček's letter, and no doubt some diplomacy on the part of Berger, was a surprising new initiative. On 23 January 1891 František Šubert (a playwright turned administrator) came to Brno to attend the Brno première of his play *The Landowner* at the Czech Theatre. After the play there was a reception at the Readers' Club at which Šubert spoke and which Janáček reported in *Moravské listy*, together with his review of *Carmen* (xv/112). It seems, too, that Šubert had a word with Janáček and that something was agreed between them.

[‡] Even before her triumph with *The Farm Mistress* Janáček had tried to get her to write something for *Hudební listy* (Preissová to LJ, 6 Feb 1888, *JODA*, PR2).

An inkling of this can be found in a letter that Janáček wrote to Mrs Bakešová two months later. The letter concludes with an offhand reference to a 'vaudeville' that he was writing with Gabriela Preissová – the beginnings of his second opera *The Beginning of a Romance* (1/3). A comment in the letter that 'Šolc wants to publish piano arrangements of the *Bouquet*' refers to the Telč-based publisher, Emil Šolc, responsible for bringing out the compilation by Bartoš and Janáček, *A Bouquet of Moravian Folksongs* (XIII/1). In 1892 Šolc would bring out a second edition of the *Bouquet* and also a volume containing Janáček's imaginative piano accompaniments for fifteen of the songs (V/2; see chap. 31). However, most of Janáček's letter is to do with the exciting prospect of his new ballet, *Rákoš Rákoczy* (1/2). The fact that Janáček gave no explanation of what he was talking about suggests that Bakešová was already apprised of the project and was simply being filled in about details:

I'm just sending the last scores to Prague.

Mrs Kusá [a leading light in 'Vesna' and owner of the block of flats where the Janáčeks lived] told me yesterday that she has already organized the purchase of the necessary material for folk costumes.

So that question is already dealt with; the costumes will be from the vicinity of Kyjov. [. . .]

As far as the libretto is concerned it doesn't matter to me who will write it. I don't need a text. The words to the songs are taken from our collection and are well known for those dances. I'm therefore not responsible for anything on that side, so I won't get mixed up in it.

The basic forms of the dances will be preserved, any variations will be justified by the need for liveliness and dramatic truth.

I'll travel to Prague for the [Easter] holidays,[5] perhaps by that time I'll get a letter from there. If there's anything new I'll tell you.

We must talk about what the second fascicle of *Moravian Dances* will contain.[9]

In the midst of all this activity, Janáček's reviewing continued: in January 1891, for instance, he published reviews of performances of *St John's Rapids* (Rozkošný), *Don Giovanni* (XV/110) and *Carmen* (XV/112), all pieces that he knew well. But his first encounter with a Tchaikovsky opera, *Eugene Onegin*, given for the first time in Brno on 21 February, produced a very different sort of review, as long as all

---

[5] Easter Sunday fell on 29 March that year.

the others put together. It consists of a scene-by-scene account of the whole opera, with attention drawn to passages that took his fancy at a first hearing. Then follows a summary of the opera's style: no leitmotifs; clear diatonic harmony; a willingness to use standard musical forms; good, striking tunes; an understanding and use of folk music. Apart from the leitmotifs no-one would disagree with the above comments, but one other point he makes stands out: the 'rhythm of the tunes is strikingly similar to the rhythm of everyday *speech*' (xv/114). This sounds like a preview of Janáček's own speech-melody theory of a few years later (see chap. 37), though from his criticisms it would appear that 'everyday speech' here means something different from the 'everyday speech' in Janáček's speech melodies. It was the second time that a Tchaikovsky event provoked a substantial article from Janáček (see chap. 23); a few years later the Brno première of *The Queen of Spades* would make an even deeper impression on him (see chap. 34).

Janáček's earlier attempts at stage works had ended in humiliating failures: *Šárka* forbidden by the librettist, the *Valachian Dances* ballet turned down by all three National Theatre conductors. If he was now returning to these genres it was because a number of factors came fortuitously together: Janáček's enthusiasm for a recent stage work (*Eugene Onegin*) coinciding with an approach from Šubert. Whereas in 1889 Janáček was trying to persuade Šubert to take a new folk ballet at the National Theatre, this time it was Šubert himself who needed something along these lines that could be put on at the National Theatre at the time of the Regional Jubilee Exhibition.

The 'jubilee' of the title was the celebration of the coronation in Prague of Leopold II in 1791 as Czech king, an event that drew attention to Leopold's submission to this courtesy, as opposed to the attitude of the present incumbent, Franz Josef, who would have nothing to do with it. This nationalist slant antagonized the Germans, who then boycotted the event, and an exhibition originally intended to commemorate Bohemian and Moravian advances in industry over the past hundred years instead went ahead as a manifestation of cultural solidarity by the Czechs. Normally the National Theatre closed for the summer, but this year it remained open from mid-May to the end of August to entertain the many visitors who came to Prague for the exhibition. A more specifically Czech repertory was appropriate, and in addition to staging revivals (for instance six of Smetana's operas, two of Dvořák's and even Bendl's *Lejla*),[10] Šubert was on the lookout for new Czech works. This is the context for a commission that this time went ahead – without a libretto, without a title and on the basis of only four dances that Berger the ballet master heard in Brno. Although Janáček had submitted most of his music by late March (as his letter above to Bakešová suggests), there was a hiatus until a scenario could be sorted out: Šubert had to write to an impatient Janáček on 27 March making clear that there could hardly be rehearsals before the text had been submitted.[11] So, meanwhile, work on the 'vaudeville' that was proposed with Mrs Preissová swung into action.

A libretto was needed and Preissová began by using her connections to try and get one. An approach to Eliška Krásnohorská, the much-maligned librettist of Smetana's later operas, triggered an immediate and negative reaction: 'I thank you warmly for the unexpected surprise and for your trust in me and for kindly sending me the interesting draft, which – as you see – I am returning.' Surely, Krásnohorská went on, Preissová remembered that after her bitter experiences she had resolved never again to write for the theatre. Krásnorhorská's letter is interesting in that it reveals that Janáček's name was current in non-musical circles beyond Moravia: 'Of Mr Janáček I have already heard that he is a solid musician; I have absolutely nothing against him.'[12]

Preissová's letter to Janáček about this disappointing outcome betrays that she had in fact already taken a hand in writing the libretto herself, though it needed to be put into verse by someone with more experience as a versifier: 'Look through the action yourself, the way I have drafted it for versification. We must wait a while in view of the mourning in Dr Rieger's household; then we'll turn to Mrs Červinková – I really did forget about her, poor thing.' Marie Červinková-Riegrová (1854–95) was the librettist of two of Dvořák's best operas, and the person to whom Krásnohorská drew attention when she herself declined. Janáček knew her slightly (he had accompanied her singing in Rožnov in 1879 at the celebration for František Palacký – her grandfather). While he was not one to be put off by any delicacy about intruding on private grief, he perhaps judged that this route sounded time-consuming. In her letter to Janáček, Preissová had asked that Janáček should not pass on the draft prose scenario to anyone else 'unless Professor Bartoš should wish to see it; I respect him so much that it was only on his account that I embarked on this',[13] and it may well have been Bartoš who came up with the final, successful suggestion:

František Rypáček, a former colleague of his at the Czech Gymnasium I, who wrote verse under the pseudonym of Jaroslav Tichý and seemed to be immediately available for and agreeable to the assignment:

Providing a text for your work [Preissová commented] is entirely your own affair – my part is simply the pleasure that you may be able to make use of the action of my story. So I consent most gladly to Mr T[ichý]'s kindly taking it on, and only if it becomes necessary to get Mrs Č[ervinková] will I offer to intercede for you.[14]

Though Tichý gratifyingly worked at the sort of speed Janáček liked, the quality left something to be desired, and when not much more than a week later Preissová received the result, she sent the libretto straight off to one of her Moravian advisers, a priest, poet and Moravian enthusiast, Vladimír Šťastný, to try and improve it: 'Mr Jaroslav Tichý has a graceful turn of phrase, quite accurate in its folk diction – only here and there would I ask you, as a brilliant poet, if you could kindly change the words underlined to something more apt. I have also tried to do a bit, but I myself am strictly a writer of prose.'[15]

In Tichý's defence it should be said that his brief was unenviable. The libretto was based on Preissová's short story *The Beginning of a Romance*, first published in the periodical *Světozor* in 1886. Preissová was from Bohemia and in 1880 had moved with her husband to Hodonín, at the time a predominantly German-speaking industrialized Moravian town (Preiss ran a sugar refinery). Accompanying her husband on business trips into the neighbouring Czech-speaking villages, she was charmed by the exotic world she discovered there, its folk crafts (embroidery, ceramics, house decoration, costumes), distinctive dialect, music and way of life. All this is recorded in her short stories, including *The Beginning of a Romance*.[16] The strength of what Preissová wrote is not in its trivial plot (a brief dalliance between the humble Poluška and her aristocratic suitor before she returns to her faithful swain Tonek) but in the opportunity it provided for detailed descriptions of the costumes and customs of Slovácko. The conflict between aristocrat male and peasant girl is handled with nicely ironic observation. Transferred to the stage, the peasants can be in folk costume, can speak in the local dialect and can perform folksongs and dances of the area, but the best part of what Preissová originally offered – irony and descriptions of folk milieu – is swept aside. Even from Preissová's description to Šťastný the project sounds perfunctory and doomed: 'The spoken dialogue is just as I hurriedly drafted it in about two hours, it was naturally more detailed.' It was also too long: 'just cut what and where it is possible! I myself have also tried cutting; perhaps the poet won't hold it against me.'[17]

Šťastný didn't spend long on it either (if he did at all). By 4 June Preissová was asking Janáček how he was getting on with it:

> I am much looking forward to *The Beginning of a Romance*. How far have you got with the work? Mr J[aroslav] T[ichý]'s versification is delightful. That it's a little strange for so many people to come together in one place in one act – don't let that bother you! After all it is a forest with footpaths crossing, where the gentry go for walks and so on; the entry of every character is justified. What about those operas where if a chorus is needed a crowd rushes on from the wings! And so on. An opera text does not call for such rigid standards as drama.[18]

According to his draft, Janáček began on 15 May, perhaps working on the overture while waiting for possible corrections from Šťastný. He had in fact only just got the ballet out of the way, sending off the 'last three numbers of music' to Šubert about then.[II]

Meanwhile a librettist had been found for the ballet, Dr Jan Herben, a Moravian working in Prague as a journalist, who had been Janáček's drama critic in *Hudební listy*. Whatever contacts between composer and librettist there may have been, no record has survived. The only known detail, gleaned from a letter Janáček wrote to Berger, was that Herben finished his task on 23 May.[19] Correspondence with Bakešová continued over more sets of dances for piano. The printing was a particular problem, especially with the four-hand arrangements.[20] With all this going on (plus of course his teaching jobs) it may seem rather surprising that Janáček was able to complete his sketch for *The Beginning of a Romance* in seven weeks, by 2 July, as he recorded on the score. That he was able to work as fast as he did was certainly helped by the fact that about half of the opera was recycled from other sources (see chap. 30).

Almost nothing survives from Janáček's first drafts of his other early operas, but in *The Beginning of a Romance* he left a unique document, a tall bound book, written in a miniature hand on blank paper with staves ruled with a rastrum. Janáček wrote his first drafts on the

---

[II] In his letter to Šubert of 29 May 1891 Janáček mentioned that he had despatched the music 'a fortnight ago' (Procházková 1992, 106).

left-hand side of each opening, corrected them, and then copied it out neatly on the right. This produced a piano-vocal score version that before the end of the year he would score for full orchestra. In the process something that had started off as a piece with spoken dialogue separating the arias, duets, ensembles and dances (this is perhaps what was intended by the word 'vaudeville') would turn into a continuously sung piece. Recitatives now replaced the spoken dialogue, though going through a 'melodrama' stage in between, with the words spoken over an orchestral background.[21]

Preissová took a lively interest and made arrangements to get to know the work as soon as it was finished, descending upon Janáček on 8 July to hear him play it on the piano.[22] She wasn't entirely happy with the results: 'it seems to me that he is composing too massively, in too classical a style – it could be lighter', as she wrote to Mrs Kusá; nevertheless, she went on, she had 'great hopes for Janáček'.[23]

While Janáček was writing his opera, the National Theatre in Prague began to make progress with the ballet and events had moved far enough by 2 June 1891 for a press release to be issued in *Moravská orlice*:

Moravian folk dances will be given on the stage of the National Theatre in Prague in the very near future in a stage setting. The overture and music for these dances comes from L. Janáček, the text accompanying the dances, of which there are twenty-seven, is by Jan Herben. The dances have been arranged by the ballet master A. Berger. The dances have already been completely rehearsed, just the writing down of the text passages has been somewhat protracted. As soon as the text is written, it will be possible to stage the dances within a few days.[24]

No title for the work was given, and when the next day Janáček wrote to the newspaper to make corrections he supplied one:

Concerning yesterday's theatre news (Moravian dances) I venture to add that the dances concerned are inserted in a scene from Slovakia under the name *The Lord of Nové Zámky* and that the text part, effectively produced by Dr J. Herben, is ready. Kindly publish this addition at a convenient moment.[25]

Janáček's title was not the final one – his ballet was presented to the world as *Rákoš Rákoczy*, a name that has given problems ever since with its mixture of Czech transliteration (*Rákoš* – i.e. Rakosh) and incorrect Hungarian (*Rákoczy*, properly *Rákóczi*). Nor did Janáček draw attention to the ethnographical mishmash: a setting in Slovácko, some dances from nearby Haná but also many of Janáček's *Valachian Dances*, recycled once more. However, events were moving fast, as a letter from Berger reveals:

The music [i.e. orchestral parts] is already being written out and today I had a big rehearsal of the dances because of the children – they are new to it. So far I still don't know whether Dr Herben has already handed over the words; he hasn't been to see me from that time, and the director has not yet told me anything more. I asked the dramaturg to evaluate it favourably after reading it.[26]

The last ploy certainly worked since the next day the ballet was accepted both by the dramaturg (the playwright Ladislav Stroupežnický, 1850–92) and by the director Šubert.[27] A week later, the text had been approved by the censor with one tiny reference to 'the emperor' removed,[28] and a contract issued in which Herben was paid 50 zl for his text while Janáček and Berger split a 150 zl advance of 4% on each performance,[29] Janáček's first theatrical royalty.¶

Against these great events, as Janáček attempted to move in more elevated circles, Bakešová's stream of letters about details in the second fascicle of *Folk Dances in Moravia* may have come as something of an irritant. In the middle of preparations for his first staged work he was expected to take decisions about whether to include more verses that had been found for some of the dances (these were in fact dance-songs with words) and what to do about the dialects (with Slovácko, Haná and Valašsko all muddled up together). Nor did Bakešová stint her robust advice about how Janáček should comport himself in Prague:

Just, I ask you, insist that you conduct the music *yourself*. They should be honoured when a composer such as yourself comes *in person*. But I know that the puffed-up, jealous [Bohemian] Czechs look on with distrust at anything that comes from Moravia and that they recognize its value only when people abroad point it out to them.[30]

Everything was coming to a head at much the same time, as Janáček's next letter to Bakešová suggests: 'Have you received the proof of the dances? Are you in agreement with the change of text? Tomorrow the 13th [July] I go to Prague for rehearsals, on the 18th it should be given in the theatre. Perhaps I'll drop by when I get back

---

¶In reality Janáček did slightly better: the advance was increased to 200 zl – i.e. 100 zl each – and the takings, by the end of September, exceeded this; he was paid an extra 17 zl 34 kr (National Theatre to LJ, 28 Sept 1891, BmJA, A 879).

and tell you how I got on in Prague.'[31] The 'proof of the dances' was presumably dealt with and, amidst all the other excitements of the time, soon forgotten about, though copies of the second fascicle of *Folk Dances in Moravia* were available later in the year.**

The Prague National Theatre was a repertory theatre with a permanent corps of actors, singers and dancers. Repertory was set only a couple of weeks ahead, according to audience demand or contingencies such as illness in the company. And if a piece wasn't ready for its designated première it was easy enough to postpone it for more rehearsals, a phenomenon that would recur in several of Janáček's mature stage works. So although, on the day that the Organ School ended its academic year, 13 July, Janáček set off for Prague, he found he had to hang around there rather longer. The première was shifted to 24 July, when at last his one-act ballet was given, in a double bill with a play by the dramaturg Stroupežnický, *The Mintmaster's Wife*, a comedy that Janáček remembered many years later when looking for a new opera text (see chap. 55).

Rákoš Rákoczy was one of four new productions given during the Jubilee Exhibition and it achieved a respectable total of eight performances. Despite the speed with which it had been put together, the theatre took some trouble staging it, casting well-known actors in the main parts, including even the choreographer Berger. An assistant had taken the rehearsals, but the performances were conducted by one of the chief conductors of the period, Mořic Anger. Naturally the Moravian newspapers were lavish in their praise. 'Splendid success', 'sold-out house', 'strong and powerful applause', proclaimed the critic standing in for Janáček in *Moravské listy*, though 'six curtain calls' at the première[32] doesn't sound all that much. Among the Prague papers, it is surprising to find not only that the famous poet Jaroslav Vrchlický covered it in *Hlas* but that he was quite complimentary about Herben's text, based on a well known poem by Vítězslav Hálek, *The Girl from the Tatras*.[33] For all that, it must be said that the libretto is a fairly slight affair, a hook for the twenty-plus folk dances, songs and choruses. Arriving in a village in Slovácko, the adventurer Rákoš is taken as the absent count and plays his part so successfully that he gets himself

---

** Janáček responded to a request from Dr Karel Pippich of Chrudim for the second fascicle, sending it on 9 December (according to his note on Pippich's letter of 7 December 1891, BmJA, A 34).

engaged to Katuška, the local beauty and the richest girl in the village. Just as the knot is about to be tied, Katuška's former sweetheart Jan Horný turns up – everyone had believed that he perished at the Battle of Leipzig in 1813. Katuška naturally marries Jan instead. Rumbled, Rákoš makes a well-timed escape.

Janáček's music found less favour with the Prague critics. Although they were not necessarily aware of the patchwork origins, some reservations were expressed about the orchestration ('more for the eye than the ear') and the fact that Janáček seemed to have learnt too little from Dvořák in this respect.[34] But eight performances was hardly a failure. Janáček could return to Brno pleased with himself, no doubt profiting from having seen one of his works performed on stage for the first time.

Once all the excitement in Prague was over, Janáček went off to Velká nad Veličkou, an ethnographically rich village in Slovácko. A local collector, Martin Zeman (see below), had written to Bartoš asking advice in his dealings with the publisher Urbánek.[35] Bartoš had passed on the letter to Janáček, who wrote to Zeman with his opinion, and also went on to express an interest in the dances of the area. Would he find Zeman at home on 17 July?[36] The plan for that day was of course overtaken by events in Prague, but was resumed in September. 'Esteemed friend', Janáček wrote to Zeman, 'I'll arrive [by train] on Tuesday morning [8 September] in Strážnice. Perhaps it will be possible to get transport [to Velká]? I look forward to getting to know you and your dances.'[37]

This is one of the turning-points in Janáček's relationship with Moravian folk music. A few months later he applied for a grant (see below) to study in more detail what he had found. His application expressed his surprise at how much more 'effective' the Slovácko dances were than those he knew from his native region, showing a completely different spirit and in particular a harmonic dimension that until then he had thought to be absent from Moravian folk music. Velká was a centre for this folk-ensemble music, boasting a particularly fine folk violinist, Pavel Trn, whom Janáček encountered in several venues. Slovácko itself was of course the region celebrated in Preissová's plays and short stories, including the one that formed the basis for Janáček's second opera, *The Beginning of a Romance*. While this opera is ethnographically uncertain (the setting unspecified, but

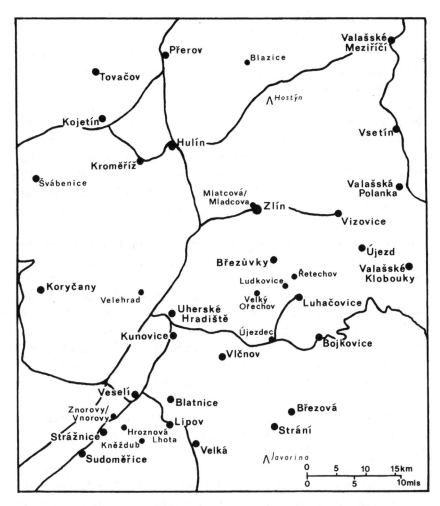

Map 3   Slovácko and part of Valašsko.

some Lachian dances used in it), in Janáček's next opera, *Jenůfa*, everything would point unequivocally to Slovácko.

Martin Zeman (1854–1919), a musically trained folksong collector and folk performer (he had studied at the Prague Organ School and was the local organist in Velká), became one of Janáček's chief folk-music associates, joining the existing team for the third and final fascicle of *Folk Dances in Moravia* (VIII/10) and organizing the Slovácko folk-music representation at the Ethnographic Exhibition in 1895. Janáček's trip in September 1891 couldn't have been for long – the new academic term was upon him – but it opened his eyes to much richer possibilities, and in the future his interest in Moravian folk music would extend from his previous tramping ground of Lašsko and Valašsko to Slovácko.

With the autumn season Janáček's reviewing activities resumed. Little stands out except for curiosities such as Ivan's Zajc's *Der Raub der Sabinnerinnen* among the routine fare of *The Bartered Bride, Dalibor, Il trovatore, The Elderly Bridegroom* (Bendl), *In the Well* (Blodek), *Die lustigen Weiber von Windsor* (Nicolai) and *La fille du régiment* (Donizetti) (xv/119–22, 124–5). Some idea of the standards involved is provided not so much by Janáček's reviews (which tried to be encouraging) as by an exchange with Dvořák at the time. As a member of the Czech Theatre Družstvo, Janáček seems to have written a letter to his distinguished friend asking whether he would allow the theatre to mount another opera of his (so far all that had been performed in Brno was the one-act *Cunning Peasant*). In principle he would be willing, Dvořák wrote back, but the tiny orchestra created difficulties: 'One would have perhaps to re-orchestrate the whole opera for small orchestra, and who would have to do that!' *The Jacobin* would be the best one to start with; *Dimitrij*, which perhaps Janáček suggested, gave 'too much work'.[38] In the event even *The Jacobin* wasn't possible since the one copy of the score was at the National Theatre in Prague and not available for copying;[39] it was a decade before Brno managed another Dvořák opera, *The Devil and Kate* in 1902.

Still haunted by his experience in Velká in September, by the autumn Janáček had formulated a specific plan of research, which he sent to the Czech Academy of Sciences in the hope of getting funding. His letter of 11 November presents a valuable summary of what he had done so far in this field and how he saw the way ahead:

I have been collecting and studying folk dances in Moravia for three years.

So far, I have got to know the region of eastern Moravia around Hukvaldy (Čeladná–Kunčice–Tichá; Mniší–Sklenov–Rychaltice; Kozlovice). [. . .]

A result of this study is also the ballet *Rákoš Rákoczy*. Until recently I didn't know the folk dances in Slovácko that are still common. And I was not a little surprised when, on my last trip, I got to know the Slovácko dances, so much more effective than the Valachian ones, and especially the dance *danaj*, whose rhapsodic form surprised me.

It's natural that in the south of Moravia there is a different spirit affecting the dance than that in the rather poor Valachian countryside.

It would be exceptionally interesting to follow the gradual transition in style of these compositions along the Moravian border from the east to the south.

Collecting folk dances is therefore extremely important since one is here at the source of *harmonic folk music*. Up till now we Czechs haven't recognized this – it was generally thought that we didn't have it. Collecting folk dances in Moravia, and it must be quick and without further delay, must therefore be our sacred duty.

After all, the cimbalom players that I got to know in Valašsko are already old people (Myška from Petřvald is around sixty years old, Mikeska in Košatka around seventy, Klepáč in Kunčice over sixty). [...]

Over the holidays (beginning on 16 July 1892)[††] I therefore want to visit Hukvaldy near Příbor and from there to undertake research trips in the direction to the north-east, to Košatka on the Odra and to Sedliště beyond the Ostravice river. [...] I have thought up a few trips to the south of Moravia, to the vicinity of Velká. It was there that I got to know the dance I've mentioned, *danaj*, with the accompaniment of two violins and bass with a bagpipe. What harmonic, contrapuntal and rhythmic forms there are, so far unsuspected in Czech folk music![40]

Three days later Janáček's application was put before a distinguished panel including Fibich and Dvořák. Sadly, they were told not to consider it since it had missed the deadline.[41] But the application letter remains a testament to Janáček's knowledge and enthusiasms of the time, and especially his growing appreciation of the folk-music-ensemble tradition in Slovácko and his discovery of the rhapsodic dance *danaj*. With it, one of the strands leading to his next opera, *Jenůfa*, had just been found.

A week or two after hearing the negative outcome,[42] Janáček had thought of another scheme to exploit his *Rákoš* success in Prague:

I have completed a one-act opera, *The Beginning of a Romance* [Janáček wrote to Šubert at the National Theatre] and I want to bring the score[‡‡] to you in the New Year.

However, I ask you respectfully for one favour. Examining [an opera] usually takes very long and I would like to avoid this long, embarrassing uncertainty. Could you speed it up so that I might go home with a decision

---

[††] The Organ School usually broke up around 15 July.
[‡‡] Presumably the full score (BmJA, A 29.920). Thus between July and December 1891 Janáček had revised the vocal score and orchestrated it.

about it? I think it could be done. I would play the work to the conductors, and for further study three or four days might perhaps suffice.

I will submit the piece to the Brno Theatre only if it stands up to the critical study of your experts. My position in the Družstvo of the Brno Theatre obliges me to do this.[43]

The last paragraph of the letter states that the reason why Janáček was taking the score to Šubert was a possible conflict of interests in Brno. As a member of the Družstvo he didn't want to submit a piece to Brno without some sort of quality assurance from elsewhere (not that in the end this stopped Janáček going ahead without it). Were Prague to make an offer at the same time, this would no doubt have been welcome, and was possibly the artful purpose of the exercise anyway, perhaps suggested by Preissová. Shortly before Janáček wrote to Šubert, she had written to him saying that she would mention the opera to Šubert, but that Janáček should stress that they mustn't take too long looking it over ('he likes to be forgetful').[44]

Janáček's reviews continued: in December a Mozart celebration on the 100th anniversary of his death (xv/127), Lortzing's *Der Wildschütz* (xv/128), Gounod's *Roméo et Juliette* on Christmas Day (xv130); in January Offenbach's *Les contes d'Hoffmann* (xv/131), *The Kiss* (xv/132), a Beseda concert (xv133), a collection of piano pieces compiled by Fibich and published by Urbánek (xv/134 and the ensuing correspondence xv/135, when Urbánek objected). This 1891–2 season was in fact the last for which Janáček wrote regular newspaper reviews, thus bringing to an end an activity that had started with the publication of *Hudební listy* in 1884. It seems unlikely that *Moravské listy* signed him off – to have one of the leading musical figures in Brno writing for it was a feather in its cap. But, as Janáček discovered during preparations to mount his new opera, reviewers make enemies. It may well be that, at the end of this season, Janáček withdrew his services in order to concentrate on his career as a composer. Or perhaps he simply got tired of trying to find something to say about the conventional fare that the Brno Theatre presented. Thereafter, his few reviews were one-off affairs, written only when the event in question was of particular significance to him.

In early 1892 a curious event took place in Hukvaldy: Janáček's sister Josefa married the teacher Jindřich Dohnal (1868–1939) on 25 January. The event was odd in that Josefa was fifty at the time and that her husband was twenty-six years younger. The event had a considerable impact on the Janáčeks: up until then, with Josefa teaching domestic science at the Hukvaldy school, she had been able to provide holiday accommodation in the family's home village. But now that she moved with her new husband to a post near Ostrava,[§§] Hukvaldy became a less attractive holiday option since any accommodation there would need to be paid for.

In February Janáček had the usual mid-academic-year break from his teaching duties and energetically set about securing a Prague performance of *The Beginning of a Romance*. Having already told František Šubert at the Prague National Theatre about the work and that he would be bringing the score with him to Prague, he now decided that the best plan was to send the score by post and, a little later, to follow this up with a personal visit. He wrote to Šubert accordingly:

I am sending the score of *The Beginning of a Romance*. I now have the half-year holiday; could you specify a time on Monday the 15th [of February] when I might play my work in its main outlines to the conductor?

I shall arrive in Prague on Sunday afternoon, if nothing upsets this plan, and I shall venture to look you up.[45]

As one can infer from Janáček's next letter to Šubert, the meeting took place as planned. The chief conductor of the Prague National Theatre, Adolf Čech, was in attendance and, according to his later note to Šubert, voiced his criticisms then and there: '*The Beginning of a Romance* in no way matches up to our view of operatic works, either in invention or in form. Furthermore, the instrumentation is, so to speak, as "elegantly" thin as that of the same composer's ballet *Rákoš Rákoczy*.'[46] Such criticisms were intended to be terminally discouraging, but Janáček did not take them this way and responded with amendments and, at the end of his February break, sent back the corrected score.[47]

Reviewing resumed with what Janáček clearly considered to be unmitigated trivia, Planquette's *Les cloches de Corneville* for the umpteenth time (XV/136 – a very short review). But then something extraordinary happened. On 3 March Brno gave the local Czech première of Mascagni's *Cavalleria rusticana*, which had been playing to enthusiastic audiences at the Prague National Theatre since January

[§§] Zdenka records 'Hulváky', now a suburb of Ostrava, but the few postcards that Josefa sent during the period came from Hrabová, still in Ostrava but a little further out.

1891. Janáček did not write at once after the première but waited to see the second performance on 8 March 1892 and the next day published his article, the last operatic review he wrote for *Moravské listy* (xv/137). Like the one he wrote on *Onegin*, his piece on *Cavalleria* is unusual for being longer than the usual paragraph or two. The opera had clearly caught his attention – partly because of its novelty as *verismo*, but also because it had something to say to him that he could put to use himself. His opening comments begin with an unidentified quotation about how some composers, having discarded the 'dust' of thousand-year-old theories, acquire so much harmonic and tonal freedom that mere mortals become dizzy listening to the results. Astonishingly, Janáček then declares that this brought Mascagni to mind.

Thereafter follows a checklist of individual numbers in the opera. Alfio's entrance song is praised for its modern harmony and 'formal perfection' (the 'exact form of a rondo' with 'ingenious' variations), Santuzza's 'No, no Turiddu – rimani' (the melodic climax of her duet with Turiddu) 'breathes tenderness'. On the debit side, Janáček considered Lola's entrance aria and Turiddu's *brindisi* 'close to triviality', though he praised the 'persuasive truthfulness' of Turiddu's farewell to his mother, 'Mamma, quel vino è generoso'.

Two things about Janáček's enthusiasm for Mascagni's one-acter are worth noting in the context of *Jenůfa*. The first is that Janáček was praising a piece cast in what was by then the oldfashioned mould of a number opera, though one tightly bonded with leitmotifs and a surprising amount of purely orchestral music. Second, that having got his checklist out of the way, he dwelt in particular on the dramatic confrontation of Santuzza and Turiddu.

From the icy calm of their first meeting there grows a destructive passion. You think there'll be an explosion at any moment, but meanwhile Lola merely feeds the glowing flames with her entrance [Lola's *stornello* interrupts the Santuzza-Turiddu duet]; Santuzza's wailing pleas, heard several times, restrain Turiddu and culminate in her unpitched cry ['quasi parlato']: 'A te la mala Pasqua, spergiuro'.

This is only a stone's throw away from similarly explosive confrontations in Act 1 of *Jenůfa*. There was, however, a more immediate consequence of his review, a letter from the singer Marie Wollnerová:

As a result of the review about my performance of the part of Santuzza in *Cavalleria rusticana*[IIII] I am forced, though most unwillingly, to return with my respectful thanks the part that through your kindness was assigned to me in the opera *The Beginning of a Romance*. Because of your attentions, I have come to the view that I would not be able to perform a part such as that of Poluška to your satisfaction with regard either to acting or to singing. I fear that my poor conception of the part would only be to the detriment of the whole opera, and I do not wish to bring any blame on myself should your opera – in every respect no doubt outstanding – not have the success in performance which you, esteemed sir, expect. Perhaps casting the part with another singer would avoid this and satisfy your refined musical taste.[48]

Apart from his leading lady walking out on him, it is also clear from Janáček's letter to Šubert below that there were other problems and delays in mounting the opera in Brno. Meanwhile things were not doing any better in Prague. Janáček had waited a month for some reaction from Šubert, but there had been silence and at the end of March he wrote to him again:

I hoped that I would get from you the answer you promised concerning *The Beginning of a Romance*.

I did not send a reminder as I wanted to invite you to the first performance in Brno. Since it has been drawn out beyond expectation here – at best they will be finished with copying out the parts only on Wednesday – and since the opera company leaves Brno next week [for its regional tour], it will probably not be performed in Brno this season.

I ask you to be so kind as to send the prompt reply you promised on the basis of the conductors' statements recommending the work for performance.

The conductor Mr Čech naturally does not see the work as an *opera* in the modern sense of the word. Then again, that was not how it was intended. Mrs Preissová called it a dramatized idyll and I wrote music to it, aspiring at least to the level of musical expression in Blodek's *In the Well*,[¶¶] which I had in mind.

I enclose the libretto; the score is at your disposal until the end of this week.[49]

Šubert took the 'end of this week' for the empty threat it was and so Janáček found himself nagging him at regular intervals throughout April.[50] Šubert had asked for formal reports from his two conductors,

---

[IIII] It seems odd that Wollnerová should have taken exception to what was an enthusiastic review. Janáček's criticism of her and the Turiddu was that their acting had not been sufficiently thought out and that their singing needed more 'gentleness' at the start: only a 'small step' prevented their performances from being 'perfect'.

[¶¶] Janáček thought surprisingly well of Blodek's one-act village comedy; see chap. 25.

Adolf Čech and Mořic Anger, and only after he had received them did he write back to Janáček, returning the score at the same time.[51] Anger correctly identified Janáček's opera as a 'pendant' to *Rákoš* (which he had conducted himself), and not really an opera at all but a compilation of songs and dances.[52] Prague had been prepared to accept *Rákoš* as such, given the need, during the Regional Jubilee Exhibition of 1891, for a work that had more ethnographic than musico-dramatic significance, but in 1892 normal operatic fare was needed, and *The Beginning of a Romance* did not fit into this category.

In Brno, on the other hand, the reason for delays over any production had nothing to do with the work and much more to do with personal antagonisms that Janáček's reviewing activities had stirred up. Since he was on the committee of the Družstvo franchised to run the theatre, there could be no question of the opera not being performed in Brno without a major fracas, so the director of the Brno Theatre, Václav Hübner, faced with rebellion from his music staff, had to resort to delaying tactics. Hübner had already mentioned to Preissová that the work needed 'deep and time-consuming study' and that the orchestra (then only twenty-four players) would have to be doubled.[53] Janáček got a full (and surprisingly frank) report only at the beginning of the next season (see below).

Janáček wrote a few more non-operatic reviews for *Moravské listy* later that spring. There were two more Brno Beseda concerts (XV/138 and XV/141), the latter, on 18 April, devoted to the music of his mentor and friend Dvořák. He wrote a review of the continuation of the *Young Violinist* series (XV/139) and there was a very substantial article on the collecting of folksongs (XV/140), so long that it was published in two instalments (16 and 20 April). It was with a review of the recital by the seven-year-old Polish pianist Raoul Kocalzski, making his début at the Reduta in Brno on 2 May (XV/142), that Janáček finally ended his activities as a regular music critic and his connections with *Moravské listy*.

Janáček's trip to Velká in September 1891 was still buzzing in his mind, in particular the folkdance *danaj* that had surprised him with its 'rhapsodic form'. He set about trying to re-create it, first in a piano arrangement (*Ej, danaj!* VIII/12), whose autograph manuscript bears a date of 2 April 1892. He wrote to Berger in Prague about it (Berger expressed enthusiasm for getting to know it, but nothing more came of this)[54] and then offered the piece to the Prague publisher Velebín Urbánek*** who, however, declined, saying that he could only publish something simpler, for instance along the lines of Dvořák's *Humoresque*.[55] Perhaps it was this rejection that encouraged Janáček to do something else with the dance. Some time before the autumn he recycled it, orchestrating it and adding a well-known folk text to turn it into a work for chorus and orchestra, *I have sown green* (III/3). Although he was unaware of it at the time, Janáček had thereby already begun work on his next opera: this choral piece and its orchestral interludes became the basis for the Recruits' Chorus in Act I of *Jenůfa*.

At the same time Janáček began to draw a line under the piano collection *Folk Dances in Moravia* (VIII/10). In a long letter in June 1892 to Lucie Bakešová he stated that he had compared all the dance material that he had assembled so far and expressed doubts about further publication of their collection. He had twenty-nine dances written out, he told her, of which twelve (i.e. the first two fascicles) had already been printed. If she were to add her material, publication would go on indefinitely and no-one would notice it. As it was, the thing was hardly selling. He had sent 100 copies of the second fascicle to the Olomouc publisher Promberger,[†††] who after a year sent them all back.[56] In the event they (Janáček, Bakešová, Běhálková and now Zeman) published a third fascicle in 1893 with another nine dances and left it at that.

Janáček's time in Velká in September 1891 encouraged him to extend his folk-music researches during the next summer to Slovácko. The fact that, with Josefa's marriage and departure, Hukvaldy holiday accommodation was no longer freely available further reinforced this trend. Details are scarce and mostly undated, and with the dismissal of his application to the Czech Academy of Sciences, any trips needed to be self-funded and thus more modest. Janáček's existing notations, however, provide evidence that some time during the summer of 1892 he

---

*** The younger brother of F.A. Urbánek, with whom he was in business most of his life. Almost all of Janáček's dealings at the time were with the older Urbánek, but in 1891 Velebín set up his own business and Janáček seems to have tried him in the hope that he might be more flexible in his approach. This proved not to be the case. As it was, Velebín Urbánek died a few months after this exchange.

[†††] Romauld Promberger, Czech publisher of books about Moravia and popular scientific handbooks (see Sedláčková 2001, fn. 32).

was in Luhačovice, where he transcribed a cimbalom-and-strings ensemble from Březůvky. He was also in Blatnice pod Svatým Antonínkem, where he took down choreographic descriptions, in Lipov, where he found a permanent ensemble of fiddle (Pavel Trn from Velká again), *kontráš*††† and bass, and Strážnice, which had a similar three-man ensemble.[57] It is possible, however, that the Blatnice, Lipov and Strážnice trips were all conducted from Velká, in search of 'variants', as mentioned in a letter to Zeman:

> I want to come for about two weeks to your region, partly for study, partly to come to an agreement with you about the guest appearance of Horňácko§§§ music at the folk concert which I have been invited to direct in November in Brno.
>
> I want to leave Brno on 1 September straight for Strážnice and stay with you in Velká. I hope that you can rent me some little room.
>
> From there I'd then explore the surrounding area in search of variants in the music and steps of the local dances.[58]

Janáček's enthusiasm for the musicians of Velká is evident in his later descriptions: 'The most important centre of the pure style of folk music in Slovácko is without doubt the small town of Velká. I have not yet come across places of similar importance in Valašsko or Lašsko.' His experiences led to writing a substantial article, *The Outlines of Musical Folk Dances in Moravia* (xv/145), which he published in the ethnographical journal *Český lid* in March 1893. The article reproduces many of his earlier cimbalom notations of dances, a total of twenty-three, including several that he used in his *Valachian Dances* (vi/4).

Janáček seems to have spent over two weeks in Slovácko: a thank-you letter to Zeman written on 20 September declared that he was writing 'on arrival' back home and apologized for the length of his stay.[59] His return to Brno was greeted by a long letter from the director of the Brno Theatre, Václav Hübner, giving a fascinating picture of the intrigues that had so far bedevilled the production of *The Beginning of a Romance*:

> Word has reached me that the Committee of the Družstvo of the Czech National Theatre in Brno is maliciously stating that it was my fault that your opera *The Beginning of a Romance* was not staged in last year's season, and

---

††† See chap. 28.
§§§ The mountainous border region of Slovácko centred on Velká.

that you are said to take the view that I am to blame for the fact that the première of the opera did not take place. [. . .]

If anyone is to blame for your opera not being performed it can only be the conductor, Mr Jílek. As soon as you kindly informed me that you were entrusting the performance of the opera to us, I definitely said to Mr Jílek that we must perform the opera this season and that it would also be an excellent enrichment of the repertory for the regional tour and a welcome piece for the box office too. Then, when we first went to your house to hear the opera, I realized from the conductor's comments that he was apparently unhappy to see that your opera was to be put into rehearsal. He did not hide such remarks even from Miss Fürstová, who was in hospital at the time and whom we stopped to see on the way to your house.

Then when we heard your opera and, still later, when he was handed the vocal score and full score, I and also doubtless other people frequently heard his fairly caustic remarks, which he did not hide, particularly from the singers, drawing attention mainly to the difficult voice parts and to the problems that the orchestra would have to overcome. [. . .] He constantly declared that he was unable to prepare it at the time and when I urged him did no more than smile or fob me off with 'So study it yourself if you know so much about it!' [. . .]

This is not slander, scandal-mongering or stirring but just an honest plea of my innocence in this matter when I state that the conductor Mr Jílek somehow intended that your opera should not reach the stage. I presume that it was in return for the fact that in his view you did not write favourably enough about him and the whole opera company in *Moravské listy*. I do not even hide the fact that he probably knew well enough – although perhaps was not himself the cause – that Miss Wollnerová returned to you her part from your opera.[60]

As long as Jílek remained chief conductor in Brno there was no progress on the production of *The Beginning of a Romance*, and a whole season passed without further activity.

Meanwhile Janáček threw himself wholeheartedly into the project that he had already announced to Zeman in August and discussed with him during his stay in September. This was the 'folk concert' given in the Brno Besední dům on 22 November 1892. The idea was to confront Brno audiences with raw traditional music and its translation into art-music arrangements. Janáček had already found what he needed, namely Pavel Trn's ensemble, and negotiations were conducted through Zeman[61] to bring Trn's folk ensemble to Brno along with a troupe of folk dancers and singers.

The 'folk concert' had three components: items performed by the

Velká musicians, a selection of Janáček's folk arrangements, and three purely art-music pieces in which Janáček conducted the Brno Theatre orchestra and an unidentified amateur chorus. The three pieces – Dvořák's overture *My Homeland* and two unaccompanied choruses by Křížkovský, *The Shepherd and the Pilgrims* and *A Thrashing* – made rather odd bedfellows with the other pieces in the concert but the close connections of both composers to Janáček suggest that these pieces were his choice.

For the folk arrangements, Janáček took two of his *Valachian Dances* (*Čeladná Dance, Furcoat*) and six items from his ballet *Rákoš Rákoczy*: two folksong arrangements for chorus and orchestra (*Musicians, what are you doing?* and *The Mosquitoes got Married*) and four dances from the Haná region (*Kalamajka, Threes, The Road* and *Triple Dance*). One further item by Janáček was new: *I have sown green* (III/3), his choral adaptation of *Ej, danaj!*

But what was exceptional about the concert, and given much attention in the local press, was the juxtaposition of Janáček's arrangements with the pieces performed by the musicians from Velká. Trn had organized a group of five musicians: himself on the fiddle, two more violins, a clarinet and a cello. Janáček had hoped for a cimbalom player as well, but although he found a suitable one during his stay in Luhačovice (Tomáš Kaláč from Březůvky, apparently willing to join the group),[62] this in the end did not happen.

There were seven dancers/singers: four women and three men. Among other things, they sang several wedding-procession songs and performed a *farmer's dance* and an *oldfashioned dance* as well as singing their own version of *Musicians, what are you doing?*, the only direct comparison with any of Janáček's arrangements. Photographs were taken by the local studio (Janáček's friend J.L. Šichan), two of which were published with a substantial report by Lubor Niederle in the January 1893 issue of *Český lid*.[63] The photographs are splendid: dancers and players are in their colourful Sunday-best folk outfits, most of them looking somewhat alarmed by this rare expedition to the Moravian metropolis (see Plate 31). The composer Vítězslav Novák (see chap. 36) was not an eye-witness himself. His corroborative detail about the cimbalom player is alas unfounded[IIIII] and the origin of the

---

[IIIII] Although Janáček tried hard to get a cimbalom player, none is depicted in the photographs and Niederle, in his report in *Český lid*, specifically regrets the absence of one.

musicians simply wrong, but his malicious account of the event never-theless rings true:

Looking at the audience flooding into the hall the dear musicians lost heart, which Janáček in vain attempted to restore with increased doses of *slivovice* – even the cimbalom player wanted to escape with his instrument under his arm. His intention was, however, thwarted in time by the alert Janáček, who locked the room. Then when the trembling Hukvaldy musicians were pushed on to the podium and displayed to the eyes and opera-glasses of the audience, they played and sang so appallingly that it was now the turn of the audience to want to escape from them.[64]

For the public it was certainly something of a disappointment: too many performances of *The Bartered Bride* with classically trained ballet dancers in fancy costumes swirling around to music played by a symphony orchestra had taken their toll. As Niederle reported, people expected something larger and more glamorous; certainly three pairs of dancers and a handful of players, however authentic, made little impact in the echoing spaces of the Besední dům. In fact things do not seem to have got going until the 'free entertainment' at the end of the concert, when the folk musicians at last let their hair down and performed with fewer inhibitions.[65]

In October 1892 Janáček had written to Martin Zeman asking him to write down the variant of a *farmer's dance* (*As we went to the feast*) that he had come across the previous month in Velká.[66] Janáček now made an arrangement for chorus and orchestra of this song (III/4) using the same forces as his *I have sown green* (III/3), premièred at the 'folk concert'. Some months later Janáček mentioned in a letter to Bakešová that he was planning a 'first suite', which he would offer to Simrock, 'the well-known publisher of Dr Ant. Dvořák'.[67] Janáček had Josef Štross copy out four of the *Valachian Dances*, though the manuscript ultimately also included his new piece *As we went to the feast*, which as a choral arrangement with a Czech text would not have been suitable for the Berlin publisher. Instead the collection, now called *Czech Dances, First Suite* (VI/9; see chap. 30), was sent to the Czech Academy to support another grant application:

The undersigned [Janáček wrote on 22 March 1893] respectfully ventures to ask for a travel grant for the purpose of collecting material in Moravia,

Hungarian Slovácko¶¶¶ and Silesia in order to get to know the harmonic aspects of Czech folk music, and for the purpose of supplementing Moravian folk collections. Last year [*recte* 1891] I ventured to turn to the esteemed presidium with a similar request but, I was told, my request arrived too late.

I support my present respectful request with a new series of Czech dances for orchestra and refer to my article on the outlines of musical folk dances in Moravia [Janáček gives publication details of xv/145] where, as an introduction, I have described the journeys that I have so far undertaken.

There can be no doubt of the importance of getting to know the harmonic aspects of folk music. It's necessary to transcribe cimbalom playing and that of the groups of folk musicians in Slovácko during the singing and dancing. It's long and difficult work, but now of the utmost urgency as both cimbalom players and folk musicians are dying out. Since my humble means aren't enough for me to travel for a long period and visit the many places of importance for this work, I turn to the Czech Academy, hoping for and trusting in its support. Should I be awarded it, I would collect the rich harmonic material again in Velká, Strážnice (and the surrounding area) and in the southern part of Těšínsko [in Silesia]. This year I should be able to devote two or even four months of my time to this work.⁶⁸

While waiting for the outcome of his application, Janáček got on with other matters. The annual report of the Brno Sokol about its public gymnastic display on 16 April 1893 includes the following item:

The performance of the physical exercises at the rally was faultless, this number being among the best. The music for the gymnastics was composed by one experienced in these matters, brother Director Janáček, to whom the Sokol gives renewed thanks.⁶⁹

The Czech gymnastic organization Sokol [Falcon] was one of the many new societies allowed by the Austrian regime in its more relaxed post-1860 policy towards the peoples of its empire. Modelled on the German physical exercise movement, the Turnverein, the Sokol was founded in 1862 ostensibly to promote physical education, though it soon became an important movement in raising Czech national consciousness, both before and after independence; the post-1918 rallies became national events, attracting huge crowds from all over the republic. Janáček was an enthusiastic Sokol supporter. He had joined the Brno I section in 1876,⁷⁰ hence the title 'brother' and the suggestion

---

¶¶¶Since 'Moravian' Slovácko is covered by 'Moravia', this unusual formulation probably means the area of Slovakia (then under Hungarian control) adjacent to Slovácko. Janáček is not known to have explored the area until 1901.

that he was 'experienced', though there are no reports of his actually taking part in Sokol exercises. What Janáček wrote (VIII/13), presumably at the request of the Moravian-Silesian District Sokol to which the pieces are dedicated, were five little pieces for piano, all beginning with a two-bar 'fanfare', and all in ABA form with repeated sections. They are all identical in length, sixteen bars, not including fanfares or repeats, and all are in a brisk, two-in-a-bar, polka style. As music for nineteenth-century aerobics they are pleasant enough, though quite devoid of any Janáček fingerprints. While they would have been fine for indoor practice, rallies were held in the open air and any piano accompaniment would not have carried, which is why arrangements for wind band were made later by Josef Kozlík and František Kmoch, perhaps in time for the Third National Sokol Rally in Prague on 29 June 1895. One puzzle is Janáček's title, *Music for Club Swinging*. Indian clubs were certainly used in Sokol exercises, though by 1900 they were confined to women's exercises (men exercised with sticks). However, the account of the 1893 rally expressly states that Janáček's music was used for *prostná*, i.e. exercising without implements: simply physical exercises.

Another commissioned piece that Janáček composed at this time was the male-voice chorus *Our Birch Tree* (IV/22), his first male chorus for five years. It was written to celebrate the twenty-fifth anniversary of 'Svatopluk', whose choir Janáček had conducted twenty years earlier. His pupil and colleague at the Organ School Max Koblížek had been music director of 'Svatopluk' since 1891 and perhaps approached Janáček for this chorus. Completed on 18 April 1893 (the date given in its publication in the *Památník Svatopluka* ['Svatopluk' Album]), it was first performed on 21 May 1893, conducted by Koblížek.

Early in July 1893 Janáček heard the outcome of his application to the Czech Academy for funds. It was negative again,[71] and presumably the long research trip that he had mentioned fell away. Nevertheless, he continued to make field trips that summer. In June 1893 he heard from Josef Pernický and František Zapletal, who sent him notes on the dance steps of local dances in the Valachian village of Jasenice.[72] Zapletal was the local teacher; Pernický the *fojt* (the village squire/mayor) and also a folk musician. Some time in the summer, probably in July after the Organ School term ended, Janáček set off for Jasenice, where he was able to add tunes to the description of the dances, as well as the names of the dancers. Although he characterized the ensemble as 'weak', he nevertheless took down four pieces for the combination of violin, clarinet, *kontráš* and bass.[73] It was an important field trip since many of the notated pieces found their way into his huge collection with Bartoš (XIII/3) and in addition, presumably that summer, Janáček worked up two of the dance notations into piano pieces, *The Cuckoo* (VIII/15) and *The Little Butcher* (VIII/14). These are both simple arrangements, preserving the keys and repetitive structures of the originals. The titles are apt and graphic, the first piece including the notes of the cuckoo call, the second the regular wide intervals imitating the motion of sawing.

Velká continued to exercise its fascination for Janáček and he returned there for a brief visit on 27 August 1893:

I am collecting evidence of the harmonic aspect of folk music [he wrote to Zeman]. Would you be so very kind as to get together in the afternoon *or perhaps the evening of Sunday 27 August*, a *hudec*, a *kontráš* and a bass player for certain? I don't want to take much down, but I want to take it down in detail. [...] What is needed is that the musicians repeat the music often, nothing more. I will reward them so that they wouldn't regret it, but I need to be certain.

Then followed various requests: could Zeman send the carriage for him from Velká (he would arrive by rail in Strážnice at noon on the 27th). So as not to inconvenience the Zemans he would stay with the Jewish lady who last year offered accommodation, and would eat at the pub. He wouldn't stay long as on 30 August he'd leave for Polanka in Valašsko.[74]

The Polanka expedition, at the invitation of the local priest, Antonín Přibyl,[75] was celebrated in an article for *Lidové noviny* (XV/143). This was a fateful moment for Janáček, his first association with the Brno journal (itself the renamed *Moravské listy*) for which he wrote for the rest of his life and from which he gathered inspiration for several of his works. It says something about his local eminence that he was asked to contribute to the first issue, on 16 December 1893. Although in a lighter style than his articles at around the same time for the specialist journal *Český lid* (XV/144, XV/145), this piece nevertheless described his main preoccupations in the field of Moravian folk music, and especially its harmonic aspects:

At the end of the summer holidays, in the month of September, I arrived in

Polanka, south from Vsetín. Here Mount Parun lords over the enchanting Valachian region, sending storms and gale-force winds into the countryside. Its peak is mostly bare, whereas many clearings are hidden away from the world in its wooded slopes. We were heading for one of these, the Verečná clearing. Although we found the cottage of the cimbalom player Jan Míčka, we had to summon the farmer from the slopes, where he was harvesting oats. He willingly exchanged his sickle for a cimbalom, sitting at the entrance of his cottage – and soon the quiet, close little valley resounded with his clanging sounds. The sun had long gone down on our way back with our good host. (xv/143)

Then followed an account of some of the local dances. Janáček was struck by the fact that although Vsetín was in Valašsko, its people wearing the distinctive Valachian folk costumes, the dancing and the music was that of Slovácko. 'How much love there is in [these dances], how much longing, happiness, and joy and – truth, always and everywhere there is truth. Also in music there is *truth*.' Janáček entitled this feuilleton *The Music of Truth*, and ended it with the provocative statement: '*how many Czech composers we have who so far have never composed the "truth"* '.

And soon Janáček was given the opportunity to do just that. Mrs Preissová, after silence in the summer, came to life again. She needed a violin teacher for her eleven-year-old son and hoped that Janáček might find one from among his Organ School pupils. At the same time, she passed on a brief news item: 'Mr J. Foerster (the younger) is writing an opera on *The Farm Mistress*. Mr Jaroslav Kvapil**** is composing the rhymes.†††† Perhaps this little bit of news will interest you, although Mr Foerster will need three years for the work.'[76] This is a very early indication of Josef Bohuslav Foerster's composition of his most celebrated opera, *Eva*, written to the text of Preissová's first play. Janáček responded promptly: Mrs Preissová's next letter (6 November) outlining arrangements for the first violin lesson, on 8 November with the third-year student that Janáček proposed, expressed the hope that she might also see Janáček at the same time. The letter goes on: 'I think that the material of P[astorkyňa] is not suitable for a musical setting – but in time we will perhaps find something more suitable'.[77] Had Janáček, between the two letters, had a brainwave about Preissová's second play, *Her Stepdaughter* (*Její pastorkyňa*), and suggested that he

****See chap. 47.
††††In the end Foerster wrote his own libretto.

might make an opera out of it? Her initially negative reaction was not an obstacle, since she seems to have been easily persuaded that *Her Stepdaughter* was suitable as an opera. This, at least, is the impression one gets from her memoir of the event, written almost half a century later:

After the composer Foerster, the highly talented, quick-tempered Moravian Leoš Janáček applied to me. He said that he had fallen in love with *Jenůfa* and already whole sentences of it rushed into his mind that he immediately dressed with his music. He did not need to put anything into verse, the words and sentences apparently spoke with their own music fully in agreement with his. We came to a happy arrangement.

True to his instincts, Janáček began to dress the action of *Jenůfa* with his heartfelt efforts. He studied the cries of young men at their folk dancing, he went off to the mill where he listened to and took down the noises of the turning and rumble of the mill wheel.[78]

The time was ripe for a new opera. In the absence of any activity at the Brno Theatre Mrs Preissová had suggested getting up an amateur performance of *The Beginning of a Romance* in her nearest town of Ivančice with local forces (maybe a 'six-piece orchestra'), conducted by the local choirmaster and stiffened with a couple of professionals from Prague.[79] Astonishingly, Janáček had agreed to this and even sent the score there.[80] Although this plan fell through almost as soon as it was proposed,[81] there was suddenly a glimmer of light in Brno: František Jílek, the hostile chief conductor who had blocked the performance of Janáček's opera, left Brno to take up a post in Sarajevo. Within a couple of months, *The Beginning of a Romance* was performed in Brno, on 10 February 1894. Thus by the time of his November contacts with Preissová, Janáček had known that his opera was to be performed soon and it was therefore sensible to plan a new one. The seeds sown by his reaction to Mascagni's *Cavalleria* and by his encounter with 'harmonic' folk ensemble music and the 'rhapsodic' dance *danaj* began to bear fruit. Janáček was now planning to 'compose the truth'.

Before then, however, there was a painful matter to be attended to in Prague:

I've got your postcard now [Janáček wrote to Zdenka and Olga from Prague at the end of December]. From it I assume that you hadn't yet got my telegram. I was at Prof. Kaufmann's again today He squirted into the hole that he made from the tooth up to my nose. I must learn to carry out this squirting myself.

I'll begin tomorrow; then they'll let me go home. Thanks to the happy chance and my desire that brought me to Prague! It would soon have turned out badly for me if I had gone on believing that idiot Dr Plenka. What will you do for New Year's Eve? From today I have a free entrance to the theatre. I've met up with Mr Mareš.†††† He was with me at the operation.[82]

During 1893, it seems, Janáček suffered from chronic infection of the facial sinuses. He was operated on by an ear and nose specialist in Prague, Dr Emilian Kaufmann, also an enthusiastic amateur musician. The operation consisted of the extraction of a tooth in the upper jaw to create a hole, into which was inserted a metal tube that then needed to be rinsed out daily (see chap. 64). As he relates, Janáček was instructed how to do this at his session the next day.

As early as 9 a.m. I was at the clinic – until 11.15! I learnt how to clean it myself. I got your letter and the postal order. In the afternoon I will be somewhere in a café and in the evening at the theatre. It's lovely weather here – but freezing! I hope that I'll be in Brno on Tuesday [1 January 1894] at four in the afternoon.[83]

†††† František Mareš (1862–1941), from 1888 director of the 'Vesna' schools in Brno. In later years he would be a supportive friend to Zdenka.

30

Folk dances in the orchestra and on stage

Janáček's *Valachian Dances* (VI/4) are not a stable, defined work but, rather, a complex of dances known always by this title until the 1920s though the selection might vary. In fact the 'complex' can be extended to take in not only other putative orchestral suites that Janáček planned in the next two years to 1893 – the Suite op. 3 (VI/6), the *Moravian Dances* (VI/7), the *Dances from Haná* (VI/8) and the *Czech Dances, First Suite* (VI/9) – but also three stage works: the ballets *Valachian Dances* (X/20) and *Rákoš Rákoczy* (I/2) and the opera *The Beginning of a Romance* I/3.

The fact that an opera is a part of this complex of many-times recycled dances is certainly the oddest fact here. In his biography Jaroslav Vogel speculated that sketches for *The Beginning of a Romance* may have existed before the completion of the Suite op. 3 (which includes several of the numbers, though without words).[1] But recycling the dances, this time into an opera, is precisely what Janáček did, and, furthermore, he hardly bothered to conceal his tracks. The manuscript libretto for *The Beginning of a Romance* has several musical incipits written against the beginnings of some of the numbers showing which existing musical materials he intended to use; the manuscripts of individual dances contain brief verbal incipits showing exactly where in the existing material he planned to place the words from the libretto. When he wrote his initial sketch of the opera, Janáček had too much music for too few words, which resulted in frequent orchestral interludes of two or four bars between lines of text; these interludes were cut in later revisions so that the opera version ended up much shorter than the original dance on which it was based.[2] Recycling doesn't account for all the musical material in *The Beginning of a*

Romance – at least half of it was specially composed – but the presence of so much recycled material, with Janáček fitting words over existing music, illuminates his priorities at the time, i.e. to promote Moravian folk music by including folk dances and folksongs in a stage work.

Janáček's relaxed attitude in this work to insertion and recycling meant that the opera became a repository for other pieces that had in some way failed to meet their target. Thus the Suite op. 3 shares not only the fourth movement (*Smoke Dance*) with the opera (used in the overture, and in nos. 8b, 9a, 9b): its first movement is the basis for no. 8a (a duet for Tonek and Poluška) and its second, slow movement for Poluška's solo no. 14a. Furthermore, the chorus for mixed voices *Our Song [2]* (IV/21), which Janáček wrote for a competition, became, through a complicated process, the cheerful finale movement no. 16.

This odd compositional approach in *The Beginning of a Romance* is a problem only if one comes to the work with a knowledge of Janáček's later operas and attempts to see it as a precursor. *The Beginning of a Romance* is a tuneful little piece that can give pleasure in a light-hearted production, but it clearly has nothing in common with the musical drama of Janáček's subsequent operas. The two ballets are a different matter, not affected by any such high-minded expectations. Both set out to be folk ballets, a more comfortable vehicle for folk material than a folk opera, and both had specially written librettos that high-lighted and maximized the dance element (folk festivities, dancing competitions, marriage celebrations, etc.).

This period of Janáček's arranging dances for orchestra and stage is brief. The various performances of the *Valachian Dances* (VI/4) range from 2 February 1889 to January 1891. By June 1891 many of its dances had been recycled into *Rákoš Rákoczy* (given at the Prague National Theatre on 24 July 1891), by which time Janáček had planned two dance suites, his Suite op. 3 (VI/6) and his *Moravian Dances* (VI/7) that also utilized the dances. Shortly afterwards Janáček completed *The Beginning of a Romance* (re-employing some of the dances) in piano-vocal score and orchestrated it by December 1891. While this opera waited in limbo for its first performance in 1894, Janáček planned two more suites: his *Dances from Haná* (VI/8) and his *Czech Dances, First Suite* (VI/9). This last metamorphosis was originally intended as something for Dvořák's Berlin publisher Simrock,[3] but in the end Janáček offered it to the Czech Academy of Sciences in March 1893 to support a grant application.[4] The changing titles are not quite as contradictory as they seem: anything Valachian can, in a more general sense, be 'Moravian', just as anything 'Moravian' can, in a more general sense, be 'Czech' (see chap. 2). And the 'Czech' of Janáček's *Czech Dances* may have been a diplomatic move on his part based on the assumption that Simrock had not heard of Moravia, and later, that the Czech Academy of Sciences, with its seat in Prague, might find 'Czech' dances more appealing than 'Moravian' ones.

And then it was all over. Although the *Czech Dances* were confidently labelled 'first suite', there was no 'second suite' and by 1894 Janáček was at work on his opera *Jenůfa* which, unlike its predecessor, included no folk dance arrangements at all, merely convincing fakes. With *Jenůfa* something else had taken over, and this early phase of Janáček's folk activity was superseded. He made just one later orchestral arrangement of a Moravian folk dance, the *Blessed Dance* (VI/11) of 1899. This couldn't be more different. Although the main tune is discernibly the same as in the earlier versions in the Suite op. 3 and *Rákoš*, the result is much more delicate, resourceful and witty, a composition in its own right rather than merely an arrangement. It came about for quite a different reason (see chap. 36) and, although perfectly satisfying its brief of providing an orchestrated Moravian folk dance for the Slavonic Beseda, it comes across almost as an ironic commentary on Janáček's previous versions.

Janáček's recycling of his dances is shown in table 30.1. Included is the final resting place for six of the dances, in the suite that Janáček made of *Valachian Dances* in 1924, with a final change of name, *Lachian Dances*, better reflecting their place of origin (see chap. 2).

The orchestral arrangements had a public impact in that they put Janáček's music before a much wider audience than he had hitherto experienced; with *Rákoš Rákoczy* he even got to Prague. However, the act of making these arrangements had virtually no impact on Janáček's style and evolution apart from allowing him to hear how his orchestral music sounded and learn a little from the experience. There is no discernible development in the arrangements between 1889 and 1894. This was in fact a completely static phase, exemplified by the constant recycling (without change) of the same materials. When Janáček came to consider them again in his old age he simply selected six, found an order for them and left it at that, a huge contrast to the complete rewriting of his early *Šárka* in 1918.

Table 30.1: The use of folkdances in Janáček's compositions

Numbers are those of the order within the individual works. None are available for vi/4.
Dances used only in *Rákoš Rákoczy* (i/2) are not included.
Putative dances in the ballet *Valachian Dances* (x/20) are not included.
Nos. 1 and 2 in vi/6 are not folk dances but are given because of their appearance in *The Beginning of a Romance* (i/3).
No. 3 of iv/9 also exists as an independent arrangement in *As we went to the feast* (iii/9).
Some dances (e.g. *Kolo* in *The Beginning of a Romance* i/3) also exist in arrangements for piano in viii/10.

VD = *Valachian Dances*	MD = *Moravian Dances*	
op. 3 = Suite op.3	HD = *Dances from Haná*	
RR = *Rakoš Rákoczy*	CD = *Czech Dances, First Suite*	
BR = *The Beginning of a Romance*	LD = *Lachian Dances*	

abbreviated title *JW number*	VD vi/4	op. 3 vi/6	RR i/2	BR i/3	MD vi/7	HD vi/8	CD iv/9	LD vi/17
date	1889–91	by Jan 1891	by 5 June 1891	by 2 July 1891	by July 1891	by 20 Nov 1892	by 22 March 1893	by 27 Oct 1924
Čeladenský [from Čeladná]	✓		9a				5	5
Dymák [*Smoke Dance*] I	✓	4	1, 6b	1			1	3
Kalamajka [i.e. from Ukrainian *kołomyka*]			11		2	1		
Kolo [*Reel*]				1				
Kožich/Kozušek [*Furcoat*]	✓		7		1		4	
Kyjový [*Club Dance*]			3					
Pilky [*Handsaw Dance*]	✓		4					6
Požehnaný [*Blessed Dance*]	✓	3	10				2	2
Rožek [*Little Corner*]			11	13	5			
Sedlácká [*Farmer's Dance*]							3	
Silnice [*Road*]			5		4	3		
Starodávný [*Oldfashioned Dance*] I	✓		3					1
Starodávný [*Oldfashioned Dance*] IIa	✓			6a				4
Starodávný [*Oldfashioned Dance*] IIb	✓							
Troják [*Triple Dance*]				6a			4	
Troják lašský [*Lachian Triple Dance*] I	✓			6b,11, 14b				
Trojky [*Threes*]			11		3	2		
unnamed movement I		1		8a				
unnamed movement II		2		14a				

31

Folksong accompaniments as
Janáček's workshop

Whereas Janáček's arranging of Moravian folk dances was a comparatively short-lived occupation that seems to have had no impact on his own compositional style, this is not true of his arrangements of Moravian folksongs for voice and piano. On the contrary, his interest here lasted many years and his experimental accompaniments can be considered to be a private workshop in which he learnt how to become a completely different composer.

Janáček's writing of piano accompaniments to folksongs began with his arrangements of *The Little Queens* (IV/20, probably by February 1889). These are little different from his arrangements of folk dances for piano (VIII/10) and would seem to be designed for the same function, i.e. of bringing folk music from the country into the town, with Janáček's piano versions supplemented by Mrs Bakešová's elaborate descriptions and diagrams of the dances (VIII/10) and dance rituals (IV/20) for interested parties to try out for themselves. The arrangements Janáček offered for *The Little Queens* are purely functional: mostly thick block chords that provide no more than a sustained accompaniment to the tune in the same rhythm (ex. 3).

In 1892 the publisher Šolc brought out a new edition of Janáček's and Bartoš's *Bouquet of Moravian Folksongs* (XIII/1), and at the same time encouraged him to make piano arrangements of some of the songs. This process seems to have gone on quietly in the background, seldom mentioned in correspondence, and is charted only by publication: a first volume of fifteen songs published by Šolc in late 1892 or 1893, a second volume of another thirty-eight published about nine years later. However, an arrangement that Janáček gave Olga in late 1896 (published in the second volume) makes it clear that after

Ex. 3

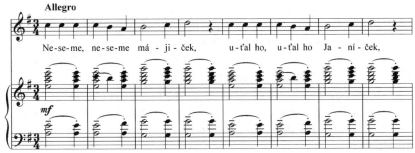

Ne-se-me, ne-se-me má - ji - ček, u-ťal ho, u-ťal ho Ja - ní - ček,

bringing out the first volume Janáček simply added more when he had the odd moment. The fact that he went on to make such arrangements over the next three decades (see table 31.1 below) suggests that he did so out of some inner compulsion, a process that, in the early years, went hand in hand with the composition of his first masterpieces in a distinctive and individual style.

In later years the motivation was perhaps different. It almost seems that, when he was frustrated in some way, Janáček would write a few more piano accompaniments to Moravian folksongs. Thus the *Hukvaldy Folk Poetry in Songs* (V/4) were written in 1898, when he had abandoned *Jenůfa* and thrown himself into other types of works before getting back to his opera. The *Six Folksongs sung by Eva Gabel* (V/9) were composed in 1909, when he was having problems with *The Excursions of Mr Brouček* and the possibility of *Fate* being performed was rapidly receding. Janáček composed the *Songs of Detva, Brigand Ballads* (V/11) while waiting for news from Prague about rehearsals for

Table 31.1: Janáček's chief arrangements of Moravian folksongs for voice and piano

JW	date	title
IV/20	1889?	*The Little Queens* (10 folk dances with songs; unison voices)
V/2	1892?	*A Bouquet of Moravian Folksongs*, vol. 1 (15 songs); retitled *Moravian Folk Poetry in Songs* in second edition (1908)
V/4	1898	*Hukvaldy Folk Poetry in Songs* (14 songs)
V/2	by 1901	*A Bouquet of Moravian Folksongs*, vol. 2 (39 songs); retitled *Moravian Folk Poetry in Songs* in second edition (1908)
V/9	1909	*Six Folksongs Sung by Eva Gabel* (6 songs)
V/11	1916	*Songs of Detva, Brigand Ballads* (8 songs)
V/13	1918	*Silesian Songs (from Helena Salichová's Collection)* (10 songs)

the recently accepted *Jenůfa*. The *Silesian Songs (from Helena Salichová's Collection)* (v/13) were written in another limbo towards the end of the First World War, with further frustrations over the staging of *Brouček*. Composing piano accompaniments to folksongs seems to have been a consoling occupation to which Janáček returned whenever he felt that he was losing his way.

Even the *Silesian Songs* of 1918 aren't quite the end of the line, as by 1922 Janáček had made another fifteen arrangements of folksongs, this time for piano solo though with the original folksong text underlaid (viii/23).

When considering the influence of folk music in art music, commentators usually point to different scale systems and rhythms. The use, for instance, of a Dorian mode, with a flattened leading note, or the Lydian mode, with its raised fourth, affects not only tunes constructed in these modes, making them sound different from those in traditional major-minor scales, but also has an impact on the tonality, affecting and loosening its harmonic functions. Moravian folk music has its Dorian, Lydian and other modes, and employs distinctive rhythms such as the Moravian mirror rhythms (long–short, short–long). It is easy enough to find examples where, one can argue, Janáček has taken note of these characteristics and employed them in his own works. However, one can also argue that apart from, say, providing a more flexible approach to melody and to harmonic function, these are almost only surface phenomena and do not constitute any sea-change in style. On the other hand the impact of Janáček's arrangements on the texture of his music was deep-seated and radical, the most important aspect of change in his music at the time.

Although in the *Bouquet* arrangements Janáček added an accompaniment for piano – taking the folksong from its folk environment into the salon by adding the salon instrument *par excellence*, the piano – what he did with the accompaniment was to try and re-create the repertory of possible folk accompaniments in the field, in a sort of folk-instrument onomatopoeia. There were essentially three instrumental possibilities: cimbalom, instrumental ensemble and bagpipes. Although Janáček was fascinated by bagpipes and sneaked imitations of them into two of his operas, they were rare in the area (more common in Slovakia or in certain Bohemian regions such as Strakonice) and their drones and decorative flourishes only occasionally figure as folk models in his piano accompaniments. The cimbalom, however, was much more common and provided its own distinctive challenge. With its two hammers it could play two notes, either struck together or in rapid alternation, thus suggesting a harmonic dimension. Players could sustain the sound by repeated hammerings (with alternating hands) and specialize in virtuosic flourishes with the hammers skittering down the strings. Ex. 4 (*Oldfashioned Dance*, which Janáček took down from Jan Myška in Petřvald) shows many of these characteristics. The nature of the instrument, however, meant that it tended to provide bursts of sound rather than something more continuous.

Ex. 4

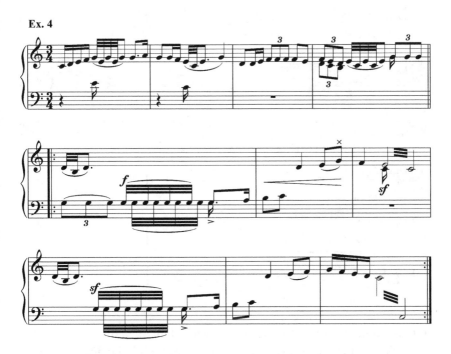

When translated into pianistic imitations this meant repeated notes (or alternating octaves), little flourishes, and many gaps, leaving the voice to deliver some phrases without accompaniment. Imitating a cimbalom became a way of freeing Janáček's style from a stodgy continuous accompaniment (as in *The Little Queens*) to one that was more gappy and independent. In no. 44 of the *Bouquet*, little bursts of sound with repeated notes show how cimbalom features can be attractively integrated into a pianistic texture (ex. 5). Accompaniments began to be

Ex. 5

witty commentaries and alternatives rather than unchallenging support systems. All these ideas began to be played out when Janáček wrote his next opera, *Jenůfa*, and he seems to have grasped that orchestra and voice could operate much more interestingly as semi-independent entities, just as voice and piano did in his folksong arrangements. And with the orchestra (more easily continuous than a cimbalom) it was possible to see the accompaniment as providing foreground structure, allowing the voice to become more independent and – after the discovery in 1897 of what Janáček would designate 'speech melody' – more speechlike.

The ensemble music of Velká provided different, equally stimulating features. The folk ensemble, playing improvised harmonies, was typically a group in which a violin (*hudec*) supplied the tune, a cello or double bass supplied the bass line, and the remaining instruments – usually a second violin – the harmony in the middle. But the middle part has a built-in disruptive element. The second violin (*kontráš*) attempts to provide a 'contrast' to the main melody, emphasizing the offbeat, putting in trills and decorations. The balance between foreground and background, between the first violin tune or voice tune and the rest, creates a tension that animates the music, and is something that Janáček seized upon in his folksong accompaniments, for instance the offbeat tugs in no. 27 of the *Bouquet* (*The Gamekeeper*) or the flashy cimbalom flourishes in no. 28 (*Uncertainty*). The tugs are a typical *kontráš* feature. Here, for instance, is a notation that Janáček made in Lipov (in 1892) where a singer is accompanied by a *hudec* playing a heterophonic version of the sung tune against a *kontráš*, with its 'energico' offbeat stresses, the so-called 'double strike' accompaniment (ex. 6).

In his own music, this *kontráš* element is transformed into disruptive

Ex. 6   Lipov (1892)

ostinatos that can threaten to derail the main melodic elements. In *Good Night* (one of the early numbers from *On the Overgrown Path* VIII/17, written in 1900 and published in 1902) there is a short, fidgety motif repeated over and over, a prelude to a very simple tune, heard at first unaccompanied and then as its accompaniment. This is an early example of the Janáček trademark of the ostinato accompaniment by a recurring three- or four-note motif (often known by Janáček's invented term *sčasovka*; see chap. 19). The disruptive effect when the accompaniment overpowers the tune is one that Janáček may have picked up from Moravian folk ensemble music: a late example is the opening of the overture to *The Makropulos Affair*, with its rumbling ostinato occasionally upsetting the lyrical melody above.

Seeing piano accompaniments as re-creations of folk-instrumental practice liberated Janáček. No longer did they need to be continuous. Unaccompanied voices were acceptable, as were solo voices with heterophonic accompaniments;* accompaniments could be unobtrusive, though occasionally *kontráš*-like counter-melodies were offered.

Janáček's arrangements presented in the first volume of the *Bouquet* (V/2) constitute the most extreme example of this liberation. A few years later, the Hukvaldy arrangements (V/4) were more conventional with only occasional hints at cimbalom imitations. And in the second volume (published in 1901) there is a distinctive difference from the outset, with folkish techniques now rubbing shoulders with more conventional types of accompaniment, sometimes within the same song. In other words the folk-imitation technique had now been thoroughly absorbed. What is astonishing is the variation from song to song. Each one is different, each one a little masterpiece. Though Janáček would go on to write extraordinary operas and all the other works of his old age, these arrangements as much as any of his own pieces show the fertile imagination of a truly creative spirit. It is a shame that these little songs have proved such bad travellers abroad.

With the changes made in Janáček's 'workshop', his orchestration stopped being over-saturated; instead it became quirky, distinctive and non-continuous, and this released something within him. His mature voice was heard.

Janáček's distinctive folksong accompaniments were noted at the

---

* i.e. a melody accompanied by what is in essence the same tune, perhaps varied or decorated.

time, for instance in the anonymous review published in *Dalibor* of his *Hukvaldy Folk Poetry in Songs* (V/4):

Janáček's arrangement sets out to be just a piano reduction of the original performance of the songs in which Valachian fiddlers with a cimbalom player, or sometimes just the last on his own, provide an accompaniment to the human voice. And he has really succeeded in this, of course rather to the detriment of the piano idiom, which however was not the aim: Janáček has captured here even those special harmonic combinations and caught in notation even that rhythmic freedom independent of the beats of the metronome but in free rhythm.[1]

This is a most perceptive comment and one that holds true not just for this collection but for all of Janáček's arrangements across the next twenty years. They came, as mentioned above, in times of confusion and uncertainty. Most suggestive of all is the last, the *Silesian Songs* (V/13). Janáček wrote these in January 1918, some months before he stopped composing *The Diary of One Who Disappeared* (V/12), which he had begun so enthusiastically in the summer of 1917. There may have been personal factors involved in his temporarily abandoning this very personal piece (see vol. ii: 1917b and 1919), but a little swig of folksong accompaniments seems to have helped him to get back to it. Its utterly individual piano texture is unthinkable without the instrumental-onomatopoeic tricks that Janáček learnt over the years.

When, a little later, Janáček came to write his *Moravian Folksongs* (VIII/23), he was able to distill, in what was his last substantial work for solo piano, a stunning evocation of both folk tune and folk accompaniment, now entirely for piano, occupying a unique space between Janáček's arrangements and original compositions.

32

1894–5

Janáček's second opera, *The Beginning of a Romance*, was performed in Brno on 10 February 1894 with the composer conducting. The short run of four performances was the only time in his life that he conducted one of his operas, in fact the only time that he conducted any opera. Although he had considerable experience as a choral conductor and some as an orchestral conductor, his presence in the pit is a surprise and perhaps reflects the difficulties that Václav Hübner had in getting Janáček's modest little work on to the stage at all. The chief conductor František Jílek had left shortly before, and maybe Janáček was catapulted into conducting it before Jílek's replacement had any time to raise objections.

The final preparations for the opera and its performances were over-shadowed by two events in Janáček's family. On 18 February his oldest sister, Viktorie Červenková, aged fifty-five, died in Hukvaldy of tuberculosis, as he learnt from a letter sent that day from her husband.[1] She and Janáček weren't particularly close – her children were nearer in age to Janáček than she was (the oldest was born two years after him) and she seems to have spent some years abroad in the United States[2] – but nevertheless it was the first death of any his siblings for a quarter of a century. And it was during this period that his daughter Olga experienced her first bout of rheumatic fever, affecting her joints and the outer covering of the heart. It lasted several months and was, in Zdenka's words, 'almost fatal', leaving her with a heart defect and a weakness that restricted her physical activities and caused considerable anxiety.[3]

Little is known about the preparations by the Brno opera house for *The Beginning of a Romance*. An undated letter from Marie

Wollnerová (who had refused to sing the part of Poluška in 1892) is probably from this period and asks, this time very politely, for a vocal score and libretto, though her pointed references to the revisions suggest that some hostility remained.[4] Janáček invited his friends and supporters to the première, among them Mrs Preissová,[5] whose short story had inspired the work, and Mrs Bakešová.[6] And, ever hopeful of a Prague production, he invited František Šubert from the National Theatre.[7] Šubert replied that he was too busy to come but would be delighted if Janáček would send the corrected score for a further appraisal.[8] Janáček did so, and at the same time suggested that the conductor Mořic Anger (who had conducted Janáček's ballet *Rákoš Rákoczy* in Prague in 1891) should come to see the next performance, on 27 February.[9] This, the fourth and final performance, was postponed until 1 March,[10] and Anger's prospective arrival was duly noted in the Brno papers,[11] as was the fact that the orchestra that evening would include a harp,[12] presumably lacking in earlier performances.

Reviews were mixed: of the two most prominent and important, that in *Moravská orlice*[13] was enthusiastic and respectful, though this is hardly surprising considering that its author, Karel Sázavský, had been one of Janáček's contributors to *Hudební listy*. The other major review, in *Lidové noviny*, was rather more reserved and confined itself to comments on the libretto.[14] The surprise, however, is that the opera was taken off after four performances. It is of course possible that Janáček's concern over his sick daughter (having lost a son only four years earlier) led to his refusing to conduct further performances, or the theatre itself may have been concerned by audience figures. A letter to Janáček from Ignát Wurm, who had not seen the work but who had had a full report from Lucie Bakešová, makes it clear that Bakešová found some passages hard-going.[15] Maybe others did too. Although the opera shares much of the same folk-dance world of the *Valachian Dances*, it uncomfortably straddles two different spheres of Janáček's activity. Moravian folk-music enthusiasts such as Bakešová were put off by its operatic elements (and the singers' tremolos), while professional musicians such as Adolf Čech and those not interested in the folk aspects found it had little to offer them (see chap. 29). At some stage Janáček himself lost faith in the work and partly mutilated the scores by tearing out pages so that when the opera was performed after his death these sections had to be reconstructed from the orchestral parts.[16] While perhaps disappointed by the mixed reception, there is an even more compelling reason why Janáček may have rejected *The Beginning of a Romance*. From November 1893 he had been considering Preissová's play *Her Stepdaughter* as the basis for his next opera (see chap. 29). Perhaps once he got down to serious consideration of what became *Jenůfa*, a much more serious and searching affair than *The Beginning of a Romance*, he began to view his cheerful little folk opera in a different light. Looking back at the opera in his seventieth year, he witheringly cast it aside, a distinction achieved by no other opera of his: 'The Beginning of a Romance was an empty comedy', he wrote, 'it was tasteless to force me to put folksongs into it. And it was after Šárka!'[17]

Ironically, at much the same time that he was having desultory dealings with Šubert over *The Beginning of a Romance*, Janáček came to play an important and extremely time-consuming part in an imaginative venture that Šubert had inspired. The public enthusiasm for the 'Czech cottage', shown at the 1891 Regional Jubilee Exhibition, had given Šubert the idea of organizing an exhibition wholly devoted to Czech ethnography. The meeting he convened on 28 July 1891 endorsed his proposal and resulted in a number of resolutions: the holding of an event in 1893, the founding of a museum to house the objects acquired for the exhibition and a society to oversee all this. Šubert's plan was realized virtually intact with the founding of a Czech Ethnographic Society (1894), the creation of a Czech Ethnographic Museum (1896) and in particular the organization of a large-scale ethnographic exhibition of the 'Czecho-Slavonic* tribe in Bohemia, Moravia, Silesia and Hungarian Slovakia'[18] which, after two postponements, was held in 1895. Such an exhibition, whose strength would be the diversity of local ethnographic traditions, needed to work intensively at a local level. Thus in a letter from the central committee of the exhibition on 23 February 1894 Janáček was invited to set up an 'Ethnographic Committee for Music in Moravia' that would prepare the musical programme of works by Moravian composers and documents relating to musical culture in Moravia.[19] The word 'ethnographic' was understood in a broader sense than today, embracing all musical aspects of the national culture including art music; nevertheless from the start

---

* A formulation of the period to indicate that all Czech culture was involved, not merely that on Bohemian soil.

Janáček realized that his most pressing need at the exhibition was to present Moravian folk music. Accordingly he took charge himself of 'folk music, dance and ceremonies', as reported in *Lidové noviny* (25 March 1894). Other people mentioned in the report were the composer Josef Nešvera (music director at Olomouc Cathedral after Křížkovský) for art music, Karel Konrád (an authority on church music) for hymn-books, and Alois Kolísek (then chaplain in Miroslav, a small town near Brno, and soon to be a functionary of the Organ School; see chap. 21) for church music.

While Nešvera, Konrád and Kolísek did indeed take on these responsibilities, Janáček seems to have had second thoughts about his own portfolio – onerous if he was to co-ordinate all the Moravian musical aspects – and wrote to both Lucie Bakešová and Martin Zeman soliciting their help. 'I have been invited by the exhibition committee', he wrote to Zeman, 'to lead the "musical section for Moravia" that would be in charge of the musical part of the exhibition as far as it concerns Moravia. I invite you to join the committee.' Zeman's task there would be to arrange folk festivities so that people would sing as if taking part in these activities as at home. There would be a committee meeting on 27 March 1894 to which he hoped Zeman could come, or at least send a brief report.[20] By the time Janáček wrote to Bakešová with the same request, his thoughts had become even clearer: 'Folksong has to be living at the exhibition. The people should sing as at home: dance songs, harvest and hay-harvesting songs, wedding and other ceremonies. It is necessary to devise a programme of such celebrations: and that will be your task.'[21]

Bakešová (in the Brno region) and Zeman (in Slovácko) applied themselves to their tasks with vigour and enthusiasm, but Janáček was never a *laissez-faire* administrator and he encouraged his forces with heavy-handed hectoring that did not always bring out the best in people. Both Bakešová and Zeman were more established figures in their field than Janáček was at this stage and responded to instructions from Brno in their different ways: Zeman by masterly inactivity and Bakešová by attempting to give as good as she got. Haná and Valašsko (Lašsko) were rather more difficult to organize since Janáček lacked figures of similar authority in these areas.

The meeting of the 'musical section for Moravia' took place on Easter Tuesday (27 March) at 4 p.m.[22] Janáček was elected chief executive, with his friends František Bakeš (Lucie's husband) as chair and František Mareš (from 'Vesna') as minutes secretary. A report that Janáček published a few months later in *Lidové noviny* to publicize their work (xv/146) shows how many interested parties he was able to assemble. In addition to those already mentioned, they included František Bartoš, Antonín Vorel (at the Brno Teachers' Institute), František Musil (organist at Brno Cathedral) as well as people further afield such as Janáček's former pupil Cyril Metoděj Hrazdira, now working as a choirmaster in Ostrava.

Janáček's committee adopted a number of resolutions. The first concerned the nature of any folk music-representation at the exhibition. The 'folk concert' in 1892 (see chap. 29) had been salutary in showing how taking folk performers and putting them in ordinary concert-giving venues inhibited the performers and misled the audience. What was needed was folk music in context; thus the music associated with ceremonies (weddings, harvest home, etc.) should be performed at re-creations of these ceremonies. It was hoped that in this way a complete picture could be built up of distinctive Moravian ethnographic regions. There would be preliminary local exhibitions, such as one planned in Velká that summer. The Ethnographic Exhibition would also include art music, and Janáček suggested at his meeting that local choirs could start rehearsing the choral works of Moravian composers such as Křížkovský and Förchgott-Tovačovský as well as living composers, so that a number of concerts could be put together from their works, something that Nešvera and Sázavský would be in charge of (and would completely fail to deliver). Similarly the Czech Theatre in Brno should be encouraged to perform operas on Moravian subjects (though apart from the scorned *Beginning of a Romance* it is difficult to know what Janáček could have had in mind). There could also be displays of folk instruments and folksong collections. While all these purely musical initiatives were going ahead, Janáček also found himself being co-opted on to a committee convened by František Bartoš on 15 April 1894 that would oversee and co-ordinate the work of all the subject committees in Moravia in preparation for the exhibition.[23]

This was not Janáček's only organizational task at the time. 'At its general assembly our society [of Czech schoolteachers from Bohemia, Moravia and Silesia] carried the motion that this year's congress should take place during the Whitsun holidays but this time on the sisterly soil of Moravia and in its main city, rich in teaching institutions, various monuments and beautiful surroundings.' This preliminary

announcement of 7 March 1894 included references to a cultural programme of events that would complement the discussions of pay,
pedagogy, pensions and other professional concerns. On Sunday and
Monday afternoons (13–14 May 1894) there would be visits to the
'famous old monastery of Rajhrad' and to the Macocha caves. And on
Sunday at 5 o'clock there would be 'an interesting concert of Brno
choral societies under the direction of Professor Lev Janáček'.[24] This
late appearance of 'Lev' (see chap. 14) is a clue to how Janáček became
involved, confirmed by the names of the local organizers, among them
the chair František Bartoš (who insisted on styling Janáček this way
long after he had ceased to do so himself). Janáček's preparations for
the 'mixed concert' requested by Jan Kapras, the local Brno executive,[25]
included commissioning the pianist Karel ze Slavkovských to play solo
piano items to illustrate dance forms[26] and writing a new chorus himself. On a blank side of a letter from Slavkovských about the concert,[27]
Janáček began putting together the final programme, a mixture of
piano and choral items. Among such familiar pieces as Dvořák's *The
Sparrow's Party* and Křížkovský's *The Love-Gift* is the first mention
of Janáček's *The sun has risen above that hill* (iv/23), for 'mixed
voices'.

Janáček's new choral piece was performed at the Czech Teachers'
Congress concert on 13 May 1894 at the Besední dům, with the composer conducting the Beseda choir (presumably a special concession on
both sides) and a baritone soloist, V. Černý. The text was a familiar
Moravian folksong found in Bartoš's 1889 collection of Moravian
folksongs and one that Janáček had taken down himself during his
field trip to Velká in the summer of 1892.[28] The presence of piano and
baritone recalls other special-occasion pieces such as the *Festive
Chorus* (iv/13) written for the opening of the new Teachers' Institute
building in 1878. *The sun has risen* has not survived in a performable
state, but from one of the dated parts that turned up in 1956 it is clear
that Janáček had completed the work before 19 March 1894.

During May 1894 Janáček made contact with folk-music enthusiasts,
soliciting collections which could be displayed at the exhibition.
Vladimír Vašátko from Horácko (an area west of Brno) sent dances
from the area;[29] Josef Válek from Vsetín wrote on 26 May to say that
he had sent his collection to the journal *Český lid*, but it had been held
up and he would ask the editor Čeněk Zíbrt about it.[30] A year earlier

Janáček had been in touch with Josef Pernický from Jasenice in Valašsko; he now wrote to him again suggesting further work together, and heard that Pernický had taken down more songs during harvesting.[31] On 31 May Janáček requested assistance from his contact in Polanka, the local priest Antonín Přibyl, in organizing folk activities in Valašsko.[32] He asked the schoolmaster Jan Richter in Petřvald to inquire whether the cimbalom player Jan Myška was still alive (he was in good health, he heard later).[33] A short letter Janáček sent in early June soliciting folksongs from the young collector Hynek Bím (1874–1958) has a significance quite beyond its simple contents: 'Counsellor[†] Bartoš and I have agreed to publish all manuscript collections of songs and dances. For a fee allow us to have your material so that the collection is complete.'[34] Just twenty years old at the time and a recent graduate of the Brno Teachers' Institute, Bím would become one of Janáček's most assiduous and useful folksong collectors. Furthermore what is mooted here, a publication of all Moravian folksongs and dances, was much too ambitious a project to be published in time for the exhibition next year, but would develop into *Moravian Folksongs Newly Collected* (XIII/3), published by Bartoš and Janáček 1899–1901.

By 17 June 1894, when the third meeting of the central committee responsible for organizing the Moravian musical contribution to the Ethnographic Exhibition in Prague was held in Brno, Janáček had made considerable progress. His report details his dealings with the above experts. There had been a few refusals: the answer from Přibyl in Polanka had been negative (his people, he said, had not wanted to take part in public displays), but help had been promised by Mr Lužný (in Kozlovice) and Mr Pernický (in Jasenice), and of course there was stout support from Zeman and Bakešová. Then followed Janáček's concrete proposals:

1. In the individual groups, from Valašsko, Slovácko, Horácko and Haná, there should be at least forty to fifty people. Thus 200 altogether.
2. A programme in each group should be elaborated, practised and performed at a rehearsal during the coming summer. Namely: *harvest home* in Kozlovice [Valašsko] and Jasenice [Valašsko]; a *wedding* in Velká [Slovácko]; *hody*[‡] in Šlapanice (Troubsko) [Brno region]. (XV/358)

[†] A courtesy title, indicating seniority, here within the school system ('school counsellor Bartoš' is the full version).

[‡] A feast or celebration, usually connected to some church event (Easter, Whitsun, patronal festival) or even a death ('wake').

Janáček also insisted that there should be firm contracts between the organizers, trainers and the director, so that workers would have the time and the means to take part in this unusual 'folk concert', and that the complete programme with a description of its songs, dances and speeches should be printed in advance. This was Janáček's preliminary budget:

200 people travelling to Prague and back @ 10 zl each	2000 zl
200 people fed and housed for three days @ 3 zl each 600 zl [daily]	1800 zl
provisional expenses (a) during practising	400 zl
(b) contribution to costumes	100 zl
(c) trainers and	
(d) travel expenses for director, etc.	200 zl
(e) printing costs	200 zl
[provisional total]	4700 zl
folk musicians	300 zl
[TOTAL]	5000 zl[§]

'The aim', Janáček wrote, 'was to give [a feast] for the eye and the ear, never seen and never heard before; the richness of the different folk costumes from Moravia should be dazzling and the whole exhibition site would resound with "Moravia". This will awake interest even in the widest circles – and [increase] box-office receipts' (XV/358).

All this work was in full flood when the summer holidays arrived, and so it was Zdenka and Olga who set off on their own on about 19 June for Hukvaldy, with Janáček due to join them later.[35] As Zdenka reported, their doctor considered Hukvaldy, with its hills, unsuitable for Olga, but Janáček 'wouldn't have it any other way'. According to a request Janáček made to the Regional School Board for financial assistance (he was retrospectively granted 40 zl), he was obliged to send the family 'to the country' as a result of his daughter's illness.[36] With Josefa no longer able to provide accommodation in Hukvaldy, they hired a room with the family of Vincenc Sládek (1865–1944), a gamekeeper and forest warden.[37] The house was on the main road to Frýdek-Místek (which was level) and with vigilance Zdenka ensured that Olga did not over-exert herself.[38] In time the Sládeks became good friends of the Janáčeks.

[§] In a letter to Zeman two months earlier Janáček said he had been given a budget of 20,000 zl for folk activities (LJ to Zeman, 2 April 1894, Uhlíková 1994, 86) and 20,000 zl seems to have been what he received in the end (LJ to Bakešová, undated, June 1895, Sedláčková 2001, no. 39).

The twelve-year-old Olga was the chief correspondent, a fact that says something both about Zdenka's frosty relationship with her husband and the developing bond between father and daughter. They arrived in a storm, Olga reported:

It's clearing up so that we are hoping for fine weather. Hrnčárek was already waiting at the station [with a carriage]. We had lunch at U Kladivy and we went on riding in the rain. The room is in the best order, heating so that it is warm. [. . .] Mummy greets you and tells you to write soon.[39]

Three days later they had settled in. It was still Olga who was writing; her letter shows a light touch and an affectionate cheekiness:

I'm healthy and cheerful and I'm drinking and eating the whole day. Mummy wanted to write to you but she's in a bad mood because it's raining. Here the weather is very changeable. Although we remembered everything nevertheless we forgot some trifles: 1. the thick little comb, which lies on the mirror; 2. steel wool in the night cupboard; 3. my prayer book in my table; 4. the measure for coffee in the larder in the kitchen; 5. the fine tea strainer, which is hanging in the kitchen; and 6. come here soon and bring these things with you. If it isn't possible then send them to us by post. The food is tasty and the first day we had nice roast chicken.[40]

Zdenka got round to writing only on 24 June, adding a few comments to Olga's next letter. Her letter is characteristically dour, telling her husband how much they were paying for their lunches and that the money would run out by the end of the month.[41]

Olga sent her greetings for Janáček's fortieth birthday, 3 July 1894: 'A pity that we can't spend that day together. On that day we'll drink an extra half pint of beer. With a hearty greeting from your well-behaved daughter Olga', while Zdenka continued with excuses for no present ('my money-box is exhausted'; 'when will you send money? I have only a little over 3 zl') and a comment on his absence ('According to your letter I judge that you probably won't be coming before the holidays').[42] Zdenka kept most of her husband's letters, but the ones from this period have disappeared and it is only from the further dispatches from his daughter and wife throughout July that one gets some idea of Janáček's movements. For instance, from the final remarks in Olga's letter of 7 July it seems that he may have made a flying visit to Hukvaldy soon after his birthday:

Today in the night and for the whole day I didn't have a temperature. We certainly hope that everything will get back to the old order. [. . .] In the afternoon we had a nice walk. We went to the 'rough beech' where they are making new benches, then to that 'forbidden path' really very, very far. It was a two-hour walk. This morning it's very beautiful and hot. We were at Rychaltice at the cemetery [where Amalie Janáčková was buried]. We're now very sad for you. How did you travel home? Happily?[43]

It was clear that the Hukvaldy holiday was doing Olga good. In her next letter she reported that her temperature was down again and that they had done a circuit of the castle. From the food she mentions (cherries, raspberries, baked fish) she seems to have had a good appetite. And, as the Organ School would break up about the middle of July, there were indications that Janáček would at last be able to join them. What would he do about the cat (a rare mention), she wanted to know: 'Perhaps put it in the concierge's little room. Or, poor thing, send it here by rail!'[44] It was during Olga's regular bulletins to her father in the summer of 1894 that her writing began changing from a child's hand, big and careful, to the characteristic fluent and rounded form of her later letters. Olga's last letter from Hukvaldy was written on 18 July, by which time she and her mother were expecting Janáček to arrive any day with final instructions issued ('send everything, don't forget anything', 'lock the flat well').[45] They had about a month together in Hukvaldy, since on 25 August Janáček had to go to Prague to report on the Moravian contribution to the exhibition.[46] He got on well there, he reported to Zeman, saying that he already had so much material planned that it would make up two complete programmes.[47] What is evident from his exchanges with Zeman is the development of a sense of theatre in the items he considered suitable for the Prague amphitheatre: it was not just the music that interested him but its visual context. For instance he singled out from Zeman's suggestions, first a scene with girls singing at the foot of the cross and, second singing and dancing round a maypole: 'For the eye what would be good would be a group of men with scythes, a group for "Hunting the King" [a traditional Moravian custom that involved many men on horseback], a group with feathers.'[48]

Presumably the whole family left Hukvaldy at the same time since on Monday 27 August the new servant, Marie Stejskalová (1873–1968), took up her duties, having been hired in June before they set off. Stejskalová was twenty-one when she arrived. She had been recommended by a friend, and was glad to exchange for domestic work her previous job as a seamstress sewing men's shirts. Although she had not been in service before, she was bright and intelligent and soon got the hang of everything. Zdenka approved of her as she was 'gentle, sensible, self-sacrificing' and did not have admirers. And even Janáček 'noticed her honesty and diligence'. It was, however, with Olga that she particularly bonded, being only nine years older.[49]

Janáček was away when Stejskalová arrived, perhaps still in Prague, or perhaps he had returned to Hukvaldy, as Stejskalová reported. In her memoirs of sixty years later she described the Janáčeks' second-floor flat as she found it. It was beautiful and big, she wrote, though without modern conveniences. Instead of a bathroom there was a single communal tap and a toilet for the tenants on each floor. All water for cooking and washing had to be carried in, and the dirty water taken out again. The pantry stood outside on the landing, beside the door, together with a tub for bathing. Olga's room led off from the lobby (which had no natural light); opposite it was the kitchen. These were independent rooms but next to Olga's room was a dining-room which led to the salon, and the salon itself led to Janáček's study. While Olga was still young her room was the family bedroom and the Ehrbar piano stood in the dining-room. Janáček composed at it during the day; at night he worked in the bedroom, but when he began working through the night, furniture (such as a bed and the piano) was shifted into his study. Heating was with tile-clad stoves.[50]

The arrival of Marie Stejskalová into the Janáčeks' household is a crucial moment in the family's history. Servants had come and gone and, apart from Vladimír's wet-nurse Cilka, had made little impact, but 'Mářa', as she was generally called, stayed with the family and survived them all. She became a good friend to Olga and a loyal support to Zdenka, whom she served until the latter's death in 1938, forty-four years later.

Some time during his summer holidays Janáček seems to have completed a 'funeral chorus' *Take your rest* (IV/24). A *terminus ad quem* date for composition is suggested by that on a set of copied parts (7 October 1894) but is contradicted by Janáček's own recollection of '1875', asserted when the chorus was rediscovered in 1925. However, Janáček's memory may have been faulty. In 1875 he had got together a group of Brno amateur singers to perform a funeral chorus by Křížkovský at Dobrovský's grave. Since Křížkovský's chorus and Janáček's share the same text, it is possible that he later conflated the two events in his mind. The constant change of metre and the harmonic confidence of the piece suggests a more experienced composer than the Janáček of 1875, preoccupied at the time with writing choruses to Latin texts. If one is looking for a reason why in 1894 Janáček would want to write a 'funeral chorus', one could speculate that the composition might have been prompted by the death of his sister Viktorie earlier that year.

Much of the rest of the year, however, was taken up with Janáček's continuing preparations for the 1895 Ethnographic Exhibition and his own theoretical writings. His article *A New Current in Musical Theory* (XV/147) was a tough one to be published in *Lidové noviny*, where it was spread over four instalments from 4 November to 16 November 1894, by far his longest article in the newspaper. One wonders what the readership made of it. Essentially, it promoted his theory of the overlapping in the listener's consciousness of two chords, the first leaving a ghost image in the mind when the second is played and creating a dissonant mix, which Janáček designated the 'chaotic moment' (see chap. 19). This became one of the cornerstones in his theory of music, and the article was partly recycled as the preface to the harmony book that Janáček now attempted to publish.

'I have finished a brief harmony treatise', Janáček wrote to the publisher F.A. Urbánek in early November 1894.[II] So far such a harmony book satisfying 'modern requirements' was lacking and he was thus offering a book of about 288 printed pages.[51] Urbánek's reply was that a book of this size was hardly 'brief'. He would have to think about it, having published books by leading theorists such as Skuherský. What sort of fee was Janáček expecting?[52] Janáček responded the next day with a hastily revised estimate of the length ('160 printed pages') and the observation that some of it was presently coming out in *Lidové noviny*.[53] This got a better response and in his next letter, almost three weeks later, Urbánek encouraged Janáček to send him the manuscript for perusal.[54]

Before then, however, Janáček had written to one of the leading Czech scholars, Otakar Hostinský, a figure of immense authority in many fields. Janáček had already clashed with him on several occasions (see, for instance, chap. 23) but this didn't prevent him from asking

---

[II]The treatise was later published as *On the Composition of Chords and their Connections* (XV/151); see chap. 36: 1897–9.

Hostinský to read his manuscript, and in particular the 'psychological parts'.[55] Hostinský, normally a most courteous and prompt correspondent, made no response at all, and throughout December Janáček reminded him with increasingly urgent missives.[56] An explanation came only at the end of the year. Hostinský had planned to read Janáček's treatise over the Christmas break, hoping to be through by Christmas Day. But hardly had the holidays started than one of his children fell ill with typhoid fever, then a second, then his wife. There was neither the time nor the opportunity to read. If Janáček could wait a little longer, he hoped at least to have dipped into it by Twelfth Night. By then Hostinský had received yet another package from Janáček, containing articles on Moravian folk music for publication ahead of the exhibition. In view of his present circumstances, Hostinský had in fact passed on official obligations elsewhere; he limited himself to the observation about the exhibition booklet that if everything that Janáček sent was printed, it would make a substantial volume of at least 128 printed pages, which would increase the price and decrease the sales.[57]

It is not surprising that the events volume had grown to such proportions. From late September Janáček had contacts with Zeman in drawing up the programme for the Slovácko contribution to the exhibition.[58] Válek had now established that Zíbrt was happy to let him put his collection of songs at the disposal of the exhibition, and so he now needed instructions about how it should be presented[59] (he sent it three weeks later).[60] A landowner, Mr Lužný, sent dances from Kozlovice.[61] Antonín Večeř sent dances from Velké Meziříčí in Horácko.[62] And above all there was Mrs Bakešová, who throughout November and December 1894 kept up a steady stream of reports on her activities, enquiries and instructions. In response Janáček was terse: 'Please kindly write a brief description of *The Little Queens* [ritual] from Troubsko as you wish it to be performed. The description and the notation will be printed, so keep the writing to one side of half a printer's sheet [*arch*, i.e. Janáček wanted no more than four printed pages]. Can I ask for it to be ready by 5 December 1894?'[63] Bakešová (not from Troubsko) presumably referred Janáček to the Troubsko schoolmaster, Konstantin Sojka; Janáček sent Sojka's version to Bakešová to look at in early December.[64]

Soon, however, there was a clash. After their 'last unhappy meeting' (Bakešová was writing on 20 December 1894) she'd gone home and brooded that while she had dealt 'openly and honourably', Janáček, 'conspiring' with the chair Dr Koudela, had wanted to 'humiliate' her. Janáček had presumably thought that she had exceeded her brief, and accordingly told her off publicly. The dispute was about whether the live Moravian folk-music contribution to the exhibition should be confined to the official 'Moravian Days' for maximum dramatic impact (as Janáček wanted) or whether, as Bakešová thought, it should be spread over the entire exhibition in a continuous programme of events:

After all I wrote to you at once about everything and it didn't occur to me to act against your will – I wanted only to tell you our view and persuade you that some of [our] folk customs and rituals should be performed outside the Moravian day [sic] in Prague. It didn't occur to me to offer the people from Troubsko anything other than what was decided on, but I thought that you would agree that the people from Šlapanice, from Ořechov [and about five other districts] should perform something characteristic and attractive either before or after the Moravian day. You, however, were of a different view and it's possible, Mr Director, that your view is a good one – but a different view could also be advantageous to the exhibition and to our nation.[65]

There was little discernible progress on *Jenůfa* in 1894. Janáček put a date at the end of Act 1 of his copy of Preissová's play, but that date (18 March 1894) is significant since it was exactly at this time that he was overtaken by organizational work for the Moravian contribution to the 1895 Exhibition. All this activity, the anxieties over Olga's health and his teaching and administrative responsibilities seem to have taken any thoughts of his next opera from the forefront of his mind. The next evidence for any work on *Jenůfa* is again in his copy of the play, where he noted that on 31 December 1894 he had completed the prelude to the opera, presumably the version for piano four hands (VIII/16) rather than the one for orchestra. This prelude has little to do musically with the opera (and was ultimately omitted) though, with its title *Jealousy*, it does allude to Laca's motivation in Act 1.

Janáček's work on *Jenůfa* continued into 1895. There is a series of dates at the ends of the last three scenes in Act 2 of his copy of the play: on scene 7 (13 January); scene 8 (15 January) and scene 9 – i.e. the end of Act 2 (17 January). There is a rather later date, 11 February 1895, at the end of Act 3. Bohumír Štědron reasonably contended that these dates could not signify just a reading of the passages concerned – the whole play could be read in a couple of hours – and that instead they suggested a systematic working through the opera with sketching or even a rough continuous draft.[66] Corroboration for this theory is provided by the survival of a single page of sketches in a rough two-stave version (i.e. the top stave for voice or orchestral tune, with harmony distributed over both staves) with decipherable fragments of Act 1 Scene 2.[67] Furthermore the next event in his copy of the play, on 16 February 1895, is a note that Janáček had begun the 'instrumentation'. So perhaps, having spent his winter working through all of the opera in some sort of sketch form with voice parts and harmonies, Janáček began that day a stage of work in which he wrote straight into full score, as was his later practice. This, at least, is what he said he did when he wrote to Otakar Nebuška many years later about the composition of *Jenůfa*: 'It should be borne in mind that I compose first in full score and do the vocal score from that; thus work on the full score was finished earlier.'[68] In the same letter to Nebuška Janáček stressed how much else he had on at the time:

For me then composition was done only on the side: being choirmaster and organist, imperial and royal music teacher at the Teachers' Institute, director of the Organ School, conductor of the Beseda Philharmonic concerts – to have at home a mortally ill daughter – and [day-to-day] life. In short it was hard to compose, and thus little was done.[69]

Janáček's list is inaccurate. He had of course long since parted company with the Brno Beseda, and although Olga's health gave cause for concern in the earlier part of 1894, it was not until the end of 1902 (when Janáček was getting towards to the end of the opera) that she could be described as 'mortally ill'. The Janáčeks' new servant Mářa Stejskalová also provided a graphic description of the early stages of work on the opera:

When I went to [work for] the Janáčeks, the master was beginning to write *Jenůfa*. [. . .] He seldom had time for it during the day, but he devoted all his free evenings to it. He rarely stayed out longer than he had to: at concerts, in the theatre, in the Readers' Club, in the Staré Brno Beseda – he never hung around anywhere, and while others went to sleep when they got home, he sat down to work. In the morning I brought a lamp into his study filled to the brim with paraffin, the next day I took it away empty. The mistress would look at it: 'He's been writing through the whole night again.' Today I find it strange that the whole of *Jenůfa* was written by the light of a paraffin-lamp.[70]

Stejskalová's list of Janáček's activities includes nothing about his part in the Ethnographic Exhibition, which rather suggests that she is recalling a later period in the genesis of *Jenůfa*. Preparations for the exhibition increasingly dominated the first eight months of 1895: it seems unlikely that after his burst of work on it during the winter of 1894–5 Janáček was able to work on the opera until after the exhibition and in particular after the 'Moravian Days' were out of the way. He was in charge of all musical aspects of the Moravian contribution, and beset by many problems. Hrazdira, for instance, was responsible for assembling information about organs, organ-builders and organists in Moravia and had taken his portfolio extremely seriously.[71] Whereas his first concern was whether Janáček intended to display old organs such as the one dating from 1567 in the wooden church in Hrušov (near Ostrava), on 9 January 1895 he wrote to say that despite putting out requests in newspapers and specialist journals for information, he had gathered only five responses.[72] Soon after agreeing to taking on the hymnbook portfolio, Karel Konrád had written to Janáček wondering if he would have the 'strength' to fulfil his obligations.[73] His fears were proved right: he died on 3 November 1894 at the age of fifty-two, leaving a hole in Janáček's team.

In December Janáček had sent to Prague contributions from his team to the publication that would explain and describe the ceremonies, rituals and customs from Moravia.[¶] This included accounts of folk customs from Valašsko (Válek and Přibyl), Slovácko (Zeman), Haná (Rudolf Reissig, see chap. 36) and the Brno region (Bakešová, Sojka and others) – all a foretaste of the demonstrations to come in August.[74] Soon Janáček was getting anxious that he hadn't received proofs: a letter to Hostinský at the end of January mentioned this as well as giving him another reminder about his harmony book, to which Hostinský had still not responded.[75] Janáček continued to bombard Hostinský with increasingly urgent reminders, for instance one on 8 February 1895:

Forgive me if this letter perhaps crosses with yours: however you would lead me into the greatest embarrassment if I didn't have my manuscript tomorrow: so I'm writing quickly to you now. If perhaps you haven't had time to page

¶Published in 1895 as *Slavnosti a obyčeje lidové z Moravy na Národopisné výstavě česko-slovanské v Praze 1895* [Folk festivities and customs from Moravia at the Czecho-Slavonic Ethnographic Exhibition in Prague 1895].

through my manuscript then please send it back without your verdict – which of course I would be extremely sorry about. Similarly we're awaiting proofs – I'd request *four* brush proofs. [. . .] Please insist on speedy printing – for we've sent the manuscripts of the arrangements and therefore the organizers have nothing to hand.[76]

Hostinský did not send his comments on Janáček's harmony book until May 1895 but presumably returned the manuscript when requested, since a couple of days after beginning the 'instrumentation' of *Jenůfa* Janáček wrote to Urbánek again about the harmony book. The first page of this long letter is missing, but on the second page he made a number of points about it: that it was directed at students without natural musical talent (e.g. at teachers' institutes) and, unlike other harmony manuals, it was not intended merely for organ students: it was brief and of general applicability. Since Hostinský seemed to have failed him, Janáček now made a new proposal: Urbánek should invite the prominent Prague theorist Karel Stecker (1861–1918) to a meeting where Janáček would explain his theories to him. He was quite convinced that Stecker would come on side and thus persuade Urbánek to publish the book. 'Please tell me your verdict as soon as possible and don't let the manuscript out of your hands until that time.'[77] Ignoring this last instruction, Urbánek immediately sent it to Stecker. If Stecker were to approve of Janáček's work then he would be happy to publish it; perhaps, he went on, Janáček might drop Stecker a line about it. Janáček did so, drafting his thoughts** on the three blank sides of Urbánek's letter.[78] In the end Stecker excused himself directly to Janáček, who when sending his letter to Urbánek pressed on with the argument that the treatise would be used at the Brno Organ School and Teachers' Institute and so the publisher wouldn't lose by publishing it. He also repeated the point he made earlier that, unlike Czech harmony books by Blažek, Gregora and Skuherský, his manual did not require any special talent in the pupil.[79] It seems that Janáček genuinely believed this and had no notion of how demanding his manual was, certainly not a volume that could be inflicted on the semi-illiterates in music that he had to cope with at the Teachers' Institute.

On 12 May Hostinský wrote an embarrassed letter to Janáček. His silence, he explained, had been caused by the previously mentioned typhoid fever in the family that then led to the death of his son. Most of

** For some of his comments, see chap. 19.

414

his comments were too late for Janáček to take much account of but enough to persuade Urbánek to proceed. All Hostinský's comments were as reasonable as one might expect from a wise and knowledgeable theorist: for instance that he felt that Janáček did not distinguish enough between the physical and psychological aspects (in later years Janáček would seek increasing support from the writings on psychology of Wilhelm Wundt) and that he reckoned that Janáček's was not the only principle of harmony, and (with a demonstration of his legendary tact) that what Janáček had written could be expressed in a more 'practical' manner.[80]

The last point seems to have gone home. Janáček asked for his manuscript back and, efficient as ever, Urbánek sent it the next day asking him to give it to a *real* expert in the language – Bartoš would be just the person. Suddenly it was all rush: they wanted to have it out by the beginning of July, so Janáček must please get it revised as soon as possible. Urbánek was, however, doubtful about this timetable: if it couldn't be achieved he would publish it in two fascicles: the first only for the Brno institutions, with a second one sent by post to those who had paid in advance for the whole work.[81]

From late February, Janáček also needed to concentrate on preparations for the Ethnographic Exhibition itself. The surviving correspondence is dominated by that with Bakešová, illuminating among other things many of the practical problems they faced in getting so many folk performers to Prague. The proposed dates for the 'Moravian Days', for instance, clashed with getting in the harvest. The second half of June, she reported, would be much better. Many workers wouldn't be able to get away at the proposed date in mid-August, and those who could might be exhausted after their labour ('several kilos lighter than before'). Bakešová went on to give a list of twenty potential participants she had assembled from her area, listing their occupations. They included a tailor, a blacksmith, a carpenter, a bricklayer and further unspecified 'workers', but the overwhelming number were farm labourers, much more difficult to get to Prague for a few days at the height of the harvest.[82] In other regions the difficulty was that half of the girls were from factories and they were getting only two days off.[83]

Bakešová and Janáček also differed over the numbers of participants. Bakešová wanted maximum impact with as many as possible, and Janáček, bearing in mind that he had to stick to a budget, tried to limit the numbers: 'I've now obtained from you, from Mr Sojka and from Mrs Lováková a list of those taking part.' From Ořechovičky (Bakešová's village) there would be twenty-four Little Queens, twenty-two youths, one organizer, seven boys. From Troubsko (Sojka's village) there would be sixteen Little Queens, ten youths, one messenger, ten musicians, two teachers, six citizens, five landowners. From Šlapanice (Lováková's village) there would be thirty-six Little Queens, four old women, one (woman) organizer.

> 76 [Little Queens] + 69 [others] = 145.
> That's an impossible number!
> Why take the Little Queens from Šlapanice when there are now suddenly twenty-four coming from Ořechovičky?
> And forty with those from Troubsko!
> Surely thirty pairs, i.e. sixty Little Queens, are redundant?
> If you really have twenty-four of them then it's enough to take another twenty from Šlapanice. And what are all those old women from Šlapanice? Surely they are also unnecessary.[84]

Janáček was not the only person who found Bakešová difficult. On 3 March 1895 her chief assistant in the area, Sojka, wrote to Janáček as follows:

> Mrs Bakešová has taken on herself all practising and costuming, as well as the general organization, therefore whenever you intend to go to Troubsko kindly agree the time and the day with Mrs Bakešová[;] the two of you together and on site would settle definitively all the shortcomings and [differences of] opinions. By way of explanation I mention that contact between me and Mrs Bakešová is completely broken off, and so I won't be able to be present there wherever Mrs Bakešová is.[85]

Tactfully Sojka seems to have intimated to Bakešová that he was withdrawing because of pressure from his employers, which led to Bakešová's tut-tutting about a 'poisonous wind from above' blowing against 'our exhibition' and the fact that a Czech teacher had to 'fear for his existence'.[86]

On 10 April 1895 Janáček was trying to coax information out of Zeman: how many people from Velká would be needed for a 'decent appearance'? Janáček needed a list so he could budget for the journey, accommodation and meals. The dates for the 'Moravian Days' (despite objections from the farming community) had been agreed with the organizers in Haná, Valašsko and Brno as 15–18 August. Could sixty people from Velká come during this period? The letter ends with a typical Janáček threat: 'If you don't answer with even a little word you'll force me to come to you for your answer.'[87]

With all this activity it is sometimes hard to remember that Janáček's heavy workload as a teacher continued, and often did not give much pleasure. On 20 March 1895, for instance, he complained at a staff meeting about a disrespectful pupil who, when invited, wasn't able to sing the second verse of the prescribed song correctly, and when given an unfavourable classification threw his songbook on to the bench.[88]

A week later (27 March 1895) the first meeting of the music section for Moravia of the Ethnographic Exhibition took place at 7 p.m. in the committee room of the Czech Readers' Club in Brno,[89] marking the beginnings of even more feverish preparations. In the spring of 1895 Janáček travelled to Kroměříž and probably to Kojetín and Tovačov for rehearsals of the Haná groups in specific ceremonies (a Haná wedding, harvest home, 'Haná rights').[90] There was another meeting of Janáček's committee on 28 April.[91]

In June Bakešová was making pleas for last-minute changes to the programme:

I arrived today from Vienna and heard that Mrs Lováková from Šlapanice was here and begged that the Little Queens could dance on 15 August, that [firstly] the girls can't stay so long in Prague and secondly they would completely spoil their white clothes. The same holds true for the Troubsko girls and for our ones [from Ořechovičky]. Why didn't we come to an agreement on this? It didn't occur to me to ask the girls whether they could stay on until the 18th.[92]

On 1 July – six weeks before the 'Moravian Days' – Bakešová suddenly had a bright idea about the people from Klobouky – so far unrepresented. They had a particularly colourful folk outfit; and wouldn't it be nice, she suggested, to have six to eight pairs of dancers from there? Much of this long letter is devoted to seeing how this could be done, and what would need to be rearranged to accommodate this sudden plan. Then came nagging enquiries as to how things were going in Kozlovice, Velká and Haná, and her objections to some of the things she'd heard via the grapevine about the Haná group.[93] Janáček must have found it all infuriating.

As preparations continued, Olga and Zdenka went to Hukvaldy again, this time on Janáček's birthday on 3 July, and in their hurry they forgot to pass on birthday greetings. In her letter a few days later Olga apologized for this and then went on to give one of her numbered lists of the items that they had forgotten, which this time included an onion-cutter (depicted in a little drawing in case Janáček had no idea what to look for), and a 'hammer for beating down a chop'.[94] A few days later there was concern for the cat and complaints that Janáček was 'stingy with writing this year'[95] but no doubt he was rushed off his feet with final preparations. He made a trip to Velká on 20 July for final rehearsals the next day, as he told Bakešová in a newsy letter, though this was upset by devastating floods in the area. In order to promote the Moravian contribution, he had got together a whole new committee that was working passionately, putting out proclamations and arranging a special train all the way from the Vlárský pass to Brno and then on to Prague. Things seemed to be worse in Vsetín (Valašsko) – total silence – so he rushed off there on Saturday. And he made tantalizing (and unexplained) allusions to arguments in Kroměříž (Haná). However, the distinguished ethnographer and architect from Slovácko, František Úprka (1868–1929), was arranging the spectacular 'Hunting the King'. Janáček would be going to Prague to view the amphitheatre, and on 28 July would be in Frenštát and then on to Radhošť for a general meeting to finalize preparations for the 'Moravian Days', now less than three weeks away.[96]

Soon after the trip to Prague Janáček wrote to Zeman about his impression of the venue, and how their plans would best fit into it. The letter is remarkable in giving some idea both of the complexities of getting together so many different groups (and the organizational problems that this would entail), but also Janáček's ever-increasing feel for the theatricality of the event:

On Sunday I was in Prague for a moment to take a look at the amphitheatre. It is of course spacious but the sound is good.

15 August. The folk musicians with the first wedding retinue go in through gate A and go round the stage in procession. The second procession enters through gate B, encountering the first retinue – contests (pp. 37–8).[††] I think that it won't last long so they could join the dance round the maypole (pp. 44, 45, 46). Before that the group of *Little Queens from Horňácko* would have reached the stage of the amphitheatre, then comes the *Haná wedding*. The Slovácko wedding, however, remains on stage and occasionally dances until everyone leaves the amphitheatre in procession.

[††] Page references to *Slavnosti a obyčeje* (see above).

Janáček went on to describe his plan for the final day, 18 August, which involved a procession to a feast (*hody* from Horácko), 'four beribboned horses', a Valachian group and a Slovácko wedding.[97]

By early August Janáček's correspondence, for example with Mrs Bakešová, was concerned not with practising the dances and organizing the folk customs, but with getting the performers to Prague: train tickets, accommodation and money.[98] Quarrels over money would blow up after the whole thing was over.

The Czecho-Slavonic Ethnographic Exhibition opened on 15 May and closed on 28 October 1895. Its two million visitors[99] were treated to a broadly conceived display of Czech life, which included reconstructions of part of the Prague Old Town, and of the humble birthplaces of some of the giants of Czech culture such as the writer Josef Kajetán Tyl and the historian František Palacký.[100] The chief focus, however, was village life, depicted in written documents such as collections of folksongs, tales and sayings, photographs of folk activities, and displays of traditional crafts such as embroidery and lace-making, pottery and basket-weaving, wood-carving and other forms of decoration. Most striking of all were the reconstructed Czech and Moravian villages that provided the backdrop for representations of agricultural work over the different seasons of the year, religious festivals and pilgrimages, village dances, etc.

The activities with which Janáček was particularly associated, the 'Moravian Days', took place in the middle of August. The live Moravian contribution began with a procession on 15 August at 10 a.m. through Prague from the Žofín island in the Vltava to the exhibition site at Stromovka. It was a colourful affair with the performers in their elaborate folk outfits, each region strikingly differentiated from the others. In the printed programme (XV/148) the order of participants is listed in eighteen numbered groups. First came the groups from Slovácko: a 'Hunting the King' procession from Kněždub and Vlčnov, reapers (for work songs) from Velká, participants in a Velká wedding on a beribboned cart, and then the remaining Slovácko people. Then followed similar groups from Horácko, Valašsko and finally Haná, a larger group mainly from the Kroměříž region, which made up a third of the ensemble with the representation of traditional ceremonies such as 'Haná rights', harvest home, spinners and the inevitable wedding. Janáček himself headed the procession. He had intended to wear Valachian folk costume but had not tried on the borrowed costume in time and found that the trousers were too small, so instead wore his *čamara*, a braided black coat.[‡‡] Zdenka took Olga to Prague – it was her first visit there – and they stood and watched the procession with pride from the Žofín bridge.[101]

Each day in the afternoon, 15–18 August, there were demonstrations of the songs, dances and ceremonies that had been assembled and practised for the exhibition. On the opening day and the final day a cross-section of all the groups performed in the exhibition amphitheatre. On 16 August there was a procession of Slovácko carnivalists through the exhibition site. The next day, 17 August, was devoted to Haná, with the 'Haná rights' group travelling on a cart through the exhibition and at 5 p.m. the other Haná groups performing in the exhibition amphitheatre; a Valachian evening was held in the Valachian village which had been assembled on the exhibition site.[102]

Janáček had done remarkably well in bringing together such a diverse and interesting range of folk performers. He had in fact done much better than his counterparts in art music. Despite the ambitious plans that had been laid as early as March 1894, the only Moravian music performed at the exhibition was in an afternoon concert on 16 August 1895 given by the Brno Beseda and the Olomouc choral society 'Žerotín'. This was offered as an addition to the usual evening concerts of the sixty-five-piece exhibition orchestra under its conductor, Karel Kovařovic, which as well as international fare presented a range of Czech music from the eighteenth century to recent works such as Novák's F major Serenade and Suk's *Winter's Tale Overture*.[103]

Buried in one of Janáček's letters to Bakešová was the comment that since the Prague committee were probably not going to publish the collected manuscript songs and dances that Janáček had acquired (e.g. from Bím) until after the exhibition, he and Bartoš intended to publish the manuscripts in their possession while the exhibition was in progress. This was yet another of Janáček's unrealistic notions. The letter is undated but seems to have been written in June. Although the exhibition went on until the end of October, it seems extraordinary that Janáček might imagine that he and Bartoš could publish within a matter of months the '500 to 600 songs' they had accumulated so far, together with anything else that Bakešová and her husband might have

---

[‡‡] The *čamara* was worn with plain black trousers, as in Janáček's wedding outfit.

to hand. He had asked all the other collectors and promised a 'splendid' fee.[104] This of course got nowhere by the planned date, but can instead be seen as one of the stages that led towards the large publication *Moravian Folksongs Newly Collected* (XIII/3), to which Janáček and Bartoš would devote years once the exhibition was out of the way.

Once back from Prague, there was still work to be done such as sorting out accounts. A letter from Janáček to the exhibition director František Šubert (30 August 1895) asking for his expenses to be settled makes it clear that he had had to pay a good deal out of his own pocket.[105] Although Janáček promptly received the requested 607 zl,[106] there were still Zeman's folk musicians to be paid, and it took many letters before Janáček was able to send him 204 zl in December.[107] Mrs Bakešová, as always, caused problems as her accounts came in late and she had seemingly overspent her budget,[108] charges that of course she vigorously denied.[109]

Janáček spent what was left of the summer in Hukvaldy. As in the previous year, Zdenka and Olga made their way back to Brno (by 7 September) for the beginning of Olga's school year, leaving Janáček on his own for a while.[110] One assumes that it was only then he was able to get back to his opera before he himself returned to Brno, but quite extraordinarily (and without any result) he seems to have planned a three-movement Organ Sonata (XI/3) at about this time. Sketches in his diary for 1895–6[111] suggest a first movement in D major in 6/4 followed by a theme and variations for the second movement, and a fugue for the third. This is a deeply puzzling development. Janáček's sonata-writing and organ-writing days were long over; maybe, like the 1908 Mass, this originated as a teaching exercise. As for *Jenůfa*, there is no further evidence of any work, though something must have been going on for him to get to the end of Act 1 early the next year (see chap. 33).

As it was, the end of the year was overshadowed by disappointments (such as the Ministry of Culture and Education turning down Janáček's application to the right and title of a 'main teacher' and the attendant regrading),[112] and yet more anxieties over Olga's health. Zdenka relates that 'in the November after the exhibition, a new blow struck. Olga got acute rheumatic fever affecting the joints again. She was in bed almost the whole winter and was very poorly. We thought then that it was the end. But in the spring, amazingly, she began to recover quickly.'[113]

33

1896

When *Jenůfa* received its Brno première in 1904, the anonymous writer of the programme (believed to be Janáček) claimed that the score of the opera had already existed in fair copy in 1897 (XV/174). This of course is nonsense. According to Janáček's dates in his copy of the play, he finished the opera only in 1903, and there is plenty of corroborative evidence to show his continuous involvement from the end of 1901 to this completion date (see chap. 42). The programme writer had quoted Karel Stecker in saying that Alfred Bruneau had been the first composer to write an opera on a prose text (in *Messidor*, 1897). Was the 1897 date for *Jenůfa* an attempt to claim that Janáček had got there first, or at least simultaneously? Or is the 'fair copy' that was claimed to exist merely that of Act 1? In the short report in *Moravské noviny* on the first performance of *Jenůfa* in the 1910–11 season, this claim is modified to state that Act 1 was complete 'before Charpentier's *Louise*',[1] i.e. by February 1900. This is more like it. In his letter to Nebuška about composing the opera, Janáček wrote: 'Between Acts 1 and 2 there was a long break. At that time I was working with Fr[antišek] Bartoš on the folksongs published by the Czech Academy'.[2] The break in writing the work that Janáček mentions is furthermore reinforced by stylistic differences between Act 1 and the next two acts.

When might Janáček's 'break' have occurred? In February 1895, the latest date in his copy of the play (apart from those in 1902–3), he recorded that he had begun the 'orchestration', and by that Štědroň and others have assumed that he meant the fully composed version in full score. Janáček's original score, if it contained any dates, might have settled the matter, but sadly was destroyed when the Janáčeks moved house (see chap. 48). The work that interrupted the composition of

Jenůfa, as mentioned to Nebuška, was *Moravian Folksongs Newly Collected* (XIII/3), which Janáček co-edited with František Bartoš. Proofs began arriving only in September 1898. Before then, however, there would have been the laborious process of deciding what to include, editing it and preparing it for the printers. This stage is mostly undocumented but a volume containing 2057 songs clearly absorbed great quantities of time from its two editors somewhere between late 1895 (once Janáček surfaced after tidying up the accounts at the end of the Ethnographic Exhibition) and September 1898. Furthermore in early 1896 Janáček was hard at work on proof corrections for his harmony manual *On the Composition of Chords and their Connections* (XV/151). By 21 March 1896 he had dealt with most of them,[3] but the process continued until 17 April, when he sent Urbánek the final complete proofs.[4] The more one considers them, the more crowded these years begin to feel, shifting the putative breaking-off point for *Jenůfa* ever earlier. A good psychological turning point presents itself in January 1896.

On 16 January 1896 the Czech Theatre in Brno gave the local première of Tchaikovsky's *Queen of Spades*. Janáček was much taken with it. Although he no longer wrote regularly as a critic, he took the trouble to write a review, published on 21 January in *Lidové noviny* (XV/149). 'Once again a genuine artistic work has shone forth', he declared; 'the genius of originality, character and truth in music has arisen for us again. In art, let us follow only such genius; and let us aim to emulate it.' In her memoirs Stejskalová emphasized that Janáček found the composition of *Jenůfa* difficult: 'Sometimes it seemed to me that the master was battling with *Jenůfa*, as if he went into the study not to compose but to fight. He got up from supper, stood and thought a moment and, really more to himself, sighed: "Lord God and the Virgin Mary, help me!"'[5] Act 1 of *Jenůfa* contains a large and crucial folkloristic scene, the Recruits' Scene, which Janáček had modelled on his earlier arrangement for chorus and orchestra, *I have sown green* (III/3). Janáček had no difficulty writing this sort of material and, with new words, remoulding it to his requirements in *Jenůfa*. The intense drama of Jenůfa's subsequent recriminations of Števa and her confrontation with Laca are arguably scenes to which Mascagni's *Cavalleria* pointed the way (see chap. 29). But with the enclosed drama of Act 2, the interaction of just four characters, Janáček was on new territory. Perhaps he began to see that *Jenůfa* could be more effective as a psychological drama, as is *The Queen of Spades*, than as a folkloristic vehicle such as he had written with his earlier *The Beginning of a Romance* and that he had begun writing in *Jenůfa*. The most plausible explanation for his abandoning *Jenůfa* was not so much the weight of his other projects but that he did not feel equipped as a composer to deal with the increasing demands of the libretto in Act 2. It may well have been the revelation of Tchaikovsky's *The Queen of Spades* that stopped *Jenůfa* dead in its tracks at the end of Act 1.

Furthermore Act 1 of *Jenůfa* contains the semblance of a number opera, with identifiable arias, duets, a trio and choruses, sometimes joined by recitative (occasionally even designated as such), i.e. much along the lines of *Cavalleria*. It does not sound at all like Janáček's description of the music of *The Queen of Spades* ('Jerky, fragmentary, it lacks tightly linked big tunes . . .').* But this description does well enough for later Janáček works, including the next two acts of *Jenůfa*. Such a radical change in style does not occur overnight, and Janáček would have needed time to reconsider his approach to composition in the light of Tchaikovsky's opera. His stopping work would seem to coincide with his encounter with *The Queen of Spades*, whose musico-dramatic language he portrayed with considerable involvement (see chap. 34). And once he stopped, he did so for several years. During this period he found time to compose other works – for instance the large-scale cantata *Amarus*, which he began in 1896. One can argue that such pieces were all part of the learning process, but it can also be suggested that to get back to his opera after a break of several years was psychologically difficult. It needed a particularly strong emotional jolt to help him do so.

Of Janáček's brothers the closest to him not only in age but also in personal sympathy was František, born two years after him. He trained as a mechanical engineer and found work in Gleiwitz, Prussian Silesia (now Gliwice, Poland), where he married a Polish woman, Marie Koziczińska, in 1883. At the end of 1895 he moved to St Petersburg to take a position as director of a machine factory. And it was from St Petersburg that a more frequent correspondence began between the two brothers, at first (on František's part) in the language of much of their education, German, then (after Leoš's reproach that 'it would be

---

* For more of this passage, see chap. 34.

shameful to forget his mother tongue') in badly spelt Czech and with the hope that Leoš would not laugh at it.[6] František's first Czech letter had been written just before the Russian New Year; in his next letter, just after the New Year, he was able to say that he had now signed a contract with his new employers, who had previously engaged him on a trial basis, and so he would be staying on in St Petersburg. He would fetch his wife at the end of February and, with the 'large flat' that he expected to have, he invited Janáček and his family to stay: 'St Petersburg is really worth looking at.' The letter goes on to mention the beautiful Orthodox choral singing in Russian churches, which František described in considerable detail, and Russian Christmas customs, of which he was rather disapproving ('everyone got drunk, including the ladies').[7]

This letter seems to have had an impact on Leoš. On 18 April 1896 his new choral work, *Hospodine!* (iii/5), was performed at a festival of Brno schools, with the composer himself conducting a mixed choir from the Brno Teachers' Institute.[†] It is based on the oldest known hymn in Czech, *Hospodine, pomiluj ny!* [*Lord, have mercy on us!*], though its hieratic chanting is Russian in effect and probably in intention (see chap. 35). It was Janáček's first venture into music that took its inspiration from Russia, a vein that proved exceptionally productive for the rest of his life. Where Janáček may have come across Russian Orthodox music is unclear, but he would have had the opportunity to hear it at the Russian Church in Prague during his student days there.

In mid-June Zdenka and Olga went again to Hukvaldy for the summer holidays.[8] In her memoirs Zdenka reports that despite the setback in Olga's health the previous winter she now (at the age of fourteen) 'began visibly to blossom both physically and mentally. She was cheerful, witty, kind, sociable' and enjoyed herself in the company of young people, which included an admirer, a German under-huntsman on the archbishop's estate. When, a month later, the Organ School broke up and Leoš joined his family in Hukvaldy, he took much pleasure in Olga's improved appearance and state of health.[9] But soon he was off to Russia, his first trip abroad since his and Zdenka's reconciliatory stay in Gleichenberg in 1884.

[†] The piece may have been performed more than once at this period, as is suggested by two different versions, the second with slightly different scoring and extending the piece by thirty-one bars.

Information on Janáček's Russian trip comes mostly from two sources: the impromptu diary he made on the endpapers and in odd spaces elsewhere of the Russian grammar that he took with him,[10] and the series of three articles that he wrote for *Lidové noviny* entitled *A Few Words from a Holiday Trip* (xv/150). The articles are dated 26, 30 and 31 July, all giving St Petersburg as a place of writing, but since Janáček had left there on 27 July, the last two reports he in fact wrote on the train as he travelled further. Focussing principally on St Petersburg, the feuilletons are arranged systematically rather than chronologically and describe Janáček's impressions on a variety of topics. Knowledge of the rest of the trip derives chiefly from the 'diary', for instance his exact timetable (table 33.1).

A journey from Moravia to St Petersburg covering roughly the same route as Janáček did would now take in Poland, Belarus, Latvia and Lithuania along the way. Janáček, however, had only one border to cross, between imperial Austria and imperial Russia. He picked up the train locally at Studénka (see Map 4; pp. 428–9) and first travelled east

Table 33.1: Janáček's train timetable for his trip to Russia, July–August 1896, according to the entries in his Russian grammar.

Studénka		5.15 afternoon	Saturday 18 July
Trzebinia	arr.	7.57 evening	
	dep.	8.14 evening	
Granica		12.00 in the night	
Warsaw	arr.	6.47 morning	Sunday 19 July
	dep.	10.10 morning	
Vilnius	arr.	9.47 evening	
	dep.	10.22 evening	
St Petersburg		6.00 evening	Monday 20 July
St Petersburg		9.00 evening	Monday 27 July
Moscow	arr.	10.10 morning	Tuesday 28 July
	dep.	9.20 evening	
Nizhny Novgorod	arr.	8.15 morning	Wednesday 29 July
	dep.	9.45 evening	
Moscow	arr.	9.20 morning	Thursday 30 July
	dep.	2.15 afternoon	
Smolensk		5.03 evening	
Brest	arr.	2.20 afternoon	
	dep.	6.00 evening	
Warsaw	arr.	10.15 evening	Friday 31 July
	dep.	12.27 in the night	
Granica		6.33 morning	Saturday 1 August
Trzebinia		8.18 morning	
Studénka		11.12 morning	

into Galicia (still in Austrian territory) in the direction of Cracow, but changed trains at Trzebinia to take the train north in the direction of Częstochowa and Warsaw. At that time the border on this line between Austrian Galicia and Russian Poland was a tiny crossing point called Granica. Forty-eight hours after he started, Janáček arrived in St Petersburg, where he was met by his brother. He spent a week there. The remaining six days were spent travelling, first via Moscow to Nizhny Novgorod for a day at the famous All-Russia Fair, and then home via Moscow (where he spent a few hours sightseeing), Smolensk and Brest to rejoin his original route at Warsaw. The concentration on St Petersburg was because he had free accommodation there at his brother's 'comfortable flat'; he spent seven nights there, and all the remaining seven nights on trains (two on the way there, five on the way back). But it is clear from his comments on Moscow that he rather regretted not spending longer there.

Janáček travelled alone. According to František's letter at the beginning of the year, the whole family had been invited and the question of them all going had no doubt been discussed.[11] Janáček's letter home to Zdenka on his first full day in St Petersburg addresses the matter: 'If I'd known how comfortably and pleasantly one travels all the way here, that it is possible to sleep the night in the carriage as at home in bed, then you could have come here too.'[12] In fact Janáček was probably better off on his own: unlike Zdenka, he spoke some Russian (see chap. 9); also, without his wife, he was more likely to strike up conversations with people – as he did on the way, for instance.

In his impressions on the journey he paid particular attention to the varying nationalities. Bohumín, though technically on Czech soil, had a 'German character' and he duly recorded the expressions 'friš [frisch] Wasser, friše Zeitung' ['fresh water, new newspaper']. But 'Třebinia' (as Janáček transcribed it) in Austrian-ruled Galicia (now part of Poland) had a 'Polish air'. His travelling companions included 'a Czech from Prague' and 'a man in the coupé with a glass of water [who] was a German Jew'. After crossing the border into Russian Poland at Granica, Janáček sensed the end of Austrian officialdom and that he was at last in a Slavonic state. 'What young men, clean, nice-looking, polite, efficient on the track.' He began to feel 'so merry: an awakening, a resurrection. I am shaking off [the bonds of] slavery! We're off. Russia!'

At Warsaw he heard the first sounds of folk music: a flute during the

Map 4 Leoš Janáček's journey to Russia in 1896.

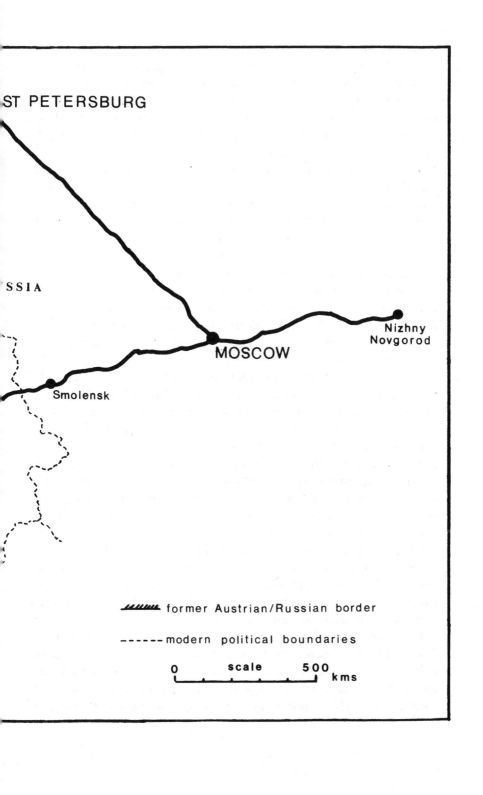

ST PETERSBURG

SSIA

Nizhny
Novgorod

MOSCOW

Smolensk

⩗⩗⩗⩗⩗ former Austrian/Russian border

------ modern political boundaries

0   scale   500
                        kms

feeding of the horses. The countryside looked like that of Moravia, but at the stations there were 'whole herds of ragged Jews'. At Grodno (now in Belarus) he encountered the first Russian in his coupé. 'I must confess that apart from words that remained in my memory from the exercises – I didn't understand. They have rapid speech and a different accent.' The Russian, Janáček proudly noted, hadn't realized that his companion was not Russian when he responded to his greeting. Then they got talking: about the Czechs, about music (his companion had known the Czech violinist, Ferdinand Laub, who had settled in Russia), about the Jewish pale of settlement. They had supper in Vilnius (now in Lithuania), where they were warned against thieves. Up at 6.15 the next morning, Janáček resumed his conversation with his Russian companion, to whom he finally said farewell on the station platform at St Petersburg, where his brother was waiting.

That same evening Janáček and his brother went to the zoological gardens and to an open-air theatre, to see a piece called *Towards the North Pole*. There Janáček was struck by the big orchestra (with six double basses) and an organ. The programme was 'absurd', but the organist played well.

On Tuesday 21 July he visited Kazan Cathedral and the Cathedral of St Isaac, and was overwhelmed by the rich decorations, the pictures made from precious stones, columns from lapis lazuli, and the diamonds in the icons. At 11 a.m. he heard a Requiem Mass in Kazan Cathedral, with four excellent singers. In his second *Lidové noviny* piece, he wrote with approval of the music heard, noting that the 'mild, indeed almost muffled tone of the choir [. . .] is distinguished appropriately from the sonorous voice of the priest', 'no interruptions, no pauses, no glaring modulations. The purely musical element does not distract one's attention nor does it put one's mind off the ceremony.' And all this was compared favourably to the 'villainous' 'roar of German mixture stops in our organs – quint stops, cornet stops, etc.'. Another impression that day was the *izvoschtchik*, the local cabman and his constant '*pozhal'te*' ['please'], another topic on which Janáček expanded in his articles.

On 22 July Janáček visited two of the islands in the Gulf of Finland: Yelagin Island, a 'wonderful excursion place' with a 'calm view of the gulf', where he heard an accordion; and then the Krestovsky Island, an excursion place 'for the higher circles', where he heard a 'weak' Russian choir. This expedition to the gulf was an event that lingered in his memory and he described it almost thirty years later in his auto-biography. Recollecting how four centuries earlier his predecessor from Hukvaldy, Jan Čapek of Sány and Hukvaldy, had stood on these shores with his Hussite armies and had taken home sea water so that the folks at home might believe they had got to the sea, Janáček himself filled a little bottle with sea water – to take to the school in his native village. At the end of the day (another memory that surfaced in his auto-biography) Janáček travelled some 28 km by train from St Petersburg to the tsar's summer palace at Tsarskoye Selo (now Pushkin) where, as the shadows deepened and the horizon darkened, he and his company got lost in the maze in the park. It was only when they heard the sounds of choral singing – the tsar's singers returning from St Petersburg – that they were able to guide themselves out of the maze by the sounds of the voices.[13]

On 23 July Janáček's only entry in his 'diary' was a digression on the sea and the appearance of the enormous surface receding into the dis-tance and blending with the horizon. According to his third *Lidové noviny* piece, however, on '11 July' (the equivalent in the Western calendar of 23 July) he visited the church at the Peter and Paul Fortress with its tombs of Russian tsars. He noted the plain inscriptions and commented on how little account Czech history books took of Russian history. At 4 p.m. in the zoological gardens he heard the military band of the 136th Tsaritsyn Infantry Regiment playing. The animals were fed at 5.30 and that was followed with various light entertainments, clowns, a ballet (*The Land of Eternal Ice*) with two hundred dancers and a hot-air balloon. Then followed light music – from all over the world, with merely two Russian items, both by Glinka.

On 24 July Janáček wrote his second (and last) letter from Russia to Zdenka and Olga, commenting on his expedition to the Gulf of Finland to get sea water. He was anxious about the journey back (by a more complicated route) and had no idea when he would return.[14] In the early evening he took a train out of St Petersburg to attend the regular orchestral concert at the Pavlovsk railway station. This was another topic that he described at some length in his final *Lidové noviny* article. The audience he reckoned to be between fifteen hundred and two thousand, made up of St Petersburg's intelligentsia who had summer dachas in the area as well as people like himself who made the two-hour train journey there. The programme, a long one conducted ('by heart') by Nikolay Vladimirovich Galkin, consisted entirely of works by Rubinstein: his Symphony no. 4, Cello Concerto no. 2, Piano Concerto no. 2, symphonic poem *Ivan the Terrible* and some songs. Rubinstein had been an early passion of Janáček's (see chap. 15) and by 1896 he still had a soft spot for his music, although he now found *Ivan the Terrible* 'garrulous' but enjoyed the Russian 'folk style' in the third movement of the Cello Concerto. He considered that the soloist, Edvard Jakobs, played with 'clarity and calm' but was icy cold: 'I want to see the marks of every note passing not only through the muscles of the fingers but also the furnace of the heart.' The concert began at eight and by ten the train that was to take them all back to St Petersburg was 'already puffing nearby'. Unwilling to miss the symphony, Janáček listened to the final movement only with half an ear, made a dash for it at the end and managed to find the last seat in the crowded train that two hours later delivered him back to St Petersburg.

On 25 July Janáček obtained his passport (presumably allowing him to travel to Moscow and Nizhny Novgorod) and saw the monastery at the Nevsky Prospekt and its cathedral with the remains of St Ivan Nevsky. The next day he attended Mass at the Catholic Kazan Cathedral and, according to his diary, 'went to get sea water'. But unless he went twice for this purpose this seems to be a mistake since, as his letter to Zdenka on 24 July confirms,[15] he had already done so on 23 July.

What is striking about the *Lidové noviny* pieces is how entirely positive Janáček is: St Petersburg is rather similar to Prague, but much bigger (he gives extensive topographical descriptions); the parks for children are wonderfully safe; the streets are spotlessly clean; cold boiled water is supplied in front of every tavern and is the responsibility of the tavern-keeper to supply; food (though coming at odd hours) is inexpensive, cabs are cheap and plentiful, the cabmen respectful, unlike the down-at-heel cabbies in Warsaw. People are polite and friendly. His only negative comments are not about St Petersburg at all but have to do with nationality: why are Czech goods described as 'Bohemian'? (the label had a pejorative sense in those days); he noted an 'ugly-looking' Korean delegation; he disliked the fact that Germans seemed to have taken over much of the music-making.

Janáček left St Petersburg on the evening of 27 July and travelled via Moscow to Nizhny Novgorod. Perhaps he had intended to write more articles for *Lidové noviny*, but knowledge of how he got on in his second week comes only from the comments in his Russian grammar and what he remembered thirty years later in his autobiography. He arrived at Nizhny Novgorod early in the morning on 29 July and bought a map and a book on the current fair – both survive in the Janáček Archive.[16] In his autobiography he remembered the 'forest of masts in the combined waters of the rivers Oka and Volga' and commented on how each warehouse was built on the first storey to save goods from the floods. He found the city more characterful than St Petersburg. This, he reckoned, was where Asia met Russia. The All-Russia Fair served as a travelling Russian school for further Asiatic regions and, as he declared in his autobiography, he was 'proud and happy at the thought that even a Slav nation was a spreader of culture!'[17]

If he found Nizhny interesting, Moscow the next day (30 July) was a revelation:

The Kremlin! – God, this fairy tale! Something so cosy, dear in its green, blue, etc. towers. Inside – all around, a beautiful view. From here Moscow is like a sea of domes – 1600. I am glad that I spent time here. Otherwise I wouldn't have seen the most beautiful bit of my journey!!!.[18]

However, he was able to spend only a few hours in Moscow: ('I have to say goodbye to dear Russia. I am sorry. It was *so nice here* [underlined three times]') and on 30 July at 2.15 he was off, travelling via Smolensk and Brest. The next day, Friday, was unlucky and at Częstochowa officials refused to let him back into Galicia. His irritated account of the incident in his 'diary' betrays a latent anti-Semitism.

Jews – a terrible number. Although I avoided them, I still fell into their hands. One rouble to the scribe, two roubles to the Jew saying that he'd showed me where to go – offering 'ladies'. They took me to lunch to a Jew – the society here! How to get further – I don't know! Perhaps my calm spirit won't desert me! Priests go walking, surely this Jewdom is hardly to their taste?!.[19]

Janáček was eventually allowed to travel home, reaching Warsaw that evening and writing the third and last of his *Lidové noviny* pieces. He arrived back in Hukvaldy on Saturday 1 August.

On his return Janáček noticed Olga's admirer and was displeased. Zdenka reports how he 'forbade Olga to go out into company where she might see the young German', and even when Leoš and Zdenka went out together in the evening, poor Olga had to stay at home, weeping with frustration at the unfairness of it all.[20] Although Janáček's reason was that she was 'too young' to have admirers, the fact that the under-huntsman was a German couldn't have helped.

Zdenka and Olga were due to leave Hukvaldy on 9 September[21] when Olga got chickenpox. Janáček had to return to his teaching, but Zdenka remained with Olga a few more weeks until she was quite well again, during which time she enjoyed frequent visits from Mr Reinoch, her under-huntsman admirer.[22] They were back by early October.[23] Janáček was glad to see his daughter again and on 5 October wrote a folksong arrangement, *Uncertainty*, into her commonplace book, which was later incorporated into the second volume of his collection *Moravian Folk Poetry in Song* (v/2).

Janáček spent all of August and half of September at Hukvaldy with his wife and daughter and, in this exceptional burst of free time, he seems to have begun writing a new work, his cantata *Amarus* (III/6). The piece was completed by May 1897, as revealed by his dealings with Dvořák about it (see chap. 36). A large-scale composition for three soloists, chorus and orchestra, lasting almost half an hour, would have taken a good while to write and would have been difficult to fit in during a busy teaching year. Support for taking its beginnings back to 1896, straight after Janáček's return from Russia, is provided by the article *How Ideas Occurred* (xv/313), which Janáček prepared for publication in the periodical *Nový život* in 1897 but which remained unpublished during his lifetime since the printing of the facsimile music examples that Janáček demanded were beyond the means of *Nový život*.[24] In it Janáček mentions 'the Slavonic sea, which I saw this year for the first time', thus supplying the starting year of composition as 1896. Furthermore Janáček alluded in the article to the 'heavy and regular breathing of my little daughter'. Had he been writing in Brno, Olga would have been sleeping in her own room; his description sounds more like the hired accommodation in Hukvaldy during the rest of the summer.

Janáček's choice of text was well in line with that of his Czech contemporaries. Jaroslav Vrchlický was one of the leading Czech poets of his day and much favoured as a supplier of oratorio texts. Bendl's *Švanda the Bagpiper* (1880) and Fibich's *Spring Romance* (1881), two particularly popular works in this genre, both had Vrchlický texts as did Dvořák's *St Ludmila* (1886), which Janáček knew well. Janáček had of course already set a poem by Vrchlický in his mixed-voice

Autumn Song (IV/14; see chap. 17). Unlike Vrchlický's *Autumn Song*, however, which elicited one of Janáček's feeblest responses, his poem about a lonely young monk confronting human love for the first time had much to say to Janáček, who had spent a lonely youth in the Augustinian monastery in Brno. In his biography of Janáček (1924), Brod reproduced a fragment of a letter, now lost, in which Janáček wrote to him about *Amarus*: 'You know, I was in the old Queen's Monastery until my teens. Those surroundings of grey corridors and a dreamy life, the monastery garden at the foot of the Žlutý kopec [Yellow Hill] in Staré Brno, the old trees, with their melancholy shade: and on top of all that, my youth! So one of my first compositions that is still generally liked, was easy to compose.'[25] And there are other poignant parallels such as Janáček's mother depositing her eleven-year-old son at the monastery in Brno just as Amarus has been left by his mother for the monks to bring up.

Janáček divided Vrchlický's poem into five movements: a short introduction; a longer second movement leading up to the angel's prophecy of when the monk Amarus will die; an even longer third movement – the climax of the work – in which Amarus is disconcerted by coming across a young couple in love and forgets his task of keeping the eternal lamp burning; a fourth movement where Amarus is discovered dead; and an 'Epilogue' with the tempo indication 'Tempo di marcia funebre'. These five movements make up a simple palindrome, working towards the long central movement in A flat minor from short, mostly orchestral outer movements in A minor. The symmetry is emphasized by a return in the final movement to material from the first, and the repetition, particularly striking in an otherwise instrumental movement, of the first-movement words for the chorus: 'Amarus jej zvali' ['They called him Amarus']. Janáček did not arrive at the symmetry of key (beginning and ending in A minor) until his late adjustment just before the unhappy première (see chap. 39) in which he removed the flats of the opening movement (originally in A flat minor) to create the more player-friendly key of A minor.

The chief protagonists are a tenor solo and chorus but in the opening movement the narrator is a baritone. Janáček's abandoning this baritone soloist after only one movement is a typical oddity, a loose end from the composition process. It is clear from *How Ideas Occurred* that the baritone was originally to have had a more substantial part, intended to 'fill out the middle section of the composition'. In line

435

with Janáček's later vocal identifications (for instance the mezzo Gypsy in *The Diary of One Who Disappeared* or the soprano Boy in *The Wandering Madman*), the words of the Angel are given to an extra soloist, here a soprano, and like the baritone abandoned after just a few lines. Janáček's choral texture is nearer Brahms and Dvořák, and indeed not much different from some of the textures in the oratorio-like third act of *Šárka*. In idiom there are undigested snatches of Janáček's Czech predecessors, not only Dvořák, but also Smetana – a suggestion of *Vltava* in the orchestral interlude before 'Šel dál a dále' (III: before figure 4) – and of Fibich (*Christmas Eve*) to the words 'U sloupu na klekátku' (III: after figure 2). Apart from the final movement, structural repetitions are neither exactly at pitch (as Janáček would favour in his later works) nor in the dominant (to give a classical key-polarity), but at the interval of a third, which provides variation without tension – a nineteenth-century commonplace from Schubert onwards and which Janáček may have known from Liszt's symphonic poems. Thus the 'Amarus jej zvali' theme, elaborated in the first paragraph of the introduction, continues in the second paragraph a third higher, but slips back, before the voice comes in, into the original key with no feeling that one has progressed at all. The choral refrains of the second movement, which provide a structural backbone, are similarly played out at third-related pitches.

Thus in many ways *Amarus* looks back rather than forward. But in the tenor part and occasionally in the orchestra there are also hints of the mature composer. The fitting of four-syllable words to four-syllable note groups in the time of three shows a type of word-setting that looks towards the characteristic patterns of his speech-melodified vocal lines. The repeated phrases, including prominent triplet groups (in the time of two), could have come straight out of Laca's Act 3 solo in *Jenůfa*; the high exultant tenor phrases and melodic passion look towards the tenor monologues of *Fate*. Above all, there are flashes of a new sort of motivic construction in which an instrumental phrase is seemingly derived from a line of the verse. Thus 'tož Amarus jej zvali' ['so they called him Amarus'] rings out towards the end of the first movement (a group of four notes played in the time of three). Janáček even alludes to such a process in *How Ideas Occurred* (xv/313): 'The musical ideas were clearly aroused by the rhythmic shapes and melodies of the poem.' However, this phrase is first heard in the orchestra in bar 8 of the piece and serves as a major theme of the orchestral introduction, thus providing one of the many vocal-instrumental puzzles that Janáček's ideas on speech melody would provoke (see chap. 37).

Amarus is a landmark piece in Janáček's development as a composer. The fact that Janáček seemed to be doing something different is perhaps the reason why he took the trouble to write about his compositional process in *How Ideas Occurred*. It was the first big work in a decade that had nothing to do with Moravian folk music and was the first, together with *Hospodine!* a little earlier that year, where his individual voice as a composer comes through (see chap. 35). It is in *Amarus* that the vocal-orchestral techniques of *Jenůfa* and his later operas begin to be forged.

34

What Janáček learnt from
The Queen of Spades

The impact on Janáček of Tchaikovsky's penultimate opera *The Queen of Spades* was both immediate – in the sense that he seems to have stopped writing *Jenůfa* – but also slow-acting: the work cast long shadows on operas that Janáček would write for the rest of his life. There were a few superficial parallels in Janáček's next opera *Fate*, for instance the unusual use of a piano on stage in Act 2 (a domestic act) echoing that in the first domestic scene in the Tchaikovsky. More substantially, however, the influence of *The Queen of Spades* can be seen in character types, in the choice of operatic conventions and in Janáček's handling of motif and structure.

In the two Tchaikovsky operas Janáček knew (*The Queen of Spades* and *Eugene Onegin*) there are a pair of women soloists, the chief one serious and a soprano, the subsidiary one cheerful and a mezzo, a scheme directly imitated in *Kát'a Kabanová*. This is the plan for *Onegin* (serious Tatyana, cheerful Olga), but the arrangement is also found in Act 1 Scene 2 of *The Queen of Spades*, where the mezzo Pauline attempts to comfort the soprano Liza, thoroughly miserable on the day of her engagement. They sing a duet together. Pauline then offers another song that reflects only too accurately Liza's mood: mournful, wide-ranging phrases ending melodramatically with the words 'a grave'. Aware that her attempts at entertainment have gone wrong, Pauline immediately follows this with a cheerful Russian 'folksong' in leader-and-chorus mode, as Janáček was to write in Act 3 of *Jenůfa* for Barena and the 'bridesmaids'. Tchaikovsky's spirited song – its nature invites dance-like gestures and energetic stage business – is cut short by the entrance of the outraged Governess: the young ladies are disturbing the household and disporting themselves in an unladylike fashion.

There is an exact parallel to this scene in the folk scene in Act 1 of *Jenůfa*, where the chorus's singing and dancing are quelled by the dramatic appearance of the Kostelnička. By the time he saw *The Queen of Spades* Janáček had already composed this passage, but the similarity of the two scenes shows what common ground there was between Tchaikovsky and Janáček, not least in their shared psychological need for heightened dramatic contrasts.

The minor figure of the Governess – a mildly comic creation – is nothing compared with Tchaikovsky's strongly drawn character of the Countess, old and imperious, commanding the younger generation with a will of iron. The Kostelnička in *Jenůfa* is much too three-dimensional (and ultimately sympathetic) to suggest a parallel, but the Countess was well remembered in later Janáček operas. In *Fate* he had introduced Míla's mother as a harridan figure who interrupts the domestic Act 2 with her mad outpourings and provides the dramatic denouement at the end of the act with her death and Míla's. There are also similarities between Tchaikovsky's Countess and Kabanicha in *Káťa Kabanová*. Kabanicha is a central, commanding matriarch who barks out orders and sarcastic comments much in the manner of Tchaikovsky's Countess. And when he came to *The Makropulos Affair* and was looking for a model of an old woman with a mysterious and glamorous past, Janáček might well have thought back to Tchaikovsky's Countess, her supernatural knowledge of three cards paralleled by Marty's knowledge of her father's long-life elixir.

Another character from *The Queen of Spades* who left his mark on Janáček's later vocal writing was Gherman (in Janáček's description 'a man with a Napoleonic profile, the soul of a Mephistopheles, and a gloomy face "as if weighed down by three murders"', xv/149). Here it was not so much his striking appearance and Byronic stance but his type of craggy, quasi-Heldentenor voice type that Janáček later espoused. Laca in *Jenůfa*, contrasted with the light lyric tenor of Števa, has something of this, but it is above all the self-obsessed tenor protagonists of later Janáček operas that look back to Gherman: Živný in *Fate*, Gregor in *The Makropulos Affair* and Luka in *From the House of the Dead*. It could also be that Janáček's later enthusiasm for children's voices goes back to the boy soldiers of *The Queen of Spades*. Although the juvenile Jano in *Jenůfa* is, according to the long-established operatic convention, composed as a *travesti* role (a young woman in breeches), and the five-year-old Doubek in *Fate* is similarly designated merely as a 'soprano', there are plenty of solo and chorus parts specifically written for children in *The Cunning Little Vixen*.

Tchaikovsky's *Queen of Spades* opens innocuously on a public park with people enjoying themselves, and a whole series of different groups is depicted (governesses with their charges, wet-nurses, boys playing at soldiers, officers). It is a colourful scene that recalls a similar opening in Bizet's *Carmen*, and provides a contrasting backdrop of normality against which the more ominous main characters stand out. Although he did not specifically mention *The Queen of Spades* in his instructions to Bartošová, this is the sort of opening that Janáček encouraged her to write for him at the beginning of *Fate*. In both operas the curtain goes up with a paean of praise to the sun, both bring the chorus together in differentiated groups and both provide a sharp contrast to the human drama that unfolds against them: Gherman's brooding, or the unexpected meeting of former lovers, Živný and Míla.

One convention in *The Queen of Spades* that influenced Janáček was the handling of simultaneous singing. By the time that Tchaikovsky wrote his opera, naturalistic conventions were becoming dominant in opera and beginning to erode the previous acceptance of the combination of solo voices in duets and trios, etc. (see vol. ii: The conventions of Janáček's operas). Tchaikovsky's response was to split his work into two modes: the decorative and the dramatic. In the decorative (which includes genre scenes such as the opening chorus, the next scene with the songs for Pauline, Liza and the women's choruses, or the eighteenth-century pastiches in Act 2) Tchaikovsky showed no inhibitions about combining voices. In the dramatic sections, however, voices are combined reluctantly if at all. An exception, in the very first scene, is the large solo ensemble bringing together Liza, her fiancé, the Countess, Gherman and others. But this is conceived 'realistically': all the characters are lost in their own thoughts and sing to themselves. What is conspicuously absent from the 'dramatic' scenes is simultaneous duet (as opposed to dialogue). The tenor and soprano, Gherman and Liza, have four encounters. In three of them they do not sing together at all, apart from single bars of high-note endings. In their final scene they sing together only for thirty bars, less than a quarter.

This is the convention that informs later Janáček operas. In Act 1 of *Jenůfa*, written before he had heard *The Queen of Spades*, the score still retains a large-scale *concertato* ensemble (for four soloists and chorus), and a trio for Jenůfa, Števa and Grandmother Buryjovka, but all of these were reduced in Janáček's later revisions (see chap. 48). The combination of solo voices in Act 2 is even more restricted (especially after Janáček's 1907 revisions) and by Act 3 almost the only combination of solo voices is the 'realistic' hubbub made up of individual reactions to the discovery of the baby's corpse. By the time of *Kát'a Kabanová*, sixteen years later, the combination of solo voices is very rare, usually incidental and fleeting, and generally has a 'realistic' justification (characters butting in on one another, speaking over one another, etc.).

While Janáček seems to have taken over these solo-voice conventions without comment, it is clear from his long review of the opera in *Lidové noviny* (xv/149) that it was Tchaikovsky's handling of the orchestra and the orchestral continuum that most fired his imagination. In his review he makes a distinction between 'invented motifs'* and 'felt motifs'. By the latter he seems to be designating something almost involuntary ('it rules with a strange force over the whole spirit, it burns in the face'), but it is the 'invented motifs' that seem to be the most useful, and which he discusses in detail. This, for instance, is his description of the famous 'tri karty' motif:

Three notes sharply etch a melodic curve: [one, then] a minor second lower, [and] a diminished fourth higher, unexpectedly changing the whole harmonic basis in a group of three or four notes, tightly bound together. [. . .] This highly ingenious motive is repeated, generally three times, and is the musical sign of the three mysterious cards and also of the Queen of Spades!

The dimensions of the melodic curve contract or expand according to the situation; but the harmonic background never loses its main identity. – This type of composition is Tchaikovsky's own; he sticks to it even where he doesn't bind the music with words, in symphonies, overtures.

These words are immensely revealing. Imagine a short motif that is word-based, distinctive and easily recognized (e.g. the 'tri karty' motif), but which can be varied ('The dimensions of the melodic curve contract or expand according to the situation') and manipulated to generate music of orchestral dimensions. Note that in all this there is not a word about singing. What Janáček is describing is a type of musical continuum in which the orchestra is dominant, and the voices added as another layer. Take, for example, the extraordinary central scene of *The Queen of Spades* when the Countess returns from the ball and is

---

* All quotations of Janáček's remarks are from his review of the opera, 21 Jan 1896 (xv/149).

confronted by Gherman, who has been laying in wait for her. It is conceived symphonically, opening with a gnawing little ostinato on the violas that is both neutral and distinctive, and which Tchaikovsky uses both for orchestral foreground and background (to the voices).

In his description of the opera (it is hard to imagine that he did not have this scene in mind), Janáček wrote: 'Jerky, fragmentary, it lacks tightly linked big tunes. The orchestra simply throws up random piercing notes in all directions. And yet the composer's highly developed musical thought weaves all these tiny particles into such a magnificent whole, with such an overwhelming effect, seldom achieved in all of musical literature.' The description fits much of Janáček's later operatic music, none better than the end of Act 1 in *Kát'a Kabanová*, where the 'tiny particles' that have been building up during the previous scene are thrillingly brought together in one of Janáček's most compelling act endings.

To see the immediate impact of *The Queen of Spades* on *Jenůfa* one needs only to look at the basically 'melodic' nature of many of the sung passages in Act 1 and compare them with what happens in Act 2, written after Janáček's encounter with *The Queen of Spades*. In Act 1 the music divides sharply into what could loosely be called 'recitative' (and Janáček does not hesitate to employ this term occasionally in this opera) and 'aria'. In a passage such as Jenůfa's opening solo one can omit the orchestral accompaniment and still retain the musical continuum. This is equally true of the 'aria' passages later in the act, for instance Jenůfa's reproaches to Števa after the *concertato* ensemble, all closely wrought out of a single four-note motif.[1] In Act 1 the musical dramaturgy is slow (much of the time the characters sing melodic paragraphs rather than sentences), and those unaware that Janáček was writing to a prose libretto might be surprised to learn this fact, given the carefully structured nature of the vocal 'arias'. This is achieved by extensive if minor surgery on Preissová's prose text, filling out or suppressing individual syllables according to metrical need, and creating a sort of quasi-verse to provide regularly structured text to fit to the regularly structured music.[2] Although there are still some set-piece arias in Act 2 (e.g. Jenůfa's Prayer to the Virgin), the general nature of the voice parts is noticeably less melodic and more declamatory, with the orchestra playing a more important part in the musical continuum.

The structural importance of the orchestra in *The Queen of Spades* is seen especially in the strong act endings: in particular the superb ending of Act 2 with its transformation of the Gherman theme set against a striding bass, or the brassy end of the canal scene with Liza's suicide. Janáček learnt fitfully from this. Although the orchestral endings of Acts 2 and 3 in *Jenůfa* are wonderfully effective, its successor *Fate* suffers from musically undistinguished and dramatically puzzling act endings. Thereafter, however, there are splendid orchestral perorations in all the later operas, where the full burden of winding up the scene to a strong conclusion is left entirely to the orchestra: the Act 1 endings of *Kát'a Kabanová, The Makropulos Affair* and *From the House of the Dead* all belong to this genre. For Act 2 endings Janáček preferred a shorter orchestral gesture – *Kát'a Kabanová* with its heavenly and poignant music, or in contrast, the trombone snarls of *The Makropulos Affair*, which gesture towards something ominous to follow. Act 3 endings, often based on a 'cathartic slow waltz' (*Jenůfa, The Cunning Little Vixen, The Makropulos Affair*), underline a change of attitude and understanding of the chief character.[3] Although Tchaikovsky does it differently, the unexpected plea for forgiveness at the end of *The Queen of Spades*, emphasized by the churchlike unaccompanied male chorus, provides an interesting parallel.

35

Pan-Slavism II

Janáček had shown an interest in Russia and Russian music for many years, but the removal of his favourite brother František to St Petersburg at the end of 1895 made much more real the possibility of his experiencing Russia for himself. František Janáček encouraged Leoš to visit Russia at the earliest opportunity, the summer of 1896, and he came back full of enthusiasm after his two-week trip (see chap. 33). The three substantial articles that Janáček published about it in *Lidové noviny* (XV/150) were the most sustained and extensive travel writing he was ever to do. They bubble over with enthusiasm for every aspect of Russian life. Critical views are muted, political aspects avoided and instead Janáček contents himself with showing an approving interest in the culture and the language, and delight in the attractive features of everyday life. Within eighteen months of his return he helped found the Brno Russian Circle (see chap. 36) and despite his limited time he served on the committee, ultimately becoming chairman (in 1910). He also helped the Russian Circle with its musical ventures. He conducted the concert in 1899 to commemorate the 100th anniversary of Pushkin's birthday, and arranged for the Russian conductor Arkhangel'sky to bring the Russian embassy choir from Vienna for a concert in honour of Gogol and Zhukovsky in 1902. When his daughter Olga got older, he encouraged her Russian aspirations and her fateful trip to Russia in 1902.

Janáček's first love among Russian musicians was Rubinstein, with whom he had once wished to study (see chap. 15) and whose music he still sought out during his 1896 trip to Russia. By then his interest in Tchaikovsky had also become important. Two of the longest reviews of opera performances he wrote were of Tchaikovsky operas, *Eugene*

Onegin in 1891 (xv/114) and *The Queen of Spades* in 1896 (xv/149). His encounter with the later opera was a turning point in his life (see chap. 34). It was after seeing it that he stopped composing *Jenůfa* and did not take it up again for five years. In October 1896 a letter to Janáček from the publisher Urbánek suggests that he had made enquiries about obtaining a copy of a 'Tchaikovsky Mass'. Tchaikovsky wrote no masses; instead Urbánek suggested Tchaikovsky's Vespers op. 52 or the Liturgy of John Chrysostom op. 41.[1] Today Rubinstein and Tchaikovsky offer an odd view of Russian nineteenth-century music: western-orientated and without any members of the 'Mighty Handful'. Some commentators have sensed an affinity between Janáček and Musorgsky, but there is no evidence of his coming across Musorgsky's music until 1910, when he commented on it in a letter to Rektorys[2] and *The Nursery* was performed at the Organ School 'sonata hours'.[3]

Janáček's preoccupation with Russian culture spilt over into his own creative work. In 1896, a few months before he went to Russia, he wrote *Hospodine!* (III/5), a strange and haunting work based on the oldest Czech hymn. Its two musical gestures are a chant to a single two-note chord (an open fifth) for the word 'Hospodine' ['Lord'] and a descending line for the subsequent words 'Pomiluj ny!' ['Have mercy on us!']. There is something hypnotic about the way these formulas are repeated over and over, shifting up and down a semitone or moving by one of Janáček's cruder modulations. What gives the piece its distinctive colour is the vocal 'orchestration': four soloists pitted against two choirs, the choirs themselves supported on the one hand by harp and organ, and on the other by a brass ensemble of trumpets and trombones. The hieratic, chord-based nature of the music suggests Russian choral music. Of course, having an accompaniment flies in the face of traditional Russian church music (and Janáček knew that Russian church choirs sang unaccompanied since František mentioned this in his letter praising the beauty of Russian church music).[4] However Janáček's accompaniment is discreet, with almost no independent life; it seems to be there chiefly for vocal support. The word-setting is distinctive, with Janáček's characteristic rhythmic groups based on the stress patterns of individual words and creating occasional clashes of three- and four-syllable groups.

What is particularly interesting, however, is that this piece, coming out of nowhere, is arguably the first piece of Janáček that sounds like the mature composer. Looking eastward had released something within him, enabling him at last to find his own voice. As soon as he returned from Russia he embarked on a far larger-scale composition, his cantata *Amarus* (III/6). This makes no attempt to sound Russian at all, but, even more so than in *Hospodine!*, the future composer had emerged. Almost every piece he wrote thereafter, including his stalled opera *Jenůfa*, took him on to a new level as a composer in whom a distinct voice was becoming more and more audible.

Three years later, a major fundraising exercise in Czech Brno for the Women's Shelter involved Janáček in writing music that was actively Pan-Slavonic. The Slavonic Beseda in January 1900 (see chap. 39) attempted to represent the major Slavonic nations through their music and dancing, and Janáček found himself writing three short dances: a Valachian *Blessed Dance* (VI/11), a *Serbian Reel* (VI/13) and a Russian *Cossack Dance* (VI/12). While the *Blessed Dance* was familiar territory for Janáček, a charming version of a well-known Moravian dance that Janáček had arranged twice before, the Russian and Serbian dances are particularly interesting in that they are deliberate exercises in pastiche and give some idea of what Janáček might have regarded as typically Russian and typically Serbian dance music. According to a note on the autograph, the *Cossack Dance* is based on a tune from Marie Veveritsa, the Russian language teacher from the Russian Circle, though Janáček would also have had access to this familiar tune from the standard collection of Russian folksongs by Ivan Pratsch.[5] What his models were for Serbian music is hard to imagine. He may have been limited to what he could glean from *Ottův slovník naučný* [Otto's encyclopedia], to which he subscribed and whose fourteenth volume, published in 1898, contained a long article on 'Jihoslavané' ['Southern Slavs']. In the ethnographical section (p. 383) Janáček would have read: 'All ceremonies are accompanied by songs to the gusle, bagpipes and other musical instruments. Gusle are very simple stringed instruments with one string.' Despite the fact that a full orchestra was available for the other pieces in the evening, Janáček restricted his *Serbian Reel* to pizzicato strings, plus two flutes and two bassoons whose trills, ornaments and sustained notes suggest the drones and characteristic decorations of bagpipe music. The pizzicato strings, however, are puzzling and hardly suggest the bowed gusle. Janáček needed to have read only a little further in *Otto* to have discovered that 'in more westerly regions another string instrument is favoured, the tambura, similar to the Italian mandolin'. Janáček's *Serbian Reel* may thus have been written to evoke the tambura and the bagpipe. Reading further in *Otto*, Janáček would have learnt that

An essential component of every festivity, family or public ceremony is the *kolo*, a very simple round dance. Men and women holding hands in a circle go, in time to the music, three steps to the left and one to the right, singing a dance-song. [. . .] The *kolo* starts in a slow tempo, becoming ever faster and more fiery, ending in a wild tempo, lasting sometimes two to three hours.

Here Janáček rather parted company with *Otto*: his *Serbian Reel* is played at a constant Allegretto and lasts for no more than two minutes.

In contrast, Janáček's *Cossack Dance* deploys the full orchestra, though also using trills and some pizzicato. It is based on the repetition of a tiny motif, just three bars, continuously repeated in different arrangements: the familiar 'changing-background' treatment of folk tunes in Russian art music from Glinka onwards. In both works the dance forms dictated repetitive structures. In the case of the *Cossack Dance* the last section is repeated three times, faster each time (the quickening tempo almost an exemplification of the description in *Otto* of the Serbian *kolo*).

The next artistic venture of the Women's Shelter, the evening for which Janáček's *Our Father* (IV/29) was written, seems, like the Slavonic Beseda, to have been another exercise in raising not only funds and but also Pan-Slavonic consciousness, this time through its *tableau vivant* re-creation of Polish paintings (see chap. 39). It could also be argued that Janáček expanded a purely Polish-inspired venture into something more Pan-Slavonic by working into his music allusions to various Slav styles. And this, it could be argued further, was part of an agenda, proudly proclaimed as early as 1885, of the eventual disappearance of separate Slavonic national styles: 'I am convinced that in time classical music will become only Slavonic and not individually Czech, Russian, etc.' (xv/65).

The third section of *Our Father*, 'Buď vůle tvá' ['Thy will be done'], for instance, is set as a melancholy Russian song in the minor key with stressed second beat, and a Tchaikovskian counter-melody on the organ (ex. 7, overleaf). The final piece 'Neuvoď nás v pokušení' ['Lead us not into temptation'] is striking for its adherence to the rhythm of the most popular of all Bohemian Hussite chorales ('Those who are

447

Ex. 7

warriors of God') (ex. 8, overleaf), although this is overshadowed by the sheer energy of the ending: the loud unison writing for organ, the typical ostinato motifs and the abrupt ending on a peal of 'Amens' suggest a much later (and equally Pan-Slavonic) Janáček – that of the *Glagolitic Mass* (III/9).

But it is the fifth section, 'A odpust' nám naše viny' ['And forgive us our trespasses'], which is particularly fascinating in the context of Janáček's 'Moravian' aspirations (see chap. 36). Though the opening suggests Dvořák in his pentatonic vein, the following entry of the

Ex. 8a

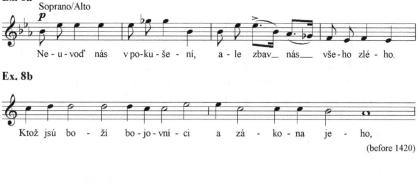

Ne - u - voď nás v po-ku - še - ní, a - le zbav_ nás__ vše - ho zlé - ho.

Ex. 8b

Ktož jsú bo - ži bo - jo-vní - ci a zá - ko - na je - ho,

(before 1420)

Ex. 9

A od-pusť nám na - še vi - ny,
[And forgive us our sins]

tenor is in a typical Moravian 'mirror rhythm' (ex. 9). For all the Pan-Slavonic aspirations of the piece, Janáček initially seems to have seen this as an opportunity to assert his Moravianness, originally calling it *Moravian Our Father*, a title used on the original score and parts.

Other 'Moravian' works from this time were the two choruses *If you only knew* and *The Evening Witch* that form part of Janáček's *Four Moravian Male-Voice Choruses* (IV/28). These two choruses, in existence by 1900, are remarkable especially because they are in dialect. This is not Janáček's short-vowel Lachian dialect, nor the Slovácko dialect of *Jenůfa*, but that of Haná, a rich farming region that takes up a large portion of central Moravia and one that would have been widely recognized as distinctively Moravian. Attractive as they are, the popularity that these pieces won with Moravian audiences from the moment they were rehearsed (by Vach's Moravian Teachers, many of whom came from Haná) has much to do with the charm of hearing a choir sing in a well-known regional dialect (a phenomenon similar to, say, Gracie Fields cultivating her native Lancashire for some of her repertory).

Janáček's climactic Moravian work, however, is *Jenůfa*. Although the play on which it was based was written by a non-Moravian, and its somewhat sporadic use of Slovácko dialect words was criticized at the time for its inconsistency, the play set out its Moravian agenda with its title (*Její pastorkyňa* – standard Czech would have rendered the second word as *pastorkyně*) and its genre description, 'a drama of Moravian country life in three acts'. Moravian atmosphere was further strengthened by the use of folksong texts and by the costumes. The region where the play is set boasts some of the most elaborate and distinctive folk costumes from the Czech lands: in a note at the end of the play Preissová allowed both 'slovenský' (i.e. from Slovácko) as well as 'ordinary country' costumes.

Many of these aspects Janáček took over when the play became an opera. The poster for the première advertised the work as a 'Moravian music drama'. Authentic folk costumes were the *sine qua non* for early productions of the opera, in Prague, in Vienna and in Berlin (courtesy of the Czechoslovak Embassy), and Janáček spent considerable energy in trying to persuade the stage director of the Prague production Gustav Schmoranz to have an authentically Moravian-looking mill in Act 1 (see vol. ii: 1916b). In setting the folksongs Janáček carefully did not exploit existing, familiar tunes – with the ballast of their possible sentimental associations – and instead composed pastiches so convincing that in the early days musicologists spent many fruitless hours searching for his sources. If nothing else this demonstrated how profoundly Janáček had absorbed elements of Moravian music through his field studies, editing and arranging. Above all, however, Janáček began to implement his new speech-melody approach that sets store by a more natural, speechlike setting of words, many of them with Slovácko dialect colouring. Although it was a process that would continue through his revisions up to 1908, it was one that he was clearly proud of and that was passed on to journalists for their pre-première publicity: 'Apart from its use of elements of a specifically Moravian nature, the work will pave the way for a particular type of word-setting, based on the melodic elements of everyday speech.'[6]

The Moravianness was stressed in a surprising way in a review published in *Hlas* at the time of the première:

The best proof of the work's Moravianness is that it is impossible, as the composer tried to, to translate it into Russian, for the Russian language is quite different in its cadence, stress and expression from our language; it would have meant composing the opera all over again.[7]

'As the composer tried to' sounds as if Janáček had had a go at translating some of the text into Russian to see how it might sound, and was soon discouraged. Since most operas do not have to be 'composed all over again' when they are translated (and *Jenůfa* later slipped into German without any compositional activity from Janáček), this statement is clearly an exaggeration, but it does indicate the extent to which *Jenůfa* was being presented as a Moravian opera at the time. This would give rise to many problems for its future (see chap. 59), problems that would later encourage Janáček to distance himself from the Moravian aspects of his music, although elements of it were absorbed into his personal musical vocabulary.

36

1897–9

In 1897 Janáček received a request that he did not act on for several years but that led eventually to one of his most individual and personal pieces of this period, his piano cycle *On the Overgrown Path* (VIII/17). Josef Vávra, a schoolmaster working in Ivančice, had conceived a series of pieces for the harmonium under the title *Slovanské melodie* and wrote to Janáček about it on 19 January:

As you were informed by the schoolteacher Mr Bím [see chap. 32], I intend very shortly to publish musical pieces devoted exclusively to performance on the harmonium.

In this matter I turn to you with the urgent request to be kind enough to support me in the intended enterprise. In the musical volumes I would like to put the most beautiful Slavonic melodies harmonized in an easy style in such a way that they would be accessible even to less experienced players. If you could kindly delight me *soon* [underlined three times] with some melodies, either arranging each song separately or grouped as a short potpourri, I would put them into print in the first volume straightaway; however I would ask for the text at the same time.[1]

In other words Janáček was invited to make folksong arrangements for harmonium, either individually or as a potpourri. The request sounds odd today in view of what Janáček ultimately made of this initiative, but in fact Vávra's request was not unreasonable: in his endeavours to promote Moravian folk music Janáček had made arrangements in many different combinations – for voice and piano, for orchestra, for piano alone. Why not for harmonium? However, Vávra's request was ignored for the time being, though Janáček kept his letter. Meanwhile a volume of Vávra's harmonium collection came out each year starting in 1897, edited by another Ivančice school-teacher, the composer Emil Kolář.

One of Janáček's pupils from the Teachers' Institute, Ezechiel Ambros, had moved in 1888 to the Moravian town of Prostějov, where for many years he was active in musical circles as a singing teacher and as choirmaster at the church and with the choirs 'Orlice' and 'Vlastimila'. He remained in contact with Janáček and was responsible for several early performances of his works. The first was probably Janáček's arrangement for chorus and orchestra, *The Mosquitoes got Married* (III/2), which he conducted in Prostějov on 2 May 1897. In an exchange of letters over the concert Ambros also enquired about the existence of Janáček's *Hospodine!* (III/5) 'with brass accompaniment', performed the previous year in Brno.[2] Janáček seems to have taken this as good evidence of public interest and wrote immediately to Urbánek,* whose preliminary edition of Janáček's harmony book (XV/151) had come out in 1896.† This was not an opportune moment, as Janáček would have realized from Urbánek's tetchy response: not only was Janáček's composition 'beyond my [i.e. Urbánek's] strength' but the harmony book was doing badly. Had Janáček introduced it at the Organ School? Urbánek had not been optimistic about sales, but he had expected that they would be better in the first year than was the case.[3]

The composer Vítězslav Novák (1870–1949) gives a revealing if jaundiced picture of Janáček at this time. Novák was in Brno on 21 March 1897 for a performance of his Quintet in A minor and after the concert was introduced to Janáček by their mutual friend Rudolf Reissig (1874–1939), who had moved to Brno in 1896 to teach at the Beseda music school. Novák describes Janáček as a 'fallen Brno giant' (i.e. no longer conductor at the Beseda) and not valued as a composer. He also characterizes him as someone with strong opinions, whether on Moravian folksong or on César Franck's chromatic harmonic style, which he allegedly regarded as emanating from Bach, via Schubert, Liszt and Wagner. Novák had different views on both topics and, as he writes in his memoirs, resolved thereafter to talk about music to

* The letter is lost but its existence can be inferred from Urbánek's reply, see below.
† The edition of 1896 gives no publisher, but since Urbánek had been in negotiation with Janáček over it throughout 1894–5 and had proposed issuing it in fascicles, of which the first would be ready by the beginning of the school year (in 1895) it may well be that Urbánek was responsible for this edition as well as that of 1897, which bears his imprint.

Janáček as little as possible.[4] Nevertheless enough common ground was established for Janáček to suggest that Novák, with his passion for Moravia, should visit Hukvaldy that summer, when the Janáčeks would be there, and the invitation was taken up.

Novák's constant belittling of Janáček in his memoirs is understandable. After Dvořák's death in 1904, Novák came to be recognized as one of the leading Czech composers of his day. In the next decade his fame continued to grow, especially in Brno, which with his friend Reissig as conductor at the Beseda became the centre of a Novák cult, culminating in the première, in Brno rather than in Prague, of his cantata *The Storm* in 1910. However, with *The Storm* Novák had peaked, and within a few years Janáček's late star began to rise. By 1946, when he published his memoirs, Novák was seventy-six, and although fêted with national honours, he must have realized at some level that Janáček, with his odd views and (in Novák's eyes) inferior technique, had somehow supplanted him.

Six days after the Prostějov concert, an important concert took place in Brno on 8 May 1897 under the auspices of the Brno Beseda. Dvořák conducted the 'Czech Philharmonic' (i.e. the orchestra of the Prague National Theatre) in performances of his Symphony no. 9 'From the New World', two symphonic poems, *The Noon Witch* and *The Golden Spinning Wheel*, and the overture *Carnival*,[‡] all recently composed. Dvořák had not been in Brno for five years, the Prague orchestra gave its services free and the concert attracted a large audience including Germans and local dignitaries. The concert made over 1700 zl, of which the profit of 800 zl was donated to the Brno Theatre fund.[5]

Janáček was there and was much taken with the symphony ('magnificent' he scrawled on his programme against the famous Largo movement)[6] but also with the symphonic poems – he published analyses of both of them later in the year (see below). The concert was perhaps not the right time for him to tell Dvořák what was on his mind, but he made an arrangement to meet his train in Brno after Dvořák's visit to Kroměříž and on his way back to Prague. But the plan went wrong: while Janáček waited at the Brno station in the morning (presumably the next day, Sunday 9 May), Dvořák's time in

[‡]The pieces were played in the order given, with an interval between the two symphonic poems. The programme is reproduced in Kyas 1995, 80–1.

Kroměříž (with his friend Dr Emil Kozánek) had been extended, and when he did pass through Brno on the afternoon train Janáček had already gone home. So instead Janáček had to write:

I wanted to ask you then for two things [. . .] First I ask you respectfully for some of your patience and time, for you kindly to look through the work that I'm sending you by post now. It is composed on a text by J[aroslav] Vrchlický and I would submit it to him if it stands up to your scrutiny. So kindly tell me the truth in a few lines without beating about the bush, simply and openly as is your habit. Of course I won't match your perfect conception – that I know. Just one thing I ask, may I have your verdict [on *Amarus*] by the end of this month?

This is the first indication that Janáček had completed his cantata *Amarus* (III/6), begun at the end of the summer 1896 on his return from Russia. Janáček's other request to Dvořák was in connection with his harmony manual *On the Composition of Chords and their Connections* (XV/151), which seven months earlier he had sent to the Czech Academy asking for financial support (the academy gave grants on the basis of works submitted). So far nothing had happened but he had heard, he said, that in March the manual had been given to Josef Förster and Zdeněk Fibich for their opinion. Perhaps, if Dvořák were in Prague, he could make inquiries that might speed things up.[7]

I'm here at Vysoká [Dvořák wrote back] and must answer your kind letter from here; not of course as is needed, it's not possible to do that well in the form of writing; but nevertheless I'd like to tell you the main things.
I've been able to look through the work only a little, because I had to leave, but from that little I can nevertheless say that you have made a substantial step forward in every respect.
The piece is interesting particularly from the harmonic respect, only I would like more *melody*, and then perhaps rather more correct declamation. [. . .]
Your composition is in Prague. My wife is there and if you want it, she'll send it to you.
I congratulate you on further work. Just go on, you are on a good path, but as I said – just a little more melody – don't be scared of it.[8]

This is a wonderfully perceptive letter. From what seems to be only a cursory inspection Dvořák was able to tell that Janáček had suddenly moved on ('a substantial step forward in every respect') and had found 'a good path'. Nor was this merely encouragement to a younger friend whom he liked. In his recollections of Janáček,

Dvořák's pupil Josef Suk mentions Dvořák showing him a passage in the score of *Amarus*:

It was very strange to me; as far as I can recall it consisted of some sort of quasi-recitative passage performed by the cello and at the same time by the flute about two octaves higher. Dvořák looked at me over his glasses and I said: 'That's strange, isn't it!' And to that Dvořák said emphatically: 'It's strange but it was written by someone who thinks with his own brain!'[9]

Armed with Dvořák's good opinion, Janáček then approached Vrchlický through his old school friend František Bílý, who had now settled in Prague as a Gymnasium teacher. (Bílý was a distinguished literary critic and knew Vrchlický.) Following Janáček's instructions,[10] Bílý called on Vrchlický but, not finding him at home, left a letter[11] and, as it seems from Vrchlický's letter, Janáček also wrote at this stage. When Vrchlický's answer came, it was affable enough: 'It greatly pleases me that you have found something in my poem *Amarus* that you recognize as suitable for being set to music. I am convinced that you have succeeded wholly and fully, and I think no intervention by others is necessary here.' And, as the letter continued, there was better to come:

Allow me to tell you that in the meeting of the Czech Academy on 1 June, at the suggestion of our referees (Messrs Fibich and Chvála), you were awarded a subvention of 200 zl for your work. Although I am not a musician, I did everything in my power to bring this about, having no inkling of your letter, which I got two days later.[12]

Either this was a coincidence or, without mentioning it in his letter to Janáček, Dvořák had put in a word about the harmony manual that led to a speedy resolution of the problem, The good news was confirmed in a letter from Bílý (10 June 1897), noting that the proposal still had to be confirmed by the Czech Academy plenum.[13] When Janáček wrote back thanking Vrchlický, he asked him to show the score of *Amarus* to Fibich.[14] Perhaps, now that Fibich appeared to be favouring him at the academy, Janáček hoped for Fibich's advocacy with his publisher Urbánek. This was something that Bílý suggested too,[15] but it was another forlorn hope: Urbánek turned down *Amarus* as 'too expensive',[16] not a consideration that prevented him from producing piano-vocal scores of Fibich's operas. Neither *Amarus* nor *Hospodine!* were published in Janáček's lifetime. *Hospodine!* had to wait until 1977.

Zdenka and Olga went for their usual Hukvaldy holidays at the beginning of July, as is clear from their birthday wishes sent to Janáček in Brno.[17] When he joined them, he was soon followed by Novák and a group of his friends and pupils. Novák's keen eye soon spotted domestic tensions. Janáček with his 'sharp temperament' appeared to be courting one of the ladies (presumably Mrs Rakowitschová) but interestingly Zdenka seemed to be keeping her end up: Janáček, Novák recalled, 'occasionally exchanged views with his similarly spirited wife'.[18] In his memoirs Novák recalled an expedition that he made on 15 August with Janáček, Reissig and two of his pupils to climb mount Radhošt'.[§] Janáček sent back two postcards from his trip, one rather a pretty card to Olga inscribed 'to my daughter at sixteen from Daddy'.[19] 15 August was Olga's fifteenth birthday (it says much for her maturity that Janáček thought of her as a year older) but presumably because of her heart condition she was not allowed on the long climb up the mountain and instead stayed at home with Zdenka. Zdenka also got a card but with no message, only Janáček's signature,[20] confirming the coolness that Novák had noticed between the couple at the time. On the journey Janáček talked, Novák recalled, about his trip to Russia the previous year and how uplifted he was by 'the thought of life in the heart of such a large Slavonic nation'.[21]

When they got back, Janáček organized a concert on 18 August involving himself, Novák, Reissig and folk musicians from the nearby village of Kunčice. Among the pieces were Novák's *Three Czech Dances* s51, played in the original version for piano duet by Novák and Janáček. Janáček seems to have taken to the pieces and included Novák's orchestral arrangement of them at a concert in Brno the next year (see below). According to Novák, the Hukvaldy concert took place in the pub 'U Uhláře', with local musicians performing the originals of some of Janáček's *Valachian Dances*. Typically, Novák added that the locals were not a patch on the folk musicians he had encountered in Velká in Slovakia.[22]

In his recollection of the Radhošt' expedition Novák recalls that at the 'Pustevně' (a folk-style 'hermitage' at the top of the mountain)

we met a young lady from Frenštát, who sang us a beautiful melancholy song, heard from a nanny in childhood. Janáček wrote down this song, saying that he would publish it in the third fascicle of Bartoš's collection of Moravian

[§] A place of pilgrimage named after a pagan god and the subject of many folk legends.

songs [*Moravian Folksongs Newly Collected* (XIII/3)]. When, however, the collection came out published by the Czech Academy, I looked in vain for that beautiful, typical Lachian song. It surprised me all the more that there were plenty of songs undoubtedly influenced by Polish and perhaps even more by Hungarian melody. I can say with a good conscience that after my own detailed comparative studies I saw in these dealings of Janáček new and serious evidence that he was not such an infallible authority in Moravian folksong.[23]

Novák's criticisms are subjective ones; he seems to have wanted to include only those songs that he thought uninfluenced by neighbouring traditions, rather than those collected on Moravian territory, which was Janáček's and Bartoš's policy.[II]

During the course of 1897 Janáček published in *Hlídka* [The sentinel] substantial analyses of Dvořák's symphonic poems *The Water Goblin*, *The Golden Spinning Wheel* and *The Noon Witch*, all based on one of the best-loved works of Czech nineteenth-century literature, Karel Jaroslav Erben's *Garland of Folk Tales*. Since its inception in 1883 as *Hlídka literární* [The literary sentinel], this monthly journal had been edited by a monk at the Benedictine monastery at Rajhrad near Brno, Dr Pavel Vychodil, and was printed on the monastery's press. The journal's contents, however, reflected its title rather than its Catholic provenance and it soon acquired a solid reputation through its articles on aesthetics and literature and a lively review section. Perhaps the church authorities wondered why they were hosting such a secular journal and in 1895 it was rebranded *Hlídka: katolická revue*. The contents, however, did not change much and Vychodil continued to attract articles from distinguished Moravian authors such as František Bartoš, František Bílý and František Rypáček. Janáček had contributed a couple of reviews in the journal's *Hlídka literární* days but his 1897 articles suggest a new initiative. The particular advantage the journal had to offer Janáček over most of his other publishing outlets was the ability of the monastery's press to set music: Janáček had used its services since 1884, for instance for printing his *Pieces for Organ* (VIII/7). His contribution was seen as a continuing commitment and his articles were given a special series title: 'Czech Musical Currents'.

[II] See for instance Bartoš's comment on the inclusion of Valachian songs: 'I've left the "Valachian dances" although they are the same as the Slovak. "Valachian" means that they are danced and collected in Valašsko and nothing else' (Bartoš to LJ, 27 March 1901, Straková 1957, 17).

The first article, in the April fascicle, on Dvořák's *Water Goblin* (xv/152), seems to have been timed to come out ahead of Dvořák's concert in Brno (8 May 1897) though curiously this was the only one of the three Erben symphonic poems Dvořák had written so far that was not included in that concert. In the June and August fascicles Janáček published analyses of the other two (xv/153, xv/154). That he intended the analyses for a lay readership (though one that could read music – each article included up to twenty music examples) is clear from the fact that they avoid harmonic or theoretical observations. Instead, Janáček wrote a type of narrative analysis particularly suitable for these works with their strong programmatic thrust. What seems to have attracted Dvořák to composing his symphonic poems on Erben was the melodramatic action, usually involving the supernatural, and the simple, folklike diction. In fact he seems to have derived many of his musical motifs from taking Erben's lines of verse and 'setting' them as if for voice. Several of these verbal tags are even written into the score. It is this aspect that seems to have intrigued Janáček. In his analysis of Dvořák's symphonic poems Janáček constantly quotes the Erben poems together with the music that seems to be derived from their words. And from time to time he commented on the connection:

The dialogue of the Water Goblin and his wife is excellently coloured and supported by the orchestra. If one speaks of *songs without words* I'd say that this was living *recitative* without words – and nevertheless intelligible. [. . .] In no orchestral symphonic poem known to me has there ever been heard such certainty, clarity and truth in the flood of motifs of 'the direct speech' of instruments, if I can call it that, as in *The Water Goblin*. [. . .] A novelty in this symphonic poem is the already mentioned 'direct speech' of the instruments. In this important part of the score the composer has adhered as closely as possible to the poem, which is the only means of making this passage intelligible. [. . .] (xv/152)

It is a strange coincidence that in his Prelude to *Jenůfa* (viii/16), written a year before the first of Dvořák's symphonic poems, Janáček seems to have done exactly the same thing: fragments of text from the folk ballad *The Jealous Man* were written into the manuscript of his version for piano duet (see vol. ii: Janáček and programme music).

In 1896 Janáček had been overwhelmed by Tchaikovsky's *The Queen of Spades* and in his review of the opera (xv/149) spent many words trying to explain how Tchaikovsky used motifs, in particular that to which the verbal phrase 'tri karty, tri karty, tri karty' [three cards] is set (see chap. 34). A year later he published his analyses of Dvořák's three symphonic poems, all based on motifs derived from speech. And a little later that year he began writing systematically into his diary the first speech melodies – as they have become called. It is going too far to posit a direct causal connection between these three events but their placing in time is suggestive. This cluster of events took place in the early part of Janáček's strange five-year sabbatical from writing *Jenůfa*. Act 1 had been written without the benefit of these insights; by the time he returned to the opera in 1901, he was a substantially different composer, with a 'method' based on speech melody (see chap. 37).

Janáček began writing speech melodies in his diary in 1897. The earliest are undated but the people mentioned (and the position in Janáček's diary) make it clear that he began writing them down during his summer holidays in Hukvaldy, i.e. in August–September 1897.[24] In this first year the speech melodies are all carefully numbered, and extra descriptive information about the speaker and circumstances is sometimes supplied. The Hukvaldy group includes children's cries ('Vinca' Sládek, the two-year-old son of the family where the Janáčeks were staying, nos. 4–7), a group of cocks ('around my house in Hukvaldy – clear, melodious like a clarinet, like a cor anglais, strange!', no. 8), a few rather prosaic words from Mrs Rakowitschová given in 'calm and melodious speech' ('it was true or it wasn't true'; 'well, it was nice', nos. 9–11) and her laughter (no. 12). The first dated speech melodies came a little later when, back in Brno on 19 September 1897, Janáček jotted down a few comments from his colleague Bartoš, clearly not refreshed after his summer break: 'this feeling, so strange', 'it's terrible', 'stakra porte' [mild expletive], 'it lasted the whole time' (nos. 17–20).

Thereafter writing down speech melodies became part of Janáček's way of life and all his diaries are full of them. When on 16 October he went to the Slovácko village of Kostice to take down folksongs, he also took down speech melodies. Having described the venue ('a beautiful village near Lanžhot. The little paintings on the houses are delightful, ornaments on the brickwork, drawn on mud moistened with a finger'), he then proceeded to recount, with appropriate speech melodies, disputes during the playing of ninepins, or the description by the chairman of the local school council of the mouth-blown type of local bagpipes.

Two speech melodies of the Kostice series turn up in Janáček's introduction to *Moravian Folksongs Newly Collected* (XIII/3). This became
a common occurrence: speech melodies noted down in the diary
sometimes became illustrative material in Janáček's published writings.

During Janáček's editorial work on *Moravian Folksongs Newly*
Collected he virtually stopped composing, though towards the end of
1897 he produced a couple of occasional works, the *Festive Chorus*
(IV/25), by 15 December 1897, and a solo song, *Spring Song* (V/3). Both
are perfunctory and undistinguished and suggest the discharge of social
obligations rather than any compositional commitment. Janáček's five-
part male voice chorus setting the words of Father Vladimír Šťastný
for the dedication of the banner of the St Joseph's Union is a simple
alternation of a vigorous opening section with a gentler, more hymnlike
section, the whole thing repeated to a second verse.

Jaroslav Tichý (i.e. František Rypáček), the librettist of *The Beginning*
of a Romance, sent Janáček his text for *Spring Song* on 23 December
1897, with the suggestion that the composer might want to work on it
over Christmas.[25] Whether he did or not, Janáček seems to have spent
little time on it. Like the *Festive Chorus*, Janáček's setting stretches
out its material with many exact repetitions. Tichý's words are an invocation to Spring, and with its dedication to the Brno 'Vesna' implies
that the work was intended for 'Vesna', with the title and subject of
the poem chosen in its honour (Vesna was the goddess of spring in
Slav mythology, the word occasionally used as poetical substitute
for the more standard word 'jaro'). Perhaps, too, with its unambitious
tessitura and the repetitions minimizing the amount of rehearsal
needed, it was originally intended for the girls at the 'Vesna' schools to
sing, though its first performers were in fact professional musicians (see
below).

The issue of *Lidové noviny* of 13 January 1898 carried the following
announcement:

Informed sources tell us that a group has been established in Brno composed
of musical experts as well as music lovers that has taken it as its responsibility
not only to maintain a large Czech orchestra [. . .] but, by the contribution
of outstanding Czech composers, especially Moravian ones, and under the
leadership of the darling of the Czech musical world, Mr Leoš Janáček, to
bring about the greatest blossoming so that Czech orchestral productions

would excel over German ones, as once used to be the case and so that we Czechs do not lag behind the Germans in every direction of cultural development. [. . .] By the endeavours of Mr Janáček, the existing orchestra of sixty men will be increased to eighty, half of which will come from the Czech Orchestra in Brno; the others would be taken from the ranks of amateurs. The following have joined this aforementioned group: Mr Leoš Janáček, Mr Emerich Beran, Mr Maxmilián Koblížek, Mr František Rund[¶] and finally the committee of the Družstvo for Maintaining a Czech National Orchestra in Brno.[26]

The Czech National Orchestra was a *cause célèbre*. In the absence of a permanent Czech orchestra in Brno, the usual solution, when an orchestra was needed, was to employ the theatre orchestra, or to build one up from military bands, amateurs, etc. But at a function on 16 May 1895 put on by the Czech Readers' Club, the enthusiastic response of the public to a rendition of the Russian national anthem had aroused the displeasure of the police authorities and brought about a ban on the use of military bands in the Besední dům. As a result the next year a society was formed under the auspices of the Readers' Club for the support of a Czech National Orchestra under the conductorship of František Rund, a 'folk conductor' from Přerov, who in 1895 had moved to Brno, where he formed a band. Support for the new orchestra was mixed and repertory was undemanding, partly because of perceived commercial pressures and partly because of Rund's limited experience. By 1898 it was time for a fresh start.[27]

The programme for Janáček's first concert, on 20 March 1898, went as follows:

Emerich Beran: National Anthem with orchestral accompaniment, conducted by the composer
Antonín Dvořák: *The Wild Dove*, symphonic poem
Bedřich Smetana: Aria from *Libuše*, sung by František Vojtěchovský, accompanied by Miss Illnerová
Leoš Janáček: *Funeral March* for large orchestra
Edward [sic] Grieg: *Norwegian Dance* for large orchestra
Vítězslav Novák: *Two Czech Dances* for large orchestra
P.I. Tchaikovsky: Serenade for string orchestra
Vítězslav Novák: *Gypsy Melodies* no. 3
Songs in national tone sung by F. Vojtěchovský accompanied by Z. Illnerová[28]

[¶] Beran and Koblížek were members of Janáček's staff at the Organ School; for Rund see above.

The format of the programme, with its interspersed songs, suggests that Janáček needed to maintain a balance between artistic ambition and popular following. What is remarkable, however, are the premières. This was the first public performance of part of Novák's *Gypsy Melodies* S50, and the first Brno performance of his *Three Czech Dances* S51.** Furthermore, under the title *Funeral March* lurked the last movement of Janáček's cantata *Amarus*. The real coup, however, was the world première of Dvořák's *The Wild Dove*. This was the fourth and last in Dvořák's series of symphonic poems based on Erben's ballads. While the earlier three had been written between January and April 1896, first performed privately at the Prague Conservatory on 3 June 1896 and published by Simrock that same year, the final symphonic poem came rather later, composed October–November 1896, and was still unperformed.

Janáček had set energetically about his task on 1 January 1898, if not earlier: the responses from Novák and Dvořák to requests for pieces to perform were both written on 3 January. Novák gave his immediate consent,[29] Dvořák was rather more cautious:

The Wild Dove has been ready for ages [about a month!] but I still *haven't heard the piece myself*, and so I must be very careful before I let it out into the world. It is planned to be rehearsed here first, at the [Prague] Conservatory, just as was the case before with *The Water Goblin*, *The Noon Witch* and *The Spinning Wheel*. If I hear the work in the month of January or February – then I would be willing to lend you the score and parts for a *public performance*, although it's only possible [to lend the score etc.], since the work hasn't yet been published. Apart from that I have one more symphonic poem [*A Hero's Song*] that is also still completely unknown here and hasn't yet even been played in Prague. So, if it's possible, I'll gladly give you one or the other.[30]

It is not known whether Janáček made further representations but a month later Dvořák mentioned in his next letter that he had 'almost decided' to allow Janáček to give a performance of *The Wild Dove*. By now, however, the grounds for his reluctance seem to be more connected with copyright and publication than with any need first to hear and possibly correct the piece. Janáček had to undertake not to let the parts and score out of his hands. Any copy that got made illegally not only contravened the law but would create unpleasantness for

---

** Or, rather, two of them; see below.

Dvořák with his publisher.[31] Three weeks later Dvořák sent the score and parts,[32] thus giving Janáček a month to study and rehearse the new work.

While preparations were getting under way for the concert, an important meeting took place in January under the auspices of the Czech Readers' Club to form a Russian Circle in Brno. In his detailed study of the circle[33] Přemysl Vrba suggested that the initiative for setting it up came from within 'Vesna', and in particular from its director František Mareš, but there was equally strong interest from other founder members such as Ferdinand Jokl from the Czech Real Gymnasium in Brno, the bookseller Joža Barvič, the medical doctor Dr František Veselý (the future founder of Luhačovice, see chap. 45) and of course Janáček himself, fired with enthusiasm after his trip to Russia in 1896. The object of the circle was to promote an interest in the Russian language, culture, music, art and science. Police permission was sought and obtained (not an entirely straightforward matter given the tense relations between Austria-Hungary and Russia) and at the first meeting at 7 p.m. on 26 January 1898 in the Besední dům, attended by some thirty people, a committee was established that included Janáček as one of its members. Language teaching was a prominent feature in its early years (but from 1901 the regular courses it held were devolved to private teaching by Marie Veveritsa). Apart from that, the circle organized public lectures (for instance one on Tolstoy on 25 May 1898), concerts, poetry and literature readings and discussions. In all of this, even the language teaching, Janáček took an active part. His passion for Russian culture is confirmed by the fact that he remained on the Russian Circle's committee until its closure during the First World War (it was briefly reconstituted in 1919), and served in various roles, culminating in his appointment as chairman in 1910. His reading in Russian literature was stimulated by the circle and led to the Russian inspiration of many later compositions.

On 6 March 1898 there was a new Janáček première in Brno, his *Spring Song* (V/3) performed by Miroslav Lazar, a frequent guest singer at the Brno Theatre under the pseudonym of Zdeněk Lev, accompanied by Hrazdira (see chaps. 27 and 32). It seems odd that, apart from folksong arrangements and the very early *If you don't want me, so what?* (V/1), this pallid little salon piece is the only work for voice and piano that Janáček wrote before his great song cycle *The Diary of One Who Disappeared* (v/12). Nevertheless he seems not to have thought ill of the piece, revising it in 1905 for inclusion in a concert put on by the Club of the Friends of Art.

The concert of the Czech National Orchestra took place in the Great Hall of the Besední dům at five o'clock on Sunday afternoon, 20 March, without either Novák or Dvořák in attendance. Novák had perhaps been hoping to come, since he wrote to Janáček about his absence only the day before. In his letter Novák is untroubled about omitting the third dance, the Furiant, thus explaining the title given in the programme: *Two Czech Dances*.[34] Hrazdira's review, which appeared in *Lidové noviny* on 24 March 1898, could hardly be objective, given his close connections with Janáček and the national aspirations of the concert. But even making allowance for this, it sounds as if it went well: 'The success of the whole concert was splendid beyond expectations. The audience, which turned up in huge numbers to the concert, made plain with its enthusiastic approval its sympathy in full measure for the noble and disinterested enterprise.' Janáček's conducting abilities were singled out for praise in the performance of *The Wild Dove*:

The performance of this symphonic poem was indeed a model one. Here everyone could clearly recognize that with such an orchestral group as constituted it will be possible to perform large pieces – and that it is possible to perform them flawlessly – indeed almost in an exemplary fashion – guaranteed by Janáček's intelligence as musician and conductor that one recognizes in every bar of a piece rehearsed by him.

On Janáček's contribution as a composer, the 'epilogue to a great scene for soloists, chorus and orchestra, *Amarus*, a poem by Jaroslav Vrchlický', judgement was however withheld until the piece could be heard as a whole, an event promised in one of the next concerts. After the *Amarus* excerpt, Janáček was presented with a laurel wreath. The success of the concert, Hrazdira suggested, removed 'at a stroke all bitterness and slights that were put in his way',[35] a formulation that perhaps referred to the unfortunate clash between this concert and one proposed by the Brno Beseda at about this time. The Beseda concert, which involved bringing the Czech Philharmonic from Prague, had to be postponed for eight months, a change negotiated with some acrimony.[36]

Janáček himself seemed pleased enough with the concert and immediately set about making arrangements to repeat it in Kroměříž, as emerges from a letter to Novák[37] and from Dvořák's response:

I am delighted to hear that it turned out so well for you. Please send me some newspaper reports. I'd have no objection to their giving *The Wild Dove* in Kroměříž but I ask you earnestly once again, don't give anyone the score or parts since I have great worries about any of it being copied! Please pay heed to this![38]

The Kroměříž concert, however, did not take place.

During 1898 Janáček continued to publish his articles in *Hlídka*, for instance a detailed analysis of Dvořák's *The Wild Dove* (xv/156), written during the time of his rehearsals of the work. It appeared in the April issue, i.e. just a little after the concert. A less characteristic contribution for the paper was a short review of Ludvík Holain's *Te Deum* (xv/157). A combination of the journal's clerical mission and his acquaintance with the composer (one of his collaborators in the 1895 Ethnographic Exhibition) perhaps explains Janáček's uncharacteristic venture into commenting on church music. Janáček the teacher is evident in his suggested corrections of a couple of stylistic infelicities such as parallel fifths, or in his noting (with approval and six examples) the variations that Holain makes on a 'fragment of a warmer tune' (which he also identifies as coming from Franz Xaver Witt's Gloria op. 12). His final verdict, however, is that the austere style of this piece, typical of Witt's Cecilian reforms of church music, denied the composer the possibility of developing a greater depth of expression.

Another publication that year was a contribution to a booklet (originally published in the periodical *Učitel*) on Hukvaldy by Eduard Vaculík. Entitled *Pod Hukvaldy se starým zámkem* [At the foot of Hukvaldy and its old castle], it consists of four sections: on the old Hukvaldy castle; on the settlement 'beneath Hukvaldy' (Janáček's contribution); on its history; and tourist information. Janáček's section (xv/158), which takes up half of the twenty-one pages, begins broadly, describing the lie of the land, then Hukvaldy and the neighbouring settlements of Horní Sklenov and Dolní Sklenov. However, the article soon slips into music, with Janáček printing thirteen folksongs and seven dances that he collected in the area. The folksongs came from two sources: four sung by Matula z pasek,[††] the remaining nine by Josef Křístek, whom Janáček describes as 'a poetic and lyrical soul', a wanderer, who sang the songs well in tune and with clear enunciation (not all singers made the transcriber's work so easy), his natural stresses being somewhat in the style of recitative. He died 'in poverty and deserted in a sheep pen at the mill in Mniší (14 August 1891)'. The songs had been collected almost a decade earlier – Janáček had given an account of them in an article published on 3 January 1891 (XV/109). If he notated the songs at pitch, which is likely, then Křístek was evidently a natural tenor: one of the songs goes up to a high B flat. The dances, which included versions of *Blessed Dance* and *Handsaw Dance*, are even earlier, played 'thirteen years ago' (i.e. 1885) by Žofka Havlová.

It was on his copy of the published article that Janáček began drafting accompaniments to the folksongs and by the end of the year he had provided them for all thirteen. They were performed on 18 December 1898 as illustrations to a lecture Janáček gave at 'Vesna', with the composer accompanying the tenor Antonín Karas and the baritone František Vojtěchovský (who had taken part in Janáček's big orchestral concert earlier in the year). Janáček's lecture was reported in some detail in *Moravská revue* (see chap. 28) and was remarkable in showing evidence of new thinking, in particular his observations of the 'close and warm relationship' between folksong and people's speech: 'The special modulations, stress and rhythmic richness of our Czech language is identical with folksong.' This, he felt, applied particularly to the eastern and southern Moravian dialects (from Lašsko/Valašsko and Slovácko). The report also mentioned that Janáček demonstrated several sentences spoken in his native Hukvaldy dialect.[39] Such thoughts came at a crucial, transitional point in his life. The previous summer he had begun systematically notating speech melody (with a great stock from Hukvaldy); within a couple of years he would write his long introduction to *Moravian Folksongs Newly Collected*, in which he attempted to give examples of the close links between observed speech melodies and Moravian folksongs.

Janáček clearly cared about these songs from his native region, ensuring that they were published a matter of weeks after the lecture

---

[††] Matula's 'surname' (from the clearings) is written lower case.

and performance. Arnošt Píša of Brno brought them out in January 1899 as *Hukvaldy Folk Poetry in Songs* (v/4) with a dedication to the 'Circle "Under the Acacia"', the group of friends (including Mrs Rakowitschová) who spent their holidays in Hukvaldy with the Janáčeks. And the next year Janáček reworked six of the songs for unaccompanied mixed chorus as *Hukvaldy Songs* (iv/27) (see below).

On 19 September 1898 František Bartoš, now retired from the Brno Gymnasium to the village of Mlatcová (Mladcova) near Zlín, wrote to Janáček:

They have finally begun! I'm sending you the first signature [i.e. large printers' sheet folded into sixteen printed pages], correct it (just the notes of course) and return it to *me* (Mlatcová, Zlín). In future they will arrange it so that they will send you a proof directly from Prague, you should then send each corrected signature as soon as possible to *me*. I will correct the text and send it to Prague. I will check the revised proof myself. Please write the number of your house for the address.[40]

And thus began the gruelling work of correcting the proofs of Janáček's and Bartoš's *Moravian Folksongs Newly Collected* (xiii/3). The two of them were at it month after month until 1901, when the 2057 songs completed publication. As a pensioner, Bartoš had lots of time to do his part and write Janáček nagging letters when he felt he was falling behind, whereas Janáček had to fit the work in with the rest of his busy life as best he could. It is a wonder that he was able to manage any composition at all during the next three years.

Janáček's contacts with Bartoš over *Moravian Folksongs Newly Collected* continued relentlessly throughout 1899. A letter sent to Janáček on 3 July 1899 gives an indication of the sort of production line that was necessary:

You haven't sent the proofs of the sixteenth signature – I've been waiting for it since Thursday [29 June, i.e. four days]! If by any chance you didn't receive it, write immediately to the Prague printers, Alois Wiesner. As I understand it, they have there only about one signature's [worth] of music print and [they] wait until the signature is printed [before beginning the next one]. Therefore don't delay, so as not to hold up the printing.[41]

What happened, then, was that a sixteen-page signature was prepared by the printers and sent first to Janáček to check the music. Janáček then sent it to Bartoš, who checked the words and returned it to the printers. A corrected proof was then sent to Bartoš, who checked it and returned it directly to the printers. The signature was printed immediately. Then the forme was broken up (so that the movable type could be re-used) and a new sixteen-page signature was prepared. At the end of the process signatures would be bound together in order. Even today one can chart the laborious process by noting the number on the bottom right of each new signature. There were seventy-five in all plus another nine for Janáček's long preface. The sixteenth signature that Bartoš was waiting for so impatiently took them to song no. 427 on p. 241. In this way they handled two signatures a month, and if Janáček was more than three days late, Bartoš immediately remonstrated. He also remonstrated with the Czech Academy to increase the pace: 'With each set of proofs I send reproachful remarks to the office of the academy to hurry up with the setting of the songs, but to no avail! If it goes on like this I, as an old man, won't see the end!'[42] Bartoš was sixty-two years old at the time and lived until 1906, by which time the volume had been published for five years.

Occasionally other matters came up in their correspondence. In his letter to Janáček of 27 January 1899, Bartoš wondered what Janáček's marking of '+' on some songs could mean, perhaps songs that particularly took his fancy? He had also received some 130 sacred songs from Martin Zeman. In assembling the collection, in which the songs are grouped by genre (ballads, love songs, wedding songs, soldier songs, humorous songs, dance-songs, etc.), he had forgotten about sacred songs but they could be put in at the end. He would send them on to Janáček to make a selection. And indeed the final 181 songs make up section XI ('religious songs'), of which a very large proportion came from Zeman. Bartoš ended this letter to his old colleague on a more personal note:

When you are parting with five krejcars for a stamp, you could surely write a little note about what you're doing, what's new in Brno, especially in the musical world, and in opera and theatre generally. In *Moravská revue* I read about an interesting and important lecture by you in 'Vesna', and that you are said to be publishing a new collection of songs with Píša.[43]

The 'new collection of songs' was *Hukvaldy Folk Poetry in Songs* (v/4), on which Janáček had based his 'Vesna' lecture (see above). Unless there are Janáček letters to Bartoš from this period that have not survived, Bartoš's request for a little personal news seems to have been ignored: Janáček was busy enough keeping up with the production line. But keep up he did, even over the summer, so that by late October 1899 they were dealing with signatures twenty-four and twenty-five, i.e. songs nos. 680–747 (pp. 369–400). And the question of the religious songs re-emerged. Zeman had taken his time about it, so it was only on 18 October that Bartoš was able to send them to Janáček. He asked Janáček to investigate whether any of them had already been published, for instance in the 'St John' *Kancionál* [hymnbook] (compiled by Vincenc Bradáč, and published in 1863–4) and to make his selection accordingly.[44] By 6 November, however, Janáček had failed to locate the *Kancionál* in Brno, and Bartoš had to give further suggestions for how he might get hold of it;[45] and then a couple of weeks later he was able to borrow a copy from his local priest and duly sent it to him.[46] Janáček, meanwhile, had managed to acquire the 'St Václav' *Kancionál český* (originally published in 1683)[47] and on 30 November, in Janáček's earliest letter to Bartoš to survive, he gave his crisp verdict on which of Zeman's songs he thought worth including. He also expressed a *cri de coeur* about the introduction and his lack of time for writing it.[48] Bartoš's response on 10 December reveals much about the way they worked and how they were remunerated:

So you see! How quickly things go when one goes to work with a will! You stipulated a month [for sorting out the spiritual songs] and you got it done in a week! But why haven't you written references to the *Kancionál* on the songs? If you have it noted, add it to the proof; I regard it as necessary (*Kancionál svatováclavský*, p...). You can work on the introduction rather slowly and comfortably, there will perhaps be time enough until Easter. In Prague they say that a general strike of compositors is being organized, which would again hold up the printing.

I was in Prague last week. I arranged that they publish the songs in one volume not, as was originally decreed, in two. The format is large, the book won't be that bulky.

I also negotiated over the fee. At first they promised me 30 zl a signature before I sent the manuscript. Then my precious friend Hattala[‡‡] suggested that 20 zl would be plenty for me, and they stuck to it and wrote it into the minutes (although Hattala, just for a simple transcription of the Alexandriad, got 40 zl a signature). I protested against this, and the chairman and executive of the third class of the academy assured us a rate of 30 zl.

[‡‡]Martin Hattala, professor of Slavonic philology at Prague University.

The director of the office told me they will pay me as soon as possible for the thirty to thirty-three signatures printed so far. I suggest that we divide the fee in three: a third for me, a third for you and a third for the contributors according to the number of songs.[49]

When Janáček replied the next day he said that he had not only noted the page numbers of the hymnbook but also the musical differences and how richly the folk versions had ornamented the old songs. And he was beginning to think about the introduction:

Can I put into the introduction some songs from Březová that I collected there? I'd like to do it during a discussion about the ways in which songs are notated in the collection.

I also have *gajdoš* [bagpiper] accompaniments that I'd like to put into the introduction.

I completely agree with your division [of the fees]. We really deserve to be paid 30 zl!

On Sunday 17 December people are coming to Brno from Strání – they will perform the 'pod šable' [sword dance] here and sing songs of the young man and his girl (ten in all). Do come – there is just as much snow here as in the village.[50]

Whether Bartoš came for the Strání concert is not known but when he next wrote to Janáček (26 December) he left the introduction to his discretion.[51] And so in his introduction Janáček included not only the Březová songs and a good sampling of bagpipe notations but also an interesting commentary on the way the folk versions of the religious songs differed from the originals.

Janáček's expedition to Březová in Slovácko had taken place over Whitsun weekend (20–2 May 1899) in the company of Alois Král (1877–1972), a recent student of his at the Teachers' Institute who had drawn his attention to the wealth of folk music in the area. In September 1898 Janáček had begun to seek information about how to get to Březová, when the *hody* [i.e. village festival] would be, and so on.[52] He was rewarded with a long letter describing both the arduous three-hour journey on foot from the railway station (but Král would send a carriage should Janáček wish to visit) and the types of folk festivities in the area.[53] Janáček's appetite was whetted and he made his expedition the next year. Information on the trip and subsequent researches comes from Janáček's correspondence with Král (some fifty letters over the next five years), from the impressive collection of fifty-one songs notated by Janáček, several with bagpipe accompaniments,[54] but particularly through a long, 100-page article *Březová Song* (XV/315). Written in Janáček's most engaging style, it describes his visit to the region, the people, the songs and the singers, and was intended for the periodical *Český lid* but for some reason not sent.[55] The reason may have been that Janáček was already worrying about the long preface needed for the *Moravian Folksongs* collection. Since in his Březová article he had described in some detail the difficulties of providing exact transcriptions (for instance giving versions in a standardized metre followed by a version trying to render exactly what was sung rhythmically), it may have occurred to him that this would fill out the preface nicely. Whatever the reason, Janáček raided his unpublished article, leaving a torso of forty-two pages, while many passages and song transcriptions on the other pages presumably found their way to the printers, incorporated into the *Moravian Folksongs* preface.[55]

Despite the continual pressure from the proofs of the folksong collection, Janáček also managed to keep going with his articles for *Hlídka* in the 'Czech Musical Currents' series. The reviews of church music that he had begun exploring the previous year with Holain's *Te Deum* continued with two more sacred works: the *Franz Josef Mass* by Josef Bohuslav Foerster which, like Holain's *Te Deum*, was written to celebrate the emperor's fiftieth anniversary in 1898, and *La risurrezione di Lazzaro*, a recent work by the young Italian composer Lorenzo Perosi, whose oratorios were just beginning their sudden wave of popularity. Janáček was polite about both works, praising Perosi's dramatic setting of the text and the fact that, seemingly unaffected by the Cecilian reforms of church music, he made use of the expressive possibilities of modern music. Foerster's *Mass* he dealt with rather more briefly, without music examples. Unlike the Perosi, this was a work written in the spirit of Witt's Cecilian reforms but, as Janáček saw it, was at least able to temper, through good Czech musicianship, the 'harshness and convulsive outbursts in harmony' that he regarded as a consequence of Witt's principles.

Both reviews were tacked on to a longer review of a work (XV/160)

---

[55] See the reprint of XV/315 in *LJOLP*, 210–17, which notes the gaps in the manuscript.

that was of much more intrinsic interest to Janáček, a commentary on Kovařovic's most popular opera, *The Dogheads*. By the time Janáček wrote his review of the score, Kovařovic's opera (1898) had already established itself as one of the most successful new Czech operas in the National Theatre repertory, with fifteen performances in its first season. Janáček may have wondered at the rise in status of the composer whom he had dismissed so ironically in his *Hudební listy* review (xv/70) in 1887 (see chap. 49). Earlier in 1899 Janáček had written, in 'Czech Musical Currents', another operatic review (xv/160) of the score of *Šárka* by Zdeněk Fibich, then at the height of his success and considered by some, despite the existence of Dvořák, as a worthy successor to Smetana. *Šárka* (1897) was showing every sign of turning out to be Fibich's most successful opera with the public. It would have been hard for Janáček not to be envious of Fibich's success with an opera with the same title and plot as his own first opera, now as good as buried in view of Zeyer's refusal to allow his setting.

This systematic, and public, immersion in the music of his Czech operatic competitors, including a review of the vocal score of Fibich's opera *Hedy* (appended in 1897 to Janáček's analysis of Dvořák's *Golden Spinning Wheel* xv/154), is unique in Janáček's oeuvre and comes at a significant moment. At a time when he had abandoned a major opera he seemed to be making a special effort to see what his more successful competitors were up to. Was he attempting to learn from them, or to satisfy himself that they were no better than he was? Janáček's review of Fibich's *Šárka* examines its final scene and remarks on the fact that there are twenty-four motifs in this scene alone. Janáček lists them, with brief comments on what they represent. It is necessary, he writes, to hear the opera and come under the spell of its effect – and this will explain the general view that *Šárka* is a great work. He goes on to say that the examples illustrate Fibich's technical facility in creating detailed and different shades of expression, with interestingly coloured orchestration. But then the criticisms begin. So many themes are a waste, he writes, and detract from the effect of the whole work. The harmony is sometimes illogical, the articulation of the music is sometimes at variance with the setting of the words. And the last, throwaway sentence is both apt and damning: 'Fibich is a contemplative soul: rhythmic wit is something he doesn't know.'

Satisfied, perhaps, that he could measure up to Fibich, Janáček then turned his attention (in xv/161) to Kovařovic. Again, he found much to like in the opera. Kovařovic is able to make charming use of folksongs and bagpipe imitations. His flair for logical harmony is remarkable (the bulk of the review is taken up with musical examples illustrating Kovařovic's mildly chromatic harmony). Such charm and well-developed use of motifs are attractive features of the entire opera (again some more examples). But – and here the knife goes in – it is not very original, and Janáček proceeds to illustrate passages that are based on Smetana's *The Kiss*. For all this, Janáček is impressed by the success of the work. He ends: 'During the performance people weep when Kozina says farewell to his family. This is to the mutual credit of the librettist and the composer.'

More reservations about Kovařovic's opera are apparent in a response Janáček made to a questionnaire about the problem of the Brno Theatre. The questionnaire had been sent to leading opinion makers in Brno (Janáček's response, xv/159, published in *Moravská revue* on 15 March, came straight after one by František Lacina, the new director of the Brno Theatre) and posed four questions. Ignoring those on matters of finance (questions 1–3), Janáček confined himself entirely to the final question, about the emergence of an individual artistic Moravian character, The melody of the Czech language, he proclaimed, had been debased through contact with German, and actors needed to purify their language by studying 'the life of the people'. Janáček, of course, had been doing just that for eighteen months now, jotting down fragments of overheard speech, and he proceeded to give a couple of examples: the drooping speech of an ill and ageing woman trudging along the street or the scherzando laughter (captured in very short demisemiquavers) of a young girl. Such insights should then be transferred to opera. There ought, he wrote, to be some difference in the speech melodies of Hanči and Kateřina (two of Kovařovic's female characters in *The Dogheads*). Kozina, the resolute and tragic hero, 'cannot after all sing in the languid melodies of modern love songs'. Studying speech melodies was thus the key to being '*genuinely Czech, genuinely Moravian*'. This is an important moment. These two tiny speech melodies were the first that Janáček published (he called them 'melodic waves' here). And the article provides the justification for studying them: it was a way of helping music to sound 'genuinely Moravian'. The question of being 'genuinely Moravian' is one that haunted Janáček for the next few years (see chap. 35).

Janáček's most important contribution to the Russian Circle in 1899 was his participation in a concert ('a festive academy') held on 7 June in the Besední dům to celebrate the 100th anniversary of Pushkin's birth. The programme of Russian literature and music included a fanfare by Lyadov, a male-voice chorus by Glinka, Balakirev's arrangements of Russian folksongs, songs by Alyab'yev and Tchaikovsky and a duet from *Eugene Onegin*, and concluded with Janáček conducting the Czech National Orchestra in Glazunov's symphonic 'essay' *A Slav Holiday*. There was also a recitation by Olga Janáčková of Pushkin's poem *The Drowned Man*, declaimed in the original Russian.[56] Such an event, so soon after Olga had begun learning Russian, is testament to her enthusiasm and progress.

The summer was spent again in Hukvaldy, joined by Janáček's brother Bedřich (who had moved that year to Warsaw) and his family. Sadly his children, who spoke no Czech, were unable to communicate with their cousin Olga, who spoke no German. Janáček's brother František called the family meetings a 'Babel-like confusion of tongues'.[57] It was perhaps the summer stay in Hukvaldy that encouraged Janáček to return to his transcriptions of Hukvaldy songs (v/4) and make further arrangements of six of the thirteen, this time for unaccompanied mixed chorus, called simply *Hukvaldy Songs* (iv/27). The autograph is dated 11 October 1899 (i.e. a few weeks after Janáček had to return to Brno for the new term) and is dedicated to the society founded by Janáček's father Jiří, the Hukvaldy Singing and Reading Club, for which they were presumably written.

On 12 September 1899 Eliška Machová, a schoolteacher and co-founder of the 'Vesna' schools for girls, founded the Women's Shelter in Brno, originally as a place for needy young women from the country seeking work in Brno, though it soon began taking in orphans and abandoned children. The Janáčeks were involved from the start – Zdenka was on the committee as treasurer and Olga took part in the fundraising activities, for example by reciting at gala musical evenings in the theatre.[58] One of the major fundraising events was a ball organized for Carnival time (January 1900), a 'Slavonic Beseda' at which characteristic dances of Slavonic nations would be performed by a total of sixty-four dancers in the appropriate costumes: a Czech polka,[||||] a Polish polonaise, a Cossack dance, a Serbian reel and a Valachian *blessed dance*. Zdenka was in charge of rehearsing the *blessed dance* and organizing the costumes, mostly borrowed from the National Theatre in Prague (though the Moravian folk costumes were made locally), and gave a spirited account of these activities in her memoirs.[59] Olga was one of the dancers. Even Janáček was drawn into proceedings, composing three of the dances: a *Blessed Dance* (VI/11), a Russian *Cossack Dance* (VI/12) and a *Serbian Reel* (VI/13; see chap. 35). He wrote the three dances over the next couple of months, beginning with the *Blessed Dance*, an arrangement of the tune that he had taken down in Kozlovice in 1885 and that had featured in several of his earlier orchestral folk arrangements. This was Janáček's last and best orchestral arrangement of this familiar tune, cleaner, sparser, with a prominent descending cello part, and an amusing repeated figure for the trombones. Earlier arrangements were in B flat but this was in G major with the original dotted version of the tune. He completed it on 22 November and then went on to the *Cossack Dance*. This rather shorter arrangement (it lasts a minute and a half, half the time of the slower *Blessed Dance*) was complete by 9 December 1899, and so Janáček continued with the *Serbian Reel*. Here the autograph is undated but it was presumably completed that month to allow time for rehearsals.

[||||] Here the two sources, Vorlová (see chap. 39) and Zdenka Janáčková (*MLWJ*), diverge. Janáčková mentions a 'polka' more than once, but Vorlová mentions 'Rimsky-Korsakov's "Rejdovák"'. It is not clear what this piece could be – Rimsky wrote no orchestral piece with this title. Could it be perhaps the *redowa* from Rimsky-Korsakov's opera-ballet *Mlada* (published in Leipzig, 1891), whose title was then confused with the Czech dance *rejdovák*? It seems odd to import a 'Czech' dance written by a Russian when there were plenty of Czech dances nearer at hand, so Zdenka's 'polka' seems more convincing, but the detailed title in Vorlová is striking.

37

Speech melody

Terminology, especially in English

Janáček hit upon his term, *nápěvky mluvy*, fairly early on.* While *mluvy* translates unproblematically into English as 'of speech', for the preceding *nápěvky*, the diminutive of *nápěvy*, there have been several translations suggested, such as 'curves of speech', 'melodies of speech', 'speech tunes', 'speech melodies', etc. To set up an opposition between *nápěv* (the singular form) and *melodie* and to assume that the different usages equate with the different usages in English between 'tune' and 'melody' is to ignore the fact that there is not much difference between the two Czech words (some dictionaries do not distinguish between meanings for them),† and what differences there are come from standardized usages within each language. Tune and *nápěv* have this much in common. (1) Tune/*nápěv* can be used in situations where a melody without words is intended: 'Do you know this tune?'; Czech folk collections, for instance Erben's, were sometimes issued with separate books of words and a supplementary book of 'tunes' (*nápěvy*). (2) Tune and *nápěv* are more demotic words than melody/*melodie* and might therefore suggest something shorter and less fancy. One hums a tune/*nápěv* rather than a melody/*melodie*. This does not seem to me sufficient reason to replace the most commonly used term 'speech melody' with the term 'speech tune' let alone to try and render the diminutive with the jaunty neologism of 'speech tunelet'.[1] If Janáček

---

* Štědroň 1966, 200, surveys the variants that Janáček employed.
† e.g. the revised version by Miroslav Barvík and Karel Tauš (1960) of Jan Malát's *Hudební slovníček* [Little dictionary of music] (Prague, 1881) explained 'Nápěv' as 'the Czech word for melody'. English 'tune' has the added complication of concepts of pitch (e.g. being 'in tune').

chose *nápěv* rather than *melodie* it might be purely because he favoured the more Slavonic of the two possibilities, a choice familiar from the technical vocabulary he used in his writings on music theory.

What is speech melody?

The concept of speech melody is in itself simple and unproblematic. From time to time Janáček would be struck by snatches of conversation around him (as well as sounds of nature) and jot them down in whatever he had to hand, usually his notebook. His notated speech melodies thus consist of short verbal phrases fitted to a 'tune' written in conventional musical notation, showing pitch, rhythm and sometimes other parameters such as dynamics. Occasionally he added comments on external circumstances.

In his writings on this topic Janáček suggested that these speech melodies provided an insight into the speaker's state of mind. They were, he said, his 'window into the human soul': 'A speech melody is a faithful momentary musical expression of a human being; it is his soul and all his being like a photograph of the moment' (xv/180; 1905).

Forget that they are called 'speech melodies' and sing one of Janáček's speech melodies just as you would any other voice line with words. The simple experiment of singing what Janáček notated will not replicate what he heard. The notes are of song, not speech, sustained in a way that speech is not. There is a world of difference between someone speaking and someone singing, and a notation for the latter is at best only an approximation of the former. What Janáček was doing was to provide a musical stylization which may well be helpful to represent and characterize a spoken phrase but it falls at the first hurdle of scientific proof ('repeatability'). Janáček was well aware of this: 'Just don't sing the speech melodies', he declared in *The Border between Speech and Song* (xv/185; 1906).‡

In later years he entered precise indications of duration, making use of Hipp's chronoscope; nevertheless such exactitude was compromised by the fact that in order to do so he needed to come home and make the timings from what he remembered.§ Janáček might well have imagined that he was being more 'scientific' than he was. There is no reason why

---

‡The versions by Iva Bittová (e.g. on Iva Bittová Classic, Supraphon SU 3371–2 931, bands 13–15) are more in the nature of creative interpretations of Janáček's notations.
§The chronoscope was not portable (see vol. ii: 1922).

people should speak in rhythms of equal-length notes (their multiples or their simple fractions) or that they should speak to pitches of a narrow range and use only the notes of the chromatic scale. As scientific data these notations say more about Janáček and his perception of the spoken phrases than about the spoken phrases themselves.

The starting date of Janáček's concept of speech melody is a matter of controversy, mostly because he supplied five different ones himself (1879, 1881, 1888, 1897, 1901),[2] four of them wrong. Whatever the vagaries of his memory, or the stages of development in his thinking that these dates may reflect, the fact remains that before 1897 there is not a single written-out speech melody; furthermore Janáček neither used the term speech melody nor wrote about his idea before this date. On the other hand his systematic notation of speech melodies can be firmly dated (the summer of 1897; see chap. 36); thereafter there are datable speech melodies for every year of his life, and within a year of 1897 he began to discuss the concept in print. In her forthright discussion of the evidence, Milena Černohorská argues that 1897 is confirmed by the trajectory of Janáček's work (especially by the word-setting in his choruses) and the stylistic break that can be perceived in his music around this date.[3] Further corroborative evidence can be adduced from Janáček's detailed published analyses of Dvořák's symphonic poems, and his emphasis on their word-based elements (xv/152–4, 156). It is also possible that Janáček took to heart Dvořák's criticism in May 1897 of his declamation in *Amarus* (iii/6) and attempted to improve it not by theoretical models, but by fieldwork, by listening to people's speech. Eighteen months later he used some of this research, quoting examples of speech melodies he had collected, in his response to a questionnaire on the Brno Theatre (xv/159); in particular he suggested that actors, if they wished to sound 'Moravian', should do similar field research.

If any date earlier than 1897 is proposed by commentators then it is usually one that equates the beginning of Janáček's interest in speech melody with the beginning of his interest in folksong. Although, like other writers, Černohorská emphasizes this connection, she nevertheless sees the speech-melody concept as a culmination of this interest rather than its starting-point. A particular red herring is the review that Janáček wrote in 1884 of a performance of Shakespeare's *Othello* (xv/40) where he rendered in music notation the pitch on which each actor most naturally and most frequently spoke. While this demonstrates a receptivity to listening to speech from a musical viewpoint, to see this as the actual starting-point of Janáček's speech-melody theories is making rather too much out of six notes (one for each actor). Janáček does not here record variations of pitch, simply a main note, and there is no insight into state of mind, one of the cornerstones of his speech-melody concept. Janáček did not follow up this lone observation until thirteen years later.

Once Janáček began writing speech melodies in his notebooks and elsewhere there was no stopping him. His attitude to what he was doing inevitably changed, as did his presentation of it to the public. In 1901, in his introduction (XV/163) to *Moravian Folksongs Newly Collected*, he quoted some ninety short speech melodies to demonstrate (as he hoped) a close relationship between informal Moravian speech, as he notated it, and Moravian folksong. The object here is related to that of the theatre questionnaire, i.e. a demonstration of Czechness (or rather, Moravianness) seen through speech, and 'formalized' into Moravian folksong.

Within a few years Janáček had found other uses for writing down speech melodies, chiefly the insight it gave him into the emotions of the speakers. At the time that he was composing *Jenůfa*, he recalled many years later, he was 'drinking in' the melodies of the spoken word:

> By stealth I listened to the speech of passers-by, I read the expression on their faces, my eyes tracked their every movement, I observed the area around the speakers, the company they kept, the time of day, lightness and darkness, coldness and warmth.
>
> I sensed a reflection of all this in the notated speech melody. How many variations of melody could be found for the same word! [. . .] But I suspected in the melody something deeper still, something that wasn't immediately apparent, that had been covered up; I sensed that in the melody there were traces of secret, inner events. In them I understood sadness as well as the outbreak of joy, determination and doubts, etc. (XV/209; 1916)

If speech melodies betrayed a speaker's state of mind, could they not be put to use in opera?

> Every person, even the most unmusical, has an intonation in his speech, which, pleasant or not, springs from a musical sensibility and, accordingly, can be carried over in its subtlest shades into musical language. In my activity as a composer I have borne in mind that a person's voice changes with every hour that passes, since he is subject to the effects of outward impressions and inward experiences. A person's feelings are always there in speech, expressed in its intonation and especially in its speed, even its pitch.[4]

1. Janáček's mother Amalie Janáčková in about 1875, aged then perhaps forty-six and, nine years after the death of her husband who left her with four young children to bring up.
2. The school in Hukvaldy where Jiří Janáček moved with his wife Amalie and five children in 1848 and where eight of his children were born, including his son Leoš (see chaps 3 and 5).

3. Amalie Janáčková (?) in about 1880, by which time she had moved to Brno to stay with her son Leoš. She died four years later.

4–5. Two of Janáček's older sisters, in about 1880: the 'gentle, kind and attentive' Eleonora (4) and the tougher Josefa (5) (see chap. 5).

6. Monks at the Augustinian monastery in Staré Brno shortly before Janáček arrived there as a chorister in 1866. The abbot, Cyrill Napp, is seated third from the left; behind him to the right is the geneticist Gregor Mendel; the composer Pavel Křížkovský is seated on the left; the Goethe expert Franz Theodor Bratránek stands in the middle; standing second from the left is the future abbot, Anselm Rambousek.

9

7

8

7–10. (Clockwise) Janáček's four surviving brothers: František (after 1897); Karel (c. 1885); Bedřich (c. 1876) and Josef (c. 1913). Apart from Karel, who followed the family tradition as a schoolteacher, they all worked abroad, Bedřich ('Fritz') in Germany and then Warsaw, František in Prussian Silesia and then St Petersburg, and Josef in Russia. Only the ne'er-do-well Josef survived his brother Leoš (see chap. 5).

10

11

12

11. Zdenka Schulzová in about 1879,
when she was fourteen. By then she had
been Janáček's piano pupil for two years;
12. Zdenka Schulzová and Leoš Janáček
a couple of days before they were married, on 13 July 1881 (see chap. 17).

13

14

13–14. The Janáčeks' children, Vladimír
and Olga, not long before their deaths,
respectively, at the age of two and a half
and almost twenty-one.

15

16

17

15. 1874, then about twenty, and thus at the time he was studying at the Prague Organ School.
16. c. 1878, the young choirmaster, a year before he studied in Leipzig and Vienna
17. 1882, a year after he married, at the time of Olga's birth.

18. c. 1886, towards the end of his term as conductor at the Brno Beseda.

19. c. 1895, at the time of the Ethnographic Exhibition in Prague.

20. c. 1900, soon to resume work on *Jenůfa*.

21. 1906, at Luhačovice drinking the healthy spa waters.

22. 1904, the portrait with which Kunc's long biographical article in *Hudební revue* (1911) was illustrated.

23. Before 1914, the illnesses of the past few years behind him.

24. Janáček with members of the Russian Circle in about 1910, taken on the balcony of the Organ School. The vice-president Dr Jan Švec is on one side of Janáček, Olga Vašková, the secretary of the society and brother of the poet Petr Bezruč is on the other.

25. Janáček with participants of the special organ course at the Organ School in 1914. Seated beside him are some of the Organ School teachers, from the left Ladislav Malý, Eduard Tregler and, far right, Bohumil Holub.

26. Karel Kovařovic, who held up the production of *Jenůfa* at the Prague National Theatre for twelve years (see chap. 49).

27. Pavel Křížkovský, Janáček's mentor at the Augustinian monastery, in 1875, by when Křížkovský had become choirmaster at Olomouc Cathedral (see chap. 8).
28. Lucie Bakešová and participants of the Ethnographic Exhibition in Prague, 1895 including (on the right) the schoolmaster Konstantin Sojka (see chap. 32).

28

29

29. Zdeněk Nejedlý, an outspoken advocate for the 'Smetana path', in 1909, the time of his first clashes with Janáček (see chap. 57).
30. František Bartoš in 1891, Janáček's superior at the Czech Gymnasium II, and with him the co-editor of the several folksong collections (see chaps. 18 and 23).

30

31. Folk musicians from Velká in Slovácko at the time of the 'folk concert' in Brno in 1892 (see chap. 29). Pavel Trn, the leader, is seated in the middle.

32. Upwardly mobile travellers to Luhačovice, from the frontispiece of František Stavěla's guidebook of 1934 (see chap. 45).

33. Camilla Urválková, who befriended Janáček in Luhačovice in 1903, the inspirer of the opera *Fate* (see chap. 44)

Comparing formalized song and informal speech brought home to Janáček how much more lifelike he found the speech melodies that he gathered from the street than anything in the concert hall:

Listening carefully to the melodies of people's speech is a good preparatory study for opera composers. Only here does one find an inexhaustible fund of true models for the dramatic melodies of Czech words.

A speech melody taken from *song* doesn't have as much life and content. [. .] A melody from a song is simply a mirror of the soul ignited chiefly by the warmth of the music, but speech melodies are a reflection of all life. (xv/172; 1903)

Janáček's first systematic printed discussion on speech melodies as such (rather than in relationship to folk music) dates from 1903 in three key essays (xv/169, xv/172, xv/173). By this time he had added considerably to his repertory by studying the Sládek children in Hukvaldy (xv/169), by noting down some sixty Russian speech melodies on the way back from St Petersburg in 1902 (see chap. 42), by keeping his notebook at the ready on holiday in Luhačovice in 1903 (xv/173) and even by taking down the last utterances of his dying daughter in February 1903 (see chap. 42).

What are speech melodies for?

It is easier to say what speech melodies are not for. They did not, for instance, serve Janáček as raw material for his compositions. On a few occasions in his discussion of speech melody, Janáček began with something he had overheard and worked it up into a little composition (*Whitsun 1910 in Prague* xv/198, 1910; *The Beginning of a Romance* xv/237, 1922; *The Mouth* xv/246, 1923), but these are simply tiny pieces to demonstrate the force of musical life that he felt in his overheard scraps of speech. With the exception of one or two special cases (for instance the quotation in *Fate* from Camilla Urválková's five-year-old son, 'Víš, co je láska?' ['Do you know what love is?']), there are no known cases of Janáček using speech melodies in a more substantial composition. It was something he was firmly against: 'Is it conceivable', he expostulated, 'that secretly I'd take these speech melodies I've collected, torn from other souls, so sensitive that they hurt, and from them "put together" my own work? How can such nonsense get around?' (xv/209).

Janáček himself seemed to be in two minds about the use of speech melodies. On the one hand there was an unspecified 'scientific' agenda

seen in his pursuing links with linguistics, by his wanting the Czech
Academy to support this work, and by the provision in his will for the
continuation of such work after his death. On the other hand was the
use he saw in it for the opera composer. In a letter to Bartoš in October
1902 he mentioned both:

You know well that in the introduction to the songs published by the academy
[xv/163] there are very many notations of speech melodies.
  Is it important also for linguistics?
  For music, especially dramatic music, one can't value it enough. Here is that
dramatic tune that Smetana was already looking for! In songs it is not so
trenchant, bare, truthful – it's already songlike there. [. . .]
  Will they trust me in the academy that I know how to listen to and notate
speech? I am asking the academy to award me a travelling scholarship (III and
IV class) to speed up the work of collecting.[5]

In his literary writings published from 1903 onwards Janáček
increasingly quoted speech examples as a means of bringing his narra-
tives and descriptions to life. *This Year and Last* (xv/180; see chap. 51),
for instance, is one of Janáček's most successful speech-melody articles,
content to do little more at first than evoke the atmosphere of the
occasion, Lidka's excitement over the Christmas tree,[||] the candles, the
reflections and her presents. In between the two groups of speech
melodies come some of Janáček's most trenchant general comments on
what speech melody meant to him: 'A speech melody is a faithful
momentary musical expression of a human being; it is his soul and all
his being like a photograph of the moment.' And from this arises its
importance to Janáček: 'The art of dramatic writing is to compose a
tune out of which, as if by magic, a human being will appear at a
certain phase of his life.'

Janáček was not content simply to theorize. He amplifies one of Lidka's speech melodies with a single chord added to it, bringing out the
unusual chromaticism of the tune ('nothing like it in a single Czech or
Moravian song'). From Lidka's fairy-story narration Janáček takes two
speech melodies (ex. 10, overleaf) and with a few deft strokes creates a
characteristic eight-bar piece for piano by expanding the first motif
melodically and harmonically, and adding the second as contrasting
punctuation between phrases (ex. 11, overleaf). It was, he said, both to

||Lidka (Ludmila Sládková) was the young daughter of the Sládeks, where Janáček
frequently lodged.

Ex. 10

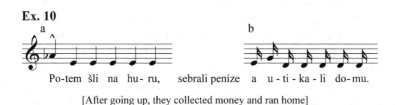

Po-tem šli na hu- ru, sebrali peníze a u - ti - ka - li do- mu.

[After going up, they collected money and ran home]

Ex. 11

show the beauty of the tune itself and the method of composition. 'The shadow of which motif should be laid on the other motive, on other motifs? For how long? When? For what reason?' 'Typical compositional form' will not provide the answers. 'The artificial web of notes should, in dramatic music, have the colour and shape, the smoothness and changeability, the suggestion of life' (xv/180).

In his review of Tchaikovsky's *Eugene Onegin* (xv/114; 1891), Janáček ventured a criticism in what is otherwise an overwhelmingly enthusiastic commentary. 'The rhythm of the tune strikingly resembles the rhythm of everyday speech.' The result, he went on, is that Onegin sings in the same manner as Tatyana, as do Olga and Lensky. Exchange their parts and the listener won't notice. It would appear that 'everyday speech' here means something different from the 'everyday speech' in Janáček's speech melodies and that, in the years between hearing *Onegin* in 1891 and formulating his theory, Janáček's perceptions of what constituted everyday speech had completely changed. Janáček's earlier understanding of the term 'everyday speech' seems to be undistinctive; only later did he widen it to something that would illuminate the soul of a character. One result of his close study of speech melody seems to be a type of ear training, a consciousness-raising exercise, from which his approach to writing differentiated voice parts would benefit. If Janáček was alert to the varying emotions expressed in speech then, it could be argued, he would be well equipped for the opposite process of expressing varying emotions when writing voice parts in his operas.

The impact of speech melodies on Janáček's music

Compare Act 1 of *Jenůfa*, written before Janáček made any speech-melody notations, with Acts 2 and 3, written after the accumulation of several hundred and after the beginnings of his comments on them, and one can see an advance in his settings of Preissová's text. Whether this is exclusively the result of his preoccupation with speech melody, or whether it is merely one of several factors in this crucial period, can only be a matter of debate.

But from this point onwards Janáček began to write operas in a very different way. The aria-recitative division that can be found in his early operas including Act 1 of *Jenůfa* falls away.[6] The voice parts that had largely sustained the melody and melodic structure no longer do so automatically, a function now often taken over by the orchestra. This allows the voice part to become irregular and more speechlike. A good way to show this is to compare the 1888 version of *Šárka* with Janáček's revision in 1918. The first date is almost a decade before his preoccupation with speech melody, the second some twenty years after he first began thinking about it. These two versions provide simple 'before' and 'after' speech-melody variants that allow a number of observations about how his vocal style changed. In general, in the 1918 version, the voice parts are speeded up by the use of smaller notes values (creating gaps between the phrases), resulting in a more irregular, speech-melodified idiom. Their range increases, they become rhythmically more varied, better reflecting multi-syllable stress patterns in Czech. Lighter off-beat starts are preferred to heavy-thump starts on the beat; final-syllable stresses (which frequently distort correct Czech declamation) are avoided; vocal phrases shrink at both ends towards a phrase climax in the middle. The emphasis in Janáček's 1918 voice parts in *Šárka* is at the middle of the phrase; the emphasis in 1888 version is at the outer ends.[7]

Although in Janáček's revision of the *Šárka* voice parts the orchestral accompaniment often stayed as it was in 1888, in operas written after speech melody one can discern an interesting new relationship between voice and orchestra. These two elements may seem to go their own way much of the time in montage-like layers, but also come together at important or emotionally charged moments.

In his examination of the impact of speech-melody theory on Janáček's operatic style, Paul Wingfield proposed a 'working theoretical model of Janáček's concept of operatic speech-melody' by examining a small sample of published speech melodies and summarizing their characteristics, and then seeing whether such features could be identified in Janáček's own post-speech-melody vocal lines. The attributes he lists are all features of a 'naturalistic' style: avoidance of repetitions of words and syllables; avoidance of melismas; avoidance of repetitions of musical motifs; a small melodic range; short note values; a preponderance of repeated notes, and so on.[8] Not surprisingly, what Wingfield concluded from the passage he then examined in *Káťa Kabanová* is that there is a continuum which stretches from 'minimally stylised speech melody' to 'maximally unrealistic vocal writing',[9] and which in the latter mode freely made use of a leitmotivic structure,[10] an approach which of course would fall foul of the rule of not repeating musical motifs.

In making his vocal lines less structured and more naturalistic Janáček was hardly doing much more than responding to trends of the time, and one wonders whether he really needed a 'speech-melody theory' to help him do so. However, the fact that it became such a dominant discourse for him for over thirty years has encouraged some scholars into making unwise claims. The use of speech melody in his music is taken for granted, albeit in cautiously general terms, for instance here by the leading Brno musicologist of the 1950s and 1960s, Jan Racek: 'The speech-melody formations in *Jenůfa* are an organic component of Janáček's musico-dramatic principles and the means of his explosive, dynamic, dramatic expression, for they determine the character of the melodic and motivic material of the opera, both vocal and instrumental.'[11]

Indeed the dangers of being specific are only too obvious. 'Is it possible to establish direct connections, affinities between the themes of Janáček's compositions and his notated melodies from the spoken language?', asks Antonín Sychra, the chief Czech musical semiotician of the period: 'There is no doubt of it. You will find proofs where the connection between Janáček's notations of speech and the themes of his compositions jump out at you at first glance.' Sychra quotes an example: four notated speech melodies of 'threats' to be compared with the vocal lines of 'threats' found in Janáček's compositions. This type of approach is compromised by the fact that the 'threat intonation' seems to be shared by other types of speech melodies that Janáček collected, as for example two phrases Janáček took down when he met Smetana's daughter (see vol. ii: 1924b), whose words have nothing to do with threats.

Sychra's method is hardly different from the more homely, traditional approach, exemplified by František Pala's studies of Janáček's operas in the 1950s, where the 'speech melodies' in Janáček's operas are quoted for their 'aptness' or their 'dramatic truth', while the author goes on to reassure the reader that the emotion expressed by the 'speech melody' is in fact just what the words might suggest.[12] There is of course no reason why there should be any connection between the literal meaning of the words and the way in which they are uttered (which appears to be a basic assumption of the Pala emotion-analysis approach). Janáček wanted to go behind the words, to the emotional state of the speaker or singer. As Gluck's celebrated example 'Le calme rentre dans mon coeur' (from *Iphigénie en Tauride*) demonstrates, there may well be a conflict between what a character says (or sings) and what he or she feels.

With the fall of the Communist administration some of the assumptions and postulates of Czech musicologists also somewhat crumbled, for instance the *intonace* theory of musical content (derived from Russian theories of *intonatsiya*, e.g. by Boris Asaf'yev), the basis for much of Sychra's work. Since then Czech musicology has taken a rather more nuanced approach to speech melody, for instance Miloš Štědroň's concentration on reported speech when examining speech melody as a concept.[13] The fascination continues, however, with several recent American dissertations devoted to the subject.[14]

Even without the urgings from Sychra, Pala and Racek, one can often be seduced by finding speechlike phrases in Janáček that appear to support a speech-melody origin. *The Evening Witch* (iv/28 no. 3), for instance, was composed by July 1900; with its partner *If only you knew* (iv/28 no. 1), it is the earliest chorus Janáček composed after beginning to write down speech melodies in 1897. It has several motifs that might seem to be derived from speech. The most striking of these is the phrase 'klekánica divá' [wild evening witch']. The musical phrase to which it is set follows the stress and rhythmic patterns of the words closely, and in order to do so, Janáček has to switch from the 3/4 metre to 7/4, an important event in the piece, marked *forte* and with the phrase repeated. However this is a strophic chorus, and while in the first verse the music fits like a glove, in the second verse the two long notes are now fitted to short vowels, and the only long vowel (the '*ná*' of '*nároči*') is fitted to one of the shortest notes (ex. 12). Janáček's musical motifs may well be word-inspired, but as soon as they are taken up in a composition and manipulated as a repeated motif they lose this connection. An examination of Janáček's sketches for his operas produces many examples where resonant verbal phrases have started off in different guises and then had different words fitted to them.[15]

Much of this, it must be said, goes back to Janáček himself. From the beginning, he placed huge emphasis on the nature of the music written in this way, wedded so closely to the words that they resist translation into another language: 'for every translation of this specifically Moravian work [*Jenůfa*] is completely unthinkable without a complete rewriting of the music which has grown organically with people's speech.'[16]

Although this might cynically be taken as an expression of Janáček's fear that *Jenůfa* would never travel, it does nevertheless touch on a

Ex. 12

fundamental problem about speech melody and its use in opera, and one that has led to the increasing proliferation of Czech-language performances of Janáček's operas by non-Czech speakers to non-Czech audiences. If there is such an intimate connection between the Czech language and Janáček's setting, bound up so much with his theories of speech melody, isn't much of this connection jettisoned as soon as the works are translated into another language? And how does this square with the fact that Janáček seems to have had no qualms about Max Brod's German translations, and never expressed any reservation about the linguistic aspects of performances of the opera that he heard in German, for instance in Vienna and Berlin? While Janáček happily gave instructions to Max Brod such as 'The same tune must have the same words beneath it',[17] there are many occasions when he did not observe this principle himself.

And what happens in Janáček's non-vocal music? Do speech melodies play any part in his instrumental music? Janáček was naturally outraged when some commentators believed his instrumental music was in some way 'invalid': 'An informative article on me was sent from Prague to the publisher Chester in London. By chance, it fell into my hands. My worst enemy could not write a worse comment. [. . .] They say that what I write for orchestra is harmed by my attitude towards the so-called speech melodies. Which means that everything in the London concert is worthless!'[18]

Something of the highly subjective nature of Janáček's speech melodies emerges when one compares the collection of folksongs and the collection of speech melodies. For folksong Janáček used a large body of collectors and, although it's clear that different collectors would undoubtedly notate in different ways, nevertheless he found it useful to employ them, and to publish the songs they collected. In May 1906 Janáček may have been surprised to receive a letter from one of his *Hlídka* readers, the parish priest and folksong collector Cyril Mašíček in the village of Vysoká Studenice near Jihlava. Mašíček wrote to Janáček to say that he would be happy to take down speech melodies for Janáček, though he would need some guidance on how to collect them systematically.[19] The next year Mašíček wrote again, this time sending some speech melodies he had collected.[20] Quite what Janáček did with them is not known: none survive with the letter, although Janáček noted on it that he had answered it. But it is significant that

Janáček did not then employ Mašíček as a collector of speech melodies, let alone edit and publish his findings. For all the 'objective', 'scientific' aspects that Janáček stressed, speech melodies in the end reflect much more of him than they did of their speakers.

38

On the Overgrown Path

With the exception of *Amarus*, none of the works Janáček wrote before returning to *Jenůfa* are large scale. Quite a few are merely occasional pieces of no particular distinction. But in around October 1900 Janáček began one of his most evocative compositions, a series of keyboard miniatures, *On the Overgrown Path* (VIII/17). Its unlikely beginning was a request for folksong arrangements for harmonium (see chap. 36). By the time Janáček had got round to attending to the request in 1900, the desired folk arrangements had turned into 'moods', i.e. short character pieces. Three were published in 1901 in the fifth volume of the harmonium series *Slovanské melodie*; two more appeared the next year. All five (together with two longer pieces which remained unpublished during Janáček's lifetime) were in existence by 1900 and make up half of what later became the first series of *On the Overgrown Path*. The remaining five were added only in 1908 and later. Although originally published as pieces for harmonium, Janáček's description of them to the critic Jan Branberger in 1908 was as piano pieces. It is arguable that he thought of them for piano from the start.

None of these five early pieces were given titles in the earliest manuscript source or when published in *Slovanské melodie* but the title of the cycle, *Po zarostlém chodníčku*, was given in *Slovanské melodie* both on the contents pages and at the head of the music. Janáček was reminded of them by a request from Jan Branberger in April 1908 for short pieces for a series that he was editing (see chap. 56). From his description of them to Branberger on 7 May as 'seven so far',[1] it is clear that he had not added any to the original seven (five published, two unpublished). But by 23 May 1908, when Janáček wrote again, he had added two more ('there are nine of these pieces').[2] Giving news of how the proposed publication was going, Branberger announced in a letter of 3 June that he liked them very much and had decided to 'write an analysis of them that would be printed on the title page'. So could Janáček please tell him something about their programmes or 'poetical relations'?[3] Janáček's first response – he probably got the letter on 4 June – was to jot down the incipits of four pieces on the fourth side of Branberger's letter with titles or descriptions.[4] Three that he quoted went into the final selection, though all the titles proposed are different from the final ones he came up with (see table 38.1). The fourth, called *A Closed Book*, bears no relation to any of the surviving pieces and seems, like one other (see below), to have fallen by the wayside. By the time Janáček had considered Branberger's request at greater leisure and written to him (on 6 June) with his comments on the pieces,[5] two of the titles he had come up with had slightly changed: *A Declaration* [*of Love*] had become *A Love Song*, and *The Bitterness of Reproach* had become *The Bitterness of Disappointment*. And neither of these was anything like the final titles (see nos. 2 and 6). At least two of the five pieces already published now had individual titles: *The Frýdek Madonna* (no. 4)* and *Good Night!* (no. 7).

The Frýdek Madonna provides a clue as to where at least some of these pieces are set. Frýdek, now half of the town of Frýdek-Místek, was a short distance from Janáček's native Hukvaldy. It has been suggested (for instance by Janáček's pupil Ludvík Kundera)[6] that the cycle, at least in part, is based on Janáček's childhood memories – he probably went to Frýdek with his parents, brothers and sisters on the annual procession to the miraculous Madonna. The piece, with its hymn tune heard at first in the distance, coming nearer, then receding again, provides an evocation of one of the more colourful events of village life in rural Moravia. But Janáček could be recalling a more recent occasion. In her memoirs Zdenka mentions a trip to Frýdek-Místek during their last stay in Hukvaldy in September 1927. 'We kept on recalling the early days there, we said to ourselves that only the two of us were left from the whole of that company, we thought of *The Frýdek Madonna* from Leoš's work, *On the Overgrown Path*'.[7] This sounds like a memory the couple shared rather than one from Janáček's

---

*Numbers are the standard numbering given in Píša's edition of 1911 of what was subsequently known as the first series.

Table 38.1: *On the Overgrown Path*, first series: evidence of date of composition of individual pieces and their titles

1900 (in Slovanské Melodie)	after 3 June 1908 (Branberger to LJ) ✓ =music quoted 'description/title'	by 6 June 1908 (LJ to Branberger) ✓ = music quoted; 'description'; ♦ title	1911 (pubd by Píša) with final no. and title
✓	✓ 'Glance to'		1. Our Evenings
✓	✓ 'Declaration' [of love]	✓ 'a love song'	2. A Blown-Away Leaf
		✓ (final 2 bars) 'A letter put away for ever'	3. Come With Us!
✓		✓✓ (opening and 'Faraway Procession') ♦ The Frýdek Madonna	4. The Frýdek Madonna
			5. They chattered like swallows
	✓ 'The Bitterness of Reproach'	✓ 'The Bitterness of Disappointment'	6. Words Fail!
✓		✓ 'Perhaps you'll hear parting in the number with the motif [. . .]' ♦ Good Night! ['the words "Good Night!" suit it']	7. Good Night!
			8. Unutterable Anguish
		'Perhaps you'll sense weeping in the penultimate number? The premonition of certain death. During the hot summer nights that angelic being lay in such mortal anguish.'	9. In Tears
✓		✓ ♦ (implicit in description): 'In the last number the ominous motif of the screech owl is heard in the intimate song of life.'	10. The screech owl has not flown away!
	✓ 'A Closed Book'		—
		✓ 'A company on an excursion is returning late. The long-drawn-out song is punctured by the terse motif of women's chattering.' (x/21)	—

childhood. Throughout the 1890s the Janáčeks spent summer holidays in Hukvaldy and could well have taken Olga to the church of St Marie for the annual pilgrimage. To Branberger Janáček described the cycle as 'memories of long ago',[8] but that was in 1908 and 'long ago' could simply refer to the years when Olga was still alive.

The five pieces published in 1901 and 1902 (together with the five added later) contain some of the profoundest, most disturbing music that Janáček had written, their impact quite out of proportion to their modest means and ambition. That they are programmatic is evident both from the cycle title and from the added individual titles; as in the case of *Amarus* there seems to be some deeply felt personal input. A few months after writing them Janáček returned to work on *Jenůfa*. The first piece, *Our Evenings*, begins deceptively – gentle, relaxed, lyrical, but what is the meaning of the violent outburst in the middle that seems to disturb the quiet family evening? Discord between husband and wife? What is the 'glance' that occurred to Janáček when he first puzzled over titles? Although the piece returns to its gentle beginnings, tensions remain not quite resolved at the end. The second piece, *A Blown-Away Leaf*, is no less puzzling. The innocent repeated tune of the opening is soon distorted by strange pauses (the metre stretched out to five beats in a bar) and broken phrases. And there are loud angry flourishes. Given the title, the piece could be mimetic: an autumn leaf, gently falling, suddenly borne away in gusts of wind. In fact the title changed. Janáček, in his account to Branberger,[9] quotes the opening of the piece, describing it as a 'declaration of love', which indeed better fits the strange eruptions of feeling.[†] Like no. 1, something that begins as a simple, lyrical piece ends up sounding edgy and ill at ease.

Such an interpretation is quite explicit in *The screech owl has not flown away!*[‡] The owl has had ominous associations from the ancient Greeks onwards and in Czech the word that Janáček uses in the title, *sýček*, is also used of someone who takes a characteristically pessimistic view of life. Janáček's composition opens with a loud flourish (of wings?) and then, against a two-note triplet tremolo, the owl's call is heard: a simple descending two-note phrase (marked 'dutě' = 'hollowly'), repeated with a drum-roll triplet – the 'musical figure of death' of Italian opera. A second section is more optimistic: a hymnlike phrase in the major key. The piece consists of the alternation of these two contrasting sections. Occasionally the opening flourish interrupts

---

[†] The Czech word *lístek* in the title is ambiguous and can also be translated as a 'short letter'.
[‡] The Czech word *sýček* is not the general word for an owl (*sova*), but one that characterizes the bird by its ominous noise and ominous association, as does the English 'screech owl'. As Jan Jiraský illustrated in a paper (Brno, December 2004), what Janáček actually imitated was the Eurasian tawny owl (*Strix aluco*).

the hymnlike section; on its last airing the latter begins to falter. It ends with the owl call, now heard very softly in the bass register. The effect is of an obsessive piece, the same material heard over and over again. Janáček wrote to Branberger: 'In the last number the ominous motif of the screech owl is heard in the intimate song of life.'[10] Janáček made it clear that this pessimistic mood was to be the final impression the listener was to take away; it was the final number in the earliest manuscript source. In his letters to Branberger in 1908 the pieces are described at random, with no indication of their respective placing – apart from the last two. Of these the screech-owl piece is referred to as the 'last number' and even when the set had expanded to ten it remained the last.

Both those published in 1902, *The Frýdek Madonna* (no. 4) and *Good Night!* (no. 7), were titled as such in Janáček's letter to Branberger.[11] The first, like the owl piece, is a simple alternation, in this case of quiet 'organ' chords and a simple childlike tune, a Marian hymn sung in procession from afar, as Janáček explained to Branberger. And as in no. 10, increasing tension comes from the juxtaposition. A huge climax to *fortissimo* for the 'organ' chords destabilizes the piece, adult doubts clouding over the innocent childlike melody of the hymn. The tune of the 'hymn' raises interesting questions. Those looking for thematic unity in the set will find a similarity of shape between the initial phrase of *Our Evenings* and the hymn of *The Frýdek Madonna*. But what appears to be the same tune is also featured in a short work for tenor, chorus, violin and piano, *Hail Mary* (II/14), fitted to the words 'Zdrávas Maria, milosti plná' ['Hail Mary, full of grace'], seemingly commissioned by Countess Serényi in 1904 (see chap. 47).

In the second number published in 1902, *Good Night!*, there is a short, rather fidgety repeated motif, a prelude to a very simple tune (heard at first unaccompanied) and then its accompaniment. 'Perhaps', Janáček wrote to Branberger, 'you'll hear parting in [it].' This, like no. 2, is one of the earliest of any of his works in which Janáček took a short motif (usually three or four notes) to provide an ostinato accompaniment, something that would become one of the hallmarks of his style. The disruptive effect when the accompaniment overpowers the tune is one that Janáček may have picked up from Moravian folk ensemble music (see chap. 31). And the technique of interrupting a lyrical tune (as in no. 10) became part of Janáček's powerful armoury of emotional effects.

In his letter to Branberger Janáček dwelt particularly on the 'pen-ultimate number' (*In Tears*). 'Perhaps you will sense weeping in it', he wrote. 'The premonition of certain death. During the hot summer nights that angelic being lay in such mortal anguish. From that time I have stopped going to the beautiful Valachian countryside for pleasure.'[12] Although the last statement is not true (unless Janáček considered his visits to Hukvaldy were no longer 'for pleasure'), this statement is the most precise programmatic indication of any in the cycle – in this case a direct reference to Olga's last summer in Hukvaldy and the 'premonition of her certain death'. This piece (no. 9) and nos. 3 (*Come With Us!*) and 6 (*Words Fail!*) were completed by 6 June 1908, when Janáček wrote to Branberger, since they are all identifiable from his descriptions. He also described one other piece (x/21) which did not make it into the published collection and which has since disappeared. Its shadowy existence is attested to only by a two-bar incipit (unrelated to any existing piece in the cycle) and the following commentary: 'A company on an excursion is returning late. The long-drawn-out song is punctured by the terse motif of women's chattering.' The description could indeed refer to the various expeditions that were made by the (women-dominated) Hukvaldy company at the time. It would seem that Janáček later substituted for it no. 5 with its related title: *They chattered like swallows*.

Nos. 5 and 3 (*Come with Us!*) are reasonably cheerful pieces, but Janáček's order for the ten published by Píša in 1911 suggests a pro-gression into increasing gloom. The last five – *Words Fail!, Good Night!, Unutterable Anguish, In Tears* and *The screech owl has not flown away!* – have titles suggestive of grief, anxiety and leave-taking, emphasizing the fact that what had been a cycle of mixed emotions in 1900 had turned much darker with Olga's illness and death.

Something of what Janáček was aiming at in this cycle can be deduced by comparing it with two numbers contained in the original manuscript sources, but which were never published during Janáček's lifetime, either in *Slovanské melodie* or in the collected first 'series' of ten pieces (1911). These are the ones published as nos. 13 and 15 of the 1942 edition, or as 'Paralipomena 3 and 2' of the 1978 Critical Edition. No. 15 may well have been rejected on the grounds of length alone – it lasts five minutes, longer than any in the first series. Both might well also have been rejected as unsuitable in a series for the harmonium because of their obvious pianistic features such as virtuoso flourishes, repeated chords and incisive dotted rhythms. The piano-harmonium comparison should not, however, be pressed too hard. Though *The Frýdek Madonna* has clear 'organ' chords that would benefit from the sustained tone of the harmonium, none of the original five work better on the harmonium than on the piano, and when publishing them explicitly for piano in 1911, Janáček made few changes that take account of the new medium.

In fact their rejection would seem to be on other grounds. Skilful and effective as they are, they lack the originality, the poetic and deep emotional content of the published pieces. No. 15, with its mazurka rhythm pounding through most bars, evokes Liszt; no. 13, with its three-beat bars divided into two, suggests Schumann. Neither sound remotely like Janáček.

39

1900–01

The Slavonic Beseda arranged by the Družstvo to raise funds for the Women's Shelter took place in the Besední dům on 10 January 1900 with Janáček conducting the Czech National Orchestra. A description in *Lidové noviny* a few days later by Zdenka Vorlová, who helped choreograph the evening, describes how the large orchestra played a Chopin Polonaise op. 40* and, emerging from the Small Hall of the Besední dům in a variety of Slavonic costumes, the dancers paraded in polonaise steps through the middle of the Great Hall. They processed twice through the hall in this way, then the Serbian group danced their *Serbian Reel*, followed by the *Blessed Dance*.

Imagine the whole scenic effect: in the middle of the hall the dashing Valach boys, and girls 'as if scattering flowers'. Along the sides, Poles, Serbs, Czechs and Russians. And now that magnificent music, Janáček's *Blessed Dance*; the whole character of beautiful Valašsko could be heard in it, but with such delicacy, strength and grace. All the groups of dancers moved as if born to it, and with each movement of the music everything got faster and faster, growing into the dizzying tempos of the piece. The *Blessed Dance* was then repeated several times and still there were complaints from the public that it was not enough, that they could have gone on looking and listening and that the whole Slavonic Beseda ought to be repeated fairly soon.[1]

If the *Blessed Dance* got 'faster and faster' at its first performance (under the composer's baton), then this was at variance with the steady Andante marking on the autograph. Perhaps Vorlová muddled it with

---

* There are two polonaises in op. 40: no. 1 in A major and no. 2 in C minor; it is not known which was performed on this occasion. There is no hint of who orchestrated it; it seems not to have been Janáček.

the *Cossack Dance*. Apart from providing the venue for three Janáček premières (and, as it happened, the final appearance of the Czech National Orchestra), the Slavonic Beseda was the scene of what in retrospect can be seen as a crucial encounter for Olga Janáčková. The next day, Zdenka recalled, Olga sat on the coal-chest drinking coffee and telling Marie Stejskalová what the previous evening had been like, how she enjoyed dancing the polka, the *Blessed Dance* and the polonaise. 'And suddenly she said to me: "Well now, Mama, you ought to know that yesterday someone declared his love for me."'[2]

In her memoirs Zdenka looked back on Olga's affairs in detail, counterpointing them with comments on her health, which, despite Zdenka's gloomy prognostications, continued to improve. By the time of the Slavonic Beseda there was no thought of Olga's not taking part in the dancing, an activity previously forbidden. In the past couple of years she had also attracted several suitors and had fallen in love herself, though the object of her affections, a young doctor, 'had not spoken' despite his being seemingly attracted to Olga. Possibly, Zdenka speculated, he was fearful about her health. This reversal had had a bad effect on Olga who, despite her many qualities and general popularity, had become hard and cynical towards further prospective suitors. She had also grown into a beautiful young woman (see Plate 14):

slender, quite tall, with exquisite small hands and feet, so tiny that she took a child-size shoe. She had a delicate complexion, a smooth skin with a hint of peach, her father's chin with a dimple. Remarkable and touching was the look from her blue eyes. Even when she laughed there was sorrow at its depth, something like a sad foreboding. Everyone liked her; everyone brightened up when they saw her. [. . .] She won people over without particularly trying to, merely by the fact that she was kind, natural and cheerful. Her dramatic talent showed itself more and more. She played in puppet theatre, she took part in presentations and amateur performances. Everywhere her deeply felt delivery achieved success, as did her melodious, resonant contralto. It was truly amazing where it came from in that slender little body.[3]

These are not just the comments of a proud mother. Vítězslav Novák, who visited the Janáčeks in Hukvaldy in the summer of 1900, was much taken with her: 'Janáček's young daughter Olenka (Olga) dazzled us. This pale blonde girl was at this time the only link between the quarrelling parents. For us then it was an experience to look on her gentle beauty.'[4]

Olga had completed her education at the local school (attached to the Women Teachers' Institute) at sixteen, but her delicate health prevented her from following the Janáček family tradition of becoming a schoolteacher. In view of her talent for languages it was decided instead that she should take the state examination and teach foreign languages, Russian in particular. So she attended the Russian Circle and learnt Russian with Professor Tacl from the Staré Brno Gymnasium.[5] She also attended the French Circle at the Staré Brno Beseda, one of Zdenka's few triumphs against Janáček's opposition. He had taken the view that Olga would get muddled if she tried to study two foreign languages at once; Zdenka regarded this objection as ridiculous in view of Olga's natural abilities, and felt that the experience would widen Olga's social circle. Their clash over this led to a 'big argument'; it was only during the Slavonic Beseda, which involved all three Janáčeks, that husband and wife became reconciled.[6]

Olga's new suitor was not to Zdenka's taste. He was Otakar Vorel, the son of Zdenka's old piano teacher Antonín Vorel and brother of Zdenka Vorlová, author of the review quoted above. He was in his early twenties and had been studying medicine in Vienna for a few years. Zdenka was unimpressed: 'Tall, thin, with a sensuous expression of the face and the beginnings of a bald patch. I didn't find him congenial. I didn't know myself what put me off him – it was something instinctive.'[7] Unwilling to antagonize her headstrong daughter, she showed mild disapproval, hoping that the affair would blow over once Vorel was back in Vienna. Instead a correspondence started up and a couple of weeks later, at the next ball, Olga and Vorel decided they would get married as soon as his studies were over. On hearing this, Zdenka insisted that Olga tell Janáček about it. Janáček knew Vorel and also disapproved of him, but his more outspoken opposition had no more effect on his daughter than Zdenka's muted reaction. But the very next day, 1 February, Janáček returned from school in great indignation, insisting on seeing Olga immediately. He had heard that Vorel had done 'something dishonourable concerning money' and ordered Olga immediately to break off all acquaintance with him. Messages via Maruška Kallusová,[†] one of Olga's friends, were sent to and fro; Vorel insisted on his innocence and Zdenka ended up having

---

[†] A few letters from Olga to Maruška Kallusová survive showing Kallusová clearly in the role of go-between (e.g. the undated letters BmJA, A 6374 and A 6376).

to go and see him herself. She was unconvinced by his explanations and told him to cease any contacts with her daughter. But he continued writing to her, and Olga, despite her father's injunction, eagerly devoured his letters.

Remarkably, Vorel's view on the affair survives: he wrote three letters in February 1900 to an unidentified friend of his in Brno. On 8 February from the General Hospital in Vienna he wrote a letter addressed 'dear friend' in which he explained that he had written a 'detailed and true' explanation to Mrs Janáčková. He asked his friend to try and discover via Maruška Kallusová how his letter had been received. If there was 'the slightest trace of mistrust' or if the Janáčeks were continuing to make enquiries about him and thus spread rumours about him, he would immediately have to break off all contacts with them, even at the expense of Olga's love.[8]

All seems to have gone well at first: on 22 February, when Vorel thanked his friend for his letter, he said that Olga was writing 'very loving letters' to him, 'almost every day'.[9] Then, according to Zdenka, Vorel wrote to Janáček, who had been kept in ignorance by wife and daughter that his instructions were not being fulfilled. In his letter Vorel 'promised that he'd stop writing to Olga until he'd finished his studies and up till then he'd entrust her to his [Janáček's] fatherly care.'[10] No letter from Janáček to Vorel has survived, but a third letter from Vorel to his friend, dated 26 February, gives a somewhat different explanation. Since the Janáčeks had forbidden contact between their daughter and him and were pretending that there was simply no 'understanding' between them, it looked to outside people as if there was something in the rumours about him; he had therefore written to Olga saying that he was mistaken about his feelings for her.[11]

The letters stopped, sending Olga into a decline, and then resumed, perhaps, as Zdenka speculated, because Olga had in some way encouraged Vorel to write. Again Zdenka colluded: 'against my own conviction and against the prohibition of my husband I continued to be Olga's confidante and shielded her.' And when, in the summer of 1900, Vorel returned for the holidays, Zdenka (or occasionally the Janáčeks' servant Marie Stejskalová, accompanied Olga on her secret assignations with Vorel, all of them terrified that Janáček would bump into them.[12]

There appear to have been contacts in Hukvaldy too: a postcard sent to Stejskalová for her name day (she was in Brno, preparing for the family's return) was signed by a number of Olga's close friends, including not only Maruška Kallusová and Josefa Jungová but also Vorel. Olga was in fine form, commenting on the good weather by making additions in pencil to the rural scene depicted on the postcard (a sun, and a hat for the man).[13] The presence of Vorel in Hukvaldy was evidently carefully calculated to coincide with Janáček's collecting trip to Kunčice pod Ondřejníkem. As a date on a sketch of a cimbalom tune shows, Janáček was there on 6 September to take down music played by František Klepáč.[14]

Janáček's Kunčice trip may have been prompted particularly by the on-going work on the preface for the *Moravian Folksongs* collection. As for proofs, these continued unabated. The good news was that Janáček was getting paid at last, as promised in Bartoš's dealing with the Czech Academy in December 1899 (see chap. 36). In a letter dated 23 February 1900 Bartoš declared that Janáček's share on the first thirty signatures was 300 zl (i. e. 600 K) plus another 20 K (as a collector), and this would be sent immediately. The bad news was that when the first volume of the collection was issued, probably in the second quarter of 1900, Janáček's name was omitted from the title page, perhaps a consequence of the project being submitted originally under Bartoš's name as a way of ensuring that it would be published (Bartoš was a member of the academy, which was obliged to publish anything submitted by any of its full members).[15] Janáček complained:

I am inexpressibly upset over the incident concerning the title page.

For years I've been taken up with the work, all my thinking relates to it – and I think also that eventually I will be able to truthfully to express something about the formation of our songs – and now this mishap.

I've asked the general secretary Dr Raýman[‡] firmly to sort it out.

It's fine for you! You are recognized in your field – but I'm fighting for recognition.[16]

It seems surprising, in view of Bartoš's comment the previous year about the collection's appearing in a single volume, that a 'first volume' was nevertheless being published in this way. Although a 'second volume' appeared when publication was complete in 1901, in practice copies of the book were usually bound in a single, though very large, volume with a new title page. Bartoš's name as the editor precedes

[‡]Bohuslav Raýman, professor of chemistry at Charles University and secretary of the third class of the Czech Academy, later general secretary.

Janáček's in slightly smaller type, responsible for the musical side. Different words are chosen to designate their respective editorial activities: 'upravil' (which has connotations of putting right) for Bartoš; 'pořádal' (which has connotations of putting in order) for Janáček. If Janáček felt aggrieved by this solution he did his best to compensate for it in the size of the introduction. While Bartoš contributed a brief preface, barely more than a page, Janáček wrote a major musicological article of 136 pages on the musical aspects (see below).

From what remains of Bartoš's and Janáček's correspondence during 1900 it is clear that the pace of proof corrections began to slow down. Although in his letter of 10 July Bartoš reminded Janáček to send the printers any change of address for the summer,[17] in his next surviving letter (19 September 1900) he complained that the printers had not been sending proofs 'for ages' and again speculated that they had something more urgent to get on with,[18] a complaint he repeated three months later.[19]

No doubt the academy would have been besieged with more complaints about the speed of the work had something else not come up to take up Bartoš's time and abundant energy. In his letter to Janáček of 10 July, he reacted to a suggestion from Emil Šolc, the publisher of the *Bouquet of Moravian Folksongs* (XIII/1), which Bartoš and Janáček had first published in 1890, for a new edition of this little volume. A second edition had come out in 1892; now Bartoš proposed an expanded edition that would include Bohemian and Slovak songs – this would do the book no harm in sales outside Moravia. The title could then become *A Bouquet of Czecho-Slavonic Folksongs.*[20] By his next letter, 19 September, Bartoš announced that there were only a few copies left of the second edition and he now made concrete proposals for expansion: twelve songs to be taken from Kadavý's *Slovak Songs* (Turčanský sv. Martin, 1880–1907), i.e. from a Slovak collection still in progress, and six from Erben's classic Bohemian collection *Czech Folksongs and Nursery Rhymes* (Prague, 1862–4). He had already had the songs copied out and wanted Janáček's approval and suggestions for any further expansions.[21] Ten days later, the additional songs had settled down to an extra twenty-five, but this, Bartoš thought, might put up the price too much (the book was used as a singing book for schools) and asked if Janáček could suggest deleting some of the longer ones.[22] Ultimately the additions were reduced to twenty-one, bringing the original total of 174 to 195, and the revised collection went off to

Šolc on 3 October.[23] Janáček meanwhile seems to have been getting on with the introduction to *Moravian Folksongs Newly Collected*. Although none of Janáček's letters to Bartoš from this period survive, a comment in Bartoš's letter of 12 December indicates that Janáček had suggested omitting discussion of dances from the introduction, a decision that Bartoš happily endorsed – he was worried that the introduction would blow up the book out of all proportion.[24]

With what appears to be a lessening load as far as *Moravian Folksongs Newly Collected* was concerned, Janáček at last began to get back to composition. In 1900 his pupil František Vojtěchovský (who had sung in various Janáček concerts, including the first performance of the *Hukvaldy Folk Poetry in Song* v/4, 1898) had moved to a new position at the Teachers' Institute in Příbor and seems to have asked Janáček if he had any choruses that could be performed. Janáček responded on 17 July 1900 with 'two little choruses';[25] a letter to Vojtěchovský two months later requested the return of the 'Haná choruses'.[26] The only choruses Janáček wrote that can be described in this way are two of his *Four Moravian Male-Voice Choruses* (iv/28), *If only you knew* and *The Evening Witch*, both composed on poems taken from Ondřej Přikryl's *Haná Songs*, i.e. written in the distinctive Haná dialect of east-central Moravia. The choruses, which were later absorbed into a collection of four published in 1906, were a new departure both in the striking setting of the words and the use of an authored text in dialect.

Little is known about the beginnings of an equally important departure in Janáček's piano music, other than that a request for harmonium arrangements of folksongs from Josef Vávra (see chap. 36) turned miraculously three years later into the stimulus for some of Janáček's finest miniatures for piano, *On the Overgrown Path* (viii/17). The nature of the work, its inspiration, its programme and titles are described in chap. 38. Seven pieces were in existence by 22 October 1900, when Vávra wrote to Janáček looking forward to receiving his 'moods'; at least some of these pieces took their inspiration from Janáček's family holidays in Hukvaldy.

In retrospect, it is clear that with such pieces as *Hospodine!* (iii/5), *Amarus* (iii/6), the Haná choruses (iv/28) and *On the Overgrown Path* Janáček had found a distinctive compositional voice and was beginning to rebuild his confidence. An important stage in his rehabilitation as a composer was of course to hear pieces in performance, particularly

Amarus, written for full chorus and soloists. Janáček had tried out the purely orchestral epilogue at his Czech National Orchestra concert in 1898. He now attempted to get a performance of the whole work and sent the score to Ferdinand Vach, with whom he had many professional dealings and who since 1895 had been working at the Teachers' Institute in Kroměříž. Vach was a highly experienced choir trainer and choral conductor, having been chorusmaster of 'Moravan', one of Moravia's leading choral societies in Kroměříž, since 1887. By the 'half-year holidays' in 1900 (i.e. February) Vach had studied the work and was full of enthusiasm, though he raised doubts over the difficult orchestral parts:

I really *very much like* your romance *Amarus* and expect that it will be a true delight not only for musicians but also for amateurs with their hearts in the right place!

I mustn't, however, deny that before I got down to a real study of the work, I had doubts that we would be able to perform at all. The chorus will be the best possible. The baritone part will be sung by Dr Alois Daněk, a solicitor in Uherské Hradiště, and for the tenor part I have invited Dr Hugo Richter, a solicitor in Lipník.

But whether our country orchestra will be up to its quite difficult role I really don't know.

I must first let you know at least about the numbers:

The orchestra is made up of amateurs plus the town band and comprises: 6 first violins, 5 second violins, 4 violas, 3 cellos, 3 double basses; 2 flutes, 2 clarinets, 4 horns, 2 trumpets, 3 trombones, 1 timpani. Oboes and bassoons we don't have at all, and also we can never get them even for big money [. . .].

Please answer me soon what you think about it yourself or whether we would be able to get them from Brno (but *good ones!!!*) – and above all not *expensive!*[27]

By the end of February, it was clear that Vach's fears were justified. Writing on Tuesday 27 February, Vach reported to Janáček that he had come away from the first combined orchestral rehearsal in despair. Although the choir was ready, the amateur orchestra, despite a rehearsal beginning at 6.30 and ending at 11.45 p.m., had not been able to go through the final movement, the funeral march, and they would probably have to omit it. Vach begged Janáček to get to Kroměříž for the first chorus and orchestra rehearsal the next day and advise them. The concert, at which a large attendance was already promised, was set for Sunday 4 March.[28]

The absence of any more letters from Vach suggests that Janáček did indeed arrive, and the decision was taken to postpone the concert until later in the spring. In his next surviving letter, Vach announced that the concert was further postponed to the autumn.[29]

But even this delay did not save the situation. *Amarus* was finally set for Sunday 2 December 1900, when it was to be performed by 'Moravan' under Vach; the concert also included Fibich's *Spring Romance*. The orchestra, however, continued to give concern and in desperation Vach suggested that the work be performed with piano accompaniment instead. At this point, just a few days before the concert, Janáček descended on Kroměříž and took over the final rehearsals himself, some of which lasted until two in the morning. Even drastic measures such as transposing the whole of the first movement from Janáček's favourite (but difficult) key of A flat minor to A minor – an instant solution that remains perpetuated in the score – and the omission of the purely orchestral funeral march did not help. Despite professional stiffening from Brno in the form of the missing oboes and bassoons, the orchestra was simply not up to it. The performance was poor and, during the orchestral interludes, Janáček painfully found himself longing for Vach's carefully prepared chorus to come and rescue the situation.[30] Almost a quarter of a century later the *Amarus* première still haunted him and in his autobiography he recorded his feelings about it: 'Oh, that I took up the baton for the première of *Amarus* in Kroměříž! I still regret it today. *Amarus* "swam". Butterflies [i.e. false notes] flew in alarm from the orchestra and chorus.'[31]

For one more year *Moravian Folksongs Newly Collected* (XIII/3) dominated Janáček's free time. He and Bartoš were, however, getting near the end of proofing the songs: on 27 March 1901 Bartoš wrote to say that there were another three or four signatures to go,[32] though the pace had now slowed down considerably: by 5 June Bartoš was again complaining about the printers not producing anything.[33] There were of course other tasks remaining before publication. On 12 August Bartoš announced that he had sent off the main index: a list of text incipits,[34] which runs to twenty pages in double columns. Bartoš took great pains over this and made a special point of differentiating texts which begin with the same words by extending them to the point where differences emerge. At this stage Janáček was working on the introduction. He appears to have sent it to the academy by early July 1901, since in his letter of 10 July Bartoš passed on the academy's comments about it: that the style would need some adjustment and that there were too many music examples,[35] the latter concerns understandable given that there is hardly a page in his 136-page 'treatise' ('rozprava', as he calls it himself on p. ii) that does not contain several. Were there even more originally, or did Janáček get his way? Work at the printers went on right to the final month of the year. On 6 December Bartoš wrote to say that he was sending the proof of Janáček's introduction to him and that he was glad all was printed;[36] the index proofs, however, were still being worked on and, as Bartoš wrote on 11 December, were 'probably printed by now'.[37] One cannot be absolutely sure that the second volume (completing the collection and including Janáček's introduction and indexes) was out by the end of the year to justify the publication date of '1901' on the title page; Bartoš received author copies only in February the next year (see chap. 42).

Janáček's introduction, *The Musical Side of Moravian Folksongs* (xv/163), was an extraordinary achievement. It is massive, detailed and utterly idiosyncratic. He divided it into seven parts: two enormous sections on rhythm and tune, then five shorter sections dealing with 'construction and typical traits', 'size of sections and length of songs', 'conspicuous features or truth in songs', 'musicians and the harmonic aspects of folk music' and, finally, 'church songs'. Janáček's individuality is evident on almost every page. What folklorist would open an account of rhythm in Moravian folksong with twenty pages of speech melodies before quoting a single folksong? While in the section on tunes there is plenty of comment on the typical melodic curves of folksongs, demonstrated with a wealth of examples (e.g. pp. lviii–lxi), this is put into a context of typical shapes in spoken speech melodies. Janáček's point about how speech melodies provided evidence of states of mind crops up in the fifth section, in which he demonstrates how sorrow, fear, warning and laughter etc. affect the character of the songs.

All this, it could be argued, is evidence of Janáček the dramatist getting in the way of Janáček the ethnographer. So it is Janáček's comments on the instrumental aspects that remain the most useful for the discipline. Folksongs are usually collected and discussed simply as tunes (without accompaniment or harmony) but, as Janáček had observed, Moravian folksong was distinctive in its range of accompaniments – bagpipe, cimbalom or instrumental ensemble – and the most valuable part of his introduction deals with these aspects and includes many of his own transcriptions. Such aspects are not confined to section 6; in his discussion of folksong tunes, a particularly fascinating passage is on how the accompanying instruments, whether bagpipe, cimbalom or violin, have affected the type of sung tune (pp. lxiv–lxxvi).

Janáček signed this preface himself and it is evident from its contents that Bartoš had very little to do with it. He consulted Bartoš about the final section, on church songs (see above), and an intriguing and typically terse account in Janáček's autobiography about their collaboration suggests that Bartoš was aware of its contents: 'Bartoš came every other day with a batch of songs. They were chosen and evaluated. At Mlatcová I read to the sick man my introduction to the bulky volume of songs. The Czech Academy published it. On the way to Zlín we parted for ever.'[38] Janáček did indeed make a trip to Bartoš's retirement home in the village of Mlatcová on Easter Sunday 7 April 1901: travel arrangements are outlined in Bartoš's letter of 5 April.[39] The chief difficulty with this account is that there is no evidence that Bartoš was unwell during 1901 (he suffered a major illness only the next year, see below). The energy of his letters suggests a particularly active sixty-four-year-old, and in Bartoš's letter of 20 March it is, instead, Janáček's health that is causing concern: 'I am sorry to hear that your health is not serving you well. At your age a fellow has to jump over nine fences in one leap. Go for lots of walks, as I do. My health, thank God, is good so far although I work lots and lots.'[40]

During 1901 Bartoš and Janáček also worked on the third edition of the *Bouquet of Moravian, Slovak and Czech Folksongs* (XIII/2), as it was finally called. Proofs arrived in March and evoked Bartoš's usual choleric response:

I have never had such a miserable printer as this famous Unie. The text is so unclear and smudged that one has to take a magnifying glass to help, they don't even have enough figures for the numbers,[§] and the music etc.! And what a wait before one gets this little signature. I've written there twice, but never anything.[41]

The result was not quite as awful as one might have expected. The third edition was completely reset, with minor style changes. 'This famous Unie' was clearly a more utilitarian printer than Jos. R.

[§] Probably a reference to the movable type from which the collection was set.

Vilímek (the publisher of the earlier editions), which had placed at the end of almost every song one of a variety of little fleurons, no doubt to complement the floral metaphor of the title. Unie had precisely one fleuron at its disposal and this is repeated ad infinitum throughout the book, which was issued in a slightly larger format and on inferior paper. That it was a careless production is evident from the pagination, which slips mysteriously from p. 20 to p. 32, although the numbers of the songs do not indicate any gaps. The process seems to have been over by the middle of the year, when Bartoš received a fee of 120 K and wondered whether it was for him alone or to be shared between the two of them.[42] Interestingly, Janáček continues to be given on the title page (as he was in the earlier editions) as 'Lev Janáček', the last time he so appeared in print.

The work on the *Bouquet* stimulated Janáček into publishing more accompaniments for some of the songs. This had always been planned: in 1892, when Janáček had published fifteen songs with accompaniments under the same title (*A Bouquet of Moravian Folk-songs*, v/2), the volume was designated 'sešit 1' ['first fascicle']. Possibly this was going on quietly anyway: the song that Janáček wrote into Olga's commonplace book, *Uncertainty* (see chap. 33), is one of the few scraps of evidence that Janáček may have been squirrelling away further arrangements during these years. The topic was discussed in his correspondence with Bartoš: 'don't forget that in the second [*recte* third] edition we also have Slovak and Czech songs, and some of these certainly deserve to be harmonized [. . .]. But don't harmonize them only for virtuosos like yourself – have a care for weaker performers.'[43] Needless to say Bartoš's advice was thoroughly ignored, whether regarding the choice of the songs or the type of accompaniment. When Šolc brought out a second volume (probably in 1901) with a further thirty-eight songs, Janáček's accompaniments remained as distinctive – and as difficult – as their fifteen predecessors.

Despite his very intensive work on the preface to *Moravian Folk-songs*, during May and early June 1901 Janáček found time to work on a new composition, *Our Father* (iv/29). The piece was prompted by further fundraising for the Women's Shelter and is his only exercise in the curious but popular nineteenth-century genre, the *tableau vivant*, in which actors silently portray a series of scenes to musical accompaniment – a remnant of this tradition survives in the 'visions' at the end of Smetana's *Libuše*. It seems to have been put together hurriedly.

Janáček was sketching it only a month before (judging from a page of sketches that he made on the verso of a letter to him dated 6 May 1901); some of the copied parts were dated the day of the first performance. The forces were modest: mixed choir and tenor accompanied by piano and harmonium. The single performance took place on 15 June 1901 in the Brno Theatre, where the tableaux were enacted by the amateur theatre club 'Tyl'.[II] The performers included two of Janáček's associates from the Organ School – Max Koblížek (conductor), and a recent graduate, Ludmila Tučková (piano) – and the tenor Zdeněk Lev (Miroslav Lazar), who had given the first performance of Janáček's *Spring Song* (v/3).

The inspiration of the piece is curious: a set of eight paintings by the Polish painter Józef Męcina-Krzesz illustrating the words of the Lord's Prayer. The pictures had been exhibited in Vienna and Warsaw in 1899 and reproduced, together with a long article about them, in the Warsaw illustrated weekly *Tygodnik illustrowany* on 28 October that year. According to Vogel,[44] this issue of *Tygodnik illustrowany* was lent by an unnamed Brno teacher to the committee of the Women's Shelter and seems to have set this strange event in motion. The originals of the painting have disappeared, probably in the Second World War, so that the black and white reproductions in *Tygodnik illustrowany* are today all that is left of Janáček's initial inspiration. Mostly depicting rather Russian-looking peasants in moments of religious awe, the paintings are an undistinguished example of late nineteenth-century sentimentalized religious art and it is difficult to see what attracted Janáček to them.

Janáček reduced the eight scenes to six, all carefully contrasted and interspersed with substantial instrumental interludes to allow for the new stage groupings to form. The first ('Our Father') is mostly a sober two-part canon, with an effective repeated unison setting of the phrase 'Hallowed be thy name'. The following numbers (based on the consecutive phrases from the prayer) all carry allusions to more popular styles (see chap. 35) and most have exactly repeated sections to ease listening (as a whole Janáček seems to have deliberately written a work with a broad appeal), or possibly to save composition time. The

[II] The Circle of Theatrical Amateurs was founded in Brno in the 1880s. In 1897 it changed its name to the Society of Theatrical Amateurs 'Tyl' (after the playwright Josef Kajetán Tyl) and frequently appeared in the Besední dům and other venues. Between 1897 and 1931 it gave over 560 performances, mainly of Czech plays.

hurried nature of the work's production may have affected Janáček's initial view of its quality. Bartoš, with whom Janáček was in regular touch at the time, complained that he had not been told that the event was taking place – otherwise he might well have attended, he wrote;[45] even more extraordinary, however, is the fact that Olga and Zdenka were not there, but had gone to Hukvaldy on the day of the première (in a joint letter they announced their arrival and enquired how it all went).[46] Nevertheless it seems to have gone well, and in her letter the next day Olga commented on an enthusiastic report from Stejskalová. Olga wrote that she had 'great pleasure in Daddy's success': Stejskalová had told her all about it and she really regretted that she hadn't been in Brno on Saturday for the performance.[47] Janáček himself seems to have been happy with it and thought well enough of it five years later to sanction a performance in Prague.

Olga went to Hukvaldy on 15 June and stayed there throughout the summer. Zdenka accompanied her, left her with her aunt and uncle (Josefa Dohnalová and her husband Jindřich Dohnal, who had moved back to Hukvaldy in 1901 when Dohnal became headmaster of the local school)[48] and then returned to Brno. On 17 June Olga wrote home under the unaccustomed heading of 'Dear Mummy and Daddy':[49] she even makes a point of stating that she had never done so before. One of the reasons for her staying in Hukvaldy on her own was that she wished to take part in some amateur dramatics there. Janáček's permission was sought and given, providing it was only a short role. His comments on this underline what he expected actors, and presumably singers, to undergo:

You know that all agitation at the present time is debilitating for you. A role in the theatre should be played *with truthfulness*, i.e. it is necessary to experience it really spiritually even on the boards: only then is the play *truthful!*

Consequently if the role is long, the scenes agitating, it becomes just as fatal as real, agitating life.¶

'Life in the theatre' took Mrs Hybnerová [sic]** down to her grave before her time.

¶Janáček's close conjunction of life and art in the theatre is reminiscent of his deeply felt reading of literature when a student in Leipzig (see chap. 15).
**Anna Hübnerová (1861–91) was an amateur actress and well-known figure in women's cultural and charitable circles. In the last year of her life she acted with the much depleted company at the Brno Theatre, playing many leading roles including those in Preissová's *The Farm Mistress* and *Her Stepdaughter*.

In that case I wouldn't advise you to play at all.
If it is a short role, relaxed – well, so be it.[50]

In the same letter of 4 July Janáček mentions that he had finished teaching and was looking forward to 'walking in the woods'. He wrote the last phrase in Russian, perhaps anticipating the arrival of his brother František from St Petersburg with his wife Marie. On 24 June František had written enthusiastically about their approaching visit. 'It's worked, I've managed to get thirty-five days leave so that, providing you'll be in Hukvaldy, we'll meet up over perhaps three weeks. Hurrah! How we will celebrate I can't even write – we simply can't wait.'[51] On 14 August, on their way back, František and his wife sent a postcard from Warsaw,[52] so it looks as though their three-week holiday in Hukvaldy began in the last week of July. Certainly they were all assembled by 2 August, when a joint expedition including František, Marie, Zdenka and Leoš sent a card from Radhošt' to Olga (left in Hukvaldy because of the steep climb).[53] It was at the family gathering in Hukvaldy that the decision was finally taken that Olga would go to St Petersburg the next year to improve her Russian.[54] The idea had been floating around for a year or two[55] but developments in Olga's relationship with Otakar Vorel seem to have precipitated the plan into action.

In her memoirs Zdenka Janáčková recalled that during 1900 and the first part of 1901 more damning evidence of Vorel's behaviour accumulated, including news that he was unfaithful to Olga. At last even Olga's feelings towards him changed and some time after the summer of 1901 she wrote to him breaking off relations. His reaction was unexpected: he said he would shoot her if he met her in the street. Although Zdenka took fright, Olga was unimpressed and she threw herself into preparing for state examinations in Russian. This was exactly what Janáček and his wife wanted for their daughter, and with the increasingly cordial atmosphere in the family that this new decision engendered, Zdenka at last confessed to her husband what had been going on and saying that Olga, of her own accord, had stopped any further contacts with Vorel. What they all feared, however, was Vorel's return from Vienna. František Janáček's invitation to spend time in St Petersburg seemed heaven-sent: it got Olga out of Brno and gave her an opportunity to improve her Russian. She would be there, it was planned, for about five months from March 1902 until the summer.

Olga redoubled her Russian studies and began to make preparations at once.[56]

And while Olga's thoughts began to turn to Russia, Janáček's returned to *Jenůfa*. Quite when is unknown. A simple voice-part sketch to words from Act 2 Scene 3 that he jotted down on the envelope of a letter sent to him in Hukvaldy by Olga on 30 December confirms that he was at work on the opera at least before the end of 1901. What with his arrangement of the Liszt Mass (XII/4, completed by early October; see chap. 18) and his heavy teaching commitments, the date may well be no earlier than November 1901.

At last he had the time: his biggest burden over the last few years, the huge folksong collection and its substantial introduction, was out of the way. If Janáček had abandoned *Jenůfa* because of inadequacies he had sensed as a dramatic composer, he had done much in the interim to put this right. A completely new development, maybe spurred on by Dvořák's criticism of the word-setting in *Amarus*, had been Janáček's exploration of speech melodies, a change signalled in his response in 1898 to the Brno Theatre questionnaire about a '*genuinely Czech, genuinely Moravian*' style, when he suggested that speech melodies showed the way to achieve this goal. It is possible that the theatrical dimension of *Our Father* provided yet another link back to the opera.

But Janáček had learnt one more important thing during the time away from *Jenůfa*, in his compositions *Amarus* and *On the Overgrown Path*. In these Janáček had composed pieces with a distinctive personal voice by writing out of his own experience. These are Janáček's first pieces – in a whole line – with a discernible autobiographical stratum. Perhaps the most compelling reason for him to get back to *Jenůfa* – after a five-year break – was the discovery of a new autobiographical link between the opera and his own life (see chap. 40).

40

Music as autobiography I

It took a long time for Janáček to find himself as a composer. Most successful composers will have written a few distinctive works by the age of thirty but Janáček only begins to sound like himself in the second half of the 1890s, when he was well into his forties. Circumstances dictated his late beginnings; none of his student works, whether liturgical in Prague or instrumental in Leipzig, show any glimmer of an individual voice. This was not their object. Janáček was learning craft and competence, the 'iron cloak' of technique that he mentions in a letter of 22–3 November 1879 to Zdenka from Vienna.[1] The early choruses are pleasant enough though they mostly stick to their Křížkovský heritage; his first opera Šárka was a fine achievement but again is an opera written consciously within a tradition. After that, much of Janáček's energies were taken up with collecting, editing and promoting Moravian folk music.

Jenůfa was the transition work, arising originally out of his enthusiasm for the folk music of Slovácko and the new verismo world that Mascagni had opened up for him in Cavalleria rusticana. But hardly had he completed an act than he came across an even more potent stage work, Tchaikovsky's Queen of Spades; after seeing it in Brno on 16 January 1896 Janáček put away his own opera for over five years. These years were not compositionally barren; once he got back from Russia in the summer of 1896 he began Amarus (III/6), a substantial cantata for chorus, orchestra and several soloists, but thereafter his time was increasingly taken up with his editorial work on Moravian Folksongs Newly Collected (XIII/3), which went on with Bartoš at an unrelenting pace over several years. It was only towards the end of 1901 that he had more time on his hands.

It is easy enough to abandon an ambitious project that is not going well, especially if one feels that one is not up to writing it. But to return to a major work abandoned for five years needs some special incentive, quite apart from having the time or feeling better equipped. By 1901 Janáček was certainly much more confident and accomplished as a composer. In two of the pieces written during his five-year sabbatical from opera, his cantata *Amarus* and the keyboard miniatures *On the Overgrown Path* (VIII/17), he had learnt one particularly important lesson. By writing from his own pain he had, in these pieces, at last composed works with a distinctive personal voice. These are Janáček's first compositions with a discernible autobiographical basis.

In this and later companion chapters, links between Janáček's works and his life will be examined. Connections between artists' lives and their works constitute a fraught and much debated area, and the easiest course is to leave them well alone. In Janáček's case this is hard to do since the connections were ones to which he continually drew attention; as I shall argue, they seem in some way to have been connections that shaped the works and explain something of his mind.

From early on Janáček found it difficult to disentangle life and art, as for instance in his extraordinarily involved reading of Bulwer Lytton's novel *A Strange Story* (see chap. 15) or his advice to Olga about how acting might affect her constitution (see chap. 39). The impact of his lived life on his works is claimed as early as 1879, for instance in a letter to Zdenka that she was the inspiration for the 'Zdenči-Leoš Fugue' (x/6 no. 14; see chap. 13); this composition, however, like all the Leipzig fugues, has disappeared and there is no mention of any such connection after Leipzig until some sixteen years later. It may well be that the concept of speech melody, wherein Janáček believed he was tapping into people's emotions and deepest feelings, had something to do with the revival of this topic. Maybe, as he thought more about it, he realized how important his own feelings could be for intensifying his musical language, for making it more direct and concrete. In the specific case of *Jenůfa*, identifying a personal link with the opera may at any rate have got him back to writing it after a five-year pause. His return to *Jenůfa* came about, I suggest, through the perception of a new autobiographical link between the opera and his own life, a link between his protective relationship to his daughter Olga and the protective relationship of the Kostelnička towards her stepdaughter Jenůfa.

The autobiographical parallels in *Amarus* and *On the Overgrown Path* are ones that Janáček himself acknowledged and pointed out to commentators. During the preparation of his Janáček biography in 1924, for example, Max Brod invited Janáček to say something about *Amarus*. Janáček responded by mentioning the connections between the story his cantata tells and his upbringing at the Augustinian monastery; a connection that made it 'easy to compose' such a piece (see chap. 33). Much earlier, when publishing five pieces from *On the Overgrown Path* in *Slovanské melodie* in 1900–01, Janáček gave nothing more away than the title. In 1908, however, when he was in negotiation with Jan Branberger over their publication with more such pieces, he was pressed into saying something about their 'poetic contents'; all sorts of recollections started tumbling out that revealed the music was prompted by 'memories of long ago'. Furthermore, many of these pieces that Janáček now added to the cycle were connected with the painful events in Hukvaldy during Olga's last summer (see chap. 38).

The most intriguing of these autobiographical connections, however, are not those to which Janáček readily conceded but in the one work where they need to be teased out – in his opera *Jenůfa*. Since January 1900 the Vorel affair had gone on in the background (see chap. 39) but, as Zdenka makes clear, it was a burden borne only by her and by Olga. Janáček expressed his views on Vorel, issued his instructions, and then ignored the problem. But by the end of 1901 the family was united in its opposition to Vorel, and had a plan for resisting his threat. Janáček, who was later to seize on the most trivial of personal connections as compositional aids, may have seen a parallel between his wayward daughter Olga, now united in policy with him, and Jenůfa after the crisis at the end of Act 1. Both Jenůfa and Olga had been 'led astray' by an unsuitable suitor (Števa/Vorel). In her dramatic entry in Act 1 the Kostelnička had made her opposition clear to Jenůfa's prospective match; so had Janáček in connection with Olga, when he had heard stories about Vorel. In both cases the match could go ahead if certain conditions were met (that Števa gave up drinking for a year/that Vorel qualified in medicine). Between Acts 1 and 2 of *Jenůfa*, Jenůfa has told her stepmother about her pregnancy (just as Olga had confessed to her father what had been going on with Vorel) and this resourceful woman conceived a plan: she announces that Jenůfa had gone off to work in Vienna, though meanwhile concealing her at home until her time for

515

delivery had come. And, in the same way, Janáček now grasped at the scheme of sending Olga to St Petersburg until the Vorel crisis had been weathered. The connections between Janáček's opera and his relationship with his daughter seem to have been understood within the family. 'My husband [Zdenka declared in her memoirs] also used to say later that his basic model for Jenůfa was his sick daughter.'[2] Stejskalová perhaps revealed more than she realized when she wrote: 'Sensitive as he was, he put his pain over Oluška into his work, the suffering of his daughter into Jenůfa's suffering. And that tough love of the Kostelnička – that's him, there is much of his own character in this part.'[3]

Janáček got back to *Jenůfa* against the background of preparations for Olga's trip to St Petersburg. When the news from there came about her illness, her recovery and her relapse this seems, if anything, to have spurred on his efforts rather than halted them. Essentially two acts of the opera were written in sixteen months, after more than five years of inactivity. And as the news got worse and worse, Janáček seems to have redoubled his effort to finish the opera so he could at least play it to his daughter on her deathbed. The work was dedicated to Olga – appropriately in Russian. When she was buried, Janáček placed the final sheet of his manuscript of the opera in the coffin.[4]

41

Janáček's finances I: to 1903

by JIŘÍ ZAHRÁDKA

The 1850s and 1860s were characterized by the economic boom of the Austro-Hungarian monarchy. In 1857 the Austrian *zlatník* [German: Gulden = florin] system was introduced. The basis of the new Austrian currency became the customs pound of 500 grams, divided according to the decimal system, from which 45 silver *zlatníky* were struck. The *zlatník* (Fl) was divided into 100 *krejcary* [German: Kreuzer]. Beside the silver *zlatník* and copper *krejcar* coins, paper banknotes were issued – the so-called *zlaté* (zl).* General economic growth was interrupted by the long-drawn-out economic crisis of the years 1873–96, with the greatest slump taking place in the 1870s. However the 1880s and the first half of the 1890s constituted a new phase of industrialization in Austria and, after overcoming the European economic crisis of the 1870s, the bases were created for the stabilization of the currency. In 1892 the modernized economy and the social advancement in the Austro-Hungarian monarchy brought about the introduction of a new, gold-based currency in which the pure content of 1 kg of gold was expressed by the value 3280 K. This was the *koruna* (K; German: Krone = crown), divided into 100 *haléře* (German: Heller = heller) and, in relation to the previous currency, worth half a *zlatník* (1 *zlatník* = 2 *koruny*). From the introduction of the new currency in 1892 to 1899 both currencies existed side by side as legal tender. From 1900 only the *koruna* was used.

---

* Czech spelling rules dictate that the abbreviation is given with a full stop (zl.). In this book, however, the abbreviation is harmonized with other currency symbols, thus omitting the full stop (zl).

The financial situation of the young Leo Janáček was very unfavourable at the time of his arrival as a chorister at the Augustinian monastery in Staré Brno in 1865. The reason for this was that his father Jiří was not well off and the family's modest financial circumstances deteriorated still further after his death in 1866. While food and accommodation were provided by the foundation, clothing and school books were paid for by his uncle, Father Jan Janáček, via Father Method Vyskočil and Father Pavel Křížkovský. In 1870 Janáček was awarded a scholarship at the Teachers' Institute. Originally 50 zl a year, it was increased to 100 zl. Two years after finishing his studies at the institute, Janáček requested the possibility of teaching without pay at the institute's practice school in order to gain the necessary work experience for getting a paid position as a teacher. His post as choirmaster in 'Svatopluk' was similarly unsalaried. So, too, were his first years of conducting the monastery choir at Staré Brno following Pavel Křížkovský, although it brought certain perks such as free lunches and suppers in the monastery refectory.

The situation at the monastery probably changed in the 1880s. A memorandum Janáček wrote in 1889 indicates that he got 170 zl from the Staré Brno monastery. It is possible that this could have been a one-off payment, for instance for the performance of festive music. The same memorandum refers to a deduction of 340 zl for the monastery, though the significance of this is unclear: was he perhaps paying for certain benefits or repaying a loan? While in Janáček literature and in the memoirs of contemporaries, the post is talked of as unsalaried, it seems probable that from 1881 Janáček was paid as choir director at the monastery. In her memoirs Zdenka Janáčková claims that from the time of their marriage Janáček was paid 15 zl a month by the Staré Brno monastery (i.e. 180 zl a year) and the sum of 170 zl from that institution in 1889 would seem to confirm this. Although the monastery account books are silent about any such sums, I have taken Zdenka Janáčková's recollection of a monthly fee of 15 zl to be valid from August 1881; only in 1889 have I made it correspond to Janáček's reference to 170 zl. There is no proof of when Janáček ended his activity in the monastery so I have taken the latest date suggested, 1891 (see chap. 10).

The overall agonizing financial situation in the first half of the 1870s for the young Janáček, who could earn money evidently only through giving private music lessons, was not resolved until he was awarded the post of provisional music teacher at the Teachers' Institute in Brno, which was accorded him in an edict of 30 August 1876. The salary at the Teachers' Institute was for many years Janáček's chief income. Although the basic pay of 800 zl a year was not large, it was increased by various additional payments such as the 'active supplement' of 240 zl a year (this seems to be some sort of personal bonus for conducting music at school church services and so on, but it is not clear whether this was a regular amount) and small extra payments for classes taught over and above the framework of his basic teaching commitment. In the school years 1876–7 and 1877–8 Janáček also taught the piano, violin and singing at the Czech Women Teachers' Institute in Brno. Here he taught for six hours a week for which he probably received some sort of payment. Since it is not possible even by analogy to estimate the relevant amount, this is not reflected in the table below. In the academic year 1886–7 Janáček began teaching singing at the Czech Gymnasium in Brno, where his first annual take-home pay was 200 zl. And evidently from 1898, when a new law was proclaimed relating to pay in education, he received 240 zl a year for four hours of teaching a week. This hourly rate was unchanged for the whole time of his work at the Gymnasium until 1902.

Janáček evidently gained further remuneration for his concert activity, articles and reviews for various periodicals. No documents survive, however, about what payment he received. Also, although his post in the Brno Beseda was honorary, from time to time his work there brought the odd small payment (100 zl each in 1878 and 1886, 50 zl in 1882).

In 1879 Janáček left to study at Leipzig and Vienna. While it is not documented whether he continued to be paid by the Teachers' Institute in 1879–80 (all classes were taken over for him by his colleagues) it is likely that he was, as Zdenka Janáčková mentions in her memoirs. There is proof that he paid for his studies in Leipzig in two instalments of 300 and 100 marks but in reality he may have paid more. In March 1880 Janáček was made a permanent teacher at the Teachers' Institute and was therefore able to claim a legal increase in his basic pay, which now became 1000 zl (a new decree in 1898 raised it further by 100 zl). The five-yearly increases of 100 zl, the so-called quinquennial supplements, followed (in 1885, 1890, 1895 and 1900). The amount was again raised by the 'active supplements', adjustments, small amounts from the examination commission and for social support (for instance in 1884 he received support for his sick mother).

After Janáček's marriage to Zdenka Schulzová in 1881 the young couple was supported for a short while by Janáček's father-in-law Emilian Schulz with a monthly amount of 25 zl, and extra payment for heating.

A further basic income came from the Organ School that Janáček founded in 1882, although he received larger amounts from it only when he retired from the Teachers' Institute. His annual salary from the academic year 1883–4 was 370 zl; that for 1890–1903 is estimated by analogy since the school records for these years have not survived.

Income from published compositions has for the most part not been recorded. In the few cases where this information is known, however, it is clear that very small amounts are involved: the publication by Winkler in 1886 of the *Four Male-Voice Choruses* IV/17, for example, brought Janáček 10 zl. One exception is the grant from the Czech Academy of Sciences in 1897 for the publication of the harmony manual *On the Composition of Chords and their Connections* (XV/151), for which he received 200 zl. Money was also remitted to him by František Bartoš for collecting and editing folksongs (in 1900 he received 600 K, in 1902 1439 K 86 h). As royalties for the ballet *Rákoš Rákoczy* (I/2) at the Prague National Theatre in 1891 Janáček received 117 zl 34 kr for seven performances (it is not known how much he received for the eighth performance; by analogy it would have been 16 zl 76 kr). On the other hand nothing is known about the financial arrangements for four performances of *The Beginning of a Romance* (I/3) at the Brno Theatre. It is, however, most likely that the amounts were negligible.

Leoš Janáček's outgoings for the period up to 1903 are largely a matter of speculation. The general family budget understandably varied according to the number of current dependents and thus was different in 1890, when the Janáčeks had two children, and different again after 1903, when they were alone again, both children having died. Examples of costs of basic foodstuff and clothing in 1883 are shown in table 41.2. Into the family budget must be taken the upkeep of the housekeeper Marie Stejskalová from 1894 and in the 1880s financial support for Janáček's mother. Two receipts have survived from 1889, when Janáček remitted 333 zl to each of his brothers František and Karel (evidently obligations connected with settling the estate of Jan Janáček). A substantial amount must have gone on visits to spas (for instance in 1888 Janáček paid out 240 zl), the trip to Russia and health treatments (Janáček's operation in 1893 cost 32 zl 50 kr). A large expense was represented by doctors' fees associated with the serious illness of his daughter Olga. The amount paid out for making copies of his compositions must also have been considerable. This work included two copies of the piano-vocal score and the first two acts of the score of his opera *Šárka*, and a copy each of the full scores of *Rákoš Rákoczy*, *The Beginning of a Romance* and *Jenůfa*. What these copyists received is not recorded, but analogous work from later periods suggests that Janáček must have paid them a total of several hundred zl by 1903.

As for tax, Janáček certainly paid it but the exact amounts are not known. For instance, for a salary in the tax band of 3600–3680 K, where Janáček would belong, the annual tax, according to the 1903 law, was 54 K. There would have been tiny amounts of further tax on receipts from compositions.

Overall it can be said that Janáček's gloomy financial situation of the 1870s improved and in the course of time corresponded to his social position as a teacher. While Zdenka Janáčková's memoirs allude to a continual financial crisis in this period, the couple's documented income doesn't suggest such an acute situation and instead indicates that Zdenka had difficulty in getting used to lower living standards than she had enjoyed with her own family, the Schulzes.

In table 41.1 the total income shown represents the lower threshold, as only documented income is given, or income that can be derived by analogy. Most of what is shown is regular income. With a few exceptions, income derived from the publication and performance of Janáček's work or from his concert activities is not shown. In summary, table 41.1 shows how between 1876, when he began to earn money, and 1903, when he was allowed to leave the Teachers' Institute on health grounds (he retired the next year), Janáček's income came above all from his activity as a teacher and only to a small degree from his compositions. By way of comparison, the annual salary of various teaching positions between 1870 and the 1890s is shown in table 41.3 alongside those of a town doctor and bricklayer.

THE BLACK RIBBON (1888–1903)

Table 41.1: Janáček's income 1876—1903

sources:

BmJA
Archiv města Brna (C.k. český ústav ku vzdělání učitelů v Brně, C.k. české státní nižší gymnázium v Brně, Český ústav pro vzdělávání učitelek, Archiv Národního divadla v Brně)
Moravský zemský archiv Brno (Varhanická škola v Brně, Augustiánský klášter sv. Tomáše na Starém Brně)
Státní ústřední archiv Praha (Archiv Národního divadla)
Archiv národního divadla Praha

(amounts are in zl to 1899; from 1900 in K)

year	Teachers' Institute	Czech Gymnasium	Organ School	Staré Brno monastery	other	total
1876	263	—	—	—	—	263
1877	1040	—	—	—	—	1040
1878	1107.95	—	—	—	100 (Brno Beseda)	1207.95
1879	1048	—	—	—	—	1048
1880	964	—	—	—	—	964
1881	1243.20	—	—	75	—	1318.20
1882	1280	—	90	180	50 (Brno Beseda)	1600
1883	1240	—	320	180	—	1740
1884	1340	—	370	180	—	1890
1885	1340	—	370	180	10 (Winkler)	1900
1886	1340	66	370	180	100 (Brno Beseda)	2056
1887	1340	200	370	180	—	2090
1888	1340	200	370	180	—	2090
1889	1340	200	370	170	—	2080
1890	1620	200	370	180	—	2370
1891	1620	200	370	180	117.34 (National Theatre, Prague)	2487.34
1892	1500	200	370	—	—	2070
1893	1472.66	200	370	—	—	2042.66
1894	1715.25	200	370	—	—	2285.25
1895	1580	200	370	—	—	2150
1896	1592	200	370	—	—	2162
1897	1540	200	370	—	200 (grant, Czech Academy)	2310
1898	1640	240	370	—	—	2250
1899	1640	240	370	—	10 (Bartoš)	2260
1900	3680	480	740	—	600 (Bartoš)	5500
1901	3680	480	740	—	—	4900
1902	3680	370	740	—	1439.86 (Bartoš)	6629.86
1903	3705.95	—	877	—	—	4582.95

Table 41.2: Examples of costs (in zl) of goods 1883

foodstuffs		clothing	
butter: 1kg	1.71	shirt	1.45–2.75
flour: 1 kg	0.21	1 pair trousers	4–9
lard: 1 kg	0.71	gentleman's suit	14–16
rice: 1 kg	0.18	overcoat	11–25
wine: 1 litre	0.15–18		

Tables 41.3: Examples of salaries 1870–90s

Year	profession, employment	annual salary (in zl)
1870	town doctor	600–1000
1871	head teacher	800
1871	teacher	600
1871	assistant teacher	360
1876	engineer, director of the Vítkovice iron works	1200 + 2000 from the prestige fund + 2% profits
1883	bricklayer	420
1888	works doctor	1900–3600
1889	general director of the Vítkovice iron works	2400 + prestige fund + 4% profits
1890s	policeman	700 + inflation supplement
1890s	state employee, 6th rank (Brno mayor)	3200–400 + 480 inflation supplement

42

1902–February 1903

In early February 1902 copies of *Moravian Folksongs Newly Collected* (XIII/3) became available: Bartoš had received twenty-four copies of the second and final volume and needed to know how many of these Janáček required.[1] In his reply – he wanted half – Janáček mentioned that he had 'written something about Pavel Křížkovský', for whose understanding it was good that their folksong collection was now available.[2] The article, a substantial piece entitled *The Importance of Pavel Křížkovský in Moravian Folk Music and in Czech Music as a Whole* (XV/166; see chap. 8), came about through 'Vesna'. On 26 February 1902 Janáček gave a lecture there with this title and it seems to have generated so much interest that he was asked to repeat it on 5 March.[3] The lecture may have been Janáček's way of drawing attention to his new folk collection, but instead of giving what could have been a boiled-down version of his long preface Janáček reminded his audience of the link between the publication of the first substantial collection of Moravian folksongs by Sušil and the creative response of the first substantial Moravian composer, Pavel Křížkovský, in his choral arrangements of some of the songs. The inference that could be made is that the new, equally substantial collection that he and Bartoš had just published might have a similar impact on Moravian composers. In fact this was happening at this very moment, with Janáček's resumption of work on *Jenůfa*.

Presumably he regarded his article as a significant statement and made sure it had wider currency by submitting it to *Český lid*, where it was processed with impressive speed. On 10 February the editor Čeněk Zíbrt acknowledged its receipt and said that he had sent it off to the printers.[4] Ten days later Zíbrt sent back the proof,[5] and a month later it was published and Janáček received his fee.[6] Janáček was doing rather well with his freelance activities. By then he had been paid the final instalment of his fee from the Czech Academy for *Moravian Folksongs Newly Collected*. In his usual punctilious way, Bartoš had sent his explanation of the accounts on 18 February, from which Janáček was to receive the total of 1427 K 11 h.[7]

The Křížkovský lecture was given again, if not as planned at 'Vesna' on 5 March then certainly at the more public venue of the Arts and Crafts Museum in Eliščina třída (now Husová) on 16 March under the aegis of the Club of the Friends of Art. This was an important point in Janáček's life. The club had begun its activities on 14 January 1900 principally to foster literature and the graphic arts – through lectures, outings, exhibitions, publications and the opening of a library and reading room. Although, according to its statutes, its aims also included 'the performance of musical and dramatic compositions' (which would have made it into a comparable outfit to the Umělecká beseda, the celebrated artistic organization founded in Prague in 1861), in the early years there was no evidence of any musical outlets and Janáček's lecture on a musical topic seems to have been the first.[8] It probably came about through his friend František Mareš, both the director of 'Vesna' and the club's first chairman. Janáček's repeat of his Křížkovský lecture was reported to be a great success and well attended.[9] And with his interest in his former teacher revived, Janáček published, in the continuing series of 'Czech Musical Currents' in *Hlídka*, a short motivic analysis of Křížkovský's chorus *The Drowned Maiden*, which appeared in the April fascicle (xv/167).

A notable development in family matters at the beginning of 1902 was the arrival in Brno of Věra Janáčková.[10] Věra was the daughter of Janáček's Prague cousin Augustin Janáček (who had died in 1900) and Josefa [Joza] Janáčková (1856–1937). At the age of eleven Věra (1891–1967) was dispatched to boarding school in Brno at 'Vesna', no doubt at Janáček's suggestion. Věra had started writing to Olga the previous autumn; although Věra and Janáček never really got on, she remained in touch until his death.

However, the big story of the time was Olga's trip to St Petersburg, which had been decided upon during the visit of František Janáček and his wife to Hukvaldy the previous summer. Having become anxious that he had no news, by 3 March 1902 František had heard from Janáček that all was going ahead as planned: 'It is excellent that your decision has not changed – I had already begun to doubt it.' In his usual practical way František had already made arrangements with a Russian language teacher, Mr Gordov, who was prepared to give Olga twice-weekly lessons until he left St Petersburg for his dacha during the summer. Mr Gordov needed information about the Austrian state examinations in Russian so that he could plan the course for her, and Janáček was asked to send information on this. František also sent practical advice for the journey:

> Further, as far as the passport is concerned don't forget that Olga will need a separate passport for herself and, naturally, confirmation from the Russian consulate in Vienna. I regard it as important to draw your attention to being careful in the carriage while travelling. At the present time one hears every-where how often people steal. [Be careful] especially while getting out at a station or leaving hand luggage without supervision and particularly don't be trusting towards your fellow travellers, as is your custom, Leo! One day you'll certainly pay for it. And you, Oluška, don't get excited, calm down, everything will be fine.

And he suggested a two-to-three-hour stop in Warsaw, where Janáček and his daughter could take a meal with Janáček's brother 'Fritz' (i.e. Bedřich Janáček), who lived near the railway station. Finally, all he needed was the date and time of their arrival.[11] On the letter Janáček jotted down the names of a couple of contacts to advise them on the Russian exams ('Kolář Josef: Russian teacher in Prague; Štěpánek Karel, teacher at the commercial academy, lecturer in the Russian language'). On 20 March Olga wrote to František in her best Russian saying when they would be arriving. What was no doubt intended as a comic formulation makes for bitter reading in the light of what happened: 'Dear uncle! If we don't die before then we will definitely arrive on Monday 24 March of our calendar, at eight in the morning. So wait for us then.'[12]

Janáček and Olga began their journey forty-eight hours earlier, their progress charted by a succession of postcards sent along the way to an anxious Zdenka. The first, postmarked 22 March, was from Přerov, only a couple of hours' travel away from Brno, where they had lunch.[13] They got to Trzebinia* that evening, and Olga announced that they were just about to cross the border and that her cough was better.[14] They arrived in Warsaw the next morning for breakfast (no mention of

* See chap. 33.

having it with Uncle Fritz)[15] and then boarded the train that would take them all the way to St Petersburg.[16] The sun was going down that evening when they passed Vilnius.[17] A final card from along the way was sent from the train as they passed the Russian town of Gatchina at seven the next morning, Monday 24 March. Gatchina presented a fairy-tale snow scene; they had slept like logs, Olga once again without coughing.[18] An hour later they were met in St Petersburg by František and warmly welcomed by his wife Marie. The next day Janáček and Olga wrote a joint postcard saying how nicely the flat was furnished, beautifully warm with no drafts, and that Olga's cough had 'definitely improved.'[19]

The continual references to Olga's cough reflect anxieties even before they left. Recounting her memoirs many years after the event, Zdenka described the time in melodramatically ominous tones:

In the early spring she began to cough so alarmingly that I took fright. I asked the doctor who was treating her what he thought about a stay in St Petersburg. He shrugged. Then I began to fear her departure, suddenly I couldn't imagine how we could live for five months so far from one another. I was dominated by a sort of presentiment that told me that the devil you know is the lesser evil than whatever awaits you in an unknown foreign country. Perhaps Olga caught it from me, perhaps she also felt something similar, but clearly she would have preferred now to remain at home. I mentioned this to my husband. He thought it was ridiculous. I began to ask him more and more urgently to leave Olga at home for me. But he was an enthusiastic Russophile and had fallen in love with the idea that Olga at any rate would be where he himself wanted to be. However, he didn't say this to me, only objecting, quite correctly: didn't I myself want Olga to be as far away from Vorel as possible? How was I to explain this dark fear of mine to him? He thought it was ridiculous, my fears sounded like feminine over-sensitivity, something to be discounted. He now got angry when I went on and on begging him. Olga said to me: 'Mamička, it's all useless. Surely you know that when Daddy's got the idea into his head, I must go, come what may.' [. . .] My husband had to pull her out of my arms when it was time to leave. I didn't have the strength to go with them to the station. It seemed to me that the world was falling apart.[20]

Janáček remained a couple of days in St Petersburg as Olga settled in. On 26 March the four of them visited the All-Russian Exhibition and all signed a reassuring postcard to Zdenka, written while they were in the café 'Paris'.[21] Two days later Janáček was off, again taking care to send a postcard to Zdenka just before he boarded the train, and mentioned that if the weather was fine he might stop off in Hukvaldy on Easter Sunday (30 March), arriving back home in Brno the next day.[22] Olga, meanwhile, started writing the 'Russian diary' that Janáček had suggested she keep during her stay in St Petersburg[23] and was reasonably punctilious about writing home. One of the highlights of her stay was a visit to the theatre to see Glinka's opera *A Life for the Tsar*, an event eagerly anticipated in her postcard of 5 April (mentioning how expensive it was and how hard it was to come by the tickets).[24] She described the event afterwards in her diary (11 April), fired with enthusiasm for the theatre, and the presence of so many 'muzhiks' in the audience, though surprisingly critical of the performance: the soprano was weak, the ladies sang Russian affectedly and as a whole it was no better than at home.[25]

Janáček's first letter written to Olga in St Petersburg is full of practical concerns about examinations and money, and provides one invaluable clue about the progress of *Jenůfa*:

I'm still waiting for Prof. Kolář's address. Write to him in Russian so he'll know at once how much you know. Tell him also that you want to take an examination of the sort that Maria K.N. Veveritsa did some time ago.

It's spring weather here but nevertheless cold. The bushes are just beginning to bud.

The theatre has left now [on its regional tour], so it's quiet.

I returned from St Petersburg in good health; they didn't have any heating on after the holidays in the school and at the institute, I caught a chill and lost my voice completely. It's better now.

I'm working very hard so that I can be finished with Act 2 by the holidays.

When it warms up where you are it will be more interesting for you to look around. So keep well and write in detail.

I wrote to your aunt and uncle at the same time as sending the money. Have you definitely got the 35 roubles? [. . .]
P.S. Do describe the Orthodox holidays.[26]

Given all the preparations for Olga's trip, the travelling and what seems like a bout of bad health, it is extraordinary to hear that Janáček was making good progress with his previously blocked opera and that he hoped to finish Act 2 by the summer holidays. But within days of writing this letter Janáček received the news not about the Russian Easter but that his daughter was in hospital with typhoid fever, then very common in St Petersburg. Her illness developed with alarming speed. In a postcard written home on 20 April she complained of pains in her head and stomach: 'it has caught me quite strongly'.[27] One tele-gram from František seems to have disappeared; but by 30 April he was able to send another saying that Olga was getting better and that a letter would follow.[28] Unless a letter has disappeared, it was only more telegrams that followed from František, one on 2 May saying that Olga was a bit better, as she had been the day before,[29] and one two days later suggesting that Zdenka come to St Petersburg.[30] Janáček responded to these the next day. He was comforted, he wrote to Olga, by the news that she was better. Although it was harder for her, he thought it best that Zdenka did not go to St Petersburg immediately (it turned out to be impossible anyway, given the slowness of the passport and visa formalities). He returned to the letter the next evening, by which time he had received a letter from František suggesting that Olga's health had been weakened in the preceding months through the efforts of sewing her outfits by day and learning Russian by night. Dismissing most of this, Janáček went on to outline his vision of Olga's future: she would not be just an ordinary teacher – she would not be up to the physical exertion – but something more interesting. So, if the doctors agreed, he suggested that she should stay in St Petersburg, not exerting herself by preparing for examinations, but instead perfecting herself in the spoken language.[31]

Two days later he wrote again, once more encouraging Olga not to slave over her books and not to overdo things by getting up too soon and returning to František's flat.[32] A week later Janáček was getting anxious that they had not heard from Olga,[33] but good news was already on the way in the form of a letter from Olga from the sanatorium. She had been allowed to get up on Monday 12 May and by 15 May (the day of her letter) she was sitting up at a little table writing a postcard to her parents. The illness, she declared, had been 'no joke' but she was drinking lots of kumis (fermented milk), beer and tea.[34] Of course it was no joke, Janáček immediately responded. But the tone of the letter, with its fussy instructions, clearly indicates that he regarded the crisis as over:

What's it like in your room? What are the sisters like attending you? I thank them that they are looking after you so nicely. [. . .] Don't forget to reward them worthily. Should I send you the standard 35 roubles now or should I wait until your uncle sends the whole bill? I'd like you *gratefully* and *properly* to take your leave from the hospital and from all who were around you. After all we can't thank them enough that they've got you well.

You shouldn't worry that I was a little disturbed by your silence of several days. After all such silence was a prelude to your illness. [. . .]

Don't have lessons from Mr Gordov until you're completely well again. When you're strong again then perhaps speaking to him won't do any harm. Chatting with the nurses has certainly helped you a lot. [. . .]

We have Whitsun holidays – with rain, cold – frost. We're still heating the house. Mother has gone off for two days to Vienna, so I'm sitting here alone.

Janáček added a postscript to this letter the next day, Whit Sunday, saying that next time he would send her a list of works of Russian literature to buy.[35]

Zdenka's absence in Vienna is another sign that she and Leoš thought that all was now well. In 1899 Zdenka's brother Leo (Leoš) Schulz had completed his schooling in Brno and, with Emilian Schulz now retired, the family had moved to Vienna where Leo began law studies.[36] If Zdenka had been to visit them before (it would be odd if she hadn't done so), this has not been recorded in any surviving correspondence or in her memoirs. Once in Vienna, however, Zdenka took her time returning, arriving back only on 21 May.[37] Once she was back in Brno Janáček, who, in her words, was 'attentive and gentle' towards her, suggested a trip to Vranov, a pilgrimage church some 10 kilometres from Brno with a well-known statue of the Virgin Mary. In her memoirs Zdenka makes a good story out of the trip to pray to the 'miraculous Madonna': that as they arrived at the church, a funeral procession was approaching – that of a young girl. Naturally she took it as a terrible omen though, with the passage of time, she linked it with the first news of Olga's typhoid fever (around 24 April) rather than with the news of her relapse.[38] The Vranov expedition is corroborated by a postcard to Olga that her parents posted on 30 May,[39] the day on which František wrote them a long letter[40] with bad news:

Again we rejoiced prematurely that Olga's health would be satisfactory from now on. Dr Botkin released her from the sanatorium because during the nice weather in the last few days she improved so much that he thought a further stay unnecessary. He advised her how to behave, what she must go on taking etc., etc. On Thursday [29 May] after lunch I brought Olga home, that night she slept heavily and got up in a good mood and cheerful, on Friday after lunch she went off to the [illegible] park, she returned also cheerfully and in a good mood and suddenly on Friday night she got ill, slept badly, got diarrhoea, her heart again was beating heavily, simply the whole thing began all over again as before – *luckily without a temperature or headache*. Naturally she remained in bed and around two after lunch I went again to get advice from Dr Botkin in the sanatorium about what to do and how to deal with her.

Dr Botkin, František went on to report, was surprised by the turn of events and promised to look in, which he did the next day (Sunday) after lunch. He said that she must stay in bed and he prescribed the same medicines as before. When František pressed him, the doctor maintained that Olga would be alright again but the changeable climate in St Petersburg was against her. Ideally she should be in the fresh air in light clothing and it would be best to get her to Hukvaldy as soon as she had recovered sufficiently. Although Dr Botkin was willing to take her back into the sanatorium, Olga herself was not keen and simply wanted to get home as soon as possible. So František advised that in 'three to four weeks' Zdenka should arrive and take her away. He would send them a telegram if there was any change for the worse. In a postscript he said that he was not telling Olga about the plan for Zdenka's trip, and asked Janáček and Zdenka not to refer to it in their letters,[41] an injunction completely ignored in Janáček's next letter.

Within a day of receiving the news, Janáček and Zdenka were off. 'Today's letter from your uncle had a terrible effect on us', Janáček wrote on Wednesday evening, 4 June.

Only from the fact that uncle wrote on Sunday, and that he hasn't so far sent a telegram, we assume, dear girl, that you're no worse. God grant that we're not disappointed. We're making quick preparations for mother to travel to you. If uncle wrote or sent a telegram that the illness has got worse then she'd leave on Thursday morning and be with you in St Petersburg on Saturday, at the same hour as we arrived. [. . .]

I'd accompany mother as far as Granica – then nothing more could happen to her in a woman's coupé. I'm writing at night. God be with you my girl. Be calm – you know what your illness is. Worrying about you and feeling with you, your Daddy, Leoš[42]

Although no further bad news came from František, anxiety seems to have energized Janáček and Zdenka to leave the next day, Thursday 5 June. Another change of plan seems to indicate further anxiety: instead of merely getting Zdenka across the border (at Granica), putting her on the St Petersburg train and then returning to Brno alone, Janáček continued with her all the way to St Petersburg, arriving on

7 June.[†] But, with teaching commitments in Brno still continuing, he needed to return home the next day. A postcard from Warsaw on 10 June charted the later stages of his return: 'I have just arrived in Warsaw [. . .] I didn't have such a comfortable journey – in particular a wretched night. But on the other hand there was a Russian gentleman's family with children and I wrote down many Russian speech melodies.'[43] Janáček had noted down six Russian speech melodies on the way to St Petersburg.[44] The fact that he wrote some ten times as many on the way back suggests both the freedom of not having to look after Zdenka and his more relaxed mood now that he had at least set eyes on his sick daughter and had left his wife to look after her.

From both his first letter written to Zdenka and Olga on his return to Brno[45] and his notebook[46] one learns that on the second night he had a place in a 'women's coupé', where his travelling companions included a Russian lady with two children (a little girl of five or six and her older brother Shura), a Bulgarian lady with an older girl, another lady, and an inspector of a Gymnasium from Moscow, a Czech by birth, who was returning to Bohemia to retire. It was, as Janáček noted, a 'very instructive journey'. The 'seventy-one' speech melodies (more like sixty)[47] that he jotted down have all the trivia of train journeys: distances, times, locations, children occupying themselves by counting or by reading (Zhukovsky in this case), the ladies fussing over tea. What was perhaps 'instructive' for Janáček was simply hearing lots of spoken Russian. The fact that he noted down isolated words and phrases rather than sentences, sometimes giving Czech equivalents or adding comments about the pronunciations, suggests an enthusiastic beginner rather than someone more linguistically experienced. Only twice in all this are there some indications of his feelings: before getting to Warsaw he records his 'hard tears for you, Olga'; and, at the end in his summary: 'What is my little soul doing in St Petersburg?'[48]

As soon as he got back to Brno, on Wednesday 11 June, he wrote to his wife: 'So I've arrived safely. The ground still wobbles beneath my feet; it's been quite a journey to travel 3000 versts [= 3201 km]. Especially when the first night I had to spend the night lying on that narrow bed by the window! There was a draft from the window, and I couldn't turn round.' The second night, as he had already reported, was better,

---

[†]A speech melody that Janáček noted in his diary, dated St Petersburg 6 June 1902 (quoted in Melnikova 1997, 342) would appear to be misdated: the Janáčeks could not have left before 5 June and the journey took a minimum of two days.

in his 'women's coupé'. Before sending the letter, however, Janáček waited for news from St Petersburg. Nothing arrived that evening and so he hung on until the next morning, when he heard that Olga still had a temperature (he reported that the letter had taken four days to arrive). At the same time as sending the letter, he told them, he was writing to Hukvaldy to make arrangements for the family to stay there when Olga was fit enough to travel.[49]

When Janáček wrote again, the weather was frightful ('terrible wind, storms and downpours are raging'; in Hukvaldy 'the whole countryside was under water!'). Janáček added that he had a guest, the Russian conductor (of the Russian embassy choir in Vienna) Anatoly Mikhailovich Arkhangel'sky. From St Petersburg there was still no 'comforting news' that Olga was out of bed.[50] The variation in Olga's temperature and the question of whether she was up and about provided the chief topics for her future letters from St Petersburg, events faithfully reflected in Janáček's almost daily replies. If there was good news from St Petersburg, Janáček would respond with general news from Brno; if the temperature was up again, Janáček would become an anxious and sympathetic father, offering advice and encouragement.

On 19 June Olga wrote that the doctors had allowed her to get up and she was just longing to return home.[51] Janáček's answer dated merely 'Sunday' (probably Sunday 22 June), provides one of the rare clues to the dating of his opera:

Dear Zdenka and Olguška

It has cleared up a little but where to go in Brno? To [illegible] – the emperor's forest[‡] – until one gets fed up with it. So I got down to work – until I finished Act 2. At least when we meet the holidays will be more pleasant for us.

I'm pleased that you're out of bed, Olga. After so many medicines your stomach won't be working properly for a while.

Do tune up the more cheerful strings – after all, the worst is behind you.

Don't forget the books!

My head, on the other hand, is as if stunned – I do so need a break now!

Well, three weeks today it [i.e. the school year] will all be over.

I wondered whether you couldn't leave on Friday – [. . .] Well, we'll see what you write to me. What are you doing today?

Máŕa [Marie Stejskalová] is cooking decently and doing her business well. [. . .]

‡ Now Wilson forest, near Staré Brno.

Well, I just hope that getting up won't do any harm.

Then it will be okay. These last days here have been a real torment for me. No work – just time ticking away.[52]

Having sent another anxious postcard on 26 June,[53] the next day Janáček was confronted with the news that Olga's temperature was up again:

Today's letter overwhelmed me as complete unhappiness. Poor thing, all that you have to go through!

Olguška, I beg you, if it's again a serious new illness, decide to go to hospital. Take a paid place so you would have the best treatment. They will perhaps allow Mummy with you?

I'm incapable of thought.

I'm prepared to take leave and come to see you.

Whether to live here in terrible agitation or with you – it makes no difference.

As soon as the illness has improved then leave there immediately.

In the present warm weather a patient too can travel by express rail if left on a made-up bed during the day.

From the fact that you, Zdenka, haven't written I see that I have nothing good to expect.

I don't want to send a telegram at night; I'll do so in the morning.

Dear Olguška, may God look after you and make you well.

Zdenka, take care of yourself at this difficult time.

In my thoughts only with you

your grieving Daddy Leoš[54]

The next day he wrote again. '(Saturday at night): I waited today for some sort of news with the morning and evening post. But nothing the whole time. [. . .] Perhaps diet will now bring down the temperature; to eat meat with a fever isn't a good idea [. . .].'[55] He continued the letter the following morning, having presumably received a telegram that Olga's temperature had now gone down:

Glory to the Lord God!

Oluška, you are fighting with nature, and you won't give up, and you'll get better, and it will be better.

I in turn [battle] with people through my thoughts and I also won't give up and we will both triumph. [. . .] Máŕa also sends greetings.[56]

Janáček's drawing of parallels between Olga's battle for health and his own creative battle is striking (see chap. 40). This relieved letter went on to mention a visit by 'Janáčková from Prague' (i.e. Joza Janáčková, perhaps visiting her daughter Věra at the 'Vesna' boarding school in Brno).

The news continued to improve, so that in his next letter three days later (Wednesday 2 July) Janáček could at last begin to make arrangements for Zdenka's and Olga's departure. And as he relaxed, he began to hand out his usual fussy instructions to both of them:

Dear Zdenka

From your letter today I judge that Olga will be out of bed next week and that you'll slowly be able to accustom her to the country air.

I think that perhaps it is agreed that we, you [plural] and I, would meet up on Sunday 13 July in Studénka?

And now I will need to know soon how much you'll need: first of all Franta [František Janáček] – 25 roubles, and for that present to the sister [i.e. the nurse] – 14 roubles? You'll both need about 50 roubles for the journey – [total] 89 R. How much will you give to Dr Botkin? And how to repay Franta and Marie? Would she like to come to Hukvaldy without Franta? [...]

Today I'm sending 100 roubles to Franta to take what belongs to him from it. Keep the rest yourself until we count it all up.

Dear Olguška

So you'll be on your feet again! Just take care now so that all ends well.

If you are going out a little then don't let uncle forget to buy

(1) the works of *Ostrovsky*

and (2) some cheap edition of *Pushkin*.

That's just that for the time being until I know how it will be with the money.

Don't forget when you are up to strength to invite Gordyeyev [*recte* Gordov] as well and say thank you to him.

But don't forget to speak in Russian now and learn the Our Father and the Creed.[57]

The next day Janáček responded to the good wishes that Olga had sent him for his birthday.[58]

Dear Zdenka and Olga

Thank you for the wishes, although otherwise I'd not myself have noticed that 'significant' day. For a long time now I've not thought about myself.

If a temperature occurs, then I put this down to your weakness and to your unsettled heart. As long as the heart responds only to drugs, my little soul, it will be necessary to keep a watchful calm. Nevertheless, I think that in a week or two perhaps, if the temperature has gone down, set out for home immediately; our dry country air will calm you down better. You mustn't be afraid of the temperature. Well-known people have had inflammation of the heart several times and lived – even to sixty-four! You, my daughter, have a long way to go still.

When you go out to town, choose a walk of a few minutes – better than a ride.[59]

In a postscript to the letter (which he continued the next day), Janáček mentioned that term at the Teachers' Institute was ending the day after (5 July), and that the Gymnasium would break up on 11 July. The Organ School term was already over. More arrangements were discussed in another letter:

I've written to Hukvaldy [to enquire] whether they would rent me the flat of the younger teacher (once he goes off on holiday). I'd move out once you'd arrived and Máňa could remain of service to you there the whole time. [. . .] On Sunday 13 July I'll therefore already be in Hukvaldy; so write there so that it will get to me.

Máňa would travel so that she would meet up with you in Studénka. According to your health I'd travel there for you – either to Warsaw or to Granica.

Let Mama get out every day; after all, she doesn't have to sit by you unnecessarily when you don't have a temperature.

Only, little soul, I know from old experience that calming one's heart takes months.

So, as soon as you feel [able?] – only when the pulse gets quiet and regular – then decide on a quick departure.

It will then be necessary for me to send (1) the doctor's fee and (2) something for the journey. I just ask to know the sum in time before leaving here. And at the worst let uncle lend it.[60]

But this optimistic tone was shattered by more bad news from St Petersburg, as is clear in a joint letter from Janáček and Marie Stejskalová. The letter, undated apart from Stejskalová's 'Monday morning', was probably written on 7 July, a few days before the end of the school term and before Janáček's departure for Hukvaldy:

Dear Olguška

I'm crushed by the repeated sad news about the fever. Ask the doctor whether they wouldn't allow you to travel in a sick state. Perhaps the different air would immediately stop the return of the fever. The journey wouldn't be bad – you could lie down. I'd come for you.

Your grieving father

Dear Madam and our dear Miss Oluška

Today we got the sad news that it's worse with Olga – the worst thing is that we're so far away. The all-powerful God will perhaps grant that we'll be fine again. [. . .] Here it's beautiful weather now, I'd also go to Hukvaldy, so we would nurse Missy and I'd remain there throughout the entire holidays. Please Madam, trust in God and he will help us; we're all quite beside ourselves here, the master wept and I don't know what to do. [. . .]

I kiss your hands many times and remain

faithful Máňa. [. . .]

[PS] I'm writing on Monday morning at 9 a.m.

Please write soon.[61]

Anxiety turned to frustration as Janáček reacted to Zdenka's reproaches in his next letter the next day: 'Don't be frightened, and let Mama leave off cursing me! Just be careful and everything will now come right. I think that you ought to throw the thermometer on the floor soon. How many times you probably had a temperature in Brno and we didn't know about it!'[62] The following evening he wrote again in reaction to more news:

Out of bed – but again a temperature of 38.1 after two days?

desperation?

cursing?

and again the old merry-go-round?

Don't extend the time out of bed *every day*. But at least *two days in succession* for the same time. I am not interested in worsening but in improvement.

He included a little domestic news, a new child at the Dresslers[§] ('They didn't even inform me of it'), and young Věra Janáčková ill and sent to recover in Štramberk. 'On Sunday morning I will leave here for Hukvaldy. I'll wait for further news from you in the morning'.[63]

It was against this background that Janáček composed much of *Jenůfa*. As we know from his letter of 22 June, one of the very few at the time where he mentions the opera, Janáček did indeed achieve his goal of completing Act 2 before the summer holidays began, and felt confident enough to pass on the act to his copyist Josef Štross, whose copy of the piano-vocal score of Act 2 is dated 7 July 1902. But instead of spending

---

[§] Dr Karel Dressler (1864–1943) was a cousin (once removed) of Janáček, the grandson of his aunt Johanka, who married the farmer Jan Dressler in Albrechtičky. Dr Dressler treated Olga in her final illness and occasionally treated Janáček.

time with his convalescing daughter as he hoped, Janáček spent the first half of the holidays waiting anxiously for bulletins from St Petersburg. At last the doctors felt Olga could risk the journey, and a telegram was sent on 11 July to say that she and her mother would leave St Petersburg on Tuesday evening (15 July). According to a follow-up letter from Olga, they would expect to meet Janáček in Warsaw on 16 July, and František would lend them money for the journey.[64]

On 13 July, all his teaching obligations at an end, Janáček left for Hukvaldy,[65] and after a day or two he travelled on to Warsaw to await his wife and daughter. Zdenka thought that she had spent seven weeks in St Petersburg watching over her daughter.[66] No doubt it seemed endless but their arrival in St Petersburg on 6 June at the beginning of Zdenka's stay is attested to by Janáček's diary, as is his arrival in Warsaw on 16 July to collect them (he recorded a 'Warsaw sparrow' and a child and its nurse in the 'Saxon Park').[67] By then Zdenka had spent five weeks and four days in St Petersburg with her ill daughter. In her memoirs Zdenka describes how they got home:

Leoš was waiting for us in Warsaw, where we arrived the evening of the next day. Olga was well, she was happy; through her Daddy a little bit of home welcomed her. We travelled on further. Late that evening her feet began to swell and hurt. In the train the next day she could hardly change out of her slippers into her shoes; during the customs inspection in Granica we almost carried her from the train and in Studénka, when we changed trains for Příbor, we really did carry her. Máňa was waiting there at the station. When she saw her 'Missy' being carried from the train to the carriage, she broke into noisy sobbing. [. . .]

No sooner had we got to Hukvaldy than we called in the local doctor, Dr Štrébl.[II] He detected that the rheumatism of the joints had returned again. He devoted so much care to Olga that she was soon walking again. But only around the house: thin, very pale, her hair fell from her head like leaves from the white birches in autumn. Her heart didn't improve, albumin appeared in her water, her kidneys started to fail. At night she had a fever, she could neither breathe nor sleep. My hope that Hukvaldy would perk her up once again, as so many times before, faded in those nocturnal vigils, where in a single rented room Máňa and I took turns watching over her. My instincts told me that this time Olga wouldn't pull through.[68]

Olga, when eventually she had the strength to write a thank-you note to her aunt and uncle in St Petersburg, was more optimistic:

[II]Dr Augustin Štrébl, doctor to the archbishop and general practioner specializing in homeopathic medicine.

After the journey I rested in bed for about a week and now I'm warming up in the sun and enjoying the view of this beloved little corner of ours – our Hukvaldy. I am convinced that the air here will cure me definitively. I thank you from my heart for everything good that you have done for me and ask you to remember well your loving niece Olga.[69]

A couple of weeks later Olga wrote again. The weather was wretched and was delaying any real improvement in her health:

So, so, it just rains and rains! We can't wait for the really nice weather. When the sun shone for a couple of days, my health improved. But now I must continually just sit in the room, I'm not allowed to go for walks as it wouldn't do me good. And how cold it is outside![70]

Zdenka's pessimism was well founded. When Janáček took himself off for a short break walking to Radhošť, all he could write on the card he sent home was 'chudák, chudáček' ('poor thing, poor little thing').[71] At the end of the summer Olga got congestion of the lungs and Dr Štrébl called for a second opinion – given by Janáček's cousin Dr Dressler, who came as if by chance from Brno. By now even the optimist Janáček realized that his daughter was mortally ill as the illness took its course: increasing dropsy, breathlessness and strain on the heart.[72] Janáček returned alone to Brno to teach – he must have been gone by 15 September since Olga wrote to him on that day[73] – and a little later he returned to fetch his wife and daughter.[74] The summer stay in Hukvaldy had not worked a miracle cure and, as the winter settled in, Olga continued to get worse. Her body went on swelling, distorting her figure and making her too embarrassed to receive friends. She was not able to get out. Zdenka records her last venture outside, a short walk across the square past the brewery towards Bauer's Ramp (i.e. towards the present Brno Exhibition grounds); she was soon overcome by lack of breath and energy. So Olga stayed at home, reading her Russian novels brought back from St Petersburg, doing the embroidery she had learnt at 'Vesna' and diverted by the purchase of a canary and a puppy, a black poodle whom Olga christened 'Čert' ['Devil'] because he kept his tongue out – as in Czech representations of devils.

In a letter of 1 November 1902 to her friend Josefa Jungová in Hukvaldy, Olga vividly evokes her state at the time. Although she seems still to think that she will recover, death haunts the letter from its opening imagery of people making their annual visit to the Brno cemetery for the All Souls' Eve ceremonies to its picture of Olga as an 'old maid' at the end.

I chose a sad day for writing – although the sun shines cheerfully in the blue sky like a fish's eye, if you look out of the window down on the street you'll see an endless line of people carrying wreaths and hurrying to visit the graves of their departed. [. . .] My God how wretched this life is and nevertheless, if death reaches out to one, one defends oneself and despairs. I experienced this myself this year and it's almost shameful how one clutches at life, but in vain – you cannot, and why in the end pretend? I'm getting better, I look better and so perhaps will get rid of this illness after all. Of course for a long time to come I won't be completely healthy, or at least as healthy as I was. Spare oneself and be patient – that's my motto. Well, fellow, suffer! [. . .] Don't think that I'm suffering because of that love, oh no. [. . .] I've come to recognize that he [Vorel] behaved wretchedly towards me and deserves nothing but derision. But I don't even feel anything for him, I'm as indifferent towards him as to the last man in the world. [. . .]

There's not much news here. From time to time Mummy has her obligatory stomach cramps and otherwise a terrible amount of work. Daddy is now always just composing and slaving away. The canary sings very sweetly and in conclusion I announce to you that I'm getting a small black poodle. You see how I am providing for myself one sign after another of an old maid.[75]

Janáček was indeed 'composing and slaving away'. Some time after his letter to Olga and Zdenka of 22 June. In addition to his teaching duties and other obligations, he had begun Act 3 of *Jenůfa*.

On 8 December the Russian Circle mounted a concert honouring the Russian writers Gogol and Zhukovsky on the fiftieth anniversary of their deaths. For the occasion the circle brought the Russian choir from the embassy church in Vienna together with its conductor Anatoly Mikhailovich Arkhangel'sky. Arkhangel'sky had visited Janáček in Brno in June while Zdenka and Olga were in St Petersburg, and throughout the autumn there was correspondence between him and Janáček in connection with the concert.[76] To publicize the event Janáček himself wrote a short piece (xv/165) in the newspaper *Hlas* (25 November 1902). Much of it was taken up with reprinting snippets from favourable foreign reviews but Janáček included some of his own reactions to the church music he had heard in St Petersburg: 'Not stifled by the roughnesses of the medieval organ, Russian choirs have developed a virtuosity of possible vocal effects. You look around you, where do these sweet chords come from?' The concert itself consisted of two 'jubilee' cantatas, one (by Arkhangel'sky) in honour of Gogol and the other (by A.V. Nikolsky) in honour of Zhukovsky. The evening was filled out with a spoken 'apotheosis to Gogol and Zhukovsky' and Russian songs and choruses.[77]

If Janáček had expected a substantial critical reaction to *Moravian Folksongs Newly Collected* (XIII/3) he would have been disappointed. In a postscript to his letter of 29 October, thus at least eight months after publication, Bartoš reported that he had not read a detailed review of the collection anywhere. There had been short news items in *Český lid* and the newspaper *Národní listy* about the first volume and a more detailed report in *Slovanský přehled* regarding the text. Janáček's long introduction had been completely ignored. The main part of Bartoš's letter concerned news of his own serious illness: 'For almost five hours I was already given up by the domestics as dead. Only the great efforts of the doctor managed to revive me. They say it was my kidneys.' This was in response to a letter from Janáček, no longer extant, in which he wrote about Olga's trip to St Petersburg and illness (Bartoš mentioned his concern and wished her a full recovery) and seems to have added that he himself was not well. Bartoš commented: 'That illness has hit you too makes me really sorry. Certainly the doctors must have said that you mustn't exert yourself mentally. Conduct yourself accordingly!'[78] The illness was not explained (nor is it mentioned elsewhere), but Janáček's workload and his anxiety over Olga no doubt contributed.

Although she helped with the household preparations for Christmas and decorated the tree, it was evident to Olga herself (Zdenka reported) that she was not long for this world. Janáček himself slipped off to Hukvaldy straight after Christmas to get away from the morbid atmosphere, and to work without such distractions on the final stages of his opera. He wrote a postcard on 27 December to say that he had arrived safely, making the journey from the station to Hukvaldy by sleigh.[79] No sooner had he gone than Olga's grandparents came to visit from Vienna – a trip arranged surreptitiously (like a previous visit in October) because of Janáček's continued hostility towards them. But the visit was overshadowed by Olga's deteriorating condition as her kidneys stopped functioning and legs began to swell with dropsy. After the Schulzes' departure Zdenka called in Dr Ervín Vašíček, chief district medical officer in Brno, who had once treated Olga and who now declared that it was the beginning of the end. Janáček himself still could not accept such a gloomy verdict. Something of his optimism is reflected in a letter that Joza Janáčková wrote to him on 16 February repeating Janáček's hope that Professor Emerich Maixner (a Prague specialist in internal diseases) would find Olga's state 'less grave' than Dr Vašíček.[80] When he finally arrived, Professor Maixner encouraged Olga to hope that she might still get to the country in the summer but he did not hide from her parents that her case was now 'completely hopeless'.[81] The sad fact is that today Olga would not have died of the effects of rheumatic fever; she would have been treated with 'large doses of aspirin or steroids' and probably cured (see chap. 43).

Up to this time Olga had slept in a small room with her mother.[82] Now she was moved into Janáček's study, where there was more air. Even so, she no longer felt the cold, while everyone else went around in overcoats. She even had a special cooling device in which cold water circulated. She was uncomfortable whether lying or sitting and had to be turned over frequently, an operation that became more laborious as her body became more and more water-logged.

As much as she could, Olga fought against her fate, doing her best to maintain her neat appearance, despite the increasing dropsy. With medical science failing her, she clutched at anything that might work. Janáček was dispatched to see a 'miracle doctor', who prescribed some types of tea – which merely increased the amount of liquid she was carrying.

On Sunday 22 February she asked to see a priest. Janáček grudgingly allowed Zdenka to go off to the monastery to fetch Father Augustin Krátký. He came, heard her confession and gave her communion and the last rites. During this event Janáček locked himself into the little room where Olga used to sleep. That afternoon, as Zdenka related, they all sat by her bed.

My husband had then just finished *Jenůfa*. During the whole time he was composing it, Olga took a huge interest in it. And my husband also used to say later that his basic model for Jenůfa was his sick daughter. Now Olga asked him: 'Daddy, play me *Jenůfa*, I won't live to hear it.' Leoš sat down at the piano and played . . . I couldn't bear it and ran off again to the kitchen.[83]

The next day, after a terrible night, Olga began to dispose of her personal possessions and make her will, duly taken down by Stejskalová. She kept only the ring she had received from her grandparents at

Christmas. She insisted on Zdenka keeping the puppy Čert in her memory, and begged Stejskalová to stay with Zdenka 'unto death'. Both wishes were respected. Čert became an important member of the household, surviving for another twelve years, and Stejskalová remained with the widowed Zdenka until the latter's death.

Olga began saying her goodbyes. That evening the Bartoš family were summoned, including Olga's contemporary Fedora Bartošová (a different family from Janáček's colleague František Bartoš). Visitors on Tuesday 24 February included her friends Mařenka and Eliška Kalussová, and the Dressler family, with the young children looking 'fearfully' at the dying Olga. Olga was now in increasing discomfort with the extra water that could not be drained off. She grew more and more breathless. In the depths of winter the windows were flung open to give maximum air; the women, who now included Stejskalová's younger half-sister, took turns in fanning her or in reviving her with vinegar when she fainted. That afternoon she began crying for her grandparents, a source of huge embarrassment for both Janáček and Zdenka in view of his continuing hostility towards them. In the end it was Stejskalová who insisted on Janáček's sending a telegram for them to come from Vienna. Janáček did so and the Schulzes were there within a few hours.

The visit was at first uncomfortable since Janáček could not bring himself even to greet them and just stood at the window of the dining room, but Olga was very happy, somewhat revived by the pills given to her earlier by Dr Dressler. Her grandparents and their son Leo sat with her for a 'long time' and then, sensing Janáček's hostility, Anna Schulzová began to make preparations to leave but it was now Zdenka who got up her courage:

I went to my husband – he was again in Olga's room – and said to him resolutely in a way that I'd seldom used with him: 'Listen, put hate aside now. Now something higher has taken over. They want to leave because of you, and Olga would like to have them here. You must control yourself. It's your duty.'

He didn't answer me, he didn't move. I left. I now thought that I'd spoken to him in vain. But after a while he went out and began talking with my brother, who was sitting in the dining room. And slowly even my parents joined in the conversation. The tension eased. We sat the whole night through and chatted. Olga was happy.[84]

On the morning of 25 February Olga began to be delirious. By now Janáček had stopped going to work. Was it in the spirit of scientific enquiry that he took down her last words and their speech melodies, or was it simply the reaction of a desperate father attempting to clutch on to what remained of his dying daughter? At first he took what he had to hand – a letter from Ladislav Holain dated 13 February – and scribbled down Olga's words and speech melodies in the available spaces.[85] Later he copied it out neatly into his notebook:

The last words and sighs of my poor Olga

She lay on the couch

1. sobbing: 'I don't want to die, I want to live!'

I ask her if she is in pain.
No, she says, she is just anxious and
2. 'such fear! –
and I'm fighting against it.'

'I've remembered that I've got to die'

3. 'I'm going to die'
(She kept on repeating this until the words were no longer intelligible.)

After the injections:
4. 'All those walks we had on the promenade!'
5. 'There is so much that (one) ought to say – and one just talks nonsense.'
(24 February 1903, 2 o'clock)
I: 'You are the loveliest of them all!'
6. She laughed happily[:] 'Try telling that to the others!'

The context for this last remark is filled out by Zdenka's recollection of the same exchange:

My husband lent over her and she said softly: 'Daddy, it's so beautiful there, there are just angels there.' And he said to her fervently: 'And you're the most beautiful angel of all.'
'Try telling that to them there, they'd laugh at you.'
Again after a little while: 'And there's Vladíček there. He's waiting for me.'
Then as if she came to her senses. She fixed her anxious gaze on my husband: 'It would be horrible, if there was nothing there.'
And Leoš gathered together all his eloquence and assured her convincingly that heaven and God existed.[86]

Janáček's notations continue:

7. 'Something will be lost – what a pity no-one will find it.'
(25 February, 2.45 p.m.)

8. 'I'm telling you that I'm better already.'
She repeated this several times to me.

When I called her twice she didn't hear me.

9. 'It gave me a fright.'

10. 'Just wait.'

11. As she received an injection (lamenting): 'Jejda'.

Her last sighs:
12. 'ah-h'.
God be with you, my soul.[87]

Zdenka described the final hours:

She stopped talking, she breathed irregularly and in fits and starts, she lay motionless. Mama didn't move from her and put the damp sponge to her lips. When towards noon [on 25 February] my family left, Olga didn't react to anything. We sat there and waited for the end. It wasn't necessary to do anything else. People continually dropped in on us, friends came, Olga's friends, no-one looked after them, no-one greeted them, no-one spoke to them. They came, they went, my husband and I, Máŕa and the Dressler women sat there the whole time and looked at Olga. After his surgery hours, Dressler came and was surprised: 'Is she still alive? What lungs she's got!'

[...]

Night again. Each lay down where he could and slept. They put me on the divan too. I didn't sleep, I listened constantly to Olga's irregular breathing.[88]

When dawn came there was another change in Olga's breathing pattern. 'Everyone who was with us in the flat came, we knelt before Olga's bed and in complete silence we waited ... The breathing stopped. It was 6.30 a.m. on Thursday 26 February 1903.'

While Zdenka and Máŕa Stejskalová and some of the other women busied themselves with preparing Olga for the coffin, Janáček gave himself over entirely to his grief. As Zdenka reported, 'He tore out his hair, crying: "My soul, my soul!"' The next day Abbot František Baŕina of the Augustinian monastery in Brno sent flowers and plants from the monastery greenhouse to decorate the room. Olga lay in her coffin 'in a grove of palms', in a white satin shroud, strewn with posies of fresh violets, and was visited by 'hundreds and hundreds of people'. Students offered to carry the coffin; Čert, who refused to stir from the body and simply howled, had to be sent away to friends. The coffin, which had stayed open all night, was eventually removed at eleven on Saturday 28 February while Zdenka's attention was distracted, to the monastery church. She merely caught a glimpse from the window 'of the black carriage slowly driving away and behind it a young girl walking all on her own, Maŕenka Kalussová'.

A large crowd turned up for the funeral that afternoon at the church of the Staré Brno monastery. Zdenka recounted how 'without tears, without feeling I walked behind the carriage up to the [teachers'] institute, where we got seated in the carriages and drove to the Central Cemetery and then afterwards behind the students who carried the coffin. Leoš walked beside me like a stranger. We didn't go arm in arm. Again, each on his own.'

When they all got back home the guests from Hukvaldy left while Zdenka's mother and brother from Vienna (her father had found the previous journey too tiring) waited for their train. Zdenka described Janáček's reaction:

My husband shut himself again in Olga's room. I heard him sobbing there. We let him be. Then he came out and joined us in the dining room and we were all together until the departure of my family. The two of us remained in the dining room on our own. Deserted, not speaking. I gazed at Leoš. He sat before me, devastated, grown thin, greying.[89]

The resentment that Zdenka had felt, her belief that Olga's death was caused chiefly by the ill-fated trip to St Petersburg, dissolved, and she clasped him round the neck. 'Perhaps he felt what was going on inside me, perhaps he was experiencing something similar; he didn't push me away but said gently: "So we will go on living this life alone now." '[90]

Janáček continued to tinker with his opera but finally put a date at the end of his copy of the play: '18 March 1903, the third week after the terrible mortal struggle of my poor Olga. Completed.' Twenty-two years later he wrote in his memoirs:

I would bind *Jenůfa* simply with the black ribbon from the long illness, suffering and laments of my daughter Olga and my little boy Vladimír.[91]

43

What Olga died of

by STEPHEN LOCK*

Zdenka's description of Olga Janáčková's illness[1] is a classic one of the evolution of chronic rheumatic heart disease. The earlier pages tell us that Olga had rheumatic fever affecting her joints and her heart (on *MLWJ*, p. 57 it is described as affecting the pericardium – the outer membrane lining the surface of the heart – and on p. 62 Zdenka speaks of 'chronic heart disease'). The later pages detail the insidious progress of heart disease leading to heart failure, congestion of the lungs, and then waterlogging of the abdomen and legs.

From a medical point of view this condition is best appreciated from descriptions in the most famous medical textbook of the times (and, for that matter, of all times), William Osler's *The Principles and Practice of Medicine*. Born in Ontario in 1849, Osler was successively professor of medicine at McGill (Montreal), Pennsylvania, Johns Hopkins Hospital (Baltimore), and Oxford, where he was Regius Professor and honoured with a knighthood. He died in 1919.

Young adults are most often affected by rheumatic fever, Osler points out, and the most frequent complication is endocarditis (inflammation of the inner lining of the chambers of the heart). The heart valves, which separate the chambers of the heart from each other, are particularly affected (and most frequently the mitral valve, which separates the left atrium from the left ventricle – respectively, the upper and lower chambers of the left side of the heart). 'In many cases,' Osler writes, 'the curtains [valves] are so welded together and the whole valvular region so thickened that the orifice is reduced to a mere chink. [. . .] Failure of compensation brings in its train the group of symptoms

* First published as 'Olga's final illness' in *MLWJ*, 255–6.

[. . .]: rapid and irregular action of the heart, shortness of breath, cough [. . .]. The liver may be greatly enlarged and in the late state ascites [fluid in the abdominal cavity] is not uncommon, particularly in children.' And Osler comments earlier in this section that with 'judicious treatment the compensation may be restored and all the serious symptoms pass away'. Later he goes on to say that: 'Patients may have recurring attacks of this kind, but ultimately the condition is beyond repair and the patient either dies of a general dropsy, or there is progressive dilatation [enlargement] of the heart, and death from asystole [cessation of the heartbeat]'. This description, from the first (1892) edition of Osler's classic textbook, emphasizes that the initial effect of disease of the mitral valve is to throw a strain on the left atrium, which becomes enlarged, and then to cause congestion of the lungs (the 'bronchial catarrh' in Zdenka's account), and ultimately the rest of the heart and the body itself. At that time the origin of the process leading to rheumatic fever was unknown; today we realize that it is due to an unusual reaction by the body to infection by the germ called streptococcus (usually a severe sore throat). Nowadays, full-blown rheumatic fever is still seen in the developing world, but in the developed world such an infection is usually nipped in the bud by treatment with antibiotics. If rheumatic fever does occur, then it can be treated with large doses of aspirin or steroids, while if rheumatic heart disease supervenes and the valves become fused or loose, then they can be split into their component parts by a surgical operation or replaced altogether with a graft or an artificial valve.

4

IN THE MISTS

(1903–14)

44

1903 (March–December)

Soon after Olga's death Janáček began to send out formal announcements, mostly a few lines of commemorative verse by his colleague František Rypáček (librettist of *The Beginning of a Romance*), printed on stiff paper surrounded by a black band:

> Young and quiet, good and gentle,
> she fell asleep like a white rose,
> a pale and lovely flower of the spring . . .
> He who has a heart and a passionate soul
> hastens to still the burning tears,
> to say comforting words:
> The Lord God suddenly beckoned.
> Holy be His will for ever.

Janáček sent this to Josefa Jungová, among others, together with one of Olga's deathbed bequests: 'Take this in memory of that poor soul who on earth had nothing but bitterness, just bitterness.'[1] To his brother Karel and his wife Anna he added a personal note: 'I forgot about the whole world when I had before my eyes the wretchedness, the terror and the anxiety of my dear Olga. She remembered you on her deathbed and greeted you for the last time.'[2] Some days later Janáček wrote an agonized letter to his Hukvaldy friend, Vincenc Sládek:

We no longer have her, our dear little heart. How she burst into bitter tears when on her deathbed she remembered you and your children! How sorry I was for her that in her youth, her beauty, her angelic goodness, her happiness, she had to take leave of all of us. How she suffered, poor thing! One can't describe it. Be so kind as, once again, to prepare your room for me, it will be our place of mourning. She was a little better in the week up to Sunday and, once again, she thought of Hukvaldy and of the holidays. But on Tuesday she began her struggle with death. How she didn't want to die; how unwilling we were to lose her. It was as if someone tore out my heart. That's how I feel now . . .[3]

On the day after the funeral, Sunday 1 March, Olga's parents went to her grave at the Central Cemetery together for the first and only time. Thereafter Janáček would visit it on Sundays, but always alone.[4] In the course of time an elaborate tombstone of white Carrara marble was erected with Olga's portrait in relief on a black marble plaque with two inscriptions: one in Czech (the first three lines of Rypáček's poem), the other in Russian by Olga's Russian teacher Maria Nikolayevna Veveritsa: 'Her spirit is where there is love and rest.'[5] Zdenka went off to her parents in Vienna, and Janáček threw himself into composition: a personal commemoration of his dead daughter. On 15 March 1903 *Moravská orlice* printed two poems in Russian (with Czech translations), 'Reminiscence of 27 and 28 February 1903'. The author was given as 'M.N.' – Maria Nikolayevna Veveritsa again; the poems were dedicated to Olga and addressed to 'Lev Grigorjevič Janáček'.* Whereas the second poem described Janáček's grief, the first was an elegy to Olga, and it was this text, in its somewhat altered Czech translation, that provided him with an appropriate compositional outlet. His *Elegy on the Death of my Daughter Olga* (IV/30) for tenor, mixed voices and piano was completed during April 1903. The words go little further than the conventional expression of grief at the death of a young girl; and the music, with its Art Nouveau, slow, curving lines, is decorative rather than tragic. It would be unkind to regard it purely as occupational therapy or displacement activity – Janáček regarded it highly enough to revise it a year later – but nevertheless it is a somewhat backward-looking piece, written too close to the event to bear the full intensity of his loss.

In her memoirs Zdenka reported that Janáček refused to take time off.[6] His going back to classes, however, placed an unbearable burden on both him and his pupils. Vladimír Mazálek, a fourth-year student at the Teachers' Institute, recalls Janáček's return after a few days, appearing before his students with a 'face of wax'. There was a death-like silence:

---

* Veveritsa made a wrong guess with the patronymic: Janáček's father was Jiří, of which the Russian form might be Georgi, Yuri or Yegor, but not Grigor.

We all remained standing because the Maestro came closer to us, which was a sign that he wanted to say something. And now a heart-rending scene took place. The Maestro wanted to speak but his throat seized up with grief and, instead of words, streams of hot tears poured out. [. . .] We stood like statues and not one eye in the whole year-group stayed dry.[7]

By March *Jenůfa* was completed and copied: the date of 18 March in Janáček's copy of Preissová's play (see chap. 42) probably refers to Janáček's checking through Štross's copy of the full score. Janáček then took the score with him to Prague, as Zdenka put it, 'in hope and fear'.[8] In 1900 there had been major changes to the management of the Prague National Theatre. Although not a musician himself, František Šubert had determined the artistic policy of the National Theatre since its opening; his chief conductor, Adolf Čech (a veteran from Smetana's day), had very little say in the choice of repertory and the engagement of singers. But the franchise that Šubert's company had held since 1881 (with uncontested renewals in 1888 and 1894) ran out in 1900 and a new company took over. Here the balance of power was rather different. Within the new company, the administrative director merely saw to the execution of the artistic director's decisions while the chief conductor had full charge of the artistic direction of the opera and ballet.[9] This new artistic director was none other than Karel Kovařovic.

Janáček could not have had worse luck. Although Šubert had turned down *The Beginning of a Romance* in 1892 and again in 1894, he had accepted *Rákoš Rakoczy* in 1891 and, as far as Janáček was concerned, had no axe to grind. But Kovařovic was another matter (see chap. 49). As Zdenka reported, Kovařovic told Janáček that he would get back to him once he had finished looking at the opera,[10] but Janáček became impatient and wrote to him hardly a month later: 'I fear writing to – you; and it is so unsettling waiting in this way. Forgive me for asking about the fate of my work.'[11] The new administrative director, Gustav Schmoranz, scribbled on the letter: 'The head of opera wishes to return to the writer his opera as unperformable here on the stage of the National Theatre.'[12] In his official letter he smoothed this out into a less brutal form, though the message was the same:

I sincerely regret that we cannot accept your opera for performance. We would wish your work to meet on the stage with complete success for you and for us, but we fear that your work would not have this type of success.

We return both the full score and the vocal score.[13]

Zdenka movingly described Janáček's receipt of this letter in her memoirs. Her husband did not have the courage to open it, so she had to read it for him, full of fear when she saw how short it was. 'It happened in the room where Olga died. My husband sat at the desk. He buried his head in his hands and broke into terrible sobbing. In a sharp fit of depression he blamed himself that he didn't know any-thing.'[14] Prague's refusal to take *Jenůfa* seriously – an attitude con-stantly upheld despite repeated challenges from Janáček and his admirers – resulted in permanent scarring: a resentment and funda-mental distrust of Prague that shaped many of his later attitudes.

Nevertheless, from this time on Janáček began to visit Prague more regularly, chiefly to get to know novelties at the theatre. His attendance at Nedbal's ballet *A Story about Honza* on 2 May[15] is inexplicable: Janáček was not interested in Nedbal,[†] nor had he shown any interest in ballet since his encounter in Vienna, 1880, with *Dyellah oder die Touristen in Indien*. But later that same month came an event that was decisive in showing him new directions that he would embrace enthusiastically in his next opera and thereafter. Charpentier's *Louise* was one of the great successes at the National Theatre. It opened on 13 February 1903 and remained in the Prague repertory until 1911, by which time it had been performed forty-eight times. Janáček saw it on 21 May, conducted by Kovařovic, and although he made no surviving written comment at the time, his enthusiasm for the work is attested to by many later statements (see chap. 46).

Another concern of the period was the preparation for a Pan-Slavonic Ethnographic Exhibition, planned to take place in St Petersburg in 1904. Janáček's energetic part in the Prague Ethnographic Exhibition of 1895 was remembered and he was appointed to take charge of the Moravian delegation. Janáček called a meeting on 9 May of a Mora-vian ethnographical committee, summoning old colleagues such as Bakešová and Zeman,[16] and new ones such as Josef Klvaňa and Josef Kretz.[17] The committee never met again and it would seem that some-thing – political pressures? – prevented any further deliberations. As it was, the exhibition itself did not take place, perhaps as a result of the Russo-Japanese conflict. All that now exists of these shadowy plans is a

---

[†]Oskar Nedbal (1874–1930), violist of the Czech Quartet (1891–1906) and conductor of the Czech Philharmonic (1896–1906) but especially known as a composer of ballets and operettas.

handwritten note by Janáček, part notes before the event, part report afterwards. The meeting itself assigned the following portfolios:

1. Moravian dialects and folk poetry (František Bartoš)
2. Folksong and dance (Leoš Janáček and Martin Zeman)
3. Folk painting (Alois Kalvoda)
4. Folk architecture (Dušan Jurkovič)
5. Embroidery and folk costumes (Josef Kretz and Josef Klvaňa). (XV/316)

The list is interesting in showing Janáček's increasing range of contacts in the Moravian ethnographic and cultural world and includes new people who would continue to play a part in his life. Dušan Samo Jurkovič (1868–1947) was a leading architect, responsible for the folk-influenced constructions in Luhačovice and Radhošt'. Alois Kalvoda (1875–1934) was a prominent painter who, for instance, suggested a new design for *Jenůfa* Act 1 in 1916. That same year Janáček took the singer Gabriela Horvátová (Kostelnička in the Prague *Jenůfa*) to see Kretz's collection of folk embroidery in Uherské Hradiště. Janáček's own survey of possible musical components for the St Petersburg exhibition included some of his discoveries made since the Ethnographical Exhibition of 1895, in particular the 'folk polyphony' that he came across in 1901 in Rovné (see chap. 53).

At about this time (Zdenka records it as 'summer', but it must have been earlier, as she had arrived in Vienna for her summer holidays by 28 May),[18] Zdenka bumped into Rudolf Kallus, a member of the Brno Theatre Družstvo, who told her that the Družstvo was upset at Prague's high-handed treatment of *Jenůfa*. He asked Zdenka to try and persuade her husband to allow the theatre to perform the opera in Brno. At first he 'would not hear of it', she reported, since he was 'too wounded by the failure'.[19]

While Zdenka went to her parents and brother in Vienna, and Stejskalová to her relatives in Matějov in the Českomoravská vysočina (i.e. the hilly borderland between Moravia and Bohemia), Janáček spent a somewhat itinerant summer. His first port of call was the mountain of Hostýn, a place of pagan and later Christian pilgrimage halfway between Brno and Hukvaldy. It was also the setting for part of *The Angelic Sonata* (1900), a novel by one of Janáček's acquaintances, the Moravian writer Josef Merhaut (1863–1907), in which a pilgrimage to Hostýn by the central couple forms a crucial incident.

The Angelic Sonata and Janáček's own trip to Hostýn left a lasting impression and twenty years later he remembered it in his auto-biography: 'I went on a pilgrimage to Hostýn, spent the night there, thoroughly bitten by insects, survived a storm, and in the darkness trod on sleepy pilgrims.'[20] The context for this account is a list of opera topics that he explored before he wrote *Káťa Kabanová*. His interest in Merhaut's novel as possible operatic material (XI/6) is attested to by annotations in his copy of the book, a sketchy scenario (written in his notebook for 1902–3 consisting of a few scene descriptions)[21] and a letter from Merhaut indicating that Janáček had contacted him about a collaboration. While expressing delight in Janáček's enthusiasm, Merhaut wondered whether it was a suitable subject for a stage work (too much lyricism, too little action). He himself was unwilling to take on writing a libretto – the work came from a creative period in his life he now regarded as over – and instead he suggested that Mr Dominík Pavlíček from *Lidové noviny* might be just the person to do it.[22] Nothing more came of it. But the plan itself reveals that just a few months after the death of Olga and the end of *Jenůfa* Janáček was beginning to turn his mind towards a new operatic project, and that furthermore he was contemplating a subject that had so many obvious connections with his own life (see chap. 52).

After Hostýn Janáček went to Hukvaldy in July, taking Olga's dog Čert with him.[23] However the weather was bad ('I got wet to the skin', Janáček wrote to Zdenka),[24] and Čert misbehaved, dispatching all the geese and hens that he came across. Janáček 'couldn't keep up paying for the damage' and had to bring Čert back to Brno, to be looked after by the caretaker of the apartment block where the Janáčeks lived.[25]

Janáček's third summer trip was by far the most important, both immediately for his next opera and more indirectly for the rest of his life. Somewhere between 11 and 15 August he went to Luhačovice. It was not his very first visit there (see chap. 45), but it was nevertheless one of his earliest to what was then still a very small resort, and it was the first trip for which considerable documentation survives. Despite his sad state – or perhaps because of it – Janáček seems to have had a relatively social time, reporting to Zdenka about various acquaintances he met there.[26] He also had his notebook at the ready to take down speech melodies. His notations formed the basis for a new article in *Hlídka* (XV/173), which, in a new vein of vivid writing, attempted to bring alive the whole scene with the copious quotation of fragments of speech captured in music. In it he described the folk music with clarinet and string bass that greeted his arrival by horse-drawn carriage, the cry of the driver halting the horse, his dealings with the housekeeper at the 'tiny Pospíšil villa' where he was staying (though to Zdenka he wrote that he was staying at the 'Spa Hotel, door 10').[27] Before it got dark there was a glance at the colourful Slanice (the local name for the spa promenade), where he was asked the time (another speech melody). And so it goes on for another eight pages with a total of fifty-nine musical snippets. The large cast of characters includes many passers-by, the spa orchestra (a loud A-major chord), Gypsy beggars, the 'temperamental' daughter of the major's wife, women trippers exploring a 'beautiful echo', their laughter when the 'echo' responded, an old lady with a limp, a young Slovak woman from Hungary, an old Jewish woman from Slovakia with a 'bubbly voice', a grumbling forester, an affected young girl with a broken umbrella, a Jewish woman talking in German. Pride of place, however, was devoted to Mrs Camilla Urválková (1875–1956, see Plate 33)[‡] and her five-year-old son: when asked by the company 'what love is?' the boy responded pertly, 'when Nana and Johan [i.e. the servants] love one another'.

In her memoirs Zdenka described Janáček's meeting with Mrs Urválková as follows:

After a short while I got a letter from him in which he told me that he'd 'found an angel just like the one that we'd buried'. And that she also had a heart defect. I thought that the 'angel' was some young girl and wrote back accordingly. But when he returned after the holidays and began telling me about this angel, it turned out to be the young and beautiful Mrs Camilla Urválková, the wife of a forest ranger from Dolní Královice. Apparently she couldn't bear to see Leoš so sad and isolated in Luhačovice. She sent him a bunch of red roses to his table. Then they got acquainted.[28]

Janáček's version of this in his autobiography helps flesh out, if rather cryptically, more of the incidental biographical background that served as raw material for his next opera, *Fate* (I/5):

And she was one of the most beautiful of women. Her voice was like that of a viola d'amore. The Luhačovice Slanice was in the scorching heat of the August sun.

[‡] Czech spelling rules have ensured that Urválková's first name is rendered in Janáček literature in a modernized form as 'Kamilla' (in Štědroň 1959b) or 'Kamila' (in Straková 1956–7). Janáček, however, addressed her as 'Camilla' in all his correspondence.

Why did she walk about with three fiery roses and why did she relate the story of her young life?

And why was its end so strange?

The 'story of her young life' (she was twenty-eight at the time) was essentially that of her relationship with the composer Ludvík Čelanský. 'Why did her lover disappear as if the earth had swallowed him up?', Janáček's questions continued, 'Why was the conductor's baton more like a dagger to the other man?'[29]

Ludvík Vítězslav Čelanský (1870–1931) was one of the restless souls in Czech music. His career as a conductor had so far taken him from Plzeň (1895) to Zagreb (1898), to Prague (1899), to Lwów (1900), to Prague again (1901), then back to Lwów (1901). Although he had begun as an opera conductor, on his return to Prague in 1901 he established the Czech Philharmonic as a fully independent body from orchestral players on strike at the National Theatre, and had gone on the next year to found the Lwów Philharmonic. Later he was director of the symphony orchestras in Kiev (1904) and Warsaw (1905). His output as a composer was slender and is now forgotten, but his one-act opera, written to his own libretto, was given nine performances at the Prague National Theatre between 1897 and 1899. It was called *Kamilla*, and its title role is alleged to be a portrait of Camilla Urválková. Depicted as attractive though superficial, the operatic Kamilla conducts an ostentatious flirtation with a visitor, causing her faithful, if sensitive, poet-lover Viktor to abandon her.

The names of the two protagonists in Čelanský's opera suggest Camilla Urválková and himself (his middle name was Vítězslav, the Czech equivalent of Viktor). By 1903, when Janáček met Mrs Urválková, Čelanský was abroad and had thus 'disappeared' again from the Czech musical scene. If his baton was 'more like a dagger to the other man', this may indicate that Mrs Urválková regarded his opera (with its unsympathetic portrayal of the title role) as a character assassination of herself and her husband. And perhaps she may even have suggested that it was Janáček's chivalrous duty, as an opera composer, to write a sequel where she might be seen in a more favourable light.

For the rest of his time in Luhačovice Janáček pursued Mrs Urválková enthusiastically. 'The most beautiful lady I have ever met', he wrote on her fan.[30] On 28 August he presented her with a copy of his *Hukvaldy Folk Poetry in Song* (v/4), which he inscribed: 'Your beauty and magnificence and the tenderness of your appearance could give birth to a joyous symphony, in which you would be celebrated. Oh, accept at least as a remembrance of the Luhačovice days this modest work of mine.'[31] On 6 September, shortly before his departure from Luhačovice, he sent her two postcards, one co-signed by two other guests ('Amazement and tribute are expressed not only by me but all of society that has fine taste and a sense for tender beauty: the devoted minister of her highness')[32] and one signed by him alone ('To the celebrated beauty Mrs Camilla, called "The Duchess" ').[33] In Přerov on his way from Luhačovice to Hukvaldy, where he was to spend a few days before returning to Brno, he sent yet another card: 'Remembering "The Star of Luhačovice". The further away, the sadder.'[34] In Hukvaldy he began a series of daily letters, written on tiny sheets of paper in a beautiful hand, clearly drafted first and then written out neatly. In the first he describes his wretched state on leaving Luhačovice, and then went on ('in tears') to recall the memories:

What a wonderfully beautiful dream it was! That sudden appearance of yours; so much bliss came flying with it, it entranced me so much that I lost all sense of time – everything became one beautiful melody that resounded so strongly during the day and didn't let me sleep at night. Hearing your laughter, your speech, the swish of your clothes, the rustle of your gracious step, smelling the scent of your body, seeing the grace and elegance of your movements – how could the whole magnificent picture not incline to me during the night!? In truth I can say that during the last fortnight I didn't know sleep.

He had, he wrote, had a 'closed heart' when he arrived in Luhačovice. But Camilla had asked him if he was unhappy, and this surprising question (no-one else had posed it) had rewakened him.[35] He had clearly fallen head-over-heels in love with her.

On a postcard from Hukvaldy depicting its ruined castle, he wrote: 'See the places from remote centuries where, in my wandering, I had constantly in my mind this proud magnificent beauty of "The Star of Luhačovice".'[36] The ringing phrase, 'The Star of Luhačovice', was not only Janáček's comment on Camilla Urválková's dazzling appearance in Luhačovice society. It was also the provisional title of his new opera, his response to Čelanský's *Kamilla*. In her letter of 2 October Urválková wrote: 'Are you working hard, how is *The Star of L[uhačovice]*? Is it finished yet? Will you dedicate it to me? At least I will have a constant reminder of those unforgettable days at

Luhačovice. My God, how time has flown!' One sentence stands out from this long letter and provided the future title of the work: 'It is that *fate* [emphasis added] that pampers you, spoils you and then casts you aside into the trap from which there is no escape.'[37]

By then Janáček was back in Brno for the entrance examinations at the Organ School, totally exhausted, as he wrote. He didn't even bother to copy out this letter neatly. He went on to say that he had also received a visit from the Brno Theatre Družstvo, asking him to let them have his opera *Jenůfa*.[38] This final pressure seems to have overcome his reluctance and plans were made to stage *Jenůfa* in the next season, 1903–4.

But for the moment, pursuing Camilla Urválková seemed to be a more pressing objective. He would be able to come to Prague any Saturday or Sunday, he promised her, an offer repeated in his next letter. Until now Urválková had been in Luhačovice, but when Janáček wrote there on 20 September, he had clearly been made aware that such flowery correspondence to a married woman would have to stop when she got home to Dolní Královice and her husband. The plan, he suggested, would be that they communicate by messages sent to a newspaper she took (today's 'small ads'): a particular form of words would announce the dispatch of a *poste restante* letter.[39] It seems unlikely that this strategy was pursued. Although it is possible that more letters from Janáček have not survived or are still in private hands (five turned up in 2004), Janáček mostly communicated thereafter with Urválková by open postcards, no fewer than three of them on 28 September, showing where he lived in Brno, what the view was from his apartment, and so on.[40]

Nevertheless the weekend-in-Prague plan was maintained. Having been so 'taken up and overworked with the final revision' of *Jenůfa*, he now wanted a break to go and see Bizet's opera *Djamileh* in Prague.[41] He did so on Saturday 3 October, later writing to tell Urválková that he had indeed been to see two operas (Bizet's one-act *opéra comique* together with Blodek's *In the Well*),[42] sitting near Urválková's '4' (i.e. her subscription box no. 4 – the lady herself had not turned up): 'Oh, it was all a magic bath of sound to my ears – that divine music.'[43] The following day he saw Bizet's *Carmen* conducted by Kovařovic before returning to Brno.[44]

Apart from trying to further his new acquaintance with Mrs Urválková, Janáček spent all his free time putting the finishing touches to the score of *Jenůfa*, thus creating the first layer of corrections in the full score copied out by Josef Štross. He had been so busy, he announced to Urválková on 28 September, that he had not even gone out for a walk since he returned.[45] One piece of luck was that Janáček's ex-pupil Cyril Metoděj Hrazdira, with whom he had kept in touch over the years, had been appointed conductor at the Brno Czech Theatre from that autumn and was thus the conductor-designate of *Jenůfa*. It meant that the new opera would be in sympathetic hands.

On 8 October the administrative director of the theatre, Alois Doubravský, wrote to Janáček about financial arrangements for staging *Jenůfa*. He agreed to his requirements regarding orchestral forces (sadly, since Janáček's letter has disappeared, it's not known what these were), suggested that he attend rehearsals (in order to give his 'advice and suggestions') and asked for Janáček to hand over the full score and piano-vocal score to the messenger that he would now send.[46] This happened the next day, as Janáček told Mrs Urválková:

Yesterday at least was one of the joyful days. I have had so few of them in my life. Perhaps that 'Highest Justice' has after all turned a smiling face towards me?

The Directorate of the National Theatre in Brno sent for the score of my opera *Jenůfa*.

When they took it away, the servant had something to carry on his shoulders! And at the same time it seemed to me as if they had taken away so many sad years from my soul.

From that moment, you know, I forgot what I had really written in this music. Empty head and then fear about Fate and also about my own fate took over in my mind.[47]

This extraordinary letter is one of the few surviving that Janáček wrote to Urválková after she left Luhačovice. It encapsulates Janáček's complex feelings as he handed over the score of the opera he had written against a background of such personal sorrow. It also goes on to announce his retirement from his post at the Teachers' Institute (a move that had been in his mind for a while, as he had mentioned to his colleague Bartoš as early as May that year);[48] and it gives the first indication of the sort of opera that he had in mind for his next work.

At the same time I am, as Imperial and Royal Music Teacher, applying to be retired, so that I can devote myself wholly to composition and to literary work. There are times approaching on the horizon for which I have waited all my life.

Shall I live to enjoy happier ones? Will my spirit be capable of more splendid work? I think so – though who knows what's going on in my brain. Things are happening so feverishly in my whole body, it seems only guesswork or a miracle can explain it. It's up to God and to fate! We make our own fates ourselves. I know that I have painted black upon black in opera; gloomy music – as was my spirit. What I'd like now is a libretto that is fresh, modern, bubbling over with life and elegance – the 'story of a child' of our time. Oh, but who will write it for me? I already have many details for it myself; I'm told that I know how to handle words – but I am diffident among literary people. And those who offer their services to me know only the coarse life of the tavern; have no notion of the spirit that blows through all of life, that it can be found quite near at hand, in ourselves, in the society well known to us – so charming, so piquant, with such surprising singing and amazing scenes. They have no notion of this, these literary people, because they don't know this life. Oh, who will write me a new libretto?[49]

In the same letter Janáček also thanked Urválková for her photograph ('Even my wife likes it. She says you are beautiful'), decorously passing on his good wishes to Urválková's husband and Zdenka's good wishes to Urválková.[50] For all Janáček's obvious infatuation, things were suddenly much better on the home front. Zdenka had even been told that Janáček and Urválková would be exchanging letters,

but that I [Zdenka] shouldn't worry because he'd give me all the letters to read. I went along with this, it really seemed to me that Leoš was now more cheerful. But this was perhaps because the rehearsals for *Jenůfa* had started. Certainly, however, he was very sweet and attentive to me. One evening he came to me in my bedroom and suggested to me that we should get together now we were so alone: that I should be his wife again. I felt bad in the child's room where everything reminded me of Olga's death – but he was my husband and I loved him. From that time we lived together again as man and wife. Later he suggested that I should go out into society with him. And I didn't deny him that either, although earlier I'd refused to go to the theatre again. He kept on corresponding with Mrs Camilla. I read the letters, there was nothing improper in them, nothing that would have made me anxious: she used to write to him about her illness, and he to her about *Jenůfa*, and about his new opera, *Fate*, which she inspired through her account of her love for the conductor Čelanský.[51]

Janáček's writings on speech melody burst forth in various publications that autumn. A letter to Bartoš[52] mentions the three different outlets he had already found: *The Speech Melodies of Children* (xv/169) in

Český lid; a shorter study, *The Melodies of our Speech with Outstanding Dramatic Qualities* (xv/172), published in the *Časopis Moravského musea*; and *My Luhačovice* (xv/173), published in *Hlídka* in November. In these writings Janáček was systematically exploring speech melodies in a range of circumstances: among children (xv/169), among holiday-makers (xv/173) and in general (xv/172). His first published references to speech melodies had been parts of broader arguments. Here, how-ever, was a series of articles whose only object was the demonstration of his new concept. The simplest essay, despite its long name, was xv/172. In a few trenchant sentences Janáček says why he was interested in speech melodies (good preparation for an opera composer; much greater variety of content and musical expression than in ordinary song). Then follow thirty-nine numbered and commented examples observed mainly on the streets of Brno.

This short article – eight pages – fared better than the much longer one that Janáček sent to *Český lid*. The editor Čeněk Zíbrt had wel-comed the latter enthusiastically ('I'll print your entire manuscript with pleasure. It's a splendid subject').[53] However, within a month Janáček was voicing his exasperation to Bartoš that Zíbrt had nevertheless decided to issue the thirty-page article in instalments. The 'tiny little thing'[54] was the first instalment of four pages published that autumn, with three more instalments in the rest of that volume. In the event the serialization went on for another two years and this undoubtedly detracted from the impact Janáček hoped it would have.

In an undated letter to Bartoš, probably sent around 24 October 1903, Janáček is more explicit than anywhere else about his health problems at the time. He had been suffering, he wrote, from inflamma-tion of the colon, which had consequently become narrow and restricted ('lots of unpleasantness!') and 'on top of all this, the old complaint' (presumably the infection of sinuses, see chap. 29). Because of all this he was seeking to retire; his pension taken at fifty (ten years early) would be low, but 'enough for me and my wife'. On a more cheerful note, the Brno Theatre was studying *Jenůfa*: 'In Prague it was thought too "Moravian"' (Janáček's interpretation; this was not offered in the official correspondence from Prague). 'I've launched now into a *mod-ern* opera. But the libretto?! If only the Good Lord had given me more poetic veins!'[55]

Within a week of writing this letter to Bartoš, Janáček had found a collaborator, but one so young and so inexperienced in theatrical craft, and indeed literary craft, that one can only assume the choice was deliberate: Janáček wanted a very junior partner, in essence an amanuensis who would simply obey his instructions. His choice fell upon one of Olga's contemporaries and friends (one of her deathbed visitors), Fedora Bartošová, then a nineteen-year-old schoolteacher working in the village of Sudoměřice, some 60 km south-east of Brno. As a poet her output had so far consisted merely of a few poems printed in a school magazine and three poems published in *Lidové noviny* on 16 February, ten days before Olga died. One can also imagine that the Olga connection was another attraction for Janáček, a way of keeping his daughter alive for him. On a trip back to Brno to visit her mother, some time between All Saints' Day (1 November) and the day Janáček left for Prague (6 November), the young Fedora was invited to come and see the composer for a 'literary conversation'. She had heard that Janáček had noticed her published poems and reportedly 'liked their form'; her first assumption was that she would be invited to write 'some song or other'.

But Janáček came up with a much greater project – something quite grandiose for me. He told me that he planned to work on an opera to be called either *The Crimson Roses* or *The Fiery Roses*. He was already thinking about the overall effects and the main characters: about Živný the composer (right from the beginning I fancied that Živný and Janáček were one and the same person), about Míla Válková (this was the beautiful lady whose photograph he had on his writing-desk), about the spa scenery of Luhačovice, which played a big part in his life. There he relived his musical inspirations, cured his physical ailments, and strengthened and stimulated his nerves, which were overwrought as is often the case with choleric people. He talked about a musical conservatory – I knew that he had in mind the Organ School, which was his pride and joy, the field in which, like the ploughman, he sowed his seeds. As he talked, his eyes sparkled and I knew that his imagination was filling out scenes from his life that he had lived through – but where the boundaries were was difficult for me to determine.

I went away enthusiastically from this first 'consultation' with Janáček, promising that I would try my best to understand him, comply with his wishes and give form to his thoughts. He himself would write the action and the individual scenes, and I would put them into verse.[56]

It was at this time that Janáček's sick leave came through. In response to the composer's earlier letter Bartoš had come back with comfort and advice. He was particularly exercised by Janáček's plan to retire early.

'I think that you have been over-hasty! Allow yourself to be talked into withdrawing your request. Ask for leave instead! The school authorities are knowledgeable in such matters and, without any difficulty, will give you leave for convalescence for a year, which you could perhaps even extend. Don't work with such haste and save yourself a little!'[57] Janáček seems to have heeded this advice since on 9 November, instead of retiring altogether, he took a year's leave from the Teachers' Institute on the grounds of ill-health.[58]

This release from the daily burden of teaching had a huge impact on Janáček's life. Suddenly he had much more time for composing and also a great deal more flexibility in his movements away from Brno. Although he remained at the Organ School, he was in charge there and could vary his timetable according to need. So on Friday 6 November he went to Prague to see Kovařovic's opera *At the Old Bleachery* (much less successful with the public than its predecessor *The Dogheads*). The next day Janáček attended a concert of the Czech Philharmonic conducted by Vilém Zemánek (1875–1922, who had recently taken over the orchestra, rescuing it from almost certain extinction) and with a distinguished soloist, the violinist František Ondříček, who played two violin concertos, Dvořák's and Beethoven's. On Sunday evening Janáček saw Vrchlický's historical drama *The Princes*. While he would normally have had to return to Brno by the night train to be ready for Monday's teaching, this time his new-found freedom enabled him to stay on: at the National Theatre on Monday 9 November (the official start of his sick leave) he heard of one of his favourite operas, Tchaikovsky's *Eugene Onegin*, conducted by Kovařovic.

The little break in Prague allowed Janáček time to think about his new opera, and on 12 November he was able to send off the first written instructions to Bartošová – 'part of a sketch until the appearance of the main character'. Seeing *Eugene Onegin* again had its consequences. One might have thought, after *Jenůfa* and its ostentatious claim about being written on a prose text, that Janáček might have wished to continue with prose, but in these instructions to Bartošová he quoted a quatrain of Pushkin's poem with the comment: 'The form of verse I have in mind is that which Pushkin uses in *Onegin*.' The letter also indicates as well how Janáček intended to work with his collaborator:

I am sending you a part of the sketch – up until the appearance of the main character.

First therefore, I ask you to provide an *overall stylization.*

Second, to develop [the draft], filling it out, *where necessary making complete changes* in those scenes based on *real life* that I have sketched with a few words. I have marked this with red pencil, 1., 2., 3.

The scene [marked with a wavy line] could close with a combination of those various voices all over the promenade: I would say a 'festive hymn' to the godlike beauty of nature.

Into this brilliance the main character would enter: *Mrs Míla Válková.* [. . .]

You know of course the overall contents, as I explained it to you when you were here; I think, therefore, that you will be able to work in stages. I would like to get on now with composing the music and therefore am sending you this section in the hope that in the stillness of your village you will soon have it done.

Please fit the underlined sentences, questions, [and] answers to the rhythm.

The music of this part is carried by a quiet conversational melody; it gets quieter during the Angelus and builds up and grows to ceremonial strength.[59]

The inspirer of the opera had also not been forgotten. The next day Janáček sent a postcard to Mrs Urválková reporting that he had a whole year's leave: 'A good chance to write the opera. I have you to thank for it. I will write to you soon.'[60] In the letter that he promised, sent a couple of days later, Janáček complained that Mrs Urválková had not sent him 'even a postcard', and mentioned delays over *Jenůfa:* 'The opera is being copied out, therefore no news from the theatre. And all that waiting, which causes one stress and irritates one unbearably. And the copying will go on for another fortnight.'[61] In fact copying and rehearsals went on simultaneously, if Janáček's later recollections to Nebuška can be trusted. According to them, police permission for the production came on 16 November,[§] rehearsals having started on 12 November.[62] Perhaps it was no coincidence that on this day Janáček sent off his first instructions to Bartošová for *Fate.* As he wrote to Urválková (15 November), 'the best cure will be to throw oneself into a new, exciting work.' The letter goes on to describe the article he had written for *Hlídka,* entitled *My Luhačovice* (XV/173):

You know: just notes, melodic fragments of speech and overheard talks. People will be amazed that I have noticed them! Mrs Koťátková, the Jewish women, the bookseller's wife, 'broken umbrella', the nightwatchman, the bakers, servant girls and so on.

[§]This date is confirmed by the police censor's note on the libretto.

Do you think that you're missing? Far from it! You are there with your husband's three 'Our Fathers' [as penance] after confession before the wedding, and your little boy with the classic answer to the question: 'What is love?' *Enthusiastic admiration is devoted to the musicality of your voice.* And that theatrical air with which you know how to talk sometimes is documented by many examples. If it interests you I'll send it to you to read when it's published. I've already had a proof.[63]

But it is the continuation of this letter that provides one of the most important moments in the history of *Fate*, with its account of Janáček's restless state of mind while taken over by the new opera, and his first attempt at a synopsis. What is clear is that he already knew the end point, so that Act 3 is given in surprising detail, in contrast to the sketchy previous two acts. It is also striking that this letter has no apparent sign of Mrs Urválková's operatic counterpart.

But I have no peace. I drive myself on and on – just as if I felt this: do it, do it while there still is time, there is so little of it!

You know that I am looking for a libretto. A modern one. I don't know a writer who would suit me. Everything is constructed, nothing is natural, completely true to life.

I know my own inner life best; unfortunately my life does not have as many romantic adventures as the stage demands.

And imagination? Let it dream up the necessary scenes!

I want to have Act 1 completely realistic, drawn from life at a spa. There is a wealth of motifs there!

Act 2 is actually to be a *hallucination*. No more reality, instead the mind, provoked almost to a nervous breakdown, propels the action further and further to the point where it is hard to say whether it's real or a hallucination, a delusion.

While the setting of Act 1 is magnificent spa scenery, Act 2 ought to reveal the extravagant interior of ladies' boudoirs, the scenery of southern landscapes.

Act 3 will be strange.

It is the great hall, the ceremonial chamber of the Conservatory. The students assemble – ladies and gentlemen. The usual student high spirits, pranks. On a wall hangs a poster of an opera – its name? I don't know yet. Perhaps *The Three Roses* or *The Angel's Song.*[II]

The students are arguing about the opera. Whether the second act was real or imaginary, the opera was downright psychopathic. It is drawn from the life

---

[II] Both titles allude to Urválková, the 'three fiery roses' that she carried, and the fact that she was 'an angel like the one we'd buried' (*MLWJ*, 97).

of the artist. Smetana heard a *single* note with elementary force in his brain – and he was ill. With my artist it will be worse. He ends his opera, with far greater agitation, at the second act. The professor asks his students: 'Suppose you were to plunge the white-hot passion of love's real pain and bliss into that frothed-up blood?'

'He might go mad', replies a student.

'They say that he went mad', points out the professor. 'His life story is not even well known – he was a mediocre composer.'

The opera would end in this way.

I am beginning work with the aid of the writer *Fedora Tálská*.[64]

'Hard to say whether it's real or a hallucination, a delusion.' It is equally hard to say how much of this was taken from life. The statement 'His life story is not even well known – he was a mediocre composer' sounds very much like an ironic comment on Janáček's own career so far. Certainly Fedora Bartošová found the boundaries between Janáček's own life and his imagined libretto 'difficult to determine' (see chap. 52). Meanwhile 'Fedora Tálská' (Janáček's muddled version of her early pseudonym, Kamila Talská) was getting on quite nicely with her daunting task. Janáček sent her his scenario in four batches between 12 November and 8 December.[65] Bartošová responded with two batches, on 25 November (Act 1) and 4 December (Act 2 Scene 1), and brought the rest back with her to Brno just before Christmas.[66] One thing that emerges from Janáček's and Bartošová's correspondence is how fluid and changeable Janáček's scenario was. A crucial early change was over the part of Živný the composer. In his instructions to Bartošová he mentioned that 'Mrs Míla Válková' (a transparent truncation of Mrs Camilla Urválková) was the main character, as corroborated by the original title *The Star of Luhačovice*. But Bartošová had her doubts: 'Some figures I see vividly before me. It is only perhaps Živný I don't know where to place. Perhaps in that category of spa visitors who observe life and are thus in the most direct contact with the audience? Is he not perhaps the *main* character?'[67] With which Janáček, when he wrote back the next day, tacitly agreed: 'From this continuation you will probably guess who is at the centre of the action.' 'I will start composing at once', he added at the end of the letter.[68]

A week later Janáček told Bartošová that he had decided not to send Act 2 in stages: 'I want you to have it whole and judge it in its finished state; [to see] whether in Act 2 there will be enough drama, strength and interest.' He was delighted with Bartošová's 'flowing verse and thoughts', but felt that she had not quite understood the 'dry, dapper solicitor', Dr Suda. He should be frivolous rather than poetical, and Janáček suggested the sort of verse that Suda should use. Janáček also mentioned that he was going off to Prague the next day, 'partly to see the doctor, but also to see *Tosca*, the latest opera'.[69] While not exactly 'the latest opera' (its première in Rome was on 14 January 1900), the performance Janáček saw on Thursday 26 November was nevertheless very soon after its Czech première, on 21 November, conducted by Kovařovic.[¶]

While in Prague Janáček sent Bartošová a postcard. Perhaps on the way he had time to reflect on how his new opera was going and what sort of timetable he had in mind for it: 'You are working so splendidly that I am getting down to sketching *Act 2* with relish. I want to be finished with the music to Act 1, let's say by June – and with the whole opera in one year's time. But that's a lot of work.'[70] In the event Janáček easily beat his Act 1 target, completing it by 22 April 1904, but finished the whole opera (in its first version) only by 12 June 1905.

A few days after his Prague trip, Janáček continued to praise Bartošová's work: 'Reading quietly through Act 1 I am, frankly, amazed by your work. I like it.' And, going back on his previous plan of sending Act 2 complete, he announced that he was sending his draft for Act 2 Scene 1: a scene in Míla's boudoir where she is seen reading a letter from Živný, who then arrives. Janáček's main anxiety, however, was that the newspapers had got on to the fact that he was writing a new opera when 'we don't know the end – everything has not yet been thought through'.[71]

'In Act 3 there is still more gradation', Janáček wrote to Bartošová. 'It would be a tangle** of laughter and surprise – so perhaps we have hit the mark! – human life is like that! I won't however send you Act 3 now – so that you can concentrate on Act 2. Even I did not know where the blow from the first act would fall, let alone from the second.'[72]

Within five days, on 8 December, Janáček had sent off his draft for Act 3 and announced that he had begun composing Act 1: 'I have shortened the first scene; it begins immediately in the full spa grounds.

[¶] Janáček's programme for the performance of *Tosca* on 26 November 1903, conducted by Karel Kovařovic, survives in BmJA (Racek 1955, 21).
** *spletna*, a word familiar from Janáček's theoretical writings, see chap. 19.

It will be more striking. But I will insert little episodes into it. Here and there you will correct the odd word for me.'[73] Janáček's passionate commitment to the project is evident from his brief postcard to Bartošová nine days later, demanding to know why she had 'gone so silent'.[74] In fact, despite her teaching commitments and having to write end-of-term school reports, Bartošová was getting on well enough. On 19 December she announced that the draft was finished, though she still had to copy it out. She would bring it with her to Brno when she returned for the school holidays.[75] It is important to stress that at this point Janáček was entirely happy with his young collaborator. Although his praise to her could perhaps be discounted merely as kindly encouragement, his own, private reactions (noted on the draft libretto) were just as enthusiastic:

1. Flowing melodious lines.
2. Fit for printing.
3. So new, new!
4. Not just the main characters are clear but also the episodic ones.
5. So much life before and after the big monologues – they can take it – Act 1! This Luhačovice!
6. For a big, even a Prague public.[76]

When the big domestic upset over Mrs Urválková happened is difficult to say. Zdenka represented it as occurring 'in the winter' and in her memoirs placed it before her account of Christmas 1903. If the incident did indeed take place before Christmas it would have been exactly when Janáček was planning his libretto and sending it to Bartošová. It would thus be fascinating to speculate – one can do no more – about how Janáček's autobiographical opera and his own life were intermingling (see chap. 52).

Zdenka, as she described it, began to get the impression that Janáček's letters from Urválková were somehow incomplete, as if 'written for me [to read]':

And something else struck me. Leoš, who was so careless and disorganized in everything, suddenly took to locking his writing-desk carefully and carrying the keys about with him the whole time. I became ever more suspicious but I said nothing to him. I was frightened of spoiling our good rapport and also I already knew from experience that he wouldn't tell me the truth if I asked directly. One morning – now in the winter – he nevertheless forgot the keys and went to get dressed in my little room. Quickly I opened his writing-desk. In the front I saw letters that I'd read with him, further back I suddenly caught sight of a pile of other letters with the same handwriting. So my suspicion about a double correspondence was correct. Quickly I took the bundle, locked the desk, and put the keys where my husband left them.

She then hid the letters in the pantry, but not for long. Janáček discovered his mistake and the disappearance of the letters almost immediately, and angrily demanded them back.

He begged, he threatened, eventually he promised me that we'd read them together. I believed him and brought the letters. He tore them out of my hand and hid them. I got angry. I told him that he was unfaithful and asked why should he come to me when he then wanted to deceive me. He didn't defend himself, he didn't make excuses, clearly he was very frightened. I never learnt why, since surely there couldn't have been anything so terrible in those letters.[77]

Zdenka's common sense about there being nothing 'so terrible' is confirmed by what has survived from Mrs Urválková – long, rambling, self-absorbed letters. Zdenka reported that she and Janáček did not speak to each other for a few days, and that Janáček went on corresponding with Mrs Urválková, though without passing on any more letters to read.

Janáček's involvement with his new opera now crowded out thoughts of the previous one, currently in rehearsal in Brno. It was only in a letter written to Mrs Urválková shortly before Christmas that Janáček expressed any idea about what was going on: 'Just the soloists and chorus know their parts from the opera and know how to perform them! The orchestra has not had rehearsals yet.' In her memoirs Zdenka recalled how her mother got an infection in the middle ear and had to have an operation, so she went to Vienna to look after her father and brother and spent Christmas with them[78] while Janáček remained in Brno and wrote to Urválková:

I received a *madonna* from my wife: a little medallion of my poor daughter; and also an embroidered cushion; I'm working all day long; so it comes in useful when for a moment it's necessary to put down one's pen and sit back.

These are sad holidays at our house: the first time left all alone. I'll go off to my native village for at least two or three days.[79]

The 'two or three days' were spent with the Sládeks, in particular observing young Lidka (not yet three) and taking down almost fifty of her speech melodies.[††] Exactly a year earlier Janáček had escaped from Brno to Hukvaldy to finish *Jenůfa*. Within two months his daughter was dead. A year later the pain was still there, captured in a card that Janáček sent Urválková from Hukvaldy on 28 December:

It is beautiful here, but sad. Some snow has fallen on the sleigh ride. A sparkling, white cover on nature: an icy wind blows into it. I'm leaving – [it's a place] where if one calls – no answer – no company.[80]

[††]Later published in *Last Year and This* (xv/180).

45

Spas, especially Luhačovice

They are an affluent and complacent couple, beaming out of the frontispiece of František Stavěla's guide to Luhačovice (1923, see Plate 32): she with her carefully cut, belted dusky-pink coat and matching gloves, he with his smart suit, tie, folded handkerchief in top pocket, and centre-parted hair. They are posed, smiling for all they are worth, in the window of a railway carriage, destination LÁZNĚ LUHAČOVICE – Luhačovice Spa. This was the desired clientèle for the Moravian spa: young, rich, beautiful, confident and no doubt upwardly mobile, the new money, the yuppies of their day.* This, rather than the more established Czech spas of Karlsbad and Marienbad, was the spa where Janáček felt most at home.

From a twenty-first-century point of view spa holidays sound impossibly remote, especially in Britain, where even in the nineteenth century the seaside holiday was beginning to replace the spa cure. Thus Bath, Leamington and Buxton became gently trapped in time to give way to the development of Blackpool and Eastbourne, with their piers, sea-front promenades, guesthouses and amusements. And today these seaside resorts have themselves fallen prey to the package holiday and cheap foreign travel. On the landlocked continent, the attractions of spas as summer holiday resorts lasted longer. Although it is said that the spa era, graced by royalty, died with Sarajevo,[1] in Bohemia and Moravia the heyday of the spas continued into the 1920s and 30s, and even after the Second World War, when the new Communist administration made spa cures available to the masses. Czech spas were

---

* As Janáček commented to Kamila Stösslová, 'I see newly rich people at lunch; they put on different clothes every day.' (12 July 1919, HŽ, no. 125).

famous. The hydropathic cures (i.e. treatments using large quantities of hot and cold water externally rather than merely drinking it or bathing in it) were devised by Vincenc Priessnitz, who opened the first water-cure institute in Gräfenberg (Lázně Jeseník), Silesia, in 1829.[2] His methods, involving wet sheets, cold douches, cold compresses, stomach packs, sweating blankets and baths of provocative hotness or coldness, spread even as far as Britain in the 1840s, to Harrogate, Matlock, Malvern and other spa towns.[3] The word 'hydro' still lingers on in names of some older buildings where hydrotherapy was practised. Several Czech spas better known through their German names, for example Karlsbad, Marienbad and Teplitz, achieved particular fame, attracting a smart foreign clientèle. Edward VII was a regular visitor to Marienbad from 1897 to 1909.[4] The high prices commanded by Marienbad and Karlsbad would have dissuaded Janáček from regular visits; so would their German orientation. He went to these spas seldom, reluctantly, and only on doctor's orders. The Moravian spa of Luhačovice was a different matter. It was nearer; it attracted a mainly Czech-speaking clientèle; and as a spa without the aristocratic, titled and royal visitors of Marienbad and Karlsbad, its prices were considerably lower.

First described in print in 1669, Luhačovice's mineral waters (recommended for digestive and respiratory problems) were exploited by its owners, the Serényi family, especially from the late eighteenth century, when a small resort began to grow up. Zdenka recalls her parents taking a trip there in 1886; she went with the young Olga to visit them and her husband,[5] his presence there confirmed by a couple of album entries (see chap. 23). According to Stejskalová, Janáček went there 'from time to time' in the 1890s[6] but only one visit is documented, in July 1892, when he made notations of cimbalom players from Březůvky and consulted a Dr Picek for his pityriasis (the flaking of dry skin).[7] It is clear from all the new developments Janáček described to Zdenka when he went there in 1903[8] that he hadn't been there for years.

In 1902 the spa of Luhačovice was acquired from Count Otto Serényi by a consortium of Moravian doctors, who set up a limited stock company and acquired most of the shares. Situated in the middle of fine countryside with many possibilities for walks and excursions, Luhačovice began to attract leading figures of Moravian cultural life and rapidly developed into a popular, mainly Czech-speaking resort. A distinctive 'Moravian' type of architecture was forged by the architect Dušan Jurkovič, who was responsible for the distinctive design of many of Luhačovice's first public buildings in a style that married Art Nouveau and Moravian folk art. From a village of 142 homes and 945 inhabitants in 1880, Luhačovice grew, by the 1921 census, to 352 houses and 1850 permanent inhabitants.[9] Its success, however, was most clearly demonstrated by the number of visitors it attracted. In 1902 there were 2024 registered visitors. This figure increased annually, especially after 1905, when the first railway came to Luhačovice. By 1926 the number was 9559, mostly from Czechoslovakia,[10] staying in 186 registered hotels and guesthouses;[11] food was provided in ten guesthouses and eight hotels, while there were also seven restaurants and wine bars. In comparison with Karlsbad (which attracted up to 70,000 visitors in the summer months),[12] this was still a small spa and this was one of its attractions: one was much more likely to bump into one's friends in Luhačovice than in Karlsbad or Marienbad.

While Olga was still alive, the Janáčeks took their holidays in Hukvaldy. But after Olga's death, Hukvaldy, which had been the scene of her sad decline, became invested with bitter memories, and in 1903, the first summer after her death, husband and wife went their different ways, she to her parents in Vienna and he to Hostýn, Hukvaldy and Luhačovice. That Janáček chose Luhačovice could have been suggested by any of his friends who were closely involved in its development, for instance its first director Dr František Veselý (1862–1923), whom he knew from the Russian Circle in Brno. Janáček's summer of 1903 set a pattern. He became one of the best-known and most faithful visitors, returning almost every summer until his death. For Janáček Luhačovice was something between a health farm and a social event. He would bump into old friends (accounts of such meetings were usually passed on to Zdenka in letters) or make new ones. One thing he discovered as early as 1886 was that a holiday spent solo in Luhačovice was ideal for amorous encounters: 'an annual conference – of beautiful women', as he recalled in his autobiography.[13] He met both his Kamilas there, Camilla Urválková in 1903 and Kamila Stösslová in 1917; the summer of 1917 and the one ten years later, when he contrived to be with Stösslová alone, were some of his happiest times in Luhačovice.

Although the years up to 1916 were increasingly better ones for Janáček's relationship with his wife, the couple continued to take holidays apart. Zdenka never went to Luhačovice nor even seems to have objected that her husband went there on his own. As for Janáček, having Zdenka around would certainly have cramped his style. The only years in which there was some question of Zdenka's coming with him were 1914, 1916 and 1918. He asked her to accompany him in the summer of 1914, soon after the outbreak of war, but she declined, feeling that she had to stay with Stejskalová in the Brno house during those unsettled times.[14] According to her memoirs, Zdenka was expecting to go to Luhačovice in the summer of 1916 after the triumph of *Jenůfa* in Prague.[15] The triumph, however, brought with it Gabriela Horvátová, and it was she rather than Zdenka who spent an ostentatiously social time with Janáček in Luhačovice that summer. In 1918 a vague invitation was offered by Stösslová; from Luhačovice Janáček sent letters to Zdenka saying how expensive it all was and recommending that she 'wait for Hukvaldy'.

To suggest that amorous adventures were the sole agenda is of course wrong. Luhačovice was known for its saline waters – the main promenade, the Slanice, was named after them – and such waters were thought to be effective for the sinusitis problems from which Janáček suffered. The fact that Janáček said little about treatments in his letters to Zdenka does not mean that he did not take cures; there are enough references to indicate that this was a routine activity, too routine, and thus uninteresting, to warrant regular reports. At the beginning of his 1903 visit he described to Zdenka what was now on offer at Luhačovice: morning and afternoon treatments, baths, inhalations, in short, he wrote, 'the activity of the big spas'.[16] In a postcard to Joza Janáčková and her daughter Věra written at the end of that same stay he mentioned that his time in Luhačovice had been necessary for 'relaxation and treatment'.[17]

There were usually at least half a dozen medical doctors resident in Luhačovice during the spa season[18] and this allowed Janáček to seek different medical opinions. In 1908, for instance, he consulted Dr F. Votruba, resident in Luhačovice 1908–10 and a former assistant of Dr Maixner (who had treated Olga). Votruba immediately diagnosed the beginnings of gout that Dr Říha in Brno had overlooked. The treatment he prescribed was mostly diet and drinking the 'strongest water from Aloiska' (one of the main springs); hydrotherapy included cold baths and 'magnetization of the left foot' every other day.[19] Other treatments that Janáček underwent (e.g. in 1921) were mud baths and electrical procedures.[20] Treatments continue to be mentioned up to Janáček's final years. He alludes to a 'schedule for treatment' to Kamila Stösslová in 1926[21] and in his final year, 1928, he seems to have taken advantage of the full range available: heated mud baths[22] and inhalation,[23] and in due course he began the 'cold water treatment: oxygen dissolved in water, paddle in warm water – then cold, then a shower'.[24] All this seems to have been directed at eliminating gout in his right foot.[25] Generally it would seem that the sinusitis problems gradually gave way to gout and rheumatic pains, all of which, it was thought at the time, could be alleviated by the spa procedures in Luhačovice (see vol. ii: Did Janáček have really gout?).

Different spas with different chemical composition of their waters specialized in treating different ailments, and doctors had their particular favourites. After Janáček's serious illness in the winter of 1912–13 his Prague doctor, Dr Jan Hnátek, recommended not Luhačovice but Karlsbad for his next summer spa trip and it was there, most unwillingly, that Janáček repaired for the summer of 1913. Presumably Dr Hnátek had in mind the reputation of Karlsbad waters for alleviating skin complaints[26] such as Janáček had suffered in 1912. After a couple of weeks there Janáček went on to the smaller (and presumably cheaper) peat-spa of Mšeno, where he contracted erysipelas, which may have provided him with an argument for not going to either spa again. There was, however, one more Bohemian spa that Janáček frequented. In 1915 František Veselý (who had presided over the early flowering of Luhačovice) took up a post in Bohdaneč. Janáček went there twice in 1915 and made brief return visits over the course of the next three years. He went there, he once announced, for his 'rheumatism'.[27] The years 1910, 1913 and 1915 were the only ones after 1903 in which Janáček did not go to Luhačovice. In 1913 and 1915 Janáček went to other spas; in 1910 the move to a new house may have precluded any financial outlay on a long spa holiday.

For several of the earlier years in Luhačovice (notably 1903–5, 1914, 1916–17) Janáček stayed in a modest guesthouse called 'Vlastimila' (in Luhačovice there were few street names and numbers, and houses were generally identified by name). In 1917, when asked by Rektorys about accommodation in Luhačovice, he described it as follows:

I usually live in Luhačovice in the villa 'Vlastimila', which belongs to Mr Pospíšil, a mechanic in Luhačovice.† It is on the edge of the Prague Quarter, the

---

† Štědroň 1939, 18, however, describes its being owned by Mrs Františka Šteflová.

first house from the Smetana House. He has flats on the first floor; small but adequate. Two of them have two rooms each; in such there is enough room for three people [Rektorys's request]. One used to pay 4 K daily for a two-room flat.

This was at the lower end of the market. Something nearer the upper end in a fashionable hotel would cost two or even four times as much. With a mere five rooms at its disposal 'Vlastimila' was one of the smallest of the Luhačovice guesthouses, and its rooms were not always available. In other years Janáček stayed in some of the larger and more central hotels owned by the Luhačovice stock company: the 'Director's House' (later the Spa Hotel), Janův dům [Jan's House] and Jestřábí [The Goshawk's]. However in 1912 he stayed for the first time in the Augustinian House, a large guesthouse owned by the Staré Brno Augustinians, and from 1918 onwards he stayed nowhere else. According to a contemporary advertisement in the 1914 edition of Balhar's guidebook, this was 'a modern, comfortably appointed house in the quiet of the forest with fifty dry, airy rooms'. It was 'ten minutes from the middle of the spa' and 'moderately priced'. That it was also 'particularly recommended to Catholic families'[29] seems not to have deterred Janáček. It had several other advantages, not least the harmonium in the chapel that Janáček was able to make use of – memorably for a try-out of the *Glagolitic Mass* (see vol. ii: 1926b).

As in most spas, the season in Luhačovice lasted essentially five months. According to Balhar it was divided into three parts: 1 May to 15 June ('spring'); 16 June to 15 August ('summer'); and 16 August to 30 September ('autumn'), with higher prices in the 'summer' and 50% price reductions on accommodation in the two outer periods. Apart from Janáček's exceptional visit in May 1904, his visits were usually later in the season. In the earlier years, while teaching at the Organ School, he would never have been able to get away before mid-July. Until 1916 he economized by fitting the trips (or at least much of them) into the 'autumn' season, but his increased wealth from 1916 allowed several July trips at the height of the season. Even then, the July trip in 1918 was undertaken only in the hope of seeing Kamila Stösslová,[30] who had gone there beforehand. Although some of the earlier visits were shorter (e.g. just a week in 1912), from 1916 onwards he aimed at a two- or three-week trip.

Getting to Luhačovice from Brno needed time and some resolve. Until 1905 the only method was by road and it is clear from a reference to the coachman in *My Luhačovice* (XV/173) that Janáček arrived by horse-drawn carriage. The opening of a rail connection in 1905 improved things considerably. The 131-km journey from Brno, however, involved changing trains at Újezdec u Luhačovic. In 1919 the fastest journey between Brno and Újezdec took 2 hours 56 minutes (and the slowest 4 hours 11 minutes) and although the remaining journey (Újezdec–Luhačovice) took only another half hour, there were only four trains a day, a number that by 1926 had been reduced to three. Even with well-planned connections one needed to allow a good four hours. In 1926 he left Luhačovice at 12.42 and would be in Brno, he told Zdenka, at 16.11.[31]

Exceptionally in 1905 Janáček called a meeting of his folksong committee at Luhačovice, and in these earlier years would occasionally use Luhačovice as a base for his own folksong collecting. In 1916 Luhačovice served Janáček as a centre for visiting nearby folkloristic attractions with Mrs Horvátová; in 1925 he took advantage of an offer of a car trip, even then something of a treat for Janáček. But generally he confined his activities in Luhačovice to treatments, walking and socializing. Photographs of him from his Luhačovice holidays (or for that matter the picture of the smart couple in the frontispiece of the Stavěla Luhačovice guide) bring home how formal it was, at least from a twenty-first-century vantage point. He always wore a tie, a suit (with a waistcoat) and a hat (either a boater or a fedora). His most informal holiday-wear is the white linen suit and cap, but even this comes with a waistcoat.[‡] A typical stay is reflected in a postcard sent to Janáček after he had left Luhačovice by the Ostrčils, with whom he had spent a happy and sociable time in the summer of 1920: 'We think of you and are missing sitting with you in the evenings and also during our walks. Yesterday we did a lovely walk according to your suggestions: [. . .] above the [Slovácká] Búda up to Řetechov and back through Pozlovice.'[32] Regular walks, a change of diet, a change of atmosphere and people: all of these were beneficial and so it was that Janáček went back time and time again to Luhačovice. The Bohemian spa of Bohdaneč, which Janáček went to several times, failed at the last instance because of the lack of friends (after he had fallen out with the Veselýs, Peška and Horvátová) and the lack of interesting surroundings

---

[‡]Photographs of Janáček at Luhačovice can be found in *IL* (plates 4, 7, 9 and 10); the same clothes are reproduced in Kožík 1983, plate 16 and in Tauber 1949, opposite p. 49.

for walks. A miserable week spent there in 1918 seems to have sealed its fate: 'I'm here, in such dead silence, in such social emptiness that if I could look at myself I'd say: What do you really want here? Completely alone! Apart from single distant acquaintance, just nobody.'[33]

Janáček did not see Luhačovice as a creative retreat and almost never composed music there. He believed in strenuous bursts of creative activity taking him to a good stopping-point in the composition, followed by thoughtful fallow periods; and the summer was for him traditionally fallow (see vol. ii: How Janáček composed operas). In later life, for instance in 1918 and 1925, there were emergencies that caused him to do some work even while on holiday. And in one case, in 1926, the weather was poor and kept him inside; as he did not like to be idle, he got down to composition (in this case the *Glagolitic Mass*). Mostly, however, the only 'work' he did was thinking. It was to Luhačovice that he took the newspaper cuttings that gave rise to *The Diary of One Who Disappeared* and *The Cunning Little Vixen*. And who knows what went on in his head at other times.

46

Louise and the hidden agenda

The starting-point of *Fate* is usually traced to Janáček's meeting with Camilla Urválková at Luhačovice in the summer of 1903 and her strange story about Čelanský's opera *Kamilla* (see chap. 44). However the inspiration for the type of opera Janáček was to write was perhaps the result of a visit to Prague earlier that year, on 21 May 1903, to see Charpentier's opera *Louise*. It made a deep impression on him and he remembered it to the end of his life.

Janáček's enthusiasm for *Louise* is documented both in his letters and in his lectures about opera at the Brno Organ School. Writing in 1924 on Janáček's attitude to opera, his pupil Václav Kaprál recalled the following comment: 'Musorgsky went from Wagnerian motifs to speech melodies, but he did not recognize their beauty. If he had, he would have stayed with them. Charpentier went to the originals.'[1] A fuller account of what is clearly the same lecture, now firmly dated to 1909 and taken down in shorthand by Mirko Hanák, was published in 1959:

From mensural music onwards the text was always put into verse. In opera there used to be only knights. Ordinary life was too small for opera. There was no real life in opera. This began only in Charpentier's *Louise*. Musorgsky's *Boris Godunov* is another example of this. Charpentier took originals (the drunk Noctambulist in *Louise*; the milkwomen call just as in Paris in the early morning) – these are correct original types [of natural speech].[2]

The first point Janáček makes is about the use of prose. Knights – a shorthand for the typical elevated, noble characters from the older traditions of opera – sing in verse, but ordinary people use prose, so that Charpentier's ordinary people in *Louise* do so too. The second is the subject matter. It is ordinary, everyday life, previously thought to be inappropriate for opera, that Charpentier uses – 'real life', as Janáček has it. And third, this 'real life' is suggested by the use of authentic street talk, what Janáček calls here Charpentier's 'originals' – in other words, Janáček's concept of speech melody.

From his naming of two specific characters in *Louise*, the Noctambulist and the Milkwoman, Janáček was speaking of Act 2 Scene 1 of the opera, the only one where these two characters occur.* This scene begins with the orchestral prelude 'Paris Awakes' and continues to depict the early morning life of Paris. Small traders, such as the Milkwoman, set up their booths; late revellers, such as the Noctambulist, return from their evening engagements. It is odd that Janáček should have mentioned the Noctambulist in this context. He is a symbolic, ambiguous figure, given to philosophizing, and someone who could scarcely be thought of as part of ordinary life or as someone who would talk in everyday speech. He has the biggest part in this scene, including a long monologue where he quotes Dante and is then energetically mocked by the more prosaic traders.

Certainly, Janáček could easily have chosen more apt examples from the other traders to demonstrate his point about Charpentier's 'originals'. His transcribed words were: 'the milk*women* call just as in Paris in the early morning'. There is in fact only one milkwoman in the score, and she certainly does not 'call her wares'. The only passage that could have suggested to Janáček that Charpentier used authentic street cries was a later part in the same scene, not involving the milkwoman at all but instead some of the other traders – the chairmender, the ragman, the artichoke-seller, the carrot-seller and others, who come together in an ingenious ensemble: an offstage chorus of recognizable street cries.[3]

But even if Janáček's memory of detail was a little hazy, his general memory of *Louise* was excellent and long-lived. A decade later, in his introductory lecture for the opening of the Brno Conservatory in 1919 (xv/220), he slipped in a characteristic aside when discussing the importance of the single note in music: 'And you, that little bee in the conservatory. Didn't Charpentier learn from you the effect of a *single* note in *Louise*?' There is no doubt what Janáček had in mind here. Charpentier was often economical with his accompaniments, and there

---

* The Noctambulist occurs again in Act 3 Scene 2, but here he is dressed and known as 'The King of Fools'.

are many effective passages in *Louise* where the voice recites against a single held note. A few years later, in 1922, Janáček tried to obtain a full score of the opera from Universal Edition, and was most put out when he learnt that none was available. 'How is it possible that the score of *Louise* is not printed! It is played all over the world! I don't need the piano score.'[4] This last sentence suggests that Janáček indeed possessed a piano-vocal score (from which his pupils studied the work), though it no longer survives with his collection of scores in the Janáček Archive.

All these references by Janáček to *Louise* provide clear evidence of something that had made a major impact on him; indeed he mentioned no other non-Czech opera so frequently and over such a long period. It is easy enough to suggest reasons for this. Here was a phenomenon to be envied: a foreign composer winning a huge success in Prague with a new work. The foreign composer, moreover, had even heard of Janáček and was well disposed towards him.[†] Furthermore the foreign composer was writing in a new way that in a couple of important respects paralleled Janáček's innovations in the work he was composing virtually at the same time – *Jenůfa*. In Charpentier's use of allegedly authentic street cries Janáček saw a step towards his own concept of speech melody. Charpentier's use of something like speech melody together with the prose libretto was a heartening validation by a fashionable and successful foreign composer of a technique that Janáček had already worked out for himself.

The aspects of *Louise* that Janáček did not discuss or write about are, however, even more interesting than the ones he did. *Louise* was the most important influence on Janáček's approach to the conventions of opera and on the formation of what we take today to be typical ingredients of Janáček's later operas. It is possible of course that several of these other ingredients came from other sources, or that Janáček stumbled upon them by himself. But the timing is suggestive. None of these techniques can be found in the operas that he wrote before he saw

---

[†]If one can rely on the account by the lawyer Rudolf Malík in a letter to Emil Šolc (who published Janáček's piano arrangements in his *Bouquet* v/2) that 'Charpentier especially asked for Janáček's *Bouquet*, from which he particularly liked some of the songs with Janáček's harmonization' (Malík to Šolc, 15 April 1904, BmJA, A 5557). The fact that this letter was found with Janáček's correspondence suggests that Šolc sent it to Janáček, who would thus have been aware of its encouraging contents.

Louise: not only *Šárka* and *The Beginning of a Romance* but also *Jenůfa*. All are usefully displayed in a single work, Charpentier's *Louise*, and all can be found in *Fate*, the opera Janáček began writing within months of seeing *Louise*, and in most of his subsequent operas. Moreover these are ingredients that Janáček did not mention at all when he talked about *Louise*. The aspects he did discuss – speech melodies, the prose libretto, everyday subject matter, and even the crucial use of the single note – can all be found in *Jenůfa*, written before Janáček heard *Louise*. Janáček was happy to draw attention to them since by so doing he was actually defending innovations that he believed to be his own discoveries in *Jenůfa*. About the others – what one might call the 'hidden agenda' – he remained silent. These aspects include the use of particular character types, of 'urban' style, of individualized songs, a specific approach to the chorus, and the use of the viola d'amore.

In the first place, Janáček may well have been drawn to *Louise* by the different world it portrays and the new types of characters in contrast to mainstream opera – not just everyday rural life as in *Jenůfa*, but a specifically urban life, with an entirely new cast of characters. The Bohemian artists (painter, sculptor, poet, songwriter, philosopher, etc.) of *Louise* may have been inspired by Puccini's Bohemians, but they are in turn reflected in *Fate* in the gathering of creative people at the Luhačovice spa. The painter Lhotský and the composer Živný in the final form of the opera are merely the remnants of a more elaborate plan. For his next opera, *The Excursion of Mr Brouček to the Moon*, Janáček chose a source that again included painters, writers, composers – and it was on his insistence that these groups were represented not only on the moon, as in the original novel by Svatopluk Čech, but that they proliferated in a more obviously Bohemian way on earth too. Málinka, carrying on with the painter Mazal to the disapproval of her elderly, respectable father – this was entirely Janáček's idea (see chap. 58) – is simply a reflection of Louise, tempted away from her father and mother by the artist Julien and the lure of his 'artistic' mode of life.

Similarly the vengeful figure of Louise's mother, who poisons Louise's hopes of reconciling her commitments to her family and to her lover, is paralleled in *Fate* by the disruptive figure of Míla's mother, who deliberately undermines Živný's attempts to lead a quiet married life with Míla. It has been suggested that Míla's mother is the descendant of the uncompromising Kostelnička in *Jenůfa* but these two characters are worlds apart. For all her fierceness and her one terrible deed, the Kostelnička is an essentially good and caring person. Míla's mother is wholly negative; the most obvious clue to her ancestry is her parody of Živný's love song, a trick she learnt from Louise's mother. Much later, Janáček chose to set another text with a disruptive mother-in-law – Kabanicha in *Káťa Kabanová*. All three characters, Louise's mother, Míla's mother and Kabanicha, are contraltos, a voice type Janáček seldom employed in his operas for major characters.

Another significant feature of the characters in *Louise* is the tender relationship between Louise and her father and the way it is destroyed by her attraction to the big city. The Prague première of Charpentier's opera took place at a time when Janáček's beloved daughter Olga (much the same age as Louise) was dying. Acutely responsive as he was to biographical echoes, Janáček may well have been reminded of his own daughter and the way that her death had taken her from him.

Fate was Janáček's first opera to employ a distinctly lighter, 'urban' style of music. The opening waltz chorus, for example, with which the opera bursts into life, suggests the efforts of a spa orchestra. It also recalls the Act 3 waltzes of *Louise*. Unlike, say, the polka, the waltz has no overt folkloristic implications for Bohemia or Moravia (see, for instance, Janáček's comments in xv/177) and has stronger associations with the town and with urban rather than folk music. Janáček used the moderately fast triple metre of the waltz to provide the structural backbone of the opening scenes of *Fate* and *Brouček*, rather as the waltz provides the backbone to much of Act 3 Scene 2 of *Louise*. There are urban-type waltzes too, in later operas such as *The Cunning Little Vixen* and *From the House of the Dead*.

In the wake of *Louise*, with its strophic serenade for Julien in Act 2 or the King of Fools' song in Act 3, Janáček was never afraid afterwards to make use of regularly structured, often strophic, songs in his operas. In *Fate* there is Dr Suda's song to the sun in Act 1 and Živný's love song in Act 2. Janáček required songs for *The Excursion of Mr Brouček to the Moon* and getting the verse texts of these songs from librettists held up the opera for years. All Janáček's later operas include such songs. They may seem at first to be a continuation of Janáček's practice of quoting folksongs or imitation folksongs in *The Beginning of a Romance* and *Jenůfa*. But there is a crucial difference in that most of the songs in these earlier operas are for chorus, not soloists, and all have a specific ethnographic function. From Dr Suda's song onwards these strophic songs are now solo songs, diegetic (i.e. part of the narrative and would be sung in 'real life') and act as a characterizing device. They are almost entirely given to subsidiary, often comic, characters – for instance Kudrjáš and Varvara in *Káťa Kabanová*, Harašta in *The Cunning Little Vixen* or Hauk in *Makropulos*.

Charpentier's example, too, seems to have suggested to Janáček other possibilities for the chorus. Choruses in Janáček's first three operas are sturdy soprano-alto-tenor-bass affairs of a fairly conventional cut. But after *Louise* there was the possibility of an 'individualized chorus'. In *Louise* Charpentier frequently brought together elaborate choral ensembles made up of many individual parts. There are some thirty-five individual characters who in the central acts come together to suggest a realistic Parisian street crowd. The opening scene of *Fate* is similarly fragmented into numerous specified individuals who combine vocally in one of Janáček's most complex choral scenes. Even more lasting an influence on Janáček was the 'symbolic' chorus, the offstage non-realistic chorus, for instance the 'voice of the forest' in *The Cunning Little Vixen* (see vol. ii: The conventions of Janáček's operas). In the final scene of *Louise*, the heroine, now back at home, is attracted away again not by the singing of her lover Julien but by the lure of the big city. An offstage chorus that cries 'O jolie!' over and over again provides a haunting audible symbol for the unseen attraction that Paris exerts on Louise.[5]

A final feature in Janáček's operas that may well have stemmed from *Louise* was Janáček's use of the viola d'amore. The first opera where this curious instrument was employed, at least in the original sketches, was *Fate*. Except for *From the House of the Dead*, it features in all Janáček's operas from *Káťa Kabanová* onwards and in several orchestral and instrumental works as well. While Janáček could have got the idea from other operas he knew such as Meyerbeer's *Les Huguenots*,[6] it is Charpentier's use of it in *Louise* that fits most closely Janáček's verbal references to the instrument and the way he employed it himself.

Of course it would be wrong to give the impression that *Louise* and *Fate* sound at all similar in terms of melodic or harmonic style. Janáček had already found his own voice in *Jenůfa* and in this respect Charpentier's music seems to have made little impact. But in other respects

Janáček's acquaintance with Charpentier's *Louise* was a turning-point in his operatic life. Important attitudes embodied in the conventions of his operas begin to occur not so much in *Jenůfa* but after his fateful encounter with Charpentier's opera *Louise*.

47

1904

Even if he had not been so sad and lonely in Hukvaldy Janáček never-theless needed to return to Brno for *Jenůfa* rehearsals – the première was only two weeks away, set for 14 January, as he announced to Urválková on his return to Brno on 3 January. While Zdenka was still away in Vienna Janáček took the opportunity to make a quick sortie to Prague to see Mrs Urválková, a trip innocently thwarted by Máŕa Stejskalová, who, on her way to the station with Janáček's case and food for the journey, went back for his travelling rug and arrived just as the train was pulling out and was met by an irate Janáček, furious that his plan had gone wrong. But it was just as well, he discovered, since when he dropped in at the Brno Theatre on the way home he found he was needed there.[1] Today it seems incredible that the tiny and under-resourced Brno Theatre could even think of putting on a work of this difficulty in a mere few weeks, and it is hardly surprising that the first performance was postponed by a week to allow time for more rehearsal.

Someone in the theatre was looking after publicity. On Saturday evening 17 January Janáček was dispatched to Prague to invite impor-tant people to the première. On the same day *Moravská orlice* ran an article about *Jenůfa*. And on the next day the Brno Družstvo invited potential reviewers, such as Dr Jan Branberger at the Prague magazine *Čas*. Despite the purely utilitarian nature of the Družstvo's letter, it contained an important statement about what was regarded as new in the opera:

On Thursday 21 January 1904 the première of Leoš Janáček's opera *Jenůfa* will be given at the Czech National Theatre in Brno. In its general conception, [artistic] tendency and manner of composition the work goes beyond the present style of music for the theatre. Apart from its use of elements of a specifically Moravian nature, the work will pave the way for a particular type of word-setting, based on the melodic elements of everyday speech. – In so doing it will achieve a special importance and this is why we take the liberty of inviting you, sir, most courteously, to visit the Brno National Theatre and hear the work.[2]

If such a statement did not come directly from Janáček himself, he had certainly briefed his friends in the Družstvo well. Much the same can be said about the article in *Moravská orlice*, where Janáček had excellent connections. The article did not hide the fact that for many listeners accustomed to a more traditional form of opera *Jenůfa* would be rather novel, and that such listeners would probably find the harmony and rhythms unusual and might not understand it at a first hearing. Such novelties arose, the article went on to explain, from Janáček's dramatic principles, which depended on the truthful capturing of life, and on psychology. Particular features were highlighted such as his conception of speech melody, his use of 'folk rhythms' and short rhythmic motifs.

Janáček's own mission in Prague failed, at least in its principal objective, as is evident from a note that he wrote there to Kovařovic:

I came to invite you to the first performance of *Jenůfa* and have learnt here that you are in poor health. I regret the fact that I cannot extend the invitation to you personally – and perhaps ask you once again if you could not, after all, make a place for my work at the Prague National Theatre as well.

I wish you a speedy recovery and I invite you to come to us in Brno – if your condition should make it at least slightly possible.[3]

Nevertheless, Janáček accomplished many other things, which he reported in a postcard sent from Prague to Mrs Urválková shortly before he left for Brno on Sunday at 11 p.m.:

I slave away in Brno for the whole of Saturday, at night there's a meeting and then the trip to Prague. I spend the whole morning inviting people. The following are coming: Preissová, the Countess Aichlburková [Aichelburg], the critic Chvála,* etc. In the evening I can't even listen in the theatre through tiredness – I should have gone to sleep straightaway.

---

*Emanuel Chvála (1851–1924) wrote reviews in *Národní politika* from 1880 to 1921; he was also a composer: his *Záboj*, 1906–7, to a text by Vrchlický, was staged at the Prague National Theatre in 1918.

His tiredness at the theatre did not perhaps much matter (Another performance of *The Bartered Bride*, conducted by the second conductor František Picka, hardly demanded one's full attention).[4] The point of the letter, however, was to persuade Urválková to join the illustrious company of the author Gabriela Preissová, the Countess Aichelburg, the critic Chvála, etc. '"For such a musician, in his bones" as I am said to be, Chvála will make arrangements to travel to Brno. Only Mrs Camilla Urválková cannot decide.'[5]

She did the next day. Illness and 'frequent attacks' would prevent her from coming.[6] When she next heard from Janáček she might well have concluded that she had decided wisely:

Today I return from the first full rehearsal of Act 1 completely fed up. There was such a wretched argument between the director [of the theatre] and the conductor that I was on edge because of it. The 'trumpeter' [Janáček's ironic quotation marks], when ticked off during the rehearsal, took it so much to heart that he got dangerously drunk. He did not recognize any 'authority'. He swore like a trooper at everyone. It was like the stone that's thrown that brings down the avalanche with it – and which would have badly damaged my première.

With difficulty they managed to sort things out and smooth them over in order to complete the rehearsal. [. . .] I'm dead tired. Drawn, pale as a paschal candle. My eyes keep closing, but yet I'm happier in this life. [. . .] God grant that all goes well on Thursday![7]

And, despite the hostility of some of the orchestral players (who let off steam by writing derisive comments in their parts),[8] it did go well. More rehearsals had been devoted to it in Brno than to almost any other opera, *Lidové noviny* reported, and so great was the advance interest that the première had been placed outside the subscription series[9] (putting an opera in the subscription series was a way of filling the house when attendance was likely to be thin). The theatre was packed and there was enthusiastic applause after the first act. Janáček, who had been lurking anxiously in the wings, had to take a bow, 'pale and agitated', as his pupil Jan Kunc recorded. Act 2, with the 'excellent' Kostelnička of Mrs Hanusová-Svobodová,[†] made an even greater impression on the audience and by the time Janáček appeared before the audience again he was 'already more cheerful and smiling'. After

---

[†]Leopolda Hanusová (1875–1941) was a leading soprano in Brno from 1898 to 1915, taking both lyrical and dramatic Smetana roles (Mařenka in *The Bartered Bride*, and the title role in *Libuše*), and other parts such as the title roles in *Rusalka*, *Tosca* and *Aida*.

the third act the response was 'unending', with Janáček taking many bows and Preissová acknowledging the applause from her box. And the celebrations did not stop there, since the Readers' Club had arranged a special reception afterwards at the Besední dům, a 'convivial evening with many toasts', as Kunc put it.[10]

On the way from the theatre in the direction of the Besední dům [*Hlas* reported on 23 January] the audience lined the street and waited impatiently for the Maestro. After servants with wreaths and bouquets had passed, their curiosity grew. As soon as the Maestro appeared with the conductor Hrazdira and the performers, the spectators called out 'sláva!' ['hurrah'] to Maestro Janáček and accompanied the composer right up to the Besední dům. The Maestro gave his thanks and made his way into the rooms of the Readers' Club.[11]

Or, if the memoirs of another Janáček pupil Václav Kaprál are to believed, he was carried on the shoulders of the soloists, still in their costumes, to the Besední dům.[12] According to Zdenka's recollection of the occasion, Janáček himself was well pleased: 'After the première when we returned home, he came to me and in my joy at the fine success of the work, which I adored, I made my peace with him.'[13]

The success had come about through a devoted and generally excellent cast and conductor, and despite an orchestra of just twenty-nine players that lacked the harp, bass clarinet and cor anglais that Janáček specified.[14] Although a producer (Josef Malý) was cited on the poster, no designer was given since there was no 'design'; they simply made do with whatever could be assembled from stock. When Janáček submitted his next opera to Brno he made a point of specifying that there should be new sets.[15]

The Brno reviews were favourable and respectful, mostly written by Janáček's former pupils. The Prague reviews were fewer and generally disappointing. Dr Branberger had turned up to write for *Čas*, where he compared Janáček unfavourably with Vítězslav Novák and dismissed him as a composer of merely local importance, though one with 'great dramatic talent and feeling for the theatre'. Unlike Smetana, Branberger continued, who had 'folksong in his inner being and wrote music naturally imbued with it', poor Janáček had had to slave away 'with ant-like industry collecting Moravian-Slovak folksongs and with an anatomical scalpel dissecting their most secret components'. Branberger hoped that 'in further works the composer would not be hampered by his theories and would never be weighed down by them in his musical flight'[16] (in this instance, at least, Janáček's declared emphasis on speech melodies, the importance of folksong and his 'new way' of writing operas had rather misfired). Emanuel Chvála was warmer in his praise in *Národní politika*. While stressing the novelty of the opera and its possible difficulty for an average audience, he noted the work's 'success, which was all-pervading and increased from act to act'. In particular he singled out the 'powerful scenes of Act 2', which 'visibly excited the audience'.[17]

A week after the première Janáček sent off a batch of reviews to Mrs Urválková with the following comment:

I know my shortcomings much better myself and could list them in more detail; I want to put things right in *The Fiery Roses*.[‡] One thing is certain – that the work is generally liked, that it's got life in it, that on the stage every word is sharp and effective, just as I emphasized it in the music. They have recognized my talents as a composer for the theatre – and in these times of Wagner, Charpentier, Dvořák, etc., etc., this is indeed significant and extremely flattering for me. As for the ovations that I experienced, it's hard for me to talk about them; I had no idea that something like this could happen. But let me be frank, you might have remembered me with at least a note – I waited – and nothing at all.[18]

Janáček had canvassed for Chvála's presence at the première in Brno, and a few days after his review appeared Janáček wrote to thank him, though the letter was mostly dominated by comments about possible revisions to his harmony manual (xv/151; see chap. 19). He also asked Chvála whether he ought to try the 'director of the Prague National Theatre' again. He gave Chvála a week to respond[19] (he didn't) and, with four performances of *Jenůfa* behind him, he tried his luck again with Kovařovic:

I don't want my renewed request that the Prague National Theatre should also grant a hearing to *Jenůfa* to be based on the most flattering Prague reviews, let alone the local ones – my only complaint is that it was unjust to turn down *Jenůfa*.

I appeal to you as a Czech composer to whom no-one wished to grant a hearing.

Because of the Moravian character of the work? So it has, mistakenly, been said. More perhaps for the all-important principle of the specific naturalism of

‡ As *The Star of Luhačovice* was now being called.

the melody – which, as it has turned out, has not been without effect or comprehension.

May I once again offer my work for performance?[20]

Kovařovic was out of town, Schmoranz explained in his response, and since it was only he, as head of opera, who could decide on operatic repertory, Janáček would have to wait.[21] Janáček gave it a couple of weeks and went to Prague to try and see Kovařovic personally. What Janáček did not realize was that Kovařovic was suffering from nervous exhaustion and had been signed off for two months.[22] Janáček timed his trip to coincide with the final rehearsals for Dvořák's latest opera, *Armida* (Dvořák had supplied the dates in his letter to Janáček of 26 February).[23] It is not clear whether Janáček attended the rehearsal on the morning of Monday 29 February (though that evening he saw a play, *For Eve*, by the Polish poet Lucyan Rydel),[24] but he was there the next day for the notorious dress rehearsal. Kovařovic was still away and had handed over the conducting of Dvořák's final opera to a deputy (František Picka), who was not up to the job. As Janáček recalled several years later: 'I never saw Dr Ant. Dvořák more irritated than at the dress rehearsal of *Armida*. And no wonder; the baton did not control the orchestral body, Mr Pták [the tenor lead] did not turn up because of illness, those taking part got out of their costumes, the rehearsal was not completed' (xv/201). The delayed première of *Armida* was postponed until 25 March.

When Kovařovic did get round to answering Janáček's letter, his answer was no more encouraging:

Director Schmoranz has given me your letter of 9 February 1904. Forgive me, but your complaints that the refusal of *Jenůfa* had been unfair and that there was an unwillingness to grant a hearing to you, a Czech composer, are not correct. Precisely because I had very serious reasons in mind and deliberated the matter with mature consideration, I became convinced that we could not accept your opera for performance. My fears continue that your work, at least on our stage and before our audience, would not meet with the complete success that we would wish both for you and for us. This is not however because of the Moravian character of the work (where do you get that impression?).

I am, however, willing to attend a performance in Brno and would be sincerely glad if the performance there taught me otherwise.[25]

Unfortunately, Janáček responded, there was illness among the cast, and it was not clear when the next performance of *Jenůfa* would be, but if Kovařovic would care to pick one of the last days of the next week, he was sure that a performance could be mounted to suit his timetable: 'I have myself twice wanted to visit you in Prague; I am therefore glad that you have decided on a visit to Brno.'[26] But Kovařovic did not respond, and so all Janáček could do was to make use of what contacts he had in Prague, such as the actress Hana Kvapilová (1860–1907), whom Janáček knew from her years at the Brno Theatre and whose husband, Jaroslav Kvapil (1868–1950), was a dramaturg at the National Theatre (and the producer of the Polish play that Janáček had recently seen there):

In less than two weeks the season will be over here. *Jenůfa* will be given once more at the most – for the ninth time – the Directorate is inviting Mr Kovařovic – I now don't even dare to write to him – he simply doesn't answer – and yet he informed me officially that he will come to one of the performances.

Is he unwell perhaps?

Do you have, Madam, any advice, how I might gain his favour?

Already a while ago, the orchestra of the local theatre has been alarmingly incomplete: the new director[§] has given notice to the horn player, the trumpet player – they are apparently not needed for the summer season.

I myself don't even go to the theatre now – I don't want to hear my own work in such a broken-down state.

And imagine a visitor who hasn't much goodwill towards me attending a 'final performance' like that![27]

Zdenka returned to her parents in Vienna for Easter and made the most of it by going there a good week earlier. On Monday 28 March – Easter Sunday fell on 3 April – she sent a buoyant postcard to Janáček depicting a pretty young lady with black stockings, violet bonnet, violet frilly skirts and a green bodice sitting on a broken egg wishing the reader 'Fröhliche Ostern!': 'So you won't be sad I'm sending you this "fešačka" ["pin-up girl"] to cheer you up. How's the libretto going? Going today to the exhibition and tomorrow to the theatre. I have a hat ordered – a terribly wide one.'[28] Zdenka seems to have come to terms with Olga's death and was clearly enjoying herself.

On 28 March, the day Zdenka wrote this card, Janáček completed his revision of his *Elegy on the Death of my Daughter Olga* (IV/30).

§ František Lacina, director for the single season 1904–5, and later in 1909–15.

Just a few days after the *Jenůfa* première he had attempted to get some new lines for *The Elegy* from Bartošová:

And now with the little verse for my poor Olga.

Life burst into flower with her only when her thoughts began to come together in one particular direction – she wanted to serve the idea of uniting all of Slavdom so far as the weak strength of a girls' schoolteacher would allow – she wanted to teach Russian. She went there for reassurance and to get to know the most powerful of the Slav nations. They saw on her brow the strange shadow of death. *In the hospital they laughed at her enthusiasm. How much she suffered!*

Apart from the terrible death, that was the most tragic thing of her life. How will you compose this into a few short lines?[29]

If Fedora Bartošová did oblige, her lines have not survived and in his revision of the piece Janáček stuck to the original words.

Janáček's affair with Mrs Urválková was nearing the end of its course. He seems to have visited her at home at Dolní Královice,[30] but soon after, as Zdenka related, 'her husband wrote to Leoš saying that he didn't want him to go on corresponding with his wife because he'd received an anonymous letter from Brno. This intervention by a decisive man achieved what I'd been vainly striving for all these months: Leoš immediately broke off correspondence with Mrs Urválková.'[31]

It is tempting to speculate that this blow might have had some impact on Janáček's current operatic project (see chap. 52). There were certainly some major changes in Act 2 at this time. Janáček explained his new ideas on the libretto in two letters to Bartošová,[32] just when his relationship with Mrs Urválková was crumbling (his last communication was a postcard sent from Warsaw on 3 May with a single word, 'Greeting').[33] Ten days later Janáček declared to Bartošová that Act 1 was now finished, so that any corrections necessary would have to be written directly into the full score; the rest of the opera would 'grow out of it'. And, somewhat belatedly, he now invited his young librettist to get to know Luhačovice and 'the "atmosphere" of the whole novel-like episode'.[34]

On about 4 May Janáček returned from Warsaw. For at the very time when he was taking sick leave from his post at the Teachers' Institute (retrospective confirmation was sent on 12 January 1904),[35] he was in negotiation with the Warsaw Conservatory over the vacant post of director. An exploratory letter to Janáček, written 'in an unofficial capacity' on 12 January 1904 by one Vsevolod´ Pavlovich´ Svyatkovsky in St Petersburg, had explained that this state-run 'Institute for Music' was looking for a new director. The previous director had been a Russian but as most of the students and teachers were Poles it was thought to be a good diplomatic move to have a Czech in this position, though one who was a 'good Slavonic patriot' and who could act as a 'mediator and conciliator in Russian-Polish relations'. Janáček, with his strong Pan-Slavonic leanings, was an ideal candidate.[36] A week later Janáček wrote to Urválková that he had 'received an offer as director of the Warsaw Conservatory – and I asked them to wait a while, that I couldn't think about it just now.'[37] The conservatory seems to have been prepared to wait a long time. According to a dated speech melody in his diary Janáček was in Warsaw on 2 May;[38] the next day he sent his final terse postcard to Urválková. That evening he went to a concert at which the death of Dvořák (who had died on 1 May) was announced. Janáček recalled this in his autobiography: 'Warsaw. Orchestral concert. Then the conductor, Mr Reznicek, appears and announces the death of Antonín Dvořák. The audience stand. In the programme they insert [Dvořák's] *Hussite Overture*.'[39]

As for his negotiations over the Warsaw Conservatory, these went wrong (he wrote in his autobiography) because he missed his appointment with the governor: it was set for eleven, but Janáček had understood 'one o'clock'.[40] In a reminiscence of Poland published in 1926 in the Polish journal *Muzyka* (xv/284), Janáček dredged up a few more details. He went to the conservatory on two days – on the first he met his potential colleagues, noted the national tensions and the general air of disarray, and was surprised that he was dealing mostly with the military (the head of the search committee was a General Bogulubow). The meeting the next day with the governor-general, Georgiy Antonich Skałon,[II] was, Janáček reckoned, to probe his political reliability; as he missed the interview, the job was not available and went instead to a local candidate, the conductor and violinist Emil Młynarski. But all this was a twenty-year-old reminiscence. In a letter to Bartoš written in July

---

[II]Janáček mentions 'general-gubernator Skałon' and yet Skałon could not have held this function at the time since he became Governor-General of Poland eighteen months later, in September 1905.

1904, Janáček mentions that 'I was to have become director of the Warsaw Conservatory but we didn't come to an agreement over my salary'.[41] This sounds more like it. Warsaw had waited four months, Janáček had taken the trouble to get there. It seems unlikely that a misunderstanding over the time of an appointment would have wrecked the whole enterprise. The salary mentioned in Svyatkovsky's letter (2000 roubles per annum, about £200 at the time) was hardly more than Janáček's combined takings from the Teachers' Institute and Organ School in 1903 (about £190). Although he could have got another 1000 roubles from teaching, Svyatkovsky wrote, Janáček really needed a substantial increase to make it worth his while moving.

Exhausted from his journey and upset by the news of Dvořák's death, Janáček went straight to Luhačovice and 'sank from sight' there, as he told Hana Kvapilová. A trip to Luhačovice in May would not have been possible while Janáček was still working at the Teachers' Institute; one wonders nevertheless what happened to his duties at the Organ School.

The death of Dvořák at only sixty-two had been a huge shock to him. Though their contacts had been fewer in recent years there was real sympathy between the two – Dvořák had been substitute father, older friend and mentor (see chap. 22). Their very last conversation had been about *Jenůfa*, as he reported to Kvapilová:

I didn't suspect that I would be speaking to him [Dvořák] for the last time when the rehearsals for *Armida* were going on. He said in the theatre at the time: '*Jenůfa* will be given!' I believe in those half-prophetic words – and think no more about it. [. . .] I will stay here perhaps for three weeks. Here of course it's still dead silence, but in luxuriant nature it is possible for me to renew my strength.[42]

About ten days after Janáček arrived in Luhačovice Bartošová joined him there, accompanied by her mother as chaperone. Many years later, in a letter to Vladimír Helfert, she described their last meeting:

In Luhačovice on 11 and 12 May 1904 we went through one or other of the scenes – and that is the last of my recollections of my work with Janáček on the libretto. I saw Luhačovice for the first time then, the scene of some of the action of the opera *Fate*. It was cold and rainy there at the time, but the young green was awakening, spring was peeping through the branches. There were only a few guests. Dr Veselý, the director of the spa at the time, smilingly gave me – the author of the libretto in which 'his' Luhačovice would live and sing – a posy of lilies-of-the-valley, and with a proprietorial gesture kept us company – Janáček, my mother and myself.

I don't know the ultimate fate of *Fate*. I don't know what form the libretto had in the end, how many acts and how many scenes, who worked on the text after me, what was omitted and what was added.[43]

It does seem odd that, having got his librettist to Luhačovice, Janáček then seems to have abandoned her. Just one impatient postcard a few months later, asking what was happening with the libretto,[44] suggests both that he was expecting more and that he did not receive it. Working presumably on his own, he completed his opera a year later (see chap. 51).

It is possible that Janáček's stay in Luhačovice in May set in motion a short occasional piece, a setting of *Hail Mary* (II/14) completed by July that year. The date of the work is attested to by a letter from Countess Serényi thanking Janáček for his work: 'I was pleasantly surprised by the beautiful *Hail Mary* you dedicated to me. I was very sorry that it was not possible to put this beautiful composition into the programme because the concert had to be given earlier, but it will certainly grace the charity concert next year.'[45] In the absence of any other information one can only guess that Janáček would have encountered the Countess Serényi during his visit to Luhačovice in May (her family had owned the spa up to 1902) and that she had requested a piece for her 'charity concert'. Janáček responded with a work for solo tenor, chorus, violin and organ (and an alternative version without chorus in which the tenor could be replaced by a soprano and the organ part by a piano). What, however, is musically intriguing is the tune: it is virtually identical with that used in *The Frýdek Madonna* from *The Overgrown Path*. If his earlier piano piece recalls a pilgrim hymn familiar from a family expedition to Frýdek with Olga (see chap. 38), then this setting of the *Hail Maria* was in origin yet another commemoration of the same event and yet another indication, like the revision a few months earlier of his *Elegy on the Death of my Daughter Olga*, that Janáček was still very much preoccupied with his dead daughter.

On 3 July 1904 Janáček turned fifty. He received some seventy cards from well-wishers, and the event was noted in a couple of newspaper articles (see chap. 50). The best birthday present was undoubtedly the grant of 400 K from the Czech Academy for the purpose of studying speech melodies in the Haná dialect – the notification was actually sent on his birthday.[46] Soon after that, husband and wife set off on their separate holidays, Janáček to Hukvaldy on 11 July, Zdenka maybe the next day to Vienna, from where she sent a querulous postcard:

I wait daily for news from you, but in vain. After all, you left earlier, so it's your turn to write. You can't surely excuse yourself through overwork. It makes me very sad but I'd rather remain quiet. Parting with Čertíček cost me tears, that poor animal felt it, he at least loves me sincerely.[47]

It's not often that Zdenka allowed her emotions to come to the surface in her postcards to Janáček. The next day, however, she received a pleasant card from him: 'I hope you arrived safely. I did also. I'm at work; I eat well and sleep. But there isn't water for bathing. Even Kamenec is full of rotting algae. And no little fishes!'[48]

One can only guess that when on 15 July 1904 Janáček remarked that he was 'hard at work', it was probably on *Fate*, the only large-scale work on which he was occupied at the time. There were, however, a couple of smaller works that might well have intruded. For instance the male-voice chorus *The Wreath* (IV/31), Janáček's reworking of a folksong collected by Antonín Pustka, dates from late 1904 to early 1905, to judge from the five-bar sketch found in Pustka's collection, which Janáček acquired some time after July 1904.[49] Another small folk arrangement was a version for piano of two familiar dances, the *Čeladná Dance* and the *Handsaw Dance*, which Janáček offered to the Brno publisher Arnošt Píša on 22 September[50] and which Píša issued the next spring under the title of *Moravian Dances* (VIII/18; see chap. 51).

Janáček stayed for almost two months in Hukvaldy. Although he announced to Joza Janáčková that he had received an academy grant 'for travelling through Haná',[51] there is no sign at all of him doing so. There was a possibility of a quick trip to Velká with Jan Kunc (who came up to see Janáček in Hukvaldy on 14 August):[52] Janáček wrote to Martin Zeman from Napajedla near Zlín on 17 August that he and Kunc would arrive the next day, and could he please find accommodation for them.[53] But something untoward seems to have happened to thwart this plan. Instead, while Kunc went on to Velká to hear the 'drawn-out songs' and the *farmer's dance*, Janáček returned to Hukvaldy: 'The journey back was a real martyrdom for me. I couldn't catch my breath. Since I didn't get better it was necessary to call the doctor. Today, Monday, there's been a turn for the better. This will

probably be the end of travelling for the moment.'[54] Zdenka returned
from Vienna on 14 September;[55] Janáček himself would have needed to
be back in Brno about then for the beginning of the Organ School
term.

He continued to make trips to Prague to go to the theatre. On 10
November he heard Mozart's *Don Giovanni*,[56] and on 14 November
he saw Alfred Capus's comedy *Les deux écoles* (in Czech translation).[57]
One assumes, moreover, that he probably had some other reason for
going there at the time. Maybe it was yet another attempt to talk to
Kovařovic, who had sent a telegram to the new director of the Brno
Theatre František Lacina on 3 October asking for a piano-vocal score
of *Jenůfa*. Lacina had written to Janáček that day asking if he should
comply.[58] Was Kovařovic still sitting on the score by mid-November
and did Janáček believe that this at last indicated some interest on
Kovařovic's part? It may not be entirely unconnected that a couple of
weeks later both Janáček and the grand-sounding Baron Pražák
(chairman of the Brno Theatre Družstvo) both wrote to a much more
eminent conductor, Gustav Mahler, then presiding over the finest years
of opera that Vienna had known. Janáček sent a self-effacing note and
a couple of reviews;[59] Baron Pražák a rather more orotund invitation,
suggesting that Mahler, if he could come to the performance of *Jenůfa*
on Wednesday 7 December, should make himself known to Director
Lacina. Pražák himself regretted that as a member of the Austrian
Reichsrat, he himself would unfortunately have to attend to parlia-
mentary business in Vienna that day.[60]

In courteous letters both to the baron and to Janáček, Mahler
explained that he could not absent himself from Vienna at the time.
'But', he wrote to Janáček, 'as I would certainly be interested nevertheless in getting to know your work I ask if some time you could send
me a piano-vocal score with a German text.'[61] And there the matter had
to rest: it would be another twelve years before *Jenůfa* was translated
into German, though Janáček had one more attempt to interest Mahler,
this time through the Czech singer Vilém Heš, who as Wilhelm Hesch
was part of Mahler's team in Vienna. In an undated letter[¶] Heš

¶The letter can be dated perhaps to the period 12–23 January 1905. The relatively short
rehearsal period for *Das Rheingold* involving Mahler began on 12 January, leading to the first
performance on 23 January 1905, by which time Heš/Hesch had to be replaced as Fafner
because of ill-health (*http://www.gustav-mahler.org/english/mahler/*); H.-L. de La Grange:
Gustav Mahler, Vienna: Triumph and Disillusion (OUP, Oxford, 1999), 77–85.

reported to Janáček that he had taken his request to Mahler, but with the preparations in progress for the new production of *Das Rheingold*, Mahler said that it was out of the question for him to get to Brno – perhaps later in the season.[62] Most surprisingly, however, it seems that Kovařovic did attend the performance, having steadfastly refused to come earlier in the year. For on the first horn part against the date of 7 December there is the following note: 'For the first time in the new season, gala performance, Kovařovic present.'[63] Sadly the gala performance did not change his mind.

48

The missing link: *Jenůfa* in 1904

Anyone comparing *Jenůfa* (1904) with Janáček's previous opera *The Beginning of a Romance* (1894) would find it hard to believe how far the composer had travelled between the two. This gulf was bridged somewhat when in place of Kovařovic's Prague 1916 version of *Jenůfa* the 'Brno 1908' version became available:[1] an attempt to rid the opera of all that Kovařovic had added, and to restore all that he had left out or changed. Instead of the romantically smooth Kovařovic version of *Jenůfa* one now had something that sounded more in keeping with the rough, colourful style of Janáček's later years. But even in the Brno 1908 version the gap between *Jenůfa* and *The Beginning of a Romance* remained huge.

One knows that *Jenůfa* was written over a ten-year period, during which time Janáček no doubt experimented and tried many things. In his last decade there are significant paper trails that lead from the first ideas in his operas to his final revisions to the copyists' scores: there is enough material here to keep a whole raft of PhD students busy following the compositional process in these operas. With *Jenůfa*, however, there is almost no paper trail.[2] Janáček's manuscript full score and piano-vocal score have never come to light, burnt in the kitchen stove, so Stejskalová recalled, when the Janáčeks moved house in 1910. Trkanová 1964, 93. All that remains are the full score and piano-vocal score made by the copyist Josef Štross, both used at the première in 1904.

It was the Czech musicologist Bohumír Štědroň who first drew attention to the significance of Štross's scores. Although Štědroň (working chiefly from the piano-vocal score) was able to point to truncated ensembles, to reprint some of the cancelled pages, and to demonstrate the rewriting of vocal lines, he was working against huge obstacles. In a sense the 1904 version no longer existed or, rather, had been buried at the bottom of a palimpsest full-score manuscript in which every subsequent revision, including Kovařovic's, had been written, leaving a confusing mixture of layers. Longer cuts were marked with cross-out signs or made by sticking pages together; smaller changes had been written on to strips of paper stuck over earlier versions or written straight on top of an earlier version that had been scratched out with a knife (though sometimes leaving a 'ghost' that could be read). Štědroň read what he could and in his book on *Jenůfa*[3] gave indications of the types of changes Janáček made. But without a full restoration of the 1904 version it was impossible to get an impression of what the opera sounded like then and how it might have worked on stage. A full restoration, however, seemed out of the question: many pages and passages were securely glued over and there were good arguments against having professional restorers attempt to open up what was already a very battered and delicate score.

Three things made a seemingly hopeless task nonetheless look feasible: the existence of a prompter's copy of the libretto from 1904 that recorded the exact verbal text (and all its repetitions); the use of fibre-optic technology to shine through stuck-over layers and reveal the notes underneath; and the existence of a motley and incomplete collection of orchestral parts that had survived from the 1904 run of performances. Admittedly, some of these orchestral parts had been brought into line with the revisions Janáček made in 1906–7 (leading to the piano-vocal score published in 1908), but since all had been discarded before Kovařovic's 1916 version what lay beneath the revised parts was easier to read than the multi-layered changes in Štross's score. It was with persistence and considerable stamina that the British musicologist Mark Audus, over a period of more than fifteen years, painstakingly reconstructed Janáček's 1904 score to a state when it could be performed. A semi-professional concert performance of Act 2 given in 2000 at the University of Nottingham encouraged the hope that all three acts could be retrieved. In 2004 Warsaw Chamber Opera staged four performances of Audus's reconstructed score allowing the opera to be heard, for the first time in a century, in much the same state as at its first performance. *Jenůfa* in its 1904 version – the missing link*

---

* The title of this chapter is taken from Audus 1996, an article on the possibility of reforging the link.

in the chain of Janáček's development as an opera composer – was now in place, and the gap between Janáček's third and second operas shortened. What still remains, however, is a learning curve more extreme than anywhere else in Janáček's output. Although Janáček made different versions of *Šárka, Fate* and *Brouček*, and tinkered in rehearsal with most of the later operas, *Jenůfa* is unique in that he heard the work several times in its early version and his revisions therefore represent a direct response to what he saw on stage. The period between 1904 and 1908 was Janáček's operatic workshop and, once one takes this into account, his astonishing growth as an operatic composer can be seen to be more gradual than hitherto realized.[†] A knowledge of *Jenůfa* in 1904 is vital to the understanding of the journey Janáček travelled in his operatic craft and in the formation of his mature style.

What strikes the listener immediately on hearing *Jenůfa* in its 1904 state is the greater presence of four-square periodicity, the 'quadratic' style of balanced and usually lyrical phrases that betrays Janáček's nineteenth-century origins. The Mayor, at his Act 3 entrance in 1904, greets the company with a jolly, regular tune in four bars that in 1908[‡] was revised to declamatory gestures, though leaving the accompaniment and the Herdswoman's vocal line largely untouched (ex. 13). In Act 2, Laca's entrance ('To jsem já tetko') – in 1908 just a few bars – was in 1904 part of a 'miniature modified da capo structure'.[4] When Laca and Jenůfa pledge their union in Act 2 they did so in 1904 with a long number, lyrically regular and repetitive. Laca sings for 38 bars on his own, Jenůfa joins him for a simultaneous duet (16 bars) until they are joined by the Kostelnička for a 22-bar 'trio'. In 1908 Janáček scrapped everything apart from a revision of Laca's first 4 bars and a truncated version of the trio. In other words, what was a self-evident 'number' (a duet/trio with simultaneous voices) has been reduced to a mere suggestion of one, though this, as Audus has shown, was a gradual process between the years 1904 and 1908.[5]

Even after such changes, there are traces in 1908 of other set numbers, but all were originally longer. In 1904 Laca's opening Act 1

[†] The 'workshop' extends back to 1903: Janáček undertook many changes to the Štross score in the lead-up to its performance in 1904, constituting the first layers of changes.

[‡] In the discussion that follows '1908' is used as shorthand for the date of Janáček's revisions which began in 1906–7 and continued into the proof corrections of 1908 and even beyond.

Ex. 13

[Mayor (Rych.): God give you happiness! Did we frighten you?]
[Herdswoman (Past.): It's just her illness!]

solo ('Vy stařenko') was more extensive and aria-like; the 'Každý párek' ensemble used to have a substantial middle section; the little stump of an ensemble for Grandmother Buryjovka and chorus ('A vy muzikanti, jděte dom') was originally a substantial piece of 43 bars; when Laca cut Jenufa's cheek at the end of the act he did so with an exciting passage of some 40 bars, reduced in 1908 to a mere 4. The most substantial cut of all is one that has now become familiar:[6] the Kostelnička's Act 1 'explanation aria' that she delivers having stopped the celebratory dancing. In 1908 this became a brief intervention. In 1904 she gave reasons for her action, which go back to her own unhappy experience of marrying a wastrel husband. The excision of this aria (75 bars) so much changes the perception of the Kostelnička that it has been increasingly included in productions of the opera, allowing a more sympathetic and three-dimensional character to emerge. Not restored in hitherto available editions, however, is its 10-bar orchestral introduction based on the *Jenůfa* 'guilt' leitmotif.

The many one-bar orchestral links between voice parts in 1908 were longer in 1904 and usually made up of two or four bars. The shortening or even omission of many of these in 1908 makes the resultant music seem less predictable and balanced but is also an indication of the fluidity that Janáček was beginning to achieve in transitions, one of his most striking attributes.

It shouldn't be thought, however, that all Janáček did was to tighten up the opera with a few cuts. Virtually every page of Štross's full score was altered, both in its orchestration and in the voice part. Even chorus pieces often sounded different: the chorus refrain to 'Daleko široko' in Act 1 used to have an arresting drone ('Ej') for the tenors and basses (instead of the tenors singing the tune with Števa), and the Bridesmaids' Chorus of Act 3 was a different piece altogether in 1904 when Barena added her catchy little descant that Janáček omitted in 1908 (the accompaniment too, was thicker and earthier). Voice parts were particularly affected, for instance to correct incorrectly stressed words: many phrases used to end, like much German-Italian music, with the final syllable of a word on the strong beat, going against natural Czech prosody, which always stresses the first syllable. But there were also many changes to provide a less regular, more lively voice part. Janáček did much the same thing in 1918 when he revised the quadratic voice parts of *Šárka* with ones that were more in keeping with the flexibility that he had acquired through his preoccupation with speech melody (see chap. 37).

Hearing the 1904 version, one sometimes wonders why Janáček needed to make quite so many changes, many of them abandoning attractive and effective music. Cutting the performing time was hardly a reason since *Jenůfa* was not a particularly long opera by the standards of the time: leaving aside the Kostelnička's aria, restoring the cuts saves some ten minutes in the first act, fewer in the others. Had there been a warmer response from Prague, Janáček might not have undertaken such an extensive revision of the score. Many of the cuts were presumably undertaken to omit verbal repetitions, something that was singled out as particularly reprehensible in Prague reviews of the Brno production.

The first impetus for cuts came from the original conductor Hrazdira, who in a letter of 11 July 1906 suggested specific tightenings-up, all of which were made as part of an early layer of cuts in performances the next season:

I think, also, that it would be in the interests of the work's dramatic flow somewhat to shorten some places. It concerns chiefly both ensembles: 'A vy muzikanti, jděte dom . . .' and 'Každý párek . . .'. It would be possible to do these very easily, I have it worked out; if it wouldn't be contrary to your thoughts I'd write out these passages and send them for you to look at. Also some orchestral interludes are a little long. [Hrazdira gives specific examples.] These are of course my suggestions and I ask for your view in this matter.[7]

In his revisions in 1906–7 Janáček took in all of Hrazdira's cuts and made more of his own. Another impetus came from the criticisms of Janáček's pupil Jan Kunc, who pointed out word-setting slips, even in the 1906–7 version (see chap. 62). Janáček's adjustments went on even into the proofs of the 1908 vocal score, where many instances of 'Je-NŮ-fa' or 'Je-nů-FA' were corrected to 'JE-nů-fa'.

All these changes were part of a continuum. Janáček's autograph has not survived, so one will never know the most interesting part of the story, but even between Štross's copying out of the full score and the first performance there was already one layer of change, and such revisions continued until 1913, with substantial stopping points in 1904 (first performance) and 1908 (publication of the piano-vocal score).

What does strike one in examining these changes is the emergence of Janáček the music dramatist, most importantly in the pacing of finales and other concerted numbers. Although ostinato accompaniments remained part of his familiar style, Janáček learnt between 1904 and 1908 how to restrict them, so that overpowering ostinato backgrounds were suppressed in favour of something simpler and less obtrusive; this allowed important words to come through (see ex. 14, overleaf). One of the glorious moments in the opera is Laca's big-hearted outburst 'Jenůfka!' when he sees Jenůfa at his second entrance in Act 2. This brief Heldentenor gesture was retained in 1908 though its lyrical continuation was speeded up, and the voice part remapped over the first

Ex. 14

[Kostelnička Buryjovka: From that moment I brought you home I sensed from your lamentations...]

four bars of the original accompaniment (ex. 15). In revising the score Janáček absorbed one of the most valuable lessons for a stage composer: how to make effective short cuts.

The 1908 version is shorter, terser and more punchy, less obviously belonging to the nineteenth century and less obviously 'folkish'. Those who know the opera from the 1908 version often feel how much the folk-music episodes in the outer acts stand out from the other material. But some of the short 'arias' that have disappeared sound, with their simple repetitions and vigorous tunes, somewhere between the overtly

Ex. 15a (1904)

Ex. 15b (1908)

[Laca: Jenůfka! God comfort you, Jenůfka!]

folk episodes and the rest of the opera. Part of the story that the revisions to *Jenůfa* tell is how Janáček modified music that was clearly modelled on Moravian folk practice into something more nuanced: a good example is the general disappearance of the 'double-stroke' accompaniments (i.e. the 'pahs' in an 'um-pah, um-pah' backing) based on *kontráš* patterns. Audus found other instances: in the prelude to

Act 3 and, with less ostensible justification in the plot, in the Act 2 scene between the Kostelnička and Števa.[8] Here Števa departed to a defiantly folksy mini-aria, which gave Janáček immense problems in revision and that did not settle down to a final version until 1916. Perhaps Janáček was attempting to make the opera less 'Moravian' and thus more acceptable to Prague (see chap. 59), but this long process was also a clarification and development of his own unique compositional style, informed by many elements of Moravian folk music and now distilled into a unique amalgam.[§]

[§] Much of this chapter is based on conversations since the early 1990s about Janáček's changes in his *Jenůfa* scores and on materials that Mark Audus kindly made available to me, now incorporated into Audus 2006.

49

Bêtes noires I: Karel Kovařovic

'Which *tune* stayed in your mind?'
'—' [i.e. no reply]
'At least which *theme*?'
'—'
'Is it the reason why the opera is dramatic?'
'—'

I would not have written 'set to music by' but 'Macháček's comedy* etc. *staged simultaneously with music*.

Both libretto and music are independent. Write a new *operetta* to this *libretto* and to this *music* some sort of *play*: full of horrible gloom, desperate screams, bodies stabbed by daggers.

Thus the *strange phenomenon* that it was *Macháček's and not Kovařovic's* 'The Bridegrooms' which made one burst out laughing several times.

[The composer's] *musical talent* is attested to by the overture, with its floods of chords and keys: which accordingly deafened one. (xv/70)

It is not surprising that Karel Kovařovic (1862–1920) took against Janáček. Janáček's review of Kovařovic's first opera, *The Bridegrooms* (given in Brno in 1887), was brief, sarcastic and disparaging, and was no doubt a shock to the twenty-five-year-old composer, who had scored a moderate success with this opera in Prague three years earlier and had hitherto enjoyed good relations with Janáček. But the revenge extracted was hardly commensurate. Kovařovic proscribed *Jenůfa* for twelve years at the National Theatre, twelve years that did untold damage to Janáček's self-esteem and which ensured that his years 'in the mists' were littered with revisions, incomplete projects and

* The play *The Bridegrooms* (1825) by Simeon Karel Macháček was the basis for Kovařovic's opera of the same name (premièred in Prague in 1884).

other signs of lack of confidence. The quick and assured creations of his final decade make an eloquent comparison.

The blow to Janáček's self-confidence was not the only damage. Kovařovic's condition of revising *Jenůfa* before finally accepting it meant – since it was then published in that form – that for some eighty years afterwards the opera was given only in Kovařovic's redaction, with its cuts and extensive reorchestration. Economics, among other factors, dictated that this is how the opera was known in Janáček's adopted home town of Brno from 1916 until January 2004.

It seems almost unbelievable that this terrible legacy was merely revenge for a bad review. This would mean an unrelenting meanness of spirit on Kovařovic's part, a meanness illustrated in the incident in 1907 when he had Janáček humiliatingly turned out from a rehearsal at the National Theatre to which a junior conductor had invited him (see chap. 55). Although, when eventually accepting the opera, Kovařovic clearly needed some sort of pretext for previously turning it down, it can be argued that the wholesale revision of *Jenůfa* was in no way directed personally against Janáček. Kovařovic did that sort of thing with the best of intentions to composers such as Dvořák (to his *Dimitrij* for instance) – it was common practice among many conductors of that period. There is also no doubt that Kovařovic, as the promoter and conductor of many foreign novelties in Prague, had first-hand practical knowledge of the latest trends and was able to apply them to his own works and to others. For instance he had rehearsed and conducted most of the sixteen Prague performances of Strauss's *Elektra* between 1910 and 1916; in comparison, Janáček's knowledge of this opera consisted of seeing it once and having a look at the piano-vocal score. Whatever one might think of Kovařovic's version of *Jenůfa*, it is a professional job by an expert musician and experienced man of the theatre.

However, the long refusal of *Jenůfa* is difficult to explain other than by ill-will. When it came to Czech novelties, the Prague National Theatre had an inclusive policy: works by Janáček's minor and long forgotten contemporaries (Váša Suk, Karel Moor, Jindřich Kàan, Adolf Piskáček, Otakar Zich, František Picka, Rudolf Zamrzla) as well as those by more experienced composers (Foerster, Ostrčil, Novák, Weis, Bendl) were performed during 1903–15 as a matter of course, but not Janáček's *Jenůfa*. Most disgraceful of all was the cynical acceptance of Nešvera's *Radhošť* as a token Moravian opera (see chap. 53): in this way it could be demonstrated that the National Theatre had done its duty to its junior sister nation Moravia.

Nor is it as though Kovařovic had merely one chance to consider the opera. He had many. Janáček submitted *Jenůfa* to the National Theatre in 1903 soon after completing the work. When Kovařovic turned it down it was taken up by Brno and staged in 1904. Janáček invited Kovařovic to the première, asking him to reconsider his verdict. It is understandable, with his professional commitments, that Kovařovic may not have been free that evening. But as someone who chose the repertory in Prague he might have thought it incumbent on him to look out for new works and take the opportunity of seeing other stagings of them. Over the run of nine performances in Brno that season, a series of invitations went out to Kovařovic asking him to name an evening and *Jenůfa* would be given in Brno especially for him. It was only at the beginning of the next season that Kovařovic got round to seeing it.

There were further opportunities for Kovařovic to change his mind after Janáček's extensive revisions to the score: in 1908, when the piano-vocal score was published and could thus be studied at leisure; in 1911, when an appeal was made by the Club of the Friends of Art to the franchise company that ran the National Theatre; and in 1915. In Bohdaneč that summer, František Veselý and his wife Marie Calma-Veselá won over both Kovařovic's friend and librettist Josef Peška and Kovařovic's hard-headed administrative director Gustav Schmoranz. So, once again, Kovařovic looked at the piano-vocal score that Schmoranz had now brought back with him. Although some passages were effective, he conceded, there were many flaws and he was 'pleased', he said, that with his verdict given all those years ago 'he had in no way done the work an injustice'.[1] Only after further hard lobbying by Peška and the Veselýs did Kovařovic finally relent. If Janáček had not had such determined friends, this might never have happened. And if *Jenůfa* had not been performed in Prague, Janáček would not have written further operas after the stalled *Brouček* (see chap 68).

Once the decision had been taken to perform *Jenůfa* in Prague, Kovařovic, as a consummate professional, threw himself into his task with immense dedication and achieved a stunning and surprising success with the opera. At first it seemed as though the old animosities between the two men had been laid aside. 'Highly esteemed friend', they would address each other in letters. But for all Kovařovic's determination to make *Jenůfa* succeed now, and for all Janáček's gratitude that it did, the relationship remained awkward, compromised by Janáček's affair with Horvátová (the subject of a careful letter to Janáček by Kovařovic, see vol ii: 1916b) and by the troubled history of Janáček's next opera, *The Excursions of Mr Brouček*. If Kovařovic did not always respond to Janáček's many letters, this may well have been a sign of overwork, but Janáček usually took umbrage and made no allowance – because of the buffetings of the past, he needed constant reassurance. Kovařovic's successor Otakar Ostrčil did much better with Janáček not because he answered more letters but because he had started off from a position of enthusiasm: kind words at the première of *The 70,000* (IV/36), an ecstatic letter after the *Jenůfa* première, his willingness to give the first performance of the problematic orchestral piece, *The Fiddler's Child* (VI/14).

Perhaps it was inevitable that Kovařovic and Janáček would not get on. Their temperaments were very different but also their musical upbringings. While Janáček was a late starter, struggling to gain a musical education while earning his living as a teacher, Kovařovic, eight years younger, had an effortless entry into his life as a professional musician. He attended the Prague Conservatory from the age of eleven, and at sixteen was a composition pupil of Fibich. He was a talented practical musician, serving as harpist at the National Theatre, the piano accompanist of leading soloists, a teacher and later director of Pivoda's singing school. But he was best known as a conductor. In his early twenties he conducted opera seasons in Brno (1885–6, where Janáček first encountered him, writing generally approving reviews in *Hudební listy*) and in Plzeň (1886–7). He made his name at the Prague Ethnographic Exhibition of 1895, where he formed and conducted the sixty-three-man orchestra. This, with the concerts he conducted of the prototype Czech Philharmonic and the success of his opera *The Dogheads* in 1898, made him a natural choice as chief conductor at the National Theatre at the change of guard in 1900. His twenty-year reign there is one of the glorious periods of the opera house in which he maintained a fine ensemble and orchestra and expanded the repertory, notably with Wagner (little cultivated before at the National Theatre), Strauss (*Elektra, Salome, Der Rosenkavalier*) and many French works (e.g. *Pelléas, Louise*), for which he had a special affinity. Janáček made special expeditions to Prague to see many of these works, and heard

Kovařovic conducting a good twenty times before *Jenůfa* was accepted there.

The job, however, took its toll. Stress played a part (Peška declared that Kovařovic's personality changed under the constant pressure, see vol. ii: 1915) and may well have been a factor in his death from cancer at the age of fifty-eight. It certainly took its toll on his compositional career. By the age of thirty-eight, when he became head of opera at the National Theatre, he had written five operas, several ballets, and a large amount of incidental music. By far his best-known work was his opera *The Dogheads*, which in 1897 won a major opera competition, squeezing Fibich's opera *Šárka* somewhat unjustly into second place. It is a skilful confection, an oldfashioned nationalist-historical opera, based on equally oldfashioned operatic conventions, derivative and eclectic in its idiom. Janáček, when he wrote about it in *Hlídka* (xv/161), was taken by its use of chromatic harmony and by its effective stagecraft. Indeed this stirring piece was still being performed in the 1980s and bears witness to a strong theatrical talent. But this was almost his swan song. After taking over at the National Theatre Kovařovic completed only one more opera, *At the Old Bleachery*, which did nothing like as well as its predecessor.

It might have seemed a bitter pill for Kovařovic to have to go on conducting performances of a work that he had so adamantly refused. But perhaps all the work that he had put into its reorchestration allowed him to think of it as 'his' work and thereby to take genuine pleasure in its success, predicting, for instance, that it would become as popular as *The Bartered Bride* (see vol. ii: 1916a). For his part Janáček showed in his letters the closeness that adversaries often can feel, and was both upset and generous when he heard of Kovařovic's final illness ('If I could give you half of my health – you wouldn't have much – but I'd give it willingly').[2] While Kovařovic was alive Janáček showed nothing but gratitude for the work that he had put into revising the opera, an attitude that changed dramatically when he discovered that Kovařovic's widow was demanding a royalty on performances of the opera (see vol. ii: 1923). When this problem had been resolved he was able again to take a remarkably balanced view, conceding, for instance in a letter to Max Brod in 1927, that when 'harming him' Kovařovic had good reason to hate him for his review of *A Way through the Window*[3] (*recte The Bridegrooms* – by then Janáček had forgotten which early opera by Kovařovic was at stake). In 1920, when

Kovařovic died, Janáček did not conceal the problems between them but, writing to Ostrčil about it, remembered him with a touching warmth of feeling:

It moved me greatly. [. . .] We knew each other from Brno days. We came into conflict here and from that time the shadows fell between us – and you know well they lay between us as late as during *Brouček*. But let's forget all that.

He worked hard, slaving away for the honour of the National Theatre. And even I at the end was grateful to him for the success of *Jenůfa* and want to remember him only well.[4]

50

Janáček at fifty

'You can look back contentedly over your life. You have not lived in vain. You have done an honest bit of work – hundreds of others cannot compare even with half of yours. And you are in the full strength of life, work gives you pleasure.' So said Janáček's schoolfriend from 1866, František Bílý, when he sent his congratulations on Janáček's fiftieth birthday.[1] Of course he was right. Compared with many others of his generation Janáček had achieved a huge amount by the age of fifty. He was best known as the founding director of the Brno Organ School, the chief musical educational institution in Moravia, in existence for over twenty years. Although he had begun to shed his other teaching commitments, and in 1903 retired early from the most time-consuming of these (at the Teachers' Institute), Janáček as pedagogue loomed large in every contemporary perception of his importance. This is certainly the main impression that anyone would have gained from the one Czech dictionary entry on him published at the time.* The unsigned, twenty-five-line article in vol. xiii of *Ottův slovník naučný* [Otto's encyclopedia] (written in fact by Josef Boleška) describes his schooling in detail and ends with his directorship of the Organ School and a brief list of published works.

This dictionary account of Janáček, published in 1898, omitted most of what by 1904 would have been an increasingly important perception: that of Janáček as folklorist. The entry in *Otto* caught the small collection that Janáček had published with Bartoš in 1890

---

* A short entry on 'Janáček, Leo' had in fact appeared in the fifth volume (on musicians and other cultural workers) of Hermann Heller's *Mährens Männer der Gegenwart* (Brno, 1892). It is reprinted, and its brief contents discussed, in Petrželka 1970.

(*The Bouquet of Moravian Folksongs* XIII/1) but it was several years too early to include the massive *Moravian Folksongs Newly Collected* (XIII/3) that Janáček published with Bartoš in 1899-1901. The pre-occupation with Moravian folk music would have been evident to Janáček's contemporaries from this collection, from his organization of activities such as the Moravian participation in the Ethnographic Exhibition of 1895, and from an increasing number of published folksong and dance arrangements. That Janáček was not merely concerned with collecting, publishing and publicizing Moravian folk music but was also thinking about its broader cultural and musical significance would have been clear by 1904 from his extensive scholarly introduction to *Moravian Folksongs Newly Collected* (XV/163) and from several journal and newspaper articles on the topic.

A more rounded and up-to-date assessment was provided on Janáček's fiftieth birthday (3 July 1904) by *Lidové noviny*, reprinted in *Moravská orlice*. Here the writings mentioned are the harmony manual (XV/151), the singing-teaching manual (XV/162), the introduction to the folksong collection (XV/163) and an 'as yet unpublished' study of form on the basis of Moravian folk music (possibly XV/314) together with unspecified articles in *Hlídka* and *Český lid*. *The Bouquet of Moravian Folksongs* is given as an example of his powerful commitment to popularizing and disseminating folksongs.

By 1894, ten years earlier, Janáček had already published almost 150 articles, mostly reviews of operas and concerts. Between 1894 and 1904 Janáček published only another twenty-five articles, but most of them were more substantial than the brief reviews in *Hudební listy*. In this ten-year period Janáček as music critic gave way to Janáček as musical thinker. Much of this was stimulated by new preoccupations: folk music was obviously important, but so were the substantial analyses of both operatic and orchestral music that for a few years he published in *Hlídka*. And there was an entirely new topic: speech melodies. There had already been references to them in the introduction to *Moravian Folksongs Newly Collected* (1901), but from 1903 Janáček published several independent studies that initiated a distinctive, if idiosyncratic, series of articles that would continue up to his death.

What is almost wholly missing in the *Otto* article is any appreciation of Janáček as a composer. By their forties most major composers have written distinctive works on which their reputations rest. Janáček's first distinctive works were written only after the age of forty-two, and then only sporadically. Thus the perception of him as a composer was naturally even more delayed. In 1898 (when he was forty-four) he is described in *Otto* as a 'Czech musician', not as a composer, and the compositions mentioned in this short article consist of only two published works, the 1885 male choruses (IV/17) and the *Valachian Dances* (VI/4), together with his one-act opera *The Beginning of a Romance* (I/3). In the fiftieth-birthday article in *Lidové noviny* the selection of compositions is greater, taking up almost a third of the biographical section, and is rather better informed. All three operas to date are listed (*Šárka* had 'remained unfinished', which is presumably how Janáček remembered it by 1904) and the section ends optimistically: 'He is now working on new operas' (note the plural). The selection of choruses understandably includes most of the published ones – the 1885 choruses (IV/17), *Our Birch Tree* (IV/22) and *The Wild Duck* (IV/18) – though it is surprising to find mention of unpublished ones such as *The sun has risen above the hill* (IV/23) and *Hospodine!* (III/5). The performances, respectively in 1894 and 1896, had left their mark. All the published folksongs and dance arrangements are listed. *On the Overgrown Path* (VIII/17) appears not by name but as 'compositions for harmonium' published in *Slovanské melodie*. Among the 'orchestral works' are the *Suite* and *Idyll* for strings (VI/2 and VI/3), the ballet *Rákoš Rákoczy* (I/2) and the *Valachian Dances* (VI/4). *Amarus* (III/6) and *Our Father* (IV/29) are both listed, the latter erroneously as a piece for choir and orchestra.

By 1904 Janáček's compositional oeuvre was of course more extensive than this list implies. Apart from apprentice works, both liturgical and chamber, there was a substantial body of over thirty male-voice choruses, most of which had been performed and some of which (notably the 1885 group) had been published. However, the arrival of a distinctive musical personality would not have been clear at the time. *Amarus* had been a disaster in Kroměříž, so embarrassingly inadequate that it was more than a decade before it was performed again. The five *Overgrown Path* pieces were published but dispersed in two volumes of harmonium music for amateurs, and *Our Father* and *Hospodine!* were written for one-off, specific occasions and had been heard once each before being put away. The only distinctive piece that could have attracted attention beyond its immediate audience was

Jenůfa, and it was this very piece whose beyond-Brno progress was thwarted by Kovařovic in Prague.

A salutary reminder of Janáček's status, as perceived even by those in Prague without an axe to grind, is the tiny entry on Janáček in a book published by the three brothers Horn in 1903, entitled *Czech Opera*. This 340-page book is a remarkably broadly conceived survey of Czech opera at the time. It consists of short articles on Czech opera composers, each headed by a photograph and rounded off with a fragment of autograph. In between are details of individual operas with cast lists and synopses. Naturally figures such as Smetana, Fibich and Dvořák dominate, accounting for twenty-seven, thirty-eight and twenty-three pages respectively. What is impressive, however, is the broad coverage of a total of thirty-eight composers. Kovařovic is there (twenty pages) but so is Janáček's pupil Hrazdira with his still unperformed *King Barleycorn* (composed 1902). That Janáček has the shortest entry among all thirty-eight composers was not a matter of bad judgement or ill-will on the part of the authors. The seven lines of information on Janáček come straight from *Otto*. There is no portrait and no concluding music facsimile because, presumably, none were forthcoming. That the usual treatment (with composition and performance details, cast list and synopsis) was not accorded to the one performed opera, *The Beginning of a Romance*, may have been because Janáček had now rejected the work and probably refused co-operation. This at least would be a reasonable inference from a rare footnote, which proclaimed that the synopsis was not given 'since it was not possible to borrow the libretto from the composer'.[†] Presumably Janáček simply ignored the Horns' request and in so doing ensured his virtual absence from their book.

For all the unfamiliarity of the image of Janáček at fifty that emerges from the *Lidové noviny* article, one thing at least was clear to its writer – that Janáček's was a very curious and utterly distinctive personality: 'There have been few artists of such rich and complicated culture as he. Deeply sensitive, with a soul of rich moods, agitated by the gentlest touch, sharply choleric at a stronger impulse, at the same time a psychologist of delicate observations with fingers more suspecting

---

[†] Janáček had taken the same attitude a decade earlier when approached by Josef Srb-Debrnov when writing his *History of Music in Bohemia and Moravia* (Prague, 1891). Janáček was characterized (p. 166, fn. 1) as 'the only one among living composers who did not comply with our request for biographical data'.

than defining.' More suspecting than defining himself, the writer had stumbled on one element of Janáček's personality that could be seen, when transposed into his music, as crucial: the mercurial changes of strongly drawn moods and emotions that in their close juxtaposition were such an important source of energy and musical character.

51

1905

Until 1905 Brno's Club of the Friends of Art (founded in 1900) had directed its interests more towards literature and the visual arts than to music, though it did organize the occasional concert, for instance of the songs, piano and chamber music by one of its members, Janáček's pupil Jan Kunc, on 26 April 1904. It was perhaps the success of this evening that led to the club's expansion, specifically to the creation of a separate musical section whose main aim would be to encourage the works of Moravian composers by performing them and publishing them. The new section was formally opened on 8 January 1905. The music committee was headed by the twenty-one-year-old Kunc; among its members were Janáček and many of his associates including Marie Kuhlová, Max Koblížek (both from the Organ School) and Ferdinand Vach.[1] Its first concerts – organized for two Sunday afternoons, 19 and 26 February, at the club's rooms at Solnoúřední (now Solniční) ulice – were intended to demonstrate the evolution of the sonata, with an emphasis on the Czech, and more particularly the Moravian sonata. Janáček appears to have written the advance publicity and maybe also drew up the programmes. His input was even greater for the club's third concert, on Sunday 9 April and described as an evening of 'Spring Songs'. Apart from one by Tchaikovsky, these were either by Bohemian composers (Novák, Dvořák and Hanuš Trneček) or by Moravians (Josef Nešvera, Antonín Hromádka, C.M. Hrazdira and František Musil).[2] Janáček's own *Spring Song* (v/3) of 1897–8 was resurrected and hurriedly revised the day before, perhaps to suit its female performer, a Miss Vytopilová (the performer of its previous 1898 version had been the tenor Zdeněk Lev).

The 'Spring Songs' concert, however, was dominated by the contribution of the Ukrainian violinist Yelizaveta Aleksandrovna Shchedrovichova. Trained in St Petersburg, she was studying at the time with the famous Czech violin teacher Otakar Ševčík, who evidently recommended her to Janáček. Janáček was much taken with her: 'It seems that all her life is directed only according to the rules of beauty. [...] She is a virtuoso of the first order whose fiery temperament is complemented by that of the poet and the painter' (xv/178). A picture of her reproduced in Kundera's study of the Club of the Friends of Art (1948) depicts a tall, rather sultry lady, full-faced with voluminous black hair, leaning moodily over an Art Nouveau screen, violin bow in hand. Janáček's enthusiasm was translated into a short newspaper article, its heading proclaiming her as an 'artistic phenomenon' (xv/178). Published in *Moravská orlice* two days after the concert, it was both a 'review' of her performance at the Club of the Friends of Art and advance publicity for a major concert (with orchestra) to be given at the Besední dům on 6 May. (She made a third appearance in Brno at a 'popular concert' on 18 May* and thereafter popped up in different Moravian towns that year and even in Vienna, whither Kunc was dispatched to 'represent' the club.)[3] For the club on 9 April she played a Tartini sonata, the Tchaikovsky Violin Concerto (with piano accompaniment) and other smaller items including a new piece by Janáček's pupil Josef Charvát called *Spring Song*, a rather perfunctory nod by the soloist in the direction of the title of the concert.

Janáček's *Moravská orlice* piece on Shchedrovichova was part of a flurry of journalism undertaken at this time. Ten days later there was his suggestion in *Lidové noviny* on how to turn the newly created Czech Brno Theatre orchestra into a permanent body (xv/179). Reading such a piece today brings home how limited any opera performances in Brno must have been at this period. Janáček was pleading here for what now seem exceptionally modest demands: pension provisions for older members, and the enlargement of the orchestra by seven players, which would bring it up to the following: strings 5/4/3/2/2, double woodwind, double brass (2 trumpets, 2 horns, 2 trombones), 1 timpani player, 1 harp. With the seven new players the number would stand at thirty-two; without the seven the theatre would be left with an

---

* Reviews of her Brno concerts were published in *Lidové noviny* on 12 and 24 May 1905.

unbalanced chamber-like combination with strings almost out-numbered by the wind and brass.

On 9 April, the same day as the 'Spring Songs' concert, Janáček published a tiny piece in *Lidové noviny* on *Why do we have so many polkas and waltzes?* (XV/177). The simpler the dance steps, the richer the musical literature, Janáček wrote. Polkas and waltzes are very simple ('even children can turn about to a waltz or a polka') and thus many famous composers have written examples. But Moravian dances are choreographically much more demanding and their complicated steps are closely wedded to well-established tunes. For instance folk dancers will dance the *Handsaw Dance* and *Čeladná Dance* only when they hear the well-known music, and the musicians will allow themselves only modest variations to these traditional tunes. In Moravia there are some three hundred such dances. What a shame, then, that people these days seem to dance only polkas and waltzes. Janáček did not go as far as making the connection, but his single paragraph in *Lidové noviny* was a well-timed puff for his latest publication, piano arrangements of the *Handsaw Dance* and *Čeladná Dance* issued by Arnošt Píša as two *Moravian Dances* for piano (VIII/18). Although the inserted slips explaining the dance steps make this look like a continuation of *Folk Dances in Moravia* (VIII/10), Janáček's motivation was rather different, judging from the explanation he gave to Píša when he handed the pieces over. The 'excellent' composer Franz Schubert, he wrote, had composed German dances, and this 'folk music' was considered so important that it was taught at music conservatories; '*I'd like these Moravian dances of ours to be a better pendant to the German ones.*' With one or two dances added a year it would, he thought, be a useful expansion of Czech piano music, quite apart from its ethnographical importance. Píša adhered to all Janáček's conditions and presumably paid him the requested 5 K per dance;[4] however the proposed annual continuation never materialized.

In one further article issued that year, *Last Year and This* (XV/180), published in *Hlídka* in March 1905, Janáček returned to the theme of speech melodies. Janáček had spent two consecutive Christmases in Hukvaldy: 1903 ('last year') and 1904 ('this'), and on both occasions he took down the words and speech melodies of young Ludmila ('Lidka') Sládková. He recorded almost a hundred of her speech melodies on these two occasions, noting how much she had grown up in between (she was not yet three in 1903). For its use of speech melodies in bringing a scene to life and its trenchant pronouncements on the essence of speech melody this is one of Janáček's most successful articles (see chap. 37).

In the early years of the century an enterprise was initiated in Vienna that would dominate Janáček's relationship to Moravian folksong for the rest of his life. Universal Edition, a new publisher created in Vienna in 1901, had in 1902 devised a grandiose plan for publishing folksongs of the entire Austrian Empire in 300 volumes, under the general title *Das Volkslied in Österreich*. From the start Universal Edition had been actively promoted by the state as a counterweight to German publishers such as Peters or Breitkopf & Härtel and, with such a grand, patriotic venture, Universal naturally applied for state support. Expert advice from the Professor of Music at Vienna University, Guido Adler, ensured that the project was approved as a 'scholarly edition' and the Austrian Minister of Culture and Education Dr Wilhelm von Hartel instructed the governors of individual regions in Austria to back Universal Edition's initiative. A newly created committee met in Vienna on 26 November 1904 and included the veteran Czech musicologist and aesthetician Otakar Hostinský representing Bohemia.[5] The next year, on 7 April 1905, Hostinský wrote to Janáček:

On Sunday I'm going to Vienna for a session of the committee for the publication of folksongs. When I was invited for the first time [on 26 November 1904], I had no idea who would be there apart from myself, and, having found no-one Czech from Moravia, I had assumed that you were invited but couldn't attend – only from the newspapers did I learn that an oversight had occurred. That was a fundamental mistake, but one without [serious] consequences. At this preliminary gathering nothing definitive was decided; but one thing seems to me to be completely assured: total autonomy for the regional – and in some cases national – committees. So we will also have complete freedom in Bohemia and Moravia either to link up for collective work, or to agree about principles and then work in parallel. [. . .] I would like to have a few words with you before the [next] session of that committee. Assuming, then, that you will be coming to Vienna this time, please allow me to make a suggestion to you: could we meet at about nine o'clock on the morning of Monday 10 April in the coffee house in the Herrengasse, which is not far from Hotel Klomser, where I shall be staying, and also not far from the ministry?[6]

But Janáček had not been invited this time either. Instead, Moravia was being represented by an obscure German choirmaster and music teacher from Brno, Viktor Zak:[7] 'I have been snooping around in all the German booksellers but none of them knew his work or had it in stock. I have written to him asking to find out he's working on.' Janáček replied thus to Hostinský, but instead of venting his anger over what could have been taken as something of a calculated insult, considering all that he had done for Moravian folksong over the past fifteen years, he simply suggested that the influential and diplomatically astute Hostinský could sort out the matter through a discreet word to the minister: 'I think it will be in the interests and to the advantage of the whole project, for which the minister Dr Hartel should be thanked. I wish you every success and ask for a brief account of the session.'[8] He may also have briefed *Moravská orlice*, since on 11 April the newspaper published a substantial, well-informed if rather chauvinistically shrill report under the heading 'A wrong not yet righted!'

Hostinský duly reported back on 10 April that there was complete support for a Czech-speaking Moravian representative. One of the German-speaking delegates, the Austrian folksong expert Dr Josef Pommer, had in fact already put Janáček's name forward but the bureaucracy had not got round to acting on it.

The result was that both in Bohemia and in Moravia there will be two independent working parties, Czech and German. So an invitation will go to you to join the committee and at the same time an invitation for you to propose the other people (about five) for the Moravian-Slavonic working party, i.e. Czechs in Moravia and Silesia. If necessary, our two working parties can come to an agreement but I think that such autonomy for Czech Moravia will be no bad thing.[9]

Janáček's invitation from Dr Hartel asking for suggestions for the formation of a working party for folksong in Moravia and Silesia arrived on 11 May. The next day Janáček wrote to Hostinský passing on this news and suggesting that he would visit him in Prague on 15 May. He would arrive at about three and hoped he could see him before going to the theatre at seven that evening.[10] In the event Hostinský met Janáček at his hotel (Victoria) soon after his arrival.[11]

By then Janáček had already written a rather peremptory note to his previous folksong colleague Lucie Bakešová, demanding a list of her publications.[12] She was baffled and sent back a perfunctory descriptive list without details. 'I don't know for what purposes you need it and I would have to put in a lot more work if I were to try and think of everything.' It was also clear that the difficulties over 1895 had not gone away: 'Joyous and not so joyous feelings swarmed out of my soul upon seeing in your hand [the word] "Ethnographic" and everything connected with it!'[13] It was only in the autumn that things began to get under way with Janáček's new and potentially enormous task. Although Zeman was designated one of the official collectors, Bakešová was not to be part of the new venture (although she would have liked to have been; see chap. 53) and Janáček's old collaborator and mentor František Bartoš, though invited, refused to come aboard, pleading age and illness.[14] He died the following year at the age of sixty-nine.

Although unrelated, two important choral events took place in 1905 that were to have a profound impact on the course of Janáček's composition and would lead to his first major breakthrough. According to Ferdinand Vach's 1924 memoir it was in 1904 that Janáček happened to hear a concert by the Moravian Teachers' Choral Society performing in Veselí na Moravě (now Veselí nad Moravou). The choir, which became the most famous Czech male-voice choir of the century, had been formed by Vach in the spring of 1903 from graduates of the Teachers' Institute in Kroměříž, where he was working at the time. After a few concerts it was organized in its final form, and with its final name, and soon established itself as a highly disciplined force with an adventurous repertory that included many contemporary Czech works. According to Vach, Janáček, who had not heard this choir before, was pleasantly surprised and immediately sent an 'interesting letter' and two unpublished choruses, *If only you knew* and *The Evening Witch* (iv/28, nos. 1 and 3),[15] the same two choruses sent, seemingly without result, to František Vojtěchovský in 1900. But, twenty years after the event, Vach's memory was in error. Janáček's first encounter with the Moravian Teachers' Choral Society took place in fact a year later, on 11 June 1905, when the choir gave a Whit Sunday concert in Veselí that included a chorus by Křížkovský.[16] That Janáček was in the area during this period is corroborated by a postcard he sent to Joza Janáčková from Hroznová Lhota, just a few kilometres away, where he was visiting an exhibition,[17] seemingly of paintings by Joža Úprka.† Although

† Born in Hroznová Lhota, Joža Úprka (1861–1940) was the model for the painter Lhotský in *Fate* and the brother of Janáček's ethnographic associate (from 1894), the sculptor and architect František Úprka.

Janáček's 'interesting letter' has vanished, Vach's thank-you note (sent on 21 June 1905) has not. It says simply: 'Many thanks [. . .] for sending the *excellent* choruses: we'll start rehearsing them at once: 1. *If Only You Knew*, 2. *The Evening Witch*. I'll return the score as soon as it's been copied.'[18]

Somewhat before this initiative another choral society, this time in Bohemia, was also beginning to explore Janáček's choruses. Unlike Vach's Moravian Teachers' Choral Society, the 'Smetana' Choral Society of Plzeň had no personal contact with Janáček and had simply acquired copies of some of the very few Janáček male-voice choruses published at the time, his *Four Male-Voice Choruses* (IV/17), issued by Winkler in Brno in 1886. On 9 March 1905 the choir's director Bohuslav Beneš wrote to Janáček: 'Towards the end of the month we will sing your magnificent chorus *Ah, the War* [one of IV/17]. Since before every concert we prepare an "introduction" to the pieces given, please allow me to ask if you could write a few lines about your beautiful chorus, which is much liked by all the singers.'[19] Janáček was delighted. The choruses had been ignored, he said, and what better introduction could there be than Dvořák's words of commendation (see chap. 23), and he trustingly sent them Dvořák's letter of 13 September 1886 plus a suggestion for dynamics.[20] Janáček was invited to the performance given in Plzeň on 25 March,[21] but Plzeň is a long way from Brno, and it would have been surprising had he gone just to hear a single chorus composed twenty years earlier. But from this tiny initiative much else followed. Later that year the Plzeň 'Smetana' went to Spa, in Belgium, to take part in a singing competition, and on 25 July performed Janáček's chorus there. This was the first performance of any Janáček work outside the Czech lands. The chorus was repeated at a 'victory' concert in Plzeň on 7 November and again in a charity concert on 15 November: *Ah the War* was clearly a hit. Janáček showed his gratitude over the next two years by writing two of his greatest male-voice choruses for the Plzeň choir, *Kantor Halfar*‡ (IV/33) and *Maryčka Magdónova* (IV/35; see chaps. 53 and 54).

Zdenka's frequent visits to Vienna continued. On 6 May she sent Janáček a postcard of the changing of the guard at the Hofburg. Was this a witty comment on the fact that her parents were moving house

‡For an explanation of the word 'kantor' see chap. 3.

the following Monday (she gave the new address), or a demonstration of loyalty to the dynasty, or a card chosen at random? Her brief message gives no clue: 'I've already got the hats and find the Dalmatian wine very tasty. What are you up to?'[22] Janáček's answer, thirteen days later – 'Nothing and [again] nothing'[23] – was not really true. In addition to any folksong work that the new working party generated, there was presumably also work on the final stages of *Fate*. In her letter to Janáček written the same day (19 May) Mrs Bakešová mentioned having heard that he was 'well and again working hard'.[24] And on 6 June Janáček's veteran copyist Josef Štross wrote the date at the end of his copy of the complete full score of *Fate*. After many years of working for Janáček it was to be Štross's last task for him. In January the next year he celebrated his eightieth birthday and presumably decided that enough was enough.

Zdenka stayed on in Vienna and in July, after the Organ School broke up, Janáček went to Hukvaldy. From there he wrote to Zdenka on 24 July:

Day after day there's a storm here. It's beautifully green here and full of fragrance. I still have my head 'all tied up' [presumably in his recently completed opera]; I go around like an idiot. I have good food here: but I *have* to speak! And I would rather be silent. Vojáček from St Petersburg invited me to Radhošt' but we sat the whole day beneath it: he couldn't get up the hill. Well, [he is] eighty![25]

'Vojáček from St Petersburg' was Hynek Vojáček (1825–1916), a Moravian (and like Janáček a former choral scholar at the Augustinian monastery in Brno), who at the age of thirty had settled in St Petersburg as a military bandmaster, bassoonist and teacher. Although he did not return regularly to his native Moravia until 1903, he was an important link between Czech and Russian musicians. He had much to offer Janáček and his Russian Circle, and he wrote over forty letters to Janáček from 1905. This unsuccessful assault on the mountain of Radhošt' was their first meeting.

Janáček may have been preoccupied after signing off his new opera, but he seemed suddenly surprisingly communicative. He sent another postcard to Zdenka, probably the next day, mentioning that he had already got soaked twice ('there hasn't been a day so far without at least one storm!'). Mushrooms were growing, there were plenty of fish. His sister Josefa was in Brno with some unspecified ailment ('from there they sent her to the clinic in Prague').[26] Three days later the weather had improved and he was having a good rest.[27] The same day he sent Zdenka some 'excellent Hukvaldy cheese'.[28] His stay in Hukvaldy continued into the next month, and he returned to Brno on the evening of 14 August. When he wrote to Zdenka two days later he told her that he had visited Olga's grave (she would have been twenty-three on 15 August). It was nice and tidy with seven posies, he said, and he had added an eighth. That day he was 'organizing everything at the Organ School' and next day he would probably leave for Luhačovice, staying in the guesthouse Vlastimila, as in the previous year.[29]

From Luhačovice, on 20 August, he reported that 'half of Brno was there' and that nothing had yet taken his interest.[30] And he was still bored six days later: 'For two days young Pergler[§] was here and attached himself to me. He's gone off now – how I heaved a sigh of relief! Boredom is said to be the best cure for nerves – which I will have like steel in a short while.'[31] Gradually his appetite for work returned, as he wrote on about 2 September,[32] now itching to return: 'I'm leaving here on Thursday [7 September] at noon. So then write now to Brno. Máŕa [Stejskalová] wrote to me that she will be in Brno on Monday. I had just one week of good weather here. I'm already looking forward to plum dumplings at home.'[33] Zdenka herself returned from Vienna on 7 September.[34] They had spent over two months apart, but had kept in touch with at least a few postcards.

Soon after his return, Janáček impatiently wrote to Hostinský demanding to know why everything seemed to have gone quiet on the folksong publication project: 'I have submitted a suggestion for the working party; the "police" investigated the people concerned before the holidays and from that time on – silence.'[35] Hostinský was not much wiser. He had heard from Hartel, thanking him for his suggestions and promising action, but Hartel had then left the ministry.[36] In fact things were going quietly ahead. As Janáček later reported to Hostinský, he had (though he did not know it at the time) already been officially appointed chairman of the working party for folksong in Moravia and Silesia.[37] His colleagues on the working party (all

---

[§] Vít (Vítězslav) Pergler, violinist and music teacher (1872–1963), the son of the prominent Brno musician, also Vít Pergler, with whom Janáček had worked in his Brno Beseda days (see chaps. 20 and 23).

Janáček's own proposals) consisted of the philologist F.V. Autrata (from the Brno Teachers' Institute) as dialect adviser, the folk-influenced architect Dušan Samo Jurkovič (see chap. 45) and Josef Vyhlídal (author of a book on Silesia) as ethnographic advisers, and Hynek Bím, C. M. Hrazdira (the conductor of *Jenůfa*) and Martin Zeman as chief music collectors.[38] Bím had begun collecting folksongs the year after he graduated from the Brno Teachers' Institute – Janáček and Bartoš included thirty-three of them in *Moravian Folksongs Newly Collected* (XIII/3) – and continued to do so while teaching at various schools in Moravia.

After Olga's death in St Petersburg in 1903, Janáček remained in contact with his brother František, but very soon František's own health began to deteriorate. Spa treatments did not do the trick and by 1904 his chief concern was to leave St Petersburg and return to his native Hukvaldy, where he bought a small cottage. In October 1905 he travelled to Prague to consult Dr Otakar Kukula,[39] professor of surgery at Charles University and one of the most eminent surgeons in Prague, who operated on him on 21 October.[40] It was not until 2 November that he discovered what the matter was. He had thought that the operation was connected with his lungs but Professor Kukula had in fact operated on his kidneys, where there had been a 'growth'.[41]

František's time in Prague coincided with stirring political events in Brno. In 1901 Czech delegates to the Viennese parliament began agitating for the realization of an old demand, the establishment of a Czech university in Moravia. Fresh impetus was given to this in 1905 when a new administration was formed in Vienna under the prime minister Paul Gautsch von Frankenthurn. Needing the support of the Czech delegates, Gautsch promised them a university in Moravia provided that they could come to an agreement with the German delegates about where it should be situated. The Czechs were overwhelmingly in favour of Brno; the Germans insisted that the establishment of a Czech university there would make further encroachments on Brno's character as a 'German' town and, in order to demonstrate that this view had popular support, called a rally of representatives of German speakers from Moravia and further afield. The 'Volkstag', as it was called, took place in Brno on 1 October 1905. The Brno Czechs organized a counter-demonstration on the same day: a rally of Czech delegates in the Besední dům. Both rallies were permitted by the authorities and led to mass demonstrations and ugly scenes between the two groups that continued into the next day. Buildings were damaged, many people were wounded and there was one fatality. The twenty-year-old František Pavlík, a joiner's apprentice from Ořechov (a village outside Brno), was killed, bayonetted on the steps of the Besední dům by one of the soldiers called in to keep order.[42]

This event had great resonance in Czech Brno. Contemporary post-cards, printed and circulated to exploit Czech sentiment, show the 'Vesna' building with windows shattered by bullet shots and guarded by Austrian troops, the restaurant 'U tří kohoutů' with its damaged picture window, the 20,000 demonstrators gathered round the station, and satirical cartoons of soldiers both marching in the pro-German procession and also breaking up the pro-Czech one. The most popular postcard, however, was the one depicting the 'murdered Fr. Pavlík' in his patriotic Sokol outfit, his young sister (in her folk costume) and his parents and their humble cottage.[43] Janáček was caught up in all this. He had been in the crowd in front of the Besední dům, unwisely doing battle with the Germans with his walking stick, and had, as František Kolář related, to be forcibly pulled inside the Besední dům when the soldiers with fixed bayonets arrived.[44] Another eye-witness (the editor of *Lidové noviny*, Arnošt Heinrich) relates how he had to calm Janáček down and prevent him from doing anything rash.[45] On the following Sunday Janáček was one of the 10,000 Czechs who demon-stratively turned up for Pavlík's funeral in Ořechov, and said a few words over his grave.[46] In October, in the still disturbed atmosphere, he sent postcards of Pavlík both to Věra Janáčková in Prague[47] and to his brother František, then in Prague and just about to undergo his operation.[48] The powerful emotions stirred up by this event gave rise the next year to a piano piece, *1.X.1905 (From the Street)* (VIII/19; see chap: 53).

At the Moravian Teachers' Choral Society Vach had been as good as his word. Janáček's two 'Haná' choruses (IV/28, nos. 1 and 3) went into rehearsal for the autumn season and were a great hit with the choir: an enthusiastic card congratulating Janáček on his 'exquisite choruses' was sent to him during rehearsals in November, signed by many members.[49] The novelty value of the Haná dialect in Janáček's setting was probably a help, and when the choruses were given their première on 26 November in the composer's presence it was in Přerov, in Haná territory. These two pieces were sung as a pair on many of the choir's tours, beginning with a performance in Vienna at the Savoy Hotel hall on 9 December that year. A card covered with signatures of the choir members sent to Janáček next day proclaimed 'complete success' in Vienna.[50]

Janáček's works featured in one more concert that year, in the Moravian town of Prostějov. On 10 December the local choral society 'Orlice' planned a concert of Moravian compositions. Originally the programme was to have included Janáček's two published *Valachian Dances* for orchestra (vi/4) but five days before the concert the director of 'Orlice', Ezechiel Ambros (see chap. 36), wrote to him saying that they were unable to perform the work. The local military band was otherwise engaged that evening and the Orchestral Association, which somehow managed to accompany Hrazdira's *Our Hymn* (for soloists, mixed choir and orchestra), could not manage Janáček's work.[51] Apart from Hrazdira's piece and a cantata by Josef Drahlovský, all the other pieces played were for more modest forces, essentially just songs or choruses. After the cancellation of the *Valachian Dances* Janáček was represented merely by three folksong arrangements, two from *Moravian Folk Poetry in Songs* (v/2, nos. 9 and 44) and one from *Hukvaldy Folk Poetry in Songs* (v/4, no. 8). 'Orlice' wrote to Janáček on 18 November, inviting him to the concert and to accompany Zdeněk Lev (Miroslav Lazar) at the piano in Janáček's harmonizations of the Moravian folksongs. 'The main rehearsal is 9 December, but it will be sufficient for you to come [just] for the concert. Accommodation, etc. will be provided. Please tell us your decision.'[52]

It is not known whether Janáček turned up (the report on the concert in *Dalibor* mentions the involvement of the composers concerned, but does not specify which of them were there),[53] though he might well have been tempted by the event, involving as it did so many composers, including several associates and pupils. The concert represents another glimmer of things to come: it was the first time that any of these songs had been performed publicly outside Brno.

For New Year Zdenka returned to Vienna and Janáček went to Prague. There was not much on and so he was reduced to attending a popular Mozart concert conducted by Oskar Nedbal on New Year's Eve.[54] He also spent time with the Prague Janáčeks. His new year greeting to Zdenka was also signed by the young Věra Janáčková.[55]

52

Music as autobiography II

On 26 February 1903 Olga Janáčková died after a long and agonizing illness. Janáček had composed half of his opera *Jenůfa* against the knowledge of his daughter's decline and put the finishing touches to it as she lay dying. Some time after 18 March he submitted the opera to the Prague National Theatre. Its swift and summary rejection (28 April) was a terrible blow to his self-confidence. The timing was devastating, just two months after Olga's death.

The fact that before the end of the year Janáček was able to begin a new opera speaks eloquently of his resilience. It could be argued that the quite different setting and subject matter of his new opera was a response to Prague's rejection of *Jenůfa*. If they don't like peasant rural stuff, if it's too 'Moravian' for them, what about an up-to-date opera with a bourgeois setting, just like Charpentier's *Louise* (then taking Prague by storm)? But just as Janáček's resumption of *Jenůfa* in 1901 seems to have been triggered by the strong autobiographical resonances between his life and his opera (see chap. 40), it may have needed the even stronger autobiographical links in his next opera to overcome the terrible blows that fate had dealt him at the beginning of 1903.

Before the idea of *Fate* came up, however, Janáček first considered Josef Merhaut's *Angelic Sonata* as a possible basis for an opera. Merhaut's novel deals with the breakdown of the marriage between Hřivna and his wife, and their joint pilgrimage to Hostýn where, after Hřivna's repentance of an extra-marital affair, the couple make peace with one another. Their reconciliation is sealed with the birth of a child who, however, dies within a year. The parallels with Janáček's own rocky marriage and their daughter's death and that of their two-year-old son in 1890 seem all too close for comfort. Nevertheless, an autobiographical impetus was one that would increasingly propel him into new compositional ventures and in this case seems to have prepared the ground for *Fate*. It can hardly be a coincidence that in the next few years, when Janáček began to write chamber and orchestral works, their programmatic backgrounds related either to marital strife (the Piano Trio x/22, after Tolstoy's *Kreutzer Sonata*) or the death of young children (*The Fiddler's Child* vi/14 or *Fairy Tale* vii/5; see chap. 60).

The extraordinary way in which *Fate* came about is described in chap. 44. In Ludvík Čelanský's opera, provocatively called *Kamilla*, the chief character (seemingly a representation of Camilla Urválková) is depicted as a heartless and superficial flirt who does not know her own mind and who thoughtlessly rejects the love of her humble and sincere admirer (Čelanský disguised as a poet). Janáček's chivalrous duty, it seemed, was to write a sequel where she might be seen in a more favourable light.

Janáček's first ideas are indeed Camilla-dominated. 'Into this brilliance the main character would enter, *Mrs Míla Válková*' goes one of Janáček's letters to his librettist Fedora Bartošová about the scenario for Act 1.[1] *The Star of Luhačovice* (i.e. Mrs Urválková) was an early, and abandoned, title for his new opera in which a composer, Živný, meets Mrs Míla Válková (the name could hardly be less disguised) in Luhačovice. Like Janáček, Živný had a daughter who had recently died. Like Camilla Urválková, Míla Válková had been in love with a composer, from whom she has had to part because of opposition from her parents. Like Mrs Urválková, she is now unhappily married with a young son.*

In the first libretto for *Fate* Act 2 opens in Míla's boudoir where she reads a letter from Živný, as perhaps Janáček imagined Mrs Urválková reading his letters. Act 2 Scene 2, set on the Dalmatian Riviera, provides a crisis when Živný and Míla, increasingly drawn to one another, encounter the fury of her jealous husband. Discovering his wife closeted in her boudoir with Živný, Válek shoots at the couple, fatally wounding Míla.

During the course of work on the opera, Janáček's friendship with Mrs Urválková came to an abrupt end when their correspondence was

---

* The early librettos of *Fate* have been expertly unravelled by Theodora Straková (1956); see also *JODA*, chap. 4.

stopped by her husband. At the same time Janáček now abandoned the dramatic conclusion to Act 2 in favour of a very different action, taken out of its exotic locale and set on home ground – a quiet domestic scene. Mr Urválek's intrusion in Janáček's life resulted in his operatic counterpart, Válek (the husband of Míla Válková), being written out of Janáček's opera.

In his letter of 10 April 1904 to Bartošová (i.e. at the time of Mr Urválek's intervention and as Janáček got to the end of composing Act 1) Janáček made the startling suggestion that Míla's young son had in fact been fathered not by Míla's husband but by Živný.[2] This change opened up a whole prehistory to their meeting at the beginning of the opera. Furthermore, the idea that Janáček was writing an opera as a corrective to Čelanský's treatment of Mrs Urválková in *Kamilla* became somehow transformed into the notion that Živný had written an opera in which he had shamed his wife and son. This is the opera that Živný now remorsefully wishes to destroy: he is seen musing about it as the (new) second act opens.

The Act 1 meeting of Živný and Míla now became the meeting of old flames. Míla's young son is their son and by Act 2 they are cosily together again, a union much disapproved of by Míla's mother. Camilla Urválková's disappearance from Janáček's life was also reflected in Míla Válková's gradual disappearance from *Fate*. Her first appearance in the opera had been stage-managed as carefully as that of Kát'a Kabanová or Emilia Marty would be, and her Act 1 duet with Živný, one of the high points of the opera, reveals them as equal partners. But by Act 2 she becomes merely a foil to Živný, and her bizarre death at the end of Act 2 removes her from Act 3. Živný, who does most of the singing in Act 2, continues in Act 3 with a vast monologue that takes up the second half. Together with Mr Brouček, he has one of the most substantial male roles in any Janáček opera. Janáček's operatic defence of Camilla Urválková became a defence of himself, and *Fate* turned into a vehicle for Janáček's own musings on the interrelationship of life and art. Instead of an act with the dramatic crisis of the shooting, Janáček wrote a new libretto. Much of it is taken up with the composer ruminating about his opera in which he had pilloried Míla (when she left him because of parental pressure) and which he now seeks to destroy.

In transferring the focus from the wronged heroine to the hero-figure of the composer, Janáček found himself writing an early example of what is sometimes called 'Künstleroper', opera about the artist. The genealogy of the German Künstleroper goes back to the figure of Hans Sachs in *Die Meistersinger*, a mouthpiece for Wagner as a composer, and not only about the correct writing of prize songs. But the idea of a composer writing an opera about his calling and containing at its centre a figure who can represent him became a familiar trope in opera between the wars. Examples range from the grand historical – Pfitzner's *Palestrina* (1917) or Hindemith's *Mathis der Maler* (1938) – to the contemporary, for example Strauss's *Intermezzo* (1924) or Krenek's *Jonny spielt auf* (1929). In all these works the composers wrote their own librettos about artists producing masterpieces (Palestrina's *Missa Papae Marcelli*, Matthias Grünewald's *Concert of Angels*) or in relation to the people around them (the little tiff between Strauss and his wife Christine, which was the subject matter of *Intermezzo*).

To mention any of these German operas is merely to draw parallels, not to suggest lines of influence. Janáček got there, quite by chance, twelve years before any of his contemporaries. If anything, influence from operas involving artists came from Puccini's *La bohème* (1896) and Charpentier's *Louise* (1900; see chap. 46). As *Fate* was unknown for decades, Janáček's German counterparts would have been unaware of his primacy in the field. Artists figure in his next opera too, *The Excursion of Mr Brouček to the Moon*. Here the satirical portraits of painters, writers and even a composer – in essence a skit on the art-for-art's sake figures of the time – come across as even more ridiculous than the solidly philistine Mr Brouček. Maybe Janáček felt that he had taken Živný (i.e. himself) too seriously and now offered a mocking corrective.

It is evident that by now a crucial element of Janáček's creativity was coming from the close connection between his life and art. *Fate* is the most overt example of this sort. Its scenario was dreamt up by Janáček himself and changed as his would-be love affair with Urválková changed. Válek was jettisoned, and Míla turned from alluring former lover to dutiful wife with harridan mother in tow. In some strange way Mrs Urválková had become transformed into Zdenka Janáčková. Although a draft letter has survived bearing witness to Janáček's hope of finding a parallel figure to Míla's mother in Brno and Prague lunatic asylums,[3] it could be argued that Míla's mother in some way encapsulated his feelings towards Anna Schulzová, including a little wishful thinking for her and her daughter (i.e. Janáček's wife Zdenka) to be out of the way.

Instead of drawing on his wide acquaintance of literary figures in Brno, Janáček selected a young and inexperienced assistant to turn his scenario into verse, perhaps to ensure that he had complete control over the product. The later, very extensive revisions to the libretto – those undertaken after Urválková disappeared from his life – were made mostly by him. With Janáček's other works the links with his own life were helpful in getting him going, in setting his creative powers in motion. Nevertheless at some stage these works took on their own independent lives, leaving behind faint traces of their autobiographical past. In *Fate* the traces are more substantial and arguably unsettle the final product. But just as Kovařovic's rejection of *Jenůfa*, freighted with autobiographical burden, was overwhelmingly upsetting for Janáček, the acceptance and subsequent non-performance of its successor *Fate*, weighed down even more with autobiographical connections, was in Janáček's words a 'spiritual torment'.[4] Somehow the two Czech opera houses in Prague had conspired to block performances of Janáček's two most recent operas, both intimately bound up with his own life. No wonder that his compositional élan ebbed away at this period: he began to lose his way and his confidence. As the title of Janáček's piano suite put it, these were years *In the Mists*.

53

1906

On Sunday 7 January at 4.30 in the rooms of the Club of the Friends of Art, Janáček presided over the first meeting of his folksong working party. He had sent the agenda to Martin Zeman on Christmas Eve:

1. Report from the leading working party.
2. Report from the representative of the Imperial and Royal Governor.
3. Discussion of the principles of the work.
4. What can Moravia and Silesia offer that is still new?
5. Plan of the [folksong-]collectors' work.
6. Any other business.[1]

Janáček had no secretary, so he would have needed to write six copies of this letter, and address them individually, to all six members of his working party (see chap. 51; an identical one went out to Hynek Bím on the same day).[2] A few days after the meeting, Zeman was in touch about his collecting plan and the budget for it,[3] and Janáček responded, inviting him to take the plan up to the autumn and to provide more detail, for example stating where and for how long he might expect to be in February, at Easter, at Whitsun, at the hay harvest and during the summer. He ought to be able to 'exact a larger sum' by noting down travel and daily expenses, as well as the costs of 'encouraging the mood for singing'.[4] This sort of exchange would have been duplicated many times over with the other collectors in his working party. With Bím, for instance, it was a lot easier since by the first day of February he had sent Janáček a detailed budget listing the places he proposed to visit in fifty-four full days and eighteen half days and cost of travel (both railway and carriage), all beautifully itemized and summarized.[5] Bím would remain Janáček's most assiduous and organized researcher over the course of the project.

As for collectors not in the working party, a few days after their meeting, Janáček wrote a note to Lucie Bakešová: 'Would you like to outline your plan for collection for this year as far as this autumn? Can you also notify me of your expenses connected with it? I have to submit a general plan so that all previous work can be subsumed into a monumental project.'[6] Bakešová replied enthusiastically on 12 January but was uncertain what exactly Janáček required of her[7] and in the end proposed visiting him on 21 January to find out more,[8] after which she wrote once again, on 25 January. Her long letter is not about the collecting of folksongs (for which Janáček's working party was chiefly set up) but about the performance of folk customs: 'The performance of children's plays here, the performance of the Shrovetide masquerades (which haven't been done for years) and then festivals with dances, "Hunting the King" in Troubsko, perhaps "The Little Queens", etc. – all this would cost several hundred zl.'[9] None of these festivities, she wrote, could take place without rehearsal and none of the participants would rehearse unless they were paid. The new feature of these enactments was that they were to be captured on camera, a consequence of the widely drawn conception of *Das Volkslied in Österreich*, which among its many progressive features advocated the collection of photographs of folk singers and musicians.[10] 'So our first work would perhaps be the masquerades at the end of February. I'll see to organizing it all and then invite you to come with a camera. I'll promise them [the participants] either money or perhaps a quart of beer (although I am definitely against drinking).'[11]

Meanwhile preparations were going ahead for the first Club of the Friends of Art concert of 1906, to present an evening of new Czech and especially Moravian music on Saturday 27 January. The club had engaged the services of the Ševčík Quartet, formed in 1900 by four of Otakar Ševčík's pupils, to play movements from recent Moravian works: trios by Jan Kunc and by Josef Nešvera, and František Musil's String Quartet. The young pianist Ludmila Tučková (1882–1960, a graduate of the Brno Organ School who was about to complete her studies at the Prague Conservatory) played movements from works by leading composers from Bohemia: Foerster's *Dreaming* op. 47, Suk's *Spring* op. 22a, Novák's *My May* op. 20 and the piano version of his *Slovácko Suite* op. 32. Today, however, the chief interest of the concert is the première of Janáček's *1.X.1905* (VIII/19), also played by Tučková. Cast in three movements, it had been written in response to the emotional turmoil of the 'Volkstag' demonstration (see chap. 51). Hearing his new piece at a rehearsal of the whole programme on Friday 26 January in the context of the elegantly polished pieces by his well-established Czech contemporaries, Janáček seems to have been dissatisfied, and the next day, when Tučková was trying out the piano before the evening performance, he took the music from her, cut out the third movement (said to be a 'gloomy funeral march') and, calling it 'vulgar', thrust it in the stove heating the room. So on that evening all Tučková could play was the two-movement torso that remained. Later that year Janáček seemed to have disliked even these two movements: after they were played informally in Prague, he allegedly cast them into the Vltava, where they floated on the water 'like white swans'.[12] Part of the mythology of the piece includes the story that Tučková, fearing that Janáček might want to destroy the remaining movements, made a 'secret' copy of them and hid it away until the composer changed his mind, but Jiří Zahrádka has sensibly suggested that she probably simply hung on to the copyist's version that she had been given in the first place.[13]

Today Janáček's action seems baffling in view of the quality of the surviving two movements. That the work is occasionally referred to as a 'sonata' goes back to Janáček's first biographer, Jan Kunc. He can be forgiven for his mistake: by 1911, when he published his long biographical article on Janáček, the music seemingly no longer existed and all he had to go on was his memory of the first performance. The erroneous genre he attached to the work reflects the perceptible sonata form of the first movement as well as the density and scale of the work. In common with Janáček's greatest works from this period (*Amarus*, *Jenůfa*, *On the Overgrown Path*) it arose out of painful personal experience. In contrast to an exquisite but emotionally lightweight piece such as Suk's suite *Spring* (the movements *The Breeze* and *Longing* were played at the Brno recital), the emotion must have seemed raw and too near the surface, and Janáček, his morale weakened by Kovařovic's refusal of *Jenůfa*, seems to have lost confidence and destroyed the work. This pattern of destroying works or compulsively revising them was one that persisted for a decade.

The 'drowning' of *1.X.1905* could well have taken place just a few days after the Brno première, for instance during Janáček's trip to

Prague of 6–11 February, when he saw two plays, *L'adversaire* by Alfred Capus and Emanuel Arène (in a Czech translation),[14] *The Lantern* by Alois Jirásek[15] and Beethoven's *Fidelio*.[16] Since none of these, and certainly not *L'adversaire*, which he attended on 6 February, fell into a 'must see' category for Janáček, it almost looks as if he was making a point of being out of Brno at the time. As an opera composer and a leading member of the Club of the Friends of Art he might have been expected to go to the club on 6 February to hear Josef Nešvera introduce his 'Moravian' opera *Radhošt'*, especially since Nešvera had recently written to him earlier, announcing when he would arrive in Brno, asking where the event would take place and what his role would be.[17] The event itself was elaborate, including not only Nešvera's introduction but excerpts sung by the cast;[18] the work was to receive its première in Brno the next day. Nešvera was Křížkovský's successor at Olomouc Cathedral, and although he was not an especially distinguished composer of operas, his *Perdita* received its première at the Prague National Theatre in 1897 and his latest opera *Radhošt'* was performed in both Brno and Prague during 1906. Neither opera could be said to have been successful (each ran for just three performances in Prague); nevertheless, the fact that Nešvera's Moravian opera *Radhošt'* had been accepted in Prague at a time when Janáček's Moravian opera *Jenůfa* had been turned down must have rankled. Janáček's trips to Prague, however, were fairly frequent at this time, for instance on 16 February to hear Massenet's *Werther*[19] conducted by Kovařovic.

Among the more curious documents of this period is a letter from Janáček to the Brno Družstvo (7 March), asking whether

the ban on wearing outdoor clothing while sitting in our theatre is absolute, especially in the case of people with rheumatism, who cannot stand the draught in our theatre. Such people would certainly not be subscribers and could not enter into our theatre as it now stands. I am personally affected by the above-mentioned belated ban, and ask you politely for reconsideration.[20]

This of course was a try-on. Although Czech theatres have always been beautifully organized and furnished with cloakrooms, so that members of the public seldom venture into the auditorium without having deposited their overcoats there, Janáček had been a committee member of the Družstvo and no doubt could have gone into the theatre in his overcoat if he had wanted to. Was this yet another excuse for missing Nešvera's opera? Were there no draughts in the Prague theatres and concert halls that Janáček had been visiting so assiduously? Whatever the reason, it provides another the first indication of the rheumatism that was to affect Janáček badly for many years. Before the end of the year the Družstvo had exacted their revenge with a pained note pointing out that Janáček hadn't yet paid his annual subscriptions for 1904–6.[21] Janáček went to Prague again on 11 March for an afternoon concert of the Czech Philharmonic with Zemánek conducting a programme of Beethoven, Mozart and Berlioz[22] followed by an evening performance at the National Theatre with Kovařovic conducting *Lohengrin*.[23]

Janáček's contacts with Bakešová over the photographing of the proposed folk customs continued. It is not clear whether he took up her invitation to go to Ořechov (a short walk from Ořechovičky, where she lived) to see the Shrovetide customs on Ash Wednesday (28 February)[24] – probably not, if his later failures to visit Bakešová are anything to go by. On 9 April, however, Janáček reported that 'we' (presumably he and a photographer) had had a successful time taking photographs at the Brno Women's Shelter, and proposed visiting Bakešová and her folk group on Easter Tuesday (17 April).[25] However this plan was soon plagued by technical problems. Janáček had been to see the photographer Klíčník, who reported that the light was insufficient to photograph movement even with a flash, and that the plan would have to be postponed until later in the year.[26] For her part, Bakešová was also experiencing difficulties. It would be impossible to perform the masquerade customs on Easter Tuesday, she wrote: 'The people taking part in it are either in Brno or working in the fields.' She suggested a postponement until 22 April, the Sunday after Easter. Furthermore, she continued, she had been planning to 'organize some plays with the girls – but it's a huge amount of work just to get them together, rehearse them and awaken the mood and atmosphere in them'. People had not been sufficiently rewarded for their part in the Ethnographic Exhibition in 1895, and this dampened enthusiasm for further work. And (she now came to the crunch), she really did not have

the appetite and enthusiasm for this big work, because you didn't suggest that I and Běhálková should be in the working party. These days there are women taking part in everything and the two of us don't deserve to be cast aside, all the more so when you know that we could indeed advance the cause. [. . .] I know that it is entirely your doing that we aren't in the working party – you didn't want to have women among you, did you?

In this long letter Bakešová went on to argue that if Janáček had really wanted her and Běhálková in his working party he could have got his way, since he commanded such authority.[27] And of course she was right: Janáček had been invited to nominate everybody in his working party. But, at least later, the membership was not all male: in 1909 Janáček brought in Františka Kyselková. His decision to exclude Bakešová was made not necessarily on the grounds of gender, but merely because their work in 1895 had been fraught with friction, and maybe he wanted more comfortable colleagues. This was not the last time Bakešová alluded to her grievance, and after the burst of activity in the first half of 1906 their contacts petered out.

On the advice of the Mayor of Ořechov (whose permission was needed for Bakešová's folk activities) the event was further postponed,[28] although Bakešová's rehearsals continued. Her letter of 23 April gives a good idea of what was involved. They had been practising seven plays daily as well as going through 'The Little Queens' three times:

Yesterday over forty girls came to me (as it was on Sunday). [. . .] Would you like to come on 29 April to have a look? Then you could judge whether it is likely to be worth coming here on 6 May. They would send horses for you and your wife to the train at Silůvky at 8.30 a.m. or at 1 p.m., as would suit you best. I must know at which time to prepare it.[29]

Janáček's response on 26 April was to the point:

I asked you for 'The Little Queens', and in one letter you say not and then in the second you promise it.

I suggest to you the following approach:

1. Work on the children's plays and 'The Little Queens'.

2. Write down the expenses carefully so that they could be paid to you on account.

3. When it's ready, give me a detailed list of what has been prepared together with a budget of expenses, and then we'll come with the photographer.

4. The clothes must be at least Sunday best. But whether it is earlier or later doesn't really matter.

5. The editing of the text depends on you.[30]

However, Janáček seems to have taken his eye off the ball towards the end of April, and Bakešová was reduced to writing increasingly insistent letters on a daily basis trying to get an answer out of him about when he would be coming.[31] That he didn't attend the preview on Sunday 29 April is clear from Bakešová's letter the next day:

It disappointed me *very much* that you and your wife did not come yesterday. It was a nice day and you could have wished yourself and your dear wife that trip into God's countryside, given us joy here, and given the children pleasure. They waited eagerly for you – for whenever they weakened or were inattentive your name was an encouragement. If you don't come to look at them then it is *the end*, I must know if the plays and 'The Little Queens' rehearsed *like this* will be enough for you or whether the movement must be very skilled. There are thirty girls. On 6 May everyone *will certainly be waiting for you* whether you are now coming with your wife or with the photographer.[32]

One reason why Janáček seems to have fallen silent at this moment was because of his involvement with the Club of the Friends of Art, which presented a 'memorial concert' for Dvořák on 30 April, the eve of the second anniversary of his death. Kundera suggests that Janáček was responsible for the rather flowery invitation that was sent out with the programmes for the concert, but he also took part as a performer. The Ševčík Quartet was invited again, playing Dvořák's E flat Quartet op. 51 and G major Quartet op. 106, and Janáček joined them in Dvořák's *Bagatelles* for two violins, cello and harmonium. The concert was completed with a selection of Dvořák's songs and his *Silhouettes* for two pianos.[33] On 27 April, a few days before the concert, Janáček published his reminiscences of Dvořák, *Dr Ant. Dvořák and Brno* (xv/181), in *Lidové noviny*. As well as describing Dvořák's links with Brno, Janáček also related how he heard about his death during his brief trip to Warsaw (see chap. 47).

There was increasingly encouraging news coming from the Moravian Teachers' Choral Society tour. On 16 April the choir, conducted as usual by Ferdinand Vach, gave the second performance in Vienna (this time at the Musikvereinsaal) of the two 'Haná choruses', *If you only knew* and *The Evening Witch* (iv/28, nos. 1 and 3). Two days later the choir performed them in Munich. On 21 April Vach wrote to Janáček to say that they had had 'enormous success' there.[34] The choruses continued to triumph in Leipzig and Nuremberg,[35] with *The Evening Witch* singled out in a review in *Signal* as having had the greatest success among all the choir's pieces in Leipzig.[36] Finally, at the end of the tour, the choir stopped off in Prague to give the première there on 29 April of these two choruses. There is no evidence that Janáček himself was present; probably he was tied up with rehearsals for the Dvořák concert the following day. Moreover, these were not the only

Janáček choruses heard in Prague that month. On 4 April* the venerable Prague choral society 'Hlahol', conducted by its conductor Adolf Piskáček (1873–1919), presented the second and third of the 1885 choruses (IV/17), *O Love* and *Ah, the War*.[37] Kovařovic had slammed the door in Janáček's face as far as opera in Prague was concerned, but the four choruses performed in Prague in a single month – two of his finest early choruses and his two most recent – were an indication that he might make some headway in other fields.

Janáček's heavy workload for the folksong project included keeping in touch with the parallel Czech working party in Prague, headed by Otakar Hostinský. With his usual energy Janáček was already further ahead than Prague. On 19 April Hostinský wrote giving the names of his working party (which had finally been approved) and asking whether the Brno group had produced any documents that might be considered by the Prague working party at its first meeting on Sunday 22 April.[38] Janáček's group had already produced a printed appeal for helpers and this was promptly sent to Hostinský.[39] More would be achieved in Vienna if the Prague and Brno groups were seen to be acting in unity, Janáček felt, and he suggested a meeting with Hostinský during his next trip to Prague, on 22 May.[40] Before then, however, there were more contacts with Bakešová. His visit to Ořechov was set for Sunday 13 May,[41] a week later than originally proposed, and in her note of 11 May Bakešová outlined the programme:

I suggest, Mr Director, that you would probably set out before 12 noon. [. . .] I think that the children will line up in our courtyard [i.e. at the Bakeš estate at Ořechovičky]. You will look them over and then [see them perform] *Smrťolka* [the personification of death], and we will all go to the school in Ořechov where there will be the carnival masks and perhaps they will perform 'The Little Queens', etc. It's all a great worry to me since my husband alarmed me by saying that it's not yet all entirely precise. You should have come earlier to have a look. Everyone is looking forward to it, the children are in ecstasy.[42]

And no sooner was this event over than Bakešová wrote again, wondering whether Janáček would like to come and photograph four or five pairs of Haná dancers in costume.[43] This initiative, however, was ignored in the wake of Janáček's next trip to Prague. He was arriving,

---

* Not 4 March as in *JAWO*, p. 114.

he told Hostinský, by express train at three o'clock on Tuesday 22 May. He had accommodation reserved at the hotel Archduke Štěpán and went on to see Hostinský that afternoon before attending the evening performance of Strauss's *Salome*;[44] the production had opened at the Prague German Theatre on 5 May, half a year after its Dresden première in December 1905. *Salome* being a short opera, Janáček afterwards went on to hear an unspecified choral concert. The last fact emerges from a feuilleton written about him and published in the Prague musical journal *Dalibor*. This anonymous article was in fact written by Adolf Piskáček, the conductor at the 'Hlahol' concert of 4 April, when Janáček's two choruses had been sung. In the feuilleton Piskáček writes that he was reviewing a concert, sitting upstairs with friends, when one of his group spotted 'Janáček from Brno' – an 'interesting head', out of which shone 'two dark and fiery eyes' and crowned with a mop of 'greying hair'. They made a point of going up to the 'Napoleonic figure' at the end of the concert. It was Strauss's *Salome*, Janáček said, that had drawn him out of his Brno retreat. At the restaurant to which they conducted him, Janáček happily imparted his views of Strauss's opera. He had been excited by it, he said, and at first 'could hardly make out anything from the flood of the orchestra' but after a while managed to follow some of the more striking motifs. He was most taken, he went on to say, by Salome's dance and by the music illustrating the 'tragic end of John the Baptist'. Conversation then turned to folk music, and Janáček became even more lively and forthcoming. He had discovered something new, something quite distinctive for which the most apt title was perhaps 'nocturne' – an unusual type of folk music in more than one voice, interestingly harmonized:

In the evening, after sunset, girls meet at the back of the cottages and one of them, the best singer, stands in front of the others leading the singing. She sings the first line and the others join in, firmly holding hands, with an unusual melody that carries over the hilltops, sinks into the valleys, and dies away in the distant, dark forest beyond the river.

And thus was captured in print the first reference to Janáček's *Folk Nocturnes* (IV/32). Although Piskáček makes it sound like a brand-new discovery, Janáček's transcriptions made in Makov near Velké Rovné in Slovakia were noted in his diary for 1901–2; dated speech melodies from the area perhaps pinpoint the exact date – 10 September 1901.[45]

Janáček returned several times to the area to verify his transcriptions, most interestingly in this connection in early June 1906, i.e. a couple of weeks after his encounter with Piskáček in Prague.[46] Quite when Janáček completed his arrangement of the seven two-part songs is unclear. In his response to Piskáček's question as to why he had not so far published them he said that he had them all written down and had already rehearsed five of them with a Brno choir in the hope of performing them in Prague.

Piskáček's feuilleton *An Evening with Leoš Janáček* (xv/182) came out in the weekly issue of *Dalibor* dated 25 May 1906, three days after their meeting. The encounter had a number of consequences. It seems that one of Piskáček's companions had been Artuš Rektorys (1877–1971), an enthusiastic music-lover (he worked all his life as an employee of a bank), recently appointed editor of *Dalibor*, who had been looking (as he later wrote in his introduction to the volume of his correspondence with Janáček) to expand the Moravian coverage of the journal.[47] Janáček's suggestion, not reported in Piskáček's feuilleton, about adding a Moravian section to *Dalibor* seemed heaven-sent. Rektorys discussed it at the meeting of his editorial board on 29 May and, once he had got the next weekly issue to bed, wrote Janáček a long letter inviting him to become editor of a Moravian supplement to *Dalibor*. Rektorys needed a brief outline of what Janáček proposed, which could be discussed in detail at his next visit to Prague, and a list of possible contributors. The publisher Mojmír Urbánek (who had taken over the journal from his father F.A. Urbánek in 1900) was willing to increase the size of *Dalibor* from the existing eight-page weekly issue to twelve pages. Janáček would be responsible not only for the extra four pages but for Moravian contributions to the usual news items on concert life, church music, reports, etc. They would have to get a move on, Rektorys added, since all this would appear in the new volume of *Dalibor*, October 1906 and onwards.[48]

At first Janáček was full of enthusiasm, jotting down a list of possible contributors on the back of Rektorys's letter and, following two meetings of local interested parties, he wrote to him with detailed proposals and conditions. These included the suggestion that the 'Brno editorial board' should in fact be the music section of the Brno Club of the Friends of Art, with perhaps a couple of extra people co-opted.[49] Rektorys agreed to most of the conditions but demurred over the composition of the Brno editorial board: he felt that it was too 'narrow' and that the Brno Beseda should be represented – he was clearly unaware of any tensions between Janáček and the Beseda. As for Janáček's enquiries about payment and expenses, these were deflected to the publisher Urbánek.[50] And here it all began to fall apart. For one thing, Janáček's ad hoc committee was hardly burning with zeal: as Kunc reported to Janáček, Hrazdira was 'a priori against' and the rest had kept silent, and Kunc himself produced a long letter with practical conditions, demanding in particular a written and notarized contract ('publishers are said to be worse than lawyers').[51] And from the other side Mojmír Urbánek pointed out in a letter to Janáček that he was enlarging the paper to twelve pages but not putting up the subscription and would therefore need to ask for Janáček's indulgence over remuneration. There would be no editorial fee (since editing would be done in Prague). Anything that Janáček wrote would be paid at 4 K a printed sheet and he would give Janáček 5 K a month for postage.[52] One can sense from Janáček's letter of conditions to Rektorys (30 July) that the whole project was beginning to seem rather more than he had bargained for, and so it was with good grace and perhaps some sense of relief that he bowed out of the enterprise: it would not be possible, he wrote, to set up an editorial board in Moravia for 5 K a month.[53] The sum is perhaps not quite so derisory as it sounds: in 1906 5 K would have paid for the postage on fifty letters (or a hundred postcards) within Austria-Hungary. Rektorys presumably reported this back to Urbánek, who doubled his expenses fee and suggested that if Janáček could rustle up 300–400 new subscribers then he (Urbánek) could improve on the 10 K. Moreover, he wrote, he had thought that Janáček would have seen the Moravian section as an excellent vehicle for promoting both himself and the Organ School, and thus that the proposal, even if modestly funded, would have been of interest to him.[54] In the end, all that came of the initiative was that Janáček was listed as being on the editorial board and sent half a dozen contributions to *Dalibor* over the next few years. Much more importantly, however, Janáček's correspondence with Rektorys continued. Rektorys became Janáček's chief (and extremely useful and reliable) Prague contact for the next eight years, during which time they exchanged over two hundred letters.

The contacts with Rektorys and *Dalibor* were not the only consequence of Janáček's meeting with Piskáček and his friends. It seems likely that Urbánek was also one of the party, unless it is coincidental that five days after the *Salome* evening Mojmír Urbánek sent off a contract to Janáček for the publication of his *Four Moravian Male-Voice Choruses* (IV/28), suggesting a fee of 50 K and six free copies.[55] By then the two Haná choruses had had considerable exposure through concerts of the Moravian Teachers' Choral Society. To these Janáček had added two more choruses, *Mosquitoes* and *Parting*, both based on Moravian folk poetry and both presumably completed some time in early 1906: *Mosquitoes* had been copied by 20 May. For Janáček the publication by Urbánek was a triumph. None of his compositions, apart from two of the *Valachian Dances* (VI/4) and his motet *Exaudi Deus (2)* (II/4) in a *Cecilie* supplement, had yet been published outside Moravia. Invited to publish Janáček's pieces (most recently *Hospodine!* III/5, *Amarus* III/6, both in 1897) F.A. Urbánek, Mojmír Urbánek's father, had always refused. But now these four choruses were in print before the end of the year.

It is clear from Piskáček's affectionate description of Janáček that he had enjoyed his contacts with him (several of Rektorys's letters to Janáček in this period have friendly postscripts from Piskáček). Another topic of conversation at the post-*Salome* meal (again not reported in *Dalibor*) appears to have been whether Janáček had any further compositions that Piskáček could perform with the 'Hlahol' choir. Janáček presumably suggested his piece written for the fund-raising concert of the Women's Shelter, *Our Father* (IV/29). Here the wheels turned rather more slowly: on 6 July, however, a member of the 'Hlahol' committee wrote to Janáček asking him to send them *Our Father* by the end of the month so that the parts could be copied during the summer vacation.[56] Since there was no question of the piece being given with the original *tableaux vivants* in this new venue, Janáček set about revising it. The original division into five sections (for the five *tableaux*) was removed and the original accompaniment for piano and/or harmonium gave way to the grander sound of harp and organ.

At the same time as Prague began to express interest in Janáček's work, preparations began to be made for the performance of his most recent opera. *Fate* (though still not called that) had been completed a year earlier: Josef Štross had signed off his copy of the full score on 12 June 1905. Over the course of the next year Janáček revised the work, though next to nothing is known about this process. By this time Fedora Bartošová was out of the picture, so Janáček either reflected alone on what he had written or discussed it with friends, and then made changes. The outcome, one year later, was a new version in which many of Štross's pages were replaced by others made by a second copyist Hynek Svozil (see table 55.1). Even before this was complete the Brno Theatre Družstvo had caught up with the news and on 16 June wrote a humble and respectful letter asking for Janáček's permission to perform the new work.[57] Janáček's letter of agreement (22 June) has not survived but is reported in the Družstvo's next letter of 9 July, full of gratitude at Janáček's decision.[58] Meanwhile, the opera had acquired its near-final title. During Janáček's rather full visit to Prague on 22 May (the *Salome* outing) he had also encountered the critic Jan Branberger and told him about his work. A month later Janáček wrote to him:

When we were on the embankment I told you that I would let you know the title of my new opera.
  Now that I am quite finished, I keep my promise.
  I think the best title is
Fatum.
  I would like to emphasize it, if appropriate, by an addition: *Slepý osud* [Blind fate].
  It is a novelistic event that I have set to music.[59]

In fact the opera could hardly have been described as 'quite finished'. According to a letter Janáček wrote to Jan Kunc on 30 July, he received the piano-vocal score from the copyist for checking on that day; the full score was still awaited.[60] By this time Janáček was already in Hukvaldy, another holiday spent separately from Zdenka, who wrote to him on 8 July announcing her safe arrival in Vienna.[61] The delay in providing the Brno Theatre with the score meant that the conductor-designate of *Fate* (Hrazdira again) had nothing to study and had instead begun taking a critical look at *Jenůfa* in the hope that he would 'be able to perform the work even better than last time. I have already secured a third flute for Brno. I hope, also, that it would be in the interests of the work's dramatic flow somewhat to shorten some places.'[62] (See chap. 48).

Janáček spent a month in and around Hukvaldy. The *Volkslied in Österreich* project and the extra funds available from it seem to have energized him into more collecting of folk material than he had done for a while. In a letter to Vach written on 28 July, just before he set off for Luhačovice, he mentioned how he had been travelling 'industriously' in search of folksong.[63] Janáček's notations of the cimbalom-playing Ignác Kotek on 27 July in Lubno survive together with his sketch of Kotek's instrument.[64] And there was more cimbalom material to be taken down in nearby Ostravice, as Janáček wrote to Zdenka around 25 July:

I arrived from Ostravice where I have found treasures of cimbalom playing. Dr Švec's[†] letter has just arrived: the purchasing contract is signed, the Greek villa is ours. There is enthusiasm about this everywhere. I have no rest. What can I do? One must finish the thing. I will go twice more to Ostravice, I want to remain at least three days in Radhošt'. How are you? Still coughing? The buzzing in my ear has already stopped a little. The weather is now hot. Perhaps I will sweat it out.[65]

The reference to the 'Greek villa' was an exciting new development for the Organ School (see chap. 21). In its twenty-four years the school had moved several times between various sets of leased rooms. Since 1896 it had been in the 'Tachovský House', a building on the corner of Jakubská ulice and Česká ulice in the very heart of Brno. According to Zdenka, Janáček did not care for these rooms, so that when a villa a few blocks out of the centre occupied by the parquet firm Haas & Kordina came up for sale, he encouraged the owner of the Organ School, the Association for the Promotion of Church Music, to make a bid for it.[66] This news of the impending move formed an important part of Janáček's report on the twenty-fifth anniversary of the school. There were other items of good news to add: in the school year of 1905–6 the Organ School had had the means to recruit students for its three-year course every year rather than every third year; there was also a new ten-month course for village organists (to improve the standards of self-taught musicians); and the Consistories of Olomouc and Brno now undertook to give preferential treatment to graduates of the Organ School when filling choirmaster posts.[67]

In addition to folk-music collecting and the new developments at the Organ School, Janáček still needed to sort out matters with the Brno Theatre over performances of his two operas. On 26 July he wrote to Antoš Josef Frýda, since 1905 the director of the Brno Theatre, proposing conditions for the performance of *Jenůfa* during the 1906–7

[†]Dr Jan Švec, a lawyer and member of the Organ School Executive Committee 1909–16, also a member of the Russian Circle (see Plate 24).

season: a 10 K fee for the season and 8 K for each performance. As for his next opera, *Blind Fate*, he would look through the scores when he got them back from the copyist (due on 7 August) and then give Frýda his thoughts.[68]

By the end of the month Janáček was feeling in need of a rest. When he wrote to Jan Kunc on 30 July (chiefly to report the breakdown of negotiations with Urbánek over the Moravian supplement to *Dalibor*) he gave an account of all that he had been doing:

I have reworked the organ and harp parts of *Our Father*.

I have written a study as a response to Dr Pommer about the collection of folksongs. In this way I want to win over the central committee.

A few journeys along the Moravian–Silesian border, together with all the worries connected with the purchase of the Greek villa – it was all too much!

On Wednesday [1 August] I'll be travelling beyond Frenštát to see the folk instrument maker of violins, cimbaloms, basses, etc. *If it's not raining, I'll certainly be at Radhošt' Pustevně*.

I arrive in Brno on 7 or 8 August. Today I received the piano score of *Blind Fate* and will begin the final revision.[69]

The trip to Radhošt' was a great success, as he wrote to Zdenka from Rožnov on 3 August: 'My nicest trip! *All alone – closest to the sky.* I want to spend the night here. What are you doing? First I passed through the clearings beneath Radhošt' in search of folksongs. Poor Olga! Why isn't she here?'[70] (Olga would have been twenty-four on 15 August, less than a fortnight away.)

It looks rather as if Janáček did not go to Brno on 7–8 August, as he had intended (Kunc reported a week later that he had not found him at home),[71] but went straight from Hukvaldy to Luhačovice for his annual holiday there. The 'List of Spa Guests' in Luhačovice has Janáček checking in at this time and staying at the Růžová villa.[72]

As one of the moving forces behind *Das Volkslied in Österreich*, the Austrian folk music expert Dr Josef Pommer (see Janáček's letter to Kunc of 30 July) had written a guide for collecting folksongs entitled *Anleitung zur Sammlung und Aufzeichnung: Fragebogen* [Introduction to collection and recording: a questionnaire], which had been sent to all the local committees; in response Janáček had come up with his own proposal, *Collecting Czech Folksong in Moravia and Silesia* (XV/183). He sent this to Hostinský in Prague[73] and also set up a meeting of his working party in Luhačovice to discuss it together with Pommer's document. Since the meeting was set for 8 a.m. on Sunday 19 August, the trip clearly involved an overnight stay in Luhačovice. At noon, according to Janáček's invitation to Martin Zeman, they would set out for Strání for an 'instructive' trip'.[74] The visit to Strání is captured on a fuzzy photograph of a Slovácko couple dancing to the accompaniment of the bagpiper Úhelný from Kopanice. Janáček in hat, dark suit and waistcoat is smiling encouragingly; at least three members of his working party, again all smartly dressed in hats and suits, can be seen on the left looking on rather glumly.[75] In his letter to Zeman, Janáček suggested that from Strání everyone could get back easily by evening trains. Expenses presumably ran to only one night in Luhačovice.

After all his exertions Janáček seems to have spent a relaxing time in Luhačovice. The following Sunday he went off again (this time to Lubina) to notate more of the bagpiper Úhelný,[76] but that seems to have been the extent of his folk-music collecting activities from Luhačovice. To Zdenka he sent only the briefest of notes telling her that he was arriving back in Brno on 1 September.[77] Hostinský wrote on 17 August to keep in touch over the Pommer document (which he regarded as 'too elementary') and mentioned Janáček's 'somewhat different standpoint in [his] brochure', which he would lay before his Prague working party after the holidays.[78] Kunc, too, had written, making a suggestion about the title of Janáček's new opera. Forget about the 'Blind' in *Blind Fate*, he suggested – it would just be the butt of jokes. *Fate* on its own said it all. And if Janáček could send him the score once the corrections were finished he would offer to make a 'proper analysis' of the work that he would publish 'in some leading Czech journal with music examples and a substantial study'.[79]

In the event Janáček got back to Brno a day earlier than expected, on Friday 31 August. He wrote to Kunc about his plans, saying that he would have the *Fate* material bound and would put in metronome marks – after that Kunc could take a look.[80] In fact, it needed rather more than mere metronome marks: there are surviving instructions from Janáček to an unnamed copyist for further work.[81] In addition to the prospect of a performance of *Our Father* in Prague that autumn Janáček now discovered that another Prague première awaited him. After studies in Leipzig, the Moravian-born conductor and composer František Neumann[‡] (1874–1929) had pursued a successful conducting career in various minor posts in Germany, Austria and Bohemia. In 1904 he was appointed second conductor in Frankfurt. However he kept close contacts with the Czech lands and in 1906 was invited by the Czech Association for Orchestral Music to conduct two concerts in Prague. On 2 September he wrote to Janáček saying that he would like to conduct a Janáček composition and asked him to send scores.[82]

Janáček was delighted and suggested the two published *Valachian Dances* (vi/4) and the unpublished Prelude to *Jenůfa* (vi/10).[83] Neumann settled for the latter and asked for performance materials.[84] Parts and a new copy of the full score were copied out in October by Janáček's new copyist, Hynek Svozil,[85] and sent to Prague. In his letter to Neumann of 21 October reporting progress on all this, Janáček looked forward to 'making Neumann's acquaintance'.[86] Although Neumann also came from Moravia, the two had never met.

When Rektorys returned from his holiday in September he learnt from Urbánek about the collapse of the *Dalibor* negotiations and suggested that as compensation Janáček be included as an 'honorary' member of the Prague editorial board.[87] Janáček agreed and, as a possible contribution to *Dalibor*, mentioned that he had already written up his principles of folksong collecting.[88] No-one but Janáček would have thought that instructions for collecting folksongs (directed both at field workers and at the various working parties of *Das Volkslied in Österreich*) might serve as an interesting general article in a weekly music magazine. But then no-one but Janáček would have written his instructions in as imaginative and creative a way. Janáček and Jiří Horák (from the Prague working party) extracted a plain list of do's and don't's fitted on to two postcards for the collectors;[89] the original instructions, sent to *Dalibor*, were however certainly of more interest than might have been expected. Janáček begins by emphasizing the creative part of the folksinger. The singer is, he wrote, 'perhaps the second, perhaps the third composer of even a well-known song'. Variants are 're-cast' in the mouths of the people. And at the end, when Janáček supplies an example, this turns into a little story about how on 17 July 1906, on a dark rainy night while he was in Hukvaldy, he heard outside the sound of drunken singers. He managed to write down the

[‡] A different František Neumann from Janáček's childhood friend; see chap. 7.

tune of the whole song but caught only some of the words. On 28 July news had got round the village that Janáček had asked the game-keeper about a song ending with these words, and a group of boys arrived to sing four verses for him. The next day a Hukvaldy resident Jan Morysak came round to supply a further two verses. Rektorys saw the value of the piece and published it in *Dalibor* in four instalments starting on 19 October as *Collecting Folksong in Moravia and Silesia* (XV/183).

On 17 September Frýda wrote to Janáček sending him 18 K for the loan of *Jenůfa* material for the season and for the first performance, which 'would inaugurate the season'. He also awaited, he said, material for *Blind Fate* (as the theatre still thought Janáček's new opera was called). The Brno Theatre inaugurated its 1906–7 season not in Brno but in Ostrava on 22 September with a performance of *Jenůfa* before returning to Brno, where it was given two more perform-ances, on 6 and 9 October. It would seem that these three 1906 performances took account of the cuts that Hrazdira had suggested to Janáček during the summer: some of the individual orchestral parts that were discarded after 1906 contain a layer of cuts that includes all those that Hrazdira proposed and thus anticipate the more extensive revisions that Janáček made to the opera later that year.[90] Although there is no evidence that Janáček heard the performance in Ostrava, he was present for at least the first of the two Brno performances, where he would have been able to make his own evaluation of whether the cuts served the work, and maybe then decided to revise the opera in a more thorough-going way (see chap. 48). Kovařovic was a lost cause, but Janáček had invited various critics and suggested to Rektorys that he come too, and bring Urbánek with him.[91] In his letter politely declining this invitation, Rektorys took up Janáček's reference to Josef Nešvera's opera *Radhošt'*, which had been performed at the Prague National Theatre on 3 October, three days ahead of the new Brno performance of *Jenůfa*; Janáček was not perhaps displeased to hear from Rektorys how Nešvera's opera weakened from act to act (and that it wasn't all that strong in the first place).[92]

'Is [Bezruč] really your brother?', Janáček wrote to Olga Vašková around 1 October. 'Please would he give me the right to compose a piece on *Maryčka Magdónova*? Moor didn't get it right. Perhaps I'd do better'.[93] Olga Vašková was the secretary of the Brno Russian Circle (see

Plate 24); her brother Vladimír Vašek (1867–1958), writing under the pseudonym of Petr Bezruč, was one of the great Czech poets of the century. His collection, published in 1903 as *The Silesian Number* (it acquired its more familiar title, *Silesian Songs*, in the enlarged edition of 1909), contains poems whose clear, bleak language paint an unsentimental picture of the harsh conditions in Czech Silesia, an area of extremes of wealth and poverty, and of linguistic conflict. It is not surprising that the poems, with their concrete language and their passionate defence of Czechdom, should have appealed to Janáček so strongly; the world in which they are set was adjacent to Janáček's birthplace, Hukvaldy. Nevertheless the act of setting such stirring narrative poems for chorus represented a huge leap from Janáček's previous choral settings, almost exclusively of folk texts (see chap. 54).

Psychologically and professionally the time was right, with the sudden interest in his choruses from three major choirs, and a Prague publisher about to publish a new set. Janáček's mention of Moor in his letter to Vašková refers to Karel Moor's melodrama setting of *Maryčka Magdónova*, first performed in Brno on 22 November 1906. Unless Janáček had seen the manuscript (he had clearly had a chat with Moor, then serving as second conductor at the Brno Theatre), his comment that he might 'do better than him' was simply a straightforward hope; in 1911 Jan Kunc was to suggest 'dissatisfaction' with Moor's setting as the impetus for his own.[94] But before Janáček composed *Maryčka*, he first completed a setting of *Kantor Halfar* (IV/33), perhaps encouraged by Bezruč's blanket permission to use his 'poems' (rather than just *Maryčka*) relayed in a letter from Olga Vašková a few days later.[95] *Kantor Halfar* was copied out by Hynek Svozil, both in score and parts by 24 October and in a second score (28 October), which Janáček sent to the 'Smetana' Choral Society in Plzeň. Sadly Bohuslav Beneš, who had so enthusiastically espoused Janáček's earlier chorus, had left Plzeň in 1905 to take up the post of school inspector in Roudnice[96] and it was only five years later (1911) that the choir eventually got round to performing the work. Seemingly without a pause Janáček then began work on *Maryčka*, completing a version some time before 11 November (when Svozil dated his copy). But suddenly Janáček changed his mind about the piece and no second copy was made. *Maryčka Magdónova (1)* (IV/34) was not sent anywhere and in March 1907 Janáček returned to Bezruč's poem to make a second, completely different version.

Janáček kept Svozil busy during October and November. Apart from the two new choruses and the extracted choral parts, Svozil also wrote out orchestral parts for the Prelude to *Jenůfa* (VI/10, on 15–18 October), which Janáček dispatched to Prague on 19 October,[97] and a few days later a newly copied full score, for which Neumann sent thanks on 27 October. In his letter Neumann suggested that Janáček write an article for *Dalibor* to draw the public's attention to this new work.[98] Janáček did so immediately (XV/184), producing a short, aphoristic piece of barely more than a column, with two short music quotations and four quotations from the folk poem *The Jealous Man*, which was its inspiration. Janáček wrote: 'For me this work was an introduction to *Jenůfa*. The same places in mountainous Slovácko, the same people – and again that unhappy excitability.' Janáček did not press the connection with *Jenůfa* any further, and in his mind seems to have detached the 'prelude' to *Jenůfa* from the opera; it was never performed with the opera in his lifetime. The explicit use of the title *Jealousy* came later, when the piece was performed again in Prague in 1917 and Janáček wrote another introduction for the programme (XV/213).

Janáček sent off his article at once to Rektorys for *Dalibor*, suggesting that it also go into the programme, if appropriate.[99] Rektorys published it as the first piece in the *Dalibor* issue of 10 November. By this time Urbánek had published the *Four Moravian Male-Voice Choruses* (IV/28), with Janáček receiving ten free copies[100] (four more than in the contract). And there was a nice surprise, namely an enquiry from the Leipzig publisher Robert Forberg as to whether Janáček would allow a German version of the two Haná choruses.[101] Following the success of the Moravian Teachers' Choral Society's tour of Germany, Forberg began publishing a series devoted to choruses sung by the choir. Janáček's two Haná choruses appeared in German in 1908 as nos. 9 and 10 in the series.

In later years Janáček would give himself deadlines: for instance, aiming to finish an act of an opera before taking a break. There is an early example of this in 1906. He had worked extremely hard in October and early November writing his first two Bezruč choruses, a major creative achievement. Two days after receiving the copy of *Maryčka Magdónova (1)*, Janáček left for Prague. This extended visit took in his two Prague premières, both at the Rudolfinum: the Prelude to *Jenůfa* (VI/10), performed by Neumann and the Czech Philharmonic on Wednesday 14 November, and *Our Father* (IV/29), performed by

'Hlahol' under Piskáček four days later. In between performances and rehearsals (the final rehearsal for the Prelude to *Jenůfa* was on the morning of the 14th, with a meeting with Neumann just before).[102] Janáček went to other events: programmes survive in the Janáček Archive for Gluck's *Orfeo ed Euridice* on 13 November[103] and Dvořák's *Dimitrij* on 15 November,[104] both at the National Theatre conducted by Kovařovic.

Neither of Janáček's premières went well. Although he had a fine orchestra (the Czech Philharmonic) and a committed conductor (Neumann), he was unhappy, as he wrote to Zdenka on 15 November, that his 'short theatrical prelude' was being squeezed in after a 'terribly long symphony' (Dohnányi's D minor Symphony op. 9).[105] The rest of the programme comprised Brahms's B flat Piano Concerto, played by Dohnányi, and one of Smetana's 'Swedish' tone poems, *Wallenstein's Camp*. Janáček's piece was by far the shortest. The performance was not helped by the copyist's having omitted expression marks in 'two prominent places', as Janáček later explained to Rektorys, thus lessening the impact the music should have had. As for *Our Father*, this had been plagued by disasters. The big tenor part was taken over at the last moment by František Pácal, and although the choir was enthusiastic, Piskáček had probably had too much going on, Janáček concluded, and had skimped on rehearsals. What would have happened, he wondered, if he had not himself played through the work with the organist, Josef Klička, and the 'two bad harpists'. Piskáček would have to do better next time: 'I think', his letter to Rektorys continued, 'he could do that with *Amarus* (words by Vrchlický, spring romance, a larger-scale piece, mixed choir, solo tenor and baritone and orchestra)'.[106] This recommendation, however, fell on deaf ears: it was another six years before *Amarus* got to Prague. What, however, upset Janáček more than the under-rehearsed and unsatisfactory performance of *Our Father* in Prague was the review by Bohuš Zázvorka in Jan Branberger's new (and short-lived) journal *Smetana*, where two choruses by Suk were praised for their clarity of organization and organically integrated united form. It went on:

This cannot be said of Mr Leoš Janáček, whose *Our Father* for mixed chorus accompanied by harp and organ has passages that have a monumental effect, but overall the work suffered from the lack of a coherent whole and did not leave the deeper and more lasting impression that a work of this serious musical theoretician would otherwise deserve.[107]

Janáček wrote angrily to Branberger:

I have said, and it is generally known, that my *Our Father* refers only to Krzesz's pictures. Why was this relationship not taken into account? On the concert platform this was completely lost. Perhaps having the pictures in the programme would have helped. I was not consulted. But why do you and Mr Zázvorka wrong me so? In Brno the work was sung to *tableaux vivants* – this is remembered to this day. Forgive me for complaining, for I know that you will agree with me that every work must be performed as the composer intended, but it should be judged from that point of view too.[108]

The brief anonymous review in *Dalibor* said virtually the same thing as Zázvorka, although muting the criticism with more positive references to the 'original harmonies' and 'unusual melodic and instrumental turns'.[109] If nothing else, Janáček's 'honorary function' on the *Dalibor* editorial board meant that his compositions generally received a reasonable press there. Piskáček's review of the Neumann concert was critical of the orchestra, of Neumann and of the programme, but Janáček himself got off lightly. The 'rhapsodically brief' nature of the overture was not entirely suited to the concert hall, Piskáček wrote, and it would have been helpful if audiences could have been informed what the piece was about (Janáček's short piece written for *Dalibor* had not got into the concert programme), although Janáček's musical 'depiction' was felicitous and the music contained interesting effects derived from its source material in the melodic elements of speech.[110] Rather more gratifying was Jaromír Borecký's amazingly prompt review of the *Four Moravian Male-Voice Choruses* (IV/28).[5] Perhaps a favourable review in *Dalibor* was a foregone conclusion since this was effectively Urbánek's house magazine. Nevertheless, in a group review of three Urbánek choral publications, Janáček's choruses head the review and occupy as much space as the review of Novák's op. 27 that follows.

On getting back to Brno Janáček sent a long letter to Rektorys (20 November) mentioning his anxieties over the Prague performances but mostly commenting on an 'irritated letter' by Zdeněk Nejedlý in *Pražská lidová revue* about the 'Moravian separatism' in Nešvera's *Radhošt'*. Only twenty-six, Nejedlý was already making his reputation

---

[5] That it was based on a proof copy is confirmed by the lack of a proper title for the work, merely *Four Choruses*.

as a trenchant and uncompromising polemicist (see chap. 57). It seemed, Janáček speculated, that Nejedlý might well have had a look at his article *Moravsky* [The Moravian way], his 'Credo' as he had previously described it.[II] 'In my manuscript *Moravsky* I surely stand for a general *Czech* position and I emphasize only Moravian peculiarities.' He had 'touched too little on one of the main points' and wanted the article back to rework and emphasize this point further.[111] For many years scholars had to assume that Janáček's 'Credo' was lost. There seemed to be no further trace of this article until in 2002 Zdeněk Mišurec published a collection of Janáček documents deposited in the Ethnological Institute of the Academy of Sciences in Prague.[112] Among them is the draft of Janáček's article *Thoughts along the Way* (xv/186). Both Mišurec's diplomatic transcription and the facsimile provided make it clear that the original title of this article was indeed *Moravsky*. This has been crossed out, together with other minor changes, and the new title substituted. Rektorys got it back the next year under its new title, and published it in *Dalibor* (see chap. 55).

On 20 October an announcement was made in the Olomouc newspaper, *Snaha*:

Janáček's new opera *Fate*, whose text contains three novel-like scenes written by the composer himself and put into verse by Miss Fedora Bartošová, has – as we already reported – been submitted for performance to the Brno National Theatre. In *Fate* Janáček continues along the road of music drama that he commenced with his *Jenůfa*. He continues to build on his basic principle of using the melody of human speech, the effect and mood of the word, to achieve dramatic thoughts expressed through the music. In this way he wants to capture and accurately depict new situations and moods that were inaccessible to old-style opera with its well-rounded melodies. Nevertheless *Fate* is melodically richer than *Jenůfa*. *Fate* will be staged probably in the middle of March next year.[113]

Quite how *Snaha* had got hold of its information is unclear but its comments were well informed and sound as if they could have been based on a briefing by Janáček. Perhaps the same information had been

---

[II] In an earlier letter (17 Oct 1906, JA iv, 27) Janáček had called *Moravsky* his 'artistic Credo'; one day later, however (JA iv, 28) he asked for it not to be printed until he had expanded it; he had sent it, he said, only because he had not expected Rektorys to print *Collecting Czech Folksong* (xv/183).

sent round to various newspapers. Věra Janáčková, for instance, wrote two days later to say that news of the submission of *Fate* to Brno had appeared in the leading newspaper *Národní politika*.[114]

However something seems to have upset Janáček: on 11 December Frýda wrote him a pained letter saying that he thought there must be some misunderstanding (Janáček had allegedly demanded the return of both *Jenůfa* and *Fate*) and asked for a personal meeting in which they could sort things out.[115] And it seems they did. On 16 January 1907 Frýda acknowledged receipt of the vocal material for *Fate*.[116] As the year came to an end Janáček found himself 'recovering', as he told Zdenka (now in Vienna for Christmas), from his overwrought nerves.[117] Hostinský wrote on 28 December, trying to co-ordinate their two folksong working parties, especially concerning the grants that they might try and extract from Vienna,[118] while Jan Kunc announced that he had posted a review of the newly published choruses[119] and told Janáček something of his new-found interest in the Russian avant-garde composer Vladimir Rebikov,[120] an interest that would rub off on Janáček during the next few years. These matters aside, Janáček was left to enjoy the snow at Hukvaldy, 'a wonderfully beautiful winter'.[121]

And perhaps, for a short while, he also enjoyed looking back at what had been an exceptionally eventful and successful year. True, Prague had not taken *Jenůfa*, but there was a new opera waiting in the wings, and Prague was suddenly seeming more receptive: after all, there had been two premières in November, a Prague publication of his choruses, and an invitation to join the editorial board of *Dalibor*. Furthermore, the fortunes of the Organ School were improving: negotiations for acquiring spacious new accommodation in the 'Greek villa' were proceeding and Janáček was already sending out postcards of the new building; 'We have a palace, now', as he wrote to Joza Janáčková.[122] And there was a new creative vigour, with two startlingly original choruses written quickly and confidently. At the age of fifty-two he began to feel that things were coming right, and this was reflected in a new mood of optimism. In his long review of the new choruses, Kunc commented on the change in the composer:

from a gloomy, untrusting pessimist as if overnight he has become an optimist, looking at the world with a merry eye, observant and understanding also the joy of life, believing in the success of truth and trusting himself above all. [. . ..] the calm of victory, freedom, the release of creative power, believing in his own importance and own strength. He is certain that the path along which he walks is the right one, that the goal pointed out is worth that effort, that his work will be recognized, understood and valued.

He is working with some sort of joyful intoxication, no longer broken by despair from the occasional failure, not consumed by the worm of doubt, not poisoned by lack of trust in his own strength. He creates quickly, certainly and easily. He is tireless.[123]

Sadly, this new creative upsurge would be crushed even more brutally by the events of the next eight years.

54

The Bezruč choruses

Until Janáček's fortunes changed with the production of *Jenůfa* in Prague in 1916 his best-known composition was his chorus *Maryčka Magdónova* (iv/35). It is a piece that makes a huge impact, one that appeals in various ways and for various reasons to a wide cross-section of audiences and that had the good fortune to be successful from its first performance. It was chiefly known through its espousal by the Moravian Teachers' Choral Society, which toured it enthusiastically throughout Bohemia, Moravia and beyond as one of its star items. 'If the Maestro', Josef Peška lamented over Kovařovic's refusal to accept *Jenůfa*, 'had heard *Maryčka Magdónova* sung by the Moravian Teachers, he would not have dismissed Janáček as a run-of-the-mill beginner.'[1] It was the one work that made people such as Peška and Rektorys realize that Janáček amounted to something. Its companion pieces *Kantor Halfar* and *The 70,000*, although cast in the same mould, had received less immediate notice, being introduced to audiences several years after they were written.

It is convenient to think of Janáček's Bezruč choruses *Kantor Halfar* (iv/33), *Maryčka Magdónova* (two completely different settings: iv/34 and iv/35) and *The 70,000* (iv/36) as forming a coherent group. Among his choruses they were written sequentially and without any others in between. All were based on poems from the same source, Petr Bezruč's collection *Silesian Number* (1903, enlarged as *Silesian Songs*, 1909). And all represented a huge advance – in size, substance and stature – on everything Janáček had written earlier for male-voice chorus. The three poems are also bound together by similar subject matter. In his collection Bezruč had dealt with the nationally oppressed Czech speakers in Moravian Silesia, an area riven with rival national claims by Germans, Czechs and Poles that were not settled until a plebiscite following the First World War, when the border between the new Czechoslovakia and the new Poland was painstakingly redrawn according to the dominance in each region of Czechs and Poles. Yet even this border was unstable, since the Sudeten Germans had their brief say twenty years later when the Munich agreement redrew the border yet again. The protagonists in all three choruses end badly, mostly by suicide. Maryčka Magdónova is the young provider for her even younger siblings after the death of her parents in colliery accidents. Gathering firewood in the grounds of the rich Austrian Marquis Géro she is apprehended; she throws herself into the waters of the river Ostravice. The schoolmaster Halfar bars himself from promotion by his commitment to his mother tongue, speaking Czech at the school where he teaches. Even his sweetheart deserts him, and he hangs himself. The ending is wonderfully ironic: as an assistant teacher he has been 'looking for a place' and in the end he finds his 'place' in a suicide's grave. The '70,000' were the minority of Czechs in Silesia who refuse to become Poles or German-speaking Austrians. There is nothing for it but to drink themselves to death.

Although the choruses now seem like a planned group, this is not what Janáček originally intended: indeed the compositional history of the pieces is rather more haphazard than such an idea might suggest. Janáček first applied for permission to compose *Maryčka Magdónova*, but by the time he got down to work on it he had already completed a setting of *Kantor Halfar*. These two choruses were written at breakneck speed: an approach to Bezruč at the beginning of October 1906, *Halfar* completed by 24 October and *Maryčka* by 11 November. But hardly had he finished this second chorus and had it copied than he had second thoughts. In the case of *Kantor Halfar* he had had a second copy made, which he sent to the choral society 'Smetana' in Plzeň in gratitude for his first foreign première (see chap. 51). But *Maryčka Magdónova [1]* languished in Brno. Janáček did not destroy this version but it never surfaced during his lifetime (it was first performed only in 1978 and was still unpublished in 2006). When in 1907 Janáček had another look at Bezruč's poem he produced a completely different chorus, with not a phrase in common.

In April 1907 Janáček sent this new version, *Maryčka Magdónova [2]*, to Plzeň. Yet despite its dedication to 'Smetana', both *Maryčka Magdónova [2]* and *Kantor Halfar* remained unperformed there. In the case of *Maryčka Magdónova [2]*, however, Janáček also sent a copy to Ferdinand Vach, the conductor of the Moravian Teachers' Choral Society. In retrospect it seems extraordinary that Janáček could have written these two visionary choruses with the Plzeň 'Smetana' in mind (a choir he had not yet heard), rather than for the Moravian Teachers – on his doorstep, trained and conducted by an old friend, colleague and supporter. Vach was cautious about *Maryčka*, rehearsing it for months and presenting it first in a Moravian provincial town before venturing to introduce it into the bigger centres of Brno, Prague or indeed Paris, where the choir was to make its début in 1908. But his care and caution paid off. *Maryčka Magdónova* was a hit from the start, with no hint in reviews that Vach's choir was not up to its demands. It soon became one of the choir's showpieces, later taken as far afield as Russia (1913) and Britain (1919). Its success led both to its early publication and to Janáček's idea of composing a further Bezruč chorus, *The 70,000*, first considered in April 1909 though not completed until December that year. Although the Moravian Teachers rehearsed it, Janáček seems to have been persuaded that it was either beyond them or in some way unsatisfactory, and he later made extensive revisions, cutting down its 334 bars to 239. Even this version did not suit Vach. The final version, complete in 1912, was first performed not by Vach and the Moravian Teachers but instead by František Spilka and the Prague Teachers' Choral Society, which gave the première in 1914. By then the Plzeň 'Smetana' had got round to giving *Kantor Halfar*, on 27 May 1911, a performance that went unnoticed by Janáček himself at the time and indeed by Janáček experts until Antonín Špelda drew attention to it in 1954.[2]

In other words, the four choruses were not conceived as a group. Although the first two (*Kantor Halfar* and *Maryčka Magdónova [1]*) were composed closely together in 1906, the others stretched out from 1907 to the revisions of *The 70,000* in 1912. *Kantor Halfar* and *Maryčka* (both versions) were composed against the background of *Fate*; *The 70,000* against *Brouček*. And their performances were spread out even more: *Maryčka [2]* in 1908, *Halfar* in 1911 and *The 70,000* in 1914; and they were given these premières by three different choral societies. The first of the choruses to be composed was the last that Janáček heard, in 1918, when finally taken up by Vach and his Moravian Teachers.

One of the secrets of the success of these choruses was a compositional strategy that was to serve Janáček well in many later works right up to *From the House of the Dead*. Apart from *Maryčka [1]*, all the choruses are bound together by an opening ritornello that returns throughout to provide coherence and stability. The ritornellos are memorable, overtly melodic and in a hymnlike style with simple harmonies and rhythms. That for *Maryčka [2]* is the most elaborate: a mechanical opening (an oscillation of two notes) followed by a slower, poignant refrain stretched out with the echoing rhythms of the name 'Ma-ryč-ka Mag-dó-no-va', a reflection of the poetic text in which every stanza but one ends with this long, haunting name. From this stable base, Janáček was able to make excursions into a far more radical musical language, with harsh harmonies and fragmented rhythms, frequent changes of tempo and character, use of ostinato accompaniments against which short vivid phrases are set in relief. If this language was disorientating for many of its listeners (and the Moravian Teachers attracted mass audiences), there were always the ritornellos to provide familiar home ground and hold the whole structure firmly together. This could be the reason why Janáček made a second version of *Maryčka* – for his first version lacks the backbone ritornello shared by all his other Bezruč settings and is a much more stop-and-start, declamatory affair, its structure driven by the words rather than by an easily grasped musical design.

Not only did the harmonies and rhythms begin to fragment, but the solid choral texture itself became increasingly broken up during the compositional span of the four choruses. *Halfar* is conducted in simple four-part texture (tenor, tenor, bass, bass) but in *Maryčka [1]* the male-voice chorus is split into eight (four tenor parts, four bass parts), to which in *Maryčka [2]* is added a solo tenor and a solo bass. *The 70,000* has even more layers of contrast: a tenor solo and a solo quartet added to the main chorus. This process is continued in Janáček's later chorus, *The Wandering Madman* (IV/43), where the voices of the madman and the little boy questioning him are individualized to turn the piece into a miniature, unaccompanied cantata.

What is clear is that Janáček was doing something quite different from his earlier works. The Bezruč choruses are dramatized choruses, little scenes brought to life through the individualization of the voice parts. The technical demands are frightening, with Janáček's use of very high and low registers: by *The 70,000* he was asking for frequent top Cs from his tenors. There are huge problems in both tuning and rhythm, for example co-ordinating simultaneous lines in different rhythms to produce a hubbub of noise. No wonder that the experienced Vach refused to touch *The 70,000* until it had been test-driven by the more adventurous Prague Teachers. There are Janáček's usual extremes of emotions thrust against one another: the declamatory (in *The 70,000* rising to almost hysterical cries) is powerfully juxtaposed against the lyrical. Interestingly, these 'male' choruses are written against type. There are very high lines and very tender moments that conventionalized musical gendering might suggest would be more appropriate to female voices. But what might otherwise be taken for *faute de mieux* forces is merely another powerful effect from Janáček's armoury of emotional ploys. Yet another is the fact that such extremes of emotion were written for unaccompanied forces: the voices are naked, exposed, vulnerable. When it was suggested in 1908 that *Maryčka* had been conceived as a piece with orchestral accompaniment (which the modest resources of the Moravian Teachers would have precluded) and that, now so successful, this might be rectified, Janáček considered the matter but in the end left the chorus just as it was. Other settings of these poems made at that time by Moravian composers were written for more elaborate forces: Karel Moor rewrote his melodrama *Maryčka Magdónova* (1905) for mixed voices and orchestra, while Jan's Kunc's setting of *The 70,000* (1907) is a cantata for eight-part choir and orchestra.

Unlike the folk texts that provided most of the words in Janáček's earlier choruses, dealing with more conventional topics, the Bezruč choruses deal with such explosive issues as genocide, ethnic cleansing and child abuse. All three Bezruč poems, furthermore, had strong autobiographical resonances for Janáček. In some ways he was the schoolmaster Halfar, clinging on to his native language just as his father and grandfather, both schoolmasters, had done; for Maryčka think of the battered women from the Brno Women's Shelter; and Janáček had himself written eloquently about the increasing Polish presence in Silesia (in xv/188). Altogether the Bezruč texts were for Janáček a heady mixture of nationalism and autobiographical resonance. It was later convenient, in communist Czechoslovakia, to emphasize the social commitment that the choice of these poems suggests. But with Janáček it is often difficult to disentangle the social and the national, or the social and the autobiographical. Janáček could identify readily enough with the underdog but it must be remembered that he held respected, secure and reasonably paid posts in education and had not starved or gone wanting since his student days.

More surprising is the way that the nihilistic messages of all three choruses run counter to Janáček's basic optimism. It could be that they reflect Janáček's depressed views at a time when his composition seemed not to be going right as far as operas were concerned. As the fate of his operas became increasingly problematic, this group of choruses became increasingly operatic in conception and realization. What is even more important about these pieces, however, is their compositional drive and maturity, which is missing from his earlier choruses. Something came alive in these works, something that pre-figures the urgency of the music of his last decade.

55

1907

Fate was in the hands of the Brno Theatre, any difficulties with the management seemed to have been resolved, and a production was planned for the current season. There is evidence that, after his sudden production of two startlingly original choruses in the autumn of 1906, Janáček's mind was beginning to turn back to opera. First, he revised *Jenůfa*. The September and October performances had been played with a series of cuts, initially suggested by Hrazdira (see chap. 53); given the respectful attitude Hrazdira had towards him, it is unlikely that these were made without Janáček's sanction. The two performances in Brno gave Janáček a chance to assess the effect of the cuts and seem to have led to a wholesale revision of the opera that incorporated all these cuts, made others, and introduced many other changes. As there was only one copy of the full score, in use in the theatre until after the second Brno performance on 9 October 1906, Janáček's revisions could have been made only after this date. Frýda's letter of 11 December 1906, referring to Janáček's request for the return of both *Jenůfa* and *Fate*,[1] may provide a start date for the revisions, but if so Janáček would have had to work very fast: according to his note at the end of Act 2 of *Jenůfa* he had corrected that act (and presumably Act 1?) by 10 January 1907. Janáček's revisions to the opera are unique: although he tinkered with his later operas during rehearsals, there is no other instance of his making a complete revision of an opera that had already been performed.* A comparison of these revisions with the 1904 version yields invaluable insights into Janáček's growing sense of musical stagecraft (chap. 48).

---

* The changes forced on him in 1925 for the Brno production of *Brouček* are hardly comparable.

Simultaneously Janáček began considering new operatic topics: a one-act comedy by a leading nineteenth-century Czech dramatist Ladislav Stroupežnický, *The Mintmaster's Wife* (1896), and Tolstoy's *Anna Karenina* (1873–6) (see chap. 59). Surviving drafts show that his plans advanced to the point of sketching a couple of scenes: seven pages for *The Mintmaster's Wife* (IX/3), twenty pages for *Anna Karenina* (IX/4). In both cases the sketches are on two staves (including the voice part on the top stave), suggesting the same sort of preliminary work that Janáček had done for *Jenůfa* before 'orchestration'. Interestingly, he tried setting *Anna Karenina* in the original Russian. According to the sketches of *Anna Karenina* (fourteen of which are dated), Janáček worked on it between 5 and 29 January 1907. *The Mintmaster's Wife* sketches are not dated, but a letter of 24 December 1906 from his schoolfriend, the literary critic František Bílý, about the rights to the play[2] suggests that he was considering this work somewhat earlier. Although Janáček received an encouraging reply from the publishers, written on 16 January 1907,[3] he was by then working on *Anna Karenina* and presumably also revising Act 3 of *Jenůfa*.

Several letters awaited Janáček's attention on his return to Brno. He answered Hostinský's letter (see chap. 53) on 6 January. Much of his reply was taken up with discussing financial aspects of the folk-song working party (he would need to submit accounts by 31 January and it was already clear to him that they were 'in debt'). But he also describes one activity during his recent stay in Hukvaldy: tracking down and notating a performance of a sacred folk play. 'During the holidays I went to see the "Three Kings". I met them in Trojanovice pod Radhoštěm up to their knees in snow and frozen but they knew their stuff.' It was a shame, he wrote, that one could collect only during the holidays and not 'wander about the whole year. Many songs escape us.'[4]

There were further encouraging signs about the production of the new opera. The director of the Brno Theatre, Antoš Josef Frýda, wrote on 16 January to say that he had received 'the vocal material' for *Fate* and wished to discuss casting. As for the Luhačovice set, he would write to Mrs Vorlová-Vlčková.[5] The latter (incidentally the sister of Olga's suitor and now a successful graphic artist) seems to have been approached to design the sets, perhaps on the basis of the 'sketches and studies' that she had already made of several buildings in Luhačovice (some of these were published as coloured postcards, which Janáček pasted into his score of *Fate*). At this stage, Mrs Vorlová-Vlčková was more concerned with the costumes:

As for costumes for the conservatory students, I will have to think more about this. It's true of course that they will wear town clothes, strikingly fashionable if possible. For the ladies I would suggest some sort of head ornament, flowers perhaps or some type of hat, especially where the action is set in the spa.

The men are more difficult; I don't know what you, Mr Director, had in mind yourself? The sort of cap that academics wear? It's difficult to think of anything different to go with the men's costumes.

However all this was rather premature. Vorlová-Vlčková needed the dimensions of the stage and above all a 'firm order' from Mr Frýda.[6] Although the report in the Olomouc paper *Snaha* had suggested a première in mid-March – and it is clear from the speed at which *Jenůfa* was staged that this might have been possible – by mid-March things had got no further. A letter from Karel Komarov, the producer-designate, written on 26 March, makes it clear from his references to rehearsals during the coming summer that the schedule had slipped and that the work would not be introduced until the 1907–8 season. It is also clear from the lack of concrete detail in Komarov's letter that negotiations with him were at a very early stage.[7] By then, however, *Fate* in Brno was doomed. Much of the success of *Jenůfa* in Brno had depended on the commitment of its conductor Cyril Metoděj Hrazdira and in February 1907 Hrazdira abruptly left the company in mid-season after disagreements with the singers. When a suggestion came later from Rektorys to submit the opera for performance elsewhere, it made perfect sense for Janáček to consider this proposal seriously.

It was early in 1907 that Janáček's most accessible article, *Alžběta* (xv/189), was published in a 'Moravian reader' edited by František Bílý. The printers (for the publisher, Emil Šolc of Telč) sent Janáček twenty-five offprints on 5 February 1907.[8] According to the preface, František Vahalík had proposed a 'historical Moravian reader' at a meeting of the Moravian-Silesian Beseda as early as January 1901. Vahalík had died shortly afterwards but the plan went ahead after much discussion (and another six years), by which time the 'historical' aspect had been watered down and, instead, over forty writers contributed articles on a variety of Moravian cultural topics: historical, biographical, ethnographic, economic, musical, literary and linguistic.

Many of Janáček's friends and associates were contributors (Bartoš, who had died in 1906, was represented by extracts from earlier work, and was also memorialized by Bílý). Surprisingly, Janáček's contribution was not on Moravian folk music (even more surprisingly this was dealt with by Adolf Piskáček, not otherwise known for any interest in the field). Janáček appears instead as a storyteller: another of his accounts of children and their speech melodies. It was entitled *Alžběta* [Elizabeth], the name of the little girl who occasionally came to play with the Sládek children in Hukvaldy. Whereas *The Speech Melodies of Children* (xv/169) and *Last Year and This* (xv/180) had simply provided examples of children's speech to exemplify his ideas on speech melodies, *Alžběta* had a much darker side: it is the account of the poverty in the area, of how Alžběta's young brother dies of hunger, while her father drinks away what little money he earns, and how her reproaches then result in her death, presumably at the hands of her violent father. The story is beautifully observed, terse and understated, a mini-drama that bears affinities with the world evoked in Bezruč's Silesian poems. As always, the scraps of speech melodies are Janáček's device to bring it alive and make it more concrete.

In Vyškov on 5 February 1907 Vach's Moravian Teachers' Choral Society gave the première of one of Janáček's newly published choruses *Mosquitoes* (from the *Four Moravian Male-Voice Choruses* iv/28) and proceeded to include it in the choir's tours that year. Meanwhile Janáček had seemingly abandoned his operatic experiments (the disquieting news about Hrazdira in February came soon after the last date entered in the *Anna Karenina* sketches) and instead had another shot at Bezruč's poem *Maryčka Magdónova* (see chap. 54). This resulted in a completely different setting (iv/35) with which he was now happy. Five days after Vojtěch Ševčík completed his copy (dated 21 March) Janáček wrote to the choral society 'Smetana' in Plzeň, asking it to accept the dedication of the new chorus.[9] The next month Janáček sent off a second copy with a dedication to 'Smetana'[10] and received a warm acknowledgement from the choir's chairman Karel Lang.[11] The choir had now been sent Janáček's two finest choruses to date, one with a dedication. However *Kantor Halfar* and *Maryčka Magdónova [2]* were of quite a different order of difficulty from the 1885 choruses, and with a couple of changes of choirmaster at the time it is hardly surprising that 'Smetana' put these complicated pieces aside. Luckily Janáček did not put all his trust in a faraway choir that he had never heard perform. According to Vach's reminiscences Janáček also sent him a copy of *Maryčka Magdónova [2]* in 1907 and played it to him on the piano. Vach liked the work, he recalled, but feared its novelty and the challenges in intonation, rhythm and dynamics that it posed. There were 'many tiring rehearsals' that almost led him to believe that it would not succeed.[12]

After the indifferent Prague 'Hlahol' performance of *Our Father* in November 1906 Janáček had suggested to Rektorys that Piskáček and the choir might redeem themselves by tackling *Amarus*. This had not happened, but the Vinohrady 'Hlahol'[†] under Milan Zuna had shown an interest. This was presumably another Rektorys initiative, and in his letter to Rektorys of 11 May Janáček enquired whether there was any news: 'He [Zuna] promised me that he would perform my *Amarus*. I sent him the orchestral score and since then I haven't had a word from him.'[13] The news came from Zuna soon afterwards saying that they could not give it at the next concert, but it would be given at the one after that.[14‡]

Janáček's only communication with Rektorys during the early part of 1907 had been to send him a copy of his new article, *Thoughts along the Way* (xv/186; see chap. 53), in which he described a field trip in 1906 to notate folk music in Lubno, Silesia, particularly that of the cimbalom player Ignác Kotek. During the period when he was at work on Bezruč's Silesian poems, Janáček began to take an interest in a region of the country he had hitherto largely ignored. The article describes how he had had to ford the river Ostravice (in which Maryčka drowns herself) and the return of the miners, black with coal dust. *Dalibor* published the article in two instalments in March 1907. Janáček's letter to Rektorys on 11 May about *Amarus* and Zuna signalled a resumption of their frequent contacts. The reason for Janáček's writing was not only for news of *Amarus* but also to express astonishment that Rektorys had given up the editing of *Dalibor* – or so

---

[†] 'Hlahol' was a popular name for Czech choral societies in the nineteenth century. Today the word can mean a (joyful) noise, clamour, chime or peal (of bells), but its evocative root goes back to the old Slavonic word for voice and language, whence the 'glagolitic' of Janáček's later Old Church Slavonic Mass.

[‡] Sadly, not even that was true. On 8 December Zuna wrote again saying that the Vinohrady 'Hlahol' could not perform *Amarus* for 'technical reasons' and so he was returning the score. The chorus had refused point blank to sing it (BmJA, A 3452).

it seemed.[15] In the notes to his edition of his correspondence with Janáček, Rektorys explained that this was simply a ploy to keep his editorial board together, unhappy at his strong support for Zdeněk Nejedlý in his latest polemic (see chap. 57).[16] As for Zuna, circumstances had changed: he had been appointed second conductor at the Vinohrady Theatre, and this would be good since the theatre was intending to give concerts as well as operas (and thus *Amarus* might have a chance there). Rektorys went on: 'Allow me to ask at the same time whether you have yet submitted any opera of yours to the Vinohrady Theatre? If not, I am most willing to take the necessary steps, and kindly ask you for news of this.' As a further encouragement, he added the postscript: 'A *fifty-piece* orchestra has already been engaged for the Vinohrady Theatre!'[17] And so began one of Janáček's most painful and humiliating experiences.

Prague at the time had three permanent opera houses: the Czech National Theatre and two German ones run by a single management, the old Estates Theatre (which had famously seen the première of *Don Giovanni* under Mozart) and a luxurious new theatre built in 1888 as a German response to the Czech National Theatre. In 1907 a second, independent Czech theatre opened in the Vinohrady suburb of Prague. Like the National Theatre its mission was to present a mixture of genres: operas and plays but not ballets in this case. The director-designate was František Šubert, who had clocked up twenty years of running the National Theatre. His chief conductor-to-be was equally experienced, if rather more restless: none other than Ludvík Čelanský, whose opera *Kamilla* had unwittingly set Janáček's *Fate* in motion (see chap. 44). In 1907, much encouraged by Rektorys, Janáček withdrew *Fate* from Brno and instead submitted it to the new Vinohrady Theatre in Prague. It was advice that Rektorys much regretted in later life (or at least in the footnotes to his edition of his correspondence with Janáček).[18] With hindsight one can see that *Fate* was never going to change Janáček's fortunes in Prague.

On hearing of Janáček's possible interest in submitting *Fate* to the Vinohrady Theatre Rektorys went straight to Čelanský, who assured him that *Fate* would be accepted as soon as Janáček sent it and that 'it would be a joy for him if its première could be earlier than in Brno'.[19] Within two weeks, by the end of May, Janáček reported to Rektorys that he had sent the score to the Vinohrady and a letter to Čelanský requesting that he look through it 'at least by Monday [3 June]' –

i.e. over the weekend – so that he would be ready and prepared for Janáček when he came to see him.[20] Rektorys reports a meeting between Čelanský and Janáček 'in the first days of June' (presumably 3 or 4 June) in the Čelanskýs' flat on Spálená ulice, where Janáček played through *Fate* to the conductor, his wife Marie and Rektorys to such an effect that they were 'all burning with enthusiasm' afterwards.[21] The rest of Janáček's Prague trip was less satisfactory. He heard Smetana's *The Devil's Wall*[22] on the Monday evening at the National Theatre, conducted by Kovařovic, but decided against staying longer to attend the next première there, Ladislav Prokop's opera *The Dream of the Forest*. But the ever-helpful Rektorys managed to negotiate with its conductor František Jílek that Janáček be allowed to sit in on a rehearsal. In a note written to Rektorys on paper from the hotel Archduke Štěpán just before he left Prague on 5 June, Janáček described how he heard Act 1 of the opera from the seat in which he had been placed but was then evicted from the theatre before the start of Act 2. In his account of the incident Janáček believed that the instructions for his removal came from the 'director', i.e. the administrative director Gustav Schmoranz.[23] As Rektorys later discovered from the hapless Jílek (a somewhat ineffective second conductor married to the star soprano Růžena Maturová), the instructions for Janáček's removal came straight from Kovařovic himself (see chap. 49).[24]

Meanwhile, as Janáček reported to Rektorys on his return to Brno, Šubert had asked Janáček to send the libretto of his new opera. The libretto existed only as text in the full score and would have to be written out by someone. And, as he gave Rektorys instructions to have this done, Janáček began to panic that František Šubert, an accomplished writer and dramatist, might judge the work purely on the basis of the libretto. 'I fear the critical spirit of "the writer Šubert"! I know that the characterization of people and action in *Fate* ought to emerge clearly from the excellent acting of the singers – and by analogy with real-life relationships.' There were scenes, for instance, that had to be suggested on stage 'by the situation or perhaps by word and movement' that in a novel would be shown in greater detail. 'It was a pity that I could not talk about it with Director Šubert, as I could with Mr Čelanský about the music.'[25] Although Rektorys did his best to reassure Janáček, he also suggested that it would do no harm to have an experienced person look at the libretto and had already approached Dr František Skácelík, a doctor by profession who was also active as a journalist and as the literary and stage critic of *Radikální listy*, and had secured his agreement. 'Dr Skácelík will give you (me, in fact) a reliable expert opinion, and will possibly help with advice.'[26] With *Fate* accepted by the Vinohrady Theatre, and a sensitive and well-disposed Prague literary critic looking through the libretto, all seemed to bode well, and Rektorys and Janáček got on with their respective summer holidays. Janáček's final letter in June to Rektorys thanked him for his efforts and also mentioned an important development in Brno, the visit on 12 June by the cabinet minister Dr Bedřich Pacák to the old Organ School and the newly acquired building on Giskrova ulice (now Kounicova).[28] The move would begin immediately, in preparation for the new academic year in September, though it would take a while for all the rooms to be suitably adapted (see chap. 21).

As in 1906, the summer gave Janáček time to search out and notate more folksongs and dances. On 23–4 June at the invitation of the teacher František Bobek he was in Valašská Bystřice, where he noted down the music for twenty-two songs whose words Bobek had already written down.[28] When he got back he assigned Hynek Bím to mopping up after him,[29] which Bím duly did in July,[30] though in the end he managed to wriggle out of his next assignment, to carry on after Janáček had 'prepared the soil' in Silesia.[32] In July, having organized the Organ School move, Janáček left for Hukvaldy, as he wrote to Zdenka (still in Brno) on 9 July.[32] His next card, sent on Sunday 14 July, was addressed to her in Vienna. He was having a miserable time, he wrote, complaining of the 'rain and the cold'.[33] A week later he was in Jablunkov, on the border between Moravian Silesia and (Hungarian) Slovakia, invited by the folksong collector Rudolf Zahradníček. His visit is corroborated by dated speech melodies (21–2 July 1907)[34] and by a card he sent the next day to Zdenka from nearby Mosty: 'Greetings from the Silesian–Hungarian border. I've prepared the soil [here] for collecting folksongs.'[35] All he did in Mosty, however, was to collect dispiriting information on the almost total Polonicization of the area. Silesia, although traditionally part of the Czech crown lands, had been disputed territory for centuries and by the time of Janáček's visit the linguistic battle, at least in Mosty, had been lost: by the time of the 1890 census, there were 1929 Polish speakers, twenty-three German speakers and two Czech speakers. The sad facts were recorded in an article which Janáček published in *Lidové noviny* at the end of the year, *Jablunkov Mosty* (xv/188). Schools, the parish priest and local officials all now did their business in Polish. The Czech postman had left, the railways were run by a Prussian-Hungarian company, and the local newspaper *Těšínské noviny* [The Těšín news] had had to move out of Těšín. Only in folksong (and Janáček quotes some in the local dialect) did Czech still survive. Even if he didn't collect songs himself, his contact there, Rudolf Zahradníček, had by the autumn collected 'forty-six songs from various places, some of which were very beautiful and valuable' (including a few in the Lydian mode). He promised to copy them out and send them to Brno in the next few days.[36]

On Monday 19 August Janáček went for his annual holiday to Luhačovice. He had wanted to stay at the Pospíšil guesthouse Vlastimila, where he had stayed in previous years, but it was full and his friend Dr František Veselý, the director of the spa, had taken him to Janův dům, as he mentioned the next day to Zdenka.[37] Later that day he wrote Zdenka a long and exceptionally interesting letter on the new headed Organ School notepaper giving the new address and even a picture of the new building. Janáček was suffering from some sort of nerve pains, which affected his getting up and sitting down but not, he wrote, his walking. The doctor had thought it was sciatica but the masseur and Janáček did not agree. Because of the pain in his neck Janáček put it down to the 'dust during the moving and talking'. He was pleased with his 'good, dry dwelling in Janův dům' ('better than in the Pospíšils', he wrote) and had 'unharnessed' himself from society. If he was well within a fortnight, he would go off for a week to Veselí na Moravě. 'It is the countryside and life that I'd need for *The Farm Mistress*.' This is one of the tantalizingly few references Janáček made to another potential opera project (xi/8), which was to set Preissová's earlier play, already the subject of a successful opera by J.B. Foerster, *Eva* (see chap. 59). He would also like to go to the distinctive Detva countryside in Hungarian Slovakia. 'A young painter is living there – he would be a good guide. It would last three to four days.' If he managed all this he would be in Brno by 12 September, depending both on the weather and on the trapped nerve (or whatever the problem was). Other news included his completion of 'that fifth article about rhythm' (see below). He had now had his say on the topic and could at last 'think of other work'. And at the end he added:

Well finally – she is here – if it matters so much to you! I think when I say this to you, that you, Zdenka, are my beloved wife, whom I'm looking forward to seeing, so proper a wife that I don't want any other than you – so maybe you can be content. I've not said that to you before.[38]

Who was 'she'? Was Camilla Urválková perhaps taking another holiday in Luhačovice? It was over three years since their last contact. The warm words to Zdenka are uncharacteristic but bespeak a level of affection that had finally been achieved four years after the death of their daughter. From her side Zdenka also records in her memoirs 'a time of peace and contentment'[39] that seems to have lasted from the conclusion of the Urválková affair in 1904 up to Janáček's infatuation with Gabriela Horvátová in 1916.

Janáček's contentment was shattered on 22 August by a report in the newspaper *Národní listy* giving a list of works acquired by the Vinohrady Theatre for its opening season: in addition to a couple of operettas, they were Puccini's *Madama Butterfly*, Giordano's *Fedora* and three Czech works: two by Karel Weis (1862–1944) and a comic opera by Jan Malát (1843–1915). Janáček's *Fate* was not among them.[40] 'I know', Janáček wrote the next day to Rektorys, 'that if you could have given me favourable news about *Fate* you would have done so long ago. Today's *Národní listy* containing the operas accepted at the Vinohrady Opera is evidently preparing me for the fate of *Fate*.' Would Rektorys please find out what was going on, he pleaded, and then report back as soon as possible.[41] Janáček was getting unnecessarily worried, Rektorys wrote in response. He had not been able to speak to either Šubert or Čelanský, and the latter was due back only 1 September. But 'it is impossible that your opera should have been refused'; Janáček should be patient 'for a few more days'. Rektorys did at least report on how Dr Skácelík's work was going: it was nearing completion, 'so he told me, while at the same time making clear how thorough were his suggestions for revisions. He's been completely taken with the idea. He regrets only that the libretto had not fallen into more professional hands.'[42]

And Rektorys was as good as his word. On 28 August Janáček wrote to him to say that Šubert, no doubt prompted by Rektorys, had now confirmed that *Fate* had been accepted at the Vinohrady Theatre. Janáček's health having presumably improved, he was leaving for Veselí on Monday 2 September: 'There is beautiful scenery there for

The Farm Mistress.' He would be back in Brno on 6 September.[43] (The proposed Detva trip seems to have been abandoned.)

With the Organ School beginning to settle into its luxurious new building, Janáček was anxious to promote it, and sent *Dalibor* an advertisement together with a 'proclamation' about its new courses.[44] Rektorys, now officially reinstated as editor of *Dalibor*, wrote back accepting both. Had Janáček heard from Skácelík yet? He was still on holiday but should be back soon, and Rektorys would chase him. Once that was done he would get Professor Karel Hoffmeister (a leading piano teacher and writer on Rektorys's editorial board) to write an analysis of *Fate*.[45]

In his long letter to Zdenka from Luhačovice (20 August) Janáček had mentioned that he had finished his series of articles on rhythm. These had been coming out in regular instalments in *Hlídka* since June under the title of *My Opinion about Rhythm* (xv/191). It says much for the indulgence of the editor, Dr Vychodil, and his remarkably open-minded attitude to what was after all a literary and philosophical journal, that he should have allowed Janáček to publish a very long (fifty printed pages) and extremely technical article, bristling with music examples, which would have been intelligible and of interest to only a tiny minority of his readership. The article shows Janáček taking his ideas of speech melody into his technical discourse about music in general, out of which arose the earliest examples of his ideas of 'rhythmic layering' (see chap. 19). Janáček's 'opinion about rhythm' was essentially a discussion of rhythm from a psychological point of view, bringing together folk music, philosophy and music theory. Its greatest significance for the development of Janáček's theoretical views, Beckerman has suggested, was in linking Janáček's ideas about the importance of rhythm to harmonic events.[46] Although Janáček told Zdenka that he had now had his say on the subject, he offered *Dalibor* a sort of postscript, *From the Practical Parts of Rhythm* (xv/192), dealing, Janáček brightly announced to Rektorys, with 'suspension-transition', analysed and discussed 'of course from a modern stand-point'. Altogether, Rektorys's invitation to Janáček to send him articles for *Dalibor* had had some curious consequences that could hardly have suited the music magazine's popular and readable image: first, the instructions for collecting folksongs (xv/192), and now a short but deeply technical article that eventually became the first part of a much longer work on music theory (xv/317). The only really suitable article

Janáček had sent him was also his shortest: the cryptic introduction to his Prelude to *Jenůfa* (xv/184; see chap. 53).

What was now causing concern to both Rektorys and Janáček was the seeming lack of activity on the part of Skácelík with *Fate*. In a letter of 11 September, Janáček urged Rektorys to get in touch – 'I am curious as to his judgement and revisions' – adding, as if it would help, the request: 'Remind him especially that the action is a real-life event.'[47] When Skácelík eventually made contact at the end of September his criticisms were devastating. They gave the first clear exposition of the problems posed by the libretto that have discouraged its staging ever since. He had read through it several times, Skácelík wrote, and made many attempts to rework scenes so that the basic plan could remain unaltered – but he had failed. His long letter explained why. He felt that the locale was emphasized out of all proportion to the action; that subsidiary events (presumably all the smaller characters in Act 1) loomed too large; that the end of Act 1 was unclear; that the beginning of Act 3 was unmotivated and came out of the blue; and that the coincidence of the storm and Živný's narration was pure chance. More drama was needed, less decoration. Despite all this, Skácelík hastened to reassure Janáček, the libretto was 'full of good things'. What was required was a poet and a practical man of the theatre. Skácelík had spoken to 'an experienced playwright', F.X. Svoboda, who was willing to read it.[48]

If Skácelík imagined that by analysing the problems and pointing to a solution (F.X. Svoboda) he had now discharged his obligations, he had underestimated Janáček's tenacity. Within days Janáček was in Prague, having set up a meeting with Skácelík at the Archduke Štěpán café for Friday 4 October at five o'clock.[49] Presumably they spent no more than an hour and a half together, as Janáček then went on to the National Theatre to see Vrchlický's play *The Trilogy about Samson* with incidental music by Foerster.[50] Quite what poor Skácelík found himself agreeing to do is unclear, but within a week Janáček had sent him new ideas for the end of Act 1. 'I come with help!', he announced on 10 October, 'I already have the music for the end of Act 1 in mind.' He then quoted two incidents in dialogue form (which eventually went into the final version of the opera): a short scene between a young girl ('Fanča') and a student; and a scene for Míla's Mother in which she looks for her daughter and discovers that she has gone off with Živný.

Janáček needed a few lines of reaction from all concerned. 'So, that's what I suggest, it would fit my music excellently. Will you do this for me, at least this, terribly soon?'[51]

On 16 October Skácelík promised to be finished 'by Sunday' (19 October).[52] Janáček waited until 22 October, when he sent him a reminder, typically impetuous and impatient, with one-line paragraphs of commands and comments:

I can hardly wait. I'm on tenterhooks.
　At least please send me your plan for the change to the end of Act 1.
　There will be time enough for the rest.
　Just so that I can work, otherwise I won't be ready.
　If I can have your suggestions then we can come more quickly to an agreement.
　So now I am waiting with certainty at least for the changes to Act 1![53]

Skácelík, of course, did nothing, and so Janáček found himself a week later doing it all himself, and sending off the results to Skácelík for approval.[54] It was early November before Skácelík sent anything – a revised version of the end of Act 1, and although he had clearly tried to be helpful, providing a section of libretto on four large sheets,[55] it was too late to be of much use, as Janáček explained in his next and final letter to him (14 November), in which he described his libretto changes to the next two acts.[56] This unfortunate pattern, with Janáček needing material far faster than it could be supplied, was to characterize his dealings with the various librettists of his next opera, *The Excursion of Mr Brouček to the Moon*. Janáček's exasperation is clear from a letter to Rektorys:

At the time of my departure from Prague I informed you that Dr Skácelík, with every sign of good will, promised me that he'd do the suggested text changes within three days.
　Today a month has already elapsed – and I have nothing.
　But I am not waiting for anything now since I am convinced that further changes could grow only on and out of the motifs of the music.
　I have done the corrections briefly myself, together with the music.[57]

By 19 November Janáček was finished with what was in essence the second large-scale revision of his opera and had sent the revised score back to Šubert, as he informed Rektorys the next day. The extent of the changes can be seen graphically from the score: newly copied sheets by a third copyist (Vojtěch Ševčík) were inserted to replace three sections (notably at the ends of Acts 1 and 2) in what was already an amalgamation of Štross's original copy together with sheets from a second copyist (see table 55.1).

As for Skácelík, Janáček wrote: 'With Dr Skácelík it would have been fine if I had been in Prague and could have chatted to him as the need arose. I am grateful for his suggestions. I have acted accordingly.' This was a diplomatic overstatement, to say the least. Skácelík contributed virtually nothing that Janáček used, apart from his initial criticisms that had encouraged the refashioning of the act endings. Janáček had now returned to his folksong work ('I've had lots of work with songs') but was intending to come to Prague on Saturday 23 November for the ceremonial opening of the Vinohrady Theatre the next day. As he told Rektorys in his letter of 20 November, he had mentioned his intention in his letter to Šubert, sent with the revised score of *Fate*.[58] Šubert had not responded, and although Rektorys encouraged Janáček to turn up anyway ('If you're there a place will be found for you. They are gentlemen at the Vinohrady – not like the National Theatre'),[59] Janáček took umbrage and stayed at home. However, Šubert's lack of response seems, in fact, to have been inadvertence or preoccupation with the opening of the theatre rather than a deliberate snub. For on 2 December he wrote an encouraging letter to Janáček: 'Please note that your opera *Fate* is already being copied. As soon as the copying is completed, steps will be taken towards the first preparations for its performance.'[60]

Table 55.1: Pages copied by individual copyists in the full score of *Fate* (BmJA, A 23.464)

copyist	Josef Štross	Hynek Svozil	Vojtěch Ševčík
Act 1	1–35		
		36–51	
	52–71		
		72–81	
	82–137		
		138–52	
			153–61
Act 2	1–42		
		43–66	
			67–73
Act 3		1–23	
			24–5
		26	
	27–101		

In the autumn of 1907 Janáček began to take advantage of the Organ School's new building. He summoned his folksong committee there on 11 October for a meeting in the 'director's office'.[61] On 5 December the Club of the Friends of Art held their first concert in the new building, which contained a small hall (the 'Dvoranka', seating about fifty). A themed concert entitled 'Nocturno', it included Beethoven's 'Moonlight' Sonata, a Chopin nocturne, pieces by Novák, Grieg and Jan Kunc, and a new Janáček première, the *Folk Nocturnes* (IV/32), the work that had featured so prominently in Janáček's interview with *Dalibor* the previous year (see chap. 53). Although the review in *Dalibor* was *parti pris*, it does nevertheless confirm that the songs made a good impression:

The event we most looked forward to was the *Moravian Folk Nocturnes*, a series of folksongs for two women's voices that breathed an atmosphere of warm, beautiful summer nights. Janáček's arrangements, which adhere faithfully in both harmony and style to the original, are masterly examples of folksong treatment. One is bound to add that the songs gained in depth of feeling and were in themselves of so interesting and rare a type that the wish to hear them again was universal.[62]

The reviewer, Karel Sázavský, had hit the nail on the head. Janáček's arrangements of these unusual two-part songs are some of his most haunting: hypnotic in their repetitions, and wonderfully evocative, even in the formal atmosphere of a concert hall.

Even more important than this première was the decision taken a couple of days earlier, at a general meeting of the Club of the Friends of Art on 2 December, that it would begin publishing music.[63] Janáček seized the moment and suggested that the first publication should be a piano-vocal score of *Jenůfa*. It was a risky undertaking, but it went ahead with breathless speed. Within a couple of weeks the Leipzig engraving firm of Engelmann & Mühlberg had been sent the Štross piano-vocal score, corrected to match Janáček's changes to the full score made the previous December and January. Daunted by the unfamiliar language, the firm asked (in a letter of 19 December) for a printed Czech libretto to help clear up dubious words.[64] None existed, of course, but this highly professional firm made a splendid and amazingly fast job of it all – the proofs began to arrive even before the end of the year.

Once again Zdenka went to Vienna for Christmas and Janáček to

Prague, arriving at the Archduke Štěpán on 25 December.[65] That evening he went to *Swan Lake* at the National Theatre[66] and the next night to Wagner's *Der fliegende Holländer*, conducted by Kovařovic.[67] Janáček did not linger in Prague, but was soon back in Brno to deal with the *Jenůfa* proofs, as we know from Zdenka's postcard sent on 31 December:

Mářa wrote today that you are home and in a good mood since the proofs have arrived. I'm pleased. You've got pleasant work and I am lazing away pleasantly – but I know that you wish me that.

So write to me soon and a happy new year. Greeting you, your Zdenka.[68]

56

1908

We are giving Haydn's *Creation*. I would like personally to secure Miss E. Destinnová for the soprano solo.

She's said to be in Prague now; I could still come to see her this week.
She's also got relatives here in Brno.
Please try and find out her address in Prague.
It won't be hard for Mr Urbánek.[1]

'Miss E. Destinnová' was Emmy Destinn (1878–1930), the most famous Czech soprano of all time. At this stage, at the age of almost thirty-six, she was at the very height of her powers, with successful débuts in Berlin, London and Bayreuth behind her and a glorious career at the New York Metropolitan Opera about to begin. It says something for Janáček's chutzpah – or maybe just his naivety – that he imagined that a personal visit to her in Prague, where she was giving a series of guest performances at the National Theatre during January and February,[2] would secure her services less than a few weeks later as the soprano in a semi-amateur performance of Haydn's *Creation* given by the Brno Organ School. Ferdinand Vach had joined the staff of the Organ School in 1906 and from that time he had mounted two large-scale choral concerts a year, mostly in local churches, though the Haydn work was planned for the Besední dům, with the band of the Brno 8th Infantry Regiment engaged as the orchestra. What Rektorys made of Janáček's request to him (sent on 7 January) one does not know: he supplied the information by return of post, mentioning that Destinn was singing three times during the next ten days and so would surely be around. The Vinohrady Theatre was due to give its first Czech première (Jan Malát's *A Merry Wooing*)*

---

* Hardly a new work, it was composed in 1899–1903 as *The Old Fools*.

on 12 January, so he suggested that Janáček could perhaps combine his visit with that.[3]

Janáček wrote to Destinn announcing his visit, as he reported to Rektorys,[4] but got back a prompt refusal ('apparently she has to return to Berlin'). He would therefore not be coming to Prague to hear Malát's opera; so maybe Rektorys, he suggested, might like to take over the good work of persuading Miss Destinn to sing in Brno: 'The concert with Haydn's *Creation* could be in three weeks' time. Wouldn't you like to see the esteemed lady for a journalist-type discussion and bring the conversation round to the concert? We would so love to hear her sing in Brno'.[5] Rektorys, as he wrote to Janáček some months later, didn't bother. The cause was lost before Janáček even began: 'You'd have to know the *background*: [. . .] more by word of mouth.'[6] The Haydn concert was postponed until 12 March, the Destinn part assigned to Leopolda Hanusová-Svobodová, the Brno Theatre's Kostelnička in *Jenůfa*.

Apart from his concerns over Vach's concert, Janáček was hard at work on the *Jenůfa* proofs. According to the printers' date stamp, he had been sent 126 pages before the end of 1907 – not quite halfway through the work. The other date stamp (10 January 1908) was on the title page, which might well have been sent with the rest of the proofs. Janáček took his proofreading seriously (he was much more cavalier in later years), making good use of this opportunity to adjust many small imperfections in word-setting so that a second round of proofs was necessary. They were completed, he wrote to Rektorys, by mid-February[7] and he was able to send out printed copies just a month later. Six hundred piano-vocal scores were printed: three hundred for members of the Club of the Friends of Art, and three hundred for sale, with Mojmír Urbánek in Prague designated on the title page as the official selling agent. The whole process of engraving, proofreading and production had been completed in less than three months, an astonishing achievement for a new work of 280 pages in what was for the engravers an unfamiliar language.

Nor was this Janáček's only publication of the time. On 23 January the Telč firm of Emil Šolc, which had published the first edition of Janáček's piano accompaniments for the Bartoš-Janáček *Bouquet* (v/2), announced that the first edition (comprising one volume of fifteen songs issued about 1892 and a second of thirty-eight songs issued about 1901) was 'completely sold out', and asked if they could go ahead with a second edition.[8] Janáček's letters to Šolc are no longer extant but the letters that Janáček received from him make it clear that he readily gave his consent and also suggested filling out the smaller first volume with some new arrangements of 'two-part evening songs'. These can be none other than the *Folk Nocturnes* (IV/32), given their première on 5 December 1907 and shortly to be performed again on 25 March 1908 by 'Vesna' pupils conducted by Max Koblížek. Šolc's letter of 28 January agreed to this proposal and asked Janáček to name his fee,[9] but twelve days later he wrote back saying that the new songs that Janáček had sent were not in the original Janáček-Bartoš *Bouquet*, and he felt they might be criticized for printing these new songs when so many from the original Bartoš-Janáček collection did not have accompaniments.[10] So the plan was dropped and the *Folk Nocturnes* had to wait another fourteen years for publication. The possible inclusion of new songs had nevertheless thrown up the question of the title of the volume, which was confusingly the same as the solo-voice edition, *A Bouquet of Moravian Folksongs* (XIII/1). The title of the 1908 edition of the songs with piano accompaniment (V/2) was now clearly differentiated as *Moravian Folk Poetry in Songs*.

Perhaps as a little celebration at having finished his *Jenůfa* proofs, Janáček went to Prague on 16 February for a lightning trip to see Puccini's *Madama Butterfly*, one of the new foreign operas being given at the Vinohrady Theatre. Although the event was mentioned in his correspondence with Rektorys,[11] there is nothing there to suggest the profound impression the work made on him. He remembered it eleven years later when, after seeing a performance in Brno, he wrote to Kamila Stösslová of it as 'one of the most beautiful and saddest of operas'. 'I am so disturbed by the opera. [. . .] When it was new I went to see it in Prague. Even now many moments still move me deeply.'[12]

If hearing *Madama Butterfly* was later to set in motion Janáček's sixth opera, *Káťa Kabanová* (see vol. ii: 1919), something that happened five days after first hearing it arguably propelled Janáček into writing his fifth opera, *The Excursions of Mr Brouček*. At his death on 21 February 1908 at the age of sixty-two, Svatopluk Čech was a distinguished and highly regarded pillar of Czech literature, well known both for his poetry and for a series of 'Brouček' novels. The first of these had been published in book form in 1888 as *The True Excursion of Mr Brouček to the Moon*, essentially a satirical tale in which the resolutely philistine Prague landlord Mr Brouček [Mr Beetle] is miraculously transported to the moon, which to his disgust he finds inhabited by aesthetes who neither drink nor eat but live off the scent of flowers and devote themselves entirely to artistic pursuits. The comic charge in the novel comes from the collision of these two diametrically opposed worlds. In its early version (published in the magazine *Květy* in 1886), Čech's novel had been essentially a literary parody of the fashionable utopian novels of the period. In 1888 the book acquired a more popular slant with the addition of social satire, in particular of the philistine attitudes of Mr Brouček. The novel was an immediate success, noticed by Janáček, who had reprinted a small section in his journal *Hudební listy* in 1888 (see chap. 24). This extract seems to have been chosen for its musical connections: the extract ends with Mr Brouček fleeing from the concert hall during a performance of *The Storm*, a composition by the lunar composer Harfoboj Hromný. There is no indication that Janáček had thought about *Brouček* since. In 1889 he had approached Čech without success for help over the text of *The Little Queens* (IV/20), and in 1895 or later he may have contemplated a setting of Čech's *Slave Songs* (there are musical annotations by Janáček, XI/4, in a copy belonging to Olga); but in the absence of other evidence it may well have been Čech's death on 21 February that recalled for Janáček his earlier acquaintance with *The True Excursion of Mr Brouček to the Moon*.

Nothing happened immediately, however. Janáček's chief concern of the moment, resulting in more tasks for Rektorys, was the proposed trip by the Moravian Teachers' Choral Society to Paris. With Vach now working for Janáček at the Organ School, and with the knowledge that the choir would perform several of his choruses in Paris, Janáček was heavily involved in the venture. The plan was that a delegation from the choir would go to Prague on 15 March[†] to seek official patronage from the Mayor of Prague, Dr Karel Groš, for the proposed tour. In a letter of 5 March Janáček asked if Rektorys could get together a few leading music journalists who could publicize the event: the choir needed publicity and sponsorship.[13] Ever helpful, Rektorys wrote back the next day having not only lined up some music critics but also secured a venue (Mojmír Urbánek's shop – Janáček had proposed 'a café'). All

---

[†] Janáček's letter says 'Sunday 16 March', but in 1908 the relevant Sunday was 15 March. In a later telegram Janáček announced their arrival on 'Sunday at 3' (JA iv, 73).

that was needed was a note from Janáček of the time and station at which the Brno delegation would arrive.[14] In a further letter fine-tuning the arrangements for the delegation's visit, Janáček slipped in another request: 'I'd like to speak to Mr Topič. I'd be glad if you could introduce me. Perhaps even on Monday morning [16 March].'[15]

Topič was the publisher of Čech's *Brouček* novels. Janáček presumably saw him on the Monday as planned but was directed to the copyright holders, the Čech heirs, in particular to Vladimír Čech and Zdenka Čechová, son and sister of the deceased. On his return to Brno, in addition to mentioning the positive attitude of Dr Groš to the Moravian Teachers, Janáček told Rektorys that he had already been to see members of the Čech family and Dr Klumpar, the lawyer who acted for them: 'according to the words of Dr Klumpar, the family would have had a conference on Tuesday' to consider Janáček's request. As usual, Rektorys was delegated to keep an eye on Janáček's affairs: 'If you can do something so that I'm granted the rights for *Brouček*, do it, but carefully. Perhaps you could ask Dr Klumpar again.'[16] For his part Rektorys had already come up with a potential librettist, perhaps to make sure that Janáček would not fall again into the hands of Brno amateurs: 'Did you acquire a libretto? [. . .] If you've got permission I'm willing to come to an agreement with Fa Presto (Mašek) to see if he'd like to do a libretto for you. You could simply put your remarks and wishes to me in a letter addressed to him and I'd explain it to him further.'[17]

Rektorys's suggestion of Mašek was not necessarily a bad choice. Karel Mašek (1869–1922) was an up-and-coming librettist who had written librettos for two recent Czech operas, by Ladislav Prokop (1873–1955) and Otakar Ostrčil (1879–1935). But a glance at Ladislav Prokop's *The Dream of the Forest* or Ostrčil's *Kunála's Eyes*, both heavy with allegoric symbolism and, in the case of the former, including 'characters' such as 'Poetry', 'Night' and 'Satyr' mingling among the human characters, reveals that Mašek's previous libretto experience little equipped him for the earthy realities of Mr Brouček. Rektorys should have known better, having published a long and enthusiastic review of the libretto of *The Dream of the Forest* sixteen months earlier in *Dalibor*.[18] Janáček might have known better too: *The Dream of the Forest* was the opera Janáček had seen in rehearsal before being evicted from the National Theatre in 1907.

Janáček's impatience to get going is evident from the letter he wrote to Rektorys on 21 March, just a few days after his Prague visit:

The Čech family were to have had a meeting on Tuesday [17 March] – and I still haven't had a line!

I beg you, I'd be eternally grateful if you could manage to get the Čech family to give me the rights for the *Excursion*.

I'm so taken with the material that it's difficult to write about it.

I've reminded both Dr Klumpar and Miss Zdenka Čechová again about the matter by letter – and all deaf.

I fear that they're at a loss [what to do] – and I don't know how to urge their agreement!

Perhaps you'll succeed!

Janáček then dealt with other matters: anxieties over the 25,000 K subsidy needed for the Moravian Teachers' Paris tour and a promise to get Rektorys a collection of reviews from the Brno *Jenůfa*. Now that the *Jenůfa* piano-vocal score had appeared and the batch of copies for sale was being sent to Urbánek, Rektorys had helpfully suggested that he might reprint some reviews in *Dalibor* to help promote the new publication.[19] But uppermost in Janáček's mind was *Brouček*, as is evident from his remark: 'So I beg you – I am waiting for news from you [saying]: *You have Brouček!!*'[20]

Janáček's plea to Rektorys was in fact answered before he had uttered it: 'You're a dear man!', Janáček wrote the same day. 'Thanks for the telegram. I will write in detail tomorrow.'[21] And the following day, Janáček did indeed do so. Since he didn't know Karel Mašek he asked Rektorys once again for his 'good offices' and then proceeded to give an outline of the libretto for Rektorys to pass on to Mašek. 'Four acts', he wrote, 'naturally suggest themselves.' The first would take place 'late on a moonlit night' with a view from the Prague Castle steps to the entrance of the street leading to the 'Vikárka', a well-known and still surviving pub opposite St Vít's Cathedral. Act 2 would take place 'on the fabulously beautiful lunar landscape with Lunobor's quaint summerhouse in the background'. Act 3 would be located in the centre of the Temple of All the Arts: a vestibule with corridors radiating out to the poets, painters and musicians. Act 4 would be back again on earth 'perhaps in the landlord's [Brouček's] room, just as they are bringing him home and he is babbling on and addressing everybody in the style of his moon adventures!' Janáček already had some of the musical climaxes in his mind: in Act 2 'Etherea would have to become noticeably aroused by the portly Brouček, pursuing him from that moment. The convulsive outbursts of Blankytný (a sonorous alto) would be a splendid end to that act!' In the next act 'the moving force would be Etherea as she flies in after Brouček; a catastrophe occurs when from one side of the door Etherea calls out "You're mine! you're mine!" and from the other Brouček is driven away by the noise of *The Storm*. He blows her away – a tragic death! In the moon acts (2 and 3) all the people involved are in continual rhythmic – i.e. *balletic* – movement. Acts 1 and 4 with their [earthbound] naturalism would make a superb contrast.' It would be necessary to fill out the 'realistic' outer acts, e.g. by introducing the innkeeper of the Vikárka, Würfl, and his staff. Act 4 needed more work: '*Could a foil to Etherea be introduced, perhaps some buxom barmaid or "domestic servant"?*'[22]

While some details changed during the composition (Blankytný became a typical high Janáček tenor, rather than the *travesti* alto specified here) Janáček held to this initial vision. The difficulty was that while there was plenty of detail in Čech's novel for Acts 2 and 3, the outer 'realistic' acts are no more than hinted at in the original novel and a librettist would have to be inventive in order to realize Janáček's needs. As is clear from his correspondence later that year, Mašek was temperamentally unsuited to bold interventions. When on 29 March he replied to Rektorys's enquiry, he wrote that he was keen to get on with his own creative work, but still 'would like to be further acquainted with the proposition concerning *Brouček*, since this material happens to be very dear to me and years ago I made a libretto from it; though at the time of course it remained unused.'[23] The next day he set out his financial conditions to Rektorys, and was also anxious to find out when Janáček would want the libretto: 'I would definitely not be able to do it soon.'[24] Rektorys should perhaps have spotted that this would be a problem – he should have remembered from the Skácelík episode over *Fate* that with Janáček speed was of the essence (see chap. 55). Nevertheless when writing to Janáček the next day and enclosing the two letters from Mašek, he commented merely that the 'conditions are completely acceptable' and left Janáček to take over the matter, suggesting a written contract and a meeting.[25]

'I'll write to Mašek at once', Janáček responded on 2 April, elated that he had now received official permission from Dr Klumpar, the lawyer representing the Čech family. 'I'd love to throw myself into the work. I'd have to cast off from myself all the weeds of everyday life.' In all the excitement about the new opera, his previous one was mentioned only occasionally: 'Mr Čelanský was in Brno. I doubt whether he'll give *Fate* before the autumn. Before he goes to Munich, he says – that's certain.'[26] Janáček's letters to Mašek have not survived, but much of what he wrote can be inferred from Mašek's reply on 4 April:

I was delighted to receive your letter and it will be an honour for me to meet you personally; surely only then will it be possible to come to a definitive agreement and decision; I'll also tell you then frankly of the circumstances that might hold up the work from my side.

[...]

My original libretto, made years ago, was written with a small, domestic production in mind, which then didn't materialize; it was divided into three acts (arrival on the moon – at Lunobor's – in front of the Temple of All Arts and departure) and was written for only four characters.

How I would visualize it today – this will become clear during our verbal negotiations.[27]

The 'verbal negotiations', however, did not take place for a couple of weeks as Janáček's next opportunity for a trip to Prague was at Easter (which fell on 19 April that year). Meanwhile Rektorys continued to inform Janáček about his interests in Prague. There was a possibility of Čelanský's conducting the Vinohrady Orchestra in Paris in a programme of Czech music that would include Janáček's Prelude to *Jenůfa*. There was also, at last, good news about *Fate*:

It will be given *for certain*. But it'll be necessary before then, however, for the ensemble to be somewhat played in so that it can overcome the enormous obstacles that lie hidden in the work. All the [performing] material has been copied out and Čelanský firmly hopes that he'll be able to perform the opera at the beginning of the autumn. He doesn't intend to go abroad and won't go anywhere. Not now, not at all. He'll stay.

The last remark was to reassure Janáček about Čelanský's restless tendencies ('this much to calm you down and [to give you] new hope'). Rektorys also proposed a 'proper advertisement' for the new piano-vocal score of *Jenůfa*.[28] Four days later, when Janáček replied to Rektorys's letter, he had not yet received the promised telegram from Čelanský about the proposed Paris orchestral concert. Furthermore the Paris choral tour by the Moravian Teachers appeared to be in jeopardy since one of the guarantors had now pulled out: 'It will be necessary to postpone the trip.' However 227 copies of *Jenůfa* had been sent off to Urbánek the day before,[29] and although Janáček did not mention it, an even more important event was taking place on 12 April: namely the première of his chorus *Maryčka Magdónova* (IV/35). It is not known whether Janáček attended it. While it seems odd that Janáček would not have the curiosity to make the trip to the Moravian town of Prostějov to hear what was after all his latest and by far his most ambitious chorus, the event went entirely unmentioned in his regular correspondence with Rektorys. It is also possible that Vach himself, ever cautious, might have discouraged Janáček from going. From Vach's memoir of 1924 it is clear that the piece gave the choir immense problems in rehearsal, and the obscure venue of the first public tryout – an out-of-the-way Moravian market town – may well be significant. Furthermore, Janáček had fallen out with the choir over the Paris trip. When he next wrote to Rektorys on 15 April he reported that although Count Seilern had saved the Paris trip with a guarantee of 20,000 K, he (Janáček) would not be going to Paris himself: he disapproved of the inclusion of Malát's chorus *Monastery Bells* ('schoolboy tastelessness') in one of the programmes. The title itself is enough to suggest what reservations Janáček might have had.[30] Nevertheless, it could surely not have helped that it was Malát's opera *A Merry Wooing* that was being given at the Vinohrady Theatre that season, and not Janáček's *Fate*. So instead of leaving with the choir for Paris, Janáček set out for Prague on Easter Tuesday (21 April), the day after the first Paris concert.

By the time he sent off a postcard to Zdenka (who was in Vienna for Easter) he had 'already studied the old castle steps' (which feature in Act 1 of *Brouček*) and had also gone to see Urbánek, who had already sent out review copies of the *Jenůfa* score to various critics and newspapers.[31] In his brief postcard to Zdenka (mentioning without further comment that he had met Franz Lehár at Urbánek's shop) there is also an indication that he had not been in good spirits: 'I'm glad that I got into a different atmosphere. Already taken out of my depressed mood by the journey.'[32] And perhaps he felt a little more confident too: that same day he sent off a postcard to his brother František announcing that 'I'm again in a new composition: *The Excursion of Mr Brouček*. That's why I travelled to Prague.'[33] He had, however, not yet seen Mašek who, as he had explained to Janáček, was tied up on Monday and Tuesday and so proposed a meeting at his home on Wednesday afternoon.[34] Janáček lingered for another day in Prague, taking in a performance of *Carmen* at the National Theatre on Thursday evening.[35] He had seen Dvořák's *Rusalka* on his first evening.[36]

During this time the Moravian Teachers continued their series of

concerts in Paris. The Prostějov tryout of *Maryčka Magdónova* seems
to have satisfied the cautious Vach, and the piece was included in the
choir's third Paris concert, given at the Théâtre du Châtelet in a programme that included pieces by Foerster, Novák, František Neumann
and Křížkovský but also, alas, Malát's *Monastery Bells*. Vach sent a
postcard to Janáček the next day reporting that the success of the
piece was '*enormous*'. On the front of the card (a nice photograph of
Saint-Germain-l'Auxerrois) Vach added: 'We've been invited to meet
Rodin – just leaving to go and see him now.'[37] Two days later, at what
was presumably intended to be a sure-fire final concert at the Théâtre
Sarah Bernhardt, the choir gave the two 'Haná choruses', *If only you
knew* and *The Evening Witch* (IV/28), interpretations that were already
well established from the choir's performances in Germany and Austria. Meanwhile Janáček's meeting with Mašek in Prague also seems to
have gone well. On 2 May Janáček got a brief note from him: 'I agree
with your division [of the action]; it will be much more compact like
this; please send me my draft (I don't have a copy) so I can work in the
new detailed scenario.'[38]

Among the review copies of *Jenůfa* that Urbánek sent out, it is odd that
none went to Jan Branberger, who wrote regularly for the periodicals
Čas and *Národní obzor*, although perhaps, given what he wrote
about the première (see chap. 47), his exclusion was not an oversight.
On 5 May he wrote to Janáček pointing out that the piano-vocal score
had just appeared. Could he be sent a copy? He 'would like to be the
first in Prague to welcome its publication'. At the same time, he
reminded Janáček that he had written to him a couple of weeks earlier
asking if he had any short compositions that could be published in the
new series he was editing.[39] Branberger's earlier invitation, written on
15 April, had come shortly before the Prague trip and, with no time to
consider it properly, Janáček had not replied. In it Branberger had
asked Janáček for a piece for piano, violin or voice of eight or sixteen
pages to be published by Bedřich Kočí in a cheap edition with a 'tasteful
cover'. The purpose of this cheap edition would be to extend the range
of good Czech music that could be played in the home.[40]

Branberger now received an immediate response. Janáček would
gladly arrange with Urbánek to have a copy of *Jenůfa* sent to him, and
then added: 'I'll also send you some of my piano pieces from the
cycle *From the Overgrown Path*.'[41] Janáček clearly had no qualms in

describing these as 'piano pieces', although their publication so far had been as pieces for harmonium. The next day he wrote again asking if he could be sent some examples of what had already come out in the series. He then continued: '*On the Overgrown Path* is a cycle of piano pieces. I'd like [eventually] to have it published as a *whole*; so far there are seven of them.' The eight-to-sixteen-page format stipulated by Branberger seemed to preclude this, so, if just one piece were to be published, Janáček wished to ensure from the outset that his right to publish the entire series together would not be affected.[42] What is significant in this letter is the number of pieces ('seven') mentioned by Janáček: he had not so far added to the original manuscript, which contained the five pieces previously published in *Slovanské melodie*, plus the two longer, unpublished pieces (see chap. 38).

Branberger, when he wrote the next day, was all co-operation. He would get Koči to send the two pieces already published by return of post. In the pipeline there were also pieces by Moor, Nešvera and Suk. Janáček could either publish a single piece, for which he would be paid 20 K, but still be allowed to publish the whole cycle elsewhere, or else Branberger would take the whole cycle, with full rights, at 25 K per seven-page fascicle.[43]

While Janáček considered these possibilities, there were signs of life from Mašek. First, a brief report on 15 May declaring that he had a new scheme for *Brouček* that he would send on Monday (18 May) 'with a suggestion for the first scene up to the flight [to the moon]'.[44] Even this brief announcement seems to have got Janáček fired up, and he jotted down a few comments on the back of the letter: 'windows closed', 'B[rouček] goes into the dark', 'a chorus from the Vikárka is singing, muffled, out of the dark'. Mašek delivered his brief portion of the libretto one day ahead of time, announcing that, 'like the poor widow', he was sending what he could before he left on holiday:

I'm working very hesitantly, trying to get round similarities in diction and to catch something of the [original] character; and even then I'm not happy with it – perhaps there's not enough time for 'maturing' and for revisions.

I'm sending Act 2 only in its main outlines, I think that changes will be necessary here. The first [act] in a little more detail – and the earth scene expanded.

I'll change things or put them into verse in accordance with your wishes (the drinking-songs?). But I'd like to say once again that I'll withdraw, renouncing all rights, should you find a suitable person to help you sooner.

And, as he signed off, he went on trying to extricate himself from something he had clearly been talked into against his will, mentioning that 'Mr Mrštík' (i.e. the Moravian playwright Vilém Mrštík) had 'greatly praised Mr Kurt (and as a writer of verse)'.[45] Janáček did not take up the Kurt suggestion for *Brouček*, but a few years later he was to set Maximilián Kurt's poem *The Čarták on Soláň* as a cantata (III/7; see chap. 62).

Mašek's libretto for Act 1 consisted of a short parting conversation on the steps of the Vikárka between Brouček and the innkeeper, Würfl, interrupted by a drinking-song from within the inn. Brouček says good night and hurries off. His subsequent eulogy to the moon was to be taken straight from Čech (Mašek here quotes the appropriate page numbers from the novel). And as he extols the virtues of a moon that lacks all the sordid complications of everyday life, Brouček is drawn higher and higher by some inexplicable force until (in the second act) he finds himself on the moon. Mašek was reluctant to introduce new elements: the drinking-chorus is the only incident not to be found in the original.[46] Undeterred by the brevity of what he had been sent, Janáček brightly announced to Rektorys that he had received the beginning of the libretto and was now immersed in 'joyful work'.[47]

Before this came, however, Janáček had begun to consider Branberger's proposition more carefully and on 23 May he sent him the entire *Overgrown Path* cycle so far. There were now as many as nine pieces, he wrote, some of which had already been published in *Slovanské melodie*. He wanted to publish them as a whole and would not want them to be broken up; perhaps they could be published in threes?[48] This was conceded: Branberger wrote on 3 June to say that Kočí would bring out the cycle 'very shortly' in three fascicles.[49] At the same time he asked Janáček for the narrative programme – 'if it has any' – or for any 'poetic reference', as he intended to write an analysis that would be printed on the title page. Janáček's swift response, sent three days later, is a unique document consisting of brief aphoristic comments on some of the pieces illustrated with short music examples (see chap. 38).

Meanwhile both Janáčeks were on their travels again. Exceptionally, Zdenka went to Prague to spend a few days with Joza Janáčková‡

---

‡A visit commemorated by a photograph showing the two of them wearing impressively large hats, as in *MLWJ*, plate 17.

and her daughter Věra. Janáček sent her two cards: one on 25 May from a local walking trip in a group that included Ferdinand Vach and his wife Karla, during which they visited Lelekovice, Vranov and Adamov,[50] and another the next day, from Vienna where – again exceptionally – Janáček had been on Organ School business. His brief card to Zdenka reports that the Organ School had been granted an advanced organ class with an organ teacher at the 'decent' salary of 5000 K.[51] The next day, 27 May, he seemed to have joined his wife in Prague where that evening he (or they) attended a performance of Nicolai's *Die lustige Weiber von Windsor* at the National Theatre.[52]

Janáček had already begun to look around for someone to take up the newly created organ post, and by 10 June had written to Rektorys telling him about it and soliciting his help in trying (through an advertisement in *Dalibor*) to track down the organist Jan Rangl, with whom Janáček had been in contact in 1907.[53] In a brief note of thanks to Rektorys (and informing him that Rangl had now been in touch), Janáček announced his holiday plans (off to Hukvaldy on 13 July) and alluded to the current state of the Mašek situation: 'Mr K.M. is too daunted by the majesty of Č. [Čech]. But we understand one another. After all, we both want the best.'[54] This was putting too optimistic a complexion on Mašek's latest note, sent after his return from holiday in Italy:

It seems to me that there is a fundamental conflict between us in how we regard the original, i.e. Čech's *Brouček*.

You place the main emphasis on the realistic, earthly side, while I would rather suppress this as much as possible and instead emphasize the poetical and satirical moon scenes.

I acknowledge your standpoint and would gladly accommodate you – but it won't work with me, for it goes against my own view.

Indeed I like the character of the Waiter very much, it is certainly most apt – but, however nice, I can't bring myself to add this part to Čech's work in addition to that of Mazal [one of Brouček's difficult tenants] at the Vikárka. Čech's Mr Brouček would never have fraternized with Mazal and sat with him in the same pub.[55]

When he next wrote, on 21 July, Mašek thanked Janáček for his 'kind notes' (one can imagine how increasingly urgent they must have sounded) and did his best to withdraw from the project entirely:

Your writing reveals an even more fundamental difference between our views, the conflict of musician and writer. For me the original work, out of which one has to create, is sacred and as far as possible inviolable; I allow only for the conversion to a stage setting – from Zeyer's novel (for Ostrčil) [*Kunála's Eyes*, 1908] I retained everything to the fullest possible extent: action, scenes, diction, and did not admit any foreign elements.

Having an affection for *Brouček*, I wanted to take on its adaptation only 'out of love' although – as you know – at the expense of other projects that I had decided on earlier, and which are more important to me.

But now I simply cannot accept your views – we are completely at odds.[56]

It was not only the collapse of Janáček's negotiations with his *Brouček* librettist that put a pall on his holiday in Hukvaldy. On 8 July Janáček wrote an angry note to Dr Jaroslav Elgart in his function as executive officer of the Brno Theatre Družstvo, withdrawing *Jenůfa* from the Brno repertory. He had been forced to do this, he wrote, because of the general choice of repertory at the theatre. 'Forgive me, but whether they now give something of mine in the Brno Theatre is of absolutely no importance to me.' And Brno shouldn't ask for any *Fate* material either.[57] In Hukvaldy things were not helped either by the weather. When Janáček sent a card to Zdenka on 23 July, it had been raining for five days.[58] His next letter, written 'in a terrible hurry' to wish Zdenka well for her birthday (30 July),[59] mentions that he had written to Mrštík, perhaps indeed to take up Mašek's suggestion that he seek advice for the *Brouček* libretto there (Vilém Mrštík's answer of 28 July was discouraging).[60] As for Mašek, he talked only of principles and didn't do anything. Janáček also had worries over the Organ School committee – only Count Belrupt, the elderly chairman who had been there since 1882 and was now retiring, really cared about the institution. There was also bad news about his brother František, who was 'in Prague for an operation' – the problem for which he had undergone operations in 1905 and 1906 seems to have returned (see chap. 51). Altogether Janáček felt 'spiritually exhausted', though he was glad of the quiet of Hukvaldy.[61] Nevertheless, the next day he made the long journey from Hukvaldy to Prague, for the première of *Maryčka Magdónova*: after its triumphant Paris tour, the Moravian Teachers' Choral Society was giving a celebratory concert in the Czech capital during the time of the Jubilee Exhibition (see below).[62] While in Prague, Janáček seems to have dropped in on Mašek who, despite his discouraging letter of six days earlier, fobbed him off with a promise that Janáček would receive a continuation in two days.[63]

Soon after his return to Hukvaldy Janáček was greeted by a letter from Dr Elgart in response to his angry one. It was partly concerned with the question of a leader for the Brno Theatre orchestra who would also be attached as a violin teacher to the Organ School: in principle the Družstvo was in favour of this joint appointment. As for the theatre orchestra, the director Frýda had guaranteed to bring it up to thirty-four players ('from his side this is a sacrifice' and a sign of good will); the conductors would be Karel Moor and Rudolf Pavlata, both of whom were well known to Janáček (Moor was the composer of another *Maryčka Magdónova*, see chap. 53; Pavlata was to join the Organ School staff in 1909): 'They will do all they can to have good players in the orchestra. You can see that we are trying gradually to raise the musical level.' All this was written calmly, rationally and gently. It was then followed by a plea:

All the harder, therefore, do I take your news that you will not allow [us] to perform *Fate*. I'm happy to believe that you – an artist ordained by God – may set little store by Brno. Your future is still to come, and it is not necessary for great men to depend on the recognition of today['s public] and Brno. – But why on earth shouldn't we, lacking a large theatre, want to satisfy our musical hunger in our humble conditions at least with illusions? True enough, you don't think it important that *Fate* be given in Brno – but we long for it! [. . .] I earnestly beg you to allow us to perform *Fate*. Mr Moor will surely take every possible care for it to turn out as decently as possible, and we would like to have it as the highlight of the spring season. By then it will be possible for the Vinohrady Theatre to lend us the score for copying, since it is quite certain that it will be given there in the autumn.[64]

It is letters like these that bring home the fact that Janáček in 1908 was not friendless. There were people such as Elgart in Brno or, for that matter, Rektorys in Prague, neither of them professional musicians, who were prepared to put themselves out to further his career. Clearly written from the heart, this appeal underlines the extent to which Elgart believed in Janáček's stature and future, and shows what he was prepared to do to smooth his passage within the restricted conditions available at Brno. It is a shame that his letter did not do the trick, for this was the last chance that Janáček had of getting *Fate* produced in Brno. If it didn't change Janáček's mind, it did at least mollify him. He relented over *Jenůfa* and perhaps would have relented over *Fate* if he hadn't begun to lose confidence:

And now about *Fate*. My esteemed friend, if I could have heard at least a rehearsal of some part of *Fate*, for instance the storm in Act 2 [*recte* 3] or anything else, and thus be convinced of the effect of at least some parts – a work one has imagined and its actual sound are sometimes far from one another – then I would say yes or no.

So please wait a bit longer with *Fate*. I have asked the director Frýda to leave *Jenůfa* in the repertory, now that the vocal score is out. After all, remember with what sort of orchestra it was performed! Première without flutes[S] and otherwise always half the colours.

I have trust also in Mr Moor, that he'll do it well.

Another thing that recommends this course of action is that many of the soloists still remember it. The producer Mr Komarov now wants to sketch its scenes in Slovakia [i.e. Slovácko]. So please put *Jenůfa* in the repertory and for *Fate* wait until I have heard at least one orchestral rehearsal.[65]

When Janáček wrote to Zdenka the day before the above it seems that both the weather and his mood had changed. The weather was now 'wonderful' and there was good news about František, recuperating in Hukvaldy: 'Franta is walking and getting stronger; after a week he has healed up and is now feeding well. They've turned his stomach inside out! – it's not cancer!' Janáček had worked out the dates for his Luhačovice holiday (16 August to 6 September), after which he would go to Prague, where *Fate* would 'certainly be in rehearsal if they stage it'. He suggested that Zdenka return to Brno by 15 August to await his arrival: 'I'm content here in the quiet, but looking forward to seeing you!'[66]

By the time he left, bringing 'a wealth of dry mushrooms, two jars of pickled mushrooms, and five jars of beans'[67] and 'a few trout',[68] he had received the Prague reviews of *Maryčka Magdónova*, which were 'marvellous', he told Zdenka. The countryside was green after the frequent showers, the weather was warm, and he had recovered mentally.[69] The news of his brother František at first seemed to be good. Earlier in the month he was walking 'hill upon hill'[70] but now there seemed to be more ominous news. In his letter of 11 August, he mentioned to Zdenka that František would stay on in Hukvaldy for another fortnight. 'We'll chat about the results.'[71]

[S] The première did include a flute, but the player had given notice by the second performance on 28 January (Němcová 1971, 118).

Although Zdenka had been detailed to return, it is clear from the addresses of Janáček's cards from Luhačovice that she remained in Vienna, so that his return to Brno was no lingering reunion but just a quick turnaround, presumably to bring back the country products and get fresh linen. By Sunday 16 August Janáček was writing from Luhačovice and had settled into Janův dům again.[72] As usual in Luhačovice, Janáček reported to the doctor on arrival:

I knew that it couldn't last long when water wouldn't go through the operated place. The hole had grown over. I had a cold all the time. It went into the neck and from there to the nose. My state and mood in Hukvaldy was therefore terrible. Here first of all, on the advice of Dr Janke, I got rid of some of the catarrh in my nose and on the vocal cords, and today he operated on me again like Dr Kaufman – but it went without pain. I had already been losing all interest in everything; I had to force myself to do everything.[73]

For all the disappointments in his work that Janáček reported to Zdenka in Hukvaldy, what was upsetting him in particular had clearly been a recurrence of the infection of his sinuses, for which he had been operated on in 1893 by Dr Kaufmann. Dr Zikmund Janke (1865–1918) was an ear, nose and throat specialist who worked both in Prague and in Luhačovice. Like Dr Kaufman, he was an amateur musician, the editor (1903–12) of a magazine for singers, *Věstník pěvecký a hudební*. Janáček's sinuses were only part of his health problems. Two days later he consulted another Luhačovice doctor, and reported the findings at length to Zdenka. Dr Votruba, 'the former assistant of Dr Maixner' (the Prague doctor whom the Janáčeks had called to examine Olga in her final days), had examined him and found signs of gout, which had gone unrecognized by 'that idiot Dr Říha' from Brno (see vol. ii: Did Janáček really have gout?). Not only his feet were affected but his neck too. Dr Votruba would be able to cure him completely. This was mostly through various spa treatments (both drinking the waters and 'magnetization of the left foot') and diet: 'in the morning milk at breakfast, at noon a little white meat, in the evening also. No beer; simply weak tea. Lots of vegetables. Little sweet fruit.'[74]

In another letter to Zdenka four days later Janáček gave more details of his life. In the 'magnificent weather' – 'really hot' – he was wearing his silk suit. He was being charged only 3 K daily for his room (although in season it should have cost 8 K), meals (lunch and supper) were 2 K each, and snacks (milk and a roll for breakfast) were 20 hellers. But altogether it was costing a lot with the spa treatments and visits to the doctor and tips. 'I will be really glad when I am a well man!' Despite having a 'huge thirst', he was avoiding beer and wine and so far had not got fed up with veal ('I eat it noon and evening'). And, for all his health problems, other things were troubling him: 'This year somehow nothing is going right.' No-one wanted to go to Brno to take up the joint post of teacher/leader of the orchestra. Vienna had gone quiet about the new organ post. 'I wander around without thoughts and ideas. I am looking forward to being at home together again.'[75]

Janáček did, however, make one important new friend, as he reported to Zdenka a week later: 'Marie Calma – such a hard name[II] [–] belongs to my latest acquaintance. But don't faint before you finish reading!'[76] Was Zdenka likely to faint because he had met another woman, or because of Marie Calma's literary fame? By 1908, she had published four collections of stories and tales, two of which she presented to Janáček during his time in Luhačovice. She also sang. A graduate of the Pivoda singing school and a pupil of Kovařovic, she had appeared as a solo soprano at the Prague Rudolfinum in 1898 at the age of seventeen. According to her reminiscences of 1938, Janáček cut open a few pages of the newly published piano-vocal score of *Jenůfa* and sat down at the piano. '"They say you sing nicely – so show us what you can do." He was surprised that I could sight-sing Jenůfa and the Kostelnička.'[77] Janáček mentioned as much to Zdenka ('She sang Jenůfa to me beautifully') and went on to describe her charms ('a gentle creature') as well as her disadvantages ('she has a mother – brr! – who praises her darling all the time'). He had been entertained 'on the cosy veranda: coffee – ice cream – grapes – peaches – *buchty*[¶] – well, useless to talk about it. It was only at the end that Dr Veselý introduced her as his fiancée!'[78] Janáček had of course known Dr František Veselý for many years (for instance through the Brno Russian Circle). This Luhačovice meeting was fateful for *Jenůfa* and for Janáček generally. A year later, Dr Veselý, having been director of the spa for seven years, returned with his new wife to Brno where the couple began actively

[II] Marie Hurychová (1881–1966) took her literary pseudonym from the song 'Ridonami la calma' by Pier Francesco Tosi (c.1653–1732). For Czechs, who pronounce 'c' as 'ts', it must have seemed odd.
[¶] Traditional yeast-raised cakes, usually with a sweet filling (curd cheese, poppyseed, jam).

campaigning for the production of *Jenůfa* at the Prague National Theatre.

In 1908 Franz Josef had been emperor for sixty years, and in Prague the event was celebrated with a Jubilee Exhibition (15 May–18 October) whose function was to demonstrate the economic development there since the Regional Jubilee Exhibition (1891). Janáček went straight from Luhačovice to Prague to see it, having sent Zdenka his 'last card from Luhačovice' on Monday 7 September.[79] He sent another from the exhibition the next day: 'There's an enormous crowd at the exhibition. I didn't get a place to sit down. Magnificent weather. But sad memories occur to me when I walk around here alone.'[80] The 'sad memories' were perhaps of the 1895 Ethnographic Exhibition when Zdenka had brought Olga on her first trip to Prague. Two days later he 'was at the magic illuminations right up to the tower'. He had looked in on the Prague Janáčeks (i.e. Věra and her mother) but their home was deserted.[81] On the Friday he brought his week away to an end with a performance of Karel Weis's German operetta *Der Revisor* (based on Gogol's *The Government Inspector*, and now given in a Czech version at the National Theatre). He was not taken with it: 'Moving witness of the Russia of the 1860s', he scribbled on the programme – which rather suggests that he had not encountered Gogol's farce before. However in Weis's musical version this 'moving witness' had been 'caricatured'. 'Laughter from pain! Music crudely folk – Viennese. Act 1 disgusting.'[82]

Back in Brno (on Saturday 12 September)[83] there were Organ School matters to attend to, for instance the unfilled post of violin teacher/orchestral leader. Rektorys wrote on 25 September with a new suggestion, and then asked how *Brouček* was doing. He also thought it would be good if Čelanský could perform *Maryčka* at the Vinohrady Theatre. Had it been originally conceived with orchestral accompaniment? Or had perhaps the fact that the Moravian Teachers had no orchestra at their disposal led Janáček to change his original plan?[84] In his reply Janáček mentioned that he still hoped for a Prague production of *Fate*. Apparently after hearing *Maryčka* in Prague Čelanský had declared that he would 'raise' Janáček with *Fate*, and Šubert, whom Janáček had encountered in Vienna, had said that it would be given in the autumn – but nothing seemed to have happened. 'Do give Čelanský a little nudge.' As for *Maryčka*:

[it] is conceived chorally. I know that there are here many ideas for an orchestra – and next week I will study the chaos of sound in Vítkovice, Moravská Ostrava and also in Staré Hamry – perhaps I will make a stab at an orchestral version too.

Since Mašek hasn't sent me a libretto I've thrown myself into smaller works. I remembered that Rodin asked the Moravian Teachers' Choral Society for Czech folksongs. They didn't know any and sang him a Croatian one! I'm writing some songs for them. Well, don't think that it is just a matter of harmonizing them!

If you see Mašek, remind him of me and my desire to have his work.

When I wanted to write to Mr Kozel [Rektorys's recommendation for the violin post], someone knocked on the door and in came Mr Dědeček [Janáček's first choice]. It's all settled.[85]

So at last Janáček had his new violin teacher. Janáček really did go off to the industrialized part of Silesia in search of possible inspiration for an orchestral setting of *Maryčka Magdónova*, telling Zdenka in a brief postcard from Ostrava on 2 October that it was 'purgatory', without a scrap of green, just black smoke and dust.[86] No orchestral version, however, came out of it and it is hard to imagine that any orchestral accompaniment or expansion could have been added to such a self-sufficient work (see chap. 54). It is extraordinary to think that Janáček was still expecting something from Mašek. As for the 'smaller works' that Janáček was getting on with, the best candidate – unless he was still tinkering with the new pieces for *On the Overgrown Path* – was a set of *Three Folksongs* for tenor, male voices and piano/harmonium, later absorbed into *Five Folksongs* (IV/37). Janáček's autograph is undated, but the set fits in well with Janáček's earlier undertaking to arrange Czech folksongs for the Moravian Teachers.

Quite apart from Mašek's inactivity (or rather Janáček's notion that he might, nevertheless, deliver the goods), *Brouček* was now bedevilled by another problem. Rektorys had received an anguished letter from the composer Karel Moor (recently appointed conductor at the Brno Theatre) asking if what he read in *Dalibor* was true about Janáček's composing a *Brouček* opera. He (Moor) had received express permission to do so from Vladimír Čech, as heir to the Svatopluk Čech estate. Rektorys went on to explain that he had eventually got hold of Vladimír Čech, who had confirmed Moor's story. Perhaps, Čech said, his aunt Zdenka Čechová had forgotten about the promise given to

Janáček. Rektorys recommended that Janáček turn to Dr Klumpar, with whom he had dealt before, for confirmation that he had the exclusive rights to a musical setting (see above).[87] In his response Janáček quoted Dr Klumpar's letter giving his consent in the name of the Čech family[88] and, armed with this, Rektorys saw Klumpar on 28 October and was able to report back to Janáček that day that Klumpar knew nothing about Moor's permission, which was invalid: permission was required from all seven members of the Čech family. Rektorys suggested that Janáček write a note to Mašek telling him 'not to interrupt his work' and a friendly but firm letter to Moor.[89]

Janáček promptly wrote in this vein to Moor, adding for good measure the misleading information that he himself had already written one act of the opera.[90] Permission or no permission, Moor went on with his operetta, which was performed in 1910, a full decade before Janáček's opera reached the stage. The advice for Mašek, however, was redundant: on the same day that Rektorys wrote, Mašek sent off his final letter to Janáček, regretting his 'rash promise' and saying that, however hard he tried, he had been unable to write a single line more of the libretto and doubted that he would be able to do so in the foreseeable future. He was living through 'terrible spiritual depression'. Someone else 'quicker and more competent' should now take up the work.[91]

Another bit of advice that Rektorys had offered Janáček in his letter of 28 October (written down the margins and overlooked in the collected Rektorys–Janáček correspondence) was to

Write a letter to the Directorate of the Vinohrady Theatre saying that it should begin rehearsing *Fate*: it was accepted a year ago now, and its production has been promised. Please don't mention any of the officials (i.e. neither Čelanský nor Šubert) in your letter. Just write a general complaint. Please inform me of the theatre's answer. I will print it in *Dalibor*.[92]

Janáček did so and received the briefest of notes from the Vinohrady administration. *Fate* had not been included in the repertory up to January 1909 and so could be scheduled to take place only after that.[93] Janáček had already reported back to Rektorys on *Brouček*. Poor Moor had been 'unscrupulously duped by director Vladimír Čech'. As for his librettist, he had finally decided to call it a day: 'Mr Karel Mašek hasn't behaved well. When I called at his house after the holidays – actually in the holidays – I was told "that I would receive a continuation in two days". *Now I'm negotiating about a continuation with the writer Holý and Dr Janke.*[94]

Josef Holý (1874–1928) was a poet and playwright of sceptical inclinations (reacting against the fashionable 'decadence' of the time). He was reasonably well known, especially after the publication in 1906 of his collection *The Adamov Forests*, which contained a poem to which the authorities took exception and resulted in his being transferred from a teaching post at a girls' lycée in Brno to a boys' school in the provincial outback of Velké Meziříčí.[95] Maybe his satirical tendencies would have suited Janáček's purposes well, but he gave Janáček a prompt and categorical no: '*I don't like the material and I have no inclination to do a libretto. If there is neither the will nor the right mood, it would not turn out well, however much I tried, and so I ask you to count me out.*'[96] Janáček had much more luck with Dr Janke. Presumably in his consultation room in Luhačovice they had talked about more than Janáček's infected sinuses:

I will at any rate have a go at the text you mentioned. There is only the question – will I be up to it? I will however do all I can to be so. I therefore intend to write a section as soon as possible and give it to you to look at – to see if it corresponds with your intentions. If you should wish some other approach do tell me your opinion quite openly, for I would want to satisfy you.[97]

On the same day that Janke wrote this letter (15 November), *Maryčka Magdónova* at last had its Brno première. It was a remarkable event in that both composer and poet were there, the latter too shy to make himself known to Janáček, who did not hear about Bezruč's presence until many years later. In an exchange of letters over his seventieth birthday, Janáček wrote warmly to the man who had inspired some of his greatest choral music:

They say we once stood next to one another – and did not know one another.
I feel that I am so close to you and yet we have never met.
Your words came as if on cue and I brought down on them a musical storm of anger, despair and pain.[98]

A month after his earlier letter (which included questions about the number of acts, etc.) Janke sent his version of Act 1 of *Brouček*. 'I am very curious to hear your judgement since it will indicate to me if I should, and if I can, continue *more or less in this vein*. For this reason I have not even begun Act 2.'[99] Dated 16 December, this second letter might not have reached Janáček in Brno. At some point Janáček went to Hukvaldy, where his brother František died on Sunday 20 December at the age of fifty-two. 'He didn't suspect death', Janáček wrote to Zdenka. 'He died quietly in the hope that he would recover. Máša will stay here. Arriving in Brno on Sunday afternoon [27 December].'[100] One can only speculate about Janáček's reaction to this event, but it would be odd if it did not affect him deeply. František was the one brother with whom he shared interests. They had spent holiday time together both in Russia and also in their birthplace in Hukvaldy, where František returned increasingly frequently for holidays and where in 1905 he had bought a small cottage,[101] in which his widow Marie ('Máša') continued to live. And there was the special bond forged by Olga's Russian trip that had ended in tragedy.

František's was not the only death that Janáček had to come to terms with at this time. A month earlier Janáček had written to Rektorys asking him to print an announcement in *Dalibor*: 'The Directorate of the Organ School announce the death of the composer, Professor František Musil. He died on Saturday 29 November 1908. One can say of him that to his last breath and in his last thoughts he devoted himself to the school.'[102] Musil was only two years older than Janáček. Much of his life he had been organist at Brno Cathedral, and from 1905 he had taught composition at the Organ School. Janáček asked Karel Moor to take his place (he did so, on a temporary basis).[103] If nothing else, this demonstrates the good feeling that existed between the two composers, despite the conflict over the *Brouček* libretto and over their respective settings of Bezruč's *Maryčka Magdónova*.

57

Bêtes noires II: Zdeněk Nejedlý

Zdeněk Nejedlý (1878–1962, see Plate 30) left his mark over an entire century of Czech music. His first book, on Fibich's stage works, was published in 1901 and although only twenty-three, he was already Dr Nejedlý, with a newly minted doctorate in Czech history from Prague University, where he had studied history and aesthetics, the latter with Hostinský. But his musical education had not been neglected. From lessons with his father, a professional music teacher and minor composer, Nejedlý had graduated to lessons with Fibich, joining the ranks of other leading young Czech musicians such as Karel Kovařovic and Otakar Ostrčil. While pursuing an energetic career as a scholar (teaching at Prague University from 1908), Nejedlý drew attention to himself as a publicist and polemicist with well-defined views on Czech music. He was seen as the natural successor to his teacher Hostinský (who died in 1910), but his strong and abrasive personality was very different from that of the emollient Hostinský. His range was huge (he wrote on many topics apart from music) and his ambitions lofty: by his death in 1962 he had published over four thousand items, including two hundred books. This literary legacy was compounded – and complicated – by his other activities. A communist sympathizer and activist, he fled to the Soviet Union at the Nazi occupation in 1938. After the war his zeal was rewarded with posts in the new Communist administration in Czechoslovakia. He was the minister of education for much of the period up to 1953 and as such exerted even greater powers. Such was his status and pervasive influence that very little critical assessment of this towering figure was possible in Czechoslovakia, not only while he was alive but for decades afterwards.

This was the person with whom Janáček began to tangle in 1906.

At the heart of their disagreement was the figure of Smetana and their different attitudes towards him. As music director at the Brno Beseda in the 1880s, Janáček had conducted a couple of Smetana's symphonic poems but performed many more works by Dvořák. This was seen as evidence of a 'Dvořák cult' in Brno, fostered by Janáček (see chap. 60); the fact that Dvořák wrote many works suitable for presentation by a middle-of-the-road concert organization and Smetana did not was not taken into account, and Janáček's attitude towards Smetana – for many the litmus-test of Czech musical nationalism – was seen as basically hostile. This was not entirely fair, but certainly in his early writings on Smetana in *Hudební listy* Janáček wrote about Smetana with cool detachment, often taking a critical stance (see chap. 25). Furthermore, Janáček also had all the wrong friends, not least Dvořák, and Smetana's opponent František Pivoda. Even before they had encountered one another, Nejedlý would have regarded Janáček as being in the wrong camp.

Nejedlý's vision of the future of Czech music was built on the legacy of Smetana and his anointed heirs, with Nejedlý himself as chief anointer. This vision was supported in practical terms by his writings on Smetana (in particular a study of his operas and a vast but incomplete biography planned in fourteen volumes), by the journal entitled *Smetana* founded in 1910 as a platform for his views, and by his books on Smetana's successors (in Nejedlý's view: Fibich, Foerster and Ostrčil). In all this Nejedlý saw himself as carrying through to its logical conclusions the battles fought in the nineteenth century for a distinctively Czech music and consolidating all that Smetana had achieved. Nejedlý was a superb polemicist who fought tenaciously – one might also say arrogantly and dirtily – for what he regarded as true causes. The difficulty with his vision was that it was an exclusive one that left little room for other composers and other views. Those composers who might be seen as rivals to Smetana and his followers were trampled on with passion or ignored in disdainful silence. The most prominent of these were Dvořák, his pupils Suk and Novák, and of course Janáček.

References to Nejedlý occur in Janáček's correspondence from 1906 onwards (for instance he noted Nejedlý's views on 'Moravian separatism' occasioned by the Prague performances of Nešvera's opera *Radhošt'* and published in the *Pražská lidová revue*, in see chap. 53). However Janáček's first real indication that he had an outspokenly hostile commentator was in 1910, when he heard Nejedlý discuss *Jenůfa* at a lecture in Prague (see chap. 60). If hearing was not quite believing (and Janáček dealt with the matter at the time by writing it up in an ironic piece in *Hlídka*, xv/198), he was able to see what Nejedlý had to say about him when the latter published his lectures the next year as a book entitled *Czech Modern Opera after Smetana*. There are six chapters, of which four are devoted to Fibich, one mainly to Foerster, and another to Kovařovic, Ostrčil and others. Dvořák, the composer of *Rusalka* (and many other operas), was simply ignored. Janáček is tucked into the Foerster chapter under 'Moravian separatism', where he is characterized as the leader of the 'separatist direction'. The aspects Nejedlý dwelt on are signalled in the book's detailed contents list: Janáček's 'naturalism' (misled by the new Russian school), 'formalism' ('decidedly a step back in Czech opera'), 'declamation' (defective) and 'speech melody' (misguided). Essentially what he was saying was that Janáček's interest in folk music took him back to a pre-Smetana era where it was thought that Czechness would be achieved by the incorporation of Bohemian folk music and that Janáček therefore had not caught up with the advances brought by Smetana. As for Janáček's speech melodies, these were virtually the same thing, Czechness by the same outdated route.

Today a map of Czech opera that ignored Dvořák and dismissed Janáček as an oldfashioned naturalist, formalist and Moravian separatist would seem to show exceptionally poor judgement. Furthermore Nejedlý's fanatical support seems to have done little for his pet causes; even before his death the operas by Fibich, Foerster and Ostrčil had become rarities in Czech opera houses. The problem was that while Smetana and Hostinský fought for the modernisms of their day (Liszt and Wagner) and for a Czech music and a Czech opera that built on this and established its Czechness through the correct declamation of the Czech language rather than the incorporation of Bohemian folksongs, Nejedlý a generation later simply repeated this formula. He espoused exactly the same causes, and was not able to see that by 1910 late Romanticism was looking distinctly oldfashioned among the new modernisms on the horizon. As Jiří Fukač makes clear in his explanation of Nejedlý's criticisms of Janáček, he had been brought up in the atmosphere of German late Romanticism and simply saw the future as a continuation of this. Mahler and Strauss were fine, maybe even Schoenberg and Berg at a pinch, but Russian and

French contributions to Modernism he simply did not understand and regarded as a backward step.[1] Nejedlý could not see that Janáček's preoccupation with Moravian folksong had nothing to do with the espousal of Bohemian folksong advocated in the 1860s but instead offered a new 'village modernism' that had elements in common with the modernisms emanating from France and Russia (see vol. ii: Janáček and Modernism). He could not see that Janáček was himself forging a new Czechness which had little to do with Smetana, and more to do with his attention to the Czech language (the ridiculed speech melodies) and to the immense riches of Moravian traditional music.

Czech commentators such as Jiří Fukač make the point that the hostility between the two was ideological rather than personal and point to the fact that after Hostinský's death, when Nejedlý took over the Bohemian section of the *Volkslied in Österreich* project, the two of them worked well together. But this is the professional alliance of rivals who make common cause against a greater evil (in this case the machinations of Vienna or, later, the niggardliness of Czechoslovak funding for folksong research). While all this went on with elaborate courtesy, Nejedlý lost no opportunity to castigate Janáček at every Prague première of his that he attended. If anything, his hostility increased in relation to Janáček's success: the huge impact of *Jenůfa* in Prague demanded a special, relentlessly hostile effort from Nejedlý (see vol. ii: 1916c). Fukač makes the point that Nejedlý was able to put his finger on many aspects of Janáček's style, good and bad,[2] but Nejedlý's comments nevertheless need to be prised away from their vitriolic discourse and seem too aggressively presented to indicate a mere difference in approach. The fact that Nejedlý's subsequent reviews of *Brouček*, *Káťa Kabanová* and *The Cunning Little Vixen* are almost interchangeable is perhaps the best indication of his method. He is less interested in the works themselves than in registering the 'defective' ideology behind them that needs to be stamped on before it can do too much damage.

Bad reviews sometimes merely increase audiences by whetting their curiosity; once it is sensed that they are ideologically driven they can simply be disregarded by those of a different persuasion. Where in the end Nejedlý caused the most damage for Janáček was not his impact on potential Janáček audiences but on official and unofficial attitudes towards him and, on the other hand, in fuelling Janáček's distrust of Prague: a Prague-Brno rivalry over Janáček has persisted to this day.*

Jarmila Procházková gives a splendid example of how official attitudes were managed when quoting the deliberations of President Masaryk's secretary about how to handle Janáček's seventieth birthday in 1924. Should perhaps the president 'remember this jubilee with a handwritten letter? The name of Janáček and its significance for our music, which penetrates also beyond the boundaries of our state, would certainly deserve such an honour.' But, as the secretary continued, everyone knows about Janáček's attitude to Smetana and, although he had softened it, he had not bothered to conceal his feelings. 'A certain group of our musicians and musical composers, the so-called Smetanists, would certainly be surprised by this and perhaps make comments on it in various ways.' So on the whole a handwritten note might cause problems and it might be better if the president simply turned up at a performance of one of Janáček's works and exchanged a few warm words.[3] This is what should have happened, except that while Janáček made his epic journey from Hukvaldy via Brno to Prague all in one day to be present at this hastily convened opportunity, the president himself fell ill and Janáček had to make do with his deputy (see vol. ii: 1924b). It says much for Masaryk's impatience with this sort of thing that when he did encounter Janáček at a later occasion he inquired directly about Dr Nejedlý and learnt from Janáček that 'he had tormented him for years'.[4]

At a less august level, this sort of deliberation was repeated at the Brno Czech Theatre in 1924 (the year of Smetana's centenary), when Janáček was invited to make a speech about Smetana: as it happened he would be on his travels that day, so the speech was submitted to be read on his behalf but was found to be unacceptable. Janáček had no trouble publishing it elsewhere (in *Lidové noviny*, xv/250; see vol. ii: 1924a). Anyone reading it today might be surprised at how warmly enthusiastic it was; Janáček's only sin, it seems, was to suggest that there could be many ways of writing Czech operas, not just the Smetana way.

---

* For instance the accusations of 'Brno-centralism' with which Jaroslav Smolka ended his review (*Hudební rozhledy*, lviii/9, 2005, 37–8) of the (Brno) edition of Janáček's literary works (*LD*), in essence a complaint that there were not more Prague authors represented in the bibliography.

At a time when Janáček had composed a masterpiece that could reasonably be expected to be performed at the Prague National Theatre, Karel Kovařovic blocked the way. The damage was immense, both to Janáček's self-esteem and to the advancement of his career when he had just reached his fifties (see chap. 49). Nothing that Nejedlý did to Janáček was remotely as harmful. In his role as arbiter of repertory at the National Theatre, Kovařovic had a stranglehold on the only reasonable route forward available to Janáček at the time as an opera composer. But once *Jenůfa* had eventually been accepted in Prague, the avenues open to Janáček multiplied. Should Nejedlý or anyone else try to block his way in Prague he could bypass Prague since his cause could now be espoused in Vienna, Berlin and beyond. Furthermore, the effects of an ideologue are double-edged. Nejedlý's anti-Janáček stance had its supporters, but it would also encourage defenders. When Nejedlý weighed in against Janáček, others took up the composer's cause. And there were significant turncoats, such as Vladimír Helfert, who went on to write the first substantial Janáček biography.

As Janáček became older and more successful he could afford to ignore Nejedlý's attacks. He reacted violently to the long review of *Jenůfa* (see vol. ii: 1916b) and the *Fiddler's Child* (see vol. ii: 1917c). After that he simply shrugged. During his seventieth birthday celebrations 'two former adversaries, Dr Helfert and Dr Axman', he told Zdenka, had 'come to confess their sins. A third, Dr Nejedlý, still remained in limbo. He will come to confession when I'm eighty.'[5]

58

1909

Janáček spent only a couple of days in Brno after his visit to Hukvaldy. In a New Year card to Rektorys (who had been expecting him to come to Prague for Christmas, as he had in previous years),[1] he announced that he would be in Prague on 2 January for a few days. While in Prague Janáček attended a performance of Smetana's *Libuše* at the National Theatre on 3 January[2] and attempted unsuccessfully to visit Jan Branberger, as is clear from a letter he wrote to him on 6 January, after his return to Brno.[3] Janáček had two reasons for getting in touch. One was to find out how Kočí's plans for publishing *On the Overgrown Path* (VIII/17) were going. Branberger's reply explains why the trail had gone cold. 'As a result of various misunderstandings', Branberger wrote to Janáček, he had broken off all contacts with the firm of Kočí. Did Janáček wish the pieces should remain with the firm 'for possible use', or should they be returned? The publishing firm of František Urbánek, to whom Branberger had also shown the pieces, 'did not show much interest'.[4]

Janáček's second reason for writing to Branberger was to get an address for Jan Heřman:

He is said to play the piano well. We would invite him to the concert in celebration of L.N. Tolstoy.

He would play something from Russian [musical] literature – and then – (whether he likes it or not) – in my work for violin, cello and piano on Tolstoy's *Kreutzer Sonata*. Do you know him?

Would you fix that for us? The Tolstoy celebration is being arranged by the Russian Circle in Brno and the Club of the Friends of Art.[5]

This is the first mention in Janáček's correspondence of an important new development, the composition of his Piano Trio (x/22). Chamber music was a genre that Janáček had not touched since his student days thirty years earlier, and perhaps the obligatory composition of chamber works at Leipzig and Vienna had given him a distaste for the genre. The last chamber piece he had written was a Minuet and Scherzo for clarinet and piano (x/19) given at a Besední dům chamber concert in 1881. Significantly, it has not survived. In his memoir of Janáček, Suk recalls that he had a 'curious attitude' towards chamber music and was thus all the more struck by an unnamed French work that the Czech Quartet was playing with the Catalan pianist Blanche Selva. 'There's something in it. It is meat-eating', Suk records his saying,[6] which implies that Janáček's view of chamber music hitherto was that it was not sufficiently red-blooded for him. The fact that it was a genre traditionally considered 'abstract' could not have helped, although there were notable Czech examples, for instance by Smetana, of pro-grammatic chamber works. When Janáček did take the plunge, all of his chamber works were programmatically inspired.

Quite when he did this is, however, difficult to say. From his letter to Branberger of 6 January it is clear that he is talking about a finished work, thus written probably in 1908, but any more precise dating is impossible. A minuted action of the music division of the Club of the Friends of Art approved Janáček's suggestion to arrange a Tolstoy celebration jointly with the club's literary division and the Brno Russian Circle. 'As a musical number a work was suggested that Director Janáček had written and which is linked to Tolstoy's *Kreutzer Sonata*.' However, the minute is undated. Although, as Helfert sug-gests, it was written 'probably in December',[7] this lack of precision together with the fact that Janáček could merely have been offering a work in progress takes one no further in dating the composition other than stating that it was begun in 1908, perhaps set into motion by Tolstoy's eightieth birthday on 7 September 1908 (Western style). Why Janáček would have been attracted to Tolstoy's embittered little novella (of which he possessed the St Petersburg 1900 edition) is also impossible to answer. It tells of the murder by Pozdznyshev of his wife, having discovered her one night with her violinist lover – there had been discord between husband and wife from the time of their honey-moon. While the 'marital discord' may have resonated with Janáček, it should also be noted that the Janáčeks were in fact getting on better than had been the case for years. It is more likely that Janáček's attraction to the material came about from its references to music and aesthetics. In his search for operatic librettos Janáček was frequently drawn to works that deal with music, musicians and artists, and from Janáček's marginal markings in his copy of the novel it can be seen that such aspects in Tolstoy's novella had taken his fancy. The most substantial passage that he marked is the one occasion when Tolstoy's speaker holds forth on the effects of music:

'They played Beethoven's *Kreutzer Sonata*', he continued. 'Do you know the first Presto? You do?', he cried. 'Ugh, Ugh! It is a terrible thing, that sonata. [. . .] They say music exalts the soul. Nonsense, it is not true! It has an effect, an awful effect. [. . .] Music makes me forget myself, my real position; it transports me to some position not my own. Under the influence of music it seems to me that I feel what I do not really feel, that I understand what I do not understand, that I can do what I cannot do. [. . .] Music carries me immediately and directly into the mental condition in which the man was who composed it. My soul merges with his and together with him I pass from one condition into another.'

Although Branberger promptly sent a contact address for Jan Heřman (Janáček's putative pianist in the première),[8] Janáček received no reply[9] and began considering other possibilities. Ever-helpful, Rektorys proposed Ludmila Prokopová, 'the best graduate of the conservatory last year, for whom I can vouch', and suggested that Janáček send her the music at once and the conditions for performance. In the same letter he also advised Janáček to withdraw his manuscript of *On the Overgrown Path* from Kočí ('expected to go bankrupt') and urged him to send his reminiscence of Smetana ('which you told me about') as an article for *Dalibor*.[10] All these suggestions went down well: 'I'll write to Miss L. Prokopová. I want to send those piano pieces *On the Overgrown Path* to Mr Moj. Urbánek. Prepare him in some way – so that he also puts something more serious into print. The little pieces are easy.'[11] Even the Smetana reminiscences were written up and sent (see below).

Meanwhile Janáček's work on *Brouček* was moving ahead. Janke had sent off his libretto of Act 1 in mid-December 1908 and was awaiting a response. Janáček's letter has disappeared but its contents can be inferred from the disgruntled letter that Janke wrote to him on 22 January 1909.[12] There had been a failure of communication. By the time he had got in touch with Janke, Janáček had completed a rough draft of Act 1, made a revised version of it and copied out the words in a libretto, which was sent to Janke as the guide he had asked for. Unless Janáček intended rewriting every note of the sung portions, it is clear that what he needed from Janke was not a new libretto but merely verbal additions for passages where he had overrun the available words and written untexted voice parts. Such places were indicated in red pencil in the libretto he sent to Janke. Janke did a great deal more. He produced a completely new piece of work full of rhyming couplets in a breezy, drinking-chorus style. Not only was this redundant (and Janáček presumably made this clear in his lost letter to Janke) but Janáček was evidently not taken with it, underlining just a couple of passages and using only a single couplet.[13]

Janke's letter of 22 January also implies that Janáček had had a new plan for the work. What it was emerges from correspondence between the two only over the next couple of months (see below). From Janke's letter of 9 February[14] (again Janáček's letter that prompted it has disappeared) and from subsequent actions, one can infer that Janáček proposed continuing on his own, since Janke now professed himself far too busy to give much help. He would nevertheless look over what Janáček produced.

Any work on *Brouček*, however, was temporarily swept aside by demands from the Organ School. For its March choral concert Vach had chosen Gounod's oratorio, *Mors et vita* (1885). The chief soloist was to be the famous Prague National Theatre soprano Růžena Maturová (Dvořák's original Rusalka, among other roles), with whom Janáček had had friendly dealings for some years; the second volume of his *Moravian Folk Poetry in Song* (v/2) had been dedicated to her in the second edition (1908). However, as Janáček learnt from the conductor František Jílek (Maturová's husband), Kovařovic was making difficulties about releasing her for the one-night engagement[15] and a new soloist needed to be found. By the time Janáček had an inspiration – to make use of his new friend from Luhačovice, Marie Calma-Veselá – a new problem had arisen. Vach had fallen ill and was unable to rehearse and conduct the concert. Janáček would have to step into the breach.[16] Although Calma was more of a lieder singer than someone used to sailing over the large forces of chorus and orchestra, she agreed and by 11 February, a few weeks before the performance on 4 March, Janáček wrote to her with suggestions about rehearsals.[17]

No sooner had he written to invite Calma-Veselá than there was a hitch over the première of Janáček's Piano Trio. On 5 February Rektorys reported that Prokopová had returned the score to him saying that the work would need considerable rehearsal and that she would be unable to come to Brno for the several days needed. Should he now pass on the manuscript to Prokopová's recommendation, Emanuel Polák, an American in his sixth year at the Prague Conservatory?[18] Janáček's telegram said an emphatic 'no'[19] and later that day* he gave his reasons in a letter: 'It is just a sketch, perhaps when after some time I look through it again, thoughts will grow in another way. So don't give it to anybody. When I come to Prague I will take it away.'[20]

Bad news lay in store. Mojmír Urbánek was no more inclined than his father František to publish Janáček's *On the Overgrown Path*.[21] And in addition to the imminent Gounod concert Janáček found more responsibilities descending upon him. His friend František Mareš had stepped down from the chair of the Club of the Friends of Art in 1906, the tenures of his two successors were shortlived and there was a vacancy again. Janáček was proposed and after some consideration he agreed. On 22 February 1909, at the general meeting at the café 'Slavia', he was appointed chairman of the whole club (i.e. not just of the music section).[22]

Late February and early March were taken up with rehearsals for *Mors et vita*. Janáček invited Calma-Veselá to come on Sunday 28 February,[23] ahead of the two orchestral rehearsals on 1 and 2 March.[24] These could not have been easy since Janáček was having to drill an ad hoc orchestra assembled from students at the Organ School and the band of the Brno 8th Infantry Regiment. But the concert went off well enough; in his words to Rektorys, the success was 'grandiose'. Calma, Janáček went on, 'sang spiritually and beautifully. It's not a big voice, but fresh, light at the top and pleasant.'[25] The soloists included a young tenor from the Moravian Teachers' Choral Society, Stanislav Tauber (1878–1959), later to become a much-sought-after soloist in *Amarus* and *The Diary of One Who Disappeared*. But it was Janáček's performance as conductor – his last public appearance in this capacity – that caught the attention of the anonymous reviewer ('-v') in *Lidové noviny* (11 March 1909):

---

* 6 February 1909, as indicated by the postmark on the envelope rather than 6 March 1909, as Janáček erroneously wrote on the letter.

The old legend of his fame as a conductor was revived – would that such a memory would return more frequently! We have not experienced a performance so exactly balanced and rehearsed to the last detail and with, we could almost say, such a freedom of interpretation since the time that Janáček exchanged his baton for a composer's pen. The suggestive force of Janáček the conductor on the performers is legendary. [. . .] If Janáček had thrown himself only into conducting he would today have an international reputation, but he has devoted all his strength, his whole being, to Moravia, and what does he have for it? More ingratitude and slights than anyone else.[26]

Once Janáček had got the concert out of the way and written his thank-you note to Calma-Veselá[27] and his glowing account to Rektorys,[28] he returned on 8 March to the vexed question of *Brouček*. His letter to Janke, the first that has survived, enclosed 'a sketch of Act 1' with various suggestions of where Janke could make additions, put passages into verse, or add 'a few juicy two- or three-syllables terms of abuse'. It is also the first evidence of Janáček's new idea that had so alarmed his collaborator. Janáček did not merely add characters to fill out the action of Act 1 (this was what had upset his previous librettist, Karel Mašek) but now made these characters mirror the moon characters in Čech's novel, who thus became dreamlike counterparts of Brouček's acquaintances on earth. According to the cast list Janáček supplied in his letter to Janke, Brouček's tenant Mazal became the equivalent of the lunar painter Blankytný, Mazal's sweetheart Málinka was Blankytný's muse Etherea and so on.[29] Janke responded with a few tentative pencil suggestions,[30] none of which was incorporated into the musical setting.

Janáček's January visit to *Libuše* in Prague had given rise to a short article, *The Podskalí Case* (XV/195), which he published in the February issue of *Hlídka*. In it he described the workers in the Podskalí district of Prague loading up vessels to go through a path cut in the ice of the frozen Vltava. Janáček took down their cries with a number of speech melodies and described their varying emotions (grumpy, threatening, etc.). 'And now to the matter', Janáček announced, 'I want to say that I did not like the performance of *Libuše* at the Prague National Theatre on 3 January 1909.' He went on to state that the yodellings of Smetana's reapers in Act 2 of *Libuše*, in comparison with the diverse emotions of the Vltava workers, were all unconvincingly the same tune. 'Art cannot be unnatural', he concluded. For the first time Janáček was using ideas drawn from his study of speech melody to criticize the lack of realism in an opera. And, while he was about it, he then went on to castigate Smetana's nature music for orchestra, which he found inappropriately noisy: 'After all, the limes just *breathe* their scent, the winds *whisper* fairy tales.' Janáček had chosen his target unwisely. To attack Smetana at the time was heresy in many Czech circles and *Libuše*, the opera that had opened the National Theatre in 1881, and which had served thereafter for many solemn national occasions, was a particularly sacred cow. From this moment, perhaps, stems the general perception of Janáček as someone firmly in the anti-Smetana camp. In the highly politicized musical environment of Prague at the time, a lack of enthusiasm for Smetana could be dangerous for a composer who had not yet established himself.

The repercussions came soon. Rektorys reported on 17 March that Rudolf Reissig (the musical director of the Brno Beseda) had requested that *Dalibor* reprint Janáček's *Hlídka* article as a way of initiating a debate about it.[31] While an article in a Brno scholarly and clerical journal made only the gentlest of waves, its reprint in a popular national musical journal would have quite a different impact. Janáček saw Reissig's move as mischief-making,[32] which was more than possible. Although Reissig had had friendly relations with Janáček for many years (including visiting him in Hukvaldy, see chap. 36) and been on Janáček's staff as a violin teacher at the Organ School since 1904, they had fallen out over Reissig's unwillingness to participate in the Organ School concerts and Reissig had been dismissed. In the light of Janáček's choleric reaction,[33] Rektorys did not reprint the article.

'I already had everything set for a quick trip to Prague', Janáček wrote to Rektorys a few days later (19 March), still seething with irritation about Reissig, 'but the main reason was removed by phone.' This is the earliest of the very few references that Janáček made to the telephone. What the business was that he transacted is not stated or inferrable, nor do we know from where such a phone call might have been made: the Brno Organ School was not one of the few Brno subscribers at the time. At least Janáček appeared to be feeling more comfortable about *Brouček*: 'At last I have a *Brouček* libretto. I think it will be good', he concluded.[34] Two days later Janáček wrote to Janke apologizing for not seeing him in Prague, and passed on a few more ideas: 'In Acts 2 and 3 please note those occasions *so frequent in a dream*, where Brouček seems to recognize Mazal in Blankytný, Würfl in Čaroskvoucí, etc. Perhaps it will occur to you to add something.

Hardly does the idea occur to Brouček than it is always suitably suppressed.' Looking further ahead, Janáček even made a few suggestions for Act 4, the epilogue.[35] Janke did not respond and so joined the ranks of Janáček's discarded *Brouček* librettists.

On 2 April the première of Janáček's Piano Trio after Tolstoy's *Kreutzer Sonata* (X/22) took place in the 'Dvoranka' [small hall] of the Organ School. Two of Janáček's Organ School staff performed, the cellist Rudolf Pavlata and the hard-gained violin teacher and orchestral leader, Pavel Dědeček. After much negotiation the piano part was taken by Růžena Fialová from Prague (who had been involved with previous Organ School ventures). The Russian Circle's planned participation in the event for some reason evaporated but the literary section of the Club of the Friends of Art was still involved, hence a lecture by Dr Miloslav Hýsek[†] on Tolstoy as part of the event. Most appropriately, Dědeček and Fialová filled out the programme with a performance of Beethoven's Kreutzer Sonata for violin and piano.[36] In view of the later disappearance of Janáček's trio, it is particularly unfortunate that there were no press reports of the concert. Almost the only account there is, apart from Dědeček's hazy memories almost forty years later,[37] was Janáček's brief but upbeat assessment to Rektorys: 'I have finished working on and tidied up the trio, of which you perhaps still have the sketch. It was given on 3 [*recte* 2] April 1909 and left a deep impression.'[38] In view of its later disappearance, it should perhaps be noted that at this stage two versions of the Piano Trio existed in several copies: Janáček's 'sketch', returned to Rektorys by Prokopová on 5 February, and a parallel version that Janáček had retained in Brno and which he later 'finished' and 'tidied up' to produce the version played on 2 April.

With the trio concert out of the way Janáček now wrote up his brief reminiscence of seeing Smetana at a concert in 1874 (XV/193; see chap. 11), which had been long-promised to Rektorys for *Dalibor*; he sent it on 10 April.[39] Although both František Urbánek and his son Mojmír had turned down the opportunity of publishing Janáček's piano cycle *On the Overgrown Path*, Janáček had also offered *Maryčka Magdónova* to František Urbánek (seemingly in a letter of 6 February giving him a one-month deadline for considering the matter). The

[†]Dr Miloslav Hýsek (1885–1957), literary historian later known for his documentary work on Moravian writers.

success the Moravian Teachers had with the piece presumably made this appear a more viable proposition to Urbánek than the piano cycle and on 14 April he wrote to Janáček offering publication. Providing Bezruč made no demands for a royalty for reproducing the words, he would pay Janáček 50 K and give him three free copies of the publication.[40] Janáček's response was to offer Urbánek, for an additional 20 K, a further Bezruč chorus, *The 70,000* (IV/36), which at the time may have been no more than a new idea – there is no evidence of Janáček working on it until later in the year (see below). But Urbánek stuck to his original offer. Janáček mentioned the good news about *Maryčka* in his letter to Rektorys the next day, at the same time announcing his planned visit to the Vinohrady Theatre on Saturday 17 April to see Karel Weis's 'folk opera' *The Blacksmith of Lešetín*.[41]

Janáček's other concerns at the time may have put his activities as chair of the Moravian Folksong Working Party on the back burner. However a change of regime in Vienna (with Dr Wiener's taking over as head of the folksong project in Vienna) precipitated an anxious letter to Hostinský,[42] to which the latter responded with one of his typical, clear, soothing notes that made the changes sound all for the better: merely a formality: the elimination of bureaucracy; besides, Janáček had always had good dealings with Wiener, hadn't he?[43] Nevertheless the changes and Hostinský's response seem to have led Janáček to call a meeting of his working party on 2 June at the Organ School.[44] The new building, with its spacious rooms and its concert hall, was already turning out to be a godsend. Meetings such as this had hitherto had to take place at the Besední dům, but most of the club activities in which Janáček was involved (such as the Club of the Friends of Art and the Brno Russian Circle) could now conveniently make use of the new facilities that Janáček had at his disposal.

Janáček made one more trip to Prague, on 12 May, when he saw *The Bartered Bride* (conducted by Kovařovic). He was so irritated by the production that he scribbled comments in his programme – about the unnecessary people on stage for the intimate scenes, the 'disgrace' of the ballet, and so on. And there is an interesting observation at the end, which gives an insight into Janáček's attitude towards the relationship between stage sets and music in opera: 'Scenes can change how they want – it doesn't harm the music.'[45]

The summer was fast approaching. Zdenka went with her family for a few weeks to the spa of Bad Ischl near Salzburg. She was there by 7 June, when Janáček sent her a postcard.[46] Janáček himself was being sent for spa treatment to Trenčianské Teplice in Slovakia, as he reported to František Vesely on 13 June. Could Vesely, with his knowledge of spas, please advise him on Czech doctors and accommodation there?[47] Vesely's reply is not extant but Janáček did not go to Trenčianské Teplice. Instead he attempted a different sort of cure. Before then, however, there was more business to attend to. Another communication from Dr Wiener in Vienna led him to consult Hostinsky again, insisting that the Vienna central committee needed a Czech on it to fight for Czech matters: after all, Austrian 'yodelling songs' and Czech songs could not be more different.[48] In July Janáček added Františka Kyselková (1865–1951) to his folksong working party. She had been involved in the 1895 Ethnographic Exhibition and in 1906 had been taken on as one of Janáček's collectors, in which capacity she turned out to be one of his most productive workers, responsible for collecting some 4600 songs.[49] On 8 July František Urbánek wrote to Janáček about the progress of the publication of *Maryčka Magdónova*. He would be getting a proof soon, but where to send it during the holidays? Urbánek also responded, in a handwritten note at the bottom of the letter, to a suggestion from Janáček that his harmony manual (XV/151, which Urbánek had published in 1897) might come out again in his 'Smetana' series. If that were the case, Urbánek commented, the book would have to be much shorter and rewritten in a popular style for amateur musicians.[50] This idea got no further but Janáček did issue a new harmony book a few years later (see chap. 62).

There are several indications that Janáček seemed to be moving towards a crisis in his health and in his state of mind. In the reminiscences she gave to Robert Smetana, Zdenka reported: 'Janáček was not ill – on the contrary – he appeared very well – but he was very tired.'[51] In a letter he wrote to Marie Calma-Veselá on 9 July, Janáček described how run down he was, having had to take on extra work at the Organ School after the death of the composition teacher František Musil, the illness of the conductor Vach and the precipitate departure of Rudolf Reissig:

You won't believe how tired I am after this [school] year. It fell to me to do the work for a dead professor and for a sick one. Unbearable.

On Monday I leave for Dr Kuthan's sanatorium to sort myself out a bit.
I'll visit Luhačovice on my pilgrimage for folksongs – but later.
When I tell you I'm not capable of working now, well, you'll certainly
believe me.[52]

Dr Kuthan's 'nerve sanatorium' was situated in Tišnov, 30 km north
of Brno, in pleasantly wooded countryside. Janáček arrived on
Monday 12 July and the next day reported on his new surroundings to
Zdenka, now back in Vienna from Bad Ischl. 'So it's like this: water
treatment as in Luhačovice. But there are just about twenty men, therefore comfortable, and is repeated many times. [. . .] The food is good,
judging by yesterday and today. I have a large, light room with all
conveniences for 81 K a week.'[53] A few days later Janáček gave more
details of the water treatment and meals. He was sprayed at 7 a.m.
directly on the backbone. At nine there was a 'brush bath' when, with
the brush in the water, they rubbed the whole body. At three the lower
part of the body was sprinkled to stimulate the blood from the head
and neck. The massage was very good; much better than 'our woman'[‡]
in Brno. In between there were meals and snacks. Lunch, for instance,
consisted of soup, roast meat with potatoes and vegetables, cheese
salad with lemon (Janáček didn't care for it) and cake. Supper was at
seven with, for example, schnitzel with lentils, butter and cheese.
Altogether, Janáček summarized,

it is a proper water cure that cannot be criticized in any way. For the seriously
ill, usually kidney disease, lameness, one cannot think of anything better.
But – expensive! For four days I have paid 65 K 2 h. It is not more expensive
in Luhačovice – where in addition there is excellent water to drink and the
warm spa.[54]

What Janáček does not say is what he did on his own initiative
in Tišnov. 'Instead of giving himself a rest in the quiet of the Tišnov
forests', Zdenka reported, 'he let himself be drawn by the slopes of the
Tišnov hills and climbed them so relentlessly and determinedly that
during the three weeks of his Tišnov stay he lost at least ten kilos in
weight.'[55] This, on top of all Janáček's worries at the Organ School,
had severe medical complications for the rest of the year. Although
Zdenka records 'three weeks', Janáček seems to have been there for
only two if he stuck to his plan for just another week announced on

[‡] Antonie Koláčná; see chap. 63.

18 July.[56] And the loss of 'ten kilos' seems somehow unlikely if, despite all the walking, he was tucking into roast meats, schnitzels and cake.

Some time in August Janáček went as usual to Hukvaldy, from where he wrote a gossipy letter to Zdenka on the 14th. It was written to entertain his wife ('so you have something to read') and included news of Mrs Jandová and her daughter at the brewery, Mr Rakowitch (who had broken his leg at the thigh and had not been able to walk since January), a Mrs Tlustá scaring the animals with her 'shocking red', and Marie Janáčková, the widow of František, who was 'putting on weight', but was well, 'everything nicely arranged in a nice cottage'. The weather was good, and Janáček had found a corner for himself in the garden where he sunbathed after lunch. And there was good news from the ministry, which had approved the proposal for all types of schools to help in the collection of folksongs.[57] Janáček himself began to go collecting again. On 19 and 20 August he spent two days collecting with Jan Juřiček in Prostřední Bečva, near Rožnov,[58] sending a greeting to Zdenka from Rožnov on the second day.[59] Then disaster struck in Vienna. Zdenka had a 'terrible attack of gallstones', an affliction from which she had suffered for the past fourteen years:

Despite the fact that I had the doctor immediately, the attack wouldn't let up. I had to have an operation. According to the law we had to have the permission of my husband. We sent him a telegram. Meanwhile they took me into a sanatorium, where I was to be operated on the next day. Leoš came at once. He was broken-hearted when he failed to catch me at my parents' house and he cried inconsolably there. When I was safely over the operation, he behaved very tenderly towards me. He remained another four days in the hotel, having meals with my parents and going round Vienna with my brother. Only when he saw that I was out of danger did he leave for Hukvaldy.[60]

All this happened between 20 August (when Janáček was in Rožnov) and 25 August, when he sent a card from Brno announcing that he had arrived safely.[61] He went on to Hukvaldy: 'There', in Zdenka's words, 'he had some heart problems, perhaps as a result of losing weight so suddenly.'[62] At this point Janáček took himself off to the spa of Teplice nad Bečvou, near Hranice. This brief venture (he was at the spa for two days at the most) is difficult to explain. It was presumably on the recommendation of friends (Mareš, Tebich) who were there at the time (see below). But if he had needed medical attention, why did he not go to a hospital? Is it a coincidence that in July he was advised to go to another Teplice, in Slovakia? Whatever the reason, the spa in Teplice could do nothing for him and sent him home. Before he went, he wrote (on 28 August) a hastily scrawled letter to Zdenka (still at the 'Hera' Sanatorium in Vienna), reporting on his problems: his heart had 'begun to play tricks in the day and at night', both missing beats and pounding as though it wanted to crash through his stomach and chest.

Today I had the chief consultant Dr Boháč examine me. He's at the local general hospital and also the spa doctor. Well, thank God, there's no heart fault.

One valve is a little fatter so more effort is needed for it to open (rheumatism crawled there from my leg – in my opinion.) Several warm baths he said, will fix it.

I asked whether here in Teplice or in Luhačovice. I'll go wherever he sends me.

Here of course it's not pleasant. When it begins to rain, there's nowhere to go other than the room. As far as guests are concerned there are just a few Jews, all unknown to me.

I'm glad that it's not worse than I'd thought!

This afternoon I'll leave for Hukvaldy. I'm already terribly dirty.[63]

Two days later Janáček wrote to Zdenka, this time from Hukvaldy. He had had a terrible journey from Teplice, having encountered both a 'mad man and a dead man' on the way – 'all too much for my nerves – this year my nerves have had no rest.' But, he went on, he was glad to hear the good news from Zdenka's brother, presumably about her continued improvement, that awaited him in Hukvaldy.[64] And from now on he wrote daily to Zdenka: on 31 August he told her that his heart trouble was over ('probably just over-excitement'); he was now sleeping well and had no pain.[65] Two days later problems had recurred during the nights: 'Always at night, towards 3 a.m., I get heart trouble, but now it's bearable. During the day of course I don't notice it.' And he did seem much better generally, taking advantage of the 'nice weather' by going for walks, though failing to find any mushrooms. He was intending to go to Luhačovice, for just a week, from Saturday 4 September, for the 'warm spa' that had been prescribed in Teplice.[66]

From Luhačovice Janáček wrote to Zdenka that he was out of danger. 'With calm everything will be put right. Kuthan['s nerve sanatorium] was not for me. I take a warm bath day after day.' And he had had a lucky escape. Typhoid fever had broken out at Teplice: 'The owner himself, [Antonín] Tebich, lies unconscious. I was told by

Mareš, who has just come from there. I've been invited today to Dr Veselý, where there will be many people. Even the Mrštík brothers have arrived.'[67] Although Janáček had only a week in Luhačovice this year, he had excellent company, with many of his friends there. On 8 September a group of them were guests of the Veselýs for Marie Calma's twenty-eighth birthday, and in the afternoon the company (which included Elgart, Kunc, Mareš and one of the Mrštíks) took a trip to Bojkovice, from where they sent a group card to Zdenka.[68] The day before, Janáček sent his longest Luhačovice letter that season to Zdenka:

I wrote to you still in the sanatorium; I imagine they'll send [the letter] on to you. Mářa [Stejskalová] is arriving in Brno on the 8th. I want to leave on the 11th [Saturday] from here. At the most I'd add on Sunday and Monday.

My heart gets calmer; I've slept now for a second night – however I'm still taking some sort of pills. [. . .] It was an overtaxed heart.

If only perhaps after Tišnov I had just sat around! But why didn't he tell me that, I would have done so.

I thought that you'd already arrive on the 12th. I know that you won't to remain in Vienna in vain. All the doctors here proclaim that it is one of the trickiest operations. What holidays we've had! God grant that next year we take a break at the seaside. [. . .]

I don't know what else I should write. I'm like a squeezed lemon. So how much will it cost – your precious stones? I'm curious, do let me know![69]

This is the first reference to any plan for taking a seaside holiday (Janáček's wish was granted in 1912). The bill for Zdenka's 'precious stones', which awaited Janáček on his return to Brno (594 K 56 h), was 'shameless [. . .] but worth it, health above everything', as he wrote on 12 September to Zdenka, now out of the sanatorium and convalescing in Vienna at her parents' house. As for Janáček, he needed calm for his heart (a heart rate of 120, 'with gaps') but although 'the treatment in Luhačovice was good, to lie in complete calm in the room is silly – better at home'. He had now organized the timetable for the new school year in such a way that he would always have the afternoons free. Mářa had put everything in order. His case, sent from Hukvaldy, had burst on the journey but everything had arrived in good order.[70]

Although Janáček seemed to be recovering, he was still concerned about his state of health, as is evident from the frequent references to it in his almost daily letters to Zdenka. On 15 September, for instance, he wrote about new treatment that he was having from his cousin Dr Dressler (see chap. 42) and it is clear that he had had quite a fright:

So now without fear. I didn't have a temperature – no pain anywhere or even a headache – it's just that the heart was beating and beating too much. I heard it all over my body – the whole person just one heart! On the advice of Dressler I put an ice pack on my heart twice a day. I summoned the old woman[§] and was massaged round the heart. Today from midnight it grew quieter and remains quiet. Even the Luhačovice doctor said that after a week's rest it would calm down. Well you know – those thoughts! I would have endured the stations of the cross –. [. . .]
I am now able to think again during the calm work on [folk] songs.
I feared that I would never finish the work.[71]

In this letter Janáček also resolved that he 'would not get angry' in the Organ School, but was worried how the student registration would go. In fact his worries began even sooner with the sudden resignation of his piano teacher, the legendary Marie Kuhlová, who had been with the Organ School since 1892, but was finding the demands of her family, children and her own private pupils too much for her.[72] Rektorys, ignored during all of Janáček's travails during the summer, was asked to find a male graduate of the Prague Conservatory to take over Kuhlová's job of eighteen hours' teaching a week at 2000 K a year.[73]

Janáček had been hoping to go and fetch Zdenka from Vienna, but his health and the overwhelming problems at the Organ School necessitated alternative arrangements, as he wrote on 19 September: 'Just come: get your brother to accompany you.' 'Vach and Mrs Kuhlová don't want to teach', he went on. The state grant had not yet been paid and the school was 'living on debts'.[74]

Rektorys had originally proposed the excellent but elusive Jan Heřman as a new piano teacher for the Organ School but by 25 September he had to conclude that his search had been in vain: there was no sign of any suitable male graduate. If Janáček would take a woman, then there was Ludmila Prokopová, Rektorys's original suggestion for pianist in Janáček's Trio.[75] Janáček seized on this possibility. They had had a woman piano teacher in the past, so why not again? Rektorys was to pass on information about conditions

---

[§] Antonie Koláčná again; see above and chap. 63.

(including taking part in Janáček's new concert series beginning in the autumn – the six 'sonata hours' concerts each year, paid extra) and opportunities for further teaching and remuneration. Janáček had a committee meeting on Friday 1 October, when the matter would be discussed. He would send a telegram with the outcome and would like the young lady to come to Brno the next day. His letter concluded:

You can have no notion how jangled my nerves have been.

Just think: last year's affair with the violin teacher [Rudolf Reissig], the death of Musil, the illness of Vach. Add to all this the teaching that I had to take over, to conduct the examinations, put on Gounod's *Mors et vita* – and on top of all this I had to compose *Mr Brouček's Excursion*, [just] the first act, four times![76]

It is quite a surprise to find any reference to Janáček's current operatic project against the background of difficulties and ill-health. The 'four times', however, is an exaggeration unless Janáček was counting the eleven pages he wrote before receiving Mašek's libretto as a separate version. He had composed an early version without the Sacristan and his daughter Málinka. Presumably he counted his revision of this as another version. Apart from a drinking-chorus and a few lines where Brouček is mocked, Mašek's libretto (sent 17 May 1908) had virtually no effect on the course of the opera. Neither did Janke's. It was during his correspondence with Janke (winter 1908–9) that Janáček himself filled out his opera with extra characters and extra action and produced a new libretto, to which he composed his third version of Act 1, perhaps complete by the time he wrote to Rektorys on 26 September 1909.[77]

One good thing that came out of the Janáčeks' bad summer was a reappraisal of their living conditions. As Zdenka recalled, the doctors advised Janáček that he should not walk too much. But the new Organ School was now even further from the Janáčeks' flat in Staré Brno and involved a walk of at least half an hour. Janáček was boycotting those trams that, under German ownership, carried only German place names (see chap. 6). Nothing was left for him but to hire a cab or move house.[78] Moving house was something that Zdenka was keen on. Although she liked their flat, it lacked electricity and running water. Various locations for new accommodation were explored but in the end Janáček found a better solution, as Zdenka explained:

In the grounds of the newly acquired building of the Organ School there were stables. They were now completely redundant. Leoš came up with the idea that it would be good to demolish them and in their place build a garden house in which the director of the school would live, paying rent for the house. The committee of the association approved Leoš's suggestion and construction began at once.[79]

There was some debate about the exact location, and in the end the house was set away from the main street by a small garden (to minimize traffic noise) and the entrance was made through the courtyard of the Organ School, from what is now Smetanova ulice. The new prospect energized the whole household. Mářa Stejskalová recalls their deliberations:

The master wanted above all a warm, light and quiet study, the mistress wanted a salon with a bay-window and a veranda at the entrance of the house, and I spoke up for a comfortable kitchen through which outside visitors wouldn't have to pass. And to the plan the master and the mistress added a little room behind the kitchen that would be mine. All three of us looked forward to the electric light and to a bathroom.[80]

The little bungalow that was built was tiny: three main rooms (salon, study and bedroom, plus Mářa's smaller room), which was one fewer than the Staré Brno flat. Building began before the end of November and was complete by the middle of 1910, by which time the original budget of 14,000 K had gone up to 20,000 K.[81]

The other good news at that time was the publication, by 30 September of *Maryčka Magdónova*. The printed version carried a dedication to Vach, a tribute to his successful espousal of this most difficult work (the manuscript dedication to the Plzeň 'Smetana', see chap. 55, had presumably been forgotten). Soon after, on 5 October, the Moravian Teachers performed the chorus again at Prostějov (where they had given the tentative première in April 1908) and, according to Janáček's pupil Ezechiel Ambros, it had 'a great and complete success. Of the whole programme it was liked the most.'[82] Another excitement was the phonograph that had been granted Janáček for his folksong research after representations in parliament. In an undated letter to Bakešová (with whom correspondence had almost dried up), Janáček announced that it was on its way from Berlin and that he would come to record 'your bagpiper'. Otherwise, he said, 'I'm not at all in a good mood.'[83]

When Janáček wrote to Rektorys at the end of the month he was more revealing about his state of mind: 'How are you? I'm in a bad way. The doctor has prescribed complete quiet – mental also. Where to get it? [. . .] I'd like to pop over to Prague but it's necessary to wait for my nerves and heart to calm down.'[84] The practical reasons for writing, however, were both to apprise Rektorys of his article on rhythm in folksong (XV/196), which was coming out in *Hlídka* (he would send it when it completed its serial publication), and to ask him to find Smetana's programme for his String Quartet *From my Life*, needed for a joint Organ School/Club of the Friends of Art concert on 14 November.

In his reply Rektorys tactfully mentioned that Janáček would find the required programme in Rektorys's book on Smetana, sent a month earlier (despite Janáček's assurances that he would get reading immediately, he clearly had not done so). Rektorys also took the opportunity of asking how Prokopová was getting on and whether Janáček was satisfied. Rektorys had, single-handed, solved Janáček's piano-teacher crisis. Ludmila Prokopová had been almost instantly installed at the Organ School exactly when needed and went on the next year to play the piano part in the première of Janáček's *Fairy Tale* (VII/5) but, unless letters have disappeared, Rektorys had no written thanks for his efforts.[85]

A week after the concert at the Organ School (at which the Smetana Quartet was played),[86] the Moravian Teachers under Vach sang *Maryčka Magdónova* in Brno for the second time. It was a triumph. *Lidové noviny* reported that

Maryčka Magdónova had such an enormous and immediate effect on the audience that it had to be repeated. It's a long time since we can remember the enthusiasm that its performance elicited. The unfeigned joyful triumph was a sign and confirmation of how much Moravians honour and respect their greatest living composer.[87]

When on 8 December Janáček thanked Rektorys for his congratulatory telegram ('an uncommon success'), he added: 'If only *The 70,000* (which I have finished) would also seize their hearts.'[88] We know from his correspondence with Urbánek earlier in the year that Janáček had contemplated (or even sketched) a setting of his third and final Bezruč chorus (IV/36) but it comes as something of a surprise that against a year full of health problems, organizational worries and generally low spirits he had gone on to complete this visionary and innovative chorus (see chap. 54). Of course one only has his word that he had 'finished' it by then, but it could not have been far off since the authorized copy of the work is dated 10 January 1910.

As Janáček had mentioned in his letter to Bakešová, a phonograph was on its way from Berlin. Ordered on 8 October, it arrived in Brno on 29 October.[89] It was put to use almost immediately by Františka Kyselková, who had discovered a woman folksinger, Eva Gabel, from Velká Slatina in Slovakia, then working as a labourer in Modřice near Brno. From Kyselková's notations of Gabel, Janáček took six songs, and by 10 December had written his characteristic piano accompaniments for them, the *Six Folksongs Sung by Eva Gabel* (V/9). For four of these songs the original Gabel recordings still survive and, for all the scratchy distance of this century-old recording, they provide a unique opportunity to compare Janáček's version with the folk original.[90] Full of enthusiasm for the new technology, Janáček wrote to Marie Calma:

A new theme. Could I invite you to us on Wednesday? I have six new folksongs harmonized – after [playing the original version on] the gramophone, which is difficult to transport, we would also sing through them.

If you agree, kindly let me know where I would find [the pianist] Dr Javůrka in order to invite him. I would await you and your husband towards 3.[91]

The Eva Gabel song harmonizations were not quite Janáček's last compositions for the year. On Christmas Eve *Lidové noviny* published a feuilleton by Janáček entitled *Early Morning Lights* (XV/194), which included a charming and gentle piano arrangement of the well-known Czech Christmas carol 'Narodil se Kristus Pán' ['Christ the Lord is born'] (VIII/20). He used this to illustrate the singing of the Sládek children, heard from outside their Hukvaldy cottage when he arrived for Christmas and looked in through the window at the Christmas tree all aglow with candles – the 'early morning lights'. The feuilleton, one of Janáček's most engaging, is a jumble of his reminiscences of the Sládek family over the years. Surprisingly (as he was generally banned from Hukvaldy), Čert the dog is described as accompanying Janáček on this visit, his growl immortalized with a 'speech melody'. A later memory alludes to the fact that that Sládek's son was not prospering in his studies:

Mrs Sládková was again lighting candle after candle but more than once she would wipe away a tear with her apron. This year Lidka stumbled again during the first verse of the carol: 'A little son is born to us, we will send him to you.'

She couldn't get to the end – for quiet grief.

The 'gentleman' [i.e. Janáček] didn't arrive either; he just sent a letter saying that '[their] son would not be a [university] student.'

Never did they put out the candles so quickly on the Christmas tree.

It was quiet and dark in the cottage when Sládek returned from the forests. The gun, thrown into a corner of the room, made a strange rattle as if to say: 'What the devil did we do to deserve this?' (xv/194)

At about the same time as writing this article, which tapped into some of Janáček's deepest and usually submerged feelings, he offered his piano cycle *On the Overgrown Path* for publication to the Brno publisher Koči. The reply came just after Christmas and was positive, though Koči asked if Janáček could wait a little while.[92] By then, however, the iron had cooled: Janáček waited until 1911 before giving it to Koči.

59

Pan-Slavism III

In 1903 Janáček submitted *Jenůfa* to Karel Kovařovic in Prague and it was turned down. The brevity and tone of the rejection (see chap. 44) did not encourage enquiry about the reasons, but nevertheless Janáček sought them from other quarters and referred to them when he wrote to Kovařovic after the successful Brno première of the opera the next year. It had been refused in Prague, Janáček declared in his letter, because of 'the Moravian character of the work' and the 'naturalism of the melody'. 'Naturalism' connected with Janáček's ideas on speech melody and was not something he wished to change: 'it has not been without effect or comprehension', he commented. But, he went on, to consider the work 'Moravian' was 'mistaken'.[1] And, just in case this accusation could be used against him in the future, he made sure his next operas and other programmatic works were set elsewhere.

In the year following his completion of *Jenůfa*, Janáček contemplated three ideas for a new opera in addition to the one that became *Fate*: Merhaut's novel *The Angelic Sonata* (xi/6, considered in June 1903), the Mrštík brothers' play *Maryša* (xi/7, considered after the première of *Jenůfa* in January 1904) and Preissová's play *The Farm Mistress* (xi/8) (considered in April 1904). The *Angelic Sonata* preceded *Fate*; the other two projects came after he had begun it. That Janáček thought of setting *The Farm Mistress* (with its familiar author and setting in Slovácko) just after he had finished Act 1 of *Fate* suggests a momentary lack of confidence in his rather strange new venture, though one that he evidently soon overcame.

Two of these plans were non-starters. *Maryša* – for which the evidence as a prospective Janáček opera is only hearsay – would never have got any further since the Mrštík brother were opposed to all operatic settings of their play.[2] And although Janáček went to the trouble of applying to the author for permission to set *The Farm Mistress* (and was granted it on 29 April 1904),[3] had he set the play he would have been intruding on a text that had already been set by Foerster as *Eva* and first performed in 1899. The popularity of Foerster's *Eva* (by far his most successful opera) might well have stood in the way of an opera by Janáček on the same text. Janáček turned away from setting *The Farm Mistress*, and presumably *Maryša* too (set in the same ethnographic region), because he would be repeating the successful formula of *Jenůfa*.[4] This is thoroughly in keeping with his cravings for 'new atmosphere' (for instance in the stage setting of the *Brouček* epilogue, see vol. ii: 1916a) and with the carefully differentiated projects of all his later operas. But another reason for abandoning all these subjects, together with *The Angelic Sonata*, was that they were all self-evidently 'Moravian'.

Fate, of course, is also 'Moravian', at least in the Luhačovice setting of its first act. But in the original draft libretto of the next act the action migrated to more exotic climes (the Croatian Riviera) and the final act could have taken place anywhere. It could also be argued that the depiction of the smart set in Luhačovice had very little to do with that town's local Moravian roots. Although folkloristic manifestations were occasionally on display in Luhačovice,[5] they do not feature in Janáček's *Fate*, and the inserted songs are not folkloristic, as they had been in its predecessor *Jenůfa*; the whole atmosphere is urban, not rural. Charpentier's Parisian-based *Louise* is the model, not Janáček's Moravian village drama *Jenůfa* (chap. 46).

Of all these unrealized operatic plans, that for *The Angelic Sonata* was the most developed. Janáček made a visit in June 1903 to the setting of its pivotal scene, the pilgrimage place of Hostýn hill in central Moravia, and sketched a scenario for a possible opera in his diary for 1902–3 (see chap. 52). The author of the novel Josef Merhaut, chief editor of the newspaper *Moravská orlice* from 1891, was one of the leading representatives of Czech Naturalism, with its emphasis on the importance of environment and heredity. Janáček had known Merhaut since the 1890s (Merhaut wrote an enthusiastic review of *The Beginning of a Romance* in *Moravská orlice*)[6] and was perhaps taken by the novel's detailed descriptions of Brno and the hostile attitude towards its Germanization (rather than its intrinsic aesthetic quality: the novel is today more interesting as social record than for its literary merit).[7]

While Janáček seems quite happy to have cast aside any narrowly 'Moravian' aspects of future work (by abandoning projects such as *The Angelic Sonata, Maryša* and *The Farm Mistress*) this did not mean that he had rejected the Pan-Slavonic roots of which such Moravian subjects were a part. The 'Moravian' aspects of Janáček's compositional work (outside the folk arrangements) were perhaps more a matter of polemics and presentation than something to be defended at all costs. Janáček's cantata, first performed in Brno in 1901 as the *Moravian Our Father*, was given in revised form in Prague in 1906: one of the revisions involved scratching out the word 'Moravian' from the title page so that the piece was renamed *Our Father*. Janáček had further cause to distance himself from things Moravian that year after reading Nejedlý's strictures on 'Moravian separatism' provoked by Nešvera's opera *Radhošt'* (see chap. 57). Soon afterwards he withdrew an article submitted to Rektorys's *Dalibor* under the title *Moravsky* [The Moravian way], resubmitting a revised version the next year as *Thoughts along the Way* (xv/186).

Moravian texts and locales continue to feature in Janáček's choral works, for instance the Bezruč choruses from 1906, but elsewhere Janáček began to move into territory that was Pan-Slavonic without being narrowly Moravian. The way forward seemed to be either going Russian (as in his next instrumental works) or going Bohemian (as in *Brouček*, with its Bohemian author Svatopluk Čech and its Prague setting). Both paths were prepared by two further, abortive operatic projects.

That Janáček even contemplated an operatic setting of Ladislav Stroupežnický's one-act *The Mintmaster's Wife* (1885) seems today puzzlingly out of character.* The play is set in the early seventeenth century, the time of the last flowering of Czech culture before the defeat of the Czechs in 1620 at the Battle of the White Mountain. The location is the rich mining town of Kutná Hora, an important centre for Czech coinage of the time. With minor exceptions its dozen characters are all from the privileged Czech bourgeois and aristocratic classes shortly before their extinction (or Germanization) by the Habsburgs; the characters' occupations, based around the mint, are denoted by specialized words that today need expert glossing.

---

* Janáček had seen the play in Prague in 1891, when it was presented as part of a double bill with the première of his ballet *Rákoš Rákoczy* (I/2).

Although one learns in the first scene about a miner trapped in the mine, the chief concern of the piece is amorous intrigue, the compromising of the local mintmaster's wife by a Falstaffian antihero, and its warm-hearted resolution. Wordy and mock-archaic, it has nothing of the earthy realism of Stroupežnický's most famous play *Our Swaggerers*. Although frequently performed up to 1939 (and characterized as late as 1941 as 'one of the most successful of our historical comedies'),[8] it is hard to see what attraction it had for Janáček. Nevertheless the fact that Janáček was considering one of the leading Prague-based dramatists is significant, and the project, which he embarked on during his Christmas break of 1906, got considerably further than the unrealized projects that cluster around the early months of *Fate*; nine pages of sketches (a single scene) survive. As it was, *The Mintmaster's Wife* was itself soon crowded out by a new operatic project the next month: *Anna Karenina* (IX/4). According to the dates on Janáček's sketches, this occupied him for a fortnight (5 to 19 January 1907). Not only are there more pages of sketches (twenty survive), but the act of extracting the text from the novel would have cost him much more effort than simply opening his copy of *The Mintmaster's Wife* and having a go at the first scene. Again the project seems misconceived. Although several composers have completed operas based on Tolstoy's novel, the condensation of such a long story into an operatic libretto would have been an exceptionally difficult task. Furthermore Janáček was attempting it in the original Russian, which in view of his imperfect (if enthusiastic) command of the language was unwise. He soon gave up. But just as *The Mintmaster's Wife* can be seen as a turning-point and possible stepping-stone (for instance to Janáček's comic opera *Brouček*), *Anna Karenina* also points the way ahead: to his next instrumental work, and to the Russian orientation of many of his later works.

Less than two years after he toyed with *Anna Karenina* Janáček returned to Tolstoy as the inspiration for his Piano Trio (X/22) after Tolstoy's novella *The Kreutzer Sonata*. And a year later this was followed by Janáček's next chamber work, the *Fairy Tale* for cello and piano (VII/5), again inspired by Russian literature, in this case Zhukovsky's epic poem *The Tale of Tsar Berendyey*. In 1915 Janáček turned to Gogol's tale *Taras Bulba* as the inspiration for his 'Slavonic rhapsody' for orchestra (see vol. ii: 1915). The only other new instrumental works of this period are the piano suite *In the Mists* (1912), the symphonic poem *The Fiddler's Child* (1913) and the Violin Sonata (begun 1914). In other words, of the six instrumental works that Janáček wrote between 1908 and 1915, half have Russian origins. Of the others, one – *The Fiddler's Child* inspired by Svatopluk Čech's poem – has Czech (but not Moravian) origins, one has an unexplained programmatic title (*In the Mists*) and the Violin Sonata alone has no programme but was said to be prompted by Russian successes at the beginning of the First World War (see vol. ii: 1914b).

As for the Russian-inspired works, all three of their authors were commemorated in events initiated by the Brno Russian Circle: the joint Zhukovsky and Gogol celebration in 1902 and Tolstoy's belated eightieth-birthday celebration in 1909. But apart from the fact that Janáček may have come across all of these works in the Russian Circle (it is known that he read *Taras Bulba* there in 1905),[9] there is an even more interesting connection between them. The plots of all three involve a family murder: a husband killing his wife (as in *The Kreutzer Sonata*) or a father killing his son. In Zhukovsky's poem the tsar finds himself having to murder his infant son as a bargain he made to kill the first creature he encounters on his return, although (since this is a fairy tale) there is a happy ending and no infanticide takes place. In *Taras Bulba* the chief character kills his younger son for taking up with a Polish woman.

It is striking that Janáček was drawn not merely to these Russian works but to works with this common 'family' thread. From today's vantage point Tolstoy's *Kreutzer Sonata* and Gogol's *Taras Bulba* are painful to read. For all its genius and intensity, Tolstoy's novella needs careful defence if it not to be read simply as a misogynist rant. Gogol's tale has none of the quirky humour of his short stories but is instead a work of unmoderated Russian chauvinism directed against another Slav nation. If Janáček was drawn to such unpleasant works, one hopes that something other than their overt message spoke to him. The parallels between the Janáčeks' difficult marriage and Tolstoy's jaundiced view of marriage reflected in his novella were not lost on Zdenka, although she denied the connection.[10] Family matters seem to cast long shadows at that time. The Piano Trio was written the same year as the last pieces that Janáček added to *On the Overgrown Path* (VIII/17), all clearly associated with Olga's death. There is an unnerving parallel between the tsar of the *Fairy Tale*, who goes out into the world to fight battles and comes back pledged to kill his infant son, and Janáček, who sets forth to conquer Prague with his operas while haunted by the memory of his two dead children.

That Janáček was attracted more by the personal issues than the shared Russian provenance is supported by the lack of any attempt to sound Russian, unlike his earlier Pan-Slavonic works such as *Hospodine!* (III/5) or his Russian pastiche for the 1900 Slavonic Beseda (VI/12). When Jan Kunc ventured to suggest that the last movement of the *Fairy Tale* was based on a Russian theme he was roundly reprimanded (see chap. 60). There are pastiches in *Taras Bulba* but these mock polonaises and mazurkas characterize, in a very superficial way, the Polish enemy not the Russians. The circle of Janáček's Russian instrumental works was closed when in 1923 he adapted his Piano Trio to become the String Quartet no. 1. Little is known about the process since the material for the trio has disappeared, but it is interesting that the subtitle 'after Tolstoy's *Kreutzer Sonata*' was retained.

As was suggested in chap. 35, looking east released something within Janáček: in his works from *Hospodine!* onwards it is possible to hear Janáček's authentic voice. In the early 1900s this Slavonic orientation was aimed at producing specifically Moravian works, resulting in the masterpieces *Jenůfa* (1904) and the Bezruč choruses (from 1906). By then Janáček had begun to retreat from such a narrow focus, a focus that appeared to upset his chances of making his way as an opera composer outside Brno. Hence his return to more general Slavonic inspiration. But influencing all of this was the need for autobiographical stimuli, something that could speak to Janáček at a very basic level and release unique aspects of his compositional identity. It is this distinctive amalgam – Pan-Slavonic and personalized – that characterizes the programmatic instrumental works of the period.

60

1910

On 19 January 1910 Otakar Hostinský died at the age of sixty-three. Although different in temperament and in their attitudes towards many aspects of Czech culture, Janáček's and Hostinský's dealings as the chairs of, respectively, the Moravian and Bohemian folksong working parties had been remarkably close and co-operative over the past five years. Janáček expressed his reaction to Rektorys in a letter the next day: 'I am sorry about Dr Hostinský; he was an honest worker. I remember him gladly and with respect. Those with great spirit depart, one after the other.' Janáček was perhaps thinking of the deaths of his mentors Dvořák (in 1904; see chap. 22) and Bartoš (in 1906; see chap. 53). That Hostinský seems to have been placed in this company is corroborated by the fact that Janáček kept Hostinský's letters separately in a folder marked 'special letters'.[1] 'I would gladly go to his funeral – but I prefer to remember everything that bound me to him when there will be quiet at his grave.' The letter went on to thank Rektorys for the 'nice review of *Maryčka Magdónova*' (another performance in Prague by the Moravian Teachers' Choral Society on 28 December) and to regret that this winter there had been no time for his usual trip to Prague: 'mountains of work lie in my way'. In addition to the concerts arranged in Brno at the beginning of February, the 'mountains' included trying to arrange for the two candidates for the Organ School's long contemplated professorship in organ (see chap. 56) to play publicly in Prague[2]

Meanwhile Janáček had completed another chamber composition. The autograph of his *Fairy Tale* for cello and piano (VII/5) is dated '10 February 1910', i.e. a little more than a year after the completion of his Piano Trio. At this stage the piece consisted of three movements. It is not known what prompted it but as a programmatic chamber work based on Russian literature it followed the path of the trio: perhaps Janáček had been taken by the sound of the cello in the trio, and wished to explore it further. Janáček's own programme, based on the epic poem *The Tale of Tsar Berendyey* by Zhukovsky, survives on a single sheet, perhaps originally attached to one of the manuscript copies of the score.* It reads as follows:

Once upon a time there lived Tsar Berendyey, who had a beard down to his knees. He had been married for three years and lived with his wife in perfect harmony; but God still had not given them any children, which grieved the tsar terribly. One day the tsar felt the need to inspect his kingdom. He bade farewell to his consort and for eight months he was on his travels.[3]

A later version, not necessarily by Janáček, clarifying the action of individual movements, was printed in the programme for a performance in Vyškov in 1912. Here the first movement was said to depict the tsar's 'calm in the shadow of grief and his unsatisfied longing for a family', the second movement his 'doubt and hope' and the third his departure on his travels.[4]

It took Rektorys uncharacteristically long to respond to Janáček's request about how to arrange for the organists to perform in Prague and, equally uncharacteristically, he had no suggestions. In the end the organists did not perform there. Rektorys had, he wrote on 16 February, been beset by 'all sorts of worries at home, in the editorial office and at work that destroy all my appetite for work'. His chief reasons for eventually writing were to get Janáček to arrange for Růžena Maturová (who had just been dismissed by Kovařovic from the Prague National Theatre) to sing in Brno, and to alert Janáček to Karel Moor's completion of his operetta *The Excursion of Mr Brouček to the Moon*. How had negotiations over this turned out in the end?[5]

When he replied two days later Janáček seemed almost unconcerned about Moor's operetta, and merely 'sorry' for Mrs Maturová, though he did comment on Kovařovic ('an evil spirit'): 'Yes, he's a conductor, but to lead such an institution to good and to the development of Czech music drama, there is something lacking – in his brain!' As for *Brouček*,

---

* As Bohumír Štědroň suggested in his preface to the Hudební matice edition (Prague, 1949).

I have not progressed further than Act 1.
Why?
Last year's drudgery almost cost me my health.
In the holidays I got heart trouble.
Now it's quietened down again, but I no longer look happily on the world!
I've just written a sort of *Fairy Tale* for piano and cello.
And now I'll make a start on Act 2 of *Brouček*.
Tregler [one of the organist candidates] played here, and well.
Don't joke with your health, it's the one thing above all.[6]

Nine days later Janáček wrote to Rektorys again. With the pianist Ludmila Prokopová installed at the Organ School and the cellist (Rudolf Pavlata) from last year's trio equally at his disposal, Janáček had no trouble finding forces to perform his new piece:

I invite you and your wife to us on 13 March. Be guests at my house.
That day we have a concert given by the second candidate for the position of professor [of organ] at the master school [see chap. 21]. At the same time Beethoven's B flat Piano Trio will be played and perhaps my *Fairy Tale* for cello and piano.
It's a Sunday, so you'll have time. Come on Saturday. Do you agree?[7]

Rektorys had to decline. With his wife broken by the death of her father, it was not a good time, he wrote,[8] so the performance on 13 March went ahead without him. It was the final concert of the six in the 1909–10 'sonata hours' series at the Organ School (see chap. 21). In addition to Janáček's *Fairy Tale* and Beethoven's 'Archduke' Trio op. 97, Jan Rangl (the second of the two contenders for the organ post) played organ works by Bach and Mendelssohn.[9] According to the reviews, Janáček introduced the *Fairy Tale* himself with a few words, saying that the composition was unfinished and that the three movements to be played represented just part of a work in progress.[10] In his review in *Lidové noviny* (17 March 1910) Jan Kunc stated that the third movement 'was composed on a Russian theme', a comment that he had to withdraw the next day after receiving Janáček's protest:

It upset me in reviews of *Jenůfa* when people wrote, wrongly, that I used music by others in it!
Now you write again about Russian speech [*mluva*] in the *Fairy Tale*. There is none there – and no foreign music at all!
You know that one must defend one's own.[11]

A week later Janáček had another première, at least a Brno one, of *Jealousy*, the prelude to *Jenůfa* (VI/10), which had been given first in Prague by František Neumann in 1906. Here it was played at the Second Symphonic Matinée Concert of the National Theatre, conducted by the cello teacher of the Organ School (and soloist in the *Fairy Tale*), Rudolf Pavlata. Surprising as it may seem, it looks as if Janáček may have been absent. A wreath had been purchased by the Brno Theatre Družstvo to present to him on stage. But according to a respectful though pained letter to him, the wreath had to be sent to Janáček's house afterwards.[12] Was the applause not enough to warrant Janáček's taking a bow; or was he showing his feelings about the absence of *Jenůfa* from the Brno stage by refusing to take a bow or even boycotting the concert?

On 18 March, in response to repeated requests for *Dalibor* articles, Janáček sent an article to Rektorys called *The Weight of Real-Life Motifs* (XV/197). This, as its subtitle ('sketches from lectures') acknowledged, was a compilation of introductory notes to the public concerts of the Organ School originally printed in the programmes.[13] The second year (1909–10) of the 'sonata hours' had been properly organized with six advertised and themed concerts at which five of Beethoven six piano trios were played by Dědeček, Pavlata and Prokopová: since writing his own piano trio Janáček had obviously got a taste for the genre. In his introductory notes for the first concert Janáček described the Adagio of Beethoven's Trio op. 1 no. 1 as having the 'emotional depth of song'; in its melody we can hear 'real-life' ['reální'] motifs. In his notes for the third concert (he wrote none for the second) he took the thought further: 'The most natural real-life motifs are *in speech melodies*.' Janáček was back on his hobby horse. By means of speech melodies 'national elements' come into the work that do not get in the way of a composer's individuality. Thereafter Janáček abandoned any pretence at saying something about the works at hand (apart from acknowledging the Russian folksong in op. 70 no. 2) and his notes continued as a serialized meditation on the relationship between speech melodies and instrumental music. Whereas speech melodies 'are so expressive that through them we grasp subjects and concepts', instrumental motifs 'grow out of a narrow field' and are 'metaphorical, not realistic'. Instrumental music has consequently got rather too far from its source (the 'real-life motifs'), and needs an infusion of real-life experience to get it back on course. 'Pluck these petals from a song and use them as the focal point of a composition. Strew them out as the form requires [. . .] a bedding consists of rose petals. Every tone that falls into its aroma exhales its fragrance. We must water instrumental motifs with Czechness – to take them to their source.'[14] Windy though some of this stuff is, it is fascinating to see Janáček grappling as a theorist with the problems of instrumental music at the very moment he was grappling as a composer with chamber works, not least the *Fairy Tale*.

'I know that it's all run together so that the odd sentence would need to be expanded on the page', Janáček commented, when offering his meditations to Rektorys.[15] Even Rektorys was unsure how to handle the article and sent it to Foerster for an opinion. On 28 March Foerster's reaction was passed on to Janáček for his consideration together with an invitation to expand it along the lines Foerster suggested (chiefly by supplying music examples).[16] The finished article, dispatched on 31 March, did nothing of the sort but, in an attempt to pin down Janáček's concept of the 'scale of emotion', merely threw in some more 'real-life motifs', speech melodies that he had taken down more than a decade earlier from Vrchlický's speech in Brno on 15 May 1898. Vrchlický began his speech in B flat major but, as he got more excited, he 'modulated' to D major.[17]

In his letter passing on Foerster's comments, Rektorys reported on further *Brouček* matters: 'In *Lumír* [a leading literary journal] I saw Holý's ballet *The Moon*, i.e. that material you told me about some time ago as an independent concept based on *The Excursion of Mr Brouček to the Moon*. You certainly didn't acquire Holý to make another lot of changes in this case, did you?[18] Holý had been one of Janáček's most emphatic non-librettists, turning down the invitation promptly and robustly ('I don't like the material and I have no inclination to do a libretto'; see chap. 56). Nevertheless it seems that Holý's contacts with Janáček were greater than surviving correspondence suggests. When Janáček responded to Rektorys's note he asked in which number of *Lumír* Holý's *The Moon* had come out (i.e. Janáček had not seen the publication) and then went on to characterize – entirely accurately – the character of its verse ('Holý wrote something other than *Brouček* – he wanted to flood me with a sea of quantitative "feet" – and even has the nerve to publish it!'). This can only mean that Janáček had seen it already in manuscript. What is interesting about Holý's *The Moon* is that it may have given Janáček the idea of linking the earth and moon characters (see chap. 58). Its chief idea is that the publican's daughter Bětuška is transformed into the moon-being Luneta during Brouček's brief sojourn on the moon – a flight of fantasy induced by his nearly drowning in a pond in which he sees a reflection of the full moon and apostrophizes on the better life up there.[19] Another fact that emerges from Janáček's letter to Rektorys (29 March) is that the circle of potential librettists was even wider than generally thought. In addition to Mašek ('for a whole year – [he] didn't have a single idea'), there were the Mrštík brothers and Elgart Sokol (all refused), Holý, an unidentified 'lady' and finally Dr Janke. 'I am going to stick to Svatopluk Čech's *Brouček* as faithfully as possible – just let all these other poets of ours leave me in peace. Everyone is buried in the mist of a narrow horizon and can never reach the sun of a new idea.'[20]

Of course it was Mašek's decision to stick to Čech 'as faithfully as possible' that had caused the rumpus in the first place. The net result of Janáček's decision to abandon further attempts to get a librettist determined the nature of the libretto for both Acts 2 and 3. His first libretto for Act 2 (written on a huge, folded sheet of wrapping paper) when compared with pp. 34–96 of his copy of the novel reveals that Janáček added nothing new: almost every word can be traced back to Čech, except for the earth-moon parallels and the operatic compression of the end of the act into a trio. The motivation here is a little different. It is Etherea's 'eloping' with Mr Brouček to the Cathedral of All Arts, hotly pursued by her lover Blankytný and father Lunobor, which brings the act to a conclusion rather than Blankytný's escorting Mr Brouček to the cathedral for a cultural tour.[21]

'A campaign is being waged against my person', Janáček wrote to Rektorys on 10 April. He had sent a letter to Hubert Doležil who in the fourth number of *Hudební revue* that year had published an article celebrating fifty years of the Brno Beseda.[22] Until then he might have regarded Doležil as a doughty defender: in his roundup of musical news for Moravia and Silesia in the February issue of *Hudební revue* in 1909, Doležil had lamented the 'unfavourable' and undeserved fate of Janáček's two operas – *Jenůfa*, fallen out of the repertory in Brno, and *Fate*, not yet produced by the Vinohrady Theatre in Prague.[23] Although Doležil described Janáček as the 'second big name' (i.e. after Křížkovský) in the history of the society, responsible for initiating its concert activities and raising its standards, he also stressed how, owing to Janáček, Brno had adopted a 'Dvořák cult'. Nothing to do, Doležil asserted, with Dvořák's foreign successes but more with Janáček's personal views 'on the key questions in Czech music at the time'. The Dvořák cult, built up 'artificially and without the composer's [i.e. Dvořák's] knowledge', was 'insincere' and revealed an 'anti-Smetana position'. This was firmly rebutted in Janáček's letter to Doležil, quoted in his letter to Rektorys:

You write a falsehood here; not only a falsehood but you besmirch my relationship to Dvořák with an indication of falsehood and lack of sincerity.

It is quite unjust to suppose that I was prejudiced against Smetana.

I have not taken the least part in those battles. The cultivation of Dvořák was incidental; every new work of his – apart from the operas – was suitable for [our] concert programmes.

Smetana, he went on, 'belongs to the theatre, where I had no authority, the second [i.e. Dvořák] to the concert platform, where I did my duty [. . .]. I have a different opinion of Smetana as a theatre composer. I am not afraid of holding to my opinion and speaking it directly. Malice is unknown to me.'[24]

Like it or not, Janáček was being sucked into the Dvořák-Smetana debates that ravaged Czech musical society in the years following Dvořák's death; the repercussions of this rift continued to be felt throughout much of the twentieth century in strangely repoliticized guises (see chap. 57). It is perfectly true, as Rektorys pointed out in a footnote to Janáček's letter,[25] that not much Smetana was played in Brno up to this time, though to imply (as Doležil did) that it was all Janáček's fault, and based on personal animosity, was an unpleasant and unfounded allegation and one with which Janáček rightly took issue.

Though placed in an awkward position since he belonged firmly to the Smetana camp, Rektorys, with all his usual decency, put *Dalibor* at Janáček's disposal. He would print Janáček's letter to Doležil, he said, and suggested that a Janáček pupil with journalistic talent could promote Janáček's thoughts on the matter: 'I would gladly give him space for this in *Dalibor*. Don't underrate such journalistic support. Today's art cannot do without it.' Janáček might even wish to 'take up the pen regularly' himself.[26] Meanwhile, Janáček had simmered down to such an extent that in reply he reduced his public letter to Doležil to a single statement: 'Leoš Janáček adds that Dvořák's works were given for their artistic value without any guile, i.e. without any animosity against B. Smetana.' 'That should be enough', Janáček commented to Rektorys, 'for with Mr Doležil it is not possible to speak about music. He has no musical education.'[27]

Ironically, while there was all this talk in Prague of a 'Dvořák cult' in Brno, Janáček's most recent successor as conductor at the Brno Beseda, Rudolf Reissig, was happily indulging in a 'Novák cult' in Brno. The climax of this was the première of Novák's cantata *The Storm*, specially commissioned for the Jubilee Concert on 17 April 1910 to celebrate the Beseda's fifty years of existence. The concert, which included Dvořák's Psalm no. 149, was a huge success. It was extensively reviewed and Novák's new work was warmly welcomed even by the Smetana lobby in Prague, despite Novák's being a former Dvořák pupil and thus not part of Nejedlý's golden succession (Smetana–Fibich–Foerster–Ostrčil).[28] Janáček's verdict was reported to be rather more negative,[29] partly perhaps sour grapes but also a clear-headed reaction to a work that for all its orchestral virtuosity has not stood the test of time. One can feel sympathy for Janáček at this juncture. Not only were neither of his two most recent operas being performed, but the chief concert-giving agency in Brno was devoting all its efforts to promoting Novák and had commissioned its jubilee cantata from him (in Prague) rather than from the older Janáček actually resident in Brno. And there was bad news on the one hopeful avenue of the last couple of years; the Moravian Teachers had begun rehearsing Janáček's latest Bezruč chorus, *The 70,000*, and had found it beyond their powers. Janáček sat in on a rehearsal and then withdrew his piece for revision.[30]

'I'd like to come to Prague for the [Whitsun] holidays', Janáček wrote to Rektorys on 7 May. 'Will you be in Prague? I want to relax a little; after all, it was some pestering! Who is now the chair of the folksong commission – after Dr Hostinský? Perhaps *Elektra* and *Quo vadis?* may be in repertory? I look forward to seeing you.'[31]

Janáček had seen Strauss's *Elektra* in 1906 and it is significant that he wanted to see it again, now produced in Czech at the Prague National Theatre. Rektorys wrote back that he could not recommend *Quo vadis?*. 'It would be a wasted evening for you if magnificent staging alone is not enough for you.'[32] It was not only Rektorys who dismissed Jean Nouguès's five-act opera *Quo vadis?*, first given in Nice in 1909. Nouguès's conventional and epigonic style has few defenders today though, as Richard Langham Smith points out, the composer was remarkably successful at getting his works performed, with over eight thousand performances in his lifetime.[33] Despite Rektorys's strictures, Janáček attended the Vinohrady Theatre's production of Nouguès's opera[34] (probably on 13 or 16 May) and was so enthusiastic about the work that he planned – though failed – to have excerpts performed later in the year at the Organ School.[35] Sienkiewicz's novel (1896) was the source of both Nouguès's opera and the later Hollywood epic, and Janáček's enthusiasm for this 'sensational and effective *verismo* opera' has been a source of embarrassment to high-minded Czech commentators ever since. Jan Racek, for instance, explains Janáček's lapse by his 'evidently' seeing the persecution of Christians in Nero's Rome as a 'symbol of the suppressed Slavonic nations, above all the Poles and Czechs'.[36] On Sunday 15 May Janáček went to an unspecified exhibition, visited the ailing (but recovering) Joza Janáčková in a sanatorium[37] and continued that evening to attend a production of Schiller's drama *Wallenstein* at the National Theatre. The evening before, Saturday 14 May, as Janáček announced to Zdenka, after *Elektra* he would be going to the 'Vikárka' pub,[38] a rare indication of his thoughts turning back to his unfinished opera.

On 27 May Zdeněk Nejedlý gave the last of his university extension lectures on Czech opera after Smetana at the Národní dům in Vinohrady. It included a short section entitled 'The problem of Moravian opera'. In the audience was one of Janáček's Moravian supporters, the cellist Antonín Váňa, who managed to take down some of the lecture in shorthand and sent it to Janáček the next day. In his lecture, as reported by Váňa, Nejedlý drew attention to the burgeoning musical life in Moravia but 'at the same time the view has appeared that Moravia needs its own [type of] opera'. This should be resisted: 'nations are coming together more and more' (for instance the north and south Germans). 'Moravian separatism must disappear and will disappear.' *Jenůfa* he regarded as an example of Moravian separatism. 'It is known', he commented, 'that Janáček was an opponent of Smetana', espoused the imitation of folksongs and now the principle of the imitation of speech – a formalist and 'purely photographic' method. 'The whole of Janáček's theory rests on a bad theory about the origin of folksongs that cannot stand up to scientific scrutiny. It is an untenable mistake.' As an example, Nejedlý played six bars from Act 1 (from p. 16 of the 1908 piano-vocal score) 'at least twice too slow'.

I don't know whether, esteemed Mr Director, you will be grateful for this; perhaps I cause you unnecessary annoyance. But I doubt that you would have got from anywhere else at least the few sentences that I've managed to take down in shorthand in case you decide to react to Dr Nejedlý's account.[39]

Janáček did 'react' to Dr Nejedlý's lecture but needed Váňa's short-hand notes only as corroborative evidence. It seems strange that Váňa had not noticed that Janáček himself was in the audience, taking down not only some of Nejedlý's words, but also his speech melodies. Perhaps Janáček, as a late arrival, was lurking at the back and after what he heard made a quick getaway. He sent his immediate reaction, while still in Prague, in the briefest of postcards to Rektorys: 'It was a string of impertinence and lack of knowledge.'[40] When he got back to Brno he elaborated further: 'I was in Prague for Dr Nejedlý's lecture. [. . .] Believe me that in [all] my life I was never more vexed than with what that gentleman awards me. The manner that he chose is his affair; but *what* he says [!]. I am answering him.'[41]

And answer him he did, in an article published in July and August 1910 in *Hlídka* entitled *Whitsun 1910 in Prague* (xv/198). It begins innocently enough with a description of Janáček's river trip on the Vltava during Whitsun weekend. Then there are the sights and sounds of Prague, all brought to life (as in the boat trip) with speech melodies: a worker with a hoist, the swish of silk clothes in the fashionable Celetná ulice (a simple octave jump for this 'instrumental motif'), a child wailing from his pram while his grandmother is distracted, an unctuous shop assistant suggesting that he might post Janáček's purchase of a large vocal score, a little girl running after her hat, clutching her doll. Janáček moves deftly on to the Vinohrady district (and in fact to his Prague trip two weeks after Whitsun). When his eyes have grown accustomed to the light in the hall he sees against the coloured wall a 'little white cloud'. Janáček took a while to under-stand the word 'un-Smetana-ish' pronounced by the 'little white cloud' in a voice that suggests water vapour rather than flesh and blood. The voice is beautifully measured – 'demigods speak like this'. 'I have found myself probably at the shrine of art and science. Oh, that I don't miss a single word!' And so it is with deep irony that Janáček characterizes

Nejedlý's manner and message. At first the 'little white cloud' is heard handing down lofty judgements on Kovařovic, whose eclecticism is his 'least sin'; the French influence provides charm, though he has doubts about *The Dogheads*. *The Grandmother* is a poor topic for an opera (how do you make an old lady sing?). But having questioned Kovařovic as a composer, the 'white cloud' goes on to commend him as a conductor – 'quite without competition'. Then it is on to Moor and Czech operetta ('nothing to do with art') and finally (in the second instalment of Janáček's article, published the next month) Moravian opera. Here the speech melodies come thick and fast: 'reject it', 'it must disappear', '*Jenůfa*, a work of oldfashioned manner', 'moving towards formalism', relying on 'bad theory', 'songs lead to curious ends', 'it is the photographic method of composition'. After that the 'white cloud' advances to the piano and with 'evident distaste' peers into a vocal score to play a few bars. Janáček describes his shame and his anger. How dare anyone publicly reproduce on a bad piano excerpts from operas, and instead of singing simply shout out the words without pitches? It is only at this stage that Janáček reveals the speaker, the place and the date. The rest of the article is devoted to an account of Nejedlý's commentary on Smetana (from his book on Smetana's operas) and the dearth of real musical comment there. Janáček's final shot is an imaginative scene of the 'white cloud' running into trouble in his ascent into heaven. Janáček will put him into *The Excursion of Mr Brouček to the Moon* (complete with speech melodies) as an example of Conceitedness and Ignorance (Janáček's capitals). If Nejedlý read any of this, it certainly did not deter him. The following year he published his book *Czech Modern Opera after Smetana*, based on his 1910 university lectures and the public lecture on 27 May, his comments on Janáček unmodified.

On 1 June Rektorys wrote to Janáček suggesting that he would visit him in Brno. His purpose was to take up a long-standing invitation but also to collect from Janáček all the letters that Dvořák had written him. Rektorys would copy them out while on holiday (for publication in a planned Dvořák memorial volume) and then return them to Janáček on the way back.[42] Janáček responded the next day in his letter commenting on the Nejedlý lecture. 'I'm looking forward to seeing you; we'll wait for you at the station. Only on that same day we're moving.'[43] In other words Rektorys had chosen the most inconvenient time possible for a visit. Rektorys acknowledged this, writing that he would change his plans: the last thing he and his family wanted to do was to trouble Janáček on such a day.[44]

Before the big move there was yet another excitement, a stormy meeting of the Brno Družstvo on 29 June at which the non-performance of *Jenůfa* was raised. Janáček was there, but left early and the chief discussion took place after his departure. The journalist Láďa Kožušníček reported to Janáček what happened next:

Yesterday, after your departure from the Besední dům, Mr Kunc asked why *Jenůfa* was not performed in Brno. Prof. Žlábek [for the Družstvo] replied that it was mainly because you yourself apparently didn't want it, and that allegedly the singers – whom the performance committee cannot order – are reluctant to sing it. [. . .] Mr Kunc remarked that you didn't want to have *Jenůfa* in Brno only under Hrazdira, who he said had performed it wretchedly. Hrazdira, however, writes to me that you and even Chvála (!) had greatly praised him after the performance, and that you were content with his performance.[45]

On 30 June *Lidové noviny* printed a somewhat cautious account of the matter, and Janáček wrote immediately to Kunc:

Thank you for the question [i.e. that Kunc had raised]. It is good that I went away, I would have been embarrassed.

If Prof. Žlábek and Dr Rudiš answered as in today's *Lidové noviny*, they did not speak the truth.

It is already the fourth year that the director wants to give *Jenůfa* – and it doesn't happen. The above-mentioned gentlemen know why.[46]

And there were further repercussions. Cyril Metoděj Hrazdira had left Brno in 1907 but evidently continued to read *Lidové noviny*. From Split (in Dalmatia) on 4 July he wrote a hurt letter to Janáček:

At the last general assembly of the Družstvo of the National Theatre Mr Kunc said publicly that you withdrew *Jenůfa* from the repertory because it was performed 'in a Hrazdira fashion'. As far as I know the withdrawal of this opera from the repertory was connected with the non-performance of your second opera *Fate* and I ask you kindly to tell me what is true in Mr Kunc's demeaning statement.

If Mr Kunc's explanation is correct and was conveyed with your consent, there was already enough time after my departure for the 'Hrazdira fashion' of performance to be exchanged for a better one.

I studied *Jenůfa* under your direction and conducted it according to your intentions; if all did not turn out according to my wishes this is the fault of other circumstances, mainly during the directorship of the infamous Frýda and company.[47]

Jenůfa had languished unperformed in Brno since 9 October 1906. Janáček's new version would of course have needed rehearsal and restudying, and after Hrazdira's departure in early 1907 there was no conductor with the energy and determination to take this on. The allegations about Janáček's dissatisfaction with Hrazdira are not corroborated elsewhere. Indeed Janáček showed every sign of having been pleased with his interpretation and in his revision incorporated all of Hrazdira's suggestions for tightening up the work. Janáček's temporary withdrawal of the music (see chap. 56) had presumably done him no favours with the management, but a major factor in the opera's non-performance seems to have been the 'reluctance of the singers' (who in 1907 had precipitated Hrazdira's sudden departure). This was confirmed by František Lacina, who had been director of the theatre at the time of the two performances in the 1904–5 season, and who replaced Frýda in 1909. Janáček had evidently written to Lacina for clarification, and Lacina responded on 5 July saying that they did not have a Jenůfa and that one singer had left the company rather than sing in Fibich's *The Tempest* and Janáček's *Jenůfa*.[48] This uncomfortable airing of differences did at least highlight the scandal and had the salutary effect that *Jenůfa*, despite the hostility of the singers, returned to the Brno repertory in the next season (see chap. 62).

Janáček may have thought (in his letter to Rektorys of 2 June) that they were moving on Friday 1 July, but according to Zdenka's later account the move happened the next day. By 10 June Janáček had given notice on the old flat although, three weeks before the move, things were far from ready: there was no heating, and the rooms had not been painted.[49] But, after much hard work on Zdenka's and Mářa's parts, the move went well enough. At first Čert disliked the new premises and found his way back to the flat in Staré Brno. However he soon settled down and became 'master of the veranda' and 'an excellent guard dog.'[50]

Once everything was in order, the Janáčeks took their holidays. Janáček himself went to Teplice for more treatment. His visit there is confirmed by a couple of postcards to Zdenka, one postmarked 18 July and saying briefly that there would be 'two cures: water and boredom'.[51] Exceptionally, Zdenka went to Hukvaldy to stay with the widowed Marie Janáčková in the cottage that František had bought. After a while Janáček joined them. It was not a happy time, Zdenka explained in her memoirs. Apart from Marie, who may have felt isolated in Hukvaldy, Janáček's sister Josefa was also unhappy. It is rather surprising that her marriage lasted as long as it did (see chap. 29), but by 1910 it was showing strains as Josefa approached seventy. According to Zdenka, her husband had been unfaithful and Josefa was in the process of leaving him, though they were officially divorced only in 1919. Zdenka found the atmosphere hard to take and went off to her parents in Vienna.[52]

During the summer there was a student performance of Janáček's Piano Trio (x/22) in Boskovice, a small town in Moravia some 30 km north of Brno. It was arranged by Antonín Váňa, the young cellist who earlier that year had sent Janáček an account of Nejedlý's lecture in Prague. On 28 July Váňa wrote to Janáček asking for a brief account of the 'contents' of the trio, which would be played in Boskovice on 14 August.[53] Evidently he had already received a set of parts and Janáček's permission. Two days after the event, Váňa wrote again to report on the trio's 'great success'.[54] This is the last attested performance of the work, now lost, though four years later Váňa made two attempts to borrow the parts again (see chap. 66).

Meanwhile much more dramatic events were taking place in Brno. While Zdenka was in Vienna and Janáček in Hukvaldy, Máňa Stejskalová was left in charge of the new house. In previous years all three members of the household went their separate ways during the summer holidays in the knowledge that a caretaker would keep an eye on the flat. Perhaps it was the novelty of the new house that made the Janáčeks feel that someone ought to take care of security when they were away, although the Organ School had it own resident caretaker, Karel Simandl. He lived on the ground floor with his family: his wife Emilie, two young sons (then aged four and three) and one-year-old daughter Emilie (Milenka). According to Stejskalová, Milenka had 'something wrong with her leg, and the doctor said she would be lame'. On 15 August, a public holiday (the Assumption of the Virgin Mary), Simandl went on a visit with the older son, leaving his wife at home with the two younger children. And, as Stejskalová reported:

Simandlová took advantage of the fact that there was no one in the school and, in the first-floor classroom behind the choir-rehearsal room, she killed Milenka, poisoning her with gas. It was already evening, I was just writing a letter to [my relations in] Matějov when she came to me and told me about it. I called one of my friends from the neighbourhood and rushed off for the police. They took Milenka to the mortuary in the hospital for an autopsy, Simandlová and her son were arrested and taken off to Cejl [i.e. the prison in Cejl street]. The next day Simandl arrived back and took the boy home, his wife remaining in jail. [. . .] Suddenly on 17 August for no reason the master arrived back. He said he had become restless in Hukvaldy, something told him that he was needed at the Organ School. [. . .] He hadn't trusted Simandlová before and had dealt sharply with her, but when he heard what she'd done, he didn't say a single word against her. Then at the trial Dr [Hynek] Bulín defended her so well that she was released.[55]

A week later Janáček was back in Hukvaldy.[56] He did not go to Luhačovice this year, the first year he had missed since 1903. He had, of course, already spent some time in Teplice on a cure and it may have been the expense that this and the new house incurred that meant he could not afford his usual stay. He returned to Brno probably on 3 September, in order to go the next day with Hynek Bím to the village of Moravec to record songs with the phonograph.[57] Soon after there was a visit to Prague to discuss the state of *Das Volkslied in Österreich* with Hostinský's successor, J.V. Dušek. Janáček told Dušek that he was getting nowhere with Dr Wiener (the chairman of *Das Volkslied in Österreich*) and he thought that Prague and Brno should act together. With Dušek's consent he would go to Vienna to see Wiener and protest at the way things were going.[58]

Rektorys had not managed to drop in on Janáček at a convenient time to pick up the Dvořák letters and, back from his summer holidays, wrote to Janáček on 28 September with 'a raft of requests': for a photograph of Janáček, the continuation (in proof) of Janáček's article about the Nejedlý lecture, and a contribution to the Dvořák memorial volume that he was editing the next year: 'As a contemporary, admirer and pioneer of the master – you can't be missing. And so I ask you to decide on a Dvořák theme yourself that you could give me for the volume.' And then there were the Dvořák letters. Could Janáček send them? 'I will copy them out and return them again to you in a perfect state as soon as possible.' And with the hope that he would see Janáček in Prague soon, he reported on what might be expected at the National Theatre: 'They are promising *Don Giovanni*, [Auber's] *Domino noir* and *Boris Godunov*' and 'a delightful little miniature', Wolf-Ferrari's *Il segreto di Susanna*.[59]

Janáček responded at once. Together with the requested picture, and the continuation of his article in brush proof, he was sending all twenty-nine of Dvořák's letters as a present. But it was the idea of a substantial article on Dvořák that had fired his imagination:

One work ought to be done.

His [Dvořák's] motivic expression is the richest, a real treasure trove of musical thoughts.

Establish its dictionary.

Organize it perhaps according to the initial interval.

In this the composer's richness and proficiency can be seen.

It will be sizable book; but it's necessary.

One values books according to new thoughts; compositions are no different.[60]

Rektorys was delighted with his unexpected cache of Dvořák letters. For the Dvořák article he wanted a 'firm promise'. The deadline was the beginning of April and the book was expected to be out in May.[61] Rektorys was an experienced editor and journalist so one has to take this astonishing schedule seriously. As it happened, however, the Dvořák memorial volume was dead in the water. Rektorys's relations with Urbánek were soon to be terminated (see below) and Dvořák's widow turned out to be uncooperative.

Janáček had meanwhile been in touch with Dr Wiener about *Das Volkslied in Österreich* and on 7 October visited him in Vienna. Back in Brno the next day he reported to Dušek in a letter about what he thought he had achieved. Wiener had agreed to the formation of a second, Slavonic executive subcommittee and this plan would be put to the central committee the next month. Before then it was important for Prague and Brno to come to an agreement. A joint meeting of both committees – not necessarily all members – should be called. Perhaps it could be in Brno, since the Moravians had 'more finished materials'.[62] And indeed in the five years so far, work had gone surprisingly well. Vysloužil records that by this stage 8000 songs had been collected from 231 locations by twenty-one collectors. Of these, 3500 had already been classified, so that a considerable part of the collection was ready for press.[63]

Meanwhile Janáček was still turning over in his mind his plan for a 'Dvořák theme dictionary', and working out how it could be done. Did Rektorys have at hand all of Dvořák's chamber, symphonic and other orchestral compositions? Janáček could get his students to do preliminary work by writing out the incipits on cards. However, this letter had a dramatic postscript: 'Now I learn you are out of *Dalibor*.'[64]

The ostensible reason for Rektorys's resignation of the editorship of *Dalibor* after seven years was given in a footnote to his edition of his correspondence with Janáček. He had refused to publish a review ('as an artistic work') of Nedbal's operetta *Die keusche Barbara*, which had been given in Czech at the Vinohrady Theatre on 14 September 1910, a year ahead of its Viennese première. Urbánek, the publisher both of *Dalibor* and of Nedbal, had understandably taken offence, and so the two parted company.[65] Despite high-minded Czech distaste for operetta, it looks as if this was just a pretext. Earlier in the year Rektorys had confessed to Janáček that he was beset with worries at *Dalibor*;[66] on 4 November a brand-new Czech music periodical started appearing in Prague called *Smetana* (the second and longer-lasting periodical with this name). Although in another footnote Rektorys declares modestly that *Smetana* was under the 'leadership of Prof. Zdeněk Nejedlý', the 'publisher and responsible editor' (as declared on the title page) was Rektorys himself. One does not invent a periodical of this size in a couple of weeks; contents, contributors and finance all need forward planning. For many months Rektorys, Nejedlý and other members of the editorial board (who included Janáček's current *bête noire* Hubert Doležil, and his later biographer Vladimír Helfert) would have been talking about the new project while Rektorys continued to edit *Dalibor*.

When Rektorys found time to write to Janáček, all he could say was that he promised an explanation about his departure from *Dalibor* by word of mouth: it was 'too long a story' to write about. The reason for his silence was that he was overworked with the founding of *Smetana*. 'At last we have a new journal that will at least be independent … Completely!'[67] Joyous though this news may have been for Rektorys (who served as publisher, editor or both for all twenty-seven years of the journal's existence), it was not good news for Janáček or for their continued friendship. *Smetana* pursued an aggressively ideological stance, one, as its title suggests, that upheld the pro-Smetana line and that was not afraid to speak ill of other, less-favoured composers, notably Dvořák. Although Janáček's correspondence with Rektorys continued for another nine years, there was much less of it, and their former ease of tone stiffened. Both men liked and respected one another but they were firmly on different sides of a deepening ideological divide. Rektorys, in particular, was aware of this and embarrassed by the conflict of loyalties. Matters were not helped either by a minor failure of communication. Janáček went to Prague on 31 October to see Dušek on folksong matters[68] and the next day attended Kovařovic's *The Dogheads* at the National Theatre, conducted by the composer,[69] but failed to meet up with Rektorys. The fact that it took him almost six weeks to tell him underlines their growing rift:

You certainly didn't get my note. I was in Prague and waited in vain for you.
What should I say about *Smetana*!
You know what I think of Dr Nejedlý and now on top of all that there is Prof. Doležil on the editorial board as a Fibich expert! [...]
[Fibich's] beauty has such an effect on people – that he feels that he also understands it! [...] To read about music – it's now sickening.

In between Janáček's sarcastic allusion to Doležil and the last sentence of the letter is a curious, fascinating but not easily intelligible paragraph that translates roughly as follows:

Through the rippling of the rhythm, harmonic conception changes its colour so many times – and these gentlemen see it only in its earliest stage of how a composer presses it into his own style, into his own picture – a picture not found in Musorgsky – and confuse it with the Smetana style, equally unclear and misty.[70]

It is infuriating that something quite so unclear should be Janáček's first attested reference to Musorgsky, a composer with whom many have seen the greatest compositional kinship. The seemingly random mention was perhaps occasioned by a short report in the first number of *Smetana*, enthusiastically looking forward to the National Theatre première of Musorgsky's *Boris Godunov*: 'Boris Godunov in particular has so much that is new in it, it overflows with such richly surprising and outright daring thoughts that in it we recognize a great spirit which anticipated the modern directions of today.'[71] And in the November issue of *Hudební revue* similar sentiments about Musorgsky were being purveyed in a substantial article by the composer and conductor Jaroslav Křička, who had spent several years working in Russia.[72]

If Janáček felt at all ambiguous about the praise lavished on a composer he had hardly heard of, Rektorys's enthusiasm in his next letter would not have helped: 'The National Theatre is planning "as a sensation" Musorgsky's *Boris Godunov*. That would be worth a trip to Prague. Will you come?'[73]

Antonín Váňa, who had written to Janáček in the summer about the Boskovice performance of the Piano Trio, wrote again on 13 November about a Moravian evening planned by a student society to take place on 24 November in the Small Hall of the Národní dům in Vinohrady, Prague. As the plans were at present, Janáček would be represented merely by folksongs, whereas his pupil Jan Kunc would have songs and a piano trio. This seemed to Váňa an absurd imbalance and so he begged that the group who had played Janáček's Piano Trio in Boskovice might be allowed to play it again in Prague. His colleagues, he wrote, had been 'so taken by your work that they want to make it the climax of the programme'. In addition they would like to perform the piano cycle *On the Overgrown Path* (viii/17) and thus, Váňa wrote, he was repeating his request to borrow the music; evidently there had been previous exchanges about this that have not survived. The programme, as he saw it, would now be:

1. Speech of Dr Hýsek about Moravian art
2. Kunc's trio
3. Your folksongs
4. Recitations from Bezruč and S.K. Neumann
5. Your piano pieces
6. Kunc's songs
7. Your piano trio[74]

It is unlikely that the above plan was realized. Váňa was assiduous at reporting back on his performances, and Janáček kept his letters. Apart from a letter four days later proposing a postponement until after Christmas,[75] there was no further mention of this concert, however, so either Janáček refused his permission, or it fell through for some other reason. One of Váňa's reassurances to Janáček was that he and his colleagues would not need for more than ten days the parts of the trio, which were then required for a performance in March 1911 under the auspices of the Umělecká beseda in Prague.[76] This is corroborated by a brief mention under the rubric of 'planned concerts' in the November issue of *Hudební revue*, where for future plans for the Umělecká beseda include a March concert of the 'Moravians L. Janáček and J. Kunc'.[77] However when it came to 1911, *Hudební revue* records all the other concerts planned by the Umělecká beseda, but not the Moravians' March concert. These planned and unrealized concerts remain tantalizing strands in the hunt for Janáček's elusive Piano Trio.

61

Janáček's knowledge of opera II
(1890–1914)

After the collapse of *Hudební listy* in June 1888 Janáček's opera reviews ceased for a while until he began writing regularly for *Moravské listy*. This was a comparatively brief period – October 1890 to May 1892 – and is surprising in that he seems not to have negotiated for himself any special conditions of service: operetta was still part of his brief (*Les cloches de Corneville* yet again) and innumerable performances of *The Bartered Bride*. The end may have been brought about when the conflict of interests between his life as an opera critic and as an opera composer became too uncomfortable (see chap. 29). After that the pattern of Janáček's opera-going changed. Much of it in the 1880s and early 1890s had been dictated by his work as a critic. Now he simply went to what interested him and was under no obligation to write about it. His final review of an opera performance was of *The Queen of Spades*, a one-off feuilleton for *Lidové noviny* in 1896, in which his captivation with Tchaikovsky's opera was abundantly clear (see chap. 34). There was a little spate of reviews in *Hlídka* of piano-vocal scores in the late 1890s in which Janáček discussed in some detail operas by Fibich and Kovařovic (see chap. 36).

Apart from his summer holidays in 1883 Janáček's opera-going had been limited to what he could pick up in the tiny Czech Theatre in Brno. But after retirement from the Teachers' Training Institute in 1903 he had more time to travel to Prague to get to know the operatic novelties given there. Indeed, after completing *Jenůfa* in early 1903, he was actively looking out for new and fashionable stimuli. These are the years when he came into contact with Charpentier's *Louise*, Strauss's *Salome* and *Elektra*, and Puccini's *Madama Butterfly*. Most of the operas he saw in Prague were at the National Theatre, but when the

Vinohrady Theatre – a competitive Czech-language venue that offered both opera and drama – opened in 1907, Janáček also went there, especially in the years when he believed that it would stage his opera *Fate*. On one rare occasion he ventured into the German Theatre in Prague, to hear Strauss's *Salome*, given there soon after its Dresden première.

Four operas stand out during the period – Mascagni's *Cavalleria rusticana*, Tchaikovsky's *Queen of Spades*, Charpentier's *Louise* and Puccini's *Madama Butterfly* – and these very different works constitute the chief non-Czech influences on Janáček as an opera composer. The first two were important for the writing of *Jenůfa* (see chaps. 29 and 34); Charpentier's *Louise* was a profound influence on Janáček's next opera *Fate* (see chap. 46) and beyond, and *Butterfly* cast long shadows on *Kát'a Kabanová* many years later. The one opera that one would have expected Janáček to know and learn from is absent. Although he was encouraged to go to Prague for the Czech première of Musorgsky's *Boris Godunov* in 1910, he did not, and he heard the opera only in 1923.

Janáček's earlier encounters with operas were documented largely by his reviews and analyses, i.e. public pronouncements in newspapers and journals. Operas he came across later are recorded in programmes that he kept, jottings in his notebooks or random comments in his letters. In a few instances, interviews extracted his views, for instance on *Salome* (see chap. 53), and much later also on *Pelléas et Mélisande* and on Wagner (see vol. ii: 1924a). Occasionally comments on operas spilt over into his general articles for *Hlídka*, for instance his comments on *Libuše* (xv/195), which got him into trouble with the pro-Smetana faction (see chap. 58). What is missing from the information here is what Janáček heard in Brno. Although, as a point of principle, he did not go to the German Theatre, he was a member of the Družstvo of the Czech Theatre for many years and would as a matter of course have attended performances. These, however, are not documented by any surviving programmes and information comes only by chance, for instance in a reminiscence by the composer and conductor Karel Moor: 'I remember vividly a performance of Smetana's *Two Widows* when on the way to "Slavia" [restaurant] after the theatre there came about a very sharp exchange of views. Janáček vehemently opposed it.'[1]

Table 61.1 should in be read in conjunction with table 25.1, where Janáček's experience of operas before 1890 is documented.

Table 61.1: Operas attended by Janáček 1890-1914

Operas mentioned in correspondence without evidence of his seeing them (either in performance or in score) are not included. Although one assumes that Janáček attended the operas he reviewed, dates are given for them only when specified in the review.

BT = Brno Theatre (Brno Provisional Theatre, National Provisional Theatre, Provisional Czech Theatre, etc.); PNT = Prague National Theatre; PVT = Vinohrady Theatre, Prague.; VS = piano-vocal score; lib = libretto

* = opera not listed in table 25.1

composer: title	original performance details	place and date of LJ's attendance	publication details of reviews by LJ; miscellaneous comments
Balfe: The Bohemian Girl	1843, London		4 Nov 1890 (XV/100)
*Beethoven: Fidelio	1805, Vienna	PNT, 11 Feb 1906	
Bendl: The Elderly Suitor	1882, Chrudim		9 Oct 1891 (XV/120)
Bizet: Carmen	1875, Paris	PNT, 4 Oct 1903 PNT, 23 April 1908	24 Jan 1891 (XV/112)
*Bizet: Djamileh	1872, Paris	PNT, 10 March 1903 (double bill)	
Blodek: In the Well	1867, Prague	PNT, 10 March 1903 (double bill)	
*Charpentier: Louise	1900, Paris	PNT, 21 May 1903	
*Donizetti: La fille du régiment	1840, Paris	BT, 24 Nov 1891	2 Dec 1891 (XV/125)
*Dvořák: Armida	1904, Prague	PNT, 23 March 1904 (rehearsal)	
*Dvořák: Dimitrij	1882, Prague	PNT, 15 Nov 1906	
*Dvořák: Rusalka	1901, Prague	PNT, 21 April 1908	
*Fibich: Hedy	1896, Prague		Aug 1897 (review of VS, XV/154)
*Fibich: Šárka	1897, Prague		Jan 1899 (review of VS, XV/160); mentioned in XV/159
Gluck: Orfeo ed Euridice	1762, Vienna	PNT, 13 Nov 1906	
Gounod: Faust	1859, Paris	BT, 27 Dec 1890	31 Dec 1890 (XV/107)
*Gounod: Roméo et Juliette	1867, Paris	BT, 25 Dec 1891	30 Dec 1891 (XV/130)
*Kovařovic: At the Old Bleachery	1901, Prague	PNT, 6 Nov 1903	
*Kovařovic: The Dogheads	1898, Prague	PNT, 1 Nov 1910	1899 (review of VS, XV/161)
*Lortzing: Der Wildschütz	1842, Leipzig	BT, 17 Dec 1891	19 Dec 1891 (XV/128)

Table 61.1:—*continued*

composer: title	original performance details	place and date of LJ's attendance	publication details of reviews by LJ; miscellaneous comments
*Mascagni: Cavalleria rusticana	1890, Rome	BT, 3 and 8 March 1892	9 March 1892 (xv/137)
*Massenet: Werther	1892, Vienna	PNT, 16 Feb 1906	
*Meyerbeer: Les Huguenots	1836, Paris	BT, 19 Nov 1890	22 Nov 1890 (xv/103)
*Mozart: Don Giovanni	1787, Prague	BT, 12 Jan 1891; PNT, 10 Nov 1904	15 Jan 1891 (xv/110)
*Nicolai: Die lustigen Weiber von Windsor	1849, Berlin	PNT, 27 May 1908	14 Nov 1891 (xv/124)
*Nouguès: Quo vadis?	1909, Nice	PVT, 13 or 16 May 1910	autumn 1910, Janáček wishes to perform excerpts in Brno
*Offenbach: Les contes d'Hoffmann	1881, Paris	BT, 16 Jan 1892	20 Jan 1892 (xv/131)
Planquette: Les cloches de Corneville	1877, Paris	BT, 24? Feb 1892	27 Feb 1892 (xv/136)
*Prokop: The Dream of the Forest	1907, Prague	PNT, 5 June 1907 (Act 1 only, rehearsal)	
*Puccini: Madama Butterfly	1904, Milan	PVT, 16 Feb 1908	
*Puccini: Tosca	1900, Rome	PNT, 26 Nov 1903	
Rozkošný: The St John's Rapids	1871, Prague	BT, 11 Jan 1891	15 Jan 1891 (xv/110)
Smetana: The Bartered Bride	1866, Prague	BT, 4 Oct 1890	8 Oct 1890 (xv/96) 12 Nov 1890 (xv/101)
		BT, 19 Dec 1890 BT, 26 Sept 1891	20 Dec 1890 (xv/106) 30 Sept 1891 (xv/118)
		BT, 5 Oct 1891 BT, 22 Oct 1891 PNT, 18 Nov 1901 PNT, 17 Jan 1904	7 Oct 1891 (xv/119) 24 Oct 1891 (xv/121)
			Nov 1911: analysis of individual numbers (xv/203)

Table 61.1:—*continued*

composer: title	original performance details	place and date of LJ's attendance	publication details of reviews by LJ; miscellaneous comments
Smetana: *The Bartered Bride*	1866, Prague	Liboc, near Prague, Šárka open-air theatre, 16 May 1913	
*Smetana: *The Devil's Wall*	1882, Prague	PNT, 3 June 1907	
Smetana: *Dalibor*	1868, Prague	BT, 13 Oct 1890 BT, 3 Oct 1891 PNT, 16 May 1911 PNT, 22 March 1912 PNT, 4 Oct 1912	15 Oct 1890 (xv/98) 7 Oct 1891 (xv/119)
Smetana: *The Kiss*	1876, Prague	BT, 26 Jan 1892	27 Jan 1892 (xv/132)
*Smetana: *Libuše*	1881, Prague	PNT, 3 Jan 1909	Feb 1909: criticism of composition (xv/195) Nov 1911: references to opera (xv/196)
Smetana: *The Secret*	1876, Prague	BT, 7 Oct 1890	8 Oct 1890 (xv/96)
Smetana: *The Two Widows*	1874, Prague	BT, March? 1908	LJ being 'vehemently opposed' (Moor 1947, 61–2)
*J. Strauss: *Der Zigeunerbaron*	1885, Vienna		13 Dec 1890 (xv/104)
*R. Strauss: *Elektra*	1909, Dresden	PNT, 14 May 1910	
*R. Strauss: *Salome*	1905, Dresden	Prague German Theatre, 22 May 1906	LJ interview (xv/182)
*Tchaikovsky: *Eugene Onegin*	1879, Moscow	BT, 24 Feb 1891 PNT, 9 Nov 1903	28 Feb 1891 (xv/114)
*Tchaikovsky: *The Queen of Spades*	1890, St Petersburg	BT, 16 Jan 1896	21 Jan 1896 (xv/149)
*Verdi: *Rigoletto*	1851, Venice		29 Oct 1890 (xv/99)
Verdi: *Il trovatore*	1853, Rome		20 Dec 1890 (xv/105)
		BT, 28 Oct 1891 BT, 27 Nov 1891	31 Oct 1891(xv/122) 2 Dec 1891 xv/125)
*Wagner: *Der fliegende Holländer*	1843, Dresden	PNT, 26 Dec 1907 PNT, 30 March 1911	
*Wagner: *Lohengrin*	1850, Weimar	PNT, 11 March 1906	
*Wagner: *Parsifal*	1882, Bayreuth	PNT, 1 Jan 1914	
*Weiss: *Der Revisor*	1907, Prague	PNT, 11 Sept 1908	
*Zajc: *Der Raub der Sabinerinnen*	1870, Berlin	BT, 4 Oct 1891	7 Oct 1891 (xv/119)

62

1911

The public meeting of the Brno Theatre Družstvo in May 1910 and its repercussions in the press had its due effect: in the next season *Jenůfa* was given five performances between 31 January and 21 April 1911. Although little was made of the fact, the performance on 31 January was the première of Janáček's new version, the 'Brno 1908' version, as it has become known, which together with a few later amendments represents the composer's final thoughts on the opera. But even this version attracted criticism. For instance Jan Kunc, having made a new study of the work, wrote to Janáček on 24 January, a week before the opening night:

Love and respect for this work, whose deeply felt emotion has again made a big impression on me and which I therefore value from my heart, makes me respectfully ask you whether you will allow me to deliver some suggestions for correcting the mistakes in declamation, quite a few of which remain even in the corrected vocal score.

Such comments, which Kunc hoped Janáček would take 'as an expression of warm sympathy', could not have helped soften Janáček's increasingly hostile view of his ex-pupil. Nevertheless he seems to have taken up the offer of a visit in which Kunc would demonstrate the word-setting mistakes he had spotted. In his letter Kunc had suggested a number of times when he was free; at the foot of the letter Janáček jotted down 'Saturday [28 January] at 4'.[1]

According to his letter, Kunc had invited various critics to the new première: Antonín Šilhan, who had just taken up his long tenure as critic at *Národní listy* (1910–41), and Otakar Nebuška from *Hudební revue*. Although Nebuška was to become one of Janáček's warmest

Prague advocates, it seems he was not in Brno for this occasion since the ten-line report that appeared in the journal was supplied by Kunc.[2] Janáček himself invited Rektorys,[3] again to no avail. The performances seem to have gone well enough. The orchestra was conducted by Rudolf Pavlata, the cello teacher at the Organ School and the cellist in both of Janáček's recent chamber premières. In his *Hudební revue* report Kunc benevolently declared it 'nice in the light of our conditions', though took issue with some of Pavlata's tempos. More worrying was the observation that, with the long gaps between them, each performance became less exact. The original, much-praised Kostelnička (Hanusová-Svobodová) was still in the cast, and the other performer Kunc singled out was Alois Fiala, whose Števa he characterized as 'psychologically well observed'. *Moravské noviny* reported twice on the occasion, the first as a brief news item (3 February), the second at much greater length (4 February). This later account was mostly about the work rather than about the performance and repeated many of the earlier claims about the opera (see chap. 47). However a couple of points were new and sound as if they could have come from a briefing with Janáček himself. One is the appropriation of a comment that Janáček had used about his speech melodies and the 'scale of feeling' to which speech melodies could be pegged. Here, however, it is the motifs taken from the speech melodies that 'do not conduct themselves according to theoretical scales but go instead with the scale of feeling'. The second point of interest was that Janáček was allegedly 'not interested in foreign recognition: because every translation of this specifically Moravian work is completely unthinkable without a complete rewriting of the music, which has grown organically from the speech of the people' (for comment on the theoretical issues this raises, see chap. 37).

One of the reasons why it was so important that *Jenůfa* stayed in the Brno repertory was that its absence there was a powerful argument for the Prague National Theatre not to accept the opera. If the Brno Theatre would not perform the work, or if Brno audiences were apathetic in their attendance, why should Prague bother? Once it was being performed in Brno, however, approaches could be made to Prague. There was clearly no point in appealing directly to Kovařovic, so a new appeal was made directly to the Společnost of the National Theatre (the company that held the franchise and which employed Kovařovic and his administrative director Gustav Schmoranz). The appeal was made on 18 February by Janáček's friend František Veselý, who had that day taken over the chairmanship of the Club of the Friends of Art after Janáček's two-year tenure. Veselý's appeal was based on the fact that the club saw in *Jenůfa* 'a work of such artistic significance that it deserves wider national attention' and that the 'still temporary' stage in Brno was inadequate.[4]

It is a shame that Veselý got going quite so quickly. Had he waited two more weeks his appeal would have come within the context of a substantial article on Janáček published in *Hudební revue*. It was the lead article that month, occupying thirteen of the seventy-three pages of the March issue, with a continuation promised (and realized) in the April issue. Divided into six sections, it was by far the most detailed information published on Janáček at the time, following his life as conductor, as theoretician and folklorist, as composer and (in the April issue) as teacher and, finally, as a personality. The article was comple-mented by a professional photograph of Janáček, carefully suited and coiffed, sitting grim-faced in an armchair and looking up at the camera rather than at the illustrated magazine he is holding (see Plate 22). And, as a very curious extra, a second plate provided a Janáček manuscript of a short Moderato for piano (VIII/21), described in *Hudební revue* as 'an example of canonic imitation written in the Organ School'. The choice of this dull (though dutifully canonic) little piece emphasizes Janáček as teacher rather than as composer, and thus goes against the thrust of the article that devotes six pages to Janáček's compositions. The author was Jan Kunc, who at the same time as attempting to correct Janáček's word-setting had devoted considerable time and effort to promoting his former teacher.

Even as Veselý's appeal was made, doubts were raised that it would do any good. Láďa Kožušníček, the maverick journalist who had reported back to Janáček after the Brno Theatre Družstvo meeting in 1910, wrote promptly to Veselý on 19 February, commiserating with him on his 'most unrewarding task – the promotion of *Jenůfa* in Prague':

Janáček has as many enemies in Prague as he has hairs on his head. Today these all know well who Janáček is – thus their hate. And in Brno itself he has few adherents. It took a lot of work to get *Jenůfa* on to the Brno stage this year. In that music meeting I heard with my own ears such disgustingly insulting comments about this masterpiece that the blood ran cold in my veins.

It is difficult to know how much of this was mischief-making. In his next paragraph, for instance, Kožušníček asserts that 'having learnt that *Jenůfa* was in rehearsal here, Kovařovic himself undermined the enthusiasm of our singers for rehearsing it, by saying that it was an eternal waste of time' (the source for this interesting information is not provided) and that, even if Veselý did manage to win over influential people at the Prague National Theatre, the work would be performed without enthusiasm and thus would end in failure.[5] Although tiresomely negative, Kožušníček's scepticism was unfortunately well founded. A week after Veselý sent his letter he received a response from the chairman of the National Theatre Společnost, Dr Jaroslav Hlava. The connection was a good one: Veselý and Hlava were friends from their university days, which explains why Veselý got a long, courteous and seemingly frank reply. It was mostly a matter of finance, Hlava declared. New operas mounted at the National Theatre constituted an 'unrecoverable loss' if they did not find favour with the general public. Kovařovic could afford one or two 'experiments' a year, and here Hlava listed some of the more fortunate works that came into this category, including works by Novák (his cantata *The Storm*, given a stage production), Foerster and Ostrčil, as well as the 'earnest cultivation' of Fibich. Now if some rich patron on Moravia were to subsidize the production, it would be a different matter. Then came the poisonous comment: 'Mr Janáček has revised his original opera, and would be willing to do so again – I think this is proof enough that it is not such a masterpiece as you imagine. Rather let Mr Janáček write something new, I will then endeavour to do something for him in the foreseeable future.' So the revision by a composer of an already staged work is automatically suspect, a comment that would apply not only to Foerster's *Jessika* (one of the so-called 'experiments') but to many mature works by highly experienced opera composers such as Verdi and Puccini. The letter, Hlava hastened to add, was not meant for public consumption. It gave as clear an indication as possible that *Jenůfa* in Prague was completely unthinkable. That was to remain the case for almost five more years.[6]

At exactly this time Janáček completed a new work, *The Čarták on Solán* (III/7). It is striking how in these years of bitter frustration over the fate of his operatic works, and at a time when his health was causing concern, Janáček's creative work contracted to one main work a year, usually written over the winter months. The previous two winters had produced his two unexpected ventures into chamber music. The new work this winter was the result of a commission, from the male-voice choral society 'Orlice' in Prostějov. Largely owing to the presence of an energetic and enthusiastic Janáček former pupil, Ezechiel Ambros, the Moravian town of Prostějov had a tradition of performing Janáček's music. More recently, the Moravian Teachers' Choral Society had taken their celebrated performance of *Maryčka Magdónova* there in 1908 and 1909 (Ambros reported that of all the works in the 1909 concert it was the most liked).[7] Ambros had stepped down from his sixteen-year tenure at 'Orlice' in 1906; his successor Vilém Steinman, vigorous, enterprising and still in his twenties, had approached Janáček at the end of 1910 for a new piece to celebrate the society's fifty-year jubilee in 1912. The result was *The Čarták on Soláň*, a cantata for tenor, male chorus and orchestra based on a poem published in 1908 by 'M. Kurt', i.e. Maximilián Kunert. Its curious title celebrates a famous inn on one of the Beskydy hills. A *čarták* was originally a wooden hut built in the border regions of Moravia against the invading Turks; in Kurt's poem this particular *čarták*, now an inn, is the setting of a brief amorous encounter against a background of vigorous folk dancing. The fact that the commission was for the male-voice 'Orlice' dictated the presence of a male chorus, but in addition Janáček had the luxury of an orchestra. Rektorys had wondered if *Maryčka Magdónova* had been conceived 'orchestrally' (see chap. 56) and in some ways *Čarták* represents an orchestral extension of Janáček's Bezruč choruses: a dramatic scene for chorus now expanded with a soloist and orchestra. Stylistically the work is a huge advance on *Amarus*, the last piece in a similar genre, and although it is short in duration (a mere seven minutes) it packs a formidable punch that makes it seem to fill a much larger space.

Janáček had released an announcement about the completion of the work in *Lidové noviny* on 19 February. Steinman discovered the fact only a month later, by which time a rival choral society, also with strong regional claims on the piece, had already appealed to Janáček to be allowed to give the first performance. On 27 February Jan Nepomuk Polášek, another of Janáček's former pupils, wrote to him on behalf of the Valašské Meziříčí Beseda asking if they might borrow the score for a performance at the end of April or the beginning of May. The text, he stressed, had been written by a resident of the town, Maximilián

Kunert; the subject itself 'comes from our region'; the town had a good male chorus, and the performance would be in the hands of the experienced chorusmaster Navrátil, uncle of the author of the text.[8] Actually, there was little contest. While Valašské Meziříčí was a small regional centre of some 3500 inhabitants at the turn of the century, Prostějov was eight times larger, a historical town with a large Jewish population and considerable cultural pretensions. In 1900 it had eighty-three Czech and forty-two German societies; 'Orlice' was one of the oldest Czech choral societies in the Czech lands.

On 18 March Steinman wrote to Janáček in terms of awed abasement:

From the daily and musical press I have read the joyful news that the chorus asked for by me* for 'Orlice', *The Čarták on Soláň*, is ready. It is indeed hard to choose the right words with which to thank you enough for the great honour that 'Orlice' has received with your work. With all my soul I want to devote myself to your work so that you will be pleased with its performance. The members of 'Orlice' have enthusiastically already studied a number of your choruses and all the more enthusiastically welcome your new work, being proud that you – our Moravian musical king – are writing for them, too. I thank you, illustrious Maestro, simply but sincerely with all my soul. I ask you urgently for news of when I could get the full score – the time for rehearsals is approaching fast. Or will it be necessary to make a copy for study? Again I ask you for a short note about what I should do next.[9]

The tone of this letter serves to remind us that, whatever Kožušníček had to say on the matter, there were people in the region who held Janáček in respect and veneration. That said, here was Janáček, approaching sixty, supplying a small regional choral society with a very short cantata for its fiftieth jubilee, while the previous year the main Brno choral society had invited an outsider, the twenty-year-younger Vítězslav Novák, to write a high-profile, large-scale choral work to celebrate the society's fiftieth birthday.

Janáček wrote back three days later to say that he would like to put the work aside for a while. Once he had 'forgotten' it he would look through it again: 'Something usually occurs to me.' He would send the

---

* Although it is clear from this formulation that the commission came from Steinman, it is not known whether he also suggested the text. It would have been unusual for Janáček to set a text selected for him. As it was, Janáček seems to have had contacts with Kunert over *Brouček* (see chap. 56) and the inn itself was well known even before the publication of Kunert's poem in 1908. Antonín Váňa had sent Janáček a postcard of it on 27 July 1907 (BmJA, A 3110).

score in a month's time.[10] True to his word, on 24 April he sent it off to Prostějov so that it could be copied.[11]

During March 1911 there were two further performances of *Jenůfa* in Brno (14 and 22 March) as well as the première of Janáček's *Eva Gabel* folksong arrangements (v/9). The latter were sung by L. Vytopilová at the Organ School on 5 March 1911, accompanied by Marie Dvořáková, who had replaced Ludmila Prokopová as the Organ School piano teacher. Janáček's visits to Prague, together with his contacts with Rektorys, had become much less frequent, but on 30 March he saw Wagner's *Der fliegende Holländer*, conducted by Kovařovic.[12] Maybe the performance in some way brought Janáček's attention back to his languishing fifth opera, *The Excursion of Mr Brouček to the Moon*. 'I come again after a long period. I'm finished with Act 2 and enclose a sketch of Act 3', he wrote to Dr Janke.[13] The letter is undated, but was presumably written in the first half of April, since Dr Janke replied on 16 April with a characteristically good-natured but nevertheless unusable attempt to satisfy the composer's latest request.[14] Janáček's letter is the only indication that he had been working on his opera and had now, three years after he started, come to the end of Act 2.

His first libretto for Act 3 was written on blank pages bound in between the printed text of his copy of Čech's novel. A second libretto, written on separate sheets, shows a considerable reorganization of the material. In this new libretto certain passages were marked with red pencil, Janáček's usual sign that he needed outside help. The first of these was the song of the patron, Čaroskvoucí, at the beginning of the act. Janáček's letter to Janke continues: 'In particular I desperately need the song: "Oh, a patron's vocation is hard"; just in the form of Čech's sonnets. Perhaps you also know some sort of "patron" from real life?'[15] Janáček did not fancy the rollicking couplets that Janke supplied and, rather surprisingly in view of his previous unhelpfulness, turned again to Josef Holý, this time supplying a prose draft of the song. And again Holý was prompt but unhelpful: maybe, he wrote, the song could stay in prose.[16]

At about this time there was an unexpected contact from the Vinohrady Theatre in Prague, still sitting on Janáček's opera *Fate*. Václav Štech, the administrator after Šubert's resignation in 1908, wrote a one-sentence letter asking for the piano-vocal score of *Jenůfa* to be sent 'so that we can give it to our experts for appraisal'.[17] This tight-lipped request does not sound like a spontaneous gesture of interest (which might be expected to be longer and more courteous) but perhaps a gritted-teeth response to an approach from the Brno Club of the Friends of Art, whose appeal to the Prague National Theatre had fallen on such deaf ears. What sparked off Štech's letter can only be a matter of speculation: it may be merely a coincidence that the day before, 21 April 1911, *Jenůfa* was performed in Brno for the final time that season.

On 16 April Janáček published a delightful autobiographical article, *Without Drums* (xv/199). It is nearest in spirit to *Early Morning Lights* (xv/194), his reminiscences of various Christmases in Hukvaldy, which *Lidové noviny* published on Christmas Eve 1909. Easter Sunday (which in 1911 fell on 16 April) provided the appropriate hook for another reminiscence: of Janáček, as a little boy, taking part in stealing the timpani from a neighbouring parish so that the High Mass in Hukvaldy on Easter Sunday could have the full complement of instruments, including drums. The incident goes back a long way, to Easter 1861 (if Janáček correctly remembered his age as 'seven') and contains some of his very few recollections that have survived of his father. Fascinatingly, in the last line of the article, Janáček offers the connection between this incident and his affection for timpani ('And this is why I never forget to write a solo for timpani'). In 1911 this was a surprising statement given that by then he had written comparatively few works that involved the timpani. But perhaps the act of pinning down this association was in some way responsible for the blossoming of timpani parts in his later operas and in works such as the *Glagolitic Mass* (iii/9) and *The Danube* (ix/7).

A month later, on 16 May, Janáček attended a performance in Prague of Smetana's *Dalibor*.[18] Who knows what may have prompted this trip to Prague on a Tuesday during term-time, to see an opera that he knew well and did not particularly like and one, moreover, conducted by the second conductor, František Picka. However, Zdenka was in Vienna at the time (she wrote on 19 May apologizing for not being back sooner);[19] maybe her absence encouraged a sudden trip to the Czech capital. Whether he took the opportunity to drop in at the Vinohrady Theatre is not known, but on 18 June he wrote to ask about the *Jenůfa* material that the company's 'experts' were appraising. His letter has not survived, but is referred to in Štech's reply, 26 June, which returned the *Jenůfa* material with the terse comment that 'it is not possible to perform *Jenůfa* on our stage'.[20] This appears to be have been the last straw for Janáček. His contacts over the stalled production of *Fate* had been surprisingly restrained in recent years but, with *Jenůfa* turned down in the most offhand way, he wrote to Rektorys. Janáček's dealings with him had shrunk to very little since Rektorys had taken over as editor of *Smetana*. Their only recent dealings had been over Janáček's letters to Dvořák, which he had presented to Rektorys in 1910, and were now needed back, at least temporarily, for their publication in *Hudební revue*.[21] Things had cooled so much between Janáček and Rektorys that, in his response, Rektorys even enquired whether Janáček wanted the letters back permanently, 'although you had given them to me'.[22] Despite the strained relationship, Janáček now wrote at length to Rektorys seeking advice on how best to proceed with *Fate*:

You know how it began with my *Fate* and the Vinohrady Theatre.

At the time I made a contract with Mr František Šubert, the piece was accepted for performance.

It is well known how afterwards it faltered at the Vinohrady Theatre. But a period of three years passed and it wasn't performed.

It seems to me that the contract with Šubert isn't even legally binding – according to what Štech has said.

So Rektorys was asked to look into the statutes of the Vinohrady company to try and discover the legal position: 'I don't want to insist on a legally enforced performance of any of my works – God forbid! – but I would like to have some light [shed on the matter] to see whether composers here were cheated. I'm sure I'm not the only one affected.'[23] Rektorys presumably replied, though no letter on this topic has survived. With or without Rektorys's help, and perhaps with some legal advice, Janáček wrote a brief, businesslike letter to the Vinohrady Theatre on 9 August aimed at bringing the matter to a head: 'I ask you to settle the matter of *Fate*, which was accepted for performance. I wish to defend my author's right if necessary by legal means, not in order to compel a production but simply to ensure the law can take its course.'[24] The theatre summer break was not the best time to write and no immediate answer was received. Perhaps Janáček did not even expect one immediately: the next day he set off for his usual summer holiday in Luhačovice.

He wrote to Zdenka on 11 August, the day after his arrival, reporting that the spa was full and that he was being put up in the hotel Jestřábí. He sounded depressed and had no idea how long he would stay. 'At least I will find some diversion', he concluded.[25] In fact the only diversion he seems to have found was a couple of folksong-collecting trips into neighbouring villages. On 20 August, for instance, he went with Hynek Bím to Velký Ořechov near Uherské Hradiště, where they notated ten mostly two-voice songs from agricultural workers from Čičmany (in Slovakia), Janáček taking down the tunes, Bím the texts.[26] The next day, 21 August, they were in Vnorovy to record songs there.[27] Bím was becoming one of Janáček's closer folksong associates and in particular was closely linked with the attempts at the time to record folksongs using the phonograph acquired in October 1909. After three weeks in Luhačovice Janáček had had enough and announced his departure to Zdenka: 'It's getting empty here with people going away. I don't know why it is that such sadness comes over my soul when one after the other people leave. I'd also prefer to leave. [. . .] On Sunday I'm going off to a nearby settlement for songs, and off [home] on Monday noon!'[28]

A couple of weeks after Janáček's return to Brno came one of the better pieces of news at this time. After the collapse of Branberger's publishing connections with Kočí in January 1909 (and with it the possibility of the publication of *On the Overgrown Path* VIII/17), Janáček had tried other publishers. He got nowhere except with the local firm in Brno run by Arnošt Píša, who in December 1909 had expressed a cautious willingness to take on the cycle providing Janáček could wait a little.[29] Perhaps he hung on in the hope of a more glamorous option, since it was almost two years before he sent the pieces to Píša, in September 1911 on his return from Luhačovice. Píša's letter of 23 September acknowledges receipt of the manuscript and repeats his willingness to publish the pieces with the one reservation (a 'respectful question') that as a layman he wondered whether the pieces weren't rather too difficult.[30] Nevertheless he asked for Janáček's conditions, and publication went ahead rapidly: the pieces were out before the end of the year.

On 30 September 1911 Janáček published in *Lidové noviny* a single piano piece described as no. 1 of a 'new series' of *On the Overgrown Path*. The music was printed from a manuscript copy headed 'On the Overgrown Path, a new series of piano pieces', which contained this and two more pieces. Janáček did not add any more after this, and made no further attempt to publish the 'new series' pieces or the two pieces from the 1900 manuscript left unpublished (see chap. 38). It is striking that none of the unpublished pieces (or the single *Lidové noviny* piece) had a title. Without the autobiographical links at which the titles hint, the rejected pieces lack something – something more than just a title – and Janáček seems to have realized this by putting them aside. Significantly, when the ten titled pieces came out at the end of the year, they were not called 'first series' (which would have been an indication that more were on the way). The omission suggests that Janáček had already taken a decision against further publication.

While the *Overgrown Path* was proceeding nicely, the news on the Vinohrady front was less good. Having had no response to his letter to Štech before leaving for Luhačovice, Janáček seems to have turned to a lawyer, Dr Adolf Stránský, who wrote to the Vinohrady Theatre on his behalf on 13 September. The reply was dated three weeks later:

In the entire theatre no-one is aware that the opera *Fate* was bought from Mr Janáček, no contract was found in the files, and also Mr Janáček, despite the fact that he was invited to, has not divulged the terms of the contract.

Thus the [music] director [of the theatre] was not even entitled to perform the work and there can be no talk of any compensation.

Should Mr Janáček wish for any agreement to this end, i.e. that the work might be performed, let him communicate his conditions and I will then ask for the decision of the Executive Committee.[31]

Things were not completely back to square one since Václav Štech clearly feared some sort of legal response and wrote privately to Janáček on 10 November suggesting a meeting at his home in Prague any time before the Vinohrady board met on 16 November, when *Fate* would be on the agenda. He was sure, Štech wrote, that as 'two authors' he and Janáček would be able to come to some agreement without recourse to the law.[32] Janáček took advice from a Brno lawyer, Dr František Pauk, and was told to go ahead with the meeting: Pauk would meanwhile hold off with the proposed court action until he had received Janáček's instructions.[33] There is no evidence that any meeting took place, except that on 6 December Štech sent Janáček a contract for signature, expressing his delight 'that it was possible to settle your case easily in this way'.[34] On 18 December, Janáček signed and dated a contract according to which the Vinohrady Theatre undertook to perform *Fate* in the winter season of 1912–13,[35] quite a long time into the future in view of the four years the work had already waited. Until that time the opera should not be performed elsewhere and should not be published.

Janáček evidently took the new Vinohrady undertaking at face value and, when he announced the publication of *On the Overgrown Path* to Rektorys on 13 December, he mentioned the new contract and its proposed performance date (optimistically truncated to 'the winter of 1912').[36] *On the Overgrown Path* had come out amazingly fast. Engraving was done by the Leipzig firm of Engelmann & Mühlberg, who were clearly maintaining the admirable turnover rate that they had displayed with the engraving of *Jenůfa*. The piano cycle, with only a few Czech words in the titles and expression marks to puzzle German engravers, and covering a span of only twenty-four pages, could not have detained them long. One tiny trace of this stage in the work's progress was a proof, dated 28 October 1911, with the comment 'Nachmalige Correctur! Píša' ['Another proof! Píša'] and corrections made chiefly by Janáček.[37] Speed perhaps dictated that there was no time for the decorative covers that Píša had chosen in previous Janáček publications (such as the *Hukvaldy Folk Poetry in Songs* V/4, the *Singing Teaching Manual* V/5 or, most recently, the two *Moravian Dances* VIII/18).[†] This time the cover consisted merely of basic information, notably the cycle title and a listing of the ten individual numbers (described as 'tiny pieces for piano') framed by a severe border.[38] According to Janáček's letters to Branberger and Rektorys of 13 December, copies arrived in Brno that day.[39] Píša promptly wrote to Janáček conceding a fee of 100 K, thanking him for the addresses of Czech critics who should be sent copies and asking for addresses of German critics.[40]

In addition to his piano cycle Janáček published five pieces of prose writing in 1911. They could hardly have been more varied as a group and illustrate well Janáček's range as a writer. *Without Drums* (XV/199), Janáček's contribution to *Lidové noviny* for Easter (see above) is pure story-telling: scenes from his childhood, aphoristically captured in a few brief lines with short-circuit jumps from one scene to another – the sort of dramaturgy Janáček increasingly favoured in his music. *In Memory of Dvořák* (XV/201), published in *Hudební revue*

[†] See illustrations in Simeone 1991, 248, 284 and 254.

in December, was Janáček's second published memoir of Dvořák (the first, xv/181, had appeared five years earlier). It pinpoints five separate recollections: at the organ bench at St Vojtěch's in Prague, Dvořák's contacts with Brno (explored more fully in xv/181), their summer ramblings in Bohemia, Janáček's last encounter with him at the dress rehearsal of *Armida* in 1904, and hearing the news of his death (during Janáček's Warsaw trip) a few months later. Coming through all this is a warm affection that was seldom on display in his writings (see chap. 22).

Besides these personal reminiscences Janáček published a preliminary version of a new *Complete Harmony Manual* (xv/202), 'drawn up according to Leoš Janáček's lectures for the use of the Organ School in Brno'. In other words this was a textbook, based on Janáček's Organ School teaching, and, like the book published by Urbánek in 1897 (xv/151), was above all concerned with the connections between individual chords, Janáček's most idiosyncratic contribution to harmonic theory (see chap. 19). The new book was shorter (it occupies 59 pages in a modern edition as opposed to the 113 of its predecessor) and this time was published 'as a manuscript' by the Benedictine Press in Rajhrad (where *Hlídka* was produced). The following year, Píša took over the publication in a revised version.

Janáček's remaining publications in 1911 encapsulate his other major preoccupations: folk music and speech melody. *Under the Sword* (xv/200) is a short piece published on 29 April in *Lidové noviny* about the ancient Indo-European origins of the Moravian sword dance. The article describes a trip to Březová, which Janáček placed in '1904', though his visit over Whitsun to Březová is reliably documented as taking place in 1899 (xv/315).[41] What brought it to mind in 1911 was an article on the sword dance by František Pospíšil, then head of the ethnographic division of the Moravian Museum in Brno; this had appeared in the February–March issue of *Národnopisný věstník českoslovanský*.

Tucked away in *Hlídka*, *Song* (xv/203) is one of Janáček's least-known articles. It is a long, rambling piece, beginning charmingly enough with a description of an old Slovak woman coming to sell her folk embroidery. Janáček was taken by this, both because it was the first time he had heard the dialect word 'pastorkyňa' (as in the Czech title for *Jenůfa*), and because it was an appropriate hook for the demonstration of speech melodies. It moves quickly on to another familiar trope, the speech melodies of children, and takes many pages before it gets to what appears to be the chief substance of the article, the clear expression of varying emotions that Janáček found in these speech melodies and the great difficulty in transplanting this clear communication on to the operatic stage. One wonders what the readers of *Hlídka* made of Janáček's analyses of *The Bartered Bride*, in particular the different song forms in Act 1: 'big rondo' (the opening number), 'small rondo' (Jeník's interlude within this), sonata form and so on; these are demonstrated with page references and lettered formulas ('hv+g+hv', 'pv+st+zv'), with the letters denoting concepts such as 'main sentence' (hv), 'gradation' (g), 'introductory sentence' (pv), 'climaxing' (st) and 'concluding sentence' (zv). If this dismayed the less musically educated reader, worse was in store on the next page, where key analyses and modulation patterns are supplied. It is difficult to know where all this is going, but one thing is clear. Zdeněk Nejedlý's dismissal of *Jenůfa*, pronounced at the public lecture that Janáček attended in 1910 and now (1911) published in Nejedlý's book *Czech Modern Opera after Smetana*, still rankled. Perhaps one of the points of this article was to show how faulty Nejedlý's analysis of *The Bartered Bride* was (denying the existence of simple song forms that Janáček had demonstrated) and thus show Nejedlý's criticisms of *Jenůfa* as equally flawed. What, for instance, Janáček complained poignantly, could Dr Nejedlý possibly have against the declamation of Jenůfa's words 'až do srdce'? Polemical prose belongs to its time and it is perhaps not surprising that *Song*, which came out in two instalments, in the November and December issues of *Hlídka*, is now forgotten. On the other hand Janáček's set of piano miniatures, *On the Overgrown Path*, which came out virtually simultaneously, has stood the test of time and, for all its modest ambitions, ranks today as one of Janáček's most haunting and profound utterances.

63

1912

Since 1907 one of the aims of the Club of the Friends of Art in Brno had been to publish new Czech compositions: in return for their subscription, members were to receive one newly published piece a year in the series Hudební moravské edice [Moravian music edition]. The publication of *Jenůfa* was deemed to constitute the club's free publications for 1907 and 1908; in 1909 the club began to contemplate its next edition. A competition was announced in June 1909 and thirty-five Moravian composers were personally invited to send compositions, either piano pieces or songs. An international jury was set up: Foerster in Vienna; the director of the Warsaw Conservatory Feliks Nowowiejski; and the Swiss writer William Ritter, who from 1909 had been a regular contributor to *Hudební revue*. The results, by the deadline of May 1911, were disappointing. Nine composers submitted pieces, of which only three complied with the conditions of the competition and none of which were thought by the judges to be worth publishing. The competition was relaunched with a new submission date of 1 November 1912.[1]

Was this the impetus for Janáček's new piano cycle *In the Mists* (VIII/22)? It seems unlikely as pieces were to be submitted anonymously and Janáček had almost revealed his authorship by sending a copy on 21 April 1911 to Jan Branberger with the request that he might give it a mention in *Čas*. Branberger's 'beautiful report' about *On the Overgrown Path* in *Čas* had led, Janáček added, to its publication.[2] However, Branberger did nothing. As late as 27 September he apologized for not yet having complied with Janáček's request, but said that his successor as music critic at *Čas*, Jindřich Pihert, would do so instead.[3] His inaction (and Pihert's), however, did Janáček a good turn, allowing him in the autumn of 1912 to submit *In the Mists* in his own competition.

Whether or not Janáček was influenced by the Club of the Friends of Art's competition, one impetus in writing *In the Mists* seems to have been the favourable response that *On the Overgrown Path* was receiving. In the months after publication in December 1911 Janáček began to get encouraging letters from admirers about it: from Ezechiel Ambros and his son Vladimír in Prostějov[4] and from the elderly Vojáček in St Petersburg (who commented specifically on nos. 1, 4, 7 and 10).[5] There were long and mostly favourable reviews in the leading musical journals: in *Smetana* by the composer Emil Axman (in the issue of 5 January, i.e. just three weeks after publication)[6] and in the February issue of *Hudební revue* by Karel Hoffmeister, the doyen of Prague piano teachers at the time.[7]

But a final trigger may well have been Debussy. In the autumn of 1911 the regular 'sonata hours' concerts at the Organ School had been upgraded to 'symphonic' concerts, given on Sundays in the concert hall in the nearby Lužánky park. These concerts were usually a mixture of chamber works with at least one symphonic work as well: during the 1911–12 and 1912–13 seasons Beethoven's first eight symphonies were performed by the orchestra of the Brno Czech Theatre, all conducted by Rudolf Pavlata.[8] However, the third concert in the 1911–12 season, on Sunday 28 January 1912, with a French theme, lacked any orchestral dimension. Stalwarts on the Organ School staff (Dvořáková, Dědeček and Pavlata) played d'Indy's Violin Sonata op. 59 and Franck's Piano Trio op. 1, and Marie Kuncová (the wife of Jan Kunc) performed songs by Duparc, Chausson, Debussy and others. Dvořáková completed the programme with piano music by Pierné, Chevillard and Debussy's *Reflets dans l'eau*.[9] Debussy was little known in the Czech lands at the time. Miloš Štědroň's list of Czech Debussy performances begins only in 1908 and is confined mostly to orchestral works performed in Prague;[10] *Reflets dans l'eau* (published in 1905), one of Debussy's first pianistic evocations of nature, may well be the first piece that Janáček encountered by this composer. Was *In the Mists*, with its rather greater sophistication than the *Overgrown Path* pieces and in particular its more pianistic texture (something Hoffmeister had criticized in his review of *On the Overgrown Path*), his response?

Given the encouraging reception of *On the Overgrown Path*, this must have seemed a good time for Janáček, with several new enquiries about performing his music. There was talk of *Our Father* (IV/29) in Prostějov,[11] and in Kroměříž conducted by Vach.[12] Dr Jaroslav Elgart, Janáček's admirer on the Brno Theatre Družstvo board (see chap. 56) and now chief surgeon at the hospital in Kroměříž, was planning a chamber concert in Kroměříž that would include both the Piano Trio (X/22) and *Fairy Tale* (VII/5).[13] There is no evidence, however, that the first of these performances took place. But others did. The Philharmonic Orchestra in the small Bohemian town of Příbram borrowed the music of Janáček's *Valachian Dances*[14] and performed the first (*Starodávný I*) in an orchestral concert on 10 March 1912 that included Dvořák, Fibich and Beethoven's 'Pastoral' Symphony.[15] And on 25 February Vach gave *Amarus* at the Brno Besední dům. Since the final orchestral movement had had to be abandoned at the first performance in Kroměříž in 1900, this Brno performance, twelve years later, was in fact the première of the complete piece. The orchestra again was mainly amateur (music teachers and others) but stiffened by wind players from the Vienna Tonkünstlerverein. The choir was an impressive new body of fifty singers, the Moravian Teachers' Mixed Choir (i.e. both men and women), which Vach had founded in 1912 and had been drilling ever since. This was their first independent outing and *Amarus* was placed in a programme of classic Czech choral-orchestral pieces: Smetana's *Czech Song* and Dvořák's *Hymnus* and *Festival Song*. In addition to approving comments on the new choir, one aspect particularly noted in reviews was the appearance as soloist in *Amarus* of the tenor Stanislav Tauber, who had sung the tenor part in Janáček's performance of Gounod's *Mors et vita* in 1909; he continued as the chief soloist in virtually all the performances of *Amarus* during Janáček's lifetime. The concert was a huge success given to a packed-out hall[16] and was repeated in the autumn in Prague. Further performances took place in 1913 in Kolín (Bohemia) and in the Moravian towns of Prostějov, Přerov and Kroměříž.[17] Meanwhile, the various performances of *Amarus* suddenly put this work on the map and laid the foundations of its later popularity with amateur choirs in Moravia.

Just as important as this rehabilitation of Janáček's major choral-orchestral work, already fifteen years old, was the first performance of its successor *The Čarták on Soláň* (III/7) in Prostějov by 'Orlice' on 23 March under Steinman. Here the work was put into the context of Smetana's *Czech Song* (as *Amarus* had been in Brno) and two further

Czech classics, Dvořák's *Te Deum* and Fibich's *Spring Romance*. It is curious that the accompanying orchestra was not the Orchestral Association that Steinman had formed the previous year in Prostějov but that of the 8th Infantry Regiment from Brno. Janáček attended rehearsals but for 'unknown reasons' was unable to attend the première.[18] In fact the première clashed with another commitment at the other end of the country, in Plzeň. To celebrate its fifty years of existence 'Orlice' was giving a high-profile concert with some of the masterpieces of Czech choral music, including a brand-new one from Moravia's leading composer; 'Hlahol' in Plzeň celebrated a similar birthday by hosting a choral competition and Janáček had been asked to be on the panel of judges. Unfortunately the competition was something of a damp squib, with the original 'international' plan downgraded to 'national' and only seven choirs (three of them local) turning up. There was presumably no chance of Janáček extricating himself from this since he was head of the six-man jury, a distinguished body that included leading choral composers and conservatory professors.[19]

On the way to Plzeň Janáček stopped off in Prague, where on Friday 22 March he heard Kovařovic conduct Smetana's *Dalibor*.[20] The next day Janáček reported his arrival in Plzeň to Zdenka,[21] and on Sunday 24 March the competition took place in the Valdek hall, with the seven choirs each singing one of the three set pieces (by Smetana, Foerster and a former 'Hlahol' director, Hynek Palla) and one own-choice piece. The victors were the Prague Teachers' Choral Society, a group that had made a considerable reputation since its first public concert in 1910. Its conductor was František Spilka, a professor at the Prague Conservatory. When the next day Janáček wrote to Zdenka from Prague that Plzeň had been hard work but that the 'new acquaintances' wouldn't do him any harm,[22] it was no doubt chiefly to Spilka that he was referring. Later that year there were contacts between Janáček and Spilka over the still unperformed chorus *The 70,000* (IV/36).

Perhaps it was during his long trip to Plzeň that Janáček had time to reflect on and write a short feuilleton for *Lidové noviny, Spring* (XV/204), published on 6 April. It begins with close observations of robins and a cuckoo in the Lužánky park, their calls all part of an evocation of spring. It then moves on to describe an old woman muttering to herself as she gathers firewood on the bank of the river Bečva.

The point of the article is to show how with their utterances both birds and humans reveal their innermost soul:

These tunes are so tenaciously attached to what prompted them, to what caused them, that when you lift the lid and uncover them, they quiver as in a draught with the same joy or with the same sorrow of your soul. *They are a comprehensible password* by which you can easily become the guest inside the soul of someone else.

The article is important as being the first of Janáček's articles to record birdsong, with its ten different short notations devoted to the robin. Almost a decade later Janáček took up bird notations in a series of articles as preparatory work for his opera *The Cunning Little Vixen*.

On 21 April Janáček sent a copy of *In the Mists* to Branberger. With an empty desk again he began to get back to *Brouček*. Janáček still needed a 'patron' song (see chap. 62). Since this song is at the beginning of Act 3, it rather suggests that he had got no further with the act than when he wrote a year earlier to Josef Holý and Dr Janke. His approach to the Moravian writer Stanislav Kostka Neumann is known only from Neumann's friendly though negative reply, on 29 April: 'Forgive me that I cannot comply with your kind suggestions: witty verse things, whenever I have tried to do them, have [always] turned out miserably. I don't know how to do them!' Neumann went on to suggest the poet and translator Josef Mach (a 'firm for jokes').[23] Janáček was getting warm. Though Mach did not help him either it was possibly through Mach that Janáček made contact with Mach's friend, the satirical poet František Gellner.

Meanwhile Janáček addressed another urgent concern, the decision by the executive committee of *Das Volkslied in Österreich* about the language in which to publish the various songs assembled. The organization had originally intended all songs, of whatever nation, to be published in German, a manifestly absurd and chauvinist notion that Janáček had fought off. As no official steps had been taken, however, he was now anxious. By strange coincidence his opposite number in Prague was now, after the death of Hostinský in 1908 and his successor J.V. Dušek in 1911, none other than Zdeněk Nejedlý, whose dismissive comments on *Jenůfa* had so roused Janáček's indignation. However, in their contacts over folksong (which continued until

Janáček's death), the two men behaved with impeccable, businesslike co-operation and courtesy (see chap. 57). In his first letter to Nejedlý, written on 5 May, just a few months after his bitter published comments in *Song* (XV/203), Janáček made no reference to their public differences but instead invited Nejedlý to enlist local parliamentarians in trying to discover why the motion to have folksongs published in local languages seemed not to have been formally adopted yet.[24] Further folksong work involved a trip to Kozlovice on 5 June to notate the Christmas plays *Valachians* and *The Three Kings*.[25] Kozlovice is just a stone's throw away from Hukvaldy, which suggests that Janáček might have taken a few days off there. If so, it would have been his only trip to Hukvaldy that year. The pattern of his trips was changing. Zdenka, on her visit to Hukvaldy in 1910, had reported how unpleasant the atmosphere had been, with Janáček's sister-in-law Marie (widow of František) feeling sorry for herself and his sister Josefa equally miserable with her marriage falling apart. There is no evidence that Janáček went there again until 1914.

Around mid-June Janáček had heard from František Gellner about *Brouček*. In 1910 Janáček had reported to Rektorys in exasperation that he was going to get on with *Brouček* on his own, simply sticking to Čech's novel. This is essentially what he did with the first two acts, extracting dialogue where it existed, and in this way composing two acts: Mr Brouček depicted on earth and among his early acquaintances in Act 1, and Mr Brouček miraculously transported to the moon in Act 2. Act 3, however, was a different matter, with Brouček shown in the midst of the moon artists, writers and composers, a scene that suggested many more opportunities for songs. Janáček needed someone to write light, rhyming verse. It was František Gellner who came to his rescue. Gellner (1881–1914) was one of the most colourful of Janáček's many *Brouček* librettists. He had published poetry from an early age but invested most of his efforts in graphic art, with studies in Vienna, Munich, Paris and Dresden. In November 1911 he returned to the Czech lands and worked for *Lidové noviny* in Brno, at first as a cartoonist and later as a member of the editorial board.[26] None of Janáček's instructions to Gellner have survived but some notion of their exchanges emerges from an undated letter from Gellner sending the patron song[27] and another, soon after (dated 17 June), sending Oblačný's recitation. Gellner's final contribution to the act was a musicians' chorus suggesting a cacophony of sound (a replacement for the symphony *The Storm* that Janáček had been attracted to when the novel first came out, and which was planned in early drafts of the work). Gellner's musicians' chorus was used as a song of praise to the patron Čaroskvoucí as Brouček makes his escape at the end of the act. Everything that Janáček needed for Act 3 was presumably received by the autumn, when Gellner next responded about the projected fourth act.

More performances of Janáček's works were being planned. In June–July there was a curious exchange between Janáček and Vach over the still unperformed chorus *The 70,000* (IV/36). On 17 June Vach wrote a tart little note saying that both he and the Moravian Teachers' archivist had considered the score of *The 70,000* to be a gift. 'Since you have now evidently decided otherwise I am sending it back *at your request*.'[28] Had Janáček's new acquaintance, František Spilka, offered to perform it? In his account of the Bezruč choruses (1953) Bohumír Štědroň reported Spilka's view that Vach had kept the chorus 'for a while' and then returned it as 'unperformable'.[29] However, a month later Janáček sent back the chorus to Vach,[30] now copied by one F. Borecký and dated 5 July 1912. So perhaps Janáček had merely retrieved the chorus for revisions (in the light of the Plzeň competition?) and, these done, sent it back to Vach? Either way, the chorus lay around unperformed and seemingly unperformable for quite some time. While there had been discussion in Janáček's correspondence with Elgart about a performance of *Fairy Tale* (VII/5) earlier that year in Kroměříž, that too had not been realized. Rather more productive was an approach from Antonín Váňa. While the summer-holidays performance in Příbram he proposed did not take place,[31] he played it a little later, at the Academic Club in the Moravian town of Vyškov on 22 September. This was only the second performance of the work, and in a new version in which Janáček's work-in-progress had been expanded to four movements.

On 23 July Lucie Bakešová wrote to Janáček after a very long gap asking if she could send two photographs she had received from Janáček of folk dances, plays and related material to the Náprstek Museum in Prague. The pictures were needed immediately and, in her forthright way, Bakešová asked for a 'prompt answer'.[32] She was not to get one: by 23 July the Janáčeks were uncharacteristically on holiday together in Croatia. Apart from family gatherings at Hukvaldy this was the first holiday that the Janáčeks had spent together for many years. In his book based on Zdenka's reminiscences, Robert Smetana devoted considerable detail to the Croatian trip.[33] He reported that the Janáčeks left by the afternoon express for Vienna 'some time' after 15 July, i.e. the end of the Organ School term. The exact day, however, is difficult to determine. On 16 July Janáček was still clearing his desk (sending off the latest version of *The 70,000* to Vach; see above). On 17 July Věra Janáčková wrote to her uncle saying that, because of doctor's orders, she was unable to accompany them.[34] If Janáček was waiting to hear how Věra would decide, the earliest the trip could have begun would have been a day or two after receiving her letter and finalizing their travel arrangements (cases were sent on in advance).[35]

In her memoirs Zdenka reported that she had been begging Janáček 'for a whole year' to see the sea. In fact the seaside plan must have been in their minds much longer. In a letter to Zdenka during September 1909, when both husband and wife were afflicted by health problems, Janáček slipped in the following comment: 'What holidays we've had! God grant that next year we take a break at the seaside.'[36] The 'seaside' did of course figure in a scheme to go to Russia in July 1912 that Janáček scribbled on the end pages of the third volume of his Tolstoy edition, an ambitious trip that took in not only St Petersburg, Nizhny Novgorod and Moscow, but also Sebastopol, Yalta and Odessa.[37] Maybe Zdenka didn't fancy this and, through the Janáčeks' contacts with the Brno Women's Shelter, found her own holiday location, the Croatian seaside resort of Crikvenica, near Rijeka. It was there that the Shelter had built a special children's home; for the Janáčeks to go there would cost, Zdenka discovered, little more than Janáček's usual summer trip to Luhačovice. The director of the Women's Shelter, Marie Steyskalová,* found them a 'cosy room with a balcony in a beautiful villa on the seafront, with a view of the beach and the sea',[38] and worked out a travel itinerary for the couple. The route went south via Vienna through the Semmering Pass into Styria, through Slovenia to Sv. Peter, where the railway line divided. The Janáčeks continued south to Rijeka and finally along the Croatian coast to Crikvenica. The route, through what are now several independent countries, was from start to finish all part of the Austro-Hungarian Empire.

---

* The spelling, but not the pronunciation, of her name is slightly different from that of the Janáček's housekeeper.

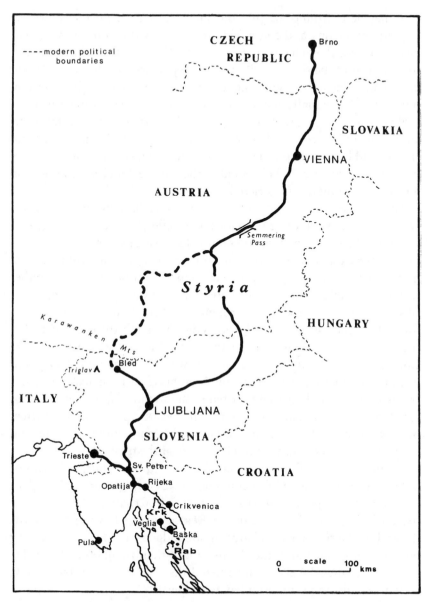

Map 5   The Janáčeks' journey to Croatia in 1912.

Somewhere around 20 July the Janáčeks set off on the afternoon express for Vienna and continued their journey the same evening. The next morning they changed trains in Sv. Peter for Rijeka, which they looked round before the afternoon departure of the steamer for Crikvenica. There they were met off the pier and taken to their accommodation.[39] Originally Janáček had expected to spend only a week in Crikvenica, planning to go on further to Kupari, a small coastal resort south-east of Dubrovnik, but after his first dip Janáček announced that they would be staying put. Janáček was much taken with the sea, going in at least twice a day. However, neither of the Janáčeks could swim and so were somewhat restricted.

The couple spent three weeks in the area, bathing and going for walks in the coastal forest Vinodol surrounding Crikvenica, and taking a trip to the island of Krk in small fishing vessels. They also took a few longer excursions by steamer, to Pula, then an Austro-Hungarian naval base, where they saw the Roman amphitheatre, and another trip around Krk, where they got off to inspect the town of Veglia.[†] On this journey they experienced rough weather, though neither of the Janáčeks succumbed to seasickness as did the rest of the passengers. On the way back the weather worsened and the ship was caught in a severe storm; it had to remain at sea since it was too dangerous to try and dock on the rocky coast. Wet through on his return, Janáček could not be restrained from lingering to listen to the sound of folksongs from an inn. On a final excursion by steamer they visited Baška, another town on Krk, eating in the Czech inn 'U Geistlichů' and looking out – in vain – for the Rektorys family on holiday there at the time.[40]

As always, Janáček took his notebook with him, jotting down not only speech melodies (an encounter on 30 July with a little girl to whom he gave a penny) but also the names in Croatian of some of the sea birds.[41] Janáček's brief card to Rektorys on 12 August, towards the end of the trip, gave a characteristic judgement: 'The sea is strong but only in surface and line. It tires more than mountains.'[42] Twelve years later, when Janáček remembered the trip in his autobiography, he reduced most of it to just a few terse lines:

Through the Alps to Rijeka and to sunny Crikvenica.

The sea. You see the shellfish deep at the bottom. An octopus with a great family of young.

[†] The Italian word for Krk. Krk/Veglia is the chief town of the island.

At noon the sun burns the beach. It sets and a golden bridge joins the shore
to the horizon.

Tolstoy's three old holy men[‡] could walk along it.

The cool in Vinodol.

A trip to the vineyards of Krk.

Women worn out with work; the comfortable fishermen.

Around Rab.[§]

To Pula to the Roman ruins; an amphitheatre.

A storm at sea.[43]

One of the themes that emerges from Zdenka's account is how
fearful a traveller Janáček was. The only reason why this exotic trip
took place at all was because of the forward planning by Zdenka and
Mrs Steyskalová. Once they had arrived in Crikvenica, the proposed
continuation to Kupari evaporated. Janáček would not hear of a
diversion to Trieste on the way back. Zdenka proposed a different
route back to Brno via the Alpine pass into Austria in the Karawanken
mountains (taking the western rather than the eastern fork at
Ljubljana), but Janáček's fear of new places prevailed so that his only
concession was to travel by steamer to Opatija, where they had a meal,
did a little sightseeing, and then went on to Rijeka by train. But on the
train to Sv. Peter they met a Czech-speaking couple who offered to
show them Trieste and so Janáček's resistance weakened and they made
an overnight stay there on 14 August. Their new friends found them
accommodation, ordered them a complicated fish meal in an *osteria*,
took them for coffee and ice cream in a café, and then on a walk
to the harbour before retiring. 'It was midnight when the Janáčeks
returned to the hotel with their companions and at five in the morning
Janáček impatiently woke up his wife again and looked round Trieste
tirelessly the whole morning.'[44] It was now 15 August and would have
been Olga's thirtieth birthday, which Zdenka remembered in one of the
churches. Emboldened by the success of the Trieste expedition, Janáček
consented to stop further in Bled, where 'they found a lovely room in
one of the villas next to the station', made a half-day trip to Vintgar
gorge with its waterfalls and visited the tiny shrine on an island in the
lake at Bled. The return trip also included a two-day stop in Ljubljana –

[‡] A reference to Tolstoy's tale *The Three Old Men* (1884), seemingly ignorant in doctrine but
so holy that they could run on the sea.
[§] A little further south, this island was presumably taken in during the Krk voyage.

'white Ljubljana', as Janáček described it in his account of the journey home, 'the castle and its guard, a Czech pensioner'.[45] Since Bled is the last town before the border on the Karawanken mountains, it sounds as if Zdenka's original return plan (the western route) prevailed. However, Smetana reports that the two-day stop in Ljubljana occurred 'after Bled', which would mean the Janáčeks' retracing their steps and then taking the eastern branch. It is possible, however, that this route through unfamiliar terrain got muddled in the telling. Janáček's own terse account in his autobiography places Ljubljana before Bled and adds a view of the Triglav mountain, visible from Bled. Back in Vienna, Zdenka remained with her parents while Janáček went on further to Brno. He could only have been there for a day or so: on 21 August 1912 he registered at Luhačovice for a week's stay.[46]

There, in a copy of *Národní listy* of 20 August, Janáček came across the welcome news that *The 70,000* was being published 'after a long delay' and reported this in a note to Zdenka.[47] Sadly the news was unfounded. It would have been odd for any publisher at this stage of Janáček's career to have taken on a still unperformed – and seemingly unperformable – choral piece. Publication was in fact nine years off. In her card Zdenka welcomed the news and said how glad she was to eat 'normally' after the exotic fare abroad.[48] Janáček's short stay in Luhačovice (he left on 28 August) is notable for its being the first time that he stayed in the Augustinian House. From 1918 he used it exclusively.

September brought the new school year in Brno and also several contacts with publishers. On 20 September Píša wrote to say that Janáček's and Bakešová's edition of *Folk Dances in Moravia* (VIII/10) was out of print. Would it be possible to reprint it?[49] It is curious that Janáček seems to have withheld permission. Did he fear further contacts with Bakešová (he had seemingly not responded to her last request, above, and perhaps felt guilty) or did he no longer stand by these arrangements? Perhaps, however, the whole matter was driven from his mind by a much more urgent crisis caused by F.A. Urbánek in Prague, about which Janáček now wrote to Rektorys on 22 September:

Help me to get out of a hole!

Has the editorial board of *Smetana* got a copy of my new work *A Complete Harmony Manual*? [XV/202].

Dr Nejedlý is not my friend, nor am I his: how he reviewed my earlier study

The Composition of Chords and their Connections [xv/151] is not important now.[II]

I'd be glad if he'd also review the *Complete Harmony Manual*.

What concerns me is whether I've written a work about harmony in a new form (text, music examples) and in thought.

Someone, you see, thinks that I'm grinding out my old stuff purely to compete with it!

One volume from the *Complete Harmony Manual* has come out so far; a second is in the press.

But a review is possible from the first volume.[50]

Rektorys, in his footnote comment on this letter,[51] explained that Urbánek was trying to get Janáček to pay 1757 K for unsold copies of the manual that Urbánek had published in 1897 because of alleged similarities with the new manual that Píša was publishing. In the end, simply to avoid a long legal battle, Janáček paid Urbánek compensation of 200 K, although he had received no fee for the book and the contents of the two volumes were quite different. When he replied to Janáček's plea, Rektorys confirmed that he had received the book (i.e. vol. i) and would pass it on to Nejedlý for review when he returned from his summer vacation.[52]

Within a week Janáček was able to send the second volume of the manual[53] and see Rektorys in person shortly afterwards on one of his now rare trips to Prague. He was going there for the weekend of 4–6 October, a trip built round the Sunday afternoon concert in the Rudolfinum of the Association of Mixed Choirs.[54] An eloquent testament to Janáček's increasingly distant relationship with Rektorys is the fact that he did not bother to mention that this Sunday afternoon concert was in fact the Prague première of *Amarus*, Janáček's largest Prague première so far. It was a repeat of Vach's concert with his new mixed choir given in Brno on 25 February, though with the Czech Philharmonic providing the orchestral accompaniment rather than the ad hoc orchestra used in Brno.[¶] Rektorys wrote back warmly: 'Will you be going on Friday evening [4 October] to hear Destinn (*Dalibor*)?

[II]It is difficult to know what Janáček may be referring to. No review by Nejedlý of xv/151 is mentioned in the comprehensive bibliography issued in his fiftieth-birthday Festschrift (Patzaková and Očadlík 1929). Nor would a review have been likely as Nejedlý, although precocious, was only eighteen at the time of its publication.
[¶]Nebuška's long report of the concert in *HR*, vi (1912–13), 92–4, makes it clear that the conductor was Vach, as at the Brno performance, not Vilém Zemánek, as cited in *JAWO*, 85.

If you don't have a ticket I will willingly place you in my seat – if you accept it as a mark of gratitude. Just say so without fuss. Then after the theatre we could speak.'[55] Arrangements needed further fine-tuning, with Janáček suggesting that Rektorys leave the ticket for him at his hotel, the Archduke Štěpán,[56] but in the end Rektorys met him at the theatre and escorted him personally to the first gallery as the *Smetana* editorial seat was a permanent, unticketed one. Presumably Janáček then met him afterwards at Šroubek's restaurant in Václavské náměstí as suggested.[57]

The Moravian Teachers' première of *Amarus* in Prague, or even just the prospect of it, seems to have generated interest in Janáček's most recent and still unperformed chorus, *The 70,000* (IV/36). On his return from Prague Janáček found a letter waiting for him from F.A. Urbánek in which the publisher offered a contract for *The 70,000*.[58] In 1909 Janáček had offered Urbánek the chorus at the same time as *Maryčka Magdónova* but Urbánek declined *The 70,000*. The success of the *Amarus* concert seems to have encouraged Janáček to raise his stakes. Not only did he refuse Urbánek's offer, but he seems to have written to František Spilka about the prospective performance of the work. In a letter of 18 October, reacting to one from Janáček, Spilka expressed surprise at Janáček's requirement of 100 K rather than the 'agreed' 50 K for the performance of *The 70,000*.[59] Whatever further negotiations took place (prompting, for instance a report in the November issue of *Hudební revue* that Spilka's Prague Teachers' Choral Society were studying Janáček's chorus),[60] it was only in spring 1914 that Spilka's group finally gave the first performance of *The 70,000* (see chap. 66).

For the third and final revision of *Fate* in 1907 Janáček had made use of a new copyist, Vojtěch Ševčík (1881–1955), a horn player in the Brno Theatre orchestra who had taken part in the Brno première of *Jenůfa*. Janáček continued to employ Ševčík at various points in the composition of *Brouček* from 1909 (Act 1) and for the later acts: there is a copy in his hand of as much of the opera as Janáček had written by 1912 (Acts 1–3). While it was were being copied, Janáček began to look ahead to the final act. 'I have read your letter', Gellner wrote to Janáček on 23 October, 'and from it it is clear to me that you are asking for a substantial piece of work from me: I don't know whether I shall be able to take on this task immediately.'[61] Instead of merely the individual songs that had been required for Act 3, Janáček now needed a whole 'epilogue' act. Further contacts between Janáček and Gellner over Act 4 took place in 1913.

On receiving Ševčík's copy of *Brouček* Janáček made extensive revisions, involving many inserted sheets, and signed the score on 5 November 1912.[62] This is an important moment in the protracted composition of the opera, the first time Janáček felt confident enough to put down a date. Presumably, while working on this, he wrote to Ševčík warning him that he would be sending him material for correction and recopying. Ševčík had by now moved to Prague. 'Just send me the music', he replied on 3 November, 'I hope that I'll somehow finish it.' What next year became even more important for Janáček than Ševčík's music copying was his position in the Vinohrady company as orchestral secretary. From here he was able to provide confidential reports about the progress of *Fate*. 'We are still not yet rehearsing *Fate*', his letter continues. 'On 25 November there is to be a première by Piskáček (the operetta conductor),** then perhaps it will be the turn of your *Fate*. At the same time accept my hearty congratulations on the great success of your *Amarus*.'[63]

If Janáček sent him *Brouček* as seems to have been promised, then Ševčík was unable to complete it. More likely, however, was that all Janáček's plans came to a halt when he suddenly succumbed to a 'strange illness'. Stejskalová described it as 'terrible rheumatism',[64] Zdenka, as reported by Smetana, as 'rheumatism or gout'.[65] In her memoirs taken down by Trkanová, Zdenka put it down to excessive bathing in the sea during their Croatian holiday.[66] Today it might be diagnosed as 'reactive arthritis' occasioned by an intestinal infection (see chap. 64). Zdenka gave a graphic description of his affliction:

His feet and his hands swelled up, he couldn't even move, he didn't sleep from November to March. Mářa and I had to turn him continually on the sheets, he was in such pain. Taking aspirin gave him some relief, otherwise nothing else was any use. At the same time he was active, he wanted to work, his pupils from the Organ School had to come to our house for lessons. They sat round his bed in the study and he taught them. Sometimes after their departure the place looked a real mess; and still worse after the masseuse. The floor was covered with stains from her ointments. Leoš loved being massaged right to the end of his life. At that time during his illness he was very keen on an old lame woman and greatly praised her expertise.[67]

** Rudolf Piskáček (1884–1940), the younger brother of Adolf (see chap. 53).

The masseuse, according to Stejskalová, was Antonie Koláčná. Born in 1877 and thus forty-five at the time, she hardly qualified as 'old'. She had attended Janáček while they were still in their Staré Brno flat but as she lived in Dvorecká (now Slovákova) ulice she was just round the corner from the new house and could come easily on demand.[68] Another treatment that seemed to have helped at this time was 'Hukvaldy honey' – bandages soaked in honey (sent by the Sládeks in Hukvaldy). According to Smetana, however, Janáček's improvement was due to Dr Stix of Panská ulice, who treated him encased in cotton wool 'with some sort of electrified magnetic implements' after which he slept well for the first time.[69] After more cotton wool and keeping to a strict diet, the swelling reduced, but all his skin peeled off. Other doctors whom Janáček consulted at the time included Dr Hora from Francouzská ulice, who prescribed compresses; Dr Jan Hnátek from Prague, consulted by post, who recommended the drug piperazine (used normally for the treatment of roundworm and threadworm infestation), of which Janáček consumed several bottles; Dr Dressler (Janáček's cousin); and Dr Jaroslav Elgart from Kroměříž. On 9 December Janáček wrote to Elgart saying that he was ill, that he could not move, the advice of the Brno doctors was not helping. Could Elgart please come and examine him?[70]

1 November was the deadline for the new Club of the Friends of Art competition. In his study of the organization (1948) Ludvík Kundera was unable to determine how many pieces were submitted this time but noted that Janáček himself intervened in two ways, by submitting his own piano cycle *In the Mists*, and by suggesting to his former pupil, Jaroslav Kvapil (1892–1958), then studying in Leipzig, that he send in some songs. Members of the club seem to have drawn up a shortlist themselves, and then sent the selected piano pieces to Karel Hoffmeister and the songs to Jan Branberger and his singer wife Doubravka Branbergerová for final adjudication. The Branbergers selected three of Kvapil's songs, Hoffmeister selected *In the Mists*. There was not enough money for printing both selections so Janáček waived his right to the immediate printing of his piano pieces and the club had Kvapil's songs printed and published in December as the free gift to its members for 1912.[71] *In the Mists* was published a year later.

In a letter to Janáček of 25 November giving his adjudication, Hoffmeister mentioned two piano cycles, *Spring Song* and *In the Mists*, stating that the latter was 'definitely much nicer' than the former.[72] This letter is the basis for the supposition that Janáček had also composed a piano cycle entitled *Spring Song*, now lost.[73] The lack of composers' names in Hoffmeister's letter was of course a result of the club's effort to keep the pieces anonymous. All the evidence points to *Spring Song* as being one of the competition entries by a composer other than Janáček. It is just as well that Hoffmeister rated Janáček's *In the Mists* more highly than the anonymous *Spring Song*. The reactive arthritis that laid Janáček up for months was quite enough bad news to be getting on with as 1912 drew to an end.

64

Janáček's illnesses I

by STEPHEN LOCK

Illness and health feature prominently in this book and others on Janáček. Thus the indexes show no fewer than forty-three entries in his wife's memoirs,[1] and over a hundred in the English edition of his correspondence with Kamila Stösslová.[2] These numbers, however, might give a false impression. Janáček lived a robustly healthy life and his troubles were minor: sinus problems, an episode of arthritis (and possibly gout, which gave intermittent problems, see vol. ii: Did Janáček have really gout?), anxiety about his heart, and recurrent bronchitis before his short-lived terminal pneumonia. Admittedly he was plump – though accounts of losing 10 kilos in a fortnight's stay in a spa (see chap. 58) are scarcely credible – but he walked many kilometres a week and was only a 'social' smoker and drinker. And this conclusion is borne out by his long life for the period (for most of the nineteenth century the predicted lifespan for a central European male at birth was under forty years, and even if he survived the dangerous childhood ailments the risks of lethal illnesses in middle life were considerable).

Janáček's ailments are summarized in table 64.1, but to a doctor three stand out as being of principal interest. In 1893 he had an operation to drain a maxillary sinus (often called the antrum of Highmore, after a seventeenth-century English surgeon). Situated in the cheekbone of either side, these sinuses are normally empty cavities filled only with air and help give resonance to the voice. Sometimes, however, like the sinuses elsewhere in the facial bones, they become infected (often in association with the common cold and tonsillitis) and full of sticky fluid. The latter accumulates because the passage that normally connects the sinus with the nose is blocked; the air in the sinuses becomes absorbed into the bloodstream and they fill with fluid, which then

Table 64.1: Janáček's illnesses 1884–1914

complaint	years	comments
Bronchitis, cough	1884, 1910	See discussion of sinus disorder above
Digestive disorders	1903	Probably spastic colon – constipation and lower abdominal pain
Ear problems	1906	Hissing sounds – probably just wax
Erysipelas (St Anthony's fire)	1913	Streptococcal skin infection (see below)
Exhaustion/depression	1908	Frequent complaint, but seems non-specific rather than psychiatric disorder
'Gout'	1908, 1914	See vol. ii: Did Janáček have gout?
Heart problems	1909	See discussion of cardiac neurosis below but note that he also complained of fast pulse rate (160) or pounding heart years later (see vol. ii: 1924b and 1927b)
Rheumatism/arthritis	1884, 1888, 1897, 1906, 1909, 1912	Seems to have taken two forms, probably non-specific muscular or connective tissue ('fibrositis') and the 'reactive arthritis' in 1912 (see above); see also Gout
Sinusitis	1893, 1903, 1908	Operation in Prague, and repeat procedure in 1908 (see above)

becomes infected by bacteria. The pain in the face may be agonizing, and not always easy to distinguish from severe toothache. Sometimes the condition can be relieved by inhalations (and especially today with antibiotics), but the infected sinus may have to be drained, temporarily by passing a wide-bore needle through the nose into the sinus, or permanently by a surgical operation.

The first such operation was devised by Karl Zeim, who had shown for the first time that infection of the sinuses originated in the nose. In 1886 he invented a procedure to drain the maxillary sinus by making a passage into the mouth after an upper canine tooth had been removed. One difficulty was that this hole tended to seal itself, and surgeons tried to prevent this by inserting a rubber plug. The latter could be removed when patients followed a subsequent suggestion by Ernest von Kuster to pass a tube up into the sinus and flush it out with fluid.

As Janáček found (see chap. 29), all this was very unpleasant, and he was also particularly unfortunate in the timing of his operation. For in the very year that Professor Kaufmann operated on him in Prague, a much better operation was described, one that persists to this day. In this, another permanent hole is made, this time into the nose, so that the sinus can drain freely and without needing any other attention. The originators of the new procedure were an American, James Caldwell, and a Frenchman, Henri Luc. Though the old operation belonged to the German school (Zeim hailed from Danzig and von Kuster from Berlin) – and surgeons tended, and tend still, to follow their national culture – the Vienna school of otorhinolaryngology, which must have influenced Prague practices, was particularly dynamic and open-minded. In 1873 the department there was the first to be established anywhere, and ten years later no fewer than a hundred postgraduate students were flocking to it from all over the world. Hence it is unthinkable that the major central European centres would not have switched to the Caldwell-Luc procedure as soon as its claims had been validated.

The second illness must have been the most alarming of the three, although paradoxically it was the most benign. In July 1909 Janáček succumbed to the many everyday difficulties he had had: he was very tired and 'run down', and went to the sanatorium at Tišnov for three weeks. A few weeks later he developed 'heart problems', ascribing these to the vigorous exercise he had taken. The symptoms were frightening, and might wake him in the middle of the night; they included a fast pulse rate, awareness of his heart pounding all over his body, and occasional dropped heartbeats. Yet he did not go to hospital, but instead took himself off to another spa, at Teplice. He stayed there only two days, probably because the symptoms were intermittent, and the chief consultant reassured him that he did not have heart disease; a few days later he was going on his usual walks (see chap. 58).

Such symptoms are quite unlike those of a 'coronary' (myocardial infarction), though this condition would not have been recognized given that it was not to be documented for another few years. Janáček, however, almost certainly had an anxiety state manifesting itself principally as a cardiac neurosis. Its textbook features include tightness in the chest, a sinking feeling in the pit of the stomach, lightheadedness, sweating, rapid pulse and awareness of the heartbeat. Similar features, lumped together as battle neurosis, have been described for centuries in soldiers, given that they interfere with the efficiency of combat troops, but, starting with the American Civil War and the Indian Frontier Wars, the emphasis has always been on the cardiac features. Thus synonyms include soldier's heart, irritable heart and disorderly action of the heart, with no fewer than 44,000 British soldiers being invalided out of the service with this diagnosis in the First World War. Nevertheless, research in 1917–18 showed that almost half of those affected had had the condition *before* they joined the Armed Forces, so that clearly it was not entirely due to the anxieties provoked by active service.

The stresses on Janáček, then, would have been likely to underlie such a cardiac neurosis. And the consultant who gave him a clear bill of health is likely to have recognized what was going on. For, starting in the 1850s, an extensive discussion had been going on in medical circles about neurasthenia, a catch-all diagnosis described by two American physicians, Silas Weir Mitchell and George Beard, and then adopted internationally. Beard, who introduced the synonym 'American nervousness', defined neurasthenia as nervous weakness produced by the frantic pressures of advanced civilization and the 'drain on the individual's nerve force'. His group of patients had consisted mainly of brain workers – sedentary, creative, educated professionals. The illness was linked to specific features of modernity: steam power, the periodical press, the telegraph, the sciences and the 'mental activity of women'. 'When civilization, plus these five factors invades any nation', Beard wrote, 'it must carry nervousness and nervous disease along with it.'

Patients could be treated by removal from home and deprivation of contact with the family, with rest and overfeeding, with four to five pints of milk a day. Around the same time as Janáček's illness, this regimen was used for Virginia Woolf (who, of course, had a much more serious bi-polar illness, characterized by extreme mania and depression) and the whole concept of neurasthenia – coupled with the late nineteenth-century ideas of degeneration and the importance of hysteria – must have been foremost in the minds of medical professionals and the educated public. For, once Beard's book had been translated into German (1881), Europeans were quick to adopt this concept, particularly its darker side, while Max Simon Nordau linked it to theories of degeneration in his book of that name published in 1893. French and German doctors attributed degeneration to poisoning of the system by alcohol, tobacco and drugs, causes very similar to those also incriminated in neurasthenia. Nevertheless, hastened perhaps by the increasingly prominent role of psychiatry in the First World War, such vagaries gradually became replaced by the theories of Freud, which hypothesized that neurosis stemmed from early sexual traumas. Freud had introduced his concepts in the 1890s, and they gradually entered medical and general thought, particularly after the first English translation of his work appeared in 1912. (In 1919, for instance, the *Saturday Review* commented that Freud's books were now 'discussed over the soup with the latest play or novel'.) Neurasthenia as a diagnosis, then, had disappeared in the USA and western Europe by the outbreak of the Second World War, though it persists in Russia, and today, 150 years after Beard, the concept of 'Russian nervousness' is still being discussed.

In 1912 Janáček developed severe and disabling arthritis, lasting from November to March. Over the years he had complained of aches and pains in his joints and neck as well as sciatica, asking if he could wear an overcoat in a draughty theatre (see chap. 53), and had even been said to have gout. Even so, there was no family history or any previous or subsequent episodes, and without the help of today's biochemical tests a diagnosis of gout was another catch-all, popular over the centuries in every country. On the last occasion, however, the symptoms were far from trivial. The pains in his hands and feet were severe, confining him to bed, keeping him awake at night, and relieved only by aspirin and massage. Fortunately the illness subsided in the spring. Traditionally retrospective diagnosis is difficult, but this episode seems most likely to have been reactive arthritis – that is, not an infection of the joints themselves, but inflammation of the joints secondary to an infection elsewhere. The latter is often in the intestine, and the provocative bacteria include those resembling some that cause gastro-enteritis, dysentery or typhoid fever.

In 1913 Janáček spent three weeks in hospital for erysipelas. Sometimes known as St Anthony's fire, this is a painful skin disease, characterized by a purplish, spreading butterfly rash over both sides of the nose and cheekbones, caused by infection by streptococci from the nose and throat and accompanied by fever, headache and vomiting. Probably this was related to the earlier problem with his facial sinuses, as was the bronchitis, which had occurred before the operation and was to persist throughout his life.

65

1913

Janáček remained ill for the early months of 1913. On his sickbed he was assailed by disturbing news of *Fate* at the Vinohrady Theatre in Prague. For instance on 4 February the administrative director of the theatre Václav Štech announced that difficulties with performing the opera had reached such a peak that he needed to talk to Janáček and would come and do so in the next few days.[1] Although the meeting seems to have been postponed (perhaps on account of Janáček's health), Janáček was soon to hear from his mole in the Vinohrady Theatre, the orchestral secretary Vojtěch Ševčík. *Fate* had not yet been handed out even to the soloists, he wrote. For the moment they were rehearsing d'Albert's *Die verschenkte Frau* and another revival of Malát's *A Merry Wooing*. An operetta was to follow, so it was beginning to look as if *Fate* would not make the 'winter season 1912–13' stipulated in the new contract. Furthermore, Ševčík wrote, members of the Družstvo wanted to cut costs by reducing the orchestra by six. The 'fifty-piece' orchestra that had been the attraction for Janáček when he submitted the opera to Vinohrady in 1907 would now comprise thirty-two players, no more than in Brno.[2] Shortly after Janáček received this letter Štech got in touch again to finalize his visit,[3] though Janáček had now become wary: in a draft letter to his legal adviser Dr Pauk he said that he had informed Mr Štech that it would be an honour to welcome him to Brno but as far as *Fate* was concerned he would act only after consulting Dr Pauk.[4] On 3 March Štech nevertheless announced his arrival in Brno the following day to see Janáček. He was not coming to negotiate, he wrote, merely to say how things were with *Fate*.[5]

Ševčík, meanwhile, continued to ply Janáček with gloomy news from the coalface. Bedřich Holeček, who had succeeded Čelanský as head of opera in 1908, had proclaimed that as long as he was conductor at the Vinohrady Janáček's *Fate* would not be given. Whether this was personal animosity towards Janáček Ševčík had not fathomed. His own theory was that Holeček was terrified of conducting a difficult new work that had never been performed elsewhere. There was now also a defeatist attitude towards Janáček's opera: people had been saying that it didn't amount to much, and this of course was affecting the attitudes of the singers. Ševčík's advice was that Janáček should not insist on a performance but wait until someone turned up who would 'take up the work with love, and who would not damn it in advance'.[6]

When Štech next wrote, on 22 March, he said that he would make 'one further attempt' to see if it was possible to put *Fate* into rehearsal. He had entrusted this task to the second conductor Rudolf Piskáček, who would report to him after the Easter holidays.[7] In his letter Štech had said he would communicate the results of Piskáček's efforts on the Tuesday or Wednesday after Easter (24–5 March). When by 26 March nothing had come from Štech, Janáček wrote to Rektorys:

I don't know if you still like me a little but nevertheless I turn to you with a request.

The conductor Holeček has refused to rehearse *Fate* – he says it would ruin the voices of the singers.

Now Director Štech has written to say that he has entrusted the piece to Piskáček. I don't know him personally and I have just got over a serious illness so I don't dare go and visit him at once.

Would you be so good as to go and instil in him a little love and devotion for my work?

It should be done at once.[8]

As usual, Rektorys could not have been more obliging:

Have no worries: I will do everything in my power gladly and willingly.

I think that the change of conductor needn't disappoint you because the change (about which you write) will be to the work's gain rather than the opposite. I will speak to Piskáček and all the soloists and sort out everything as if you were present.

I would wish from my heart that you'll be happy with the performance. Let's keep up our hopes; I don't want to take away hope from you. [. . .]

See you then at the happy première![9]

Did Rektorys really believe that *Fate* could be rescued at this stage and that there would be a 'happy première'? As an experienced music journalist and journal editor he would have been well abreast of the musical gossip of the time. It would have been cruel to have buoyed up Janáček's hopes if he knew otherwise; perhaps, however, Rektorys, without whose encouragement *Fate* would never have been submitted to the Vinohrady in the first place, was deluding himself. He did not do so for much longer. It was Dr Pauk who first broke the news to Janáček:

In connection with your opera *Fate* I have heard from the director, Mr Štech, that it is impossible for the directorate to stage your opera *Fate* since during the rehearsals undertaken by the second conductor all the soloists proclaimed that the opera puts such demands on them that they are unable to cope with them.

Kindly let me know whether you wish me to proceed with an action against the directorate.[10]

The next day Rektorys himself confirmed this: 'I delayed [writing] so that I should not be the first who had to give you such unpleasant news.' Furthermore, as Rektorys had gathered, Štech was anticipating a lawsuit and had statements taken down from the soloists. 'If it comes to a lawsuit – Štech told me that he has already received notification from your solicitor – I can only advise you to be very careful in your choice of expert advisers.' Of the possibilities that Janáček might consider, Rektorys advised against Čelanský ('too *parti pris*') and against the director of the Prague Conservatory, Jindřich z Albestů Kàan ('too set in his ways').[11]

There are times when things are so awful that one just tries to push them out of one's mind. If Janáček felt that way then he would have been happily distracted by a couple of rare successes. The day after getting Rektorys's letter he had a note from Vach, who had successfully given a third performance of *Amarus* with his new choir in the Bohemian town of Kolín.[12] A few days later Janáček, now presumably well enough to venture further afield, travelled to Olomouc, where he heard for the first time a performance of his cantata *The Čarták on Soláň* (III/7). The performance, given on 13 April, was conducted by Rudolf Pavlata, who from 1911 had taken over the Olomouc choral society 'Žerotín'. Pavlata had already established himself as an excellent choral conductor, and with his experience of conducting *Jenůfa* in Brno (see chap. 62) and his part in the premières of two Janáček chamber works (see chaps. 58 and 60), his insight into performing Janáček's works was unrivalled at the time. Reality, however, broke in on Janáček's return with a note from Rektorys asking for news of *Fate*.[13] This time Janáček replied within a matter of hours:

Forgive me for not answering you any earlier. You know what a mood I am in – three years I compose the work – five years it lies around in the theatre with a contract binding them to perform it for me.

I still don't know what I'll do. If there's no sure way of convincing the soloists of their dishonour to their profession I won't launch into a lawsuit, for on top of all this to pay out expenses, which could amount to 1000–2000 K, that would be too much.

And to gamble the thing on the expert opinion of 'specialists', that I won't do. This is really a personal matter – I won't be instructed in such things – by anyone.

I'll let you know when the thing becomes a little clearer.[14]

· There is interesting proof that Janáček was nevertheless prepared to gamble. In a letter to Alois Doubravský, Leopolda Hanusová-Svobodová (who had sung the first Kostelnička in *Jenůfa*) revealed that she had studied the part of Míla with Hrazdira and was sorry when Janáček withdrew his opera from Brno:[15] through Doubravský (the administrative director of the Brno Theatre at the time of the première of *Jenůfa*) Janáček seemed to be assembling evidence to contradict the Vinohrady view that *Fate* was unsingable.

The best confirmation that Janáček had recovered from his debilitating illness was his composition of a new work. On 28 April he wrote to Vilém Zemánek as conductor of the Czech Philharmonic in Prague, the orchestra that had taken part in the Prague première of *Amarus* on 6 October 1912, shortly before Janáček fell ill: 'I was glad that, after the performance of my *Amarus* in the autumn, you asked me to write something orchestral for the [Czech] Philharmonic. I have done so: *The Fiddler's Child* [VI/14] is finished.'[16]

One door had shut; another had opened. When, however, had he written this new piece? Asked for composition dates for *Brouček*, Janáček told Otakar Šourek that what became Act 2 (i.e. Act 3 in the plan so far, with Brouček's escaping back to earth) was complete on 12 February 1913.[17] From the manuscript it is clear that he had in fact completed this act earlier, on 5 November 1912, but that he was also in negotiation with Vojtěch Ševčík for copying further corrections. Does the date 12 February 1913 record the end of this process and thus a psychological turning-point? Just as Janáček abandoned *Jenůfa* for several years while he poured his energies into other activities, now he put *Brouček* aside and got on with other types of work. He already had a flattering commission on the table – an orchestral piece for the Czech Philharmonic – and this rather than the final act of *The Excursion of Mr Brouček to the Moon* is what occupied Janáček after 12 February, as soon as his health and mood allowed him to work again: he had indeed completed *The Fiddler's Child* by the time he wrote to Zemánek on 28 April.

Brouček, however, had not been completely forgotten. In April–May Janáček was in negotiation with Gellner over a libretto for the epilogue act.[18] Furthermore, for the inspiration for his new orchestral piece Janáček returned to the author of his *Brouček* novels, Svatopluk Čech, whose ballad *The Fiddler's Child* had been published in 1873. It tells the story of the village fiddler who has died in poverty, leaving only a violin and a child. During the night the ghost of the musician returns and retrieves both the violin and the soul of the child. Like some of the pieces composed when Janáček broke off from *Jenůfa*, it is a work with deeply personal resonances. It was fitting that a performance of *Amarus* had prompted it: both works depict the reconciliation in death of a parent with a child. In the first he mourned his own lonely orphan-like childhood; in the second, Janáček, himself from a line of village musicians, may have had in mind the deaths of both his children.

'Perhaps you'll notice the theme of the fiddler', Janáček wrote to Zemánek, 'his child, the mayor, perhaps in the four violas the soul of our history: suffering, feeling.' These instrumental associations were to grow considerably by the next year, in the short article that Janáček published about the piece (xv/206). Janáček accompanied this letter with the full score, copied by Ševčík, and a promise of parts when they were ready. 'Do one thing for me', he concluded his letter to Zemánek, 'let me hear the work if only at a rehearsal play-through. That will be enough for me.'[19] Ironically, this is precisely all he got.

With *The Fiddler's Child* out of the way – Janáček's longest independent orchestral work so far – his mood lifted. On 9 May he wrote (and dated) an introduction for his harmony manual (xv/201), appended to the second volume, and planned a trip to Prague with Zdenka. Its chief purpose was to visit Dr Jan Hnátek, one of the doctors he had consulted during his illness and who now prescribed a spa stay in Karlovy Vary.[20] That year the National Theatre had been allowed to give performances in the spring and summer in the large open-air theatre Šárka (in Liboc, on the western outskirts of Prague), and Janáček asked for Rektorys's help with a couple of tickets for the opening performance of *The Bartered Bride* on 16 May:[21] they would be staying at the hotel Archduke Štěpán from 15 May.* Perhaps while in Prague Janáček took the opportunity of dropping in on Zemánek. Otherwise it is hard to explain the unsolicited letter of reassurance that Zemánek wrote on 22 May declaring that Janáček's 'disquiet' was unnecessary: he had invited Janáček to write the work, he would be studying it during the summer holidays and was looking forward to scheduling it in due course.[22]

Fate continued its grim story. Janáček had decided to go ahead with a court case and, as he was informed by Pauk, the first hearing was set for 4 June in Prague at 9 a.m. at the Imperial and Royal Law Court in Prague.[23] A report in *Národní politika* summarized the course of events so far:

Mr Janáček submitted his opera *Fate* to the Vinohrady Theatre in 1907, when it had already been accepted by the Brno National Theatre for performance. The Vinohrady Theatre accepted it for performance, demanding, however, that the opera must receive its première on the Vinohrady stage, whereupon Mr Janáček withdrew the score from the Brno National Theatre. When by 1911 the opera still had not been performed and thus Janáček, according to the law, resumed his right to dispose of his work and to demand compensation, further negotiations took place, during which the Vinohrady Theatre undertook to perform the work in the winter season of 1912–13. However, the opera has not yet been performed because, as the Vinohrady Theatre contends, it makes such demands on the soloists that it is beyond their powers. But Mr Janáček states that the opera can be performed without problems and that, during the study of the opera by the Brno National Theatre, it had not created difficulties for the soloists or for the conductor. So Mr Janáček initiated an action at the Regional Court, demanding that within fourteen days after the judgement, the [Vinohrady] Družstvo begin preparations for performing the opera and that it be given on the stage of the Vinohrady Theatre within six months. It is of interest that Mr Janáček has expressly refused financial compensation.[24]

---

* In her memoirs Zdenka wrote that the trip was on 'St John's day'. There are many St Johns in the Czech calendar. It is clear from references in the Rektorys correspondence that this was St John of Nepomuk (16 May) rather than St John the Baptist (24 June) as suggested in *MLWJ*, 115.

The last point is the important one. At this stage Janáček was not interested in money, only in hearing his work performed. His plea to Zemánek for at least a play-through of *The Fiddler's Child* is in the same vein. Now that Janáček's dispute with the Vinohrady Theatre was public knowledge, others began writing about it. Rektorys published a feuilleton in the newspaper *České slovo* (17 June), giving a straightforward account of the events so far and expressing astonishment that in the days of Strauss, Mahler and Novák the theatre seemed incapable of mounting a work that had already been put briefly into rehearsal in Brno without any great difficulty. Janáček thanked him for his support two days later at the same time as sending him 'the first complete copy' of his harmony manual (XV/202) with its new preface.[25] On 27 June Čelanský, who had been conducting at the Apollo Theatre in Paris from 1909, suddenly re-emerged to tell his part of the story in an interview in *Národní obzor*:

Leoš Janáček belongs among the unrecognized [Czech] composers. [. . .] This is why his opera *Fate* was accepted although at first glance it gave the impression that it would not be a box-office success. Since the opera is very interesting, it was worth a try. Six years ago the Družstvo of the Vinohrady Theatre agreed to stage the work on my recommendation.

In my first year I could not proceed right away with the rehearsal of such a difficult opera. [. . .] If the Družstvo is to stage such an opera, and is not to bleed to death, the conductor has to allocate his time. I wanted to rehearse the opera *Fate* between the preparation of other operas, not wanting to narrow the repertory and wanting to be thorough. So I postponed rehearsing *Fate* until the next year, when the members of the theatre would be played in.[26]

The interview was not just interesting information for a curious public. Eighteen days after it was published Čelanský was reinstated as chief conductor at the Vinohrady Theatre. Negotiations were presumably under way beforehand and Čelanský would have realized that his return to the Vinohrady also meant a return to the unsolved problem that he had left behind in 1908. Clearly, he was already looking ahead and attempting to mend fences.

'What a surprise from the Vinohrady Theatre!' Janáček wrote to Rektorys on 17 July. 'I'm curious what Čelanský will do now. I am going to Karlovy Vary – in truth unwillingly. I would rather go south – but one is fearful of this Balkan theatre [of war].'[27] The Second Balkan War between Serbs and Bulgarians had broken out that month and although this did not so far affect Austrian Croatia, it seemed wiser to postpone a repeat trip to Crikvenica. But Karlovy Vary was not a congenial destination for Janáček; as 'Karlsbad' he considered it a 'German' spa (see chap. 45).

The courts had allowed the Vinohrady Družstvo until 27 August to prepare its defence.[28] Meanwhile, however, Čelanský got to work with an energetic attempt to get Janáček to withdraw his case. The opera was difficult, he wrote. 'Just think how many rehearsals I would need if I wanted to give your opera even half decently. And I don't want to do it badly.' If Janáček continued to insist that *Fate* be performed 'as quickly as possible' it was bound to end in tears. Instead Čelanský suggested the following:

Withdraw your suit and announce this to the executive committee, mentioning that you will submit your opera once again for performance.

In this way you will ease my position to the point that I will be able undisturbed to spread out my work [over a period of time] on your opera.

I advise you sincerely as your friend, and as a man who wants to help you.[29]

Janáček must have mentioned that he was off to Karlovy Vary as Čelanský's original letter had been sent there and returned to him. Janáček seems to have got to the spa only by 25 July, as confirmed by a postmarked card sent to Zdenka that day, complaining about the weather.[30] He remained there for another fortnight. He wrote to Zdenka again on 6 August describing the company in the spa (which included the Veselýs, who also signed the card) and hoped that he would leave in good health.[31] This, however, was clearly not the case. Two days later, on 8 August, he was on his travels – not back to Brno but to the village of Mšeno, which contained a peat spa. A new colleague at the Organ School, the violin teacher Ladislav Malý (1885–1937), Pavel Dědeček's successor, had recommended it,[32] presumably from present experience: Janáček's card sent to Zdenka on arrival was signed also by Malý.[33] It was, Janáček wrote to Zdenka, a 'pleasant retreat'. More ominously, as Janáček wrote to Veselý, 'even here as in Karlovy Vary I am seized by a fever every third day. I will be glad when this wretched wandering is finished.' And then, it all came out in his postscript: 'Čelanský has not scheduled *Fate*. This is now a spiritual torment for me.'[34] Physical torments were not far behind. The next day Janáček developed erysipelas ('St Anthony's fire'; see chap. 64) over his whole body. He was taken to the nearest hospital, in Roudnice, and there he remained at least until 26 August, when he wrote to Veselý again thanking him for his sympathy and 'intercession' (according to Stejskalová, Veselý kept in touch with the Roudnice doctors throughout Janáček's stay there).[35] By then he was ready to be discharged ('They have bathed me, so they will soon release me')[36] but the hospital did not want him to make the journey on his own and had one of their doctors accompany him to Brno. Janáček and the doctor were welcomed by Stejskalová with a lunch of baked pigeon: one of two pairs that they kept in the loft of the Organ School.[37]

Meanwhile there were further developments on both *The Fiddler's Child* and *Fate*. Zemánek wrote on 18 August saying that *The Fiddler's Child* had been scheduled for the next season. But he had clearly taken fright at conducting the piece himself:

Because I fear, however, that I won't manage immediately to be able to capture the identity and the individual character of the work I would make it a condition that you, esteemed Mr Director, rehearse and conduct it. As an experienced and well-tried conductor it would certainly not give you problems. You can have as many rehearsals as you need.[38]

Janáček responded from his hospital bed in Roudnice and presumably made much of his poor health (his letter has not survived but its contents can be inferred from Zemánek's reply). Although he had conducted Gounod's *Mors et vita* to considerable acclaim (see chap. 58) he had nevertheless done so on home ground with sympathetic forces. The Czech Philharmonic was quite another matter. Zemánek, however, saw through his excuse and was completely unswayed by the promise of a dedication:

Thank you for the dedication of *The Fiddler's Child*. Because the piece would be performed in the second half of the season, by which time you will certainly be well again, you'll be able to conduct it yourself. I ask you for this most respectfully: it would be a great pleasure for us to welcome you into our season not just as a composer but also as a conductor.[39]

Čelanský was equally unbending. On 26 August, i.e. a day before the case was meant to resume in court with the Vinohrady Theatre's defence, Čelanský wrote again. While offering sympathy (and even the services of a 'marvellous visiting foreign doctor' who would examine Janáček free of charge), he nevertheless stuck to his original proposal. It is easy to disparage his negotiations with Janáček merely as a soft-cop technique to get the Vinohrady Theatre off the hook. (If Janáček were to go along with what was suggested he would be throwing away all his cards and any means of legal redress.) Neverthe-less Čelanský's arguments could well have been meant genuinely and are sound ones: a performance brought about only through legal com-pulsion is bound to fail. If, as suggested in his previous letter, Janáček withdrew his suit and then resubmitted his opera, 'but without specify-ing a performance date', Čelanský would give his promise

that I will look to perform your opera well from an artistic point of view and, as far as possible, soon.

You, on the other hand, with such an accommodating stance – which in the end everyone will understand given the present change in direction in the opera [at the Vinohrady Theatre] – will gain the sympathy of the committee and of the public, because your work will be performed by me voluntarily and not under duress.

All this time Zdenka had been in Vienna, anxiously waiting for reports from Roudnice (since Janáček's illness was infectious she had not been allowed to visit). With Janáček back home, she now returned. Smetana describes her first sight of her husband: 'She saw him sitting in the garden house, sad, miserable, thin and completely yellow, and when the couple met, Leoš Janáček broke down at the memory of what he'd been through during his illness.'[40] In her memoirs she recalled: 'Although he was weakened, Leoš didn't let up and soon began to walk about. From that he got spasms in his leg, he had to lie or at the most sit.' Zdenka was also laid up by tearing a ligament, so

we sat opposite one another for whole days like two invalids, but we felt good together and were cheerful. I remember how we laughed when [František] Bílý, my husband's colleague from his school days, came to visit us, and neither of us could move.[41]

Stejskalová saw this moment as a turning-point in Janáček's health. Her comments also provide an explanation for the familiar later appearance of Janáček:

From the time of that illness, the master began to fear for himself and take more care. Not that he would have kept to a diet; he still insisted on good food. But he began to go for lots of walks, he invited the masseuse ever more frequently and feared every ache and pain. He suffered with his teeth a lot at that time. Also he began to lose his hair. He went immediately to consult Dr Dressler. He advised some sort of lotion and the master thereafter always moistened his hair with it. It helped; his hair seemed to thicken even more and took on that lovely white colour admired by everyone and about which so much was written. It shone around the master's head like white fire. Dr Dressler now had the master under constant observation and we also began to take care of him like a precious ointment. For food we chose the very best; when the temperature fell a little we made a fire for him in the study, when he sweated we immediately got him a dry, warmed shirt.[42]

Čelanský's letter seemed to have done the trick, or so he thought. On 1 September he sent off another letter declaring his happiness that Janáček's 'non-artistic quarrel' could now 'end artistically'.[43] At the same time he enclosed a letter from the head of the executive committee of the Vinohrady Theatre for Janáček to sign. It proposed that Janáček withdraw his suit, that he would receive 250 K expenses and that the theatre would endeavour to perform *Fate* at a time 'when circumstances allow'.[44] One doesn't know on what Čelanský based his optimistic conclusion: a letter with Janáček's agreement, or sheer bravado? Whatever the case, Janáček now dug his heels in. A longer, more hectoring letter from Čelanský written on 14 September makes it clear that Janáček did not intend being fobbed off with 250 K expenses and a non-binding promise. Janáček, Čelanský wrote, was not dealing with him as sincerely as Čelanský had dealt with him. Instead of settling the matter privately (which his letters to Čelanský suggested), he was continuing to employ Dr Pauk to deal with the theatre.

Why do you trust lawyers more than a fellow artist who knows well what it means to write a big three-act opera and then to have to beg for its performance somewhere?

[. . .] in your own interest – sign the attached letter for me and simply tell your legal representative that you are withdrawing your suit.

Don't you know how to read between the lines? Please, I beg you earnestly, read all my letters again and you must surely understand![45]

Janáček's hesitations, though perfectly understandable, were futile. Pauk and his opposite number acting for the Vinohrady Theatre negotiated an adjournment of the case for a year (it was due to come to court on 27 September),[46] and Čelanský sent a brief take-it-or-leave-it letter for Janáček to sign, inviting him again to withdraw his suit.[47] Surprisingly, this worked. Perhaps his previous 'we-two-artists' approach had irritated Janáček's. Next, on 18 October, Čelanský sent a curt letter confirming Janáček's withdrawal of his suit 'whereby the whole matter is concluded'. But he could not resist expressing his irritation that all his personal appeals had been in vain: 'The Directorate of the Opera regrets only that on your side matters did not rest with the first pronouncement suggested by the Directorate.'[48] Very soon Janáček had confirmation from his Vinohrady contact Vojtěch Ševčík that he had probably done the right thing:

I am still in the theatre, but terrible conditions prevail. [...] No-one knows what will happen or how, and the whole staff is in fear that it will be shut in the spring.

There are too many bosses and no-one's doing anything together. It is said that Mr Čelanský has to go at the New Year and perhaps Holeček is returning.

While Mr Čelanský is here we're giving nothing other than *Butterfly*, *Carmen* and now *Hänsel und Gretel* – that's everything, we don't have anything else, and we're not rehearsing anything.[49]

Čelanský clung on beyond the New Year, but finally left on 1 May 1914: his second tenure at the theatre had lasted barely a year.

In comparison with this long-drawn-out and painful affair other matters must have seemed trivial. It is understandable that, while it was going on, an approach from the Brno Beseda for permission to perform the well-received *Čarták on Soláň* the following April was refused.[50] Janáček had not forgotten his quarrel with the Beseda. Nor was he any more receptive to an approach a week later from Otakar Nebuška (see below) on behalf of Hudební matice to publish *The 70,000*, the second such offer from a publisher in less than a year. Nebuška, as he wrote, was responding to Janáček's letter of 31 August asking when *Hudební revue* would be getting round to reviewing his harmony manual. Yes indeed, *Hudební revue* had received both volumes, and it was only the indisposition of Professor Stecker that had delayed the review. But Janáček's letter had reminded Nebuška of something else. As far as he knew, Janáček's chorus *The 70,000* did not have a publisher. 'To leave your work further unpublished or at least unsecured would be a sin.' How would Janáček feel about a 10% royalty and an advance of 50 K?[51] In 1907 Hudební matice, the musical press of the Umělecká beseda [Artists' Club], had been reconstituted and under Nebuška's energetic leadership it became in the next decades one of the most important publishers of modern Czech music (including much of Janáček's). However, Janáček appears not to have been tempted at this stage and *The 70,000* remained unpublished.

Amarus continued to make its rounds, now triumphant in Kroměříž, the scene of its unsuccessful first performance, as Elgart recalled in his letter of congratulations.[52] *Maryčka Magdónova* continued its world-wide success when Vach and the Moravian Teachers took it to Russia in December.[53] And there was a new première. On 7 December Marie Dvořáková performed *In the Mists* for the first time, in Kroměříž; Janáček was not there but Elgart wrote a warm note describing the event.[54]

Work on the Moravian contribution to *Das Volkslied in Österreich* continued. A draft contract drawn up by Universal Edition with an addendum dated 16 December 1913 makes it clear that the Imperial and Royal Ministry of Culture and Education was continuing to underwrite the project while Universal Edition's responsibility was concerned with its publication, undertaking to issue at least two volumes a year of the projected three hundred volumes.[55] For his part Janáček drafted a substantial preface of thirty printed pages for the Moravian contribution, dated 29 September (*Folksong* XV/323), chiefly concerned with the origin of folksongs and their social function. Since the preface was set in galley and even page proofs (with linguistic corrections by Janáček's working-party colleague F.V. Autrata),[56] it would appear that publication was then thought to be imminent.

1914 was the year in which Bayreuth's monopoly on performing *Parsifal* expired. Although the copyright had already been breached in America and a few rogue European capitals, in January 1914 a rash of productions sprang up throughout the world. Prague was in the front line with two rival productions on 1 January: in German at the German opera house (beginning at 5 p.m.) and in Czech at the National Theatre one hour earlier. Although he had shown only limited interest in Wagner so far, Janáček's curiosity was whetted by the advance publicity and Rektorys was once again approached: 'Is it possible to get into the National Theatre for the performance of *Parsifal* on 1 January 1914? Would you kindly get me any sort of ticket?'[57] And, as usual. Rektorys obliged, writing on 22 December to say that he had a ticket for him.[58] Thus equipped, Janáček planned a New Year trip to Prague, staying as usual at the Archduke Štěpán.[59] Veselý had written to him (a letter that has since disappeared) and Janáček responded on 28 December, proposing a visit on New Year's Eve. It is a letter that sums up Janáček's feelings about the fate of his works at this juncture, half a year before his sixtieth birthday.

Do not think that it would be possible to smooth the path for *Jenůfa*. I know very well that I stand alone in my musical feeling. I cannot attach myself to anyone. I am difficult to understand and – in Prague [–] there is no need for anyone to exert themselves over it.

After all in Brno I sit like a magpie only in my own nest [i.e. he doesn't get about]. Dr Elgart from Kroměříž is perhaps one other who is favourable to my works.

I know who decides who can go higher and who cannot have his place in the sun.

[. . .]

I'll come to you towards five on New Year's Eve – but spare me any kind of debates about the subjects you raised [i.e. plans for the further promotion of *Jenůfa*]. Prague will have an opportunity to hear *The Fiddler's Child* and in the autumn perhaps *The Eternal Gospel* – that's enough for me. Rather make it possible for our Miss M. Dvořáková to play in the Prague Chamber Society, she plays my *In the Mists just as it ought to be* [Janáček's emphasis].[60]

In the year that Janáček had given up with *Fate* at the Vinohrady Theatre and abandoned *Brouček*, he was pinning his hopes on his new orchestral piece and, it seems, was writing a new cantata, *The Eternal Gospel* (III/8), following the triumphant progress of *Amarus*.

66

1914a (January to 28 July)

From Prague Janáček wrote a brief note on New Year's Day to Zdenka letting her know that he would be back on Saturday 3 January. He had been to see the Veselýs three times and had slept ten hours on New Year's Eve. *Parsifal*, still to come that afternoon, went unmentioned.[1]

'During the study of your chorus *The 70,000*' (IV/36), Spilka wrote from Prague on 21 January, 'I have come to the realization that it is necessary to give the audience in good time a comprehensive analysis of this work in which the composer's ideas and means are seen in the appropriate light.' In comparison with the other choruses to be sung in the same concert (by Adolf Piskáček, Suk, Smetana, Vomáčka, Novák, etc.) Janáček's work was demanding: 'Even an expert does not get at a first hearing all that is sung simultaneously, let alone the layman.' It would be best, Spilka went on, if Janáček would write such an analysis himself.[2] When such requests were made Janáček usually complied, though the enigmatic comments that he offered were sometimes more revealing about his own psychology than about the pieces they were meant to illuminate. This is presumably what the Prague Teachers' Choral Society concluded on receipt of Janáček's letter of 29 January containing a brief account of his chorus (xv/324). It was not printed in any of their programmes but instead festered in the society's archive until published in 1971.[3] This was a shame. Although compact and cryptic as ever, Janáček's 'analysis' would have provided the listeners with some of the themes and their words (the theme of the 'chief culprit', Marquis Géro, is memorably characterized as a 'poisonous bubble' continually wandering through the texture). Janáček's scene-setting – the 'cloud of steam and fiery glow' of the Těšín furnaces – recalls his comments to Zdenka (October 1908) about the 'purgatory' of his visit to the industrialized part of Silesia (see chap. 56). That visit failed to kindle the suggested orchestral version for *Marycka Magdónova* (IV/35) and seems instead to have inspired his final Bezruc setting, *The 70,000*, composed the next year. Janáček's account of this chorus is of images wafting through the 'coal dust and sulphurous air', the clinking of glasses, and the suppression of all finer feelings, replaced by cries of desperation.

Even before these thoughts were dispatched, there was another similar request, this time from the journal *Hudební revue* for an analysis of *The Fiddler's Child* (VI/14), due to be performed soon by the Czech Philharmonic.[4] Janáček got to work immediately: his comments were printed in the January–February fascicle, which came out early in February. What is memorable about this brief article (XV/206) is its emphasis on orchestration, signalled in the subtitle: 'some remarks about the instrumentation on its first performance at a concert of the Czech Philharmonic'. More than any other composition by Janáček until his last opera, *From the House of the Dead* (I/11), *The Fiddler's Child* depends on the symbolization of particular instruments – a point on which Janáček insisted in his article. The solo violin, heard at the outset, is the fiddler, his life and death, his sorrows and pleasure; the subdivided violas represent the poor of the village; the sick child is suggested by the oboe. The all-powerful mayor is represented by the cellos and basses, the people's fear of him by the bass clarinet, the harshness of his decision by the trombones. At any one point one particular instrument, Janáček explains, is 'constantly the bearer of the same, in many cases the only, musical mood'. This is an astonishing statement for someone who hitherto had put so much emphasis on speech melodies as a conveyor of musical meaning. As it is, his themes do not always stick to these instruments; nevertheless this statement provides evidence of a shift in his attitude towards the expressive powers of the orchestra and its colours. At the end of the article there is a startling insight into Janáček's reaction to the Beethoven trios that had been performed at the Organ School in 1909–10: the migration of themes between the violin, piano and cello had 'disconcerted' him; too much routine in these compositions, he concluded tartly.

The 'symphonic' concerts organized by the Organ School from October 1911 in the Lužánky hall continued into a third season,

1913–14, the orchestral component now generally consisting of a symphonic poem (Saint-Saëns, Berlioz, Dvořák, Smetana) and a violin or piano concerto. For the third concert of the season, on Sunday 24 January, the orchestral works, again conducted by Pavlata, were Tchaikovsky's Violin Concerto (played by the Organ School's new violin teacher, Ladislav Malý) and Dvořák's *Water Goblin*. Apart from Rachmaninoff's Fantaisie-Tableaux for Two Pianos op. 5, the chamber works were two recent winners of the Club of the Friends of Art competitions – the Romance for violin and piano* by Eduard Tregler (teacher at the Organ School that academic year) and the Brno première of *In the Mists* (VIII/22). It was played by Marie Dvořáková, who had given the première in Kroměříž the previous month. Sadly, there were no reviews. Although Kunc published a brief report of the first two orchestral concerts in *Hudební revue*, this event was passed over. From his comments to Veselý in 1913, however, Janáček seemed pleased with the way Dvořáková played the piece.

Altogether it promised to be a time full of premières, with that of *The Fiddler's Child* planned for March and *The 70,000* included in the Prague Teachers' 'Czech ballad' concerts in the spring. On 2 February the conductor of the Czech Philharmonic, Dr Vilém Zemánek, wrote to Janáček that *The Fiddler's Child* was scheduled for Sunday 8 March.[5] On 25 February Janáček sent a newly revised score and parts to Prague. Since those for the solo violin and the four solo viola parts had tricky intonation problems, he asked in his letter to Zemánek for the parts to be given out to the players ahead of time and that he be allowed a special rehearsal with these players.[6] And with this new Prague première looming it seemed time to effect closure at the Vinohrady Theatre. On 28 February, three days after he dispatched the *Fiddler's Child* material to Prague, Janáček wrote to the Vinohrady asking the directorate to return that for *Fate*. This letter is referred to in one from the administrative director Dr František Fuksa when he returned the score on 2 March. No doubt it was with some relief that Fuksa noted (presumably repeating a statement by Janáček) that the composer 'no longer had any interest in its performance'.[7]

By then, however, the Czech Philharmonic Concert with *The*

---

* As given in *JKPU*, 131; *JVŠ*, 64–5 places the Tregler in the fourth concert, on 14 February 1914.

Fiddler's Child had shifted on a week, to Sunday 15 March.[8] As Janáček described it after the event to the Prague critic and composer Emanuel Chvála, the schedule agreed was that the special rehearsal (for the solo strings) would place take on Thursday 12 March, to be followed by two full rehearsals on Friday and Saturday before the concert on Sunday.[9] However, a letter from Zemánek dated 10 March mentions that the special sectional rehearsal had been scrapped, downgraded to a slot during the 'last interval' on the Friday rehearsal.[10] The Friday rehearsal was a disaster. It began at 5.30 with Janáček soon discovering that the violin soloist did not know his part, and that the four solo violas were 'terrible'. He spent his ninety minutes simply trying to teach them the notes. There was no time to do more as the rehearsal for the last movement of Beethoven's Ninth Symphony (with chorus and soloists) was to follow. Beethoven's Ninth dominated the Saturday morning rehearsal. Janáček's turn eventually came at 12.15. After an hour, members of the orchestra proclaimed that they were too tired to carry on and with the concert the next day there was no more rehearsal time. Despite Zemánek's promise that Janáček could have 'as many rehearsals' as he wanted, Janáček's sensible request for a separate rehearsal for the solo strings had been over-ridden and, as a whole, rehearsal time had been compromised by Zemánek's own rehearsals for Beethoven's Ninth. The brief account of all this that Janáček scribbled in his notebook mentions that at the end he thanked the players for their work and asked Zemánek to withdraw the piece from the next day's concert. The orchestra, he wrote, banged their approval. Later, he wrote, he was visited by a deputation from the orchestra, 'ashamed at the disgrace that they had experienced [i.e. that they had been incapable of playing the piece]'.[11] To Zdenka Janáček sent a cryptic postcard stating that 'many times in life one makes a mistake'. To take charge of the rehearsal would have needed 'superhuman' powers.[12]

Janáček's original instincts to try and wriggle out of conducting the concert himself (see chap. 65) had probably been right. It is significant that the choral concerts put on by the Organ School in the first decade of the century had been left to Vach, and the symphony concerts in the second decade to Pavlata. Although Janáček had taken up the baton when there was nothing for it (replacing Vach for the première of *Amarus* and in Gounod's *Mors et vita*, or trying to kick-start the Czech National Orchestra in 1898), it was not his natural habitat and any good results achieved seem to have come out of his musicianship rather than any technique or talent as an orchestral trainer.

As soon as Janáček got back to Brno, on 16 March, he wrote to Zemánek asking for *The Fiddler's Child* to be rescheduled together with the introduction to Act 3 of *Fate*.[13] Zemánek readily agreed though again insisted that Janáček conduct the pieces himself and specify how many rehearsals would be needed 'so that the unlovely case of *The Fiddler's Child* won't be repeated'.[14] Janáček responded that the Act 3 prelude to *Fate* had a male chorus but he would invite the Prague Teachers' Choral Society, so as not to tax the Czech Philharmonic.[15] His generally resigned attitude to what could be regarded as a further Prague humiliation is reflected in a letter he wrote to Emanuel Chvála a couple of days later. He repeated that he bore no malice towards Zemánek and quite understood how much time was needed to conduct Beethoven's Ninth from memory. All that was wrong was that insufficient time had been left for rehearsing a difficult piece with 'possible problems in intonation'.[16]

Zdenka meanwhile had gone off to Vienna and when Janáček wrote to her on 23 March he mentioned that he was 'at work', so busy that he had not been able to read 'his bible'.[17] Quite what the 'bible' might mean is impossible to say. It is easier to speculate about what Janáček had been working on. For a start there was a long, untitled article (xv/325) of thirty-eight pages, which bears two dates: 8 March 1914 (halfway through) and 26 June 1914 (end), which means that he was devoting at least some time to this during the *Fiddler's Child* débâcle. This unpublished article is essentially a reflection on words and the psychology of speech, and the way that speech reflects feeling and different forms of feeling. And at the same time as this Janáček appears to have been putting the finishing touches to a new oratorio, *The Eternal Gospel* (III/8). There is remarkably little evidence for dating it: no dates in scores, no references in correspondence apart from that in his letter to Veselý of 28 December 1913 (see chap. 65). When in 1917 its first conductor Jaroslav Křička introduced the work with an article in *Hudební revue*, he provided a composition date of 1913.[18] This makes sense as a beginning date and is corroborated in the letter to Veselý. What with the Prague National Theatre's refusal to stage *Jenůfa* and the Vinohrady Theatre's refusal to stage *Fate*, opera was clearly blocked. But after many years of lying unperformed, his oratorio

Amarus, under Vach, was suddenly winning enthusiastic and respectful notices all over the country. Its successor, *The Čarták on Soláň* (III/7), had already had successful performances in Prostějov and Olomouc, and interest had been expressed in performing it in Brno. The time seemed ripe for another choral and orchestral work.

What is rather harder to understand is why Janáček chose this particular text. That the words are by Jaroslav Vrchlický, the author of the *Amarus* text, provides some explanation, in the sense that Janáček wished to capitalize on the success of his previous large-scale cantata by adhering to a tried and trusted model: mellifluous words by the same eminent author (who had given his permission last time, though by 1913 he was dead), a multi-movement work with a dominant part for tenor (maybe by now Janáček had Stanislav Tauber specifically in mind), substantial chorus work (for the many Czech choral societies) and a smaller part for soprano. But why these particular words? They came from Vrchlický's collection *Frescoes and Tapestries* (1891) which included a seventy-line poem, *The Eternal Gospel*, based on the millenarian writings (collectively known as *Evangelium aeternum*) of Joachim of Fiore (*c.* 1130/5–1201/2). The poem, one of Vrchlický's attempts at evoking a medieval world, is essentially a poetic exposition of Joachim's revelation of three ages of increasingly spirituality: the age of the Father will pass; even that of Christ and the love of one's neighbour will pass; it will give way to the third age, that of the Holy Spirit and love towards all creation. At first sight this overtly religious text seems an odd choice for a fervent agnostic. The progression towards the 'third age' of the Holy Spirit is perhaps the key. The 'love of all creation' expounded in the final part is not far away from the pantheistic philosophy of love and renewal that is expounded in *The Cunning Little Vixen* and in Janáček's explanation of the composition of the *Glagolitic Mass* (see vol. ii: 1927c).

We sang *The 70,000* in Benešov on Wednesday. At the end of the chorus several moments of dead silence ensued. Suddenly however there erupted directly from the audience elemental and enormous applause – it led me to suspect that we had plucked at the right string. I don't know whether we'll please you, but this much I'm sure of, that it will be the jewel of the choir's spring concert. [...] would be happy if you could come.[19]

Thus František Spilka described the first performance of *The 70,000* to Janáček. It had taken place on 25 March (just ten days after the planned but unrealized première of *The Fiddler's Child*) at Benešov, a small town 38 km south of Prague. Like the Moravian Teachers, the Prague Teachers conducted their experiments well out of the limelight. But this experiment had clearly worked, and the new piece was included in the high-profile and vigorously trailed 'Czech ballad' concert in Prague by the Prague Teachers on 4 April. It took place amid the splendours of the Obecní dům [Municipal House], an architecturally striking complex built between 1905 and 1911 and one of the most stylistically unified expressions of Czech Art Nouveau. Its Smetana Hall, seating 1200, was a welcome addition to Prague's concert spaces and was to be the scene of several important Janáček premières. *The 70,000* was the first. Janáček was there himself and reported his success in a smug postcard to Vach (who had declined the work because of its difficulty)[20] and in another to Zdenka, revealing that in conversations there he had been letting off steam about his feelings over the *Fiddler's Child* fiasco ('Zemánek is universally condemned').[21]

Another person present at the concert was Otakar Ostrčil, who made a point of congratulating Janáček during the interval,[22] thus initiating a friendship that was artistically important for both parties. Ostrčil (1879–1935) went on to become one of the chief Czech opera conductors in the first half of the twentieth century, presiding from 1920 until his death over a glorious period at the National Theatre that included several Janáček premières. As a composer (a pupil of Fibich) he had already had important successes, including two well-regarded operas given at the National Theatre. Despite this, he continued to earn his living as a teacher of Czech and German until 1919. He honed his considerable skills as a conductor in amateur groups such as the Prague Orchestral Association, which he conducted from 1908; in 1914 he took over at the troubled Vinohrady Theatre.

In addition to attending the première of *The 70,000*, Janáček had made use of this trip to Prague to consult his doctors, Dr Výmola and Dr Hnátek. Dr Výmola, whom he saw on the Saturday afternoon before the concert, proclaimed that his nose ailment would cure itself – he needn't go to Karlovy Vary.[23] According to the letter he wrote to František Veselý on his return to Brno, Janáček visited Dr Hnátek on Sunday for his yearly checkup, thus preventing a visit to the Veselýs ('there was no time other than to get to the station and be in Brno that night'). As for the première of *The 70,000*, Janáček reported to Veselý, it had been a 'penetrating success' (one wonders why the Veselýs seem not to have been there), 'perhaps it will open the door a little for me'. And there was just a flash of hope that things might change at the National Theatre: 'I heard the rumour that Dr Kramář[†] will perhaps take over [as administrative director] – but again with Kovařovic.'[24]

Despite his assurances about Janáček's nose ailment, Výmola seems to have insisted on Janáček's coming to Prague again so he could have another look. Thus on Wednesday–Thursday 15–16 April, Janáček returned, visiting Výmola at 4.30 on the Wednesday afternoon. This is clear from Janáček's letter to Rektorys on 14 April proposing a meeting.[25] In Rektorys's response, a note left at Janáček's hotel as suggested, there is an intriguing instruction to Janáček to deliver 'the score' to Rektorys's place of work at the bank. Rektorys's notes to the edition of his correspondence with Janáček state that the score in question was *The Eternal Gospel*.[26] Later, in his letter of 11 May (see below), Rektorys mentions Ostrčil's favourable reaction to the work. Rektorys was presumably the go-between, passing on the score to Ostrčil, to whom, perhaps, Janáček had mentioned his latest large-scale work at the Prague Teachers' concert earlier that month. All this means that Janáček must have completed the new cantata a good month before its delivery to Rektorys in mid-April (to allow for a copy to be made and corrected). It also means that it was inconveniently in the wrong hands when yet another conductor began to show interest in performing a choral piece by Janáček. This was Jaroslav Křička, conductor since 1911 of the Prague 'Hlahol' choral society. He had, perhaps, also heard the recent Prague première of *The 70,000* and was looking to perform something by Janáček for chorus and orchestra, as he wrote to Janáček in his letter of 6 May.[27] Janáček consulted Rektorys about this on 10 May[28] and received a detailed and immediate response the next day:

At once, as soon as I got your letter, I went to Ostrčil and am passing on completely frankly the result of my intervention.

Ostrčil definitely likes your *Legenda* [i.e. *The Eternal Gospel*] and has proclaimed it to be a very interesting work although it differs considerably from his own style as a composer.

According to my conviction it would not even be necessary to do much to persuade him to agree to perform your work. But the situation is changed by your letter today.

[†]Karel Kramář (1860–1937), a leading politician of the time, who served briefly as the first prime minister of independent Czechoslovakia (1918–19).

The problem, Rektorys went on to say, was that whereas *The Eternal Gospel* was eminently suited to the choral society 'Hlahol', Ostrčil's Orchestral Association would need to involve an independent chorus to perform Janáček's cantata. It usually collaborated with 'Hlahol' but it was already in its debt since it had recently performed Berlioz's *Lélio* with the society. Altogether, Rektorys concluded, it would be best to accept Křička's offer and 'to reserve for Ostrčil perhaps a future, purely orchestral work of yours for which the Orchestral Association will not need any forces other than its own. As soon as *The Fiddler's Child* comes out in print please send it to me and I'll give it to Ostrčil.' Even if Janáček did not want to part company with the Philharmonic over *The Fiddler's Child* (by allowing Ostrčil's orchestra to give the première) he could write his next work 'calmly with the consciousness that Ostrčil *will* conduct it. I myself will promote it with all my strength.'[29]

Janáček did as suggested, asking Rektorys now to pass on the score of *The Eternal Gospel* to Křička.[30] Rektorys's reference to *The Fiddler's Child* coming out in print was not just a flattering prediction: it is evidence that the Club of the Friends of Art's plan to honour Janáček's approaching sixtieth birthday by publishing the work was already under way and that Janáček had mentioned it when he saw Rektorys. Seizing the moment, Janáček also suggested that Křička look at other possible works: *The Čarták on Soláň* and *Fate* (presumably the choral opening of Act 3, provisionally agreed with Zemánek as an item in a future Czech Philharmonic concert, with the Prague Teachers providing the men's voices). This emerges from a letter from Spilka to Janáček, saying that he had handed over these works to Křička as requested. He could also tell Janáček of the continuing triumph of the Prague Teachers with *The 70,000*: 'With joy I can tell you that in all twenty-two concerts we sang your chorus *The 70,000* with complete success. We'll now approach the study of *Maryčka* with great delight.'[31]

In her memoirs, Zdenka Janáčková's recollection of 1914 was dominated by the outbreak of the First World War and its conjunction with the ill-fated Sokol rally in Brno, organized to celebrate over fifty years of the Sokol movement there and featuring a 'display of the habits and customs of the Moravian people'.[32] Through the involvement of friends such as the Dresslers' daughters (who were constantly rehearsing) both Janáčeks were caught up in the excitement about an event planned as a provocatively Czech demonstration in what was still a German-dominated city. All three members of the household – the two Janáčeks and Stejskalová – wanted to attend the rally but were nervous about leaving the house empty, especially since the Organ School caretaker and his family would also be at that event. As it was spread over two days, however, they took turns – or at least the women did. Zdenka would stay at home on the first day, and Stejskalová on the second. Janáček would go for both days.

Thus on Sunday 28 June Janáček and Stejskalová set out for the Královo Pole stadium on the outskirts of Brno and watched the opening display of men's gymnastics. But instead of the women's gymnastics that should have followed there was merely a 'strange silence'. After some time it was announced that Archduke Franz Ferdinand, the heir to the Austrian throne, and his wife had been assassinated. The rally was abandoned and everyone was sent home. The next day's celebration was cancelled, or at least postponed.[33]

This is the strange context for Janáček's sixtieth birthday, on 3 July. Significantly, in her memoirs dictated to Trkanová, Zdenka ignores the birthday altogether. Robert Smetana whose book is also based on Zdenka's recollections, does at least refer to it and to Janáček's reluctance to celebrate this birthday. Smetana relates how, when Janáček got to hear of preparations at the Organ School, he at first forbade any festivities but in the end allowed staff and students from the Organ School and members of the Russian Circle to bring their gifts and good wishes. In return he took the Organ School teachers and their wives out to dinner at the Lužánky restaurant, bringing them back afterwards to his garden to enjoy wine and biscuits until late into the balmy summer evening. Smetana ascribed Janáček's unwilling attitude in part to his bitterness at lack of recognition.[34] However, ten years later, when Janáček was famous and recognized, he likewise did his best to avoid any celebration. In 1914 Janáček would certainly have been discouraged by the collapse of his career as an operatic composer and by the recent *Fiddler's Child* fiasco in Prague. Friends and well-wishers, however, sent respectful and affectionate greetings; there were several articles in the local newspapers commemorating the event. The generous gesture of the Club of the Friends of Art to publish a miniature score of *The Fiddler's Child* was going ahead; a letter from the engravers Röder in Leipzig on 20 June reporting that the score could be delivered only in a fortnight[35] suggests that it was intended to come out on the day itself, though in the end publication was delayed until the autumn (but see vol. ii: 1914b). And there was some hope even for *Fate*. One of the birthday letters, from Karel Komarov, the original producer-designate of *Fate* in Brno, mentions that Janáček had 'graciously favoured the Brno Theatre' with *Fate* for the 1914–15 season, and as Komarov was negotiating a return to Brno he was hoping to have the honour of staging it.[36]

And, for the moment, even the Sokol rally looked hopeful. The authorities gave permission for it to go ahead, on 12 July, a magnificently warm day with everyone in their finery, including Janáček in his cream tussore suit made of raw Indian silk (brought back from Russia), silk cap and white shoes, Zdenka in a white frock and panama hat. This time, however, festivities were brought to an end by the weather. No sooner had the event begun than the heavens opened with a violent storm and cloudburst. Once again the proceedings were halted, and bedraggled participants made their way home in their ruined outfits, much to the mirth of the Brno Germans.[37]

The Janáčeks started their summer as if nothing were amiss. While Zdenka stayed at home in Brno, Stejskalová went off to relatives in Koválovice and Janáček went to Hukvaldy on 16 July.[38] From Hukvaldy Janáček wrote to Veselý on 17 July ('I am here for a moment in the forests beneath Hukvaldy. It is nice weather and warm') and, astonishingly, despite the increasingly tense international situation, he was planning a return visit to Crikvenica, this time with a possible extension to the Montenegrin capital of Cetinje.

I want to go to Cetinje. I read your wife's [verbal] pictures of your journey [published in the magazine *Zvon* in May and June 1914] but I'd like to have a practical description as well so that I would get there safely and without long enquiries.

Be so kind and describe the whole tour to me. Also I'd like to know approximately how much it costs.

From what place does one leave by motorcar to Cetinje? Do Austrian boats from Trieste stop there? [...] How for instance does one get from Dulcinje‡ to Cetinje? I'd like to leave from Brno on 5 August.[39]

Three days later, things were even further advanced, as he reported to Zdenka:

It's gorgeous weather here and unaccustomed heat. I have written to Crikvenica that we'll accept. Also to Věra [this time coming with them]. I walk

‡Probably Ulcinj (Italian, Dulcigno), a harbour town in Montenegro.

contentedly in the woods; I really feel healthier than I have ever felt in Hukvaldy. Without a coat for the first time. Little post arrives – still nothing for the second day. [. . .] You are probably baking in Brno![40]

According to his diary, Janáček went to Valašská Bystřice for a few days on 24 July with the painter and architect Dušan Jurkovič to photograph 'the song environment'.[41] Against this nonchalant background events in Vienna were unfolding rapidly. Austria-Hungary sent its ultimatum to Serbia on 23 July 1914, demanding a reply within forty-eight hours. Serbia accepted most of the Austrian demands within the given time but the Austro-Hungarian government nevertheless ordered a partial mobilization on Saturday 25 July, news that Zdenka, on her own in Brno, read in the newspaper the next day. On Monday Stejskalová returned, frightened by what was happening, and Zdenka wrote to her husband telling him to come home. According to her memoirs, Janáček answered that 'he wouldn't dream of it, that he wouldn't let his holidays be ruined.'[42] However, only a matter of hours after the arrival of his letter, Janáček himself arrived, 'red-faced and puffing in exasperation, carrying his cases in both hands and with his hat pulled right to the back of his skull, always a sign that the Maestro was in the worst mood'.[43] His abrupt and reluctant departure from Hukvaldy seems to have been because of the rumour that civilians would not be able to travel by train, and so there was a possibility that he might not be able to get back to Brno, where he would be needed at the Organ School.[44] Austria declared war on Serbia on Tuesday 28 July.

67

Janáček's finances II
(1904–14)

by JIŘÍ ZAHRÁDKA

The beginning of the twentieth century was characterized by the strengthening of the Austro-Hungarian economy. A second phase of industrialization within the Czech lands took place resulting in a rapid development of industry and extensive building of the new industrial concerns. This favourable economic development ended with the First World War. From 1 January 1900 only the new currency based on the *koruna* (K) [crown] was in use.

In the academic year 1903–4 Janáček took sick leave (evidently paid) from the Teachers' Institute beginning on 9 November 1903 (awarded as late as 12 January 1904 by a decree of the Imperial and Royal Ministry of Culture and Education). He proceeded to permanent retirement by a decree of the ministry of 14 September 1904. His basic pension (2200 K in 1903) was based on his yearly salary, which with five quinquennial increments (of which the fifth was awarded after calculating his pension) brought it up to 2600 K. This evidently remained unchanged until 1919, when Janáček began to work in the state education system again. A further, substantial source of income in the years 1909–14 arose from teaching at the Organ School and from his role as director. After retiring from the Teachers' Institute Janáček could devote himself wholly to this institution and increasingly also to composition. His income from the Organ School came from two sources (as director and as teacher) and varied each year. For example as director of the Organ School in 1904 Janáček was paid 200 K a year, 400 K in 1905, 600 K in 1906, 900 K in 1907; in further years this amount settled down at 600 K annually. His teaching income at the Organ School varied according to the number of hours he taught. Thus in the first half of 1904, before retiring from the Teachers' Institute, Janáček received a monthly salary of 96 K for teaching; in comparison the highest monthly income for teaching at the Organ School he received was 291 K in 1914. In written documents there are several references to *bytné* [living allowance]. This appears for first time in 1905, when in February and March the amount of 64 K 80 h was entered, and for the second time a year later, when two amounts of 111 K are entered. Since there is no further mention of this type of income, it has not been the included in the final calculation.

From 1913 until his death Janáček also drew a pension from the savings bank, where the annual amount of 800 K was fixed; in the year 1913 he got an extra amount of 136 K 45 h from life insurance.

Janáček also received income, if not for the moment a great deal, from the performance of his works. Thus for example in the year 1904 he was paid 146 K for the staging of *Jenůfa* at the Brno National Theatre (ten performances at 12 K, two performances on tour at 8 K and 10 K for the loan of the full score). This amount is partly derived by analogy. (In comparison Karel Kovařovic received 14 K per performance of his opera *The Dogheads* in Brno.) In 1906 for *Jenůfa* in the same theatre Janáček received 46 K (one tour performance at 8 K, two performances in Brno at 14 K, 10 K for the loan of the full score). In 1911 he seems to have received about 70 K for five performances and in the year 1913 the amount of 12 K is entered for a single performance. In the case of his opera *Fate* Janáček wanted to sue the Vinohrady Theatre for breach of contract and demanded the payment of 3000 K. In the end, an out of court settlement took place by which Janáček was paid 387 K 80 h.

Similarly Janáček did not receive substantial sums from publishers at this point: the most he got was 1000 K for publication of the piano-vocal score of *Jenůfa* by the Club of the Friends of Art in 1908. Further amounts are shown in table 67.1. It is not known, however, how much he got for the publication of *Moravian Dances* (VIII/18, Píša 1905), the piano cycle *On the Overgrown Path* (VIII/17, Píša, 1911), *In the Mists* (VIII/22, Píša 1912) or for his *Complete Harmony Manual* (XV/202, Píša 1912). A further source of income came from a study grant from the Czech Academy of Sciences in 1904 for 400 K.

The composer's expenses in the years 1904–14 were evidently much the same for anyone of his social standing. (Examples of costs of basic foodstuffs and clothing in 1906 are shown in table 67.2.) In addition to

Table 67.1: Leoš Janáček's income 1904–14

sources:

BmJA

Archiv města Brna (C.k. český ústav ku vzdělání učitelů v Brně, Archiv Národního divadla v Brně)
Moravský zemský archiv Brno (Varhanická škola v Brně)
Nadace Leoše Janáčka (documents from the Městské divadlo na Královských Vinohradech)
amounts are in K

year	salary	pension	Organ School	other	total
1904	Teachers' Institute: Jan–Oct 2920	(Nov–Dec) 424	1332.80	400 (Czech Academy of Science grant), 146 (*Jenůfa* 1/4 performances by the Brno Theatre)	5222.80
1905	—	2660	2520	—	5180
1906	—	2660	2452.24	50 (IV/28, Urbánek), 46 (1/4, performances by Brno Theatre)	5208.24
1907	—	2660	2888.50	—	5548.50
1908	—	2660	2721.90	1000 (1/4 publication by Club of the Friends of Art)	6381.90
1909	—	2660	2399	—	5059
1910	—	2660	3256.60	—	5916.60
1911	—	2660	3876	70 (1/4, performances by Brno Theatre)	6606
1912	—	2660	3919.60	—	6579.60
1913	—	2660 + 800 (pension from savings bank)	3720	136 (life insurance) 50 (deposit for choruses HMUB) 387.80 (out of court settlement with Vinohrady Theatre) 12 (1/4, performance by Brno Theatre)	7766.25
1914	—	2660 + 800 (pension from savings bank)	2546	74.75 (fee from *HR*)	6043.75

Table 67.2: Examples of costs (in K) of goods in 1906

foodstuffs		clothing	
milk, 1 litre	0.30	1 shirt	2.40
flour, 1 kg	0.28	gentleman's suit	24–48
butter, 1 kg	2–2.42	1 pair shoes	12
beef, 1 kg	1.27–1.78		
1 goose	8.14–11		

the usual outgoings on food, clothing and rent (in the years 1910–14 Janáček paid 600 K a year to the Association for the Promotion of Church Music in Moravia for his house behind the Organ School), there was also the standard maintenance of a housekeeper and regular stays in spas. Further expenditure came from undoubtedly substantial amounts for copying compositions (for example copying the full score of *Fate* in 1905 cost perhaps 167 K). Two substantial, documented expenses stand out: contributions to life insurance in 1908 (141 K 40 h) and in 1912 (707 K 44 h). Janáček paid out further amounts for health treatment, for instance in the year 1909 for staying in Kuthan's sanatorium for heart problems (166 K) and in 1910 in the hospital in Roudnice nad Labem, where he was treated for erysipelas (he paid Dr Dvořák 200 K). Janáček made a one-off payment to the publisher F.A. Urbánek who had published his manual *On the Compositions of Chords and their connections* (xv/151) in 1897 (in 1912 Janáček published his *Complete Harmony Manual* xv/202 with another publisher for which Urbánek demanded compensation). Janáček's tax burden was evidently tiny: it is documented that he paid tax on his Organ School earnings of about 41–4 K a year.

In general it can be stated that in the years 1904–14 Janáček's financial situation constantly improved (for comparison the annual salaries of other workers and professions in the years 1904–10 are given in table 67.3). This was because of a generally high state pension and income from the Organ School. The bulk of his income continued to derive from his teaching activities (rather than from his compositions), and although even here there was an increase, in relation to his overall earnings, it remained in the minority.

Table 67.3: Examples of salaries, 1904–10

Year	Profession, Employment	Annual salary (in K)
1910	worker	800
1910	mechanic at brickyard	840
1910	master blacksmith	1080
1910	clerk	1080
1904	9th grade of state employee (main teacher at a Teachers' Institute)	2000
1904	1st grade of state employee (chief financial adviser)	24,000

68

Janáček at sixty

Janáček, as Robert Smetana reports, was reluctant to do much about celebrating his sixtieth birthday (see chap. 66). Presumably reflecting what Zdenka and Máŕa had told him, Smetana put this down to a feeling of embitteredness at the lack of recognition. Ten years earlier everything had seemed so promising. His fiftieth birthday had been celebrated six months after the triumphant première of *Jenůfa* in Brno. A few years later, the Organ School had acquired its final and splendid new building, and, with yearly intakes of students (rather than every three years), it was a much more vibrant affair with a higher profile, mounting several series of public concerts. And the Janáčeks themselves had moved into a newly built house on the premises, wonderfully handy and with all the modern conveniences. Janáček's life, too, was less stressed, his teaching concentrated entirely on the Organ School, which gave him more time for his own work.

It was during this decade that his writing of unaccompanied male-voice choruses climaxed with the three Bezruč choruses in which powerful words were united unforgettably with music of high voltage and startling innovation (see chap. 54). And although extremely taxing, one of these works, *Maryčka Magdónova*, had found its ideal interpreter in Vach's Moravian Teachers, who had toured it throughout the Czech lands and beyond. The success of the work was confirmed by the huge number of performances, the many letters that Janáček received about it and the shrewd calculation by F.A. Urbánek to publish it, although hitherto he had turned down every composition that Janáček had offered him. After its disastrous first performance twelve years earlier, *Amarus* (III/6) had been rehabilitated and taken round the country. On the basis of its Prague showing the Czech Philharmonic commissioned a new orchestral piece from Janáček, *The Fiddler's Child* (VI/14). The extended decade up to 1914 was the period of Janáček's finest piano music, his finest choral music, his increasing interest in chamber music and a new short choral-orchestral piece, *The Čarták on Soláň* (III/7), which revealed a completely different world from that of *Amarus* and constituted a significant step forward. In public terms Janáček was still the best known musician in Moravia: the head of its chief music-teaching institution and a prominent writer on music theory; the leading figure, after Bartoš's death, in Moravian folk-music research, now funded on a regular basis by Austrian state funds; and a much respected conductor when he chose to take up the baton.

However the years since Janáček's fiftieth birthday could also be construed as profoundly unhappy and frustrating. Bartoš and Dvořák, the two mentors to whom he felt nearest, both died during this decade, as did his younger brother František, the only one of his siblings close to him, the one whom he had seen and corresponded with regularly. Above all, what became abundantly clear to Janáček in this decade, despite his local fame and some compositional successes, was how much his career as a composer was stalled. *Jenůfa* should have opened doors elsewhere, but neither the Prague National Theatre nor the Vinohrady Theatre would have it. Even in Brno its survival in the repertory after Hrazdira's departure had been a matter of pressure from Janáček's adherents rather than its being a natural part of the repertory. Worse still, *Fate* had got nowhere at all. Its staging at the Vinohrady Theatre had been promised for years but in the end Janáček had ignominiously to take away his unperformable opera. Inevitably this had repercussions on his further operatic plans. *Brouček*, begun enthusiastically in the year in which *Fate* seemed set to be performed and in which *Jenůfa* was published, was continually slowed down, first by libretto problems but more and more by despair. If Prague would not perform *Jenůfa* or *Fate*, was there any point in writing any more operas? With three of the four acts of *Brouček* finished, he simply put it away. As an opera composer Janáček, at the age of sixty, had failed.

From this viewpoint the decade after 1904 looks like a wasteland for Janáček in terms of progress and confidence. Here was a composer in his fifties who should have been at the height of his powers. Instead with Janáček one observes a series of works that he revised or even destroyed, actions which suggest great uncertainty about where he should be going. His two piano suites of the period seem to say it all:

from the 'overgrown path' (VIII/17) he then blunders around 'in the mists' (VIII/22). The list of destroyed works begins with the piano piece *1.X.1905* (VIII/19) – whose final movement Janáček publicly burnt and whose remaining two movements he scattered on the Vltava – and continues with the Piano Trio (X/22). The list of revised works includes *Jenůfa* (revised in 1906–7), *Fate* (two substantial revisions), *Brouček* (constantly revised), *Maryčka Magdónova* (a completely new version), *The 70,000* (IV/36) (withdrawn for a year or two), *Our Father* (IV/29), the *Fairy Tale* and *The Čarták on Soláň*. The list of abandoned works includes the most substantial: *Brouček*. Wherever Janáček turned it seemed to go wrong. Productivity narrowed down about one piece a year, a sad reflection on his state of mind.

And, as the years marched on, Janáček's health gave way. His fifties began with his taking early retirement from the Teachers' Institute because of chronic ill-health. They ended with some of the worst health problems that he had experienced, culminating in painful and persistent rheumatism, which stopped him working for several months. The breakdown in health as he approached sixty seems to mirror the breakdown in his confidence. He no longer believed that *Jenůfa* or *Fate* would be given in Prague; there was no point in finishing *Brouček*. As Janáček wrote to František Veselý in 1915, 'I no longer valued my works – just as I did not value what I said. I did not believe that sometime someone would notice anything [of mine].'[1]

Understandable as it is, Janáček's stark assessment of his life as a composer was too bleak. For a start it is mistaken to regard the revision of pieces as inherently negative (as did Dr Hlava from the National Theatre; see chap. 62). It is only by experimenting that a composer's range extends. The fact that Verdi, after a whole string of masterpieces such as *Rigoletto, Il trovatore* and *La traviata*, could go back to the drawing-board with works as experimental as *Don Carlos* bespeaks growth not atrophy, let alone incompetence. Whatever the slow-down of pace and the uncertain results, Janáček was growing throughout his fifties so that, when the conditions were right after 1916, his career took off as if he were a new composer, with incredible panache and success. And, when one looks a little more closely at the list of revised, lost and abandoned works, it is clear that this picture too is misleading.

The only mature composition where there is reasonable proof that Janáček tried to destroy it is *1.X.1905*. Perhaps, as was suggested earlier (see chap. 53), Janáček was disconcerted by the context in which its rehearsals and first performance took place. The other Czech piano pieces played at the same concert were written by established composers for the piano, writing with considerable sophistication and surface gloss; Janáček's work is much more earthy and gutsy, and today this aspect is valued more than the superficial trappings of piano-friendly technique. Janáček, too, eventually saw it this way and sanctioned the performance and publication of the piece in 1924 when the copy that Ludmila Tučková had held on to turned up. One simply does not know whether he destroyed his Piano Trio. He reported to Rektorys after its first performance that it was well received. He lent performance materials to Antonín Váňa for a second performance. After that the trail goes cold. The fact that the highly successful String Quartet no. 1 in 1924 shares the same title – and apparently some of the same material – suggests that he saw at least something in the work. One can argue that just as he revised *Fairy Tale* for publication in 1923, he revised the Trio in the same year but rather more drastically, reshaping it as a string quartet (see vol. ii: 1923).

As for the works that he revised, it seems entirely positive that he did so. Many of them were early attempts in new genres, and few composers get things right first time. Performances are useful in showing a composer what works and what doesn't. The *Fairy Tale* for cello and piano, only Janáček's second chamber piece of his mature years, was presented virtually in a workshop performance, with the composer announcing that he might add more movements at some stage (and at its performance two years later in Vyškov it did indeed have one more). In genres where Janáček had composed more and had considerable on-the-ground experience with conducting his male-voice choirs, there were fewer problems, even in the experimental Bezruč choruses. *Kantor Halfar* was left unrevised. With *Maryčka Magdónova* Janáček wrote a version, but then had second thoughts (without even hearing the work performed) and simply wrote another – a reinterpretation of the same material, one could say. And this second version, although taking Vach's choir to the edge of its abilities, did work and was a huge success from the moment it was given. Much of the excitement in Janáček's music stems from its difficulty; *The 70,000* was the only choral piece where Janáček's imagination and boldness outstripped the performance realities of the time and he took it back to the drawing-board.

It is with the operas that the biggest picture of revision and lack of confidence remains, a picture compounded by several false starts. This is not unreasonable. Operas are complicated, multi-dimensional works that need above all a context of stage experience. Sadly Janáček did not have the opportunity of hearing *Šárka* in performance and learning whatever lessons he might have taken from it. With his second opera, *The Beginning of a Romance*, he realized immediately after the première that this was not the way forward for him and withdrew the opera after only a few performances. From this point of view it is then quite miraculous that *Jenůfa* worked as well as it did, especially when, more than any other single work of Janáček's, it had been plagued by self-doubts that blocked it for five years.

Whereas the problems with *Jenůfa* were essentially ones of craft-learning and tackling more demanding subject matter, the problems with the next two operas were ones of librettos. And in *Fate* there was a nearness to real life that occasionally stood in the way of Janáček's taking an objective view of what he had produced (see chap. 52). The painful lesson that needed to be learnt in both these operas was that his conception of opera was so original that he really could not expect effective help from librettists. In *Brouček*, for instance, the long gestation of the Moon Excursion is explained not by writer's block, state of health or outside commitments, but mostly by his not having a satisfactory libretto. A huge amount of time was lost on librettists – trying to find suitable ones and then trying to get them to write what he wanted. It was only in 1912, after four years, that he at last discovered an amenable librettist in František Gellner, by which stage Janáček had discovered that he could get by on his own. Not much – apart from a demand for his works – was needed to awaken the seemingly effortless productivity of his final fourteen years. However, neither Janáček nor his commentators realized that at the time.

One of the reports of Janáček's sixtieth birthday was in the journal *Moravskoslezská revue*. According to a note by the editor in the next number, Janáček had been asked to write something for the journal to provide in his 'jubilee year', a 'picture of his personality and aspirations of an important representative of Moravian culture'. What the journal got, and published on 20 November, was a seven-page article entitled *From a Literary Mood* (XV/207), which had nothing to do with Moravian culture but instead reflected Janáček's latest preoccupation with his speech-melody theory: the relationship between individual phon-emes that make up a single syllable. This is simply a footnote to previ-ous work but one that became increasingly unclear as Janáček waded further into the subject with diagrams and a new nomenclature. Per-haps even he sensed that this might be inappropriate for the general reader and preceded this theoretical discourse with something quite different, charming and homely: an account of an orphaned blackbird, sadly wandering around the Janáčeks' garden. His siblings had all died (the most enterprising had drowned himself, the weakest had been frozen to death) and his parents had been shot by a neighbouring 'German gardener'. *Moravskoslezská revue* may have wanted a picture of a leading representative of Moravian culture, but what it got was more autobiographical than anyone intended. In 1913 Janáček had declared that he was stuck in his own nest 'like a magpie'. Now, it seems, he was the sad and lonely blackbird going on singing his song – an image that reflected his increasingly isolated position in Czech musical culture, and one made even more forlorn by the outbreak of the First World War.

Notes

1: Images of Janáček

1 *JODA*, JP135.
2 *JODA*, LB2.
3 Jascha Hoeinstein interviewed by Alan Blyth on BBC radio (1970), reproduced on UKCD2036 (Unicorn-Kanchana Records 1990; originally issued 1975); edited version, *The Gramophone* (1970), Nov, 768 and 775.
4 Weyr 2001, 313.
5 Löwenbach 1933, 188.
6 Trkanová 1964, 74.
7 *MLWJ*, 8–9.
8 Černík 1933.
9 'Hudba: k padesátým narozeninám Leoše Janáčka' ['Music: on the fiftieth birthday of Leoš Janáček'], *LN* (3 July 1904).
10 Weyr 2001, 313.
11 LJ's personal files in Archiv Zemského národního výboru, S–3, quoted in Štědroň 1947a, 144.
12 LJ's personal files in Archiv Zemského národního výboru, S–3, quoted in Štědroň 1947a, 142.
13 *JODA*, BR71.
14 *JODA*, BR86.
15 Mikota 1933, 192.
16 Weyr 2001, 316.
17 Personal communication (1980).
18 Kožík 1983, 130.
19 Personal communication (1980).
20 Weyr 2001, 317.

2: Nations and languages

1 LJ to Jan Mikota, 18 April 1926 (*LR*, 183–4).
2 Quoted in Pernes 1996, 93.
3 František Čapka: *Dějiny Moravy v datech* [The history of Moravia in dates] (CERM, Prague, CERM, 2001), 17–20 ;–: *Morava* [Moravia (Libri, Libri, 2003), 18–25.
4 Pernes 1996, 70–1.
5 Pernes 1996, 72.

6 Pernes 1996, 85–6.
7 Pernes 1996, 85.
8 Pernes 1996, 17.
9 Pernes 1996, 81–4.
10 *LJPT*, 43.
11 Pernes 1996, 118–19.
12 'Praha', *OSN*, xx (1903), 488.
13 Kuča 2000, 171.
14 Pernes 1996, 97–8.
15 *LJPT*, 60.
16 Pernes 1996, 111.
17 Pernes 1996, 83.
18 *LJPT*, 57ff.
19 Pernes 1996, 23.
20 Compiled from *Chambers Dictionary of Etymology*, ed. Robert K. Barnhart (Chambers, Edinburgh, 1988) and Jiří Rejzek: *Český etymologický slovník* (Leda, Prague, 2001).
21 For instance Josef Jungman: *Slownjk česko-německý* [Czech-German dictionary] (Josefa wdowa Fetterlowá, 1835–9); *RSN* (1860–74).
22 'Lach', *OSN*, xv, 1900.
23 Procházka 1948, 18.
24 Procházka 1948, 9–17.
25 *LJPT*, 49, fn. 3.
26 *IB*, 21.
27 Veselý 1924, 16.
28 Friedrich Janáček to LJ, 21 Feb 1895 (BmJA, A 1376).
29 e.g. František Janáček to LJ, St Petersburg, 26 Nov 1895 (BmJA, B 1415).
30 František Janáček to LJ, St Petersburg, 10 Jan 1896 N.S. (BmJA, A 5108).
31 Přibáňová 1984, 135.
32 *MLWJ*, 61–2.
33 Kunc 1911, 188.
34 LJ to ZJ, 22 July 1907 (BmJA, A 3939).
35 *MLWJ*, 165.
36 LJ to Mikota, 22 June 1925 (original in LA PNP; copy in BmJA, D 1631).

3 : The Janáčeks

1 *LJPT*, 9–15.
2 Přibáňová 1984, 130–1; see plate 4 for facsimile of the birth register.
3 *LJPT*, 17.
4 *LJPT*, 16.
5 *ŽJJ*, 13.
6 Trojan 2000.
7 *ŽJJ*, 30–31.
8 *ŽJJ*, 51.
9 *ŽJJ*, 33.
10 Veselý 1924, 15.
11 e.g. LJ to Horvátová, 22 Dec 1917 (JA vi, 47–8).
12 *LJPT*, 43.
13 *LJPT*, 42.
14 *ŽJJ*, 31.
15 *LJPT*, 30–4.

16 Vašek 1930, 17, presumably on the basis of Josef Janáček's recollection.
17 ŽJJ, 28–9.
18 See ŽJJ for details.
19 Janáček's recollection given to Brod (Brod 1924, 14).
20 Vašek 1930, 17, presumably on the basis of Josef Janáček's recollection.
21 Janáček so described his father in xv/291.
22 LJPT, 36.
23 LJPT, 37–8.
24 ŽJJ, 29.
25 LJPT, 38.
26 LJPT, 38–9.
27 LJPT, 37.

4: Hukvaldy

1 RSN, iii (1863), 965.
2 BH, 13, 14.
3 BH, 16.
4 LJ to KS, 5 Aug 1918 (HŽ, no.77).
5 LJPT, 35.
6 OSN, xi (1897), 855.

5: Childhood (1854–65)

1 BH, 23.
2 Based on Přibáňová 1984.
3 MLWJ, 48 and 175.
4 Vašek 1930, 16.
5 Přibáňová 1984, 133.
6 LJPT, 39.
7 Přibáňová 1984, 136.
8 Přibáňová 1984, 136.
9 Josefa Janáčková to LJ, 25 Oct 1884 (BH, 33).
10 Brod 1924, 14.
11 Kniha školou povinných dětí v Hukvaldech 1860 [School book of compulsory child (attendance) in Hukvaldy 1860], quoted in LJPT, 49, fn. 3.
12 Veselý 1924, 15,
13 Listed in LJPT, 39.
14 LJPT, 49.
15 BH, 22.
16 Veselý 1924, 16.
17 Veselý 1924, 15.
18 Veselý 1924, 16.
19 Veselý 1924, 15, 16.
20 LJPT, 51–2, especially p. 51, fn. 1.
21 Veselý 1924, 21.
22 LJPT, 52.
23 ŽJJ, 59.
24 LJPT, 30–2.
25 Eichler 1904, 37.
26 Vašek 1930, 24.
27 Veselý 1924, 19.

6:   Brno I: 1860–1914

1 Kuča 2000, 518.
2 Kuča 2000, 271; additional information from Milena Flodrová.
3 Flodrová 2003, 24; Dřímal and Peša 1973, 30; Kuča 2000, 148, 283.
4 Flodrová 2003, 28–9; Dřímal and Peša 1973, 40–2; *JKPU*, 23–4; Šujan 1928, 420–1, 428–9.
5 Dřímal and Peša 1973, 52–3; Flodrová 2003, 27; Kuča 2000, 119; Šujan 1928, 412.
6 Bajgarová 2005, 121–35; Flodrová 2003, 26 and 27; *LJPT*, 182–52; Štědroň 1938.
7 Bajgarová 2005, 121–35; *SČHK*, 80.
8 Dřímal and Peša 1973, 48–51; Pernes 1996, 114–15, 118–20, 125–6.

7:   From schoolboy to schoolmaster: Brno 1865–74

1 See illustrations in Kožíšek 1938, 176–7.
2 Henig 2000, 23.
3 Henig 2000, 26.
4 Iltis 1932, 47.
5 'Napp, Cyrill. Fr.', *OSN*, xvii (1901), 1035.
6 Henig 2000, 24–5.
7 Sehnal 1980.
8 'Napp, Cyrill. Fr.', *OSN*, xvii (1901), 1035.
9 Kožíšek 1938, 176.
10 Kožíšek 1938, 177.
11 Eichler 1904, 37–8.
12 Henig 2000, 24.
13 *LJPT*, 54, fn. 1.
14 Veselý 1924, 23–8.
15 Veselý 1924, 28.
16 Veselý 1924, 22.
17 K. Mach: *P Paul Křížkovský u.d. kirchliche Knabengesang*, 1936, 11), quoted in *LJPT*, 70, fn. 2.
18 Vašek 1930, 39.
19 Eichler 1904, 19.
20 Veselý 1924, 21.
21 Eichler 1904, 37–8.
22 Veselý 1924, 21.
23 *ŽJJ*, 85.
24 Eichler 1904, 37.
25 LJ to Jan Janáček, 21 June 1866 (*ŽJJ*, 73).
26 *LJPT*, 52.
27 Přibáňová in *ŽJJ*, 69, quoting records in the Archiv města Brna.
28 Veselý 1924, 21–2.
29 Šujan 1928, 410.
30 Veselý 1924, 22.
31 Veselý 1924, 26–7.
32 Veselý 1924, 28.
33 Their stance is confirmed by the memoirs of Jan Havlíček, who attended the Old Brno Realgymnasium (*LJPT*, 319, fn. 1).
34 LJ to Jan Janáček, after 1 March 1867 (*ŽJJ*, 74).
35 Veselý 1924, 23.
36 Zatloukalová 2001, i, 181–7.

37 Veselý 1924, 23.
38 Veselý 1924, 23.
39 Přibáňová in *ŽJJ*, 70.
40 LJ to Jan Janáček, between 5 and 12 June 1867 (*ŽJJ*, 74–6). The comment 'geschikt' is on the original letter, BmJA, B 1325.
41 Vašek 1930, 33.
42 Křížkovský to his mother and family, 15 Dec 1867 (Eichler 1904, 40).
43 Eichler 1904, 41.
44 Křížkovský's letter home 15 Dec 1867, quoted in Eichler 1904, 41.
45 Reprinted in English translation in Stern and Sherwood 1966, 1–48.
46 Henig 2000, 239–48.
47 LJ to Jan Janáček, 21 March 1868 (*ŽJJ*, 76–8).
48 Přibáňová in *ŽJJ*, 70.
49 Přibáňová 1984, 135.
50 LJ to Jan Janáček, after 5 July 1868 (*ŽJJ*, 78–9).
51 LJ to Jan Janáček, 19 Aug 1867 (*ŽJJ*, 80).
52 Vašek 1930, 38, from information supplied by the Augustinians from the 'book of the foundation'.
53 *LJPT*, 56.
54 Eichler 1904, 44.
55 LJ to Jan Janáček, 26 May 1869 (*ŽJJ*, 80–2).
56 Named in Eichler 1904, 45, including Janáček as an alto.
57 LJ to Jan Janáček, 26 May 1869 (*ŽJJ*, 80–2).
58 Facsimile in *ŽJJ*, 75.
59 LJ to Jan Janáček, 6 Aug 1869 (*ŽJJ*, 82–4; facsimile of original reportion *ŽJJ*, 75).
60 LJ to Jan Janáček, 14 Aug 1869 (*ŽJJ*, 84).
61 *BH*, 29.
62 I am indebted to Milena Flodrová for this information (Archiv města Brna).
63 Drlíková 2004, 11.
64 Bártová 1998, 131.
65 *LJPT*, 270.
66 Přibáňová in *ŽJJ*, 70–71.
67 *CO*, xv.
68 *JVD*, 24–5.
69 Neumann 1940, 81–3.
70 BmJA, A 23.540, facsimile in *JAWO*, 154.
71 Veselý 1924, 29.
72 *LJPT*, 72.
73 Catalogue of pupils quoted in. Přibáňová's preface to Janáček's letters to his uncle in *ŽJJ*, 70.
74 Eichler 1904, 49.
75 Eichler 1904, 49.
76 Drlíková 2004, 11.
77 *LJPT*, 72.
78 *LJPT*, 72, fn. 1.
79 *LJPT*, 72, fn. 1.
80 *LJPT*, 90.
81 *LJPT*, 74.
82 *LJPT*, 195.
83 Křížkovský to Schulz?, 12 Jan 1874 (*LJPT*, 77–8).

84 Eichler 1904, 51.
85 LJ to Ministry of Culture and Education, 31 Jan 1874 (*LJPT*, 73, fn. 2).
86 *LJPT*, 78, fn. 5.
87 Transcribed in *LJPT*, 73.

8: Pavel Křížkovský

1 Veselý 1924, 37–8.
2 *MLWJ*, 28.
3 Straková 1959, 170.
4 *LJPT*, 52–3.
5 Eichler 1904, 1.
6 *DHM*, 156–8.
7 J. Vysloužil: 'Sušil, František', *NG*2.
8 Kunc 1911, 121.
9 Žalud to LJ, 28 Jan 1880 (*LJPT*, 317, fn. 2).
10 Eichler 1904, 85.
11 Eichler 1904, 87.
12 Eichler 1904, 87.

9: Pan-Slavism I

1 Kohn 1960, ix.
2 Erickson 1964, 4.
3 Kohn 1960, 1–68.
4 Burghauser 1961, 6.
5 Kohn 1960, 77.
6 'Duma', *RSN*, ii, 346–7.
7 *LJPT*, 339–41.
8 Burghauser 1991, 86.
9 *LJPT*, 253–4.
10 Veselý 1924, 159; Brod 1924, 73.

10: Early professsional life: before Prague (1874–4)

1 *LJPT*, 178, fn. 9, quoting information from Bohumír Štědroň.
2 Eichler 1904, 56.
3 'Svatopluk' minutes for 20 Aug 1872, quoted in *LJPT*, 180, fn. 7.
4 *LJPT*, 179, fn. 1.
5 BmJA, Z10, 113–14. The 170 zl is not far from Zdenka's '15 zl a month' (i.e. 180 zl).
6 MO (1 Sept 1876) about the bishop's interdict, quoted in *LJPT*, 179.
7 *MLWJ*, 28.
8 *LJPT*, 186–94.
9 *LJPT*, 194–5.
10 *LJPT*, 196–7.
11 *LJPT*, 197.
12 *LJPT*, 200–1.
13 Information compiled by Helfert in *LJPT*, 199–200, fn. 5.
14 *LJPT*, 197.
15 MO (see *LJPT*, 201).
16 *LJPT*, 197, fn. 2 based on 'Svatopluk' minutes.

17 *LJPT*, 198–9.

18 *LJPT*, 198, fn. 2.

19 Quoted in *LJPT*, 333.

20 *LJPT*, 331, fn. 2.

21 *LJPT*, 332–3.

22 František Sušil, ed: *Moravské národní písně s nápevy do textu vřaděnými* [Moravian folksongs with tunes includes with the texts] (Karel Winiker, Brno, 1860), no. 214.

23 *MO* (29 April 1873) quoted in *LJPT*, 331.

11: Musical studies: Prague 1874–5

1 *LJPT*, 328–9.

2 Ludvová 1989, 36–7.

3 Srb 2004, 46; Kuča 2000, 271.

4 *OSN*, xii (1908), 488.

5 Kuča 2000, 271.

6 *Kalendář českých hudebníkův*, iv (1886), 49.

7 *Dalibor* (15 Aug 1874), 263, quoted in *LJPT*, 99, fn. 2.

8 Brod 1924, 16.

9 Veselý 1924, 32.

10 xv/275.

11 Veselý 1924, 32.

12 *Kalendář českých hudebníkův*, iv (1886), 49. The information derived from this source comes from a later period, but the regulations probably did not change much.

13 *Kalendář českých hudebníkův*, iv (1886), 49.

14 *LJPT*, 78.

15 *LJPT*, 81–6.

16 *Kalendář českých hudebníkův*, iv (1886), 49.

17 The following paragraph draws information and views from Ludvová 1989, 39–41 and Jiří Fukač: 'Skuherský, František Zdeněk', *NG2*.

18 Ludvová 1989, 40.

19 *LJPT*, 81.

20 Veselý 1924, 31.

21 *LJPT*, 80, fn. 1.

22 Novák 1980, 90, quoted in Ludvová 1989, 40.

23 *LJPT*, 87–8.

24 Ludvová 1989, 40.

25 *LJPT*, 90, fn. 2.

26 *LJPT*, 101.

27 *LJPT*, 88.

28 Janáček's progress in reading and some of the annotations are described in *LJPT*, 91–5; see also Beckerman 1994, 21–4.

29 'Janáček and the Herbartians', Beckerman 1994, 15–24.

30 Beckerman 1994, 23.

31 Veselý 1924, 47.

32 *LJPT*, 91, fn. 1.

33 *LJPT*, 91, fn. 1.

34 *LJPT*, 333.

35 *LJPT*, 78, fn. 5.

36 *LJPT*, 79.

37 *LJPT*, 79.

38 *LJPT*, 79.
39 *LJPT*, 88, fn. 3.
40 *LJPT*, 91, fn. 1.
41 Brod 1924, 17.
42 Ludvová 1989, 39.
43 *LJPT*, 79.
44 *LJPT*, 89.
45 Certificate dated 24 July 1875, quoted in *LJPT*, 89, fn. 3.
46 List of pupils in Prague Organ School, quoted in *LJPT*, 89.
47 Certificate dated 7 Nov 1875, quoted in *LJPT*, 102, fn. 2.
48 Ministerial decree of 30 Aug 1876, quoted in *LJPT*, 102.
49 *LJPT*, 102.
50 *LJPT*, 103, fn. 3.
51 *LJPT*, 108.
52 *LJPT*, 103–7 provides examples of his work.

12: Early professional life: after Prague (1875–9)

1 *LJPT*, 289, fn. 3.
2 *LJPT*, 293, 294–5.
3 *LJPT*, 295.
4 'Svatopluk' minutes, quoted in *LJPT*, 205.
5 *LJPT*, 214.
6 List assembled from *LJPT*, 206–10.
7 Štědroň 1947d.
8 Hans Klotz/Theodor Wohnhaas: 'Steinmeyer, G.F.', *NG*2.
9 Veselý 1924, 40.
10 *LJPT*, 109, fn. 1.
11 LJ to ZS, 12–13 Feb 1880 (*IB*, 178).
12 Veselý 1924, 40.
13 Sázavský 1900, 1.
14 *LJPT*, 214.
15 Based on Sázavský 1900, 136–9.
16 *LJPT*, 343–4.
17 LJ to ZS, 20–1 Feb 1880 (*IB*, 192).
18 Brod 1924, 73.
19 *LJPT*, 334, fn. 10.
20 Přibáňová 1987, 206–7.
21 Veselý 1924, 156.
22 Miloš Štědroň: [liner notes], *Čekám Tě: Janáček Unknown [1]*, Supraphon 11 1878–2 931 (Prague, 1994).
23 *LJPT*, 204–5.
24 *LJPT*, 179.
25 The summary below is based on *LJPT*, 255–6 with extra details (such as the dates of the 1878 concerts) from Kyas 1993a.
26 Facsimile in Kyas 1993b, 236.
27 *LJPT*, 219.
28 Kyas 1993a.
29 Kyas 1993a, 37.
30 LJ to ZS, 11–12 Nov 1879 (*IB*, 84–6).
31 LJ to ZS, 9 Oct 1879 (*IB*, 37–8), 14 Oct 1879 (*IB*, 43–4).

32 Kyas 1993a, 40–1.
33 Kyas 1993a, 41.

13: The Schulzes

1 An English translation was published as *My Life with Janáček* (= *MLWJ*) in 1998.
2 See *MLWJ*, xvi.
3 *LJPT*, 270.
4 *MLWJ*, 1.
5 Štědroň 1947a, 144.
6 Personal communication from Dr Svatava Přibáňová on the basis of examining the Teachers' Institute archives.
7 *MLWJ*, 2.
8 *MLWJ*, 3–4.
9 *MLWJ*, 6–7.
10 *MLWJ*, 8.
11 *MLWJ*, 8–9.
12 *MLWJ*, 9.
13 *MLWJ*, 10.
14 LJ to ZS, 28 April 1880 (*IB*, 219–20).
15 *MO* (27 April 1879), quoted in *LJPT*, 275.
16 *LJPT*, 274.
17 *MLWJ*, 11.
18 *MLWJ*, 10.
19 LJ to ZS, 23 June 1879 (*IB*, 245).
20 *MLWJ*, 12.
21 *MLWJ*, 12.
22 *MLWJ*, 12.
23 *MLWJ*, 29.
24 Smetana 1948, 25.
25 LJ to ZS, 8 Sept 1879 (*IB*, 246).
26 *LJPT*, 253 and many later accounts.
27 LJ to ZS, 8 Sept 1879 (*IB*, 246).
28 *MLWJ*, 13.
29 LJ to ZS, 27–8 Jan 1880 (*IB*, 152–3).
30 LJ to ZS, 24–5 Nov 1879 (*IB*, 101–3).
31 For example LJ to ZS, 29 Nov 1879 (*IB*, 107–9).
32 *MLWJ*, 13.
33 LJ to ZS, 23–4 Oct 1879 (*IB*, 57–8).
34 LJ to ZS, 2–3 Dec 1879 (*IB*, 113–14).
35 *MLWJ*, 14.
36 LJ to ZS, 28 April 1880 (*IB*, 219–20). [db12999].
37 *MLWJ*, 14–15.
38 LJ to ZS, 11–12 Jan 1880 (*IB*, 131).
39 LJ to ZS, 12–13 Feb 1880 (*IB*, 177–8).
40 Sázavský 1900, 139.
41 LJ to ZS, 8–9 Jan 1880 (*IB*, 125–6); 9–10 Jan 1880 (*IB*, 126–9).
42 *MLWJ*, 14–15.
43 LJ to ZS, 17–18 Jan 1880 (*IB*, 138–9).
44 LJ to ZS, 20–1 Feb 1880 (*IB*, 187–92).
45 *MLWJ*, 10.

46 *MLWJ*, 15.
47 LJ to ZS, 27–8 May 1880 (*IB*, 235–6).
48 LJ to ZS, 31 May 1880 (*IB*, 239–40).
49 Smetana 1948, 25.

14: What's in a name? Leo, Lev and Leoš

 1 Bauerová 1992, 190; Pracný 269–70.
 2 Knappová 1996, 122.
 3 LJ to ZS, 12 April 1880 (*IB*, 207–8).
 4 Amalie Janáčková to LJ, undated, about 17 April 1882 (*ŽJJ*, 89–90); undated, April 1883 (*ŽJJ*, 93); undated, 11? April 1884 (*ŽJJ*, 95).
 5 Leo Schulz to LJ, 9 April 1910 (BmJA, A 4099), 9 April 1911 (BmJA, A 4099).
 6 Věra Janáčková and others to LJ, 9 April 1915 (BmJA, A 2239).
 7 Patrick Hanks and Flavia Hodges: *A Dictionary of First Names* (Oxford University Press, Oxford, 1990), 202 and 204; Knappová 1996, 122.
 8 *ŽJJ*, 89–95.
 9 *MLWJ*, 14.
10 LJ to ZS, 8 Jan 1880, 6 p.m. (*IB*, 125).
11 LJ to ZS, 8 Jan 1880, 8 p.m. (*IB*, 125–6).
12 LJ to ZS, 11–12 Jan 1880 (*IB*, 131).
13 LJ to ZS, 29–30 Oct 1879 (*IB*, 66–7).
14 *Dalibor*, i (1879), 264 (under 'Drobné zprávy').
15 LJ to Vlk, 22 Feb 1880 (*LJPT*, 224, fn. 5).
16 *JVD*, 36.
17 *LJPT*, 243.
18 *Dalibor*, v (1883), 298.
19 BmJA, D 38 (facsimile in Straková 1975, unpaginated).
20 Bártová 1998, 134.
21 e.g. Josefa Dohnalová to ZJ, 21 Aug 1919 (BmJA, A 5701).
22 ZJ to Joza Janáčková, 1 Jan 1906 (BmJA, A 6389).
23 LJ to ZJ, 24 July 1921 (BmJA, B 1373).

15: Musical studies: Leipzig 1879–80

 1 LJ's personal files in Archív Zemského národního výboru, S–3, quoted in Štědroň 1947a, 141.
 2 LJ to ZS, 24–5 Jan 1880 (*IB*, 146–8).
 3 Skuherský to Schulz, 12 April 1879 (*LJPT*, 110).
 4 LJ's personal files in Archív Zemského národního výboru, S–3, quoted in Štědroň 1947a, 141.
 5 *LJPT*, 111, fn. 3.
 6 LJ's personal files in Archív Zemského národního výboru, S–3, quoted in Štědroň 1947a, 141.
 7 *OSN*, xvi (1900), 83, gives population for 1875 as 200,149.
 8 *LJPT*, 111, fn. 4.
 9 LJ to ZS, 20–1 Feb 1880 (*IB*, 187–92).
10 *LJPT*, 111, fn. 4.
11 Mrs Kaluschka to the Schulz family, 30 Sept 1879 (*IB*, 247).
12 LJ to ZS, 1 Oct 1879 (*IB*, 28).
13 BmJA, E 1228–E 1351.
14 LJ to ZS, 1 Oct 1879 (*IB*, 28).

15 Racek 1977, plates 1–2.

16 LJ to ZS, 1 Oct 1879 (*IB*, 28).

17 LJ to ZS, 5–6 Dec 1879 (*IB*, 117–18).

18 LJ to ZS, 8–9 Dec 1879 (*IB*, 121–2).

19 LJ to ZS, 15–16 Jan 1880 (*IB*, 135–6).

20 LJ to ZS, 23–4 Feb 1880 (*IB*, 195–6).

21 LJ to ZS, 9 Oct–10 1879 (*IB*, 38–9).

22 LJ to ZS, 4–5 Dec 1879 (*IB*, 116–17).

23 LJ to ZS, 9 Oct–10 1879 (*IB*, 38–9).

24 LJ to ZS, 16–17 Oct 1879 (*IB*, 47–8).

25 LJ to ZS, 1 Oct 1879 (*IB*, 28).

26 LJ to ZS, 20–1 Nov 1879 (*IB*, 96–7).

27 *LJPT*, 118.

28 LJ to ZS, 8–9 Jan 1880 (*IB*, 125–6).

29 LJ to ZS, 6–8 Nov 1879 (*IB*, 79–81).

30 e.g. LJ to ZS, 16–17 Oct 1879 (*IB*, 47–8); 25–6 Oct 1879 (*IB*, 60–1); 6 Nov 1879 (*IB*, 78–9).

31 LJ to ZS, 14 Feb 1880 (*IB*, 179–80).

32 LJ to ZS, 15 Feb 1880 (*IB*, 180–1).

33 LJ to ZS, 29–30 Oct 1879 (*IB*, 66–7).

34 LJ to ZS, 13–14 Nov 1879 (*IB*, 87–8).

35 LJ to ZS, 18–19 Jan 1880 (*IB*, 139–40).

36 LJ to ZS, 1–2 Feb 1880 (*IB*, 160–1).

37 LJ to ZS, 29–30 Oct 1879 (*IB*, 66–7).

38 LJ to ZS, 26–7 Oct 1879 (*IB*, 61–3).

39 LJ to ZS, 23–4 Nov 1879 (*IB*, 100–01).

40 LJ to ZS, 17–18 Jan 1880 (*IB*, 138–9).

41 LJ to ZS, 18–19 Jan 1880 (*IB*, 139–40).

42 LJ to ZS, 19–20 Jan 1880 (*IB*, 140–2).

43 LJ to ZS, 21–2 Jan 1880 (*IB*, 143–4).

44 LJ to ZS, 11–12 Feb 1880 (*IB*, 174–6).

45 LJ to ZS, 16–17 Jan 1880 (*IB*, 136–8).

46 LJ to ZS, 18 Nov 1879 (*IB*, 94–5).

47 Reproduced in *IB*, 32.

48 e.g. LJ to ZS, 16–17 Jan 1880 (*IB*, 136–8).

49 LJ to ZS, 7–8 Feb 1880 (*IB*, 169–70).

50 LJ to ZS, 16–17 Nov 1879 (*IB*, 91–2).

51 LJ to ZS, 12–13 Nov 1879 (*IB*, 86–7).

52 LJ to ZS, 21–2 Oct 1879 (*IB*, 54–5).

53 LJ to ZS, 15 Feb 1880 (*IB*, 180–1).

54 *LJPT*, 118, fn. 5.

55 *MLWJ*, 13; at 4.90 zl (*OSN*, viii, 154) this would be 98 zl, or 196 Marks.

56 LJ to ZS, 21–2 Oct 1879 (*IB*, 54–5).

57 LJ to ZS, 5 Nov 1879 (*IB*, 76–7).

58 George B. Stauffer: 'Leipzig, §II, 5: Education', NG2.

59 LJ to ZS, 30–31 Oct 1879 (*IB*, 67–8).

60 LJ to ZS, 21–2 Nov 1879 (*IB*, 98–9).

61 LJ to ZS, 14 Oct 1879 (*IB*, 43–4).

62 LJ to ZS, 10–11 Feb 1880 (*IB*, 173–4).

63 LJ to ZS, 7–8 Oct 1879 (*IB*, 34–7).

64 LJ to ZS, 17 Feb 1880 (*IB*, 183).

65 LJ to ZS, 11–12 Nov 1879 (*IB*, 84–6).

66 LJ to ZS, 2 Oct 1879 (*IB*, 29).

67 BmJA, Z1: 'Leipzig Diary', no. 7.

68 LJ to ZS, 14–15 Oct 1879 (*IB*, 44–6). [db12267].

69 Veselý 1924, 41–2.

70 LJ to ZS, 19–20 Nov 1879 (*IB*, 95–6).

71 LJ to ZS, 21–2 Nov 1879 (*IB*, 98–9).

72 LJ to ZS, 22–3 Nov 1879 (*IB*, 99–100).

73 LJ to ZS, 11–12 Nov 1879 (*IB*, 84–6).

74 LJ to ZS, 7–8 Feb 1880 (*IB*, 169–70).

75 LJ to ZS, 20–1 Feb 1880 (*IB*, 187–92).

76 LJ to ZS, 3–4 Feb 1880 (*IB*, 165–6).

77 LJ to ZS, 25–6 Nov 1879 (*IB*, 103–4).

78 *LJPT*, 136, fn. 1.

79 LJ to ZS, 4–5 Nov 1879 (*IB*, 74–5).

80 LJ to ZS, 2 Oct 1879 (*IB*, 29).

81 LJ to ZS, 16 Oct 1879 (*IB*, 152–3).

82 LJ to ZS, 13–14 Jan 1880 (*IB*, 133–4).

83 LJ to ZS, 15–16 Oct 1879 (*IB*, 46–7).

84 *LJPT*, 122, fn. 3.

85 LJ to ZS, 21–2 Oct 1879 (*IB*, 54–5).

86 LJ to ZS, 5–6 Nov 1879 (*IB*, 77–8).

87 LJ to ZS, 1–2 Nov 1879 (*IB*, 70–1); 2–3 Nov 1879 (*IB*, 73–4).

88 LJ to ZS, 22–3 Jan 1880 (*IB*, 144–5).

89 *LJPT*, 115.

90 LJ to ZS, 20 Oct 1879 (*DZ*, 60–3).

91 LJ to ZS, 9 Oct 1879 (*IB*, 37–8); 11–12 Oct 1879 (*IB*, 41–3).

92 LJ to ZS, 5–6 Dec 1879 (*IB*, 117–18).

93 LJ to ZS, 13–14 Jan 1880 (*IB*, 133–4).

94 LJ to ZS, 14 Feb 1880 (*IB*, 178–9).

95 LJ to ZS, 20–1 Feb 1880 (*IB*, 187–92).

96 Robert W. Wason: 'Paul, Oscar', *NG*2.

97 LJ to ZS, 3 Oct 1879 (*IB*, 30–31).

98 BmJA, Z1, no. 7 gives the op. 32.

99 LJ to ZS, 10–11 Oct 1879 (*IB*, 40–1).

100 BmJA, Z1, unnumbered, between nos. 36 and 37.

101 LJ to ZS, 27–8 Oct 1879 (*IB*, 63–4).

102 LJ to ZS, 13–14 Jan 1880 (*IB*, 133–4).

103 LJ to ZS, 3–4 Feb 1880 (*IB*, 165–6).

104 LJ to ZS, 16–17 Feb 1880 (*IB*, 182–3).

105 LJ to ZS, 9 Oct 1879 (*IB*, 37–8).

106 *IB*, 36, fn. 22 provides dates for Grill's retirement and death.

107 LJ to ZS, 9–10 Oct 1879 (*IB*, 38–9).

108 See for instance the Christmas assignment jotted down in BmJA, Z1, between pp. 36–7.

109 LJ to ZS, 13 Oct 1879 (*DZ*, 44–6). [NB the German original for this letter has disappeared and its text is available only in the Czech translation published in *DZ*].

110 LJ to ZS, 15–16 Oct 1879 (*IB*, 46–7).

111 LJ to ZS, 23–4 Oct 1879 (*IB*, 57–8).

112 LJ to ZS, 20 Oct 1879 (*DZ*, 60–3); see fn. 109.

113 LJ to ZS, 26–7 Oct 1879 (*IB*, 61–3).
114 LJ to ZS, 2–3 Nov 1879 (*IB*, 71–2).
115 LJ to ZS, 10–11 Nov 1879 (*IB*, 83–4).
116 LJ to ZS, 26–7 Nov 1879 (*IB*, 103–4).
117 LJ to ZS, 3–4 Dec 1879 (*IB*, 114–15).
118 LJ to ZS, 10–11 Dec 1879 (*IB*, 123–4).
119 LJ to ZS, 14–15 Jan 1880 (*IB*, 134–5).
120 LJ to ZS, 2–3 Nov 1879 (*IB*, 71–2).
121 LJ to ZS, 29–30 Oct 1879 (*IB*, 66–7).
122 *LJPT*, 127–8.
123 LJ to ZS, 23–4 Oct 1879 (*IB*, 57–8).
124 *LJPT*, 127.
125 LJ to ZS, 11–12 Jan 1880 (*IB*, 131).
126 LJ to ZS, 2–3 Nov 1879 (*IB*, 73–4); see also *JAWO*, x/8, nos. 1–3.
127 *JAWO*, x/8.
128 LJ to ZS, 6 Nov 1879 (*IB*, 78–9).
129 LJ to ZS, 18–19 Nov 1879 (*IB*, 94–5).
130 LJ to ZS, 6 Nov 1879 (*IB*, 78–9).
131 LJ to ZS, 25 Jan 1880 (*IB*, 148–9).
132 LJ to ZS, 19–20 Jan 1880 (*IB*, 140–2).
133 LJ to ZS, 11–12 Jan 1880 (*IB*, 131).
134 LJ to ZS, 19–20 Jan 1880 (*IB*, 140–2).
135 LJ to ZS, 31 Jan 1880 (*IB*, 158–9).
136 LJ to ZS, 15–16 Feb 1880 (*IB*, 180–1).
137 LJ to ZS, 14–15 Jan 1880 (*IB*, 134–5).
138 LJ to ZS, 11–12 Jan 1880 (*IB*, 131).
139 LJ to ZS, 4–5 Feb 1880 (*IB*, 166–7).
140 LJ to ZS, 28–9 Jan 1880 (*IB*, 153–5).
141 LJ to ZS, 31 Jan–1 Feb 1880 (*IB*, 159–60).
142 LJ to ZS, 8–9 Feb 1880 (*IB*, 170–2).
143 LJ to ZS, 7–8 Feb 1880 (*IB*, 169–70).
144 LJ to ZS, 22–3 Feb 1880 (*IB*, 193–5).
145 LJ to ZS, 21–2 Feb 1880 (*IB*, 192–3).
146 LJ to ZS, 25 Jan 1880 (*IB*, 148–9).
147 LJ to ZS, 28–9 Jan 1880 (*IB*, 153–5).
148 LJ to ZS, 29–30 Jan 1880 (*IB*, 155–6).
149 LJ to ZS, 12–13 Feb 1880 (*IB*, 177–8).
150 Zellner to LJ, 14 Feb 1880 (BmJA, D 3).
151 LJ to ZS, 15–16 Feb 1880 (*IB*, 180–1).
152 LJ to ZS, 30 Jan 1880 (*IB*, 157–8).
153 LJ to ZS, 22–3 Feb 1880 (*IB*, 193–5).
154 LJ to ZS, 23–4 Feb 1880 (*IB*, 195–6).
155 LJ to ZS, 21–2 Jan 1880 (*IB*, 143–4).
156 LJ to ZS, 25 Jan 1880 (*IB*, 149–50).
157 LJ to ZS, 31 Jan 1880 (*IB*, 158–9); 10–11 Feb 1880 (*IB*, 173–4).
158 LJ to ZS, 14–15 Feb 1880 (*IB*, 179–80).
159 LJ to ZS, 18 Feb 1880 (*IB*, 184–5).
160 LJ to ZS, 8–9 Feb 1880 (*IB*, 170–2).
161 Veselý 1924, 41–2.
162 LJ to ZS, 10–11 April 1880 (*IB*, 206–7).

16: Musical studies: Vienna 1880

1 'Vídeň', *OSN*, xxvi, 656.
2 *MLWJ*, 5.
3 LJ to ZS, 2–3 April 1880 (*IB*, 198–9); 3–4 April 1880 (*IB*, 199–200).
4 LJ to ZS, 8–9 May 1880 (*IB*, 227–8).
5 LJ to ZS, 5 April 1880 (*IB*, 200–1).
6 LJ to ZS, 2–3 April 1880 (*IB*, 198–9).
7 LJ to ZS, 4 May 1880 (*IB*, 221–2); 6–7 May 1880 (*IB*, 225–6).
8 LJ to ZS, 1 April 1880 (*IB*, 197–8).
9 LJ to ZS, 1 April 1880 (*IB*, 197–8).
10 LJ to ZS, 9–10 April 1880 (*IB*, 205–6).
11 LJ to ZS, 9–10 May 1880 (*IB*, 228–9).
12 LJ to ZS, 23 April 1880 (*IB*, 215).
13 e.g. LJ to ZS, 4–5 May 1880 (*IB*, 222–3).
14 LJ to ZS, 26 April 1880 (*IB*, 218).
15 LJ to ZS, 1 April 1880 (*IB*, 197–8).
16 LJ to ZS, 3–4 April 1880 (*IB*, 199–200).
17 LJ to ZS, 9–10 April 1880 (*IB*, 205–6).
18 LJ to ZS, 5–6 April 1880 (*IB*, 201–2).
19 LJ to ZS, 13 April 1880 (*IB*, 208–9).
20 LJ to ZS, 5 April 1880 (*IB*, 200–1).
21 LJ to ZS, 1 April 1880 (*IB*, 197–8).
22 *IB*, 263.
23 LJ to ZS, 8–9 April 1880 (*IB*, 204–5); teachers added.
24 LJ to ZS, 5–6 April 1880 (*IB*, 202–3).
25 LJ to ZS, 21 April 1880 (*IB*, 212).
26 See facsimile, *IB*, 262 and Krones's discussion of the conservatory rules on main and subsidiary subjects, *IB*, 263–4.
27 LJ to ZS, 6–7 May 1880 (*IB*, 225–6).
28 LJ to ZS, 5 April 1880 (*IB*, 200–1).
29 LJ to ZS, 13 April 1880 (*IB*, 208–9).
30 LJ to ZS, 14–15 April 1880 (*IB*, 210–11).
31 LJ to ZS, 1 June 1880 (*IB*, 241).
32 LJ to ZS, 1–2 June 1880 (*IB*, 241–2).
33 LJ to ZS, 26–7 May 1880 (*IB*, 233–4).
34 LJ to ZS, 2–3 April 1880 (*IB*, 198–9).
35 LJ to ZS, 5–6 April 1880 (*IB*, 202–3).
36 LJ to ZS, 6–7 April 1880 (*IB*, 203–4).
37 LJ to ZS, 2–3 April 1880 (*IB*, 198–9).
38 LJ to ZS, 3–4 April 1880 (*IB*, 199–200).
39 LJ to ZS, 9–10 April 1880 (*IB*, 205–6).
40 LJ to ZS, 7–8 May 1880 (*IB*, 226–7).
41 LJ to ZS, 21–2 April 1880 (*IB*, 212–14).
42 BmJA, Z2 (diary for 1880), 42–54.
43 Dates of individual songs and arguments for the total number that Janáček set are given in *JAWO*, 312–14.
44 LJ to ZS, 7–8 May 1880 (*IB*, 226–7).
45 LJ to ZS, 10–11 May 1880 (*IB*, 229–30).
46 LJ to ZS, 23 April 1880 (*IB*, 215).
47 LJ to ZS, 23–4 April 1880 (*IB*, 216).

48 LJ to ZS, 26 April 1880 (*IB*, 218).
49 LJ to ZS, 7–8 May 1880 (*IB*, 226–7).
50 LJ to ZS, 10–11 May 1880 (*IB*, 229–30).
51 LJ to ZS, 11–12 May 1880 (*IB*, 230–1).
52 LJ to ZS, 24–5 May 1880 (*IB*, 232–3).
53 LJ to ZS, 23–4 April 1880 (*IB*, 216).
54 LJ to ZS, 11–12 May 1880 (*IB*, 230–1).
55 LJ to ZS, 7–8 May 1880 (*IB*, 226–7).
56 *LJPT*, 169, fn. 1.
57 LJ to ZS, 8–9 May 1880 (*IB*, 227–8).
58 LJ to ZS, 26–7 May 1880 (*IB*, 233–4).
59 LJ to ZS, 28 May 1880 (*IB*, 236).
60 LJ to ZS, 29 May 1880 (*IB*, 237).
61 LJ to ZS, 30–1 May 1880 (*IB*, 238–9).
62 LJ to ZS, 24–5 April 1880 (*IB*, 217).
63 LJ to ZS, 24–5 May 1880 (*IB*, 232–3).
64 LJ to ZS, 27–8 May 1880 (*IB*, 235–6).
65 LJ to ZS, 1–2 June 1880 (*IB*, 241–2).
66 LJ to ZS, 30–1 May 1880 (*IB*, 238–9).
67 LJ to ZS, 31 May 1880 (*IB*, 239–40).
68 *IB*, 266.
69 *IB*, 265.

17: June 1880–December 1881

1 LJ to ZS, 1–2 June 1880 (*IB*, 241–2).
2 LJ to ZS, 30–1 May 1880 (*IB*, 238–9).
3 LJ to ZS, 1 June 1880 (*IB*, 241).
4 LJ to ZS, 1–2 June 1880 (*IB*, 241–2).
5 LJ to ZS, 30–1 May 1880 (*IB*, 238–9).
6 *LJPT*, 225.
7 *LJPT*, 171, fn. 2.
8 I am grateful to Milena Flodrová for this information (Archiv města Brna).
9 *MLWJ*, 15–16.
10 *MLWJ*, 15–16.
11 e.g. LJ to Alois Vlk, 22 Feb 1880 (*LJPT*, 224, fn. 5).
12 Based on Sázavský 1900, 139–47 and programmes in BmJA.
13 *LJPT*, 239, fn. 4.
14 *LJPT*, 243.
15 *LJPT*, 214.
16 *LJPT*, 351, fn. 2.
17 *MO* (8 Jan 1881), quoted in *LJPT*, 242, fn. 3.
18 *LJPT*, 242, fn. 5 summarizing the Beseda minutes.
19 *LJPT*, 242.
20 *LJPT*, 242.
21 *LJPT*, 115, fn. 1.
22 *MLWJ*, 16.
23 *MLWJ*, 16.
24 *MLWJ*, 17.
25 *MLWJ*, 17.
26 *MLWJ*, 19.

27 Lord Lytton [Edward Bulwer Lytton]: *A Strange Story* (Routledge, London, n.d.), 69.
28 *MLWJ*, 20.
29 Mrs Kaluschka to the Schulz family, 30 Sept 1879 (*IB*, 247).
30 Smetana 1948, 27.
31 LJ to ZS, 25 Jan 1880 (*IB*, 148–9).
32 *MLWJ*, 20.
33 *MLWJ*, 22.
34 *MLWJ*, 20–1; *LJPT*, 324.
35 *MLWJ*, 31.
36 Smetana 1948, 28.
37 *MLWJ*, 23.
38 Smetana 1948, 27.
39 *MLWJ*, 24.
40 LJ to ZS, 13 Feb 1880 (*IB*, 177–8).
41 *MLWJ*, 25.
42 *MLWJ*, 26.
43 *MLWJ*, 25–6.
44 *MLWJ*, 27.
45 *MLWJ*, 37.
46 *MLWJ*, 27.
47 *MLWJ*, 27–8.
48 *MLWJ*, 32–3.
49 *MLWJ*, 26.
50 *MLWJ*, 29.
51 *Allgemeine Wohnungs-Anzeiger* (Brno 1881), 102, quoted by Přibáňová in *ŽJJ*, 85.
52 *ŽJJ*, 85.
53 I am indebted to Svatava Přibáňová for this information (Archiv města Brna).
54 LJ to ZS, 25–6 Oct 1879 (*IB*, 60–1).
55 Amalie Janáčková to LJ, before 9 Oct 1879 (*ŽJJ*, 89).
56 LJ to ZS, 25 Jan 1880 (*IB*, 148–9).
57 *MLWJ*, 33.
58 *MLWJ*, 33–4.
59 Amalie Janáčková to LJ, undated, Dec 1881 (*ŽJJ*, 89).
60 LJ to KS, 14 Feb 1921 (*HŽ*, no. 169).
61 *MLWJ*, 34.
62 *MLWJ*, 30.
63 *MLWJ*, 31.

18: Janáček as teacher

 1 Vysloužilová 1976, 214.
 2 Bártová 1998, 131.
 3 *LJPT*, 271.
 4 Štědroň 1934, 316.
 5 Personal communication from Jiří Zahrádka, whose researches on the matter continue.
 6 Bártová 1998, 131–2.
 7 Vysloužilová 1976, 214; Bártová 1998, 133.
 8 Bártová 1998, 131.
 9 Vysloužilová 1976, 214.
10 Černík 1933, reprinted in *JVD*, 37–8.
11 ves 1942.

12 BmJA, Z4 (1881–2).
13 BmJA, Z9 (1887–8).
14 Bártová 1998, 132.
15 Bártová 1998, 133.
16 Bártová 1998, 132.
17 Kunc 1911, 185–6.
18 LJ's personal files in Archiv Zemského národního výboru, S–3, quoted in Štědroň 1947a, 142–3.
19 Bártová 1998, 133.
20 LJPT, 272.
21 Vysloužilová 1976, 215.
22 Vysloužilová 1976, 215.
23 Černík 1933.
24 Sís 1940.
25 Straková 1957, 3.
26 Štědroň 1947b, 228.
27 BmJA, Z12 (notebook for 1890–1).
28 BmJA, Z13 (notebook for 1891–2).
29 Štědroň 1947b, 235.
30 Štědroň 1947b, 238–9.
31 Štědroň 1947b, 224.
32 Štědroň 1947b, 224.
33 Štědroň 1947c, 94.

19: Janáček as music theorist

1 HTD.
2 HTD, i, 47–51; Beckerman 1994, 133–6.
3 Beckerman 1994, 48–50.
4 Kulka 1990, 16.
5 Beckerman 1994, 36–7, 41, 53, 57, 104ff.
6 Chlubna 1924, especially 78.
7 Hanák 1959, especially 156–62.
8 Kulka 1990, 35.
9 Kunc 1911, 187.
10 HTD, i, 22 quoted in Eng. trans. in Kulka 1990, 27.
11 Organ School's annual reports of 1902 and 1915 quoted in JVŠ, 33.
12 Kulka 1990, 27.
13 xv/202, iii, quoted in Eng. trans. in Kulka 1990, 27.
14 Beckerman, 1994, 98.
15 Volek 1961, 237–8.
16 Vogel 1981, 161–3.
17 Blatný 1969.
18 Kunc 1911, 125.
19 Kulka 1990, 23.
20 Beckerman 1994, 134.
21 David Pountney: 'Producing Kát'a Kabanová', in Tyrrell 1982, 184–98, especially 186–8.
22 Kulka 1990, 24.
23 Kulka 1990, 25.
24 LJ to Brod, 2 Aug 1924 (JA ix, 164–5).

20: 1882–summer 1884

1 *MLWJ*, 35.
2 Application cited in Štědroň 1947a, 142.
3 *MLWJ*, 35.
4 Štědroň 1947a, 142.
5 *JVŠ*, 19.
6 *MLWJ*, 35–6.
7 LJ to Brno Beseda, 31 July 1871 (BmJA, B 2182).
8 BmJA, JP 23 and JP 24.
9 *LJPT*, 243.
10 *LJPT*, 231.
11 Sázavský 1900, 160.
12 Lehner to LJ, 22 Nov 1881 (BmJA, B 767).
13 Lehner to LJ, 5 Jan 1882 (*LJPT*, 318, fn. 1).
14 *MLWJ*, 19.
15 *MLWJ*, 36.
16 *MLWJ*, 37.
17 LJ to ZS, 19 Oct 1879 (*DZ*, 60–3) [the German original has disappeared].
18 Amalie Janáčková to LJ, 7 Dec 1882 (*ŽJJ*, 90).
19 Amalie Janáčková to LJ, undated, after 7 Dec 1882 (*ŽJJ*, 91).
20 Amalie Janáčková to LJ, undated, about 20 Dec 1882 (*ŽJJ*, 91).
21 Amalie Janáčková to LJ, undated, late? Dec 1882 (*ŽJJ*, 91–2).
22 Racek 1955, 18, fn. 20.
23 Racek, 1955, 18.
24 *MLWJ*, 40–1.
25 *MLWJ*, 41.
26 LJ's personal files in Archiv Zemského národního výboru, S–3, quoted in Štědroň 1947a, 142.
27 LJ's personal files in Archiv Zemského národního výboru, S–3, quoted in Štědroň 1947a, 142–3.
28 LJ's personal files in Archiv Zemského národního výboru, S–3, quoted in Štědroň 1947a, 144.
29 LJ's personal files in Archiv Zemského národního výboru, S–3, quoted in Štědroň 1947a, 144.
30 *MLWJ*, 40–1.
31 *MLWJ*, 42.
32 *MLWJ*, 43.
33 *ŽJJ*, 86.
34 *MLWJ*, 42.
35 LJ to Srb-Debrnov, 1 Sept 1883 (Prague, Narodní muzeum: Muzeum české hudby).
36 BmJA, J III, 25, quoted in preface to edition by Jan Trojan (Supraphon, Prague, 1979).
37 K. Baedeker: *Southern Germany and Austria [...]: handbook for travellers* (Karl Baedeker, Leipzig, 6/1887), 281.
38 Dvořák to LJ, 24 July 1883 (*ADKD*, i, 359–60).
39 Dvořák to LJ, 19 Aug 1883 (*ADKD*, i, 360).
40 *ADKD*, x, 359.
41 *LJPT*, 354.
42 Dvořák to LJ, 2 Sept 1883 (*ADKD*, i, 361–2).
43 *MLWJ*, 43–4.
44 Amalie Janáčková to LJ, undated, April 1883 (*ŽJJ*, 93).

45 *MLWJ*, 42.
46 *MLWJ*, 44–5.
47 LJ's personal files in Archiv Zemského národního výboru, S–3, quoted in Štědroň 1947a, 144–5.
48 LJ's personal files in Archiv Zemského národního výboru, S–3, quoted in Štědroň 1947a, 144–5.
49 *MLWJ*, 45.

21: The Organ School

1 Smetana 1948, 35.
2 Smetana 1948, 35.
3 *JVŠ*, 20.
4 *JVŠ*, appendix e, 141.
5 *JVŠ*, 21–2.
6 *JVŠ*, appendix e, 141.
7 *JVŠ*, 21–2.
8 *JVŠ*, 23–4.
9 *JVŠ*, 25.
10 *JVŠ*, opposite p. 25.
11 *JVŠ*, appendix e, 141.
12 Veselý 1924, 30.
13 *LJPT*, 109, fn. 1.
14 LJ to ZS, 29 Nov 1879 (*IB*, 107–9).
15 LJ to ZS, 26–7 Oct 1879 (*IB*, 61–3).
16 Organ School annual report for 1881–2, quoted in *LJPT*, 276 fn. 1; *LJPT*, 278.
17 *LJPT*, 278.
18 *MO* (8 June 1881), quoted in *LJPT*, 278.
19 Lists of functionaries and committee members are given in *JVŠ*, 137–8.
20 *Dalibor*, v (1883), 298.
21 Chmelíček to LJ, 5 July 1885 (BmJA, B 772).
22 *JVŠ*, 27.
23 *JVŠ*, 18.
24 *JVŠ*, 106.
25 *JVŠ*, 109.
26 *JVŠ*, 24.
27 *JVŠ*, 108.
28 *JVŠ*, 108–9.
29 *JVŠ*, 26.
30 *JVŠ*, 15.
31 *LJPT*, 278.
32 *JVŠ*, 29.
33 *JVŠ*, 30.
34 *JVŠ*, 30.
35 *JVŠ*, 20.
36 *Dalibor*, v (1883), 298. Helfert corrects Žalud's date on *LJPT*, 281, from 18 to 19 July.
37 See *JVŠ*, appendix e, 141, with chart of student numbers.
38 *JVŠ*, 32.
39 See the list of teachers in *JVŠ*, appendix e, 139.
40 *JVŠ*, 39.
41 *JVŠ*, 40.

42 *JVŠ*, 41.
43 *JVŠ*, 48.
44 *JVŠ*, 48ff.
45 *JVŠ*, 43.
46 *JVŠ*, 42.
47 *JVŠ*, 139–40.
48 *JVŠ*, 125–6 provides a full list of choral performances.
49 *JVŠ*, 125, 127–32 provides a full list of chamber and symphonic concerts organized by the Organ School, together with Janáček's introductions for the 1909–10 series, pp. 133–6.
50 *LJPT*, 280–1.
51 *JVŠ*, 55.
52 *JVŠ*, 53.
53 *JVŠ*, 56.
54 *JVŠ*, 56–7.
55 *LJPT*, 280.
56 Kunc 1911, 187.
57 Kunc 1911, 186.
58 Kvasnica 1974, 172–4.
59 Chlubna 1955, 57.

22: Antonín Dvořák

1 Burghauser 1991, 86.
2 Veselý 1924, 38–9; italics as in the original.
3 *LJPT*, 237.
4 LJ to ZS, 6 Nov 1879 (*IB*, 78–9).
5 LJ to ZS, 18 Feb 1880 (*IB*, 185–6).
6 LJ to ZS, 28 May 1880 (*IB*, 236).
7 Květ 1946, 49.
8 Inferred from the comment 'Dvořák, Prague' jotted down on p. 476 of LJ's copy of Helmholtz's *Die Lehre von den Tonempfindungen*.
9 LJ to ZS, 20–1 Feb 1880, 21–2 Feb and 22–3 Feb (*IB*, 187–95).
10 Dvořák to LJ, 31 March 1882 (*ADKD*, i, 297).
11 LJ to Šubert, ?3 Oct 1889 (Prague, Státní ústřední archiv v Praze, fond Reg. Národního divadla v Praze, D–148, i, 228).
12 Štědroň 1958, 107; unverified.

23: Autumn 1884–Summer 1888

1 Amalie Janáčková to LJ, undated, April 1883 (*ŽJJ*, 93).
2 Amalie Janáčková to LJ, undated, after 10 July 1883 (*ŽJJ*, 93).
3 Amalie Janáčková to LJ, undated, winter 1883–4 (*ŽJJ*, 93).
4 Amalie Janáčková to LJ, undated, about 11 April 1884, and 21 April 1884 (*ŽJJ*, 95).
5 František Janáček to LJ, 6 May 1884 (BmJA, A 5102).
6 Bedřich Janáček to LJ, 5 May 1884 (BmJA, B 1800).
7 Bedřich Janáček to LJ, 29 May 1884 (BmJA, A 3675).
8 *ŽJJ*, 86.
9 Amalie Janáčková to LJ, undated, beginning? of Oct 1884 (*ŽJJ*, 95).
10 Josefa Janáčková to LJ, 25 Oct 1884 (BmJA, B 1245).
11 *MLWJ*, 46.
12 *LJPT*, 245.

13 Josefa Janáčková to LJ, 23 Nov 1884 (BmJA, A 4654).
14 *MLWJ*, 46.
15 *MLWJ*, 46.
16 *MLWJ*, 46.
17 *MLWJ*, 31.
18 LJ to ZS, 15–16 Oct 1879 (*IB*, 46–7).
19 *MLWJ*, 31.
20 *LJPT*, 244.
21 LJ to ZS, 28–9 Nov 1879 (*IB*, 107).
22 *LJPT*, 233.
23 *Dalibor*, vii (1885), 103.
24 ský [Karel Sázavský?]: 'Dopisy z Brno II' [Letters from Brno II], *Dalibor*, vii (1885), 103.
25 LJ to F.A. Urbánek, 20 June 1885 (*LJPT*, 351, fn. 2).
26 F.A. Urbánek to LJ, 24 Aug 1885 (BmJA, B 11). db13324.
27 Josefa Janáčková to LJ, 15 June 1885 (BmJA, A 4655).
28 *LJPT*, 281, fn. 3.
29 BmJA, JP 35.
30 Josefa Janáčková to LJ, 15 June 1885 (BmJA, A 4655).
31 Janáček's notes of the meeting and report to the Brno Beseda, quoted in *LJPT*, 296, fn. 2.
32 *LJPT*, 236.
33 Herben to LJ, 2 Dec 1885 (BmJA, A 13).
34 Kosmák to LJ, 22 Oct 1885 (BmJA, A 4843) and 18 Nov 1885 (BmJA, A 4844).
35 Dvořák to LJ, 4 Jan 1886 (*ADKD*, ii, 120).
36 Brno Beseda minutes, summarized in *LJPT*, 238; fn. 1.
37 Brno Beseda minutes, summarized in *LJPT*, 246.
38 BmJA, A 42822.
39 BmJA, uncatalogued.
40 *MLWJ*, 47–8.
41 Knittl to LJ, 6 Sept 1886 (BmJA, A 3385), thanks Janáček for sending a copy.
42 Pivoda to LJ, 5 Oct 1886 (BmJA, B 1149).
43 Dvořák to LJ, 13 Sept 1886 (*ADKD*, ii, 177–8).
44 *LJPT*, 271, fn. 1.
45 Brno Beseda minutes (6 Oct 1886), summarized in *LJPT*, 245.
46 Casimir Hofmann to LJ, 17 Dec 1886 (BmJA, A 14).
47 Gregor Benko: 'Hofmann, Josef (Casimir)', *NG2*.
48 Brno Beseda minutes, summarized in *LJPT*, 229.
49 LJ to Hostinský, ?25 Feb 1886 (Mišurec 2002, 10); Hostinský to LJ, 26 Feb 1886 (Mišurec 2002, 84); LJ to Hostinský, ?28 Feb 1886 (Mišurec 2002, 11).
50 LJ to Hostinský, Sept 1886 (Mišurec 2002, 12).
51 Veselý 1924, 69.
52 Dvořák to LJ, 3 Oct 1887 (*ADKD*, ii, 264).
53 Dvořák to LJ, 25 Oct 1887 (*ADKD*, ii, 269).
54 *LJPT*, 243.
55 *JODA*, SR10.
56 *LJPT*, 246.
57 *LJPT*, 246–7 (especially 247, fn. 1 quoting minutes); *LJPT*, 312, fn. 3.
58 LJ to Váňa, 1 June 1888 (*LJPT*, 247, fn. 2).
59 Brno Beseda to LJ, 8 June 1888 (BmJA, D 10).
60 *LJPT*, 281, fn. 2.

24: *Hudební listy*

1 *LJPT*, 232, 268, 295.
2 Brno Beseda minutes, quoted in *LJPT*, 295.
3 *LJPT*, 296–7, identifies these writers from the symbols used.
4 *LJPT*, 296, fn. 2, 297.
5 *LJPT*, 297, identifies the symbol used by Žalud.
6 *LJPT*, 297.
7 Pivoda to LJ, 2 Feb 1885 (BmJA, B 1143).
8 *LJPT*, 312, fn. 2.

25: Janáček's knowledge of opera I: up to *Šárka*

1 Many of his comments are reproduced in Racek 1936, 10–12.
2 *CO*, 57.
3 *LJTP*, 263.
4 *LJPT*, 267.
5 *CO*, 264–6.
6 Racek 1936.

26: Janáček's first opera: *Šárka* in 1887–8

1 Respectively Storch, Prague, 1884, and Storch, Prague, 1885; Straková 1955a, 418.
2 'Abenderragové', *OSN*, i (1888).
3 BmJA, Z 6, quoted in Straková 1955a, 418–19.
4 *JODA*, 1–3.
5 *CO*, 104–11.
6 Štědroň 1986.
7 *JODA*, SR8.
8 *JODA*, SR10.
9 *LJPT*, 366ff.
10 *JODA*, SR27.
11 Zeyer to LJ, 10 Nov 1887 (*JODA*, SR9).
12 Zeyer to LJ, 17 Nov 1887 (*JODA*, SR11).

27: Summer 1888–1890

1 *MLWJ*, 49.
2 *MLWJ*, 48–50.
3 *MLWJ*, 55.
4 LJ's personal files in Archiv Zemského národního výboru, S–3, quoted in Štědroň 1947a, 144–5.
5 *Moravské noviny* (17 Jan 1889), quoted in Procházková 1992, 313.
6 *Moravské noviny* (21 Jan 1889), quoted in Procházková 1992, 314.
7 *Moravské noviny* (16 Feb 1889), quoted in Procházková 1992, 314.
8 *Moravské noviny* (20 Feb 1889), quoted in Procházková 1992, 314.
9 LJ to Šubert, 21 Feb 1889 (Pala 1955, 73–4).
10 LJ to unknown woman [? Marie Pospíšilová], undated, ?December 1889 (Ambros 1929, 24–6).
11 Šubert to LJ, 28 Feb 1889 (Pala 1955, 74).
12 Šubert to LJ, 5 March 1889 (Pala 1955, 74–5).
13 LJ to Šubert, ?7 March 1889 (Pala 1955, 75).
14 LJ to Šubert, undated, after 10 March 1889 (Pala 1955, 75).

15 National Theatre to LJ, 11 March 1889 (Pala 1955, 75).
16 Kosmák to LJ, undated, ?after 14 March 1889 (Straková 1955a, 422).
17 Kosmák to LJ, undated, ? early April 1889 (Straková 1955a, 422).
18 LJ to Šubert, undated, about 1 April 1889 (Pala 1955, 76–9).
19 LJ to Šubert, undated, about 1 April 1889 (Pala 1955, 76–9).
20 Berger to LJ, 10 April 1889 (BmJA, A 3391).
21 Šubert to LJ, 13 May 1889 (Pala 1955, 79).
22 *Dalibor*, xi (1889), 235.
23 *Hlas* quoted in *Dalibor*, xi (1889), 235.
24 LJ to Šubert, undated, about 1 June 1889 (Pala 1955, 80).
25 *LJPT*, 282.
26 *MLWJ*, 50–1.
27 OJ to ZJ, undated, ?28 July 1889 (BmJA, A 5455).
28 *MLWJ*, 51.
29 LJ to Šubert, undated, summer 1889 (Prague, Státní ústřední archiv v Praze, fond Reg. Národního divadla v Praze, D–148, i, 226).
30 Šubert to LJ, 26 Sept 1889 (Pala 1955, 80).
31 LJ to Šubert, undated, ?Dec 1889 (Prague, Státní ústřední archiv v Praze, fond Reg. Národního divadla v Praze, D–148, i, 228).
32 LJ to Urbánek, 5 Dec 1889 (BmJA, D 1547).
33 Urbánek to LJ, 7 Dec 1889 (BmJA, B 15).
34 Bursík & Kohout to LJ, 7 Dec 1889 (BmJA, B 101).
35 LJ to Šubert, 14 Dec 1889 (Prague, Státní ústřední archiv v Praze, fond Reg. Národního divadla v Praze, D–148, i, 229).
36 M. Horský: review in *Moravské listy* (29 Dec 1889), reprinted in Procházková 1992, 316.
37 *MO* (5 Jan 1890), reprinted in Procházková 1992, 317.
38 Wurm to LJ, 9 Jan 1890 (BmJA, B 760).
39 Wurm to LJ, 13 Jan 1890 (BmJA, A 3373).
40 Bártová 1998, 132.
41 *MLWJ*, 51.
42 Bursík & Kohout to LJ, 3 March 1890 (BmJA, B 17).
43 Bursík & Kohout to LJ, 10 March 1890 (BmJA, B 18).
44 LJ to Bakešová, undated, after 10 March 1890 (Sedláčková 2001, no. 4).
45 Bursík & Kohout to LJ, 18 April 1890 (BmJA, B 20).
46 *BH*, 40.
47 *BH*, 40.
48 Bursík & Kohout to LJ, 3 April 1890 (BmJA, B 19).
49 *MLWJ*, 51–2.
50 *MLWJ*, 52–3.
51 Beseda minutes, quoted in *LJPT*, 248.
52 Beseda minutes, quoted in *LJPT*, 248.
53 *MLWJ*, 55–6.
54 Listed in Sázavský 1900, 148–9.
55 *MLWJ*, 56.
56 *MLWJ*, 56.
57 LJ to KS, 21 May 1927 (*HŽ*, no. 446).
58 BmJA, Z6, 79.
59 Vogel 1981, 93.

28: Janáček as musical ethnographer

1 LJ to ZS, 11–12 Jan 1880 (*IB*, 131).
2 Straková 1957, 3–4.
3 A reminiscence of Bartoš's pupil Jan Zachoval, quoted in Straková 1957, 3.
4 Vychodil to LJ, 1 Sept 1886 (BmJA, B 13).
5 Brno, Ústav pro etnografii a folkloristiku Akademie věd České republiky, A 1397.
6 Vysloužil in preface to *LJOLP*, 38, fn. 7; Procházková 1998d, 125.
7 *LJOLP*, 104.
8 *LJOLP*, 48.
9 *LJOLP*, 38.
10 LJ to Zeman, undated, Oct 1892 (Uhlíková 1994, 83).
11 For an example, see *LJOLP*, 38.
12 Plocek 1998.
13 Smetana 1948, 18.
14 Procházková 2004.
15 *LJOLP*, 37.
16 LJ to Bím, 3 June 1894 (Toncrová 1999, no.1).
17 *Moravská revue*, ed. Jaroslav Tůma (1899), 62ff, reprinted in *JLOLP*, 593–5.
18 See Vysloužil's description in *JLOLP*, 75.
19 *LJOLP*, 31, fn. 5.
20 Hrabalová 1988; Procházková 1998c, 113.
21 *LJOLP*, p. 35, fn. 5; Vysloužil 2004.
22 *LJOLP*, 33, fn. 4.
23 *LJOLP*, 33.
24 I. Pratsch and N.A. L´vov: *Sobraniye narodnïkh russkikh pesen s ikh golosami* [Collection of Russian folksongs with vocal parts] (Schnoor, St Petersburg 1790, enlarged 2/1806).
25 *LJOLP*, 73, fn. 4 provides a list of Russian collections in Janáček's library.
26 Procházková 1998c, 114–15.

29: 1891–3

1 LJ to Bakešová, undated, before 7 Jan 1891 (Sedláčková 2001, no.7).
2 *Moravské listy* (8 Jan 1891), quoted in Procházková 1992, 104.
3 *MO* (9 Jan 1891), quoted in Procházková 1992, 104.
4 LJ to Šubert, undated, after 7 Jan 1891 (Pala 1955, 74).
5 'Vesna' chronicle, quoted in *LJOLP*, 52, fn. 1.
6 Procházková 1992, 104–5.
7 Kodl 1929, 90.
8 *MO* (13, 15 and 17 Jan 1891), quoted in Procházková 1992, 105.
9 LJ to Bakešová, undated, about 20 March 1891 (Sedláčková 2001, no.8).
10 *CO*, 50.
11 Šubert to LJ, 27 March 1891 (Pala 1955, 82).
12 Krásnohorská to Preissová, undated, before 1 April 1891 (*JODA*, PR3).
13 Preissová to LJ, 2 April 1891 (*JODA*, PR4).
14 Preissová to LJ, 5 April 1891 (*JODA*, PR5).
15 Preissová to Šťastný, 13 May 1891 (*JODA*, PR6).
16 *JODA*, 22–3.
17 Preissová to Šťastný, 13 May 1891 (*JODA*, PR6).
18 Preissová to LJ, 4 June 1891 (*JODA*, PR7).
19 LJ to Berger, undated, about 26 May 1891 (Procházková 1992, 106).
20 LJ to Bakešová, undated, May 1891 (Sedláčková 2001, no. 10).

21 Tyrrell 1967, 264–5.
22 Preissová to LJ, 7 July 1891 (*JODA*, PR10).
23 Preissová to Kusá, undated, after 24 July 1891 (*JODA*, PR11).
24 *MO* (2 June 1891), quoted in Straková 1955a, 425.
25 *MO* (3 June 1891), quoted in Straková 1955a, 425.
26 Berger to LJ, 5 June 1891 (Procházková 1992, 106).
27 Indications on the title page of the libretto with its original title *Pán na Nových Zámcích*, quoted in Procházková 1992, 106.
28 M. Malura: *Lašské tance Leoše Janáčka* [Janáček's Lachian Dances] (diploma dissertation, Brno 1960), quoted in Procházková 1992, 106.
29 Prague, Státní ústřední archiv v Praze, fond Reg. Národního divadla v Praze, D–148, i, 245.
30 Bakešová to LJ, 19 June 1891, with postscript 24 June (Sedláčková 2001, no. 11).
31 LJ to Bakešová, undated, 12 July 1891 (Sedláčková 2001, no. 12).
32 *Moravské listy* (29 July 1891), quoted in *JVD*, 124–5.
33 Vrchlický's review, *Hlas* (after 24 July 1891), quoted in Procházková 1992, 108.
34 For example in the German newspaper *Politik*, quoted in Procházková 1992, 108.
35 Zeman to Bartoš, 11 June 1891 (BmJA, B 23).
36 LJ to Zeman, 24 June 1891 (Uhlíková 1994, 82).
37 LJ to Zeman, 6 Sept 1891 (Uhlíková 1994, 82).
38 Dvořák to LJ, 11 Nov 1891 (*ADKD*, iii, 101).
39 Dvořák to LJ, 27 Nov 1891 (*ADKD*, iii, 105).
40 LJ to Czech Academy of Sciences and Arts, 17 Nov 1891 (*LJOLP*, 515–16).
41 *ADKD*, x, 101.
42 Czech Academy of Sciences and Arts to LJ, 5 Dec 1891 (BmJA, C 4).
43 LJ to Šubert, undated, after 17 Dec 1891 (*JODA*, PR13).
44 Preissová to LJ, 16 Dec 1891 (*JODA*, PR12).
45 LJ to Šubert, undated, early Feb 1892 (*JODA*, PR19).
46 Čech to Šubert, undated, before 2 May 1892 (*JODA*, PR25).
47 LJ to Šubert, undated, after 15 March 1892 (*JODA*, PR20).
48 Wollnerová to LJ, 13 March 1892 (*JODA*, PR17).
49 LJ to Šubert, undated, about 28 March 1892 (*JODA*, PR21).
50 See *JODA*, PR22–4.
51 Šubert to LJ, 2 May 1892 (*JODA*, PR27).
52 Anger to Šubert, undated, late April 1892 (*JODA*, PR26).
53 Preissová to LJ, 25 March 1892 (*JODA*, PR18).
54 Berger to LJ, 5 May 1892 (BmJA, A 38).
55 Urbánek to LJ, 11 July 1892 (BmJA, B 26).
56 LJ to Bakešová, 8 June 1892 (BmJA, A 6574).
57 *LJOLP*, 98, 105, 114; Procházková 1998d, 126.
58 LJ to Zeman, undated (Uhlíková 1994, 82).
59 LJ to Zeman, 20 Sept 1892 (Uhlíková 1994, 83).
60 Hübner to LJ, 5 Sept 1892 (*JODA*, PR28).
61 See his letters to Zeman of ?Oct, 1, 4 and 8 Nov 1892 (Uhlíková 1994, 83–4).
62 LJ to Zeman, 20 Sept 1892 (Uhlíková 1994, 83).
63 *Český lid* (1892–3), 431–3, reprinted in *LJOLP*, 517–19.
64 Novák 1946, 92.
65 *Český lid*, ii (1892–3), 433, reprinted in *LJOLP*, 519.
66 LJ to Zeman, undated, Oct 1892 (Uhlíková 1994, 83).
67 LJ to Bakešová, undated, Feb or March 1893 (Sedláčková 2001, no. 18).

68 LJ to Czech Academy of Sciences, 22 March 1893 (Procházková 1992, 110); two sentences not in Procházková taken from *JVD*, 73–4.

69 Quoted by Štědroň in the introduction to his Hudební matice edition of viii/13 (1950).

70 Štědroň in introduction to Hudební matice edition of viii/13 (1950).

71 Czech Academy of Sciences to LJ, 2 July 1893 (Procházková 1992, 111).

72 *LJOLP*, 100.

73 *LJOLP*, 100–1.

74 LJ to Zeman, 23 Aug 1893 (Uhlíková 1994, 85).

75 *LJOLP*, 111, fn. 3.

76 Preissová to LJ, 1 Nov 1893 (*JODA*, JP4).

77 Preissová to LJ, 6 Nov 1893 (*JODA*, JP5).

78 *JODA*, JP3.

79 Preissová to LJ, 13 Nov 1893 (Straková 1958, 159).

80 Inferred from Preissová's letter to LJ, 11 Dec 1893 (Straková 1958, 159–60).

81 Preissová to LJ, 11 Dec 1893 (Straková 1958, 159–60).

82 LJ to ZJ and OJ, undated, 30? Dec 1893 (BmJA, A 4899).

83 LJ to ZJ and OJ, undated, 31? Dec 1893 (BmJA, A 4900).

30: Folk dances in the orchestra and on stage

1 Vogel 1981, 107.

2 Tyrrell 1967, 252–6.

3 LJ to Bakešová, undated, after 10 Feb 1892 (Sedláčková 2001, no.18).

4 LJ to Czech Academy of Sciences, 22 March 1893 (Procházková 1992), 110.

31: Folksong accompaniments as Janáček's workshop

1 *Dalibor*, xxi (1898–9), 44.

32: 1894–5

1 Ondřej Červenka to LJ, 18 February 1894 (BmJA, A 4846).

2 See Přibáňová 1984, 133.

3 *MLWJ*, 57.

4 Wollnerová to LJ, undated, Nov 1893 (*JODA*, PR29).

5 Preissová to LJ, 4 Feb 1894 (*JODA*, PR30).

6 LJ to Bakešová, undated, Feb 1894 (BmJA, A 5497).

7 LJ to Šubert, undated 5? Feb 1894 (*JODA*, PR31).

8 Šubert to LJ, 6 Feb 1894 (*JODA*, PR32).

9 LJ to Šubert, undated, 25? Feb 1894 (*JODA*, PR34).

10 Šubert to LJ, 26 Feb 1894 (*JODA*, PR35).

11 Quoted in Straková 1958, 161.

12 Nováková 1956, 69.

13 Karel Sázavský in *MO*, 13 Feb 1894 (*JODA*, PR33).

14 Straková 1958, 162.

15 Wurm to LJ, 9 March 1894 (Straková 1958, 162–3).

16 *JODA*, 39–40.

17 *JODA*, PR42.

18 Zíbrt 1892.

19 *LJOLP*, 55.

20 LJ to Zeman, 9 March 1894 (Uhlíková 1994, 85).

21 LJ to Bakešová, undated, 20? March 1894 (Sedláčková 2001, no. 21).

22 LJ to Hrazdira, 23 March 1894 (BmJA, A 54).
23 Bartoš to LJ, 10 April 1894 (Straková 1957, 7).
24 Spolek ústředních českých učitelů, leaflet, 7 March 1894 (BmJA, B 1163).
25 Kapras to LJ, 28 Feb 1894 (BmJA, D 13).
26 K. ze Slavkovských to LJ, 7 March 1894 (BmJA, A 50); LJ to ze Slavkovských, undated, 15? March 1894 (BmJA, A 6255).
27 K. ze Slavkovských to LJ, 16 March 1894 (BmJA, A 55).
28 *LJOLP*, 115–16.
29 Vašátko to LJ, undated, May 1894 (BmJA, A 56).
30 Válek to LJ, 26 May 1894 (BmJA, A 57).
31 Pernický to LJ, undated, June 1894 (*LJOLP*, 101).
32 *LJOLP*, 524, fn. 3.
33 *LJOLP*, 524, fn. 2.
34 LJ to Bím, 3 June 1894 (Toncrová 1999, no. 1).
35 ZJ and OJ to LJ, 19 June 1894 (BmJA, A 3662).
36 Janáček's personal files in Archiv Zemského národního výboru, S–3 (Štědroň 1947a, 145).
37 *BH*, 37.
38 *MLWJ*, 58.
39 OJ to LJ, 19 June 1894 (BmJA, A 3662).
40 OJ to LJ, 22 June 1894 (BmJA, A 3665).
41 OJ and ZJ to LJ, 24 June 1891 (BmJA, A 3648).
42 OJ and ZJ to LJ, 1 July 1894 (BmJA, A 3647).
43 OJ to LJ, 7 July 1894 (BmJA, A 3664).
44 OJ to LJ, 10 July 1894 (BmJA, A 3660).
45 ZJ and OJ to LJ, 18 July 1894 (BmJA, A 3661).
46 LJ to Zeman, 5 Aug 1894 (Uhlíková 1994, 86).
47 LJ to Zeman, undated, Oct? 1894 (Uhlíková 1994, 87–8).
48 LJ to Zeman, 5 Aug 1894 (Uhlíková 1994, 86).
49 *MLWJ*, 58–9.
50 Trkanová 1964, 21.
51 LJ to Urbánek, undated, before 6 Nov 1894 (BmJA, A 6833).
52 Urbánek to LJ, 6 Nov 1894 (BmJA, A 71).
53 LJ to Urbánek, 7 Nov 1894 (BmJA, A 6834).
54 Urbánek to LJ, 26 Nov 1894 (BmJA, A 68).
55 LJ to Hostinský, 22 Nov 1894 (Mišurec 2002, 13).
56 LJ to Hostinský, two letters, undated, Dec 1894 (Mišurec 2002, 14–15).
57 Hostinský to LJ, 27 Dec 1894 (Mišurec 2002, 84–5).
58 Zeman to LJ, 27 Sept 1894 and 11 Dec 1894 (Uhlíková 1994, 86–7, 88)
59 Válek to LJ, 12 Oct 1894 (BmJA, A 62).
60 Válek to LJ, 3 Nov 1894 (BmJA, A 66).
61 Lužný to LJ, 12 Dec 1894 (BmJA, A 72).
62 Večeř to LJ, 30 June 1894 (BmJA, A 59)
63 LJ to Bakešová, undated, Nov? 1894 (BmJA, A 5501).
64 LJ to Bakešová, undated, 1? Dec 1894 (Sedláčková 2001, no. 24).
65 Bakešová to LJ, 20 Dec 1894 (Sedláčková 2001, no. 25).
66 *ZGJ*, 60–1.
67 BmJA, A 30.380.
68 LJ to Nebuška, 22 Feb 1917 (*JODA*, JP9).
69 LJ to Nebuška, 22 Feb 1917 (*JODA*, JP9).

70 *JODA*, JP6.

71 Hrazdira to LJ, 8 March 1894 (BmJA, B 29).

72 Hrazdira to LJ, 9 Jan 1895 (BmJA, A 77).

73 Konrád to LJ, 5 April 1894 (BmJA, B 36).

74 *LJOLP*, 56 provides a fuller description.

75 LJ to Hostinský, 30 Jan 1895 (Mišurec 2002, 15).

76 LJ to Hostinský, 8 Feb 1895 (Mišurec 2002, 18).

77 LJ to Urbánek, undated, before 19 Feb 1895 (BmJA, A 6755).

78 Urbánek to LJ, 20 Feb 1895 (BmJA, A 82).

79 LJ to Urbánek, undated, before 27 April 1895 (BmJA, A 6835).

80 Hostinský to LJ, 12 May 1895 (Mišurec 2002, 86–7).

81 Urbánek to LJ, 13 May 1895 (BmJA, B 41).

82 Bakešová to LJ, undated, May? 1895 (Sedláčková 2001, no. 32).

83 Bakešová to LJ, 22 July 1895 (Sedláčková 2001, no. 45).

84 LJ to Bakešová, undated, May? 1895 (Sedláčková 2001, no. 33).

85 Sojka to LJ, 3 March 1895 (Sedláčková 2001, fn. 92).

86 Bakešová to LJ, undated, about 28 Feb 1895 (Sedláčková 2001, no. 27).

87 LJ to Zeman, 10 April 1895 (Uhlíková 1994, 90–1).

88 Bártová 1998, 133.

89 LJ to Bakeš, undated, March? 1895 (BmJA, A 5478).

90 *LJOLP*, 104.

91 LJ to Zeman, 20 April 1895 (Uhlíková 1994, 92–3).

92 Bakešová to LJ, undated, June 1895 (Sedláčková 2001, no. 38).

93 Bakešová to LJ, 1 July 1895 (Sedláčková 2001, no. 43).

94 OJ to LJ, 7 July 1895 (BmJA, A 3646).

95 OJ to LJ, 11 July 1895 (BmJA, A 3659).

96 LJ to Bakešová, 24 July 1895 (Sedláčková 2001, no. 46).

97 LJ to Zeman, undated, 31? July 1895 (Uhlíková 1994, 95–6).

98 e.g. Bakešová to LJ, 4, 5, 11, 12? (2 letters) August (Sedláčková 2001, nos. 47–51)

99 Horák 1933, 412–14.

100 Efmertová 1995, 393–6.

101 *MLWJ*, 60–1.

102 Daily programmes are given in xv/148.

103 'Kovařovic, Karel', *ČSHS*.

104 LJ to Bakešová, undated, June? 1895 (Sedláčková 2001, no. 39).

105 LJ to Šubert, 30 Aug 1895 (*LJOLP*, 54).

106 Exhibition committee to LJ, 7 Sept 1895 (BmJA, B 43).

107 LJ to Zeman, 11 Dec 1895 (Uhlíková 1994, 100).

108 LJ to Bakešová, undated, Sept? 1895 (Sedláčková 2001, no. 55).

109 Bakešová to LJ, 23 Sept 1895 (Sedláčková 2001, no. 56).

110 ZJ and OJ to LJ, 7 Sept 1895 (BmJA, A 5440).

111 BmJA, Z17, 74–5.

112 LJ's personal files in Archiv Zemského národního výboru, S–3, quoted in Štědroň 1947a, 145.

113 *MLWJ*, 61.

33: 1896

1 'S.', *Moravské noviny* (4 Feb 1911).

2 LJ to Nebuška, 22 Feb 1917 (*JODA*, JP9).

3 LJ to Urbánek, undated, by 21 March 1896 (BmJA, A 6836).

4 LJ to Urbánek, undated, before 17 April 1896 (BmJA, A 6837).

5 *JODA*, JP6.

6 František Janáček to LJ, 10 Jan 1896 (BmJA, A 5108).

7 František Janáček to LJ, 24 Jan 1896 (BmJA, D 1227).

8 OJ and ZJ to LJ, 17 June 1896 (BmJA, A 3653).

9 *MLWJ*, 61.

10 F. Vymazal: *Rusky v desíti úlohách* [Russian in ten exercises] (Telč, 1896) [BmJA, JA-III-55], transcribed in Racek 1936, 22–5. Vrba 1959 reproduces much of this material together with material from the feuilletons.

11 František Janáček to LJ, 10 Jan 1896 (BmJA, A 5108).

12 LJ to ZJ, 21 July 1896 (BmJA, A 4902).

13 Veselý 1924, 44–5.

14 LJ to ZJ and OJ, 24 July 1896 (BmJA, A 4903).

15 LJ to ZJ and OJ, 24 July 1896 (BmJA, A 4903).

16 Vrba 1959, 471, fn. 69.

17 Veselý 1924, 43–4.

18 LJ's 'diary', quoted in Racek 1936, 24.

19 LJ's 'diary', quoted in Racek 1936, 25.

20 *MLWJ*, 61–2.

21 OJ to Stejskalová, 29 Aug 1896 (BmJA, A 5729).

22 *MLWJ*, 62.

23 OJ to Josefa Jungová, 4 Oct 1896 (BmJA, A 6190).

24 Karel Dostál-Lutinov to LJ, 12 Feb 1897 (BmJA, A 122).

25 Brod 1924, 38; cf. similar letter to Linda (1924), quoted in Vogel 1981, 125.

34: What Janáček learnt from *The Queen of Spades*

1 See *CO*, 283–6 for an analysis.

2 *CO*, 283, 285–6.

3 Tyrrell 1987.

35: Pan-Slavism II

1 Urbánek to LJ, 30 Oct 1896 (BmJA, A 105).

2 LJ to AR, 11 Dec 1910 (JA iv, 145).

3 *JKPU*, 128.

4 František Janáček to LJ, 24 Jan 1896 (BmJA, D 1227).

5 I. Pratsch and N.A. L'vov: *Sobraniye narodnïkh russkikh pesen s ikh golosami* [Collection of Russian folksongs with vocal parts] (Schnoor, St Petersburg 1790, enlarged 2/1806).

6 Brno National Theatre to the music critic of *Čas*, 18 Jan 1904 (*JODA*, JP25).

7 *Hlas* (24 Jan 1894), quoted in Němcová 1974, 142.

36: 1897–9

1 Vávra to LJ, 19 Jan 1897 (BmJA, A 166).

2 Ambros to LJ, 2 Feb 1897 (BmJA, A 121).

3 F.A. Urbánek to LJ, 24 Feb 1897 (BmJA, B 51).

4 Novák 1946, 90–1.

5 *Dalibor*, xix (1896–7), 222–3.

6 Reproduced in Kyas 1995, 81.

7 LJ to Dvořák, undated, 11? May 1897 (*ADKD*, viii, 60).

8 Dvořák to LJ, 21 May 1897 (*ADKD*, iv, 89–90).

9 Květ 1946, 49.
10 LJ to Bílý, 24 May 1897 (*SKV*, B/1, ix).
11 Bílý to LJ, 31 May 1897 (BmJA, A 3367).
12 Vrchlický to LJ, 8 June 1897 (*JVD*, 104–5).
13 Bílý to LJ, 10 June 1897 (BmJA, A 3368).
14 LJ to Vrchlický, 12 June 1897 (*SKV*, B/1, ix).
15 Bílý to LJ, 7 July 1897 (BmJA, A 3366).
16 F.A. Urbánek to LJ, 11 Jan 1898 (BmJA, A 132).
17 ZJ and OJ to LJ, 2 July 1897 (BmJA, A 3655).
18 Novák 1946, 91.
19 LJ to OJ, 15 Aug 1897 (BmJA, A 5568).
20 LJ to ZJ, 15 Aug 1897 (BmJA, B 981).
21 Novák 1946, 91.
22 Novák 1946, 91.
23 Novák 1946, 91.
24 All speech melodies from 1897 are printed in Štědroň 2000, some in facsimile, all in transcription.
25 Rypáček to LJ, 23 Dec 1897 (BmJA, A 4888).
26 *LN* (13 Jan 1898), quoted in Procházková 1995, 93.
27 Procházková 1995, 91–3.
28 Procházková 1995, 96, fn. 13.
29 Novák to LJ, 3 Jan 1899 (Lébl 1964, 59, fn. 9).
30 Dvořák to LJ, 3 Jan 1898 (*ADKD*, iv, 111).
31 Dvořák to LJ, 2 Feb 1898 (*ADKD*, iv, 117).
32 Dvořák to LJ, 24 Feb 1898 (*ADKD*, iv, 122).
33 Vrba 1960; subsequent information from there.
34 Novák to LJ, 19 March 1898 (BmJA, A 135); extract printed in Lébl 1964, 59, fn. 9.
35 *LN* (24 March 1898), quoted in Procházková 1995, 93.
36 Procházková 1995, 93.
37 LJ to Novák, undated, 21? March 1898 (Lébl 1964, p. 50, fn. 9).
38 Dvořák to LJ, 23 March 1898 (*ADKD*, iv, 126).
39 *Moravská revue*, ed. Jaroslav Tůma (1899), 62ff, reprinted in *LJOLP*, 593–5.
40 Bartoš to LJ, 19 Sept 1898 (Straková 1957, 7).
41 Bartoš to LJ, 3 July 1899 (Straková 1957, 9).
42 Bartoš to LJ, 27 Jan 1899 (Straková 1957, 8).
43 Bartoš to LJ, 27 Jan 1899 (Straková 1957, 8).
44 Bartoš to LJ, 18 Oct 1899 (Straková 1957, 10).
45 Bartoš to LJ, 6 Nov 1899 (Straková 1957, 11).
46 Bartoš to LJ, 23 Nov 1899 (Straková 1957, 11).
47 Bartoš to LJ, 26 Nov 1899 (Straková 1957, 11).
48 LJ to Bartoš to LJ, 30 Nov 1899 (Straková 1957, 11–12).
49 Bartoš to LJ, 10 Dec 1899 (Straková 1957, 12).
50 LJ to Bartoš, 11 Dec 1899 (Straková 1957, 12–13).
51 Bartoš to LJ, 26 Dec 1899 (Straková 1957, 13).
52 LJ to Král, 27 Sept 1898 (BmJA, A 5510).
53 Král to LJ, 30 Sept 1898 (BmJA, B 58).
54 *LJOLP*, 96–8.
55 *LJOLP*, 210, fn. 1.
56 Vrba 1960, 80.
57 *BH*, 48.

58 *MLWJ*, 67.
59 *MLWJ*, 67–8.

37: Speech melody

 1 As proposed in Beckerman 1994, 133.
 2 1879 in xv/306 (1928); 1881 in LJ to UE, 25 Nov 1925 (BUE, 72); 1888 in xv/272 (1924); 1901 in xv/209 (1916).
 3 Černohorská 1957.
 4 Janáček reported in *Neues Wiener Tagblatt* (12 Feb 1918), reprinted in *BUE*, 80.
 5 LJ to Bartoš, undated, Oct 1903 (Straková 1957, 24).
 6 Tyrrell 1995.
 7 *CO*, 296; see pp. 292–7 for specific examples.
 8 Wingfield 1992, 289.
 9 Wingfield 1992, 298.
10 Wingfield 1992, 294–5.
11 This passage on Czech views of speech melody in the 1950s and 1960s is based on Tyrrell 1973; see there for notated examples and sources of the quotations.
12 See for example Pala 1955, 144–9.
13 Štědroň 1998, 157–224; extracts in English in Štědroň 1999.
14 Christiansen 2002; Pearl 2005.
15 Tyrrell 1969.
16 Based on an interview with Janáček printed in *Moravské noviny* (4 Feb 1911).
17 LJ to Brod, 9 Jan 1927 (JA ix, 219).
18 LJ to Newmarch, 10 April 1926 (Fischmann 1986, 102–3).
19 Mašíček to LJ, 2 May 1906 (BmJA, A 290).
20 Mašíček to LJ, 24 Jan 1907 (BmJA, A 5653).

38: *On the Overgrown Path*

 1 LJ to Branberger, 7 May 1908 (BmJA, B 1433).
 2 LJ to Branberger, 23 May 1908 (BmJA, B 1435).
 3 Branberger to LJ, 3 June 1908 (BmJA, B 809).
 4 Branberger to LJ, 3 June 1908 (BmJA, B 809).
 5 LJ to Branberger, 6 June 1908 (*LD*, ii, 98–9).
 6 Kundera 1955, 314–15.
 7 *MLWJ*, 213.
 8 LJ to Branberger, 6 June 1908 (*LD*, ii, 98–9).
 9 LJ to Branberger, 6 June 1908 (*LD*, ii, 98–9).
10 LJ to Branberger, 6 June 1908 (*LD*, ii, 98–9).
11 LJ to Branberger, 6 June 1908 (*LD*, ii, 98–9).
12 LJ to Branberger, 6 June 1908 (*LD*, ii, 98–9).

39: 1900–01

 1 Zdenka Vorlová in *LN* (16 Jan 1900), partly reprinted in Procházková 1992, 165.
 2 *MLWJ*, 68.
 3 *MLWJ*, 62–3.
 4 Novák 1946, 106.
 5 *MLWJ*, 62.
 6 *MLWJ*, 65 and 68.
 7 *MLWJ*, 68–9; the following account is based on Zdenka's memoirs.

8 Vorel to unknown man, 8 Feb 1900 (BmJA, A 6295).

9 Vorel to unknown man, 22 Feb 1900 (BmJA, A 6296).

10 *MLWJ*, 70.

11 Vorel to unknown man, 26 Feb 1900 (BmJA, A 6297).

12 *MLWJ*, 70-1.

13 OJ to Stejskalová, 8 Sept 1900 (BmJA, A 5743).

14 *LJOLP*, 104-5.

15 Straková 1957, 29, fn. 49.

16 LJ to Bartoš, undated, June? 1900 (Straková 1957, 14).

17 Bartoš to LJ, 10 July 1900 (Straková 1957, 14-15).

18 Bartoš to LJ, 19 Sept 1900 (Straková 1957, 15).

19 Bartoš to LJ, 12 Dec 1900 (Straková 1957, 16).

20 Bartoš to LJ, 10 July 1900 (Straková 1957, 14-15).

21 Bartoš to LJ, 19 Sept 1900 (Straková 1957, 15).

22 Bartoš to LJ, 29 Sept 1900 (Straková 1957, 15-16).

23 Bartoš to LJ, 3 Oct 1900 (Straková 1957, 16).

24 Bartoš to LJ, 12 Dec 1900 (Straková 1957, 16).

25 LJ to Vojtěchovský, 17 July 1900 (BmJA, A 6568).

26 LJ to Vojtěchovský, 23 Sept 1900 (BmJA, A 6570).

27 Vach to LJ, undated (BmJA, A 4752).

28 Vach to LJ, 27 Feb 1900 (BmJA, A 156).

29 Vach to LJ, 4 May 1900 (BmJA, A 157).

30 Kašlík 1936, 15.

31 Veselý 1924, 46-7.

32 Bartoš to LJ, 27 March 1901 (Straková 1957, 17).

33 Bartoš to LJ, 5 June 1901 (Straková 1957, 18).

34 Bartoš to LJ, 12 Aug 1901 (Straková 1957, 19).

35 Bartoš to LJ, 10 July 1901 (Straková 1957, 18-19).

36 Bartoš to LJ, 6 Dec 1901 (Straková 1957, 20).

37 Bartoš to LJ, 11 Dec 1901 (Straková 1957, 18).

38 Veselý 1924, 38.

39 Bartoš to LJ, 5 April 1901 (Straková 1957, 17).

40 Bartoš to LJ, 20 March 1901 (Straková 1957, 16-17).

41 Bartoš to LJ, 20 March 1901 (Straková 1957, 16-17).

42 Bartoš to LJ, 10 July 1901 (Straková 1957, 18-19).

43 Bartoš to LJ, 20 March 1901 (Straková 1957, 16-17).

44 Vogel 1981, 152.

45 Bartoš to LJ, 10 July 1901 (Straková 1957, 18-19).

46 OJ and ZJ to LJ, 16 June 1901 (BmJA, A 3474).

47 OJ to LJ and ZJ, 17 June 1901 (BmJA, A 3476).

48 *BH*, 37.

49 OJ to LJ and ZJ, 17 June 1901 (BmJA, A 3476).

50 LJ to OJ, 4 July 1901 (BmJA, A 5826).

51 František Janáček and Marie Janáčková to LJ, 24 June 1901 N.S. (BmJA, A 4063).

52 František Janáček and Marie Janáčková to LJ, 14 August 1901 (BmJA, A 1604).

53 LJ and others to Olga, 2 Aug 1901 (BmJA, A 6532).

54 *MLWJ*, 72.

55 Zlámalová 1999, 34-5.

56 *MLWJ*, 71-2.

40: Music as autobiography I

1 LJ to ZS, 22–3 Nov 1879 (*IB*, 99–100).
2 *MLWJ*, 84.
3 *JODA*, JP7.
4 Or said he did, in a letter to Otakar Šourek, 3 March 1920 (*LR*, 143).

41: Janáček's finances I: to 1903

42: 1902–February 1903

1 Bartoš to LJ, 8 Feb 1902 (Straková 1957, 20).
2 LJ to Bartoš, 8 Feb 1902 (Straková 1957, 21).
3 'Vesna' committee minutes, quoted in *LJOLP*, 87.
4 Zíbrt to LJ, 10 February 1902 (BmJA, A 3392).
5 Zíbrt to LJ, 20 Feb 1902 (BmJA, A 164).
6 Zíbrt to LJ, 20 March 1902 (BmJA, A 168).
7 Bartoš to LJ, 18 Feb 1902 (Straková 1957, 21).
8 *JKPU*, 13–14.
9 *JKPU*, 22.
10 Věra Janáčková to LJ, 2 Jan 1902 (BmJA, A 3650).
11 František Janáček to LJ, 3 March 1902 N.S. (BmJA, B 1429).
12 OJ to František Janáček, 20 March 1902 (BmJA, A 5397).
13 LJ and OJ to ZJ, 22 March 1902 (BmJA, A 3807).
14 LJ and OJ to ZJ, 22 March 1902 (BmJA, A 3766).
15 LJ to ZJ, 23 March 1902 (BmJA, A 5444).
16 OJ to ZJ, 23 March 1902 (BmJA, A 3787).
17 LJ and OJ to ZJ, 23 March 1902 (BmJA, A 5435).
18 LJ and OJ to ZJ, 24 March 1902 N.S. (BmJA, A 5436).
19 LJ and OJ to ZJ, 25 March 1902 N.S. (BmJA, A 5443).
20 *MLWJ*, 72–3.
21 LJ and others to ZJ, 26 March 1902 N.S. (BmJA, A 3765).
22 LJ to ZJ, 28 March 1902 N.S. (BmJA, A 5438)
23 Zlámalová 1999, 35–6.
24 OJ to LJ, 5 April 1902 (BmJA, A 1755).
25 Zlámalová 1999, 35–6.
26 LJ to OJ, 17 April 1902 (BmJA, A 3501).
27 OJ to LJ, 20 April 1902 (BmJA, A 3500).
28 František Janáček to LJ, 30 April 1902 [receipt date of telegram] (BmJA, D 1281).
29 František Janáček to LJ, 2 May 1902 [receipt date of telegram] (BmJA, D 1280).
30 František Janáček to LJ, 4 May 1902 [receipt date of telegram] (BmJA, D 1282).
31 LJ to OJ, 5–6 May 1902 (BmJA, A 3535).
32 LJ to OJ, 8 May 1902 (BmJA, A 3457).
33 LJ to OJ, 14 May 1902 (BmJA, A 3456).
34 OJ to LJ, 15 May 1902 N.S. (BmJA, A 3506).
35 LJ to OJ, 17–18 May 1902 (BmJA, A 3455).
36 *MLWJ*, 73.
37 ZJ to LJ, 20 May 1902 (BmJA, A 2097).
38 *MLWJ*, 73.
39 LJ and ZJ to OJ, 30 May 1902 (BmJA, A 5571).
40 František Janáček to LJ, 1 June 1902 N. S. (BmJA, B 1425).
41 František Janáček to LJ, 1 June 1902 N. S. (BmJA, B 1425).

42 LJ to OJ, 4 June 1902 (BmJA, A 3564).
43 LJ to OJ and ZJ, 10 June 1902 (BmJA, A 3509).
44 Melnikova 1997, 340–2.
45 LJ to ZJ and OJ, 11 June 1902 (BmJA, A 3502).
46 Melnikova 1997, 342–51.
47 See Melnikova 1997, 342–51.
48 Melnikova 1997, 351, 352.
49 LJ to ZJ and OJ, 11–12 June 1902 (BmJA, A 3502).
50 LJ to ZJ and OJ, 'Friday', 20–1? June 1902 (BmJA, A 3757).
51 OJ to LJ, 20 June 1902 N. S. (BmJA, A 3469).
52 LJ to ZJ and OJ, 'Sunday', 22? June 1902 (BmJA, A 3470).
53 LJ to OJ, undated, postmarked 26 June 1902 (BmJA, A 3471).
54 LJ to OJ and ZJ, 'Friday', 27? June 1902 (BmJA, A 3565).
55 LJ to OJ and ZJ, 'Saturday, at night', 28? June 1902 (BmJA, A 3566).
56 LJ to OJ and ZJ, 'Sunday morning', 29? June 1902 (BmJA, A 3566).
57 LJ to OJ and ZJ, 'Wednesday afternoon', 2? July 1902 (BmJA, A 3485).
58 OJ to LJ, 1 July 1902 (BmJA, A 3503).
59 LJ to OJ and ZJ, 'Thursday evening 2/VII 1902', *recte* 3 July 1902 (BmJA, A 3492).
60 LJ to ZJ and OJ, undated, 5? July 1902 (BmJA, A 3494).
61 LJ and Stejskalová to ZJ and OJ, 'Monday', 7? July 1902 (BmJA, A 3571).
62 LJ to OJ, undated, 8? July 1902 (BmJA, A 3567).
63 LJ to ZJ and OJ, 'Wednesday–Thursday', 9–10? July 1902 (BmJA, A 3568).
64 OJ to LJ, 12 July 1902 N.S. (BmJA, A 3487).
65 LJ to ZJ and OJ, undated, 9–10? July 1902 (BmJA, A 3568).
66 *MLWJ*, 75.
67 Melniková 1997, 352.
68 *MLWJ*, 75–6.
69 OJ to František Janáček and Marie Janáčková, 30 July 1902 (BmJA, A 5395).
70 OJ to František Janáček and Marie Janáčková, 14 Aug 1902 (BmJA, A 5398).
71 LJ to ZJ, postmarked 23 Aug 1902 (BmJA, A 6637).
72 *MLWJ*, 77.
73 OJ to LJ, 15 Sept 1902 (BmJA, A 3488).
74 *MLWJ*, 77.
75 OJ to Jungová, 1 Nov 1902 (Zlámalová 1999, 37–9).
76 Vrba 1960, 81, fn. 51.
77 Vrba 1960, 81.
78 Bartoš to LJ, 29 Oct 1902 (Straková 1957, 22).
79 LJ to OJ, postmarked 27 Dec 1902 (BmJA, A 3479).
80 Joza Janáčková to LJ, 16 Feb 1903 (BmJA, A 4653).
81 *MLWJ*, 80.
82 The following account is based entirely on Zdenka's memoirs (*MLWJ*, 80–93).
83 *MLWJ*, 84.
84 *MLWJ*, 88.
85 Facsimile in Novák 1957, 142–3.
86 *MLWJ*, 88–9.
87 Facsimile in Štědroň 1966, 219 and 221; Štědroň 1972, Plate 19.
88 *MLWJ*, 89.
89 *MLWJ*, 93.
90 *MLWJ*, 93.
91 Veselý 1924, 94.

43: What Olga died of

1 In *MLWJ*; the page references that follow are to this source.

44: 1903 (March–December)

1 For instance in LJ to Josefa Jungová, undated (BmJA, A 6239).
2 LJ to Karel Janáček and Anna Janáčková, undated (BmJA, A 5430).
3 LJ to Sládek, 7 March 1903 (*JVD*, 149).
4 *MLWJ*, 95.
5 *MLWJ*, 94.
6 *MLWJ*, 95.
7 Mazálek 1914, 1000.
8 *MLWJ*, 96.
9 *CO*, 44–5.
10 *MLWJ*, 96.
11 LJ to Kovařovic, 27 April 1903 (*JODA*, JP14).
12 Schmoranz to LJ, 28 April 1903 (JA vii, 16).
13 Schmoranz to LJ, 28 April 1903 (*JODA*, JP15).
14 *MLWJ*, 96.
15 Racek 1955, 21.
16 LJ to Bakešová, 5 May 1903 (Sedláčková 2001, no. 66); LJ to Zeman, 5 May 1903 (Uhlíková 1994, 101).
17 Klvaňa to LJ, 7 May 1903 (BmJA, A 169); Kretz to LJ, 7 May 1903 (BmJA, A 169).
18 LJ to ZJ, 28 May 1903 (BmJA, A 3757).
19 *MLWJ*, 97.
20 Veselý 1924, 96.
21 Straková 1955a, 426–7.
22 Merhaut to LJ, 4 June 1903 (BmJA, B 768–9).
23 LJ to ZJ, undated, 17? July 1903? (BmJA, A 3868).
24 LJ to ZJ, undated, postmarked 31? July 1903 (BmJA, A 3851).
25 *MLWJ*, 97.
26 LJ to ZJ, 19 Aug 1903 (BmJA, A 6638).
27 LJ to ZJ, 19 Aug 1903 (BmJA, A 6638).
28 *MLWJ*, 97–8.
29 Veselý 1924, 94–5.
30 Štědroň 1959, 160.
31 LJ to Urválková, 25 Aug 1903 (Štědroň 1959, 160).
32 LJ to Urválková, 6 Sept 1903 (Štědroň 1959, 164).
33 LJ to Urválková, 6 Sept 1903 (Štědroň 1959, 164).
34 LJ to Urválková, 9 Sept 1903 (Štědroň 1959, 164).
35 LJ to Urválková, undated, 9? Sept 1903 (BmJA, no shelfmark assigned).
36 LJ to Urválková, 12 Sept 1903 (Štědroň 1959, 165).
37 Urválková to LJ, 2 Oct 1903 (BmJA, E 1134).
38 LJ to Urválková, undated, 16? Sept 1903 (BmJA, no shelfmark assigned).
39 LJ to Urválková, 20 Sept 1903 (BmJA, no shelfmark assigned).
40 LJ to Urválková, 25 Sept (one card), 28 Sept (three cards) 1903 (BmJA, A 6154–7)
41 LJ to Urválková, 3 Oct 1903 (Štědroň 1959, 165–6).
42 Racek 1955, 21.
43 LJ to Urválková, 9 Oct 1903 (Štědroň 1959, 167–8).
44 Racek 1955, 21.
45 LJ to Urválková, 28 Sept 1903 (Štědroň 1959, 165).

46 Doubravský to LJ, 8 Oct 1903 (*JODA*, JP19).
47 LJ to Urválková, 9 Oct 1903 (Štědroň 1959, 167–8; extracts in *JODA*, JP20 and OS6).
48 LJ to Bartoš, undated, 24? Oct 1903 (Straková 1957, 24).
49 LJ to Urválková, 9 Oct 1903 (*JODA*, OS6).
50 LJ to Urválková, 9 Oct 1903 (Štědroň 1959, 167–8).
51 *MLWJ*, 98.
52 LJ to Bartoš, undated, 24? Oct 1903 (Straková 1957, 24).
53 Zíbrt to LJ, 14 Sept 1903 (BmJA, A 175).
54 LJ to Bartoš, undated, 24? Oct 1903 (Straková 1957, 24).
55 LJ to Bartoš, undated, 24? Oct 1903 (Straková 1957, 24).
56 Bartošová to Helfert, 4 Dec 1933 (*JODA*, OS8).
57 Bartoš to LJ, 27 Oct 1903 (Straková 1957, 24–5).
58 Štědroň 1959, 179, fn. 28.
59 LJ to Bartošová, 12 Nov 1903 (*JODA*, OS9).
60 LJ to Urválková, 13 Nov 1903 (Štědroň 1959, 179).
61 LJ to Urválková, undated, 15? Nov 1903 (Štědroň 1959, 169–74).
62 LJ to Nebuška, 22 Feb 1917 (BmJA, D 1569).
63 LJ to Urválková, undated, 15? Nov 1903 (*JODA*, OS3, OS7).
64 LJ to Urválková, undated, 15? Nov 1903 (*JODA*, OS03, OS7).
65 LJ to Bartošová, 12, 17 and 29 Nov and 8 Dec 1903 (*JODA*, OS9, OS11, OS15 and OS18).
66 *JODA*, 115.
67 Bartošová to LJ, 16 Nov 1903 (*JODA*, OS10).
68 LJ to Bartošová, 17 Nov 1903 (*JODA*, OS11).
69 LJ to Bartošová, 25 Nov 1903 (*JODA*, OS13).
70 LJ to Bartošová, 26 Nov 1903 (*JODA*, OS14).
71 LJ to Bartošová, 29 Nov 1903 (*JODA*, OS15).
72 Bartošová to LJ, 3 Dec 1903 (*JODA*, OS17).
73 LJ to Bartošová, 8 Dec 1903 (*JODA*, OS18).
74 LJ to Bartošová, 17 Dec 1903 (*JODA*, OS19).
75 Bartošová to LJ, 19 Dec 1903 (*JODA*, OS20).
76 LJ's comments written on a letter from Bartošová (*JODA*, OS21).
77 *MLWJ*, 98–9.
78 *MLWJ*, 99–100.
79 LJ to Urválková, undated, 23? Dec 1903 (*JODA*, JP22).
80 LJ to Urválková, 28 Dec 1903 (Štědroň 1959, 180).

45: Spas, especially Luhačovice

1 Křížek 2002, 217.
2 Křížek 2002, 72.
3 Hembry 1997, 165, 176–8, 182–5.
4 Křížek 2002, 207.
5 *MLWJ*, 47.
6 Štědroň 1939, 16.
7 Picek to LJ, 12 July 1891 (BmJA, A 44).
8 LJ to ZJ, 18 Aug 1903 (BmJA, A 3868).
9 Jančar 1988, 17.
10 Balhar 1927, 85.
11 Listed in Stavěla 1932, 91–106.
12 Lažnovský 1926, 93.

13 Veselý 1924, 69.
14 *MLWJ*, 122.
15 *MLWJ*, 127.
16 LJ to ZJ, undated, postmarked 19 Aug 1903 (BmJA, A 6638).
17 LJ to Joza Janáčková and Věra Janáčková, undated, postmarked 1 Sept 1903 (BmJA, A 6312).
18 Balhar 1927, 93.
19 LJ to ZJ, 18 Aug 1908 (BmJA, A 4948).
20 LJ to ZJ, 24 July 1924 (BmJA, B 1373).
21 LJ to KS, 15 Aug 1926 (*HŽ*, no. 407).
22 LJ to KS, 7–8 July 1928 (*HŽ*, no. 705).
23 LJ to KS, 2–3 July 1928 (*HŽ*, no. 701).
24 LJ to KS, 16 July 1928 (*HŽ*, no. 712).
25 LJ to ZJ, 6 July 1928 (BmJA, A 5060).
26 Cmunt 1949, 167.
27 LJ to Věra Janáčková, 20 June 1918 (BmJA, B 2335).
28 LJ to Rektorys, 3 May 1917 (JA iv, 171).
29 Balhar 1914.
30 LJ to KS, 4 June 1918 (*HŽ*, no. 62).
31 LJ to ZJ, 21 Aug 1926 (BmJA, A 5017).
32 Ostrčils to LJ, 3 Aug 1920 (JA ii, 43–4).
33 LJ to KS, 3 Sept 1918 (*HŽ*, no. 83).

46: *Louise* and the hidden agenda

1 Kaprál 1924, 65.
2 Hanák 1959, 171
3 Gustave Charpentier: *Louise*, piano-vocal score (Paris: Heugel, 1907), 14–18.
4 LJ to UE, 7 Nov 1922 (*BUE*, 197).
5 *Louise*, piano-vocal score, 382–8.
6 See 'Janáček and the viola d'amore' in Tyrrell 1982, 154–61.

47: 1904

1 *MLWJ*, 100.
2 Brno Theatre Družstvo to Branberger, 18 Jan 1904 (Němcová 1974, 139).
3 LJ to KK, 17 Jan 1904 (*JODA*, JP24).
4 Racek 1955, 22.
5 LJ to Urválková, 17 Jan 1904 (Štědroň 1959, 181).
6 Urválková to LJ, 19 Jan 1904 (Štědroň 1959, 181).
7 LJ to Urválková, undated, 19? Jan 1904 (*JODA*, JP26).
8 Some quoted in Němcová 1974, 139.
9 Němcová 1974, 138.
10 Kunc 1933.
11 Němcová 1974, 140–1.
12 *JODA*, JP30.
13 *MLWJ*, 100.
14 Němcová 1971, 117–18.
15 LJ to Brno Theatre Družstvo, 9 Oct 1905 (*JODA*, OS39).
16 Branberger review in *Čas*, 24 Jan 1904, quoted in Němcová 1974, 142–3.
17 '-la' [Chvála]: review in *Národní politika*, 27 Jan 1904, quoted in Němcová 1974, 143–4.
18 LJ to Urválková, 28 Jan 1904 (Štědroň 1959, 182).

19 LJ to Chvála, 1 Feb 1904 (Prague, Narodní muzeum: muzeum české hudby).
20 LJ to KK, 9 Feb 1904 (*JODA*, JP35).
21 Schmoranz to LJ, 11 Feb 1904 (*JODA*, JP36).
22 Němeček 1968, i, 106.
23 Dvořák to LJ, 26 Feb 1904 (*ADKD*, iv, 266).
24 Racek 1955, 21.
25 KK to LJ, 4 March 1904 (*JODA*, JP37).
26 LJ to KK, 10 March 1904 (*JODA*, JP38).
27 LJ to Kvapilová, undated, after 15 April 1904 (*JODA*, JP39).
28 ZJ to LJ, 28 March 1904 (BmJA, A 2470).
29 LJ to Bartošová, 27 Jan 1904 (BmJA, A 5805).
30 Straková 1957, 139.
31 *MLWJ*, 100.
32 LJ to Bartošová, undated, 10? and 12? April 1904 (*JODA*, OS23–4).
33 LJ to Urválková, 20 April 1904 (Štědroň 1959, 183).
34 LJ to Bartošová, undated, 22? April 1904 (*JODA*, OS25).
35 Štědroň 1959, 179, fn. 28.
36 Svyatkovsky to LJ, 12 Jan 1904 N. S. (BmJA, B 72).
37 LJ to Urválková, undated, 19? Jan 1904 (Štědroň 1959, 180–1).
38 Melniková 1997, 354.
39 Veselý 1924, 45.
40 Veselý 1924, 45.
41 LJ to Bartoš, undated, after 5 July 1904 (Straková 1957, 25–6).
42 LJ to Kvapilová, 9 May 1904 (*JODA*, JP40).
43 Bartošová to Helfert, 4 Dec 1933 (*JODA*, OS28).
44 LJ to Bartošová, 2 July 1905 (BmJA, A 5813).
45 Leopoldina Countess Serényi to LJ, 22 July 1904 (BmJA, A 230).
46 Czech Academy to LJ, 3 July 1904 (BmJA, C 277).
47 ZJ to LJ, undated, receipt postmark 16 July (BmJA, A 1598).
48 LJ to ZJ, 15 July 1904 (BmJA, A 3911).
49 Novák 1962.
50 LJ to Arnošt Píša, 22 Sept 1904 (BmJA, A 6088).
51 LJ to Joza Janáčková, undated, postmarked 18? July 1904 (BmJA, A 6314).
52 Kunc to LJ, 9 Aug 1904 (BmJA, A 2028).
53 LJ to Zeman, 17 Aug 1904 (Uhlíková 1994, 101).
54 LJ to Kunc, undated, postmarked 22 Aug 1904 (BmJA, A 6134).
55 ZJ to Joza Janáčková, 12 Sept 1904 (BmJA, A 6383).
56 Programme in BmJA.
57 Racek 1955, 22.
58 Lacina to LJ, 3 Oct 1904 (*JODA*, JP41).
59 LJ to Mahler, 5 Dec 1904 (*JODA*, JP42).
60 Pražák to Mahler, 5 Dec 1904 (Blaukopf 1979, 286).
61 Mahler to LJ, 9 Dec 1904 (*JODA*, JP44).
62 Heš to LJ, undated, Jan? 1905 (BmJA, A 4706).
63 Kašlík 1938, 6.

48: The missing link: *Jenůfa* in 1904

1 Leoš Janáček: *Jenůfa: Její pastorkyňa: brněnská verze (1908)* [*Jenůfa: Her Stepdaughter*: Brno version (1908)], ed. Charles Mackerras and John Tyrrell (Universal Edition, Vienna, 1996).

2 A lone, much reproduced sheet of sketches with fragments of Act 1 Scene 2 (BmJA, A 30.38) is all there is, apart from a few jottings in Janáček's copy of Preissová's play.
3 Štědroň 1972.
4 Audus 2006.
5 Audus 2006.
6 It was published for the first time in the Dürr 1969 full score (Universal Edition), which in all other respects embraced Kovařovic's version.
7 Hrazdira to LJ, 11 July 1906 (BmJA, B 83).
8 Audus 2006.

49: Bêtes noires I: Karel Kovařovic

1 Schmoranz to Peška, 29 Sept 1915 (*JODA*, JP62).
2 LJ to KK, 22 Nov 1919 (JA vii, 84).
3 LJ to Brod, 22 May 1927 (JA ix, 225).
4 LJ to Ostrčil, 6 Dec 1920 (JA ii, 47).

50: Janáček at fifty

1 Bílý to LJ, 3 July 1904 (BmJA, A 203).

51: 1905

1 *JKPU*, 23–32.
2 *JKPU*, 35–8.
3 LJ to Kunc, 15 Nov 1905 (BmJA, A 6135).
4 LJ to Píša, 22 Sept 1904 (BmJA, A 6088).
5 *BUE*, 13; Toncrová 1995; Nigel Simeone: 'Universal Edition', NG2.
6 Hostinský to LJ, 7 April 1906 (Vysloužil 1958, 172–3).
7 *LJOLP*, 57–8.
8 LJ to Hostinský, 9 April 1905 (Mišurec 2002, 22).
9 Hostinský to LJ, 10 April 1905 (Vysloužil 1958, 173).
10 LJ to Hostinský, 12 May 1905 (Mišurec 2002, 23).
11 Hostinský to LJ, 15 May 1905 (Vysloužil 1958, 173).
12 LJ to Bakešová, undated, before 19 May 1905 (Sedláčková 2001, no. 68).
13 Bakešová to LJ, 19 May 1905 (Sedláčková 2001, no. 69).
14 Bartoš to LJ, 17 May and 20 Aug 1905 (Straková 1957, 26).
15 Vach 1924.
16 Report in 'Koncertní ruch' [Concert activity], Veselí na Mor., *Dalibor*, xxvii (1904–5), 266; Helfert 1923, 114.
17 LJ to Joza Janáčková, 15 June 1905 (BmJA, A 6321).
18 Vach to LJ, 20 June 1905 (*VDKS*, 122).
19 Beneš to LJ, 9 March 1905 (BmJA, A 233).
20 LJ to Beneš, 11 March 1905 (Špelda 1954, 645).
21 Plzeň 'Smetana' to LJ, 17 March 1903 (BmJA, D 792).
22 ZJ to LJ, 6 May 1905 (BmJA, A 1594).
23 LJ to ZJ, 19 May 1905 (BmJA, A 3842).
24 Bakešová to LJ, 19 May 1905 (Sedláčková 2001, no. 69).
25 LJ to ZJ, 24 July 1905 (BmJA, A 3900).
26 LJ to ZJ, undated, 25? July 1905 (BmJA, A 3906).
27 LJ to ZJ, 28 July 1905 (BmJA, A 3816).
28 LJ to ZJ, 28 July 1905. (BmJA, A 3812).

29 LJ to ZJ, 16 Aug 1905 (BmJA, A 3849).
30 LJ to ZJ, 20 Aug 1905 (BmJA, A 3885).
31 LJ to ZJ, 26 Aug 1905 (BmJA, A 3930).
32 LJ to ZJ, undated, 2? Sept 1905 (BmJA, A 3903).
33 LJ to ZJ, 5 Sept 1905 (BmJA, A 3845).
34 ZJ to LJ, 7 Sept 1905 (BmJA, A 1590).
35 LJ to Hostinský, undated, before 31 Oct 1905 (Mišurec 2002, 24).
36 Hostinský to LJ, 1 Nov 1905 (BmJA, A 3357).
37 LJ to Hostinský, 13 Dec 1905 (Mišurec 2002, 25).
38 JA iv, 22, fn. 19.
39 František Janáček to LJ, 11 Oct 1905 (BmJA, A 1383).
40 František Janáček to LJ, 21 Oct 1905 (BmJA, A 1588).
41 František Janáček to LJ, 2 Nov 1905 (BmJA, A 5120).
42 Dřímal and Peša 1973, 66.
43 *BSP*, iii, 451–62.
44 Grufik 1974, 21–2.
45 Arnošt Heinrich: 'Brněnská vzpomínka' [A Brno reminiscence], *LN* (1 Oct 1925), quoted in Zahrádka 2005, 24.
46 Grufik 1974, 21–2.
47 LJ to Věra Janáčková, undated, 13? Oct 1905 (BmJA, A 6273).
48 LJ to František Janáček, 19 Oct 1905 (BmJA, A 4898); *BH*, 59.
49 PSMU to LJ, 2 Nov 1905 (BmJA, A 2931).
50 PSMU to LJ, 10 Dec 1905 (BmJA, A 1730).
51 Ambros to LJ, 5 Dec 1905 (BmJA, A 239).
52 'Orlice' to LJ, 18 Nov 1905 (BmJA, D 62).
53 Reports under 'Dopisy [Letters]: Prostějov', and 'Koncertní ruch [Concert activity]: Prostějov', *Dalibor*, xxviii (1905–6), 27–8, 29.
54 Racek 1955, 22.
55 LJ to ZJ, 31 Dec 1905 (BmJA, A 3722).

52: Music as autobiography II

1 LJ to Bartošová, 12 Nov 1903 (*JODA*, OS9).
2 LJ to Bartošová, undated, 10? April 1904 (*JODA*, OS23).
3 LJ to an unknown doctor, undated (*JODA*, OS30).
4 LJ to František Veselý, 8 Aug 1913 (*JODA*, OS99).

53: 1906

1 LJ to Zeman, 24 Dec 1905 (Uhlíková 1994, 103).
2 LJ to Bím, 24 Dec 1905 (Toncrová 1999, no. 9).
3 Zeman to LJ, undated, after 7 Jan 1905 (Uhlíková 1994, 103–4).
4 LJ to Zeman, undated, Jan? 1905 (Uhlíková 1994, 104).
5 Bím to LJ, 1 Feb 1906 (Toncrová 1999, no. 10).
6 LJ to Bakešová, undated, before 12 Jan 1905 (Sedláčková 2001, no. 70).
7 Bakešová to LJ, 12 Jan 1906 (Sedláčková 2001, no. 71).
8 Bakešová to LJ, 20 Jan 1906 (Sedláčková 2001, no. 72).
9 Bakešová to LJ, 25 Jan 1906 (Sedláčková 2001, no. 73).
10 Toncrová 1995, 247.
11 Bakešová to LJ, 25 Jan 1906 (Sedláčková 2001, no. 73).
12 *JKPU*, 41–2.
13 Zahrádka 2005, 27.

14 Racek 1955, 23.
15 Programme in BmJA.
16 Racek 1955, 22.
17 Nešvera to LJ, 2 Feb 1906 (BmJA, A 3336).
18 *JKPU*, 43.
19 Racek 1955, 22.
20 LJ to Brno Theatre Družstvo, 7 March 1906 (Firkušný 1938, 131).
21 Brno Theatre Družstvo to LJ, 11 Nov 1906 (BmJA, D 1164).
22 Racek 1955, 23.
23 Racek 1955, 22.
24 Bakešová to LJ, 25 Feb 1906 (Sedláčková 2001, no. 74).
25 LJ to Bakešová, 9 April 1906 (Sedláčková 2001 no. 76).
26 LJ to Bakešová, undated, April 1906 (Sedláčková 2001, no. 77).
27 Bakešová to LJ, undated, before 13 April 1906 (Sedláčková 2001, no. 78).
28 Bakešová to LJ, 13 April 1906 (Sedláčková 2001, no. 79).
29 Bakešová to LJ, 23 April 1906 (Sedláčková 2001, no. 81).
30 LJ to Bakešová, 26 April 1906 (Sedláčková 2001, no. 82).
31 Bakešová to LJ, 27, 29 and 30 April 1906 (Sedláčková 2001, nos. 83–5).
32 Bakešová to LJ, 30 April 1906 (Sedláčková 2001, no. 86).
33 *JKPU*, 42–3.
34 Vach to LJ, 21 April 1906 (BmJA, A 1759).
35 PSMU to LJ, 25 April 1906 (BmJA, A 1760).
36 Vach to LJ, 27 April 1906 (BmJA, A 2952).
37 Lichtner 1911, ii, 78.
38 Hostinský to LJ, 19 April 1906 (Vysloužil 1958, 173–4).
39 LJ to Hostinský, 20 April 1906 (Mišurec 2002, 26–7).
40 LJ to Hostinský, 6 May 1906 (Mišurec 2002, 30).
41 LJ's expenses list, quoted in *LJOLP*, 110.
42 Bakešová to LJ, 11 May 1906 (Sedláčková 2001, no. 88).
43 Bakešová to LJ, 18 May 1906 (Sedláčková 2001, no. 89).
44 LJ to Hostinský, 21 May 1906 (Mišurec 2002, 30).
45 *LJOLP*, 46–7, 108.
46 *LJOLP*, 47.
47 JA iv, 11.
48 AR to LJ, 31 May 1906 (JA iv, 12).
49 LJ to AR, 11 July 1906 (JA iv, 15–16).
50 AR to LJ, 19 July 1906 (JA iv, 17–19).
51 Kunc to LJ, undated, after 15 July 1906 (BmJA, A 4840).
52 Urbánek to LJ, 27 July 1906 (JA iv, 18, fn. 15).
53 LJ to AR, 30 July 1905 (JA iv, 20).
54 Urbánek to LJ, 31 July 1906 (JA iv, 20, fn. 16).
55 Urbánek to LJ, 30 May 1906 (BmJA, B 1016). [db5552]
56 'Hlahol' to LJ, 6 July 1907 (BmJA, D 714).
57 Brno Theatre Družstvo to LJ, 16 June 1906 (*JODA*, OS32).
58 Brno Theatre Družstvo to LJ, 9 July 1906 (*JODA*, OS33).
59 LJ to Branberger, 24 June 1906 (*JODA*, OS34).
60 LJ to Kunc, 30 July 1906 (BmJA, A 6143).
61 ZJ to LJ, 8 July 1906 (BmJA, A 1729).
62 Hrazdira to LJ, 11 July 1906 (BmJA, B 83).
63 LJ to Vach, 28 July 1906 (BmJA, A 6653).

64 *LJOLP*, 105; see also *LJOLP*, plate no. 14.

65 LJ to ZJ, undated, postmarked 25? July 1906 (BmJA, A 3778). [d3832]

66 *MLWJ*, 101.

67 *JVD*, 80–2.

68 LJ to Frýda, 26 July 1906 (BmJA, A 5449).

69 LJ to Kunc, 30 July 1906 (BmJA, A 6143).

70 LJ to ZJ, 3 Aug 1906 (BmJA, A 3751).

71 Kunc to LJ, 13 Aug 1906 (BmJA, A 264).

72 Štědroň 1938.

73 LJ to Hostinský, 3 Aug 1906 (Mišurec 2002, 31). [2046]

74 LJ to Zeman, 13 Aug 1906 (Uhlíková 1994, 105).

75 Picture reproduced as no. 10 in *LJOLP*.

76 Notations made in Lubina, 26 Aug 1906, quoted in *LJOLP*, 107.

77 LJ to ZJ, undated, postmarked 23? Aug 1906 (BmJA, A 3919).

78 Hostinský to LJ, 17 Aug 1906 (Vysloužil 1958, 175).

79 Kunc to LJ, 13 Aug 1906 (BmJA, A 264; extract in *JODA*, OS37).

80 LJ to Kunc, undated, postmarked 27 Aug 1906 (*JODA*, OS38).

81 LJ to unknown male copyist, undated, Sept? 1906 (BmJA, A 5450).

82 Neumann to LJ, 2 Sept 1906 (BmJA, A 3453).

83 LJ to Neumann, 4 Sept 1906 (Štědroň 1941, 59).

84 Neumann to LJ, 2 Oct 1906 (BmJA, A 3421).

85 *JAWO*, vi/10.

86 LJ to Neumann, 21 Oct 1906 (Štědroň 1941, 59).

87 AR to LJ, 11 Sept 1906 (JA iv, 20–2).

88 LJ to AR, 12 Sept 1906 (JA iv, 22).

89 Facsimile in Toncrová 1995, 253.

90 Audus 2006.

91 LJ to AR, 1 Oct 1906 (JA iv, 25).

92 LJ to AR, 4 Oct 1906 (JA iv, 25–6).

93 LJ to Vašková, undated, 1? Oct 1906 (*VDKS*, 122).

94 Kunc 1911, 133.

95 Vašková to LJ, 5 Oct 1906 (BmJA, A 5914).

96 Špelda 1954, 645, fn. 2.

97 LJ to Neumann, 21 Oct 1906 (Štědroň 1941, 59).

98 Neumann to LJ, 27 Oct 1906 (BmJA, A 3418).

99 LJ to AR, 30 Oct 1906 (JA iv, 30).

100 M. Urbánek to LJ, 10 Nov 1906 (BmJA, B 804).

101 Forberg to LJ, 9 Nov 1906 (BmJA, B 85).

102 Czech Philharmonic to LJ, 13 Nov 1906 (BmJA, D 709).

103 Racek 1955, 22.

104 Racek 1955, 22.

105 LJ to ZJ, 15 Nov 1906 (BmJA, A 3785).

106 LJ to AR, 25 Nov 1906 (JA iv, 34–5).

107 *Smetana*, i (1906), 285.

108 LJ to Branberger, 4 Dec 1906 (BmJA, A 5134); Eng. trans. (misdated) in *LR*, 88–9.

109 *Dalibor*, xxix (1906–7), 91.

110 *Dalibor*, xxix (1906–7), 80.

111 LJ to AR, 21 Nov 1906 (JA iv, 31–2).

112 Mišurec 2002, 122–47.

113 *Snaha* (Olomouc, 20 Oct 1906).

114 Věra Janáčková to LJ, 22 Oct 1906 (BmJA, A 1726).
115 AR to LJ, 23 Nov 1906 (JA iv, 182).
116 Frýda to LJ, 16 Jan 1907 (*JODA*, OS42).
117 LJ to ZJ, undated, postmarked 28? Dec 1906 (BmJA, A 3880).
118 Vysloužil 1958, 176–7.
119 It appeared in Lidové noviny, 17 Dec 1906.
120 Štědroň 1998, 75.
121 LJ to ZJ, undated, postmarked 28? Dec 1906 (BmJA, A 3880).
122 LJ to Joza Janáčková, 4 Oct 1906 (BmJA, A 6326).
123 *LN* (17 Dec 1906).

54: The Bezruč choruses

1 Peška to Schmoranz, 3 Oct 1915 (*JODA*, JP63).
2 Špelda 1954.

55: 1907

1 Frýda to LJ, 11 Dec 1906 (BmJA, D 719).
2 Bílý to LJ, 24 Dec 1906 (Straková 1955, 432).
3 František Sekanina to LJ, 16 Jan 1907 (Straková 1955a, 432–3).
4 LJ to Hostinský, 6 Jan 1907 (Mišurec 2002, 32–3).
5 Frýda to LJ, 16 Jan 1907 (*JODA*, OS42).
6 Vorlová-Vlčková to LJ, 3 Jan 1907 (*JODA*, OS41).
7 Komarov to LJ, 26 March 1907 (*JODA*, OS43).
8 Felix Cammra to LJ, 5 Feb 1907 (BmJA, D 68).
9 LJ to 'Smetana', 26 March 1907 (Špelda 1954, 646).
10 LJ to 'Smetana', 11 April 1907 (Špelda 1954, 646).
11 Lang to LJ, 19 April 1907 (BmJA, D 70).
12 Vach 1924, 38.
13 LJ to AR, 11 May 1907 (JA iv, 38–9).
14 Zuna to LJ, undated, after 11 May 1907 (BmJA, A 4747).
15 LJ to AR, 11 May 1907 (JA iv, 38–9).
16 JA iv, 38, fn. 37.
17 AR to LJ, 14 May 1907 (JA iv, 39).
18 JA iv, 40, fn. 41.
19 AR to LJ, 17 May 1907 (*JODA*, OS46).
20 LJ to AR, 29 May 1907 (*JODA*, OS47).
21 JA iv, 41, fn. 43.
22 Racek 1955, 23.
23 LJ to AR, 5 June 1907 (JA iv, 43).
24 JA iv, 43, fn. 45.
25 LJ to AR, 8 June 1907 (*JODA*, OS49).
26 AR to LJ, 11 June 1907 (*JODA*, OS50).
27 LJ to AR, 15 June 1907 (JA iv, 48).
28 *LJOLP*, 98.
29 LJ to Bím, 25 June 1907 (Toncrová 1999, no. 32).
30 Bím to LJ, 20 July 1907 (Toncrová 1999, no. 36).
31 LJ to Bím, 29 July 1907; Bím to LJ, 31 July and 7 Aug 1907 (Toncrová 1999, nos. 37, 38 and 43).
32 LJ to ZJ, undated, postmarked 9? July 1907 (BmJA, A 3867).
33 LJ to ZJ, 14 July 1907 (BmJA, A 3852).

34 *LJOLP*, 100.

35 LJ to ZJ, 23 July 1907 (BmJA, A 3749).

36 Zahradníček to LJ, undated, postmarked 14? Sept 1907 (BmJA, A 1389).

37 LJ to ZJ, 20 Aug 1907 (Racek 1941).

38 LJ to ZJ, 20 Aug 1907 (BmJA, D 1207).

39 *MLWJ*, 101.

40 *Národní listy*, 23 Aug 1907 (*JODA*, OS54).

41 LJ to AR, 23 Aug 1907 (*JODA*, OS55).

42 AR to LJ, 26 Aug 1907 (*JODA*, OS56).

43 LJ to AR, 28 Aug 1907 (JA iv, 51).

44 LJ to AR, 7 Sept 1907 (JA iv, 52).

45 AR to LJ, 10 Sept 1907 (JA iv, 52–3).

46 Beckerman 1994, 44.

47 LJ to AR, 11 Sept 1907 (JA iv, 53–4).

48 Skácelík to LJ, 27 Sept 1907 (*JODA*, OS58).

49 Skácelík to LJ, 2 Oct 1907 (BmJA, A 1724).

50 Racek 1955, 24.

51 LJ to Skácelík, 10 Oct 1907 (*JODA*, OS59).

52 Skácelík to LJ, 16 Oct 1907 (*JODA*, OS60).

53 LJ to Skácelík, 22 Oct 1907 (*JODA*, OS61).

54 LJ to Skácelík, 28 Oct 1907 (*JODA*, OS62).

55 Straková 1956, 228–9.

56 LJ to Skácelík, 14 Nov 1907 (*JODA*, OS65).

57 LJ to AR, 3 Nov 1907 (*JODA*, OS63).

58 LJ to AR, 20 Nov 1907 (JA iv, 64–5).

59 AR to LJ, 21 Nov 1907 (JA iv, 65).

60 Šubert to LJ, 1 Dec 1907 (*JODA*, OS68).

61 LJ to Bím, 2 Oct 1907 (Toncrová 1999, no. 46).

62 *Dalibor*, xxx (1907–8), 91.

63 *JKPU*, 55.

64 Engelmann & Mühlberg to Josef Kuhl, 19 Dec 1907 (BmJA, A 3958).

65 LJ to ZJ, undated, postmarked 25 Dec 1907 (BmJA, A 3798).

66 Racek 1955, 24.

67 Racek 1955, 24.

68 ZJ to LJ, 31 Dec 1907 (*JODA*, JP50).

56: 1908

1 LJ to AR, 7 Jan 1908 (JA iv, 66).

2 Němeček 1968, i, 216.

3 AR to LJ, 8 Jan 1908 (JA iv, 67).

4 LJ to AR, undated, 9? Jan 1908 (JA iv, 67).

5 LJ to AR, 11 Jan 1908 (JA iv, 68).

6 AR to LJ, 4 March 1908 (JA iv, 68–9).

7 LJ to AR, 5 March 1908 (JA iv, 70–1).

8 Šolc to LJ, 23 Jan 1908 (Koukal 1998, 367).

9 Šolc to LJ, 28 Jan 1908 (Koukal 1998, 368).

10 Šolc to LJ, 9 Feb 1908 (Koukal 1998, 369).

11 LJ to AR, 9 Feb 1908 (JA iv, 68).

12 LJ to KS, 5 Dec 1919 (*HŽ*, no.145).

13 LJ to AR, 5 March 1908 (JA iv, 70–1).

14 AR to LJ, 6 March 1908 (JA iv, 71–2).
15 LJ to AR, 12 March 1908 (JA iv, 73).
16 LJ to AR, 18 March 1908 (JA iv, 74–5).
17 AR to LJ, 17 March 1908 (JA iv, 73–4).
18 *Dalibor*, xxix (1906–7), 59–60. The review is unsigned but was reprinted with Rektorys's name in a booklet in which the composer supplied an analysis of the opera (Prague, 1907).
19 AR to LJ, 20 March 1908 (JA iv, 76).
20 LJ to AR, 21 March 1908 (JA iv, 77–8).
21 LJ to AR, 21 March 1908 (*JODA*, BR8).
22 LJ to AR, 22 March 1908 (*JODA*, BR9).
23 Mašek to AR, undated, postmarked 29? March 1908 (*JODA*, BR10).
24 Mašek to AR, 30 March 1908 (JA iv, 179–80).
25 AR to LJ, 31 March 1908 (JA iv, 82–3).
26 LJ to AR, 2 April 1908 (JA iv, 84).
27 Mašek to LJ, 4 April 1908 (*JODA*, BR13).
28 AR to LJ, 8 April 1908 (JA iv, 85–6).
29 LJ to AR, 12 April 1908 (JA iv, 86–7).
30 LJ to AR, 15 April 1908 (JA iv, 87–8).
31 Urbánek to LJ, 15 April 1908 (BmJA, A 3432).
32 LJ to ZJ, 21 April 1908 (Racek 1955, 24).
33 LJ to František Janáček, 21 April 1908 (BmJA, A 5100).
34 Mašek to LJ, 15 April 1908 (BmJA, A 3555).
35 Racek 1955, 24.
36 Racek 1955, 24.
37 Vach to LJ, 28 April 1908 (BmJA, A 1396).
38 Mašek to LJ, 2 May 1908 (JA v, 17).
39 Branberger to LJ, 5 May 1908 (BmJA, B 817).
40 Branberger to LJ, 15 April 1908 (BmJA, D 698).
41 LJ to Branberger, 6 May 1908 (BmJA, B 1432).
42 LJ to Branberger, 7 May 1908 (BmJA, B 1433).
43 LJ to Branberger, 8 May 1908 (BmJA, B 818).
44 Mašek to LJ, 15 May 1908 (JA v, 17).
45 Mašek to LJ, 17 May 1908 (*JODA*, BR15).
46 *JODA*, 167–8.
47 LJ to AR, 20 May 1908 (JA iv, 88–9).
48 LJ to Branberger, 23 May 1908 (BmJA, B 1435).
49 Branberger to LJ, 3 June 1906 (BmJA, B 809).
50 LJ to ZJ, 25 May 1908 (BmJA, A 3870).
51 LJ to ZJ, 26 May 1908 (BmJA, A 3758).
52 Racek 1955, 24.
53 LJ to AR, undated, by 10 June 1908 (JA iv, 91).
54 LJ to AR, 8 July 1908 (JA iv, 92–3).
55 Mašek to LJ, 4 July 1908 (*JODA*, BR18).
56 Mašek to LJ, 21 July 1908 (*JODA*, BR21).
57 LJ to Elgart, 8 July 1908 (Firkušný 1938, 132).
58 LJ to ZJ, 23 July 1908 (BmJA, A 3874).
59 LJ to ZJ, 25 July 1908 (BmJA, D 1209).
60 Mrštík to LJ, 28 July 1908 (Racek 1940, 27).
61 LJ to ZJ, 25 July 1908 (BmJA, D 1209).

62 Racek 1955, 24.
63 LJ to AR, 1 Nov 1908 (*JODA*, BR27).
64 Elgart to LJ, 29 July 1908 (*JODA*, OS73).
65 LJ to Elgart, 31 July 1908 (Firkušný 1938, 132–3).
66 LJ to ZJ, 30 July 1908 (BmJA, D 1208).
67 LJ to ZJ, undated, postmarked 5? Aug 1908 (BmJA, A 3854).
68 LJ to ZJ, undated, postmarked 11 Aug 1908 (BmJA, A 4946).
69 LJ to ZJ, undated, postmarked 11 Aug 1908 (BmJA, A 4946).
70 LJ to ZJ, undated, postmarked 5? Aug 1908 (BmJA, A 3854).
71 LJ to ZJ, undated, postmarked 11 Aug 1908 (BmJA, A 4946).
72 LJ to ZJ, 16 Aug 1908 (BmJA, A 4947).
73 LJ to ZJ, 16 Aug 1908 (BmJA, A 4947).
74 LJ to ZJ, 18 Aug 1908 (BmJA, A 4948).
75 LJ to ZJ, 22 Aug 1908 (BmJA, A 4949).
76 LJ to ZJ, 28 Aug 1908 (*JODA*, JP54).
77 *JODA*, JP55.
78 LJ to ZJ, 28 Aug 1908 (*JODA*, JP54).
79 LJ to ZJ, undated, postmarked 7 Sept 1908 (BmJA, A 6647).
80 Racek 1955, 24.
81 LJ to ZJ, 10 Sept 1908 (BmJA, A 3761).
82 Racek 1955, 24.
83 LJ to ZJ, 10 Sept 1908 (BmJA, A 3761).
84 AR to LJ, 25 Sept 1908 (JA iv, 94).
85 LJ to AR, 26 Sept 1908 (JA iv, 94–5).
86 LJ to ZJ, undated, postmarked 2 Oct 1908 (BmJA, A 3840).
87 AR to LJ, 26 Oct 1908 (JA iv, 96).
88 LJ to AR, 27 Oct 1908 (JA iv, 97).
89 AR to LJ, 28 Oct 1908 (JA iv, 97–8).
90 LJ to Moor, 29 Oct 1908 (Moor 1947, 67–8). [d3520]
91 Mašek to LJ, 28 Oct 1908 (*JODA*, BR23).
92 AR to LJ, 28 Oct 1908 (*JODA*, OS76).
93 Vinohrady Theatre to LJ, 4 Nov 1908 (*JODA*, OS 77).
94 LJ to AR, 1 Nov 1908 (JA iv, 99–100).
95 'Josef Holý', *LČL*.
96 Holý to LJ, 8 Nov 1908 (*JODA*, BR28).
97 Janke to LJ, 15 Nov 1908 (*JODA*, BR29).
98 LJ to Bezruč, 1 Oct 1924 (Veselý 1924, tipped in as facsimile).
99 Janke to LJ, 16 Dec 1908 (*JODA*, BR30).
100 LJ to ZJ, undated, after 20 Dec 1908 (BmJA, A 3904).
101 *BH*, 59.
102 LJ to AR, 30 Nov 1908 (JA iv, 101–2).
103 JA iv, 102, fn. 135.

57: Bêtes noires II: Zdeněk Nejedlý

1 Fukač 1963b.
2 Fukač 1963b.
3 Dr J. Říha's memorandum, quoted in Procházková 1990, 174–5.
4 Janáček comments in his notebook BmJA, Z60, quoted in *HŽ*, 133–4, fn. 274.
5 LJ to ZJ, 15 July 1924 (BmJA, B 1376).

58: 1909

1 LJ to AR, 30 Dec 1908 (JA iv, 103).
2 Racek 1955, 25.
3 LJ to Branberger, 6 Jan 1909 (BmJA, B 1437).
4 Branberger to LJ, 10 Jan 1909 (BmJA, B 815).
5 LJ to Branberger, 6 Jan 1909 (BmJA, B 1437).
6 Květ 1946, 50.
7 JA iv, 116, fn. 161.
8 Branberger to LJ, 10 Jan 1909 (BmJA, B 815).
9 LJ to AR, undated, after 10 Jan 1909 (JA iv, 103–4).
10 AR to LJ, 21 Jan 1909 (JA iv, 104–5).
11 LJ to AR, 22 Jan 1909 (JA iv, 105).
12 Janke to LJ, 22 Jan 1909 (*JODA*, BR31).
13 *JODA*, 172–3.
14 Janke to LJ, 9 Feb 1909 (JA v, 12).
15 Jílek to LJ, 17 Jan 1909 (JA iv, 106, fn. 146).
16 LJ to Calma-Veselá, 4 Feb 1909 (JA viii, 19–21).
17 LJ to Calma-Veselá, 11 Feb 1909 (JA viii, 21).
18 AR to LJ, 5 Feb 1909 (JA iv, 106–7).
19 LJ to AR, 6 Feb 1909 (JA iv, 107).
20 LJ to AR, 6 Feb 1909 (JA iv, 109).
21 Urbánek to LJ, 9 Feb 1909 (BmJA, D 700).
22 *JKPU*, 87.
23 LJ to Calma-Veselá, 13 Feb 1909 (JA viii, 22).
24 LJ to Calma-Veselá, 11 Feb 1909 (JA viii, 21).
25 LJ to AR, 7 March 1909 (JA iv, 110).
26 *LN* (11 March 1909), reprinted in JA iv, 113, fn. 157.
27 LJ to Calma-Veselá, 7 March 1909 (JA viii, 22).
28 LJ to AR, 7 March 1909 (JA iv, 110).
29 LJ to Janke, 8 March 1909 (*JODA*, BR33).
30 Janke to LJ, 17 March 1909 (JA v, 12).
31 AR to LJ, 17 March 1909 (JA iv, 111).
32 LJ to AR, 17 March 1909 (JA iv, 112).
33 LJ to AR, 17 March 1909 (JA iv, 112–13).
34 LJ to AR, 19 March 1909 (JA iv, 113–14).
35 LJ to Janke, 21 March 1909 (private archive).
36 *JKPU*, 47–8.
37 Wingfield 1987a, 233–4.
38 LJ to AR, 9 April 1909 (JA iv, 115–16).
39 LJ to AR, 10 April 1909 (JA iv, 116).
40 Urbánek to LJ, 14 April 1909 (BmJA, A 402).
41 LJ to AR, 15 April 1909 (JA iv, 117).
42 LJ to Hostinský, 5 May 1909 (Mišurec 2002, 41).
43 Hostinský to LJ, 7 May 1909 (Vysloužil 1958, 177–8). [d8257]
44 LJ to Zeman, 7 May 1909 (Uhlíková 1994, 108).
45 Racek 1955, 25.
46 LJ to ZJ, 9 June 1909 (BmJA, A 3709).
47 LJ to Veselý, 13 June 1909 (JA viii, 23).
48 LJ to Hostinský, 17 June 1909 (Mišurec 2002, 42).
49 Plocek 1998b, 129–33.

50 Urbánek to LJ, 8 July 1909 (BmJA, D 697).
51 *MLWJ*, 102.
52 LJ to Calma-Veselá, 9 July 1909 (JA viii, 23–4).
53 LJ to ZJ, 13 July 1909 (BmJA, A 4952).
54 LJ to ZJ, 18 July 1909 (BmJA, A 4953).
55 Smetana 1948, 34.
56 LJ to ZJ, 18 July 1909 (BmJA, A 4953).
57 LJ to ZJ, 14 Aug 1909 (BmJA, D 1210).
58 *LJOLP*, 95.
59 LJ to ZJ, 20 Aug 1909 (BmJA, A 3869).
60 *MLWJ*, 102–3.
61 LJ to ZJ, 25 Aug 1909 (BmJA, A 3776).
62 *MLWJ*, 103.
63 LJ to ZJ, 28 Aug 1909 (BmJA, A 4954).
64 LJ to ZJ, 30 Aug 1909 (BmJA, A 4955).
65 LJ to ZJ, 31 Aug 1909 (BmJA, A 3753).
66 LJ to ZJ, 2 Sept 1909 (BmJA, A 4956).
67 LJ to ZJ, undated, postmarked 5? Sept 1909 (BmJA, A 3859).
68 LJ and others to ZJ, undated, postmarked 9? Sept 1909 (BmJA, A 3717).
69 LJ to ZJ, undated, postmarked 7 Sept 1909 (BmJA, A 4957).
70 LJ to ZJ, 12 Sept 1909 (BmJA, A 4958).
71 LJ to ZJ, 15 Sept 1909 (BmJA, A 4960).
72 *JVŠ*, 86.
73 LJ to AR, 18 Sept 1909 (JA iv, 119).
74 LJ to ZJ, 19 Sept 1909 (BmJA, B 1332).
75 AR to LJ, 25 Sept 1909 (JA iv, 120).
76 LJ to AR, 26 Sept 1909 (JA iv, 121).
77 *JODA*, 175.
78 Smetana 1948, 34–5.
79 *MLWJ*, 104.
80 *MLWJ*, 105.
81 Smetana 1948, 36.
82 Ambros to LJ, 5 Oct 1909 (BmJA, A 1766).
83 LJ to Bakešová, undated, after 8 Oct 1909 (Sedláčková 2001, no. 92).
84 LJ to AR, 28 Oct 1909 (JA iv, 122–3).
85 AR to LJ, 29 Oct 1909 (JA iv, 123–4).
86 *JVŠ*, 127–8.
87 *LN* (26 Nov 1909), quoted in JA iv, 124, fn. 173.
88 LJ to AR, 8 Dec 1909 (JA iv, 124).
89 Toncrova 1998, 140.
90 A CD version is supplied with Plocek 1998.
91 LJ to Calma-Veselá, undated, after 10 Dec 1909 (JA viii, 25).
92 Kočí to LJ, 27 Dec 1909 (BmJA, B 798).

59: Pan-Slavism III

1 *JODA*, JP35.
2 Racek 1940, 63, fn. 4.
3 Preissová to LJ, 29 April 1904 (BmJA, A 3460).
4 LJ to Alois Mrštík, 20 June 1920, Racek 1940, 38.
5 Stavěla 1932, 39–44.

6 Extract in *LR*, 63; *JVD*, 101.

7 Robert B. Pynsent: 'Nationalist Naturalism: Josef Merhaut's Brno', paper presented at the Janáček conference: London, 1999.

8 Václav Müller: 'Ladislav Stroupežnický', *České umění dramatické* [Czech dramatic art]. ed. František Götz and Frank Tetauer (Šolc & Šímáček, Prague, 1941), 137.

9 Vrba 1960, 77–8.

10 *MLWJ*, 196.

60: 1910

1 JA iv, 125, fn. 176.

2 LJ to AR, 20 Jan 1910 (JA iv, 125).

3 Quoted in preface to Hudební matice edition (Prague, 1949).

4 *SKV*, E/2, ix.

5 AR to LJ, 16 Feb 1910 (JA iv, 126).

6 LJ to AR, 18 Feb 1910 (JA iv, 127).

7 LJ to AR, 27 Feb 1910 (JA iv, 128).

8 AR to LJ, 3 March 1910 (JA iv, 128).

9 *JVŠ*, 127–8.

10 *SKV*, E/2, ix.

11 LJ to Kunc, undated, after 17 March 1910 (BmJA, B 2197).

12 Brno Theatre Družstvo to LJ, 20 March 1910 (Firkušný 1938, 136).

13 Reprinted in *JVŠ*, 133–6.

14 Translated in Beckerman 1994, 49.

15 LJ to AR, 18 March 1910 (JA iv, 129).

16 AR to LJ, 28 March 1910 (JA iv, 129–30).

17 LJ to AR, 31 March 1910 (JA iv, 131–2).

18 AR to LJ, 28 March 1910 (JA iv, 129–30).

19 *JODA*, 176.

20 LJ to AR, undated, postmarked 29 March 1910 (*JODA*, BR39).

21 *JODA*, 178.

22 Doležil 1910.

23 Hubert Doležil: 'Morava a Slezsko' [Moravia and Silesia], *HR*, ii (1909), 70–2 (includes section on 'Janáčkovy zpěvohry' [Janáček's operas], 71–2.

24 LJ to AR, 10 April 1910 (JA iv, 132–3).

25 JA 132, fn. 188.

26 AR to LJ, 11 April 1911 (JA iv, 133).

27 LJ to AR, 13 April 1910 (JA iv, 134).

28 Lébl 1964, 135–7.

29 Lébl 1964, 133, fn. 7.

30 Blažek 1971.

31 LJ to AR, 7 May 1910 (JA iv, 134).

32 AR to LJ, 9 May 1910 (JA iv, 135).

33 R. Langham Smith: 'Nouguès, Jean(-Charles)', *NG2*.

34 Racek 1955, 25.

35 LJ to AR, 10 June 1910 (JA iv, 137–8).

36 Racek 1955, 25, fn. 51.

37 LJ to ZJ, undated, postmarked 15? May 1910 (BmJA, A 3794).

38 LJ to ZJ, undated, postmarked 14? May 1910 (BmJA, A3793).

39 Váňa to LJ, 28 May 1910 (BmJA, A 337).

40 LJ to AR, 28 May 1910 (JA iv, 135).

41 LJ to AR, 2 June 1910 (JA iv, 136).
42 AR to LJ, 1 June 1910 (JA iv, 135–6).
43 LJ to AR, 2 June 1910 (JA iv, 136).
44 AR to LJ, 9 June 1910 (JA iv, 137).
45 Kožušníček to LJ, undated, 30? June 1910 (BmJA, A 4849).
46 LJ to Kunc, 30 June 1910 (BmJA, B 2198).
47 Hrazdira to LJ, 4 July 1910 (BmJA, A 339).
48 Lacina to LJ, 5 July 1910 (BmJA, D 82).
49 LJ to AR, 10 June 1910 (JA iv, 137–8).
50 *MLWJ*, 106.
51 LJ to ZJ, undated, postmarked 18 July 1910 (BmJA, A 3893).
52 *MLWJ*, 108.
53 Váňa to LJ, 28 July 1910 (BmJA, A 3428).
54 Váňa to LJ, 16 Aug 1910 (BmJA, A 3420).
55 Trkanová 1964, 71.
56 LJ to ZJ, 25 Aug 1910 (BmJA, A 3830).
57 LJ to ZJ, undated, Sept? 1910 (BmJA, A 3946).
58 *LJOLP*, 60.
59 AR to LJ, 28 Sept 1910 (JA iv, 139–40).
60 LJ to AR, 29 Sept 1910 (JA iv, 140–1).
61 AR to LJ, 5 Oct 1910 (JA iv, 141–2).
62 LJ to Dušek, 8 Oct 1910 (Mišurec 2002, 45–6).
63 Vysloužil 1955, 248, fn. 8.
64 LJ to AR, 11 Oct 1910 (JA iv, 143).
65 JA iv, 141, fn. 200.
66 AR to LJ, 16 Feb 1910 (JA iv, 126).
67 AR to LJ, 26 Oct 1910 (JA iv, 143–4).
68 Vysloužil 1955, 247, fn. 5.
69 Racek 1955, 25.
70 LJ to AR, 11 Dec 1910 (JA iv, 145).
71 *Smetana*, i (1910–11), 15.
72 J. Křička: 'O Musorgském a jeho "Borisu Godunovu"' [About Musorgsky and his *Boris Godunov*], *HR*, iii (1910), 452–60.
73 AR to LJ, 21 Nov 1910 (JA iv, 144–5).
74 Váňa to LJ, 13 Nov 1910 (BmJA, A 3431).
75 Váňa to LJ, 17 Nov 1910 (BmJA, A 347).
76 Váňa to LJ, 13 Nov 1910 (BmJA, A 3431).
77 *HR*, iii (1910), 495.

61: Janáček's knowledge of opera II (1890–1914)

1 Moor 1947, 61–2.

62: 1911

1 Kunc to LJ, 24 Jan 1903 (BmJA, A 349).
2 *HR*, iv (1911), 281–2.
3 LJ to AR, 15 Jan 1911 (JA iv, 146).
4 *JKPU*, 77–8.
5 Kožušníček to Veselý, 19 Feb 1911 (JA viii, 29–32).
6 Hlava to Veselý, 25 Feb 1911 (*JODA*, JP57).
7 Ambros to LJ, 5 Oct 1910 (BmJA, A 1766).

8 Polášek to LJ, 27 Feb 1911 (BmJA, B 116).
9 Steinman to LJ, 18 March 1911 (BmJA, A 354).
10 LJ to Steinman, 21 March 1911 (*SKV*, B/3, xi).
11 LJ to Steinman, 24 April 1911 (BmJA B 2389).
12 Racek 1955, 26.
13 LJ to Janke, undated, April 1911 (*JODA*, BR42).
14 Janke to LJ, 16 April 1911 (BmJA, B 1583).
15 LJ to Janke, undated, April 1911 (*JODA*, BR42).
16 *JODA*, 178–80.
17 Štech to LJ, 22 April 1911 (BmJA, D 710).
18 Racek 1955, 26.
19 ZJ to LJ, 19 May 1911 (BmJA, A 3207).
20 Štech to LJ, 26 June 1911 (BmJA, D 711).
21 LJ to AR, 20 May 1911 (JA iv, 146).
22 AR to LJ, 22 May 1911 (JA iv, 147).
23 LJ to AR, 29 June 1911 (*JODA*, OS78).
24 LJ to Vinohrady Theatre, 9 Aug 1911 (*JODA*, OS79).
25 LJ to ZJ, 11 Aug 1911 (BmJA, A 3891).
26 *LJOLP*, 99.
27 *LJOLP*, 116.
28 LJ to ZJ, undated, postmarked 2? Sept 1911 (BmJA, A 3912).
29 Píša to LJ, 27 Dec 1909 (BmJA, B 798).
30 Píša to LJ, 23 Sept 1911 (BmJA, D 701).
31 Dr Miřička (for Vinohrady Theatre) to Stránský, 4 Oct 1911 (*JODA*, OS80).
32 Štech to LJ, 10 Nov 1911 (*JODA*, OS81).
33 Pauk to LJ, 11 Nov 1911 (BmJA, A 3445).
34 Štech to LJ, 6 Dec (*JODA*, OS83).
35 Vinohrady Theatre to LJ, 18 Dec 1911 (BmJA, C 172).
36 LJ to AR, 13 Dec 1911 (JA iv, 148).
37 BmJA, A7428, quoted in *SKV*, F/1, 142.
38 Simeone 1991, 226.
39 LJ to Branberger, 13 Dec 1911 (BmJA, B 1441); JA iv, 148.
40 Píša to LJ, 14 Dec 1911 (BmJA, D 219).
41 xv/315; see *JLOLP*, 214.

63: 1912

1 *JKPU*, 61–2.
2 LJ to Branberger, 21 April 1912 (BmJA, B 1442).
3 LJ to Branberger, 27 Sept 1912 (BmJA, B 113).
4 Ezechiel Ambros to LJ, 30 March 1912 (BmJA, A 3427); Vladimír Ambros to LJ, 29 March 1912 (BmJA, A 3202).
5 Vojáček to LJ, 16 Feb 1912 N.S. (BmJA, A 2750).
6 *Smetana*, ii (1911–12), 152–4.
7 *HR*, v (1912), 177.
8 For programmes see *JKPU*, 129–31.
9 *JKPU*, 129; Štědroň 1998, 64.
10 Štědroň 1998, 64.
11 Ezechiel Ambros to LJ, 10 Jan 1912 (BmJA, A 365).
12 Vach to LJ, undated, Jan? 1912 (BmJA, A 4558).
13 Elgart to LJ, 19 March 1912 (BmJA, B 339) and undated (BmJA, A 4536).

14 Příbram Philharmonic to LJ, 17 March 1912 (BmJA, D 92).
15 *HR*, v (1912), 365.
16 See for instance Kunc's view in *HR*, vi (1912), 356–7.
17 'Moravský smíšený sbor učitelský', *ČSHS*.
18 SKV, B/3, xi.
19 Machoň 1912.
20 Racek 1955, 26.
21 LJ to ZJ, 23 March 1912 (BmJA, A 3916).
22 LJ to ZJ, 25 March 1912 (BmJA, A 3917).
23 Neumann to LJ, 29 April 1912 (JA v, 26).
24 LJ to Nejedlý, 5 May 1912 (Mišurec 2002, 46).
25 *LJOLP*, 103.
26 *LČL*, i, 795–7.
27 Gellner to LJ, undated, before 17 June 1912 (*JODA*, BR47).
28 Vach to LJ, 16 June 1912 (BmJA, A 376).
29 Štědroň 1953a, 248, fn. 28.
30 LJ to Vach, 16 July 1912 (BmJA B 2460).
31 Váňa to LJ, 5 July 1912 (BmJA A 380).
32 Bakešová to LJ, 23 July 1912 (Sedláčková 2001, no. 93).
33 Much of what follows comes from Smetana 1948, 43–9; for a more detailed redaction see *MLWJ*, 111–14.
34 Věra Janáčková to LJ, 17 July 1912 (BmJA, A 5712).
35 Smetana 1948, 44.
36 LJ to ZJ, undated, postmarked 7 Sept 1909 (BmJA, A 4957).
37 Quoted in Vejvodová 2004, 26.
38 Smetana 1948, 44.
39 Smetana 1948, 44.
40 LJ to AR, 12 Aug 1912 (JA iv, 150).
41 Melnikova 1997, 356.
42 LJ to AR, 12 Aug 1912 (JA iv, 150).
43 Veselý 1924, 70–1.
44 This and further quotations from Smetana 1948, 48–9.
45 Veselý 1924, 71.
46 Štědroň 1939.
47 LJ to ZJ, undated, postmarked 21? Aug 1912 (BmJA, A 3811).
48 ZJ to LJ, 25 Aug 1912 (BmJA, A 2832).
49 Píša to LJ, 20 Sept 1912 (BmJA, D 93).
50 LJ to AR, 22 Sept 1912 (JA iv, 150–1).
51 JA v, 151, fn. 213.
52 AR to LJ, 25 Sept 1912 (JA iv, 151).
53 LJ to AR, 1 Oct 1912 (JA iv, 152).
54 LJ to AR, 30 Sept 1912 (JA iv, 152).
55 AR to LJ, 2 Oct 1912 (JA iv, 152).
56 LJ to AR, 3 Oct 1912 (JA iv, 152).
57 AR to LJ, 4 Oct 1912 (JA iv, 153).
58 Urbánek to LJ, 3 Oct 1912 (BmJA, D 87).
59 Spilka to LJ, 18 Oct 1912 (BmJA, B 713).
60 *HR*, vi (1912–13), 110.
61 Gellner to LJ, 23 Oct 1912 (*JODA*, BR50).
62 Tyrrell 1968, 120–2.

63 Ševčík to LJ, 3 Nov 1912 (BmJA, A 441).
64 Trkanová 1964, 72.
65 Smetana 1948, 51.
66 *MLWJ*, 114.
67 *MLWJ*, 114.
68 Trkanová 1964, 73; see also *MLWJ*, 114.
69 Smetana 1948, 51–2.
70 LJ to Elgart, 9 Dec 1912 (BmJA, A 6544).
71 *JKPU*, 62–3.
72 Hoffmeister to LJ, 25 Nov 1912 (BmJA, B 133).
73 *JAWO*, 350.

64: Janáček's illnesses I

1 *MLWJ*.
2 *IL*.

65: 1913

1 Štech to LJ, 4 Feb 1913 (JA iv, 188).
2 Ševčík to LJ, undated, postmarked 20 Feb 1914 (*JODA*, OS88).
3 Štech to LJ, 28 February 1914 (BmJA, D 799).
4 LJ to Pauk (draft letter), 1 March 1913 (Straková 1956, 241).
5 Štech to LJ, 3 March 1913 (JA iv, 189).
6 Ševčík to LJ, undated, after 3 March 1913 (*JODA*, OS89).
7 Štech to LJ, 22 March 1913 (*JODA*, OS90).
8 LJ to AR, 26 March 1913 (JA iv, 153–4).
9 AR to LJ, 27 March 1913 (JA iv, 154).
10 Pauk to LJ, 5 April 1913 (*JODA*, OS91).
11 AR to LJ, 6 April 1913 (*JODA*, OS92).
12 Vach to LJ, 7 April 1913 (BmJA, A 2519).
13 AR to LJ, 13 April 1913 (BmJA, A 6607).
14 LJ to AR, 14 April 1913 (*JODA*, OS93).
15 Svobodová to Doubravský, 16 April 1913 (BmJA, A 3931).
16 LJ to Zemánek, 28 April 1913 (*SKV*, D/6, ix).
17 LJ to Šourek, 20 Feb 1920 (JA iv, 169).
18 Gellner to LJ, 23 May 1913 (*JODA*, BR51).
19 LJ to Zemánek, 28 April 1913 (*SKV*, D/6, ix).
20 *MLWJ*, 115.
21 LJ to AR, 9 May and 11 May 1913 (JA iv, 156).
22 Zemánek to LJ, 22 May 1913 (BmJA, D 678).
23 Pauk to LJ, 27 May 1913 (JA iv, 189).
24 'Ze soudní síň: spor skladatele Janáčka a Městským divadlem na Král. Vinohradech' [From the court room: the dispute between the composer Janáček and the Town Theatre in Král. Vinohrady], *Národní politika* (4 June 1913), partly quoted in Straková 1956, 243–4.
25 LJ to AR, 19 June 1913 (JA iv, 157).
26 *Národní obzor* (27 June 1913), extract in *JODA*, OS70.
27 LJ to AR, 17 July 1913 (JA iv, 158).
28 Pauk to LJ, 10 July 1913 (JA iv, 190).
29 Čelanský to LJ, undated 18? July 1913 (*JODA*, OS98).
30 LJ to ZJ, 25 July 1913 (BmJA, A3861).
31 LJ to ZJ, 6 Aug 1913 (BmJA, A 3920).

32 Trkanová 1964, 73.
33 LJ to ZJ, undated, 8 Aug? 1913 (BmJA, A 3862).
34 LJ to Veselý, 8 Aug 1913 (JA viii, 33).
35 Trkanová 1964, 73.
36 LJ to Veselý, 26 Aug 1913 (JA viii, 34).
37 Trkanová 1964, 73.
38 Zemánek to LJ, 18 Aug 1913 (JA iv, 163, fn. 230).
39 Zemánek to LJ, 29 Aug 1913 (JA iv, 163, fn. 230).
40 Smetana 1948, 53.
41 *MLWJ*, 116.
42 Trkanová 1964, 74.
43 Čelanský to LJ, 1 Sept 1913 (Straková 1956, 248).
44 Dr Karel Marek to LJ, 1 Sept 1913 (*JODA*, OS101).
45 Čelanský to LJ, 14 Sept 1913 (Straková 1956, 249–50).
46 Pauk to LJ, 20 Sept 1913 (JA iv, 190).
47 Čelanský to LJ, 24 Sept 1913 (*JODA*, OS104).
48 Čelanský to LJ, 18 Oct 1913 (*JODA*, OS105).
49 Ševčík to LJ, undated Dec? 1913 (Straková 1956, 251).
50 LJ to Pražák, 13 Sept 1913 (*SKV*, B/3, xi).
51 Nebuška to LJ, 18 Sept 1913 (BmJA, D 110).
52 Elgart to LJ, 21 Sept 1913 (BmJA, B 122).
53 Vach to LJ, 18 Dec 1913 N.S. (BmJA, A 1433) and 17 Dec 1913 N.S. (BmJA, A 1433).
54 Elgart to LJ, 8 Dec 1913 (BmJA, B 114).
55 *BUE*, 187–8.
56 BmJA, S10–12.
57 LJ to AR, 15 Dec 1913 (JA iv, 159).
58 AR to LJ, 22 Dec 1913 (BmJA, A 6609).
59 LJ to Veselý, 28 Dec 1913 (JA viii, 35–6).
60 LJ to Veselý, 28 Dec 1913 (JA viii, 35–6).

66: 1914a (January to 28 July)

1 LJ to ZJ, undated, postmarked 1? Jan 1914 (BmJA, B 961).
2 Spilka to LJ, 21 Jan 1914 (BmJA, B 124).
3 Blažek 1971, 112–13.
4 Zubatý to LJ, 26 Jan 1914 (BmJA, D 102).
5 Zemánek to LJ, 2 Feb 1914 (BmJA, D 111).
6 LJ to Zemánek, 25 Feb 1914 (*SKV*, D/6, x).
7 Fuksa to LJ, 2 March 1914 (*JODA*, OS106).
8 Zemánek to LJ, 22 April 1914 (BmJA, B 834).
9 LJ to Chvála, 20 March 1914 (Pn, MČH).
10 Zemánek to LJ, 10 March 1914 (BmJA, D 114).
11 JA iv, 164, fn. 229.
12 LJ to ZJ, undated, postmarked 14? March 1914 (BmJA, A 3771).
13 LJ to Zemánek, 16 March 1914 (*SKV*, D/6, x–xi).
14 Zemánek to LJ, 17 March 1914 (JA iv, 163, fn. 230).
15 LJ to Zemánek, 18 March 1914 (BmJA, B 753).
16 LJ to Chvála, 20 March 1914 (Pn, MČH).
17 LJ to ZJ, undated, postmarked 23 March 1914 (BmJA, A 3901).
18 Křička 1917.
19 Spilka to LJ, 27 March 1914 (BmJA, B 748).

20 LJ to Vach, 5 April 1914 (BmJA, A 3934).
21 LJ to ZJ, undated, postmarked 4? April 1914 (BmJA, A 3767).
22 JA ii, 13, fn. *.
23 LJ to ZJ, undated, postmarked 4? April 1914 (BmJA, A 3767).
24 LJ to Veselý, 8 April 1914 (JA viii, 37–8).
25 LJ to AR, 14 April 1914 (JA iv, 159).
26 JA iv, 160, fn. 224.
27 Křička to LJ, 6 May 1914 (BmJA, A 418).
28 LJ to AR, 10 May 1914 (JA iv, 160).
29 AR to LJ, 11 May 1914 (JA iv, 160–2).
30 LJ to AR, 12 May 1914 (JA iv, 162).
31 Spilka to LJ, 23 May 1914 (BmJA, B 125).
32 Trkanová 1964, 75.
33 *MLWJ*, 116–19.
34 Smetana 1948, 58–9.
35 Röder to Barvič & Novotný, 20 June 1914 (BmJA, A 4853).
36 Komarov to LJ, 3 July 1914 (*JODA*, OS107).
37 *MLWJ*, 119.
38 *MLWJ*, 120.
39 LJ to Veselý, 17 July 1914 (JA viii, 38–9).
40 LJ to ZJ, 20 July 1914 (Racek 1941).
41 *LJOLP*, 98.
42 *MLWJ*, 120.
43 Smetana 1948, 60.
44 Trkanová 1964, 77.

67: Janáček's finances II: 1904–14

68: Janáček at sixty

1 *JODA*, JP111.

Bibliography

The purpose of this bibliography is to provide full details of the sources consulted in writing this volume. It begins with a list of abbreviations covering periodicals, dictionaries and frequently cited works, followed by an alphabetical listing by author.

ADKD Milan Kuna, ed.: *Antonín Dvořák: korespondence a dokumenty: kritické vydání* [Antonín Dvořák: correspondence and documents: critical edition], 10 vols. (Editio Supraphon/Bärenreiter, Prague, 1987–2004)

BH Jarmila Procházková and Bohumír Volný: *Born in Hukvaldy* (Moravian Museum, Brno, 1995) [Eng. trans. of *Narozen na Hukvaldech* (Moravské zemské muzeum, Brno, 1994)]

BmJA Janáček Archive, Brno, Hudební oddělení Moravského zemského muzea [Music Division of the Moravian Regional Museum]

BSP *Brno: Staré pohlednice/Alte Poskarten/Old Postcards*, ed. Vladimír Filip, 14 vols. (Josef Filip, Brno, n.d.)

BUE Ernst Hilmar, ed.: *Leoš Janáček: Briefe an die Universal Edition* (Hans Schneider, Tutzing, 1988)

ČMM *Časopis Moravského musea/muzea: vědy společenské* [journal, 1901–]

CO John Tyrrell: *Czech Opera* (Cambridge University Press, Cambridge, 1988)

ČSHS Gracian Černušák, Bohumír Štědroň and Zdenko Nováček: *Československý hudební slovník: osob a institucí* [Czechoslovak music dictionary: people and institutions], 2 vols. (Státní hudební vydavatelství, Prague, 1963–5)

DHM Jiří Sehnal and Jiří Vysloužil: *Dějiny hudby na Moravě* [The history of music in Moravia], Vlastivěda moravská: země a lid, xii (Muzejní a vlastivědná společnost v Brně, Brno, 2001)

HL *Hudební listy* [journal, 1884–8]

HM	*Hudební matice* [publisher]
HR	*Hudební revue* [journal, 1908–20]
HTD	Leoš Janáček: *Hudebně teoretické dílo*[Music theory works], ed. Zdeněk Blažek
	i: *Spisy, studie a dokumenty* [Writings, studies and documents] (Supraphon, Prague, 1968)
	ii: *Studie, Úplná nauka o harmonii* [Studies, Complete harmony manual] (Supraphon, Prague, 1974)
HV	*Hudební věda* [journal, 1961–]
HŽ	Svatava Přibáňová, ed.: *Hádanka života: dopisy Leoše Janáčka Kamile Stösslové* [The riddle of life: the letters of Leoš Janáček to Kamila Stösslová] (Opus musicum, Brno, 1990; Eng. trans. as *Intimate Letters*; see *IL*)
IB	Jakob Knaus, ed.: *'Intime Briefe' 1879/80 aus Leipzig und Wien* (Leoš Janáček-Gesellschaft, Zürich, 1985)
IL	John Tyrrell, ed. and trans.: *Intimate Letters: Leoš Janáček to Kamila Stösslová* (Faber & Faber, London, 1994) [Eng. trans. abridged, of *HŽ*]
JA	Janáčkův archiv, first series, general editors Vladimír Helfert (JA i) and Jan Racek (JA ii–ix)
JA i	Artuš Rektorys, ed.: *Korespondence Leoše Janáčka s Artušem Rektorysem* [The correspondence of Leoš Janáček with Artuš Rektorys] (HM, Prague, 1934) [enlarged 2/1949 = JA iv]
JA ii	—: *Korespondence Leoše Janáčka s Otakarem Ostrčilem* (HM, Prague, 1948)
JA iii	—: *Korespondence Leoše Janáčka s F.S. Procházkou* (HM, Prague, 1949)
JA iv	—: *Korespondence Leoše Janáčka s Artušem Rektorysem* (HM, Prague, 1949 = enlarged second edition of JA i)
JA v	—: *Korespondence Leoše Janáčka s libretisty Výletů Broučkových* [The correspondence of Leoš Janáček with the librettists of *The Excursions of Mr Brouček*] (HM, Prague, 1950)
JA vi	—: *Korespondence Leoše Janáčka s Gabrielou Horvátovou* (HM, Prague, 1950)
JA vii	—: *Korespondence Leoše Janáčka s Karlem Kovařovicem a ředitelstvím Národního divadla* [The correspondence of Leoš Janáček with Karel Kovařovic and the directorate of the National Theatre] (HM, Prague, 1950)
JA viii	Jan Racek and Artuš Rektorys, ed.: *Korespondence Leoše Janáčka s Marií Calmou a MUDr Františkem Veselým* (Orbis, Prague, 1951)
JA ix	—: *Korespondence Leoše Janáčka s Maxem Brodem* (Státní nakladatelství krásné literatury, hudby a umění, Prague, 1953)

JAWO   Nigel Simeone, John Tyrrell and Alena Němcová: *Janáček's Works: a catalogue of the music and writings of Leoš Janáček* (Oxford University Press, Oxford, 1997)

JKPU   Ludvík Kundera: *Janáček a Klub přátel umění* [Janáček and the Club of the Friends of Art] (Velehrad, Olomouc, 1948)

JODA   John Tyrrell: *Janáček's Operas: a documentary account* (Faber & Faber, London, 1992)

JVD   Bohumír Štědroň, ed.: *Janáček ve vzpomínkách a dopisech* [Janáček in reminiscences and letters] (Artia, Prague, 1946; rev. Eng. trans., 1955; see *LR*)

JVŠ   Ludvík Kundera: *Janáčkova varhanická škola* [Janáček's Organ School] (Velehrad, Olomouc, 1948)

LA PNP   Literární archiv Památníku národního písemnictví v Praze [Literary archive of the Memorial collection of national literature, Prague]

LČL   Vladimír Forst and Jiří Opelík, ed.: *Lexikon české literatury: osobnosti, díla, instituce* [Dictionary of Czech literature: people, works, institutions], 3 vols. (Academia, Prague, 1985–)

LD   Leoš Janáček: *Literární dílo (1875–1928)* [Literary works (1875–1928)], ed. Theodora Straková and Eva Drlíková, 2 vols. (Editio Janáček, Brno, 2003)

LJOLP   Jiří Vysloužil, ed.: *Leoš Janáček o lidové písni a lidové hudbě* [Leoš Janáček on folksong and folk music] (Státní nakladatelství krásné literatury, hudby a umění, Prague, 1955)

LJPT   Vladimír Helfert: *Leoš Janáček: obraz životního a uměleckého boje*, i: *V poutech tradice* [Leoš Janáček: a picture of struggle in life and art, i: In the bonds of tradition] (Oldřich Pazdírek, Brno, 1939)

LN   *Lidové noviny* [daily newspaper, 1893– (with interruptions)]

LR   Bohumír Štědroň, ed.: *Leoš Janáček: Letters and Reminiscences*, trans. Geraldine Thomsen (Artia, Prague, 1955) [rev., in Eng., of *JVD*]

MLWJ   Zdenka Janáčková: *My Life with Janáček: the memoirs of Zdenka Janáčková*, ed. and trans. John Tyrrell (Faber & Faber, London, 1998)

MO   *Moravská orlice* [daily newspaper, 1863–1943]

MSN   *Masarykův slovník naučný* [Masaryk's encyclopedia], 7 vols. (Československý kompas, Prague, 1925–33)

NG2   ed. Stanley Sadie and John Tyrrell: *The New Grove Dictionary of Music and Musicians*, second edition, 29 vols. (Macmillan, London, 2001)

OM   *Opus musicum* [journal, 1969–]

OSN   *Ottův slovník naučný* [Otto's encyclopedia], 28 vols. (J. Otto, Prague, 1888–1909)

RSN   Frant. Lad. Rieger, ed. (from vol. iii with J. Malý): *Slovník naučný* [Encyclopedia], 11 vols. (I.L. Kober [Kober & Markgraf in vol. i], Prague, 1860–74)

SČHK	Jiří Fukač and Jiří Vysloužil, ed.: *Slovník české hudební kultury* [A dictionary of Czech musical culture] (Supraphon, Prague, 1997)
VDKS	Bohumír Štědroň, ed.: *Leoš Janáček: vzpomínky, dokumenty, korespondence a studie* [Reminiscences, documents, correspondence and studies] (Supraphon, Prague, 1986)
ŽJJ	Vincenc Janáček: *Životopis Jiříka Janáčka* [The autobiography of Jiří Janáček], ed. Jiří Sehnal; with Leoš Janáček: *Dopisy strýci/Dopisy matky* [Letters to his uncle/Letters from his mother], ed. Svatava Přibáňová (Opus musicum, Brno, 1985)
Ambros 1929	Emanuel Ambros: 'Z korespondence Leoše Janáčka' [From Leoš Janáček's correspondence], *Tempo*, ix (1929–30), 24–6
Audus 1996	Mark Audus: 'Chybějící pojítko: rekonstrukce Její pastorkyně z r. 1904' [The missing link: a reconstruction of the 1904 *Jenůfa*], *OM*, xxviii (1996), 186–96
Audus 2006	—: *The 1904 Version of Janáček's 'Jenůfa': sources, reconstruction, commentary* (doctoral dissertation, University of Nottingham, 2006)
Bajgarová 2005	Jitka Bajgarová: *Hudební spolky v Brně a jejich role při utváření 'hudebního obrazu' města 1860–1918* [Music societies in Brno and their role in creating a 'musical picture' of the town 1860–1918] (Centrum pro studium demokracie a kultury, Brno, 2005)
Balhar 1914	Jak. Balhar: *Průvodce Lázněmi Luhačovicemi na Moravě a 75 výletů do okolí* [A guide to Luhačovice spa in Moravia and 75 excursions into the surrounding countryside] (F. Hložek, Luhačovice, rev. 3/1914)
Balhar 1927	— and others: *Lázně Luhačovice 1902–1927* [Luhačovice spa 1902–27] (n.p., n.d. [Luhačovice, 1927])
Bártová 1998	Jindřiška Bártová: 'Leoš Janáček, c.k. učitel hudby' [Leoš Janáček, imperial and royal music teacher], *OM*, xxx (1998), 131–9
Bauerová 1992	Anna Bauerová: *Tisíc jmen v kalendáři* [A thousand names in the calendar] (Šulc, Prague, 1992)
Beckerman 1994	Michael Beckerman: *Janáček as Theorist* (Pendragon Press, Stuyvesant, NY, 1994)
Beckerman and Bauer 1995	Michael Beckerman and Glen Bauer, ed.: *Leoš Janáček and Czech Music: International Conference at St Louis, Missouri 1988* (Pendragon Press, Stuyvesant, NY, 1995)
Blatný 1969	Josef Blatný: 'Janáček učitel a teoretik' [Janáček: teacher and theoretician], *OM*, i (1969), 97–100
Blaukopf 1979	Kurt Blaukopf: 'Gustav Mahler und die tschechische Oper', *Österreichische Musikzeitschrift*, xxxiv (1979), 285–8
Blažek 1971	Vilém Blažek: 'Neznámé marginálie Leoše Janáčka' [Unknown marginalia concerning Leoš Janáček], *OM*, iii (1971), 112–13
Brod 1924	Max Brod: *Leoš Janáček: život a dílo* [Life and works] (Hudební matice Umělecké besedy, Prague, 1924; Ger. original, Wiener

Philharmonischer Verlag, Vienna, 1925, enlarged Universal Edition, Vienna, 2/1956)

Burghauser 1961   Jarmil Burghauser, ed.: Antonín Dvořák: *Dimitrij: kritické vydání* [*Dimitrij*: critical edition (of the libretto)] (Státní hudební vydavatelství, Prague, 1961)

Burghauser 1991   Jarmil Burghauser: 'Dvořákova a Janáčkova Dumka' [Dvořák's and Janáček's dumka], *Hudební rozhledy*, lxiv (1991), 86–9

Černík 1933   Jos. Černík: 'Vzpomínání na Leoše Janáčka' [Remembering Leoš Janáček], *LN* (12 Aug 1933); partly reprinted in *JVD*, 37–8; Eng. trans. in *LR*, 30–1

Černohorská   Milena Černohorská: 'K problematice vzniku Janáčkovy teorie
1957   nápěvků' [On the problems of the origin of Janáček's speech-melody theory], *ČMM*, xlii (1957), 165–78

Černohorská   —: 'Nápěvková teorie Leoše Janáčka' [Leoš Janáček's speech-melody
1958   theory], *ČMM*, xliii (1958), 129–44

Chlubna 1924   Osvald Chlubna: 'Teoretické učení Leoše Janáčka' [The theoretical teaching of Leoš Janáčka], *Hudební rozhledy*, i (1924–5), 57–63, 77–78, 114–16, 129–32

Chlubna 1955   —: 'Janáček – učitel' [Janáček as teacher], *Musikologie*, iii (1955), 51–8

Christiansen   Paul Victor Christiansen: *Leoš Janáček's Conception of Speech Melody*
2002   (doctoral dissertation, University of California at Davis, 2002)

Cmunt 1949   Eduard Cmunt and others: *Almanach lázní Československé republiky* [Almanach of spas of the Czechoslovak Republic] (Balneologický ústav Karlovy university v Praze and Balneologické oddelenie Štátného zdravnotne-sociálneho ústavu v Bratislavě, Prague, 1949)

Dřímal and Peša   Jaroslav Dřímal and Václav Peša, ed.: *Dějiny města Brna* [The history of
1973   Brno], ii (Národní výbor města Brna/Blok, Brno, 1973)

Drlíková 2004   Eva Drlíková, ed.: *Leoš Janáček: život a dílo v datech a obrazech/ chronology of his life and work* (Opus musicum, Brno, 2004)

Efmertová 1995   Marcela C. Efmertová: *České země v letech 1848–1918* [The Czech lands in the years 1848–1918] (Libri, Prague, 1998)

Eichler 1904   Karel Eichler: *Životopis a skladby Pavla Křížkovského* [The biography and compositions of Pavel Křížkovský] (Knihtiskárna benediktinů rajhradských, Brno, 1904)

Erickson 1964   John Erickson: *Panslavism* (The Historical Association, n.p., 1964)

Firkušný 1938   Leoš Firkušný, ed.: 'Dopisy Leoše Janáčka z archivu Družstva Národního divadla v Brně' [Janáček's letters from the archive of the Družstvo of the National Theatre in Brno], *Musikologie*, i (1938), 130–9

Fischmann 1986   Zdenka E. Fischmann, ed.: *Janáček–Newmarch Correspondence* (Kabel Publishers, Rockville, Maryland, 1986)

Flodrová 1984   Milena Flodrová, Blažena Galasovská and Jaroslav Vodička: *Seznam ulic města Brna s vývojem jejich pojmenování* [Catalogue of streets of the town of Brno with the evolution of their naming] (Muzejní a vlastivědná společnost, Brno, enlarged 2/1984); for continuation see Zřídkaveselý 1996

Flodrová 2003   Milena Flodrová: *Brno v proměnách času: malá zamyšlení* [Brno in the changes of time: brief reflections (Šimon Ryšavý, Brno, 2003)

Fukač 1963a   Jiří Fukač: 'Kritický vztah Zdeňka Nejedlého k Leoši Janáčkovi' [Zdeněk Nejedlý's critical relationship to Leoš Janáček], *Sborník Václavkova Olomouc 1963*, 239–50

Fukač 1963b   —: 'Leoš Janáček a Zdeněk Nejedlý', *Sborník prací filosofické fakulty Brněnské university*, F7 (1963), 5–29

Grufík 1974   Fr. Grufík [= Fr. Kolář]: 'Vzpomínka na Leoše Janáčka' [A reminiscence of Leoš Janáček], *Luhačovický zpravodaj* (1974), Aug, 20–2

Hanák 1959   Mirko Hanák: 'Z přednášek Leoše Janáčka o sčasování a skladbě' [From Leoš Janáček's lectures about *sčasování* and composition], *Leoš Janáček: sborník statí a studií* (Hudební rozhledy, Praha, 1959), 137–74

Helfert 1923   Vladimír Helfert, ed.: *Památník Pěveckého sdružení moravských učitelů: vydaný k jubileu jeho dvacetileté činnosti r. 1923* [Memorial volume of the Moravian Teachers' Choral Society: published on the jubilee of its twenty-year activity] (PSMU, Brno, 1923)

Hembry 1997   Phyllis Hembry, ed. L.W. Cowie and E.E. Cowie: *British Spas from 1815 to the Present: a social history* (Athlone Press, London, 1997)

Henig 2000   Robin Marantz Henig: *A Monk and Two Peas: the story of Gregor Mendel and the discovery of genetics* (Weidenfeld & Nicholson, London, 2000)

Hornové 1903   Václav, Antonín and Josef Hornové: *Česká zpěvohra* [Czech opera] (Grosman & Svoboda, Prague, [1903])

Hrabalová 1988   Olga Hrabalová: 'Leoš Janáček o třídění moravských lidových písní' [Leoš Janáček on the classification of Moravian folksongs], *Náropísné aktuality*, xxv/4 (1988), 217–27

Iltis 1932   Hugo Iltis: *Life of Mendel*, trans. Eden Paul and Cedar Paul (Allen & Unwin, London, 1932, reprinted 1966)

Jančář 1988   Antonín Jančář: *Luhačovice: průvodce* [Luhačovice: a guide] (Olympia, Prague, 2/1988)

Jančář 2000   Josef Jančář and others: *Lidová kultura na Moravě* [Folk culture in Moravia], Vlastivěda moravská: země a lid, x (Muzejní a vlastivědná společnost v Brně, Brno, 2000)

Kaprál 1924   Václav Kaprál: 'Janáčkův poměr k opeře' [Janáček's attitude to opera], *Hudební rozhledy*, i (1924–5), 63–6

Kašlík 1936   Hynek Kašlík: 'Leoš Janáček – dirigent' [Leoš Janáček – conductor], *Hudební věstník*, xxviii (1935); xxxix (1936); reprinted as booklet, Prague, 1936, in Knihovna Unie čsl. hudebníků z povolání

Kašlík 1938   —: 'Retuše Karla Kovařovice v Janáčkově opeře Její pastorkyně' [Karel Kovařovic's 'retouchings' in Janáček's opera *Jenůfa*], *Hudební věstník*,

	xxxi (1938), 112–13, 130–1, 142–3, 159–60; reprinted separately (Unie čes. hudebníků z povolání, Prague, 1938)
Knappová 1996	Miloslava Knappová: *Jak se bude Vaše dítě jmenovat?* [What will your child be called?] (Prague, Academia, 1996)
Knaus 1982	Jakob Knaus, ed.: *Leoš Janáček-Materialien* (Leoš Janáček-Gesellschaft, Zürich, 1982)
Kodl 1929	Al. Kodl: 'Janáček a Písek' [Janáček and Písek], *Otavan*, xii (1929), 90–2, 123–4
Kohn 1960	Hans Kohn: *Pan-Slavism: its History and Ideology* (Vintage Books, New York, 2/1960)
Koukal 1998	Petr Koukal: 'Korespondence nakladatele Emila Šolce s Leošem Janáčkem' [The correspondence of the publisher Emil Šolc with Leoš Janáček], *Vlastivědný sborník vysočiny: oddíl věd společenských*, xi (1998), 363–75
Kožík 1983	František Kožík: *Po zarostlém chodníčku* [On the overgrown path] (Vyšehrad, Prague, 3/1983)
Kožíšek 1938	Alois V. Kožíšek, ed.: *Brno: město a okolí* [Brno: town and surroundings] (Národohospodářská propagace Českolovenska, Brno, 1938)
Křížek 2002	Vladimír Křížek: *Obrazy z dějin lázeňství* [Pictures from the history of the spa] (Avicenum, Prague, 2/2002)
Krones 1984	Hartmut Krones: 'Leoš Janáčeks Studienaufenthalt in Wien', *Österreichische Musikzeitschrift*, xxxix (1984), 657–61, reprinted in *IB*, 363–7
Kuča 2000	Karel Kuča: *Brno: vývoj města, předměstí a připojených vesnic* [Brno: evolution of the city, suburbs and attached villages] (Baset, Prague–Brno, 2000)
Kulka 1990	Jiří Kulka: *Leoš Janáček's Aesthetic Thinking* (Academia, Prague, 1990)
Kunc 1911	Jan Kunc: 'Leoš Janáček', *HR*, iv (1911), 121–34, 185–9
Kunc 1933	—: 'Vzpomínky na premiéru Její pastorkyně' [Reminiscences of the première of *Jenůfa*], *Divadelní list Zemského divadla v Brně*, ix (1933–4), 74–81; abridged in *JVD*, 153–5
Kundera 1955	Ludvík Kundera: 'Janáčkova tvorba klavírní' [Janáček's piano works], *Musikologie*, iii (1955), 306–29
Kvasnica 1974	Rudolf Kvasnica: 'Leoš Janáček jako učitel ve vzpomínkách Rudolfa Kvasnici' [Janáček as teacher in the reminiscences of Rudolf Kvasnica], *OM*, vi (1974), 172–4; Ger. trans. in Knaus 1982, 65–7
Květ 1946	J.M. Květ, ed.: *Živá slova Josefa Suka* [Josef Suk in his own words] (Prague, 1946)
Kyas 1993a	Vojtěch Kyas: 'Janáček se neměl o koho opřít?' [Did Janáček have no-one to lean on?], *OM*, xxv (1993), 33–42
Kyas 1993b	—: 'Slavná hudební rodina Nerudů' [The famous Neruda musical family], *OM*, xxv (1993), 228–41

Kyas 1995   —: *Slavné hudební osobnosti v Brně/Berühmte Musikpersönlichkeiten in Brünn (1859–1914)* (Opus musicum, Brno, 1995)

Lázně 1927   *Lázně Luhačovice 1902–1927* [The spa of Luhačovice 1902–27] (Ředitelství Lázní Luhačovic, Luhačovice, 1927)

Lažnovský 1926   Bohuslav Lažnovský: *Průvodce po Československé republice* [A guide to the Czechoslovak Republic] (Orbis, Prague, 1926)

Lébl 1964   Vladimír Lébl: *Vítězslav Novák: život a dílo* [Vítězslav Novák: life and work] (Československá akademie věd, Prague, 1964)

Lichtner 1911   Rudolf Lichtner, ed.: *Památník zpěváckého spolku Hlaholu v Praze vydaný na oslavu 5otileté činnosti 1861–1911* [Memorial volume of the choral society 'Hlahol' in Prague published in celebration of fifty years of activity 1861–1911] (Hlahol, Prague, 1911)

Löwenbach 1933   Jan Löwenbach: 'Clona se rozvírá a uzavírá' [The curtain opens and closes], *Sedmdesát let Umělecké besedy 1863–1933*, ed. František Skácelík (Umělecká beseda, Prague, 1933), 187–9

Ludvová 1989   Jitka Ludvová: *Česká hudební teorie novější doby 1850–1900* [Czech music theory: the more recent period 1850–1900] (Academie, Prague, 1989)

Machoň 1912   Josef Machoň: 'Pěvecké zápasy v Plzni' [Singing competitions in Plzeň], *HR*, v (1912), 334–7

Mazálek 1914   Vladimír Mazálek: 'Veselé i trpké chvíle mistrovy: vzpomínka k šedesátinám mistra Leoše Janáčka' [The maestro's merry and bitter moments: memoir for the sixtieth birthday of Maestro Leoš Janáček], *Věstník Ústř. spolku jednot učit. na Moravě*, xiii/41 (10 July 1914), 999–1000

Melnikova 1997   Marina Stejskalová-Melnikova: 'Janáčkova sbírka ruských nápěvků mluvy' [Janáček's collection of Russian speech-melodies], *HV*, xxxiv (1997), 333–57

Mikota 1933   Václav Mikota: 'Leoš Janáček a Hudební matice', *Sedmdesát let Umělecké besedy 1863–1933*, ed. František Skácelík (Umělecká beseda, Prague, 1933), 190–4

Mišurec 2002   Zdeněk Mišurec, ed.: *Leoš Janáček: korespondence a studie z dokumentačních fondů Etnologického ústavu AV ČR v Praze* [Leoš Janáček: correspondence and studies from the documentary funds of the Ethnographical Institute of the Academy of Sciences of the Czech Republic in Prague] (Academia, Prague, 2002)

Moor 1947   Karel Moor: *V dlani osudu: vzpomínky českého hudebníka* [In the hand of fate: the reminiscences of a Czech musician] (Janata, Nový Bydžov, 1947)

Nejedlý 1911   Zdeněk Nejedlý: *Česká moderní zpěvohra po Smetanovi* [Czech modern opera after Smetana] (n.p., n.d. [Prague, 1911])

Němcová 1971   Alena Němcová: *Profil brněnské opery v kontextu s dějinami českého divadla v Brně v letech 1894–1904* [A profile of the Brno opera in the context of the history of the Czech theatre in Brno 1894–1904] (doctoral dissertation, University of Brno, 1971)

Němcová 1974 —: 'Brněnská premiéra Janáčkovy Její pastorkyně' [The Brno première of Janáček's *Jenůfa*], *ČMM*, lix (1974), 133–46; Ger. trans. in Knaus 1982, 7–22

Němcová 1994 —: 'Horňácké vzory Janáčkovy Její pastorkyně' [Horňácko models in Janáček's *Jenůfa*], *OM*, xxvi (1994), 57–67

Němeček 1968 Jan Němeček: *Opera Národního divadla v období Karla Kovařovice 1900–1920* [The opera of the (Prague) National Theatre in the time of Karel Kovařovic 1900–20], 2 vols. (Divadelní ústav, Prague, 1968–9)

Neumann 1940 Augustin Neumann: *Z pamětí rodiny Neumannovy z Olešnice na Moravě* [From the family memoirs of the Neumanns from Olešnice in Moravia] (Augustin Neumann, Brno, 1940)

Novák 1946 Vítězslav Novák: *O sobě a o jiných* [About myself and others] (Jos. R. Vilímek, Prague, 1946)

Novák 1957 Přemysl Novák: 'Její pastorkyňa – dílo bolestí' [*Jenůfa* – a work of pain], *Slovenská hudba*, i (1957), 142–4

Novák 1962 —: 'Vznik Janáčkova sboru Vínek' [The origins of Janáček's chorus *The Wreath*], *Hudební rozhledy*, xv (1962), 367–70

Nováková 1956 Eva Nováková: *Opera v Prozatímním divadle v Brně v letech 1884–1894* [Opera in the Provisional Theatre in Brno 1884–94] (diploma dissertation, University of Brno, 1956)

Orel 2003 Vítězslav Orel: *Gregor Mendel a počátky genetiky* [Gregor Mendel and the beginnings of genetics] (Academia, Prague, 2003)

Pala 1953 František Pala: 'Janáček a Národní divadlo' [Janáček and the National Theatre], *Hudební rozhledy*, vi (1953), 882–91

Pala 1955 —: 'Jevištní dílo Leoše Janáčka' [The stage works of Leoš Janáček], *Musikologie*, iii (1955), 61–210

Patzaková and A.J. Patzaková and Mirko Očadlík, ed.: *Sborník prací k padesátým*
Očadlík 1929 *narozeninám profesora dra Zdeňka Nejedlého* [Festschrift for the fiftieth birthday of Professor Dr Zdeněk Nejdlý] (Borový, Prague, 1929)

Pearl 2005 Jonathan Geoffrey Secora Pearl: *The Music of Language: the notebooks of Leoš Janáček* (doctoral dissertation, University of California at Santa Barbara, 2005)

Pečman 1973 Rudolf Pečman: 'Leoš Janáček a některé směry moderního divadla (myšlenky a glosy)' [Leoš Janáček and some trends of modern theatre (thoughts and glosses)], *Na křižovatce umění: sborník k poctě šedsátin prof. dr. Artura Závodského, DrSc.* [At the crossroads of art: volume in honour of the sixtieth birthday of Prof. Dr Artur Závodský, DrSc.], ed. Zdeněk Srna and Jiří Krystýnek (Universita J.E. Purkyně, Brno, 1973), 353–8

Pečman 1978 —: 'Disjunkce estetických názorů a skladebného díla Leoše Janáčka'

[The disjunction between Janáček's aesthetic outlook and his music], *OM*, x (1978), 175–8

Pernes 1996   Jiří Pernes: *Pod Moravskou orlicí aneb Dějiny Moravanství* [Under the Moravian eagle, or A history of Moravianness] (Barrister & Principal, Brno, 1996)

Petrželka 1970   Ivan Petrželka: 'První slovníkové heslo o Leoši Janáčkovi' [The first dictionary article about Leoš Janáček], *OM*, ii (1970), 169–70

Plocek 1998   Jiři Plocek and others: *Nejstarší zvuková záznamy moravského a slovenského lidového zpěvu (z folkloristické činnosti Leoše Janáčka a jeho spolupracovníků/The Oldest Recordings of Moravian and Slovak Folk Singing (on folkloristic activities of Leoš Janáček and his collaborators)* (Gnosis, Brno, 1998), incl. 'Janáček's most important collaborators', 129–38 [Czech version, 30–6]

Plocek 2002   Jiř Plocek: *Folklorní mapa Moravy* [A folklore map of Moravia] (Gnosis, Brno, 2/2002)

Pracný 1994   Petr Pracný: *Český kalendář světců* [A Czech calendar of saints] (EWA, Prague, 1994)

Přibáňová 1984   Svatava Přibáňová: 'Nové prameny k rodokmenu Leoše Janáčka' [New sources for Leoš Janáček's family tree], *ČMM*, lxix (1984), 129–37

Přibáňová 1985   —, ed.: *Dopisy strýci/Dopisy matky* [Letters to his uncle/Letters from his mother], see *ŽJJ*

Přibáňová 1987   —: 'Neznámý slavnostní sbor Leoše Janáčka z roku 1878' [An unknown festive chorus by Leoš Janáček from 1878], *ČMM*, lxxii (1987), 205–14

Přibáňová 1998   —: 'Přehled inscenací jevištního díla Leoše Janáčka z let 1894–1998' [A survey of stage productions of Leoš Janáček's works 1894–1998], in S. Přibáňová and Z. Lederová-Protivová: *Svět Janáčkových oper/The World of Janáček's Operas* (Moravské zemské muzeum and others, Brno, 1998), 97–126

Procházka 1948   Jaroslav Procházka: *Lašské kořeny života i díla Leoše Janáčka* [The Lašsko roots of the life and work of Leoš Janáček] (Okresní a místní rada osvětová ve Frýdku–Místku, Frýdek–Místek, 1948)

Procházková 1990   Jarmila Procházková: 'Prezident a skladatel' [President and composer], *OM*, xxii (1990), 168–82

Procházková 1992   —: 'Janáčkovy tance: České, Moravské, Valašské, Lašské, Hanácké a Národní' [Janáček's dances: Czech, Moravian, Valachian, Lachian, Haná and folk], *OM*, xxiv (1992), 311–18; xxv (1993), 104–11, 164–71

Procházková 1995   —: 'Leoš Janáček a Česká národní kapela v Brně' [Leoš Janáček and the Czech National Orchestra in Brno], *OM*, xxvii (1995), 91–6

Procházková 1998a   —: 'Leoš Janáček jako organizátor orchestrálních koncertů v Brně 1889–1914' [Leoš Janáček as organizer of orchestral concerts in Brno 1889–1914], *OM*, xxx (1998), 50–59

Procházkova 1998b —: 'Janáček's folkloristic activites in the period context', in Plocek 1998, 102–112 [Czech version, Plocek 1998, 7–15]

Procházková 1998c —: 'Theoretical aspects of Janáček's folkloristic activities', in Plocek 1998, 112–16 [Czech version, Plocek 1998, 15–18]

Procházková 1998d —: 'A survey of Janáček's collecting activities', in Plocek 1998, 125–9 [Czech version, Plocek 1998, 26–9]

Procházková 2004 —: 'Hudební stránka Janáčkových folklorních záznamů' [The musical side of Janáček's folkloristic transcriptions], OM, xxxvi (2004), 20–6

Racek 1936 Jan Racek: 'Z duševní dílny Leoše Janáčka' [From Janáček's spiritual workshop], Divadelní list Zemského divadla v Brně, xi (1935–6); reprinted as booklet (Hudební archiv zemského musea, Brno, 1936)

Racek 1940 —: Bratří Mrštíkové a jejich citový vztah k Leoši Janáčkovi a Vítězslavu Novákovi [The Mrštík brothers and their emotional relationship with Leoš Janáček and Vítězslav Novák] (Moravské kolo spisovatelů v Brně, Brno, 1940)

Racek 1941 —: 'Janáček v přírodě a na cestách' [Janáček in nature and on his travels], Časopis turistů, liii (1941), 79–80

Racek 1955 —: 'Leoš Janáček a Praha' [Janáček and Prague], Musikologie, iii (1955), 11–50

Racek 1977 — : 'Janáčkův studijní pobyt v Lipsku' [Janáček's study trip to Leipzig], ČMM, lxii (1977), 75–82; originally published as 'Janáčeks Studienaufenthalt in Leipzig in den Jahren 1879–1880', 1843–1968: Hochschule für Musik Leipzig (Leipzig, 1968), ed. M. Wehnert, J. Froner and H. Schiller, 187–99

Sázavský 1900 Karel Sázavský: Dějiny filharmonického spolku Beseda brněnská od r. 1860–1900 [The history of the Brno Beseda Philharmonic Society from 1860 to 1900] (Beseda brněnská, Brno, 1900)

Schánilec 1961 Josef Schánilec: Za slávou: čtení o českých hudebnících v Rusku [After glory: reading about Czech musicians in Russia] (Svět sovětů, Prague, 1961)

Sedláčková 2001 Simona Sedláčková: Vzajemná korespondence Lucie Bakešové s Leošem Janáčkem [The correspondence between Lucie Bakešová and Leoš Janáček] (bachelor dissertation, Masaryk University, Brno, 2001)

Sehnal 1980 Jiří Sehnal: 'Das Musikrepertoire der Altbrünner Fundation unter Cyril Napp (1816–1818)', Sborník prací filosofické fakulty Brněnské university, H15 (1980), 63–78

Simeone 1991 Nigel Simeone: The First Editions of Leoš Janáček: a Bibliographical Catalogue (Hans Schneider, Tutzing, 1991)

Sís 1940 Vladimír Sís: 'Mr Professor L. Janáček' [Mr Professor Leoš Janáček], Národní listy (15 Aug 1940), reprinted in JVD, 42

Smaczny 1994 Jan Smaczny: 'Daily repertoire of the Provisional Theatre Opera in

Prague: chronological list', *Miscellanea musicologica*, xxxiv (1994), 9–139

Smetana 1948 — Robert Smetana: *Vyprávění o Leoši Janáčkovi* [Stories about Leoš Janáček] (Velehrad, Olomouc, 1948)

Šourek 1954 — Otakar Šourek: *Život a dílo Antonína Dvořáka* [The life and works of Antonín Dvořák], i–ii (Státní nakladatelství krásné literatury, hudby a umění, Prague, rev. 3/1954–5), iii–iv (ibid, rev. 2/1956–7)

Špelda 1954 — Antonín Špelda: 'Leoš Janáček a Plzeň' [Leoš Janáček and Plzeň], *Hudební rozhledy*, vii (1954), 645–7

Špelda 1969 — —: *Hudební místopis Plzeňska* [A musical topography of the Plzeň region] (Plzeň, 1969)

Srb 2004 — Vladimír Srb: *1000 let obyvatelstva českých zemí* [1000 years of population of the Czech lands] (Karolinum, Prague, 2004)

Stavěla 1932 — František Stavěla: *'Průvodce' Lázní Luhačovic* [A 'guide' to the spa of Luhačovice] (Stavěla & Siegl, n.p., 1932–3)

Štědroň 1934 — Bohumír Štědroň: 'Leoš Janáček na učitelském ústavu v Brně' [Leoš Janáček at the Teachers' Training Institute in Brno], *Tempo (Listy Hudební matice)*, xiii (1934), 314–20

Štědroň 1938 — 'Janáček jako Sokol' [Janáček as Sokol], *LN* (3 July 1938)

Štědroň 1939 — —: *Leoš Janáček a Luhačovice* (Luhačovice, 1939) [reprinted from annual news of Městská spořitelna v Luhačovicích]

Štědroň 1941 — —: 'Leoš Janáček a František Neumann', *Smetana*, xxxiv (1941–2), 58–60, 72–4, 89

Štědroň 1947a — —: 'Leoš Janáček na učitelském ústavě' [Leoš Janáček at the Teachers' Institute], *Rytmus*, xi/9–10 (1947–8), 140–5

Štědroň 1947b — —: 'Janáček, učitel zpěvu' [Janáček: teacher of singing], *Ročenka Pedagogické fakulty Masarykovy university v Brně za rok 1947*, 223–40

Štědroň 1947c — —: 'Janáček, upravovatel Lisztovy mše' [Janáček: the arranger of a Mass by Liszt], *Cyril*, lxxii (1947), 90–4; Ger. trans. as 'Leoš Janáček und Ferenc Liszt', *Sborník prací filosofické fakulty Brněnské university*, F7 (1963), 139–43

Štědroň 1947d — —: [report on findings in the Augustinian monastery], *LN* (4 Nov 1947)

Štědroň 1958 — —: 'Antonín Dvořák a Leoš Janáček', *Musikologie*, v (1958), 105–23

Štědroň 1959 — —: 'K Janáčkově opeře Osud' [Janáček's opera *Fate*], *Živá hudba*, i (1959), 159–83

Štědroň 1966 — —: 'K Janáčkovým nápěvkům mluvy: zárodky jeho operního slohu' [On Janáček's speech melodies: the germs of his operatic style], *Sborník pedagogické fakulty University Karlovy k šedesátým nározeninám Prof. Dr. Josefa Plavce* (Universita Karlova, Prague, 1966), 197–235

Štědroň 1972 — —: *Zur Genesis von Leoš Janáčeks Opera Jenůfa* (University J.E. Purkyně, Brno, enlarged 2/1972)

Štědroň 1986   Miloš Štědroň: 'Janáček a Zeyerův verš v opeře Šárka' [Janáček and
                Zeyer's verse in the opera *Šárka*], *Sborník prací filozofické fakulty
                brněnské univerzity*, H21 (1986), 41–48

Štědroň 1998   —: *Leoš Janáček a hudba 20. století: paralely, sondy, dokumenty* [Leoš
                Janáček and the music of the twentieth century: parallels, soundings,
                documents] (Masarykova univerzita and others, Brno, 1998)

Štědroň 2000   —: 'Janáčkovy nápěvky mluvy: imprese – stereotyp – výsledky analýz?'
                [Janáček's speech melodies; impressions – stereotypes – results of
                analyses?], *HV*, xxxvii (2000), 140–56

Stern and   Curt Stern and Eva R. Sherwood, eds.: *The Origin of Genetics: a Mendel
Sherwood 1966   source book* (W.H. Freeman, San Francisco and London, 1966)

Straková 1955a Theodora Straková: 'Janáčkovy operní náměty a torsa' [Janáček's
                operatic subjects and fragments], *Musikologie*, iii (1955), 417–49

Straková 1955b —: *Pavel Křížkovský: tvůrce české hudby z ducha lidového* [Pavel
                Křížkovský: the creator of Czech music from folk spirit], exhibition
                catalogue, (Moravské museum v Brně, Brno, 1955)

Straková 1956   —: 'Janáčkova opera Osud' [Janáček's opera *Fate*], *ČMM*, xli (1956),
                209–60; xlii (1957), 133–64

Straková 1957   —, ed.: *František Bartoš a Leoš Janáček: vzájemná korespondence*
                [František Bartoš and Leoš Janáček: correspondence] (Krajské museum v
                Gottwaldově, Gottwaldov, 1957)

Straková 1958   —: 'Setkání Leoše Janáčka s Gabrielou Preissovou' [The meeting of Leoš
                Janáček with Gabriela Preissová], *ČMM*, xliii (1958), 145–63

Straková 1959   —: 'Neznámé nástrojově skladby Leoše Janáčka' [Leoš Janáček's
                unknown instrumental works], *ČMM*, xliv (1959), 163–78

Straková 1975   —, ed.: *Iconographia janáčkiana* [Janáček iconography] (Moravské
                muzeum, Brno, 1975)

Šujan 1928   František Šujan: *Dějepis Brna* [The history of Brno] (Musejní spolek,
                Brno, enlarged 2/1928)

Tauber 1949   Stanislav, Tauber: *Můj hudební svět* [My musical world] (Vladimír
                Hapala, Brno, 1949)

Toncrová 1995   Marta Toncrová: ' "Das Volkslied in Österreich": aneb Ke zrodu Ústavu
                pro etnografii a folkloristiku v Brně' ['Das Volkslied in Österreich', or the
                birth of the Institute for ethnography and folklore studies in Brno], *OM*,
                xxvii (1995), 242–53

Toncrová 1998   —: 'Phonograph in folkloristic work of Leoš Janáček and his
                collaborators', in Plocek 1998, 138–46 [Czech version, Plocek 1998a,
                37–46]

Toncrová 1999   —: *Korespondence Leoše Janáčka s Hynkem Bímem* [Leoš Janáček's
                correspondence with Hynek Bím] (doctoral dissertation, Masaryk
                University, Brno, 1999)

Trkanová 1964   Marie Trkanová: *U Janáčků: podle vyprávění Marie Stejskalové* [At the

Janáčeks: after the account of Marie Stejskalová] (Panton, Prague, 2/1964)

Trojan 2000   Jan Trojan: *Kantoři na Moravě a ve Slezsku v 17.–19. století: jejich sociální postavení, společenská funkce a význam ve vývoji národní hudební kultury* [Kantors in Moravia and Silesia in the 17th to the 19th centuries: their social standing, function in society and importance in the evolution of national musical culture] (Muzejní a vlastivědná společnost v Brně, Brno, 2000)

Tyrrell 1967   John Tyrrell: 'The musical prehistory of Janáček's *Počátek románu* and its importance in shaping the composer's dramatic style', *ČMM*, lii (1967), 245–70

Tyrrell 1968   —: 'Mr Brouček's Excursion to the Moon', *ČMM*, liii–liv (1968–9), 89–122

Tyrrell 1970   —: 'Janáček and the speech-melody myth', *Musical Times*, cxi (1970), 793–6

Tyrrell 1973   —: 'Janáček's speech-melody theory: claims and conclusions', *Music and Word: Brno 1969: Colloquia on the History and Theory of Music at the International Musical Festival in Brno*, iv, ed. Rudolf Pečman (International Musical Festival, Brno, 1973), 175–82

Tyrrell 1982   —: *Leoš Janáček: Káta Kabanová* (Cambridge University Press, Cambridge, 1982)

Tyrrell 1987   —: 'The cathartic slow waltz and other finale conventions in Janáček's operas', *Essays on Drama and Music in Honour of Winton Dean*, ed. N. Fortune (Cambridge University Press, Cambridge, 1987), 333–52

Tyrrell 1995   —: 'Janáček's recitatives', in Beckerman and Bauer 1995, 3–19

Uhlíková 1994   Lucie Uhlíková: 'Leoš Janáček a Martin Zeman: vzájemná korespondence' [Leoš Janáček and Martin Zeman: mutual correspondence], *Národopisná revue*, iv (1994), 77–112

Vach 1924   Ferd. Vach: 'Vzpomínky' [Reminiscences], *Hudební rozhledy*, i (1924–5), 38–9

Vašek 1930   Adolf E. Vašek: *Po stopách dra Leoše Janáčka* [In the tracks of Dr Leoš Janáček] (Brněnské knižní nakladatelství, Brno, 1930)

Vejvodová 2004   Veronika Vejvodová: *Leoš Janáček: Živá mrtvola: geneze, analýza, edice* [Leoš Janáček: *The Living Corpse*: genesis, analysis, edition] (bachelor dissertation, Masaryk University, Brno, 2004)

ves 1942   ves [pseudonym; author unknown]: 'Janáček na učitelském ústavě' [Janáček at the Teachers' Institute], *LN* (12 Aug 1942)

Veselý 1924   Adolf Veselý, ed.: *Leoš Janáček: Leoš Janáček: pohled do života a díla* [Leoš Janáček: a view of the life and works] (Fr. Borový, Prague, 1924)

Vogel 1981   Jaroslav Vogel: *Leoš Janáček: Leben und Werk* (Artia, Prague, 1958; Czech original, Státní hudební vydavatelství, Prague, 1963; Eng. trans. as *Leoš Janáček: a Biography*, Orbis, London, enlarged 2/1981)

Volek 1961   Jaroslav Volek: *Novodobé harmonické systémy z hlediska vědecké filosofie* [Modern harmonic systems from the standpoint of scientific philosophy] (Panton, Prague, 1961)

Vrba 1959   Přemysl Vrba: 'Janáčkova první cesta do Ruska roku 1896' [Janáček's first trip to Russia in 1896], *Slezský sborník*, lvii (1959), 464–72

Vrba 1960   —: 'Ruský kroužek v Brně a Leoš Janáček' [The Russian circle in Brno and Leoš Janáček], *Slezský sborník*, lviii (1960), 71–85

Vysloužil 1955   Jiří Vysloužil, ed.: 'Z korespondence k Janáčkově hudebně folkloristické činnosti' [From Janáček's correspondence about musical folklore activities], *Musikologie*, iv (1955), 246–53

Vysloužil 1958   —, ed.: 'Z korespondence Otakara Hostinského Leoši Janáčkovi' [From the correspondence of Otakar Hostinský to Leoš Janáček], *Musikologie*, v (1958), 171–80

Vysloužil 1992   —: 'Leoš Janáček und Wien', *Studien zur Musikwissenschaft*, xli (1992), 257–85

Vysloužil 2004   —: 'Leoš Janáček: čtenář Sušilových Moravských národních písní' [Leoš Janáček: reader of Sušil's Moravian folksongs], *OM*, xxxvi (2004), 27–9

Weyr 2001   František Weyr: *Paměti*, ii: *Za Republiky (1918–1938)* [Memoirs, ii: During the (First) Republic (1918–38)] (Atlantis, Prague, 2001)

Wingfield 1987a   Paul Wingfield: 'Janáček's "Lost" Kreutzer Sonata', *Journal of the Royal Musical Association*, cxii (1987), 229–56

Wingfield 1987b   —: 'Janáček V mlhách: towards a new chronology', *ČMM*, lxxii (1987), 189–204

Wingfield 1992   —: 'Janáček's speech-melody theory in concept and practice', *Cambridge Opera Journal*, iv/3 (1992), 281–301

Wingfield 1999   —, ed.: *Janáček Studies* (Cambridge, 1999)

Zahrádka 2005   Jiří Zahrádka: '1.X.1905: mýtus a skutečnost Janáčkem zničené skladby' [1.X.1905: the myth and reality of Janáček's destroyed composition], *OM*, xxxvii (2005), 23–5

Zatloukalová 2001   Jarmila Zatloukalová: *Brněnské divadlo: repertoár v letech 1848–1914* [Brno theatre: repertory in the years 1848–1914], 2 vols. (Archiv města Brno, Brno, 2001–2)

Zíbrt 1892   Z [Čeněk Zíbrt]: 'Národpisná společnost a národopisná výstava českoslovanská v Praze' [The Ethnographical Society and the Czecho-Slavonic Ethnographical Exhibition in Prague], *Český lid*, i (1892–3), 104–6

Zlámalová 1999   Nora Zlámalová: 'Olga Janáčková – dcera skladatele' [Olga Janáčková – the daughter of the composer], *OM*, xxxi (1999), 30–41

Zřídkaveselý 1996   František Zřídkaveselý: *Nové a změněné názvy ulic v městě Brně 1984–1996* [New and changed names of streets in the town of Brno 1984–96] (Muzejní a vlastivědná společnost, Brno, 1996)

General Index

This index excludes all references to Janáček's compositions and writings, which are the subjects of separate indexes. Publishers, newspapers and periodicals are listed under the their own names but performing organizations and venues are listed under their town or city. References to Janáček's works are abbreviated to *JW* numbers (see next indexes). Titles of Czech works are given in English (as elsewhere in the book); the original Czech titles have been included in square brackets. Janáček's contacts with others are dealt with under the person concerned.

Austria – *Continued*
  October diploma, 37, 80
  post-1860 freedoms, 380
Autrata, František V., 633, 815
Axman, Emil, 716, 782

Bach (American student in Leipzig),
  143
Bach, Johann Sebastian
  biographical notes copied by LJ, 97
  keyboard; Concerto for two
    harpsichords, 270–1; Inventions,
    157; Organ prelude *Gottes Sohn
    ist kommen* BWV, 703, 147;
    Preludes and Fugues (*Das
    wohltemperirte Clavier*), 93, 158;
    Toccata, Adagio and Fugue BWV,
    565, 103; Toccata in C, 270;
    unspecified prelude, 150
  other works; *Actus tragicus*, 148;
    choruses, 114 critical edition, 157
  harmonic style, 453
  Leipzig connections, 14, 139
Bach, Wilhelm Friedemann, 120
Bad Ischl, 726–7
Bakala, Břetislav, 337
Bakeš, František, 322–3, 401, 648
Bakešová, Lucie, Plate 28
  lecture at 'Vesna', 356
  The Little Queens [Královničky],
    322
  and LJ: I/3, 399; advice to, 364;
    collaboration, 323–4, 642;
    contacts over Ethnographic
    Exhibition, 401, 404, 410–11,
    413, 415–17, 419–21, 645;
    correspondence, 332, 355, 358,
    360, 362, 364, 375, 379, 418–19,
    628, 631, 642, 646, 733; folksong
    collecting, 420, 642; Folksong
    working party, 628–9; I/3, 399;
    Pan-Slavonic Ethnographic
    Exhibition, 556; photographing
    folk rituals, 345, 642, 645–8, 787;
    relationship, 323, 401, 410–11,
    416, 629, 646, 792; resentment at

exclusion from Moravian folksong
  working party, 645–6
rehearses dances, 322
Bakunin, Mikhail, 79
Balakirev, Mily Alekseyevich, 475
Balcárek, Matouš, 253
Balfe, Michael William
  The Bohemian Girl, 303, 335,
    764
Bargiel, Woldemar, 120
Bařina, František, 248, 546
Bärman (student in Leipzig), 143
Baroch, Mr (violinist), 51–2
Bartók, Béla, 15, 347
Bartoš, František, Plate 29
  as director of Czech Gymnasium II,
    212, 214; retirement, 213, 341,
    468
  as ethnographer;, 340, 352;
    bowlderizing tendencies, 352;
    views on Lachs, 16
  illness and death, 507, 541, 629,
    743
  and LJ: advice on harmonizing V/2,
    508; advice on health, 507, 541;
    author copies of XIII/3, 524;
    Bartoš speech melodies notated by
    LJ, 460; consulted by LJ about
    speech melodies, 482; consulted on
    preface to XIII/3, 507;
    correspondence, 468–70, 502–3,
    507, 541, 564–5, 598; at Czech
    Gymnasium II, 211–13, 279, 340;
    and Ethnographic Exhibition, 402;
    fees for XIII/2, 508, 520; fees for
    XIII/3, 470–1, 501, 520, 522, 525;
    friendship, 340, 469; and IV/29,
    510; as LJ's mentor, 834; LJ's
    obituary notice, 350; LJ's visits,
    507; Pan-Slavonic Ethnographic
    Exhibition, 557; proofs of XIII/2,
    507; proofs of XIII/3, 423,
    468–71, 501–2, 505–6; subscriber
    to *Hudební listy*, 340; suggested as
    linguistic advisor for XV/151, 415;
    title page of XIII/3, 501–2; V/2,

508; views over LJ's retirement,
563, 566–7; what Bartoš called LJ,
136, 403
and others; Preissová, 357, 360;
Zeman, 366
writings and editions; *Dialektologie
moravská*, 17; *Moravian
Folksongs Newly Collected*
[Národní písně moravské v nově
nasbírané] (1889), 136, 349, 403;
other writings, 292, 458, 675;
XIII/1, XIII/2 and; XIII/3.
See under Index of Janáček's
compositions: XIII/3
Bartošová, Fedora, 440, 543, 566–8,
570–2, 597, 599, 637–8, 652, 663
Bártová, Jindřiška, 136, 208–9
Barvič, Joža, 464
Baška, 790
Bath, 575
Battle of the White Mountain, 11,
739
Baur, Antonio
Dyellah oder die Touristen in Indien,
173, 556
Bayreuth, 688, 766, 815
Bazin, François-Emanuel-Victor, 114
Beard, George, 801–2
Becker, Albert, 148
Beckerman, Mike, 97, 123n., 215–17,
221, 682
Bečva river, 784
Beethoven, Ludwig van
chamber; Piano Trio op. 1 no. 1, 746;
Piano Trio op. 70 no. 2, 746; Piano
Trio op. 97 (Archduke), 745; piano
trios, 746, 818; String Quartet op.
18/6, 120; String Quartet op. 131,
152; String Quartet (unspecified),
113–14; string quartets, 180;
violin pieces, 114; Violin Sonata in
F op. 24 ('Spring'), 120; Violin
Sonata in c minor op. 30/2, 158;
Violin Sonata in A op. 47
(Kreutzer), 719, 724; violin
sonatas, 152

church music; Mass in C, 54; masses
(unspecified), 60, 70; *Missa
solemnis*, 51, 54, 113, 115, 121,
126, 148, 168, 231; other, 48
Fidelio, 644, 764
orchestral; *Egmont* music, 172;
Piano Concerto no. 1, 189; Piano
Concerto no. 4, 149; Piano
Concerto no. 5 ('Emperor'), 150,
158–9; symphonies nos. 1–8, 254,
782; Symphony no. 1, 47;
Symphony no. 3 ('Eroica'), 47,
149, 152; Symphony no. 6
('Pastoral'), 152, 783; Symphony
no. 8, 152; Symphony no. 9,
820–1; unspecified, 645; Violin
Concerto, 567
piano; Sonata in C minor
('Moonlight'), 686; sonatas, 25,
34; symphonies arranged for piano
duet, 64, 91, 93
Běhálková, Xavera, 323, 356, 375,
645–6
Bellini, Vincenzo
Norma, 303
Beloveža, 345
Belrupt-Tissac, Jindřich Count, 248,
701
Bendl, Karel
choruses, 86, 109–10, 114, 188–9,
235
operas, 299, 614; *The Elderly Suitor*
[Starý ženich], 299, 303, 368, 764;
Lejla, 303, 308, 360
other works; songs, 209; *Švanda the
Bagpiper* [Švanda dudák], 434
Beneš, Bohuslav, 630, 659
Benešov, 822–3
Bennett, William Sterndale, 154
Beran, Emerich, 253, 462
Berg, Alban, 713
Berger, Augustin, 325–7, 356–7, 360,
362–5, 374
Berlin, 22, 111, 143, 231, 280, 282,
306, 379, 387, 450, 488, 688–9,
716, 733, 735, 765–6, 800

Janáček, Leoš – *Continued*
  trips abroad – *Continued*
    532, 536, 538, 597–8, 647, 779;
    Yelagin Island, 430
  trips within Czech lands; Adamov,
    700; Blatnice, 376; Bohdaneč, 579,
    581–2; Bojkovice, 730; Březová,
    471; Frenštát, 418, 655; Hostýn,
    557–8, 577; Hroznová Lhota, 629;
    Hukvaldy, 273, 286, 321–2,
    406–7, 421, 425, 433–4, 457,
    511–12, 528, 536–8, 541, 558,
    561, 573–4, 590, 601–2, 626,
    631–2, 653, 657, 664, 673, 679,
    701–3, 710, 717, 728–9, 755, 757,
    786, 827–8; Husinec, 238, 259,
    261; Jasenice, 381; Karlovy Vary,
    809–10; Karlsbad, 579; Karlštejn,
    261; Kozlovice, 786; Kroměříž,
    417, 504–5; Lelekovice, 700;
    Lipov, 376; Lubina, 656; Lubno,
    676; Luhačovice, 275–8, 376, 481,
    558–61, 577–9, 582–3, 599–600,
    632, 653, 655–6, 680, 703–6,
    729–30, 775–6, 792; Mosty, 679;
    Mšeno, 579, 810; Olomouc, 198,
    805; Ořechov, 648; Orlík, 238,
    261; Ostrava, 707; Ostravice, 654;
    Plzeň, 784; Polanka, 382–3;
    Prachatice, 238, 259, 261; Prague,
    230–1, 237–9, 259, 261–2, 265,
    274, 282, 297, 315, 358, 364, 371,
    384, 418–19, 555–6, 562, 566–7,
    571, 583, 590–1, 595, 602, 616,
    628, 635, 643–5, 648–50, 653,
    660, 683, 687, 690, 695–7, 700–1,
    706, 717, 722, 725, 750–2, 757,
    760, 773–4, 784, 793, 807–8,
    815–17, 820, 823–4; Prostějov,
    635; Prostřední Bečva, 728;
    Radhošť, 418, 511, 539, 631,
    654–5; Roudnice, 810–12;
    Rožnov, 655, 728; Strání, 656;
    Strážnice, 366, 376, 382; Teplice,
    755; Teplice nad Bečvou, 728;
    Těšín, 817–18; Tišnov, 727;

Trojanovice, 673; Valašská
  Bystřice, 679, 828; Velká, 366,
  368, 376, 382, 418; Velký
  Ořechov, 776; Veselí, 629, 681;
  Vienna, 679, 687; Vnorovy
  (Znorovy), 341–2, 776; Vranov,
  700; Vsetín, 418; Vysoká, 238–9,
  241, 259, 261, 265
and Warsaw Conservatory;
  interviewed for post of director,
  598–9
Janáček, Vincenc (LJ's uncle), 25–7, 35
Janáček, Vladimír (LJ's son), 32, 81,
  283, 285, 320–1, 329, 335–7, 355,
  357, 545, 547, Plate 13
Janáčková, Amalie (LJ's mother), Plates
  1 and 3
biography, 26
after 1866, 200
in Brno; accommodation, 186; hires
  rooms to students, 200; keeps
  house for LJ, 229; leaves Brno,
  201; pension arrangements, 200;
  possibility of living with LJ and
  Zdenka, 201–2
dispute with Eleonora, 229
illness and death, 266–8; grave,
  273
and LJ: announces his engagement,
  191; attendance at wedding,
  195–6; attitude to separation from
  Zdenka, 230, 241–2;
  correspondence, 201, 231; does
  not return to live with LJ, 236–7;
  final letter, 266–7; his financial
  support for, 166n., 199, 229, 520;
  minimal contacts when LJ in
  Leipzig, 201; name for him, 135;
  relationship, 200–2; unhappy that
  she cannot live with him, 230
in Příbor, 200
in Švábenice, 229
Janáčková, Anna (Karel's wife),
  553
Janáčková, Anna (LJ's grandmother),
  27

overerture to *A Winter's Tale*
[Pohádka zimního večera], 420
Suk, Váša
Sullivan, Arthur, 140
Suppé, Franz
Boccaccio, 269, 306
Donna Juanita, 269, 306
Der Gascogner, 269, 306
Sušil, František, 65, 72–3, 76, 89–90,
340, 348–9, 352, 524
Svatopluk (ruler of Great Moravia), 59
Švec, Jan, 654, Plate 25
Svendsen, Johann, 140
Světozor (journal), 361
Svoboda, F.X., 683
Svozil, Hynek, 653, 657, 659–60, 685
Svyatkovsky, Vesvolod′ Pavlovich′,
598–9
Sychra, Antonín, 486–7
Sychrov, 240

Tacl, František, 499
Tartini, Giuseppe, 625
Tauber, Stanislav, 254, 581n., 721, 783,
822
Tchaikovsky, Pyotr Il′ych
church music, 445
Eugene Onegin, 81, 358–9, 372, 438,
445, 475, 483–4, 567, 766
orchestral; 1812 overture, 282–3;
Piano Concerto no. 1, 282–3;
Romeo and Juliet overture, 282–3;
Serenade for strings, 188, 226,
462; Violin Concerto, 282, 819
The Queen of Spades, 359, 423–4,
438–43, 445, 459–60, 513, 762–3,
766
songs, 475
Swan Lake, 687
Tebich, Antonín, 728–9
Telč, 358, 674, 689
Teplice nad Bečvou, 728–9, 755, 757,
800
Teplice (Slovakia), 729
Teplitz (Teplice), 576 (*see also* České
Teplice)

Terchová, 346
Těšín, 17, 23, 680, 817
Těsnohlídek, Rudolf, 3–4
Thaler, Aurelius, 45
Thurn-Wallessin Foundation, 46–8
Tichá u Frenštátu, 344
Tichý, Jaroslav, 272, 290, 361–2, 461
(*see also* Rypáček, František)
Tišnov, 39, 727, 730, 800
Tlustá, Mrs, 728
Tlusťák, Rainer, 276
Tochavice, 238
Tolstoy, Lev Nikolayevich, 62, 464,
637, 673, 717–19, 724, 740–2,
788, 791
Topič (publisher), 692
Tovačov, 88n., 417
Tovačovský, Arnošt. See under
Förchtgott-Tovačovský, Arnošt
Tregler, Eduard, 745, 819, Plate 25
Treiber, Wilhelm, 149
Trenčianská Teplá, 39
Trenčianské Teplice, 726
Trieste, 791, 827
Triglav, 792
Trkanová, Marie, 795, 826
Trn, Pavel, 344–5, 366, 376–8,
Plate 31
Trneček, Hanuš, 624
Trojan, Jan, 24, 119
Trojanovice, 345, 673
Troubsko, 404, 410–1, 416–17, 642
Trzebinia, 426–7, 526
Tučková, Ludmila, 509, 642–3, 836
Turnverein (German gymnastics
organization), 380
Tygodnik illustrowany (Polish journal),
509
Tyl, Josef Kajetán, 419, 509n.

Učitel (journal), 466
Úhelný (bagpiper, 345, 656
Uherské Hradiště, 504, 557, 776
Újezdec u Luhačovic, 581
Ulcinj (Dulcigno), 827n.
Unie (publisher), 507–8

Index of Janáček's compositions

The arrangement and numbering of this list is based on that in *JAWO*, where full details of dating, publication, performance etc. can be found.

Works are given in the English translations used throughout the book, followed by original titles in square brackets

stage works

I/1 Šárka: Bakala's rediscovery of, 337; composition history, 281, 283, 286, 298, 307–9, 311–14, 322, 339; consultation with Dvořák, 261–2, 312, 314; libretto, 309–11; LJ unable to learn from hearing it performed, 837; LJ's recollection in, 1904, 621; manuscript materials, 521; orchestration, 323; place within LJ's oeuvre, 217, 279, 314–16, 436, 513; revisions and versions, 312–14, 388, 484–5, 606, 608; set numbers, 311–14; VI/5 as extra overture?, 337–8; Zeyer's ban, 315–16, 319, 359

I/2 Rákoš Rákoczy: plot, 365–6; production in Prague, 365–6; title, 363; recycling of musical numbers, 386–9; composition history, 358, 363–4; in context of Regional Jubilee Exhibition, 359–60, 365, 374; invoked by LJ for grant application, 368; invoked by LJ in promoting I/3, 369; listed in *Lidové noviny* article (1904), 621; manuscript copies, 521; production in Prague, 388, 399, 555, 739n.; recycling of musical numbers, 378, 386–8; royalties, 520

I/3 The Beginning of a Romance [Počátek románu]: Brno première, 298, 373, 376–7, 384, 398–9; comments by Prague conductors, 371, 374; compilation and recycling, 374, 386–7, 389; composition history, 358, 362–3, 369, 371; ethnographic aspects, 366, 386–9, 400, 402, 424; finances, 520; later mentions, 621–2; libretto and plot, 310, 360–2; LJ's attempt to get performed in Prague, 301, 369–71, 373–4; LJ's later repudiation, 400, 837; place in LJ's oeuvre, 604; Preissová's attempt to get performed in Ivančice, 384

Index of Janáček's writings

Writings are given with original title first and an English translation supplied in square brackets.

For full details of original and subsequent publication, and English and German translations, see the list in *JAWO*, on which this is based. Since then, Janáček's 'literary works' (i.e. those not concerned with folk music or theoretical matters) have been published in a modern critical edition (*LD*); some important English translations have been made available for the first time in Michael Beckerman, ed.: *Janáček and his World* (Princeton University Press, Princeton and Oxford, 2003).